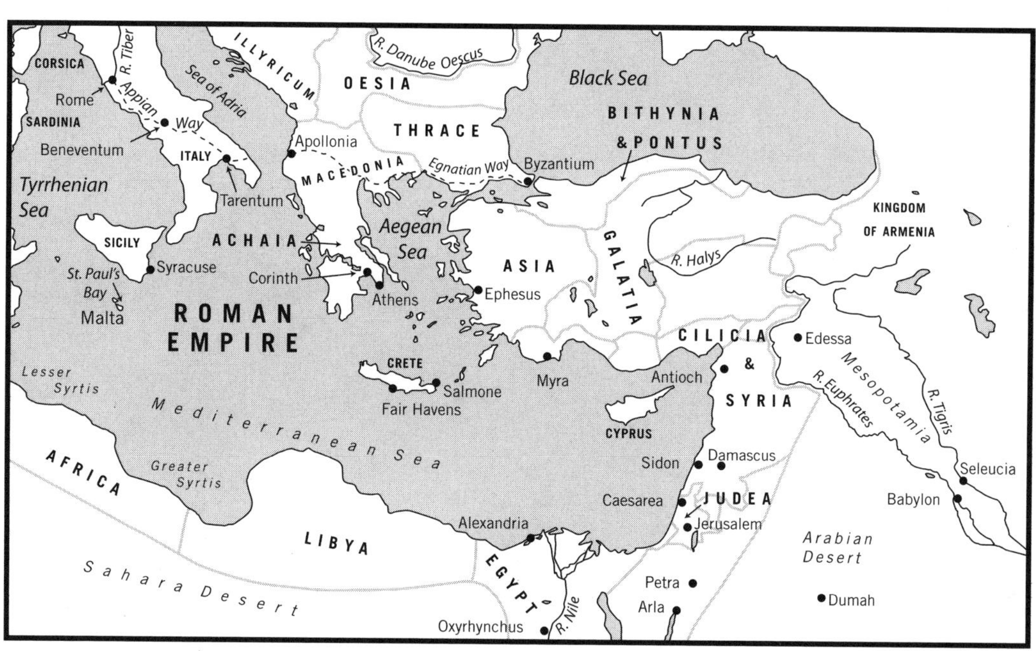

MAP 1: The Mediterranean Region in the First Century.

AN INTRODUCTION TO THE
New Testament

AN INTRODUCTION TO THE

New Testament

History, Literature, Theology

M. EUGENE BORING

First edition
Published by Westminster John Knox Press
Louisville, Kentucky

12 13 14 15 16 17 18 19 20 21—10 9 8 7 6 5 4 3 2 1

Book design by Drew Stevens
Cover design by Dilu Nicholas
Cover illustration: © *Zadvinskiy/istockphoto.com;* © *Paolo Cipriani/istockphoto.com;*
© *Enviromantic/istockphoto.com*

Library of Congress Cataloging-in-Publication Data

Boring, M. Eugene.
An introduction to the New Testament : history, literature, theology / M. Eugene Boring.
p. cm.
ISBN 978-0-664-25592-3 (alk. paper)
1. Bible. N.T.—Introductions. I. Title.
BS2330.3.B67 2012
225.6'1—dc23

2012013171

PRINTED IN THE UNITED STATES OF AMERICA

♾ The paper used in this publication meets the minimum requirements
of the American National Standard for Information Sciences—Permanence
of Paper for Printed Library Materials, ANSI Z39.48-1992

Westminster John Knox Press advocates the responsible use of our natural resources.
The text paper of this book is made from 30 percent post-consumer waste.

Most Westminster John Knox Press books are available at special quantity discounts
when purchased in bulk by corporations, organizations, and special-interest groups.
For more information, please e-mail SpecialSales@wjkbooks.com.

Contents

List of Illustrations

Maps

Figures

List of Text Boxes

Preface

THIS BOOK HAS BEEN WRITTEN FROM THE following perspectives and convictions:

The New Testament is a book of history. It is not a book of ideas, ideals, and inspirational religious principles, but narrates and interprets the events in the life of Jesus and his followers who became the early Christian community. The New Testament is more (not less) than a history book in that it interprets these events as revelatory acts of God for the salvation of the world. In their interpretations of history, New Testament authors use the ideas of their world (Jewish and Gentile, religious and secular). Each writing of the New Testament is embedded in its own history, the story of the early church. The New Testament as a whole has a history of collection, transmission, translation, and interpretation. The New Testament not only communicates a story; it has its own story. For such texts, historical insight is an appropriate and necessary element in authentic understanding.

Study of the New Testament requires hands-on critical method. As a history book, the New Testament requires critical method. "Who wrote what, when, where, to whom, and why" are unavoidable issues for historical understanding, even if these questions cannot always be definitively answered. This book does not attempt to work through every point in methodological detail, but from case to case intends to provide enough specifics to illustrate evidence and argument. At four points, standard issues of New Testament introduction are treated in extensive excursuses exploring the evidence and arguments on which typical scholarly conclusions are based: the literary unity of 2 Corinthians, pseudepigraphy, the Synoptic Problem, and the markings of parallels in the Synoptic Gospels. Instead of merely providing students the results of "what scholars think," the evidence and arguments are given that allow students to judge for themselves the degree of confidence we may have about such conclusions, and what difference they make theologically. Students who follow the details of evidence and argument enhance their ability to navigate and evaluate the ocean of secondary literature about the New Testament, and develop their own skills as interpreters of the New Testament.

"Begin at square one; go a long way." This book is intended for the beginning student, presupposing only serious interest in the subject matter, but no prior experience in detailed Bible study. It is a fairly technical book, reflecting much of the history and present state of New Testament research. I have sometimes retained citations in Greek, as a reminder that engagement with the New Testament is cross-cultural study and that those who want to understand it need to enter its linguistic world. The book is completely understandable by those with no Greek or Hebrew; everything is translated, often also transliterated to facilitate pronunciation. I have in mind the kind of readers one often finds in seminary and the pastorate, many of whom are second-career students without

an undergraduate major in religious studies or biblical languages. While presuppositions are minimal, the book attempts to lead the student toward an in-depth understanding and competence as an interpreter of the New Testament.

The New Testament is a book of faith and theology. New Testament authors express their faith that God acted in the life of Jesus and events in the early church. When faith expresses itself in conceptual, linguistic form, the result is theology, "faith seeking understanding," in Anselm's historic phrase. While faith and theology are not the same thing, there can be no thinking about the faith, no communication of faith, apart from theology. "Theology" does not refer only to abstract systematic second- and third-level discourse, but to first-level discourse, to any articulation of the faith. The New Testament is thus a thoroughly theological book. This means that to understand the New Testament in its own terms requires theological reflection, whether or not its readers share its faith or theology. An introduction to the New Testament must itself be in some sense theological, even if only at the descriptive level.

The New Testament is essentially composed of Letters and Gospels. The historical process that led to the formation of the canon resulted in a New Testament composed of only two types of literature. This is still reflected in the liturgical reading of Scripture, in which all New Testament texts are either "Epistle" or "Gospel." This bipartite generic structure of the New Testament has often been noted. However, so far as I know, this book represents the first effort to structure an introduction to the New Testament along these lines. This is in step with early Christian history and theology; there is also a pedagogical reason. The Letters are treated first, in the historical order argued here, 1 Thessalonians–2 Peter. Only then do we turn to the Gospels and Acts. About midway in the course, students begin to notice that there was an extensive tradition, complete in itself, of expressing the faith entirely within the confines of the epistolary genre. They become aware that they have studied most of the books of the New Testament without encountering a single story about Jesus. They come to the later, parallel genre of Gospels with new eyes, new questions, new insights. Near the end of the course they see Epistle and Gospel combined—for the first time—in the Johannine community, the prolepsis of the New Testament canon.

There is a narrative substructure of the New Testament and its theologies. Both Letters and Gospels share a common foundation: narrative. All New Testament documents confess faith within a narrative framework. The Gospels and Acts are obviously narrative. But the Epistles are also a narrative genre; each letter functions by projecting a narrative world. This book is in step with this narrative mode, is itself a kind of narrative. It tells the story of New Testament, from pre-Christian Judaism, through Jesus, the early church, Paul and the letter tradition, Mark and the Gospel tradition, to the combination of Letters and Gospel in the Johannine community. This involves (re)construction of a plausible story line, as does all history. The alternative is to study New Testament documents as free-floating texts not tied to history. As the New Testament is a story, or collection of stories within a larger story, so this book is a narrative. It tells the story of the New Testament.

New Testament theology is best done as diachronic exposition of texts. This book is a synthesis of the traditional genres *Introduction to the New Testament* and *Theology of the New Testament*. New Testament theology is interwoven into the narrative presentation of the formation of the New Testament. Instead of attempting topical essays under rubrics such as the "Christology" and "Ecclesiology" of each book or the New Testament as a whole, an *Exegetical-Theological Précis* of each New Testament document presents its theology structured in the mode of the text itself. The New Testament's own theologizing is in the narrative mode. The appropriate way to grasp the theology of each book is by working through each text in its own genre and structure.

The New Testament is the church's book. Much of the above is summed up in this familiar phrase, which, of course, is not original with me.[1] Fifty years ago I was impressed by the central importance of this hermeneutical key in Leander Keck's Vanderbilt lectures. Another of my teachers, Fred Craddock (also a student of Keck), often refers to the essential dialogue between Book and Community. The Community needs the Book as norm and anchor point; the Book needs the Community as its context for understanding. I owe Keck, Craddock, and all my teachers an incalculable debt, as I do to all my long-suffering students, from whom I also learned much. I dedicate this book to the students in my "Introduction to the New Testament" classes at the Graduate Seminary of Phillips University (1967–1986), and Texas Christian University and Brite Divinity School (1987–2006).

Over the years my understanding of the New Testament has been broadened and deepened by dialogue about the substance of this book with numerous colleagues and students. I value especially what I have learned from Leander Keck, Fred Craddock, Russell Pregeant, Udo Schnelle, David Balch, and William Baird, both from their writings and from personal conversations. I am deeply grateful to the editorial and production staff of Westminster John Knox Press, who have provided not only professional expertise, but counsel and encouragement. As this project comes to its conclusion, I offer heartfelt thanks to Jon L. Berquist, who was Executive Editor for Biblical Studies at Westminster John Knox Press when he invited me to write this book in 1994 and accompanied it along the way with many helpful conversations; to Marianne Blickenstaff, Acquisitions Editor for Biblical Studies at WJK, who shepherded it through the final editorial process, and to Julie Tonini, Director of Production, both of whom handled a large and complex manuscript; and to Daniel Braden, Managing Editor, for his editing advice. I am also grateful for the sharp-eyed reading of the penultimate draft by Jerry L. Coyle, Bobby Wayne Cook, and James E. Crouch, whose diligence resulted in numerous suggestions incorporated in the present text, and especially to Victor Paul Furnish, who read the sections on Paul and the Pauline epistolary tradition and offered many valuable suggestions. But, as is rightly said, none of the above should be held accountable for the book's defects, for which I alone take credit.

1. Cf., e.g., Willi Marxsen, *The New Testament as the Church's Book?!* trans. James E. Mignard (Philadelphia: Fortress Press, 1972); Sandra Schneiders, *The Revelatory Text: Interpreting the New Testament as Sacred Scripture*, 2nd ed. (Collegeville, MN: Liturgical Press, 1999), chap. 3, "The New Testament as the Church's Book."

ACKNOWLEDGMENTS

M. Eugene Boring: Statue of Pontius Pilate, Arch of Titus, Masada, altar inscription at Perga, Delphi, Mithras altar, model of mystery cult, reconstructed *stoa*, ascension of deified Caesar, Augustus inscription, Miletus city gate, wealthy home, Antioch of Pisidia, Corinth temple, Corinth bema, carved footprint, Hierapolis, Sergius Paulus inscription, Nike, island of Patmos, model of Pergamum. Used by permission.

British Library Board: Page from Codex Sinaiticus. Used by permission.

German Bible Society: Gospel of John in Nestle-Aland, *Novum Testamentum Graece*, 27. Used by permission.

Holy Land Photos: Miletus inscription. Used by permission.

Münster Institute: Dr. Marie-Luise Lakmann of the Institut für Neutestamentliche Textforschung, critical apparatus of Acts 1:1 in the process of revision, Dr. Klaus Wachtel of the Institut für Neutestamentliche Textforschung. Used by permission.

David Padfield: Roman theater in Caesarea, Caesarea Philippi, relief on the Arch of Titus, Qumran Cave 4, Sepphoris, relief at Thessalonica, votive offerings, temple of Apollo, Roman road, prison at Philippi, Via Egnatia, ruin of Roman forum at Philippi, Roman forum at Philippi, relief of Beroean couple, temple warning inscription, Sardis, Ephesus, Smyrna, Thyatira. Used by permission.

John Rylands Library, University of Manchester: Papyrus 52 fragment. Used by permission.

William O. Walker Jr.: M. Eugene Boring and Bruce M. Metzger

Abbreviations

AB	Anchor Bible
Abraham	Philo, *On the Life of Abraham*
ABRL	Anchor Bible Reference Library
Ag. Ap.	Josephus, *Against Apion*
Alleg. Interp.	Philo, *Allegorical Interpretation*
Ant.	Josephus, *Jewish Antiquities*
ANTC	Abingdon New Testament Commentaries
Apol.	Justin Martyr, *Apologia*
ASNU	Acta seminarii neotestamentici upsaliensis
ASV	American Standard Version
AV	Authorized Version
B	Codex Vaticanus
b.	Babylonian tractate (of the Talmud)
Bar	Baruch
B. Bat.	*Bava Batra*
BCE	before the Common Era
BETL	Bibliotheca ephemeridum theologicarum lovaniensium
BJRL	*Bulletin of the John Rylands University Library of Manchester*
BZNW	Beihefte zur Zeitschrift für die neutestamentliche Wissenschaft
CBQMS	Catholic Biblical Quarterly Monograph Series
CD	Cairo Damascus Document
CE	Common Era
CEB	*The Common English Bible*
Chr	Chronicles
CJA	Christianity and Judaism in Antiquity
Clem.	*Clement*
Col	Colossians
Cor	Corinthians
D	Bezae Cantabrigiensis
Dan	Daniel
De Princip.	Origen, *De principiis*
Deut	Deuteronomy
Did.	*Didache*

Eccl	Ecclesiastes
EDNT	*Exegetical Dictionary of the New Testament*. Edited by H. Balz, G. Schneider. ET. Grand Rapids, 1990–1993.
EKKNT	Evangelisch-katholischer Kommentar zum Neuen Testament
Ep.	Seneca, *Epistulae morales*
Ep. Brut.	Cicero, *Epistulae ad Brutum*
Eph	Ephesians
Esd	Esdras
Exc.	Excursus
Exod	Exodus
Ezek	Ezekiel
FGH	Farrer-Goulder Hypothesis
fig.	figure
FRLANT	Forschungen zur Religion und Literatur des Alten und Neuen Testaments
Gal	Galatians
GCS	Die griechische christliche Schriftsteller der ersten [drei] Jahrhunderte
Gen	Genesis
GTA	Göttinger theologischer Arbeiten
Heb	Hebrews
Heir	Philo, *Who Is the Heir?*
Hist. eccl.	Eusebius, *Historia ecclesiastica*
HNTC	Harper's New Testament Commentaries
Hos	Hosea
HTS	Harvard Theological Studies
HUT	Hermeneutische Untersuchungen zur Theologie
ICC	International Critical Commentary
Ign. *Eph.*	Ignatius, *To the Ephesians*
Ign. *Phld.*	Ignatius, *To the Philadelphians*
Ign. *Pol.*	Ignatius, *To Polycarp*
Ign. *Rom.*	Ignatius, *To the Romans*
Ign. *Smyrn.*	Ignatius, *To the Smyrnaeans*
Isa	Isaiah
Jas	James
JBL	*Journal of Biblical Literature*
Jdt	Judith
Jer	Jeremiah
Josh	Joshua
JSNTSup	Journal for the Study of the New Testament: Supplement Series
Jub.	*Jubilees*
Judg	Judges
KEK	Kritisch-exegetischer Kommentar über das Neue Testament (Meyer-Kommentar)
Kgs	Kings
KJV	King James Version
LCL	Loeb Classical Library

Lev	Leviticus
Life	Josephus, *The Life*
LJS	Lives of Jesus Series
LXX	Septuagint
Macc	Maccabees
Mal	Malachi
MAs	Minor Agreements
Matt	Matthew
Mic	Micah
MT	Masoretic Text
NAB	*The New American Bible*
NACSBT	New American Commentary Studies in Bible and Theology
NASB	*New American Standard Bible*
NEB	*The New English Bible*
NICNT	New International Commentary on the New Testament
NIGTC	New International Greek Testament Commentary
NIV	*New International Version*
NJB	*The New Jerusalem Bible*
NovTSup	Novum Testamentum Supplements
NRSV	New Revised Standard Version
NT	New Testament
NTL	New Testament Library
NTS	*New Testament Studies*
Num	Numbers
ÖTK	Ökumenischer Taschenbuch-Kommentar
Pet	Peter
Phil	Philippians
Phlm	Philemon
Pol. *Phil.*	Polycarp, *To the Philippians*
Prov	Proverbs
Ps (Pss)	Psalm(s)
Pss. Sol.	*Psalms of Solomon*
Q	*Quelle* (source)
Rab.	*Rabbah*
REB	*The Revised English Bible*
Rev	Revelation
Rom	Romans
RSV	Revised Standard Version
Sam	Samuel
SBLDS	Society of Biblical Literature Dissertation Series
SBLSBL	Society of Biblical Literature Studies in Biblical Literature
SBLSBS	Society of Biblical Literature Sources for Biblical Study
SIG	*Sylloge inscriptionum graecarum*. Edited by W. Dittenberger. 4 vols. 3rd ed. Leipzig, 1915–1924
Sir	Sirach
SNTSMS	Society for New Testament Studies Monograph Series

SP	Sacra pagina
TDNT	*Theological Dictionary of the New Testament*. Edited by G. Kittel and G. Friedrich. Translated by G. W. Bromiley. 10 vols. Grand Rapids, 1964–1976.
TEV	*Today's English Version*
T. Levi	*Testament of Levi*
t. Suk.	*Tosefta Sukkah*
Thess	Thessalonians
THKNT	Theologischer Handkommentar zum Neuen Testament
Tim	Timothy
TNIV	*Today's New International Version*
TNTC	Tyndale New Testament Commentaries
TOB	Tobit
TUGAL	Texte und Untersuchungen zur Geschichte der altchristlichen Literatur
2DH	Two-Document Hypothesis
2GH	Two-Gospel Hypothesis, also known as Griesbach Hypothesis
2SH	Two-Source Hypothesis
War	Josephus, *Jewish War*
WBC	Word Biblical Commentary
Wis	Wisdom of Solomon
WMANT	Wissenschaftliche Monographien zum Alten und Neuen Testament
WUNT	Wissenschaftliche Untersuchungen zum Neuen Testament
Zech	Zechariah
ZNW	*Zeitschrift für die neutestamentliche Wissenschaft und die Kunde der älteren Kirche*

1
What Is the New Testament?

THE NEW TESTAMENT IS THE SELECTION OF early Christian writings that became part—but only part—of the Christian Bible. To open its pages is to enter a story that has been underway a long time, the next-to-last act of a drama approaching its climactic scene, a story that claims to communicate the meaning of the universe and every human life. To be sure, it is not necessary to read this assortment of letters and narratives as Holy Scripture. The same collection of texts can legitimately be called *Selections from the Religious Literature of Antiquity* or some such, and still be read with horizon-expanding educational value. The New Testament is certainly a cultural treasure, the most influential single book in shaping the literature, art, and philosophy of Western civilization. But almost everyone who studies these texts reads them as part of the Christian Bible, as the "New Testament." To understand why the Bible itself (both Old Testament[1] and New Testament) speaks of a "new testament," we must attempt to understand the Bible's covenant language from the inside. What does it mean to call this collection of documents the "New Testament"?

1.1 "Testament"

A powerful king in the ancient Near East sends an army during the night to surround a town some distance away. In the morning, the king's messenger speaks to the surprised townspeople: "I am your new king. You are my people. This is my covenant with you. I will protect you from your enemies, and guarantee your peace and prosperity. From now on, you must obey the following laws . . ." The people had no voice, no vote, in the decision to become part of the realm. They do have a choice in how they will respond.

Terminology. English translations of the Bible use the terms "testament" and "covenant" interchangeably. "Old Testament" and "New Testament" mean the same as "Old Covenant" and "New Covenant" (see the title page of the New Testament in the RSV and NRSV). Contemporary English uses both "covenant"

1. Jews, of course, do not refer to their sacred Scripture as the "Old Testament," a designation these writings first received as part of the Christian Bible. I follow the model of Sandra Schneiders, Walter Brueggemann, and numerous others who speak of "Jewish Scriptures" when referring to the Bible of the Jews, ancient and modern, and "Old Testament" when speaking of the first part of the Christian Bible (Schneiders, *The Revelatory Text: Interpreting the New Testament as Sacred Scripture*, 2nd ed. [Collegeville, MN: Liturgical Press, 1999], 6; Brueggemann, *An Introduction to the Old Testament: The Canon and the Christian Imagination* [Louisville, KY: Westminster John Knox Press, 2003], 1–3). For a collection of essays that discuss this issue from a variety of perspectives, see Roger Brooks and John J. Collins, eds., *Hebrew Bible or Old Testament? Studying the Bible in Judaism and Christianity*, CJA 5 (Notre Dame, IN: University of Notre Dame Press, 1990).

and "testament" in nonbiblical contexts, but only in restricted senses: "covenant" is used as a synonym for "contract," and in the traditional marriage ceremony, where it is bilateral and voluntary; "testament" is found in the phrase "last will and testament," where it is unilateral and imposed. The biblical meaning of the terms cannot be determined on the basis of English usage, but by their usage in the biblical texts. The term consistently used for "covenant" in the Old Testament is בְּרִית (*berith*); in the LXX and New Testament, it is διαθήκη (*diathēkē*). The New Testament's covenant language, like much of its theological terminology and conceptuality, is derived from the Old Testament. Although ancient Israel could speak of a "book of the covenant" (e.g., Exod 24:7; 2 Chr 34:30–31; 1 Macc 1:57), the covenant itself was not a book, but an act binding together two parties.

Unilateral. Covenant terminology was already present in the ancient Near East prior to and alongside Israel, who adopted the term in both its secular and sacred aspects. In the Old Testament, covenants are basically of two kinds, those between humans and those between God and humans. Human covenants were often bilateral, reciprocal, mutual—like "covenant" in the traditional wedding ceremony (see, e.g., 1 Kgs 15:19, where *berith* is a negotiated treaty translated "alliance"; *diathēkē* of 1 Macc 11:9 is mutual and bilateral). However, even on the human level, covenants are often from the superior to the inferior partner. The covenant was thus unilateral and unnegotiated, like our use of "testament" in English, but not like our marriage "covenant." A covenant was not a contract, not even a sacred contract. In the *berith* between Jonathan and David (1 Sam 18:3), "Jonathan (the royal son) made a covenant with David (commoner, shepherd) that day," not "Jonathan and David made a covenant." The royal covenant in which a covenant is granted/imposed on the inferior by the superior serves as the model for understanding the relationship between God and Israel. It is not a matter of equal partners, in which each freely chooses and negotiates the terms. In the Bible, God always speaks of "my covenant" (56 times), never of "our covenant." Thus, in the key text Jeremiah 31:31–34 cited in Hebrews 8:8–12, God is the subject throughout, who makes the covenant and speaks of "my" (not "our") covenant.

Event. In the Bible, the divine *berith* is an event, not an ideal or principle. The covenant is a gracious act of God, taken at the divine initiative for the benefit of humanity. It is often associated with deliverance, validation of life and security, total well-being and peace, *shalom* (שָׁלוֹם), that is, it is a *saving act.* The fundamental saving act of God for Israel in the exodus was then read back into the story of Abraham and Noah, and was seen as the paradigm for God's dealing with the world as a whole. The Old Testament authors began with the historical act of God in creating Israel by delivering them from Egypt and graciously granting them the covenant—including its obligations—and then used this as their model for understanding the relation of the Creator to the whole creation. Here and elsewhere in biblical theology, act is primary to being, history to ontology, particular to universal. The Bible is not a discussion of God's being, but the testimony to God's acts.

Indicative and imperative. God's grace precedes and is the basis for the call to human responsibility, also in the Old Testament covenant. Judaism understood this. Grace precedes demand; God's redemptive, covenant-making act precedes human response. Yet the covenant calls for human response, and requires it. The good news of God's saving, covenant-making act (indicative) carries with it the demand for human response (imperative).

Community. The covenant is not with individuals but with the people of God. Whenever the covenant is made with one person (Noah, Abraham, David, the Servant of Second Isaiah), the individual represents a community. The chosen people are the people of the covenant, who have been constituted what they are by God's act. This community is charged with a mission, to be the means of God's blessing of all (Gen 12:1–3), to be a light to the nations. (Isa 42:6). Thus, in later Israelite history, the covenant with Israel is understood in terms of a covenant with David and his descendants, the means of God's blessing for the whole world (e.g., 2 Chr 7:18; 13:5; 21:7; 23:3; Ps 89:3; Isa 55:3; Jer 33:21).

Already/not yet. This means there is an already/not yet dimension to Israel's covenant language from the beginning. God is already and eternally Lord and king of the universe, God's own creation. But the creation has rebelled against its Creator, and God's rule is not yet fulfilled within the rebellious creation. In the same way, God's covenant with the faithful covenant people already exists in this world, but at present it is still partial, fragmentary, and looking for a future consummation. The covenant is not static, not complete, but awaits an ultimate fulfillment. One of the pictures of the consummation of God's purpose at the end of history is the renewal of the covenant, involving a renewal of humanity, for which God takes the responsibility (Jer 31:31–33).

Unilateral faithfulness, unconditional love. God's covenant is unilateral, and cannot be nullified from the human side. Like a will, the covenant is simply there by imposition of the one who made it. The covenant people can ignore it or refuse to live by the responsibilities to which it calls them. This is the only sense in which human beings can "break" God's covenant. They cannot break it in the sense of revoking, annulling, or destroying it. This could be done only by the covenant's Maker. The faithfulness of God calls for human response, but is not conditional on it. Even though human beings are unfaithful, God remains faithful (Lev 26:44–45; Judg 2:1; Isa 54:10; Jer 33:19–21; Ps 89:19–45).

The covenant and the book. As the redemptive act of God—past, present, and future—the covenant has signs that bear witness to its reality and meaning. Some are *nonverbal* signs, such as the rainbow (Gen 6:18; 9:9–16), circumcision (Gen 17:11–13), and the ark of the covenant that accompanied Israel in their journey and made God's holy presence tangible and real (Exod 26:34; Deut 10:8; 1 Sam 4). The "blood of the covenant" (Exod 24:8; Zech 9:11), the covenant bread (Lev 24:5–8), and the wine of the covenant (Deut 7:12–13) point to its reality. There are also *verbal* witnesses to the covenant, the tables of the commandments and the book of the law, called the book of the covenant (e.g., Exod 24:7; Deut 29:21; 31:26; 2 Kgs 23:3; cf. 1 Macc 1:56–57). The book is not the covenant, but the book is placed in the ark, witnesses to the meaning of the covenant, and makes it tangible and real (Exod 24:7; 25:21).

1.2 "New"

THE BARRAGE OF ADVERTISING HYPE FOR the "new and improved" version ("14 percent stronger") is not the context in which the Bible's language of newness can be understood. Just as "testament" must not be defined in terms of contemporary English usage, so "new" must not be understood in terms of contemporary culture, where "new" is a generally positive relative term and "old" tends to mean "outmoded, relatively inferior." The Jewish Scriptures use the language of newness in an absolute sense, as a term for God's eschatological fulfillment of the divine promises. Thus Second Isaiah, on the basis of God's covenantal faithfulness, calls for Israel to perceive the "new thing" that God is about to do (Isa 43:19)—not the negation of the past, but its eschatological fulfillment. Ezekiel speaks of God's intention to implant a new heart and new spirit within his people (Ezek 11:19; 18:31); God does not give up on sinful people who have violated the covenant, but takes responsibility for recreating them according to the ultimate divine purpose. Third Isaiah looks forward to "new heavens and new earth" in which God's righteousness dwells (Isa 65:17; 66:22). This means not that the Creator abandons the "old" creation, but that he brings it to ultimate fulfillment.

When Paul uses the language of "new creation" to speak of the saving event of Jesus Christ (2 Cor 5:17; Gal 6:15), this does not mean the rejection of the present creation but its redemption. When John pictures ultimate salvation as the descent of the "new Jerusalem" (Rev 3:12; 21:2), this means both continuity and discontinuity with present Jerusalem. In all these illustrations, "new" is not a relative term, but an eschatological one. In the biblical thought world, the new does not supersede the past relatively, but fulfills it absolutely. It is not the abolition of the old but its eschatological renewal.

1.3 "New Testament"

JEREMIAH SPECIFICALLY PICTURES THE eschatological fulfillment of God's purposes as the making of a new covenant, that is, the eschatological renewal of God's covenant with Israel (Jer 31:31–34). This vocabulary is not repeated elsewhere in the Old Testament as the expression of Israel's eschatological hope, but the idea is reflected (cf. Ezek 16:60, 62; 34:25; 36:26; 37:26; Isa 54:10; 55:3; 61:8, and 42:6; 49:8, where the Servant is representative of the covenant).

The Jewish sectarian community at Qumran, contemporary with Jesus and the early church, understood the events of their own history as God's eschatological act of the renewal of the covenant. The Dead Sea Scrolls show that they understood the reality that was happening in their midst, with the arrival of the Teacher of Righteousness, as the fulfillment and climax of God's covenant with Israel, and regarded themselves as the people of the new covenant (see, e.g., CD 6:19; 8:21; 19:33; 20:12 [Bar 2.35?; *Jub.* 1:22–24?]). The members of the Qumran community were Jews who interpreted their own experience in terms of their Scriptures and God's covenant with Israel. Their language of the new covenant was not a rejection of the old covenant or a claim that it had been superseded.

Analogous to the hermeneutical perspectives of Qumran, the early Christian community interpreted the event of Jesus of Nazareth as God's definitive revelatory and saving event, saw this Christ event as the fulfillment of God's purposes for the world, God's eschatological renewal of the covenant. Thus the earliest document that reports Jesus' eucharistic words presents him as speaking of his own body and blood as the expression of this new covenant (1 Cor 11:23–26). Covenant language occurs often in the New Testament, with "new covenant" found seven times: Luke 22:20; 1 Cor 11:25; 2 Cor 3:6; Heb 8:8, 13; 9:15; 12:24. The new covenant is often implied, however, even where "new" is not made explicit. Paul, for example, clearly thinks in these categories (e.g., Gal 4), though he uses the phrase "new covenant" only twice (1 Cor 11:25; 2 Cor 3:6). Covenant connotations are also present in the language of kingship (cf. 1.1 above). Jesus spoke often of the kingdom of God, rarely of the covenant.

Two concluding notes

1. Even though the covenant was never a book, but God's saving act that founded a community, we now rightly use "New Testament" to refer to a book, a collection of documents. When the Christian community refers to part of its sacred Scripture as the "New Testament," this is only a shorthand way of saying *the collection of documents that bear authentic witness to the meaning of the Christ event, God's saving act of eschatological renewal of the covenant with Israel.* In the New Testament, "New Covenant/Testament" never refers to a book. This vocabulary began to be used in the late second century (Irenaeus, *Against Heresies* 4.9.1), as the church began to select those documents that bore authentic witness to God's act in Christ. By the early third century, Origen could refer to the "divine Scripture" as composed of the "Old Testament" and the "New Testament" (*De Princip.* 4.11, 16).

2. The preceding discussion should make clear that Christians need not hesitate to use

the terminology of "New Testament" and its corollary "Old Testament" to refer to the two sections of the Christian Bible. The terminology does not imply that the "new" supersedes the "old," or that it is "better" in some relative sense (cf. "old friend" does not refer to one now superseded by some "new friend"). Christians confess that God's act in Jesus Christ is the eschatological event. One way this is expressed is the declaration that God's covenant with Israel has been eschatologically renewed, and that believers in Jesus as God's messiah are incorporated into this covenant by God's gracious act. The church's traditional language of "Old Testament" and "New Testament" is an affirmation that both Testaments have a common origin and center, that the God who definitively acted in Jesus Christ is none other than the God of Israel, the covenant God who is faithful to his promises of eschatological fulfillment. Since this terminology has sometimes been misunderstood to imply supersession or the devaluation of the Old Testament, some contemporary interpreters prefer to use such terms as "Hebrew Bible" for the Old Testament and "First Testament" and "Second Testament" for the two sections of the Christian Bible. While rightly wanting to avoid being offensive, such modern substitutions are themselves problematic: "Hebrew Bible" excludes not only the Aramaic portions of the Jewish Scriptures, but some of the apocryphal/deuterocanonical books, not written in Hebrew but considered to be part of the Old Testament by the majority of Christians in the world. The term "Hebrew Bible" likewise ignores the reality of the Greek Septuagint (LXX) as a parallel version of the Jewish Scriptures for many centuries (see below § 4.3.1). "First/Second Testaments" are subject to the same kind of relativizing misunderstanding as "Old/New." "First" and "second" in biblical terminology are not positioned on a relativizing scale, but "second" means "ultimate," beyond which there cannot be a "third," or "fourth" (e.g., 1 Cor 15:45–47; Heb 8:7; 10:9; Rev 20:6). In Christian faith, the New Testament is not a beta version of the "old," but the omega of which the "old" is the alpha (Rev 1:8; 21:6; 22:13). The texts Christians have traditionally called the Old Testament certainly belong to the Jewish community as sacred Scripture, but in a Christian context, or in the context of the Christian Bible as a whole, to speak of "Jewish Scriptures" seems to deny that the Old Testament is also Christian Scripture—in fact the original and primary Bible of the Christian Church.

1.4 The New Testament as Epistle and Gospel

IN TERMS OF LITERARY GENRE, THE NEW Testament contains only a narrow selection of the types of literature produced in early Christianity (see below §2.1 on the formation of the canon). Early Christians made collections of Jesus' sayings, parables, and miracles; they wrote church constitutions to regulate church order and made lists of church laws; they composed myths explaining the origin of evil in a world presumably created and governed by the one almighty God; they assembled collections of Christian hymns and wisdom sayings. None of these were finally included in the Bible. The New Testament contains only texts related to two broadly defined literary genres, both related to particular people and particular situations: *letters* addressing certain groups of Christians, dealing with particular problems in early Christianity, and *narratives* about particular groups of people. It is important from the outset to see that all the books that made the canonical cut are, in one way or another, *narrative*. The Gospels and Acts are obviously narratives; it is often not noticed that letters, including Revelation, are also a kind of narrative. Letters are a narrative genre that presupposes and projects a narrative world (§10.2.4). All New Testament texts are this-worldly narratives that deal with transcendent events and perspectives. There seems to have been an implicit, intuitive, theological force at work in those movements within

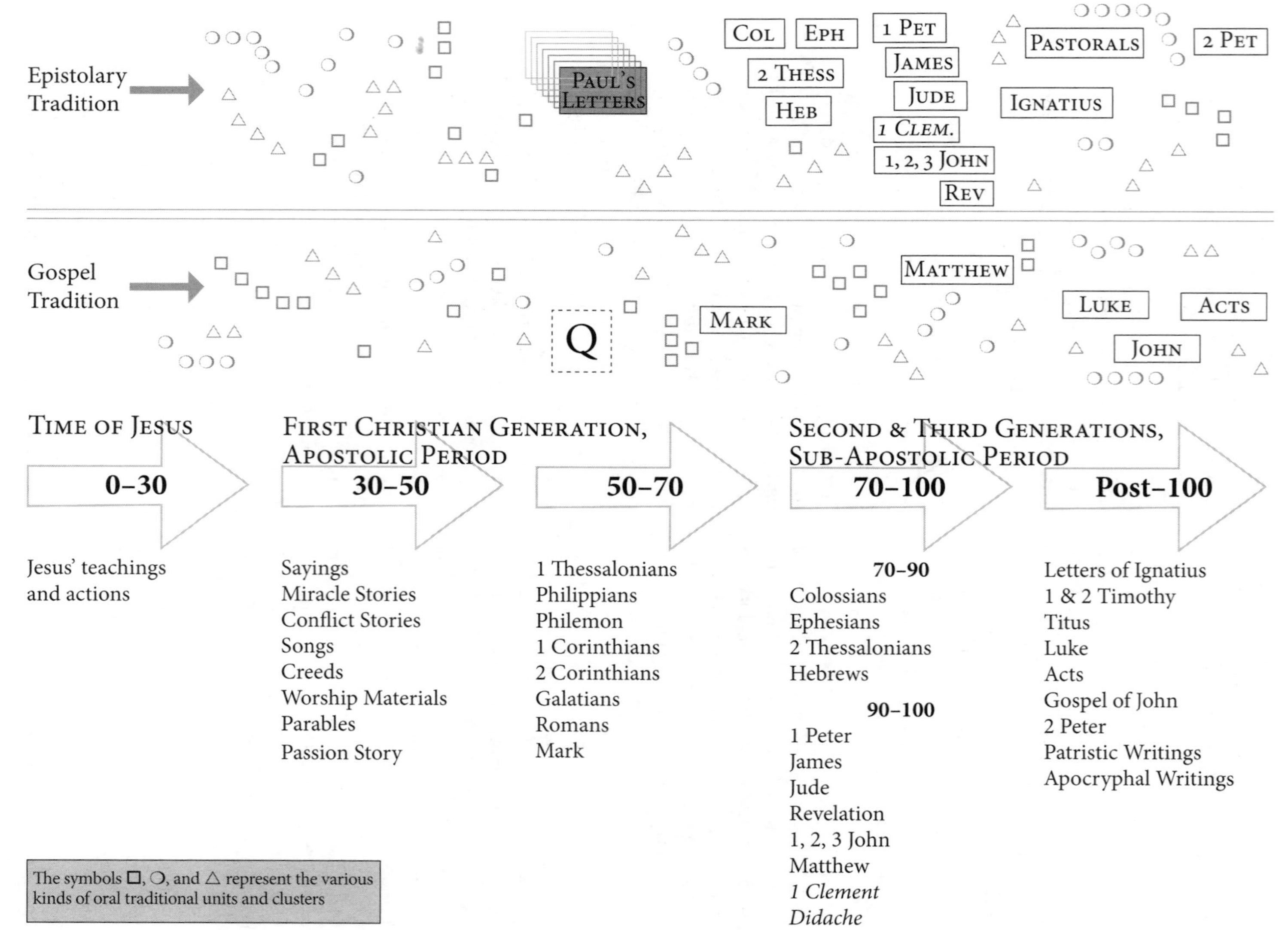

BOX 1: Formation of the New Testament

early Christianity that became the mainstream, a noncoercive force that tended toward the writing of confessional documents of the Christian faith in the narrative mode expressed in only two genres, Letters and Gospels.[2] There was an "epistolary pressure" for the church to adapt writings to the epistolary form (§10.2.1), to confess its faith in God's act in Christ by writing Gospel-like narratives, and finally to accept only such documents into the canonical Scriptures. Believers speak of this theologically as the work of the Holy Spirit (see §§2.2, 5.1.4).

It is historically appropriate and hermeneutically helpful to bring this bipartite, Letter/Gospel structure of the New Testament into sharp focus. This twofold division is represented in our earliest canonical collection, represented in the two codices of the Chester Beatty Papyri 𝔓[45] (containing the Four Gospels and Acts) and 𝔓[46] (containing the Letters of Paul). The church exercised a true intuition and insight when at an early period it designated all liturgical readings from the New Testament as either Epistle or Gospel.

In early Christianity, the two genres traveled in separate channels: the origin and transmission of Gospels (and Acts) were later and different from that of the letters.

Letters were primary, both in origin and collection. One can read all of Matthew–Acts without ever supposing that there was another genre of Christian confession at work in the church, just as one can read all the Epistles with no hint that there are Gospel documents that narrate the "life and teachings of Jesus." The genres did not easily mix. Here are two distinct types of Christology, two different approaches to addressing the meaning of Christian faith and life. In the final phase of New Testament history, the Johannine community was the first to bring Letters and Gospels together, but even there the genres were kept distinct. The Christian community finally united them in one Bible.

1.4.1 The Two Fundamental Genres of New Testament Literature Are Both Narrative Forms

The literary genres appropriate to a historical faith are narrative accounts concerned with concrete events, not philosophical discussions concerned with abstract ideas. The common denominator of Letters and Gospels is that both are narrative forms. This is a fundamentally Jewish mode of theologizing, different from the propositional, discursive thinking expressed in the logic of the Greek world. Both Letters and Gospels project a narrative world larger than the plotted narrative they directly present. New Testament documents address their readers as living their lives within the narrative worlds they project, whether or not the readers see their own lives in this perspective. Narrative implies ethic. The Letter or Gospel challenges its readers to accept the narrative world it projects as the real world, to accept that story as their own story, and to live accordingly. The New Testament does not meet its readers with a moralistic list of "ought" and "should," but with a strange, new world.[3] The structure of the narrative world projected by the New Testament documents constitutes a silent, persistent call for conversion, the reconfiguring of one's own narrative world that makes sense of one's life.

1.5 The New Testament as Narrative: History, Stories, and the Story

AS A BOOK OF FAITH, THE NEW TESTAMENT narrates events in the real world of space and time, understood as God's saving acts in history. The New Testament is a history book in

2. Acts is volume two of a Gospel; Revelation is a letter. All New Testament documents fit within the broad categories of Letter and Gospel. See the introductions to each genre and each book below.

3. Cf. Karl Barth, "The Strange New World within the Bible," in *The Word of God and the Word of Man*, ed. Karl Barth (New York: Harper & Bros., 1957), 28–50.

FIGURE 1: In 1961 Italian archaeologists unearthed a statue of Pontius Pilate in Caesarea, the capital of the Roman province of Judea. PHOTO CREDIT: M. EUGENE BORING.

at least three senses: (1) the central figure of the New Testament is a historical figure; (2) like the Bible as a whole, the New Testament is about this-worldly history; and (3) the Bible projects a macronarrative that embraces its individual stories in a comprehensive whole.

1.5.1 The Central Figure of the New Testament Is a Historical Figure, a Human Being Who Lived and Died in the World of Actual History.

Luke 3:1–2 sets the beginning of his narrative of Jesus' mission in the realities of political history:

> In the fifteenth year of the reign of Emperor Tiberius, when Pontius Pilate was governor of Judea, and Herod was ruler of Galilee, and his brother Philip ruler of the region of Ituraea and Trachonitis, and Lysanias ruler of Abilene, during the high priesthood of Annas and Caiaphas . . .

Jesus was born during the reign of Herod the Great, who had been installed and backed by the Romans. Jesus lived and worked in Galilee under the Roman lackey Herod Antipas, and was executed by Pontius Pilate, the Roman governor of Judea (see fig. 1). Such a narrative projects a different world from "once upon a time . . ."

1.5.2 From Beginning to End, the Bible is about This-worldly History.

The Bible as a whole is not a book of timeless principles, of casuistic law, or otherworldly mythology. The Bible contains laws, wisdom materials, poetry, hymns, and the like, but everything is set in a narrative framework. Thus the Ten Commandments are not presented as abstract laws or ideals to be striven for, but are prefaced with "I am the LORD your God, who brought you out of the land of Egypt, out of the house of slavery" (Exod 20:2). All readers of the Bible know that it is mainly composed of stories: Adam, Eve, and the snake; Cain's murder of Abel; Noah and the flood; Moses and the exodus from Egypt; David and Goliath; Daniel in the lions' den; the baby Jesus and the magi; Jesus healing a blind man; Peter denying Jesus while the rooster crowed; Jesus executed by the Roman authorities; the appearance of the risen Jesus to the women running to tell the disciples on Easter morning; Paul preaching in Athens; Peter miraculously delivered from prison. Not all readers recognize, however, that the Bible not only contains a multitude of stories, but as a whole, from Genesis to Revelation, can be read as one Great Story.

1.5.3 The Bible Projects a Macronarrative that Embraces its Individual Stories in a Comprehensive Whole.

The plethora of local and micronarratives are subsumed under one great metanarrative, a drama in five acts. The biblical narrative begins with the creation of this world, with a pointed lack of interest in what went on in the heavenly world prior to creation, and concludes with the end of this world, but without describing what sort of things will occur in the age to come. Even when "otherworldly" events occur, they occur in this world. The New Testament world includes stories of angels and demons and of the acts of God. But these are acts of God in *this* world, between creation and eschaton, not myths of the goings-on in the transcendent world before, after, and above history. Here is a streamlined, rough-and-ready outline of the encompassing biblical drama (see Box 2).

BOX 2: The Bible as a Historical Narrative in Five Acts

I. ***Creation* (Genesis):** The one God created all that is.

II. ***Covenant* (Exodus–Malachi):** When creation was spoiled by rebellious humanity, God created a people, Israel, to be God's agents and witnesses, and bearers of the promise of God's present-and-future salvation.

III. ***Christ* (Matthew–John):** The definitive event of all history is the act of God, in the person of his Son the Messiah, to accomplish salvation and mediate reconciliation.

IV. ***Church* (Acts–Jude):** God has continued Israel's mission in the church by creating an inclusive community from all nations, to be witnesses and agents of his saving act already accomplished for all people.

V. ***Consummation* (Revelation):** God will bring history to a worthy conclusion, when the creation, which de jure belongs to God's kingdom, will de facto "become the kingdom of our Lord and of his Christ, and he will reign forever and ever" (Rev 11:15).

The New Testament presupposes and retells its own variation(s) of Israel's and Judaism's grand narrative of universal history from creation to eschaton. To say "New *Testament*" (=New *Covenant*) or "Jesus is the *Christ*" is to place each paragraph of its contents within the sweep of this macronarrative.

1.6 For Further Reading

Covenant and New Covenant

Behm, Johannes. "καινός, καινότης, ἀνακαινίζω κτλ. (new, newness, renew)." In *Theological Dictionary of the New Testament*, edited by Gerhard Kittel and Gerhard Friedrich, 3:447–54. Grand Rapids: Eerdmans, 1964–1976.

Brooks, Roger, and John J. Collins, eds. *Hebrew Bible or Old Testament? Studying the Bible in Judaism and*

Christianity. CJA 5. Notre Dame, IN: University of Notre Dame Press, 1990.

Goldingay, John. "Covenant, OT and NT." In *New Interpreter's Dictionary of the Bible*, edited by Katherine Doob Sakenfeld, 767–78. Nashville: Abingdon Press, 2006.

Mendenhall, George E., and Gary A. Herion. "Covenant." In *The Anchor Bible Dictionary*, edited by David Noel Freedman, 1:1179–1202. New York: Doubleday, 1992.

General and Comprehensive Works on the New Testament

Achtemeier, Paul J., Joel B. Green, and Marianne May Thompson. *Introducing the New Testament: Its Literature and Theology*. Grand Rapids: Eerdmans, 2001.

Boring, M. Eugene, and Fred B. Craddock. *The People's New Testament Commentary*. Louisville, KY: Westminster John Knox Press, 2004.

Brown, Raymond E. *An Introduction to the New Testament*. Anchor Bible Reference Library. New York: Doubleday, 1997.

Bultmann, Rudolf. *Theology of the New Testament*. Translated by Kendrick Grobel. 2 vols. New York: Scribner, 1951.

Carson, Donald A., and Douglas J. Moo. *An Introduction to the New Testament*. 2nd ed. Grand Rapids: Zondervan, 2005.

Childs, Brevard S. *The New Testament as Canon: An Introduction*. Philadelphia: Fortress Press, 1984.

deSilva, David A. *An Introduction to the New Testament: Contexts, Methods, and Ministry Formation*. Downers Grove, IL: InterVarsity Press, 2004.

Ellis, E. Earle. *The Making of the New Testament Documents*. Leiden: Brill, 2002.

Holladay, Carl R. *A Critical Introduction to the New Testament*. Nashville: Abingdon Press, 2005.

Johnson, Luke Timothy. *The Writings of the New Testament: An Interpretation*. Rev. ed. Minneapolis: Fortress Press, 1999.

Koester, Helmut. *Introduction to the New Testament*. Vol. 2, *History and Literature of Early Christianity*. Foundations and Facets. Philadelphia: Fortress Press, 1982.

Kümmel, Werner Georg. *Introduction to the New Testament*. Translated by Howard Clark Kee. 2nd ed. Nashville: Abingdon Press, 1975.

Marshall, I. Howard. *New Testament Theology: Many Witnesses, One Gospel*. Downers Grove, IL: InterVarsity, 2004.

Marxsen, Willi. *Introduction to the New Testament: An Approach to Its Problems*. Translated by G. Buswell. Philadelphia: Fortress Press, 1970.

Matera, Frank J. *New Testament Theology: Exploring Diversity and Unity*. Louisville, KY: Westminster John Knox Press, 2007.

Powell, Mark Allen. *Introducing the New Testament: A Historical, Literary, and Theological Survey*. Grand Rapids: Baker Academic, 2009.

Pregeant, Russell. *Engaging the New Testament: An Interdisciplinary Introduction*. Minneapolis: Fortress Press, 1995.

Schneiders, Sandra. *The Revelatory Text: Interpreting the New Testament as Sacred Scripture*. 2nd ed. Collegeville, MN: Liturgical Press, 1999.

Schnelle, Udo. *The History and Theology of the New Testament Writings*. Translated by M. Eugene Boring. Minneapolis: Fortress Press, 1998.

———. *Theology of the New Testament*. Translated by M. Eugene Boring. Grand Rapids: Baker Academic, 2009.

Spivey, Robert A., D. Moody Smith, and C. Clifton Black. *Anatomy of the New Testament*. 6th ed. Minneapolis: Fortress Press, 2010.

Strecker, Georg. *Theology of the New Testament*. Translated by M. Eugene Boring. New York: De Gruyter, 2000.

Wright, N. T. *The New Testament and the People of God*. Vol. 1, *Christian Origins and the Question of God*. Minneapolis: Fortress Press, 1992.

2

Formation: "The New Testament as the Church's Book"

DISCLAIMERS: BY CALLING THE NEW TEStament the church's book, I do not intend anything esoteric, smug, or off-putting; in the first place, I intend only to express a historical reality. The expression is somewhat analogous to referring to the Qur'an as Islam's book, or to the Jones family album as the Joneses' book. It is not necessary to belong to the Islamic community or the Jones family to read their significant texts with insight and appreciation. But Muslims and the Joneses read their books with different eyes than others, and see things there that others do not see. Those who would understand these texts must hear the voices of those who confess them as their own faith. Hearing the confession in its own terms is indispensable to understanding, whether or not interpreters share this confession—though the texts are written by authors who believe they are witnessing to ultimate truth, and call readers to share that confession, written for "insiders" but always indirectly calling "outsiders" to share the "insider" perspective.

By "church" I do not mean any particular institution or denomination, but I do mean the publicly recognizable ecumenical community of Christian faith that exists around the world and through the centuries. I do not mean the individualistic admirers of Jesus or advocates of private "spirituality" who contrast these with "institutionalized religion"—though they too, of course, have every right to study and evaluate the New Testament on their own terms. By the common phrase "the church's book," I do not mean that the New Testament is the church's property and subject to the church's understanding, as if the church can hear from it only that which does not challenge its own dogmas, ideologies, and presuppositions. Nor do I intend to suggest that only those in the Christian community have a right to interpret it.

The New Testament can in fact be legitimately interpreted in a variety of ways. What one gets from it depends to a great extent on what one is looking for. Linguists can study it as representing samples of Hellenistic Greek, analyzing its vocabulary and grammar and locating its various documents at the appropriate place in the development of the Greek language. Sociologists can study the family and social structures reflected in its writings, their power structures, and the various ways first-century Mediterranean communities came to terms with them, as important windows into the Hellenistic world. Historians of religion can examine it for the light it sheds on the status of religious institutions in the first-century Mediterranean world, including the new Christian group. Representatives of various ideologies (e.g., nationalism, cosmopolitanism, racism, antiracism, feminism, antifeminism, militarism, pacifism, communism, capitalism) can comb the New Testament texts for data relevant to their own beliefs, as can advocates of every Christian denomination and sect. The perspectives are overlapping, and some bring to light data that might be missed, important for any understanding of the New Testament. But all bring their own agenda to the text, and none purport to interpret the New Testament in terms of *its* agenda (on "agenda," see below §5.1.4). To interpret the New Testament as the *New Testament* means to attempt to understand it from the point of view of the community for which it became the foundational and normative set of documents that bear authentic witness to the meaning of God's eschatological, covenant-renewing act in Jesus Christ.

No one today receives the documents of the New Testament directly from the hands of the authors. In notes for a 1940 lecture to pastors, Dietrich Bonhoeffer reminded them, "One cannot overlook the reality that between us and the Bible stands the church, a church that has a history."[1] The reader who wants to understand the Bible cannot disdain church history. The New Testament is the church's book in the sense that it has been *written*, *selected*, *edited*, *transmitted*, *translated*, and *interpreted* by the Christian community. These statements need to be grasped as an integrated group and then explored one by one (see Box 3).

BOX 3: The Church's Book

—The New Testament is the church's book in the sense that the church *wrote* it.
—The New Testament is the church's book in the sense that the church *selected* it.
—The New Testament is the church's book in the sense that the church *edited* it.
—The New Testament is the church's book in the sense that the church *preserved* and *transmitted* it.
—The New Testament is the church's book in the sense that the church *translated* it.
—The New Testament is the church's book in the sense that the church *interprets* it.

1. Dietrich Bonhoeffer, *Reflections on the Bible: Human Word and Word of God*, trans. M. Eugene Boring (Peabody, MA: Hendrickson, 2004), 90.

2.1 The New Testament Is the Church's Book in the Sense that the Church *Wrote* It.

JESUS WROTE NOTHING IN THE NEW TEStament, nor is there any suggestion in the Gospels that Jesus instructed his disciples to record his words or deeds. In terms of authorship, the New Testament is not Jesus' book.

Nor is the New Testament the apostles' book. There is a real sense in which the whole of the New Testament is apostolic, in that it represents the faith of the "one holy catholic and apostolic church" of the Nicene Creed. But the documents of the New Testament do not come to us exclusively from the hands of the apostles. Titles of New Testament documents attribute them not only to the apostles Matthew, John, Peter, and Paul, but also to Jesus' brothers who did not belong to the group of the Twelve apostles (James and Jude), and to the nonapostles Mark the companion of Peter and Luke the companion of Paul.

The present titles of all New Testament books were given to them not by their authors but by the later church. In the community of faith, people write anonymously. We do not know, for instance, who wrote most of the Old Testament books, which are anonymous, presented in the name of the community itself, not as the product of an individual author. The New Testament is Jewish on this point, not Greek or Roman, where individual authorship was important for establishing the authority or reputation of a literary work. One-third of New Testament books are anonymous: the four Gospels and Acts, Hebrews, 1–3 John. Of the eighteen books attributed to particular authors, only seven are undisputed. From the time of Jesus to the earliest Gospel's portrayal of his life and teaching, the message from and about Jesus was transmitted not by a few illustrious individuals, but in the worship, preaching, teaching, and life of the community of believers (see below §19.3). Taken as a whole, the New Testament does not represent the product of a few brilliant individual writers, but the faith statements of the Christian community. Said theologically, the New Testament documents derive from the work of the Spirit of God at work in the Christian community as a whole. The New Testament is the church's book because the church wrote it.

2.2 The New Testament Is the Church's Book in the Sense that the Church *Selected* It.

THE CHURCH HAS ALWAYS HAD A BIBLE, but it has not always had a New Testament. The New Testament is the church's book as *part* of the canon of its sacred scripture.[2] The church was born in the matrix of Judaism, which by the first century CE had a solid core of normative documents on the way to becoming a closed, official canon. The first followers of Jesus that became the earliest church found themselves in a community that already reverenced a collection of texts as Holy Scripture. As Christian leaders and teachers composed texts that became authoritative within the church, they were added to the developing canon of Judaism; they did not replace it as an independent Christian canon.

Early Christianity produced much literature, much more than is included in our New Testament. We are aware of at least sixty-three documents that circulated as "Gospels" in the early church, as well as numerous "Acts," "Epistles," and "Apocalypses." This is not new or suppressed information, despite the sensationalizing claims sometimes made about the "lost books of the Bible."[3]

Our New Testament is thus a selection made by the Christian community from a much larger pool of writings. Much of the New Testament was composed by the end of the first century CE, all of it by the middle of the second century. Though functioning as normative texts, the collection did not attain canonical status until generations later. The selection was not firmly fixed until the fourth century CE, and even then the decision was not absolute in all branches of Christianity. At first, it was not clear which authors and documents could be trusted as authentic interpreters of the faith. One thinks of the churches addressed in Revelation at the end of the first century, who had to decide between competing "apostles" and "prophets" (Rev 2:2, 20; 16:13; 18:20; 19:10), or the situation in Corinth, in which the church had to decide whether Paul or his rivals were true apostles representing Jesus (2 Cor 10–13). That we have Revelation and not the writings of John's opponents, that we have Galatians and 2 Corinthians and not the writings of Paul's opponents, shows that the church affirmed and selected these writings of Paul and John.

To read the New Testament is to enter into a decision already made by a particular community of faith. The selection was a gradual process in which some books came to be acknowledged by what became the mainstream of the whole church, and others were neglected or intentionally excluded. The formation of the Christian Bible is illuminated by a sketch of the history of this process.

2.2.1 Historical Sketch

The Jewish Scriptures as the Bible of Earliest Christianity

The church lived for generations without a New Testament, but was never without a Bible. The Christian community began in Judaism and assumed the authority of the Jewish Scriptures from the beginning, as had Jesus. From the beginning, early Christianity assumed without

2. The most significant exponent of this point of view in the last generation was Brevard Childs. A thorough review of Childs's contribution, with bibliography, is provided by Daniel R. Driver, *Brevard Childs, Biblical Theologian: For the Church's One Bible* (Grand Rapids: Baker Academic, 2012).

3. These documents are readily available, with critical introductions. The best collection in English is Wilhelm Schneemelcher, ed., *New Testament Apocrypha*, trans. R. McL. Wilson, 2nd ed., 2 vols. (Louisville, KY: Westminster John Knox Press, 1991).

argument that its own story was in continuity with the story of Israel and that Israel's Scriptures were normative for the life of the church. One of the earliest fragments of Christian tradition, which Paul received from the pre-Pauline church only a few years after Jesus' crucifixion, twice declares that the Christian gospel is "according to the Scriptures" (1 Cor 15:3–5). Marcion's challenge to this in the second century (see below) was considered an aberration, and was rejected by the developing protocatholic church.[4]

The Jewish Scriptures themselves were the result of a long process of selection, so that all the New Testament authors did not necessarily work with the same understanding of which books are to be considered Scripture.[5]

Early Christianity thus lived for more than a century with the Jewish Scriptures as its only Bible. The New Testament as a book is not necessary for the existence of the church, and is not its foundation or constitution. For the first four Christian generations, the church had as its Bible the Jewish Scriptures, which it interpreted in the light of the Christ event, the eschatological renewal of God's covenant with Israel (cf. §1.3 above and §9.2.2 below). The church also had its growing collection of authoritative Christian documents, but these were not placed alongside the Jewish Scriptures as "Old Testament" and "New Testament" until late in the second century. When this did happen, the New Testament did not become *the* canon for the church. The New Testament has always been a part of the Christian Bible only in combination with the Old Testament. In the church, these two collections of writings can never be separated from each other and interpreted independently of one another. In the Christian community, the Old Testament has always been interpreted in the light of the Christ event; the New Testament has always been interpreted in the context of and in continuity with the Old Testament.

Earliest Christian Community

New Testament documents were not available for individual, private perusal, nor were they intended for such reading. The Scriptures were appropriated by being read aloud and heard in the Christian community with one's fellow believers, in the context of worship. One went to church to hear the Bible. This reading-in-worship was part of the selection process, and a criterion for the later formation of the canon.

1 Clement (ca. 95 CE)

Clement, a leader in the Roman church at the end of the first century CE, still reflects the perspective of the New Testament itself. He knows Paul's writings and Hebrews, but reflects no knowledge of the Gospels or Acts, though Mark, and perhaps other Gospels, were in circulation by Clement's time. Yet it is clear that by "Scripture" Clement means the Jewish Scriptures; there is as yet no Christian New Testament. Clement cites Romans, 1 Corinthians, and Hebrews, but never as "Scripture."

2 Peter and the Pastorals (ca. 100–150 CE)

Second Peter, among the latest New Testament documents to be written (ca. 130 CE; see below §18.3), seems to place (some of) Paul's letters on a par with "the other scriptures" (3:16). This statement makes clear that by this

4. The phrase "catholic church" was first used in extant literature about 110 CE by Ignatius of Antioch, *Smyrneans* 8:1. The group of churches that became "mainline Christianity" in the second century called itself "catholic" (="universal"). I use "protocatholic" for this emerging mainstream.

5. Our New Testament documents make several citations from and allusions to "Scriptures" not finally adopted as canonical in Judaism, and thus not appearing in the Christian Old Testament. A complete list is found in Barbara Aland, Kurt Aland, Eberhard Nestle, and Erwin Nestle, eds., *Novum Testamentum Graece*, 27th ed. (Stuttgart: Deutsche Bibelgesellschaft, 1994), 800–806. As examples, see Matt 2:23; Luke 11:49; John 7:38; 12:34; 19:28; 20:9; 1 Cor 2:9; Jas 4:5; Jude 14–16.

time Paul's writings were considered authoritative in some streams of early Christianity outside the Pauline tradition itself. The author of 2 Peter seems to have a "canonical" interest, since he purges his sources of statements that could rank *1 Enoch* as "Scripture" (cf. Jude 11–14; 2 Pet 2:14–17). First Timothy 5:18 cites the saying of Jesus in Matthew 10:10//Luke 10:7 along with Deuteronomy 25:4, and may include both under the rubric of "Scripture."

Justin (ca. 150 CE)

Justin Martyr, a Christian philosopher from Samaria who taught in Rome about the middle of the second century (martyred 165 CE), cites Scripture often. Each of his seventy-six explicit citations or allusions refers to the Old Testament as his written authority. He understands them allegorically as teaching the doctrines of the Christian faith, for the Logos, the Word of God as the preexistent Christ, speaks in them (e.g., *1 Apol.* 36–38). He establishes points of Christian doctrine, and even events in the life of Jesus, on the basis of (his interpretation of) the Old Testament, not from Christian writings.[6] Justin is acquainted with several Christian documents, which he regards as important and authoritative. He indicates that the Gospels ("Memoirs of the Apostles") were read in Christian worship alongside "the Prophets," that is, the Jewish Scriptures (*1 Apol.* 66–67). Yet he has no list of authoritative Christian writings, and gives no indication that there is anything like a "New Testament" as part of the Christian Bible.

Marcion (ca. 150 CE)

Marcion too was a teacher in the Roman church, a contemporary of Justin. He understood himself to be a radical follower of the Pauline gospel of grace, which compelled him to reject the God of the Jewish Scriptures as a different God from the God of Jesus and Paul. He did not accept the Jewish Scriptures as authoritative for Christians, but he did not reject the concept of sacred Scripture as such. Some Christian writings had been steadily growing in authority (see above), without having their official status clarified and designated. Marcion was apparently the first to make a particular set of Christian writings the norm of Christian faith. His twofold canon was the "Gospel" (a form of the Gospel of Luke) and the "Apostle" (ten Pauline letters, without the Pastorals or Hebrews). This bipartite canon corresponded to the Torah and Prophets considered Scripture by Judaism and the church. Like them, it consisted of narrative, recounting the saving acts of God (Torah/Gospels), and discursive documents delineating the meaning of the saving event and the human response it requires (Prophets/Epistles). The later catholic church was basically to accept Marcion's understanding of the canonical shape of the church's New Testament, Gospel and Epistle.

Marcion's influence was widespread. One aspect of catholic Christianity's response was to reaffirm the role of the Old Testament as Christian Scripture within the church, and to clarify the status of Christian documents that had long been considered authoritative. *In the wake of Marcion, the church discovered that it had a canon, but rejected Marcion's canon as too narrow.* The Christian Bible includes, and must include, the Old Testament. The Christian Bible includes, and must include, documents that bear authentic witness to the meaning of God's eschatological renewal of the covenant, the New Testament. This New Testament includes, and must include, more than one Gospel, and a plurality of Epistles representing more than one apostle. The church's intuition—believers would say "guided by the Holy Spirit"— constituted a limited pluralism as normative. More than one thing is acceptable, but not just anything. The remaining issue was to determine the boundaries of this pluralistic canon.

6. E.g., he knows that the colt on which Jesus rode into Jerusalem was found "tied to a vine" not because this detail occurs in any Gospel, but from Gen 49:11 (*1 Apol.* 32).

Irenaeus (ca. 180 CE)

The line of development leads directly from Marcion to Irenaeus, bishop of Lyons in the last quarter of the second century. His multivolume *Refutation and Overthrow of Knowledge Falsely So Called* (*Against Heresies*) is no longer content to defend orthodox faith on the basis of the Old Testament alone. He distinguishes the Old and New Testaments, regarding both as Christian Scripture. In defense of the catholic faith he quotes, interprets, and appeals to New Testament documents, explicitly naming them, defending their authenticity, and arguing that they are normative for Christian faith. For Irenaeus, the church already has a canonical core accepted by all catholic Christians—four Gospels and Acts, plus the letters of Paul—but its edges are not firm, and its authority is far from universally acknowledged. Irenaeus has a "New Testament," but no fixed list.

Gospels, Pauline Letters, Acts and Catholic Letters as Three Separate Preliminary Collections Later United

We ought not to suppose that the canon was formed on one great day when some pope, bishop, or council chose, from the vast sea of early Christian writings, the twenty-two letters and five narratives that became the twenty-seven books of the New Testament canon. The Pauline letters were the first to be collected and circulated, apparently as a corpus of seven letters, or letters to seven churches. With the later inclusion of secondary Pauline writings and Hebrews, the Pauline corpus became a fourteen-letter authoritative collection. The use of seven and its multiples is not accidental, but reflects the symbolic meaning of seven as "complete."

As a counterpart and complement to this exclusively Pauline collection of fourteen letters, a collection of seven Catholic Letters was made that included the letters of the three "pillar apostles" James, Peter, and John (see Gal 2:6, 9), framed by the letters of James and Jude, the brothers of Jesus, all presumably representing the Jerusalem Christianity in tension with Paul. The collection was assumed to be composed by authors who, unlike Paul, had known the earthly Jesus. This collection was later prefaced by the book of Acts, in which Peter and Paul are two complementary leaders of early Christianity. Still later, this fourfold Gospel collection, which had a separate history, was combined with the two epistolary collections to form the New Testament canon.

Muratorian "Canon" (ca. 200 CE?)

In 1740 a fragment from an ancient Christian list of accepted books was discovered embedded in a codex from the seventh or eighth century CE. Until recently, most scholars were convinced that the fragment comes from Rome, about 170–200 CE. An alternative view argues the list derives from fourth-century Eastern Christianity.[7] The list begins in mid-sentence, and its abrupt conclusion may mean that the ending is lost as well. Since Luke is the first Gospel mentioned (as "the third book of the Gospel"), the initial sentence fragment apparently referred to Matthew and Mark. The list continues with John, Acts, thirteen letters of Paul (excluding Hebrews), Jude, 1 and 2 John, the Wisdom of Solomon, and the Apocalypses of John and Peter (with the comment that not everyone accepts them). There is no reference to James, 1 and 2 Peter, or 3 John. Gnostic,

7. See, e.g., A. C. Sundberg Jr., "Canon Muratori: A Fourth-Century List," *Harvard Theological Review* 66 (1973): 1–41. Sundberg's arguments are effectively met by Everett Ferguson, "Canon Muratori: Date and Provenance," Studia Patristica 17, pt. 2, ed. Elizabeth A. Livingstone (Oxford Pergamon, 1982): 677–83. According to the careful study of Peter Lampe, the extant Latin translation may have been made later than the third century and outside Rome, but it is clearly a translation of a Greek text made in Rome before 200 CE (Peter Lampe, *From Paul to Valentinus: Christians at Rome in the First Two Centuries*, trans. Michael Steinhauser; ed. Marshall D. Johnson [Minneapolis: Fortress Press, 2003], 145).

Marcionite, or Montanist writings are categorically rejected.

Eusebius (ca. 325 CE)

Eusebius (*Hist. eccl.* 3.25) distinguishes four classes of Christian writings for which normative claims had been made:

1. "Recognized" (*homologoumena*, "confessed" by the catholic church as representing Christian truth): Four Gospels, Acts, Paul's Epistles (no number named), and one Epistle each bearing the name of Peter and John. Eusebius notes that some also place Revelation in this group.
2. "Disputed" (*antilegomena*, "spoken against" by some and accepted by some): James, Jude, 2 Peter, 2 and 3 John.
3. "Spurious" (*notha*, "not genuine"): *Acts of Paul*, *Shepherd of Hermas*, *Apocalypse of Peter*, *Epistle of Barnabas*, the *Didache*. Eusebius indicates that some place Revelation and the *Gospel of the Hebrews* here. This is a somewhat peculiar and imprecise category, containing books considered orthodox but still not canonical, showing that Eusebius and early Christianity did not consider the emerging canon to include all that was worth reading.
4. "Heretical" (*hairetikos*, i.e., divisive, representing another faith than that of the catholic church): As samples of a larger group he names the *Gospels of Peter*, *Thomas*, and *Matthias*, the *Acts of Andrew*, and the *Acts of John*.

In Eusebius's day, at the time of the legalization of Christianity and the Council of Nicaea, the church throughout the empire already had virtually the same collection of authoritative documents, but some books remained disputed. Hebrews was early "recognized" in the East, but continued to be "disputed" in the West; the opposite situation prevailed for Revelation: the Western churches accepted it early, but it continued to be disputed in the East for generations.

Codex Alexandrinus (ca. 400 CE)

This major manuscript of the whole Bible is a codex (bound book) that includes all the books of the present New Testament canon, as well as *1 and 2 Clement*, books included by numerous Coptic manuscripts, and a Syriac manuscript as late as the twelfth century.

Codex Sinaiticus (ca. 350 CE)

This codex, a well-written parchment manuscript of both the Old Testament and the New Testament, represents the Bible of some large church about the middle of the fourth century. It is one of our major witnesses to the text of the New Testament. The New Testament contains the standard twenty-seven books, plus the *Epistle of Barnabas* and the *Shepherd of Hermas*, with no indication that the latter two belong to a separate category. Hebrews is located between 2 Thessalonians and 1 Timothy.

Athanasius (367 CE)

The bishop of Alexandria followed the local tradition of writing, shortly after Epiphany, a Festal Letter to the Egyptian churches and monasteries informing them of the date of Easter for that year, which thus also fixed the dates of other Christian festivals. Such letters were the occasions for other edifying instructions. In Athanasius's Thirty-Ninth Festal Letter (367 CE), he gave his episcopal declaration on the list of canonical documents in the Christian Bible. His list of New Testament books is—for the first time in extant records—exactly the same as our present New Testament. Both the Old Testament and the New Testament have a penumbra, a list of books valuable for edification but not considered canonical.[8] But the list

8. For the Old Testament: Wisdom of Solomon, Wisdom of Ben Sirach, Esther, Judith, and Tobit. For the New Testament: *Didache* and *Shepherd of Hermas*.

of canonical books themselves appears crisp and firmly established. Only minor variations persisted after Athanasius.

This brief survey has illustrated (1) that it was important in the life of the early church to establish the canon; (2) that this was a gradual process; and (3) that it was never completed consistently and absolutely. Each of these points has its own theological significance. What does it mean for the Christian community to have a canon? If it is so important, why isn't the canonical list clear and consistent?

2.2.2 Theological Reflections

What Does It Mean to Have Such a Historically Ambiguous Canon?

This question must be preceded by a consideration of what it means to have a canon at all. "Canon" comes from the Greek κανών (*kanōn*), itself a loanword from Hebrew קָנֶה (*qaneh*). Both words mean "reed," and were used in the sense of "stick," "walking stick" (cf. Eng. "cane," from the same root), and especially "measuring stick," "yardstick," "ruler." The canon is thus the norm by which other things are measured. To claim that the biblical documents are canonical does not mean that all divine revelation is contained within them, but that this collection of documents is the normative collection by which other claims are measured. To have a canon means that the Christian community acknowledges it has been given a norm for its own testimony to the faith.

Were There Criteria Used in "Closing" the Canon?

The canon gradually emerged, and the church found itself gradually acknowledging that some documents functioned as authority for what could be counted as God's revelation, and other documents could not be so regarded. This process was not random or arbitrary. But did the church apply specific criteria to determine its selection?

1. *Inspiration*. The church has always regarded the Spirit of God as at work in the process by which its Bible came to be. The later church regarded the canonical books as inspired by the Holy Spirit in a way that noncanonical books were not. However, this is an ex post facto judgment about books that had already been acknowledged as canonical, not a criterion by which canonicity could be determined in the first place.

2. *Liturgical reception by major churches*. Documents were accepted as canonical partly on the basis that leading Christian communities had adopted them as authoritative documents to be read in worship. In the synagogues from which earliest Christianity originated, the reading from specific documents in the worship service affirmed them as Holy Scripture. The earliest churches not only continued this practice, but alongside "the Law and the Prophets" began to read the letters from Paul and other Christian leaders, which were written for this purpose. At first, such letters were not considered on a par with Scripture, but represented the homily or "word of exhortation" that would have been delivered by an apostolic preacher, had he or she been present. After the apostolic period this practice continued, and Christian documents read aloud in worship began to be accepted as on a par with Scripture (see 2 Pet 3:15–16). It was then that the issue of which documents legitimately could be read as part of the Christian liturgy became an important issue. This distinction continues in the contemporary church. Edifying texts (e.g., Abraham Lincoln's *Gettysburg Address*, Martin Luther King Jr.'s "Letter from Birmingham Jail") might be read in a worship service, but not from the lectern as Holy Scripture, as the norm and basis for the church's proclamation. For us, the question of which books can be regarded as Scripture is settled by looking at a printed Bible. Any Bible that has "extra" books printed would be immediately

obvious. For the early Christians, "publication" was a matter of books being read in the common worship. This was not done casually. Today, we *look* between the covers of a *book*. The earliest Christians *listened* for what was read in *church*.

3. *Date, purported or real.* In general, earlier books were considered to be more authoritative than later ones. To be accepted as canonical, a document had to have some claim to mediate the meaning of the original revelatory events. A document known to have been written in the third century, for example, could never have been acknowledged as canonical. The Muratorian Canon respected the *Shepherd of Hermas* as valuable, but not canonical, because "it was written in our own time." Yet date was not the determining criterion, as if all the documents finally accepted as canonical were earlier than all those rejected. *First Clement*, for example, is almost certainly earlier than 2 Peter, yet the former never became canonical, while the latter did.

4. *Authorship, purported or real.* It is not the case that documents of apostolic authorship were accepted and documents not written by apostles were rejected. On any understanding of authorship, the church accepted into its canon documents for which apostolic authorship was not claimed (Mark, Luke, Acts). Presumed apostolic authorship was validated by the theological content of the document, not vice versa. In the late second century Serapion, bishop of Antioch, heard that the *Gospel of Peter* was being read in the church at Rhossus, in his diocese. Serapion registered no objection, since he had never read the *Gospel of Peter*. Upon visiting the congregation and learning the contents of the document purportedly written by the apostle Peter, he rejected it on the basis of its theology, without raising the question of authorship per se. His judgment was that since its content did not represent the apostolic faith, it was not by Peter (Eusebius, *Hist. eccl.* 6.12).

5. *Theological adequacy.* "Authorship" was thus a designation, conscious or not, for the church's judgment as to whether the document in question represented the apostolic faith, that is, its theological adequacy as an interpretation of the meaning of the Christ event. Attribution or denial of apostolic authorship was not primarily a historical claim, but a theological one. In the case of Hebrews, for example, despite initial reservations in the Western churches, the document was finally accepted on the grounds that the ecumenical church acknowledged its implicit claim to communicate the word of God and to represent the apostolic faith.[9]

These developments in the final stages of the canonizing process are not merely the church's defense mechanism. The canon was not formed only as a reaction to Marcion, Montanus, and other movements judged later to be heretical. The formation of the canon was not primarily reactive, but proactive, as the church sought for adequate means to express its own developing faith. The fixing of the canon in the fourth century represents the culmination of the struggle already begun in the first century to discern true from false apostles. The canon is thus one manifestation of the "one, holy, catholic, apostolic church" affirmed in the Nicene Creed about the same time as the final defining of the canon.

The Christian community had more or less intuitive reasons for accepting some books and rejecting others (theologically said: the *sensus fidei* of the church as it makes its journey through history under the guidance of the Holy Spirit). In establishing the canon, the church recognized that it was grasped by the Word of God and the understanding of the Christian faith that came through these documents, and that it had no higher "criteria" by which to

9. Cf. Luther's often-cited dictum, "Whatever does not teach Christ [*was Christum treibet*] is not apostolic, even though St. Peter or St. Paul does the teaching. Again, whatever preaches Christ would be apostolic, even if Judas, Annas, Pilate, and Herod were doing it" (cited from Martin Luther in Heinrich Bornkamm and Karin Bornkamm, *Luthers Vorreden zur Bibel* [Frankfurt am Main: Insel, 1983], 216–17).

prove to itself or to outsiders that some books belonged "in" and others remained "out."[10]

This in turn means that, although there has never been an official action that closed the canon, the canon is by definition closed. To speak of reopening the canon implies that we claim to have in hand criteria by which to judge that some books should be added (and that some present ones should be removed). This would mean that our own criteria, not the Bible (either in present or projected form) function for us as canon. As the apostles are a closed circle, so the canon is a closed book. The New Testament canon bears witness to the apostolic faith. The apostolic faith is the canonical faith. The New Testament is the church's book in the sense that the church selected it.

2.3 The New Testament Is the Church's Book in the Sense that the Church *Edited* It.

THE PRESENT FORM OF THE NEW TESTAMENT is an anthology composed of twenty-seven documents written over a period of about a hundred years in a variety of locations in the Mediterranean world. This has profound implications for interpretation. When reading a letter of Paul, for instance, we can only read it as part of a collection, selected and edited by the Christian community, which is very different from the situation of its first readers. The New Testament did not come together by itself, but is the result of an editorial (redactional) process. What is involved in editing such a book?

1. *Collection and copying*. The scattered documents were at first collected into small collections. Paul's letters were the first to be collected. Churches such as Corinth would already have more than one letter of Paul's, and would be aware that he had written to other churches. Churches in the Pauline tradition came to regard all Paul's letters as addressed not only to their original addressees, but to the wider church (see 1 Cor 1:1–2; Col 4:16). Marcion's writings indicate that by about 140 in Rome, ten Pauline letters were known as a collection. The Muratorian Canon, probably also representing the Roman church about 200 CE, includes the Pastorals, making a Pauline collection of thirteen letters. The papyrus codex 𝔓[46] shows that by about 200 a codex of Pauline letters was circulating containing all the traditional Pauline letters except the Pastorals. Our present collection is the end product of a process that included smaller prior collections: the Pauline Letters, the Gospels, the Catholic Letters (prefaced by Acts).

2. *Labels, titles, and concluding notes*. The documents were originally without titles. In the process of collection and editing, the documents were given titles that may or may not represent original authorship, readership, and literary genre. The author of the Gospel of Mark, for instance, begins at 1:1 with his own title, just as Matthew 1:1 represents the original author's title. The titles—"According to Mark," "According to Matthew," with their elaborations such as "The Gospel according to Saint Matthew"—were added in the process of editing and canonization. Concluding "amen," benedictions, and notes about the writing of the document may sometimes have been added to individual writings in the process of combining them into an anthology. This is often suggested, for example, concerning Romans 16:25–27.

3. *Order*. Someone, or some group, placed the books in their present order beginning with Matthew and ending with Revelation. All known manuscripts of the whole New Testament begin with the Gospels and have Revelation at or near the end, but otherwise there is considerable variety. Both Gospels and Epistles are preserved in a variety of orders. The present

10. Cf. Karl Barth, *Church Dogmatics*, I/1, *The Doctrine of the Word of God*, trans. G. T. Thompson (Edinburgh: T. & T. Clark, 1963), 111–24, and Luke Timothy Johnson's "Canonical Theses," in "The Authority of the New Testament in the Church: A Theological Reflection," in Charles R. Blaisdell, ed., *Conservative Moderate Liberal: The Biblical Authority Debate* (St. Louis: CBP Press, 1990), 87–118.

order of the Pauline letters is determined by their relative length, with letters to churches preceding letters to individuals. Though Luke and Acts represent two volumes of a single work, Acts was early separated from Luke and became the initial narrative framework for the collection of the Catholic Epistles. In the formation of the whole New Testament from smaller collections, Acts remained separated from Luke and became the transition narrative to the epistolary literature as a whole. While many ancient manuscripts, but not all, have something like the present order of books, the first canonical list that agrees with our present New Testament lists the books in a different order. Through the centuries, there have been only minor variations in the order of New Testament books.

4. *Editorial combinations*. It is likely that either prior to or in the process of their collection, some letters or letter fragments were editorially combined to form our present letters. Many scholars believe, for example, that our present 2 Corinthians is composed of more than one letter; a smaller number argue the same for Philippians (see introductions to 2 Corinthians and Philippians).

5. *Glosses and annotations*. The collectors and editors made explanatory comments or glosses to make the particular details of the original letters more understandable or more relevant to a wider readership than originally intended, or to harmonize what was said with other documents in the collection (possible examples: 1 Cor 1:2b; 14:34–36; Rom 7:25b).

6. *Interpolations*. More extensive additions to the original documents, called interpolations, may have been made in the process of editing. For example, 2 Corinthians 6:14–7:1 is sometimes regarded as a post-Pauline addition that became a part of the letter at the point when it was edited into the Pauline corpus.[11]

7. *Word, verse, and chapter divisions*. The original authors did not write in chapters and verses; these formal markers were later placed in the text to facilitate reference. In the fourth century, Bishop Eusebius devised a numbering system of dividing the pericopes (paragraphs) in the Gospels to facilitate reference and comparison; his numbers are found in the margins of many later manuscripts, and still indicated in some printed editions of the Greek New Testament. Sometime after the fourth century, divisions somewhat corresponding to later chapter divisions and lectionary sections were marked. It was not until the early thirteenth century, however, that Stephen Langdon, archbishop of Canterbury, made our present chapter divisions. Since they often do not come at appropriate points in the structure of the text, and since he is reported to have done some of the work while on a trip, presumably on horseback, it has been suggested that some of the present chapter divisions are the result of marking the text while bumping along in the saddle. The 1551 edition printed by Robert Stephanus introduced the present verse divisions (adopted for the first time by an English translation in the 1560 Geneva Bible)—again not always corresponding to the literary structure of the text.

It is not so well understood that not only chapter and verse divisions, but sentence and even word divisions, are not original but are editorial decisions made much later. Our earliest manuscripts are without accents, punctuation marks, or spaces between the words, as were the original texts. So long as the original Greek of the texts continued to be a living language and the mother tongue of the reader who was interior to both the language of the text and its meaning, this rarely presented a problem. Modern native speakers of English, for example, have little difficulty in correctly understanding

11. That interpolations exist in the present form(s) of the New Testament is almost universally acknowledged. The extent of such interpolations, and of our ability to identify them, is a disputed point among critical interpreters. See William O. Walker Jr., *Interpolations in the Pauline Letters*, JSNTSup 213 (Sheffield: Sheffield Academic, 2001).

a text such as the following, printed in the style of our oldest Greek manuscripts:

> TWINKLETWINKLELITTLES
> TARHOWIWONDERWHATYO
> UAREUPABOVETHEWORLDSO
> HIGHLIKEADIAMONDINT
> HESKY

As long as the reader already knows the content, "what the text is supposed to say" is clear because he or she belongs to the community in which the text is living tradition. Even in such situations, however, there is sometimes ambiguity and the possibility of misunderstanding: SHEISNOWHERE can be read more than one way.

Sometimes differences in English translations are the result of different editorial decisions on how the letters of the Greek manuscripts should be divided into words, or how they are to be punctuated (e.g., John 1:3–4). These manuscripts had already been edited when they became the basis for modern printed editions of "the" Greek New Testament. We thus do not and cannot receive New Testament texts from the hands of their original authors in their original form; we receive them in an edited form from the hands of the church. Who were these "editors" responsible for the formation of the New Testament as one book? They are entirely anonymous; we do not know the name of a single individual who contributed to this process. Many scholars believe there is good evidence that already in the New Testament period there were such groups as a "Pauline school," a "Matthean scribal community," and a "Johannine school" that cultivated the developing tradition and played a role in the formation and editing of the documents that eventually became our New Testament (see the introductions to Matthew, the deuteropauline letters, and the Johannine texts below).

2.4 For Further Reading

Gamble, Harry Y. *Books and Readers in the Early Church: A History of Early Christian Texts*. New Haven, CT: Yale University Press, 1995.

———. *The New Testament Canon: Its Making and Meaning*. Philadelphia: Fortress Press, 1985.

Knox, John. *Marcion and the New Testament: An Essay in the Early History of the Canon*. Chicago: University of Chicago Press, 1942.

McDonald, Lee Martin. *The Formation of the Christian Biblical Canon*. Revised and expanded edition. Peabody, MA: Hendrickson, 1995.

McDonald, Lee Martin, and James A. Sanders, eds. *The Canon Debate*. Peabody, MA: Hendrickson, 2002.

Meade, D. G. *Pseudonymity and Canon: An Investigation into the Relationship of Authorship and Authority in Jewish and Earliest Christian Tradition*. WUNT 39. Tübingen: Mohr, 1986.

Metzger, Bruce M. *The Canon of the New Testament: Its Origin, Development, and Significance*. Oxford: Oxford University Press, 1987.

Miller, John W. *The Origins of the Bible: Rethinking Canon History*. New York: Paulist Press, 1994.

Schneemelcher, Wilhelm, ed. *New Testament Apocrypha*. 2nd ed. 2 vols. Louisville, KY: Westminster John Knox Press, 1991.

von Campenhausen, Hans. *The Formation of the Christian Bible*. Translated by John Austin Baker. London: Adam & Charles Black, 1972.

3

Textual Criticism: From Manuscripts to Electronic Text

THE NEW TESTAMENT IS THE CHURCH'S book in the sense that the church *preserved* and *transmitted* it.

3.1 Materials for Reconstructing the New Testament Text

NO ORIGINAL DOCUMENT (TECHNICAL term "autograph") of any New Testament writing has been preserved. The oldest extant fragment of a New Testament document is Papyrus 52 ($\mathfrak{P}^{52}$), a tiny (2.5″ × 3.5″) remnant of a papyrus codex containing John 18:31–33 on the obverse and 18:37–38 on the reverse side, copied between 125 and 175 CE.[1]

This is our only fragment of a manuscript of the New Testament certainly from the second century, with six more being dated about 200, and twenty-eight from the third century. The majority of our manuscripts are from the fourth century and later. We have a rich treasure of ancient manuscripts of the New Testament from which our present text is reconstructed. Of the countless manuscripts of the Greek New Testament that existed in antiquity, more than 5,000 Greek manuscripts have survived the ravages of time and persecution. Most of these are only fragments, while others contain the complete text. In addition, there exist thousands of manuscripts of early versions in a variety of ancient languages into which the Greek texts had been translated, and thousands of quotations of the New Testament from patristic writers. This is far more material than is available for any other ancient author. We have only a few hundred ancient copies of Homer's *Iliad*, and the first six books of Tacitus's *Annals* are dependent on a single manuscript. The data base for reconstructing the text of the New Testament may be summarized as follows:

127 papyri	mostly fragmentary	2nd to 8th century
320 uncials (majuscules = capital letters)	mostly fragmentary; some are whole Bibles	4th to 15th century
2,903 cursive (minuscule = small letters)	many fragmentary; often whole books or whole Bible	9th–18th century
2,445 lectionaries	sections arranged for liturgical reading	4th–13th century, mostly late

1. Previously often dated "ca. 125 CE," this fragment can no longer be confidently dated so early. Ca. 150 is more probable, as late as 175 quite possible. See discussion and bibliography in Udo Schnelle, *Das Evangelium nach Johannes*, 3rd rev. ed., THKNT 4 (Leipzig: Evangelische Verlagsanstalt, 2004), 8, and D. C. Parker, *Codex Sinaiticus: The Story of the World's Oldest Bible* (London: The British Library, 2010), 101.

FIGURE 2: A fragment of a manuscript called Papyrus 52, containing a few lines from the Gospel of John, is the oldest New Testament document ever found. It was copied sometime between 125 and 175 CE. REPRODUCED BY COURTESY OF THE UNIVERSITY LIBRARIAN AND DIRECTOR, THE JOHN RYLANDS LIBRARY, THE UNIVERSITY OF MANCHESTER.

The entire New Testament is found in none of the papyri, only three uncials (א, A, C), and fifty-eight minuscules. Two more uncials and one hundred forty-seven minuscules have the whole New Testament except for Revelation—reflecting the late reception of Revelation into the canon in some circles (see above).

The total of 5,795 Greek manuscripts or fragments thereof is amplified by more than 10,000 manuscripts in Latin, Coptic, Syriac, Armenian, Georgian, Ethiopic, Gothic, Slavonic, and other languages. Greek had been the language of the New Testament world, but by the end of the second century, New Testament documents were being translated into other languages. The translations thus sometimes represent an earlier form of the Greek text on which they were based (technical term *Vorlage*, exemplar) than surviving Greek manuscripts. In addition, there are thousands of quotations of the Greek New Testament in the writings of the church fathers, again sometimes reflecting a different and earlier Greek text than our extant manuscripts. Unfortunately, however, we do not have the original text of any of the translations or of the patristic writings, each of which must be reconstructed on the basis of its own textual history.

The academic discipline devoted to the study of the available manuscripts and the texts they contain, the history of the transmission of these texts, and the attempts to establish the earliest recoverable text is called *textual criticism*. Since the nineteenth century, textual scholars ("text critics") have traditionally divided the mass of materials into categories or families or stemma representing the patterns of textual variations they manifest and their presumed genealogical relationships. Most of the later manuscripts, which had been somewhat standardized into a full text incorporating many later readings now known not to be original, are called the *Koine* ("common," also called *Syrian*, *Byzantine*, *Imperial*, or *Majority* text type). The pattern represented by the great uncials from the fourth and fifth centuries CE, now deemed one of the most reliable text types, is called *Alexandrian* (or *Hesychian*). B. F. Westcott and F. J. A. Hort, pioneer textual scholars of the nineteenth century, designated this text type as *Neutral* because they believed it was relatively uncontaminated and free of theological tendentious readings. The *Western* text type was so designated because it was often represented by quotations in Western church fathers, but it is now known that it was widespread. It is represented especially by Codex Bezae, some Old Latin (pre-Vulgate), Syriac, and Armenian translations, as well as quotations in Western church fathers (Cyprian,

Augustine). Some scholars have identified a Caesarean text type, and with less confidence, a Jerusalem text. The identification of text types is a very specialized and complex discipline. Only the *Alexandrian, Koine, and Western* types are now generally accepted. We now know that there are no pure text types, but that there has been much cross-fertilization among the postulated types. Most manuscripts have a checkered ancestry rather than representing one pure type. Each postulated type includes both earlier and later readings. Some of the more important Greek manuscripts for reconstructing the New Testament text:[2]

— $\mathfrak{P}^{45}$ and $\mathfrak{P}^{46}$ The *Chester Beatty papyri* are in the Chester Beatty Library, Dublin, the Austrian National Library, Vienna, and the University of Michigan Library at Ann Arbor. $\mathfrak{P}^{45}$ is from the early third century and $\mathfrak{P}^{46}$ is even earlier, about 200 CE. $\mathfrak{P}^{45}$ contains parts of all the Gospels and Acts, with a mixture of Alexandrian, Caesarean, and Western readings. This is our oldest manuscript representing a collection of Gospels. $\mathfrak{P}^{46}$ contains the Pauline letters (including Hebrews, which it places immediately after Romans), but breaks off at 1 Thessalonians, and is thus missing 2 Thessalonians, Philemon, and the Pastorals. This is our oldest manuscript of a Pauline collection.

— $\mathfrak{P}^{52}$ The *Rylands papyrus* is our oldest extant fragment of a New Testament document (see above). It was rediscovered and published in 1935.

— $\mathfrak{P}^{66}$, $\mathfrak{P}^{75}$ *Bodmer Papyri II, XIV, XV* are in the Bodmer Library in Geneva. $\mathfrak{P}^{66}$ contains John 1:1–21:9 with lacunae; $\mathfrak{P}^{75}$ Luke 3:18–18:18; 22:4–24:53 with lacunae; John 1:1–15:8 with lacunae. $\mathfrak{P}^{66}$ is dated about 200, $\mathfrak{P}^{75}$ from the early third century. The Bodmer Papyri were rediscovered only in the 1950s, and confirmed that the Alexandrian text type represented by א and B (fourth century) was not the result of fourth-century editing, but represents an earlier text type. Here and elsewhere in this discussion, the difference between the date of a *manuscript* and the date of the *text* it contains must be kept in mind. While an early manuscript cannot have a late form of the text, a relatively late manuscript can represent an early form of the text, if the exemplar from which it was copied was early.

— א or 01 *Codex Sinaiticus* This manuscript is named from the monastery at Mt. Sinai where Constantine von Tischendorf rediscovered it in his visits of 1844 and 1859. He designated it by the first letter of the Hebrew alphabet א (*alef*) to signify the importance he attached to it (A was already taken). It contains both the LXX and New Testament. The manuscript is on parchment, beautifully printed, and in the judgment of most scholars represents one of the most accurate witnesses to the original text. Copied in the fourth century CE, it is the earliest extant manuscript that contains all the present books of the New Testament; it also includes the *Epistle of Barnabas* and the *Shepherd of Hermas*, with no indication that they are not part of the canonical New Testament. Codex Sinaiticus is now generally available in a beautifully printed facsimile edition reproducing high-definition photographs of the original manuscript (Peabody, MA: Hendrickson Publishers, 2010) and can be examined online at codexsinaiticus.org.

— B or 03 *Codex Vaticanus* This manuscript derives its name from the Vatican library where it has been housed at least since 1481 (except for a brief period while Napoleon removed it to Paris). It was not made fully available to scholars until the late nineteenth century (see figs. 7 and 8). It includes the LXX and the New Testament to Hebrews 9:14, the latter part of the codex having been lost and replaced in a much later hand. We thus do not know whether, like

2. In the standard abbreviation system used for identifying ancient New Testament manuscripts, papyri are numbered consecutively by the date of their discovery; uncials are indicated by capital letters or Arabic numerals prefixed by a zero; minuscules are designated by Arabic numerals.

Sinaiticus, it originally included Christian documents finally not considered canonical. The manuscript was copied in Egypt in the fourth century CE and, like Sinaiticus, is judged to represent an early version of the text.

— D or 05 *Codex Bezae* This codex from the late fifth or early sixth century originally contained the Gospel and Acts/Catholic Epistles in Greek and Latin on facing pages. Much of Acts and almost all the Catholic Letters have been lost. While ℵ and B represent the Alexandrian textual tradition, D represents the Western text, noted among other things for its lengthier readings. The Western text of Acts, for example, is 8.5 percent longer than the Alexandrian text (see the footnotes in NRSV in Luke 22–24 for samples of Western readings, and further discussion below in the introduction to Acts, §24.4).

— W or 032. *Codex Freerianus or Washingtonius* Now in the Freer Gallery of the Smithsonian Institution in Washington, DC, it is one of the few major New Testament manuscripts now accessible in North America. It contains the four Gospels in the Western order (Matt, John, Luke, Mark) except for the missing pages Mark 15:13–38; John 14:25–16:7. It represents a mixture of text types, indicating that various parts of the manuscript were copied from manuscripts of different origins and dates: the Alexandrian text type is found in Luke 1:1–8:2 and the Gospel of John; the Byzantine ("Koine," "Majority Text") type is found in Matthew and Luke 8:3–24:53; the Western text is found in Mark 1:1–5:30, with the Caesarean text in Mark 5:31–16:20. The manuscript also has independent readings, the most famous one found in Mark 16:14:

> And they replied saying, "This age of lawlessness and unbelief is under Satan who by means of unclean spirits does not allow people to comprehend the true power of God; so reveal your righteousness now." And Christ answered them, "The limit of the years of the authority of Satan is fulfilled; but other horrors draw near and for the sake of those who sinned I was delivered to death that they might return to the truth and sin no more, so that they might inherit the spiritual and incorruptible glory of righteousness which is in heaven."

— Family 1, Family 13. Generally speaking, the mass of later minuscule manuscripts is not as valuable as the earlier papyri and uncials for purposes of textual criticism, since they represent the copying and proliferation of earlier copyists' errors. In some identifiable instances, however, a group of later manuscripts appears to have been copied from an early and more reliable exemplar (see note on $\mathfrak{P}^{66}$, $\mathfrak{P}^{75}$ above). These are often cited as a group. Family 1 (*f*1) represents minuscules numbered 1, 118, 131, 209, 1582, and others. Family 13 (*f*13, also labeled ϕ, for Ferrar, who first identified it) represents manuscripts 13, 69, 124, 174, 230, 346, 543, 788, 826, 828, 983, 1689, and 1709. Though both families are composed of late manuscripts, they often preserve an early form of the text.

3.2 Variations and Their Causes

NO TWO OF THE MORE THAN 5,000 GREEK manuscripts of (parts of) the New Testament are exactly alike. The same is true of the additional thousands of early translations and patristic citations. No one knows how many textual variations are contained in our extant manuscripts. The standard critical edition of the Greek New Testament (Nestle-Aland, *Novum Testamentum Graece*, 27th edition, 1998) averages listing about twenty-five variations per page (see fig. 3).

A very rough calculation would suggest that the footnoted critical apparatus of the 680 pages of Greek text documents about 17,000 variations (see figs. 3–5). This is only a selection of what is considered the more significant variations for purposes of textual criticism. If every variation in spelling and orthography,

⸀ΚΑΤΑ ΙΩΑΝΝΗΝ⸁

1 III **1** Ἐν ἀρχῇ ἦν ὁ λόγος, καὶ ὁ λόγος ἦν πρὸς τὸν θεόν, 1J 1,1s; 2,13 Gn 1,1 · Ap 19,13 ·
καὶ θεὸς ἦν ὁ λόγος. **2** οὗτος ἦν ἐν ἀρχῇ πρὸς τὸν θεόν. 17,5 | Prv 8,22s
3 πάντα δι᾿ αὐτοῦ ἐγένετο, καὶ χωρὶς αὐτοῦ ἐγένετο ⸀οὐδὲ Sap 9,1 Ps 33,6 1K 8,6 Kol 1,
ἕν⸁⁚. ὃ γέγονεν⁚¹ **4** ἐν αὐτῷ ζωὴ ⸂ἦν, καὶ ἡ ζωὴ ἦν τὸ φῶς 16s H 1,2 Ap 3,14 | 5,26 1J 1,
⸋τῶν ἀνθρώπων⸌· **5** καὶ τὸ φῶς ἐν τῇ σκοτίᾳ φαίνει, καὶ 2 · 8,12! | 3,19; 12,35 Is
ἡ σκοτία αὐτὸ οὐ κατέλαβεν. 9,1
2 III **6** Ἐγένετο ἄνθρωπος, ἀπεσταλμένος παρὰ ⸂θεοῦ, ⸆ Mc 1,4p
ὄνομα αὐτῷ Ἰωάννης· **7** οὗτος ἦλθεν εἰς μαρτυρίαν ἵνα 5,33
μαρτυρήσῃ περὶ τοῦ φωτός, ἵνα πάντες πιστεύσωσιν δι᾿ Act 19,4
αὐτοῦ. **8** οὐκ ἦν ἐκεῖνος τὸ φῶς, ἀλλ᾿ ἵνα μαρτυρήσῃ περὶ 20; 5,35
τοῦ φωτός.
3 III **9** Ἦν τὸ φῶς τὸ ἀληθινόν, ὃ φωτίζει πάντα ἄνθρω- 8,12! Mt 4,16 1J 2,8 · 3,19; 11,27!
πον, ἐρχόμενον εἰς τὸν κόσμον. **10** ἐν τῷ κόσμῳ ἦν, καὶ 3-5; 14,17 1K 2,8 1J 3,1
ὁ κόσμος δι᾿ αὐτοῦ ἐγένετο, καὶ ὁ κόσμος αὐτὸν οὐκ ἔγνω.
4 X **11** εἰς τὰ ἴδια ἦλθεν, καὶ οἱ ἴδιοι αὐτὸν οὐ παρέλαβον. 5,43
12 ὅσοι δὲ ἔλαβον αὐτόν, ἔδωκεν αὐτοῖς ἐξουσίαν τέκνα G 3,26 E 1,5 1J 3,1 ·
θεοῦ γενέσθαι, τοῖς πιστεύουσιν εἰς τὸ ὄνομα αὐτοῦ, 20,31 1J 5,13!
13 ⸀οἳ οὐκ⸁ ἐξ αἱμάτων οὐδὲ ἐκ θελήματος σαρκὸς ⸋οὐδὲ 3,5s 1P 1,23
ἐκ θελήματος ἀνδρὸς⸌ ἀλλ᾿ ἐκ θεοῦ ⸂ἐγεννήθησαν. 1J 4,7! Jc 1,18
5 III **14** Καὶ ὁ λόγος σὰρξ ἐγένετο καὶ ἐσκήνωσεν ἐν ἡμῖν, 1T 3,16 Kol 1, 22! · PsSal 7,6
καὶ ἐθεασάμεθα τὴν δόξαν αὐτοῦ, δόξαν ὡς μονογενοῦς Ez 37,27 Ap 21, 3 · 2P 1,16s
6 I παρὰ πατρός, πλήρης χάριτος καὶ ἀληθείας. **15** Ἰωάννης 1J 1,1 · 2,11! L 9, 32 · 3,16! · 17!
μαρτυρεῖ περὶ αὐτοῦ καὶ κέκραγεν λέγων· ⸀οὗτος ἦν ὃν
εἶπον·⸁ ὁ ὀπίσω μου ἐρχόμενος ⸆ ἔμπροσθέν μου γέγονεν, 27.30 Mt 3,11!

Inscriptio: ⸀ευαγγελιον κ. I. 𝔓$^{66.75}$ (A) C D L W^{s} Θ Ψ *f*^{1} 33 𝔐 vg^{ww} ¦ αγιον ευ. κ. I. (28) *al* ¦ *txt* (א B)

¶ **1,3** ⸀ουδεν 𝔓^{66} א* D *f*^{1} *pc*; Cl$^{ex\ Thd}$ | ⁚† – *et* ⁚¹. א^{c} (Θ) Ψ 050^{c} *f*$^{1.13}$ 33 𝔐 sy$^{p.h}$ bo ¦ *txt* 𝔓^{75c} C D L W^{s} 050*. *l* 2211 *pc* b vg^{s} sy^{c} sa; Ptol^{Ir} Theoph Ir^{lat} Tert Cl Cl$^{ex\ Thd}$ Or (*sine interp. vl incert.* 𝔓$^{66.75*}$ א* A B Δ *al*) • **4** ⸂εστιν א D it vg^{mss} sa?; Ptol^{Ir} Ir^{lat} Cl^{pt} Or^{mss} ¦ – W^{s} | ⸋ B* • **6** ⸂κυριου D* | ⸆ην א* D* W^{s} sy^{c}; Ir^{lat} • **13** ⸀ουκ *et* ⸂εγεννηθ- D* ¦ qui non *et* natus est b; (Tert) ¦ *txt* 𝔓^{66vid} א B^{2} C D^{c} L W^{s} Ψ *f*$^{1.13}$ 33 𝔐 sy$^{p.h}$ (*sed* εγενηθ- 𝔓^{75} A B* Δ Θ *pc*) | ⸋ B* • **15** ⸀ουτ. ην ο ειπων· א^{1} B* C*; Or ¦ ουτ. ην א* | ⸆ος א* W^{s} c

FIGURE 3: The beginning of the Gospel of John as it appears in Nestle-Aland, *Novum Testamentum Graece*, showing textual variations in the critical apparatus. Nestle-Aland, *Novum Testamentum Graece*, 27th Revised Edition, edited by Barbara Aland, Kurt Aland, Johannes Karavidopoulos, Carlo M. Martini, and Bruce M. Metzger in cooperation with the Institute for New Testament Textual Research, Münster/Westphalia, © 1993 Deutsche Bibelgesellschaft, Stuttgart. Used by permission of German Bible Society. PHOTO CREDIT: M. EUGENE BORING.

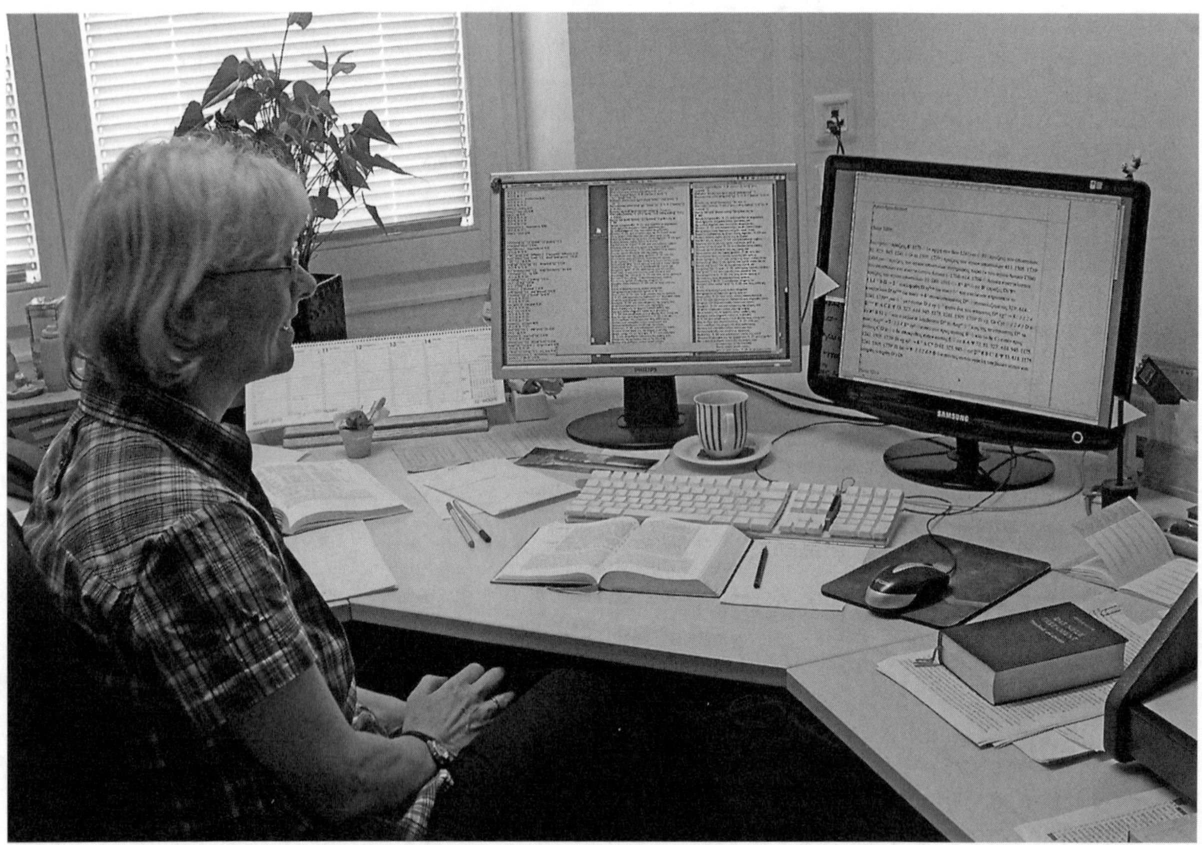

FIGURE 4: Dr. Marie-Luise Lakmann of the Institut für Neutestamentliche Textforschung, Münster, editing the critical apparatus of Acts 1:1 for Nestle-Aland 28. PHOTO CREDIT: M. EUGENE BORING. USED BY PERMISSION OF MÜNSTER INSTITUTE.

and all the obvious scribal blunders, were listed, for every available manuscript, the number of variations would certainly go into the hundreds of thousands. Some variations are simple: some manuscripts contain a particular word and others do not; some have the singular and others have the plural of the same word, and the textual scholar must only decide which of the two forms represents the earlier reading. Other variations are more complex, involving combinations of vocabulary, form, grammar, and word order. The phrase in Colossians 2:2 translated in the NRSV as "God's mystery, that is, Christ himself," occurs in fifteen quite different forms in the manuscripts, several of which involve different meanings from that represented in the NRSV.

The significance of this vast number and complexity of variations should neither be exaggerated nor minimized. On the one hand, in regard to exegetical and theological significance, most of the variations are minor, indeed trifling. The vast majority consists of differences in spelling, word order, use of pronouns for nouns or vice versa, synonyms for the same word, and other such variations that make no difference in the meaning. Their importance pertains entirely to the technical purpose of charting the history of the manuscript tradition, that is, which manuscripts and families

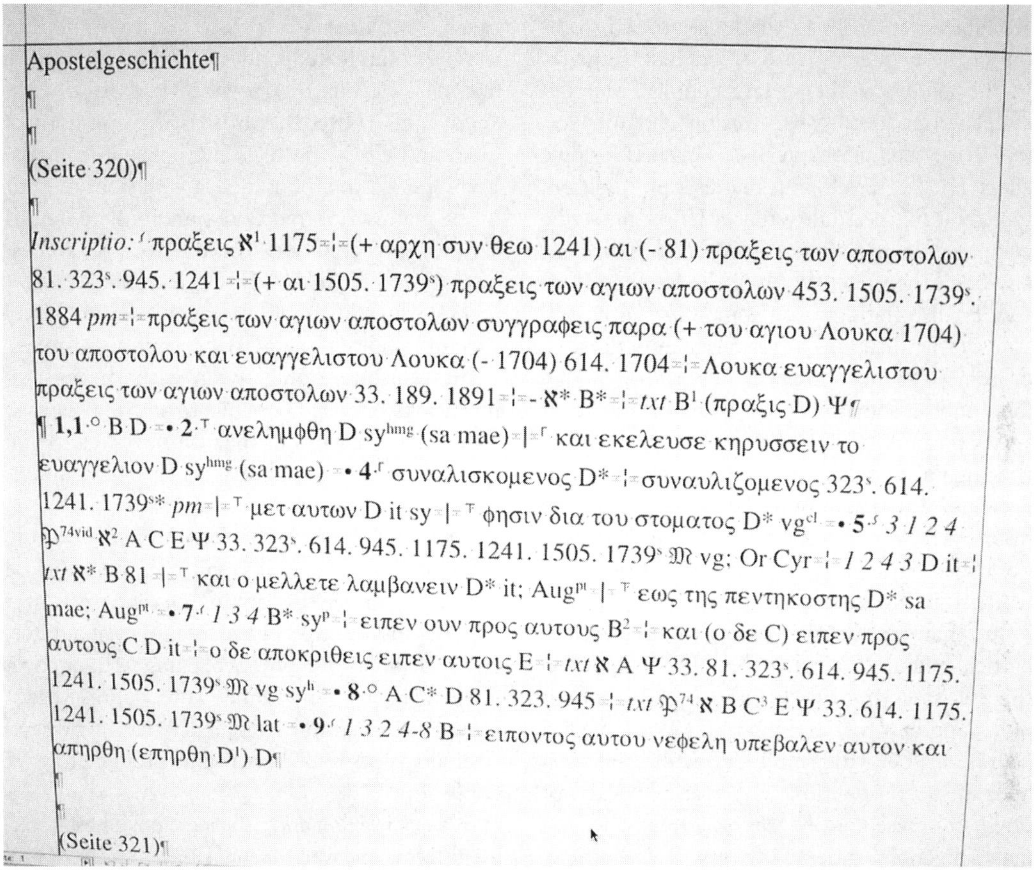

Apostelgeschichte¶

¶

¶

(Seite 320)¶

¶

Inscriptio: ʼ πραξεις ℵ¹ 1175 ¦ (+ αρχη συν θεω 1241) αι (- 81) πραξεις των αποστολων 81. 323ˢ. 945. 1241 ¦ (+ αι 1505. 1739ˢ) πραξεις των αγιων αποστολων 453. 1505. 1739ˢ. 1884 *pm* ¦ πραξεις των αγιων αποστολων συγγραφεις παρα (+ του αγιου Λουκα 1704) του αποστολου και ευαγγελιστου Λουκα (- 1704) 614. 1704 ¦ Λουκα ευαγγελιστου πραξεις των αγιων αποστολων 33. 189. 1891 ¦ - ℵ* B* ¦ *txt* B¹ (πραξις D) Ψ¶

¶ **1,1** ° B D • **2** ᵀ ανελημφθη D sy^hmg (sa mae) | ʳ και εκελευσε κηρυσσειν το ευαγγελιον D sy^hmg (sa mae) • **4** ʳ συναλισκομενος D* ¦ συναυλιζομενος 323ˢ. 614. 1241. 1739ˢ* *pm* | ᵀ μετ αυτων D it sy | ᵀ φησιν δια του στοματος D* vg^cl • **5** *ʃ 3 1 2 4* 𝔓^74vid ℵ² A C E Ψ 33. 323ˢ. 614. 945. 1175. 1241. 1505. 1739ˢ 𝔐 vg; Or Cyr ¦ *1 2 4 3* D it ¦ *txt* ℵ* B 81 | ᵀ και ο μελλετε λαμβανειν D* it; Aug^pt | ᵀ εως της πεντηκοστης D* sa mae; Aug^pt • **7** *ʃ 1 3 4* B* sy^p ¦ ειπεν ουν προς αυτους B² ¦ και (ο δε C) ειπεν προς αυτους C D it ¦ ο δε αποκριθεις ειπεν αυτοις E ¦ *txt* ℵ A Ψ 33. 81. 323ˢ. 614. 945. 1175. 1241. 1505. 1739ˢ 𝔐 vg sy^h • **8** ° A C* D 81. 323. 945 ¦ *txt* 𝔓^74 ℵ B C³ E Ψ 33. 614. 1175. 1241. 1505. 1739ˢ 𝔐 lat • **9** *ʃ 1 3 2 4-8* B ¦ ειποντος αυτου νεφελη υπεβαλεν αυτον και απηρθη (επηρθη D¹) D¶

¶

¶

(Seite 321)¶

FIGURE 5: The critical apparatus of Acts 1:1 in the process of revision. This is a close-up of the material being edited by Dr. Marie-Luise Lakmann. PHOTO CREDIT: M. EUGENE BORING. USED BY PERMISSION OF MÜNSTER INSTITUTE.

are related to others. On the other hand, many variations are dramatic and crucial for understanding the text. Here are some well-known examples:

The ending of the Gospel of Mark. The manuscripts manifest six different endings, as indicated in the text and footnotes of the NRSV and other modern translations, with internal variations also found within each of the different endings.[3] One's judgment as to whether Mark ended his story at 16:8, or whether the original ending is lost or retained in one of the versions of the Markan ending now preserved in many manuscripts, profoundly influences how one understands the meaning of Mark's resurrection story and the story line of the Gospel of Mark as a whole (see below §21.7), as well as the literary history and interrelations of the Gospels in the earliest period.

3. Here and elsewhere in discussing the manuscripts data for particular texts and how it is evaluated by textual scholars, the reader is encouraged to examine Bruce M. Metzger, *A Textual Commentary on the Greek New Testament*, 2nd ed. (Stuttgart: United Bible Societies, 1994). For Mark 16, a full and interesting discussion is found in David C. Parker, *The Living Text of the Gospels* (Cambridge: Cambridge University Press, 1997), "The Endings of Mark's Gospel," 124–47.

The ending of Paul's letter to the Romans. There are fifteen variations in the location and wording of the benedictions that conclude Romans. In the middle of the second century, Marcion circulated an expurgated version of Paul's letters that ended at chapter 14. This had a ripple effect on the developing manuscript tradition, including the possibility that a Christian scribe composed the benediction now found as the conclusion of the present form of the letter in standard English translations (Rom 16:25–27 as well as five other locations in various manuscripts).

Some variations are still important, though more subtle, sometimes consisting of a word or two important for understanding the meaning of the original text. In Ephesians 1:1 the words "in Ephesus," found in most manuscripts, are missing from several key witnesses. If the original text did not contain them, this would be additional evidence that the letter was originally an encyclical rather than representing itself as addressed to a particular church, a matter that also impinges on the issue of authorship. In John 7:52, two of our oldest and best witnesses, $\mathfrak{P}^{66}$ and $\mathfrak{P}^{75}$, have the definite article with "prophet," while the mass of manuscripts do not. If the article was not originally present—one Greek letter—the text makes a general statement, but with the article, John refers to *the* eschatological prophet, a specific christological hope of first-century Judaism. Another significant one-word variation is found in Matthew 27:16, where some manuscripts and ancient versions have "Barabbas" and others "Jesus Barabbas"—the reading now adopted as original in Nestle-Aland^{27} and several English translations (TEV, NAB, NRSV, REB, *Die Bibel* [1984 revision of the Luther Bible], and the 1976 and 1991 editions of the *Modern Hebrew New Testament*). So also in 1 John 5:18, the difference between the KJV and the NRSV is not only a matter of interpretation and translation, but of the text that is to be translated. Again, the variation consists of only one letter of one word. If ἑαυτόν (*heauton*) is read, the meaning is clearly "but he that is begotten of God keepeth himself" (KJV); the believer is the one "begotten of God," and as such guards himself from the Evil One. But if αὐτόν (*auton*) is read, the interpretation is more complicated, and the Greek text may be understood to mean "He who was born of God keeps him" (NRSV); Christ is the one born of God, and Christ protects the believer from the Evil One. Of the thousands of variations present in the manuscript tradition, hundreds are significant for interpretation—on the average, at least one or two per page of the Greek text.

How did all this variation come about? Many variant readings seem to be simply mistakes, entirely unintentional. Even with the best of intentions, it is impossible to copy a passage of any length without making mistakes. Some types of unintentional mistakes are so common they have been classified:

Omission: A word, phrase, sentence, or whole paragraph is accidentally omitted, then may be noticed later by the original scribe or a later copyist, and inserted in the margin or at a different location in the sentence, paragraph, or page.

Dittography: The same word, phrase, sentence, or paragraph is copied twice; if noticed later, attempts to correct it may produce further confusion.

Homoioteleuton and *homoioarcton*: These technical terms, meaning "same/similar ending," and "same/similar beginning" respectively, designate a phenomenon contributing to errors of the types "omission" and "dittography," when the scribe's eye skips from a word that ends a line to a different line ending with the same word, causing him to omit or duplicate all the material in between.

A *marginal gloss* intended to comment on or explain the text is taken by a later scribe to be a part of the text itself, and is so copied. In the age of printing, marginal comments are easily distinguished from the original text, but when everything was handwritten, this was not the case, and the line between "text" and "annotation" was thin.

Especially in parallel accounts of similar events and sayings in the Gospels, many alterations were the result of *harmonization*. The scribe might replace the reading of one Gospel by another, or blend the parallel versions in the Gospels into one reading that existed in none of them. Thus some of the Old Latin manuscripts used in North Africa, cited by Augustine and adopted by Jerome in the Vulgate, combine the account of Judas's death in Matthew 27 (he hanged himself) and Acts 1 (he fell down and burst open). This harmonized rendering, found in no Greek manuscript, was adopted in the 1582 Rheims-Douay translation that became the standard Roman Catholic Bible for more than three centuries, but it is not followed by any modern Catholic or other translation.

Some mistakes are matters of hearing: the lector dictates the text to be copied, and words that sound alike are confused (e.g., English "there" and "their"). From Byzantine times on, the Greek words for "we" and "you" sounded very much alike (although spelled differently, ἡμεῖς, ὑμεῖς = *hēmeis, humeis*). There are thus numerous instances in which some manuscripts read "we" and others read "you."

Many mistakes were simply the result of careless or tired scribes. On the other hand, some readings were introduced intentionally. This does not necessarily mean that the scribes purposely falsified the text; they sometimes changed it sincerely believing that they were restoring or preserving the correct reading, or that the current normative interpretation needed to be built more explicitly into the text. The text may pose theological or other difficulties. The scribe thus "corrects" it to what he regards as the true reading. Of numerous examples, we may mention Luke 1:3, where most manuscripts read "it seemed good to me" to write the Gospel on the basis of his oral and written sources. Other manuscripts have "and the Holy Spirit" after "me." It thus seems that the original author wrote "me," which seemed defective to some scribes, who added "and the Holy Spirit" on the analogy of Luke's own report in Acts 15:28. The scribe assumes that the exemplar from which he is copying has already been corrupted, because it disagrees with texts he already regards as authoritative. Alternatively, the scribe possesses more than one exemplar of the document he is copying. Since they do not agree exactly, the scribe combines the different readings into a new, expanded version of the text that preserves both versions—thereby assuring himself that within this conflated version he has preserved the true text.

3.3 Textual Criticism—In Quest of the "Original Text"

THE PROBLEM OF ESTABLISHING THE EARliest recoverable text of the New Testament is constituted by the dual facts that (1) all the original documents are lost or destroyed, and (2) of the surviving manuscripts (5,000+ Greek manuscripts, 10,000 ancient versions, thousands of quotations in the church fathers), no two are exactly alike. If we had the original documents, or if all our manuscripts agreed, there would be no problem. We would simply print this text as "the Greek New Testament." For us to have a New Testament at all, we must either (1) adopt one manuscript as "the original" and consider all others as corruptions, or (2) reconstruct the earliest recoverable form of the text on the basis of the numerous differing manuscripts.

Textual scholars attempt to determine the earliest attainable form of the text. Textual criticism is both science and art. The scholar must analyze all the data and argue on the basis of objective evidence and the accepted rules and principles of the discipline. While textual criticism can never be reduced to mechanics—a computer is now an invaluable tool, but cannot be programmed to reconstruct the original text—there are a number of overlapping and somewhat conflicting rules that serve as guidelines for reconstructing the text. Among such fundamental guidelines we may list these:[4]

4. See Kurt Aland and Barbara Aland, *The Text of the New Testament: An Introduction to the Critical Editions and to the Theory and Practice of Modern Textual Criticism*, trans. Erroll F. Rhodes, 2nd ed. (Grand Rapids: Eerdmans, 1989), 275, "Twelve Basic Rules of Textual Criticism."

1. Older manuscripts are generally more valuable than later ones. Distinctions must be made, however, between the date of the manuscript and the date of the text it represents. Codex Regius (L), for example, is a manuscript from the eighth century, but it was copied from a very old manuscript, agreeing with manuscripts from the fourth century, and thus represents a very old text. Related to this is the fact that the early translations of the New Testament into Latin, Coptic, and other languages were made from manuscripts older than any we now possess. While retranslation into the Greek text they presumably used (technical term: *Vorlage*) is a tricky business, some evidence is quite clear. The Latin Vulgate, for instance, was based on Greek manuscripts more than a thousand years older than those used by the translators of the 1611 King James Version, and does not contain the concluding doxology in the Matthean Lord's Prayer ("For thine is the kingdom . . .").

2. A few manuscripts from diverse geographical origins may be more important than a larger number from the same area.

3. Manuscripts must be weighed rather than merely counted. The number of manuscripts supporting a particular reading may be important, but their age and the quality of their text are more important than their number. In Mark 7:19, for example, the dominant reading numerically is that which is translated in the KJV as "purging all meats." This is the reading of several hundred manuscripts, most of them late minuscules. But the uncials ℵ, A, B, E, F, G, H, L, S, X, Δ, and some of the church fathers support a slightly different reading that means "Thus he declared all foods clean." The eleven manuscripts and three church fathers represent a reading older and more widely attested than the hundreds of later manuscripts that represent basically one text type.

4. One aspect in evaluating the potential significance of each manuscript is sorting them out genealogically, attempting to determine which family (*stemma*, pl. *stemmata*) each represents. Readings are then evaluated in terms of which stemma they represent, not merely as representatives of a particular manuscript. If 500 manuscripts have been copied from a single exemplar, they can only be counted as one "vote" in deciding on the original reading. If another manuscript is the sole representative of its exemplar, the "vote" is one to one, not 500 to one. Yet the whole concept of "text families" is being reevaluated in current research, and there is less confidence in this approach than fifty years ago (see above).

5. All things being equal, the shorter reading is to be preferred (since the manuscripts tended to expand with time). But scribes also abbreviated and omitted, so this rule cannot be applied mechanically.

6. All things being equal, the more difficult reading is to be preferred (since scribes would more likely "correct" what appeared to them to be mistakes rather than invent them).

7. The reading that can most plausibly explain the derivation of the other readings is most likely to be original. Again, such judgments call for reconstructing the genealogy into which the manuscript fits.

The above rules are mostly concerned with external criteria (age, geographical distribution, and genealogical relation of manuscripts) and the probabilities of transcriptional transmission (scribal practices, types of error). But internal criteria (context, style, vocabulary, theology of the author) must also be taken into consideration. From what we otherwise know about the author, which of the available readings is he most likely to have written? The criterion of *coherence* also plays a role here. Assuming that no New Testament writer wrote nonsense, every reconstruction must yield a text that makes sense. What makes sense to the modern critic and what made sense to the ancient author may not be the same, however.

It will be seen that these "rules" will sometimes conflict with each other (e.g., the shorter reading may also be attested only late, and be unable to explain the other readings as deriving from it). Each possible reconstruction must be

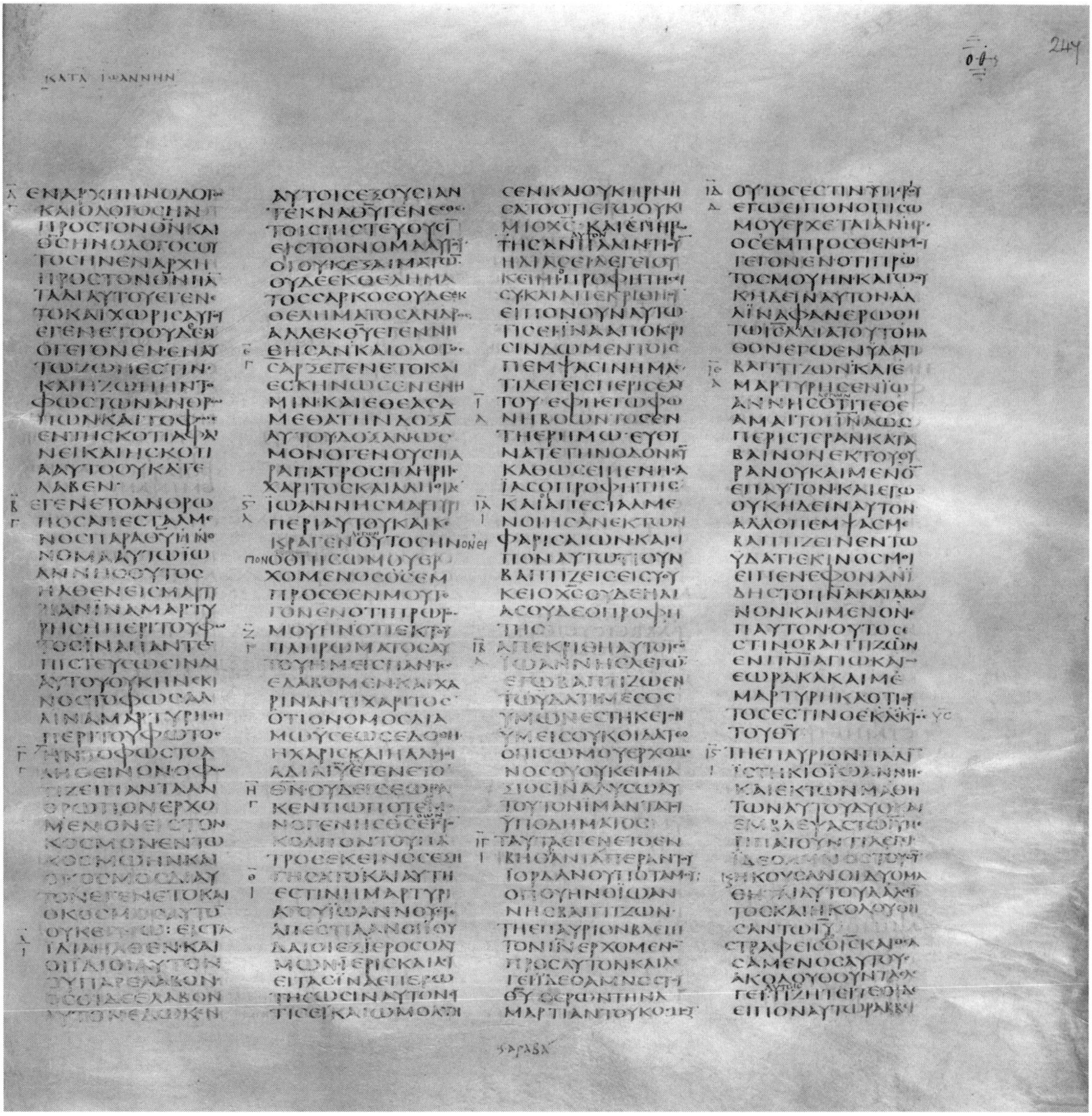

FIGURE 6: Page from Codex Sinaiticus, showing John 1.

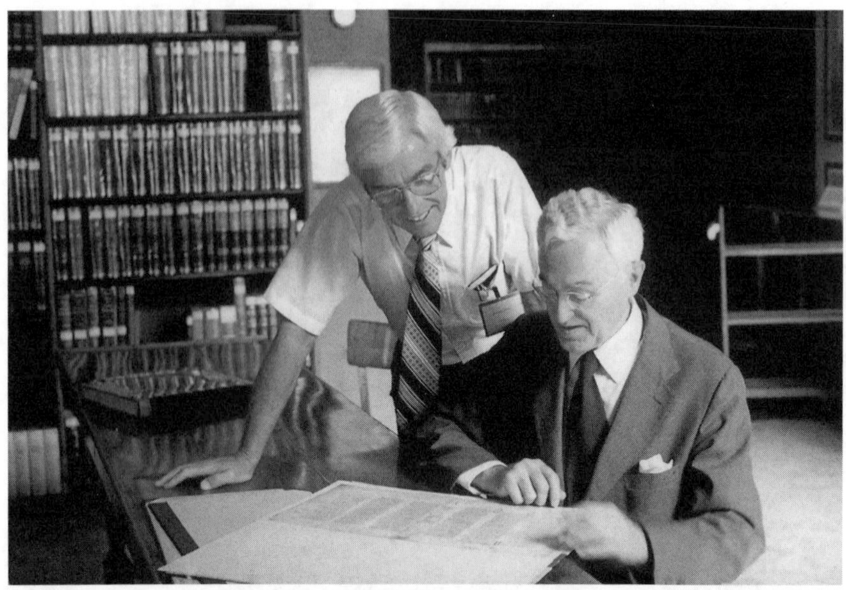

FIGURE 7: M. Eugene Boring (left) and Bruce M. Metzger (seated) examining the text of Hebrews in Codex Vaticanus in the Vatican Library, 1981. Metzger obtained permission to examine the codex, because he wanted to personally examine a text where the original had been erased and a correction made over the erasure. PHOTO CREDIT: WILLIAM O. WALKER JR. USED BY PERMISSION OF WILLIAM O. WALKER.

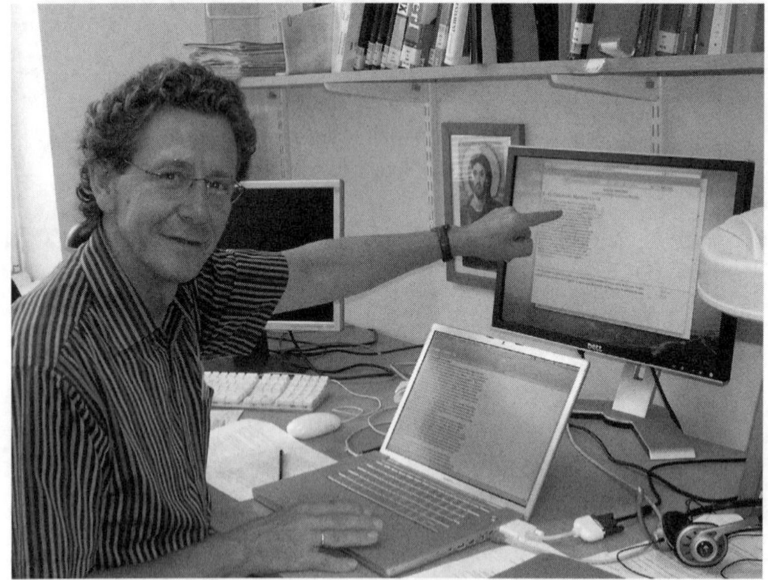

FIGURE 8: Dr. Klaus Wachtel of the Institut für Neutestamentliche Textforschung, Münster, working on the text of Codex Vaticanus of Matthew 1:1-10. PHOTO CREDIT: M. EUGENE BORING. USED BY PERMISSION OF MÜNSTER INSTITUTE.

weighed and balanced against other possibilities. Thus most contemporary textual scholars use the methodological approach now often called "reasoned eclecticism." Both external and internal evidence is considered, and every instance of variation is evaluated in its own terms as a discrete problem to be solved, with the primary guideline being to prefer the reading that best accounts for the others. Although numerous Greek New Testaments have been edited and published by individuals, the kind of judgments called for in reconstructing the original text are best made by small, qualified groups. Both the Nestle-Aland *Novum Testamentum Graece* and the United Bible Society's *Greek New Testament* have the same international and ecumenical editorial committee.

3.4 Results: The Modern Printed Greek New Testament(s)

THE INVENTION OF PRINTING MEANT THAT, for the first time in history, thousands of identical copies of the New Testament could be produced. The first printed Greek New Testament was completed in 1514 as part of the comprehensive project of Cardinal Ximenes of Spain to print a Bible containing the Hebrew, Latin, and Greek text in parallel columns. This project was carefully done, involving the work of several scholars under Ximenes' supervision, but its actual publication was delayed until 1522 by several factors, including the delay of papal permission until borrowed manuscripts were returned to the Vatican. Thus the first Greek New Testament actually to be published was edited by Desiderius Erasmus in 1516. Erasmus's first edition was hastily and poorly done, containing many editorial and printer's errors. It was based only on the few manuscripts available to him in Basel, not one of which contained the whole New Testament. Erasmus was aware that there were earlier and better manuscripts, but the pressure to produce the edition quickly did not allow him the time and travel necessary to access them. The primary basis of his edition was one twelfth-century manuscript of the Gospels and one twelfth-century manuscript of Acts and the Epistles. For Revelation, his only available Greek manuscript was incomplete, lacking the final six verses—which Erasmus did not hesitate to retranslate into Greek from the Vulgate. Since all Erasmus's manuscripts were late, they contained all the expansions and modifications of the late medieval textual tradition. Erasmus's text went through several editions in which many of the original typographical errors were corrected, but it was basically his text that became the standard Textus Receptus (Received Text) on which the 1611 King James Version was based, and remained the standard printed Greek text until the critical editions of the nineteenth century.

The late eighteenth and nineteenth centuries brought the rediscovery of much more ancient and better manuscripts, such as the great uncials Vaticanus (B) and Sinaiticus (א), and the birth of the modern discipline of textual criticism. These discoveries led to the publication of such critical editions as J. J. Griesbach (1775), Tischendorf (1869–1872), Westcott and Hort (1881), and the first edition of the text that was to become the foundation of all modern texts, that of Eberhard Nestle (1898). The Textus Receptus was seen to represent a late and corrupt version of the original texts, and critical versions of the text were published that were closer to what the original authors had written. Westcott and Hort's Greek text, for instance, differed from the Textus Receptus used in 1611 by the King James Translators in about 5,800 readings, about 25 percent of which substantially modify the understanding of the subject matter.[5]

Of the more than a thousand editions of the Greek New Testament that have appeared since 1514, no two are *exactly* alike. Current textual criticism has seen a merging of editorial boards and a corresponding convergence of results, so that for the first time in history, practically all students of the New Testament worldwide use exactly the same text.[6] This is a "working" text, however, with the important variants listed in the apparatus at the bottom of the page, so that every exegete can come to appreciate the history of the text and make his or her own informed decisions as to the form of the text to be interpreted.

5. Frederic G. Kenyon, *Our Bible and the Ancient Manuscripts* (London: Eyre & Spottiswoode, 1958), 312–13.
6. Kurt Aland and Barbara Aland, eds., *Novum Testamentum Graece*, 27th ed. (Stuttgart: Deutsche Bibelgesellschaft, 1993); Kurt Aland, Barbara Aland, J. Karavidopoulos, et al., eds., *The Greek New Testament*, 4th ed. (Stuttgart: United Bible Societies, 1993).

Two major projects are currently in progress: the International Greek New Testament Project (IGNTP), which has been located at various American universities, and the *Editio Critica Maior* of the *Institut für Neutestamentliche Textforschung* in Münster, Germany. Installments of each project have been published, but in each case the completed multivolume work will not be available for many years. Their results will trickle down into the manual editions of the United Bible Societies and Nestle-Aland.

3.5 Implications for Translation

BEFORE THE TRANSLATOR CAN MAKE AN English translation of the New Testament, he or she must decide which text to translate. Some differences between English translations are due not to differences in translation theory or variations in how the original text is understood, but to a different choice in which text is to be translated in the first place. Thus, in Luke 2:14 the difference between "on earth peace, good will toward men" (KJV) and "on earth peace among those whom he favors" (NRSV) is that the KJV is a faithful translation of what we now know is not the oldest and best Greek text. The NRSV and practically all modern translations translate the earlier form of the text, almost certainly closer to what the author originally wrote. Likewise, in Romans 8:28 the difference between "all things work together for good" (KJV, NAB, NRSV) and "in everything God works for good" (RSV; cf. TEV, NIV) is not based on a different understanding of the same Greek text, but represents a different judgment as to the original wording of the Greek text.

3.6 Theological Implications

WE ARE THUS RELATIVELY CERTAIN, OFTEN virtually certain, of the original wording of our New Testament documents—but, in the nature of the case, never absolutely certain. Several times per page, there is a degree of uncertainty as to the original text. Through the centuries, the church has lived with this uncertainty. The church never made a "master copy" of its New Testament against which all manuscripts and printed editions could be checked for absolute accuracy. In Christianity, the divine Word did not become a book. "The Word became flesh and lived among us" (John 1:14). In Jesus Christ, the absolute divine Word was understood to have entered into the realm of "flesh," that is, into the relative and ambiguous world of human existence. The New Testament, by its very form, bears witness to this faith (see on John 1:1–18 below).

3.7 For Further Reading

Aland, Kurt, and Barbara Aland. *The Text of the New Testament: An Introduction to the Critical Editions and to the Theory and Practice of Modern Textual Criticism*. Translated by Erroll F. Rhodes. 2nd ed. Grand Rapids: Eerdmans, 1989.

Ehrman, Bart D. *Misquoting Jesus: The Story behind Who Changed the Bible and Why*. San Francisco: HarperSanFrancisco, 2005.

Kenyon, Frederick G. *Our Bible and the Ancient Manuscripts*. London: Eyre & Spottiswoode, 1958.

Metzger, Bruce M. *A Textual Commentary on the Greek New Testament*. 2nd ed. Stuttgart: United Bible Societies, 1994.

Parker, David C. *An Introduction to the New Testament Manuscripts and Their Texts*. Cambridge: Cambridge University Press, 2008.

———. *The Living Text of the Gospels*. Cambridge: Cambridge University Press, 1997.

4

LXX to NRSV: No Translation without Interpretation

4.1 The New Testament Is the Church's Book in the Sense that the Church *Translated* It.

THE NEW TESTAMENT WAS WRITTEN IN Koine (common) Greek and understood by most of the literate population of the Hellenistic world. Modern Greek is the direct descendant of Koine Greek, but the Greek language has changed enough through the centuries so that today Greek Christians need the ancient text to be updated into modern Greek for it to be properly understood.[1] There are about 6,800 living languages in the world. As of the year 2000, the whole Bible has been translated into 371, the NT into another 960, portions into another 902.[2]

4.2 The Task of Translation

WORDS. TRANSLATING THE GREEK TEXT OF the New Testament into a modern language is not simply a mechanical process of replacing each Greek word with the appropriate English word. Most words in both Greek and English have more than one meaning. Words have sets of meanings and semantic fields, not single, univocal meanings. Very few words have precisely the same meaning or sets of meanings in any two languages. A word might have only a narrow range of meaning in Greek, but a wide range of meanings in English, or vice versa. The Greek word ἄνωθεν (*anōthen*) can mean "again" (as clearly in Gal 4:9) or "from above" (as clearly in John 3:31). In John 3:3, 7 the author has chosen this word in order to present these two alternative understandings: Jesus intends "from above," but Nicodemus understands "again." Here the translator is in a quandary, for there is no English word that has these two meanings. While the Greek reader can perceive the word as again/from above, the English translator must choose between them.

Structure. Translation can rarely be word for word, since no two languages are structured exactly alike. Greek varies the form of the same word (inflection) to indicate its grammatical function; English relies primarily on word order and the addition of extra pronouns and auxiliary verbs to achieve the same result. Thus, for example, "they may be praised" in the NRSV of Matt 6:2 is one word in Greek, δοξασθῶσιν (*doxasthōsin*). Greek has a definite article but no indefinite article; English has both. Thus every "a" or "an" in the English New Testament has been "added" to the Greek. Greek and English use the definite article in very different ways, so that to translate every Greek article by "the" would be confusing, misleading, or incorrect. As in English, Greek sometimes has the verb

1. The New Testaments placed in Greek hotel rooms by The Gideons International have two columns of Greek text, the ancient Koine text and a modern Greek version.
2. Bruce M. Metzger, *The Bible in Translation: Ancient and English Versions* (Grand Rapids: Baker, 2001), 8.

understood, implied by the context. Thus 2 Timothy 3:16a has no verb, but one must be supplied for the sentence to make sense in English. Translations differ as to where the verb is to be supplied, depending on how the translator interprets the sentence.[3] *In order to translate at all, words must be added to, and omitted from, the original text.* Some translations have attempted to indicate where they have added words not in the original, but this is impossible to carry out consistently in practice, and also has the unfortunate result of seeming to emphasize the words in the translation not in the original text. Here and elsewhere, there can be *no translation without interpretation.* There are hundreds of instances that illustrate that because of the differences in linguistic structure between source and target language, no translation can be word for word, and no translation can claim to indicate those places where it is not. While some translations are closer to the wording of the original text than others, this does not necessarily mean that they are more "accurate." Thus there is not, cannot be, and should not be any such thing as a "literal translation." A translation that follows the wording of the Greek text very closely may be inaccurate, while a translation that rephrases and adapts the Greek linguistic structure to English may be very accurate. Likewise, the line between "translation" and "paraphrase" is not as clear as is often assumed to be the case.

4.3 History of Biblical Translation

SEVERAL INSIGHTS AND ISSUES REGARDing the process and significance of translation may be illustrated by sketching a brief history of the English Bible. We must begin with the history of translation within the biblical period itself. It is not the case that the Bible was first completed and the issue of translation arose only later.

4.3.1 Translation in the Jewish Community

The Old Greek/Septuagint (LXX)

The Jewish Scriptures were written in Hebrew (except for small sections in Aramaic), the common language(s) of the people at the time they were written. During the Hellenistic period (roughly 300 BCE–300 CE), most Jews in both the Diaspora and Palestine no longer spoke or understood Hebrew. Beginning in the third century BCE and extending over a period of some generations, the sacred text was translated into Greek. These translations later came to be more or less standardized into "the" Septuagint (LXX).[4] The name means "Seventy," and derives from a legendary story, slightly different versions of which are extant in *The Letter of Aristeas*, Philo (*On the Life of Moses* 2.41), and later authors. Some versions of the legend explain that, to prevent collaboration, each of the translators was placed in a small telephone-booth-like cubicle until he had completed the translation of the whole Bible (actually, the original LXX was only of the Pentateuch; other books were translated piecemeal later). When the results were compared, all seventy-two translations agreed word for word, thus demonstrating that the translation (and not just the original) was verbally inspired!

All the factors involved in making a translation were at work in the formation of the LXX:

1. "The" LXX has a history. It was not translated all at once, but by a variety of translators

3. Thus the KJV, NIV, NRSV and CEB insert "is" before "inspired," so that the sentence declares all Scripture to be inspired. The ASV, RSV, and other translations place the "is" after "inspired," so that the sentence makes a statement about all inspired Scripture, namely that it is profitable. The first interpretation declares all Scripture to be inspired, the second does not, but makes a statement about all inspired Scripture. The NASB, which claims to be a literal, word-for-word translation, inserts "is" in the first position, without indicating that a word has been "added."

4. It is misleading to speak of "the" LXX, as though there were a single translation that came into being at a particular point in time. A variety of Greek translations originated from a number of different translators over an extended period, using different translation theories and translating from different Hebrew texts. For a clear and helpful introduction, see Karen H. Jobes and Moises Silva, *Invitation to the Septuagint* (Grand Rapids: Baker, 2000).

with differing levels of competence and theories of what a translation should be, from very literal to free paraphrase. During the first and second centuries CE, new translations were made and previous translations revised, sometimes so completely that the results could be considered different translations, and circulated under the names of Lucian, Aquila, Symmachus, and Theodotion. Scholarly literature sometimes uses "LXX" as an umbrella term for all the Greek translations of the Bible in that period, just as one might refer to the "English Bible" in contrast to the Vulgate—but this would include a variety of translations and versions, with a long and colorful history.[5]

2. The various translators had to choose a Hebrew text to translate. Since different versions of the Hebrew text circulated prior to its standardization in the second century CE, their choice did not always correspond to the version of the Hebrew text that later became canonical. Thus, for example, the LXX version of Jeremiah is one-eighth shorter than the present Hebrew text, and has a different arrangement of the materials.

3. The LXX translators had to decide on the actual words represented by the Hebrew consonantal text, which was not supplied with vowel points until generations later. Of course, the translators stood in a living tradition of how the text was to be pronounced and understood—but the tradition had numerous variations that had not yet been standardized. In some places, they decided, or accepted decisions already made in their tradition, to read the Hebrew text differently from the way that was finally accepted in the form that finally became the standard text of the Jewish Scriptures, the Masoretic Text (MT). For example, in Genesis 47:31 the unpointed Hebrew text had a word, מטה, that could be understood either as "bed" (מִטָּה *mittah*) or "staff" (מַטֵּה *matteh*) depending on how it was vocalized. The Masoretes pointed the text to mean *bed;* the LXX translators understood the word to mean *staff*. Hebrews 11:21 follows the LXX of Genesis 47:31, "bowing in worship over the top of his *staff*." There are numerous such instances.

4. Hellenistic Jews had not only to translate the Hebrew language into Greek, which had a different linguistic structure, but also to translate the ancient Hebrew thought forms into the thought world of Diaspora Judaism in a way that did not mislead the Hellenistic reader. Words such as בְּרִית (*berith*, covenant, treaty) had a different semantic field and set of associations than any corresponding Greek word. When *berith* was translated by διαθήκη (*diathēkē*), the Greek word for "will," "testament," and "covenant," some possibilities for meaning were left behind, and new ones were added on. The Hebrew idiom "sons of God," the divine beings of the heavenly court (בְּנֵי אֱלֹהִים), if translated literally, would have been widely misunderstood (as is still the case in English). The LXX translators sometimes chose ἄγγελοι (*aggeloi*, angels) as less subject to misunderstanding—but this inevitably introduced new possibilities for misunderstanding (e.g., Job 1:6; 2:1; 38:7; contrast Gen 6:2, 4). The revelation of the name of God in Exodus 3:14, literally translated as "I am who I am" or "I will be who I will be" is rendered in the LXX as ἐγώ εἰμι ὁ ὤν (*egō eimi ho ōn*, I am the One Who Is, The Being). The personal name of God in Hebrew (יהוה, YHWH) is related to an action verb, "he-causes-to-be," presenting the dynamic name of God as the One who acts in history. The Greek translation makes it into abstract, static participle, "Being," more recognizable and acceptable to the Greek mind. The LXX is more amenable to being understood in terms of Greek philosophical categories of being, while the Hebrew text is more orientated to the God who acts in history.

The LXX was widely used in the Hellenistic world (including Palestine) in the time of Jesus

5. In this book, unless otherwise indicated, "LXX" is used in this broad sense, "the" LXX that one finds in the modern critical texts (Alfred Rahlfs and Robert Hanhart, eds., *Septuaginta: Id est Vetus Testamentum graece iuxta LXX interpretes*, 2 vols. [Stuttgart: Deutsche Bibelgesellschaft, 2006] and the *Göttingen Septuagint* edited by Robert Hanhart, 9 vols. 1966–2003).

and the early church. Most of the citations of the Old Testament found in the New Testament are from the LXX—though other translations are represented as well. The New Testament authors used as their Bible a translation that had already interpreted the original texts. This can be important for grasping how New Testament authors understood their Bible, in those numerous places where the text cited in the New Testament (based on the LXX) is different from the reading in our English Bibles (based on the MT). Thus the interpretation in Matthew 1:22–23 presupposes the LXX translation that reads παρθένος (*parthenos*, virgin) while the Hebrew text of Isa 7:14 reads עַלְמָה (*'almah*, young woman).

Targums (Targumim)

Like the Jews of the Diaspora and Greek-speaking Jews living in Palestine, indigenous Jews in Galilee and Judea no longer spoke Hebrew as their native tongue.[6] Although Greek was the standard language for government administration throughout the Near East, Aramaic was the dominant language of everyday life for much of the eastern Mediterranean, including first-century Palestine. According to the Gospels, Jesus and his disciples spoke Aramaic (see, e.g., Mark 5:41; 7:34; 14:36; 15:22). The sacred language of the Hebrew Bible was understood by rabbis and scholars, and the Scripture was read forth in the synagogue liturgy in the original text. A translation was then provided so that the Scripture reading could be understood. At first these were ad hoc and piecemeal, but they were later standardized: for the Pentateuch we have the Babylonian *Targum Onqelos* and the Jerusalem *Targum of (Pseudo-)Jonathan*; for the Prophets the *Targum of Jonathan*. *Onqelos* became the more-or-less official paraphrase, and after the invention of printing, it was normally printed alongside the Hebrew text.

6. The New Testament sometimes refers to the common language of first-century Palestine as Hebrew (John 19:20; Acts 21:40; 22:2), but by this they mean Aramaic, a related language.

Fragments from Qumran show that some written Targums already existed in the first century CE and before (*Targum of Job* from Cave 11). From the available Targums, the discerning student can gain an impression of the way the Hebrew Bible was translated and interpreted in the synagogue in the time of Jesus and the early church. It is clear that the line between translation, paraphrase, and extended interpretation was very fluid. Worshipers in the synagogue received the Bible in a form already translated and interpreted. For example, the Jerusalem Targum on Numbers 11:27 says, "At the end of the days Gog, Magog, and their host will come against Jerusalem" (cf. Rev 20:8). Here and elsewhere, New Testament authors sometimes base their interpretation of the Old Testament not on the Hebrew (or LXX) texts themselves but on the expanded translation/interpretation proclaimed in the Targum. When the early Christians began to formulate their Scriptures in Greek, and later Christians translated them into other languages, they entered into a long tradition already present and "authorized" by their Bible.

4.3.2 Early Christianity to the Reformation

The Bible of Greek-speaking Christianity remained the LXX, but as the Christian faith spread through the Mediterranean world, it was translated into several other languages, the most important ones for our purposes being Latin, Coptic (the language of Egyptian Christianity), and Syriac. Latin became the most important of these in the ancestry of the English Bible. A variety of Latin translations developed. Since the copying of manuscripts was not controlled, the cross-fertilization of manuscript traditions resulted in a large variety of corrupt texts. As Latin replaced Greek in Western Christianity, it became important to have an accurate and authoritative translation. In the late fourth century Pope Damasus I commissioned Jerome to make an authoritative translation of the whole Bible. His translation became known as the

Vulgate (*vulgar*, i.e., *common*), because it was in the common language of the people. Jerome originally used the LXX for his translation of the Old Testament, as the old Latin translations had done, but later consulted the Hebrew texts. As is typically the case for new translations, the Vulgate was opposed by many (including Augustine) who had become accustomed to the Old Latin translation, which had already been the Bible of the Latin church for generations. Despite this initial suspicion and opposition, the Vulgate became the standard Bible of Western Christianity for more than a thousand years. Over the centuries it too became corrupt in the process of copying, so that many versions of the Vulgate existed in the Middle Ages.

The Renaissance and Reformation brought dramatic changes in the translation, circulation, and interpretation of the Bible. The Council of Trent (1545–1563) authorized a revision of the Vulgate that was declared to be the standard, authentic text of the Bible. The invention of printing with movable type (Gutenberg 1453) meant that for the first time thousands of exact copies of the same text could be reproduced. Latin was no longer a living language, and was read only by the educated. For the most part, common people could not read the Bible for themselves, nor hear it read in their own language in the liturgy of the church. However, prior to and during the Reformation, numerous translations of the Bible were made in the vernacular, most based on the Vulgate rather than the original languages. At least nineteen German translations of the Bible or parts thereof had appeared prior to Martin Luther, but his own translation of the whole Bible into German, made from the original Hebrew and Greek, quickly became "the" Bible of German-speaking Protestantism (New Testament 1522, whole Bible 1534). The new emphasis on the Bible as the norm for church teaching and Christian life, in conscious contrast to ecclesiastical tradition and the teaching office of the church, meant that it was now more important to define the exact limits of the canon. Protestantism mostly followed Martin Luther's lead in returning to the Hebrew Bible of Palestinian Judaism, thus relegating to the margin or rejecting entirely the deuterocanonical books found in the LXX and Vulgate but not in the Hebrew. Since early Christianity had not done this, this meant that the New Testament contained quotations and allusions to documents no longer regarded as canonical.

4.3.3 The English Bible

Pre–King James Version

The King James Bible of 1611 was not the first English Bible, but came at the climax of a long and controversial development. Among its predecessors:

William Wycliffe, 1382, 1388. There had been fragmentary paraphrases and glosses of parts of the Bible into English as early as the ninth century, but the first complete translation of the Bible into English was made under the influence and encouragement of the Oxford scholar and reformer William Wycliffe (1330–1384). Guided by Wycliffe's leadership, his students and associates made a relatively literal translation of the Latin Vulgate into English. Though Wycliffe was condemned for heresy, for two centuries his translation was the only English Bible and exerted great influence on the developing English language (as Luther's translation did for German) and on all subsequent English translations.

William Tyndale, 1526. Though opposed by the church authorities, William Tyndale (ca. 1492–1536) published his translation of the New Testament from exile in Germany. Copies were smuggled into England. The Old Testament was almost completed before he was executed for heresy in 1536. A reversal in the church situation when Cromwell came to power meant that the Tyndale Bible could be freely circulated. While influenced by Wycliffe, it was a fresh translation that bypassed the Vulgate and was made directly from the Hebrew and Greek texts. Its clarity and vividness had great influence on subsequent English translations. The New Testament order of books followed that of Martin Luther, who had separated Hebrews, James, Jude, and Revelation in a secondary category at the end of the New Testament, almost as an appendix.

Miles Coverdale, 1535. Coverdale's translation was partly influenced by Tyndale. Though it received no official royal approval, its circulation in England was not opposed, and it was the first complete English Bible to be printed and circulated. Coverdale followed the Vulgate order of books rather than that of the Hebrew Bible, and for the first time printed the Apocrypha as a separate appendix. Coverdale's translation of the Psalms was incorporated into the *Book of Common Prayer*, where it remained until the 1979 revision.

"Thomas Matthew," 1537. Published under a pseudonym (it was still dangerous to translate the Bible in England), this translation was heavily influenced by Tyndale.

The Great Bible, 1540. This Bible was called "great," that is, "large," because of its size (10″ × 15″). This was the first "authorized" English Bible, that is, the first version officially approved by ecclesiastical and government authorities. It was a revision by Miles Coverdale, based on several previous translations, primarily that of "Thomas Matthew." The Great Bible returned to the "standard" order of New Testament books now found in our Bible (see on Tyndale above).

Various printer's editions, 1547–1553. During the brief reign of Edward VI, when it was legal to publish the Bible apart from ecclesiastical regulation, publishers took advantage of the occasion to produce fourteen editions of the whole Bible and thirty-five editions of the New Testament. These were mostly reprints of the versions of Tyndale, "Thomas Matthew," and Richard Taverner, but were intentionally blended into "new" versions with tendentious annotations. Bible publishing was becoming a profitable business, and lack of control allowed it to become market-driven.

Geneva Bible, 1560. The restoration of Roman Catholic authority in England made biblical translation by unauthorized individuals once again a dangerous venture. The new English translation produced by Protestant scholars exiled in Geneva became the Bible of the English Reformation. For over a century it was among the most influential English Bibles, appearing in over 180 different editions. It was the Bible of Shakespeare and Milton, of the Pilgrims who came to America, and of King James himself. The Geneva Bible was the first to introduce numbered verses (numbered chapters had been introduced in the thirteenth century). While this facilitated the location of biblical references, the printing of every verse as a separately numbered paragraph contributed to the false impression that biblical documents are collections of individual verses rather than coherent unified texts. Likewise, the Geneva Bible was the first to introduce the misconceived idea of italics for words "added" to the original texts, a practice continued by the KJV and some of its successors.

Bishops' Bible, 1568. Partly to counteract the Protestant Geneva Bible, which was very popular among the people, but not officially authorized by the established church, a revision of the Great Bible was issued; its translators were exclusively bishops. It was the second English Bible "authorized to be read in churches."

Rheims-Douay, 1582–1610. The changing politico-religious situation meant that now Roman Catholics found themselves persecuted in England. Some scholars found refuge in Douay (Douai) across the channel in France, and for the first time produced an English Bible sponsored by the Roman Catholic Church. The translation was made from the Vulgate rather than the original languages. Its relatively literal Latin-like English was difficult to understand, but in succeeding generations it was revised several times and remained the standard Roman Catholic English Bible until the twentieth century.

King James (Authorized) Version, 1611

We have seen what a large number of English Bibles had been produced from the beginnings under Wycliffe in 1382, through the turbulent times of the Reformation in England, until the reign of James VI of Scotland, who became James I of England. James had a personal interest in producing a standard Bible for the English-speaking church and in 1604 convened a conference of both Anglican and Puritan clergy. As a result, a translation committee of fifty-four (extant lists name only forty-seven) leading scholars and churchmen was appointed and instructed.[7] They were to use the best available Hebrew and Greek texts (not the Vulgate) as the basis of their work. They were not to make a fresh translation, but to revise previous translations, chiefly the Bishops' Bible of 1568; thus the AV or KJV is a *version* (of previous translations), not itself a *translation*.

The work was well done. The task was divided among six panels of translators (three for the Old Testament, two for the New Testament, one for the Apocrypha), but the whole group reviewed and passed on the work of each panel. Their results were expressed in the vivid and clear English of the Elizabethan age, unsurpassed in style and beauty, and destined to have a formative effect on the developing English language. It was a fairly literal translation, but the translators explicitly rejected the idea that the same Greek or Hebrew word should always be translated by the same English word. The translators adopted the practice of the Geneva Bible of printing each verse as a separate paragraph, and indicating words "added" to the original text by printing them in italics. When it appeared in 1611, the elaborate title page declared the version to be: "The Holy Bible, Conteyning the Old Testament, and the New: Newly Translated out of the Originall tongues: & with the former Translations diligently compared and revised, by his Maiesties speciall Commandement. Appointed to be read in Churches."

In fact, though the king had sponsored the production of the new version, it was never officially authorized either by the king or any ecclesiastical body. Nevertheless, the work became known as the "Authorized Version" (AV) or "King James Version" (KJV), and was gradually accepted by Protestant English-speaking Christianity as simply "the Bible." This it remained for three centuries.[8] The reader should note that this was a relatively late development in the history of the English Bible. It is not the case that the King James Version was the "original" English Bible that was "changed" by later translations. In 1600, there were many English Bibles on the scene; in 1700, mainly one.

KJV to NRSV

The KJV itself was never a single text, but from the beginning had a variety of wordings. A 1613 revision of the original 1611 edition included more than four hundred changes. There were further revisions in 1629, 1638, 1762, and 1769, and printers and publishing houses continued to quietly amend the text, so that the editions almost universally accepted as "the" Bible differed from each other, from various earlier editions of the AV, and from the 1611 "original." By the nineteenth century, two major developments made it clear that the version of the KJV then current needed to be officially revised. First, new discoveries brought to light older manuscripts of the New Testament than those used by the KJV translators, so that advances in textual criticism meant the available Greek New Testament was closer to the original documents than the Greek New Testament that had been translated in the KJV. Second, the English language continued to change. Not only did the "thee and thou" style of Elizabethan English no longer represent everyday speech, but hundreds of words in the Bible were no longer understandable, or were misunderstood, by the ordinary reader (e.g., "wot" for "knew," "conversation" for "manner

7. The original preface, "The Translators to the Reader," is a classic statement of the translators' principles. Now seldom printed in the KJV Bible itself, it is available in a 1997 reprint from the American Bible Society and online.

8. But not immediately. In 1620 when the Pilgrims came to the New World, they apparently brought only the 1560 Geneva Bible, which had already become traditional. The 1611 KJV was still "too modern."

of life," "ass" for "donkey"). Words that were understandable but no longer common English style gave the Bible a look and feel it did not originally have ("begot"; "and it came to pass"; "which" referring to persons, as in "Our Father which art in heaven").

Revised Version (RV) and American Standard Version (ASV)

To overcome the difficulties and respond to the needs cited above, during the eighteenth and especially the nineteenth centuries, several translations of the whole Bible, and especially of the New Testament, were made by various individuals and privately published. Some of these were idiosyncratic, some were marked improvements on various aspects of the KJV, and some were both. None of them had any "authorized" standing, and none caught on, as "the" English Bible. The need was apparent for the church itself, represented by its official bodies, to make an up-to-date translation or revision. A proposal was introduced in the British churches in 1870 that resulted in the Revised Version (RV). The New Testament was published in 1881, and the whole Bible in 1885. American scholars had been included, in the hope of producing one Bible for the English-speaking world. The Americans were not always pleased with the majority decisions of the committee, however, particularly in view of differences between British and American English, and proposed about six hundred modifications. By agreement, an edition with the renderings preferred by the American scholars could be published after twenty years, which resulted in the American Standard Version (ASV) of 1901.

Like the RV, the ASV was not a fresh translation, but a revision of the KJV in the light of later manuscripts, advanced knowledge, and the changing English language. In many respects it was a very accurate translation, a vast improvement on the KJV, and became the accepted text in academic circles. Two major weaknesses were that it attempted to be a very literal translation ("good Greek but poor English") and that it retained the archaic "thee and thou" style of the KJV. While it was an immediate publishing sensation—some newspapers printed the entire New Testament as a supplement on the day it appeared—the initial interest quickly subsided, and in the popular mind the KJV continued to be "the" Bible for most of the English-speaking world.

Revised Standard Version (RSV)

To prohibit pirated and altered editions circulating under the title "American Standard Version," the text was copyrighted, and designated the "Standard" version to distinguish it from other versions that appeared in the meantime claiming to be the "American Revised Version." In 1928 this copyright was transferred to the International Council of Religious Education, an association of the appropriate boards of more than forty major denominations in the United States and Canada, which was incorporated into the National Council of Churches' Division of Christian Education after its formation in 1950. The Council assumed responsibility for the continued revision of the ASV and formed an ecumenical Standard Bible Committee for this purpose. After much deliberation it was decided that a thorough revision of the ASV was needed.

Thirty-seven scholars served as members of the translation committee, along with a fifty-member advisory board representing all cooperating denominations (and one Jewish scholar). The New Testament was published in 1946 and the whole Bible in 1952. It was not a new translation but a thorough revision of the KJV and ASV, eliminating their archaic language and other problems. The appearance of the Revised Standard Version (RSV) precipitated a furor of excitement among some readers, who charged it with being a "communist-inspired" "infidel" version, but it quickly became the Bible in mainstream American Protestantism. A second edition of the New Testament appeared in 1971, with minor revisions and improvements continuing to be made. The version was also well received among Roman Catholics. An adjustment in the way in which the apocryphal/deuterocanonical books were printed as a separate section, and a few footnotes representing alternate translations, eventuated in an edition of the RSV—the *Common Bible*—officially acceptable to Protestant, Catholic, and Orthodox. By 1977, for the first time since the Reformation, there existed a truly ecumenical version of the English Bible blessed by these three branches of the worldwide church.

New Revised Standard Version (NRSV)

In the light of new manuscript discoveries that further clarified the original text of the Bible, increased insight into the meaning of biblical texts as the result of biblical scholarship, continuing changes in the English language, and increased desire for inclusive language, in 1974 the Standard Bible Committee was charged by the National Council of Churches to make a thorough revision of the RSV. The ecumenical committee held two one-week meetings per year until the work was completed in 1989. Hundreds of passages were changed in order to render the meaning of the original Greek text more accurately, in more natural English, and less subject to misunderstanding, especially when read orally in worship. (See samples in Box 4.)

Some remaining archaisms were eliminated: "Behold" occurs 142 times in the RSV New Testament, never in the NRSV, being omitted or replaced with "look," "see, "suddenly," and the like. "Whence" or "whither" (nine times RSV New Testament) became "where," "where . . . from," or other equivalents in contemporary English.

The grammatical constructions of the Greek New Testament were more precisely rendered. For instance, the Greek form of posing a question often indicates whether a positive or negative response is expected (see Box 5).

The most distinctive change in the NRSV, however, was its use of gender-neutral English language referring to people when the original texts clearly meant to include both male and female. The Greek language, ancient and modern, uses grammatically masculine terms in a generic sense (e.g., "man," "brother"), as English once did. Increasing sensitivity in the

BOX 4: Examples of Clarification from RSV to NRSV

	RSV	*NRSV*
John 2:15	And making a whip of cords, he drove them all, with the sheep and oxen, out of the temple.	Making a whip of cords, he drove all of them out of the temple, both the sheep and the cattle.
Luke 22:35	"Did you lack anything?" They said, "Nothing."	"Did you lack anything?" They said, "No, not a thing."
2 Cor 11:25	Once I was stoned.	Once I received a stoning.
2 Pet 2:16	A dumb ass spoke with human voice.	A speechless donkey spoke with a human voice.

BOX 5: Greek Questions that Anticipate a Particular Response

	RSV	*NRSV*
Matt 9:15	And Jesus said to them, "Can the wedding guests mourn as long as the bridegroom is with them?	And Jesus said to them, "The wedding guests cannot mourn as long as the bridegroom is with them, can they?"
John 21:5	Jesus said to them, "Children, have you any fish?"	Jesus said to them, "Children, you have no fish, have you?"

BOX 6: Rephrasing with Gender-inclusive Language

	RSV	*NRSV*
Matt 4:4	Man shall not live by bread alone.	One does not live by bread alone.
Matt 6:30	O men of little faith	You of little faith
2 Cor 10:17	Let him who boasts, boast of the Lord.	Let the one who boasts, boast in the Lord.
Rev 2:29	He who has an ear, let him hear what the Spirit says to the churches.	Let anyone who has an ear listen to what the Spirit is saying to the churches.

English-speaking world to this issue meant that what was originally intended inclusively was now heard exclusively. Consequently, the committee received a mandate from the National Council of Churches that "in references to men and women, masculine-oriented language should be eliminated as far as this can be done without altering passages that reflect the historical situation of ancient patriarchal culture."[9] The committee decided not to use the "her/his" terminology that had become common, but to achieve the goal of inclusiveness in language by changing active verbs to passives, singulars to plurals, third-person pronouns to second-person pronouns (which are gender-neutral in English) and by various kinds of rephrasing that still preserved the original meaning. Some samples are in Box 6.

The response to the NRSV was overwhelmingly positive—though some were suspicious of the new version. To the extent that there can be an authorized translation in today's ecclesiastical scene, the NRSV is the translation most widely authorized by the churches. Thirty-three Protestant denominations, the American and Canadian Conferences of Catholic bishops, and the Greek Orthodox Church have all given it official blessing.

The NRSV represents the legacy of the King James tradition. The NRSV is a revision of the RSV, which was a revision of the American Standard Version, which was a revision of the 1881 Revised Version, which was a revision of the 1611 KJV. But the KJV had been informally and unofficially revised numerous times between 1611 and 1881. Moreover, the KJV itself was not the beginning, but the end of a process—it was the revision of the Bishops' Bible, a revision of the Great Bible (under the direction of Miles Coverdale), which was a revision of "Matthew's Bible," which was a revision of Tyndale. There is thus an unbroken chain extending from Tyndale through the KJV to the NRSV, the contemporary representative of this tradition. As a revision of the RSV, the NRSV remains copyrighted by the National Council of Churches.

Other Church-Sponsored Translations

As a representative sample, we have looked at one stream of biblical translation in some detail. The history of the English Bible includes other significant streams of church-sponsored translation alongside the KJV–NRSV tradition, which we can here only mention:

— *The New English Bible–Revised English Bible.* In 1946 the Church of England was joined by several other British Protestant church bodies, as well as Roman Catholic observers, in proposing an entirely new translation, not a further revision of the 1881 Revised Version. The New Testament of the NEB appeared in

9. From the preface of the NRSV, "To the Reader."

1961, slightly revised when it was included in the whole Bible published in 1970. A thorough revision appeared in 1989 as the *Revised English Bible* (REB), which has become the standard Bible in the United Kingdom and some other English-speaking parts of the world.

— *The New American Bible*. American and British Roman Catholics had also long acknowledged the problems involved in continuing to use an archaic English translation. In 1943 Pope Pius XII issued his famous encyclical on biblical studies, encouraging Catholic scholars to work from the original texts rather than the Vulgate and to take account of modern literary criticism. Thus in 1944 a group of Catholic scholars, at the invitation of the Bishops' Committee of the Confraternity of Christian Doctrine, began work on the first American translation of the Bible made directly from the original languages. After the Second Vatican Council's directive that translations be produced "in cooperation with separated brothers," Protestant scholars were included in the translation team. The work was completed in 1970, adapting some of the earlier work on the New Testament already published in 1941 (but that had been based on the Latin Vulgate). The translation was called *The New American Bible* (to be distinguished from the *New American Standard Bible*). Especially in the New Testament, neither the translation nor the copious notes were abreast of current scholarship, so that in 1978 a major revision was commissioned. The results were published in 1986, along with improved introductions and notes. The preface explains the general adherence to traditional gender-specific language. While many readers would have preferred a more inclusive translation policy analogous to the NRSV, the NAB is an accurate and readable translation. The *Catholic Study Bible*, an annotated version with an extensive "Reading Guide," introductions, and notes, is a splendid translation and resource for Bible study.

— *The Jerusalem Bible–New Jerusalem Bible*. The *Bible de Jérusalem* is so named because it originated as a project of the French Dominican biblical scholars located at the École biblique de Jérusalem under the leadership of Roland De Vaux, one of the pioneers in research on the Dead Sea Scrolls. Their extensive series of biblical commentaries that included a new translation from the original languages was compressed into one volume that appeared in 1956. An English edition, the *Jerusalem Bible*, based on the original languages but with the French translation and notes in view, was made by twenty members of the British Catholic Biblical Association. When it appeared in 1966 it was thus the first Roman Catholic translation of the whole Bible in English made directly from the original languages instead of the Latin Vulgate. Its readability, accuracy, and comprehensive introductions and notes, as well as its approval by church authorities, made it a favorite among British and American Roman Catholics, as the French translation had become in French-speaking countries. An updated edition of the *Bible de Jérusalem* appeared in 1973, and its corresponding English version in 1985, the *New Jerusalem Bible*.

Private, Denominational, Institutional, and Commercial Translations

In every period, some individuals and groups have been dissatisfied with the "authorized" translations. There are several overlapping reasons for this: (1) The process of official revision sometimes lags behind the discovery of new manuscripts and advances in textual criticism, the insights of biblical scholarship into the meaning of the ancient texts, and the churches' need for the Scripture to speak in understandable contemporary language. This was the case during the Reformation, for instance, when Luther's and other translations into the vernacular made the Bible more accessible to the laity. (2) Various individuals and groups have felt that the "standard" translations did not adequately reflect political or theological views they assumed to be in the Bible. (3) The standard translations were too liberal or conservative for the group's interests. (4) Ecclesiastical "power structures" responsible for the standard translations were suspect in some circles, both conservative and liberal. (5) The profit motive and marketing considerations also play a role, sometimes the major role. Bible publishing is an enormously lucrative business, so that publishers have an economic interest in having their own versions/translations/editions of the Bible.

This combination of reasons has produced hundreds of different English translations of the New Testament. The thirty-seven years between 1952 and 1989 (RSV to NRSV) saw the publication of twenty-six translations of the whole Bible and an additional twenty-five translations of the New Testament, that is, more than one new translation of the New Testament per year. Several more have been added to the list since 1989, and new translations and versions are marketed every year. In the typical religious bookstore or website, the uninitiated reader is met by a bewildering variety of translations and annotated versions of the Bible. Currently, at least 140 English translations and versions of the New Testament are available (sixty English translations of the whole Bible, another eighty of the New Testament). Of these, we will only briefly note the most successful in marketing terms, *New International Version* (NIV) and its most recent competitor, *The Common English Bible* (CEB).

The New International Version (NIV). The RSV was met with suspicion and skepticism by many religious conservatives, who considered it to be too influenced by the liberal theology and critical biblical scholarship of the translators. Dissatisfaction with the RSV led to the appointment of committees by the Christian Reformed Church (1956) and the National Association of Evangelicals (1957) that resulted in a new translation representing exclusively conservative scholarship. The New Testament was published in 1973 and the whole Bible in 1978 as a "Modern and Accurate Phrase for Phrase English Translation," that is, it abandoned the claim to be a word-for-word, literal translation. The NIV has been widely accepted among evangelicals as "the" Bible and has sold more than 150 million copies. The translation committee was composed of ninety-nine persons of a variety of denominations, ninety of whom were from North America, three from England, and three each from Australia and New Zealand, presumably the basis for calling it the "international" version. The preface declares that they were all "committed to the authority and infallibility of the Bible as God's word in written form."[10] The NIV follows an eclectic reconstructed Greek text, but still agrees with the NRSV in forty-five of forty-six places where verses and phrases of the Textus Receptus are omitted or relegated to the margin. It sometimes adopts a disputed textual reading, thereby avoiding a problem for the claim that the Bible is infallible.[11] Many of its renderings are accurate and felicitous and were later adopted by the NRSV.

Responding to continuing changes in the English language and culture, a full-scale new revision was completed in 2001, the *Today's New International Version* (TNIV). Many changes were mere updating into contemporary English (Mary is no longer "with child" but "pregnant"). Avoidance of gender-inclusive language had become a hallmark of the NIV, but this was adjusted to more recent sensitivity in

10. Nonetheless, as Metzger, *Bible in Translation*, 141, points out, the NIV was thus severely criticized by fundamentalists and the most conservative evangelicals, since it "translated" words not in original texts and did not translate some words found there. See, e.g., Robert P. Martin, *Accuracy of Translation and the New International Version* (Carlisle, PA: Banner of Truth Trust, 1989), 19–67, and Earl D. Radmacher and Zane C. Hodges, *The NIV Reconsidered: A Fresh Look at a Popular Translation* (Dallas: Rendención Viva, 1990), 25–130.

11. E.g., in John 7:8, by reading οὔπω (not yet) instead of οὐκ (not, as in the NRSV), the NIV avoids a clash with 7:10. This has now been changed in NIV 2011, so that the current version adopts the same Greek text and translation as the NRSV.

the TNIV, as can be seen from the comparisons in Box 7 (Rom 12:6–8).

The inclusive language of the TNIV proved to be problematical for some evangelicals, and its publication was suspended in view of marketing considerations. The 2011 updated NIV partially rescinds its gender-neutral language. An illustrative example from Gen 1:26 is in Box 8.

The Common English Bible (CEB). While a number of factors and motivations are at work in this most recent project, the CEB can be thought of as the response of a "mainline" church publishing house to the success of the NIV and frustration over copyright fees for use of the NRSV. The CEB is a project of Abingdon Press, a publishing imprint of the United Methodist Publishing House and affiliated with the United Methodist Church. Neither this denomination nor any other provides financial support or directly oversees the publishing activities of Abingdon Press. As sponsors for the new translation, Abingdon Press formed the Common English Bible Committee and an alliance of denominational publishers called the Church Resources Development Corporation. These publishers have played a minimal role in the project and seem to have been enlisted for purposes of consultation and promotion. Abingdon Press will receive most of the financial benefits. The denominations with which they are affiliated played no role at all.

To date, the procedure used in translating and assembling the final text has not been published. Conversations with translators and public presentations and discussions at the Society of Biblical Literature indicate that the translation of each book was farmed out to an individual translator, whose work was reviewed by a colleague, then evaluated by an editor for reading level, then by "readability groups," and given its final revision by the editorial committee. This committee then smoothed out some of the differing styles and perspectives of the individual translators and decided on the final text.

BOX 7: Comparison of Romans 12:6–8

NIV	*TNIV*	*NRSV*
We have different gifts, according to the grace given us. If a man's gift is prophesying, let him use it in proportion to his faith. If it is serving, let him serve; if it is teaching, let him teach; if it is encouraging, let him encourage; if it is contributing to the needs of others, let him give generously; if it is leadership, let him govern diligently; if it is showing mercy, let him do it cheerfully.	We have different gifts, according to the grace given to each of us. If your gift is prophesying, then prophesy in accordance with your faith; if it is serving, then serve; if it is teaching, then teach; if it is to encourage, then give encouragement; if it is giving, then give generously; if it is to lead, do it diligently; if it is to show mercy, do it cheerfully.	We have gifts that differ according to the grace given to us: prophecy, in proportion to faith; ministry, in ministering; the teacher, in teaching; the exhorter, in exhortation; the giver, in generosity; the leader, in diligence; the compassionate, in cheerfulness.

BOX 8: Comparison of Genesis 1:26

NIV	*TNIV*	*NIV 2011*	*NRSV*
Then God said, "Let us make man in our image,	Then God said, "Let us make human beings in our image,	Then God said, "Let us make mankind in our image,	Then God said, "Let us make humankind in our image,

Individual translators did not have the opportunity to approve the editorial changes in their own work, nor did the group of translators as a whole review the whole work. The translation is thus basically an anthology of individual translations, reviewed and edited by a small committee.

Among the features emphasized in the publishers' promotion:

(1) It is an *inclusive* translation. The 120 translators include men and women who represent twenty-two faith traditions and cover much of the ethnic, racial, and liberal-to-conservative spectrum. In some places, gender-inclusiveness is obtained by using "he or she" for the generic masculine singular Greek pronoun (e.g., Rom 7:1); elsewhere, "they" or "their" plays this role (e.g., "each one will receive their own reward" [1 Cor 3:8]). Sometimes the effort to use gender-inclusive language seems to be at cross-purposes with this effort toward readability, for example, in Nehemiah 10:36, "firstborn sons" becomes "oldest offspring of our children." In Genesis 1–3, "Adam" has become "the human being," resulting in such translations as "the LORD God fashioned a woman and brought her to the human being" (Gen 2:22).

(2) It is a *readable* translation, with seventh-grade reading level as the goal (NRSV: eleventh-grade level). It was market-tested by seventy-seven reading groups and revised (by the editors, not the translators) in the light of their feedback. Venerable vocabulary unfamiliar to modern readers has disappeared or been minimized: "Son of Man" has become the "Human One" (though in Matt 16:28 the Human One still comes in *his* kingdom); the "Law" (*Torah*) has become the "Instruction." On the other hand, such renderings as "immigrant" for *gēr/paroikos* (גֵּר/πάροικος), traditionally "sojourner" or "alien," improve both readability and accuracy.

(3) It uses *contemporary speech*, including contractions, except "in divine or poetic discourse." Though God doesn't use contractions, angels (Luke 1), Satan (Job 1), and the risen Jesus do ("I've received all authority in heaven and on earth" [Matt 28:18]).

For many readers within the Christian community the main question raised by such translations is not how best to translate this or that phrase, but how best to deal with the complexity of issues associated with authority, responsibility, and legitimacy. For most readers, even those with some knowledge of Greek or Hebrew, the English translation *is* the Bible. They rightfully ask who it is that hands them a book with the claim that it is Holy Scripture, and by what authority they do so. Such translations as the CEB will continue to keep alive the question of the relationship between commercial success in the religious marketplace and legitimacy in the community of faith as Holy Scripture.

4.3.4 "Which is the Best Translation?"

We are happily past the time when the church had one officially approved translation, and those who introduced new translations could be burned at the stake for corrupting the faith by their innovations. These times must never return, and will not. Yet the issue remains. Can any individual, group, or business select the books they think should be in the Bible, translate them in accord with their own understanding and purpose, and have the result accepted as "the Bible"? Who gets to say, and on what criteria?

The above discussion suggests three overlapping criteria in evaluating translations:

1. Based on Oldest and Best Manuscripts

Translation and textual criticism are inseparable. No translation of the New Testament can be better than the reconstructed Greek text on which it is based. The best reconstruction of the Greek New Testament must be based on the oldest and best manuscripts and the best methods of textual criticism (see §§3.1–3.3). This cannot be the work and judgment of one individual, but must represent the combined efforts of qualified and authorized scholars. While the late and corrupt Textus Receptus (see §3.4 above) still has some advocates among conservative Bible readers, practically all translations of the twentieth and twenty-first century are based on the latest critical texts such as Nestle-Aland[27], the best available reconstruction of the lost original texts.

2. Contemporary Language

Biblical texts originally spoke in the language and idiom of their own time. As the English language changes, biblical translations must also change to preserve the ancient meaning in contemporary language. Virtually all translations of the last hundred years meet this criterion. Even advocates of the *King James Version* have mostly switched their allegiance to the upgraded *New King James Version*, which uses contemporary English. Yet just what constitutes "contemporary language" continues to be an issue. The New Testament is an ancient collection of texts, from another culture, expressed in a vocabulary and conceptuality not easily grasped by modern English readers, who are mostly not able to determine whether or not what they are reading accurately represents the Greek text. In the interest of readability or sales, should this inherent difficulty be mitigated by "dumbing down" the text to everyday speech so that readers are "more comfortable" with it? In the case of, for example, Shakespeare or the Constitution of the United States, we ask the readers to make the intellectual effort required to understand important texts from another time and place, and would resist rephrasing them in street language.

3. Committee Translation Commissioned by (Major, Responsible Segments of) the Ecumenical Church

No one person knows enough, or is unbiased enough, to translate the Bible adequately for the whole church. A large committee, qualified in the biblical languages and their interpretation, representing a variety of cultural settings, theological streams, and denominational loyalties, by working together and comparing their results, will tend to cancel out individual and denominational biases, and produce a translation representing the best insight into the meaning of Scripture for the whole church. Such a translation must represent internal discussion and consensus among a broad spectrum of the translators, not an anthology of individual translations of particular books. Such a process requires several years of intensive work by a large number of people; it is very expensive. It is a project to be guided by the church as a whole, working through its corporate structures. Yet the worldwide church is not structured in such a way as to authorize Bibles for all Christians. No group or individual can presently speak for all English-speaking Christians.

All translations and versions are thus somewhere on the spectrum between purely individual translations and translations that are universally and officially approved by the church. At one end of the spectrum, there are purely individual translations, but they would not continue to exist unless they were received by some elements of the community of Christian faith. On the other hand, no version of the Bible can claim official approval by the whole church. Yet there are representative groups in various denominations and councils of churches that are ecumenically oriented, and have the interests of the whole church at heart. The Roman Catholic Church and the Greek Orthodox Church have clear means of authorizing a particular translation. For Protestantism, councils of churches such as the National Council of the Churches of Christ in the USA and similar structures in other countries play an important role in protecting the Bible from purely publish-for-profit, theological, or ideological motives. Sponsorship by such groups is important in legitimizing any translation or version.[12] The commercial success of such

12. The role of individual translations in some situations is not to be minimized or discounted. The example of Luther's German translation is often cited. The individual must sometimes oppose constituted ecclesiastical authorities. Yet Luther's translation quickly became a committee translation authorized not just by the

translations as the NIV and the CEB (the latter still to be determined) raises the issue of the relation between the church, denominational publishing houses, and the commercial presses. Who has the right to hand a book to the church, and to purvey it in the marketplace, with the claim "This is a Bible"?

Most modern translations of the New Testament can be read and studied with profit by the inquiring student. The discerning student will not approach the variety of translations and versions as though it were a cafeteria; "I *like* the way this translation handles this verse" is hardly a usable criterion for the validity of one translation over another. While insight can be gained from numerous translations, the following are among those that meet the criteria discussed above, and can form a trustworthy basis for preaching and teaching in the church:

— *NRSV* American mainline Protestantism with an ecumenical orientation

— *NAB* American Roman Catholic translation with an ecumenical orientation

— *REB* British Protestantism with an ecumenical orientation

— *NJB* British Roman Catholicism with an ecumenical orientation

4.4 For Further Reading

Ackroyd, P. R., and C. F. Evans, eds. *The Cambridge History of The Bible*. 3 vols. Cambridge: Cambridge University Press, 1963–1970.

Jobes, Karen H., and Moises Silva. *Invitation to the Septuagint*. Grand Rapids: Baker, 2000.

Lewis, Jack P. *The English Bible from KJV to NIV: A History and Evaluation*. 2nd ed. Grand Rapids: Baker Book House, 1981, 1991.

McGrath, Alister. *In the Beginning: The Story of the King James Bible and How It Changed a Nation, a Language, and a Culture*. New York: Random House, 2001.

Metzger, Bruce M. *The Bible in Translation: Ancient and English Versions*. Grand Rapids: Baker, 2001.

Metzger, Bruce M., Robert C. Dentan, and Walter Harrelson. *The Making of the New Revised Standard Version of the Bible*. Grand Rapids: Eerdmans, 1991.

individual Luther, but by a major stream of the institutional church, and has been revised several times by church commissions, so that the present form of the Luther Bible represents the community, not just Luther the individual.

5
The Interpreted New Testament

5.1 The New Testament Is the Church's Book in the Sense that the Church *Interprets* It.

Working Definitions. The terms "exegesis," "hermeneutics," and "interpretation" are used with varied and overlapping meanings. For purposes of communication, I adopt the following working definitions: *Exegesis* (from the Greek ἐξήγησις [*exēgēsis*, explication, explanation], literally a "leading out" of the meaning) refers to the process of recovering the ancient meaning in its own historical setting, "what it meant." *Hermeneutics* (from the Greek ἑρμηνεία *hermēneia*, interpretation, translation from one language to another) refers to the process of translating the ancient meaning, originally expressed in its own language and worldview, into the language and conceptuality of another time, so that that original meaning can be understood in a different setting within a different worldview. *Interpretation* refers to both aspects, the whole task of discovering the original meaning and translating it into modern categories. Thus *interpretation* is the comprehensive term that embraces the historical *exegesis* and the contemporizing *hermeneutics*.

Written and oral "texts." Although the following discussions refer to "readers" and the interpretation of "texts," the modern reader should keep in mind that this is a conventional way of referring to ancient compositions that were mostly written to be read aloud. Israelites, Jews, and early Christians received these "texts" orally, in the context of community. In oral presentation, there is always already an interpretation, generated by selection, emphasis, tone of voice, and community context. Further: the texts were read forth in the assembly—the synagogue or church—as *wholes* or extensive, continuous segments. The issue was rarely the meaning of a particular "verse" or sentence, but the shaping of community life by the common experience of hearing together extensive readings from their sacred writings. The New Testament is the church's book because it is heard together as the worshiping community.

5.1.1 Interpretation: Necessity, Nature, Value

The traditional doctrines of *sola scriptura* ("the Bible alone") and *the perspicuity of Scripture* ("the Bible is clear in itself") have generated two popular protests against interpretation: (1) "I don't want an interpretation of the Bible. I just want the Bible." (2) "I don't want anybody to tell me how to interpret the Bible; I just want to interpret it for myself." Each of these protests expresses reverence for the Bible and is usually made by those who affirm the Bible's authority and want to appropriate its message rather than a secondary substitute.

1. The first objection is misleading, however, in that it supposes a clear distinction can be made between the Bible's own message and

secondary interpretations. We have already seen that every translation is an interpretation, just as is every reading of the ancient Greek text. So also is every oral or silent reading of the text an interpretation. This becomes immediately clear when one hears the text read aloud by someone else, for no two people will give exactly the same intonations and emphases. Interpretation is not a barrier between reader and text, but the means that facilitates a hearing of the text. Without interpretation, texts are merely letters on the page, and Mozart's music or Shakespeare's drama are inkblots frozen on silent paper. To be sure, it is these notes of Mozart and these words of Shakespeare that are to be interpreted; the interpreter cannot substitute other notes or words, or make them say just anything. Nonetheless, it is by interpretation, and only so, that the text regains its living voice. Interpretation is not an evil, not even a necessary evil, but an indispensable ally in hearing the text.

2. The second protest acknowledges the necessity of interpretation, but disdains the presumed efforts of *other* people or communities to tell me how *I* should interpret it: "To be sure," says the objector, "texts must be interpreted, but I will make my own interpretation without interference from anyone else." The first objection resists interpretation, the latter resists dogma as limiting the individual's own interpretation. The reality, however, is that all interpretation, of the Bible and everything else, is done from within an interpreting community and is influenced by the perspective of the community. The appropriation of every text, every statement of the meaning of a text, has already been interpreted in a provisional sense. This received interpretation may indeed be modified by further study, but this study too will be influenced by the community in which one stands, the lenses through which one sees, the commitments one already inevitably has. To be aware of this is to be a more competent and responsible interpreter.

5.1.2 All Interpretation Is *Perspectival,* from within an *Interpreting Community.*

Along with most scholars of all perspectives and persuasions, I consider it an illusion to suppose that the Bible can be read with total objectivity, from some neutral, uninvolved standpoint that transcends the human perspective. No one approaches the Bible (or any other text) as a tabula rasa. Every reader views the Bible through a particular set of lenses. These lenses both facilitate and condition seeing. Without these lenses, no one could see at all. Yet all lenses are shaped by the particular setting of the reader—the overlapping and interpenetrating social, economic, political, religious, gender, and racial aspects of every standpoint. In order to see at all, each person must stand somewhere and view reality from a particular perspective, through a particular set of eyes. This necessity of a particular standpoint does not mean that interpretation is individualistic, but precisely the opposite. An intrinsic aspect of every particular standpoint is that it is not purely individualistic, but belongs to and is shaped by community.

Human Existence as Such Is Linguistic and Hermeneutical.

One becomes human by being socialized. The chaos of sense experience must be organized and interpreted before the existent being can think and function as a human being. This includes the acquisition of language, which is acquired historically in a particular social context; it is not innate. A couple who adopts a newborn infant from Poland does not need to worry that they will not be able to understand Polish. If the couple is Hungarian, the baby will grow up speaking and thinking as a Hungarian; if the couple is American, the baby will grow up as an American—not as generically "American," but within some particular American community context. This acquisition of language includes not only vocabulary and grammar, but the genres and thought patterns that make communication possible in a particular culture.

No one can be generically human, only particularly so. One cannot belong to the human race in general; one's belongingness to humanity as a whole is always by belonging to some subdivision of humanity. No one speaks "human"; everyone speaks some particular human language—Spanish, Norwegian, English, Arabic. Every human being speaks and thinks in a particular language that has developed in history, which forms and conditions the possibilities of understanding and communication. This takes place only in community.

All Interpretation of Texts, of the Bible or Otherwise, Takes Place in Community.

Each community, and the texts written from within it, can be studied and analyzed from the outside by interested spectators. There is certainly an important sense in which such spectators can understand and appreciate the texts of a community to which they do not belong, and can respect and value the community itself. As a non-Muslim, I can study the Qur'an and understand much about it—especially if I am willing to learn Arabic well and immerse myself in the history and culture in which the Qur'an was written and has been interpreted. A Christian cathedral can be analyzed, even admired, from the outside, from the analytical spectator's standpoint. Explanations of the history of architecture, pointing out the various stages of construction, the differences between Gothic and Romanesque, and the details of constructing stained-glass windows, can be very helpful to uninformed insiders, who come to the cathedral to worship. But there is a sense in which the beauty of a cathedral, what a cathedral actually *is*, can be grasped only when one enters to worship, to sit quietly and pray or listen to the organ. Those who regularly do this as part of a worshiping community do not claim that they have grasped something, but that they have been grasped by the Reality represented by the cathedral (see the various translations of Phil 3:12, in which being grasped, grabbed by the risen Christ is Paul's point).

One can readily think of secular illustrations of the point as well: there is a sense in which books about Mozart and his music cannot be understood by nonmusicians, or by rock musicians who simply disdain classical music; similarly, lovers of Mozart who disdain rock music cannot really understand it. The nonmusician who wants to understand Mozart will seek out books written by musicians who claim to hear and appreciate something nonmusicians do not hear, even if he or she is dubious about the claim. Capitalists who want to understand the literature of communism will not only read the literature of other capitalists, but the literature of convinced communists. This is simply a matter of good historical method: all literature is written within and for an interpreting community, and there are dimensions of understanding that can be perceived only from within that community.

Thus, to claim that "The New Testament is the church's book in the sense that the church interprets it" is not necessarily dogmatism, but a particular instance of the hermeneutical project in general that applies to all texts, without exception. All interpretation represents some dimension of community interpretation, which individuals bring with them even when interpreting a text (or anything else) "privately." Thus *which* community/communities form the context(s) of interpretation, consciously or unconsciously, becomes a crucial issue. Through the centuries, the Christian community has claimed, in various ways, that the Bible can be truly understood only within the worshiping community of Christian faith. We will now briefly trace the outline of how this insight has worked out in the life of the Christian community.

5.1.3 The Ongoing Historical Stream of Interpretation

Interpretation and Reinterpretation within the Bible Itself

Reinterpretation within the Old Testament. To enter into the world of the Bible is to step into a lively, continuing stream of interpretation and reinterpretation. Placing constellations of books together and in a particular order is already an act of interpretation.[1] Deuteronomy represents a later reinterpretation of the legislation in Exodus. The final form of the texts of the Pentateuch represents the interpretation of earlier traditions and sources—including Deuteronomy. The books of Chronicles are explicitly reinterpretations of earlier documents, including Samuel and Kings. Most of the prophetic books were not written all at once by a single author, but represent an ongoing stream of prophetic reinterpretation. The language of Hosea, for example, was meant quite literally in its original proclamation; the accusation of harlotry was a protest against Baalism, the fertility religion attractive to the Israelites of the northern kingdom. This language was taken up a generation later in Judah, where the threat of Baalism and fertility religion was no longer the danger, and applied metaphorically. The language already had this metaphorical capacity, or this would not have been possible.[2] Such reinterpretation is occasionally made explicit, as when Jeremiah's prophecy that the exile would last seventy years is reinterpreted in Daniel as seventy weeks of years, that is, 490 years, in order to make the prophecy relevant for the later writer's own time (see Jer 25:11–12; Dan 9:1–27). This dynamic process of retelling and reinterpretation continued alongside the composition of the Jewish Scriptures, and after they were completed.

Biblical interpretation in early Judaism. It is clear that the rabbis came to the biblical text with their own convictions derived from tradition, and sought to ground them in the authoritative scriptural text. They read the text in the light of the fundamental convictions of their faith, one of which was that every word and letter of Scripture is given by God and theologically important. In a classic example, the Midrash on Genesis 2:7 points out that the verb for "and-he-formed" is spelled with a double *yod* (י), only here in the twenty-eight occurrences of this form in the MT (וַיִּיצֶר *wayyitser* rather than the usual וַיִּצֶר *wayitser*). Since every letter and minor variation of the sacred text has significance,[3] the doubling of the yod here must have significance. Since the noun יֵצֶר (*yetser*) begins with a yod, and can mean "imagination, inner impulse," the meaning must be that human beings were made by God with two impulses, the good *yetser* and the evil *yetser*, and that human beings are responsible to choose the good. By ingenious exegesis, this later doctrine is discovered in the text of the Bible.

The rabbis brought their deep concerns about the salvation of non-Israelite peoples to their interpretation of Scripture. God is the God of all peoples, but God has chosen only Israel to be the covenant people; only Israel has the Torah, the divine promises, and the temple ritual that mediates God's forgiveness. What about the others? Johanan ben Zakkai's interpretation of Proverbs 14:34 provided the answer: *Righteousness exalteth a nation, but the*

1. This is one of the points of canonical criticism. Placing James in the same New Testament canon as Romans, for instance, causes them to be interpreted in relation to each other. Placing James at the head of the collection of Catholic Epistles (instead of, e.g., between Matthew and Mark) is already an interpretation. The early church's separation of Acts from the Gospel of Luke and placing it prior to the Pauline letters or the Catholic Letters gives a different interpretation of both Acts and the letters. See Robert W. Wall, "A Unifying Theology of the Catholic Epistles," in *The Catholic Epistles and Apostolic Tradition*, ed. Karl-Wilhelm Niebuhr and Robert W. Wall (Waco: Baylor University Press, 2009), 13–42, and "The Priority of James," 153–60.
2. Cf. Brevard S. Childs, *Introduction to the Old Testament as Scripture* (Philadelphia: Fortress Press, 1979), 378–79.
3. In the New Testament, cf., e.g., Matt 5:18, and Paul's argumentation in Gal. 3:16.

kindness of the peoples, is sin (i.e., a sin offering). This means that just as the sin offerings make atonement for Israel, so good deeds, deeds of kindness, make atonement for the heathen. Here it is not clear whether it is the Gentiles' own good deeds, or the faithfulness of Israel in performing acts of charity, but the point of this Scripture is clear: God has provided a way for righteous Gentiles to be saved, just as God has provided for faithful Israelites to be saved.[4] So also, the Genesis Midrash reads Genesis not as ancient history, but as telling the story of Israel in the here and now and dealing with Jewish concerns in the Roman era. In Genesis, Esau rules, but Jacob possesses the birthright; in the interpreter's time, Rome rules, but Israel has the promise of God. By imaginative exegesis, Esau is made to represent Rome, the last of the four empires found in Daniel 2 and 7; this whole history is presumed to be known to the patriarchs and to Moses. That Esau is the brother of Jacob means that Rome is the brother of Israel. Esau/Rome now rules as the last empire, but what comes after that? The promised age of Israel's glory. Israel thus said to Rome, "Yes, you are part of Israel, the rejected part." "That concession—Rome is a sibling, a close relative of Israel—represents an implicit recognition of Christianity's claim to share the patrimony of Judaism, to be descended from Abraham and Isaac."[5] This is something of a counterpart of Paul's labored interpretation of Scripture in Romans 9–11, but from the other side—a Jewish view of the universal grace of God, claiming that Esau/Rome/Christianity is finally part of the one family of God and will be included in God's final redemptive act.

Some of this exegesis seems arbitrary or even frivolous to the modern reader, but the rabbinic tradition was devoted to the idea that every word and letter of Scripture was filled with divine meaning and therefore developed strict procedures and methods for deriving contemporary meaning from the ancient text. Rabbi Hillel, an older contemporary of Jesus, is credited with developing seven rules of interpretation that became traditional; these were later refined and expanded to thirteen, then to thirty-two. The lists included such principles as attending to the context, interpretation of an unclear passage by a clear one, and—most famous of all—*qal wahomer* ("light and heavy," *a minore ad maius*), that is, inference from the lesser to the greater. If something was prohibited on the Sabbath, for example, it was also prohibited on the greater festival days, even if not specifically mentioned in the biblical text. Such rules were not applied mechanically. In fact, the actual rule that guided interpretation was the dynamic tradition of the faith community; the rules sometimes functioned as rationalizations in the best sense of the word, providing justification for the interpretations provided by the living voice of tradition.

Allegory emerged within Judaism as a method of biblical interpretation during the Second Temple period. In allegorical interpretation, the literal meaning of the text is denied, and elements of the text are understood to represent other realities. While there is some allegorizing in the biblical interpretation of Palestinian Judaism, it was especially in the Greek-speaking Diaspora that the Greek methods of allegorizing were applied to the Bible. These methods had already been developed by streams of Greek philosophy, especially in Athens and Alexandria, as a way of making the classical Homeric stories of the gods acceptable to later generations who found their conduct unreasonable and immoral. In such traditions, the *Iliad* and *Odyssey* were not understood as recounting literal events, but as pointing to philosophical truths and providing directions for the moral life. This style of interpretation had been underway in Alexandria for generations and was a commonplace

4. For elaboration and documentation, see Jacob Neusner, *First-Century Judaism in Crisis: Yohanan ben Zakkai and the Renaissance of Torah* (Nashville: Abingdon Press, 1975), 124.
5. Jacob Neusner, *The Way of Torah: An Introduction to Judaism*, 3rd ed. (Belmont, CA: Wadsworth, 1979), 58, who elaborates the point.

when Philo came on the scene. He did not invent it, though it is mostly through his writings that later Christians have become aware of this method. In the second century BCE, the *Letter of Aristeas* not only gives an interesting, legendary account of the origin of the LXX, but provides examples of allegorical interpretation. An educated, thoughtful person might wonder why the eternal God stipulated that the only ritually clean animals available for Israelite consumption are those that have cloven hoofs and chew the cud (Lev 11; Deut 14:6). Surely the divine Legislator did not make this distinction arbitrarily. The reflective interpreter can perceive that the hoof is the *supportive foundation for the animal*, and that *dividing* is a kind of discrimination, a sorting out. Thus the text is offering directives for rational *discrimination* that *supports* the ethical life. This interpretation is confirmed by thinking more deeply about the true meaning of *chewing the cud*, which has nothing to do with bovine gastronomy but pictures meditative reflection on the Torah.

Philo of Alexandria's extensive writings stand in this stream of Jewish interpretation of the Scriptures, which understands every word of the sacred text as charged with profound, allegorical meaning. Philo disdains literal interpretation as failure to recognize the depth of Scripture and the majesty of God. When one reads that God had planted fruit trees in Eden, for instance, it is silly to suppose that this refers to a literal reality. The text of Genesis must really be speaking of "the paradise of virtues, implanted by God in the soul" (*On Planting* 8–9). Philo was bothered that anyone would think the eternal God was concerned to record in the Scripture the petty quarrels between two women, and finds the deeper allegorical meaning: It is not women who are spoken of, but two types of virtue and educational accomplishments. Hagar, the concubine, represents the mind that exercises itself in elementary studies, and Sarah, the wife, represents the mind contending for the higher prize of virtue (Philo, *On the Preliminary Studies* 11–180). "When, therefore, you hear that Hagar was afflicted by Sarah, you must not suppose that any of those things befell her, which arise from rivalry and quarrels among women; for the question is not here about woman, but about minds; the one being practiced in the branches of elementary instruction, and the other being devoted to the labors of virtue" (Philo, *Prelim. Studies* 180).[6]

Philo's interpretation was not considered arbitrary but followed conventional rules (*Abraham* 15). Scripture itself has shown that the literal sense cannot be accepted when, for example, (1) a text says something unworthy of God—that God has hands and ears, and all other anthropomorphisms; (2) a text contradicts another text when taken at the literal level, for example, that Cain acquired a wife, and built a city, when the whole human race consisted of one family of three people; (3) a text is obviously not meant literally, such as the talking snake of Genesis 3.

Traditional Jewish interpretation in the New Testament. The early Christians not only adopted the Jewish Scriptures as their own, but adopted and adapted some of the later interpretations that had become traditional as the basis for their own Christian reinterpretation. Thus, for example, when Paul interprets the rock that brought forth water in the wilderness for the thirsty Israelites (Num 20:2–13) as referring to Christ, he indicates that this was not a one-time event, but that the rock followed them and gave them water throughout the wilderness wanderings—as does Christ for his people (1 Cor 10:4). That the rock followed Israel is not in the Old Testament, but is found in later Jewish interpretation contemporary with Paul (see *t. Suk.* 3:11).

When New Testament authors interpret the Bible, their interpretations would have seemed appropriate in their own historical settings, for they generally shared the perspectives and some of the methods of contemporary Jewish interpreters. In each case, the fundamental

6. The student of the New Testament might compare Paul's interpretation of the Sarah/Hagar story in Gal 4:21–31.

convictions of faith are brought to the Scripture, not merely derived from it. For Christians, this meant an intensive rereading of their Bible in the light of their conviction that Jesus of Nazareth is the Messiah, and that God has raised the rejected Messiah to be Lord of all (see below §9.2.2).

Continuing reinterpretation in the New Testament. This ongoing process of reinterpretation in the New Testament includes the interpretation of earlier Christian traditions and documents by later ones: Paul himself sometimes reinterprets his earlier compositions, as his later letters clarify misunderstandings generated by his earlier writings (e.g., 1 Cor 5:9–11; the reinterpretation of 1 Cor 12–14 in Rom 12–14). Acts and the later Pauline tradition reinterpret the earlier Pauline writings (see §§15, 16, 23 below). The latest writing of the New Testament warns against the misinterpretation of Paul's letters, which are indeed difficult to understand and are not of "private interpretation," but can be rightly understood only within the ongoing mainstream Christian community (2 Pet 3:16; see below §18.3).

5.1.4 Interpretation of the New Testament in Church History

The history of the copying of the text is itself part of the history of its interpretation. Especially in the precanonical period, copyists sometimes made additions and modifications to the text to clarify the meaning or to "correct" what they assumed were transmission errors. A study of such variations is a helpful window into how the text was understood at a particular time. Indeed, this is a major contribution of textual criticism. The discipline is devoted not only to reconstructing the earliest form of the text possible but to illuminating its history. The Western text provides an outstanding example. Already in the second century, an extensive series of changes were made, constituting a new edition of the text, often with hermeneutical commentary built in. Thus, of numerous examples, the D text's version of the "Apostolic Decree" in Acts 15:20, 29 understands the ritual laws in an ethical sense. Prohibitions against the pollutions of idols, things strangled, blood, and prohibition of marriage with relatives within prescribed boundaries—all matters of ritual purity—become rules against idolatry, fornication, and murder, to which the Golden Rule is added. The D manuscript representing the Western text is something of a Christian midrash, updating the meaning of the text and building its contemporary interpretation into the text itself.

When the New Testament canon was closed, the New Testament entered into the stream of Christian history as part of the Christian Bible. The modern reader of the New Testament cannot circumvent this history but stands within a centuries-long stream of interpretation shaped by the Christian community's ongoing dialogue with Scripture. This does not mean that the contemporary reader must uncritically accept previous interpretations as authoritative, but it does mean that contemporary readings will be influenced, positively and negatively, by the ways the Bible has been previously interpreted. A very rough outline of some main turning points in this history may be briefly sketched.

Irenaeus, Tertullian, the rule of faith, and the ecumenical creeds. Heated struggles within the early Christian community made it painfully clear that, even when the church had a Bible, authentic theology could not be defined merely by quoting Scripture. Both "orthodox" and "heretic," as they were later to be called, appealed to the same Bible. The role that the interpreting community and its perspective played in each interpretation needed to be made more explicit. This occurred gradually, but came to an important focus in the work of Irenaeus of Lyons (ca. 130–200 CE). Irenaeus not only argued for the validity of the church's choice of four Gospels and other books as authoritative, but proposed that the Scriptures could only be rightly understood within the catholic church that stood in the tradition of the original apostolic interpreters. The oral tradition received from the apostles, formulated in the rule of faith, is the authoritative guideline for proper interpretation of Scripture. A more hard-line formulation of this approach was developed by Tertullian of Carthage (ca. 160–240). Tertullian's more legal approach—he was probably a lawyer by profession—argued that the Scriptures are the property of the developing mainline orthodox church and that outsiders to this community have no right to interpret them.

After Constantine's Edict of Toleration, which allowed the church throughout the Mediterranean world to organize and conduct its business publicly, the Nicene-Constantinopolitan Creed (325/381) and the Chalcedonian Creed elaborated the earlier Old Roman and Apostles' Creeds. One of the main functions of such creeds was to provide firm guidelines for the interpretation of Scripture. Although there was still considerable latitude for variety of interpretation within what had become the Catholic Church, no interpretation could be considered valid that violated the basic tenets of the creeds. The first article, that there is one God who is the Creator of all things, meant that any gnosticizing interpretation that regarded the material world as the bungled creation of a lesser deity must be erroneous. Likewise, the Chalcedonian formulation that adequate christological language must affirm the full humanity and true divinity of Jesus Christ excluded any interpretation of the Gospels or Paul's letters that dualistically portrayed a heavenly divine Christ as a separate being from the suffering and dying human Jesus (see the sketch of Gnosticism below, §9.2.2).

Allegory and the gap between past and present, literal and spiritual. The problem is the interpretation of the meaning of a document written for one situation but being read in a later, different situation. While this problem had been encountered in the ongoing reinterpretation within the Jewish Scriptures and in Judaism (see §5.1.3, §7.6), it became critical when the early Christians adopted these Scriptures as their own and read them from the perspective that the hopes and promises of the Jewish Scriptures had found their definitive fulfillment in Jesus Christ. The hermeneutic that made this possible was often articulated as various forms of typology and allegory that saw more than one level of meaning in the texts of Scripture. While, to be sure, the text on its surface, literal level may have been talking about some particular event in Israelite history not directly relevant to Christian faith, the deeper, spiritual meaning at another level was seen to be teaching Christian truth. Jewish, pre- and para-Christian readers saw only the surface meaning and missed the depth of truth in the text that is visible only through eyes of faith illuminated by the Holy Spirit.

Some early and medieval Christian teachers refined the art of allegorical interpretation to a fine point, discovering all the depths and subtleties of Christian theology beneath the surface of the Old Testament. The prophecies were understood in terms of Jesus and Christian history and the laws seen as "types" (models and prototypes of Christian doctrine). By means of the allegorical method, every sentence, even every word, of the Old Testament could be made to yield Christian teaching. It is easy enough to find bizarre examples of such interpretation, which was far removed from the original meaning: "The girl [Rebekah] was very fair to look upon, a virgin, whom no man had known" (Gen 24:16) means that Christ is the husband of the soul when it is converted, Satan becomes the husband of the soul when it falls away.[7] Practically every piece of wood in the biblical story could represent some aspect of the Christian understanding of the cross of Jesus. The Song of Solomon, at the surface level, is erotic poetry celebrating sexuality as part of the goodness of creation; Bernard of Clairvaux (1090–1153) interpreted it in

7. Origen, *Hom.* in Rom vii. §8, cited in Frederic W. Farrar, *History of Interpretation* (Grand Rapids: Baker, 1979), 199. Farrar delights in showing the foibles of allegory, and provides many examples of this "dreary irrelevance" (p. 204). For a more up-to-date and more positive appropriation of allegory that incorporates but goes beyond historical criticism, see the works of Brevard Childs, especially *Biblical Theology of the Old and New Testaments* (Minneapolis: Fortress Press, 1992) and *The Struggle to Understand Isaiah as Christian Scripture* (Grand Rapids: Eerdmans, 2004).

eighty-six sermons as an allegory of the love of Christ for the church, discovering the whole of Christian theology embedded in this book.

We should not, however, think of allegorical interpretation as a trivial pursuit occupying second-rate minds. Some of the church's greatest thinkers saw it as the key to unlocking the profound mysteries of the faith God had revealed through the Scriptures to those who were willing to learn. Augustine (354–430 CE) had too philosophical a mind and was too honest to pretend that he believed the Bible literally. He was able to become a Christian only after discovering the allegorical method. For numerous other thoughtful Christians, allegory made it possible to uphold the rationality of Christian faith.

To be sure, not all Christian interpreters through these early and medieval centuries of Christian history interpreted the Bible allegorically. Early on, the Antioch school represented by Theodore of Mopsuestia (ca. 350–428 CE) argued for a common-sense, historical meaning of Scripture, in opposition to the Alexandrian school represented by Origen's (ca. 185–254 CE) sophisticated allegorizing methods. Thomas Aquinas (1225–74), the greatest medieval Christian thinker, insisted on the literal meaning as basic to all other interpretations. The great variety of biblical interpretation during these centuries was held together not by a particular hermeneutical method, but by church tradition that provided firm guidelines for interpretation, whatever methods were utilized. Scripture and Tradition were a symbiotic unity that guided the church on its pilgrimage through history—but this unity became unraveled by parallel developments during the sixteenth to eighteenth centuries: the religious revolution of the Reformation and the secular and scientific revolution of the Renaissance Enlightenment.

The Reformation

When some sixteenth-century reformers left or were excluded from the Roman Catholic Church, they mostly saw themselves as rejecting the human traditions that had led the church astray and returning to the Bible as the sole source of authority (*sola scriptura*). Of course, they brought some elements of tradition with them, and the new Protestant communities generated new traditions as guidelines for biblical interpretation, reflected in the Protestant creedal statements and in the later dogmas of Protestant scholasticism. The continuing links between church and state in Europe led to religious wars and persecutions of one group of Christians by another, but when the new *sola scriptura* perspective was transplanted to North America, the separation of church and state allowed each denomination to flourish to the extent that it could appeal to the populace. All claimed that the Bible was the supreme authority, interpreting it according to their own tradition, but understanding themselves to be guided by the "Bible alone."

Since "human tradition," specifically Roman Catholic tradition, had been rejected, various streams of Protestantism devised their own methods of implementing the general Protestant claim that "the Bible is its own interpreter." The effort was to restore the Bible to the people, without the intervention of either clergy or tradition. Despite this "Bible only" claim, the historic denominations that saw themselves as standing in the tradition of the Reformation continued to be guided by the tradition of the larger church as adapted by the particular denomination. Within these denominations, the ecumenical creeds, the mainstream patristic traditions, and the continuity of the church's authorized ministry through the centuries continued to be affirmed in each denomination's distinctive manner, and the Bible was acknowledged as the sole authority and interpreted within this framework. The numerous denominations and sects that did not acknowledge their place in this history tended to reject the whole history of the church as a decline, perversion, or apostasy from its original purity, and to claim that they had returned to the original faith and church as set forth in the Bible.

This whole discussion, sometimes conducted in a brotherly spirit and sometimes with arrogance and acrimony, took place within a shared commitment that the Bible was to be understood as literally true and authoritative in every respect. The only issue was how to interpret and apply this universal norm. Despite their differences in interpretation, all denominations understood the Bible to be the same kind of book. The divisions were between denominations, not within them. This situation was to change radically by incursions of the "modern" approach to the Bible advanced by the Renaissance and Enlightenment. This approach began about the same time as the Reformation and proceeded along a parallel track with the growth of Protestantism, but it did not become critical within most churches until the nineteenth century.

The Renaissance and Enlightenment

Prior to the sixteenth century, most Christian readers of the Bible perceived themselves to live in the same world as those who wrote the Bible. There was no major gap between what they read in the Bible and the way they understood their own world. The dawn of modern science—geography, astronomy, geology—and an approach to historical thinking that was critical and analytical, rather than accepting the authority of tradition, showed that many accepted traditions were demonstrably false. The discovery of the New World across the Atlantic, the invention of the telescope that facilitated study of the planets and stars, and the revolutionary new insights of Copernican astronomy in which the sun—not the earth—is the center of the solar system created a troublesome gap between the world of the Bible and the world of everyday experience. Educated people began to perceive that the earth is much older and the universe unimaginably larger than the cozy biblical world in which they had previously lived.

The Enlightenment of the seventeenth and eighteenth centuries expanded the Renaissance perspectives (one could also say its focus), emphasizing human reason and individualism rather than biblical and ecclesiastical authority as the arbiters of truth. Ancient documents were examined for their authenticity; some survived critical examination and some did not. Such critical sifting was able, for instance, to separate the authentic writings of Plato from later documents written in his name. Another famous and significant example is the Donation of Constantine, a document on which the medieval church had relied for its authority, in which the emperor Constantine transfers authority over Rome and western Europe to the pope. Renaissance scholars demonstrated, on the basis of vocabulary, style, and anachronistic historical references in the document, that it could not have been written earlier than the eighth century. This approach to ancient texts was vigorously carried forward during the Enlightenment, which continued to examine the historical authenticity of ancient documents. This rise of historical consciousness within the church of the nineteenth and twentieth centuries turned out to be the greatest turning point—and divisive issue—in biblical interpretation since the church's use of the allegorical method.

Historical (Higher) Criticism and the Churches' Response

Historical criticism or "the" *historical-critical method* is in reality a cluster of methods used to study a text historically. The most basic method is textual criticism, sometimes called "lower criticism" because of its foundational character, which attempts to restore the earliest recoverable form of original texts that are no longer extant (see above, §3.3). "Higher criticism" is that cluster of methods that seeks to understand the text in its original context. Historical study of texts typically explores the following issues:

— *Authorship/authenticity*. Who wrote the text? Based on internal and external evidence, was it written by the person to whom it is traditionally attributed?

— *Language*. Was the text written in the language of its extant forms, or do we have a translation of a text originally written in a different language?

— *Genre*. Which literary genres were current when a particular document was composed? How were they understood, adopted, and adapted by the biblical authors?

— *Date*. When was the text written?

— *Provenance*. Where was the text written?

— *Addressees*. Who were the readers intended by the author?

— *Social, religious, and political setting*. Interpreting a text historically means understanding it in terms of its own world, which in turn requires exploration of its social, religious, and political context. *Social-scientific* approaches, sometimes seen as a separate discipline from historical criticism, emphasize the importance of social structure in understanding the historical context, for example, how parents would understand their role, how marriage and family were understood, how employment and the slavery system worked, how the patronage and honor/shame culture influenced authors and their texts. *History of religion* (*Religionsgeschichte*), likewise sometimes seen as a discipline distinct from historical criticism, investigates the religious thought of the New Testament within the context of religious options available in the historical context.

— *Orality, form criticism*. Were there units of oral tradition used by the author and/or incorporated into the sources he or she used? What types (forms, subgenres) were these, and where and how did they function in the life of the community (*Sitz im Leben*, setting in life)?

— *Sources*. What sources did the author use? Are these still extant, so that the author's selections and modifications can be determined?

— *Tradition history (Traditionsgeschichte)*. Tracing the trajectory of a unit of tradition through its various reinterpretations in the oral period through the sources that may have included it to the extant form found in the New Testament is called Tradition Criticism or Tradition History.

— *Redaction criticism and composition criticism*. How did the author select, arrange, and modify the materials available to him or her to produce the document in its present form? Editorial analysis is also called Redaction Criticism (*Redaktion* is the German word for editing). The author's distinctive theology could be seen by the way he had selected, arranged, and modified his sources. Redaction criticism flourished in the decades just after World War II and made important contributions, especially in refocusing hermeneutical attention on the final form of the text. As biblical authors came to be seen less as collectors and editors but as authors in their own right, redaction criticism modulated into composition criticism.

— *Unity, integrity*. Is the extant document a unity as composed by the original author, or is it a later editorial combination of documents? Related to both textual criticism and unity is the question of interpolations: has a later editor or scribe inserted word, sentences, or paragraphs into the original?

— *Reception*, Wirkungsgeschichte *(history of effects), history of interpretation*. The historical study of a document includes the history of its effects, how it was received and the response it generated, the effects it had in later history. Even though it may be that the contemporary interpreter does not simply adopt an interpretation from among those discovered in the history of interpretation, such study tends to break up the crust of the interpreter's own interpretation and open up the possibility of a fresh hearing of the text. *Wirkungsgeschichte* belongs in the tool kit of all who want to understand the Bible.

The application of this cluster of methods to biblical documents attempted to set each text in its own context and allow the interpreter to hear it as it was originally intended. This same process tended to remove the text from the world of the modern reader, who, for example, no longer lived in a world where animal sacrifice and demon possession were assumed as constituent elements in the life world. Modern readers of the Bible who appropriated the insights of historical criticism found that they had a new grasp of what the biblical texts originally *meant*, but that what these texts might *mean* now became problematic. "What it meant" could now be established with relative confidence; "what it means" was another issue.[8]

A key figure in attempting to hold together ancient and modern meaning, combining the insights and conclusions of modern critical study and the religious meaning of the Bible for Christian faith, was Friedrich Schleiermacher (1768–1834). He argued that Bible scholars must also be theologians, that theologians must be Bible scholars, and embodied this model himself. For some who followed in Schleiermacher's train, historical criticism was emancipating, a breath of fresh air that freed both Bible and reader from oppressive dogmas. The text could once again speak its own message to its own time and place, launched into a different world than that of the reader, to be overheard by the emancipated reader who was free to listen in on the ancient conversation without imposing later dogmatic meanings on the biblical texts.

Frederick W. Farrar, beloved exponent of historical criticism within the church of the late nineteenth century, represented this perspective. His history of biblical interpretation regards the whole history of the Bible in the church until his present, enlightened time, as basically a "history of errors."[9] Farrar was an extremely popular teacher and preacher within the church, a respected Cambridge scholar who served as Dean of Canterbury. His 1874 *Life of Christ* was widely read as a summary of warm-hearted evangelical-liberal piety that allowed his readers to accept the results of historical criticism while continuing to affirm the "essential truths" of the Bible. Even though the Bible is now seen as written to other people, in another time and place with different worldviews than the modern, scientific perspective of our own time, "there is not the slightest practical difficulty" in distinguishing this temporal husk from the abiding truth of the Word of God.[10] This older, reductionistic, liberal hermeneutic of the late nineteenth and early twentieth centuries was very popular among the churches that could no longer affirm biblical literalism and the pre-critical traditions about how the Bible had been composed. For such people, historical criticism was a liberating, positive influence that allowed them to continue to affirm the biblical faith and interpret the Bible as a guide for the church and the Christian life.

For other people within the church, historical criticism posed a threat to the faith itself. For them, believing the "truth of the Bible" was inseparably bound to affirming traditional views of authorship and date of the biblical texts. The doubts that historical scholarship cast on these traditional views were understood as rejecting the faith itself. In such circles, historical study was considered the enemy, and traditional views were reasserted as orthodoxy. The nineteenth- and early-twentieth-century dispute over higher criticism of the Bible, sometimes called the "modernist controversy," not only caused deep rifts between denominations that generally accepted the results of higher criticism and those that did not, but occasioned tensions and even splits within particular denominations.

Though higher criticism had a polarizing effect within the Christian community, by no means all advocates of the traditional faith rejected historical criticism in toto. While fundamentalists and extreme conservatives made it a mark of authentic faith to reject "modernism"

8. Classically expressed by Krister Stendahl, "Biblical Theology, Contemporary," in *Interpreter's Dictionary of the Bible*, 1:418–432.

9. Farrar, *History of Interpretation*, 8.

10. Ibid., 430–31. These are the last words of the book.

and "higher criticism" and to reassert the verbal inspiration and infallibility of the biblical revelation, many moderate and evangelical Christians found they could incorporate the less radical methods and conclusions of the critics into their theology. By no means was the old liberal hermeneutic as advocated by, for example, Adolf Harnack in Germany, Frederick W. Farrar in Britain, and Harry Emerson Fosdick in America the only means of coming to terms with higher criticism. Various hermeneutical streams illustrated that historical criticism could become the basis for a fresh appropriation of the message of the Bible within the church. These included the various forms of dialectical theology (neo-orthodoxy) and existentialist interpretation represented in varying ways by, for example, Karl Barth, Rudolf Bultmann, and Paul Tillich, and the salvation-history and biblical theology approaches represented, for example, by Oscar Cullmann, Leonhardt Goppelt, and George Eldon Ladd.

The Roman Catholic Church offers a good example of the adoption of historical criticism as a method appropriate and helpful for faithful interpretation of the Bible in the church. At first suspicious and hostile to critical methods, during the pontificate of Pius XII the church leadership completely reversed its previous position. The encyclical *Divino Afflante Spiritu* of 1943 commended the modern critical tools of biblical exegesis to Roman Catholics, and subsequent directives of the Pontifical Biblical Commission granted complete freedom (*plena libertate*) with regard to earlier restrictions, so that Catholic interpreters could follow historical research to whatever conclusions it led. This meant that Roman Catholic scholars quickly adopted the critical positions on authorship, date, and source analysis long affirmed by their Protestant and secular counterparts. In our own generation, Roman Catholics such as Raymond E. Brown, John P. Meier, and Joseph A. Fitzmyer have pursued historical-critical studies of the New Testament in a way that has won the respect of the whole spectrum of the academic world, and have done so while combining historical method with theological concern and integrity.[11]

An important new factor in the twentieth century was that critical biblical study increasingly moved from the church into the academy. Historical criticism became ever more specialized, with scholars tending to identify themselves as, for example, "archaeologists," "form critics," "source critics," or "history of religion" specialists, often also narrowing their focus to only one biblical author or group of texts—Pauline scholars, Gospel scholars, Psalms specialists, and the like. In the academic setting, biblical scholarship itself became increasingly isolated from hermeneutical and theological concerns, as well as from the practical concerns of interpretation in the educational and preaching ministries of the church. These were left to be carried on by other specialists in the academic world or by seminary teachers of the practice of ministry. The move of biblical scholarship into the secularized university also generated a number of new methodological approaches that opened up new dimensions of meaning in the ancient texts, but were unconcerned with or actively hostile to the theological interpretation of the Bible as the church's Scripture.

The Explosion of Recent Methodological Approaches

Prior to about 1970, the spectrum of hermeneutical options for interpreting the Bible was often portrayed as two competing and somewhat hostile camps: "traditional" vs. "higher

11. Two of the numerous products of recent Roman Catholic scholarship that make the results of historical-critical study of the Bible available not only to experts but to the church at large: Raymond E. Brown, Joseph A. Fitzmyer, SJ, and Roland E. Murphy, eds., *The New Jerome Biblical Commentary* (Englewood Cliffs, NJ: Prentice-Hall, 1990) and Donald P. Senior, Mary Ann Getty, Carroll Stuhlmueller, and John J. Collins, eds., *The Catholic Study Bible. The New American Bible: Including the Revised New Testament Translated from the Original Languages with Critical Use of All the Ancient Sources* (New York: Oxford University Press, 1990).

criticism," or "conservative" vs. "liberal." One either utilized historical criticism or did not, and this alternative shaped much of what else one might do with the Bible. In the last generation, the methodological explosion has generated a large number of additional methods, sometimes as refinements or complements to historical-critical methods, sometimes as alternatives to historical interpretation. Some of the more recent methods will be simply listed here, without any attempt at categorizing or integrating them. A representative and overlapping catalogue of recent methods would include these:[12]

— *Literary criticism*. One of the most significant and illuminating recent approaches is the application of literary criticism to biblical texts. In a previous generation, Bible scholars used the label "literary criticism" for a branch of historical criticism that studied the literary connections between texts, that is, source analysis. Now literary criticism refers to the group of disciplines that study the Bible as classical literature, using the methods that have become common in studying other literature. While historical criticism had been concerned with the world behind the text, literary criticism is concerned with the story world within the text. The question is not "what are the stages by which this text came to be?" or "what happened in actual history?" but "what happens in the narrative world within and projected by the text?"

— *Narrative criticism, narratology*. In this subheading of literary criticism, the Bible is approached with the same standard issues addressed when studying other narrative literature (e.g., Shakespeare, Steinbeck), for example, characterization, point of view, type of narrator, the distinction between real author and implied author. The Bible is, in fact, fundamentally narrative. While it contains numerous other genres (law, poetry, oracle, wisdom instruction, etc.), these are all included within the framework of one grand narrative that stretches from creation to eschaton (see above §1.5.3). Jesus followed the Jewish insight that the ultimate truth of God is best communicated not as law or philosophy, but as story. Although the literature of early Christianity manifests a great variety of genres, all the documents that were ultimately canonized belong, in one way or another, to the encompassing narrative genus (see §1.5). Narratological methods and insights have thus become very important in New Testament interpretation.

— *Canonical criticism*. Canonical criticism represents an attempt to combine historical criticism with a thoroughly church-oriented affirmation of the Bible as the canon for the community of faith. The modern champion of this approach is Brevard Childs (1923–2007), who understands his approach to be not anticritical but "postcritical," accepting but going beyond critical methods and results. Though recent as a self-conscious hermeneutical method, this approach claims to recover the church's ancient approach inherent in the formation of the canon. It is important to inquire into the significance of canonical order and location; though Matthew was written after Mark, what does it mean that it precedes Mark in the canon?

It is a valid point of canonical criticism that "individual writings did not circulate as such; the atomism that considers individual writings in isolation from their canonical collections is a modern critical convention."[13] Each text

12. More complete catalogues, with more extensive summaries and bibliographies detailing the elements and procedures of each method, are found in Paula Gooder, *Searching for Meaning: An Introduction to Interpreting the New Testament* (Louisville, KY: Westminster John Knox Press, 2009), who discusses twenty-three methods; W. Randolph Tate, *Biblical Interpretation: An Integrated Approach*, 3rd ed. (Peabody, MA: Hendrickson, 2008), 277–342, and in the relevant articles in John H. Hayes, *Dictionary of Biblical Interpretation* (Nashville: Abingdon Press, 1999). A helpful anthology containing chapters illustrating the application of a variety of recent methods to the interpretation of the Gospel of Mark is provided by Janice Capel Anderson and Stephen D. Moore, *Mark and Method: New Approaches in Biblical Studies*, 2nd ed. (Minneapolis: Fortress Press, 2008).

13. Robert W. Wall, "Acts and James," in Karl-Wilhelm Niebuhr and Robert W. Wall, eds., *The Catholic Epistles and Apostolic Tradition* (Waco: Baylor University Press, 2009), 134.

had its concrete set of meanings for its original situation. But when Matthew, Romans, 2 John, and so on began to be circulated for the church as a whole, they did not circulate individually. Someone decided the grouping and order, and this influences the meaning. There is a sense in which canonical criticism is an extension to the New Testament as a whole of the insights of redaction criticism vis-à-vis form criticism: not the individual unit or document in their original contexts is decisive, but the final form of the text. The final form of the text is its canonical form in its canonical context.

— *Structuralism*. Based on the linguistic philosophies of Ferdinand de Saussure and the anthropological theories of Claude Lévi-Strauss, structuralism finds meaning neither in the historical events behind the text nor in the content of the text itself, but in its *deep structure*. These structures are common to all human societies and to language itself, of which each particular language and composition is a specific manifestation. Authors must work within these general constraints, of which they are mostly unaware. Since authors and readers have internalized these deep structures and can only write and read within their constraints, to understand a text does not mean understanding the author's intention, but to discover the deep structures coming to expression in the particular use of narrative and language. Charting a particular narrative on the grid of these deep structures lets the reader see what is really going on in the text, and facilitates understanding at the deepest level, which is quite unrelated both to actual history outside the text and to the particular events within the text or the author's intended meaning.

— *Reader response criticism*. This approach argues that meaning is neither behind nor within the text, but in front of the text, in the interaction between text and reader. There is no meaning "in" the text to be discovered, for the text embodies a very large number of potential meanings, but none of them is "the" meaning of the text. Meaning does not exist until an actual reader interprets it; the reader is the cocreator of meaning. The reader's response does not *reproduce* a meaning buried in the text waiting to be discovered, but *produces* meaning that did not previously exist, as the reader's response is combined with the potential of the text. In its extreme form, the text actually contributes nothing but the occasion, and the reader produces all the meaning.[14]

— *Rhetorical, social-rhetorical criticism*. Though in modern American culture the term "rhetoric" has sometimes developed a bad reputation, understood as insubstantial or deceitful fluff that avoids or conceals one's real intent, rhetoric in the ancient world was simply the art of skilled communication and persuasion. Rhetoric was a matter of advanced, "graduate level" education, a skill needed by good leaders. There were rhetorical handbooks on effective communication that both exhibited and nurtured such skills and developed the expectations of educated people as to what a good speech or composition should be. The analysis of the strategies of communication built into a text can facilitate the reader's understanding of not only *what* it means, but *how* it means, how it leads the reader to a conclusion. Socio-rhetorical criticism explores these literary and compositional features that signal how they function within the whole social matrix, including the intertextual (relation to other texts and subtexts within the culture) and ideological relationships.

— *Postmodern interpretation*. The term *postmodernism* is used in a variety of senses in the fields of art, architecture, and other cultural realms. In theology and hermeneutics it generally defines itself over against the "modernist" era of biblical interpretation dominated by the historical-critical method, which in turn defined itself

14. "It has been said of Boehme that his books are like a picnic to which the author brings the words and the reader the meaning. The remark may have been intended as a sneer at Boehme, but it is an exact description of all works of literary art without exception" (Northrop Frye, *Fearful Symmetry: A Study of William Blake* [Princeton, NJ: Princeton University Press, 1974], 427).

in contrast to precritical traditionalist views. Postmodernism rejects what it assumes to be the claim of historical criticism to study the Bible objectively with the goal of recovering the ancient meaning of the text. A central characteristic of much postmodernist thought is the rejection of metanarratives, grand narratives of the great scheme of things, which have a legitimating function and are used to impose the will of one group on another.[15] Biblical interpretation must renounce absolutes and the claim to objectivity, must abandon all grand schemes of universal history, and must accept the fragmentary, relative, contextual, and subjective nature of all claims to truth. While my purpose in this survey is not to critique the array of modern methodological proposals, here one must at least ask whether the New Testament can be *understood*—we are not talking here about believing or disbelieving its claims—apart from its own Christ-centered, creation-to-eschaton metanarrative, shared in one way or another by all its authors. One must also ask whether postmodernism itself can be understood—again, whether one believes or not—apart from its own metanarrative by which it defines itself, the precritical/modern/postmodern schema of universal history. One may even ask whether there is not a metanarrative presupposed by every human effort to find meaning in life, by fitting the little story of each life into some larger narrative that gives it meaning.

— *Deconstruction.* Following Jacques Derrida, the French philosopher often regarded as the patron saint of deconstruction, this approach emphasizes that careful analysis of texts—any texts—reveals that all texts are inherently ambiguous, metaphorical, with gaps that must be filled in by the reader in order to have any meaning at all. Texts give us the dots, but not the lines that connect them into meaningful wholes. Careful study of texts reveals their gaps—the resultant ambiguity making the search for "the" meaning of a text misguided and useless—and emphasizes the freedom of the reader in creating meaning.

— *Demythologizing and existential interpretation.* The term *demythologizing* was made popular a generation ago and is in fact rarely used today, but variations of the same hermeneutical approach continue to be used. Whereas the older liberalism peeled away and discarded the mythological layers of the Bible in order to get to the "eternal truths" they contained, Rudolf Bultmann and his later followers saw the biblical myths as themselves the vehicles of Christian truth. Although he believed modern interpreters could no longer accept the mythological form of the New Testament message, the myth should not be discarded, but interpreted, translated into the categories that modern human beings could understand and accept. Bultmann, dependent on the existentialist philosopher Martin Heidegger, believed that the personal, existential concerns and faith of the biblical authors are the same as those of modern human beings, and that their communication of the Christian faith in the mythological form of their times could be translated into the existential categories of self-understanding that could address modern human beings with the same gospel proclaimed by the early Christian preachers.

— *Postcolonial, liberation theology, imperial criticism.* The liberation theology of the decades following the 1960s called for reading the Bible as a resource for establishing justice and resisting oppression. This theology, emanating from theologians in both the developing countries and those oppressed by the social structures of the industrialized nations, emphasized the

15. Jean François Lyotard, *The Postmodern Explained: Correspondence, 1982–1985*, trans. Don Barry (Minneapolis: University of Minnesota Press, 1993), 19. "Simplifying to the extreme, I define postmodern as incredulity toward metanarratives. . . . Where, after the metanarratives, can legitimacy reside?" (Jean François Lyotard, *The Postmodern Condition: A Report on Knowledge*, trans. Geoffrey Bennington and Brian Massumi [Minneapolis: University of Minnesota Press, 1984], xxiv–xxv).

stream of biblical tradition, including the mission of Jesus of Nazareth, that resisted imperial oppression. Recent postcolonial interpretation and imperial criticism analyze the political assumptions of both biblical writers and their later interpreters, often contrasting the kingdom of God with this-worldly empire. In New Testament studies, this approach pays close attention to the stance of biblical authors to the Roman Empire—do they resist its oppression and exploitation of the poor, or do they accommodate the revolutionary Christian message to the elite power structures?

— *Feminist and womanist criticism.* The Bible was written within a patriarchal culture, to people who shared this assumed perspective, and through the centuries it has mostly been interpreted from a male point of view, whether consciously or not. Feminist criticism and hermeneutic wants to expose and correct this distorted point of view. It sometimes proceeds as though the biblical faith itself supports the feminist agenda, although it has been obscured by male interpreters. The hermeneutical task is then to recover the original meaning of the text before it was distorted by patriarchal interpreters.

Other feminist authors consider the real culprit to be the Bible itself. Jesus established a "discipleship of equals" that provided a "critical feminist impulse" (Schüssler Fiorenza), but this was obscured or reversed by the New Testament authors and the male bishops who selected the canonical documents. The oppressive, patriarchal orientation of the biblical authors must be exposed and corrected by the norm of "women's experience." *Womanist* hermeneutic takes this perspective further and focuses particularly on the experience of black women, who have not been sufficiently considered by the white feminist movement and almost entirely neglected by the liberation impulse in black liberation theology, which is orientated to black males.

— *African American, Hispanic, and other variations of culture criticism.* The general principle is that one always reads and interprets from a particular social location that tends to make one blind to how the same text is heard within other social locations. The experience of minority groups in the United States becomes the lens for exposing and correcting the inherent racism, conscious or otherwise, inherent in the way the Bible has been read in American churches. African American criticism is one of several approaches emphasizing that texts, interpreters, and their interpretations are always enmeshed in cultural forces and can unconsciously become their agents (gay, lesbian, queer theory; child abuse, children's rights; environmental concerns).

Churchly Interpretation

How does the interpreter within the church who regards the Bible as Holy Scripture respond to this cafeteria of methodological options, whether as minister charged by his or her ordination to be a responsible interpreter of Scripture for the community of faith, or as lay believer who wants to read the Bible as guide for life and action and as the vehicle of the Word of God? Churchly interpretation is not an alternative to the methodological approaches listed above. Each of these methods can help the interpreter hear something in the biblical text that is really there, something that he or she might have otherwise missed. Those who stand within the Christian community and interpret the New Testament as sacred Scripture can consider the value of each of the newer methods and utilize several of them in discovering the contemporary meaning of Scripture for Christian faith, and can do so without surrendering or compromising the confessional stance of the Christian community that the Bible is the vehicle of the Word of God. The inseparable issues revolve around *agenda* and *conversation/dialogue*.

Agenda and Dialogue

Agenda is a Latin word, the plural of *agendum*, which is the gerundive form of the verb *agere*, meaning *what ought to be done*. It is a neutral term, and need not be understood in the sinister or manipulative sense of "hidden agenda." The issue of *agenda* transcends that of *method*; agenda is not merely another method, but programmatically establishes how the method or methods are to be used. Every reader approaches the text with a particular agenda or set of agendas. I may be a racist or antiracist, a pacifist or a militarist, a feminist or male or female chauvinist, a nationalist or one with a commitment to the larger human community. My agenda is what I am concerned with, what I consider important and true and how to implement it, that-which-is-to-be-done. I have my agenda, and I cannot do otherwise. "Let the one who is without an agenda cast the first stone."[16]

Does the Bible itself have an agenda? If so, what is it, and how does it get into the conversation? It would, of course, be a grand oversimplification to speak of "the" agenda of the Bible, and yet one can ask what the Bible, taken as a whole, is *about*, just as one can ask this question of any book or text of the Bible. A biblical text is not about deep literary structures, or social relationships in the Mediterranean world, not about racism or antiracism per se. There is a sense in which the Bible as a whole, in its present shape given by the community of faith through the centuries, is about "God." Yet, insiders to the Jewish and Christian communities would not state it this way, with "God" in quotes, but say straightforwardly that the Bible is about the living God who spoke through the prophets and who continues to speak through the Scriptures, the God whose reality is known in worship and service.

Christians would say all this from the perspective of faith that sees the definitive revelation of this God in Jesus Christ. That the Bible is *about* God and the plan of God for this world is the overarching agenda that holds the variety of biblical documents together. Within this encompassing framework, each of the biblical writers and texts has its own agenda or set of agendas, its own theological expression of this agenda, its own perspective on this agenda that permeates and underlies the whole. Interpreters inevitably bring their own agenda to the text; an essential aspect of any interpretation that wants to understand the biblical text is to ask for the text's own agenda, to inquire what it is really *about*, how the text's own agenda gets into the dialogue between text and reader. Critical methods allow the interpreter to come within hearing distance of the text, to listen to it in its terms, and to enter into serious conversation with the text.

16. I do not know the source of this variation on John 8:7; I first heard it from N. T. Wright.

On Attaining a Wholesome "Second Naiveté"

Much of the preceding can be summed up and pulled together under the rubrics provided by Paul Ricoeur, who charts the larger history of the church's dealing with the Bible, and the personal history of many individuals, in the progression *First Naiveté//Critical Distance//Second Naiveté*.[17]

First naiveté. The church, and many individuals, first began to read the Bible with a wholesome naiveté, without pursuing critical questions, but entering into the story world and experiencing one's own life story in continuity with the biblical story. Readers did not raise the questions of whether the biblical stories "really happened just as they were told" and whether biblical books were written by the authors traditionally assigned to them. There was no gap between the world of the Bible and the reader's own world. The Bible spoke directly to the reader, who heard it as the Word of God. Moses, Jesus, and Paul spoke directly to the reader. *The Bible was written to us*.

Critical distance. Historical-critical study allowed the Bible to be heard in its own situation, in its own historically conditioned terms. Isaiah

17. Paul Ricoeur, *The Symbolism of Evil* (Boston: Beacon Press, 1967), 351–52.

spoke to the people of Judah in the eighth century BCE, and one of his later disciples, whose oracles are also included in the book of Isaiah, spoke to the exiled Judeans in Babylonia two centuries later. Paul wrote to the Corinthians in 53–55 CE, but I am not a Corinthian and live more than nineteen centuries later. In many ways I can understand Isaiah of Jerusalem, his later disciple Second Isaiah, and Paul of Tarsus better than my precritical predecessors, but their writings no longer speak directly to me, and what it might mean to call the Bible the Word of God is not nearly so clear as it once was. A cardinal principle of critical study is this: *The Bible was not written to us*.

Some readers, frightened by or misinformed about the results of critical study of the Bible, attempt a retreat to precritical naiveté. There may be a wholesome instinct here, for if people in the community of faith must choose between reading the Bible in a way that allows it to speak to us, and reading it in a way that distances it from us, as merely another book of ancient history, the believing community understandably chooses the former. Other readers simply abandon their previous naive reading, some with reluctance but compelled by honesty, some with celebration and relief.

Still other readers, who have had difficulty with precritical literal understandings of the Bible and have always experienced it as something of an alien book, welcome critical studies as liberating, allowing them to understand the Bible in its original meaning, but are no longer compelled to try to hear it as somehow the word of God. Unfortunately, these various types of readers sometimes become stuck in this second level.

Second naiveté. Ricoeur commends going beyond critical distance once again (or for the first time) to experience the Bible as having a message that addresses the modern reader. This is not the same as going back to a first naiveté—which is difficult to do in any case. The insights of critical study are retained, but they facilitate coming within hearing distance of the message of the text, rather than erecting a barrier between text and reader. In this second naiveté, readers within the community of faith who hear the Bible as Holy Scripture affirm both: *The Bible was not written to us//The Bible was written to us*.

This is not mere double talk or dialectical mumbo jumbo. The key is the word *us*, which refers to the community of faith. Those who see themselves as members of the ongoing people of God, the community of faith of the Old and New Testaments, know that they are not eighth-century Judeans or first-century Corinthians ("not written to us"). Yet they belong to the same community of faith that has persisted through the centuries and around the world ("written to us"). This community, with its ongoing interpretation of its sacred texts, bridges the gap between "what it meant" and "what it means," interpreting to later generations of believers the revelatory words and insights of previous generations. This is part of what it means to claim that *the New Testament is the church's book because it interprets it for us and with us*.

Again, this does not mean that the individual reader of the Bible merely accepts the interpretations of church authorities. In this view, each reader can and must struggle with the texts and attempt to hear and understand them in a personal and existential way, using the whole range of exegetical and hermeneutical tools. But all interpretation takes place within a community.

We interpret for ourselves. // We do not interpret by ourselves.

5.2 For Further Reading

Ackroyd, P. R.; et al., eds. *The Cambridge History of the Bible*. 3 vols. Cambridge: Cambridge University Press, 1963–1970.

Anderson, Janice Capel, and Stephen D. Moore. *Mark and Method: New Approaches in Biblical Studies*. 2nd ed. Minneapolis: Fortress Press, 2008.

Baird, William R. *History of New Testament Research*. 3 vols. Minneapolis: Fortress Press, 1992, 2002, 2012).

Elliott, John H. *What Is Social-Scientific Criticism?* Minneapolis: Fortress Press, 1993.

Epp, Eldon J., and George W. MacRae, eds. *The New Testament and Its Modern Interpreters*. Atlanta: Scholars Press, 1989.

Farrar, F. W. *History of Interpretation*. Grand Rapids: Baker, 1979.

Fowl, Stephen E., ed. *The Theological Interpretation of Scripture: Classic and Contemporary Readings*. Cambridge: Blackwell, 1997.

González, Justo L. "How the Bible Has Been Interpreted in Christian Tradition." In *The New Interpreter's Bible*, ed. Leander Keck, 1:83–106. Nashville: Abingdon Press, 1994.

Grant, Robert M., and David Tracy. *A Short History of the Interpretation of the Bible*. 2nd ed. Philadelphia: Fortress Press, 1984.

Hayes, John H. *Dictionary of Biblical Interpretation*. Nashville: Abingdon Press, 1999.

McKnight, Edgar V. *What Is Form Criticism?* Philadelphia: Fortress Press, 1969.

Perrin, Norman. *What Is Redaction Criticism?* Philadelphia: Fortress Press, 1969.

Petersen, Norman R. *Literary Criticism for New Testament Critics*. Philadelphia: Fortress Press, 1978.

Powell, Mark Alan. *What Is Narrative Criticism?* Minneapolis: Fortress Press, 1990.

Stendahl, Krister. "Biblical Theology, Contemporary." In *The Interpreter's Dictionary of the Bible*, edited by George Arthur Buttrick and Keith Crim, 1:418–32. Nashville: Abingdon Press, 1962.

Tate, W. Randolph. *Biblical Interpretation: An Integrated Approach*. 3rd ed. Peabody, MA: Hendrickson, 2008.

6
The New Testament within the Hellenistic World

6.1 The New Testament as History

A text from the first century is like a door between two rooms, an opening through which to look into another culture, a different world. However, if we look at the door without going through it, we see only how the space for the door fits into the decor of the room on our side of the door—with all the cultural assumptions and social configurations of our time and place. We see it only in the context of the world we inhabit. Instead, we need to imaginatively walk through the opening into the world on the other side of the door, into the very different cultures of first-century Palestine and the Roman Empire—and then turn and look at the space for the door (the text) in the context of the decor of the first-century Mediterranean time and place.[1]

To set New Testament documents within their historical context, the reader needs a basic grasp of the following periods:

— The Hellenistic world from Alexander to Hadrian

— Judaism within the Hellenistic world

— Jesus within Judaism

— The story of the early church from Jesus to Paul, when early Christian history first becomes directly visible from primary sources

— The story of the early church from the earliest extant Christian document (1 Thess) to the latest document included in the New Testament (2 Pet).

1. David Rhoads, *Reading Mark, Engaging the Gospel* (Minneapolis: Fortress Press, 2004), 141.

6.2 The Hellenistic World from Alexander to Hadrian

THE PEOPLE OF ISRAEL, AT HOME IN THE small strip of arable land connecting Asia and Africa, had for centuries been familiar with the struggle to come to terms with the great powers that surrounded them—Egypt, Assyria, Babylon, Persia. As a coastland, Israel had cultural and commercial contacts for generations with Macedonia, Greece, and other Western countries, but the empires that dominated its life had all been Eastern powers, and Israel had always found it necessary to accommodate its fragile existence to its location between the great powers of Asia and Africa. When Alexander, young king of Macedonia, in 333 BCE set out eastward with his disciplined troops to conquer the Persian Empire, the Jewish people in Palestine were faced with a new reality. They were on the border of the grand East/West conflict, and had to decide how to live as the covenant people they believed God had called them to be (see maps 1 and 3).

Within ten years, Alexander's spectacular military conquest carried him through Greece and Asia Minor, down the Mediterranean coast through Palestine and into Egypt, then eastward through Persia to the border of India. All this was not mere personal ambition, but a continuation of the generations-long conflict between Greece and Persia, the effort of the outnumbered Greeks on the western edge of the great empires to escape from the Persian threat once and for all. For Alexander, his conquest was much more than a string of military victories that imposed Greek rule on the conquered countries. With the missionary zeal of an enlightened Westerner, he saw himself as bringing the blessings of Greek civilization to the "barbarians" of the East.

6.2.1 Hellenization

Alexander had been taught personally by Aristotle, had absorbed and idealized Greek language and culture, and saw this heritage as the means of uniting the world under the banner of Greek civilization. He encouraged his soldiers to marry local women and settle down in the conquered lands. His strategy was to found new cities and refound old ones on the Greek model, with new leadership eager to cooperate with the new world power. The *gymnasium*—a combination of school, athletic field, intellectual center, and elite cultural club—became both symbol and means of advancing Greek culture. The presence of new gymnasia and Greek theaters in every urban center emphasized that the wave of the future lay with those who adopted Greek language, dress, and perspectives. Whether people favored it or not, Greek currency, measures, weights, and business procedures became the norm.

Under the leadership of Alexander's successors, the new city of Alexandria, with its new library, became the world center of Greek scholarship. Scholars from Athens relocated to the new intellectual center, which drew philosophers, rhetoricians, artists, and educators from throughout the Mediterranean world. Rural areas and villages were not so deeply affected, but in the towns and cities those who wanted to get ahead adopted the Greek ways and sent their children to schools where they could learn Greek, which had become, in the somewhat unified and simplified Koine (common), the *lingua franca* of the Mediterranean world.

"Common" means not only "less nuanced and sophisticated," in contrast to the subtleties of classical Greek, but "common to all people," the common denominator linguistic glue that held the empire together and allowed it to function. Courses in "Greek as a Second Language" became popular—and necessary, if one wanted to succeed. In some ways, Hellenistic (Koine) Greek became more specific than classical Greek, since those who learned it as a second language had to spell out grammatically what had been clear to native speakers who understood its nuances. It was in this widely understood Greek that all the documents of the New Testament were written. This new amalgamation of West and East came to be called the Hellenistic world.[2] *Hellenic* would be authentic Greek; *Hellenistic* meant the Grecianization of the conquered territories (cf. the "Americanization" of much of the world conquered by American forces after the Second World War, when adopting Western dress and learning English became keys to upward mobility throughout the Western world). Alexander slept with two items under his pillow: a short sword and a copy of Homer's *Iliad.* He conquered by the sword, and spread Greek culture. The sword finally failed, as Rome outsworded the Greeks. But Greek culture prevailed and overcame Rome. Paul's letter to the *Romans* was written in *Greek.*

2. The effects of Hellenization and some Jewish responses to it are vividly portrayed in 1 and 2 Maccabees and indirectly reflected in Daniel. Martin Hengel, *Judaism and Hellenism: Studies in Their Encounter in Palestine during the Early Hellenistic Period,* trans. John Bowden (London: SCM Press, 1974), documents and illustrates in overwhelming detail the cultural forces of Hellenization in Palestine, especially its linguistic dimension.

The Jewish people of Palestine accepted Alexander without resistance—in contrast, for instance, to Tyre, which resisted and was defeated only after a brutal seven-month siege. When Alexander came on the scene, Palestinian Jews had been exercising a limited local autonomy as a part of the Persian Empire; with the defeat of Persia they exchanged one overlord for another and began to adjust to Greek ways. When Alexander died in Babylon in 323 BCE, his successors (*Diadochoi*) continued his policies. As the strategically desirable corridor and buffer state, Judea came alternately under the control of the Syrian Seleucids to the north and the Egyptian Ptolemies to the south (see Dan 11:5–9).

The series of wars—five in the third century—and political intrigues and power moves from all sides did not alter the gradual process of Hellenization in Palestine, for both the Seleucids and Ptolemies were Greek states in the tradition of Alexander. The subtle but constant pressure of Hellenization, often supported by the local aristocracy, continued without regard to whether Judea was under Ptolemaic or Seleucid political domination. The many Hellenistic cities in Palestine meant that traditional Jewish communities were becoming a shrinking proportion of the population in their own homeland. During the third century BCE Judea shared the general restlessness of the peoples of the East under the Macedonian yoke, sometimes expressed in eschatological hopes. By the second century BCE, Judeans joined in active resistance, manifest in the riots in Egypt, Persia, and elsewhere. By and large, however, the gradual Hellenizing development would have continued unabated, encouraged by reform-minded priestly leadership in Jerusalem. Sirach (Ecclesiasticus), written about 180 BCE, is a good illustration of the kind of Judaism that was open to the new developments in the Hellenistic world while remaining true to its own traditions. Politically, Judea was coming more and more to resemble a typical Hellenistic territory, with Jewish faith adapting to Hellenistic ways of thinking and practice. But then occurred a critical series of polarizing events that were to shape Jewish history—including that of Jesus and the early church—for all time to come.

6.2.2 The Maccabean Crisis

In 175 BCE, Antiochus IV Epiphanes (the name means "[God] Manifest") became the Seleucid ruler in Antioch, with Judea part of his empire. In need of money, he dismissed and exiled Onias III, the authorized Zadokite high priest who defended the traditional faith, and appointed Onias's brother Joshua, a Hellenizer who adopted the Greek form of his name, Jason. The high priesthood was hereditary and had been passed from father to son for centuries. When Israel was without a king and dominated by foreign powers, the high priest was recognized as God's designated leader for the people, not only for religious affairs. The pious in Israel regarded the transformation of the high priesthood into an office subject to appointment by foreign kings and bribery by unfaithful Jews as representing the lowest point of apostasy. Jason had offered Antiochus a large sum of money for the office—to be raised by increased taxes on the people. However, he was later outbid by Menelaus, an even more radical supporter of the Hellenizing program.[3] With Menelaus's personal supervision, Antiochus's troops plundered the temple.

The goal of the "progressive" group, almost entirely priests, was to transform the Jewish temple state (*ethnos*) into a regular Greek *polis*, in which citizenship would belong to a limited group with Greek education and aspirations. The masses, especially in the rural areas, were

3. To some considerable extent, the Hellenizing Jewish leaders seem to have seen themselves not as rejecting the traditional faith, but as reformers who were bringing Judaism up to date, and thus considered themselves faithful Jews (so, e.g., Elias Bickerman, *From Ezra to the Last of the Maccabees* [New York: Schocken Books, 1962], 93–182). The authors of 1 and 2 Maccabees and Daniel and the Qumran Essenes saw them as out and out apostates, as has much of the later Jewish and Christian interpretation.

to be left aside, effectively demoted to the status of outsiders in their own country. The situation should thus not be romanticized, as though it was only the "evil empire" of the Antiochenes against the faithful Jews. The struggle was not a united Jewish community loyal to the ancestral faith versus the pagan overlords, but a conflict internal to Judaism as well. And this fierce internal struggle was not merely between faithful and apostate Jews, but expressed the intense debate concerning what it meant to be a faithful Jew: to hold fast to the old ways or to adapt theology and practice to the emerging cultural reality. It was during this period that the term Ἰουδαϊσμός (Judaism) originated as a designation for the religion of Jews self-consciously devoted to loyalty to the law, distinguishing themselves from other Judeans, Palestinians, and those they considered apostate Jews (2 Macc 2:21; 8:1; 14:38). The early Christians and authors of New Testament texts would face analogous situations. What does it mean to be faithful? When is adaptation a way of preserving the tradition, and when is it a betrayal of the faith?

In 168 BCE Antiochus continued his attempt to expand his empire into Egypt. In a famous and symbolic scene, on his second foray into Egypt he was met by the representative of the new world power emerging on the western horizon, the Roman legate C. Popillius Laenus. In the name of the Roman Senate, the Roman legate ordered Antiochus to withdraw. When Antiochus responded that he would think it over and then decide, the Roman officer drew a circle in the sand around him, with the words ἐνταῦθα βουλεύου (*entautha bouleuou*, decide in this circle). Antiochus backed off and started back north with his army. Jewish leaders in Jerusalem, misunderstanding the situation as the military defeat of Antiochus, began an internal struggle for power, with the supporters of Menelaus fighting those of the ousted Jason. Antiochus, in turn, understood this as a full-scale revolt, responded with great violence in which his soldiers killed many Jews, looted the temple treasury, demolished the city walls, and erected a citadel called the Acra in the old city of David.

Antiochus decided the problem was rooted in the Jews' religion and that, in the interest of law, order, and modern civilization, their primitive religion should be abolished. He forbade observance of the Sabbath and the practice of circumcision, executed mothers who allowed their babies to be circumcised, made it a capital crime to possess a copy of the Jewish Scriptures, and converted the temple into a Hellenistic shrine devoted to the Olympian Zeus. Swine were sacrificed on a new altar built over the old one. This "desolating sacrilege" defiled the holy place and made it impossible for Jews to worship there.[4] Jews were forced not only to abandon their observance of the Torah, but to demonstrate their patriotism and loyalty to the government by participating, under pain of death, in the worship of Zeus. The aristocratic "reform party" among the Jerusalem priestly leadership seems to have encouraged these measures as a step in bringing Judea and Judaism into the modern world. These events and images, ineradicably burned into Jewish consciousness, were destined to play a continuing role in the future religious thought of both Judaism and Christianity.

When the Syrian officer charged with enforcing the law came to the village of Modein, twenty miles northwest of Jerusalem, Mattathias, a priest loyal to the traditional faith, killed both the officer and the Jew who was about to offer the pagan sacrifice. This triggered an all-out revolt, in which numerous Jews fled to the hills to join the guerilla army.[5] Mattathias

4. Traditionally translated "abomination of desolation" (KJV), the phrase is better rendered "desolating sacrilege" (RSV, NRSV). The sacrilegious act ("abomination") defiled the temple and meant the cultic acts could no longer be carried out, so the temple was deserted, became desolate ("of desolation"). See 1 Macc 1:54; Dan 11:31; 12:11; Mark 13:14, Matt 24:15.

5. The situation should not be romanticized, as though it was only the evil Antiochenes against the faithful Jewish population. Judas and his militia killed not only Syrians

died soon afterward, but was succeeded by his son Judas, nicknamed "the Maccabean" (apparently "the hammerer"). Under his leadership battles were won, and the temple was cleansed and rededicated, an event still celebrated at Hanukkah.

The revolt begun in order to achieve religious freedom expanded its goal to achieving political independence. Judas sent an embassy to Rome, which negotiated a treaty securing Roman support against the Seleucids (1 Macc 8:1–32). The revolt finally succeeded, and the Hasmoneans (as Judas, his brothers, and their descendants were now called) became the priestly rulers of the country. Not only religious faith but social factors internal to Judean life played a role. The Maccabees were rural priests who drew support from the countryside against the urban priests. When they came to power, they expelled or killed many of the "old guard," replacing them with people like themselves. Judas's brother Jonathan, though not of the Zadokite line, became high priest in 153 BCE and was recognized as head of the Jewish people by the Seleucid court. At his death, the priesthood passed to his brother Simon. Under his leadership, the Roman Senate recognized the independence of Judea in 139 BCE. Simon's son John Hyrcanus ruled 134–104. His sons Aristobulus I (104–103) and Alexander Janneus (103–76) called themselves not only high priests, but kings.

The Hasmoneans, who had begun as champions of the "true patriotism and religion" of rural Judea, established themselves as the new aristocracy, petty kings in the grand Hellenistic style, with standing armies of hired mercenaries. They annexed neighboring non-Jewish territory when they were able—always with the support of and under the watchful eye of Rome.

but compromising Jews, and the battles in Judea were as much a civil war as a revolt against foreign oppression. Nor should "religious liberty" be understood in the later sense of equal freedom for all religions. Jews were fighting for freedom to practice Judaism, not for general religious toleration.

The Empire from the Birth of Jesus to the Bar Kokhba Revolt

Jesus lived in Galilee, ruled by a puppet king of Rome, and was killed in Judea, a Roman province administered by a Roman governor. Early Christianity developed, and all the documents that became the New Testament were written, within the Roman Empire (see Box 9).

6.2.3 The Coming of the Romans

In 66–62 BCE the Roman general Pompey carried out a successful campaign in the east, resulting in the incorporation of Syria as a province of the Roman Empire and establishing a permanent Roman military presence in eastern Asia Minor. In Judea, the death of the reigning Hasmonean ruler, Salome Alexandra, precipitated a struggle between her two sons for the right of succession. Both Hyrcanus II and Aristobulus II appealed to Pompey for Roman support—as did a delegation from the Jewish people, who wanted to be rid of the Hasmoneans, now regarded as neither legitimate Zadokite high priests nor Davidic kings. Pompey decided for Hyrcanus, though denying him the title of king, but Hyrcanus had to enforce the decision with military subjugation of Jerusalem and Judea.

Roman pacification had come, and the relative independence of the Hasmonean era was gone. Though Judea retained some local government, the proconsul of Syria, already a Roman province, was given authority to exercise general supervision over Judea. Rome had come to stay.

The Decapolis, a league of ten Hellenistic cities in the Jordan valley, was formed about this time. Independent of their Jewish environment, they were loosely allied with each other and directly subordinate to the Syrian governor. All but Scythopolis were on the east side of the Jordan, where they played the strategic role of warding off Arab and Parthian threats from the east and promoting Hellenistic city life in the area. They were Gentile to the core, powerful cities oriented to the Roman world, grateful to

Box 9: The Roman Empire from the Birth of Jesus to the Bar Kokhba Revolt

27 BCE–14 CE Octavian (Caesar Augustus)

Herod the Great
Birth of Jesus
Judea becomes Roman province

14–37 CE Tiberius

Mission of Jesus
Beginning of church
Call of Paul to be an apostle

37–41 CE Gaius Caligula

Attempt of the emperor to place his statue in the Jerusalem temple
Early mission of Paul

41–54 CE Claudius

Expulsion of Jews (including Jewish Christians) from Rome
Later mission of Paul; Pauline letters

54–68 CE Nero

Persecution of Christians in Rome
Revolt in Judea

68–69 CE Galba, Otho, Vitellius

Year of tumult with three emperors

69–79 CE Vespasian

Destruction of Jerusalem and the temple
Gospel of Mark

79–81 CE Titus

Later New Testament writings

81–96 CE Domitian

Later New Testament writings

96–98 CE Nerva

Later New Testament writings

98–117 CE Trajan

Revolts and tumults among Jewish population
Later New Testament writings

117–138 CE Hadrian

Revolt in Palestine led by Bar Kokhba
Probable composition of the latest New Testament documents

Pompey and the Romans for liberating them from the tyranny of Jewish and Nabatean kings. They generally supported the empire, and could become aggressively anti-Jewish with minimal provocation.

In the civil war that broke out in 49 BCE between Pompey in the East and Julius Caesar in the West, Pompey was defeated and killed. After his victory, Julius Caesar came through Palestine and Syria and confirmed the Hasmonean Hyrcanus as "ethnarch of the Jews" (not "king"). Antipater, an Idumean who had been consolidating his power in Judea, had been Hyrcanus's sponsor and advisor, the real power behind the throne. Julius Caesar made Antipater a Roman citizen and procurator of Judea, with both military and political power. During the internal struggles that followed the assassination of Julius Caesar in 44 BCE, Antipater adroitly managed to stay on the winning side, as did his son Herod, who inherited the leading role in Judea when Antipater was killed in 43 BCE.

6.2.4 Herod the Great (74–4 BCE)

The Parthians, heirs of Persia on the eastern border of the Roman Empire, wanted control of Palestine and supported Herod's rival, the Hasmonean Antigonus, as their puppet king. Herod went to Rome and was appointed king of Judea by Anthony and Octavian, but he had to conquer his "own" kingdom in a bloody war. Herod was considered an outsider, an Idumean half-Jew who wanted only to reign as a Hellenistic monarch under Roman control. Like Antipater, Herod owed everything to the Romans and thus gave them wholehearted support. Herod's supporters were to be found mainly among the Gentile and nonindigenous settlers in Samaria and Idumea, and among the Hellenizing Jews who saw the future of Palestine as a Hellenistic Roman state. Despite Herod's marriage into the Hasmonean family in an effort to establish his legitimacy, the Jewish population continued to regard him as an Idumean usurper and

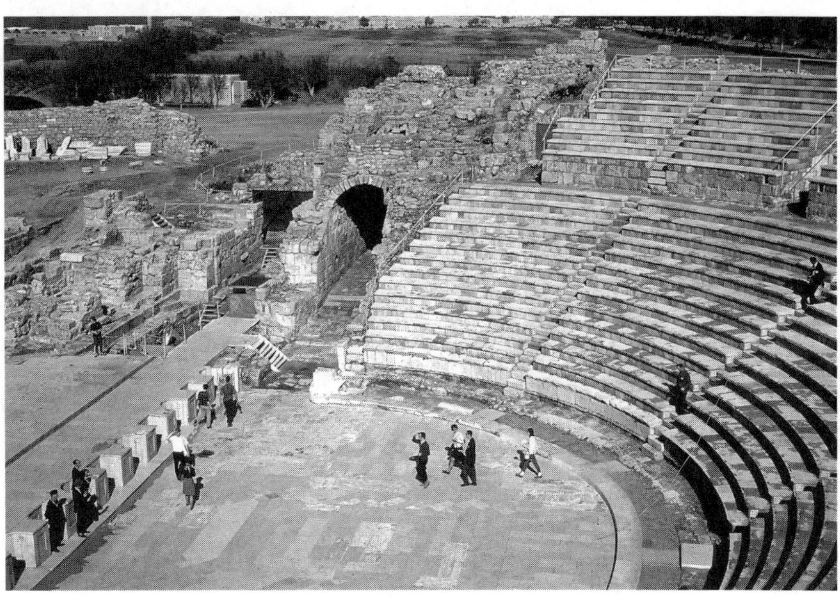

FIGURE 9: Roman Theater in Caesarea. USED BY PERMISSION OF DAVID PADFIELD.

interloper, who had destroyed the legitimate Hasmonean dynasty in a personal power grab and ruled only with Roman support.

This popular assessment was correct. Herod was a brilliant and energetic leader, who in fact did much for the economy of Palestine by his extravagant building projects, including his rebuilding the coastal town Strato's Tower into a splendid seaport named Caesarea in honor of his sponsor.

Likewise, his reconstruction of the temple in Jerusalem made it one of the most magnificent buildings in the empire. Nonetheless, his kingdom was in all respects like the numerous other client kingdoms under Roman sovereignty. He could rule like an independent king within his own territory, so long as his decisions did not impinge on broader Roman interests. Thus he could not have an independent foreign policy; he could not make treaties with other rulers or conduct military operations beyond his own borders without the consent of Rome. This represented a change in the broad Roman policy in effect throughout the Hasmonean times, during which the Romans had an alliance with the Jewish people, conducted through the Roman Senate and the Jewish people as represented by their high priest. Now, neither Rome nor Herod regarded the Jewish people as a political entity. Rome dealt directly with Herod, and Herod with Rome.

Herod's main obligation to Rome, aside from keeping the peace and providing a stable buffer state against the Parthians, was the annual raising of a considerable tribute. Rome thought of the land as belonging to the emperor, who leased it to the client king on condition of payment of tribute. Herod was thus faced with the constant responsibility of paying his Roman overlords. This required the extraction of exorbitant taxes of numerous varieties from the population, rich and poor alike, estimated at 30–40 percent, not counting tithes and religious taxes. This, in turn, required a stable and functioning economy; it was to Herod's advantage to promote peace and prosperity in his own realm, and he did so. He resettled peasants who had lost their land and helped them become

FIGURE 10: Caesarea Philippi. USED BY PERMISSION OF DAVID PADFIELD.

productive farmers again—who could pay the needed taxes. He helped cities rebuild and become prosperous, and he founded new cities. His building projects maintained employment and promoted the development of skilled workers. At the end of his reign the economic situation of the people as a whole was better than at the beginning.

From the perspective of skillful political and economic success, the title "Herod the Great" had some justification. Herod maintained good relations with his Roman overlords, especially Octavian/Augustus, and sent his sons Alexander and Aristobulus to Rome to be educated and groomed for future leadership. In Palestine, however, Herod ruled with intrigue and terror, brutally eliminating real and suspected political opposition, and killing several of his ten wives and numerous sons whom he considered potential threats. Reflecting Herod's lip service to Judaism that included abstinence from pork, Augustus allegedly remarked in a caustic wordplay that works only in Greek, "It is better to be Herod's pig (ὗς *hus*) than his son (υἱός *huios*)."

When Herod died in 4 BCE, his sons quarreled over the succession and went to Rome to plead their respective cases before Augustus. At home, disturbances and revolts broke out among elements of the exploited population of Palestine. A delegation from the people had also gone to Rome to plead that the country be placed under direct control of Rome, rather than being subject to any of the Herods. Meanwhile, Varus, governor of Syria, pacified the Palestinian countryside with brutal force, crucifying two thousand of the rebels. Augustus denied the title king to any of Herod's sons, dividing Herod's territory among them. *Philip* was appointed ruler of the territory north and east of the Sea of Galilee and conducted himself as a typical Hellenistic client ruler, building a temple to Augustus at the ancient shrine city of Banias, which he renamed Caesarea Philippi (Philip's Caesarea).

Herod Antipas, the "King Herod" of the Gospels, was made ruler of Galilee and Perea. His official title was tetrarch, literally "ruler of a fourth part," but the word simply meant "prince." He comported himself royally and was popularly known as the king. He founded new cities and rebuilt others, all in the Hellenistic style. The ancient Sepphoris, less than four miles northwest of Jesus' hometown of Nazareth, was rebuilt as a shining example of the new culture, complete with a palace and a theater that seated three thousand (see Josephus, *War* 2.511; *Ant.* 18.27, and fig. 15). Sepphoris was apparently Herod's initial headquarters, but the capital was later moved to the new city, Tiberius, named after the emperor, which Herod built on the southwest shore of the Sea of Galilee. Here too, despite Herod's provision of a synagogue, the city was built in the Hellenistic style, with a Greek stadium, and Herod's palace splendidly decorated with animal images. Herod chose the spot for its beauty and personal convenience (it was near the warm springs of Hammath) and as an administrative center for the profitable fishing business, but without regard to traditional Jewish sensitivities. The new city was located on an ancient cemetery. This not only showed disdain for Jewish tradition, but made everyone entering the city ritually unclean, so that no orthodox Jew could voluntarily live and work there. Herod colonized the city by force, resulting in a mixed population of Gentiles and lapsed or compromised Jews.

Though Rome was the power behind the "throne" of "king" Herod, Galilee was not directly under Roman rule in the time of Jesus. The tax collectors of the Gospels, seen in terms of Jesus' historical setting, were not collecting Roman taxes; the centurion of stories from Jesus' Galilee mission (Matt 8:5–13) would not have been a Roman soldier but an officer of Herod Antipas's army, which included local Gentiles and non-Jews from Syria. The census narrated in relation to Jesus' birth (Luke 2) would not have affected Herod's Galilee. The situation was different in Judea.

As ethnarch over Judea, Samaria, and Idumea, *Archelaus* was awarded the heartland of his father's kingdom, which included the major cities of Jerusalem, Samaria, Caesarea, and Joppa. He was the least competent of Herod's sons. His oppressive measures were so unbearable that a Jewish delegation sent to Rome was able to persuade Augustus to replace him. His rule came to an end after ten years (4 BCE–6 CE), and his territories were placed under direct Roman administration as a province of the empire. In preparation for the new tax program in which taxes would be paid directly to Rome, Quirinius, Octavian's legate in Syria, took a census of the property of the Jews in Judea.

This precipitated armed resistance by Judas the Galilean and his followers, which exhibits the solidarity felt by Galilean Jews with Jerusalem and Judea, for the census did not directly affect Galilee. The attempted revolt was quickly put down. Except for a brief interregnum when all Herod the Great's territories were restored to his grandson Herod Agrippa I (41–44 CE), Judea remained a Roman province until the outbreak of the revolt in 66 CE.

6.2.5 Judea as Province, 6–66 CE

From the beginning of Roman rule, Judea was considered a strategic territory and potential trouble spot and thus became a province with a governor of equestrian rank and the title of *praefectus*. The governors were later called procurators, since their chief responsibility was the procuring of Roman taxes. This included, however, a strong emphasis on the maintenance of law and order and a stable political and economic situation. While some governors attempted to implement Rome's rule with sensitivity to local customs and religious traditions, the fifth procurator, Pontius Pilate (26–36 CE), was so ruthless that he was suspended from his post.

The census of 6 CE tangibly brought every resident of Judea under the direct fiscal and legal authority of Rome, precipitating the revolutionary movement begun by Judas of Galilee. Judas and his followers claimed that acceptance of the Roman yoke violated the fundamental convictions of Jewish faith, for Jews could worship only the one God and must resist both the introduction of Roman images they considered idolatrous and the claims by and about the emperors to divinity. They also saw, correctly as it turned out, that acceptance of direct taxation from the Romans would lead to slavery of the population when the taxes could not be paid. Judas and his followers attacked the Roman fort in Sepphoris but were defeated. Judas was killed, and his followers were dispersed (Acts 5:37; Josephus, *War* 2.117–18; *Ant.* 18.1–10, 23–25). The movement he had begun smoldered underground, broke out afresh from time to time, and eventually became the Zealot movement that led to the disastrous war of 66–70 CE.[6]

6.2.6 The Revolts of 66–70 and 132–135 CE

As the rebel movement gained influence, conditions in Palestine deteriorated. The chaos preceding the war is illustrated by events in the brief interregnum between the departure of Festus (60–62) and Albinus's assumption of office (62–64). The high priest Ananus exploited the absence of a procurator to impose the death penalty on a number of his opponents, including James the brother of Jesus, the leader of the Christian group in Jerusalem (Josephus, *Ant.* 17.10–7.278–84; *War* 4.3.60–65). If not illegal, this was at least ill-advised—for the Romans seem to have reserved the right of capital punishment for themselves—and the new governor Albinus deposed Ananus.

When the revolt was signaled by the cessation of the daily temple sacrifices made for the emperor,[7] Nero sent Vespasian, his best general, to take command of the Roman armies charged with quelling the revolt. Many of the outnumbered and overwhelmed Jewish rebels fought bravely, but their efforts were practically nullified by internal struggles among rival Jewish claimants to leadership. Nero's suicide in 68 turned Vespasian's attention toward Rome and his own ambition to be emperor. He left his son Titus in Jerusalem to continue the siege, waited out the tumultuous year of 69 in Egypt, taking control of the Roman food supply while the three other contenders for the throne were killed (Galba, Otho, Vitellius). Vespasian was then proclaimed emperor by the legions. Amid great bloodshed and terrorism, in which the numbers of those crucified by the Romans grew into thousands, Titus completed the subjugation of Jerusalem in 70 CE, destroyed the temple, and celebrated his triumphal procession in Rome the next year (see figs. 11–12).

At Vespasian's death, his son Titus became emperor (79–81 CE), succeeded by Domitian (81–96), Titus's brother, the third member of the Flavian dynasty. In Domitian's latter days, his increasing insistence on his own deity (see on the emperor cult, §9.2.2 below) and interest in purifying the empire of foreign cults brought pressure on the growing Christian movement. During Nero's time, Christians in Rome had already come to the attention of the empire as a group separate from Judaism. Nero blamed the great fire of 64 CE on them and with the approval of much of the population had large numbers of Christians in the city of Rome arrested and condemned to terrible deaths. During the whole period in which the church was growing and documents that became the New Testament were being written, the Christian community lived a harassed and fragile existence within the Roman Empire, but there was no systematic, empirewide persecution or attempts to

6. The war began in 66 CE; Jerusalem and the temple were destroyed in 70, which effectively ended the war. Pockets of resistance continued (as at Masada) until 74, but the war is conventionally designated as 66–70.

7. The Jewish leaders in Jerusalem had successfully maintained their view, backed up by the people's readiness for martyrdom, that they could not participate in emperor worship by offering sacrifice *to* the emperor as a god, but demonstrated their loyalty to Rome by offering a daily sacrifice *for* the emperor. The cessation of sacrifice was a symbolic act, the equivalent of lowering the Roman flag and raising the rebel banner over Jerusalem.

FIGURE 11: The Arch of Titus in Rome, depicting the Roman emperor's victory over Judea. PHOTO CREDIT: M. EUGENE BORING.

FIGURE 12: Relief on the Arch of Titus in Rome, depicting the sacking of the temple in Jerusalem in 70 CE. Note the seven-branched menorah. USED BY PERMISSION OF DAVID PADFIELD.

eliminate Christianity until the third century under the emperors Decius and Diocletian.

The Flavian dynasty came to an end with Domitian's death. His successors Nerva (96–98 CE) and Trajan (98–117 CE) saw both violent suppression of some Jewish riots against Roman policies and sporadic actions against Christian leaders. The catastrophic war of 66–70 CE inhibited, but did not destroy, the rebellious movements among the remnants of Jewish militants, some of which were fueled by eschatological fervor and messianic hopes. Yet the hope for rebuilding Jerusalem and the temple and the establishment of God's rule through a messianic deliverer persisted, as documented, for instance, in the synagogue prayers and *Sibylline Oracles* from the time.[8]

Revolutionary disturbances continued among some Jews in North Africa after 70 CE. A general rebellion in 114–117 CE that involved most of the Jewish population of Egypt and Cyprus under the messianic claimant Andreas Lukas was suppressed only with great difficulty. Many Alexandrians were killed early in the revolt, and Egyptian Judaism was eventually all but destroyed. Hadrian's (117–138 CE) plan to purify Rome of religiously and culturally backward groups included a ban on circumcision and the transformation of Jerusalem into a temple city dedicated to Jupiter. This precipitated another revolt in Judea, led by Simeon ben Kosiba, known popularly as Bar Kokhba ("Son of the Star," the "Star-Man" deliverer predicted in Num 24:17). Bar Kokhba was proclaimed as the Messiah by the revered Rabbi Akiba. Again, the Jews fought courageously, but Roman power triumphed in 135 CE after desolating the whole of Judea in a bloody and costly campaign. Many of the surviving Jews were sold into slavery, Jerusalem became Aelia Capitolina, and Judea became the Roman province Syria Palaestina. Jews were forbidden to enter the city under pain of death.

6.3 For Further Reading

Barrett, C. K., ed. *The New Testament Background: Selected Documents*. 2nd ed. New York: HarperOne, 1995.

Boring, M. Eugene, Klaus Berger, and Carsten Colpe. *Hellenistic Commentary to the New Testament*. Nashville: Abingdon Press, 1995.

Carter, Warren. *The Roman Empire and the New Testament: An Essential Guide*. Nashville: Abingdon Press, 2006.

Ferguson, Everett. *Backgrounds of Early Christianity*. 3rd ed. Grand Rapids: Eerdmans, 2003.

8. See, e.g., Andrew Chester, "The Parting of the Ways: Eschatology and the Messianic Hope," in *Jews and Christians: The Parting of the Ways*, ed. James D. G. Dunn (Grand Rapids: Eerdmans, 1992), 239–58.

7

Palestinian Judaism within the Hellenistic World

WHILE THE NEW TESTAMENT CANNOT BE understood apart from the Old Testament, the student interested in understanding the New Testament cannot go directly from the biblical text to the early Christian writings, but must also be informed by the Judaism that emerged in the intertestamental period. Five brief illustrations: (1) In the Old Testament, the term "Messiah" refers primarily to the anointed king of Israel or Judah, and is never applied to the savior figure expected in the eschatological future. The Judaism of the first century CE had no contemporary Jewish king, and after 70 CE applied messianic terminology to a variety of figures still to come. (2) The concept of resurrection is almost totally absent from the Jewish Scriptures, barely making it into the latest book (Dan 12:2–3). Yet when the New Testament opens, resurrection is a commonly accepted idea in first-century Judaism, not introduced by Jesus and his followers, but assumed by friend and foe alike (Mark 6:14; John 11:24). (3) When the New Testament cites the Jewish Scriptures, it often gives a version of the text different from what we find in our Old Testament, and sometimes cites books not found in our Old Testament. Thus, for example, Matthew 1:23 cites Isaiah 7:14 in a form not found in the Hebrew text, Matthew 2:23 cites a text of uncertain provenance not found in our Old Testament at all, and Jude 14–15 cites *1 Enoch* 1.9. (4) Stories and events are understood in terms of later interpretations, not only as found in the Jewish Scriptures (see above §5.1.3, below §9.2.2). (5) The Old Testament knows of tabernacle and temple, but no synagogues. When the New Testament opens, the synagogue is central in Jewish life.

7.1 Key Primary Sources

IN ADDITION TO THE LATER BOOKS OF THE Old Testament (Haggai, Zechariah, Ezra, Nehemiah, Daniel), the Apocrypha/deuterocanonical books, and the New Testament itself, the following primary sources are the basis for our understanding of early Judaism:

7.1.1 Josephus

Josephus (37–ca. 100 CE) was a young priestly aristocrat of Jerusalem who was charged with commanding Jewish troops in Galilee at the beginning of the 66–70 war.[1] His troops were defeated and he surrendered, ingratiating himself with Vespasian by predicting that the victorious general would be the next emperor. Josephus assisted Vespasian in the defeat of the Jews and returned with him to Rome where he

1. The definitive edition in English is the Loeb Classical Library, with Greek and English text on facing pages (ten volumes). The eighteenth-century translation of William Whiston, often reprinted and still available, is inaccurate and to be avoided.

FIGURE 13: Masada, showing the ramp constructed by the Romans to attack the walled fort atop the plateau. PHOTO CREDIT: M. EUGENE BORING.

was provided an apartment and generous pension that allowed him to write and publish. His works are in four categories:

The Jewish War, seven volumes written in Aramaic in the mid 70s CE, translated and published in Greek, covers the war in Palestine in great detail, concluding with the mass suicide at Masada in 74 and prefaced by an extended introduction beginning in Maccabean times (see fig. 13).

Jewish Antiquities, twenty volumes written in Greek (with scribal assistance) near the end of the first century CE, presents a history of the Jewish people from its origins until the eve of the revolt. The first ten volumes are essentially a paraphrase of the biblical story, but Josephus's additions and modifications allow the modern reader to see how Jewish history and religion were perceived by some cosmopolitan Jews in the first century. The remainder is based on a number of sources, most no longer extant, including the history of the Jews by Nicholas of Damascus, court historian to Herod the Great.

Life, an autobiographical work appended to the *Antiquities*, deals with the six months of Josephus's conduct just prior to and during the war.

Against Apion, Josephus's last work, is a defense of the Jews that responds to charges and misunderstandings.

7.1.2 Philo

Philo was a well-educated, prominent member of the Jewish community in Alexandria.[2] His native language and thought patterns were Greek, and his literary ambition was to interpret Judaism in Greek terms in a form attractive to the Hellenistic world. His writings are mostly detailed allegorical interpretations of the Pentateuch, including the *Questions and Answers*, the *Allegorical Interpretations*, and the *Expositions*. Among his important nonexegetical works are *That Every Good Person Is Free* (including a description of the Essenes), *On the Contemplative Life* (including a description of

2. The definitive edition in English is the Loeb Classical Library, with Greek and English text on facing pages (twelve volumes).

the Therapeutae), and his *Life of Moses*. While Philo is a representative of the intellectual elite, he must have been considered a good representative of Judaism by the large Jewish population of Alexandria, for he represented them in an embassy to the emperor Claudius to protest against the violation of their rights.

7.1.3 Pseudepigrapha

The term "pseudepigrapha" has become in practice a catchall designation for all early Jewish writings that do not belong to any of the other categories: canonical Scripture, the Apocrypha/deuterocanonicals, Josephus, Philo, Dead Sea Scrolls, Rabbinica.[3] The label refers literally to writings with a false title, that is, not actually written by the author to whom they are attributed. The designation is unfortunate and derives from the title of an early collection of such documents,[4] now replaced in English by the expanded collection edited by James H. Charlesworth, *The Old Testament Pseudepigrapha*. This two-volume anthology contains a total of sixty-three texts representing a variety of literary genres. Among those most important for New Testament studies are these:

Jubilees, composed about 150 BCE, is a rewriting of the narrative of Genesis–Exodus, reporting among other things the instructions God gave to Moses during the forty days on Mt. Sinai that are not recorded in the Bible. It is concerned with circumcision, ritual purity, Sabbath laws, and tithes. It advocates a solar calendar rather than the standard lunar calendar, thus making the festivals fall on different days from the calendar of conventional mainstream temple Judaism. The parts of sixteen copies found in the Qumran library show it was very popular among some streams of Second Temple Judaism.

Testaments of the Twelve Patriarchs, like the works of Josephus, Philo, and much of the Pseudepigrapha, was preserved not by Judaism but by the church. Sometimes, as in the case of the *Testaments*, these originally Jewish documents were revised and expanded to give a Christian message or perspective. These twelve separate compositions (*Testament of Judah*, *Testament of Levi*, etc.) represent each of the twelve sons of Jacob as addressing his family just prior to his death and "predicting" the future, especially the eschatological events, while warning against vices and encouraging obedience to the law.

First Enoch is composed of separate compositions that Qumran fragments show had an independent existence before being combined into the "Book of Enoch." The earliest parts of this lengthy and complex compilation of traditions derives from pre-Maccabean times; its latest sections may come from the first century CE. Each of the five booklets into which the final version was edited is represented as revelations made to Enoch (Gen 5:18–24). Since he was taken to heaven without dying, he is an especially appropriate figure to speak from the perspective of the heavenly world. He predicts, in transparently symbolic language, the history of the world to the real author's own time. Especially important for New Testament interpretation is the section called *Similitudes* or *Parables* (chaps. 37–71), which portrays a heavenly figure, the Son of Man, who will come at the end of history and exercise God's judgment. No fragments of the *Similitudes* were found at Qumran, which may mean that this text was composed later or that the Covenanters rejected its theology. The fourteen manuscripts from Qumran containing works from the Enoch literature testify to its popularity among some streams of Second Temple Judaism.

Psalms of Solomon, written about 50 BCE, attacks the "sinners" of the Jerusalem temple leadership, who have profaned the temple, and

3. The best edition in English is James H. Charlesworth, ed., *The Old Testament Pseudepigrapha* (2 vols.; Garden City, NY: Doubleday, 1985).
4. R. H. Charles, ed., *The Apocrypha and Pseudepigrapha of the Old Testament in English*, vol. 2, *Pseudepigrapha*, 2 vols. (Oxford: Clarendon Press, 1964; originally published 1913).

looks forward to a militant messianic figure who will purge the temple and defeat the Romans.

Testament of Moses (also called *Assumption of Moses*), written in the first century CE in its present form, portrays Moses' final speech to Joshua, predicting the history of the world from the time of Adam until the end. God will establish an apocalyptic kingdom (chap. 10) accompanied by cosmic phenomena, but will do it directly, with no reference to a Messiah.

The Life of Adam and Eve was interwoven with another apocalyptic work, the *Apocalypse of Moses*, in a complex literary history. Although the Genesis 1–3 story of Adam and Eve had little direct effect on the Old Testament, it was profoundly influential on some of the literature of Second Temple Judaism, generating a number of apocalyptic works. When Adam and Eve learn that they are going to die, they predict the whole future history of the world until the resurrection, and indicate that their sin is the cause of all human woes.

Sibylline Oracles are collections of oracles purportedly uttered by the aged prophetess (the Sibyl) and officially collected, preserved, and interpreted by the Roman Senate. The official collection was lost in a fire that destroyed the Temple of Jupiter in 83 BCE, but was later restored from scattered collections. This later anthology includes insertions by Jewish authors, some claiming to foretell eschatological events, others reflecting historical events of the Second Temple period. In the standard Roman collection, Books 3–5 are mainly Jewish and reflect the period between the Maccabees and Bar Kokhba. The *Nero redivivus* legend appears strikingly in 5:137–54. The "great king of Rome" who "murdered his mother" flees from "Babylon" (=Rome) and takes refuge with the Parthians. He will return in the last days to take vengeance on Rome, which had rejected him. This legend lies behind the imagery of Revelation. The *Sibylline Oracles* were taken very seriously, since they often purported to predict the political future. The emperor Augustus, for instance, edited the Roman collection and had hundreds of them destroyed (Suetonius, *Augustus* 31.1).

2 Esdras/4 Ezra, an originally Jewish apocalypse text (chaps. 3–14) written in the 90s of the first century CE, was supplemented by Christian additions (chaps. 1–2, sometimes called *5 Ezra*; chaps. 15–16, *6 Ezra*). In Roman Catholic tradition, the book has often been circulated along with the canonical documents but—in contrast to the Apocrypha/deuterocanonical books—never achieved canonical status in either Judaism or Christianity. The book, which depicts Ezra lamenting the destruction of the temple and pondering the justice of God by which only a very few will finally be saved, addresses the situation of post-70 Palestinian Judaism. Ezra receives a revelation comprising seven visions filled with symbolic imagery showing that the time is short. The eschatological drama will involve the Son of God, who is identified with the Messiah (2:47), and a figure like the Son of Man who comes with the clouds of heaven (13:1–4).

7.1.4 Dead Sea Scrolls

In 1947 Bedouin shepherds accidently discovered a cache of scrolls in a cave at Qumran near the Dead Sea. The scrolls had been deposited there by a Jewish sectarian group for safekeeping as the Roman army approached in 68 CE (see fig. 14). Relatively few whole manuscripts have been recovered from the Qumran caves. Decomposition and destruction by treasure hunters through the centuries have reduced most of the original manuscripts to "the world's greatest jigsaw puzzle," consisting of more than 15,000 fragments. Nonetheless, painstaking reconstruction has pieced together larger units representing a total of more than 850 manuscripts that have been identified from the eleven caves investigated at Qumran, representing about 660 different works. The process of analysis and publication has been complex and slow, sometimes giving rise to unwarranted suspicion and speculations that the unpublished

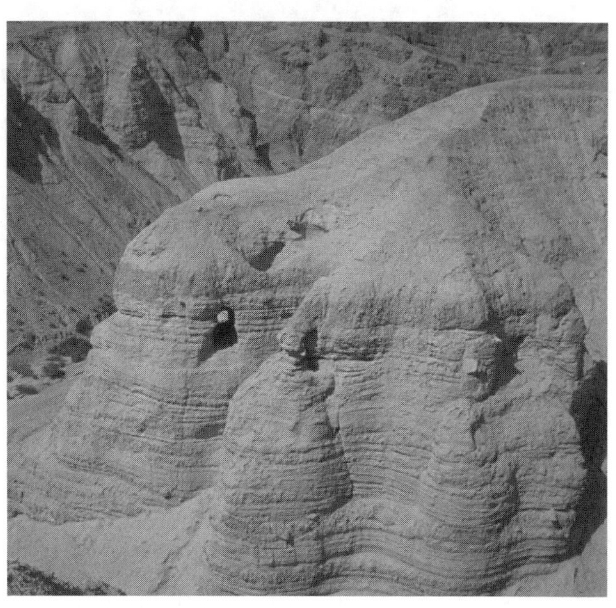

FIGURE 14: Qumran Cave 4. USED BY PERMISSION OF DAVID PADFIELD.

scrolls contained secret information that religious or academic authorities wanted to suppress. Since June 1993, every manuscript and fragment has been published and is publically available. Counting the manuscripts that have been lost or destroyed, the Qumran library must have consisted of more than a thousand scrolls. Only nine scrolls, about 1 percent of the total manuscripts identified, have more than half of their original content. Of the about 660 manuscripts whose content and genre we can recognize, about 200 are of biblical texts. Numerous others are manuscripts of works that were already known. There are manuscript fragments of about 120 different works that were previously completely unknown to us. This means that we know something of the genre and contents of more than half of the original contents of the library.

Enough has been preserved to make it virtually certain that the Qumran library was strictly Essenic, containing no works from Pharisees, Sadducees, or pagan authors. Likewise, the Qumran library included no biblical books that appeared after about 150 BCE and thus appeared only in the later LXX and Vulgate (1 and 2 Maccabees, Judith, Wisdom of Solomon). Nonetheless, what we learn from the scrolls is enormously illuminating, not only for the Essene community, but for many other aspects of Second Temple Judaism. Of primary interest are the more than twenty-five compositions by members of the sect. Of these, the most important for New Testament studies are these:

1QS Rule of the Community, Manual of Discipline The *Rule* occurs in multiple copies and recensions, perhaps reflecting various subgroups within the sect and different stages in its life (which lasted more than two hundred years). The oldest manuscript of the *Rule*, found in Cave 4 (4QSe), is dated on paleographical grounds before 100 BCE and thus was probably composed between 150 and 125 BCE, perhaps by the Teacher of Righteousness, the founder of the sect. The rules and procedures are for the Essenes in general, not just for the Qumran group, and throw much light on the Essenes' self-understanding and theology.

1QpHab The Habakkuk Commentary The cache of manuscripts includes seventeen verse-by-verse commentaries on biblical books in the *pesher* style, citing a phrase from the Bible followed by an interpretation in terms of the contemporary history of the sect. The *Habakkuk Commentary* is one of the more revealing of these commentaries. A brief section of the biblical text is quoted, followed by "Its pesher (interpretation) is . . ."; then the biblical text is interpreted as referring to events contemporary with the life of the Qumran community. Here is one example of many, from 1QpHab, the Habakkuk commentary. On Habakkuk 1:4–5:

> ["For the wicked man hems in] the righteous man." [The "wicked man" refers to the Wicked Priest, and "the righteous man"] is the Teacher of Righteousness. [. . .] ["There] fore judgment comes out [perverted." This means that . . .] not [. . .] [. . .] ["Look, traitors, and see,] [and be shocked—and amazed—for the Lord is doing something in your time that you would not believe it if] told."
>
> [This passage refers to] the traitors with the Man of the Lie, because they have not [obeyed the words of] the Teacher of Righteousness from the mouth of God. It also refers to the trai[tors to the] New [Covenant], because they did not believe in God's covenant [and desecrated] His holy name; and finally, it refers [to the trai]tors in the Last Days. They are the cru[el Israel]ites who will not believe when they hear everything that is to c[ome upon] the latter generation that will be spoken by the Priest in whose [heart] God has put [the ability] to explain all the words of his servants the prophets, through [whom] God has foretold everything that is to come upon his people and [the Gentiles].[5]

The Essenic group at Qumran believed they were the Community of the New Covenant, promised by God at the end of history (Jer 31:31–34), and they reread all Scripture in the light of what they believed God was doing in their present situation. The meaning was not determined by asking what the original author meant, but was given by divine inspiration to the leader of the group, revealing that the Scripture spoke directly to and about the community of the last days.

CD Damascus Document (CD="Cairo Damascus") Like 1QS, this document portrays something of the early history and rules of the community, referring to "Damascus" as the place of the community's "exile" after separating from the Jerusalem temple. It is not clear whether this is intended literally or symbolically. This is the only document directly associated with the community that was known prior to the 1947 Qumran discoveries. It was discovered in 1896 in the Geniza (consecrated storage room for discarded sacred texts) of the synagogue in Old Cairo. Its significance was not appreciated until it was related to the Qumran discoveries.

1QM War Scroll This text, found in several variations, gives instructions for a ritualistic eschatological battle the Qumran community expected to occur soon, with the Romans on one side ("the sons of darkness") and the heavily outnumbered Qumran warriors ("the sons of light"), assisted by angels, on the other. At the end of seven periods of battle, God finally gives the victory to the faithful Qumran community.

1QH Thanksgiving Hymns One of the seven original scrolls from Cave One at Qumran contained compositions similar to the biblical thanksgiving hymns in the Psalter, and was given the name *Hodayot* ("Thanksgivings"). Several other copies were later found in other caves, as well as copies of similar works composed by members of the community. All reveal the theology and fervent piety of the

5. The translation is from *Qumran Non-biblical Manuscripts: A New English Translation* based upon the book *The Dead Sea Scrolls: A New English Translation*, edited by Michael O. Wise, Martin G. Abegg Jr., and Edward M. Cook (New York: HarperCollins Publishers, revised 2005), as transcribed in *Accordance Bible Software*. ©2009 by Michael Wise, Martin Abegg Jr., and Edward Cook. Used by permission of HarperCollins Publishers.

community; some were probably composed by the Teacher of Righteousness himself.

11QT The Temple Scroll Written before the destruction of the second temple in 70 CE, this longest of the Dead Sea Scrolls is devoted to detailed descriptions of the new temple the Qumran community expected to replace the existing temple. It explicates both the different architecture, different cultic calendar, and different personnel for the eschatological temple, illustrating how important the temple was in the theology of the cult. The world could not be rightly related to God unless and until there was an authentic temple cultus. The formula sometimes used, "And I [God] said . . ." shows the community regarded the document as divinely inspired.

4QMMT Halakic Letter This lengthy document, perhaps written by the Teacher of Righteousness himself to the existing temple authorities, spells out the differences, calendric and otherwise, between the Qumran Essenes and the priests in charge of the Jerusalem temple. It calls on them to reform their practice in conformity with the Qumran community's interpretation and thus legitimize the present temple practice. Like the *Temple Scroll* and *Jubilees*, 4QMMT advocates a 364-day solar calendar that places the festivals on different days than those practiced according to the Jerusalem lunar calendar, and again illustrates how indispensable it was for the community's theology to have the temple functioning properly.

4QShirShabb Angelic Liturgy,* or *Songs of the Sabbath Sacrifice Pre-Qumran, perhaps as early as the third or fourth century BCE, this text, found in several fragmented copies, gives a detailed description of the heavenly liturgy that is simultaneously celebrated with the worship conducted in the earthly temple. The prayers, hymns, and blessings prescribed for each Sabbath are listed, along with the angels responsible for each worship service and the appropriate vestments.

4Q246 The "Son of God" text Interpretation of this fragmentary text is disputed, but it refers to someone to come who will be called "Son of God" and "Son of the Most High," apparently referring to the expected eschatological warrior king, the Davidic Messiah.

7.1.5 Rabbinica

All the rabbinic literature was written down after the New Testament period, but it represents firm oral tradition, much of which was current in the first century CE.[6] The major types and designations important for New Testament students are these:

Targumim. A Targum (pl. Targumim) is an Aramaic paraphrase of the Hebrew text (see above §4.3).

Midrashim. A midrash (pl. midrashim) is a commentary on the biblical text. There are two main types: (1) *Halakic Midrashim*, interpreting the legal sections of the Bible resulting in laws about how one should live (*Halakah* means "walk," i.e., the way one should live); (2) *Haggadic Midrashim*, dealing with the narrative sections of the Bible (*Haggadah* means "story").

Mishnah. The oral tradition was edited and written down about 200 CE. Unlike the Midrashim, the Mishnah does not follow the order of the biblical text, but is a compilation of sixty-three Tractates arranged in six divisions: (1) *Zeri*, "Seeds," dealing with agricultural laws, tithes, and the like; (2) *Moed*, "Set Feasts," dealing with the Sabbath, the Passover, and other festivals and related matters; (3) *Nashim*, "Women," dealing with domestic issues; (4) *Nezikin*, "Damages," dealing with oaths, civil law, and related matters; an especially important unit of this section is *Aboth* or *Avoth* (The Fathers), distinct from all the rest in

6. English translations of the most important primary texts can be found in Herbert Danby, *The Mishnah* (London: Oxford University Press, 1958); Isidore Epstein, *The Babylonian Talmud*, Quincentenary ed. (London: Soncino Press, 1978). For the Targums on the Pentateuch, see the five-volume series edited by Alexander Sperber, et al., *Targum Onkelos* (New York and Denver: KTAV, 1982–1998).

that it deals with the transmission and authority of the tradition itself, and the basic principles of the major rabbis; (5) *Qodashim*, "Hallowed Things," providing regulations for offerings and cultic procedures; (6) *Tohoroth*, "Cleannesses," dealing with matters of purification. The *Mishnah* represents the period of Tannaitic Judaism; "tannah" (תנה) is the Aramaic word for "repeat"—this is the period when the tradition was (orally) repeated; instruction and transmission was by repetition.

Tosephta. The unofficial version of the Mishnah, containing extraneous materials, some of which are early and useful for documenting the Judaism of the New Testament period.

Gemara. The Gemara (Completion) is an Aramaic commentary on the Mishnah, compiled by the Amoraim ("speakers," "interpreters"). The Gemara is to the Mishnah as Midrashim are to the Bible. As the Mishnah represents Tannaitic Judaism, the Gemara represents the Amoraic, post-Mishnah period.

Bariata. Earlier traditions included in the Gemara.

Talmud. The combination of the Mishnah and the Gemara produced the Talmud, the repository of ancient Jewish tradition.

7.2 The Temple, High Priest, and King

THERE WERE MANY SYNAGOGUES, BUT only one temple.[7] Even though in modern times "temple" has sometimes been used as part of the name of a local synagogue, temple and synagogue were entirely distinct institutions. The first temple had been built by Solomon as the successor to the tabernacle (1 Kgs 5–8). It endured from the tenth century BCE until its destruction by the Babylonians in 587 BCE. The second temple, begun in 520 and dedicated in 516 BCE, existed continuously until its destruction by the Romans in 70 CE. It was remodeled several times during these almost six centuries, but even the grandiose reconstruction by Herod the Great that in fact made it a new building was considered the continuation of *the* temple.

The temple was the center of economic and political life, especially of Jerusalem and Judea. Its treasury was the depository not only for the temple and national funds but for the assets of the wealthy, local and international. Rich depositors were naturally concerned for its stability. It was the largest employer in Judea. Under the supervision of Herod the Great, and then under the direction of the Romans, the high priests continued to exercise a leading political role, mediating between the Romans and the people at large. Although the high priest was supposed to be a lifetime appointment, the fact that Josephus can list twenty-eight different persons who held the office from the reign of Herod until the temple's destruction shows how politicized the office had become. The biblical model, in which the high priest's tenure was for life and then passed from father to son, was abolished by Herod, who appointed high priests at will, as did the Romans after him.

The temple was also associated with the kingship. In the days of Jesus and the early church, Israel's kingship had been taken away by Gentile powers, and internal leadership of the people was vested in the high priest. But the temple had been conceived originally by the great king David and built by his son Solomon. The Hasmonean priests had assumed the royal office, but both their priesthood and kingship had, in the eyes of many Jews, turned out to be illegitimate. The hope for a future king included the hope for a restored and cleansed temple; the hope for an authentic temple and priesthood was inseparable from the hope for the coming of the true king, the Messiah.

7. During the Second Temple period, other temples outside Jerusalem were in fact constructed: at Elephantine in Egypt in the sixth century BCE, the Samaritan temple in the fourth century BCE, the temple of the deposed high priest Onias at Heliopolis/Leontopolis ca. 165 BCE, and the Tobiad temple at Araq el-Emir in Transjordan in the second century BCE. None of these was ever a serious competitor with the Jerusalem temple, which was always regarded by practically all Jews worldwide as *the* temple.

The temple, celebrated in the psalms as the earthly dwelling place of the God who was creator of heaven and earth and Lord of all nations, was the center of the earth and the cosmos, the life-giving umbilical cord where heaven and earth met. In the temple the authorized priests carried out the rituals and sacrifices commanded by God through Moses. Daily sacrifices were offered for the people and, in Jesus' day, for (but not to!) the Roman emperor. Individuals brought their gifts and sacrifices to be dedicated to God. Once each year, on Yom Kippur, the Day of Atonement, the high priest enacted the sacrifice that made God's forgiveness effective. For some Jews, the present temple was defiled by an illegitimate priesthood and by Israel's sins, and one aspect of the future hope was the cleansing of the present temple or establishment of the true temple, in which God would truly reign from Zion. For many Jews, it was unthinkable that the temple could be destroyed. How could Judaism continue to exist if there were no temple?

7.3 The Synagogue

ONE TEMPLE, MANY SYNAGOGUES. THE temple was clearly grounded in the Bible and the ancient history of Israel. The synagogue originated in the postbiblical period, sometime after the destruction of the first temple, as a response to the Diaspora situation. Not only were there many synagogues; there were many kinds of synagogues, with a variety of social roles and settings, expressing the faith of Israel within different types of architecture and with a variety of rituals. Although we can readily speak of "the" temple, we cannot speak of "the" synagogue of first-century Judaism, as though all synagogues represented a single type. *Temple* designated a building; *synagogue* means simply "gathering," "assembly," and only gradually assumed a somewhat uniform institutional type. This process was not yet complete in pre-70 Palestinian Judaism, where synagogues did not, for the most part, have a distinctive building. Not all synagogues were alike, but represented various manifestations of worship gathering, school, and community center.

As the temple was a formal cultic institution, centered on priesthood and sacrifice, the synagogue was an informal noncultic institution, led by laymen and oriented around word and teaching. In contrast to temple Judaism, synagogue Judaism was a religion of the book. The emphasis on Scripture required a literate constituency. While Samuel Sandmel's insistence, "Wherever there was a synagogue, there was a school,"[8] may overstate a valid point, the synagogue clearly played a major role not only in promoting a knowledge of the Bible and Jewish tradition among the literate elite, but also in cultivating literacy among the common folk. Jesus and (some of?) his disciples, who did not belong to the literate upper classes, would probably have learned to read the Bible in Hebrew in the synagogue school.

Jews who did not live in Jerusalem or its environs visited the temple only on major pilgrimage festivals, if at all. The local synagogue, on the other hand, was the center of community life, with regular services every Sabbath for worship and instruction. We have no clear and complete description of a first-century synagogue service, but it apparently consisted of recitation of the Shema ("The Lord is one . . ."), the saying of prescribed prayers, the recitation or singing of psalms, readings from the Law and the Prophets, with a homiletical interpretation of one or both texts, and a closing blessing by a priest or prayer by a layman.

During the New Testament period, the Roman government regarded the synagogue as belonging to the category of *collegia* and *thiasoi* of other national and religious groups, and extended formal protection to them as

8. Samuel Sandmel, *Judaism and Christian Beginnings* (New York: Oxford University Press, 1978), 144. The point is elaborated and documented by Hengel, *Judaism and Hellenism*, 1:82.

authorized associations. Jews were allowed the right of assembly, the right to administer their own finances, including the collection and transmission of the annual temple tax to Jerusalem, jurisdiction over and discipline of their own members, and freedom from military service and participation in the imperial cult.

7.4 Sadducees to Sicarii: The Pre-70 Spectrum of Palestinian Judaism

UNITED BY THEIR BASIC CONFESSION OF the one God who had chosen Israel, who had revealed the Torah to Moses, and who had led and preserved Israel through the centuries as recounted in the Scriptures, Jews expressed and practiced their faith in a variety of ways.

Wanting to explain his ancestral religion to his Hellenistic readers in a positive perspective, Josephus presents the various streams of contemporary Judaism as though they were "philosophical schools of thought" corresponding to Greek philosophical schools (*War* 2.119–66; *Ant.* 13.171–73; 18.11–24; *Life* 2.10). Three times he lists these, not always in the same order or with the same descriptions, as *Essenes*, *Pharisees*, and *Sadducees*. In *Life* 10, Josephus claims to have spent some time with each of these groups, and then to have studied three years with an ascetic teacher, Bannus, who belonged to none of them. In *Antiquities* 18.23, Josephus adds another faction he designates only as the "fourth philosophy," obviously referring to the Zealots, who agree with the Pharisees in all items of doctrine but believe in armed revolt and led the rebellion against the Romans.

First-century Palestinian Judaism included a large number of groups, schools of thought, and streams of tradition, not just the three or four mentioned by Josephus and the New Testament. Among these are Samaritans; John the Baptist and his followers, along with other sectarian baptizing movements in the Jordan valley; Jesus and his followers; Pharisees; Sadducees; Essenes; Therapeutae; Zealots; Sicarii; Hellenists; and *'am ha'aretz* (people of the land). The groupings are not all of the same kind. Just as it would be erroneous to describe "the" American political spectrum as composed of Republicans, Democrats, Rotarians, and the American Legion, so the Jewish groups are heterogeneous and not mutually exclusive.[9] Each group had both a changing history and an internal variety at any particular time. Not all the groups were official organizations with fixed membership lists; they were more like overlapping schools of thought. It would be possible for individual Jews to "belong to" or be influenced by more than one group. They should not be thought of in terms of the denominational structure of American Protestantism. The majority of first-century Palestinian Jews did not "belong" to any of the groups at all. Of the total population of about a million inhabitants, the combined membership of the main groups totaled no more than 12,000. Since these would all be adult males, if wives and children are counted, the total membership of the three or four parties mentioned by Josephus combined would still be only around 5 percent of the population. Some Jews may have been mainly influenced by only one group; the religious views of most were probably influenced by the cross-currents emanating from more than one source.

All the groups, movements, and streams of tradition contended for some form of theocratic rule, but they advocated different options for how the God's rule was to be implemented. These options may be represented by brief descriptions of the traditional groupings within the spectrum of pre-70 first-century Palestinian Judaism.

7.4.1 Samaritans

Samaria is the hill country between Galilee in the north and Judea in the south. But just as *Jews* (=*Judeans*) came to mean those who belong to Jewish religion and/or culture regardless of

9. Cf. Sandmel, *Judaism and Christian Beginnings*, 154.

geography or ethnicity, so by New Testament times *Samaritan* could refer to a religious community centered in Samaria, but not confined to this region. They sometimes called themselves *Jews/Judeans, Hebrews* (Josephus, *Ant.* 11.340–44), or *Israelites* (Delos inscription, 150–50 BCE). They had their own temple with its own cultus and priesthood, which they believed to be the only authentic temple of the ancestral and biblical God. They had their own version of the Scripture, the same five books of Moses used by Jerusalem Jews, but edited to show that the true temple is in Samaria. That the Samaritans considered only the Pentateuch to be Scripture suggests that the formation of the Samaritans as a separate community occurred when the "Jewish Bible" still consisted of only the five books of Moses. Like Jerusalem Judaism, they had a Diaspora, so that Samaritan communities could be found in such places as Rome, Thessalonica, and on the island of Delos.

The Samaritans are known to us from references in the New Testament, Josephus, and other ancient literature, but principally from their own writings, including their version of the Pentateuch. In their self-understanding, they represented the original Israelites, descendants of the Joseph tribes, who had persisted in faithful worship of God from the beginning. They understood the term "Samaritan" to refer not merely to their city or region; they derived it from שׁמר *shamar* ("keep"). They were those who did not apostatize, but "Keepers," those who kept the Torah. After the exodus and the conquest of the promised land, Israel originally worshiped God in Samaria. When, under David and Solomon, the cult moved to Zion, this was, in Samaritan perspective, never YHWH's intent. The true place of worship was thus a fundamental bone of contention between Samaritans and Jews (see John 4:20).

The Samaritans considered themselves to be the remnants of the old, pre-Davidic kingdom of Israel. Many ancient Jews considered the Samaritans to be the descendants of the foreign settlers the Assyrians had relocated after they had destroyed and depopulated Samaria in 721 BCE. They were thus disdained as a syncretistic mixture both racially and theologically. This legendary view is already found in 2 Kings 17:24–28, is repeated in Josephus, and is occasionally still found even in scholarly writings. Other legends have grown up: Jews supposedly did not travel through Samaria, but made a wide detour.[10] Accordingly, Jesus is supposed to have illustrated his lack of prejudice by going through Samaria (Luke 9:51–53; John 4:4). The antipathy and suspicion between Jews and Samaritans was, of course, the necessary background for understanding Jesus' story of the Good Samaritan (Luke 10:25–37).

7.4.2 Hellenists and Hellenistic Jews

There is a sense in which most Jews in the first century CE, whether in the Diaspora or Palestine, could be described as Hellenistic Jews, that is, participating to some extent in what had become the international culture of the Mediterranean. Just as "Americanization" became a global influence after World War II, affecting even those who opposed it and advocated loyalty to the ancestral ways, so Palestine was to some extent Hellenized, and the older rigid distinction between "Palestinian" and "Hellenistic" Judaism can no longer be maintained. Nonetheless, within Palestine there were some who resisted and some who continued to be more open to the wider world of Hellenizing influences, due to cultural momentum or to the personal conviction that the way forward for Judaism was to come to terms with the dominant culture and politics. In the Hellenistic cities along the Mediterranean coast (Caesarea Maritima and Ptolemais, the nearest port city to the Galilee of Jesus' day), there was intensive interchange between traditional Judaism and Hellenistic language, culture, and politics.

10. That this is pious legend is confirmed by Josephus, *Ant.* 20.6.1 = 118, who indicates that most Jews followed the direct route between Judea and Galilee.

The cities of the Decapolis, in the heartland of Judaism, were centers of Hellenistic culture (see above §6.2.3). The new cities in Galilee founded or rebuilt by Herod Antipas in the Hellenistic style (Sepphoris, Tiberias) had at least a veneer of Hellenistic culture.

Though they apparently formed no organized party, some Jews were specifically identified as *Hellenists* (Acts 6:1; 9:29; 11:20). These were evidently Jewish people in Palestine whose first language was Greek, who did not understand the local Aramaic, and who lived in the Greek style. They were apparently Diaspora Jews who had moved or returned to Judea to be near the sacred city, to retire, die, and be buried there. One might compare them to English-speaking Jews of our own time who move to Israel for religious reasons. Such Jews tended to live in their own enclaves, to continue to speak Greek, and to have their own synagogues, even in Jerusalem, in the shadow of the temple (Acts 6:1, 9; a *Greek* inscription belonging to a synagogue has been found in Jerusalem). They were called *Hellenists*, "Greek speakers," in contrast to the native Judean population whose mother tongue was Aramaic. There was continuing tension between the Greek-speaking Hellenists and local Aramaic-speaking Jews.

7.4.3 Essenes, Therapeutae, Qumran Covenanters

The English term "Essenes" is a transliteration of the Greek Ἐσσηνοί of disputed derivation. It may correspond linguistically to the Hebrew and Aramaic words for "pious." If so, the term may have been used in a wider, generic sense for several groups and movements, as well as for a specific group. Though not mentioned in the New Testament, the specific group known as Essenes is documented in Josephus, who treats it at greater length than any of the other Jewish "philosophical schools of thought" he catalogues (see above), and in Philo (*Good Person* 12–13, 75–91 and *Hypothetica* 11.1–18). Pliny (the Elder), an officer under Titus in the Roman subjugation of Judea, toured the Dead Sea area and later reported his impressions of the Essenes on the west bank in his *Natural History* (5.25). If, as is now generally assumed, the sectarian monastery-like community at Qumran were Essenes, the Dead Sea Scrolls provide primary sources written by Essenes and numerous books they valued and preserved, and they are by far our best source for portraying the life and thought of the Essenes.

According to the most probable and widely accepted theory, the history of the Essene community at Qumran unfolded as follows: In protest against what they regarded as the illegitimate Hasmonean priesthood that had assumed control of the temple, its cultus, and its calendar, about 150 BCE a group withdrew and, after a period of indecision, founded a community led by the מֹרֶה צֶדֶק (*Moreh Tsedek*, the Right Teacher or Teacher of Righteousness). They considered their own community the provisional true temple of the interim period and awaited the eschatological restoration of the true temple in which they would be the authorized priests. In the meantime, they conducted their own life according to the laws of temple purity and their alternative calendar for the festivals. They had two meals in common every day, preceded by a ritual bath and conducted in a state of ritual purity. They had no slaves, renounced private property, and lived simple, austere lives devoted to a rigid schedule of Bible study. There was some variety in their theology and community structure. One group of Essenes lived at Qumran. These were mostly single males who had left their families temporarily or permanently. Some scholars argue the Qumran Essenes were celibates who replenished the population of the sect by adopting male children[11] into the community and by accepting

11. This view is based on secondary reports in Philo and Josephus. It has not been confirmed by archaeology, for some graves of women have been found at Qumran, and nothing in the rules of the community in the recovered scrolls refer to celibacy of the members or adoption of children into the community.

applicants after an extended period of probation. Archaeology (size of the assembly and dining room; number of graves in the cemeteries) suggests the average population of full members and novitiates as about two hundred Covenanters, with about fifty of them full members.

The Qumran contingent of Essenes was only a small minority of the whole sect. The majority of the Essenes—Josephus says they numbered about four thousand—apparently lived in enclaves throughout the land, some or all of them permitting marriage and living among the population, but not participating in its common life. The relation of the Qumran community to the sect as a whole is unclear. Some scholars consider it the "headquarters" of the larger group, while others argue it was the sect's "publishing house," devoted to preparing leather scrolls and copying the Bible and key sectarian texts for use throughout the land. The Jerusalem priests considered them heretics and sometimes persecuted them, sometimes grudgingly cooperated with them, while the Essene sectarians denounced the Jerusalem priests as liars and profaners of the temple.

When the Romans approached in 68 CE, the Qumran Covenanters carefully sealed their scrolls in large pottery containers and hid them in the nearby caves, where they remained until accidentally discovered in 1947. The sectaries then marched out courageously to meet the Roman armies in what they believed was the final battle of history, confidently expecting the divine intervention that would restore them to their position in the renewed temple in Jerusalem. The Qumran group was destroyed by the Romans. Numerous other Essenes perished in the war and ensuing chaos. The remainder seem to have dissolved into the general population, and the Essenes as a distinct group disappeared from history.

While the Essenes are not typical of first-century Judaism and had minimal direct effect on its life and thought, their scrolls provide the interpreter of the New Testament with one tiny window into the world of Jesus and the early church—often as a reaction to what became the major streams of Judaism. Among the insights derived from a study of the Dead Sea Scrolls that illuminate the history and theology of the New Testament writings, we may list the following:

- The use of Scripture at Qumran gives insight into the course of canon formation, which was still in process at the time (see below). The Dead Sea Scrolls contain no reference to canonical lists, which would be anachronistic, but do have parallels to New Testament phrases such as "the Law, the prophets, and the Psalms" (Luke 24:44). The fact that the Essenes wrote commentaries on the Psalms, for example, shows that the Psalter belonged to the group of documents considered authoritative Scripture.
- The biblical texts used at Qumran give valuable insight into textual history. For instance, when New Testament citations from the Old Testament differ from the Masoretic Text and/or the LXX as previously attested, we see that the New Testament authors were not always changing the text, but sometimes were following a different textual tradition available to them and now attested at Qumran.
- The Qumran community understood that God's eschatological act had been initiated in their own history and would soon be consummated as the eschatological event. They saw this eschatological renewal of the covenant as already beginning and regarded themselves as the people of the new covenant (e.g., CD 6:19; 8:21; 19:33; 20:12).
- The Qumran community interpreted the Scripture as a whole as eschatological prophecy and saw its predictions as being fulfilled in their own time. They reread all of Scripture from the point of view that God's definitive eschatological act was occurring in their own history.
- Even before the destruction of the temple, they understood themselves, the community itself, to be the true temple. For instance, although

tables and furniture existed at Qumran, the full members of the community took their meals together while seated on the bare floor of the assembly hall, as though they were pilgrims in the outer court of the temple in Jerusalem.

The Qumran scrolls provide the modern student with an enormously valuable window into one small group of Jewish dissidents. Despite more than a generation of intensive study, it is still not clear how typical the Qumran Covenanters were of similar movements.

7.4.4 Sectarian Baptizing Movements

There were other nonconformist groups, alienated from both temple and synagogue, who formed sectlike communities, with a variety of water purification rites. Josephus claims that during his religious quest as a youth, he spent three years with a desert ascetic teacher named Bannus, who practiced a rigid discipline involving purifying lustrations (Josephus, *Life* 2.11). Some scholars make "Essene" a generic term for these groups or speak of a general group of "baptist sects" in the Jordan valley.[12]

John the Baptist does not belong within the organized religious groups such as the Pharisees, Sadducees, and Essenes. But neither was he merely a solitary individual preacher. Those who believed his message and were baptized by him did not automatically become members of a Baptist sect, but returned to their ordinary lives. Yet it is also the case, the details of which remain unclear, that some of those he baptized became a continuing community with a particular discipline and instruction in matters such as a fixed form of prayer, apparently remaining with him during his life and enduring after his death (Mark 2:18; Luke 7:18–20; 11:1; Acts 18:24–19:7). The movement begun by John is rightly seen within the context of a series of renewal movements within Judaism that came into being after the Roman takeover in Palestine. Yet John and his movement appear to have had distinctive importance. Of apocalyptic baptizing preachers, only he is mentioned in Josephus, and only he directly affected Jesus, early Christianity, and the New Testament. The term "the Baptist" ὁ βαπτιστής (*ho baptistēs*), itself a translation of Hebrew הטובל or Aramaic מטבלא, is found in both the New Testament and Josephus as a title for John but is used of no one else in all ancient literature.

Like the symbolic acts of the Old Testament prophets, John's demeanor, dress, and baptism carried a symbolic message. John seems to have deliberately stationed himself on the east side of the Jordan near a well-traveled road leading into Judea, calling for a new entrance into the promised land. He calls Israel to see themselves not as "already there," but in prospect, needing to go into the Jordan again by being baptized. His baptism thus functions like proselyte baptism, though it was not based on it. Proselytes baptized themselves; John was the first to baptize others (hence the title). The Jewish practice of baptizing proselytes is clearly documented only after John's time. Yet the symbolism is similar: empirical Israel is not yet the true Israel and, like the Gentiles, needs to make a fresh entrance into the land and be incorporated into the true, renewed covenant people ready to meet their God.

John proclaimed the near advent of the judgment of God, in flaming fire destroying those who were not prepared, and urged people to repent and be baptized in preparation for the coming judgment. He expected a transcendent figure to appear in the near future to exercise God's final judgment, but it is not clear whether this would be God himself, or, more likely, a human figure endowed with God"s power, the Mighty One, the One to Come (Matt 3:1–10; 11:1–3; Luke 3:1–9; 7:18–20). The figure John expected has some similarity to the Son of Man expected in some streams of apocalyptic eschatology (see below §7.7.3). John himself may not

12. For a survey, see Kurt Rudolph, "The Baptist Sects," in *The Cambridge History of Judaism*, ed. W. D. Davies and Louis Finkelstein (Cambridge: Cambridge University Press, 1984), 471–500.

have been clear as to the identity of the coming Judge.

7.4.5 Zealots, Sicarii, the "Fourth Philosophy," "Social Banditry," and Other Revolutionary Militarist Movements

The term "Zealot," capitalized as the name of a specific organized group, is found twice in standard English translations of the New Testament: Luke 6:15 and Acts 1:13. Each time, it refers to Simon the Zealot as one of Jesus' twelve disciples. The Greek term ζηλωτής (*zēlōtēs*) is found not only here, but also in Acts 21:20; 22:3 and Galatians 1:14 as a general, nontechnical term for those who are zealous for the law and Jewish tradition (probably its meaning in Acts and Paul), and in 1 Corinthians 14:12; Titus 2:14; and 1 Peter 3:13 for Christians who are zealous for spiritual gifts and good deeds. Though the term *Zealot* can be properly applied only to one of the military groups in the latter days of the 66–70 revolt, it has become a general, though inaccurate, term for the variety of resistance movements in Palestine from the time of the imposition of direct Roman rule in Judea in 6 CE to the catastrophic war of 66–70 CE. These groups shared the common goal of overthrowing Roman rule, but the movements were never united under a single name, leader, program, or theology, and often fought with each other and their fellow Jews who favored cooperation with the Romans. In general, these movements can be thought of as continuing the early days of Maccabean resistance,[13] the militaristic right wing of the spectrum of Jewish efforts to come to terms with pagan political, cultural, and religious domination.

Josephus, who claims to have always favored orderly cooperation with Rome, pictures the Zealot movement in a consistently bad light. He uses the noble term "Zealot" for them only in the *War*, in his later writings speaking of them only disdainfully as brigands and bandits (λησταί *lēstai*)—one person's freedom fighter is another person's terrorist. Josephus is probably correct in locating the beginning of the movement in the action of Judas the Galilean and his followers, who resisted the Roman census of 6 CE.[14] Josephus also refers to Judas as the leader of a "school of thought," the "Fourth Philosophy," and calls him a σοφιστής (*sophistēs*), a teacher (*War* 2.118). Although it is certainly true that the social distress and chaos of much of this period generated robber bands, it is also true that many of the groups in the resistance movement acted on the basis of particular understandings of the Scripture and Jewish tradition. Apocalypticism (see below) flavored much of the movement. Like the Covenanters of Qumran, they could hardly have thought that their own little armed bands could defeat the Roman legions, but acted on the conviction that if they were faithful to the covenant, God would intervene and establish the promised eschatological kingdom. The leaders of some of the groups saw themselves as messianic figures, claiming to be the promised eschatological prophet or king.[15] It is in this context that Jesus' and early Christianity's talk of messiahship and kingdom of God must be understood, both in comparison and contrast. The message of the revolutionary leaders was clear, and they backed it up with their willingness to die for it: the covenant people of the one true God are called to establish the peace and justice of God's kingdom not by withdrawing from political life into a secluded monastic setting where they would study, pray, and wait for God to act—as among the Essenes and other versions of apocalypticism—but by military violence. "God helps those who help themselves." "If we launch out in faith and begin the war, God will finish it."

13. So, for example, Hengel, *Judaism and Hellenism*, 1:227.

14. Josephus, *Ant.* 18.23. See above under Herod the Great and Luke 2:1–2; Acts 5:36–37.

15. This situation is reflected in Mark 13:22; Acts 5:36; 21:38; Josephus, *Ant.* 17.278–85; 20.97–98; *War* 2.433–34, 261–62. For thorough and detailed discussion, see Richard A. Horsley and John S. Hanson, *Bandits, Prophets, and Messiahs: Popular Movements in the Time of Jesus* (Minneapolis: Winston Press, 1985).

7.4.6 Herodians

This group was identified in some way with Herod Antipas, the puppet king of Galilee (see above §6.2.4), but the relation is not clear. Josephus refers to them (*War* 1.319), as does Mark 3:6; 12:13 (Matt 22:16). They may have been simply members of the Herodian court or household, but the Latin formation *Herodiani* (Greek Ἡρῳδιανοί) seems to be parallel to party names such as *Augustiani*, which would suggest they were active partisans of the Herodian "kingship." This could be understood in a traditional patriotic sense (advocating a Jewish king rather than Roman rule), or in an anti-traditional sense (supporting Herod's own Hellenistic and Roman regime rather than more right-wing religiopolitical movements such as the Zealots).

7.4.7 Sadducees

The Sadducees are the most difficult of the groups to describe. We have no texts in which the author identifies himself as a Sadducee, no source explicitly composed from a Sadducean point of view, no post-70 CE group that claims to be the heirs of the Sadducees. They are mentioned in the Gospels, Josephus, and rabbinic literature—all hostile sources. In the Gospels, they are the priestly opponents of Jesus, instrumental in his death. Josephus portrays them as not believing in "fate," that is, divine providence, but emphasizing human responsibility, and as rejecting the doctrines of immortality, resurrection, and postmortem rewards and punishments. They are wealthy, have a following among the wealthy elite rather than the common people, and (sometimes) belong to the ruling elite themselves, but are constrained to rule in accord with the dominant doctrine of the Pharisees. In their conduct with each other, they are somewhat boorish (*War* 2.119–66; *Ant.* 13.173; 18.16–17). In later rabbinic Judaism, the Sadducees get a bad press; they are regarded as heretics and hardly belonging to Judaism. The etymology of the name is disputed, but it is most likely related to Zadok (Sadducee=Zadokite), who established what became the line of authentic priests in the time of Solomon (1 Kgs 1:8, 34, 38–39). In first-century Judaism, the Sadducean group would thus have represented the priestly party of the Jerusalem temple, understanding themselves to be the authentic priests in the Hasmonean line.

Inferences from this minimal and prejudiced textual base have produced a picture of the Sadducees in which they represented the local ruling elite under the supervision of the Romans. They were conservative religiously in that they rejected the progressive oral tradition of the Pharisees (see below), the new apocalyptic doctrines such as resurrection, and the later biblical books in which these doctrines were found. There is scant evidence for such a neat and consistent picture. There were probably Sadducees who had some of these features, and Jews who had some of them who were not Sadducees. Nonetheless there were overlapping groups of first-century Jews and Jewish tradition with these characteristics:

— *Cooperation with the Romans, implementing and sharing their rule.* In any colonial or imperial political structure, the ruling power needs local leaders who can maintain the law and order necessary for collection of taxes. Some of the local leadership will see that this is for the good of all and will cooperate. One way of doing this is to restrict "politics" to one area of life and "religion" to another, which allows cooperation in the "secular" realm while maintaining purity in the "religious" realm.

— *Accepting only the Pentateuch as "canonical."* There was no fixed canon accepted by all Jews during the first century CE. It has often been assumed that the Sadducees accepted only the five books of Moses as canonical, while Pharisees accepted the later prophetic and apocalyptic books. It seems to be clear that some first-century Jews regarded only the Pentateuch/Torah as sacred Scripture and others affirmed a more extensive "canon," but there is no clear evidence identifying the Sadducees with the former and the Pharisees with the latter.[16] The important point here is that it was in fact the later prophetic and apocalyptic books that provided pictures of a coming eschatological kingdom, resistance to earthly empires, and resurrection of the dead. Such books could fuel the fires of political rebellion and were resisted by Jewish groups that saw the way forward for God's people in terms of submission and cooperation rather than rebellion.

— *Rejection of the oral tradition of the Pharisees*. The oral tradition of the Pharisees attempted to bring the whole of life under the sway of the divine revelation at Sinai (see below). Some of those who rejected the Pharisees' oral traditions may have wanted to find a "secular" sphere for which the *revealed* truth of the Torah gave no specific directions, thus allowing cooperation with the Romans without violating the Bible.

7.4.8 Pharisees

The Pharisees are the Jewish group most frequently mentioned in the New Testament, the group that apparently had the most influence on Jesus, early Christianity, and the New Testament. They too are a difficult group to describe.[17] Both the nature of the group and its theology seem to have changed over the course of their history, so that descriptions of the group at one time do not necessarily apply to a different period. According to Josephus, the Pharisees first emerge on the historical stage in the time of the Hasmonean king John Hyrcanus (134–104 BCE, see above). They had no political power of their own but as members of the retainer class were influential in shaping the policies of the king.[18] They lost his support, and his son Alexander Janneus had many of them put to death because of their political intrigues. Alexandra, his widow and successor, restored the Pharisees to political power, so that they became the real power behind the throne. By the first century CE, the New Testament depicts the Pharisees no longer as a political interest group (though see their collaboration with the Herodians, Mark 3:6; 12:13). As the opponents of Jesus, the New Testament portrays them as primarily interested in matters of purity, fasting, and Sabbath observance, and charges them with advocating the "traditions of the elders" rather than the "Word of God" found in the Bible.

For our purposes in this volume, there are three points on which there is widespread agreement:

1. *The Pharisees represented a centrist, lay movement respected by broad streams of the population.* In contrast to the Essenes, they did not withdraw from everyday life to cultivate their own holiness and await the apocalyptic act of God. In contrast to the Zealots, they did not actively resist the Roman government or call the populace to armed rebellion. In contrast to the Sadducees, they did not collaborate with the Romans and help implement their rule in the pre-70 period. Though a relatively small group—Josephus gives their number at around six thousand—they were highly respected, the "leading school" (*War* 2.162) that "have the masses on their side" (*Ant.* 13.288).

2. *The Pharisees were lay advocates of the holiness of the whole people of God in every aspect of its life.* Although priests could be Pharisees, the Pharisees were basically a lay movement. As the temple was the realm of the priests, the synagogue was the domain of the Pharisees'

16. The Qumran Essenes reproached the Sadducees because they recognized only the Torah as divine revelation, and not the prophets who had revealed what is coming on this last generation of human history (1QpHab 2.9–10; cf. Josephus, *Ant.* 18.16).

17. The primary difficulty has to do with sources: our earliest sources are the New Testament documents and the contemporary writings of Josephus.

18. Anthony J. Saldarini, *Pharisees, Scribes and Sadducees in Palestinian Society: A Sociological Approach*, Biblical Research Series (Grand Rapids: Eerdmans, 2001), 4–5, 37–48, and passim.

activity—though there is no evidence that they were in charge of it. They took seriously the biblical vocation of Israel *as a whole* to be a priestly community (Exod 19:6), and seem to have attempted to apply the rules of temple and priestly purity to the life of all Jews. They thus advocated a kind of "priesthood of all believers." They were unwilling to mark off a part of life as a particular sacred zone, leaving the rest free of cultic and ritual restraints, which would allow free collaboration with the Roman authorities, but argued for the sanctification of all of everyday life. They thus elaborated rules that covered every aspect of personal and social life, with the intent of specifying how Israel could be a holy people whose every move was in conformity to the revelation of God at Sinai.

3. *The Pharisees were champions of oral tradition as the means of this sanctification.* As a lay movement, the Pharisees were concerned to authenticate a chain of tradition that ignores the priesthood. A key Mishnah text *Aboth* (also transliterated *Avoth*, "the Fathers") begins: "Moses received the Law from Sinai and committed it to Joshua, and Joshua to the elders, and the elders to the Prophets, and the Prophets committed it to the men of the Great Synagogue."[19] The tractate proceeds by naming sixty teachers of the law who lived between 60 BCE and 200 CE, the time when the oral tradition contained in the Mishnah was written down. The list includes only one priest, Simeon the Just. The point: the authentic tradition has been handed down by the lay teachers, not the priests. The means of transmission was oral tradition.

The modern discussion of religious tradition has often been influenced by the Protestant perspective on the post-Reformation debate concerning Scripture and tradition. In this debate, Scripture is presented as good, the original divine revelation, and tradition is understood to be later human additions to Scripture, and therefore bad. The reality is that no religious community can live by *sola scriptura*, but every religious community has, and must have, tradition in order to function. This simple example is much discussed in the rabbinic tradition: the Decalogue commands that no work be done on the Sabbath day. Severe punishment results from its violation. In order to fulfill this command, what constitutes "work" must be defined, and the beginning and ending of "Sabbath" must be specified. The Scripture itself does not do this, nor can it be left to individual interpretation. Thus the scribal teachers discussed the ways the biblical commands could be implemented and specified their results in great detail.

"The Pharisees have delivered to the people a great many observances handed down by their fathers, which are not written in the law of Moses" (Josephus, *Ant.* 13.297). However, the Pharisees did not understand their tradition to be later human additions to an original divine deposit. Assuming here that the later rabbinic tradition somewhat represents the views of first-century Pharisees on this point at least, the Pharisees believed that God had not left to human discretion the specific information and directives necessary to implement the law, but had given the requisite knowledge along with the law itself. "A certain Gentile came to Shammai and asked him, 'How many Torahs have you?' 'Two,' he replied, 'the Written Torah and the Oral Torah'" (*b. Shab.* 30b).

The written law was inscribed by Moses in the Pentateuch, but the oral law, *also given directly by God to Moses on Sinai*, was handed on through a chain of authorized teachers. The rabbis did not doubt, of course, that particular traditions had emerged in the teaching of particular rabbis, but regarded rabbinic discussion as only the rediscovery and further transmission of what had been originally given on Sinai. Oral tradition was not in opposition to written Scripture, but its necessary complement. It is reverence for the written Scripture and the desire to put it into practice that requires the oral Torah and its authorized bearers and interpreters such as Shammai. The later rabbinic portrayal of the

19. Danby, *Mishnah*, 446.

two Torahs, the oral and written, guaranteed by a firm chain of oral traditional links from Moses to their own time is probably more specific and detailed than that which was common in the first century. There can be no doubt, however, that in the days of Jesus and earliest Christianity the Pharisees were advocates of the authority of traditions not found in the written Torah.

In effect, the concept and content of oral Torah, developed by lay teachers such as Pharisees associated with the synagogue, circumvented the Sadducean authority of the priests associated with the temple. Thus, with the destruction of the temple and the dissolution of priestly authority, there was already in place a powerful way for reconstituting Judaism and carrying it forward.

7.4.9 "People of the Land," *'am ha'aretz,"* "the Common people," "Common Judaism"

"People of the land" is a common Old Testament designation (fifty-two times) for local residents of Israel or other countries and/or the common people in contrast to their rulers (e.g., Gen 23:7; 2 Kgs 11:14). After the return of a relatively small number of Jews from Babylon, tensions developed between the returnees and the local population (e.g., Ezra 4:4). The returned exiles emphasized genealogical and ritual purity and were suspicious of resident Jews on both counts. The term thus developed pejorative overtones in later Jewish tradition, including the Mishnah, which discourages association with the *'am ha'aretz* (*Demai* 2.2–3). The term is thus not the name of a particular party, but neither is it a romantic designation for the "common people" of simple piety who disdained the sophisticated theology of their religious leaders. The term is a reminder, however, that the great mass of people in first-century Palestine represent a generic Judaism that, without subscribing to the program of a particular group, shared the basic tenets of "common Judaism": faith in the one God who tolerated no rivals or images; a sense of election as God's people; orientation to the temple and the Torah, especially observance of circumcision, the Sabbath, the food laws, and the major festivals.[20]

7.5 Prophecy and the Spirit

PROPHETS ARE CHARISMATIC, INSPIRED figures who do not derive their authority from Scripture, institution, or tradition but speak their message as given directly by God. The later rabbinic view was that prophecy had ended in the time of Ezra or Alexander and would not return until the eschatological age (e.g., *Song of Songs Rab.* 8.9–10; *Numbers Rab.* 15.10; *b. Yoma* 9b, 21b; *t. Sota* 13.2; *Aboth* 1). This view contributed to the writing of revelatory (apocalyptic) literature in the name of past heroes from Adam to Ezra, who was the last to whom prophetic powers could be attributed. Thus Daniel, composed by an anonymous author in Maccabean times, was written in the persona of a figure in the sixth century BCE. It was written too late to be included among the Prophets in the developing canon but was later included among the Writings. While some first-century Jewish teachers held the view that prophecy and divine inspiration had ceased with Ezra, this dogma has sometimes been accepted at face value and generalized to include all first-century Judaism (hence the later idea of the "four hundred silent years" between Malachi and John the Baptist).

In actuality, there were numerous prophetic figures in first-century Judaism.[21] Although Josephus sometimes seems to accept the rabbinic theory that prophecy was limited to the biblical

20. The term "common Judaism" in this sense has been made current, especially by E. P. Sanders, *Judaism: Practice and Belief, 63 BCE–66 CE* (London: SCM Press, 1992), Part II, along with the fundamental pattern of the Jewish religion as "covenantal nomism" (ibid., 75, 236, and passim).

21. For documentation, see M. Eugene Boring, *The Continuing Voice of Jesus: Christian Prophecy and the Gospel Tradition* (Louisville, KY: Westminster John Knox Press, 1991), 51–57, and the literature given there.

period (*Against Apion* 1.40–41), contemporary Jewish prophets in fact play a prominent role in his history (*War* 1.78–80; 2.112–13; 2.159; 2.259–63; 6.283–88; 6.300–309; *Antiquities* 13.311–13; 14.172–76; 15.3–4; 15.370; 17.345–48; 20.97–99; 20.168–72). A prominent example is Joshua (Jesus) ben Ananiah, an unlettered peasant who claimed a direct revelation from God, an oracle of doom against Jerusalem that he began to proclaim constantly against the city, in the style of the Old Testament prophets. Despite insults, arrest, and torture, he continued to repeat his oracle until the last days of Jerusalem in 70, when he was killed by a Roman projectile (*War* 6.300–309). The Qumran מֹרֶה צֶדֶק (*moreh tsedek*, Teacher of Righteousness) is an inspired, prophetic figure who interprets the Scripture in the power of the Holy Spirit and whose teaching is directly "from the mouth of God" (1QpHab 2.2–3), so that "What comes out of his mouth is the word of God"(1QH, trans. Gerd Jeremias). There was no "prophetic party" in first-century Judaism; the prophetic phenomenon was experienced across party lines, and a variety of groups claimed prophetic authority for their views and programs. John the Baptist and Jesus stand within this stream of first-century Judaism. Like the Teacher of Righteousness, they were opposed by the institutionalized authorities.

7.6 The Spectrum of Eschatological, Messianic, and Apocalyptic Hope

THE LANGUAGE AND IMAGERY THAT COMmunicated the hope of Israel was not a matter of speculation but of trust in the goodness and faithfulness of God. In oversimplified terms, the conceptual moves that generated the language of eschatology, apocalyptic, and messianism were generated by Israel's faith in one God, the Creator, who is just, powerful, and loving. But how, then, can there be so much evil in the world? Israel did not discuss the problem of evil in philosophical terms but responded in characteristic narrative terms, out of their conviction of the faithfulness of God: the world is a story, God is the author, and the story isn't over yet. "Why doesn't God destroy evil?" "He will." Israel's trust in the faithfulness of God generated their language of hope for the ultimate future.

Since scholarly discussion has not developed a consistent set of definitions for key terms, it is important to avoid semantic confusion by defining how the terms are used in this book. The following definitions would find broad, but not universal, agreement:[22]

— *Providence*. The term is derived from the Latin *pro* (before) and *video* (see), and refers to seeing what is before one, looking out ahead. Practically all Old Testament and Jewish thought affirms the providence of God, that history is not rushing on blindly out of control, but is under the direction of the sovereign God.

— *Eschatology*. The term represents the Greek ἔσχατος (*eschatos*, last), and refers to the ultimate end of things. Eschatology is a particular kind of thought within the doctrine of providence. God is not only guiding history, but will bring it to a worthy conclusion. All eschatological thought is providential, but not all understandings of providence are eschatological. Eschatology can be personal, referring to the ultimate goal of the individual's life (what happens when we die), or historical and cosmic, referring to the ultimate goal of the world and history, the meaning of the "end of the world." Since biblical theology is concerned with God as the Creator of the universe and the Lord of history as a whole (not merely of individual souls or particular nations), most biblical eschatological thought is expressed within this cosmic framework that embraces all history. Eschatology speaks of the end, but it is a meaningful end,

22. For elaboration, see M. Eugene Boring, *Revelation*, Interpretation (Louisville, KY: Westminster John Knox Press, 1989), 35–41, in broad agreement with John J. Collins, *The Apocalyptic Imagination: An Introduction to Jewish Apocalyptic Literature*, 2nd ed. (Grand Rapids: Eerdmans, 1998), 1–23.

the end of a *story*. Thus narrative, not metaphysical speculation, is its biblical mode.

— *Apocalyptic*. The term is derived from the Greek verb ἀποκαλύπτω (*apokaluptō*, reveal), and means literally the removal of a veil or covering. Just as eschatology is a particular kind of thinking about God's providence, so *apocalyptic* is a particular kind of eschatology. An *apocalypse* is a text belonging to a particular literary genre. *Apocalypticism* refers to sociological phenomena reflecting apocalyptic thought. Apocalyptic thinking cuts across party lines and is not to be identified with any particular Jewish group. Some members of all the groups (with the probable exception of Sadducee types) embraced various aspects of apocalyptic thought.

Apocalyptic thought did not fall out of the sky ready-made, but is the process of a long and complex period of development. While it is true that throughout its history Israelite and Jewish thought adopted and adapted elements from its religious surroundings, the basic core of apocalyptic thought is in continuity with and derived from its Israelite heritage.[23]

The common denominator of apocalyptic thought is that the ultimate victory of God will be brought about by God's initiative, when God's power is revealed from the transcendent world. It need not be thought of as the dissolution of the space-time world—ancient Judaism and Christianity hardly thought in these categories—but it is more than a social revolution. It involves the resurrection of the dead, in more than a metaphorical sense. It involves both continuity and discontinuity with the present order of things. Apocalyptic thought does not necessarily require the imagery of the literal destruction of the present world, the "end of the world" in astrophysical terms, but it does mean the end of the world as we know it and a reordering of power and relationships.

The continuation of apocalyptic thought in formative Judaism and emerging Christianity. In Second Temple Judaism, during the time of Jesus, the beginnings of the church, and the formation of the New Testament, apocalyptic eschatology was a vigorous element in broad streams of Jewish life and theology. For a few generations after 70, some Jews continued to cultivate the apocalyptic hope, which fueled the fires that led to the Bar Kokhba revolt. After the catastrophic failure of the two revolts against Rome, the Jamnian scribes and their rabbinic successors (see §7.7) turned away from apocalyptic visions that had contributed to the revolutionary fervor, with the result that the apocalypses, Jewish and Christian, were preserved by Christians. Christians sometimes expanded and modified the Jewish apocalypses, giving them a Christian orientation and interpretation (e.g., 4 Ezra). Apocalyptic tradition is not marginal in the New Testament, but pervasive. Whoever would understand the New Testament must become interior to the thought world of apocalypticism. This is the case not only for Paul, the Synoptics, and Revelation, where it is conspicuous, but as undercurrent or dialogue partner in New Testament documents generally and a key issue in the discussion of the mission and message of Jesus. Apocalyptic is not limited to apocalyptic books such as Revelation, nor to apocalyptic passages such as the "Little Apocalypse" of Mark 13 and its parallels in Matthew 24 and Luke 21, but is the overarching framework for much of New Testament thought, which is either expressing, reinterpreting, or reacting to apocalyptic ideas. For those who want to understand the New Testament, understanding apocalyptic thought is not optional.

7.6.1 Typical Features of Apocalyptic Eschatology

The following list of typical and overlapping features characterizes apocalyptic thought taken as a whole, though not every apocalypse manifests every feature.

23. See, e.g., Paul D. Hanson, *The Dawn of Apocalyptic* (Philadelphia: Fortress Press, 1975), and Collins, *Apocalyptic Imagination*, 19–42, and the literature they list.

— *Crisis literature*. Apocalyptic literature is often described as generated by and emerging from crisis situations. It is true that some apocalypses, such as Daniel and Revelation, were written in times of persecution and political turmoil, but it is by no means true that all apocalyptic literature was composed by the persecuted and oppressed. There is a sense, however, in which all apocalyptic writings reflect a crisis situation—the theological crisis of attempting to make sense of the justice of God in purely this-worldly terms.

— *Universal, cosmic scope*. Just as Genesis 1–11, the story of universal beginnings, is concerned with God the creator of the whole world and lord of all history, so the apocalyptic writers looked beyond the covenant history of Israel to universal history. They were concerned not only with Israel's future, but with the goal and end of all things. Thus several apocalyptic writings are attributed to universally human figures such as Adam and Enoch, who lived prior to Abraham, Moses, and the covenant history of Israel.

— *Divine intervention to bring this world to a worthy conclusion*. The apocalyptic thinkers emphasized discontinuity with the present, rather than continuity. God's salvation will come at the end of history, not by gradual growth from within history, but by a cataclysmic intervention from beyond this world. This cosmic drama need not mean the destruction of the present cosmos, nor does it imply that the change would be instantaneous; in Jewish apocalyptic thought the coming end typically means the radical transformation of *this* world, which occurs in the final period of history. Jewish apocalyptic thought is not typically "otherworldly" in the sense that it disdains the present world and seeks escape into some other world. This is Gnosticism, not apocalyptic theology. Gnosticism is world-denying, but apocalyptic thought is world-affirming. It is precisely because Jewish apocalyptic thinkers affirmed this world as God's good creation that they held on to their faith that God would redeem the world, though they saw no way that God's salvation could occur by developments within this world.

— *The imminent end*. For most apocalyptic thought, the projected end was to come soon, as the solution to the troubles experienced in the present. The time of the end was not a matter of speculation, but an expression of the intensity of hope and encouragement for those experiencing the terrors of the present. The nearness of the end was encouragement to persevere, not abstract calculation.

— *Penultimately pessimistic, ultimately hopeful*. Apocalyptic literature is not optimistic in the sense that it bases its favorable view of the future on observable evidence in the present world. The apocalyptists were pessimistic about human ability to bring in the final rule of God, but their pessimism was penultimate. Ultimately, they were optimistic, in the sense that they affirmed the confident hope in the ultimate faithfulness of God.

— *Angels*. Earlier Israelite thought already had the concept of angels, but in apocalypticism angels become more numerous, receive names and ranks, and exercise key functions in the divine administration of the universe. Earthly institutions have heavenly, angelic counterparts. God does not act so directly as in earlier Israelite thought, but works through angelic intermediaries. God the creator is ultimately responsible for the whole universe, but not directly responsible for everything that happens in it. God has assigned the details of world management to angels, who sometimes overreach their authority or fail in their responsibilities. God will hold them accountable at the final judgment (Isa 24:21–22; 1 Cor 5:3; Jude 6). God's revelation is not directly intelligible, but requires angelic interpretation, and the *angelus interpres* becomes a standard character in the apocalyptic revelatory configuration.

— *Demons and Satan*. Earlier Israelite thought had little place for evil spirits and demons. God the creator was in charge of the whole cosmos and ultimately responsible for everything in it, including evil. Without abandoning its core faith in the one God, Second Temple Judaism began to attribute evil to secondary demonic powers who were still ultimately under God's sovereignty. Such evil spirits were the *direct* cause of evil, and the one God was only indirectly responsible, though still ultimately so. The figure of the Satan, thought of originally as a member of the heavenly court and the divinely authorized prosecuting attorney (see Job 1–2), gradually became the commander in chief of the demonic world. Thus questionable acts originally attributed to God are later attributed to Satan (2 Sam 24:1 vs. 1 Chr 21:1).

— *Dualism.* It is only in a qualified sense that we can speak of the dualism of Jewish apocalyptic, which never surrendered its fundamental monotheistic faith. Yet there is a kind of dualism characteristic of apocalypticism, a dualism that thinks in terms of this world and the beyond, in both spatial and chronological terms. Spatially ("vertically"), the heavenly world stands in contrast to this evil material world. Chronologically ("horizontally"), this evil age stands in contrast to the world to come.

— *Pseudonymous authorship.* No Jewish apocalypse was written in the author's own name. Each was attributed to some venerated ancient figure. All were presented as written in the time of Ezra or before, since it was often assumed that prophetic revelation came to an end in the time of Ezra. Several were attributed to figures who lived in the earliest days of the human race—Adam, Enoch, or Noah—and thus before the world's decline. Enoch and Elijah, both of whom were taken to the heavenly world without dying, were favorite authors, since they could communicate the heavenly realities by direct experience.

— *Deterministic view of history.* In contrast to the prophets, who emphasize human responsibility for the political future and call for decision, the apocalyptists emphasize the sovereignty of God in such a way that human decisions are no longer open. Things are not out of control, and God has a plan for the world: this is the message of comfort and hope, but its conceptual byproduct, taken as objectifying language, is that world history is already predetermined and can only run its course. Yet, in biblical apocalyptic, this view is affirmed only dialectically. For instance, the dialectical combination of divine sovereignty and human responsibility in Daniel brings together the stories of decision and faithfulness of chapters 1–6 with the deterministic apocalyptic visions of chapters 7–12.

— *Prewritten history.* The real author of an apocalyptic text has a message for his own time, but in the apocalyptic framework this had to be presented as the "prophecy" of the postulated author, who "predicts" the history from the time of the postulated author to the real author's own time. The retrospective view of the real author and his own historical locus becomes clear at the point where he ceases to look backward and report events with relative accuracy, and begins to look forward and predict his own actual future, at which point his predictions become vague or erroneous.

— *Mysterious, esoteric character.* The apocalypses are revelatory of divine wisdom that cannot be attained by human research and insight. Why things are as they are, and what the future holds, are mysteries preserved in the divine realm: God knows, humans do not know and cannot know. But chosen humans can be given a vision of the divine world or taken there personally, where they can learn the divine mysteries, which may be portrayed as inscribed in heavenly scrolls or tablets. The apocalypses function to encourage suffering human beings who despair of finding meaning in the events of this world. The world is not meaningless, but its meaning cannot be discovered; it must be revealed.

— *Symbolic language.* It is universally recognized that the transcendent realities about which the apocalyptic writers speak cannot be expressed in the conventional language of literalism. The visionary apocalyptists refined and developed a kind of metaphoric, mythical, symbolic language already at home in Israel's biblical and theological tradition.

7.6.2 Apocalyptic and Empire

Apocalypticism has sometimes been seen as otherworldly, a flight from the realities of practical politics into a heavenly or internal spiritual world. But apocalypticism is essentially political, this-worldly, unwilling to surrender Israel's faith in the one true God who is finally the God of justice, unwilling to assign ultimate power to the penultimate unjust powers of this world. The book of Daniel, the first full-blown apocalypse, originated in the crucible of imperial persecution, unmasking imperial power as anti-God and essentially dehumanizing, protesting the claims of human imperial power and presenting an alternative vision of God's rule as the ultimate kingdom.[24] Daniel proclaims that the will of God is to deliver humanity from such oppression and set people free for the kind of life the Creator wills for them (σωτηρία *sōtēria*, salvation; ζωή *zōē*, life). Daniel's visions portray the march of human empire from Babylon through Persia to Alexander and his Greek successors, and promise that God's own empire will soon smash the earthly empires and establish God's justice (Dan 2, 7). This did not happen, but the failure of God's kingdom to appear in history did not destroy the faith expressed in this theology. When the Roman Empire succeeded the Greeks, Jewish apocalyptic teachers reconfigured the imagery so that Rome was the final earthly empire, soon to be replaced by God's empire.[25]

In the apocalyptic thought of the New Testament, the conflicts between the people of God and earthly powers are the concrete foreground conflicts representing the ultimate conflict between God and Satan. The outcome of this conflict is not in doubt, but already decided in the Christ event. Three important qualifications are important in advance of interpreting particular New Testament texts or documents expressed in apocalyptic language.

1. It is important to understand that, although there is an inseparable political dimension to apocalyptic thought, apocalypticism cannot be reduced to political protest literature. In New Testament apocalyptic thought, the ultimate conflict is not between God and Rome, but between God and Satan. There is indeed a fundamental conflict between the values and way of life embodied in Jesus and his disciples and the values and way of life represented by this-worldly empire. But the this-worldly enemy is not the ultimate enemy. Just as the followers of Jesus or the church is not the kingdom of God, so the Roman Empire is not the kingdom of Satan. Paul Minear has pointed out that this conceptuality prevents us from demonizing our own political opponents, who are in fact themselves God's beloved creatures and who are themselves victims of demonic power, as are all humans.[26] All expectations that God will finally destroy human empires cannot be greeted with vindictive glee by those who have accepted Jesus' command to love the enemy and who believe in the God who impartially loves those who respond and those who do not (Matt 5:43–48).

2. The biblical understanding of monotheism and creation means that apocalyptic dualism is finally penultimate, that all things are

24. For a helpful summary portrayal of imperial government as essentially oppressive, see Warren Carter, *The Roman Empire and the New Testament: An Essential Guide* (Nashville: Abingdon Press, 2006).

25. Βασιλεία (*basileia*) is translated by both *empire* and *kingdom*; *kingdom of God* and *empire of God* are exactly the same in Greek. In 2 Esdras 11:1–12:15, the author explicitly reinterprets the previous vision of Daniel so that Daniel's final vision of the last earthly empire is the Roman Empire of the author's own time. The divine interpreter clarifies that "the fourth kingdom that appeared in a vision to your brother Daniel . . . was not explained to him as I now explain to you" (12:11–12).

26. Paul S. Minear, *New Testament Apocalyptic*, Interpreting Biblical Texts (Nashville: Abingdon Press, 1981), 108.

finally in one hand. The evil empire cannot ultimately exclude even itself from the redeeming love of God, and the followers of Jesus who rightly oppose imperial injustice must not self-righteously look down on imperialists as ultimately "them" (see on Col 1:15–20; Eph 1:3–23).

3. The confession that Jesus is the definitive revelation of the character of God means that the apocalyptic act of God that finally overthrows evil and establishes God's justice, though expressed in the language and imagery of imperial violence, is not merely the replacement of earthly imperial violent power with heavenly imperial violence. The use of such language and imagery is ironic and inescapable—the only language and conceptuality we have to express God's acts is this-worldly language and conceptuality. To speak of "winning" and "conquering," even of "ruling," inevitably brings with it the connotations of earthly rule and power. Yet the early Christians believed that the definitive revelation of God in Jesus means that the ultimate power of the universe is self-giving love as manifest in the life and death of Jesus, and that this power shall ultimately prevail.

This is a christological redefinition of "winning," not a divine stamp of approval on human means of conquest. To speak of the "empire of God" is not merely a borrowing of this-worldly imagery to communicate God's rule, for the God of this empire is the one revealed in Jesus. In the light of the Christ event, imperial language is transformed in the process of borrowing it. This is analogous to New Testament christological language in general. To say *Jesus* is the Christ does not merely identify Jesus in terms of traditional (violent!) imagery, but redefines "Christ" in terms of who Jesus actually was (see on Rev 5).

7.6.3 "The One to Come"—Varieties of the Messianic Hope

Christians have sometimes pictured "the" Jews of the first century as waiting for "the" Messiah, but rejecting Jesus because he did not fit their (mistaken) understanding of what the Messiah should be. In this view, the Jews all believed that God would send a future Messiah, shared a common idea of the role and function of this Messiah, and thus rejected Jesus because he did not fulfill this hope. There are two fundamental problems with this stereotype:

1. As we have seen, the broad spectrum of types of Judaism makes it difficult to speak of what "the" Jews believed about their hopes for the future. To be sure, an orientation to the future was a fundamental perspective of most first-century Judaism, but a messianic figure was not integral to this hope as such. Many Jews, perhaps most, expressed their hopes for the ultimate fulfillment of God's purposes for Israel and the world without reference to a Messiah. Most Jewish religious texts, ancient and modern, including those oriented to the future, have nothing to say about a specific messianic figure. Later rabbinic writings in the Talmud make relatively frequent reference to the Messiah, but the whole corpus of the Mishnah, which includes practically all the traditions from the first century CE and earlier, has only two such references. The view that the messianic hope was an essential element in all first-century Judaism, in which Jews universally cherished the hope of a future Messiah, is a stereotype created by later Christians. There is increasing reluctance in academic circles to use "messianic" as a catch-all term for all Jewish hopes for future salvation.

Recent scholarship may have overreacted to this stereotype. In the days of Jesus and early Christianity, many Jews would have expressed their faith in a way that included a climactic future act of God involving a savior figure sent and empowered by God. The very early Christian formulation of the question of John the Baptist, "Are you the one who is to come, or shall we wait for another?" (Matt 11:3//Luke 7:19, a Q text), would have been meaningful to many first-century Jews.

2. Yet, among Jews who hoped for such a future divinely sent deliverer, there was much

variety in how they conceptualized and articulated this hope. There was no single set of beliefs about "the" Messiah. There were two major types: (a) the hope for a this-worldly figure, a human being authorized and empowered by God, representing the prophetic, eschatological hope, and (b) a transcendent, heavenly being who would erupt into this world from beyond, representing the apocalyptic hope. Since one aspect of early Christian faith involved interpreting the significance of Jesus by applying traditional messianic titles to him, we will here explore the spectrum of Jewish messianic hopes by briefly discussing the messianic titles available to Jesus and the early Christians.

Christ (מָשִׁיחַ, χριστός, anointed)

The Hebrew word מָשִׁיחַ (transliterated *mashiach*, Anglicized as Messiah) is an adjective derived from the verbal root מָשַׁח (*mashach*, anoint), with a passive meaning, *anointed*. Anointing with oil was part of the inauguration ritual for *kings* (e.g., 1 Sam 10:1; 16:13; Ps 2:2; 18:50), for *priests* (e.g., Exod 30:30–31; 40:15; Lev 4:3, 5; 2 Macc 1:10), and for *prophets* (e.g., 1 Kgs. 19:16; Isa 61:1; Ps 105:15). The Dead Sea Scrolls show that this threefold understanding of the Messiah as anointed prophet/priest/king was quite alive in some streams of first-century Judaism. This became the classical Christian paradigm for explicating the office of Jesus Christ in some streams of later Christian theology. The LXX regularly translates מָשִׁיחַ (*mashiach*) with the Greek χριστός (transliterated *christos*, anglicized as "Christ"), an adjective belonging to the class of verbal adjectives ending in –τος. Such adjectives have the meaning of the past participle of the cognate verb, such as ἀγαπητός (*agapētos*, beloved), ἐκλεκτός (*eklektos*, elected), εὐλογητός (*eulogētos*, blessed), and διδακτός (*didaktos*, taught). This is analogous to such adjectives as chos*en*, appoint*ed*, authoriz*ed*, empower*ed*. The passive form and meaning is here theologically important. To designate someone Messiah/Christ/Anointed One does not claim they are something extraordinary in and of themselves, but that they have been anointed by God. To confess that Jesus is the Christ is not a claim about Jesus, but about God as the one who has chosen, authorized, and empowered Jesus. The "point of Christology" is that it does not answer the question "Who is Jesus?" but "Who is God?"[27]

In the Hebrew Scriptures, the term מָשִׁיחַ (*mashiach*) always refers to present or past anointed ones, mostly for the king or priest. Strictly speaking, it is thus incorrect to speak of the "messianic hope" in the Old Testament, especially in the exaggerated traditional sense that supposes the Old Testament is essentially a book of hopes and predictions of a coming Messiah. There was, however, an important stream of Old Testament theology that, disappointed with the actual Judean kings, saw the eschatological hopes of Israel as soon to be fulfilled in the birth or inauguration of a new king, to whom extravagant titles were applied (e.g., Ps 2; Isa 9:1–7; 11:1–9).

In Second Temple Judaism, after the Judean monarchy had ceased to exist, such texts were reinterpreted and became elements of the "messianic hope." This cluster of messianic images and concepts was no longer bound strictly to the מָשִׁיחַ (*mashiach*) terminology. This means that leaders of Jewish movements that appeared sporadically 6–66 CE, protesting Roman rule and/or current Jewish leadership, are rightly regarded as expressions of the messianic hope, even though they rarely claimed the title itself.[28]

27. See Schubert M. Ogden, *The Point of Christology* (San Francisco: Harper & Row, 1982).

28. Although only Jesus of Nazareth is known to have explicitly been associated with the messianic title during this period (and after him, no one until Simeon ben Kosiba in 132 CE), numerous messianic leaders and claimants may be listed: John the Baptist, Judas the Galilean, Simon, Athronges, Eleazar ben Deinaus, Alexander, Menahem, Simon bar Giora. See, e.g., N. T. Wright, *Jesus and the Victory of God*, vol. 2 of *Christian Origins and the Question of God* (Minneapolis: Fortress Press, 1996), 110.

Messianic King

The messianic hope continued to be expressed as the hope for a future king. Such hopes were subversive of the present ruler. For anyone to claim, or have others claim for him, that he was the divinely appointed king of the endtime was a call to revolution against the current government. Such claims were dealt with harshly.

Son of David

The eschatological king was often considered to be a descendant of David, a rightful heir of the original David who had freed Israel from its enemies and brought peace and prosperity. This hope is classically expressed in *Psalms of Solomon* 17:21–32, written about 50 BCE after the Roman takeover of Judea.

> 21 See, Lord, and raise up for them their king,
> the son of David, to rule over your servant Israel
> in the time known to you, O God.
> 22 Undergird him with the strength to destroy the unrighteous rulers,
> to purge Jerusalem from gentiles
> who trample her to destruction;
> 23 in wisdom and in righteousness to drive out
> the sinners from the inheritance;
> to smash the arrogance of sinners
> like a potter's jar;
> 24 To shatter all their substance with an iron rod;
> to destroy the unlawful nations with the word of his mouth;
> 25 At his warning the nations will flee from his presence;
> and he will condemn sinners by the thoughts of their hearts.
> 26 He will gather a holy people
> whom he will lead in righteousness;
> and he will judge the tribes of the people
> that have been made holy by the Lord their God.
> 27 He will not tolerate unrighteousness (even) to pause among them,
> and any person who knows wickedness shall not live with them.
> For he shall know them
> that they are all children [υἱοί *huioi*, sons] of their God.
> 28 He will distribute them upon the land
> according to their tribes;
> the alien and the foreigner will no longer live near them.
> 29 He will judge peoples and nations in the wisdom of his righteousness. Selah.
> 30 And he will have gentile nations serving him under his yoke,
> and he will glorify the Lord in (a place) prominent (above) the whole earth.
> 31 And he will purge Jerusalem
> (and make it) holy as it was even from the beginning,
> (for) nations to come from the ends of the earth to see his glory,
> to bring as gifts her children who had been driven out,
> and to see the glory of the Lord
> with which God had glorified her.
> 32 And he will be a righteous king over them, taught by God.
> There will be no unrighteousness among them in his days,
> for all shall be holy,
> and their king shall be the Lord Messiah.[29]

While we do not know how typical such a view of the Messiah was, it was a noble hope, reinterpreting such texts as Isaiah 9 and 11 to point to a future reign of peace and justice. The Messiah through whom this will be accomplished is a human being, chosen and empowered by God to establish God's just rule for all peoples, with Israel at the center. *Psalms of Solomon* 17 is also important in that, in addition to *Messiah*, it uses two other terms that were to become central in New Testament Christology.

29. Cited from Charlesworth, ed., *Pseudepigrapha*, 2:665–67.

The term *"Lord"* (κύριος *kurios*, also transliterated *kyrios*) is used for the Messiah (v. 32), and the term *"son(s) of God"* appears—but for faithful Israel of the messianic times, not of the Messiah himself (v. 27).

Son of God

Second Temple Judaism did occasionally refer to the coming Messiah as Son of God. This is in continuity with the biblical (not pagan) understanding of the term. In the Bible's extensive use of the language of sonship, it is important to bear in mind the usage of the term "son" in Hebrew (and other Semitic languages). In addition to the primary English meaning of the word "son," that is, male biological offspring, the Hebrew noun בֵּן (*ben*) is used in a number of ways alien to English usage. One of the most important and most common usages of "son" in Hebrew is with the cluster of meanings, "belonging to a category," "having the characteristics or quality of," "member of a guild, order, or class," or "part of, belonging to a set," as illustrated by the following literal translations. Sparks from a campfire can be called "sons of the fire" (Job 5:7), arrows are "sons of the bow" (Job 41:28), those who belong to a prophetic guild or group are "sons of the prophets" (1 Kgs. 20:35; Amos 7:14), and exiles are "sons of the exile" (Ezra 4:1). A person's age is given as being "a son of x-number of years" (Gen 5:32, "a son of five hundred years"). A strong man is a "son of strength" (1 Sam 14:52). The Egyptians are "sons of Egypt" (Ezek 16:26), and the Israelites are "sons of Israel" (Exod 1:12 and more than 1,300 times in the Old Testament). In such expressions, the primary reality is the nation, the people of Israel, and the individual Israelites, male and female, are its "sons." *Belonging to a category* is the essential idea.

Thus the Hebrew term בֶּן־אֱלֹהִים (*ben-Elohim*, son of God) might mean any of these:

— The people of Israel (Exod 4:22).

— True eschatological Israelites, Israel as Israel was meant to be, what Israel will be in the messianic age (*Pss. Sol.* 17:27).

— The ideal Israelite, that is, a truly righteous person (Wis 2:10–20).

— The Judean king. Adopted by God at the coronation ritual (Ps 2:7; cf. 2 Sam 7:14), the Judean king was considered the son of God in a special sense, but the title had no biological or metaphysical connotations.

— Divine beings, members of the heavenly court. Without compromising Israel's conviction that there is only one God, Genesis 6:1–4 refers to members of the heavenly court as "sons of God," that is, beings that belong to the divine world. The LXX would later translate such terms with ἄγγελος (*angelos*, angel). The prosecuting attorney of the heavenly court, the satan (accuser), was such a "son of God" (Gen 6:2, 4; the same phrase in Job 1:6 is rendered "heavenly beings" in the NRSV).

Priest

Priests were also anointed for a special function of mediating between God and the world. Like the king, the high priest in particular was known as the מָשִׁיחַ (*mashiach*), "the anointed one" (Lev 4:3, 5; Dan 9:25, 26). After the exile, when the kingship no longer existed, the high priests were the ruling powers, under their imperial overlords. When the kingship was briefly restored under the Hasmoneans (priests who belonged to the Levitical rather than the Davidic line), some Jews reinterpreted the messianic hopes in terms of a future priestly ruler and a restored, authentic temple (e.g., *T. Levi* 18; 4Q541; 4QT Levi 1). The mysterious figure of Melchizedek, the priest-king of Genesis 14:18–20 and Psalm 110:1–7, was reinterpreted in terms of the future messianic hope.

Prophet

Moses, the original savior figure of Israel, had promised that after his death God would raise up a "prophet like Moses" as Israel's guide (Deut 18:15–18). This text originally referred to the line of prophetic figures to whom Israel was to look for divine guidance (rather than witches and soothsayers), a kind of charismatic leadership in contrast to the dynastic claims of the Judean monarchy. After the exile, Second Temple Judaism sometimes pictured the expected future deliverer as a prophetic figure, the "eschatological prophet," who would be the divinely authorized spokesperson for the last days, clarifying disputed points of Torah and declaring the ultimate will of God. A variation of this hope is the expectation that Elijah would return just before the end to prepare the way. This view was based on Malachi 3:1–2; 4:5–6 and reinforced by the story that Elijah did not die but was taken bodily to heaven (2 Kgs 2:11). In the Old Testament and Jewish hope, however, Elijah is not the Messiah, nor does he prepare the way for the Messiah, but he is the final prophet before the advent of the Lord God.

Lord

The Hebrew אָדוֹן (*Adon*), Lord, was used for the king and other powerful figures. In the form אֲדֹנָי (*Adonay*), my Lord, it became a proper name for God in Jewish tradition, a substitute for the sacred name יהוה that was not pronounced. This meant that a term used for God could be used for the king, including the eschatological messianic king. When the LXX regularly translated the sacred name יהוה (*YHWH*) as κύριος (*Kurios*, Lord), used for royal and other respected figures, the linguistic transition from earthly ruler to divine being was greatly facilitated (cf. *Pss. Sol.* 17:32, cited above).

Servant

Since the Lord's anointed king (מָשִׁיחַ, *mashiach, messiah*) could also be called God's servant (עֶבֶד, *ebed*), as in Psalm 132:10 and 2 Chronicles 6:42, it was possible to refer to the coming Messiah as God's Servant. A few scholars have argued that the Suffering Servant figure of Isaiah 53 was already interpreted in pre-Christian Judaism as a messianic figure. The contrary move seems to have been the case: in the Targum of Isaiah 53, the servant of God is a powerful figure who makes the enemies of God's people suffer for their sins against Israel. Rather than interpreting the Messiah as one who suffers for the sins of others, the Targum reads the features of the royal national Messiah into the figure of the servant, so that he becomes a triumphant, conquering figure.

Son of Man

Some streams of Second Temple Judaism expressed their hopes for the future in terms of an apocalyptic figure called the *Son of Man* who would come from heaven to establish God's kingdom, raise the dead, and be instrumental in the Last Judgment (*1 Enoch* 37–71; Dan 7; strikingly absent from Qumran documents, though they were apocalyptists who affirmed Daniel). The New Testament Gospels use this term as the most common designation for Jesus, where it occurs eighty-two times, always as Jesus' own self-designation. The origin, history, usage, and meaning(s) of this phrase is one of the most disputed issues in the study of Second Temple Judaism and the New Testament. These are main points to be kept in mind:

— The phrase originated in the Semitic languages Hebrew and Aramaic and is not originally a Greek phrase native to the New Testament. "Son of Man" thus sounded as strange in Greek ears as it does to those who speak English.

— בֵּן (*ben*, Hebrew) and בַּר (*bar*, Aramaic) have a variety of meanings. The phrase "son of man" in Hebrew or Aramaic means "belonging to the category 'human being,'" an individual member of the human race. It is thus used more than ninety times in the Old Testament to mean "human being," especially in contrast to God.[30]

30. In the interests of gender-inclusive language, the NRSV often renders the phrase "mortal" when referring to humans, and "human being" in reference to the heavenly figure of Dan 7, never translating it in the Old Testament literally as "son of man." This makes it difficult for the English reader to see the biblical connotations of

— In Daniel 7, the seer is given a vision of the succession of world empires in which the traditional four oppressive empires are represented in mythological form as wild animals, while the final kingdom of God is represented by a human figure—a "son of man" (Dan 7:13).

— In some streams of Second Temple Judaism, the Son of Man of Daniel 7 was seen as more than a symbolic human figure parallel to the beastly figures, and came to be regarded as an actual heavenly being already present in the divine world (*1 Enoch* 37–71). God would send this Son of Man at the end of time to raise the dead, execute the divine judgment, and inaugurate God's kingdom.[31]

— It is thus paradoxical that, among the messianic images and vocabulary available to Jesus and the church in the first century, in Second Temple Judaism "Son of God" would normally be understood as a *human* royal figure, the divinely sent Davidic Messiah, while "Son of Man" could be used of a *divine* being, the heavenly figure who would descend at the end of time to establish God's justice. In Judaism, the "Son of God" hope was prophetic-eschatological, in continuity with the present world and bringing it to fulfillment; the "Son of Man" hope related to the apocalyptic view that divine deliverance would come from the transcendent world, in discontinuity with present history.

We have a spectrum composed mostly of overlapping clusters of images. Messianic imagery, vocabulary, and traditions were often combined. Thus, for example, Zechariah 4:14 proclaims two anointed ones (literally "sons of oil"), the messianic king and priest. The Qumran Covenanters expected three messianic figures, the Messiah of Aaron (the priestly Messiah), the Messiah of Israel (the Davidic Messiah, subordinate to the priest), and the eschatological Prophet (1QS 9.11; 1QSa 2.12–14; 4Q249 fragments 1–3). There was no uniform picture or nomenclature for the expected savior figure. Sometimes the different titles were combined and used interchangeably, as in *1 Enoch* 37–71, in which the same messianic figure is called the Messiah, the Elect One, the Righteous One, and the Son of Man; but it is the latter image that fills in the content of what the savior figure is to do. In 2 Esdras 7:28; 12:32; 13:37, 52, Son of God, Son of Man, and Messiah are interchangeable designations for the same figure, but here the role is a combination of the expectations associated with each term. Sometimes the hope was expressed in general terms, as the hope for a mighty one sent by God without further specification, "the one who is to come," but a particular set of expectations was still involved (Matthew 11:3//Luke 7:19).

It is within this complex matrix of Second Temple Judaism that the life and death of Jesus, early Christianity, and the New Testament documents are to be understood.

7.7 Jamnia and the "Parting of the Ways"

FOR PALESTINIAN AND DIASPORA JEWS alike, the destruction of the temple and the holy city in the revolt of 66–70 was the great turning point in their religious and personal history. Second Temple Judaism comes to an end, and the development of rabbinic Judaism begins. Jesus, earliest Jerusalem Christianity, and Paul lived prior to this transition; most of the New Testament was written during or after it. The war was a watershed event, marking the beginning of the "parting of the ways" that resulted in Judaism and Christianity becoming two separate religions.

There was a rich variety in the spectrum of pre-70 Judaism. So far as we know, the Essenes disappeared as an organized party in the war of 66–70; there is no reference to them in New Testament or rabbinic literature, no trace of

the phrase when Son of Man is used as a christological title in the New Testament.

31. A clear and concise discussion of the relevant texts is provided by Collins, *Apocalyptic Imagination*, 173–94.

them anywhere after 70. Militant groups such as the Zealots and Sicarii were decimated by the Romans and discredited among the people—but the embers of revolution remained, to flame forth repeatedly until finally extinguished in the Bar Kokhba rebellion of 132–35. The Sadducees, bound closely with the temple cultus, practically disappeared as a party with the destruction of the temple. Though the office of high priest was gone, numerous priests remained throughout the country, but they had lost much of their power.

The Pharisees became the dominant influence in postwar Judaism, so that there is a sense in which all Judaism that survived is Pharisaic Judaism. There was indeed a power shift, but Pharisaic Judaism did not immediately become the "normative" Judaism of the synagogues. We should rather think of an extended period after the 66–70 war, stretching to the time of the codification of the Mishnah about 200 CE, as the period of "formative Judaism." During this time the pre-70 Pharisaic party competed with the remnants of other Jewish groups that had survived the war (priestly, scribal, apocalyptic, Christian, to some minor extent even Samaritan, Sadducean, and Zealot) and finally established itself as the definitive element in that kind of rabbinic Judaism that became "normative."[32] They did not assume general leadership of Palestinian Judaism by default, however—the Romans chose them as the group with whom they would work in rebuilding the country and reestablishing Roman order.

Pharisees assumed the previous Sadducean role: "we will cooperate with you, the Romans, in matters of political rule, and promise no rebellion; you will give us the right to determine the religious life of the people." Even so, post-70 Judaism should not be thought of as simply the direct continuation of pre-70 Pharisaism. While it is probable that much of the rabbinic leadership came from Pharisaic groups and continued to propagate the Pharisaic perspective and traditions, there is no evidence that the Pharisees survived the war as an organized, coherent group. It was, nonetheless, primarily the Pharisaic influence that determined the shape of Judaism after the war. The generative center of this influence was the rabbinic academy at Jamnia.

7.7.1 The Academy at Jamnia

During the last days of the war, Johanan ben Zakkai, a leading teacher among the Pharisees, escaped the doomed city and, with Roman permission, established an academy for study of the Torah at Jamnia (Jabneh, Yavneh) near modern Tel Aviv. Jamnia functioned as the new spiritual center of emerging rabbinic Judaism in the period between the 66–70 and 132–35 wars. The academy was not a council on the model of the later ecumenical church councils, but a center for study of the Torah and for making crucial decisions about the life of Judaism in the absence of temple, cultus, Sanhedrin, and high priest. The academy had no means of promulgating or enforcing its decisions. Jamnia's only authority was its prestige and power of persuasion.

7.7.2 A More Institutionalized Rabbinic Leadership

At Jamnia, the sages did not automatically assume leadership of the continuing Jewish community in Palestine or elsewhere. In Palestine, the priests still thought of themselves as leaders of the people; in the Diaspora, local leadership continued as before. Only little by little, over a period of generations, did the rabbinic

32. For a variety of perspectives on this complex history, see E. P. Sanders, Albert I. Baumgarten, and Alan Mendelson, eds., *Jewish and Christian Self-Definition*, vol. 2, *Aspects of Jewish Self-Definition in The Greco-Roman Period*, 1st American ed.; 2 vols. (Philadelphia: Fortress Press, 1980); Jacob Neusner, "The Formation of Rabbinic Judaism: Yavneh (Jamnia) from A.D. 70 to 100," in *Aufstieg und Niedergang der römischen Welt*, ed. Joseph Vogt, Hildegard Temporini, and Klaus Haacker (Berlin: De Gruyter, 1979), 3–42; Shaye J. D. Cohen, *From the Maccabees to the Mishnah* (Philadelphia: Westminster Press, 1987), 214–31.

group attain their status as *the* authorities in Judaism, by gradually incorporating local leaders into their movement. Sometime during this period, the ordination of rabbis became more institutionalized. In the pre-70 days of John the Baptist and Jesus, there was no formal ordination, and one's acceptance as a teacher and rabbi was a matter of personal ability, charisma, and informal community validation. Whoever gained a following as a religious teacher was a rabbi to their followers, and there were no generally accepted standards or procedures. In the reconstitution of Judaism during the Jamnia period, "rabbi" became a more official title, but there were still no standards or procedures that prevailed throughout Judaism. In 30 CE, John the Baptist and Jesus could be considered rabbis; in the period after 70 they would not have qualified.

7.7.3 An Increased Sense of an Authoritative Canon

It has sometimes been supposed that the canon of the Hebrew Bible was "established" at Jamnia. It is true that at the beginning of the Jamnia period there was a central core of sacred writings consisting of the Torah, the former and latter Prophets, and a variety of Writings including the Psalter; but there was no firm canonical list accepted by all Palestinian Jews, not to speak of the wider range of texts considered sacred by Diaspora Judaism (see above 2.2.1). Neither Josephus nor any other first-century Jew used the word "canon," but by about 100 CE, Josephus could assume it as commonly accepted that the Jewish Scriptures contained the same twenty-two books as at present, which he divided into five books of Moses, thirteen books of prophets, and four other books of hymns and instructions (Josephus, *Ag. Ap.* 1.8, §§38–41; these twenty-two books of the Hebrew Bible, differently divided and arranged, are the thirty-nine books of the Christian Old Testament). Second Esdras (4 Ezra) 14:37–48 designates two categories of sacred books, the twenty-four inspired books given to everyone (presumably the same as Josephus's twenty-two, divided differently), and an additional seventy books intended only for "the wise among the people." Many of these were presumably included in the categories later called Apocrypha and Pseudepigrapha. Some early rabbis referred to the "Law, Prophets . . . , [and] Sacred Writings" (*B. Bat.* 14b; cf. Luke 24:44, "law, prophets, psalms"). Jews of the Diaspora used the somewhat expanded canon of the LXX.

By the end of the Jamnia period, around 200 CE, with the codification and publication of the Mishnah, this list was relatively fixed, and the documents it included had attained an increased degree of verbal sanctity. This is illustrated by the fact that manuscripts of biblical documents at Qumran deposited in 68 CE manifest some variety in their textual form, while those from Khirbet Mird about sixty-five years later have a precisely uniform text, that of the later Masoretes. The standardization of the text that occurred in these two generations argues for a sharpened sense of canonical status. Debates were carried on as to which books "defile the hands," that is, have a unique divine inspiration and authority that communicates powerful divine holiness by touch. None of the books now contained in the Pseudepigrapha were included; conspicuously absent were the numerous apocalyptic texts that had fanned the flames of insurrection and led to two disastrous wars. The new Christian texts such as the Gospels and several Jewish Christian (or Christian Jewish) texts had to be clearly excluded. Some books such as Ezekiel that were eventually accepted into the canon were still considered marginal, and their authority was vigorously debated. Yet there never was a day when the "council" of Jamnia decided precisely which books should be in the Bible and which not, and borderline cases such as Ezekiel continued to be argued for some time.

Thus both early Judaism and early Christianity were establishing their own identities at about the same time, partially in reaction to each other. One dimension of this was the firming up of canonical boundaries on both sides. Early Christianity ended up accepting more books into its Old Testament than post-70 rabbinic Judaism's definition of canonical writings. When Christianity became predominately a Gentile, Greek-speaking community, its Bible became the LXX, which included several documents not accepted into the canon of Palestinian Judaism.

7.7.4 Synagogue Judaism Replacing Temple Judaism

When the temple was destroyed, what remained was synagogue Judaism (see above on nature of "the" synagogue). The transition was smoother and less critical than might have been expected, since for many Jews the synagogue had functioned as the central focus of community and religious life long before the temple ceased to exist. But with the demolition of the cult, the cessation of daily sacrifice, and the impossibility of the annual Day of Atonement ritual, the Torah's commands regarding sacrifice and atonement had to be rethought. The Jamnia sages provided a satisfying, twin-pronged answer:

1. Sacrifice was spiritualized, internalized, ethicized, individualized, as expressed in a saying of Johanan ben Zakkai cited in *Avot of Rabbi Nathan* 4.21: "For we have another atonement, which is like sacrifice, and what is it? Deeds of loving-kindness, as it is said, *For I desire mercy and not sacrifice* (Hos 6:6)." The rabbis taught that every Jew must pray twice daily (morning and afternoon), since prayer corresponded to the Tamid sacrifices. The regularity of daily sacrifice in the temple was transferred to prayer (cf. Luke 1:10; Acts 3:1). Daniel 1–6 indicates that already in Maccabean times it was understood that prayer had replaced sacrifice for Diaspora Jews, so it was a small step to make *synagogue prayer* the continuing substitute for *temple sacrifice*.

2. When it was no longer possible actually to perform the sacrificial rituals commanded in the Torah, loving devotion to the *study* of the rules of sacrifice, and of the Torah in general, was substituted for the performance of the commanded rituals. As the temple had been the place of ritual and sacrifice administered by priests, the synagogue became the place of the book, the place of study, and the sage replaced the priest.

7.7.5 The Birkath ha-Minim

According to a variety of traditions, during the Jamnia period one of the traditional synagogue prayers was reformulated to include a "blessing" (=curse) against the מִנִים (*minim*, separatists, heretics). The Palestinian recension of this benediction:[33]

> For apostates may there be no hope,
> And the arrogant kingdom uproot speedily in our days.
> May the nozerim (Christians) and the minim (heretics) perish in an instant.
> "May they be blotted out of the book of the living,
> And may they not be written with the righteous" (Ps 69:28).
> Blessed art thou, O Lord, who humblest the arrogant.

The later church fathers understood this to be directed against Christians, and thus claimed that Christians were cursed in the Jewish synagogues.[34] It has been argued by some Christian and Jewish historians that this prayer served as a tool in ferreting out Christian Jews in the synagogue (who, of course, could not participate in this part of the liturgy)

33. Solomon Schechter, "Geniza Specimens," *Jewish Quarterly Review* 10 (1896): 656–57, cited from Philip S. Alexander, "The 'Parting of the Ways' from the Perspective of Rabbinic Judaism," in *Jews and Christians: The Parting of the Ways*, ed. James D. G. Dunn (Grand Rapids: Eerdmans, 1992), 7.

34. Justin, *Dialogue with Trypho* 16, 47, 96, 137; Origen, *H. Jeremiah* 10.8.2; Epiphanius, *Panarion* 29.9.1; Jerome, *Epis. August.* 112.13.

in order to force them out of the synagogue.[35] The wording of the prayer was changed over time, due in part to fear of Christian reprisals, so that the original wording is disputed. It is not clear that it originally included a specific reference to Christians; it may have been directed against any group considered heretical by the Jamnian leaders.[36] It is thus an oversimplification to regard the Birkath ha-Minim as proof that, for example, the Christians in Matthew's and John's churches had been officially excluded from formative Judaism, and to interpret these Gospels as the responses of an excommunicated group to Jamnia. The influential view argued by Davies and Martyn saw the expulsion as official, as happening in the 80s, and as intended to be comprehensive: the Jamnia decree was to be enforced by local synagogues and *gerousiai* (sanhedrins, local Jewish councils). Many scholars would now see the expulsions for which Matthew and John provide historical evidence as local and episodic, not a general, official rejection of Christianity by Judaism. In this view, the "parting of the ways" came some time after the New Testament period, and the conflicts reflected in the New Testament are the early signs of the approaching storm. Nonetheless, the evidence is clear that there were deep tensions between formative Judaism and the emerging institutional church, which had its own sense of identity, structures, and procedures for excommunication and promulgating new authoritative teachings over against formative Judaism (see, e.g., Matt 18:15–20).

35. E.g., W. D. Davies, *The Setting of the Sermon on the Mount* (Cambridge: Cambridge University Press, 1966), 256–315; J. Louis Martyn, *History and Theology in the Fourth Gospel* (New York: Harper & Row, 1968), 37–62 (the 2003 third edition of Martyn's work nuances his view and brings it up to date without essentially changing it); Robert Kysar, *John The Maverick Gospel*, 2nd ed. (Louisville, KY: Westminster John Knox Press, 1993), 21–24.

36. See Reuven Kimelman, "Birkath ha-Minim and the Lack of Evidence for an Anti-Christian Jewish Prayer in Late Antiquity," in Sanders, ed., *Jewish and Christian Self-Definition*, 2:245–68.

7.7.6 Jewish Persecution of Early Christians?

There was no extensive or systematic persecution of Christians by Jews. Historically, there were instances of Jewish persecution of some early Christians—that is, of Jewish Christians who were still within the synagogue structure and subject to its discipline—and Jewish cooperation with or manipulation of the Roman government to secure the condemnation and execution of Christians (see 2 Cor 11:25; Acts 26:10; John 16:2).[37] Such instances of Jewish persecution of Christians were not a matter of one religion or race oppressing another or of outsiders interfering in the religious practices of another group; that is, they were not at all like the later Christian pogroms against the Jewish community. Such texts as Matthew 10:17 and 23:34 reflect an internal struggle of Jew vs. Jew, analogous to the internal conflicts among Christians of the Reformation period.

7.7.7 When Did the "Parting of the Ways" Take Place?

The above discussion makes it clear that there was no particular date—or decade or generation—in which a definitive separation between formative Judaism and emerging Christianity took place. The process was sometimes a matter of perception, with members of the Christian community regarding themselves as still insiders to Judaism, but not being so perceived by (some elements of) the Jewish community itself. From one point of view, whether one belonged to Judaism could be objectively determined: after 70, Rome had

37. James the brother of Jesus and leader of the Jerusalem church was condemned and executed in 62 CE in Jerusalem for "violation of the Torah" (see above, §6.2.6). In the 132 CE rebellion, the Jewish leader Bar Kokhba executed those Jewish Christians who refused to deny that Jesus was the Messiah (Justin, *Apology* 1.31.6; *Trypho* 46.1, 47.1; 39.7; see C. K. Barrett, *The Gospel of John and Judaism*, trans. D. Moody Smith [Philadelphia: Fortress Press, 1970], 10). The issue was not Torah observance, but messianic confession; Bar Kokhba claimed that he was the Messiah.

decreed that Jews throughout the empire must pay to Rome the annual tax previously paid to the temple. The procedures for the collection of this tax were reformed by the emperor Nerva, Domitian's successor, in 96 CE. At this time, the government became more aware than they had been previously that people of non-Jewish origin could become Jews, and thus liable to the tax, and that members of the Jewish community could avoid the tax by renouncing Judaism, thus declaring in effect that they were apostates or adherents to some other religion. This made it clear that Christians, if they did not pay the tax, were not Jews. It would remain unclear, however, how this would affect the religious self-understanding of Christians who saw themselves as heirs of the biblical promises and in some sense the "new Israel," and how they would be regarded by insiders to the Jewish community.

7.8 For Further Reading

Charlesworth, James H., ed. *The Messiah: Developments in Earliest Judaism and Christianity*. Minneapolis: Fortress Press, 1992.

———, ed. *The Old Testament Pseudepigrapha*. 2 vols. Garden City, NY: Doubleday, 1985.

Cohen, Shaye J. D. *From the Maccabees to the Mishnah*. Philadelphia: Westminster Press, 1987.

Collins, John J. *The Apocalyptic Imagination: An Introduction to Jewish Apocalyptic Literature*. 2nd ed. Grand Rapids: Eerdmans, 1998.

———. *The Scepter and the Star: The Messiahs of the Dead Sea Scrolls and Other Ancient Literature*. New York: Doubleday, 1995.

Danby, Herbert. *The Mishnah*. London: Oxford University Press, 1958.

Dunn, James D. G., ed. *Jews and Christians: The Parting of the Ways*. Grand Rapids: Eerdmans, 1992.

Martinez, Florentino Garcia, and W. G. E. Watson. *The Dead Sea Scrolls Translated: The Qumran Texts in English*. 2nd ed. Grand Rapids: Eerdmans, 1996.

Hanson, Paul D. *The Dawn of Apocalyptic*. Philadelphia: Fortress Press, 1975.

Hengel, Martin. *Judaism and Hellenism: Studies in their Encounter in Palestine during the Early Hellenistic Period*. Translated by John Bowden. London: SCM Press, 1974.

Horsley, Richard A., and John S. Hanson. *Bandits, Prophets, and Messiahs: Popular Movements in the Time of Jesus*. Minneapolis: Winston Press, 1985.

Minear, Paul S. *New Testament Apocalyptic*. Interpreting Biblical Texts. Nashville: Abingdon Press, 1981.

Mowinckel, Sigmund. *He That Cometh: The Messiah Concept in the Old Testament and Later Judaism*. Translated by G. W. Anderson. Biblical Resource Series. Grand Rapids: Eerdmans, 2005.

Neusner, Jacob. *First-Century Judaism in Crisis: Yohanan ben Zakkai and the Renaissance of Torah*. Nashville: Abingdon Press, 1975.

———. "The Formation of Rabbinic Judaism: Yavneh (Jamnia) from A.D. 70 to 100." In *Aufstieg und Niedergang der römischen Welt*, edited by Joseph Vogt, Hildegard Temporini, and Klaus Haacker, 3–42. Berlin: De Gruyter, 1979.

Nickelsburg, George W. E. *Jewish Literature between the Bible and the Mishnah*. Philadelphia: Fortress Press, 1981.

———. *Resurrection, Immortality, and Eternal Life in Intertestamental Judaism*. HTS 26. Cambridge: Harvard University Press, 1972.

Saldarini, Anthony J. *Pharisees, Scribes, and Sadducees in Palestinian Society: A Sociological Approach*. Biblical Resource Series. Grand Rapids: Eerdmans, 2001.

Sanders, E. P., Albert I. Baumgarten, and Alan Mendelson, eds. *Jewish and Christian Self-Definition*. Vol. 2, *Aspects of Jewish Self-Definition in the Greco-Roman Period*. 1st American ed. 2 vols. Philadelphia: Fortress Press, 1980.

Sandmel, Samuel. *Judaism and Christian Beginnings*. New York: Oxford University Press, 1978.

Schäfer, Peter. *The History of the Jews in the Greco-Roman World*. New York: Routledge, 2003.

Schiffman, Lawrence H., ed. *Texts and Traditions: A Source Reader for the Study of Second Temple and Rabbinic Judaism*. Hoboken, NJ: KTAV, 1998.

Stegemann, Hartmut. *The Library of Qumran, on the Essenes, Qumran, John the Baptist, and Jesus*. Grand Rapids: Eerdmans, 1998.

VanderKam, James C. *The Dead Sea Scrolls Today*. Grand Rapids: Eerdmans, 1994.

———. *An Introduction to Early Judaism*. Grand Rapids: Eerdmans, 2001.

Vermès, Geza., ed. *The Dead Sea Scrolls in English*. 4th ed. London: Penguin Books, 1995.

8
Jesus within Judaism

ALL THE NEW TESTAMENT DOCUMENTS are decisively shaped by the events of the life and death of Jesus. If Jesus had been different, early Christianity and the New Testament would have been different. A historical understanding of the New Testament thus requires that we look, at least briefly, at what can be confidently said about the "historical Jesus." One might justifiably ask why the following section about Jesus is relatively brief, in contrast to the preceding extensive section on Judaism. There are two reasons for this: (1) We have no written records from Jesus himself, but there is an extensive collection of primary sources on which to base our picture(s) of Second Temple Judaism. (2) Study of the historical Jesus is a field of research in itself, which can properly be undertaken only after one has made a thorough study of the New Testament and other relevant ancient literature. The fact that the Gospels are later interpretations strongly influenced by Christian theology makes it difficult to read the life of Jesus "as he really was" off the surface of the New Testament documents. A depiction of the historical Jesus thus should properly follow an introduction to the New Testament, rather than precede it. The beginning student is advised to skim through the following sections and return to considerations of the historical Jesus after digesting the introductory issues connected with New Testament history and literature.

8.1 Terminology

SCHOLARLY STUDY OF THE JESUS WHO WAS really "back there" behind the Gospels uses a number of overlapping terms, which might be sorted out as follows:

The real Jesus. Jesus as he really was, prior to anyone's interpretation of his significance, would include all that he said, did, and thought. There was, of course, such a Jesus, just as every person who has ever lived was such a reality. *This* Jesus existed, but he is forever lost to later generations. Any representation of the "real Jesus" will necessarily be a selection and an interpretation.

The historic Jesus. Not everything Jesus said and did made an impact on those about him. Those things about Jesus that made him a significant figure to his contemporaries, his "impact," caused some words and deeds to be remembered and formulated into narratives. Such a Jesus can be called the *remembered Jesus*,[1] if it is kept in mind that all such remembering already includes interpreting Jesus within some presupposed framework. Jesus as he was remembered will always be (much!) less than Jesus as he actually existed.

1. So James D. G. Dunn, *Jesus Remembered*, vol. 1 of *Christianity in the Making* (Grand Rapids: Eerdmans, 2003).

The historian's Jesus. Given sufficient data, historians can use generally accepted historical methods to construct the major outlines and significant features of any figure who has had an impact on history. In the case of Jesus of Nazareth, the product of such historical study results in what can be said, with relative probability, of his life and mission. This product of "Jesus research" is often called the *historical Jesus*, but might better be designated the *historian's Jesus*.

The historical Jesus. In the wake of Albert Schweitzer's epoch-making *The Quest of the Historical Jesus* (see below), it has become conventional to use *historical Jesus* somewhat loosely as a general designation for the pre-Easter Jesus as he actually was, the Jesus who can be distinguished from the variety of later interpretations. Keeping the above nuances in mind, the present volume will use "historical Jesus" in this sense. Some discussions contrast the "Jesus of history" and "Christ of faith," but using these phrases uncritically tends to suggest that each is a known datum that can be contrasted with the other, and that one, the "Jesus of history," is a matter of objective fact, while the "Christ of faith" is (only) subjective belief. The matter is much more complex. So also, the "pre-Easter Jesus" is often contrasted with the "post-Easter Christ" as a general distinction between the Jesus who actually lived about 30 CE and Jesus as he was interpreted by later Christians as their risen Lord. The attempt to identify and construct the historical Jesus has extended through several phases.

8.2 Phases of the "Quest of the Historical Jesus"

1. *PRE-QUEST AND "FIRST NAIVETÉ."* WHAT became known as the quest of the historical Jesus is a relatively modern, post-Enlightenment phenomenon. From the first to the eighteenth century, the Gospels were read as though they were transparent windows through which the reader looked to see Jesus as he actually was. The idea of distinguishing between the 30 CE Jesus of history and the 70–120 CE Jesus of the Gospels hardly occurred to anyone. The reader entered into the story world of each Gospel without distinguishing it from the historical world of Jesus. Of course, discrepancies between the Gospels were noticed, but it was assumed that they could be harmonized, and that each Gospel simply reported the story of Jesus as it actually occurred. Such an uncritical, precritical reading has been called, without patronizing or condescension, *first naiveté* (see §5.1.4 above). Historical critical study of the Bible posed severe challenges to this way of reading.

2. *The Old Quest.* The first full-scale effort to recover the historical Jesus was made by H. M. S. Reimarus, whose lengthy manuscript was published in 1778 after the author's death, at first without revealing his name.[2] Reimarus made an absolute distinction between Jesus' own intention and that of his disciples after his death. Jesus had intended to found the kingdom of God by military power. After his execution by the Romans, his disciples stole the body, claimed God had raised him from the dead, and founded a new religion. Reimarus was posthumously attacked by the orthodox, and his work hardly convinced anyone, but his new approach had driven a wedge between the historical Jesus and the New Testament's pictures of Jesus. The awareness of this gap now called for historical studies that would show what sort of continuity or discontinuity existed between the Jesus of 30 CE and the later Christian portrayals. The nineteenth century saw a large variety of such efforts, by believer and nonbeliever alike, portraying Jesus in various guises: the rationalist teacher of an ethical ideal, a Jewish Zealot freedom fighter, a romantic Zorba-like lover of

2. See recent English translations: Hermann Samuel Reimarus and George Wesley Buchanan, *The Goal of Jesus and his Disciples*, trans. George Wesley Buchanan (Leiden: Brill, 1970); Charles H. Talbert, ed., *Reimarus: Fragments*, trans. Ralph S. Fraser, LJS 1 (Philadelphia: Fortress Press, 1970).

nature who celebrated life, a member of a secret Jewish cult, a good Pharisee who debated with other teachers, and numerous other constructions. The history of this study was chronicled by Albert Schweitzer in 1906 in a large volume entitled *Vom Reimarus zu Wrede: Eine Geschichte der Leben-Jesu-Forschung* (From Reimarus to Wrede: A History of Research on the Life of Jesus). The English translation of 1910 bore the title *The Quest of the Historical Jesus*, and the label "quest" became attached to the whole project of Jesus research.

As an aspect of nineteenth-century liberal Christianity's effort to interpret the Christian faith in terms of the modern world, something of a consensus on what the historical Jesus was really like had been attained: a teacher of idealistic ethics whose essential message was "the fatherhood of God and the brotherhood of man," the commandment of love, and the infinite value of the human soul. Jesus did not preach about himself but about God and his kingdom; it was the early church, after Easter, that focused its message on Jesus himself. Apocalyptic eschatology and miracles were mostly later Christian accretions to the tradition that could be stripped away to reveal the real Jesus. After a "Galilean springtime" in which his message was well received, Jesus journeyed to Jerusalem to confront the religious establishment with his message. He was killed, but his message lives on in the lives of his followers, who, with the intrusion of many new elements, became the church.

Schweitzer showed that the liberal construction, like the other nineteenth-century efforts to recover the historical Jesus, was without historical foundation. Each scholar had created Jesus in his own image. For Schweitzer, the only two legitimate options available at the beginning of the twentieth century were that of William Wrede ("thoroughgoing skepticism") and his own proposal ("thoroughgoing eschatology"). Both Wrede and Schweitzer rejected the nineteenth-century "lives of Jesus," but for very different reasons. Wrede's principal work, *Das Messiasgeheimnis in den Evangelien* (*The Messianic Secret in the Gospels*),[3] argued that the editorial work of the Gospel writers, beginning with Mark, was so extensive that one could hardly discern the historical figure behind the theological imagery of the Gospels. Schweitzer argued that the historical Jesus was in fact only too clear, but had been avoided because the actual Jesus recovered by historical study could not be integrated into modern conceptions. Schweitzer had been persuaded by the revolutionary study of Johannes Weiss, who argued that Jesus did not teach idealistic truths about an inward spiritual kingdom of the heart but saw himself as the herald of the apocalyptic kingdom that would soon break in from heaven and transform the world.[4] Historical study revealed Jesus to be an eschatological prophet who believed he was the Messiah designate, whose ultimate role in human history would soon become visible to all at the coming of the apocalyptic kingdom of God, when Jesus would be identified with the heavenly Son of Man. For Schweitzer, Jesus' radical ethic was intended to be obeyed literally, but only as an "interim ethic" that could be strictly followed only in the brief time between his preaching and the approaching end. When the end did not appear as expected, Jesus went to Jerusalem to force God's hand by suffering the torments of the "messianic woes" himself, saving his people from them, and thus clearing away the last obstacle to God's eschatological intervention. The kingdom did not come, and Jesus died in despair. Such a historical Jesus was both mistaken and irrelevant; this Jesus could not be translated into modern categories. Schweitzer himself adopted a kind of Christ mysticism; it is not the historical Jesus or the Jesus of the

3. Not translated into English until 1971, William Wrede, *The Messianic Secret*, trans. James C. G. Greig, Library of Theological Translations (London: James Clarke, 1971).

4. The first German edition of 1892 was a small volume of sixty-five pages. The second, expanded edition of 1900 was first translated into English in 1971: Johannes Weiss, *Jesus' Proclamation of the Kingdom of God*, trans. Richard H. Hiers and David Larrimore Holland, LJS (Philadelphia: Fortress Press, 1971).

New Testament who can be Lord and Savior to modern human beings, but the "spirit of Jesus" that can still call people to heroic discipleship. Wrede and Schweitzer, in their different ways, had together effectively ended the quest for the historical Jesus.

3. *No quest.* While some scholars continued along the lines of the old quest, attempting to preserve confidence in a historical Jesus who could be the foundation of the church's faith (or show that it was a colossal mistake), most twentieth-century New Testament scholarship in the period between the two world wars abandoned the effort to recover the historical Jesus. This move was encouraged by three further developments: (a) World War I had brought an end to the optimistic and idealistic liberal Christianity of the nineteenth century for which the liberal lives of Jesus had served as model. (b) The work of form criticism (see below §19.3), studying the individual units of tradition from which the Synoptic Gospels are composed, showed that their arrangement is the result of the editorial work of the Gospel writers and that their content often reflects the *Sitz im Leben* (setting in life) of the early church. Thus neither the outline of the Gospel story nor the content of the material reflects the life of Jesus directly. This means it is very difficult to excavate beneath the Gospels and discover "what really happened" in the life of Jesus. (c) Dialectical theology (neo-orthodoxy), the influential theology that replaced liberalism as the dominant theological model in much of Protestantism, had little interest in the historical Jesus behind the Gospels. This theology was based on the kerygmatic message about Jesus of the New Testament and tended to consider efforts to recover a historical Jesus as an illegitimate quest for historical data as the basis or support for faith. This kind of kerygmatic theology was represented in different ways by, for example, Karl Barth, Rudolf Bultmann, and Paul Tillich. In this view, faith is generated by encountering the Word of God mediated by biblical preaching, not by the probabilities and uncertainties of historical research. As expressed by Bultmann, the earlier quest was both historically impossible and theologically illegitimate. This does not mean that scholars of this era believed that nothing reliable could be known about Jesus. Bultmann himself wrote a substantial Jesus book, but it was nothing like the old liberal lives of Jesus.[5]

4. *New Quest.* A famous 1953 essay by Ernst Käsemann, himself a prominent member of the "Bultmann school," argued that Christian theology could not live indefinitely if severed from its roots in the historical Jesus. While there could be no return to the methods and goals of the nineteenth-century quest, it is both historically possible and theologically legitimate—even necessary—to explore what can be known about Jesus as he really was. While Christian faith cannot be proven by the ever-changing results of historical study, such study can never be irrelevant for a faith that is based not on an idea or ideal, but on a historical event. A "New Quest of the Historical Jesus" was launched, mostly by members of the Bultmann school who wanted to show historical continuity (not identity) between the message of Jesus and the message of the early church. The most significant product of the New Quest was Günther Bornkamm's *Jesus of Nazareth*, considered by many scholars of the 1960s and 1970s as the best portrayal of Jesus and his message. Already Bultmann had argued that, while Jesus did not make messianic claims for himself, as he announces the immediate approach of the kingdom of God, "his call to decision implies a Christology."[6] The New Quest sought to expand this Bultmannian approach, attempting to provide a more substantial base in the life and message of Jesus for the later church's more explicit theology. As dialectical theology waned as the

5. Rudolf Bultmann, *Jesus and the Word*, trans. Louise Pettibone Smith and Erminie Huntress Lantero (New York: Scribner, 1958).
6. Rudolf Bultmann, *Theology of the New Testament*, trans. Kendrick Grobel, 2 vols. (New York: Scribner, 1951), 1:43.

dominant theological paradigm, the Jesus of the New Quest declined with it.

5. *Third Quest.* The recent phase of Jesus research, begun in the 1980s in North America and the United Kingdom, has generated much interest in both academy and church, as well as within the general public. While the New Quest was closely bound up with a particular theological perspective, prominent especially in Germany, the Third Quest has a broader scope and wider range of goals, not consistently related to one theological program, and sometimes claims to be explicitly atheological or antitheological. This resurgence of interest in the historical Jesus has been characterized by four features: (a) The Third Quest tends to utilize a wide range of sources extending beyond the canonical New Testament. The *Sayings Source Q* has been analyzed more carefully, with some scholars arguing for an early wisdom stratum devoid of eschatology and pointing to a noneschatological Jesus. The *Dead Sea Scrolls* contain nothing about Jesus, but have thrown new light on the world in which Jesus lived. *Noncanonical Gospels*, known for some time, have been reevaluated by some scholars, who argue that some of them, particularly the earliest strata of the *Gospel of Thomas* and the *Gospel of Peter*, preserve more accurate representations of Jesus than the canonical Gospels. (b) Alongside theology, sometimes with the claim to be nontheological, the perspectives and methods of literary criticism and the social sciences have been brought to bear on Jesus research. This in part reflects the shifting of the center of gravity of Jesus study from theological seminaries to secular departments of religion and history. (c) The Third Quest has generally emphasized the Jewishness of Jesus. Previous research had frequently contrasted Jesus with his Jewish context, sometimes using Judaism as a foil for Jesus or Christianity. The *criterion of dissimilarity*, which considered material to be from the pre-Easter Jesus of history if it did not fit either in Judaism or Christianity, was often used in the New Quest. This criterion has mostly been replaced by the *criterion of plausibility*—authentic material must plausibly fit within Judaism and present Jesus as a figure from whom the Christian faith could develop. (d) The Third Quest has become an umbrella term for a scholarly movement already disintegrating. It has generated a broad range of disparate pictures of Jesus, among which may be listed the *Hellenistic Cynic sage* who subverts conventional wisdom, with no religious or political program (Burton L. Mack); the *Jewish Cynic peasant* who opposed the Roman Empire and championed the poor (John Dominic Crossan); a *Jewish "spirit person,"* a social prophet and subversive sage attempting to replace the Jewish purity system (Marcus Borg); *egalitarian prophet of feminine Wisdom* who understood himself as child and spokesperson of Divine Sophia, challenging patriarchal power structures and founding an egalitarian community in which women were the primary leaders (Elisabeth Schüssler Fiorenza); *eschatological prophet of the present and coming kingdom of God* (John P. Meier and several others); *prophet of imminent restoration eschatology*, announcing the regathering of the twelve tribes of Israel and a new or renewed temple that would form the center of a new religious and social order on an eschatological plane (E. P. Sanders; differently, N. T. Wright).

8.3 A Summary Sketch of What We Can Know about the Historical Jesus

THE FOLLOWING LIST IS PROVIDED AS A brief guide to the student who has appropriated an informed impression of Second Temple Judaism and wonders what sort of thumbnail sketch of the life and message of Jesus can be reliably presented before proceeding to the study of the early church and the New Testament writings. To be sure, Jesus was a *complex* and *dynamic* figure who cannot be summarized in a list. The following catalogue of key features is no substitute for the intricate interplay of pictures of

FIGURE 15: Sepphoris, a Hellenistic city near Jesus' hometown of Nazareth, has recently been excavated. USED BY PERMISSION OF DAVID PADFIELD.

Jesus within and between the Gospels. Here I will not present evidence and arguments for the validity of the various points of my summary, or dialogue with scholars advocating other views or emphases. This information can be found in the sources devoted explicitly to the quest of the historical Jesus listed at the end of this chapter, and the bibliography they provide.

1. *Jesus existed.* Today no responsible historian doubts the existence of Jesus as a historical figure. It is certain that the man Jesus was born and lived in Palestine in the first part of the first century of the common era, and was killed in Jerusalem about 30 CE.

2. *Jesus grew up in Galilee in a pious family of modest means.* Jesus' family was of the tribe of Judah and of Davidic descent. He had four brothers and at least two sisters. Jesus grew up in the village of Nazareth, two hours' walk from the Hellenistic city of Sepphoris (see fig. 15), but there is no indication that he ever visited it. It is not clear whether he attended a local school; his father taught him the Scripture and traditions of Judaism. Jesus was at home among the vast majority of Galileans, who were pious Jews, not lax in their practice, attending the festivals in Jerusalem.

During Jesus' whole life, Galilee was under the rule of Herod Antipas, with Rome as the power behind the throne. Though not officially recognized as a king by Rome, Herod was locally considered the king. In contrast to Judea, which had been a Roman province since 6 CE, there were no Roman soldiers or tax collectors in Galilee. While some revolutionary sentiment smoldered beneath the surface, Jesus grew up and conducted his mission in a context of relative peace and stability. In typical Jewish fashion, he was taught a trade by his father. Τέκτων (*tektōn*), usually translated *carpenter*, could also refer to construction workers in general. He was by no means wealthy, but there is no reason to exaggerate his poverty.

3. *Jesus was a Jew, though his place on the spectrum of Judaism is unclear.* He was clearly no Sadducee. Though a few scholars have attempted to present him as a Zealot (an anachronism in any case) or Essene, their arguments have been unconvincing. Jesus' belief in the resurrection, angels, demons, and his affinities with

apocalyptic thought means that theologically he stood close to the Pharisees on some issues—hence his conflicts were especially with this group. He was certainly not a member of the Pharisee party. He rejected their understanding of ritual purity as applied to Israel as God's holy people, the Sabbath, and the food laws, and their understanding of oral tradition that legitimated the purity system. Jesus was a Jew, but, like the vast majority of first-century Palestinian Jews, he did not belong to a particular group.

4. *Jesus was baptized by John the Baptist and was associated with John's movement for a while.* About 28 CE Jesus left his home and journeyed south to be baptized by John, never to return to his village life as a carpenter. He may have experienced some sort of prophetic call in association with his baptism; his life was never to be the same. Like some others, Jesus may have remained with John for a while and considered himself John's disciple in a special sense. He came to regard John as the greatest among the prophets, unsurpassed by any human being (Matt 11:7–11). It is not clear whether Jesus began his own mission of preaching while John was still alive, or whether it was John's violent death that triggered the beginning of Jesus' independent work (cf. the conflicting pictures of, e.g., Mark 1:14–15 and John 1:19–3:30).

John the Baptist is the one person who had the greatest single influence on Jesus' own mission and message. Though Jesus' message shifted the focus and emphasis of John's message of judgment, he retained John's apocalyptic framework, including his conviction that the end of the present age was near. The principal difference between Jesus' and John's understanding of the impending act of God is their respective understandings of where they stood on God's eschatological timetable. John stood immediately before the coming end ("five minutes to twelve"). For Jesus, the expected future is already beginning in his preaching and acting ("it is striking twelve"). Jesus did not abandon John's message of judgment, but shifted the focus to the mercy of God that is already available and present in Jesus' own mission.

5. *Jesus called disciples to share his mission.* Jewish teachers and rabbis had disciples, students who applied to follow a revered teacher. Jesus, on the other hand, took the initiative, analogous to God's calling the Israelite prophets. Multitudes responded positively to Jesus' message and followed him in some sense, but remained at home at their normal work. Within this larger circle was a particular group who followed him in the literal sense, leaving family, work, and property to become itinerant messengers with Jesus. Scandalously in that setting, this number included women, as well as people of questionable associations such as Levi the publican. Jesus and his entourage traveled from village to village. He sometimes sent disciples on mission trips. Paradoxically, Jesus both called people to radical obedience *and* celebrated table fellowship with all sorts of disreputable people.

Within this inner group was a still narrower circle, the Twelve. The formation of the Twelve was a symbolic prophetic act, the proleptic reconstitution of eschatological Israel. Jesus announced that the time of exile was over, that the time of the eschatological regathering of the people of Israel, the Grand Homecoming, was about to take place. The choice of twelve, instead of eleven with himself as the twelfth, shows that he saw himself as the creator of the community he was calling into being, not a part of it. Choosing twelve is an unmistakable indication that he had no intention of separating his group from Israel as an independent, discontinuous sect. The Twelve would have leadership roles in the restored people of Israel (Matt 19:28; Luke 22:30). Thus Jesus did not found a church, a new religion, or even a movement in the conventional modern sense. The community of disciples he called together around himself was the nucleus of what would become the church after his death. He spoke of this community as a new family that took priority even over their families of flesh and blood, and he gave them a ritual prayer, a covenantal meal, and a job. During the (brief) interval after his death but before the end, they were to engage in mission. Jesus' call to decision implied an ecclesiology.

6. *Jesus functioned as a teacher and preacher.* He was called "rabbi," but this was an informal title. Jesus had no rabbinic training or ordination, which did not yet exist in an official sense. He spoke with authority, but his authority was the direct authority of a prophet, not derived from tradition or institutional status. Jesus' teaching brought him into disputes and conflicts with other religious teachers, especially the Pharisees. Jesus regarded the Torah as from God and did not set it aside or reject it, but he interpreted it with sovereign freedom. His stance toward the Torah was paradoxical and unsystematic. Ethically, his teaching radicalized the Torah, calling for even stricter obedience to its intent; ritually, he relaxed its stipulations in view of the present-and-coming kingdom.

The double commandment of love for God and neighbor was central in Jesus' teaching about the will of God. Jesus renounced violence and retaliation, taught and lived out the universal and unconditional love of God, without conditions and without boundaries. Jesus never left the land of Israel, and conducted no mission to Gentiles in or outside the land. But his proclamation of the boundless love of God, his acceptance of outcasts and affirmation of Samaritans, his affirmation that God justifies and accepts sinners, the absence of the doctrine of the election of Israel from his core preaching—all these provided points of contact within his ministry for the later Gentile mission of the church.

7. *Jesus' message and ministry was entirely focused on the present-and-coming kingdom of God.* "Kingdom" (מַלְכוּת *malkuth*, βασιλεία *basileia*) can be understood and translated either in the dynamic sense of "reign," "rule," "exercising kingly power" or in the territorial sense of "kingdom," "realm." The English word "dominion" has something of the same twofold aspect. "The reigning presence of God"[7] captures both the dynamism and personal dimension of the phrase, which is about Someone, not an abstraction or principle. In the phrase "kingdom of God," "kingdom" means primarily "rulership," God-acting-as-king, the act of ruling, not the territory over which God rules. "Kingdom of heaven," used only by Matthew in the New Testament, substitutes "heaven" for "God" for reverential reasons, and means exactly the same as "kingdom of God." Traditional adoption of Matthew's terminology has often misunderstood it as referring to a place, "heaven," and encouraged the false idea that Jesus' message was primarily about "going to heaven."

Jesus was not the first to speak of the kingdom of God. Both the Jewish Scriptures and various streams of Second Temple Judaism had used the concept and language of God as king: the present king who rules the universe, the king over his own people who were called to take upon themselves the "yoke of the kingdom" by obeying God's revealed will in the Torah, the king who would act in the future to establish justice and make his legitimate kingship known to all the world. The kingdom was not a "concept" but a *symbol*—a tensive symbol that evoked the mythical drama of God the Creator who has been active in history to preserve his people, and who will soon act definitively at the denouement of history to defeat the powers that have held the world captive and reassert his rule over the rebellious creation.[8]

Jesus was the first to make the kingdom of God the focus of his life, message, and mission in a distinctive way. There is a sense in which the whole of Jesus' life can be comprehended under this one rubric. The distinctive aspects of the kingdom of God as proclaimed and lived out by Jesus may be summarized as follows:

a. *Theocentric.* Jesus saw himself having a unique role in God's eschatological plan that was rapidly coming to fulfillment, but he did not proclaim himself. The kingdom is God's kingdom, not Jesus'.

7. Francis J. Moloney, *The Gospel of Mark: A Commentary* (Peabody, MA: Hendrickson, 2002), 49 and passim, so translates ἡ βασιλεία τοῦ θεοῦ, *hē basileia tou theou.*

8. For elaboration of tensive vs. steno-symbols, see M. Eugene Boring, "The Kingdom of God in Mark," in *The Kingdom of God in 20th-Century Interpretation*, ed. Wendell Willis (Peabody, MA: Hendrickson, 1987), 131–46.

b. *Not yet/already*. Jesus expected the soon coming of God's eschatological kingdom, living in the reality of the dawning new age himself and calling others to share this vision of reality and this life. There is an ineradicable future element to Jesus' proclamation of the kingdom, as illustrated in the petition in the Lord's Prayer, "thy kingdom come" (Matt 6:10), the "has come near" (but not yet arrived) of Mark 1:15, the not-yet-fulfilled future expectation of many parables, the crisis and judgment still to come (e.g., Mark 13:28–29; Matt 7:24–27; 25:1–11), the dramatic reversal that will occur at the eschaton but has clearly not yet occurred (e.g., Luke 6:20–23). Jesus did not spell out the details and schedule of the coming end in the style of some apocalyptic visionaries, but he does have some apocalyptic traits: he expects the ultimate act of God to include the fulfillment of Israel's hopes for a regathered and reunited people of God, the coming of the Son of Man, the resurrection of the dead and the Last Judgment, and the transformation/restoration of this world to be the world as God created it to be. This new world does not mean the destruction of the present space-time universe, but neither is it merely a matter of social revolution. While Jesus' hope for the kingdom was very this-worldly—"thy will be done *on earth*"—it involves a transformation of the world as we know it. The kingdom of God will bring justice and shalom to humanity, but, even more fundamentally, it will be the vindication of God. God's name (=God's reality), presently trivialized, besmirched and abused, will be hallowed. God will be holy and just, and will be seen to be so. Jesus expected this grand consummation of God's purpose for history, the kingdom of God, to come soon—so soon that its presence and power were already active.

It is also undeniable that Jesus proclaimed and lived out the present experience of the kingdom, which was not only a matter of future hope. While the kingdom has (only) come near, the time is (already) fulfilled (Mark 1:15). His disciples already see what the prophets had only hoped for (Matt 13:16–17; cf. 12:41–42). That people are being healed, demons are being cast out, and the poor have good news preached to them means the kingdom is already present in power (Matt 12:28; cf. 11:4–6). The not yet/already dynamic of the kingdom should not be quantified, as though Jesus preached that the kingdom was "partly" present and "partly" to come. A better analogy that has become traditional in Jesus research is that of the *dawn*: Jesus lives in the dawn of the kingdom: it is not yet daylight, but the night is already passing away, and people are called to orient their lives to the new day that is already dawning, rather than to the darkness that is already vanishing.

c. *Alternative empire*. The term commonly translated "kingdom" (βασιλεία) is the same word translated "empire." To speak of the present and coming kingdom of God is to proclaim an alternative to the existing power structure. Jesus did not directly challenge the Roman Empire, but his life and message presented a clear alternative picture of how life and the world might be ordered that could be ignored by neither friends nor foes.

d. *Salvific miracles*. "What really happened"—whether Jesus "really worked miracles," that is, whether the transcendent power of God appeared in history and was actually at work in Jesus' mission—is something that the historian, qua historian, cannot answer. But all historians acknowledge that Jesus was believed to work miracles, that sick and demonized people came to him and went away whole. Even Josephus's brief summary calls Jesus "a doer of startling deeds" (παραδόξων ἔργων ποιητής, *paradoxōn ergōn poiētēs*, Josephus, *Ant.* 18.3). Jesus' exorcisms and other powerful deeds were not a separate aspect of his mission but a dimension of his experience of the kingdom. While miracle workers were common in the ancient world, Jesus' powerful saving acts were not merely an instance of a general phenomenon.

More miracles are attributed to Jesus than to any other ancient figure, but the difference is not merely quantitative. Jesus was distinctive in that he placed his miraculous activity in the comprehensive context of the inbreaking of God's kingdom. Jesus' miracles should not be treated as a separate category, but in integral relation to his proclamation of the kingdom, his parables, his table fellowship. Jesus' exorcisms and healings were not merely the release from bondage of a few tormented individuals but the battle line on which the power of God was overcoming the power of Satan. Jesus' real enemy was not Rome or the religious establishment, but the ultimate power of evil that had usurped God's creation and victimized the world, including Rome and the religious authorities.

e. *Compassion and acceptance.* Jesus' message and ministry were expressions of radical inclusiveness. Like the Cynics, he paid little attention to normal social and ritual boundaries. He included women and children in a way shocking to people of conventional sensibilities. He associated with those normally excluded from the people of God—the leprous, those sick with defiling diseases or bleeding that made them ritually unclean, the "publicans and sinners" regarded as defiling the holy people and impeding the final coming of God's kingdom. Jesus touched them, ate with them, celebrated with them the presence of God's kingdom.

Unlike that of the Cynics, Jesus' inclusiveness was not a matter of philosophical truth or his personal ideological understanding of tolerance and acceptance, as opposed to racism and bigotry. Jesus' inclusive table fellowship was an experiential acting out of God's acceptance in the here and now, an inclusiveness integral to God's character and coming kingdom. It was a matter of good news about an event, not good advice based on a theory.

f. *Parables.* Jesus' proclamation of the kingdom was indirect. He never explains what the kingdom is, never presents a list of principles that define the nature of the kingdom. He mediates the reality of the kingdom by telling stories, a particular kind of stories. Jesus' stories are neither illustrations of general principles nor allegories of Christian doctrine—though they were later understood as such. The best-known definition of Jesus' parables is that of C. H. Dodd:

"At its simplest a parable is a metaphor or simile drawn from nature or common life, arresting the hearer by its vividness or strangeness, and leaving the mind in sufficient doubt about its precise application to tease it into active thought."[9]

The parable begins as a narrative set in this world, the everyday world of common experience. It is not a fable in which foxes talk or a mythical story about angels and demons, nor is it a specifically religious story; almost all the parables have a secular plot about ordinary things. The story draws the hearer-readers in, then takes an imperceptibly strange turn, presenting the world in a way that challenges conventional, commonsense wisdom. The parable does not make its "point" directly, but "teases" the mind into active thought. Hearer-readers must decide whether to remain spectators or to participate in the story, that is, to take a stand. Jesus' parables were—and are—bothersome, for those who hear them must decide whether to stay in their conventional everyday world or enter into the new world opened up by the parable.

The parables are not illustrations of a manageable "point" that can then be integrated into the hearer's everyday world. Rather, they threaten and overturn that world. Parables strike softly at the core of our secure world, the narrative world that all human beings necessarily create to make sense of our lives. Parable subverts world, indirectly threatening it, undermining it from within and upsetting it before we are aware of what is going on. Each person has constructed or adopted an assumed (mythical) framework of truth by which we usually live, within which we evaluate everything else. When we receive new insights and data, we integrate them into the old paradigm, the framework of reference that makes sense of the world and our place within it. We are usually unaware of the framework

9. C. H. Dodd, *The Parables of the Kingdom* (New York: Scribner, 1961), 5.

itself; it is just "the way things are." We resist, at the deepest level, any tampering with the framework, and defend ourselves against direct attacks. Jesus' proclamation of the kingdom, the new reality of God's-world-already-breaking-in, *subverts* this world by telling stories. We enter into the narrative world of the parable, and then discover that we have a decision to make about what is real and what Reality requires of us. We often don't like this.

8. *Jesus' understanding of his own role in the plan of God.* Two particularly important issues are inherent in the question of Jesus' own self-understanding: his "messianic consciousness" and his understanding of his death.

a. Messianic self-designations? Shortly after the Easter events, the early church used various titles to express Jesus' significance (e.g., Christ, Lord, Son of God, Son of Man; see above §7.6.3). Jesus' own use of such designations, and/or his response to others' presumed use of such titles in speaking to or about him, remains uncertain. His message was focused on God and God's kingdom; his mission was not an effort to get people to believe particular things about himself, to "become Christians," or to confess faith in *him*. This did indeed occur in the Christian community after Easter. It does seem clear, however, that Jesus attributed key significance to himself in God's redemptive act. The response to Jesus' message/person would be the criterion of acceptance or rejection in the judgment soon to come. We can clearly see the development and increased use of christological titles attributed to Jesus in the growth of the Gospel tradition (cf., e.g., Mark 8:27–30 and Matt 16:13–20). Whether the beginnings of such specific christological language were already present during the ministry of the historical Jesus continues to be a disputed point in Jesus research. It is not likely that Jesus used such titles as "Christ," "Lord," or "Son of God" explicitly with reference to himself, though enthusiastic followers may have used these titles for him. There is no scholarly consensus about Jesus' use of "Son of Man" terminology. This is the most common christological designation for Jesus in the Gospels. The designation is found in all streams of the Gospel tradition (Mark, Q, M, L, Matthew, Luke, John). The usages fall quite neatly into three groups, which do not overlap: the Son of Man who is present and acts with authority, the Son of Man who will suffer and die in Jerusalem, and the Son of Man who will come on the clouds at the end of history. It does seem that Jesus used the term in some way with reference to himself, in some way associating himself with God's eschatological representative through whom judgment and salvation will be effected. Since "Son of Man" is itself a teasingly ambiguous term that can mean "a human being," "a man such as I am," as well as the eschatological deliverer reflected in Daniel 7:13 and the Enoch tradition (see above §7.6.3), Jesus may have used the term indirectly and provocatively of himself, just as he spoke of the present-and-coming kingdom of God indirectly in parables.[10] This somewhat vague conclusion is the best that historians can presently do, perhaps because of the limitations of historical data and methods, perhaps because Jesus himself used such designations, if at all, in an ambiguous manner that called for the hearer's own decision. None of the traditional christological categories seemed entirely acceptable to him. In Eduard Schweizer's oft-quoted statement, Jesus was "The Man Who Fits No Formula."[11]

b. Jesus' understanding of his death. Early Christianity confronted the reality of Jesus' crucifixion retrospectively as a given and developed a variety of ways of expressing their faith that Jesus' death was not meaningless tragedy, but the saving act of God. Jesus confronted the reality of his coming death prospectively, not as a given, but as a destiny he could choose

10. Petr Pokorný and Ulrich Heckel, *Einleitung in das Neue Testament: Seine Literatur und Theologie im Überblick* (Tübingen: Mohr Siebeck, 2007), 408.

11. Eduard Schweizer, *Jesus*, trans. David E. Green (Macon, GA: Mercer University Press, 1987), 13. The German text "*der Mann, der alle Schemen sprengt*" might be translated "The man who explodes all categories."

or reject, and without specific theological meaning attached in advance. How did he understand it? *Two extremes of the spectrum of possibilities can be immediately dismissed: (1) Jesus saw no particular meaning in his death.* Jesus was unfortunately caught up in some disturbance in Jerusalem and executed by the Roman authorities as a trouble-maker. *(2) Jesus saw in advance all the details of his death, believed it was necessary for the salvation of the world, and gave his disciples detailed predictions of these events and their meaning. He then acted out his part in this pre-written drama of salvation.*

Any perception of Jesus' own understanding of the meaning of his death must see it in continuity with his life and mission. Jesus' life and death form a coherent whole. Jesus' view of himself as standing in the line of Israel's prophets, as their definitive climax and fulfillment, must have included the very real possibility that, like other faithful prophets, he would suffer and die in fulfilling his mission. It was a destiny he could have refused but chose to accept. He went to Jerusalem with full awareness of this reality.

Jesus' "Palm Sunday" procession into Jerusalem was a symbolic action like that of the Old Testament prophets, a very serious form of "street theater." So also his action in the temple was not a ritual "cleansing," but a symbolic act of "destruction" that brought the present temple to an end, in preparation for the final advent of God's kingdom. Jesus' words about the temple were brought up at his trial and were part of the case against him (Mark 14:58). Likewise, Jesus' last meal with his disciples was not only a continuation of the table fellowship that had characterized his ministry, but a symbolic meal to be repeated by his disciples, uniting them during the (brief) interval between his death and the coming of the kingdom. On the night before his death, Jesus knew that he would die before the full and final advent of God's kingdom and that his disciples would be left to carry on his mission. He did not despair but expected to be vindicated, and interpreted his death as part of the saving eschatological act of God. Jesus was arrested that same evening, and the next day was condemned and crucified.

9. *Jesus was crucified by the Roman provincial government.* The most certain historical fact about Jesus is that he was officially executed by the Roman authorities as a threat to Roman rule in the province of Judea. There are no extant records of his trial and execution in the Roman archives. Josephus's brief notice, though later edited by Christians, is widely accepted as having an original core something like the following:[12]

> At this time there appeared Jesus, a wise man. For he was a doer of startling deeds, a teacher of people who received the truth with pleasure. And he gained a following both among many Jews and among many of Greek origin. And when Pilate, because of an accusation made by the leading men among us, condemned him to the cross, those who had loved him previously did not cease to do so. And up to this very day the tribe of Christians (named after him) has not died out. (Ant. *18.63–64)*

In agreement with the Gospels, Josephus reports that it was not the Jewish people as a whole, but "the leading men among us" who initiated Jesus' arrest and turned Jesus over to the Roman governor for trial and execution. The Romans were responsible for the death of Jesus, but the Jewish leadership was involved. Why would the Jewish leaders be concerned to get Jesus out of the way, and why would the Romans cooperate and execute Jesus as a criminal, dangerous to the state? Another quotation from Josephus, this one in regard to John the Baptist, also throws light on the death of Jesus. Commenting on the defeat of Herod Antipas by the Nabatean king Aretas, Josephus writes:

12. As reconstructed in Dunn, *Jesus Remembered*, 141, which omits only the most obvious Christian additions. The final reference to "Christians" may also be an interpolation. For the unedited version, see the Loeb Classical Library edition, 9:49–51.

> To some of the Jews the destruction of Herod's army seemed to be divine vengeance, and certainly a just vengeance, for his treatment of John, surnamed the Baptist. For Herod had put him to death, though he was a good man and had exhorted the Jews to live righteous lives, to practice justice toward their fellows and piety towards God, and so doing to join in baptism. . . . When others too joined the crowds about him, because they were aroused to the highest degree by his sermons, Herod became alarmed. Eloquence that had so great an effect on mankind might lead to some form of sedition, for it looked as if they would be guided by John in everything they did. Herod decided therefore that it would be much better to strike first and be rid of him before his work led to an uprising, than to wait for an upheaval, get involved in a difficult situation, and see his mistake. (*Ant. 18.116–18*)

If this was the way John had been regarded and dealt with, it was even truer of the way Jesus was seen by both Jewish and Roman authorities. Jesus had been baptized by John, spoke highly of John, and to some extent continued his mission. He attracted great crowds. He had organized a parade into Jerusalem, a demonstration that somehow involved claims to kingship. He precipitated some sort of disturbance in the temple. While the Gospel accounts of Jesus' arrest and trial are influenced by later Christian interpretations concerned to show the divine meaning of his death, it requires little imagination to see that both Jewish and Roman leadership, responsible for law and order, especially in the volatile situation of the Passover festival, would decide that the better part of political valor was to eliminate a single potential terrorist before terrible things happened that would result in the death of many people, rather than later regret that they had not done so (see John 11:49–50). Both Roman and Jewish leaders knew Jesus was not guilty of being a revolutionary in the straightforward, criminal sense; but he *attracted crowds* who were not so nuanced in their understanding. The Romans were not the last imperial power to decide it is better to arrest, torture, and kill a few terrorist suspects in the name of national security than to let them continue their work and possibly cause the death of thousands.

What the historian, qua historian, can say about Jesus ends with his crucifixion by the Romans. But the story of Jesus did not end with his death. Within a few days, his small band of followers was convinced that God had raised him from the dead, that Jesus had appeared to them, and had charged them with a mission to the world. The resurrection as such is a transcendent event, a matter of faith, beyond the realm of historical research. Both the resurrection event and the resurrection faith of the disciples will be treated in the next section.

8.4 For Further Reading

Borg, Marcus. *Jesus: Uncovering the Life, Teachings, and Relevance of a Religious Revolutionary*. New York: HarperCollins, 2006.

Boring, M. Eugene. "The 'Third Quest' and the Apostolic Faith." *Interpretation* 50/4 (Oct. 1996): 341–54.

Bornkamm, Günther. *Jesus of Nazareth*. Translated by Irene and Fraser McLuskey and James M. Robinson. New York: Harper & Row, 1960.

Bultmann, Rudolf. *Jesus and the Word*. Translated by Louise Pettibone Smith and Erminie Huntress Lantero. New York: Scribner, 1958.

Crossan, John Dominic. *The Historical Jesus: The Life of a Mediterranean Jewish Peasant*. San Francisco: HarperSanFrancisco, 1991.

Dunn, James D. G. *Christianity in the Making*. Vol. 1, *Jesus Remembered*. Grand Rapids: Eerdmans, 2003.

Keck, Leander. *Who Is Jesus? History in the Perfect Tense*. Columbia: University of South Carolina Press, 2000.

Meier, John P. *A Marginal Jew: Rethinking the Historical Jesus*. Anchor Bible Reference Library. 4 vols. New York: Doubleday, 1991–2009.

Sanders, E. P. *The Historical Figure of Jesus*. New York: Penguin Books, 1993.

Schweitzer, Albert. *The Quest of the Historical Jesus: A Critical Study of Its Progress from Reimarus to Wrede*. Translated by W. Montgomery, John Bowden, J. R. Coates, et al. "First Complete" edition. Minneapolis: Fortress Press, 2000.

Theissen, Gerd, and Annette Merz. *The Historical Jesus: A Comprehensive Guide*. Minneapolis: Fortress Press, 1998.

Weiss, Johannes. *Jesus' Proclamation of the Kingdom of God*. Translated by Richard H. Hiers and David Larrimore Holland. Lives of Jesus Series. Philadelphia: Fortress Press, 1971.

Wright, N. T. *Jesus and the Victory of God*. Minneapolis: Fortress Press, 1996.

9
Jesus to Paul

9.1 The First Christian Generation, 30–70 CE

CHRISTIAN HISTORY BEGAN WITH A SMALL group of Jesus' followers in Jerusalem in 30 CE, shortly after the execution of Jesus. The first generation ended in 70 CE with the destruction of Jerusalem and the temple by the Roman armies. By this time, thousands of Jesus' followers were scattered across the empire, having formed churches in many of the major cities of the Mediterranean, including Rome, where they had suffered persecution under Nero in 64 CE. In 49 CE, Christians in Rome were not distinguishable from Jews and were forced to leave the city when Claudius expelled Jews from Rome (Acts 18:2). By 64 CE, Nero's police could identify Christians as a group distinct from Jews.

What had begun as a sect within Judaism had become a predominantly Gentile religion in tension with the Judaism from which it sprang. The decade of the 60s saw the death of several major leaders of the first generation, including Peter, Paul, and James the brother of Jesus. Second Temple Judaism came to a formal end with the destruction of the temple, and the "parting of the ways" between Christians and Jews received momentum from the catastrophe of 66–70, as both Jews and Christians solidified their identity as distinct groups.

The year 70 CE formed a watershed in the development of Christian writings. Beginning about 50 CE, the Pauline letters inaugurated the epistolary mode of confessing the faith in what became the canonical tradition. A new phase of Christian literature began about 70 CE with the Gospel of Mark, a new literary genre that inaugurated the second generation with the Gospel mode of confessing the faith. We may thus distinguish three phases:

— 30–50, Jesus to Paul, Jerusalem to Corinth; no Christian writings from this period are preserved.

— 50–70, Corinth to destruction of Jerusalem; the Pauline Aegean mission; the Pauline letters were written during this time.

— 70–120, the letter tradition continues, the Gospel tradition develops, other genres of Christian literature emerge.

9.2 The First Twenty Years: Jesus to Paul, Jerusalem to Corinth

THERE ARE TWO HISTORICALLY FIRM points: (1) Jesus is crucified by the Romans in Jerusalem about 30 CE. (2) Paul writes from Corinth to the church he had founded in Thessalonica, about 50 CE. There is a vast difference between these two scenes. In the first, a Jewish prophet is executed by the Romans, and his few followers are scattered. In the second, a Christian missionary who had never known the historical Jesus writes in Greek from a major Greek city to one of numerous new Christian congregations scattered about the Mediterranean, composed mostly of Gentiles. This letter, known to us in the New Testament as *1 Thessalonians*, is the earliest extant document of Christian literature (see §11.1 below). For a modern reader to open 1 Thessalonians is to step on a moving train that has been underway for some time. An understanding of the letter requires an awareness of what had happened in the twenty years since the death of Jesus.

9.2.1 Sources for This Period

If Christians wrote anything during the first twenty years of church history (as they almost certainly did), none of their writings have come down to us, except as they may be embedded in later documents. Any construction[1] of what happened in the life of the Christian community between 30 CE Jerusalem and 50 CE Corinth is a matter of inferences from secondary sources. We have both Christian and non-Christian sources.

Non-Christian Sources for Earliest Christianity

It is a surprise to many people to learn that there is only minimal reference to Jesus and early Christianity in non-Christian sources, and that the brief comments that have been preserved are all incidental and late. The earliest are from the end of the first century (Josephus) and early decades of the second century (Tacitus, Suetonius, Pliny the Younger). Paul is not mentioned in any secular source of the first two centuries. Josephus (*Ant.* 18.63–64) barely mentions Jesus, refers to Christians only once at most (see §8.3), and reports the execution of Jesus' brother and other Jews by the high priest Ananus in 62 on the charge that they were violators of the law, without indicating that James was the leader of the Jerusalem church.

Tacitus (*Annals* 15.44.2–5) reports that Nero blamed the great fire of 64 in Rome on the Christians and had them arrested and killed. Tacitus, no admirer of Nero, does not lament the persecution of Christians, whom he regards as merely another example of Oriental superstition. His report reveals that there was a substantial Christian population in Rome in the 60s and that Roman Christians were distinguishable from Jews by that date.

Suetonius (*Divus Claudius* 25.4) briefly mentions that Claudius expelled the Jews from Rome, apparently in 49 CE, because they were making disturbances at the instigation of a certain "Chrestus." This is probably his misunderstanding of problems caused in the synagogues of Rome by Christian Jews evangelizing in the name of Christ (*Chrestus*, a Greek name common among Romans, was pronounced the same as *Christos*=Christ).

Pliny the Younger (*Epistles* 10.96; for the text, see below §26.1.4), the newly arrived governor of Bithynia, finds that Christians in his jurisdiction have been accused as criminals but does not know how he should proceed. His letter to Hadrian and the emperor's response are illuminating on the legal and social status of Christians in the early second century.

It is revealing that, in all the vast literature of the Greco-Roman world, these four—and possibly a few other possible indirect allusions[2]—are the only references to Christians and

1. While there are events that are really "back there" prior to their memory and documentation in texts, there is no *history* until some human being selects, interprets, and constructs the connections between past events, thus constructing history. See especially Udo Schnelle, *Theology of the New Testament*, trans. M. Eugene Boring (Grand Rapids: Baker Academic, 2009), 26–33.

2. Cassius Dio, writing ca. 200 CE, reports that in 96 CE the emperor Domitian executed Flavius Cemens and his wife Flavia Domitilla on the charge of "atheism," related to their "Jewish ways," which may reflect their conversion to the Christian faith (67.14.1–3). In the early second century, Epictetus referred to the philosophy of "the Galileans," apparently meaning the Christians. None of these offer any solid data for reconstructing the history of earliest Christianity.

Christianity in the first hundred years after the death of Jesus. The earliest event referred to is the expulsion of Jews from Rome in 49 CE. There is thus no trace at all of Christianity's first twenty years outside the church's own writings. Although we have no direct Christian sources from this period, there are three types of secondary sources, all written later, from which a picture of this period can be constructed.

Christian Sources for the History of Earliest Christianity

Paul's Letters and Their Traditions

Although Paul's earliest letter was written in 50 CE, his letters sometimes refer directly to events in his own past or incidentally provide information valuable for constructing the history of the church in the years prior to 50 CE (e.g., Gal 1:11–2:14; 2 Cor 11:32–33). Paul's letters can be examined minutely for the *narrative world* they project, even when Paul is not consciously relaying material about earlier Christianity. Paul also sometimes explicitly cites materials he has received from earlier Christians, such as the eucharistic tradition of 1 Corinthians 11:23–26 and the creedal statement of 1 Corinthians 15:3–5. In addition, there are numerous passages that can be identified with more or less confidence in which Paul is citing or alluding to earlier Christian tradition (e.g., the hymn of Phil 2:6–11 and the creed of Rom 1:3–5). All such traditional materials can be used to fill in the picture of pre-Pauline Christianity.

The Gospels, Acts, and Their Sources

The Gospels, though written decades later than the 30–50 CE period, contain materials that not only go back to the pre-Easter life of Jesus, but also reflect the modifications and expansions of these materials during the earliest life of the church. A discussion of how these materials were handed on is found below in the introduction to the Gospels, §19.3. Here it is only important to note that critical study of the Gospels is an important resource for constructing the life of the earliest churches. Especially important is that collection of materials in the hypothetical source known to New Testament scholarship as Q. If Q existed, it is not only a valuable source for the message of the historical Jesus but provides the historian an indirect view into one group of Jesus' disciples in Palestine in the first generation after his death (see below Exc. 3.5).

Acts portrays the origin of the Christian community as a single story line, beginning in Jerusalem on the day of Pentecost fifty days after Jesus' crucifixion, through its expansion and conflicts in Jerusalem, Judea, and Syria, as it struggles to grow from a Jewish sect into a universal religion. However, Acts was written at or after the turn of the century, by someone who was not an eyewitness of the earlier history he recounts. The author had access to and included some earlier traditions, probably including written sources, but he views them through the lens of a later Christian generation, writing for the edification of his own time rather than to provide a comprehensive and accurate history of the earliest times. Acts is important for constructing the history of the Pauline mission but must be used with critical caution in writing the history of the early Christian community from Jesus to Paul. (For a more extensive discussion of the value and limitations of Acts as a historical source, see below §23.3.)

9.2.2 Jesus to Paul—Key Events

Resurrection

Historically, it is not possible to move directly from "the life and teaching of Jesus" to the earliest church. Jesus had not proclaimed himself or called for a confession of faith in himself; his proclamation was focused on the coming kingdom of God. The first Christians proclaimed (God's act in) Jesus and called for faith in him. *Something happened* to generate this transition from Jesus the proclaimer of the kingdom of God to Jesus the proclaimed. In the New Testament and Christian history, this "something" is called the resurrection.

Conceivably, there may have been some of Jesus' followers who did not know about, or did not believe, the message of the resurrection. One can imagine that there were those who, like John's disciples (or those of Martin Luther King Jr.) were inspired by Jesus' person, his cause, and/or his way of life and resolved to continue it. But if there were such followers of Jesus, they did not become part of the early church, and their writings, if there were such, did not find their way into the New Testament.

The resurrection of Jesus is central to Christian faith and the New Testament. That God raised Jesus from the dead is the implicit—and often explicit—presupposition of all the New Testament writings. The resurrection is thus in a different category altogether from, for example, Jesus' miraculous conception, which is never referred to again after the birth stories in Matthew and Luke; and Jesus' identity or saving significance is never related to or based on these stories. The resurrection is not merely another example of the stories of miracles Jesus had performed, not even his last and greatest. The resurrection is primarily a claim about *God*, so that "who raised Jesus from the dead" becomes the new, defining characteristic of God (e.g., 1 Thess 1:9–10; Gal 1:1; 2 Cor 4:14, Rom 4:24; 6:4; 8:11; 10:9; Eph 1:20; Col 2:12; 1 Pet 1:21).

This is not the place to attempt anything like a full-scale discussion of the resurrection (see *For Further Reading* below). Here I will merely list some major points necessary for understanding the New Testament affirmations of the resurrection of Jesus, without documenting all the nuances and alternatives to the view here presented.

— The resurrection was *an event*. The Christian faith did not begin with a great new idea, insight, ideal, or teaching, but with something that happened. The formation and continuation of the Christian community was not dogged determination on the part of the disciples to hold on to Jesus' ideals, but their response in faith to God's act in raising Jesus from the dead. From the beginning, Christian faith was not good advice, but good news.

— The event was understood as an act of God, not as Jesus' final accomplishment. The resurrection is the act of God for the Jesus who suffers the victimization of a truly human death and enters into the realm of death as powerless as any other human being. The early Christian faith in the resurrection was about God, not something extra about Jesus.

— The resurrection was a unique, transcendent event. If it happened, it was a unique act of God, impinging on this world, but not locatable in this world the way space-time events can be located. It is thus not the kind of event that, in itself, can be studied by historians. The resurrection is a matter of God's act perceived by faith. Historians cannot deal with such events, but only with those who believed them and the effects of their belief.

— From the very beginning, the event was an interpreted event. As the act of God, it could be perceived and appropriated only in terms of the conceptuality of those who believed it, concepts they already had. Though we can separate event and interpretation for purposes of discussion, in historical reality these two are inextricably interwoven. It is not possible that some of Jesus' followers first came to believe the event had happened, and then, as a second step, interpreted it in certain ways. The interpretation was built into the perception.

— The concept of resurrection was already present in Jewish faith when Jesus appeared, and was a commonplace in the theology of the Pharisees (e.g., Dan 12:2; Mark 12:18–27; John 11:17–24). Jewish faith in the resurrection was not a theory about the immortality of the human soul but a way of affirming the faithfulness of God when there appears to be no way in this world that God can vindicate his faithful people. Thus the affirmation that God had raised Jesus was not merely a claim that the disciples had recovered their idealism, or that something spectacular had happened to Jesus, but testimony to the act of God.

— The resurrection was perceived and interpreted in a (limited) variety of ways, all of them within the general framework of apocalyptic thought. Some streams of late Old Testament and early Jewish faith pictured God's victory at the end of history as involving the resurrection of the dead, God's final victory over the enemies of life, and the vindication of God's faithful people (see above §7.6). It is very important to see that for the early Christians, the resurrection was not merely a spectacular thing that God did for Jesus, but represented the leading edge of this eschatological event, the beginning of the new age. God raised Jesus from the dead as the "firstfruits" of the complete harvest that was soon to come (1 Cor 15:20–23). Thus resurrection faith is not merely believing that a dead body came back to life, or that the tomb was empty on Easter morning.

— Since the resurrection affirms the transcendent act of God, every expression of the resurrection carries the same problem of all God-talk: speaking of the otherworldly in this-worldly terms; that is, it involves the use of mythological language. To guard against misinterpretation, it is helpful to point out some things resurrection faith is not:

— Resurrection faith is not a belief in immortality, a belief that Jesus' "immortal soul" somehow "survived death."

— Resurrection faith is not merely the subjective experience of the powerful memory of Jesus living on in the hearts of his disciples, or the belief that Jesus still calls people to commit themselves to his cause. The resurrection is not only an experience that happened to the disciples; it happened to Jesus, prior to and apart from the disciples' experience, for which it was the generating cause.

— Resurrection faith has nothing to do with ghosts, channeling, séances, and various parapsychological phenomena.

— Resurrection faith is not a matter of resuscitation, a restoration to this-worldly life, like the amazing recoveries that have sometimes happened on the operating table.

— The resurrection faith did not originate by adapting the mythical ideas associated with the dying-and-rising fertility gods of antiquity, though the imagery associated with these myths could be used in expressing the Christian faith.

— It was Jesus who was resurrected by God. The issue was not "whether there is life after death," but the faithfulness of God to the life Jesus had lived. It was the person of Jesus that was raised up,[3] not merely his teachings or his cause. Jesus had embodied the will of God, had represented what a truly human life in service to God was intended to be. The institutions of this world, secular and sacred, had rejected this life in the most shameful and cruel way imaginable. The resurrection meant that God had vindicated and affirmed this life, this person, as the initial installment on God's re-creation of humanity and the world.

The resurrection can be affirmed, as in creeds and songs, without narrating or picturing it, that is, without claiming to conceptualize or express what is meant by the act of God in raising up Jesus. But when narrated, as in the stories of Easter morning found in the Gospels, the stories that express the Easter faith portray it with different chronologies, locations, and casts of characters. In Mark three women go to the tomb, and there are no appearances (16:1–8; [16:9–20 is a later addition]). In Matthew two women go to the tomb; Jesus appears to both and then later to all the apostles in Galilee. In Luke three named women go to the tomb

3. This is the point of New Testament declarations that Jesus' "body" was raised. In such statements σῶμα (*sōma*) refers to the person, the self, not to "flesh and blood" (see, e.g., 1 Cor. 15:35–50, esp. 15:50).

(plus other unnamed women), and there are no appearances to women. Jesus appears to two disciples (not apostles) on the road to Emmaus, who later learn that Jesus had already appeared offstage to Simon Peter; then Jesus appears to all the apostles in Jerusalem. All this is on Easter Sunday, and in Luke there are no Galilean appearances. In John, Jesus appears to Mary Magdalene alone on Easter Sunday morning, then to ten disciples (without Thomas) that evening, then to the eleven disciples one week later, all in Jerusalem. In the epilogue/appendix of John 21, Jesus then appears to seven disciples in Galilee. In Mark and Matthew, Jesus' first appearance to the disciples is in Galilee, with no room for Judean appearances (Mark 16:7; Matt 28:16–17); in Luke and John, Jesus appears to all the disciples (except Thomas) in Jerusalem on Easter Sunday.

— Stories of discovering the empty tomb are one way of expressing faith in the resurrection, but resurrection faith is not to be identified with faith in an empty tomb or with any particular way of conceptualizing the post-Easter body of Jesus. To emphasize that the Risen One transcends all human and earthly modes of reality, Paul makes no reference to an empty tomb, declares that the resurrection is not a matter of flesh and blood (1 Cor 15:35–57, esp. v. 50), and declares that wanting to know "how it happened" and "what kind of body" is involved is an expression of arrogant human foolishness (1 Cor 15:35–36). To emphasize that the resurrection really happened, that the risen Jesus was not a ghost, Luke portrays a "flesh and bone" Jesus who eats fish (Luke 24:36–43). These are only two modes of the NT's manifold witness to the resurrection. These different ways of conceptualizing and narrating the resurrection faith are not to be harmonized; each points beyond itself to the transcendent reality of God's act in raising Christ from the dead. Resurrection faith is not identical with affirming the historical factuality of any of the Gospels' resurrection stories. The story is the vehicle of the faith, but is not to be identified with it.

Emergence of the Christian Community—From Jesus Movement to Church

During the twenty years between the resurrection of Jesus and the writing of 1 Thessalonians, the *Jesus movement* became a *church*. For purposes of discussion in this context, both terms need to be defined. During his ministry, Jesus did not found a church or call people to become members of an institutionalized religious group. Neither did he found a movement in the modern sociological sense (e.g., labor movement, civil rights movement, antiwar movement, environmental movement, feminist movement).[4] These movements are focused on a cause, and the cause endures apart from the initial leader. Some contemporary interpreters have preferred "Jesus movement" as a secular alternative to "church," but Jesus founded neither in the modern sense. The only movement involved in Jesus' own terminology was a movement back to God ("repent"), which meant a movement in the direction of one's fellow human beings ("love your neighbor"). His language was "kingdom" and "discipleship." He was not dispensable to his movement. The religious and political authorities did not consider Jesus to have founded a movement independent of himself and did not pursue his followers after his death. He announced the coming kingdom of God that was already making itself known in his miracles, and called disciples to follow him.

When Jesus led his band of followers to Jerusalem, we do not know exactly what they were anticipating, but it was apparently some dramatic manifestation of the kingdom

4. Cf. Leander Keck, *Who Is Jesus? History in the Perfect Tense* (Columbia: University of South Carolina Press, 2000), 48–49. "Jesus movement" is not a recent coinage. Johannes Weiss and others used it early in the twentieth century (see, e.g., Johannes Weiss, *Earliest Christianity: A History of the Period A.D. 30–150*, trans. Frederick C. Grant, 2 vols. [New York: Harper, 1937, 1959], 14, 19, 45).

of God. Jesus' arrest and execution were the shattering of their hopes, and they fled back to Galilee (Mark 14:50; 16:7). There they experienced the appearances of the risen Jesus. The first appearance was to Peter (1 Cor 15:5), who then played the leading role in regathering and reconstituting the group of the Twelve (Mark 16:7; Luke 22:31–32; Acts 1). Some disciples soon made their way back to Jerusalem, probably with great apocalyptic excitement: the resurrection of Jesus meant that the grand eschatological drama that would bring in God's kingdom of justice and peace was already beginning, and they likely expected the consummation, and the return of Jesus, to take place in Jerusalem. There other disciples experienced the Easter revelation, including James the brother of Jesus, who had not been a disciple during Jesus' ministry (1 Cor 15:7; Mark 3:21; John 7:1–5).

There is much that we do not know about this earliest period, making it difficult to imagine the life of the nascent Christian community. How many disciples were there who made the move to (temporarily?) resettle in Jerusalem? How and where did they live, and with what means of support? How did they understand themselves, and how did they express their new understanding of Jesus, in the light of their resurrection faith? How were they organized, if at all? After numerous converts to the new movement were baptized, how were they instructed in the new faith? What were its essentials, and who did the instructing? Our only narrative of this period (Acts) was written two generations later, tends to picture the earliest days of Christianity in terms of the churches of its own time, and is not interested in providing answers to our historical curiosity. While we cannot write a detailed, chronological history of the first two decades of the life of the church, we can portray several key developments that occurred during this period as a whole, events and developments that were already shaping the life of the church by the time Paul wrote to the Thessalonians in 50 CE.

The Earliest Christian Confession and the Formation of the Earliest Christian Community

In the first few weeks after Jesus' death, his Galilean followers and new adherents in Judea formed a distinct religious community in Jerusalem, based on their conviction that God had raised up Jesus as the promised Messiah. We do not know the terminology in which the earliest Christian confession was made. Very early, he was confessed as "Christ" and "Son of Man." The church began as a particular group within Judaism, where faith was never thought of only as an individualistic personal relation to God; no Jew, then or now, thinks of God as "my personal savior" apart from the relation to the whole community of faith. It is modern Western society that conditions people to contrast a personal spirituality with "institutionalized religion." Jews thought of belonging to the people of God, established by God's saving acts, with a mission from God to this world.

How did the earliest believers in Jesus as the Messiah think of themselves, and how were they seen by their fellow Jews? Of one thing we may be sure: they did not understand themselves to be members of a new religion, belonging to the "church" in contrast to "Judaism." Like Jesus, the original disciples were all Palestinian, Aramaic-speaking Jews, and understood themselves as a special group within Judaism. They continued to worship in the temple, which became the focus of their own life, and observe the regular hours of prayer (Acts 2:46–3:1).

Like Pharisees, Sadducees, Essenes, and the disciples of John the Baptist, their fellow Jews would have seen them as a sect (αἵρεσις *hairesis*) within Judaism, but not necessarily with the negative overtones of this term in English. While continuing to attend the synagogues and to worship in the temple, these first disciples also formed distinctive small congregations that met in private homes. Like the Qumran Essenes, they saw themselves as the eschatologically renewed Israel, but—in contrast to Qumran—not as the true Israel in an exclusive sense. A rough analogy might be the formation of charismatic groups within mainline Protestant denominations, who continue to participate in the life of their local congregation and to think of themselves as loyal members of their denomination, but who also meet in small groups in people's homes to celebrate the renewed life of the Spirit they experience.

A central aspect of their new self-understanding was that the eschatological gift of the Spirit was powerfully present in their midst. The Holy Spirit, the spirit of prophecy, understood by some streams of Jewish tradition to have ceased in the time of Ezra, was expected to reappear in the final period of history. This Spirit, already active in the ministries of John the Baptist and Jesus, had now called the eschatological community into being. The church was not the project of perceptive disciples who saw in Jesus what the Jewish leaders had missed, not a "worthy cause" created by interested human beings concerned to continue Jesus' program. The initiative was from God's side. God had raised up Jesus and sent the Spirit. This awareness was accompanied and reinforced by signs, including especially the rebirth of prophecy, charismatic gifts of healing, and glossolalia—the latter a distinctively Gentile expression of the Spirit.

The rebirth of prophecy is especially significant. God had spoken directly to Israel through the prophets. Now Jesus as exalted Lord acts with divine authority, sending the Spirit and speaking through the mouths of prophets. This is an astonishing development. In the Old Testament and Jewish history, some figures are taken to heaven (Enoch, Elijah), but it is God alone who speaks through the prophets. In earliest Christianity, the *Spirit*-inspired prophets communicate the word of *God* as the exalted *Christ* speaks through them.[5] The risen Jesus not only appears in visions but speaks through his chosen prophets, assuming the role previously occupied by God alone. This explosion of charismatic phenomena in which the risen Lord speaks from heaven is related to the Easter phenomena, and provides a middle term between Jesus the pre-Easter proclaimer and the post-Easter Jesus proclaimed by the church: Jesus the self-proclaimed, who speaks from heaven through his prophets.[6]

What did they call themselves? The earliest community in Jerusalem did not use the term "Christians," which did not appear on the scene until Antioch in the 40s (according to Acts 11:26), as a label applied to the new group by outsiders. The term is not found in Paul but first begins to appear in literature at the end of the first century and the beginning of the second century.[7] Likewise, "disciples" is used in the Gospels and Acts, but nowhere else in the New Testament (strikingly absent in Paul!). The term seems to have been used during Jesus' ministry and reintroduced by Luke in Acts, but it does not seem to be a self-designation of the earliest church.

The earliest Christian community seems to have adopted a distinctive usage of Jewish nomenclature. (1) They referred to themselves as a/the "church," the same term used of the people of Israel in their Bible: קהל (*qahal*, congregation), often translated as ἐκκλησία (*ekklēsia*, assembly, church) in the LXX.[8] In this earliest

5. This modulation of the Spirit who speaks in the church into the voice of the risen Christ, which in turn modulates into the voice of God, is still seen in our one clear example of Christian prophecy in the New Testament, the book of Revelation (e.g., Rev. 2–3, where the message of the risen *Christ* is called "what the *Spirit* says to the churches," and all is considered the word of *God*). For elaboration, see M. Eugene Boring, "The Voice of Jesus in the Apocalypse of John," *Novum Testamentum* 34 (1992), and Boring, *Continuing Voice of Jesus*.

6. For a detailed argument, see "Christian Prophecy and the Origin of Christology," in M. Eugene Boring, *Sayings of the Risen Jesus: Christian Prophecy in the Synoptic Tradition*, SNTSMS 46 (Cambridge: Cambridge University Press, 1982), 239–50.

7. In the New Testament, only Acts 11:26; 26:28; 1 Pet 4:16. Then in Josephus (perhaps once, *Ant.* 18.64), Ignatius, Pliny the Younger, Tacitus, Suetonius.

8. קהל *qhl* is also translated as συναγωγή (*sunagōgē* synagogue). The New Testament authors make remarkably little use of "synagogue" as a Christian term (only Jas

period, "church" was not contrasted with Israel, but identified with it. In the Hellenistic world, ἐκκλησία (*ekklēsia*) was also used of the secular assembly of citizens that made political decisions for the city (Acts 19:39). Thus *ekklēsia*, "church," had overtones of both the continuing people of God one read about in the Scripture and the assembly to which Christians belonged that had an alternative vision of the political and social world. (2) They applied the biblical term ἅγιος (*hagios*, holy), used sparingly of Israel, to themselves as the holy community of the last days. As God is holy, so God called his people to be holy (e.g., Exod 19:6; Deut 7:6; often in the Holiness Code of Lev 17–26). Paul still uses this term when referring to the Jerusalem church (1 Cor 16:1; Rom 15:26), and often addresses the Christian communities he has founded as "saints," that is, the holy ones of the eschatological community. (3) The earliest Christians also probably referred to themselves as the people of the Way (Acts 9:2; 18:25–26; 19:9, 23; 22:4; 24:14, 22).

How and when did they worship, and what rituals did they celebrate? In Luke's picture of earliest Christianity (Acts 1–6), there is no temple polemic. Galilean disciples, or some of them, resettle in Jerusalem and are constantly in the temple, apparently in expectation of the eschatological events soon to transpire there. As observant Jews, the new Christian community continued to worship in temple and synagogue and to participate in Jewish rituals and festivals, including observance of the Sabbath (Saturday).

By the time the Pauline letters were written, churches were worshiping on the Lord's Day, the first day of the week (Sunday; see 1 Cor 16:2; Acts 20:7; Rev 1:10). While we have no documentation on the details of how the transition was made, we may readily imagine that when the Sabbath ended at dusk on Saturday, the community of believers in Jesus would make their way to their own gatherings in people's houses (see Acts 2:46–47), where they would worship with Christian songs and prayers (such as the Lord's Prayer and the sort of hymns and prayers found in the canticles of Luke 1–2). In Jewish reckoning in which the new day began at sunset, this late Saturday evening worship was on Sunday, the first day of the week (cf. Acts 20:7).

Like the disciples of John the Baptist, Jesus' followers had their distinctive form of prayer (cf. Luke 11:1–4). So also, the baptism of new believers was a distinct, public identification with the new community. During Jesus' ministry, he had preached and taught but had not established a distinct new community set apart by baptism.[9] By Paul's time, both baptism and the eucharistic meals were firmly established as Christian tradition and practice and could be assumed. Jesus had practiced a distinctive table fellowship that included notorious sinners (Mark 2:15–16; Luke 7:34) and had celebrated a solemn, festive Last Supper with his disciples (Mark 14:22–26 par.). This inclusive, festive table fellowship continued in the earliest church, with some variety in the ways it was understood theologically.

What structure and offices did they have? Luke pictures the church as from the beginning directed by the Twelve apostles resident in Jerusalem, who supervised not only the local congregation but the new mission churches in other cities (Acts 2:42; 4:32–37; 6:1–6; 8:1, 14–17; 9:26–28; 11:1–18). This idealized theological portrait of a united church ruled by apostolic authority from Jerusalem is not the whole picture. After the number of the Twelve is restored by choosing a successor for Judas and their number is listed, most of them are never mentioned again (Acts 1:12–26). Three of the disciples first

2:2). The earliest Christians apparently did not think of themselves as only a "Christian synagogue" in Judaism, analogous to other distinctive groups that did so describe themselves (see Acts 6:9).

9. John 4:1–3 locates baptism as a ritual already practiced during the ministry of Jesus, but is ambivalent about whether Jesus himself had baptized. The Synoptic Gospels know nothing of this. Luke–Acts portrays baptism as a new practice introduced in the earliest Jerusalem church, Acts 1:5; 2:38–41.

called by Jesus seem to have formed an inner circle: Peter, James, and John. Later, James the brother of Jesus, with Peter and John, constitute a three-person leadership group called the "Pillars" (Gal 2:9, playing a role in the renewed people of God analogous to Abraham, Isaac, and Jacob, sometimes called the "Pillars" of Israel).

According to Acts, at first Peter plays the leading role, but is later replaced by James (Acts 12:17; 15:13; 21:18; cf. Gal 1:19; 2:12). Historically, the respective leadership roles of Peter and James in the earliest days are far from clear; they may have been overlapping or competitive. "Elders" emerge in the Jerusalem church as leaders alongside the apostles, but how they were related to the apostles, Peter, and James is not clear (Acts 11:30; 15:6, 22–23). Parallel to these leaders from Palestinian Jewish Christianity, Luke also indicates that there were Greek-speaking Jewish Christians in Jerusalem who had their own structure (Acts 6:1–6; see below on the Hellenists). While Luke pictures these as a later and subordinate group of leaders established by apostolic initiative, the Seven of the Hellenists seem to have been parallel to the Twelve of the Hebrew (=Aramaic-speaking) Christians. In addition to this variety of official leadership, from the very beginning there were charismatic church leaders, inspired by the Spirit, who were not authorized by any institutional structure (Acts 2:17–18; 8:4–8, 39–40; 11:27–29; 13:1–3). Thus, by the time Paul writes 1 Thessalonians, the church, though understanding itself as one Christian community, was already struggling with issues about how to manifest this unity and carry on its mission.

Expansion of the Christian Community

Mission was inherent in the community's being from the beginning. Already in the pre-Easter ministry of Jesus, he had sent his disciples to proclaim the message of the kingdom of God. Being a disciple of Jesus was not an individual, private affair, but incorporation into the renewed people of God and participation in its mission. The church quickly expanded not only numerically but geographically and across cultural, religious, and ideological boundaries. By the time Paul wrote 1 Thessalonians, the church had spread from Jerusalem through parts of Syria and Asia Minor to Macedonia and Greece. Since Luke focuses exclusively on the church's western mission from Jerusalem to Rome and on Paul as the leading missionary in this movement, the modern reader tends to forget that the church expanded in other directions. There are incidental NT references, however, to numerous Christian communities outside the orbit of the Pauline mission. Only rarely giving us any details of how they got there, Acts mentions churches not only in Jerusalem and Judea, but in Lydda, Joppa, the Plain of Sharon, Caesarea (Acts 9 and 10), Samaria, and Galilee (Acts 8; 9:31; 15:3), Damascus (9:19); in the rest of the province of Syria, including the "Phoenician" cities, Antioch (11:20), Tyre (21:3–14), Sidon (27:3), Ptolemais (21:7); in Cyprus (11:20; 13:4–13) and Cilicia (Gal 1:21; Acts 9:30; 11:25). The Christian message seems already to have been received as far away as Cyrene (Acts 6:9; 11:20), and Christian leaders from Alexandria are mentioned (Acts 18:24–25). When Paul finally arrives in Italy, there are Christians already in Puteoli (Acts 28:13) as well as Rome itself.

This expansion was facilitated by the Pax Romana, the Roman peace that made transportation and communication possible throughout the empire. The Greek language had become the lingua franca for most of the Mediterranean world, so that Christian preachers could communicate their message in Greek wherever they were and be understood by most of the population of all social strata. The Jewish Diaspora had already responded to the longing of many Gentiles for a monotheistic faith with a high ethical standard and had unintentionally prepared the way for Christian preachers, providing a point of contact for their message that the Messiah expected by Judaism had come and that the promises of the Jewish Scriptures were being fulfilled.

Before proceeding, we must ponder what it meant that the Christian faith, born in the bosom of traditional Palestinian Judaism, now encounters the wider Hellenistic world and learns to conceptualize and express its faith in a radically different culture and language. Of course, Palestine itself was considerably Hellenized, and Christians did not first encounter Greek thought, language, and culture beyond the borders of Palestine. Diaspora Judaism already represented the extension of what had been Palestinian Judaism into the Hellenistic world, where it adopted and adapted Greek language and thought forms (cf. §9.2.2 below, "Hellenistic [Diaspora] Judaism"). Jesus himself never left the land of Israel; neither he nor his disciples conducted a mission to Gentiles. Jesus had certainly met individual Gentiles and Hellenized Jews, but he had launched no Gentile mission.[10] During his ministry he invited all Israel, but no Gentiles.

There were elements of continuity between Jesus' Palestinian mission and the Hellenistic mission of the post-Easter church.[11] His proclamation of the boundless love of God, his acceptance of outcasts and affirmation of Samaritans, the absence of the doctrine of the election of Israel from his core preaching—all these provided points of contact within his ministry for the later Gentile mission of the church.

In the Palestinian Jewish context, the mission of the earliest Christians was to proclaim the Christian faith to people who were already worshipers of the one true God, people who already had Scripture and tradition that taught them monotheism, the pattern of God's mighty acts in history, the covenant faith of the God of Israel, who required an ethical life in accord with the law of Moses. Many of these already hoped for a dramatic eschatological event that would establish God's kingly rule in this world—often involving a messianic savior figure (see above §7.6.3). Within this context, the mission of the earliest Christians was to convince their fellow Palestinian Jews that this hoped-for event had happened, that the Messiah had appeared in history as Jesus of Nazareth, who would shortly return in glory as the Son of Man to establish God's eternal kingdom. The original Jewish hearers of the Christian message were not asked to "convert" in the sense of leaving their ancestral faith, but—*as Jews*—to believe that God was acting to fulfill their Jewish hopes (Acts 28:20).

But when Christian missionaries move into the larger world, how is the Messiah to be proclaimed where a Messiah is not expected? Such Jewish terms as "kingdom of God," "Son of Man," "resurrection," and even "Christ" were hardly understandable in the Greco-Roman world outside Palestine, while much in Hellenistic culture was alien to the Palestinian Jewish tradition in which Christianity was born. *Unlike the situation in Jewish Palestine, in the wider Hellenistic world the early Christian missionaries were in fact calling for a conversion.* In Palestine the Jesus movement could appeal to Israel's tradition as common ground that brought certain practices within Israel under the judgment of the one God worshiped by both themselves and their hearers. In the wider world, the Christian movement appeared as a new religious group intruding as an alien element into the dominant religiocultural ethos of the Greco-Roman world. On pagan soil, the Christian message represented an exclusive, intolerant claim that was new to most hearers. But what did this mean? Must Gentiles first become monotheistic, Torah-observant Jews who are expecting a Messiah, so that the Messiah can be preached to them? Or can Christian faith be proclaimed to them in their terms, so that they can become

10. In the Matthean tradition, Jesus was remembered as explicitly forbidding the Gentile mission during his lifetime, so that it was only at the command of the risen Jesus that his disciples carried his message to the Gentiles (Matt 10:5; 28:16–20). Likewise in Luke–Acts, the command to go to all nations is first issued by the risen Lord (Luke 24:47), with the post-Easter church only gradually coming to the realization of its commission to the whole world, under the guidance of the Holy Spirit (Acts 1–15).

11. Later Gentile Christianity continued to use some Aramaic expressions from the ministry of Jesus and the earliest Palestinian church: *Marana tha, abba, amen*. Stories and sayings of Jesus played an important role in some (not all!) streams of Hellenistic Christianity.

full members of the redeemed people of God without becoming Jews prior to or as part of their conversion to the Christian faith? *This issue, in its many dimensions, was the most theologically problematic and emotional issue faced by the first generation of Christians*.

It is thus helpful to make a pause in the narrative here and ponder the nature of this new context in which the early Christians wanted to communicate their faith. For purposes of analysis, we need to think of four stages, though the synchronic messiness of actual history did not unfold in this neat diachronic fashion:

— Hellenistic Gentile Religion

— Hellenistic Judaism

— Hellenistic Jewish Christianity

— Gentile Churches

Hellenistic Gentile Religion

"Then Paul stood in front of the Areopagus and said, 'Athenians, I see how extremely religious you are in every way'" (Acts 17:22). The earliest Christians did not enter a religious vacuum, but encountered a world with deep religious convictions and a vibrant spirituality. Early Christian missionaries did not enter an irreligious world trying to get people to be religious; they were not purveyors of "spirituality" but announcers of good news in a world already "extremely religious," (see fig. 16). The world addressed by the Christian message already believed, prayed, sacrificed, formed religious communities, had sacred times, places, rituals, myths, and stories that gave meaning to their lives. Religion was not a separate aspect of life that could be abstracted and discussed as a thing itself but was embedded within the whole world of social, political, economic, and family life. What was this religious world like?[12]

Religion is always a varied and concrete, particular phenomenon that resists generalizing summaries. Ponder how difficult it is to generalize about Christianity in North America; imagine trying to summarize the religious landscape of twenty-first-century America to a visitor from Mars or from the forty-first century. While keeping this in mind, we attempt a brief sketch of the main categories and features of Hellenistic religious life:

The Classical Cults Devoted to the Traditional Gods of Greece and Rome

Every town of any size had a variety of temples, ancient and beautiful, where the classical gods were worshiped.[13] A revered priestly staff carried on the worship in an official, formal sense, under government sponsorship and with broad community support. It was a function of the state, for the welfare of the state, and contributed to the sense of belonging. The good of the community depended on its faithful maintenance. For many people, these traditional practices did not offer a personal religion with a satisfactory theology, ethic, or help for life's problems but, rather, represented the orderly world to which they belonged (see fig. 19).

The practice of animal sacrifice was virtually universal, not only in the traditional public religion, but also as a central element in family and personal devotion to the gods (see fig. 17).

Most public functions and private associations and clubs involved some sort of sacrifice. The slaughter of animals for food was generally

12. Among the numerous resources helpful in understanding the world of Hellenistic religions, see especially: Everett Ferguson, *Backgrounds of Early Christianity*, 3rd ed. (Grand Rapids: Eerdmans, 2003); Hans-Josef Klauck, *The Religious Context of Early Christianity: A Guide to Graeco-Roman Religions*, trans. Brian McNeil, ed. Fortress Press (Minneapolis: Fortress Press, 2003), each with extensive bibliographies. For annotated collections of primary sources from the Hellenistic world that illuminate particular New Testament texts, see M. Eugene Boring, Klaus Berger, and Carsten Colpe, eds., *Hellenistic Commentary to the New Testament* (Nashville: Abingdon Press, 1995); C. K. Barrett, ed., *The New Testament Background: Selected Documents*, 2nd ed. (New York: HarperOne, 1995).

13. The reader is reminded that in such contexts, "cult" refers to structured religious practice of a group, especially its worship, and does not carry the negative connotation of popular parlance.

FIGURE 16: An altar inscription at Perga, "To the Holy and Righteous One," illustrates the religious terminology of the Hellenistic world also found in the New Testament (see Acts 3:14). PHOTO CREDIT: M. EUGENE BORING.

FIGURE 17: A relief at Thessalonica portrays the emperor and his family sacrificing to the gods. USED BY PERMISSION OF DAVID PADFIELD.

a ritual act involving the gods (see fig. 17). The sacrifice was typically followed by a festive meal. Modern readers of the Bible are sometimes acquainted with animal sacrifice only as an Old Testament and Jewish institution, but wherever the Christian faith went, it found the practice and theology of sacrifice as a pervasive element in the culture. Jewish and biblical religion actually manifested less sacrificial ritual than the Hellenistic world in general, since in Judaism sacrifices were offered only at the temple and were not part of daily community life.

The understanding of sacrifice in the ancient world was deeply rooted and complex, from time to time involving the intertwined motifs of gift or bribe to the Deity, community fellowship meal, scapegoating and removal of personal and/or community guilt, a ritualization of slaughter and acknowledgment of the sacredness of life, the ritual venting or sublimation of violence and anger. Pagan religion had long been aware of the concept of the φάρμακος (*pharmakos*, scapegoat), the person killed or driven out to save the city.

The old local gods had continued to be worshiped, but the wider vision of the world given by Alexander's conquests placed them in a new perspective. As the Roman Empire gradually annexed the Mediterranean world, the old gods of Greece were fused with the Roman pantheon, so that, for example, Zeus was identified with Jupiter, Hermes with Apollo, and Artemis with Diana. While much of the older religion continued among the masses, some among the more educated and sophisticated had devised a kind of religious rationalism. It is true enough that in popular religion the gods look and act like human beings, and people of simple faith regarded the statues of the gods with superstitious awe and the gods themselves as only more powerful versions of themselves, with the same

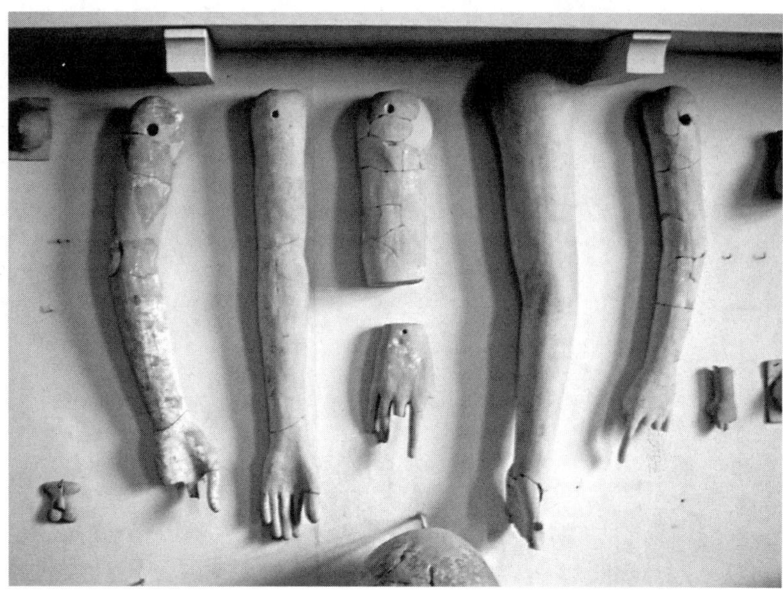

FIGURE 18: Votive offerings to the gods for healing. USED BY PERMISSION OF DAVID PADFIELD.

emotions, loves, hates, and foibles (only writ large). Yet it is also true that, from the Pre-Socratics to Pliny, thoughtful believers in the gods had warned against confusing the image with the reality, rejecting the identification of the unimaginable Deity with the statues in the temples. Many thoughtful people understood the variety of gods to be expressions of one Supreme Being.[14]

Popular Folk Religion

Alongside the traditional religion and its worship of the classical gods was a wide variety of religious expressions, ranging from crude superstitions and beliefs in witches and goblins to more sophisticated understandings, from purely personal and individual beliefs and practices to organized and traditional cultic communities.

Hearth and home. Religion was not only public, political, and community-centered, but a matter of family and the home. The paterfamilias presided at family worship as priest. Many homes had a family shrine and niches for a variety of gods.

Magic and astrology. Popular belief in the power and influence of stars, planets, and comets was surrounded by a religious aura. While disdained by the intellectual elite, the more refined forms of reflection on the patterns of

14. "Thou, O Zeus, art praised above all gods: many are thy names and thine is all power for ever.
The beginning of the world was from thee: and with law thou rulest over all things.
Unto thee may all flesh speak: for we are thy offspring.
Therefore I will raise a hymn unto thee: and will sing of thy power.
The whole order of the heavens obeyeth thy word: as it moveth around the earth:
With little and great lights mixed together: how great thou art, King above all forever.
Nor is anything done upon earth apart from thee: nor in the firmament, nor in the seas:
Save that which the wicked do: by their own folly.
But thine is the skill to set even the crooked straight: what is without fashion is fashioned and the alien akin before thee.
Thus hast thou fitted together all things into one: the good with the evil:
That thy word should be one in all things: abiding for ever.
Let folly be dispersed from our souls: that we may repay thee the honor, wherewith thou has honored us:
Singing praise of thy works forever." (Cleanthes, third century BCE)

FIGURE 19: Temple of Apollo in Corinth, Greece. USED BY PERMISSION OF DAVID PADFIELD.

the starry universe were also met with mingled respect and fear. Eastern religions that had migrated westward were especially appreciated as representing ancient wisdom in coming to terms with the potentially malevolent powers of the universe, though sometimes suspected as too foreign and rejected as not truly Roman. In some circles, we find elaborate theologies and philosophies in which the seven planets were understood to determine human destiny, sometimes correlated with the seven elements of the universe, the *stoicheia*, which also correspond to the seven Greek vowels. These views could be elaborated in terms of simple folk belief and magic spells, in which pronouncing α ε η ι ο υ ω (a e ē i o u ō) in the proper combinations had religious power, and as profound philosophical meditations relating the elemental structures of the universe to numbers and syllables. Most people believed that their lives were subject to various personalized forces in the universe and that one needed powerful rituals and formulas in order to cope.

Demigods, immortals, heroes, "divine men," and savior figures. In the Greco-Roman world, the boundaries that separated human beings and the gods were not firm. Gods could assume human form, and human beings could be spoken of in terms of deity. Wandering preachers and miracle workers could be regarded as gods (see Acts 14:8–20; 28:1–6).

The gods could disguise themselves in human form, visiting human beings to check up on their morality, as in the popular tale in which only Philemon and Baukis offer hospitality to two needy strangers when everyone else in town had rejected them—only later to learn that they were entertaining Zeus and Hermes (in the Roman version, Jupiter and Mercury).[15]

There were two basic categories of divine beings. Some gods had always been gods and had never lived a human life (though they might appear on the earth disguised as humans). Other gods had once lived human lives, even if they were born of divine-human unions, and first became gods by being exalted to the heavenly world, changed from mortals into immortals because of their beneficent acts in

15. Ovid, *Metamorphoses VII*.

behalf of humanity. Zeus and Apollo belonged to the former category, Heracles and Dionysus to the latter. There was also a class of outstanding human beings who, though less than gods, were so filled with divine power that they were more than human. The term θεῖος ἀνήρ (*theios anēr*, "divine man") was sometimes used of such people.

Among the best-known of these was Apollonius of Tyana, an itinerant preacher, religious reformer, and miracle worker who lived in the first century, but whose biography was not written until more than a hundred years later.[16] Apollonius was born in a miraculous manner, of a human mother and the god Proteus. He called people to abandon their dissolute, materialistic life and devote themselves to higher values. Moving and detailed stories are told of how he cast out demons, healed the sick, and raised the dead. Like Pythagoras and Iamblicus, he calmed the waves of flood and sea in order to grant safety to those in danger. He walked among wild animals, and they did not harm him. He was considered by some to be one of the gods and did not reject the idea.[17]

It is difficult for a storyteller or biographer to describe the departure of such a person from the human scene. He certainly cannot suffer and die like ordinary human beings. Philostratus reports that after Apollonius had become famous, the emperor Domitian resolved to destroy him. Of his own accord, Apollonius allowed himself to be arrested and tried in Domitian's court. However, he confided to his disciples: "I myself know more than mere men do, for I know all things . . . and that I have not come to Rome on behalf of the foolish will become perfectly clear; for I myself am in no danger with respect to my own body nor will I be killed by this tyrant" (LCL). During his trial, Apollonius removes his shackles at will. After hearing Apollonius's defense, Domitian declares that he will not condemn him. But Apollonius considers this a ruse and responds, "Give me my freedom, if you will, but if not, then send someone to imprison my body, for it is impossible to imprison my soul! Indeed, you will not even take my body, for [quoting Homer, *Iliad* 22.13] 'you cannot kill me since I am not a mortal man,' and, saying this, he vanished from the courtroom, suddenly appearing to his disciple Damis and a friend in another town" (7.5 LCL). Philostratus proceeds to relate various conflicting accounts of the supposed "death" of Apollonius, attaching the most credence to those stories in which he enters the temple of one of the gods and then vanishes, amid the chorus of heavenly choirs singing "Come up from earth, come to heaven, come."

Oracles and revealers. Practically all levels of society believed in communication of divine wisdom and counsel from the divine world. There were numerous fortune-tellers and wandering prophets inspired by various gods, and the will of the gods could be determined by casting lots or by studying the pattern of the flights of birds and the entrails of sacrificial animals. There were also numerous shrines in which the gods revealed their message more or less directly. Of these, by far the most famous and respected was the oracle at Delphi (see fig. 20).

This pilgrimage site was visited by the whole range of society from peasants to kings, who sought the divine word on all matters from success in love and business to the propitious time for beginning a war. The shrine existed over several centuries. How the oracles were actually delivered was understood in a variety of ways. According to some, the Pythia, the priestess of the revelatory god Apollo, responded to queries in glossolalia-like incomprehensible phrases, either because she breathed the vapors from the opening in the rock (yet to be identified by archaeology) or because such language was induced by traditional expectations

16. Philostratus, *The Life of Apollonius of Tyana*, trans. F. C. Conybeare, 2 vols., LCL (Cambridge: Harvard University Press, 1969).

17. In his forty-fourth letter to his brother Hestiaeus, he complains, "Other men regard me as the equal of the gods, and some of them even as a god, but until now my own country alone ignores me, my country for which in particular I have striven to be distinguished" (LCL).

FIGURE 20: Delphi, the location of the most-respected oracle in the Greco-Roman world. PHOTO CREDIT: M. EUGENE BORING.

FIGURE 21: Mithras altar in Rome. PHOTO CREDIT: M. EUGENE BORING.

and psychology. These utterances were then "interpreted" into comprehensible speech by cult functionaries called προφῆται (*prophētai*, prophets).

The Mystery Cults

There were mystery cults related to several deities (Demeter, Dionysus, Orpheus, Attis, Isis, Mithras), with a long and changing history and some variation from locale to locale.

Some generalizations can be helpful in understanding the whole spectrum:

1. The mysteries were secret. This is the meaning of μυστήριον (*mystērion*, mystery). "Mystery" does not mean "difficult to understand," but "concealed from outsiders." The mysteries were open for all to join (though initiation was expensive), but the initiates learned secrets that must not be shared with outsiders.

2. The mysteries had initiation rites, often with a purifying ritual involving water. There was a disclosure, in dramatic form, of the mystery of the cult. There was impressive solemn symbolism in word, actions, vestments, and ceremony.

3. Some of the mysteries created a fellowship in which all shared. Modern readers need to remember that one did not *belong* to the state religions. They were simply there as an important part of community life. But in the mysteries, membership was by choice. There was a sense of acceptance, of belonging, of sharing something in which others did not participate. Distinctions between slave and free, rich and poor, male and female did not count within the common bond of the initiates (though payment of a considerable fee was required in advance, which would have eliminated many aspirants). The crowd in the procession on the occasion of Lucius's initiation into the Isis cult consisted of "throngs of those initiated into the divine mysteries, men and women of every rank" (Apuleius, *Metamorphoses* 11.10).

FIGURE 22: Model of mystery cult center at Elysius, near Athens. PHOTO CREDIT: M. EUGENE BORING.

4. The mysteries were based on a somewhat common mythology. While there is some variation in characters and plot, the story generally involved the following pattern:

a. The divine husband (or child) is tragically trapped and killed by the powers of evil. Since the stories are not dealing with mortals, "killed" is understood in the sense in which gods can die—a banishment to the nether world, which affects the seasons. In such language, the transcendent powers are pictured in human terms.

b. The wife (or mother) grieves over the loss for a period (thus winter).

c. The husband, son, or daughter is restored to the divine wife or mother, and new life begins. The lord worshiped in the cult is thus a "dying and rising" god corresponding to the annual cycle of the seasons.

5. Deliverance, salvation, was the goal of the mysteries. The old classical gods were themselves subject to μοῖρα (*moira*, fate), and to εἱμαρμένη (*heimarmenē*, destiny). When classical religion and philosophy declined, *Moira* and *Heimarmenē* themselves became gods, evil powers before which one was helpless. But in the mystery cults, initiates believed that the lord of the cult had broken through, was delivered, and could deliver others, in this world and the next. This salvation gives joy and peace of mind now and a blessed immortality hereafter.

6. Deliverance was sought by union with the deity. The story of suffering, dying, rising became the story of the devotee. In initiation, the suppliant reenacts the story of the god. In communion meals the lord of the cult is present, and sometimes is symbolically eaten. (One can understand Christian objections to fellow members of the church continuing to participate in such meals; see 1 Cor 8:7–10; 10:27–30.) Thus in the Orphic cult, Zagreus (Dionysius), a son of Zeus, is killed by the Titans and eaten by them. Zeus calls him back to life, takes him to heaven, and gives him the kingdom. Human beings are descended from the Titans; they have some divinity in them. After being initiated and learning the story that establishes their identity, members of the Orphic cult recapture

the moment of divinity in the symbolic meal. In the ecstatic worship of some Orphic cults, a living bull was torn apart and the bloody flesh was eaten, the devotees taking the life of the god into themselves. Sacred meals were involved in the cult of the Magna Mater (the Great Mother), and the liturgical confession was pronounced: "I have eaten from the drum, I have drunk from the cymbal."

7. The mystery cults appealed to the emotions, giving a sense of personal relationship to the deity. The vastness and impersonality of the post-Alexander empire had caused individuals to see their lives as embedded in a cosmos that was no longer home. In the mysteries, initiates rediscovered a warm, snug place in the world. One can think of the variety of expressions of Christianity: some are stirred by the vastness and richness of Roman Catholic tradition and ritual, others by "my personal Lord," whose presence I feel in my heart and in the warmth and enthusiasm of local congregation. Both experiences were already present in Hellenistic religion.

8. The mystery cults involved conversion, personal transformation. In Apuleius's story of Lucius in the *Metamorphoses* (*The Golden Ass*), Lucius is fascinated by magic, dabbles in the occult sciences, and is accidentally transformed into donkey; but he is delivered from his subhuman state and restored to his true self by Isis. His petition had concluded, "Restore me to my own self as Lucius" (cf. the lost son, living among the swine, who "comes to himself" in Jesus' story, Luke 15:17). He refers to being "born again" (*Metam*. 11.21), and hears from Isis the reassuring words, "There is now dawning for you, through my providence, the day of salvation" (*Metam*. 11.2, 5). This is a true conversion: Lucius is restored to his authentic self in this world, devotes his life to Isis, and will continue with her in a blessed immortality beyond death. The Roman government came to regard the Isis cult as a political threat, but efforts to stamp it out were a failure, for the followers of Isis would accept martyrdom rather than abandon her worship.[18]

9. The mystery cults had obvious similarities and points of contact with early Christianity. These similarities were noted by the church fathers (e.g., Justin Martyr, ca. 150 CE, and Tertullian, ca. 200 CE). They explained that Satan, knowing that Christianity would win over multitudes of people, planted counterfeit religions that would look like the real thing, in order to confuse people—an explanation that shows they considered the similarities between the mystery cults and developing Christianity to be close enough to make them nervous and to call for an explanation.

Modern scholars have responded to these similarities in three ways:

1. The *history of religions school* (*die Religionsgeschichtliche Schule*). The early days of rigorous study of the religions of the ancient Near East and the Hellenistic world emphasized the genetic relationship between Greco-Roman religion and Christianity, especially the mystery cults. In its most extreme form, Paul was regarded as an initiate into one of the mysteries who transformed Jesus' own Jewish faith into a Hellenistic cult, with Jesus' Jewish religion becoming a Greco-Roman religion about him. Jesus was understood in the role of the cultic dying-and-rising lord, and the church as a Christian mystery cult.[19] This approach to New Testament theology was often associated with the theological liberalism developing about the same time, which contrasted the religion *of* Jesus with the religion *about* him.

2. The *conservative reaction* to this approach is represented by J. G. Machen's *The Origin of*

18. See Howard Clark Kee, *Miracle in the Early Christian World. A Study in Sociohistorical Method* (New Haven, CT: Yale University Press, 1983), 128–31.

19. See, e.g., Wilhelm Bousset, *Kyrios Christos: A History of the Belief in Christ from the Beginnings of Christianity to Irenaeus*, trans. John E. Steely (Nashville: Abingdon Press, 1970; first German edition 1913), influential on an earlier generation of scholars.

Paul's Religion,[20] which pointed out many contrasts between early Christianity and the mysteries and argued that early Christian faith and theology had nothing to do with mystery cults.

3. There is now a broad consensus among scholars that both 1 and 2 were respectively a too hasty acceptance and rejection of the potential value of the study of Hellenistic religions for insight into early Christianity and the New Testament. The early Christian missionaries did indeed adopt and adapt many motifs and practices from this world, which was their own thought world. *In interpreting the New Testament, there is always a need to distinguish Christianity as a religion from the gospel as the proclamation of God's saving act.* The communication of the gospel will always necessarily make use of human religious thought and practice, and not only as a negative reaction. Every response to the gospel is a religious response, expressed in a particular theological thought and language, but Christians should not confuse the religious response and its theological expression with the thing itself. Early Christianity as a religious response to the gospel had much in common with other religions of the day.

There were also significant differences. I will not attempt to catalogue them here, but two are particularly important:

1. Christianity had as its Lord one who was a *recent, remembered, historical human being*. Jesus Christ was not the personification of the forces of nature, not a mythical being slain by another mythical being, but an Aramaic-speaking Galilean Jew who died on a real historical cross. The resurrection was a once-for-all, unique act of God, not part of the annual cycle of nature. None of the devotees of Isis, for example, thought of her as one who had entered this world as a truly human being and died a truly human death. Isis was and remained a divine being, and this was her power to save. The difference between the mystery cults and the Christian gospel can be expressed in one word: *Jesus*.

2. In Christianity, theology and mythology are the foundation for an *ethical style of life*. In the mystery cults, initiation was the means of overcoming fate and death and guaranteeing a happy immortality, but it had little to do with the conduct of one's personal life, one's relations to one's neighbor, and the mission of God in the world.

Popular Philosophical Movements That Functioned as Religions

Acts 17 pictures Stoic and Epicurean philosophers of Athens engaging Paul on religious issues. Hellenistic popular philosophy is often, and rightly, discussed under the heading of Hellenistic *religion*. By "philosophy" in this context, we do not mean only, or primarily, the academic discussion of philosophy in the classroom, but, rather, something like "philosophy of life" in the modern context. Alternatively, one might think of the way the "free enterprise system" sometimes functions in American culture, not as an abstract economic theory, but as a practical way of life with deep religious associations. The philosophy the early Christian missionaries encountered was personal and practical. Neither the classical religion of the temples nor the pop-folk religion was essentially related to ethics and values, to the question of how to live one's life. This role was played by philosophy.

Stoic-Cynic philosophy. Classical Stoicism looked to Zeno as its founder, who had taught in the *stoa* (porch, colonnade) of the Agora in Athens (see fig. 23).

Zeno divided philosophy into three interrelated areas: *logic*, the study of how to know; *physics*, the study of all reality; *ethics*, the study of how to live. By the first century, much of Stoic thought had blended with a popular version of Cynic thought. The Cynics looked back to Diogenes as one of their heroes. He had rejected the norms and expectations of conventional

20. J. Gresham Machen, *The Origin of Paul's Religion* (James Sprunt Lectures delivered at Union Theological Seminary in Virginia) (Grand Rapids: Eerdmans, 1925).

FIGURE 23: Reconstructed *stoa* of the Agora in Athens, where Zeno taught Stoic philosophy. PHOTO CREDIT: M. EUGENE BORING.

society and lived "according to nature," thus the nickname "dog" (κύων *kyōn*, adj. κυνικός *kynikos*, from which Cynic is derived).[21] This was the point of contact between the two philosophies that facilitated their fusion in popular thought. While Stoics and Cynics could use the conventional language of the gods, the underlying philosophy was profoundly atheistic. Nature itself, the immanent Reason that pervaded all nature, was the only "god." This "deity" was benevolent, for the universe functions rationally, and the Reason that indwells all nature is akin to human reason. The good life is to live in accord with this Reason, to go with the flow of Nature—which in any case cannot be resisted.

The *Discourses* of Epictetus (ca. 55–135 CE) and the *Meditations* of the emperor Marcus Aurelius (121–180 CE) are among the best-known classical examples, but then as now the personal religion of the individual who simply wants to live with internal peace of mind found popular expression. The Cynics' disdain for conventional values fit well into this philosophy. The image of Diogenes, who lived on the streets and slept in a tub, carefree and enjoying life, was admired by many who had no intention of following him literally. In a famous legend, Alexander the Great came to pay his respects, stood over Diogenes as he sunbathed in his tub, and greeted him with, "I am Alexander: ask what you will, and I will give it to you." Diogenes responded, "Move out of the sun." The Stoic-Cynic preachers did not drop out of society but understood themselves to be sent by the gods to call others to the good and simple life. They could be seen on the street corners in every Hellenistic town, with their characteristic cloak, staff, and beggar's bag containing all their earthly possessions, berating the population for their false way of life. Both Stoics and Cynics proclaimed the gospel of liberation, a kind of internal freedom that could neither be granted nor taken away by society and its rulers.

21. Thus "cynic" does not have its modern English connotations (skeptic, one who believes all people are motivated only by self-interest, etc.), just as "Stoic" in the ancient context meant far more than its modern English counterpart.

Epicureanism. Just as first-century Stoics and Cynics should not be defined by what these terms have come to mean in modern English, so "Epicurean" does not mean superficial hedonism. Epicurus was a serious philosopher of the classical period who, after seeing much of the Mediterranean world as a soldier, settled in Athens in 306 BCE and founded a school that met in his quiet garden (κῆπος *kēpos*). As the *stoa* (porch) designated stoicism, the *garden* was often used to designate Epicurus's disciples and their tradition. Epicurus too offered freedom from anxiety. In contrast to the Stoics, he did not assure his disciples that the capricious, powerful, and often malevolent personal gods did not exist. The gods existed, but they dwelt in their own world apart and did not interfere with the human world. In this world, all that exists is atoms and the void; atoms randomly collide and merge into the elements of this world. There is nothing to hope from it, but also nothing to fear from it. There is no reason to live in fear of the gods or to attempt to placate them. There is nothing to fear in death. The good life is to live quietly, to be disengaged from society and its misconceptions, to avoid the media and keep a low profile.

Middle Platonism. Plato's famous Academy of the fourth century BCE had declined, but Platonic thought experienced a revival in the first century CE, in its renewed form expressing the central ideas of (1) a dualism between the reality of ideas and the transience of the material world, (2) the transcendence and eternity of the ideal world, and (3) the immortality of the soul. This complex of ideas formed the background and substratum of much enlightened thought of the first two centuries CE, expressed in such varied figures as the Jewish Philo of Alexandria and the Christian apologist Justin. Perhaps the single most helpful source for shedding light on the thoughtful, philosophical context of Hellenistic religious life into which early Christianity entered is the writings of Plutarch, whose life almost exactly spans the period in which the New Testament was composed (ca. 50–120 CE). Plutarch discusses the nature of religion, ethics, and the gods; the interrelations of myth and history; theories of life after death and the meaning of immortality; and numerous other topics that illuminate the world in which the early Christians attempted to express their faith.

The Skeptics. Mixed in with the urbane questioning of the conventional system of classical religion and its gods was a variety of popular philosophers such as Aristophanes (446–ca. 386 BCE), whose plays (e.g., *The Birds*, *The Frogs*, *The Clouds*) lampooned the gods and replaced "Zeus" with "nature."

The Emperor Cult

Alexander's conquests gave the world a glimpse of how big and diverse it was. Local gods and local rulers could now appear rather petty as one attempted to come to terms with such a world. The concept of the divine ruler, long at home in the East, proved valuable to both ruler and subjects in integrating their lives into the larger vision of the world. Alexander's dramatic conquests seemed to demonstrate his divine status, and he was somewhat surprised to find himself hailed in the East as a god. He found the acclamation politically useful and seemed to warm to it personally. After he conquered Egypt and founded the city of Alexandria, he made a pilgrimage to the oracle of Zeus-Ammon at the oasis of Siva in the Libyan desert, where he was greeted by the prophetic spokesperson for the god as "Son of God" (παῖς Διός *pais Dios*).

When the cloak of empire passed to the Romans, this veneration of the divine ruler was transferred to the emperor. In the West, the typical pattern was to distinguish between the living man and his guiding spirit (*genius*), who was then deified at his death. Among famous last words are those of Vespasian, who, as he lay dying, said—but we do not know in what tone of voice— "*Vae, puto deus fio*" (Dammit, I think I am becoming a god).

In the East, the tradition of worshiping the living emperor continued, sometimes despite

FIGURE 24: Ascension of the deified Caesar. PHOTO CREDIT: M. EUGENE BORING.

the resistance or reluctance of the emperor himself. Augustus tolerated this veneration and utilized it politically.[22] ΣΩΤΗΡ (*SŌTĒR*, Savior) appeared frequently on temples and altars. Virgil could celebrate Augustus's reign with such lines as "This is a man, who was long promised to the fathers, Caesar Augustus, Son of God and bringer of the golden endtime" (*Aen.* 6.791). The 9-BCE inscription from Priene in Asia Minor concludes with the line that "the birthday of the god Augustus was the beginning for the world of the good tidings (εὐαγγέλιον *euangelion*, gospel) that came by reason of him."

Examples could be multiplied from coins and inscriptions, but we mention here only the 49-BCE inscription from Ephesus:

> The cities in Asia and the [communities] and the country districts [honor] Gaius Julius, son of Gaius, Caesar, Pontifex Maximus, Imperator and consul for the second time, descendant of Ares and Aphrodite, the god who has appeared visibly [θεὸν ἐπιφανῆ *theon epiphanē*, God manifest] and universal savior of the life of human beings.

Two of the later emperors (Caligula and Domitian) took their own deity seriously and insisted that it be generally acknowledged. Caligula attempted to have his image placed in the temple in Jerusalem; Domitian required that all, including his family members, address him as "my lord and my god"; had those put to death who booed his team in the arena; promoted the imperial cult; and may have actively insisted that recalcitrant groups such as Christians demonstrate their loyalty by participation in it.

With these few exceptions, we should not see emperor worship as a requirement imposed from the top down by megalomaniacal rulers, but as a grassroots movement expressing gratitude for the peace and prosperity Rome had brought to

22. A readable account of the all-pervasive Augustan imperial propaganda in the first century is provided by John Dominic Crossan and Jonathan L. Reed, *In Search of Paul: How Jesus's Apostle Opposed Rome's Empire with God's Kingdom; A New Vision of Paul's Words and World* (New York: HarperSanFrancisco, 2004), esp. chaps. 1 and 3. For technical details and abundance of historical and archaeological support, see esp. S. R. Price, *Rituals and Power: The Roman Imperial Cult in Asia Minor* (Cambridge: Cambridge University Press, 1984).

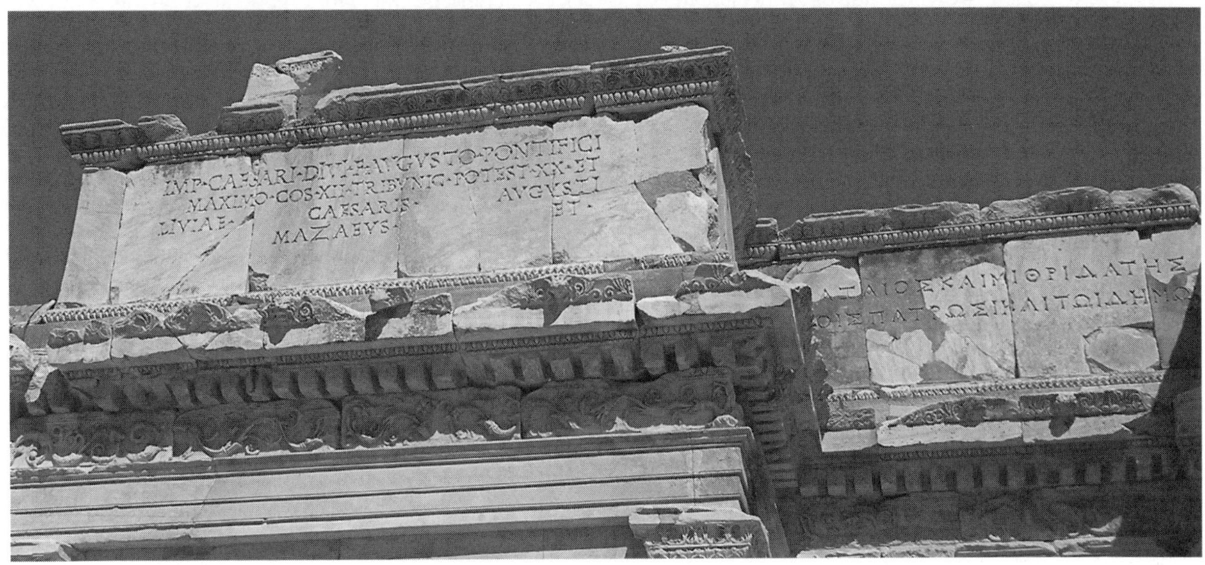

FIGURE 25: A Latin inscription that reads in part: "From the Emperor Caesar Augustus, the son of the god, the greatest of the priests . . ." PHOTO CREDIT: M. EUGENE BORING.

the world. Worship was not demanded by the emperors but freely offered by the population, as a response to the benefactions of Rome. Sailors landing in Mediterranean ports gave thanks in local temples to Augustus, who had driven pirates from the seas and made the Mediterranean a Roman lake. Especially in Asia Minor, the emperor cult was all-pervasive, supported by local officials as a way that cities and villages could integrate their own locality and past into the wider world. Cities vied for the privilege of constructing temples to the divine Caesar, which were staffed with impressive priests, equipped with solemn liturgies and mythologies, and thronged by the population. Rome, the goddess Roma, and the emperor were symbols of the unity and stability of the world in a vast universe of pluralities always threatening to return to chaos. Festivals were the chief manifestation of the cult, involving the whole community, rich and poor. The main sacrifice was in the temple or public square, but homeowners sacrificed to or for the emperor as the procession passed their houses. "All members of the community were expected to participate in the imperial cult."[23]

However, in the first century the expectation was not a requirement imposed by the government, but the general expectation of the community. Participation in the emperor cult was mostly considered a matter of patriotism and support of the common good; "worship" of the Caesar was not exclusive, did not compete with other religious loyalties, and to many citizens was something like saluting the flag and reciting the pledge of allegiance—which could (and can) be done as conventional ritual or with religious fervor. It could be added on to whatever other religious commitments one had. The Romans could not understand why anyone would object to the practice, and were suspicious of groups that did.

There were two groups for which this was a problem. *Jews* could not acknowledge the emperor as a god or participate in his worship. Jewish martyrs had shed their blood in resisting

23. Price, *Rituals and Power*, 114.

such worship during Maccabean times (see above §6.2.2). By the first century they had demonstrated that they were a stable, ancient group with venerable traditions, not subversive of the government or dangerous to the general welfare. They had worked out an arrangement with the empire: twice every day, sacrifices were offered for (not *to*) the emperor in the temple in Jerusalem.

The *Christians* at first were seen as a subgroup within Judaism, and did not come into direct conflict with the emperor cult. By the time of the great Roman fire of 64 CE, Roman authorities could distinguish Christians from (other) Jews, and only the former were blamed for the fire. Christians were arrested and cruelly executed on the charge of arson, not because of resistance to the emperor cult. This was the first official move of the empire against the Christians. In the crisis of Domitian's reign (ca. 95 CE), the pressure to worship the emperor played a role. About fifteen years later, Pliny's letter to Trajan shows the confused but hostile situation in Bithynia, and tells us that the stance of Christians to emperor worship played a role in how they were regarded by the state. Those accused of being Christians were asked to invoke the Roman gods and to offer sacrifice to the image of the emperor; those who refused were executed (see below, §26.1.4). Here we see how church and empire regarded each other after three generations of Christian mission and growth. This polarization did not exist at the beginning of the Christian mission, but the potential was there from the first.

(Proto-) Gnosticism

The English word "knowledge" is derived from γνῶσις (*gnōsis*, the initial *g* is silent, analogous to the initial *k* in "knowledge").[24] The adjective is γνωστικός (*gnōstikos*, gnostic), which has no direct English counterpart, but could be translated "good at knowing," "knowledgeable," with the positive overtones of "scientific," in contrast to the "unscientific" views of the populace. A gnostic was one who knew, at a deep level, beyond the superficial understandings of common people. In religious perspectives, such knowledge provided understanding of the ultimate mysteries of human existence. These questions are representatively expressed in a quotation from Theodotus, a second-century gnostic teacher:

> Who were we?
> What have we become?
> Where were we?
> Whither have we been thrown?
> Whither are we hastening?
> Whence have we been set free?
> What is birth, what is rebirth?[25]

If you had gone into Antioch or Corinth in the earliest days of the Christian mission (30s-50s CE) and asked for directions to the local Gnostic congregation, you would simply have received a blank stare. Though its roots are earlier, what came to be known as Gnosticism did not become a distinct, identifiable movement with its own institutions and literature until the second century CE. Among the sources in which Gnosticism first appears as an identifiable religious and philosophical movement are Irenaeus's five-volume work *Against Heresies* (ca. 185 CE), Tertullian's *Prescription against Heretics*, his *Against the Valentinians*, his *Against All Heresies*, and *The Five Books against Marcion* (ca. 200–10 CE), and Hippolytus's *Refutation of All Heresies* (ca. 210–30 CE). While these descriptions of the Gnostics are all from hostile witnesses in the protocatholic church, the authors cite extensive quotations from the Gnostic teachers' own writings, the originals of which are mostly now lost to us. Clement of Alexandria, more sympathetic to a Gnostic perspective

24. There is no universally accepted definition of "Gnosticism." The term is used in a wide variety of ways. The following discussion would find wide, but not total, resonance.

25. As quoted by Clement of Alexandria, *Excerpta ex Theodoto* 78.2.

on Christian faith, also gives valuable material about Gnostic teachers he considers objectionable and dangerous (ca. 200 CE).

Until recently, historians had very limited primary sources for the study of Gnosticism. In 1945 a chance discovery of part of an ancient library near Nag Hammadi in Upper Egypt provided some primary sources composed by Gnostics themselves. The collection of thirteen codices contained over fifty texts, including the *Gospel of Thomas*, the *Gospel of Philip*, the *Gospel of Truth*, and *The Sophia of Jesus Christ*, as well as a few non-Gnostic texts such as Plato's *Republic* and a collection of wisdom sayings, *The Sentences of Sextus*. No manuscripts of the New Testament or of orthodox patristic texts were included. The manuscripts themselves are written in Coptic and date from the fourth century CE but are mainly translations of earlier documents mostly written in Greek. The original date and language of some of the texts continues to be disputed, but in any case the collection provides our earliest and best primary sources for describing ancient Gnosticism.[26]

Gnostics could give profound and detailed explanations to questions that trouble the heart of every simple believer: If there is one good God who created the world and is responsible for everything, how does it happen that we live in a world that includes much evil and innocent suffering? Why are some people ill at ease in the world, troubled about the meaning of life and their own role in the great scheme of things, longing for serenity and salvation, while others, animal-like, seem to seek only physical enjoyment, with no fear of death or interest in what might lie beyond it? I am torn in different directions; how can I know my own true identity and how I should live my one and only life in this world? As is the case with the mystery cults, there is variety among the specific Gnostic groups, but a basic general pattern can be discerned, which is summarized here.[27]

There is an explanation for the evil in the world, but it requires deep philosophical study, involving an understanding of what happened in the transcendent world of true being prior to the creation of this world. The creation of the material world was, in fact, a tragic mistake. The outline of this theosophy, as taught by the followers of Valentinus in the second century, can be summarized, without the details and philosophical subtleties, as follows:

I. God is the Ultimate One, the All, the Unknown, the Unnameable, the Unimaginable, the Perfect One, dwelling in the transcendent realm far beyond anything the human mind can conceive. Then whence evil? This God, of course, has Reason and Thought. Gnostic philosophers can explain this inner self-contemplation of the Eternal One, as a series of contrasting pairs: Abyss and Silence, Mind and Truth. This first Tetrad is followed by a second, Word and Life, Anthropos and Ecclesia. Together, these form the Ogdoad, the Eight, thought of as a series of emanations from the divine mind. These are followed in turn by a series of Ten, then a series of Twelve, a total of thirty Aeons in the eternal world that comprise the Totality, the Fullness of divine being.

II. In terms of grammatical gender, each pair is male and female (e.g., Word/*Logos* is masculine, while Life/*Zōē* is feminine). While each pair interacts to generate further reality, this is understood as at the furthest pole from physical reproduction. All this is within the profound depths of the Eternal Divine Mind. In a Gnostic school, the explanation of these first two points would require much time and discipline, and it was not for the lazy, timid, or

26. After some delay and intrigue, the documents were reliably translated into English and are available in James M. Robinson, Richard Smith, and Coptic Gnostic Library Project, *The Nag Hammadi Library in English*, 4th rev. ed. (Leiden and New York: Brill, 1996).

27. For a detailed, sympathetic, and nuanced exposition of the Gnostic faith and its understandings of salvation, see Hans Jonas, *The Gnostic Religion*, 2nd. rev. ed. (Boston: Beacon Press, 1963), esp. "Part Two—Gnostic Systems of Thought," 101–238.

intellectually challenged. Those who repudiated it or simply did not understand it thereby demonstrated their unworthiness, and that they were incapable of redemption. Those who pursued demonstrated that they were in fact Knowers, Scientists of Reality.

III. Yet all was not well within the Pleroma. Sophia (Wisdom), according to her very being, was properly inquisitive and wanted to know her own origin. This is the nature of true wisdom, to pursue its own origins. She could not be faulted for this, and yet it is not possible, even in the transcendent world, to truly know the Unknown Father. Thus a crisis had arisen in the Pleroma, for which no one could be blamed—certainly not the One True God, the Unknown Father. And yet the disruption could not go unremedied. The now-tainted version of Sophia is expelled from the Pleroma, with true Sophia remaining, and the equilibrium within the Transcendent Mind was restored.

IV. Outside the Pleroma, the expelled Sophia is called Achamoth.[28] She has conceived (note that also in English, this word can have a purely mental as well as a biological meaning) and now brings forth her child as a kind of deformed abortion. He is called "Father" and "King," and does not know his own origin. Though the product of a catastrophic mistake, now corrected within the Pleroma, he supposes that he is the only existent Being and proceeds to create the physical universe. Thus matter and physical reality (ὑλή, ψυχή *hylē, psychē)* come into being. The origin of the material universe and the evil inherent within it can thus be explained. The physical cosmos is not the creation of the One True God and was never intended by the Ultimate One, but is the product of a divine being considerably downscale from Ultimate Reality, the "god of this world" (cf. 2 Cor 4:4: Satan, the demonic power who in Paul's view is the source of this world's evil was, in the Gnostic view, actually the world's creator).

V. How do human beings fit into this grand story of origins? Most of them are simply the products of the Demiurge, the "Creator," "Father," and "King" who is responsible for this world. They are composed only of matter and/or soul; they are material or psychical beings who only belong to this world. They do not wonder about their origin, are happy in this world, can never move beyond it, and will perish with it.

VI. Others are uncomfortable in this world, have the deep feeling that they do not belong here, that they belong to another order of existence than that of cows and rocks. The Valentinian Gnostics have yet more to explain. In the process of the expulsion of Sophia from the Pleroma, some of the transcendent reality, called Spirit, was imparted to Sophia and continued even in her expelled version Achamoth, in her offspring Father/King, and filtered down into his creation. Thus the present world not only is composed of its main elements matter and soul, but also contains fragments of the divine Spirit from the eternal world within the Pleroma. These eternal sparks of divine reality are the interior selves of some human beings, who are trapped in a world in which they do not belong and in which they are not at home. They have a longing for the other world but do not know the source of this longing or what it means. Their birth in this world was a going to sleep of the divine spark within them, and they wander about dissatisfied and numbed. They can be awakened from this sleep only by knowledge of their divine origin.

VII. No one could have discovered this knowledge. It was revealed from heaven. The preexistent Christ, who belonged to the Pleroma,

28. Sophia is the Greek word for wisdom, Σοφία; *Achamoth* is derived from the Hebrew word for wisdom, חָכְמָה. The reader is reminded that the above summary is only of one stream of Valentinian Gnosticism. In related forms of the myth, Sophia brings forth a lion-headed serpent called Yaltabaoth, who ignorantly supposes he is the only god, creates the world, and exclaims, "I am God and there is no other besides me," i.e., the Old Testament YHWH (cf. Isa 45:5).

saw the distressed state of those sparks of divine being longing to return to their true home, and he had compassion on them. He descended through the various aeons, layers of reality, and planetary spheres, disguising himself by uniting with the human being Jesus, delivered the saving knowledge to trusted disciples, separated from Jesus at the crucifixion, and returned to the heavenly world.

VIII. This knowledge is what the Gnostic teacher can provide. It is not mere information, but saving knowledge. If I sense my own alienation in this world and wonder why, and am willing to engage in long-term disciplined study (of which this outline is only the most meager summary), I can learn who we were, what we have become, where we were, how it is that we have been thrown into this existence, where we are going, and where our deliverance comes from. I can learn what birth is and what rebirth is. I can discover who I truly am. This knowledge is salvation.

IX. Gnostic believers who have become aware of their true being must express this in the way they *live*. Gnostic groups developed lifestyles that corresponded to the reality of their true spiritual selves. These lifestyles tended in two different directions. Some Gnostic believers lived an ascetic lifestyle, rejecting all pleasures of the flesh, showing their superiority to bodily existence by keeping the flesh under rigid control and disdaining all fleshly delights. Other Gnostics manifested their spiritual inner being in a libertinism that showed their contempt for this world and its conventions, living in freedom from all this-worldly laws and expectations, allowing the body of flesh to do whatever it desires, since nothing the body does can stain the eternal inner self.[29] Strangely enough, sometimes the two tendencies were combined, with Gnostic believers practicing both ascetic superiority over the world and libertine disdain for its conventions.

When did such Gnostic views originate? The summary above represents a late form of Gnosticism, already combined with elements of Christianity, articulating the meaning of Christian faith within the framework of Gnostic philosophy. Were these views already available as part of the religious world into which the first Christian missionaries entered? There are three basic views of this issue:

1. The church fathers of the second and third centuries understood the Gnosticism they opposed as a perversion of orthodox Christianity. Jesus and the apostles had established what came to be mainline orthodox Christianity at the beginning, and the Gnostics had distorted it by combining it with Hellenistic philosophy and mythology. Some modern scholars continued to follow this basic approach, considering Gnosticism to be the "acute Hellenization of Christianity."[30] In this view, Gnosticism is a later derivative of Christianity that was disowned by the parent.

2. In the early twentieth century, the German history of religions school developed a theory of Christian origins that is the polar opposite of the traditional view: an original Gnosticism that existed prior to and alongside Christianity was adopted and adapted by some early Christians as a way of expressing their faith. While the Christian form of Gnosticism that includes a role for Jesus and the church is obviously later, the understanding of human existence and the pattern of the preexistent divine redeemer who descends to bring saving knowledge was already

29. The heresiologists among the church fathers claimed that Gnostic Christianity promoted licentious behavior, a view already present in some New Testament authors' claims about their proto-Gnostic opponents (1 Cor. 6:9–20; Jude 14–23; 2 Pet. 2:1–22; the opponents opposed in the Pastorals include both ascetics [1 Tim. 4:1–5] and licentious libertines [2 Tim. 3:1–9]). The Nag Hammadi documents uniformly advocate an ascetic ethic, providing no support for a libertine ethic among Gnostics represented by these texts.

30. Adolf von Harnack, *History of Dogma*, trans. Neil Buchanan, 7 vols., Theological Translation Library (New York: Russell & Russell, 1958), 1:226.

there for the Christians to adopt and adapt, and continued alongside Christianity as one of its chief competitors.

3. Each of these views is now regarded by the majority of scholars as dogmatically based and stretching the evidence to fit the preconceived theory. Gnosticism cannot be reduced to a late Christian heresy, nor was there a fully developed Gnostic mythology that could be adopted by early Christian thinkers. In particular, there was no ready-made Gnostic redeemer myth already available to Christian thinkers, who supposedly adapted it in order to interpret the Christ event.[31] There were elements of what was to become Gnosticism already present in the first century, for example: (1) the Gnostic mood of alienation, of not being at home in the world; (2) the dualistic understanding of reality, especially the body-soul dichotomy; (3) the understanding of salvation as deliverance of my true self from its worldly and fleshly prison; (4) a disdain for this imperfect world of ambiguity and relativity and a lust for the absolute; (5) especially, the idea that there were spiritual beings who belonged to the divine world of transcendent perfection who could assume human form and impart secret knowledge to the chosen few.

Thus, here as elsewhere, the early Christian missionaries faced the double task that involved (1) adopting and adapting (sometimes unconsciously) the thought forms of their world in order to communicate their message and (2) trying to avoid misunderstandings that resulted when their hearers and converts too readily "understood" the Christian message in terms of their own previous religious conceptuality. In all this, we should not understand the missionary situation as though these ideas of Hellenistic religion were external to the missionaries themselves, which they only adopted and adapted as a missionary and communications strategy. These ideas did not invade the church "from outside." New converts brought such ideas with them as a part of their thought world, understanding the meaning of the Christian confession in these terms from the beginning. They were also already an inherent component of the thinking of the missionaries themselves.

The church was able to make this adaptation to the world of Hellenistic thought because of the essentially historical, act-centered character of its own faith. It was not purveying a certain abstract metaphysical idea about the nature of God or the character of the good life, but was proclaiming the saving act of God, which by its very nature can be perceived anew in each new situation and expressed in the thought forms appropriate to that situation. The church did not announce good ideas, but good news. While this good news cannot be proclaimed in some "pure" form uncontaminated by theology—the proclamation of the gospel is always necessarily done in terms of some theology— the church knew from the beginning the difference between gospel and theology and could adapt theologically without surrendering the gospel.

Hellenistic religions were polytheistic, sometimes with a tendency toward monotheism. This means that they were tolerant and nonexclusive. Only Judaism and Christianity were monotheistic in the exclusive sense and were thus condemned as intolerant. When Christians were persecuted, it was not because they would not deny their own faith, but because they would not add another faith to their own religion—which they could not do and remain Christians. *This* intolerance was what made Jews and Christians so odious to their Roman neighbors, and why they were disliked and suspect for their standoffishness and were called "enemies of the human race."[32]

31. This was a keystone in the interpretation of Rudolf Bultmann, whose interpretation was influential in the middle third of the twentieth century. See especially Bultmann, *Theology of the New Testament*.

32. Cf. N. T. Wright's reflections on mission as key component in early Christianity: "Why then did early Christianity spread? Because early Christians believed that what they had found to be true was true for the whole world" (N. T. Wright, *The New Testament and the People of God*, vol. 1 of *Christian Origins and the Question of God* [Minneapolis: Fortress Press, 1992], 360). Their faith was not true just "for them," while other people could have their

Hellenistic (Diaspora) Judaism (Also, see above, §7.4.2)

When, in the 30s and 40s CE, the early Christian missionaries first entered the towns and cities of the Hellenistic world, they were the newcomers, and their message was new. They found there not only the variety of Greco-Roman religions, but Jewish synagogues, congregations of Jewish believers who for generations had maintained the biblical faith and Jewish traditions throughout the Hellenistic world. Since the exile in the sixth century BCE, most Jews had lived in the Diaspora. In the first century CE, of 4.5 million Jews worldwide, fewer than 15 percent lived in Palestine. The Mediterranean world was polka-dotted with Jewish synagogues; many large cities had a sizable Jewish population. More Jews lived in Alexandria than in all of Palestine. Nonetheless, Diaspora Jews were a minority wherever they lived, and it was there, in the Diaspora, that Judaism was under the greatest pressure, internal and external, to accommodate itself to the surrounding world.

What was Hellenistic Judaism like? As a loose analogy, one might think of the Jewish community in a contemporary urban center in North America. They belong to a particular religious community and identify themselves with historical Israel of the Bible and Jewish tradition, but are Americans and think of themselves as such. They speak English, as their ancestors have done for generations. They may attend the synagogue, and, in varying degrees and traditions, maintain Jewish traditions at home.

Thus the vast majority of Diaspora Jews thought of themselves as belonging to historical Israel, but they were generally integrated into the prevailing Greco-Roman culture, spoke Greek as their native language, worshiped in the local synagogue, and maintained Jewish tradition in their family life. They mostly lived in their own neighborhoods—not in ghettos, but in close association with predominately Jewish neighbors. They enjoyed toleration and religious freedom almost everywhere, and were excused from military service because of their insistence on Sabbath observance and kosher food. They were specifically excused from participation in the cult of the emperor.

Community structure varied from place to place, but often there was a local Jewish council (γερουσία, *gerousia*) where matters of Jewish religious law could be settled and discipline could be administered so long as it did not violate Roman law. The large Jewish population of Alexandria seemed to have been organized into a πολίτευμα (*politeuma*), almost a state-within-a-state. Since their freedom and legal status had been obtained through struggle and sacrifice and had to be maintained with care, Diaspora Jews were concerned not to permit internal disorder and tumult that might draw the attention of the Roman authorities.

Many Jews were caught in the crosscurrents of wanting a degree of assimilation within the wider culture, but resisting assimilation as a dimension of their self-understanding as the covenant people called to witness to all nations to the reality of the one God. In particular, this sense of vocation and group identity was expressed in maintaining the boundary-marking rituals of circumcision, Sabbath keeping, and the food laws. While some Diaspora Jews were themselves neglecting the observance of these laws and/or interpreting them in a nonliteral sense, others saw their strict observance as their mission and responsibility in preserving the covenant faith. The more extreme of these saw themselves as "zealots" in the tradition of the biblical Phinehas and the Maccabean martyrs and resisted any dilution or compromise of the traditional Jewish practice. The stage was set for conflicts with Jewish Christian missionaries who proclaimed that Gentiles could become full members of the covenant people without adhering to these laws.

How did Hellenistic Judaism understand its faith? We have a variety of windows into the

own gods. Monotheism carries with it this kind of missionary imperative, this kind of intolerant exclusivism.

thought world of Hellenistic Judaism. The LXX not only provides numerous illustrations of interpreting Hebrew thought in Greek categories (see above, §4.3.1), but contains several books composed in Greek by Hellenistic Jews, giving the modern historian direct access to the ways that some Jewish thinkers who thought and wrote in Greek expressed their faith (Wisdom of Solomon; 2, 3, and 4 Maccabees). Hellenistic Jews produced a varied and extensive literature, including poetic, historical, and religious writings. This is illustrated by the fact that in the first century BCE a Gentile editor, Alexander Polyhistor, assembled an anthology of excerpts from Jewish writings called *About the Jews*. His work included selections from Demetrius the Chronographer, Eupolemos, Artapanus, Aristeas, Cleodomus-Malchus, Pseudo-Eupolemos, Philo the Poet (not to be confused with the later Philo of Alexandria), Theodotus the Poet of Samaria, Ezekiel the Tragedian, Aristobulus the Philosopher. Most of these writings have perished, and we would not know them, had not Alexander preserved excerpts from their works. They are the tip of a much larger iceberg. For our purposes, the extensive writings of Josephus, Philo, and the LXX provide revealing glimpses into the variety of ways Hellenistic Jews understood their faith. Here we can give only a few illustrations:

— The author of the *Wisdom of Solomon* had already taken massive steps toward interpreting Jewish theology and ethics in traditional Greek terms. Plato's definition of the four cardinal virtues had become classic: self-control, prudence, justice, courage. These are now taken to be good Jewish ethics, with the declaration that "nothing in life is more profitable for mortals than these" (Wis 8:7).

— *Josephus* explained the Pharisees, Sadducees, Essenes, and "Fourth Philosophy" (Zealots) in terms of Greek philosophical schools, distinguished by their varying doctrines of fate and free will (see above, §§7.4.3–7.4.8). Here we see an educated Palestinian Jew with an insider's understanding of biblical and traditional institutions and concepts. He intentionally interprets them to outsiders in their categories, aware of and accepting the distortion that is necessarily involved in order to communicate at all.

— Josephus refers, in good Greek style, to the soul "imprisoned within a mortal body and tainted with its miseries," which will be "freed from the weight that drags it down to earth and clings about it, and the soul is restored to its proper sphere" after death (*War* 7.344, 346). Is this also a matter of accommodation, expressing the authentic Jewish view of resurrection within the Greco-Roman understanding of immortality? Or has Josephus himself accepted the Greek way of expressing the Jewish hope?

— *Fourth Maccabees* is emphatic in its argument that the Jewish martyrs endured torture and death because of their belief in the immortality of the soul, and expresses the doctrine in a way that would have been readily understood by the Stoicism popular in the Hellenistic world (see, e.g., 9:22; 14:5; 15:3; 16:13; 17:12; 18:23). This general viewpoint is shared by the *Wisdom of Solomon*, where immortality, but not resurrection, is affirmed. Here we seem to have clear instances of the Jewish hope for life beyond death expressed in the Greek conceptuality of the immortality of the soul. The authors seem not only to have adopted Greek concepts for purposes of communication, but to have internalized them as their own way of expressing the Jewish faith. Yet even here, the idea of the preexistence of the soul is lacking, and eternal life is seen as the gift of God, not something that is ontologically inherent in being human as such. Thus the final words of 4 Maccabees did not declare that the faithful Maccabean martyrs had merely sloughed off their fleshly body so that their immortal soul could return to God, but they "*received* pure and immortal souls *from* God" (18:23).[33]

33. For a detailed and nuanced treatment of the contrast between "immortality" and "resurrection," see George W. E. Nickelsburg, *Resurrection, Immortality, and Eternal Life in Intertestamental Judaism*, HTS 26 (Cambridge:

— *Philo* is our most extensive, and most spectacular, example of the efforts of Diaspora Judaism to interpret the faith in Greek categories. He was a fierce advocate of the literal observance of the traditional laws, but he nonetheless interpreted them in a nonliteral manner, accommodating them to the Greek understanding of natural law. Philo saw the world through Middle Platonic lenses, and argued that, when properly understood, Moses teaches the Platonic worldview and ethic. The deeper meaning of the biblical ritual laws is always concerned with how the individual's mind or soul can prevail over the passions of the flesh and attain the freedom of the truly spiritual person, with immortality as the reward. Moses was the original revealer of divine wisdom, had lived before Plato, who had in fact derived his philosophy from the law of Moses! Plato was simply Moses speaking Attic Greek, and Moses himself was interpreted in the Greek categories of the Hellenistic θεῖος ἀνήρ (*theios anēr*, divine man).

Missions, proselytes, and God-fearers. Modern Judaism is not "evangelistic," does not seek converts. Hellenistic Judaism was not only open and inviting to its Gentile neighbors, but sometimes carried on an active mission (see Matt 23:15; Acts 2:10; 6:5), understanding its covenant responsibility to be the "light to the nations" (see Isa 42:6; 49:6). When it is called a missionary religion, the phrase must be understood differently from the later Christian usage. The Jews did not send out missionaries into the unbelieving world expressly to proselyte among the heathen. They were already there, settled by the thousands in innumerable towns and cities across the Mediterranean world, and they did missionary work by living out their faith in ways attractive to thoughtful Gentiles.

The Jewish advocacy of monotheism, when taken seriously, carries with it a missionary imperative—the one God is the God of all peoples, and they must know this and acknowledge God as God. Jewish monotheism, ancient tradition, and high ethical standards (e.g., they did not abandon unwanted babies to die by exposure) was very attractive to many Gentiles, and many became proselytes. For others attracted to Judaism, circumcision and the food laws were a deterrent; the number of women converts far exceeded that of male proselytes.

Diaspora Judaism developed an alternative method of participating in Jewish life without becoming a full convert: the concept of the "God-fearer." The term means "worshiper of God," that is, the one true God proclaimed by Judaism. Such people had abandoned pagan polytheism, forming a penumbra around the synagogue acquainted with biblical teaching and Jewish tradition, a kind of associate membership and prospect list of people who attended the synagogue but had not formally become proselytes (see fig. 26). Acts represents Cornelius as such a person (Acts 10:1–3) and pictures Paul, preaching in the synagogue, addressing his hearers as "Jews and God-fearers" (Acts 13:16, 26). Though in the New Testament only Acts speaks of such a category, the existence of such a class, distinguished from both ethnic Jews and ex-Gentile proselytes who had been converted to Judaism, now seems to be confirmed by inscriptions from Miletus and Aphrodisias.[34]

Harvard University Press, 1972), esp. the appendix responding to Oscar Cullmann, *Immortality of the Soul; or, Resurrection of the Dead? The Witness of the New Testament* (London: Epworth, 1958). N. T. Wright argues for an integrated understanding in which all mainstream Jews actually believed in a future resurrection, with references to immortality understood as referring to the intermediate state between death and resurrection (N. T. Wright, *The Resurrection of the Son of God*, vol. 3 of *Christian Origins and the Question of God* [Minneapolis: Fortress Press, 2003], 162–81).

34. See Boring, Berger, and Colpe, eds., *Hellenistic Commentary*, §507. See also the inscription in the Miletus theater, "Jews and Godfearers," designating a seating section corresponding to other ethnic, social, and professional groups. On such occasions, God-fearers were publicly identified as included among Jews, though distinguished from them. The issue continues to be disputed (see concise discussion and full bibliography in Richard I. Pervo, *Acts: A Commentary*, Hermeneia [Minneapolis: Fortress Press, 2009], 332–33). I use "God-fearer" as a general term

FIGURE 26: An inscription from the theater in Miletus indicating reserved seating for God-fearers in the Jewish section. PHOTO CREDIT: HOLY LAND PHOTOS.

Such a group proved to be a fertile field for the first Jewish Christian missionaries, who offered full participation in the covenant people of God without circumcision or the ritual laws. The conflicts that erupted after the incursion of Christian missionaries into the synagogue are thoroughly understandable. We ought not to suppose, however, that when God-fearers became Christians, it was with a sense of relief that they could now become full members of the people of God without the burden of the law and circumcision. Such Gentiles who had been attending the synagogue were attracted to Judaism and were willing to be publicly identified with it despite the social problems it might cause them. Their conversion to the Christian faith did not necessarily diminish their loyalty to Judaism, where they had already learned the Bible and the traditions of Israel. Such Gentile Christians may have been among the chief advocates of retaining Jewish traditions and identity within the church.

Hellenistic Jewish Christianity in the Earliest Church—the Hellenists (see above §7.4.2 *Hellenists*)

When Greek-speaking Diaspora Jews migrated to Jerusalem, for example, because of family connections, for business reasons, or to settle or retire in the Holy Land for religious reasons, they found themselves in a strange environment where they could not understand the language, where their own Greek language and Hellenistic ways did not always commend them to local religious Jews.[35] As it turned out, these

for Gentiles who were attracted to Judaism's monotheism and ethics, as typified by Cornelius in Acts 10, who may have attended the synagogue without becoming proselytes. I am not arguing or presupposing that "God-fearer" was a technical term for a clearly defined and widely recognized status of almost-Jews or wannabe-Jews.

35. See Karl Löning, "The Circle of Stephen and Its Mission," in *Christian Beginnings: Word and Community from Jesus to Post-Apostolic Times*, ed. Jürgen Becker (Louisville, KY: Westminster John Knox Press, 1993), 103–31; James G. D. Dunn, "The Hellenists and the

FIGURE 27: Miletus city gate, now reconstructed in Berlin Pergamon museum. PHOTO CREDIT: M. EUGENE BORING.

Hellenists in Jerusalem were to play an important role in the formation and expansion of early Christianity. Some were converted to the Christian faith in the earliest days of the church. While some Hellenists had presumably moved to Jerusalem to be near the temple, they found they were not always welcomed by other Jews, and some became alienated from the temple and its sacrificial system. In their previous Hellenistic context, they had become accustomed to interpreting the Torah in a spiritual sense that no longer absolutized the literal observance of the sacrificial system of the temple, and now such converts understood their new Christian faith in a way that relativized the law. The Messiah had made God's forgiveness available on an entirely different basis than the temple's sacrificial cult; the heavenly Son of Man would soon return, and the eschatological conversion of the nations to the one true God would be a reality that would no longer require strict Torah observance. They had not known Jesus in Galilee, had become members of the Christian community on the basis of the post-Easter kerygma, and knew Jesus only on the basis of the church's proclamation. As they had had their own Greek-speaking synagogues within Judaism, so now they had their own Greek-speaking house churches within the new Christian community, where they celebrated the Lord's Supper, received instruction in their new faith, and launched their mission to the world. Such seems to have been the Hellenists' understanding of the new faith, as they lived in uneasy tension with their native Palestinian, Aramaic-speaking brothers and sisters in the new Christian community who continued to worship in the temple and adhere strictly to the law.

Luke's history of the earliest days of the church was written later to emphasize its unity and harmony, minimizing its internal conflicts and concerned to show that such problems emerged only gradually and were peacefully resolved by apostolic leadership (e.g., Acts 6:1–7). Thus, in Acts, when the Hellenists complain about the neglect of their widows in the charitable distributions of the church, the

First Outreach," in James D. G. Dunn, *Beginning from Jerusalem* (Grand Rapids: Eerdmans, 2009), 241–321.

apostles appoint a commission of seven men from the Hellenist group to supervise this distribution. But the extensive description of the testimony and death of a leading member of this group, Stephen, portrays him as anything but an administrator of welfare funds. He is a miracle worker and especially a powerful, Spirit-filled preacher, performing the "ministry of the word," which Luke had just specifically assigned to the Twelve. The seven are leaders of a special segment of the community. They, and not the native Aramaic-speaking apostles, are driven from Jerusalem by the Jewish authorities.[36] It seems that the Hellenists criticized the Mosaic law and the temple cult in a provocatively different way from the main body of Aramaic-speaking disciples represented by the Twelve apostles. From the very beginning, this initial diversity generated a variety of ways in which the new faith was understood, and the seeds of internal conflict were present from the earliest days. The controversy about Christian observance of the Torah continued, with deep and wide-ranging effects in the growing Christian movement.

Gentile Churches

Some Hellenistic Jewish Christians in Jerusalem interpreted the new faith in Hellenistic categories. It is they who were persecuted by the local Jewish authorities, not because they were Christians, but because of their dangerous views about Torah and temple.[37] The Aramaic-speaking Jewish Christians were not persecuted but remained in Jerusalem, abiding by the Torah and loyal to the temple (Acts 6:8–8:1). The missionaries outside Jerusalem included the Hellenists who had been driven out. Philip, one of the original seven leaders, went to Samaria (Acts 8:1–13) and was later instrumental in the conversion of an Ethiopian eunuch. This government official in the service of the queen was returning from his pilgrimage to Jerusalem—a pilgrimage made even though he could not worship in the temple or be fully accepted into the Jewish community (not because of his nationality, but because he was a eunuch). Both Samaritans and the physically mutilated were excluded from mainstream Judaism but welcomed by the Jewish Christian Hellenist missionaries.

As the displaced Hellenists resettled outside Jerusalem, they proclaimed their new faith in the Greek-speaking synagogues. Here they sometimes found a (minimal) positive response and a few converts among the Jews, but mostly experienced rejection. The God-fearers proved to be a more fertile field. This initial "mission to the Gentiles" at first meant the *dropping* of what had been an insuperable barrier *within* the synagogue, a barrier that had prevented people who were already attracted to monotheism, Scripture, and the Jewish perspective on the world and life from becoming full members of the covenant people of God. When members of this group became believers in Jesus as the Messiah, they sometimes found after a while that they had to withdraw from the synagogue or were excluded from it.

Then *this* group made the most radical revolutionary move of all and began to communicate their new faith to Gentiles who had not previously been associated with the synagogue at all. Predominantly Gentile churches came into being. By the time our earliest Christian document was written, people who had never had any association with Judaism were being won to the new faith (1 Thess 1:9–10). Their conversion did not involve first becoming Jews; they were accepted into the new Christian communities without circumcision. This was a momentous step the modern reader must ponder at length in order to understand and appreciate its historical and theological significance.[38]

36. Marcel Simon, *St. Stephen and the Hellenists in the Primitive Church* (New York: Longmans, 1958).

37. This Hellenistic interpretation of Christianity had already taken place prior to the conversion of Paul. It was not Paul who replaced the "simple Jewish faith of Jesus" with a Hellenistic religion about him; when Paul was converted, he became a member of a church that was already thoroughly Hellenized.

38. To get an impression of what this momentous step meant, the modern reader might reflect on such biblical

Thus, for the first time, communities of baptized-but-uncircumcised Christian believers came into being, composed of people who were not Jews. Gentile Christianity was born, generated by unknown Hellenistic Jewish Christian missionaries. Acts' later retelling of this expansion credits the conversion of the first Gentiles to the apostle Peter and reports that it received official approval from the apostolic leadership in Jerusalem (Acts 10–11). But, having made this point clear, the author also indicates, almost incidentally, that the first missionaries to Gentiles were in fact these anonymous Hellenists (Acts 11:19–26). Luke here telescopes the widespread Hellenists' mission that resulted in the formation of Gentile churches into one dramatic scene in which Peter—for Luke the primary apostle in the earliest days of the church—plays the leading role.

Students of the New Testament should note carefully that this history demolishes the romantic idea that "toleration" and "inclusiveness" was first proclaimed by *Jesus*. This revolutionary new development was a matter of the Holy Spirit at work in the life of the church, not the program of the individual hero Jesus. Nor was it the work of Paul.

The House Church

The dynamics that shaped the new movement were not only theological, but also social and political, and these sociopolitical forces both facilitated the church's mission and made it problematic.[39] A social reality especially crucial for understanding the nature of early Christianity was the formation of house churches. Acts 2:42 portrays the followers of Jesus not only as continuing to worship in temple and synagogue, but as meeting in private homes, but this may be the author's retrojection of the situation of his own time into the earlier history. We can be confident that by the time of the Pauline mission reflected in the earliest Christian documents, it was common to refer to "the church in the house" of someone (1 Cor 16:15, 19–20; Rom 16:3–5, 23).

As the church became more distinct from the synagogue, the house church, presumably developed in earlier phases of the Gentile mission, increasingly became the primary form of congregational life. Here the word was proclaimed, the sacraments were celebrated, hospitality was extended to traveling disciples and missionaries. In the Pauline mission, the house church became an aspect of missionary strategy.

Paul and his colleagues did not preach on street corners or go door to door or even village to village. They established house churches that became the centers of mission work to which people were invited and attracted, and that generated other such house churches. That the congregations met in private homes would encourage the informality and sense of belonging and equality that was inherent in family life. At the same time, it tended to reinforce the patriarchy of family structure in the Hellenistic world. The atrium of a large home could accommodate thirty to fifty people; sometimes there would be more than one such congregation in a city (fig. 28). In such cases, it would be difficult for the congregations of individual house churches to meet in plenary session and easy for party lines and factionalism to develop.

How should we imagine the social interaction of these house churches with the surrounding world? How did their neighbors view them? On the one hand, they must have generated some suspicion. Worshipers at Roman temples gathered outside, in front of the temple; the temple was for the deity, not the worshipers. New religious groups whose meetings were not conducted in public were viewed with suspicion. On the other hand, the modern reader should not imagine the early Christian house churches in terms of contemporary North America or Europe, where there is a vast contrast between informal (and often suspect) religious "fringe"

texts as Gen. 17:9–14 and the martyr stories of 1 and 2 Maccabees, attempting to appreciate what Israel's martyrs had died for and how this was seen by devoted first-century Jews.

39. See Roger W. Gehring, *House Church and Mission: The Importance of Household Structures in Early Christianity* (Peabody, MA: Hendrickson, 2004), and the bibliography he provides.

FIGURE 28: One of the numerous large, wealthy houses excavated recently in Ephesus. Homes like these could accommodate many people, and the households of wealthy Christians became the meeting places for house churches. PHOTO CREDIT: M. EUGENE BORING.

groups that meet in private homes and the impressive architecture of "mainline" churches, synagogues, and mosques. In the ancient world, there was already a long tradition of private religious associations, groups of initiates and philosophical schools that met in the commodious homes of patrons.

In the first century, the synagogue was not usually a traditional building with a distinctive architecture, on the public square "next door to the Zeus temple," but was in the residential section inhabited by Jews, and their meeting places were not conspicuous. Gentile neighbors were in fact sometimes suspicious of them, but Jews had been around a long time, long enough to allay some of these suspicions. So long as the church was a movement within or a subgroup of the synagogue, it had an established place in the social structure. As the early Christian movement became increasingly Gentile and left or was expelled from the synagogue, the house church became the standard social structure for the new communities of believers.

The contemporary reader, especially in Europe or North America, must resist the pressure to think of "house church" in terms of modern one-family houses, in which people of different socioeconomic classes are geographically segregated, with the wealthy upper classes living in large homes in one part of town, poorer people in their own smaller homes in other parts, the very poor in tenements in a poverty-stricken inner city. In such settings, poor people may visit wealthy neighborhoods—where they are noticed as "out of place." They may admire, envy, and resent the elegant homes they see. Wealthy people may visit poor neighborhoods, either on social visits or slumming expeditions. But at the end of the day, each returns to his or her place, and social boundaries are marked by residential areas.

In Hellenistic cities, we should rather think of society as composed of a large number of overlapping pyramids, with each pyramid containing the whole gamut from very rich to very poor, with the patron at the peak of each pyramid, and the emperor as the chief patron at the top of them all. In large cities, rich and poor lived together in large city-block *insulae* ("islands"), all in the same large building complex that included the elegant apartment of the owner/patron; his or her extended family; shops and small offices where his employees, retainers, and slaves lived; with small living quarters attached in a loft or back room. Distinctions between social classes were very rigid, and each one "stayed in his place," but the separation was not geographical. All lived under one roof, and the distinctions were maintained by social rituals rather than geographical space. Paul would have worked at his trade (tentmaker, leatherworker) in one of these shops and would have slept in the loft or adjoining room, in close physical proximity to both slaves and wealthy property owners, in a social situation where all understood the rules and lived by them, without giving a thought that it could or should be otherwise.

In situations where all or most of the disciples belonged to the lower social classes—as was typically the case—a "house church" would be a "tenement church," meeting in a small room that could accommodate no more than ten or twelve people. When wealthy people were converted, their more spacious homes with dining rooms and atriums could accommodate larger groups. Thus Prisca and Aquila were apparently business people of some wealth, Phoebe apparently had employees and slaves, and Philemon had a house served by slaves, with more than one guest room. Such economically powerful people were accustomed to acting as patrons, just as others were accustomed to ordering their lives in regard to their standing with their patron. The structure of the patriarchal family was accepted by all, considered just as "natural" and unquestionably "the way things are" as private property, the market economy, and the distinction between first class and economy class on jetliners are assumed by most modern residents of North America.

The social barriers that were considered absolutely normal by all concerned were now called in question by the new egalitarian *koinonia* of the Christian community. When, for instance, a church met in the spacious house of the patron, which rules and conventions apply? Is the group a household or a religious institution? While the house churches provided the setting for redemptive Christian freedom of the "discipleship of equals,"[40] in which there was no longer Jew or Gentile, slave or free, male or female (Gal 3:27–28), it also was the setting for tensions and disputes that were often more sociological than doctrinal. In any case, theological understanding of the new faith could not be abstracted from the social realities in which it was lived out.

Formation of Distinctive Traditions and Theologies

In the twenty years between the death of Jesus and the writing of (what became) the first New Testament book, early Christian thinkers

40. Cf. Elisabeth Schüssler Fiorenza, *Discipleship of Equals: A Critical Feminist Ekklesiology of Liberation* (New York: Crossroad, 1993).

developed distinctive ways of expressing their new faith. In order to clarify its own faith, instruct its new members, and communicate this faith to others, early Christianity generated and handed on a number of new theological traditions. This did not happen all at once or uniformly among the whole Christian community, or in a straight-line diachronic development. Here we will survey and summarize some of the kinds of theological developments that took place between the initial formation of the new faith in 30 CE immediately after Easter and Paul's first letter to the Thessalonians about 50 CE. When Paul began his mission, norms for the faith and standard rituals for expressing it had already been worked out in the early Christian community, norms that were acknowledged as valid in the church beyond Jerusalem and Judea. These earliest ways of thinking about the meaning of the Christ event were generated by Jesus' followers in the early days and years of the church, on the basis of their experience of the risen Christ, their community life in the power of the Holy Spirit, and the traditions and materials from which they could draw in formulating their new faith. From the very beginning, early Christianity had three main categories of materials that influenced how they understood their new faith: (1) Jewish tradition, both Palestinian and Hellenistic, (2) the Bible, both Hebrew and its Greek translations, (3) traditions from and about Jesus.

1. Jewish Tradition, both Palestinian and Hellenistic

Whether Palestinian or Hellenistic, the earliest Christians were Jews, and that not merely as an incidental fact, a given of their historical situation. They were intentionally, self-consciously Jews, who did not understand themselves as persons who had seceded from Judaism or been converted to another religion, but as those who celebrated the climax and fulfillment of the hope and history of Israel. Their faith was expressed in the eschatological and messianic categories already present in Jewish tradition, transformed in the light of their faith that Jesus is the risen Lord.

2. Christological Interpretation of (Jewish) Scripture

The church did not have a New Testament for a long time, but it always had a Bible. The earliest Christians inherited a Bible by virtue of being Jews. They did not decide whether or not to have a Bible; it was a given from the very beginning. The church did not merely adopt a book that was in the public domain—the book came with its self-understanding as Israel. The earliest Christians did not make independent canonical decisions about which books they would "accept" in "their" Scripture; they accepted the canon of Jewish Scriptures that was still in process of formation, with its ambiguities and fuzzy edges (see above, §2.2.1). That Scripture played a normative rule in the new community was assumed without dispute, and did not become a problem until the second century (Marcion!). This was not true only in the original Palestinian Jewish setting. As the church spread in the wider Hellenistic world, and Christian congregations became primarily Gentile, this self-understanding continued. Gentile Christians soon came to understand that, by being incorporated into the covenant people of God, they had become heirs of the Jewish Scriptures, saw their own story as the continuation of the biblical story, and understood their life together in the church as directed by the word of God in Scripture.

In Judaism, as in the Bible itself, Scripture continued to be authoritative for the community as it moved through history and faced new situations by a continuous process of reinterpretation. In reinterpreting their Bible, early Christians were continuing Israel's dialogue with Scripture. They understood that with the coming of the Messiah and the eschatological age, the community's dialogue with Scripture now reached a definitive climax. Just as the Qumran community found new meanings in the Scripture on the basis of their conviction that the eschatological times had begun and they were living in the last days, so with the early Christians—including their use of some of the same texts (e.g., Isa 40:1–3). There is no doubt that the early Christians read their Bible with new eyes, found meanings there that were not the original historical meaning. They did not begin with the biblical texts and ask if Jesus fulfilled them, and then, finding predictions of Jesus there, came to believe in Jesus as the Messiah. The process was exactly the reverse: they began with their Christian faith, generated by God's act in Jesus, by the resurrection, by the work of the Holy Spirit in the community and in their own lives; they then found this faith confirmed, illustrated, and given content by their new reading of the Bible.[41] It was the Christ event, the Christian faith brought to the texts, that allowed Christian teachers to read them as predicting the Christ event. This is paradigmatically illustrated in the scene of Acts 8:26–35. The Ethiopian already has the Bible, reads it sincerely, but does not understand it. Philip, the Christian evangelist, brings his faith to the text, and proclaims the Christian faith from it. The text of itself did not testify to Jesus or generate Christian faith.

The modern reader may gain an impression of some of these developments from the following examples:

— The general conviction could be expressed that the Christ event—Jesus' life, death, and resurrection—was "according to the Scripture," without giving any details (1 Cor 15:3–4).

— Specific events in Jesus' life could be seen as explicitly predicted in the Old Testament. The first New Testament instance (Isa 7:14=Matt 1:22–23) represents a very common occurrence.

— The new faith could be expressed in terms of biblical statements and language without explicitly claiming that the biblical promises or predictions were now being fulfilled. This too is very common in the New Testament. The author of Revelation, for instance, never once explicitly cites his Bible, yet there are about five hundred allusions and echoes of biblical language and phraseology in his twenty-two chapters. Since the New Testament authors do not often indicate they are alluding to the Scripture, such allusions are often missed by modern readers unless their minds are already steeped in biblical texts (e.g., Matt 5:5=Ps 37:11).

— Details of Jesus' life and death could be filled in from Scripture texts. Thus Mark 15:34 portrays Jesus' last words from the cross as a citation from Psalm 22:1, while Luke 23:46 draws from a different Psalm (31:5) to represent Jesus' last prayer. Psalm 22 and other psalms of the suffering righteous person vindicated by God were particularly rich sources for portraying the passion story.

— The Scripture could be cited as very words of Jesus. Hebrews 10:5, for example, quotes Psalm 40:6–8 as the words of Jesus "when he came into the world." It is not clear whether the author is thinking of what the heavenly Christ says as he enters this world or whether the author of Hebrews thinks of these as words of the earthly Jesus—in either case, they come from his christological reading of his Bible, not from historical memory of something said by Jesus of Nazareth (see also Heb 2:11–13, where three Old Testament texts are cited as sayings of Jesus or the transcendent Christ).

— Biblical models could be adopted as a way of telling the Jesus story (typology). Jesus becomes the "new Adam," "new Moses," or "new David," and the church becomes a "new Israel," and its

41. Paul is an example of those Jews who had studied the Scriptures their whole life without seeing it filled with prophecies of the coming Messiah. He did not recognize Jesus as Messiah on the basis that he fulfilled biblical prophecies. But, as pictured in Acts, when he was converted by his encounter with the risen Christ, he came to believe that scales had fallen from his eyes (Acts 9:18) or a veil had been lifted from his reading of the Bible (2 Cor 3:12–18). He read the same texts, but he now saw them in terms of his new faith in the crucified and risen Lord.

opponents become contemporary versions of God's enemies in the Bible. Without claiming specific texts as "predictions," Christian teachers see Jesus or the church as already anticipated in their Bible (e.g., Gen 1–3 and Rom 5:12–21; Exodus–Numbers and 1 Cor 10:1–10).

— Biblical stories are allegorized to represent Christian realities (e.g., the story of Abraham, Sarah, and Hagar is understood in terms of the church's view of Jewish and Gentile Christianity, Gen 16–21=Gal 4:21–31). In neither typology nor allegory is the reality of the original biblical story denied, but what it was "really" talking about is explicated from the perspective of the Christian interpreter.

— Early Christian teachers both adopted texts from Judaism that had already been understood messianically and discovered new texts not previously understood as referring to the Messiah. Such texts were apparently copied out into collections that circulated independently, apart from their original contexts. No such Christian "testimony books" have survived, but circumstantial evidence of their existence has been strengthened by the discovery of such collections of messianic texts at Qumran.[42]

— In interpreting the biblical texts, Christian authors occasionally changed the text they were citing to bring out more clearly the meaning they saw from the Christian perspective. Some alterations are seemingly minor, but hermeneutically significant. For example, in the first biblical citation in Matthew, the "you" of Isaiah 7:14 (both MT and LXX) becomes "they," understood as a periphrasis for "God." Thus the Bible is understood to say that God will name the baby Emmanuel, not that the parents will do so. In the Bible, the verb "name" is often understood as meaning "constitute," "designate the reality of." When "name" is understood in this way, Matthew's initial biblical quotation means, "God will constitute this child as God-with-us; he will represent God's presence among humanity." This is an important Matthean theme of which the author was already convinced; he has changed the biblical text he is quoting to make this meaning clear. Similarly, the imperative "Strike the shepherd" of Zechariah 13:7 becomes the first-person indicative in the quotation in Mark 14:27, "I [God] will strike the shepherd," to make clear that Jesus is not merely the victim of human injustice, but that the death of Jesus is God's act: God is present and active in the event of Jesus' crucifixion. Like Jewish translators and copyists, Christian scribes copying the LXX (which was transmitted exclusively by Christians after the Jewish community abandoned it) very occasionally changed the text of the LXX itself (not just in Christian documents citing it) to make their interpretation clearer. They did this in the conviction that they were either correcting the text to its original form, or that their new reading was in fact the original, divinely intended meaning.[43] While questionable from a modern historical perspective, in which a premium is placed on the exact citation of sources, such hermeneutical moves were quite in accord with biblical interpretation in first-century Judaism, as documented in the Qumran texts.

3. *Traditions from and about Jesus*

Whatever messianic ideas the disciples had entertained prior to Jesus' death, his execution had made it clear that he was not the Messiah they were hoping for (see Luke 24:21). The resurrection had radically reversed this judgment, but now the meaning of messiahship had to be rethought from the ground up. The church does not, or does not only, continue Jesus' proclamation; it proclaims Jesus himself. The proclaimer

42. For a brief summary of the hypothesis, see Harry Y. Gamble, *Books and Readers in the Early Church: A History of Early Christian Texts* (New Haven, CT: Yale University Press, 1995), 27, and the literature he gives. Such books of testimonies seem to have existed in the earliest period, but (like the hypothetical Q document) are among the lost items of early Christian writings.

43. Jobes and Silva, *Septuagint*, 297 and elsewhere.

becomes the proclaimed, the message of Jesus becomes the message about Jesus, believing in response to Jesus becomes believing in Jesus (=God's act in Jesus).

The impact was immediate; the conceptual and theological fallout extended over some time. This transition from what-Jesus-said-and-did to what-God-did-in-the-Christ event was at first done in intuitive, unreflective ways. The earliest church lived in the excitement and fervor of their experience of the risen Christ and of the Spirit; they were not conducting seminars on philosophical theology or discussion groups on Christology or eschatology. It never entered their minds but that they continued to be worshipers of the one true God. The relation of the risen Jesus to this one God was not a conceptual problem for them, but the conviction that God had not let the cross be the end of Jesus, that the Jesus to whom they were devoted had been exalted to the presence of God in a unique way, meant that faith had to be fundamentally rethought.

When we separate their thought into discrete topics for purposes of discussion (Christology, soteriology, eschatology and the like), we are using the later rubrics of Christian theology only for the modern reader's convenience in perceiving the contours of the thinking of the earliest Christians. In reality, their thoughts of God, Christ, Israel and the church, the law, and eschatology were interwoven into one dynamic whole. Since the resurrection experiences evoked an immediate rethinking of the meaning of Jesus' identity and the meaning of his life and mission, we will begin with Christology. We do not know what sort of christological affirmations about Jesus were already present in the pre-Easter period (see above §8.3), nor do we know which of the christological titles already present in Judaism (see above §7.6.3) played a role in the earliest post-Easter reconfiguration of the disciples' faith.

Here is a plausible scenario: Jesus had used the designation *Son of Man* in a provocatively ambiguous way (or ways). As a result of the resurrection, it was now clear that Jesus himself is the transcendent Son of Man (Dan 7:9–14), who has already been present on earth, spoken and acted with authority, suffered, died, and been raised by God—and who now reigns with God's authority from heaven, and will shortly return in power to establish the kingdom of God. Jesus' resurrection was not merely something special that happened to him—it was the firstfruits of the harvest that signaled the beginning of the eschatological age (1 Cor 15:20–23), with the general resurrection soon to follow at the parousia.

The risen Jesus not only appeared to chosen disciples, but continued to speak from heaven in the words of charismatic prophets. The risen Lord, speaking in the first person, identifies himself as the transcendent Son of Man. Jesus himself had often used this self-designation, it designated a heavenly figure, and it can be found in the Bible. These three points (Jesus' own usage, Son of Man as transcendent figure that Jesus was now believed to be, and searching the Scriptures for categories by which to interpret the dramatic visionary event) all point to Son of Man as the earliest christological title.[44] Continuity with the pre-Easter Jesus is provided by the Son of Man designation. Thus the proclaimer of the kingdom of God becomes the self-proclaimed from heaven, and then is proclaimed by other Christian preachers. Perceiving Jesus as the exalted Son of Man became the theological gateway to understanding him as Messiah, Lord, and Son of God, so that other christological titles were applied to him. This process did not take long. Very early, the affirmation of Jesus as the Christ became the, or a, central Christian confession (see on 1 Cor 15:3–5 below).

44. Martin Hengel and Anna Maria Schwemer, *Paul between Damascus and Antioch: The Unknown Years*, trans. John Bowden (Louisville, KY: Westminster John Knox Press, 1997), 103, rightly argue that confession of Jesus as Son of Man belongs within the earliest Jerusalem circle of Hellenist Christians. See the detailed argument in Boring, *Sayings of the Risen Jesus*, 239–50.

We can speak with some confidence about two early streams of christological tradition: (1) traditions *about* Jesus that focused on the Christ event as a whole, with emphasis on the death and resurrection and minimal reference to Jesus' life and teachings, and (2) traditions (purportedly) *from* Jesus in the form of reports of particular sayings and deeds. The present state of research does not allow us to sort out this development in terms of particular persons or groups. We do not know how these two streams of christological thought were related in the very earliest days of the Christian movement.

How can we determine what Christian materials were handed on and around in the time prior to our extant written documents? For the Pauline churches, we can fairly often recognize that Paul is quoting traditional materials. He sometimes explicitly tells us so (1 Thess 4:15–17; 1 Cor 11:23–26; 15:3–5). There are numerous places where Paul and other writers cite or allude to liturgical, catechetical, and other early traditions without explicitly saying so. Throughout the Pauline corpus and later New Testament writings, these can be identified with considerable probability by form criticism, just as in a modern letter quotations or allusions from a hymn, creed, or fragment from a traditional liturgy can be identified by meter, rhyme, style, and vocabulary. No modern reader would have any difficulty in sorting out Psalm 23 or the Lord's Prayer if they were cited in a letter, even if not set apart by font, parentheses, or quotation marks, and even if the reader is not directly familiar with these biblical texts. In addition to the explicit citations of tradition mentioned above, other traditional materials embedded in later texts that have been identified by scholars, with more or less probability from case to case, are 1 Thessalonians 1:9–10; 4:16–17; 5:8; 1 Corinthians 1:30; 6:11; 8:6; 12:3, 13; 16:22; 2 Corinthians 1:21–22; Romans 1:3–4; 3:23–26; 4:24–25; 6:3–4; 10:9; Philippians 2:6–11; Galatians 3:27–28; 4:6; Colossians 1:15–20; Ephesians 4:4–6; 5:14; 1 Timothy 3:16; 6:15–16; 2 Timothy 1:9–10; 2:11–13; Titus 3:4–7; 1 Peter 1:18–21; 2:21–25; 3:18–19; 1 John 4:7–10; Revelation 4:11; 5:9–10; 5:12–14. Moreover, it is probable that some extensive topical discussions (e.g., "wisdom," 1 Cor 2:6–3:1; "love," 1 Cor 13:1–13) and midrashic expositions of Scripture texts (e.g., 1 Cor 10:1–21; 2 Cor 3:7–18; Gal 4:21–31) are not ad hoc compositions, but represent the products of exegetical discussions among Christian teachers within the pre-Pauline and Pauline traditions. While some such traditions originated in later New Testament times, some were certainly composed prior to our earliest New Testament document and represent the thought, life, and worship of the earliest church. As an example of such material, we will briefly examine one key text, 1 Corinthians 15:3–5:

I.

A. ὅτι Χριστὸς ἀπέθανεν	that Christ died
B. ὑπὲρ τῶν ἁμαρτιῶν ἡμῶν	for our sins
C. κατὰ τὰς γραφὰς	according to the Scriptures
D. καὶ ὅτι ἐτάφη	and that he was buried

II.

A. καὶ ὅτι ἐγήγερται	and that he was raised
B. τῇ ἡμέρᾳ τῇ τρίτῃ	on the third day
C. κατὰ τὰς γραφὰς	according to the Scriptures
D. καὶ ὅτι ὤφθη Κηφᾷ	and that he appeared to Cephas

Clearly, Paul does not compose this creedal statement as he is writing 1 Corinthians. He identifies this statement as a summary of the εὐαγγέλιον (*euangelion*, gospel, good news) he had preached on his initial visit to Corinth. The creedal statement is not an identification formula applying messianic titles to Jesus, such as "Jesus is the Christ" or "Jesus is the Son of God," but is a narrative that presupposes this identification and declares the act of God in the Christ event. Jesus is passive, and God is the actor. The narrative is retrospective on Jesus' life, speaking only of his death and resurrection, with nothing of the "life and teaching of Jesus." The bare-bones structure is seen in the pair of verbs that introduce their respective units, representing the event and its historical confirmation:

ἀπέθανεν / ἐτάφη	died/was buried
ἐγήγερται / ὤφθη	was raised/was seen (=appeared)

Each unit is then elaborated with two lines of theological interpretation and validation that maintain the parallel structure of the units, giving the following pattern repeated in each of the two sections:

A = event

B = interpretation

C = theological validation

D = historical validation

Paul received this creed as normative tradition, presumably when he was converted, probably from the church in Damascus or Antioch (see Gal 1:17; Acts 11:25–26).[45] The creed appears to have been composed in Greek, which by no means precludes its having been composed in the earliest Jerusalem community, whence it was transmitted as part of the earliest tradition to other churches. It probably did not originate among those earliest Jewish Christians who continued to participate in the temple ritual, including its regular sacrifices and the Day of Atonement, but could well have come from the Jerusalem Hellenistic Christians who were alienated from the temple.[46] This would take us back to within a year or two of the birth of the Christian faith, and would make this creed the oldest Christian confession.

Alongside creedal and hymnic summaries of the meaning of the Christ event, the new Christian community communicated its faith in the form of stories and sayings from the life of Jesus. Many of these were later preserved, elaborated, and interpreted in the Gospels. The Gospels themselves represent a new literary genre introduced in second- and third-generation Christianity, but they contain materials from the earlier period in which the Christian tradition was transmitted primarily as oral tradition (see below §§19–20). Such sayings and stories from the Jesus tradition, like the creedal and hymnic materials, pointed to the church's faith in God's act in the Christ event as a whole. They were not transmitted as a connected story of the "life of Jesus" but as individual units of teaching and kerygmatic material. For discussion of the types of material and their function, see below §19.3.1.

Opposition and Conflict in Earliest Christianity, 30–50 CE

Jesus was a controversial figure, often in conflict with elements of the Jewish leadership. With the complicity of some of them, Jesus was executed by the Romans as a potential political troublemaker. Between Jesus' death in 30 CE and the writing of the earliest extant Christian document in 50 CE, Jesus' followers were embroiled in various conflicts that shaped the character of the movement. From our later

45. Hengel and Schwemer, *Between Damascus and Antioch*, 99, argue the form and content of the creedal text goes back to the earliest church in Jerusalem, transmitted to the Damascus disciples, and this is where Paul received it, immediately after his baptism ca. 33 CE.

46. Dunn, *Beginning from Jerusalem*, 232–35, gives a full discussion of how difficult it is to see the Jerusalem Christians "also" believing in the atoning death of Jesus, while actively participating in the temple cult of atonement. The Hellenistic churches and Paul could recite the creed of 1 Cor. 15:3 without conflicting with their own understanding of the temple cultus.

perspective, we can distinguish between (1) secular, political conflicts between early Christians and the Roman authorities, and (2) religious conflicts of two types: (a) external conflicts between Christians and Jews, and (b) internal conflicts among Christians themselves.

Conflicts between Christians and Their Greco-Roman Context

The Roman authorities had officially executed Jesus as a potential threat to the state. But the Romans did not pursue Jesus' followers. Having disposed of their leader, the Romans did not attempt to stamp out the movement he had initiated. This was analogous to the government's response to the disciples of John the Baptist; once John was out of the way, the potentially troublesome movement had been nipped in the bud, and John's followers were not molested unless, on other grounds, they ran afoul of the state. So also with Jesus' followers; it would be a serious historical mistake to portray the Roman authorities as opposed to the church from the very beginning. Christians were not recognized as a group distinct from Judaism until decades later. The first official Roman persecution of Christians was 64 CE, limited to the city of Rome. Christians were charged with arson; Christian faith as such was not a crime. In the early second century, Roman governors were still unclear as to the identity of Christians and how they should be dealt with legally (see §26.1.4).

Though it was not illegal to be a Christian and there was no comprehensive official Roman persecution, from the earliest days Christians were subject to harassment and mistreatment by their Gentile neighbors and by local officials, which sometimes became lethal (Mark 13:9; Acts 16:19–24). Thus, when Paul writes our first extant Christian document, some Christians had already met death because of their faith (1 Thess 2:14).

Conflicts between Christians and Jews

The Acts account of Christianity's earliest days in Judea is filled with efforts by the Jewish authorities to suppress the new movement. This was seen as an internal conflict among Jews, not as a clash between two religions. Peter and John are arrested and brought before the Sanhedrin but released (4:1–22). The temple officials arrest the two apostles, briefly imprison them, threaten them, have them beaten, and then release them (5:17–42). Stephen is arrested and brought before the Sanhedrin, gives a fiery speech, and is killed, but this seems to be mob violence rather than an official execution (6:8–7:60). Then follows a persecution of the Hellenist group among the Christians, and they are forced to leave Jerusalem. They are pursued, brought to trial, and convicted, and some of them are killed (8:1–3; cf. 9:1; 22:4; 26:10). After Saul has switched his loyalty to the new Christian group, attempts are made on his life by Hellenistic Jews in both Damascus and Jerusalem (9:23–25, 29).

It is not only the religious authorities in Jerusalem who use violence in their opposition to Jesus' followers. Herod Agrippa I (41–44 CE) has James the brother of John arrested and executed. This was not because James confessed faith in Jesus, but because he was not loyal to (the dominant understanding of) the Jewish law. James the brother of Jesus, the leader of the Jerusalem church, was not touched by Herod, for he was known as a fierce advocate of the law. Herod needed to exhibit his piety and signal his devotion to traditional Jewish religious values, and thus officially eliminates one of the leaders of the new sect, who has been one of the original disciples of Jesus. He then proceeds to arrest Peter, who escapes only by divine intervention (12:1–11). Apparently Herod fears the potentially destabilizing factor the Christian movement would have in the Diaspora and the resulting problems for Jewish relations with Rome, and moves against those segments of the church that are open to Gentiles and thus causing trouble with strict Jews and some Jewish Christians. In the Acts narrative of Paul's mission journeys, it is mainly the Jews who oppose his work, frequently with violence (13:50–52; 14:5, 19–20; 17:5–9, 13). This Jewish opposition to the Christian movement, though narrated from the perspective of Luke's later theological purpose, finds support in other New Testament data that indicate Jewish opposition to the early Christian movement, official and unofficial, sometimes to the point of lethal violence (1 Thess 2:14–15; 2 Cor 11:24–25; Mark 13:9; Luke 6:22; John 16:2; see also §7.6 above).

Why did official Judaism present such violent opposition to the new sect? There were legal and theological issues. It was not just that the Jewish leaders opposed the scandalous idea proclaimed by the Christians, that God had raised up a crucified itinerant preacher, who had not been a qualified teacher of the Torah but only a manual laborer, and made him to be the Messiah. To be sure, they rejected this proclamation, but such ideas were not in themselves illegal or essentially dangerous. After the initial confrontations, the body of Christian Jews in Jerusalem remained largely undisturbed; their confession of Jesus as Son of Man or Messiah was controversial and rejected by most as terribly mistaken, but was in itself no reason for persecution.

The principal problem was that the followers of Jesus were understood to practice a dangerous, deviant form of Judaism that compromised the law and thus the essential nature and mission of the Jewish people. The new Christian movement threatened Judaism's whole symbolic universe, and this evoked persecution. Jews subjected other Jews who subverted the law to severe discipline, sometimes exacting the death penalty when they had the authority and power to do so (2 Cor 11:24–25; 1 Thess 2:14–16). The Dead Sea Scrolls indicate that the official high priest in Jerusalem had attempted to kill the leader of the Qumran community, regarded as a deviant group that threatened the very being of Judaism (1QpHab 8.17; 9.9; 11.4–8).

While the theological issues were real and important, the primary reason for Jewish violence against early Christians probably had to do with Judaism's effort to maintain its own precarious place in a fragile political world. The scene in Antioch of Pisidia exhibits a paradigmatic case (Acts 13:14–52). We know from history and archaeology that the Jewish community in Antioch was a respected and successful group, not to be thought of as backstreet or ghetto. This perception was endangered by large numbers flocking to this new group claiming to represent Judaism, "taking over the synagogue," endangering their always fragile status with the prevailing authorities, and was "likely to send a shiver up and down many a spine, since it could so easily be represented as in direct antithesis to the loyalty owed to the emperor."[47] In particular, the *Edict of Claudius* in 49 CE expelling the Jews from Rome (Acts 18:2) would have had far-reaching effects on the early Christian mission. If the emperor and the capital city were reacting negatively to Judaism as such, Jews throughout the empire had to take care not to allow Jews with radical views to upset the fragile balance Judaism was trying to maintain with the empire.

Acts 16:20–21 illustrates the situation perfectly: "When they had brought them before the magistrates, they said, 'These men are disturbing our city; they are Jews and are advocating customs that are not lawful for us as Romans to adopt or observe.'" The missionaries are not said to be *Christians*, but *Jews*, and are giving to the Jewish community in Philippi, which had struggled to gain social acceptance, a bad name they did not deserve. Understandably, Jews objected to Christians—especially if they were Gentiles—causing problems for the Jewish community, and would want to clarify: "*They* do not belong to *us*."[48]

Conflicts within the Christian Movement

The transition from the time of Jesus to the time of the church did not unfold smoothly. There were conflicting views of what it meant to be a follower of Jesus (see above on the Hellenists, §7.4.2). It was not yet clear what would become "mainline" or "orthodox" Christianity, the protocatholic church of the second century.

47. Ibid., 426, 430.
48. Cf. the later resentment of this from the Christian side, Rev. 2:9; 3:9.

Many of the internal conflicts were interwoven with the life and mission of Saul, the zealous Jewish Pharisee of Tarsus who became Paul the Christian missionary.

The most famous and influential view of the conflicts over Paul's apostolate is that of Ferdinand Christian Baur, who taught at Tübingen in the mid-nineteenth century and whose followers came to be known as the "Tübingen School." Baur's hypothesis was that Paul and his associates preached a completely different gospel from that of Peter, James, and the other apostles, producing rival groups of churches. He expressed the dynamics in terms of Hegel's dialectical philosophy of history:

Thesis: Petrine Christianity, based on loyalty to the law, represented by, for example, the Gospel of Matthew.

Antithesis: Pauline Christianity, based on freedom from the law, represented by Paul and his followers.

Synthesis: The protocatholic church of the second century, which brought the two together after their deaths and their battles were over, looked back upon both of them as heroes of the one great church. (Acts is a representative of this kind of Christianity.)

Baur thus saw all Paul's opponents as a single, unified group, sponsored by the Jewish Christianity of Jerusalem led by Peter and James, and applied the term "Judaizers" to them all. Although the model has continued to be useful, subsequent research has shown that it is a grand oversimplification that attempts to conform all the data to one unified theory.[49] It should not be assumed in advance, however, that all who opposed or were suspicious of Paul's message and mission should be lumped into one category, as though there was a single group of Paul's "opponents" with a single agenda. We will treat these conflicts in the context of his story.

49. The Baur model was renovated in the early twentieth century by Walter Bauer. See Walter Bauer, Georg Strecker, Robert A. Kraft, and Gerhard Krodel, eds., *Orthodoxy and Heresy in Earliest Christianity*, trans. Paul J. Achtemeier, et al., 2nd ed. (Philadelphia: Fortress Press, 1971), and the evaluations of this renovation in Thomas A. Robinson, *The Bauer Thesis Examined* (Lewiston, NY: Edwin Mellen Press, 1988).

9.3 For Further Reading

Resurrection and the Formation of Christology

Avemarie, Friedrich, and Hermann Lichtenberger, eds. *Auferstehung=Resurrection: The Fourth Durham-Tübingen Research Symposium; Resurrection, Transfiguration, and Exaltation in Old Testament, Ancient Judaism, and Early Christianity*. WUNT 135. Tübingen: Mohr, 2001.

Bousset, Wilhelm. *Kyrios Christos: A History of the Belief in Christ from the Beginnings of Christianity to Irenaeus*. Translated by John E. Steely. Nashville: Abingdon Press, 1970.

Davis, Stephan, Daniel Kendall, and Gerald O'Collins, eds. *The Resurrection: An Interdisciplinary Symposium on the Resurrection of Jesus*. Oxford: Oxford University Press, 1997.

Fuller, Reginald H. *The Foundations of New Testament Christology*. New York: Scribner, 1965.

Hahn, Ferdinand. *The Titles of Jesus in Christology: Their History in Early Christianity*. Translated by Harold Knight and George Ogg. New York: World, 1969.

Hurtado, Larry W. *Lord Jesus Christ: Devotion to Jesus in Earliest Christianity*. Grand Rapids: Eerdmans, 2003.

Wright, N. T. *The Resurrection of the Son of God*. Vol. 3 of *Christian Origins and the Question of God*. Minneapolis: Fortress Press, 2003.

Early Christianity

Balch, David L., and Carolyn Osiek. *Families in the New Testament World: Households and House Churches*. Louisville, KY: Westminster John Knox Press, 1997.

Brown, Raymond E. "Not Jewish Christianity and Gentile Christianity but Types of Jewish/Gentile Christianity." *Catholic Biblical Quarterly* 45 (1983): 74–79.

Brown, Raymond E., and John P. Meier. *Antioch and Rome: Cradles of Catholic Christianity*. New York: Paulist Press, 1983.

Conzelmann, Hans. *History of Primitive Christianity*. Translated by John E. Steely. Nashville and New York: Abingdon Press, 1973.

Crossan, John Dominic. *The Birth of Christianity: Discovering What Happened in the Years Immediately after the Execution of Jesus*. San Francisco: HarperSanFrancisco, 1998.

Dunn, James D. G. *Beginning from Jerusalem*. Vol. 2 of *Christianity in the Making*. Grand Rapids: Eerdmans, 2009.

Gehring, Roger W. *House Church and Mission: The Importance of Household Structures in Early Christianity*. Peabody, MA: Hendrickson, 2004.

Goulder, Michael. *A Tale of Two Missions*. London: SCM Press, 1994.

Simon, Marcel. *St. Stephen and the Hellenists in the Primitive Church*. New York: Longmans, 1958.

Theissen, Gerd. *The Religion of the Earliest Churches: Creating a Symbolic World*. Minneapolis: Fortress Press, 1999.

Weiss, Johannes. *Earliest Christianity: A History of the Period A.D. 30–150*. Translated by Frederick C. Grant. 2 vols. New York: Harper, 1937, 1959.

Religion in the Hellenistic World, Gentile and Jewish

Boring, M. Eugene, Klaus Berger, and Carsten Colpe, eds. *Hellenistic Commentary to the New Testament*. Nashville: Abingdon Press, 1995.

Jonas, Hans. *The Gnostic Religion*. 2nd. rev. ed. Boston: Beacon Press, 1963.

Klauck, Hans-Josef. *The Religious Context of Early Christianity: A Guide to Graeco-Roman Religions*. Translated by Brian McNeil. Edited by Fortress Press. Minneapolis: Fortress Press, 2003.

Price, S. R. *Rituals and Power: The Roman Imperial Cult in Asia Minor*. Cambridge: Cambridge University Press, 1984.

Robinson, James M., Richard Smith, and Coptic Gnostic Library Project. *The Nag Hammadi Library in English*. 4th rev. ed. Leiden and New York: Brill, 1996.

Tcherikover, Victor. *Hellenistic Civilization and the Jews; with a Preface by John J. Collins*. Reprint of 1959 ed. Peabody, MA: Hendrickson, 1999.

10
Paul and His Letters

10.1 Paul's Life and Mission to 50 CE: A Preliminary Sketch

WHILE THE GENERAL OUTLINE OF PAUL'S life is clear, the detailed chronology, sometimes important for interpreting the letters, is a complex matter upon which scholars are not united. The sketch presented here has widespread, but not unanimous, support (cf. §13.3.3).

10.1.1 Birth and Early Life

Birth. When Paul writes to Philemon about 52 CE, he refers to himself as πρεσβύτης (*presbytēs*), commonly translated "old man" (Phlm 9; so NRSV, TNIV). When the Acts narrative represents him as present at the death of Stephen in the early 30s, he is called a νεανίας (Acts 7:58; *neanias*, young man). A document circulating under the name of Hippocrates refers to a person in the twenty-two to twenty-eight age bracket as a νεανίσκος (*neaniskos*, young man), and uses πρεσβύτης (*presbytēs*) of a man aged fifty to fifty-six, prior to the diminished powers of "old age," which begins at 57. Some authors used νεανίας (*neanias*, young man) as the stage after the νεανίσκος, *neaniskos*, about twenty-nine to thirty-five. On this basis, Paul would have been born about 1–5 CE, was in his early 30s when he first appears in Acts, in his 50s when he wrote the extant letters, and about 60 when he died.

Education and training. Greek was clearly Paul's mother tongue. Just as the Diaspora Jew Philo can refer to Greek as "our language" (*Prelim. Studies* 44), so Paul functions in Greek as a native speaker. More precisely, his vocabulary and typical metaphors point to an urban setting. He is a Diaspora Jew who grew up in a large Hellenistic city. Paul himself never mentions his hometown, but Acts reliably supplies the missing information. Paul hails from Tarsus in Cilicia, "an important city" (Acts 9:11; 21:39; 22:3), the capital of the Roman province of Cilicia.

Tarsus was a famous university town, where Stoicism was the dominant philosophy. There is no indication that Paul received a higher education in the Greek academic setting, but he was clearly not isolated, ghettolike, from the main stream of Greco-Roman culture, and he learned at least the basics of the rhetorical skills that were part of every Greek education. In his own self-understanding, it was even more important that he belonged to a traditional Jewish family where the ancient traditions and language were preserved, "a Hebrew of Hebrews" (Phil 3:5), that is, he not only knew Greek but was conversant, perhaps fluent, in the Aramaic of Palestine and the Hebrew of the Scriptures. He was not a proselyte, but a born Jew whose family had been Jewish for generations. He knew something of rabbinic and scribal theology and biblical interpretation, and may have studied in Jerusalem, as pictured in Acts (22:3). He was a Pharisee, whose zeal for the ancestral traditions drove him to surpass many of his contemporaries (Gal 1:14). That his numerous biblical citations are typically from the LXX makes it clear, however, that the Greek translation of the Hellenistic synagogue remained his Bible.

Though he belonged to the literate minority that could compose complex documents in Greek, he learned a trade, and could support himself at manual labor (1 Thess 2:9; 1 Cor 4:12; 9:6; 2 Cor 11:27). Paul himself never describes the nature of his work. Acts calls him a σκηνοποιός (*skēnopoios*, traditionally "tentmaker") but the term also can mean "leather worker" or "linen worker"; Tarsus was well known as a center of the linen industry. Paul was not an independent businessman with his own firm, but a handworker who leased temporary space, or worked at his craft for others, probably as one who sewed together sun awnings or tents for private customers.[1] It was not an occupation of high social status.

Roman citizen? Acts represents Paul as a citizen of both Tarsus and the Roman Empire (Acts 21:39; 22:25–29; 23:27); his Roman citizenship plays a large role in the narrative of Acts (16:35–40; 25:11–12, 21; 26:32; 28:19). Since this way of representing Paul was important to the author of Luke–Acts, and since Paul never refers to himself as a Roman citizen, numerous Pauline scholars doubt its historicity, while others consider the Acts tradition to be correct on this point. However, the only explanation for Paul's being taken to Rome for trial, rather than having his case settled in Judea, seems to be that he was indeed a Roman citizen. Only citizens could appeal to the emperor (Acts 25:11; see Pliny the Younger, *Letters* 10.96).

Married? We have no information on Paul's marital status. The Paul who writes the New Testament letters was not married, has no wife to accompany him on his mission trips (1 Cor 9:5), and recommends that those among his readers who are unmarried remain so, just as Paul himself is unmarried (1 Cor 7:7–8). Paul may have been a widower. However, there are good reasons to suppose that Paul—like Jeremiah, who was something of a model for Paul's own apostolic vocation—understood his vocation to be a (prophetic) renunciation of marriage.[2] There are also Hellenistic models for remaining unmarried in the service of a higher calling.[3]

10.1.2 Paul the Persecutor

Acts depicts Paul as a zealous opponent of the early Christians, intent on destroying the new movement (Acts 8:1–3; 9:1–2; 22:4–5; 26:9–11). Paul confirms this picture, describing himself as a zealot for the ancestral faith, bent on destroying the church (1 Cor 15:9; Phil 3:6; Gal 1:13).[4] This characterization became legendary and integral to the later view of Paul, preserved in the later letters written in Paul's name (1 Tim 1:13–16). Paul did not instigate the conflicts, nor was he the principal ringleader among the

1. So Lampe, *Paul to Valentinus*, 187–89, with evidence. Cf. Ronald F. Hock, *The Social Context of Paul's Ministry: Tentmaking and Apostleship* (Philadelphia: Fortress Press, 1980).

2. So, e.g., Hengel and Schwemer, *Between Damascus and Antioch*, 95.

3. Cf. Epictetus, *Diatr.* 3.22.69, who thinks of the Cynic as a messenger from the gods, a scout in military service. While Epictetus argues that in principle there is no reason for the Cynic to remain unmarried, "in view of how things are at the present, and the situation at the front, the Cynic must be unhindered from placing himself entirely in the service of God, must be able to travel freely among people without being hindered by bourgeois obligations, unbound by personal connections. If he contracted such obligations and violated them, he would no longer have the character of an honorable man; if he maintained them, it would destroy his mission as the messenger, scout, and herald of the gods." Cf. Paul in 1 Cor 7:26–29.

4. Paul's later statements that he "persecuted the church" are from his perspective as missionary to the Gentiles. At the time, Paul saw himself as a zealous opponent of a deviant Jewish group he was determined to stamp out. He did not oppose "the church" as such, and did not harass the initial majority of Jewish Christians who continued to keep the law.

persecutors. The initial clash was not between Jews and Christians per se, but represents a cleavage among the Hellenist Jews in Jerusalem. The point at issue was the Hellenists' relaxation of the Torah, and then the Hellenistic Jewish Christians' Gentile mission, which welcomed into the covenant people of God even those who did not keep the law (see above, §9.2.2). This fundamental objection was exacerbated by the scandalous, blasphemous claim that one who had died under the curse of the law (Deut 21:23; Gal 3:13; cf. 1 Cor 1:23) was God's Messiah. Paul's zeal for the law, modeled on the zeal of Phinehas, who killed those who violated the covenant and encouraged others to do so (Num 25:1–13; see also Ps 106:28–31; Sir 45:23–24; 1 Macc 2:26, 54; 4 Macc 18:12), caused Paul himself to advocate disciplinary violence and even the death penalty for those who were profaning the covenant and hindering the mission of the holy people of God (Acts 26:10). After Paul had become a missionary for the Christian movement, the same Hellenistic Jews to which he had belonged attempted to kill him (Acts 9:29).

Acts indicates that Paul was an authorized representative of Jerusalem Judaism, sent to stamp out the new deviant messianic movement in Damascus (Acts 9:1–2). Paul himself does not give the location of his persecution of Christians, but the sequence "persecuting the church" . . . "I went away into Arabia" . . . "I returned to Damascus" clearly implies Damascus to be the locus of the persecution (Gal 1:13–17). Paul never indicates he persecuted the church in Jerusalem or Judea, or that he was sent from Jerusalem to Damascus. That Paul was "unknown by sight" to the churches in Judea (Gal 1:22), as well as the difficulty of imagining that Jerusalem priests had authority to arrest and extradite members of Jewish synagogues in Damascus, suggests that Paul was living in Damascus at the time, and that Damascus was the only place he persecuted the church. It seems that Paul did not know Palestinian Jewish Christianity, but was keenly aware of the Hellenistic Christians who were active and disruptive in the synagogues of Damascus, and he attempted to eradicate this danger to the faith. Acts and Paul's letters agree that Damascus was the location for the life-changing event in the life of Paul that was to have unimaginable consequences for the church and for Western civilization.

10.1.3 Call to Apostleship

In or near Damascus about 33 CE, Saul the zealous persecutor of Jewish believers in Jesus who were relaxing the law and the traditional Jewish boundaries, convinced that he was doing the will of God, was encountered by the risen Christ (1 Cor 9:1; 15:8; Gal 1:15–16; Acts 9:1–8; 22:6–11; 26:9–18). Paul had never seen Jesus during his earthly life. Paul describes the encounter with the risen Christ as something that happened ἐν ἐμοί (*en emoi* variously translated: "in me" KJV, NJB, NIV, TNIV; "to me" RSV, NAB, NRSV; "in and through me" REB). Acts calls it a "vision" (Acts 26:19). Yet the event cannot be reduced to psychology. Neither Paul himself nor the Acts narratives intend to represent the event as merely Paul's subjective experience, just as neither intends to portray the event as something that can be described in the categories of the space-time world.

Paul did not understand the event as the climax of his own religious quest. He was already secure and confident of his relation to God, sure that he was doing God's will. The unexpected initiative came from Christ; it was Christ who "apprehended" Paul (Phil 3:12 κατελήμφθην *katelēmphthēn*, laid hold of, grabbed), not the other way around. Paul identified his call as God's revelation to him of Jesus Christ as Lord (Gal 1:12, 16), expressed with verbs of seeing in 1 Corinthians 9:1 and 15:8. Paul believed that something beyond himself had happened to him: the crucified, accursed blasphemer whose followers he had been persecuting had been vindicated by God and raised to the heavenly world, and had now appeared to Paul and called him to be his follower and apostle. Paul never doubted the reality of this event, and it turned his life around.

The experience is often called Paul's "conversion," and it was indeed a conversion in the sense that it effected a deep personal transformation in Paul's life, a total reversal in his perspective and sense of values (see Phil 3:4–11). It was not a conversion in the sense that Paul converted from one religion to another. He did not see himself as leaving Judaism and joining Christianity (though see Gal 1:13). He always considered himself a Jew, but now came "to realize that the very group he had been persecuting as an aberrant form of Judaism was indeed the true way of Judaism after all."[5] Paul's own term for the experience is "call." At Damascus, the risen Christ not only called Paul to be a Christian believer, but called him to be an apostle—the apostle to the Gentiles. We do not have his immediate understanding, interpretation, and reflections on this experience. His earliest letter, written about seventeen years after the encounter, expresses his sense of a special apostolic call (1 Thess 2:7), which was intensified in his later writings documenting his clashes with those who disputed the authenticity of his apostleship (esp. 2 Cor 10–13; Gal 1–2). Paul described the experience in images and languages taken from the call stories of Israel's prophets (Jer 1:5; Isa 49:1), and henceforth understood himself as apostle, called like the prophets to be a spokesperson for the risen Christ.[6]

Paul as apostle. The English word "apostle" is the transliteration (not translation) of the Greek word ἀπόστολος (*apostolos*), which had an entirely secular meaning: one sent as an authorized representative of some other person or group. It thus can be translated as "delegate," "deputy," "messenger," "ambassador," "representative," or any other commissioned person. Thus Jesus can be called God's apostle (Heb 3:1), and those commissioned to particular tasks by the churches are called apostles. In Philippians 2:25, Epaphroditus is called ἀπόστολος (NRSV "messenger"; see marginal note). In 2 Corinthians 8:23, the duly elected representatives of the churches of Asia, Macedonia, and Achaia who would accompany Paul on his trip to Jerusalem are called ἀπόστολοι (*apostoloi*, NRSV "messengers"). In Acts 14:4, 14, Barnabas and Paul are called ἀπόστολοι, that is, authorized missionaries of the Antioch church (see Acts 13:1–3). In the first generation of Christianity, the term ἀπόστολος quickly developed a more narrow, technical meaning: those who had been chosen directly by Jesus Christ, either during his earthly life or by a special appearance after the resurrection, to be the authorized interpreters of what became the "apostolic faith." The adjective ἀποστόλικος (*apostolikos*, apostolic) used in this sense is found in second-century patristic writings, but not in the New Testament.

Paul always understood himself to have been called directly by the risen Christ. He served for several years as a missionary authorized by the church in Antioch, and perhaps already in Damascus. There are no extant letters from Paul during this time, nor references to such. He apparently did not use letters as a means of mission instruction and direction during this period. After Paul's break with the Antioch church and the beginning of his Aegean mission, it became important to him to emphasize that his authorization as an apostle did not depend on human authority.

10.1.4 Paul in Damascus and Arabia

Paul was converted into the Hellenistic church. Although as a persecutor he had surely known something about the faith and practice of the community he was persecuting and its crucified

5. L. Michael White, *From Jesus to Christianity* (San Francisco: HarperSanFrancisco, 2004), 157.

6. Beverly Roberts Gaventa acknowledges that, while Paul was not converted from one religion to another, to exchange "conversion" for "call" goes too far. "Conversion" is still appropriate, of which "call" is an essential element, but the best term is "transformation," which does not devalue Paul's previous life and commitments but incorporates them into the transformed new life. See Beverly Roberts Gaventa, *From Darkness to Light: Aspects of Conversion in the New Testament* (Philadelphia: Fortress Press, 1986), 38–40.

leader, it was at Damascus that he was baptized and in the community of Christians at Damascus that he received the insider's view of what it meant to be a Christian. There he received some of the earliest Christian traditions. Even if Paul had previously been in Jerusalem and knew something of the church there, it was in Damascus that his understanding of everything was turned upside down—he would have said "right side up"—and that he became a representative of the Hellenistic church.

Following his conversion, Paul went immediately to Arabia. We do not know how Paul at first understood the relation of his personal encounter with the risen Christ and his sense of mission, whether he went to Arabia purely with a sense of personal apostolic commission or as a missionary of the Damascus church. Since "Arabia" was used in several geographical and political senses in the first century, we cannot be certain what he intended, but the strong probability is that he refers to the part of the Arab kingdom of Nabataea contiguous with Damascus. Here were numerous thriving Hellenistic cities, including the capital Petra—now a tourist attraction, then a thriving center of commercial, cultural, and political activity. Paul says not a word about his activities there or how long he stayed. He apparently went alone, supported himself by his craft, and almost certainly began immediately to work as a missionary to Gentiles. Contrary to the schematized Acts picture, *this* was Paul's "First Missionary Journey." We do not know why he chose Arabia, but presumably it was not merely geographical convenience. Since he returned to Damascus, he may have operated as an agent of a mission that was already underway, sponsored by the Damascus church.

The Pharisee and intense student of the Scriptures now saw everything in a new eschatological light. Despite the hostilities that already prevailed between Jews and Arabs in the first century, the Arabs were regarded by many Jews as Ishmaelites, and thus also children of Abraham. The issues of Sinai, circumcision, Hagar, and the eschatological role of this people with roots in the patriarchal promises may already have weighed heavily in the thinking of the new convert. These issues came to the surface in Paul's later intense debate with the Christian teachers troubling the Galatian churches (Gal 3–4; see below, §13.1). In any case, this earliest phase of Paul's mission preaching must have been a period of intense rethinking of his theology that influenced his later thought.

There are no later references to churches that Paul established during this time; his efforts may have been fruitless. Presumably his preaching to Gentiles caused disturbances within the Nabatean Jewish community, Paul came to the attention of the Arab king's deputies as an undesirable outside agitator, and after an unspecified time in Arabia (it may have been relatively brief) he returned to Damascus (Gal 1:15–17). There his troubles with the Nabateans continued, and he was sought for by the Nabatean ethnarch in Damascus, probably the ruler of the Nabatean business colony there. Paul was forced to flee the city under cover of darkness, let down unceremoniously in a basket through an opening in the wall (2 Cor 11:32–33; Acts 9:23–25). This must have happened before the death of Aretas IV in 40 CE.[7]

10.1.5 Jerusalem #1—Visit with Peter (Gal 1:18)

After his ignominious escape from Damascus, Paul went to Jerusalem (Gal 1:18–24; 2 Cor 11:32–33; Acts 9:26–30; cf. 22:17). This was certainly his first visit to Jerusalem after his conversion, and—depending on whether Paul had studied there during his youth—perhaps his first visit ever. Since Paul's later rivals in Galatia were suspicious of him as only a secondary apostle, who had received whatever authority he had from the original Jerusalem apostles, it was important for him later to insist in his letter to

7. For a full discussion of the chronological issues involved, see Rainer Riesner, *Paul's Early Period: Chronology, Mission Strategy, Theology*, trans. Douglas W. Stott (Grand Rapids: Eerdmans, 1998), 80–89.

the Galatian Christians that he had been called directly by the risen Lord, that he had had only minimal contact with the Jerusalem church, had already been an apostle for some time, and had long since formulated the fundamental content of his apostolic message when he made his first visit to Jerusalem. He spent only fifteen days there, and the only church leaders he consulted were Peter and James the brother of Jesus.

The author of Acts, on the other hand, interested in emphasizing the continuity between Paul and the Jerusalem church, presents quite a different picture from Paul's own: After his conversion, Paul went to Jerusalem after "some days" (not three years); Barnabas introduced him to all the apostles (not *other* apostles; Acts does not consider Paul to be an apostle); Paul became a public figure in Jerusalem, speaking out boldly and debating with the Hellenist Jews (Acts 9:26–30). Paul's own account is clearly to be preferred, though told from his own perspective and in the interest of his own self-understanding as an apostle independent of Jerusalem.

As historians, we would love to know what transpired during those fifteen days in Jerusalem. The stories and sayings of Jesus we find in the Gospels are virtually absent from Paul's letters. Those who argue that material from and about the ministry of the pre-Easter Jesus was important in Paul's own theology and mission point out that he had ample opportunity to learn the "life and teaching of Jesus" from one of the original disciples and from Jesus' own brother.[8] There is no doubt that Paul had the opportunity. The question is whether he had the motive—or whether he did more talking than listening. Sayings from and stories about the earthly Jesus were not central to Paul's understanding of the faith.

Though Paul had a different experience and theology, the importance that he attached to staying in communication with the Jerusalem church and its leaders is evident. While he did not consider his apostolate to be dependent on their authorization, he did not think of himself as establishing a cluster of independent congregations unrelated to the larger church. Paul always considered his mission to be part of the one mission of the one church, and thus regarded it as vitally important to stay in communion with the "mother church" and its leaders in Jerusalem (see, e.g., Gal 2:2). Paul was not a missionary loner with his own project, but wanted to remain in association with the original Twelve and their spokesman and leader of the Jerusalem church, Simon Peter.

10.1.6 Paul in Syria and Cilicia (and Galatia?) ("First Missionary Journey"?)

When Paul left Jerusalem for "Syria and Cilicia" (Gal 1:21), we enter a period of twelve to fourteen years of which little is known in detail. Acts 9:28–30 tells of Paul escaping a plot against his life in Jerusalem, returning to Tarsus, and then, after an indefinite period, being brought to Antioch by Barnabas. He works with Barnabas for a year in the Antioch church, and is sent with him to Jerusalem to bring an offering to the Jerusalem Christians who are suffering from the famine. They return to Antioch and, again after an indefinite period, are sent as missionaries to Cyprus and towns in the southern part of the Roman province of Galatia: Perga, Antioch, Lystra, Derbe.

It is the problem caused by the formation of Gentile churches on this trip—the traditional "First Missionary Journey" of Paul in the Acts story—that causes the Antioch church to send Paul and Barnabas to Jerusalem to confer with the leaders there (Acts 13–14).

Paul himself refers to this period as working in Syria and Cilicia, with no further details (Gal 1:21), though his reference in 2:11 seems to indicate that (Syrian) Antioch was the, or a, focal point of his work during that period. He probably worked as a missionary under the

8. E.g., Wright, *Jesus and the Victory of God*, 134, 633, and passim; Dunn, *Beginning from Jerusalem*, 367–69 and passim; Hengel and Schwemer, *Between Damascus and Antioch*, 144–50.

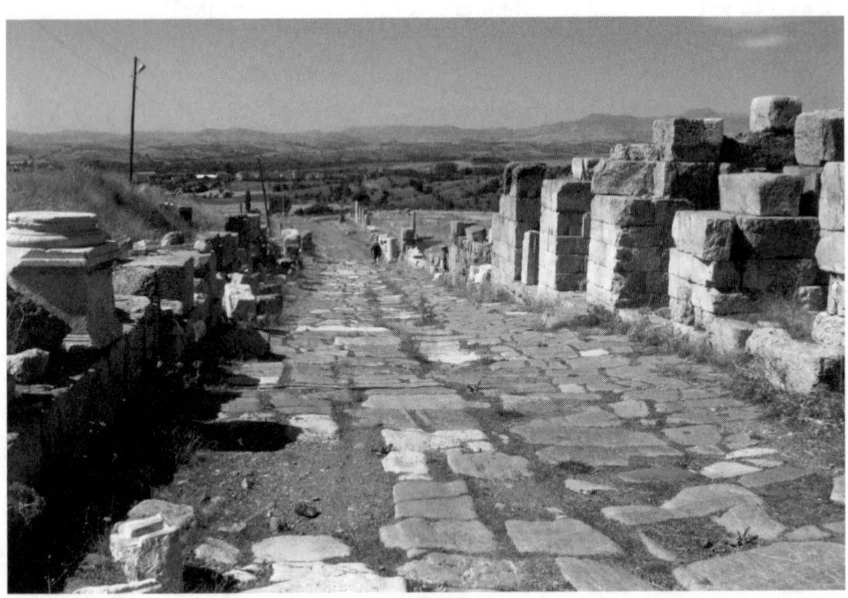

FIGURE 29: Main street of Antioch of Pisidia. The stone remains of vendors' stalls line each side of the road. Paul worked in shops like these to support himself during his missionary travels. PHOTO CREDIT: M. EUGENE BORING.

auspices of the Antioch church but is reluctant to make this clear after his break with Antioch, and with rival apostles undermining his work in the Aegean area by claiming that he is only a secondary missionary who derived his authority from others. This period can hardly have been the time when the churches of Galatia were established, since in Galatians 1:21 Paul would surely have said "among you," "I came to you Galatians," rather than the distancing "I went into the regions of Syria and Cilicia"—not to speak of the fact that Syria and Cilicia are distinct from Galatia both geographically and politically.

It is difficult to harmonize Paul's brief account with the Acts picture, in which Luke has used some traditional materials to schematize a First Missionary Journey in terms of his own theology. Acts portrays Paul in Tarsus, then Antioch (Syria), then Cyprus and cities in Lycia, Pamphylia, Pisidia, and Lycaonia, the latter two regions being in the southern part of the Roman province of Galatia (though Acts does not refer to Galatia). Paul refers only to Syria and Cilicia. A Pauline mission to Cyprus is difficult to fit into Paul's own summary, as well as clashing with Luke's earlier report that the island had already been evangelized by Hellenist missionaries from Jerusalem (Acts 11:19; see Rom 15:20). The date of Paul's letter to the Galatians, whether or not it was written to churches established during this period (the "South Galatian Theory," see below §13.1.2), and how Acts 16:6 and 18:23 are to be understood, all impinge on how the chronology of this period is understood. Acts and Paul's own writings converge, however, in portraying Antioch as the locus of the next crucial phase of Paul's work.

Paul and the Antioch church. Antioch was a large, cosmopolitan city with a population of 300,000–600,000, the third largest city of the empire after Rome and Alexandria. The city contained a large Jewish population and numerous synagogues. The new church was an innovative, integrating Christian community that began among the Gentile God-fearers in the synagogues, but then formed its own congregations of (mostly) Gentile Christians. Here the church was for the first time recognized as a distinct religious community separate from the synagogue, not a subset within Judaism, and for the first time its members were called "Christians" (Acts 11:26).

There is no indication that the followers of Jesus in Antioch were expelled from the synagogues, but their separation must have involved tensions with the large Jewish community in the city. Their new situation called for Christians to think through their relation to Judaism and the Jewish Scriptures, and their continuing self-understanding as the covenant community of Israel. Such questions did not first arise with the destruction of the temple in 70 CE and the reconstitution of Judaism at Jamnia in the generation following.

Though all were rooted in the original Jerusalem church, four "branches" of early Christianity are already discernible in Antioch: (1) the more traditional, rigid position from Jerusalem represented by James the brother of Jesus;[9] (2) the more moderate Jerusalem-Judean tradition represented by Peter, (3) the Hellenist group, originally also from Jerusalem, but who had been carrying on a mission to Gentiles in which the requirements of the law were relaxed, represented by Stephen and Philip; (4) the stream of Gentile Christianity represented by Paul's mission in Arabia, Damascus, and Cilicia, now in conjunction with the mission experience of Barnabas. During this dynamic, creative period, all four streams interacted with each other, regarding each other as all belonging the one church, the eschatological people of God, a unity in diversity, but constantly engaged in a struggle to maintain this. Both Peter and Paul have connections with all four streams.

This was a formative period for what came to be identified as "Pauline" theology: Antioch receives Jerusalem traditions, both Aramaic and Greek, with varying degrees of loyalty to traditional interpretations of the Torah and temple, reflecting some of the spectrum of theological beliefs and practices of the Jerusalem church. This period was characterized by a dialogue from which Paul received and to which he contributed. Much of what later emerges in 1 Thessalonians and later Pauline writings was hammered out during this dynamic, formative period. When the New Testament opens with 1 Thessalonians, we already have the results of this years-long integrative process. We cannot determine precisely *how* much, but we know that considerable elements of the Christology, soteriology, mission theology, thinking about the relation of the church to the synagogue, sacramental theology, and such were formulated during this period. Thus even key "Pauline" terms such as ἐν Χριστῷ (in Christ) are sometimes found in *traditional* sections of Paul's letters (e.g., 1 Thess 4:16). So also, at Antioch, there must have been dialogue on the role of the Jesus tradition, that is, the tradition of the sayings and deeds of the pre-Easter Jesus. Peter and James and their followers may have represented an emphasis on Jesus' own sayings and stories about the earthly life of Jesus, as an important means of communicating the gospel; Paul and his colleagues made only minimal use of these materials.

When Paul broke with the Antioch church, he left behind this approach focused on sayings and incidents from Jesus' life, but its influence continued in other descendants of this early Antioch matrix. Matthew later represents the Antiochene life-of-Jesus tradition associated with Peter and James and is a bit anti-Pauline. But in the 40s, these two traditions, the kerygmatic tradition focusing on the cross and resurrection, and the life-of-Jesus tradition, lived alongside each other, with some cross-fertilization. We cannot now tell whether such elements contained in Paul's later letters represent Paul's original contribution *to* what became Antiochene theology, or whether he received them *from* the Antioch church. In any case, when we begin to read Paul's letters, we must not suppose that everything *we* read there for the first time is original with Paul.

9. The position of James himself is not always to be identified with those who cited his authority. See, e.g., Wilhelm Pratscher, *Der Herrenbruder Jakobus und die Jakobustradition*, FRLANT 139 (Göttingen: Vandenhoeck & Ruprecht, 1987), 80–102.

10.1.7 Jerusalem #2—The Council (Gal 2:1–10; Acts 15:1–29)

The establishment and growth of predominately Gentile Christian congregations precipitated a crisis in the young, newly integrated church. The issue was not "Judaism" versus "Christianity." All parties agreed on the vital importance of believers in Jesus belonging to the covenant people of God. The issue was whether it was still necessary to keep the law of Moses to be included in eschatological Israel, the elect community of the end time, and how continuity was to be maintained with the covenant people of God represented in the Scripture and contemporary Judaism. The issue became focused on one question: should circumcision continue as a general requirement, as it had been the boundary marker since the time of Abraham (Gen 17:11) between those inside God's covenant and those outside? Said otherwise, can one become a Christian without becoming an observant Jew? Proponents of both sides met in Jerusalem. The unity of the one church was at stake. Would there be one church or separate churches of Jewish Christians and Gentile Christians?

We have two accounts of the Jerusalem Council (Gal 2; Acts 15).[10]

1. In both Galatians and Acts, the issue is whether Gentile Christians must be circumcised and keep the law of Moses (Gal 2:3; Acts 15:1).
2. Both Galatians (2:2) and Acts (15:2, 31, and implied throughout) consider the approval of the Jerusalem church and its apostolic leadership as vitally important.
3. Both Galatians and Acts assume that "salvation for those who believed in Jesus was attained only in continuity with Israel."[11]
4. In Galatians, the Council visit is Paul's second visit to Jerusalem after his conversion (Gal 1:18; 2:1). In Acts, it is his third visit (9:26–30; 11:30; 15:2).
5. In Galatians, the Council visit is fourteen (or seventeen) years after his conversion (Gal 2:1). This is compatible with Acts' chronology, though Luke does not locate it precisely (see on Acts 15:7).
6. In Galatians, Paul is accompanied by Barnabas and Titus, an uncircumcised Gentile Christian who becomes a test case of the issue that occasioned the Council (Gal 2:1, 3). Acts nowhere mentions Titus, and Paul is accompanied only by Barnabas (Acts 15:2).
7. In Galatians, Paul goes to the meeting "by revelation," that is, at the direct command of the risen Christ received in a vision or prophetic oracle (Gal 2:2). In Acts, he is sent as a delegate of the Antioch church (Acts 15:2).
8. In Galatians, Paul represents the left wing, Peter is the moderate, and James represents the right wing. In Acts, Paul makes no speech, Peter represents the Pauline left wing (Acts 15:7–11), James is the moderate (Acts 15:13–21; cf. 21:17–25), and the Christian Pharisees represent the right wing (Acts 15:5).
9. In Galatians, Paul as an apostle has a private meeting with the "Pillars" of the Jerusalem church: James, Cephas (Peter), and John (Gal 2:2, 9). In Acts, Paul meets with the apostles, elders, and the whole church (Acts 15:4), and Paul is pointedly not an apostle (see on Acts 14:4, 14).
10. Paul speaks of those Jerusalem leaders who advocate circumcision and keeping the law as "false brethren" (Gal 2:4); Acts speaks of them as "believers who belonged to the sect of the Pharisees" (Acts 15:5).
11. In Galatians, Paul sets before the group the gospel that he preached among the Gentiles (Gal 2:2). In Acts, he and Barnabas rehearse the signs and wonders that God had worked

10. As elsewhere, I am here assuming the majority view that the Jerusalem trip of Gal 2 is to be identified with that of Acts 15. For alternative views, see the introduction to Galatians below.
11. Udo Schnelle, *Apostle Paul: His Life and Thought*, trans. M. Eugene Boring (Grand Rapids: Baker Academic, 2005), 126.

during their mission (Acts 15:12), but Peter is the spokesperson for the Pauline gospel (15:11).

12. In Galatians, Paul insists that his own view carried the day and that the Jerusalem leaders added nothing to him (Gal 2:6, 10). In Acts, the "Apostolic Decree" is formulated (Acts 15:23–29), and Paul willingly delivers it to the Antioch church and his own mission churches (15:30; 16:4).

13. In Galatians, the only request made by the Jerusalem leaders is that Paul "remember the poor" (Gal 2:10), that is, that he take up an offering from the Gentile churches for the poor Christians of Judea. There is no reference to this in Acts 15, but see 24:17.

14. Galatians speaks of a division of labor in which Paul will go to the Gentiles and the Jerusalem leaders to the Jews (Gal 2:9), while Acts knows of no such arrangement.

The comparison thus reveals numerous agreements, but also significant disagreements, some of which may be only a matter of emphasis and perspective, while others resist harmonization (esp. #4, #8, and #11). The most likely solution to the central focus on the Apostolic Decree in Acts 15 and its absence in Galatians 2 is that Luke has combined the accounts of two separate events in his sources into one grand scene (see his composition of the Gospel, comments on Luke 1:1–4). The Jerusalem Council on which Paul reports dealt with circumcision and keeping the law. A later meeting in Jerusalem, at which Paul was not present, would have then dealt with the question of dietary rules in the Antioch church, probably as a result of the dispute Paul reports in Galatians 2:11–14. This would explain both Paul's lack of reference to the Apostolic Decree in Galatians 2:1–10 and why even in Acts he seems to be informed of it for the first time in 21:25 (see also 1 Cor 8–10, esp. 10:25).

Luke seems to have taken the accounts of two separate meetings and reformulated them into a ideal portrayal of how differing groups in the church work through their difficulties with mutual respect and a concern to maintain the unity of the one church of God: Jewish Christians do not insist on circumcision and keeping the Mosaic law for Gentile Christians, and Gentile Christians agree to keep a minimum of the ritual law for the sake of church unity and mission. Luke's narrative in Acts 15 provides a model of decision making for maintaining the unity of the church under the guidance of the Holy Spirit, a model he holds up as valuable for later generations of Christians. While it contains historical materials, precision in reporting historical detail is not its function or main point, and in fact it contains serious historical inaccuracies.

In Paul's later memory and interpretation, the principal result of the conference was the recognition of his apostleship and of the law-free Gentile mission. Two parallel missions would be conducted, with Peter the leader of the Jewish mission and Paul the leader of the mission to the Gentiles. This was probably not understood in ethnic terms, as though Paul agreed never to preach to ethnic Jews like himself. Rather, the Council recognized the inclusive mission of Paul, in which churches of Jews and Gentiles could be united in the one church that did not require Gentiles to be circumcised and keep the Jewish law, alongside the mission to Jewish people who need not abandon the Torah in order to become disciples of Christ.[12]

10.1.8 Antioch Confrontation and Separation

The Jerusalem Council had preserved the unity of the new movement by recognizing the parallel existence of two forms of Christian mission within the one church. It had dealt with entrance requirements and had authorized the inclusion of Gentile Christians within the one

12. As argued by, e.g., John Painter, *Just James: The Brothers of Jesus in History and Tradition* (Minneapolis: Fortress Press, 1997/1999), 61–62: "To the Gentiles" (εἰς τὰ ἔθνη *eis ta ethnē*) of Gal. 2:8 means "to [all] nations, including Jews."

church of Jewish and Gentile Christians without the requirement of circumcision. The leaders of both sides were apparently pleased to settle this potentially divisive issue without schism, and they did not press for a resolution of other issues that were bound to emerge—how Jewish and Gentile Christians could live and work together in one congregation, respecting the convictions of both, without violating the conscience of either. This issue soon came to a head in the Antioch incident, as it has come to be called, in a confrontation between Peter and Paul. It is reported only in Galatians 2:11–21. In Acts, Peter drops out of the story after the Jerusalem Council, never to appear again. The leadership of the Jerusalem church is assumed by James the brother of Jesus, a proponent of strict observance of the Jewish law (see §18.1 below).

The situation in Antioch on the relations of Gentile Christians, Jewish Hellenist Christians, and Hellenistic Jews was complex and cannot be completely reconstructed.[13] The Hellenist Christians had been accepted into the synagogue as "Messianic Jews," and their Gentile converts could be regarded as God–fearers, who were not full Jewish converts but participated in the life and worship of the synagogue. They could eat together by themselves, without keeping the kosher food laws, but they could not eat with Jewish Christians and non-Christian Jews in the synagogue unless they became full Jews, that is, were circumcised and kept the food laws. When the Antioch church became predominately Gentile, such restrictions were abandoned; otherwise, the church could not even celebrate the Eucharist together. Peter, Barnabas, and other Jewish Christians continued the practice of the Antioch church in which all Christians, Jewish and Gentile, ate together. Then "certain people came from James," who insisted that Jewish Christians must continue to maintain the Jewish way of life, including the purity laws related to food: Jews may not eat with Gentiles as a matter of ritual purity (Gal 2:12). This was not a matter of bigotry or religious snobbishness; from their theological perspective, it was inherent in the vocation of Israel, the people of God, to remain faithful to the covenant and its stipulations, for which Israel's martyrs had died. They did not claim that *Gentile* Christians need live by these laws, but insisted that when *Jews* became Christians, they were not free to violate them. This meant that Jewish Christians could not continue the table fellowship with Gentile Christians, and some withdrew, including Peter and Barnabas.

13. Raymond Brown has warned against using the labels "Jewish Christian" and "Gentile Christian" indiscriminately. Rather than speaking of "Gentile Christianity" and "Jewish Christianity" as though there were only two clearly distinct groups, he proposes a typology of four categories:

— Group One consists of Jewish Christians and their Gentile converts who insisted on full observance of the Mosaic Law, including circumcision, for those who believed in Jesus. In short, these ultraconservatives insisted that in order to become Christians, Gentiles had to become Jews (so the Galatian rival missionaries, see below).

— Group Two consists of Jewish Christians and their Gentile converts who did not insist on circumcision but did require converted Gentiles to keep some Jewish observances. One can speak of this as a mediating view, inclined to see a value in openness (no demand of circumcision) but preserving some of the wealth of the Jewish Law as part of the Christian heritage. Peter and James are both in this group, though there is variety here; note Paul somewhat sarcastically lumps them together in Gal. 2:6, 9, 12. Both were to the right of Paul, but James was further right from Peter.

— Group Three consists of Jewish Christians and Gentile converts who did not insist on circumcision and did not require observance of the Jewish (kosher) food laws. Paul did not require Christians to abstain from food dedicated to idols (1 Cor. 8), a requirement imposed by James according to Acts 15:20, 29. Paul is the main New Testament spokesperson for this liberal attitude.

— Group Four consists of Jewish Christians and their Gentile converts who did not insist on circumcision or observance of the Jewish food laws and who saw no abiding significance in Jewish cult and feasts; the "Hellenists" of Acts 6 represent this category (Raymond E. Brown and John P. Meier, *Antioch and Rome: Cradles of Catholic Christianity* [New York: Paulist Press, 1983], 2–7; Raymond E. Brown, "Not Jewish Christianity and Gentile Christianity but Types of Jewish/Gentile Christianity," *Catholic Biblical Quarterly* 45 [1983]: 74–79).

The Antioch incident had some relation to the Apostolic Decree. At some point this minimalist compromise was promulgated (see above). It may have been a disputed point, or *the* bone of contention, at the Antioch incident that caused the separation between Paul and Silas, on the one side, and Peter and Barnabas, on the other. We have only Paul's side of the story. In his version of the incident, he soundly denounced and defeated the compromising Peter and "even Barnabas," his former colleague in the Gentile mission. Since Peter remained in Antioch, and Antiochene Christianity turned away from its previous radical openness, in the direction of the more conservative Jacobite Jewish Christianity of Jerusalem, it appears that Paul lost the debate and decided he could no longer participate in the Antiochene mission program. Peter would remain in Antioch, and Paul would leave.

10.1.9 The Aegean Mission (roughly "Second and Third Missionary Journeys")

The movement into the Aegean was not the "second missionary journey" in a series emanating from Jerusalem and Antioch, but a fresh beginning after Paul's break with Peter, Barnabas, and the Antioch church. The author of Acts characteristically downplays any theological disunity at Antioch and portrays the split between Paul and Barnabas as a personal matter involving their previous associate John Mark (Acts 15:36–41). Paul chooses Silvanus ("Silas" in Acts) as his new coworker, a Jewish Christian and prophetic leader in the Jerusalem church who is affirmative of the Gentile mission. The two missionaries set out along the land route from Syria through Cilicia, visiting congregations previously established. At Lystra, Timothy is converted by Paul (1 Cor 4:17; according to Acts, had Timothy already been converted in the 14:8–20 first mission journey?). At Paul's invitation, Timothy joins the mission team. Guided by divine revelation (Acts 16:6–10), they are led to Macedonia. Acts represents the author of the "we-source" as joining them at Troas, so the mission team is composed of Paul, Silvanus, Timothy, and the author of Acts.

The Aegean mission represents a new missionary strategy on Paul's part. Paul's plan of action is not to try to visit each town and village separately, but to establish a mission center in major metropolitan areas, especially provincial capitals, from which his missionary team and the new converts could evangelize neighboring regions. From such centers (Philippi, Thessalonica, Corinth, Ephesus), Paul's plan is to evangelize the surrounding region with the distinctively Pauline gospel, establishing a symbolic and functional beachhead for the dissemination of the faith and the gathering of the eschatological community. After having established such mission centers in key locations, Paul can think of his work as "done" for a major geographical area and move on to other fields (see Rom 15:18–24). Previously, he had evangelized as the missionary sent out by a major mission center. He made "missionary journeys," accompanied by a senior colleague such as Barnabas, and returned to report to the church that had sent him. This was clearly the case for Antioch and may have been the case for Damascus as well. So long as Paul understood his own commission and theology to be in harmony with the church that sent him, his consciousness of being personally sent and called by the risen Christ did not constitute any problem for his serving as missionary delegate of a central church. The Antioch incident changed this situation. Henceforth Paul would not function as the representative of a mission center, making "missionary journeys" in its behalf, but would found new mission centers in major cities.[14] Henceforth, he needed to be absolutely clear that as an ἀπόστολος (apostle, one who

14. The traditional terminology of numbered "missionary journeys" is problematic in any case, suggesting that Paul's normal state was to be settled in Antioch, from which he made three extended mission trips (see the maps in most Bibles). Rather, after his conversion and particularly after the Antioch incident, his normal state was to be traveling in the Aegean, settling down temporarily in Corinth and Ephesus, which he interrupted to make a trip (possibly two) to Jerusalem.

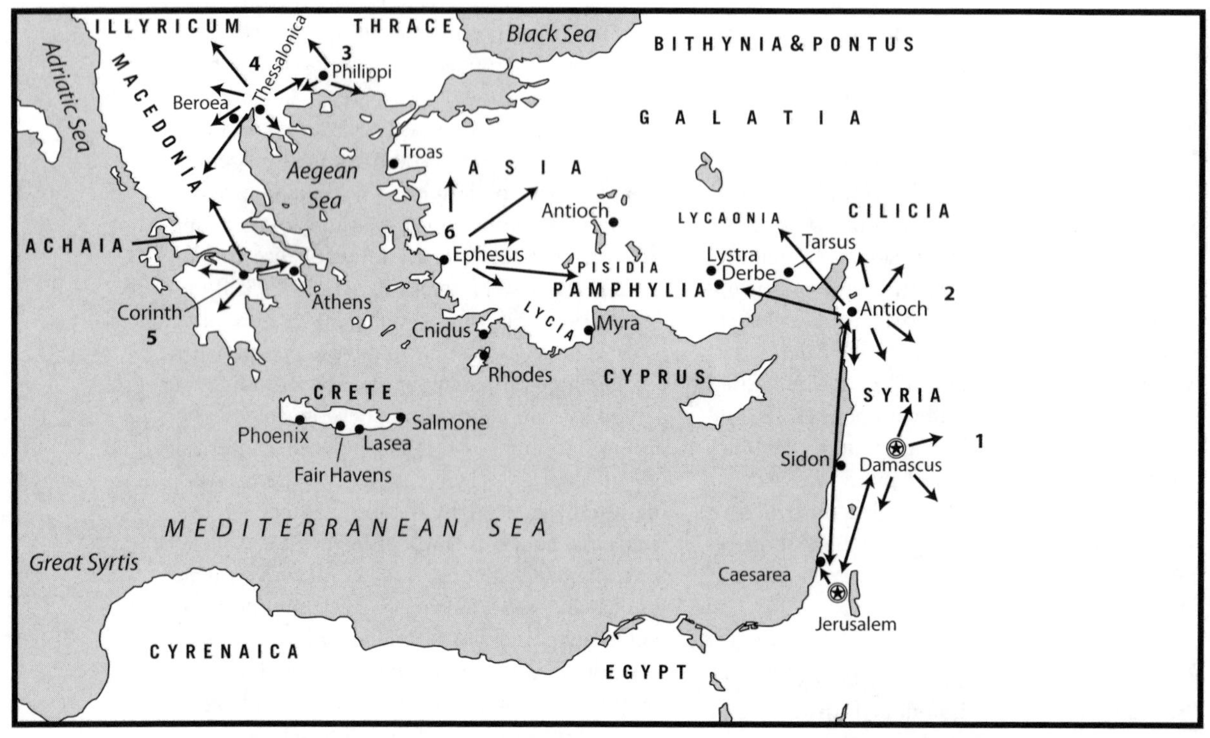

MAP 2: Though Paul maintains contact with Jerusalem, he minimizes contact with both Antioch and Jerusalem. Paul writes that he makes two trips to Jerusalem, from Damascus and Antioch (Gal 1–2), then a final trip to bring the offering (2 Cor 8–9; Rom 15). After the break with Antioch, he founds mission centers in major cities and provincial capitals: Philippi and Thessalonica (Macedonia), Corinth (Achaia), and Ephesus (Asia). There was, perhaps, another brief trip to Jerusalem (recounted in Acts 18:21–23), though this trip is more likely a Lukan construct. This reconstruction of the shape of Paul's missionary career is in contrast to the traditional three "missionary journeys," based on Acts.

is authorized and sent, missionary) he is the authorized representative of the risen Lord, and that he is more than one who has been authorized by other human beings (see Gal 1:1 and discussion above, "Paul as apostle.").[15]

15. Paul's use of ἀπόστολος (*apostolos*), insisting that his apostleship is not by human commission, is contrasting himself not only with Peter and the Twelve, but with his own prior work as a missionary-apostle in the sense of a delegate from a church (Acts 14:14; 2 Cor 8:23), as Paul had been in Antioch. In the Aegean mission, Paul rejects not only the claim that he got his message from the Twelve or Peter, but that he was authorized by a church, such as Antioch. From this time on, "apostle" has a more independent meaning than previously: my gospel doesn't come just from the church tradition I was taught at Antioch, but directly from Christ.

The mission team begin a new church in Philippi, where Paul and Silvanus are arrested, beaten and briefly imprisoned by the local authorities.

Upon their release, they and Timothy journey to Thessalonica, where, amid tumult and trouble, they also successfully establish a new congregation. When the missionaries are forced to leave Thessalonica, they preach and win converts in Beroea, and when Paul must flee from there, he leaves Silvanus and Timothy behind and journeys to Athens, then to Corinth. There, in cooperation with Priscilla and Aquila (recently arrived from Rome as a result of Claudius's expulsion of the Jews), he begins a new Christian congregation. When he is joined by Silvanus and Timothy, who arrive from Macedonia with the good news that the church in Thessalonica is flourishing despite its persecution, he (and Silvanus and Timothy) write the encouraging and clarifying letter to them which comes into the Christian Bible as 1 Thessalonians, the earliest extant Christian document. Though the Acts account of this phase of the "Second Missionary Journey" has some legendary features and minor conflicts with what can be gleaned from Paul's letters, its major outlines are confirmed (Acts 16:20–24=1 Thess 2:2).

Since the only New Testament documents we have from this period are Paul's own letters, and since from this time on, the Acts account is devoted exclusively to Paul, the New Testament reader receives the impression that the whole mission of the church was henceforth dominated by Paul. The modern reader must remember there were other streams of Christian mission in progress alongside him and in other parts of the Mediterranean world, the products of which we do not see until the later New Testament writings, or have been lost to us. Nonetheless, it was the work of Paul that was formative for the later church, and we justifiably focus our attention on him and his work—as did the New Testament authors.

The period of Paul's Aegean ministry, ca. 48–56 CE, roughly equivalent to the Acts' second and third missionary journeys, was indeed a crucially important time for the Pauline mission, early Christianity, and the formation of what came to be the New Testament. All Paul's extant letters probably come from this period.[16] The Aegean mission was an independent Pauline mission in the sense that Paul was no longer operating as a representative of the Antioch church, and did not consider himself subordinate to the Jerusalem "Pillars." After the break with Antioch, he never again goes back to either city to report, only visiting Jerusalem at the close of his mission work in the East, to bring the offering he had promised, as a symbol of the unity of the one church. Even after the dispute at Antioch that led him to break with both Barnabas and Peter, he speaks respectfully of each of them as colleagues in the church's larger mission (1 Cor 3:5–9, 21–23; 9:5–6; 15:2–11). He is aware that others might see the apostles representing the authority of Jerusalem and Antioch as rivals, but was intensely concerned that the churches of the Aegean mission manifest their unity with the larger church by sending their symbolic—and substantial—offering to Jerusalem. He never thought of himself as independent of Jerusalem, or of the church as a whole.

Despite Paul's passionate ecumenism, a Jerusalem group associated with James[17] sooner or later launched a countermission to Paul's, challenging the legitimacy of his apostleship and insisting that Gentile members of his mission congregations must be circumcised and adopt other identity marks of the covenant people prescribed by the Torah, i.e., in effect become practicing Jews. This was not only their sincere theological conviction, but had an important political dimension, intended to maintain the goodwill of the empire toward the Jewish Diaspora (see §9.2.2, "Conflicts between Christians and Jews"). This countermission of the "circumcision party" is certainly important for understanding Galatians, Philippians, and Romans, and perhaps for the earlier mission and letters as well.

16. Of the seven undisputed Pauline letters (see §10.2.1), the possible exceptions are Philippians and Philemon, if they were written from Rome, and Galatians, if written prior to the Jerusalem Council. See the introductions to each book.

17. This was not necessarily the position of James himself, or of the whole Jerusalem church. No New Testament evidence suggests James advocated the circumcision of *Gentile* Christians. See Pratscher, *Herrenbruder Jakobus*, 80–102.

10.2 Introduction to the Epistles

10.2.1 Letters in the New Testament and Early Christianity

For the early Christians, the letter form quickly became the most important literary genre for communication and instruction. Of twenty-seven New Testament documents, twenty-two are in the letter form; of 680 pages of Greek text in Nestle-Aland[27], 272 pages (40 percent) are letters. Acts contains letters and indicates that the early church developed a network maintained by letters (Acts 15:23, 30; 18:27). In what became mainstream Christianity, for the first one hundred years the letter form dominated Christian writing. The narrative genres of Gospels and Acts appeared after the letter form was well established, and the new genre was not immediately accepted by all Christians. This early dominance of the letter form is a striking, unanticipated fact. In no other religious community have letters become sacred Scripture or played such a formative role.

Paul was the decisive influence. Christian tradition has assigned fourteen canonical letters to Paul: Romans, 1 and 2 Corinthians, Galatians, Ephesians, Philippians, Colossians, 1 and 2 Thessalonians, 1 and 2 Timothy, Titus, Philemon, Hebrews. All except Hebrews have "Paul" as their first word, representing themselves as written by Paul himself. Since in the ancient world letters were sometimes composed in the name of a famous teacher of the past, it is not immediately clear which of these were written by Paul himself and which may have been composed in his name by later disciples (see Excursus 2 after §14.2). After a long period of careful study and debate, a widespread consensus has emerged among contemporary critical scholars:

— Seven undisputed letters acknowledged by all as written by Paul himself: Romans, 1 and 2 Corinthians, Galatians, Philippians, 1 Thessalonians, Philemon.

— Two disputed letters, considered by some critical scholars to be authentically Pauline: Colossians, 2 Thessalonians.

— Four disputed letters, regarded by the majority of critical scholars as written after Paul's time by his disciples: Ephesians, the Pastorals (1 and 2 Timothy, Titus). Historical scholarship is now unanimous that Hebrews was not written by Paul.

Paul did not understand himself to be writing sacred Scripture, nor were his letters regarded as such by the congregations that received them. They were more, however, than personal letters. They were written by one who understood himself to be an apostle called and authorized by the risen Christ. They were directed to the community of faith, intended to be read in worship. As they were circulated among the churches and read in the worship service alongside the Scripture, they gradually assumed the status and function of Scripture (see 1 Thess 5:27; Col 4:16; 2 Pet 3:15–16).

After Paul's death, his students continued to use the letter form as the primary means of Christian instruction, composing letters in his name. In some cases, the letter form was only superficially imposed on other types of content. *Ephesians* is more like a tract, clothed in epistolary form though lacking most of the features of a real letter. The *Pastoral Epistles* present instruction about church life and order and warnings against false teaching in the form of personal letters to Timothy and Titus. Later Christian teachers outside the Pauline school tradition (see below §17.1.1) were familiar with the apostolic letter read as part of the liturgy in the congregations to which they belonged, and adopted the letter form as the vehicle of their instruction, though their compositions were not typically letters in the real sense. Early Christians composed many other kinds of texts, but *all* the documents finally included in the New Testament canon except the Gospels and Acts are presented in the letter form. *Hebrews* is a sermon, but equipped with an epistolary ending. *James* is a collection of Christian wisdom instruction, but is presented as a letter. *First and Second Peter* closely imitate the Pauline letter form, even in details. First Peter is a real letter, but 2 Peter belongs to the testament genre, the last speech of a beloved figure of the past—in the New Testament it assumes the form of a letter. Of the Johannine letters, *2 and 3 John* are real letters, but *1 John* is a theological tract on which the letter form has been imposed. *Jude* is nonletter content inserted into a minimal letter framework. *Revelation* is mostly visionary apocalyptic material, including prophetic messages from the risen Christ to the seven churches, but the whole is placed in the conventional framework of a Pauline letter, using Paul's characteristic forms. The author of *1 Clement* places his instruction to the Corinthian church in the form of a letter. So also *Barnabas*, with no formal epistolary features, was called a letter in the second century and was included in the Sinaiticus manuscript of the New Testament as the *Epistle of Barnabas*. There are numerous other examples.

Why this extensive adaptation of the letter form and multiplication of letters in the Christian tradition, why this "epistolary pressure" to write in the letter form and to impose this form even on nonepistolary material, and why its dominance in the New Testament? (See above §1.4.) It is easy enough to see that, once the letters of Paul were circulated and became a normative form of church networking and Christian instruction, the literary form would be imitated and letters would be written in the name of Paul and other apostolic figures. But why did the letter form become established in the first place? Why did, for example, lists of sayings of Jesus (such as Q and the *Gospel of Thomas*), essays and meditations on Christian doctrine (such as the *Gospel of Truth*), or guidebooks of church order (such as the *Didache*) not become more integral to developing mainline Christianity and end up in the New Testament?

Why letters?

The primary reason for the importance of letters in the New Testament canon is their theological appropriateness as expressions of the Christian faith. This is a matter to which we must return below, but first it is necessary to explore the form and function of the Pauline letters against their historical background of letter writing in antiquity.

10.2.2 Letters in the Ancient World

Paul did not invent the letter form. Early Christianity was born in a letter-writing culture. It was Paul, however, who transformed the conventional Hellenistic letter form into a vehicle of Christian instruction and made it a standard genre of early Christian communication. Paul and the early Christians adopted a this-worldly cultural form that functions on the horizontal plane of history. The New Testament letters are not vertical "letters from heaven," although this genre existed in the Hellenistic world.[18] Even the messages to the seven churches of Revelation 2–3, though presented as messages dictated by the risen Christ, are in the framework of a this-worldly letter: not "heavenly Jesus to earthlings," but "John to the churches."

We have more than 14,000 examples of ancient letters. Most are brief private letters recovered from the dry sands of Egypt, but hundreds are from collections of literary letters that circulated in the ancient world, readily available to all educated people. Hans-Josef Klauck lists thirty-eight such freestanding collections of Greek letters, as well as numerous letters quoted, embedded, or summarized in other literary works, and a comparable number of Latin collections and letters, as well as copious

18. From ancient Egypt to Paul's own time, there were letters from the gods delivered directly to earthlings. See Adolf Deissmann, *Light from the Ancient East: The New Testament Illustrated by Recently Discovered Texts of the Graeco-Roman World*, trans. Lionel R. M. Strachan (New York: Doran, 1927), 244–45, 374–75, and Hans-Josef Klauck, *Ancient Letters and the New Testament: A Guide to Context and Exegesis* (Waco, TX: Baylor University Press, 2006), 352–53.

examples of letters from the Old Testament, Jewish, and other ancient literature. This array of ancient letters provides an extensive grid against which to examine and compare New Testament letters:[19]

Real and Literary Letters

Not all letters are of the same type. We may begin by considering two examples that represent opposite poles of a spectrum.

Real letters. The following one-page letter from a sailor in the Roman grain fleet to his brother is a real letter, intended to be read only by his family. One copy was written and delivered. We have the original.

> Irenaeus to Apollinarias his dearest brother many greetings. I pray continually for your health, and I myself am well. I wish you to know that I reached land on the sixth of the month Epeiph and we unloaded our cargo on the eighteenth of the same month. I went up to Rome on the 25th of the same month and the place welcomed us as the god willed, and we are daily expecting our discharge, it so being that up till today nobody in the corn fleet has been released. Many salutations to your wife and to Serenus and to all who love you, each by name. Good-bye. Mesore 9. *(Papyrus BGU 27, from the 2nd cent. CE; trans. LCL)*

Literary letters. Seneca, Roman philosopher and statesman (ca. 4 BCE–65 CE), a contemporary of Paul, wrote hundreds of letters; a collection of 931 letters was published after his death. No doubt he too wrote brief personal notes like the one above, but these are mostly lost. Preserved in Seneca's literary legacy is a collection of 124 letters in twenty volumes, written to his friend Gaius Lucilius, a person we know actually existed. Whether the letters addressed to him are real letters is another question. Even if actually delivered, it is clear that as Seneca writes he is composing not just for Lucilius. He expects the letters to be published and writes with posterity and a general readership in mind: "I am working for later generations, writing down some ideas that may be of assistance to them" (*Ep*. 8.2; cf. 21.5). His literary letters are more like books or essays than real letters. The letter form is a literary device and has a fictive character. A real letter is composed for a particular person or limited group sharing a common history, known to the author and addressing the particularities of their concerns. A literary letter is like a book, in that the author does not know the readers personally, but it is written for whoever is interested. Seneca acknowledged this difference, already expressed by the most important letter writer of classical antiquity, Cicero (106–43 BCE): "I have one way of writing what I think will only be read by those to whom I address my letter, and another way of writing what I think will be read by many" (*Fam*. 15.21.4).

Terminology. These two types of letters have been designated by various pairs of contrasting labels: "real/non-real," "private/"public," "non-literary/literary," "letter/epistle." The pioneering work on New Testament epistolography by Adolf Deissmann popularized the distinction between *epistles* and *letters*. Prior to Deissmann, New Testament letters had mostly been interpreted as doctrinal treatises in letter form. His research in the rich finds of papyrus letters, written by everyday people in everyday language, convinced him that Paul's letters were informal communications written for particular occasions and addressees; they were not literary productions (which Deissmann designated "epistles"), but real letters.[20]

19. Among the more helpful books that set New Testament letters in their Hellenistic context: William G. Doty, *Letters in Primitive Christianity* (Philadelphia: Fortress Press, 1973); Stanley K. Stowers, *Letter Writing in Greco-Roman Antiquity* (Philadelphia: Westminster Press, 1986); Klauck, *Ancient Letters*.

20. Adolf Deissmann, *Paul: A Study in Social and Religious History*, trans. William E. Wilson (New York: Harper, 1957), 7–26; Deissmann, *Light from the Ancient East*, esp.

Deissmann's contribution is extremely important, but, in regard to interpreting Paul's letters, his either/or approach exaggerated the polarities between literary and real letters. Paul, and especially the later Pauline tradition, represents something of a middle way between these polarities. None of Paul's letters is exclusively to individuals; all are to churches and intended to be read in worship, and thus have a certain public character. They are to particular churches with particular problems, not to the church in general, and are thus somewhere between public and private, literary and nonliterary letters. Except for Philemon, Paul's letters are much longer than the typical Hellenistic letter, incorporating and revising traditional material, dealing with themes that far transcend the typical personal letter, and sometimes utilizing rhetorical forms and structures. Deissmann was absolutely right, however, that Paul did not compose doctrinal treatises in the form of letters, and that Paul's letters manifest many of the characteristics of real letters.

Paul's letters as real letters. In the Hellenistic world, two oft-repeated characterizations of real letters are important for understanding Paul's writings: (1) Letters mediate the presence of the writer to the distant reader. The letter is not only a substitute for, but is the bearer of, the living voice of the writer. Paul wanted to be present and address his readers face to face. His second choice was to send a delegate who represented him. When neither of these options was possible, his third option was the letter: his oral message is inscribed on papyrus, and when it is read forth to the assembled house-church congregation, it is Paul's voice that they hear. (2) A real letter thus is part of a conversation; it represents half a dialogue. It is not a monologue, launched into the void and complete in itself, but part of a conversation that takes the particular readers seriously. Even though the letter itself was a written text, the oral/aural medium of communication must be kept clearly in mind. The author dictated the letter to a scribe or secretary, speaking as he would speak to the addressees. The "readers" were in fact hearers, as the letter was read forth in the congregation. All reading was, in fact, an oral/aural experience; even private reading was a matter of reading aloud and hearing what one read.[21]

146–251: "The letter is a piece of life; the epistle is a product of literary art" (230).

Mechanics and Practicalities

Literacy. The process by which letters were composed in the Hellenistic world illuminates the Pauline letters. The proportion of the general population that could read and write has been variously estimated, with about 10 percent being a common figure. "Literate" is itself a term with a broad definition. Not only was there a wide range of reading levels among those who could read at all, but, then as now, there was little correlation between the ability to read and competence in writing. Among those who could write, very few could compose complex sentences and documents such as Paul's letters to the Romans. It was thus normal, even for people who could read and write well, to employ skilled friends or professional scribes to do the actual composition of a letter, and then at the end to take the pen in hand to write the final words as a kind of personal signature (see 1 Cor 16:21; Gal 6:11; Col 4:18; 2 Thess 3:17; Phlm 19).

Coworkers, scribe, secretary. Although Paul himself takes responsibility for what appears in the letters, most appear as the product of joint authorship, with the names of his coworkers appearing with his own name in the initial greeting, and with an alternation between "we" and "I" in the body of the letter. This is

21. See Acts 8:30, Philip *hears* the Ethiopian official reading to himself; John 8:8–9, those around Jesus *heard* what he had written on the ground, i.e., it was *read* aloud. Augustine marveled that Ambrose *read* silently. Cicero is purported to have said: "I am sorry I have not responded to your letter sooner, but I have had a sore throat . . ." See Doty, *Letters*, 7.

an indication that Paul's letters, though direct and personal, are also intended to represent the Pauline mission and missionary team to the churches. Only once does the name of the scribe appear (Tertius, in Rom 16:22), but Paul clearly made use of scribal help in his other letters. In the Hellenistic world, the role of the scribe/secretary could range from that of the mere recorder who wrote word for word what the author dictated, through varying degrees of editorial and compositional help, to actually composing the letter in the name of and at the behest of the author.

In Paul's case, the process of composition would normally involve conversation among Paul, his coworkers, and the scribe, the composing of a rough draft and settling on the final wording, and the transcribing of this to a finished document, which would be checked over by Paul before releasing it for delivery. Writers of longer letters typically made copies which they retained for future reference, and Paul may have done this as well. Yet, examples of broken grammar and allowing erroneous statements to stand even when corrected shows that Paul's letters sometimes represent his original unedited dictation (cf., e.g., 1 Cor 1:14–15).

Letter types, use of rhetorical forms. Paul's letters, like other extensive Hellenistic letters, do not simply ramble on, but give evidence of careful structure. We do not know whether Paul had formal training in rhetoric, but he does manifest some awareness of rhetorical form. We should not imagine, however, that as he composes, he is following a rigid outline, as though he said to himself, "Well, now, I've finished part 3.a—on to 3.b" (so Doty, *Letters*, 28). There were various types of Hellenistic letters, each type manifesting certain conventional forms. Stowers discusses thirteen different types of letters, including friendship letters, letters of praise and blame, letters of recommendation, and letters of consolation.[22] These conventions undoubtedly had an effect on the structure and style of Paul's letters, but it has not proven helpful to apply the canons of letter writing to the interpretation of individual documents, as though Paul said to himself in each case, "Now I'm going to write a letter of defense and follow its specific pattern" (or whatever the occasion called for).

Likewise, since there are points of contact between composing a persuasive letter and preparing a good speech, the conventions of the various types of rhetoric can sometimes be illuminating in seeing what Paul is doing and how he is composing a particular letter or letter section. Again, however, the insights of such rhetorical analysis cannot be applied rigidly in interpreting Paul's letters; only minimal agreement exists among those who emphasize rhetorical analysis as a major key to understanding Paul.[23] Paul is aware that he is going a new way, and that in part he must build the road as he goes. While he makes use of previous patterns, adapting them to his own purpose, his aims are not best expressed by attempting to fit his letters into previous categories. The one word that probably best characterizes Paul's letters is *pastoral*. There had been nothing previous quite like them.[24]

Dating. Affixing the exact date to a letter was not part of the prescribed form. Letters were ordinarily not dated, though official royal letters might be. Sometimes the date, but not the year, is given, more or less incidentally (see example above; Mesore [June] 9, but no year). No New Testament letter is dated; perhaps the original included a date extraneously, on the back or outside, but none of the copies we have are dated. Would that they were—it would clarify several issues of New Testament chronology and exegesis.

22. Stowers, *Letter Writing*, 49–174.

23. The parade example is Hans-Dieter Betz's application of rhetorical analysis to Galatians, which has generated mixed reviews and considerable debate. See below, §13.1.4. See also the thoughtful discussion of the rhetorical category to which the Thessalonian letters belong in Abraham J. Malherbe, *The Letters to the Thessalonians: A New Translation with Introduction and Commentary*, AB 32B (New York: Doubleday, 2000), 96, 359–61.

24. See Abraham J. Malherbe, *Paul and the Thessalonians: The Philosophic Tradition of Pastoral Care* (Philadelphia: Fortress Press, 1987), 77–78 and passim.

FIGURE 30: Roman road near Tarsus in Turkey. By the time of Paul, the Romans had built a system of roads that facilitated travel throughout the empire. USED BY PERMISSION OF DAVID PADFIELD.

Composition and delivery. There were a good system of Roman roads that expedited travel throughout the empire and an efficient postal service, but it was available only for government business. Writers of private correspondence had to find their own means for delivering their letters. For the wealthy, a slave could be dispatched with the letter, perhaps waiting to bring the response by "return mail." Paul and most others were dependent on finding someone going to the neighborhood of the addressee. Paul typically sent his letters by one or more of his coworkers who were traveling on missionary business, or specifically to deliver his letters—interrelated tasks in Paul's view.

Since letters, like all ancient texts, were composed without punctuation marks, and without spaces between sentences and words, reading the letter aloud to the congregation involved some preparation and interpretation. In the best case, someone who knew the author of the letter and had been present, or even involved in, the writing of the letter served as its oral interpreter to the congregation. The meaning, tone of voice, and emphasis of the author could be explained in the process of delivering the letter. The papyrus scroll itself, far from being an inert object, then became a factor in a more dynamic process of human communication that linked author and hearer-readers in one community.

The amount of time, work, and expense involved meant that letter writing was not a casual process. Romans, Paul's longest letter, would have required many days of full-time work by a professional scribe, costing the modern equivalent of about $2,000 for materials and labor.[25] In the case of Romans, dealing with this expense is most easily explained by the detail Paul reveals in 16:2, that Phoebe "became a benefactor [προστάτις patron] of many and of myself as well."[26] Robert Jewett argues that Tertius may well have been the slave or employee of Phoebe, would have accompanied her to Rome, and would have been the one who read the letter aloud to the assembled house churches (a woman of Phoebe's social class would not have done this herself). Mentioning Tertius implies he is authorized to expand on the letter's

25. E. Randolph Richards, "Letter," in *New Interpreter's Dictionary of the Bible*, 3:640.

26. Robert Jewett, *Romans: A Commentary*, Hermeneia (Minneapolis: Fortress Press, 2007), 22.

contents and explain it to the hearers. In the case of Romans, this means that "Tertius and Phoebe were engaged in the creation, the delivery, the public reading, and the explanation of the letter."[27]

Collection, preservation, editing. Composers of literary letters written with an eye to later publication, even if they were "real" letters actually sent to friends, normally kept their own copies, which they might continue to edit and revise. Such editing, whether done by the original author or later, sometimes involved combining two or more independent letters into one. "In Cicero's letter exchange with Brutus two letters of Cicero and one of Brutus may be shown to be redactional compositions in each case from two independent letters (*Ep. Brut.* 1.2.1, 3–6; 1.3.1–3, 4; 1.4.1–3, 3–6)."[28] Sometimes a letter written over a longer period of time gives evidence of the different sections, their relative date and occasion; in effect a secondary combination of different letters by the original author became the "original" version sent to the first readers.

Again, the Ciceronian collection provides an example. In a letter addressed to Cicero by M. Caelius Rufus, the author refers to what he "wrote above," and describes how the situation had changed in the meantime. A certain political figure had behaved dishonorably, but he "had not [yet] done this when I wrote the earlier part of the letter" (*Ad familiars* 8.6.5). Cicero's trusted private secretary Marcus Tullius began to edit these copies for publication, combining them with other letters of Cicero he obtained from correspondents. It is thus not always clear what goes back to Cicero's own collecting and editing and what is to be attributed to the later editor. In some published letter collections, these edited versions of the original author's letters were combined with later fictive letters written in his name, adapting his teaching to a later situation. The key examples are the collections of letters from Plato and Ignatius, and the Cynic Epistles attributed to Diogenes. There is general agreement that historical criticism has succeeded in sorting out the authentic letters written by Plato and Ignatius from those of their later disciples.

In all this, possible parallels to the Pauline letter corpus are evident. Previous generations of scholars thought in terms of "the" original of each letter, but it is reasonable to suppose that Paul may have kept copies of his letters, revising them himself and reissuing them in more than one version. On the arguments pro and con as to whether the present form of various Pauline letters represents editorial combinations of more than one letter, see the introductions to Romans, Philippians, and especially 2 Corinthians. On the inclusion of pseudepigraphical letters in the Pauline corpus, see Excursus 2 after §14.2, and the introductions to 2 Thessalonians, Colossians, Ephesians, and especially the Pastorals.

10.2.3 Form and Structure of Pauline Letters

Paul's letters manifest an identifiable form that is more or less consistent through all his letters, a form that consists of Paul's own transformations of the conventional Hellenistic letter. Typical letters in the Hellenistic world consisted of three parts: introduction, body, and conclusion, each of which might be subdivided as follows:[29]

I. Introduction
   A. Prescript (Greeting), in three stereotypical parts: A to B, greetings
      1. sender: *superscriptio*
      2. addressee: *adscriptio*
      3. greeting: *salutatio* (χαίρειν, *chairein*, greetings, lit. "rejoice")
   B. Proem (Thanksgiving), which may consist of one or more of the following:

27. Ibid., 23.

28. Klauck, *Ancient Letters*, 163. The following illustrations are also from Klauck, who provides a fuller discussion and more examples.

29. See esp. ibid., "Standard Letter Components," 17–42, and Doty, *Letters*, "The Form of the Pauline Letters," 27–43.

1. prayer-wish (εὔχομαι, *euchomai*, I pray)
2. thanksgiving (εὐχαριστῶ *eucharistō*, I give thanks)
3. intercession, remembrance (μνείαν ποιούμενος, *mneian poioumenos*, making remembrance) before the gods
4. expression of joy (χαρά, ἐχάρην, *chara*, *echarēn*, joy, I rejoice)

II. Body
- A. Body Opening, sometimes with conventional formula such as "I want you to know"
- B. Body Middle: information, instruction, request, recommendation, exhortation
- C. Body Closing: summary exhortations, travel plans

III. Conclusion
- A. Epilogue: concluding exhortations, future plans
- B. Postscript
  1. greetings from those with the writer, to those with the reader
  2. farewell (ἔρρωσθε *errōsthe*, lit., be strong)
  3. final words in author's own hand
  4. date

Paul makes the following distinctive transformations:

I. Introduction: Prescript (Greeting). The conventional "A to B, greetings" may be seen in Acts 15:23; 23:26; James 1:1. Paul's prescripts follow the same threefold pattern as typical Hellenistic letters, but are generally longer, often dramatically so (see Rom 1:1–7!). This is not Pauline wordiness, but theological transformation of conventional phraseology. He often identifies himself and his readers with theological terminology, identifying both his and their role in the eschatological plan of God, for example, using "apostle" as a frequent term for himself, "saints" or "church" for his readers.

The most significant transformation is Paul's replacement of the colorless *chairein* with his distinctive "grace and peace to you." Paul originated this phrase. It is found nowhere in literature except in Paul's own writings and in literature dependent on him. Those who have often heard this phrase in worship or seen it in Christian literature may have had their senses dulled by familiarity, but it is a striking opening greeting, laden with theological overtones. The Greek infinitive *chairein* functions as a weak imperative of the word for "rejoice," but in conventional letters the meaning is practically irrelevant. The word functioned as a greeting, like "Hi" or "Hello," without reference to meaning. For it, Paul substitutes a similar word from the Christian language of faith, χάρις (*charis*, grace). Paul combines this with the key term used in the greetings of Jewish letters, the rich word שָׁלוֹם, *shalom*, usually translated "peace," but connoting much more than the lack of hostilities: wholeness, soundness, the goodness of things when they are as the creator intended them.

We might suppose that in this simple greeting Paul combined the Christian Greek *charis* with the Jewish *shalom* with the intention of symbolizing the two worlds that he integrated in his own person: the Jewish Christian apostle to the Gentiles, who saw his ministry as bridging the gap and breaking down the walls between these two groups. This may be going too far, but we can be sure that he created and intentionally used this formula that became his trademark, and expected his hearer-readers to ponder the significance of this new language.

Proem (Thanksgiving). Paul likewise expands the second part of the letter opening and fills it with new meaning. What was conventionally a brief phrase expressing the writer's wish for the reader's good health or a stereotyped prayer of thanksgiving to the gods becomes a full-bodied theological declaration that often anticipates and prepares the way for the themes to be developed in the body of the letter.[30]

30. The classical work is Paul Schubert, *Form and Function of the Pauline Thanksgivings*, BZNW 20 (Berlin: Töpelmann, 1939), but see also Robert W. Funk, *Language, Hermeneutic, and Word of God* (New York: Harper, 1966), 254–70.

II. Body. Paul structures the main body of his letters according to his understanding of the gospel and the Christian life. The primary element in his thought is the conviction that God has acted in Christ for the salvation of the world. God's act calls for human response; God's grace calls for human gratitude. The Christian life is not a new law, not a moralism, but is the grateful response to the saving act of God. Thus the body of Paul's letters revolves around two poles, typically separated into two distinct sections. The primary pole explicates the saving act of God and its meaning, in the indicative mode; the secondary pole spells out the response of faith in a series of imperatives. These may be expressed in a series of descriptive complementary pairs, inseparable and dynamically related:

God's act	//	human response
Grace	//	gratitude-faith, thus
χάρις as-God's-grace	//	χάρις as-human-gratitude
Theology	//	ethics
Indicative	//	imperative
Kerygma	//	didache
Euangelion	//	parenesis
"What?"	//	"so what?"

Neither element can stand alone. The left column taken by itself results in theological abstraction. The right column in isolation results in legalistic moralism. Taken together, the two poles correspond to the shape of covenant commitment in the Old Testament and the Bible as a whole: God's gracious act makes authentic human response both possible and necessary. This pattern is seen most clearly in the Decalogue (Exod 20:2–17), prefatory to the book of the covenant, 20:22–23:33, which begins, "I am the LORD your God, who brought you out of the land of Egypt, out of the house of slavery // [therefore] you shall have no other gods before me."

In Paul's letters, this structure is most visible in Romans, his longest and most systematic letter, written to a church he did not found and to which he had never been, a letter in which he could express the structure of his own thought most clearly. Chapters 1–11 represent God's act, chapters 12–16 human response. The transition is marked by the "I appeal to you *therefore*" (οὖν) of 12:1. Other more or less clear examples are 1 Thessalonians 1–3 / 4–5 and Galatians 1–4 / 5–6. Though the indicative/imperative dialectical structure of Paul's thought remains evident in 1 and 2 Corinthians as well, the literary pattern is obscured in 1 Corinthians by the serial treatment of particular problems, and in 2 Corinthians by the fact that the present form of the letter is the result of a later editorial process. The deuteropauline Colossians 1–2 / 3–4 and Ephesians 1–3 / 4–6 pick up the Pauline pattern.

III. Conclusion. Paul's transformation of the closing section is less dramatic than in the other sections, but he still remolds the conventional formulae to express his own theology. He often sends greetings from his coworkers, and greets particular people in the congregation to whom he is writing, strengthening the network that bound together the scattered congregations and their sense of mutual solidarity in the one body of Christ. He never uses the conventional *errōsthe*, but includes a blessing and sometimes other liturgical expressions appropriate to the worship setting in which the letters would be read. His announcement of travel plans that include visiting the congregation he addresses is not mere information, but the promise—or threat—that the written text that mediates his apostolic word will soon be replaced by his personal presence. The eschatological tone interwoven throughout much of the letter is emphasized at the end—the parousia of the Lord and the apostle's impending visit to the congregation are not unrelated.

10.2.4 Theological Perspectives on the Letter Form

We now return to the question introduced above: how to account for the preponderance of letters in the New Testament, and the "epistolary pressure" that caused the early church to write letters, to force nonletter material into the letter form, and to include, along with the Gospels, only letters in the New Testament (see above §1.4). Four characteristics make letters the appropriate vehicle for the Christian faith.

Particularity, Finitude, Affirmation of Relativity, Incarnation

Real letters (as distinct from books and literary letters) are not general, but written by a particular person or persons to particular people and deal with particular situations. The letters to the editor of a national publication are not real letters. Though they may deal with particular situations important to the publication's readers, they are addressed to a general public, not to particular persons. Real letters are essentially particularistic and situational. Rather than stating grand general truths, they fully enter into the particular situation of their readers. If Paul had mistakenly sent the letter to the Galatians to the Christians in Thessalonica, they and we would understand it entirely differently—even though it would contain exactly the same words.[31]

This *scandal of particularity* is inherent in the Christian faith. The early Christians did not believe that God became incarnate in humanity in general, or in some abstract principle, but in one particular Aramaic-speaking Jew, born in an obscure land under Roman rule, crucified under the local governor Pontius Pilate. This particularity is related to the essential character of human life. No one lives in general; every human life is unique. The letters of the New Testament are appropriate to the incarnation.

The Community and Its Mission

Related to the particular character of New Testament letters is their orientation to community. There are no letters to individuals in the New Testament. Even Paul's letter to Philemon includes "Apphia our sister, Archippus our fellow soldier, and the church in your house"; 3 John is not strictly only to Gaius (see v. 15). The pseudepigraphical letters to Timothy and Titus are in reality addressed to the wider Christian community, as is made clear by the concluding verbs in the plural (see below §16.1.2). A letter assumes a common community experience, evoked in Paul's letters by such expressions as "as you yourselves know" and "as you remember" (see, e.g., the concentration of such phrases in 1 Thess 2:1, 2, 5, 9, 11; 3:3, 4).[32] A real letter can say "we" in a meaningful sense, can address the readers in the second person singular or plural, whether or not the author knows the readers personally, for it assumes a shared history and concerns.

In the New Testament, even letters addressed to a particular readership are also projections of the sender's purpose into the wider world. And the author/sender is himself sent, intensely conscious that his message does not originate with himself. The New Testament letters represent a segment of God's mission into the world: God ⇒ Christ ⇒ Apostle ⇒ Letter ⇒ Church ⇒ World. Letters are appropriate to apostolicity, to communicating the apostolic faith (on apostolicity, see below §§10.1.3 and 13.2).

Narrative World, Human Existence, and Ethics

Letters project a narrative world that is important for their interpretation. "Letters have stories."[33] The letter represents a segment of a

31. Victor Paul Furnish, *The Moral Teaching of Paul: Selected Issues*, 3rd ed. (Nashville: Abingdon Press, 2009), 16, citing Willi Marxsen.

32. See Calvin Roetzel, *Paul: The Man and the Myth* (Minneapolis: Fortress Press, 1999), 76.

33. Norman R. Petersen, *Rediscovering Paul: Philemon and the Sociology of Paul's Narrative World* (Philadelphia: Fortress Press, 1985), ix, 2. On the narrative world of epistolary literature, see M. Eugene Boring, "Narrative Dynamics in 1 Peter: The Function of Narrative World," in *Reading 1 Peter with New Eyes: Methodological Reassessments of the Letter of First Peter*, ed. Robert L. Webb and Betsy Bauman-Martin, Library of New Testament

narrative line shared by author and reader(s). This becomes important in studying the Pauline and other New Testament letters: *to understand a letter, one needs to recognize the narrative in which it is embedded and which it projects, for the letter is a narrative form.* The brief letter to Philemon provides a clear example (see §11.3 below).

Human existence has an essentially narrative character. Human beings exist diachronically, in space and time. To be human is to have a story. As a human being, I do not exist as a timeless essence, but as a sequence of events in space and time. As a human being, my story is not something optional or extra that I as a human self "have." I am my story. Just as I am not an immaterial "soul" that exists encased *in* a material body, but exist *as* a body, so I do not only *have* a story, but in my essential being I *am* a story, and do not exist as a human being apart from the narrative that defines my being.

The little narrative that defines my life is a segment of a larger story. My self-understanding is shaped by how I see this larger symbolic universe that gives meaning to my little life. When I am addressed by a letter, as a narrative form, the letter projects a narrative world that I am challenged to see as the real world, the world that actually defines my existence.

New Testament letters are written to instruct the readers on how to live in the light of Christian faith. These letters are permeated with parenesis that seem to present this instruction directly: "Do this." "Don't do that." However, just as Hebrew wisdom materials and the Christian Sermon on the Mount are heard differently when read within their canonical narrative contexts, so paraenetic materials are heard differently when read within their epistolary setting—which is a narrative context. The reader does not merely look at the command or exhortation and decide whether or not to do it, not even on the basis of weighing the arguments or authority expressed in the letter's discourse.

Studies (Edinburgh: T. & T. Clark, 2007), 7–40 and the bibliography there provided.

Rather, readers of letters are addressed as though they actually lived within a particular narrative world that undergirds a way of life represented by the commands and exhortations. As in Jesus' parables, the low-key penumbra of the narrative world projected by the letter is presented as the real world. The discourse of the letter does not so much preach, but quietly assumes without fanfare that the world it represents is the real world, and that the readers live within it. Through this subtle, nonmanipulative pressure, readers are indirectly challenged—"forced" is not too strong a word—to decide on the reality of the narrative world projected by the letter.

Like preaching, the surface of the epistolary form itself is direct (second person!), and the parenesis of its content is direct. The narrative world projected by the letter's discourse is indirect. The readers' assumed symbolic universe is challenged, indirectly and subliminally, by an alternate vision of how things are and what life is about. A narrative approach allows the reader to hear the letter's parenesis as more than a list of commands. Without directly instructing the reader about it, the letter simply assumes an alternate vision of reality, a larger story that embraces the reader's life story. There is a parabolic dimension to New Testament letters, as there is to Gospels.

10.3 The Letters of Paul

SINCE LETTERS ARE A NARRATIVE FORM embedded in a particular history, when studying a series of related letters, it is helpful to know their chronological order. In the case of the seven undisputed letters of Paul, the relative order of four letters is evident and agreed upon by all: 1 Thessalonians ⇒ 1 Corinthians ⇒ 2 Corinthians ⇒ Romans. Of the other three letters, it is clear that Galatians is prior to Romans, but how much earlier is disputed. The place of Philippians and Philemon within this chronology is also a matter of continuing debate. In the chronology argued for in this book, we will begin with 1 Thessalonians, then study Philippians and Philemon, then the Corinthian correspondence, and conclude with Galatians and Romans.

10.4 For Further Reading

Paul's Life and Mission to 50 CE: A Preliminary Sketch

Hengel, M., and A. M. Schwemer. *Paul between Damascus and Antioch: The Unknown Years*. Translated by John Bowden. Louisville, KY: Westminster John Knox Press, 1997.

Riesner, R. *Paul's Early Period: Chronology, Mission Strategy, Theology*. Translated by Douglas W. Stott. Grand Rapids: Eerdmans, 1998.

Introduction to the Epistles

Doty, W. G. *Letters in Primitive Christianity*. Philadelphia: Fortress Press, 1973.

Klauck, H.-J. *Ancient Letters and the New Testament: A Guide to Context and Exegesis*. Waco, TX: Baylor University Press, 2006.

Richards, E. R. "Letter." In *The New Interpreter's Dictionary of the Bible*, edited by Katherine Doob Sakenfeld, 3:638–41. Nashville: Abingdon Press, 2006.

Stirewalt, M. L. *Paul, the Letter Writer*. Grand Rapids: Eerdmans, 2003.

Stowers, S. K. *Letter Writing in Greco-Roman Antiquity*. Philadelphia: Westminster Press, 1986.

11
Letters of the Early Aegean Mission

11.1 Interpreting 1 Thessalonians

11.1.1 Thessalonica

Thessalonica was a large, sophisticated, commercially and politically important city, the capital of the Roman province of Macedonia—and thus an ideal location for a Pauline mission center representing the strategy of Paul's Aegean mission. Population estimates in Paul's time range from 30,000 to 100,000. Thessalonica was not a Roman colony, but had been a loyal Roman community for two centuries when Paul arrived. Even after Macedonia became a Roman province, Thessalonica remained a free city, ruled in the Greek style and maintaining its Greek cultural heritage, and did so by its alliance with and loyalty to Rome. It was a prosperous city with a good harbor, advantageously located at the head of the Thermaic Gulf, at an important station on the strategic east-west Egnatian Way. This ancient superhighway was the all-weather road built by the Romans that connected Rome and points further east, facilitating both rapid troop deployment and commercial traffic. Paul chose Thessalonica as an evangelizing center for Macedonia, and the church there played this role in his mission strategy.

Religion in Thessalonica manifested the usual array of Greco-Roman cults (see above §9.2.2), but two stand out: the emperor cult associated with the goddess Roma and the local cult of the Cabiri. Paying due respect to such cults was not only a matter of religious conviction, but important as a manifestation of civic loyalty and allegiance to the Roman Empire. The Jewish community of Thessalonica had long since learned how to negotiate its precarious way in a pagan city. Not only the authorities but the local population would be suspicious of any group that might upset the symbiosis and balance of competing powers that made life good for all. Though Paul and his few dozen converts would not seem to pose a threat in this large city, his message of an alternate king and kingdom could be perceived by both Jews and Gentiles as upsetting this fragile stability, and they would be resisted, even with violence.

11.1.2 Historical Setting, Context, Situation

For the setting of 1 Thessalonians in the larger narrative of early Christian history, see above §10.1. The narrative world projected by the letter itself largely agrees with that of Acts 16–17. The following story can be constructed with some confidence:

1. Paul, Silvanus, and Timothy arrived in Thessalonica about 50 CE, after having been arrested and mistreated in Philippi (1 Thess 2:2; cf. Acts 16:11–40; on the chronology, see §13.3.4).
2. They were the first Christian missionaries in the city. They remained for some time, and

founded a church, which became a mission center for founding other churches (1 Thess 1:8). Acts 17:1–10 reports that they were forced to leave after three weeks, but Paul's own letters indicate a longer time, perhaps about three months. The congregation at Philippi repeatedly sent Paul financial help while he was in Thessalonica, a typical round trip of ten days (Phil 4:15–16). Paul also indicates that while in Thessalonica, he supported himself by working with his own hands (1 Thess 2:9).

3. Troubles in Thessalonica forced the missionary team to leave. Paul's preaching typically generated conflicts with the synagogue, as indicated by Acts and confirmed by his own letters (2 Cor 11:24; Acts 13–14, 17–18). The hostilities that had caused Paul to leave continued to plague the new converts, who suffered abuse because of their new faith. It was a tumultuous time (Acts 17:6, "these men have turned the world upside down"), in which Jews opposed the new group, not only on the basis of religious convictions, but as a matter of political and social prudence—if others regarded the new Christian group as a party within Judaism, the Jews' own precarious economic and social position was endangered. Likewise, citizens grateful for the order, peace, and prosperity brought by Rome resisted what appeared to be a subversive cult undermining loyalty to the empire by preaching another king and an alternative kingdom (Acts 17:7–8).

4. After Philippi and Thessalonica, Paul's next main mission center was Corinth, which he reached after mostly unfruitful efforts in Beroea and Athens (Acts 17:10–18:1; 1 Thess 3:1). From Athens, Paul sent Timothy back to Thessalonica to check on the church, and went ahead to Corinth alone. There, in collaboration with Prisca and Aquila, who had just arrived from Rome under the pressure of Claudius's decree (see above §9.2.1), he founded a new church and mission center.

5. When Paul was rejoined by Timothy and Silvanus, he (and they) wrote in response to the issues and questions he received in Timothy's report. First Thessalonians does not specify its place of origin, but it fits best into the early period in Paul's year-and-a-half stay in Corinth, about 50 CE (see 2 Cor 11:8–9; Acts 18:5). Most constructions of the history of early Christian literature consider 1 Thessalonians to be the earliest New Testament document, and thus the earliest extant piece of Christian writing.[1]

Early Pauline thought? First Thessalonians is thus a document of "early Pauline thought."[2] This should not be misunderstood, however, as though it is the product of a neophyte missionary-theologian, advocating rudimentary ideas the more mature Paul will later abandon. This approach has sometimes been advocated in explaining Paul's "early" eschatology expressed in 1 Thessalonians, with its expectation that Jesus will soon return (1 Thess 4:13–5:11), as though this was an aspect of the immature Paul that he later outgrew. This view is sometimes supported by pointing to the relaxing of the eschatological hope in the later letters (Colossians, Ephesians, the Pastorals). However, though these letters do represent a modification of the eschatology found in Paul's own letters, they were probably not written by Paul himself. Moreover, the expectation of the near parousia is not merely Paul's early, provisional view, but an integral element in his theological thought still found in his last letter, whether Romans or Philippians is considered latest (Rom 13:11–14; Phil 3:20; 4:5). Paul wrote 1 Thessalonians about seventeen years after his conversion, after he had been instrumental in the founding of several churches, as the work of a seasoned missionary and mature theologian.

1. Other (less likely) claims to be the earliest extant Christian writing have been made for Galatians, 2 Thessalonians, Hebrews, James, and Jude (see introductions to each book).
2. Earl Richard, "Early Pauline Thought: An Analysis of 1 Thessalonians," in *Pauline Theology I: Thessalonians, Philippians, Galatians, Philemon*, ed. Jouette M. Bassler (Minneapolis: Fortress Press, 1991), 39–51.

There is a real sense, however, in which 1 Thessalonians represents the early period of Paul's own distinctive theology. Paul considered his break with Antioch and the launching of the Aegean mission a major turning point, something of a fresh start, marked by a new missions strategy of which he was the principal architect. The Aegean mission was the principal period of Paul's own missionary work, so that he could refer to the first church founded during the Aegean mission as the "beginning of the gospel" (ἀρχῇ τοῦ εὐαγγελίου, *archē tou euangeliou* Phil 4:15). It seems that the launching of the Aegean mission was also the inauguration of a new strategy of communication and instruction represented by the Pauline letter, of which 1 Thessalonians is the first. In regard to Pauline theology, this means that the later developments in Paul's thought, hammered out in response to later crises, cannot be used to explain the theology of 1 Thessalonians, which is based on and expresses its own coherent theology.

11.1.3 The Church in Thessalonica

First Thessalonians is our earliest extant document that provides a window into what the earliest Christian congregations were like. Acts 17:1–9 presents a very brief description of the founding of the church, containing some reliable information, but also heavily influenced by Luke's own later perspective and theological interests.

The letter itself is addressed to a church of Gentile Christians (1:9–10), which may have contained a Jewish minority.[3] While it is likely that, following Paul's typical practice, he found many of his converts among the God-fearers, the Gentile penumbra of the synagogue, even they would hardly be described as those who had responded to Paul's preaching by turning from idolatry to serve the one true God.

We have no way of estimating the size of the Thessalonian church, but judging from the indications of the size of other Pauline congregations, when Paul wrote 1 Thessalonians the congregation probably numbered dozens rather than hundreds.[4] It was large enough, however, that some leaders had emerged (5:12–13). No offices or orders of ministry are mentioned. Leadership was apparently informal and charismatic. The church is acquainted with Christian prophets and other expressions of the work of the Spirit in its midst (5:19–22), and must be admonished neither to reject nor uncritically accept the declarations of those who claim to speak by the inspiration of the Holy Spirit. Despite its small size and lack of firmly institutionalized structure, we should not think of the new church as merely a small group of enthusiasts enjoying their new spirituality. The little church in Thessalonica was willing to suffer for its faith (1 Thess 1:6; 2:14) and to share their faith with others. It became a mission center from which other congregations were founded and became well known among the network of new churches (1 Thess 1:8–9).

The church was founded on the Pauline kerygma. It was the message proclaimed by Paul and his associates that the Thessalonian converts heard as the word of God (1 Thess 2:13). What was the content of the Christian preaching and teaching, which caused such a change in the lives of the new believers, and caused them to be suspect and harassed by their neighbors? First Thessalonians is our only direct source for answering this question. They only knew what Paul and his coworkers had taught them—no other Christian teachers had been to Thessalonica when Paul writes this letter. Of this, *we*

3. Acts typically represents Paul as beginning his mission preaching in the synagogue, being rejected, and only then going to the Gentiles (13:13–48; 14:1–7; 18:1–11; 19:8–10). Paul's experience in Thessalonica is portrayed in the same stereotypical pattern (17:1–9). Looking back from the end of the first or beginning of the second century CE, Luke portrays the history of each local church as reflecting the history of the whole church: the Christian message was in fact at first proclaimed to the Jews, but by Luke's time the church had already become primarily a Gentile Christian community.

4. Again, Luke's later picture tends, for his theological reasons, to portray the earliest churches in biblical proportions as numerically strong, but his figures are difficult to accept as accurate history (see below, §23.3.4).

only know what can be inferred from the letter, and this is risky and certainly incomplete.

Since the letter is not primarily a didactic letter, we may surmise that most of what Paul alludes to had already been taught while he was present. This would include the proclamation of the one true God in contrast to lifeless idols (1:9), who sent his Son to die for us (5:10), who raised him from the dead (4:14), and who will come again soon for the salvation of believers (5:9). While he was with them, Paul had also given them ethical instruction, and they had become imitators of Paul and of the Lord (4:1–2; 1:6). Whether this means that Paul taught his new converts the elements of the "life and teaching of Jesus" is a moot point (see §18.4.1 below), but there is no indication in 1 Thessalonians that he had done so.

This argument from silence must not be used uncritically, however. The letter refers to neither baptism nor the Eucharist, and has no explicit references to the Old Testament. Yet it would be a mistake to infer that Paul's church-founding proclamation and teaching had not included these constituent elements of Christian instruction. Paul is writing from Corinth. First Corinthians clearly indicates that during his church-founding visit there he taught the new converts specific creedal, catechetical, and liturgical traditions (1 Cor 11:2, 23–25; 15:3–5). Presumably Paul did this in every church (see 1 Cor 4:17).

11.1.4 Unity, Interpolations

There is a broad, but not universal, consensus that we have Paul's letter essentially as he wrote it. A relatively few scholars have explained the perceived duplications, the overlappings, and the extensive thanksgiving section as the result of a post-Pauline editor combining two or more letters. Such hypotheses have not survived critical examination, and interest in such partition theories has waned, with practically all scholars now regarding the letter as a unity.

A related, but different, issue is that of *interpolations*—whether the original letter, composed as a unity, subsequently received one or more brief interpolations. The passage 2:14–16 has sometimes been regarded as a post-Pauline interpolation, and there are some weighty arguments for this view: (1) the fragment seems to interrupt the context and to be out of place, comparing the Thessalonians' problems in their Macedonian context to earlier problems of the church in its Judean context; (2) only here does Paul claim that the Jews killed Jesus; (3) the charge that the Jews "displease God and oppose everyone" sounds like the common Gentile charge against Jews for their "clannishness, standoffishness," taking care of each other but otherwise "haters of the human race," a charge that Paul, himself a Jew, would not likely repeat; (4) the announcement that God's wrath has come on the Jews "at last" or "to the full" can be heard as a retrospective anti-Jewish interpretation of the 70 CE destruction of Jerusalem, and in any case is hard to reconcile with Paul's more positive perspective on God's final acceptance of the Jews in Romans 11.

On the other hand, there is no manuscript evidence for an interpolation, and there are cogent responses to each of the above objections: (1) Closer study shows that the passage is in fact integrated into its context in terms of both content and syntax (see recent commentaries). (2) The Jews who "killed Jesus and the prophets" reflects both the Deuteronomistic theology of history in which rebellious Israel killed the prophets and the inner-synagogue struggles against Jewish Christians in Judea (see §7.7.6). The analogy is not between Gentiles and Jews, but between Macedonians who persecute the church in Thessalonica and Judeans who persecuted the church in Judea. (3) Paul, like the biblical prophets, may indeed take up Gentile charges against the Jews; as a Jew he participated in the harsh language used in internal Jewish conflicts (cf. Qumran!).[5] (4) If one looks for an event in which a Christian

5. For an extensive discussion with numerous illustrations, cf. Luke Timothy Johnson, "The New Testament's Anti-Jewish Slander and the Conventions of Ancient Polemic," *JBL* 108, no. 3 (1989): 419–41.

interpreter could have seen God's wrath falling on unfaithful Jews, one need not wait until the 70 CE catastrophe; there were disasters aplenty in Paul's own time that could have been so understood, for example, the famine in Judea or the expulsion of Jews from Rome under Claudius that had just occurred as Paul writes. Paul probably does not have a particular historical event in mind, however. As later in Romans, Paul more likely thinks of the rejection of the gospel as itself an expression of God's wrath. Moreover, the ambiguous Greek clause may be translated "God's wrath [the final judgment] is about to come upon them," or "God's wrath has come upon them until the end." The prevailing tendency of recent scholarship is to regard the passage as originally written by Paul and part of 1 Thessalonians.[6]

11.1.5 Structure and Outline

The first three chapters constitute a long thanksgiving, including autobiographical reflections on Paul's experience with the Thessalonians, concluded with a transitional prayer. The purpose is to establish the relationship between Paul and the readers, the basis of the instructions to follow. The parenesis proper, with the characteristic οὖν (*oun,* therefore), as in Romans 12:1, Galatians 5:1, begins at 1 Thessalonians 4:1.

1:1	Greeting
1:2–3:13	Thanksgiving/Body: Thanksgiving to the God Who Calls the Church and Keeps It Holy until the End
1:2–10	The Thessalonians' reception of Paul's gospel
1:2–5	Work, labor, hope
1:6–10	Imitators of the Lord and of Paul
2:1–12	Apostolic missionaries worthy of God
2:13–20	God's word and human opposition
3:1–10	Timothy brings good news
3:11–13	Transitional summary and prayer
4:1–5:22	The Life to Which Christians are Called
4:1–12	A life pleasing to God
4:13–5:11	The coming of the Lord
5:12–22	Life in the Christian community
5:23–28	Concluding Greetings, Adjuration, Benediction

6. Among those who continue to argue for an interpolation are Walker, *Interpolations*, 210–20, and Earl J. Richard, *First and Second Thessalonians*, SP (Collegeville, MN: Liturgical Press, 1995), 119–27, each with additional bibliography.

11.1.6 Exegetical-Theological Précis

1:1 Greeting

The inclusion of Paul's two coworkers does not mean the letter is written jointly by three people, but that Paul as the author speaks for his colleagues; they have read his letter and stand behind it, but Paul is the author. Likewise, the repeated "we" sometimes includes his fellow missionaries (e.g., 1:2, 4, 5), but is also used as an epistolary we, equivalent to "I" (2:18; 3:2 "we sent" is the same as 3:5 "I sent"). Only here (and 2 Thess 1:1) does Paul give himself no title. "Apostle" is found only in 2:7, in the plural, in its nontechnical sense "missionary." Paul's authority and apostleship are not an issue in his letter to the Thessalonians.

1:2–3:13 Thanksgiving/Body: Thanksgiving to God Who Calls the Church and Keeps It Holy until the End

In 1 Thessalonians, the thanksgiving modulates into the body of the letter in such a way that it is difficult to separate them. Since 1 Thessalonians is not primarily a didactic letter, the first section of the letter body generally devoted to theological teaching is subsumed under the more personal and worshipful thanksgiving. This section as a whole then forms the basis for Paul's paraenetic instructions in chapters 4 and 5.

1:2–5 Work, labor, hope Paul is grateful that the new, struggling congregation not only has survived, but continues its mission to others. The triad "faith, love, hope" here expresses the conviction that permeates the whole letter: the lives of the new Christians in Thessalonica have been incorporated into the time line of God's saving program for all history: the past event of God's act in Christ and God's call of the Thessalonians, their present existence as mediators of God's love, and their confident hope of God's future to be manifest at the parousia.

1:6–10 Imitators of the Lord and of Paul Paul is grateful that the suffering they have experienced because of their commitment to God has not caused them to abandon the faith. In this they have become imitators of Paul and of Jesus himself. Such imitation of a beloved and respected teacher was highly regarded in the Hellenistic world. In turn, the new Thessalonian Christians have become models to be imitated throughout Macedonia and Achaia. Other churches report to Paul the authentic conversion of the Thessalonians, described by Paul in language from an early creedal statement utilizing three verbs expressing the human response to God's act: they *turned* to God from idols, to *serve* a living and true God, and to *wait* for his Son from heaven (note again the tripartite past/present/future structure of faith). God's saving act points to both past and future: God *raised* Jesus from the dead, the Jesus who *will deliver* us from the coming eschatological wrath. These highly charged apocalyptic phrases signal a major concern of the letter to be developed later (4:13–5:11).

2:1–12 Apostolic missionaries worthy of God Paul here seems to be defending himself: his work among them was not a matter of deceit, impure motives, or trickery, and his preaching was not motivated by flattery or greed. On the contrary, he worked with his own hands to support his mission among them. It has sometimes been argued that the Thessalonians had become suspicious of Paul, tending to classify him among those traveling teacher-philosophers who cultivated and exploited a local group of adherents and then moved on. This would be a misunderstanding, however. Numerous parallels illustrate that making claims about one's own competence and honesty was the conventional style in the letters and writings of Hellenistic philosopher-teachers who wished to distinguish themselves from those unqualified traveling teachers interested in themselves rather than those they instructed. In Paul's situation, *not* to make such conventional claims would raise questions among the Thessalonians about his own sense of authority and calling. The letter is not an apologetic writing, but a letter of friendship in which Paul gives thanks for the readers and cultivates the continuing relationship with them. This, and not apostolic authority, is the basis for the instructions he will give in 4:1–5:11.[7] Paul's apostolic authority is not disputed but assumed by both author and readers, so that he can use ἀπόστολος (*apostolos*) in its general sense of "missionary," including both Silvanus and Timothy. Paul's lack of hierarchical, authoritarian thinking is also manifest in his mixture of family metaphors: he is not only both father (2:11) and nurse-mother (2:7), but brother, baby; when he had to leave the community, he was "orphaned"—he, and not they, was in the situation of the child bereft of parents (2:17).

Corresponding to the conventions of Hellenistic culture, Paul expresses his gratitude not to the readers, but to God for them.[8] This is also a theological point: God is the one who has chosen the Thessalonians and called them into the church, as it is God who calls them into his kingdom and glory, shortly to appear in its fullness at the return of Christ. Paul gives thanks to the God who called them to faith. Paul saw

7. See especially Malherbe, *Thessalonians*, 133–63 and passim.
8. In the Hellenistic world, saying "thank you" *to* someone meant something like "the matter is finished, we are even, we need have no further dealings with each other," obviously something entirely different from its meaning in modern North American culture. Thus there are *no* "thank yous" on the horizontal level in the entire New Testament, where the numerous expressions of thanks are always directed to God. See, e.g., Bruce J. Malina, *Windows on the World of Jesus: Time Travel to Ancient Judea* (Louisville, KY: Westminster John Knox Press, 1993), xi–xiii.

his mission, and the life of the church generally, as taking place within competing transcendent force fields. God elects (1:4), calls (2:12; 4:7; 5:24), works within the Christian community (2:13), directs the mission of the church (3:11), teaches believers (4:9), and sanctifies. But Satan blocks the way (2:18); every departure from the faith was not mere human foible, but succumbing to "the tempter" (3:5). Within the context of struggling transcendent powers, Christians must make their own decisions and accept responsibility for them. But the initiative is with God.

2:13–20 God's word and human opposition Paul is thus grateful that they received his message not as his own word, but as God's word, which continues to be effective in them. They need this assurance, for they have suffered for their faith at the hands of their Macedonian neighbors. They are not alone in this suffering. Not only are they imitators of Christ and of Paul and the other missionaries in this regard (1:6); they are imitators of the parent church in Judea that suffered at the hands of their Judean neighbors. While Paul's statements in 2:14–16 can unfortunately be read as an expression of and encouragement to anti-Judaism (see above, and §7.7.6), in their context they are intended to encourage the new Thessalonian Christians by exhibiting their continuity with the original church in Judea and their place in the ongoing history of God's saving acts. God's people suffer as inherent in their calling, as manifest in the prophets, Jesus, the original church, and Paul himself.

3:1–10 Timothy brings good news Paul does not include these paragraphs as items of a travelogue, but in order to give yet another reason for his thanksgiving. He had been worried that the faith of the Thessalonians might have withered under the duress they were experiencing, and sent Timothy to encourage them and to report on their status. Paul understands the gospel not as an abstraction, nor as merely an individualistic personal relationship with God, but as bound up on the horizontal level with particular human beings called into the Christian community and joined together in mission. The Thessalonians' continuing steadfast faith in the gospel is inseparably identified with their trust in Paul, who had brought the gospel to them, just as his own relation to God is inseparably bound up with their continuing faith in the gospel. Their steadfastness in the faith is a life-and-death matter, not just for themselves, but for Paul's status when they all stand before God at the parousia.

3:11–13 Transitional summary and prayer Paul brings this section to a close with a prayer that both sums up the whole section 1:2–3:13 and, by its eschatological perspective, forms the transition to the subject matter of the parenesis beginning at 4:1. For Paul as for Jesus, responsibility to God is summed up in the love command, a love directed not only to the insiders of one's own congregation, but outward to the whole church and to all people as God's creatures (cf. 5:15). The final phrase of the prayer points to the parousia of the Lord Jesus with all his ἅγιοι (*hagioi*), literally "holy ones," which could refer to the angels that will accompany the Son of Man at his parousia (Matt 13:41; 16:27; 25:31; Mark 8:38; Luke 9:26; 12:8). However, elsewhere Paul always has a negative view of angels, uses the word ἅγιοι to mean *saints*, and in 1 Corinthians 6:2–3 the "holy ones" are members of the Christian community contrasted with "angels" at the Last Judgment. Paul is therefore probably referring to the members of the Christian community who have died, whom the Lord Jesus will bring with him at his return (4:14).

4:1–5:22 The Life to Which Christians Are Called

In typical Pauline fashion, the section of practical instructions and exhortations (parenesis) follows and is based on the didactic, more theological section (see §10.2.3 above).

4:1–12 A life pleasing to God As is the case with biblical ethics in general, Paul's ethic is explicated as doing God's will. As for Jesus, so also for Paul, right living is a matter of responsibility to God and care for others, love for God and love for the neighbor. While Paul had been with them on the founding visit, he had taught them how they "ought to live and to please God" (4:1). This way of life is summarized as holiness and love. Paul applies holiness initially to sex ethics. The Greek phrase also includes justice in business and social dealings. That the Thessalonians are "taught by God" to love refers to God's act in Christ, to God's word that came through the preaching and conduct of Paul and his colleagues as they did their missionary work in Thessalonica, and to the charismatic teachers and prophets among them who continue to communicate God's word to them. The focus of this teaching is Christian love, not only for the members of their own congregation, but beyond. Love is here identified with the concrete acts essential for the Christian mission: upholding the work of other congregations and missionary preachers with prayer, financial support, and opening one's home to traveling missionaries such as Paul, Silvanus, and Timothy.

The exhortation to live quietly, mind your own affairs, and do manual labor (as Paul himself had done while among them, 2:9) has been explained primarily in two ways. Although Paul himself does not relate this instruction to the eschatology of the "idlers," it has sometimes been argued that, on the basis of superheated expectations about the Lord's return, some had given up their regular jobs and become loafers dependent on the church. Alternatively, Paul is seen as warning against those who are taking advantage of the church's compassionate hospitality that provides for the needy, especially if they are retiring from ordinary work in order to enter the contemplative life and live off the handouts of others, on the model of the Cynic wandering preachers. But the conduct of the new Christian converts is not merely a matter of personal piety; they are called to represent the Christian faith by living in a manner that can be commended by outsiders (v. 12). Though they will encounter harassment and ostracization because of their Christian faith, they are to live honorably in the eyes of their non-Christian neighbors and manifest love for them.

4:13–5:11 The coming of the Lord This is not the "eschatological section" as though Paul now says, "I would now like to turn to a new topic and explain a few things about the return of Jesus." The letter and Paul's theology are permeated with eschatology throughout; it is the horizon of all his thinking. It is important, however, to note the location of this explication of what will occur before and at the time of the parousia: these instructions are in the practical Part Two, not doctrinal speculations on "what happens when we die" or "teaching about the end."

This section is *pastoral care for a grieving community*. Some members of the church have died, and the congregation was apparently distressed about their fate. Would they be excluded from participation in the glory of Christ's return, or does their death in advance of the parousia indicate that they were not believers after all? Paul's answer is clear: those who have died will not be left out, for God will bring them "with" Jesus at his return. Exactly what this means is not so clear. If the "holy ones" of 3:13 refers to Christians who have died, they are in heaven now and will return with Jesus. This way of conceiving the eschatological events clashes with the following verses, in which the dead believers will be raised and go to meet the returning Jesus—but Paul is concerned with pastoral care, not conceptual clarity. Paul's purpose is not to give *information* on "where are the dead," but to give *assurance* that all believers will be included in God's final triumph. In communicating this assurance, Paul may utilize more than one image, even conflicting images, in expressing his faith.

Paul reassures his readers by citing a "word of the Lord"—not a traditional saying of the historical Jesus, but a revelation from the risen Jesus expressed in conventional apocalyptic imagery. This may be a saying of an anonymous post-Easter Christian prophet, or a revelation that had come directly to Paul. The Antioch church, to which both Paul and Silvanus had once belonged, had such prophets in its leadership (Acts 11:27–29; 13:1–3). The oracle's content portrays the returning Jesus in the imagery of the visit of a Hellenistic ruler; this is the primary meaning of *parousia*. The loyal subjects go out to welcome the king, queen, or governor, and usher him or her into their city; this reception and procession back into the city is expressed by the term ἀπάντησις (*apantēsis*, "to meet the Lord," NRSV).[9] Paul's point: those who have died will not miss out on this ultimate triumph of Christ, but will be raised first, to join living believers who will go out to meet the returning Lord. Paul expects to be among that number, when the saints go marching in.

5:12–22 Life in the Christian community Congregational leaders are to be respected (5:12–13). It is the community as a whole, however, that is to exercise pastoral care, encourage the weaker members, and warn the ἄτακτοι (*ataktoi*, disorderly). Are these the ones ignoring the church's leadership? Are they those who had quit their jobs and become busybodies? The community has charismatic leadership, Spirit-inspired prophets and teachers. Their instructions are neither to be disdained nor blindly obeyed. The community as a whole, empowered by the Spirit of God, is to test purported revelations and to decide what is valid and what is not (see on 1 John 4:1–3 below).

9. This is very different from the modern misunderstanding expressed in the doctrine of the "rapture," in which believers are snatched up into the atmosphere and then taken to heaven. Here, the picture is of Jesus who returns to earth, his followers going out to welcome him and join him in his triumphal return to reign in this world. Ἀπάντησις, *apantēsis* is found elsewhere in the New Testament only in Matt 25:6 and Acts 28:15; the cognate verb is found in Mark 14:13 (cf. Luke 17:12). In each case, the meaning is clearly "go out to meet and bring back with."

5:23–28 Greetings, Adjuration, Benediction

Paul expects the letter to be read aloud to the congregation during its worship service. He concludes by again taking up the worshipful tone of the long thanksgiving in 1:2–3:13, with the confident prayer that the God who called them will bring his purpose for them to completion at the appearance of Christ. The letter was more than a personal communication to friends. The strongly worded adjuration of 5:27 instructs them to have it read aloud to the whole church as a part of worship. Here begins a tradition that was carried on in 1 Corinthians 14:37–40 and through the formation of the Pauline corpus. Disputes about what is authentic apostolic faith are settled by apostolic writings, so that already in our earliest New Testament document begins a trajectory that leads to the New Testament canon.

11.2 Interpreting Philippians

SOMETIME AFTER WRITING 1 THESSALONIANS, Paul left Corinth and established a new mission center in Ephesus, where he worked for three years. During his Ephesian ministry, Paul wrote 1 and 2 Corinthians, and probably also Philippians, Philemon, and Galatians, though the date and relative order of these are disputed. In Ephesus he came into conflict with the authorities and seems to have been imprisoned for a time, perhaps more than once.

Authorship and destination of Philippians are unproblematic. The letter was written by Paul to the church in Philippi.

11.2.1 Philippi: City and Church

Philippi was already an ancient city in Paul's time, founded about 356 BCE by Philip II of Macedon, father of Alexander the Great. The city was located on the Via Egnatia, the main traffic artery connecting the east and west of the

FIGURE 31: Ruins of a prison at Philippi. Paul's incarceration may have been in a setting such as this. USED BY PERMISSION OF DAVID PADFIELD.

FIGURE 32: The Via Egnatia at Philippi. USED BY PERMISSION OF DAVID PADFIELD.

Roman Empire, about ten miles inland from the port city of Neapolis (see fig. 33).

While it manifested the typical spectrum of Hellenistic religions, including the older fertility gods of the native Thracian population, the Roman imperial cult was very strong in Philippi. In 42 BCE Octavian and Anthony defeated Cassius and Brutus, the assassins of Julius Caesar, on the plains of Philippi, ending the Roman Republic and founding the Empire. Octavian became the deified Caesar Augustus, and Philippi proudly became a Roman colony

FIGURE 33: Roman forum at Philippi. USED BY PERMISSION OF DAVID PADFIELD.

that was a focal point of the blend of patriotism and religion expressed in the Caesar cult. Many of the city's 10,000 inhabitants were Roman citizens, with the same legal status as though they lived in Rome itself (see figs. 33–34).

The church at Philippi was the first Christian congregation in Europe. The story of its founding is anecdotally but reliably recounted in Acts 16:16–40: Paul, Silas, and Timothy are guided by the Spirit to Philippi, where they preach, baptize, and found a new Christian community. Acts indicates they were accompanied by the author of the "we-source" (possibly Luke), which begins at Acts 16:11 and continues through the account of founding the church at Philippi. Lydia, a God-fearer (or perhaps a Jew), becomes the first convert and the leader of a house church (Acts 16:14–15, 40). Paul and Silas run afoul of the authorities and are beaten and imprisoned overnight, during which they experience an earthquake and the conversion of their Roman jailer and his family (16:25–34). None of these events or people is mentioned in Philippians, but 1 Thessalonians 2:2 confirms the missionaries' mistreatment at Philippi just before coming to Thessalonica. During Paul's founding visit and after his departure, the church developed several leaders: Lydia, Euodia and Syntyche, Clement, the anonymous "beloved yokefellow," and "the rest of the fellow workers," 4:2–3.

11.2.2 Date and Provenance: The Setting in Paul's Life

The issues of the date, place of origin, and setting in Paul's life and ministry are interrelated and will be discussed together. Philippians has traditionally been included in the four prison epistles, written from Rome in the last period of Paul's life (Acts 28). The following arguments are given for a Roman provenance:[10]

1. *Tradition:* Acts pictures Paul in prison in two places from which he could have written

10. Udo Schnelle, *The History and Theology of the New Testament Writings*, trans. M. Eugene Boring (Minneapolis: Fortress Press, 1998), 130–33.

FIGURE 34: Ruins of the Roman forum at Philippi. USED BY PERMISSION OF DAVID PADFIELD.

a letter to Philippi: Rome (Acts 28:16–31) and Caesarea (Acts 23:31–26:32). Caesarea has occasionally been defended as the place of origin,[11] but the distance involved, and Paul's future plans, make Caesarea an unlikely location. The Marcionite Prologue (ca. 200 CE) already suggested a Roman provenance, a tradition that continued through Eusebius (*Hist. eccl.* 3.15.1), an annotation in the fourth-century Codex Vaticanus, and into modern times.

2. *"Roman" references:* The reference to the praetorium/imperial guard (Phil 1:13) and to "the emperor's household" (Phil 4:22) would be appropriate to Rome.

11. For recent arguments in favor of Caesarea, see Gerald F. Hawthorne, *Philippians*, WBC 43 (Waco, TX: Word Books, 1983), xli–xliv, and Marion L. Soards, *The Apostle Paul: An Introduction to His Writings and Teaching* (New York: Paulist Press, 1987), 33–34, 113–14.

3. *Lack of reference to the offering* indicates a time after the trip to Jerusalem to deliver the offering (cf. Exc. 1, §13.3.4).

4. *"Developments" in Paul's Christology, eschatology, and ecclesiology* point to a time late in Paul's career. Thus the advanced Christology (preexistence), the presumed fading of his earlier expectation of the near parousia, and the reference to bishops and deacons (Phil 1:1) represent a time after the Aegean mission. The letters from the Aegean mission portray a church led by charismatic leadership without firm structure. Philippians illustrates a transitional point toward the post-Pauline development of church officers reflected in the Pastorals and Ignatius.

5. *The moderate, humane prison conditions* described in Acts would allow for Paul to be cared for by his friends, as indicated in Philippians, and to write such a letter, and thus point to a Roman imprisonment.

Many scholars, however, consider the case for Ephesus more convincing, for the following reasons:[12]

1. *The arguments for a Roman provenance are not compelling.*

On #1 above: Paul himself refers to several imprisonments not mentioned in Acts (2 Cor 6:5; 11:23–25). The demonstrable incompleteness of the Acts narrative means the historian need not try to fit the letters into specific locations mentioned in Acts. The tradition of a Roman origin of some or all of the prison letters is likely an inference from Acts rather than independent tradition.[13]

On #2 above: The praetorium refers to the governor's official residence in provincial cities, as, for example, in Jerusalem (Mark 15:16; John 18:28), not only to the Roman headquarters in the capital city. (However, this may apply only to imperial provinces, and Asia was a senatorial province.) "The emperor's household" was likewise a general term that included the thousands of slaves and freedmen in the employ of the emperor, who managed his holdings throughout the empire, and came to mean something like "civil service." "Caesar's household" was represented in every major city of the empire. These references thus do not necessarily point to Rome, but indicate that Paul and his message have become known, and in some cases respected, even by government employees.

On #3 above: The lack of reference to the offering in Philippians does not require a Roman, post-Jerusalem provenance. Other viable explanations include the composition of the letter before (rather than after) the offering became a lively issue in the Aegean mission (see §10.1.9). The offering is mentioned in all the undisputed letters except 1 Thessalonians, Philemon, and Philippians. The nature of the letter to Philemon makes discussion of the offering inappropriate. First Thessalonians lacks reference to the offering because it was written early in the Aegean mission, and the same may well be the case with Philippians. In any case, nothing is proven by the argument from silence, which can cut both ways.

On #4 above: The "development" of Paul's theology manifest in his extant writings is a fragile base for charting the chronology of the letters. Paul clearly adapts his theology from one situation and letter to another as appropriate to changing situations, but it did not "develop" from "primitive" to "more sophisticated." He already has a sophisticated Christology of preexistence from early in the Aegean mission (e.g., 1 Cor 10:4, 9), and his latest letter still expects the parousia to occur soon, whether this be Romans (Rom 13:11–12) or Philippians (Phil 1:6; 2:16; 4:5). How to translate and understand the reference to bishops and deacons is itself a disputed point (see below). However the terms are understood, they refer to a unique situation in Philippi, not to a progressive development in Paul's own thought, as though he is implementing something new. In any case, the letters of the Aegean mission indicate some internal structure within his charismatic congregations, without using the specific designations current in Philippi (see 1 Thess 5:12–13; 1 Cor 12:28; 16:16). Plotting "the" development of Paul's thought is a complex of interrelated issues; depending on the topic, Philippians can be located at more than one point on the presumed "trajectory" of such developments (see 13.1.2).

On #5 above: The picture of Paul's moderate prison conditions in Rome (Acts 28:16–31) expresses Luke's general view of how Paul was

12. The classical case was made by George S. Duncan, *St. Paul's Ephesian Ministry: A Reconstruction with Special Reference to the Ephesian Origin of the Imprisonment Epistles* (London: Hodder & Stoughton, 1929). See also Victor Paul Furnish, *II Corinthians*, AB 32A (Garden City, NY: Doubleday, 1984), 122–23; most recently, John Reumann, *Philippians: A New Translation with Introduction and Commentary*, AB 33b (New Haven, CT: Yale University Press, 2008). Arguments against an Ephesian imprisonment and for the traditional Roman provenance of Philippians and Philemon, with further bibliography, are listed in Schnelle, *New Testament Writings*, 131.

13. On the problematic nature of early Christian traditions regarding date, authorship, and provenance of New Testament documents, see Exc. 3.1.

treated by Roman authorities. Even if accurate in details, we do not know that this was the only time he was imprisoned under such circumstances as to permit writing letters. If Paul was a Roman citizen, his situation as a prisoner in Ephesus would be no more severe than in Rome.

Thus the arguments for a Roman provenance for Philippians are not compelling.

2. *The distance factor and travel time involved favors Ephesus over Rome.* The letter to the Philippians presupposes seven[14] trips between Philippi and Paul's place of imprisonment: (1) They hear that he is in prison. (2) They send a gift through Epaphroditus (4:18; see also 2:25; 4:14). (3) Epaphroditus remains with Paul, but the Philippians hear that he is critically ill (2:26–30). (4) Paul sends Epaphroditus back to them, with the letter conveying his gratitude (2:25, 28). (5) Paul sends Timothy to Philippi, (6) who returns with news from the church for Paul. (7) If Paul is released in the near future, as he anticipates, he will come to Philippi himself (1:26; 2:23–24). These seven trips, already made or anticipated in the near future, make it difficult to imagine the letter as written from Rome. The eight hundred miles one way, Rome–Philippi, would require five to seven weeks, a three-month round trip, while Ephesus–Philippi would require two or three weeks for each round trip.

3. *Paul's future plans.* Paul hopes to be released and to visit the Philippians in the near future (1:21–26; 2:24). But after Rome, Paul planned to go further west, to Spain, not to return to visit churches in the east, where he considered his work complete (Rom 15:22–24).

4. *The probable relation of the letters to the Philippians and to Philemon fits Ephesus better than Rome as the provenance of both letters.* The letter to the Philippians seems to have a close relation to the letter to Philemon. In both letters he is in prison, in moderate circumstances that permits him to receive gifts to be served by his friends and to continue some aspects of his ministry. On Philemon as written from Ephesus, see §11.3.4.

5. *Early Christian tradition testimony to an Ephesian imprisonment.* The "Marcionite Prologues" (ca. 200 CE) state there was an Ephesian imprisonment and that Colossians was composed there—though Philippians and Philemon are assigned to Rome. This indicates that there was an older tradition of an Ephesian imprisonment, which was later partially accommodated to the Acts tradition of Roman imprisonment.[15] In the third century CE, Origen argues Philippians was written between 1 and 2 Corinthians, that is, not from Rome but Ephesus. The *Acts of Paul and Thecla*, though legendary, continues the tradition that Paul was imprisoned in Ephesus, as do the *Acts of Titus* and Hippolytus's *Commentary on Daniel.* All these may be inferences from 1 Corinthians 15:32 rather than independent tradition, but show that Christian authors of the second and third centuries had no hesitation in reaffirming this tradition.

6. *Paul's statements suggesting and compatible with an Ephesian imprisonment.* In 1 Corinthians 15:32, writing from Ephesus, Paul refers to having "fought with wild animals" at Ephesus, that is, being condemned to the arena. Though the expression is metaphorical, it is a metaphor for a reality—he was imprisoned in Ephesus, chained to a guard,[16] and felt that he had already received the death sentence (see 2 Cor 1:8–9; 4:7–12). In Philippians 1:19–30, Paul writes of the prospect of his imminent execution, suggesting it comes from the same situation of which he speaks in the Corinthian letters. In Romans 16:3, 7, written from Corinth, Paul refers to experiences in

14. If Philippians is a composite of more than one letter, the number of trips increases. Reumann (like several others) argues for three letters, which calls for twelve trips (Reumann, *Philippians*, 7).

15. John Knox, *Marcion and the New Testament: An Essay in the Early History of the Canon* (Chicago: University of Chicago Press, 1942), 43–44.

16. Ignatius, on his way in Roman custody to Rome to be martyred, speaks of his guards as "leopards." This is, to be sure, metaphor, but points to the reality of his imprisonment and imminent death (Ign. *Rom* 5).

prison, apparently recent, that would point to Asia (=Ephesus).

Some of Paul's statements to the Philippians imply an earlier date for the letter than is compatible with a Roman provenance, but fit the Ephesian location. In 4:10 the statement that "now at last you have revived your concern for me" implies some time since receiving their last gift. For Ephesus, this would be a year or more; for Rome, it would mean ten years or more, and would seem to imply a strange set of circumstances: the Philippians had repeatedly helped Paul early in his Aegean ministry, then had not done anything for him for ten years, during which time he was imprisoned several times in the Aegean area, and then suddenly sent him a gift in Rome. An Ephesian provenance implies appropriate continuity, a Roman provenance does not.

So also the statement of Philippians 1:30—the Philippians once saw Paul in trouble when he was with them, and now hear about his troubles—implies temporal proximity between Paul's imprisonment when he was with them at the founding of the church (Acts 16) and the imprisonment he now suffers, not two incidents separated by twelve years. If Philippians was written from Rome, Paul had been back to Philippi at least twice in the meantime, but this comment sounds as though he had not been in Philippi since the founding visit—therefore from Ephesus.

7. *The group of people with Paul as he writes Philippians (and Philemon) correlates better with Ephesus than with Rome.* As Paul writes Philemon, with him are Timothy, Mark, Luke, Aristarchus, Epaphras, and Demas (Phlm 1, 23–24). Apart from the prison epistles themselves, and the possible identification of the author of the we-source of Acts with Luke, there is no evidence that any of these were in Rome. Epaphras is probably a shortened form of Epaphroditus (Phil 2:25; 4:18), so Epaphras is a firm link between the two letters.[17] Thus, all the evidence that indicates Philemon was written from Ephesus also applies to Philippians (see §11.3.4).

In 2 Corinthians 1:1, Timothy is traveling with Paul from Ephesus through Macedonia, that is, he has been with Paul in Ephesus. In Philippians 1:1, Timothy is with Paul as he writes, indicating the same situation as 2 Corinthians 2:13; 7:7–16, after Titus had already been sent to Corinth. Paul's expressed intention to come to Philippi if his life is spared (Phil 2:24) corresponds to the fact that Paul did go to Macedonia after leaving Ephesus (2 Cor 1:8–9; 2:12–13; 7:5). Then Paul's plan to follow Timothy from Ephesus to Philippi as soon as possible (Phil 2:19–24) corresponds to the presence of both Paul and Timothy in the greeting of 2 Corinthians 1:1. In 1 Corinthians 4:17; 16:10; Acts 19:22, Timothy's trip from Ephesus through Macedonia to Corinth corresponds to Paul's hope to send Timothy to the Philippians in Philippians 2:19. The references to Timothy all fit into the Ephesian ministry, but there is no evidence that Timothy was ever in Rome (apart from the references in the prison letters, if understood to be from Rome). The possibility that Philippians is a combination of more than one letter makes it difficult to chart a chronology of Paul's Ephesian imprisonment.[18]

8. *Changes in Paul's situation and related rhetorical strategies in his letters suggest that Philippians is relatively early.* The following data, combining changed circumstances and changes in Paul's thought, suggest that Philippians was written early in the Aegean mission:

17. So already William M. Ramsay, *The Cities of St. Paul: Their Influence on His Life and Thought* (Grand Rapids: Baker, 1907), 207. Cf., more recently, Crossan and Reed, *In Search of Paul*, 274–76. Epaphras (Phlm 23; cf. Col 1:7; 4:12) is the short form of the name Epaphroditus (Phil 2:25; 4:18), like Silas/Silvanus, Prisca/Priscilla. Philippians indicates Epaphroditus is from Philippi; the deuteropauline Colossians calls him "one of you," i.e., from Colossae (4:12). But if Paul is not the author of Colossians, neither is Colossae the destination. Both author and readers belong to the fictive world of the letter; Colossians cannot then be used as evidence the letter to Philemon was sent to Colossae.

18. Reumann, *Philippians*, 16–18, makes a detailed attempt. The structure is fragile.

— The offering. In the chronology here followed, from 1 Corinthians on, Paul refers to the offering in every letter. This had not yet become a live issue when Philippians was written.

— The "doctrine" of justification by faith. There is no reference to this conviction, which became a cornerstone of Pauline theology, in 1 Thessalonians or Philemon. In Philippians 3:7–10, it emerges briefly for the first time, in response to the rumored claims of the rival apostolate, which is not yet an actual threat. This theology becomes more explicit in 1 and 2 Corinthians, though it is not yet a fundamental issue, then emerges as a major emphasis in Galatians and Romans. Philippians appears to stand early in this development.[19]

— Defense of his apostleship. Paul stakes out his apostolic claim in the first line of every undisputed letter except 1 Thessalonians, Philemon, and Philippians. From the day of his call, Paul was conscious of his commission to be an apostle. However, it does not become crucial to emphasize this until he is confronted by the rival apostles during the Aegean mission. In 1 Thessalonians, Philippians, and Philemon, Paul manifests no deep sensitivity about his apostolic status, but it is probable that early in the Aegean mission the threat of the rival apostles/missionaries was not yet serious. Beginning with 1 Corinthians, Paul asserts his apostleship in the opening words of the letter, and one can trace an increasing explicitness and intensity in the debate about apostleship from 1 Corinthians through 2 Corinthians, Galatians, and Romans. By this criterion, Philippians appears to be prior to 1 Corinthians.

— Explicit use of Scripture. From his earliest days, Paul's mind had been saturated with the language and imagery of Scripture, manifest in the unselfconscious way he alludes to biblical phrases and images in every letter, earliest to latest. The earliest letter, 1 Thessalonians, contains at least nineteen such allusions, and Philippians and Philemon contain at least eleven. Yet no explicit appeal to Scripture is made in these letters. This first occurs in 1 Corinthians, which is massively permeated with Scripture—ninety-seven references, twenty of which are explicit to scriptural authority—and continues in every letter after that. It seems that just as Paul began to make explicit appeal to his apostolic authority in 1 Corinthians, he did the same with regard to biblical authority. Both moves seem to have been in response to the rival mission based in Jerusalem that disputed both Paul's apostleship and the validity of his gospel as representing the biblical faith. These phenomena support the view that Philippians and Philemon were written relatively early in the Aegean mission, after 1 Thessalonians but prior to 1 Corinthians, about 52–53 CE.

11.2.3 Genre

The rhetorical handbooks of the Hellenistic world discuss a letter type known as the "friendship letter" (see above §10.2.2), with which Philippians exhibits some similarities and points of contact. While Paul did not slavishly follow a conventional rhetorical model, the letter does manifest the warmth and personal touch of the ἐπιστολὴ φιλική (*epistolē philikē*, friendship letter). Paul's phraseology would be recognizable to the Philippians as expressions of the Hellenistic ideal of friendship. The key word κοινωνία (*koinōnia*, sharing, having in common, 1:5; 2:1; 3:10; 4:15) represents this ideal; it was axiomatic for this ideal that true friends have all things in common. The joyful friendship expressed in Philippians is not sentimentality, but the bond of sharing a common calling and task, for which both Paul and the Philippians are willing to suffer.

11.2.4 Literary Unity

It is inherently likely that Paul *wrote* more than one letter to the Philippians. He was on very good terms with the church, maintaining a deep, ongoing relationship with them that

19. Cf. Schnelle, *Apostle Paul*, 465–68, for a different reading of this data that places Philippians last.

makes it unlikely that he wrote only one letter to them. The reference in 3:1 to "writing the same things" may well refer to one or more previous letters, rather than to what he has already written in the canonical letter. The Philippian Christians had repeatedly sent money to him early in his Aegean ministry; it is unlikely that the "thank-you letter" that is our Philippians was the only such letter he wrote to them. Second Corinthians 8:1–5 reflects information about the Macedonian churches Paul has in Ephesus that indicates lively communication with the churches of Macedonia.

Early in the second century, the letter of Bishop Polycarp of Smyrna to the Philippians refers to the "letters" Paul wrote them, evidence that more than one letter to the Philippians was known, perhaps even circulated. Thus, whether canonical Philippians is one letter or composite, it probably does not represent all Paul's correspondence with Philippi, and is another indication of how fragmentary our knowledge is. Not everything Paul wrote was included in the Pauline corpus as edited by the church (1 Cor 5:9!). This is another reminder that we receive our New Testament from the hands of the church.

It is thus very likely that Paul wrote more than one letter to the Philippians. The question remains, however, whether the canonical letter is one of those letters, or an editorial combination of more than one. There is some evidence for the latter possibility. Partition theories have appealed to the following data:[20]

— The phrase at 3:1, "Finally, my brothers and sisters," seems to signal the conclusion of the letter, but it is only halfway through the present text, which continues for another two chapters.

— The sharp change of tone at 3:2, "Beware of the dogs, beware of the evil workers," which continues with defensiveness and sarcasm against rumored enemies, seems out of place in a letter otherwise permeated with joy and affirming great confidence in the Philippians. Nothing in the first two chapters prepares for this unexpected outburst. Thus 4:4 seems to be the natural continuation of 3:1, with 3:2–4:3 a discordant insertion.

— In the present form of the text, which is a letter of gratitude for the Philippians' gift, the expression of gratitude comes very late (4:10–20), when it would have been more appropriate early in the letter. The actual thanksgiving for the Philippians' gift is missing from the thanksgiving section of the present letter, 1:3–11.

— The present form of the letter seems to have two different concluding admonitions, 4:4–7 and 4:8–9.

— The section 4:10–20 appears to be a tightly written coherent unit in itself, a separate letter of thanksgiving.

These and other data have convinced a number of scholars that canonical Philippians is an editorial combination of two or three letters. This conclusion, however, is far from unanimous. In this book, we will interpret Philippians as a single letter written from prison early in Paul's Ephesian ministry, open to the possibility that it represents more than one letter.

11.2.5 Structure and Outline

1:1–2	Greeting
1:3–11	Thanksgiving
1:12–26	Paul in prison; the gospel flourishes nonetheless
1:27–30	Précis and appeal
2:1–4:1	Keys to unity: humility and obedience
2:1–4	Call to unity
2:5–11	Christ event as paradigm
2:12–18	Humility and obedience as the church's mission mandate
2:19–3:1a	Timothy and Epaphroditus as models

20. Only a summary of evidence and arguments can be given here. For a more complete discussion of how such arguments work, see Excursus 1: The Unity of 2 Corinthians and Partition Theories of the Pauline Letters, in §12.2.

3:1b–4:1	Paul himself as model
4:2–9	Climactic appeal for unity
4:10–23	Thanks and conclusion

11.2.6 Exegetical-Theological Précis

1:1–2 Greeting

Paul refers to himself as apostle in the prescript of every undisputed letter except 1 Thessalonians, Philippians, and Philemon. In these letters, the legitimacy of his office is not in dispute. By referring to himself and Timothy as δοῦλοι (*douloi*, slaves), Paul is not being ostentatiously humble. A slave's status depended on that of his master; Paul is slave of Christ. The reference to ἐπίσκοποι καὶ διάκονοι (*episkopoi kai diakonoi*, overseers/bishops and assistants/deacons) is unique in the undisputed letters. The Philippian church seems to have developed some structure beyond the purely charismatic leadership found in Corinth, but the words should not be understood in the later sense of firm ecclesiastical offices. However, the NRSV margin, "overseers and helpers," is probably too informal. As in Romans 16:1, "deacon" seems to refer to a definite, commissioned office or function of ministerial leadership, and "bishop" probably refers to the leader of a particular house church. They probably were responsible for administering the church's funds. Since Paul had received a gift through their agency (4:10–18), he makes particular reference to them in the greeting. Paul is not giving instructions on general church organization, as though other churches had, or should have, such officers. This development in the Pauline tradition comes later, in the Pastorals.

1:3–11 Thanksgiving

This section sounds notes that will be developed in the body of the letter: Paul's gratitude for the church's partnership in supporting his missionary preaching from the earliest days of his work in Macedonia and Achaia (1:5; 4:15–16) and especially the deep theme of abiding joy that resonates throughout the letter, though written from a prison (1:4, 18; 2:2, 17, 18, 28, 29; 3:1; 4:1, 4, 10). The letter is not devoted to eschatological instruction, but the hope for the soon coming of the Lord appears often (2:10–11, 16; 3:20–21; 4:5), and is anticipated in the thanksgiving (1:6, 10).

1:12–26 Paul in prison; the gospel flourishes nonetheless The structure of the body of the letter is unclear; it does not follow the typical bipartite kerygma/parenesis pattern fundamental to Paul's thought and some of his letters (see §10.2.3). In the present form of the letter, whether or not Paul's own, this initial section of the body of the letter places Paul's own situation in a larger theological context: the progress of the gospel in the mission of the church as a whole. Paul celebrates that the gospel continues to be preached, even by those with mixed motives.

Paul's situation is grave; he could be condemned to death. He is unafraid; in fact, dying and being with Christ would be better for him personally than to continue his life in this world. Yet Paul wants to be spared to continue his mission, believes that he will be, and looks forward to seeing his beloved brothers and sisters again in Philippi. None of this is an individualistic meditation on the relative happiness of "dying and going to heaven" versus the values of earthly life. Paul's point of orientation is the Christian mission; he evaluates everything from the perspective of the gospel of God's saving act in Christ and the role he has been called to play in this mission.

1:27–30 Précis and appeal These verses, one long sentence in Greek, represent a hinge in the letter's structure, shifting from indicative to imperative and concentrating several themes that are later elaborated:

— Conduct yourselves as citizens of the realm to which you belong, which means to live in a manner appropriate to the gospel. Πολιτεύεσθε (*politeuesthe*, NRSV "live your life") means to live in accordance with the political realm to which one belongs. Philippi was a Roman colony, where Roman citizenship was the valued and prevailing norm. Diaspora Jews in such cities had their own πολίτευμα (*politeuma,* political unit) that granted status and protection under the law. Christians belong ultimately to another realm, God's kingdom already revealed in Christ, soon to be manifest to all; they are a "colony of heaven" (NRSV "our citizenship is in heaven"), an outpost of God's present-and-coming reign (3:20). This could bring harassment and persecution, as it had for Paul.

— There are threats and opposition, against which the Philippian Christians are to struggle and stand fast, even suffering for the faith.

— The appeal to unity woven into the remainder of the letter first becomes explicit here. Differing responses to the threat of persecution was probably one of the divisive issues. The "one Spirit" is not merely an irenic attitude, but the one Spirit of God that unifies the church (1 Cor 12:4–13).

— The soon-to-be-manifest victory of God will reveal that they have been on the right side.

— Paul himself is an example of such suffering, but—as is to be shown immediately—in this he is only following the master paradigm provided by the Christ event.

2:1–4:1 Keys to Unity: Humility and Obedience

2:1–4 Call to unity Paul calls the church to unity so that it may present a unified front to its opponents and offer a unified witness to the world (2:1–4, 12–16a). "Humility" and "obedience" are concretely embodied in the Christ event (2:5–11) and are to be lived out in the Philippians' own experience, just as they are already manifest in the lives of Paul (2:16b–17 [extended in 3:1b–4:1]) and his coworkers Timothy and Epaphroditus (2:19–30).

2:5–11 The Christ event as paradigm Paul here quotes a pre-Pauline hymn. He does so, however, not to present some speculative reflections on Christology, but as the basis for his appeal to practical Christian living. He challenges Philippian believers to renounce the attractive option of holding on to or trying to attain status that would protect them from suffering. Their individual decisions affect the unity of the congregation and its mission. Divisiveness is brought about by party spirit and self-seeking. The example of Christ makes this impossible for his followers. This is not a matter of ethical idealism, we-should-all-really-be-more-humble-as-Jesus-was, but a call to orient one's life to the act of God in Christ. While the precise structure of the hymn is disputed, the drama to which it points is clearly three acts:

— The curtain opens on the first act in the heavenly world, where the preexistent Christ shares the divine reality.[21] The action quickly moves to this world, however. Neither here nor elsewhere does Paul or the New Testament indulge in curiosity or speculation about the nature of the transcendent world and events that transpired there. The New Testament is a very this-worldly book. The first and only action of the preexistent Christ is expressed in one verb: the preexistent one, existing in the mode of divine reality and equality with God, did not regard this divine status as something to be held on to, but emptied himself, that is, divested himself of his divine status (ἐκένωσεν, *ekenōsen*; on kenosis Christology, see below, §20.1.2).

21. Μορφή (*morphē*, form) has a broad semantic field, but here "form" does not connote mere external appearance; the term here refers to intrinsic reality, not manner of appearance but mode of being. Cf. Ernst Käsemann, "A Critical Analysis of Philippians 2:5–11," *Journal for Theology and the Church* 5 (1968): 45–88, who rightly insists, however, that Paul's discussion is not directed to the divine and human natures of Christ, but to the decision of Christ to empty himself and become an obedient servant; Paul's point is not what Jesus *was* but what he *did*.

— Having divested himself of the divine mode of being, Christ entered the human mode of being, taking the form of a slave. Here, human existence as such is seen as slave existence. Human life, however exalted, is enslaved to transcendent powers over which the human self has no control. Humans do not decide to be born, cannot decide not to die, and in the interim are subject to superior powers beyond themselves. In becoming human, Christ enters this realm of slavery, and thus becomes a slave himself.[22] "Taking the form of a slave . . . in human likeness . . . in human form" means he really became a human being, not that he merely assumed human appearance. The same vocabulary is used for his humanity as for his divinity. As he truly shared the divine, so now he shares the reality of human existence. In this human realm, Christ is obedient, that is, to God. This obedience knows no bounds, but extends to the point of death, even the shameful death on a cross (the final phrase is often considered a Pauline addition to the hymn).

— In entering the human world, Christ gave up his divine power. He could not and did not "rise from the dead" by his own superhuman power, any more than other human beings can do this. He had committed himself in obedience to God, and God did not let the cross be the end of the matter. God acted and not only restored Christ's original status, but raised him up (literally, superexalted) him, so that all creation should/will/does confess Jesus Christ as Lord. The scene of universal acknowledgment of Jesus as Lord is not an alternative to or in competition with worship of the one God, but is "to the glory of God the Father." The scene is not placed in a temporal framework, but the Greek subjunctive construction with ἵνα (*hina*) cannot be taken in the English sense of "should," implying hope and obligation but not reality—as though all creation should do this, but most in fact will not. In this scene, the whole creation is portrayed as finally doing what it should, bowing in adoration to its Creator and Redeemer.

This three-act divine-human-divine drama has overtones in which Jesus is presented as the truly human being, made in the form/image of God like Adam (v. 6). But unlike the first human pair, who rebelled against God because they wanted to be like God (Gen 3:5), Christ did not grasp after deity, but was obedient in a truly human manner. In Philippi, proud colony of Rome, where the imperial propaganda and emperor cult were omnipresent, the One who *is* truly God acts as Deity in a radically different manner than the "divine Caesar."

2:12–18 Humility and obedience as the church's mission mandate Paul has cited the hymn not to teach Christology but to call the Philippians to the steadfastness and unity that will equip them for mission. As Christ obeyed, so they are to obey, as Paul himself is already modeling this obedience (the point will be elaborated in 3:1b–4:1). Such obedience calls for giving up self-serving attitudes and acts, but it is not grim: the vocabulary of joy spontaneously reappears four times in verses 17–18.

2:19–3:1a Timothy and Epaphroditus as models This transitional paragraph provides information for the Philippians about the travel plans of Paul and his associates, but it is not merely incidental that he describes them in terms of orienting their lives by the "mind of Christ" portrayed in the preceding hymn. They too have divested themselves of their previous positions and have not sought their own welfare, but have entered another realm of service.

22. It must be emphasized that this does not mean that, among humans, Jesus adopted a modest attitude, that he served others as a slave, like the Suffering Servant of Isa 53 or the humble servant of the Fourth Gospel, who washes the disciples' feet in John 13. In this hymn, human existence per se is slave existence. No other human being freely chose this existence; we find ourselves here without any vote in the matter. For us, human existence is *Geworfenheit* (thrownness, Martin Heidegger). But the Preexistent One *decided* to enter this realm. The human choice is not whether or not to be a slave, but whom to serve (so Paul in Rom 6:12–23).

The previous language of "slavery" (v. 22) and "death" (vv. 27, 30) reverberates though this report. Timothy and Epaphroditus model the christomorphic life to which Paul calls the Philippians. Such self-sacrifice occurs not only in hymns, but in concrete lives.

3:1b–4:1 Paul himself as model The sharp warning tone and abusive language introduced here, in a letter that otherwise speaks of joy and affection, has been taken as evidence that Philippians is composite. Another, perhaps more likely possibility, is that the "dogs, evil workers, those who mutilate the flesh" are not actual opponents at work among the Philippians, but a rhetorical enemy constructed by Paul. Such people are real opponents elsewhere in the Aegean mission, so they are on Paul's mind as a potential threat in Philippi, but do not seem to be actually troubling the congregation in Philippi—at least not yet. Paul uses them as a rhetorical foil for his own credentials and the portrayal of himself as the third model of the humility/obedience pattern as the basis for his call to unity.[23] God-fearers who had become Christians were under pressure to become full Jews, members of a legally recognized religious community, as the way to avoid suffering (see 1:29–30). The message is: stand firm, you are called to suffer, take me as an example; I was already a full Jew with supreme credentials, but am now suffering for the gospel. The extravagant and harsh rhetoric found in this chapter was conventional and expected; not to lambast one's opponents, supposed or real, was taken to be an admission of the weakness of one's own position.[24]

The abusive language of verses 2 and 19 is not randomly chosen, but is the ironic reversal of the claims of Paul's rivals. "Dogs" are unclean (but his challengers emphasized their own ritual purity). "Workers" was a quasi-technical term for Christian ministers and missionaries. His rivals claimed to be such workers, but Paul categorizes them as workers of evil. They required circumcision (*peritomē*) as the mark of the covenant, but in a sarcastic wordplay Paul lampoons their stance as "mutilation" (*katatomē*). In verse 19, the opponents make their "belly" (food laws) into something divine, and their "shame" (genitals, i.e., circumcision) into something glorious. These local Jews and Jewish Christian missionaries, who potentially threaten the church's faith, boast of their biblical and traditional Jewish qualifications as authentic representatives of the faith.[25]

Paul counters that he too has such qualifications, that he in fact had outstanding credentials, but voluntarily gave them up—just as the preexistent Christ did not hold on to his transcendent perquisites. Paul's identity, and the gospel he preaches, mean accepting and participating in God's own righteousness, made real for human beings in the Christ event. Those who see themselves in this way are freed from the efforts to establish themselves and their own image. This is what God has done in the cross of Christ. Human striving after self-image and prestige is the enemy of the cross of Christ, and the reason for the divisive spirit plaguing the church at Philippi.

"Heavenly citizenship" (3:20) is not a Gnosticlike appeal to separate oneself from "earthly things" and be aloof to this-worldly life. The noun πολίτευμα (*politeuma*), usually translated "citizenship," has a double connotation. Since Philippi was a Roman colony with numerous Roman citizens, Christians are reminded that their ultimate loyalty is to the kingdom of God, not to any earthly empire. The term also has a more specific meaning relevant to the situation

23. This point is developed in Carolyn Osiek, *Philippians, Philemon*, ANTC (Nashville: Abingdon Press, 2000), 79–95.

24. See, e.g. Johnson, "Anti-Jewish Slander," 419–41.

25. Others understand "their god is their belly, their glory is their shame" (3:19) as pointing to libertine gnosticizing types, who see themselves as already belonging to the heavenly world, advocating a mixture of spirituality and lax morals, so that Paul is struggling on two fronts (e.g., Pokorný and Heckel, *Einleitung*, 277–78, and the literature they give).

in Philippi and the present context. *Politeuma* is used for the separately incorporated Diaspora Jewish associations that had privileged legal status in Roman cities. Jewish and Jewish Christian associates of the new Christian converts, especially those who had previously been God-fearers attending the synagogue (and who may have continued to do so), would encourage them to become full Jews, where they would enjoy the legal protection of belonging to the Jewish *politeuma*. In this context of warning his readers against those who encourage circumcision, this temptation to abandon Christian faith by conversion to Judaism was probably uppermost in Paul's mind.

4:2–9 Climactic Appeal for Unity

Paul has carefully laid the groundwork and worked up to this point. He brings his appeal for unity to a climax by specifically naming the two leaders who are having a divisive influence on the congregation: Euodia and Syntyche. *They* are not Paul's opponents; their names are (both!) enrolled in heaven in the book of life; they have struggled alongside Paul in the work of the gospel. Paul specifically designates them, along with Clement, as "fellow workers," a semi-official term for ministers and church leaders. They may, like Phoebe of Cenchreae (Rom 16:1), function as διάκονοι (*diakonoi*, deacons) and would be included in the group of deacons greeted in 1:1. They may well be house-church patrons who exercised leadership in the congregations that met in their respective homes. If so, they may be included among the ἐπίσκοποι (*episkopoi*, overseers) greeted in 1:1.

Previous generations of interpreters unconsciously assumed church leadership to be all male, so that the dispute between Euodia and Syntyche was simply a minor personal disagreement between two women. We now see that Paul considers them leaders in the church, and thus with major potential for creating disunity. His appeal to them is on the model of the preexistent Christ, Paul's coworkers Timothy and Epaphroditus, and Paul himself, to exercise their leadership in the proper direction and maintain the unity of the congregation.

4:10–23 Thanks and Conclusion

Paul concludes on the note with which he began, his thanksgiving for their continued support of his Aegean mission from its earliest days in Macedonia. In some situations such as Corinth, Paul had refused church support and insisted on supporting himself (1 Cor 9:3–18), so as not to be misunderstood as obligated to powerful patrons. It was a mark of the special relationship between him and the Philippian congregation that he gladly accepted their support and gives thanks to God for it and them.

11.3 Interpreting Philemon

11.3.1 Genre

Philemon is a *letter*, not an essay on "Christian Perspectives on Slavery" or the like. It is in fact the New Testament's parade example of the Hellenistic letter form, being more like other extant examples of first-century letters than any other New Testament document. Although the most personal of Paul's extant letters, it is nonetheless an apostolic and churchly letter, not an individualistic private note. The letter is addressed not only to Philemon, Apphia, and Archippus, but to "the church in your house" (v. 2). While the English "you" may be singular or plural, Greek second-person pronouns are number-specific. In Philemon, the plural is found in verses 3, 22, and 25 and singular in the body of the letter; the personal address in the singular is framed by the community plural. The personal appeal to Philemon is not only on a one-to-one basis between Paul and Philemon; the congregation is addressed, and Paul's appeal to Philemon is made within the context and in the hearing of the whole church. Although Paul does not use the word "apostle," his apostolic authority is evident (vv. 8, 21).

That the letter was preserved in the Pauline collection and later canonized reveals that it was always read as a churchly document. Paul may well have written personal letters, but we have none in the New Testament.[26] If it were only personal correspondence, we would not have it.

11.3.2 Authorship

That Philemon is an authentic letter of Paul was practically undisputed in the ancient church. This has been challenged only by a few critics in the early days of the Enlightenment, when all ancient documents were questioned, and by F. C. Baur and a few of his followers in the nineteenth-century Tübingen school. The letter is now universally accepted as an authentic letter of Paul.

11.3.3 Occasion

As a letter, Philemon must be interpreted within the story line of which it is a part and the narrative world it projects. The story reflected in the letter has traditionally been constructed by combining data from Philemon, Colossians (with which it is closely related in some way), Ephesians, and Acts. Since Colossians and Ephesians are often considered deuteropauline, and Acts is not always historically accurate, it is best initially to consider Philemon alone. The letter itself presents the following data:

— Paul is in prison (vv. 1, 9–10, 13, 23). The location is not given. With him are Timothy (v. 1), Epaphras, Mark, Luke, Aristarchus, and Demas (vv. 23–24). Only Epaphras is called a "fellow prisoner."

— Philemon is the leader of a house church (v. 2). The location is not given. Paul and Philemon apparently know each other well; Paul was influential in the conversion of Philemon, may have been directly involved (v. 19), and probably worked with him as a missionary ("coworker," v. 1).

— Onesimus is apparently the slave of Philemon. This has occasionally been contested,[27] on the basis of verse 16, which could be understood to mean that Onesimus is the biological brother of Philemon. On this understanding, Philemon has treated him more like a slave than a brother, and now, since Onesimus has been converted, is urged to treat him as both a natural brother and as a brother in the faith (see John 15:15). In antebellum America, this interpretation was sometimes advocated in order to avoid finding slavery approved in the New Testament. However, the overwhelming thrust of the letter argues for the traditional interpretation: Onesimus is Philemon's slave.

— Onesimus is absent from his master's household, has fallen into his disfavor, and needs someone to intercede for him. The nature of his problem is not clear. It is not said that he is a runaway or that he has done anything illegal.[28] Though this is the traditional view and may be correct, it was not advocated in the ancient church until Chrysostom in the late fourth century, who exploited the homiletical potential of this view he apparently introduced.[29] That Onesimus may be indebted to

26. The letters of 1 and 2 Timothy and Titus are not exceptions; see §16.1.2. Third John is a churchly letter written to an individual church leader, preserved in the New Testament only in conjunction with the church letters 1 and 2 John.

27. A. D. Callahan, "Paul's Epistle to Philemon: Toward an Alternative *Argumentum*," *Harvard Theological Review* 86 (1993): 357–76.

28. John Dominic Crossan, *God and Empire: Jesus against Rome, Then and Now* (New York: HarperCollins, 2007), 161–62, points out there were two modes of flight, permanent and temporary, depending on the slave's intention. Permanent flight was a crime with terrible punishments: branding or disfigurement, condemnation to the mines, or public execution by fire, arena, or cross. If Onesimus had done this, it would have been foolish for him to come to Paul in prison, endangering his own life and guaranteeing Paul's execution. But temporary flight for refuge to seek the intercession of a friend was perfectly legal.

29. White delineates the three possibilities, and opts for the third: (1) runaway slave returned; (2) troubles between

Philemon (vv. 18–19) may mean that he has deprived him of his services for some weeks (if he is a runaway or Paul has detained him), that he has stolen something or been accused of thievery or pilfering, or that he has in some way mismanaged his master's property (see, e.g., Matt 18:23–25). However, if Onesimus had stolen something or otherwise harmed or wronged his master, one would expect some reference to his repentance.

— Onesimus has come into contact with Paul, who has converted him (v. 10). There is no indication that as a runaway he had been apprehended and thrown into jail with Paul. If this were the case, the authorities would return him to his master. Paul, probably a Roman citizen, is apparently incarcerated in a type of imprisonment that allowed him to have visitors and write letters; apprehended runaway slaves were dealt with more harshly. The letter provides no information on how Paul and Onesimus met—whether it was fortuitous, or whether Onesimus had sought Paul out. If Onesimus is not a runaway but is in trouble with his master, he may have sought out a friend of his master (*amicus domini*) to intercede for him. We have such a letter of intercession from Pliny the Younger to Sabinianus, pleading the case of a freedman servant who had wronged him.[30] It is probable that Onesimus had heard Philemon speak of Paul as a revered friend and coworker, and sought him out to intercede for him.

— Paul writes to Philemon and the church in his house, and sends the letter with Onesimus. There is no reference to anyone accompanying him or to visiting other churches en route.

The narrative world projected by the letter produces a coherent picture in itself, though it does not specify either its place of origin or the location of its addressees.

The traditional scenario. By combining this information with data from other New Testament documents and traditional elements, the following scenario has emerged, which has become the traditional view: Onesimus is the slave of Philemon, who lives in Colossae (Col 4:9). The church there had been founded by Epaphras, an associate of Paul's, though Paul himself has never been there (Col 1:7; 2:1; 4:12). Paul, at the end of his career, is imprisoned in Rome. Onesimus steals something from his master and runs away, finds his way to Rome, where he fortuitously encounters Paul. Paul converts him and sends him back home. The letter to Philemon was written at the same time as Colossians and Ephesians, and was sent along with them, in the company of Tychicus (Col 4:7, 9; Eph 6:21–22). Some scholars continue to affirm precisely this picture.[31]

An intriguing *variation of this traditional view* has been advocated by Edgar J. Goodspeed and his student John Knox, who developed the arguments of earlier scholars.[32] In the Goodspeed-Knox construction, Philemon responded positively to Paul's plea, did the "more" implicit in Paul's request (Phlm 21), and granted

Onesimus and Philemon, seeks Paul as intermediary; (3) Onesimus sent with gift to Paul in prison (as Epaphroditus had done for the Philippians), Paul had detained him, this had created awkwardness (White, *Jesus to Christianity*, 194–97).

30. Cited in full in Latin and English by Eduard Lohse, *Colossians and Philemon: A Commentary on the Epistles to the Colossians and to Philemon*, trans. William R. Poehlmann and Robert J. Karris, Hermeneia (Philadelphia: Fortress Press, 1971), 196–97. The essay of Peter Lampe has been influential in redirecting scholarly opinion away from the "runaway slave" hypothesis toward the view that Philemon is an intercessory letter similar to that of Pliny. See Peter Lampe, "Keine 'Sklavenflucht' des Onesimus," *ZNW* 76 (1985): 135–37.

31. E.g., Luke Timothy Johnson, *The Writings of the New Testament: An Interpretation*, rev. ed. (Minneapolis: Fortress Press, 1999), 383–91.

32. Edgar J. Goodspeed, *An Introduction to the New Testament* (Chicago: University of Chicago Press, 1937), 109–24, 210–39; Edgar J. Goodspeed, *The Meaning of Ephesians* (Chicago: University of Chicago Press, 1933), 1–75; John Knox, *Philemon among the Letters of Paul: A New View of Its Place and Importance*, rev. ed. (New York: Abingdon Press, 1935, 1959); John Knox, "Introduction and Exegesis of Philemon," in *Interpreter's Bible*, ed. George Arthur Buttrick (Nashville: Abingdon Press, 1957), 11:555–61.

Onesimus his freedom. The young Christian later went to Ephesus, the provincial capital, where he continued the work of the Pauline mission, eventually became the bishop of Ephesus, was instrumental in collecting and editing the Pauline letters, and composed Ephesians as a cover letter for the collection (see §15.2.1). Onesimus was still there about 110 (ca. fifty-five years later), when Ignatius of Antioch, en route to his martyrdom in Rome, met with him in Smyrna. Goodspeed considers the ancient tradition that identifies Bishop Onesimus of Ephesus with the Onesimus of Philemon as historically valid, though not demonstrable.

Neither the construction of Goodspeed nor that of Knox has been widely accepted, having generally been considered too imaginative, speculative, and ingenious, and being dependent on the view that Paul is the author of both Philemon and Colossians and that they were written at the same time. Critical study has advanced since Goodspeed's day; each of the elements of his scenario must now be reexamined (see §§15.1, 15.2).

11.3.4 Date, Provenance, and Addressees

Date, provenance, and addressees are all linked and must be treated together. In the letter itself, there is no indication of the location of the church and household to which it is addressed. If Colossians is written by Paul or contains reliable historical tradition on this point, then recent critical exegesis is correct in interpreting the data to mean that Onesimus is the slave of Philemon from Colossae and Archippus is a member of the Colossian church; the letter is thus directed to Philemon and the church in his house, with Apphia and Archippus (Col 4:9, 17). Philemon was a personal convert of Paul's (Phlm 19), and worked with him as a fellow evangelist and missionary (Phlm 1; the quasi-technical term "coworker" used for Philemon, also used for Mark, Aristarchus, Demas, and Luke, v. 24; and "partner" in v. 17). According to Colossians, Paul had not been to Colossae (Col 1:4, 9; 2:1); so Philemon would have been converted by Paul elsewhere, or Philemon 19b means simply that Philemon became a Christian under the influence of the Pauline mission. If Colossians and Ephesians are both pseudonymous and derive their information about Onesimus and his connections entirely from the letter to Philemon (and oral tradition about Paul), we cannot use them to locate the church to which Philemon and Onesimus belong.

Paul is in prison as he writes (vv. 1, 9, 13, 23). Presumably the recipients knew where. It is likely that Paul was incarcerated at some time during the course of his work in *Ephesus* (see §11.2.2). If so, there are good reasons to regard both Philippians and Philemon as having been written from Ephesus; this is now the majority view of critical scholars. (1) If Onesimus is from Colossae, it is easier to picture Onesimus as traveling from Colossae to Ephesus (120 miles, six days), than from Colossae to Rome (1,000 miles, many weeks). (2) It has been argued that Rome would have been the more likely goal of a "runaway slave," who would presumably want to put as much distance between himself and his master as possible; but Ephesus was also a large city some distance from Colossae, and would provide a safe refuge for a runaway. In any case, it is not at all clear that Onesimus was a runaway, nor that he is from Colossae (see above). (3) The Roman provenance is dependent on the picture of Paul in Acts, which is demonstrably not historically reliable about such data. (4) Paul expects to be released and visit Philemon in the near future (v. 22). But after Rome, Paul planned to go westward to Spain, not return to visit churches in the east (Rom 15:22–24). (5) If the Onesimus of Philemon is the same person as the Onesimus who was later bishop of Ephesus (see above), the "Ephesian connection" would fit into the presumed scenario: Philemon sends Onesimus back to Paul *in Ephesus* to help him in his missionary work, where he becomes a leading figure in the Ephesian church. Since after Paul's death Ephesus probably continued as the center of the Pauline school where Paul's letters were collected, edited, and circulated, this scenario centered in Ephesus would help account for the inclusion of the small letter of Philemon in the collection—which it was from the very first.

If written from Ephesus, the date of Philemon is about 54, and it is among the earlier of Paul's extant letters. If written from Caesarea, it was written about 58. If written from Rome, it is among the last of Paul's letters and is to be dated about 61 CE (see 13.3.3).

11.3.5 Slavery in the Ancient World and in the Early Church

For whatever reason, the slave Onesimus had separated from his master on problematical terms, had become a Christian under Paul's tutelage, and now returns with a letter from Paul pleading for reconciliation and acceptance. We modern readers find this scene difficult to imagine; we must struggle against reading into the text our later sensibilities, in which it is very difficult to think of Christian slave owners and to imagine Christians who did not protest against slavery as a social institution. Yet such historical imagination is the presupposition of reading this text with understanding.

We begin with a brief summary of the nature of slavery in the Hellenistic world. Slavery was a social institution almost universally accepted in the world of the New Testament. Estimates of the proportion of the slave population in the Roman Empire range from 25 percent to 50 percent. In some parts of the empire, the majority were slaves.[33] Slavery meant that one person was owned by another; it was a matter of property and property rights. Slaves could thus be bought and sold, rented, and given to others as gifts. Slaves had no social status and few legal rights. While most slaves were treated humanely, they could be abused, and were sexually available to their owners. One could become a slave by being born of slave parents, by being exposed as a baby, by being kidnaped by pirates, by being a prisoner of war, or by selling oneself into slavery to pay one's debts. Most slaves in the first century had been born as slaves and had a well-defined place in the household and social structure. Many slaves were well educated and constituted a significant element of the managerial class (as, for example, in the stories of Jesus in Matt 18:23–35; 24:45–51 and Luke 16:1–13; some translations soften the picture by rendering the word as "servant" rather than the more accurate "slave"). It was to the owner's advantage to provide education for his or her slaves, since this enhanced both their usefulness and their value. Slaves could be bought out of slavery by others or could accumulate enough money to purchase their own freedom. Slaves had some limited legal rights; for example, if their master treated them too harshly, they could demand to be sold to another master. Some slaves were paid wages, with which they purchased their freedom; some even owned their own slaves.

Slavery was not a matter of race; slaves could not be recognized as such on the street. While the slave's life was usually not easy in the ancient world, modern readers should not read into the New Testament the terrible pictures of the enslavement of Africans by Europeans and Americans in the eighteenth and nineteenth centuries. There was not always a wide gap in the New Testament world between slaves and free. Most slaves were humanely treated by their owners, and the modern reader should not assume that every slave wanted to be free.[34]

33. Raymond F. Collins, *I & II Timothy and Titus: A Commentary*, NTL (Louisville, KY: Westminster John Knox Press, 2002), 302: "the vast majority . . . —perhaps in excess of ninety percent in some of the urban centers of the empire."

34. On slavery in the Hellenistic world, see S. Scott Bartchy, *Mallon Chresai: First-Century Slavery and the Interpretation of 1 Corinthians 7:21*, SBLDS 11 (Missoula, MT: Society of Biblical Literature, 1973); David L. Balch and Carolyn Osiek, *Families in the New Testament World: Households and House Churches* (Louisville, KY: Westminster John Knox Press, 1997), 174–92, and especially Jennifer A. Glancy, *Slavery in Early Christianity* (Oxford: Oxford University Press, 2002), and the bibliography they provide.

While a few philosophers taught the essential equality of all human beings, slave or free, even they did not advocate abolition of slavery as an institution, and practically everyone accepted slavery as a given and necessary part of the social and economic order. The question was hardly raised in the ancient world, just as in a capitalist culture the legitimacy of the institution of private property is assumed, and the injustice brought about by private property is rarely discussed. In the first-century world, some members of the Jewish sect of the Essenes rejected slavery as such (Josephus, *Ant.* 18.1.5 §21; Philo, *Contempl. Life* 9 §70–71; cf. Philo, *Good Person* 12 §79), just as they rejected other social institutions such as marriage. They rejected neither slavery nor marriage as a social institution for the public at large, but as the practice of some members of their own sect.

There were no protests against the institution of slavery as such in the Hellenistic world. The gladiatorial war against Rome led by the escaped gladiator slave Spartacus in 73–71 BCE was not an attempt at social revolution, just as the war of independence fought by the American colonists was for their own freedom, not an attempt to abolish the institution of monarchy as such in other parts of the world. The early Christians did not form a sect that withdrew from the world, but put their faith into practice within society as it existed.

We know that Paul's gospel and theology proclaimed that among those who were baptized into Christ, the social distinctions between male and female, Jew and Gentile, slave and free no longer counted (Gal 3:27–28). The letter to Philemon gives us our only direct window into a first-century Christian household with slaves, our only picture of what this baptismal formula meant in practice. Among the things we learn:

1. A master could be converted without the household slaves becoming Christian. We do not know if there were other slaves in Philemon's household who became Christian; we know that Onesimus did not do so until his later encounter with Paul. Whatever "household conversions" might mean, they did not always remove the option of personal choice as to whether or not one became Christian.

2. When the head of a household became Christian, he or she was under no pressure to free slaves when converted. Philemon the slave owner was Paul's coworker, a leader in his own congregation, loved and respected in the wider church. If becoming a Christian meant to Paul or Onesimus that a Christian could not or should not be a slave owner, this fundamental tenet of the faith would have been known long before Philemon was written; it would not first come up indirectly in the letter to Philemon.

3. When either slave or master is converted, it was not merely a personal transaction between the individual and God. The new Christian now lived in a different world (2 Cor 5:17); their old world simply could not continue as before. Now that Onesimus has become a Christian, he is a brother to whom Philemon cannot relate in merely worldly terms (Phlm 16). Whether this *should* have already come up when *Philemon* became a Christian is not addressed in this letter.

4. This fundamental change that came about when either slaves or masters were converted did not mean a protest movement against slavery as an institution. Cain Hope Felder, African American New Testament scholar, insists that "Paul's letter to Philemon does not focus on the issue of slavery. . . . its message is about reconciliation."[35] He also points out that this does *not* mean that Paul "approves the institution of slavery." The institution of slavery was a given element in the social fabric of the Roman Empire, just as it was an unquestioned aspect of the social world of the Old Testament, like private property in capitalist North America of the twenty-first century. The subject of slavery in the abstract never enters Paul's mind or that of his readers as an issue one can either

35. Cain Hope Felder, "The Letter to Philemon," in *New Interpreter's Bible*, ed. Leander Keck, *The New Interpreter's Bible* (Nashville: Abingdon Press, 2000), 886–87.

approve or disapprove. The same is true of Jesus of Nazareth. To ask whether or not Paul and Jesus approved of slavery is to force a modern perspective on a different time and culture.

This does not mean that Paul privatizes or individualizes the ethical issues involved. Paul writes not only to Philemon but to the church; the issue is not between Philemon and Onesimus alone. An analogy from 1 Corinthians 6:1–11 is helpful at this point. There, Paul was not concerned to reform the Roman system of civil justice, but this did not mean he was unconcerned with issues of justice among Christians. Rather, what was dealt with in the civil courts was to be settled by Christians in their own corporate life.

5. Here we are neither accusing or defending Paul's stance toward the social institutions of his own day. It is too easy to take cheap shots at his "acceptance" of slavery from the safety of our later liberated perspective. And how shall we respond to Jesus' "acceptance" of slavery? Our task is neither to condemn nor to justify, but to understand. Two important considerations come to bear on this point. One is the matter of *political power*. The early church had none. It was a tiny minority, suspect in the eyes of the larger society. The second factor is *eschatology*. While there are no expressions of Pauline eschatology in this brief letter (even the typical "hope" is missing from the usual faith/hope/love triad of v. 5), we know that Paul's mission is constantly carried out within the horizon of the expected parousia. Whoever takes eschatology seriously must allow it to influence his or her understanding of Christian social responsibility. For Paul, the world is simply not going to last long enough to make it worthwhile to engage in efforts to change its social institutions, even if he had been able to effect social change or felt obligated to do so (see 1 Cor 7:17–31).

Still and all, we should not imagine Paul or other early Christians as thinking to themselves, "We would like to abolish slavery, but we have no political power, and Christ is coming back soon anyway, so we will just have to adjust to the status quo." The option of expressing Christian faith in terms of active political responsibility in behalf of more just social institutions did not appear on their mental screen. Modern Christians need to understand this stance in order to understand the New Testament, but we who live in a different political situation with a different eschatology cannot uncritically adopt it as our own. Acknowledging and understanding that Jesus, Paul, and the early church took no overt steps against institutionalized social evils is no reason to condemn first-century believers, to remold them into our own image, or to use the response to their social situation as justification for inaction in our own.

6. The issue remains: what does Paul expect from Philemon in regard to Onesimus, now that both are Christians? What is the "duty" (τὸ ἀνῆκον, *to anēkon*, better translated as "the appropriate thing"), the "even more than I say," that Paul urges on Philemon (vv. 8, 21). Some have argued that this is a covert demand that Philemon "do the Christian thing" and free his slave.[36] It is possible that in this instance Paul is asking for the slave's manumission, not because he affirms abolition as a general principle (1 Cor 7:21–24!), but because he has found Onesimus to be a helpful assistant (vv. 11–14), either personally (prisoners needed help in prison, which did not provide food and clothing to prisoners) or as an associate in his missionary work he continued to direct even from his prison cell.

Even though Paul would not violate Philemon's property rights without his consent, he wanted Onesimus back with him—either by Philemon's freeing him and asking him to return to Paul as a free man, a voluntary helper in Paul's missionary work, or by Philemon's sending him back as still Philemon's slave, Philemon's contribution to the Pauline mission, or even by giving him to Paul as a slave. In a

36. Most insistent in this regard is the careful and helpful study of Petersen, *Rediscovering Paul*. Petersen argues that Philemon must free Onesimus, and that if he does not, it is the community's duty to expel him—the leader in whose house the church met! (99–100, 268–70, 287).

patron/client society, a freed Onesimus would still be attached to Philemon's household as his freedman/client.[37] We do not know the results of this letter, but the fact that it has been preserved indicates that Philemon responded to Paul's appeal in some way, and that Onesimus rejoined Paul as his coworker in the gospel. For possible further developments, see the Introduction to Ephesians.

11.3.6 Structure and Outline

The letter follows the typical Pauline adaptation of the standard form of the Hellenistic letter (see §10.2.3):

1–7	Letter Opening
1–3	Greeting
4–7	Thanksgiving
8–22	Letter Body
8–21	Paul's request
22	Paul's anticipated arrival ("Apostolic Parousia")
23–25	Letter Closing
23–24	Greetings
25	Benediction

11.3.7 Exegetical-Theological Précis

The letter is not a casual composition. Paul writes both to persuade Philemon and to commend Onesimus; the document resembles both the conventional letter of request and the letter of recommendation. Artfully composed and not without wit, the letter represents Paul's indirect but powerful appeal to Philemon to receive his slave back as a Christian brother. The prescript (vv. 1–3) greets both the individual Philemon and the church meeting in his house (the "you" of v. 2 is singular, that of v. 3 plural). The thanksgiving section (vv. 4–7), while following the conventional form, is also sincere, and prepares the way for the request to come: Philemon is known as a loving person who cares for "*all* the saints" (v. 5), including the community of faith to which the slave Onesimus now belongs. That "the hearts of the saints" have been refreshed by Philemon (v. 7) prepares for the appeal for Onesimus, Paul's own "heart" (v. 12).

Paul could command as an apostle, but prefers to appeal on the basis of Christian love (vv. 8–9)—not an emotional attachment to Philemon or sentiment for Onesimus, but the new reality that pervades the Christian community to which both Philemon and Onesimus now belong. Paul speaks as an "old man"[38] and as a "prisoner." He makes his appeal for the bondsman Onesimus as one who is himself in bonds (see also v. 23).

11.4 For Further Reading

Best, E. *A Commentary on the First and Second Epistles to the Thessalonians*. Black's New Testament Commentaries. London: Adam & Charles Black, 1972.

Duncan, G. S. *St. Paul's Ephesian Ministry: A Reconstruction with Special Reference to the Ephesian Origin of the Imprisonment Epistles*. London: Hodder & Stoughton, 1929.

Felder, C. H. "The Letter to Philemon." In *The New Interpreter's Bible*, edited by Leander Keck, 11:881–905. Nashville: Abingdon Press, 2000.

Fitzmyer, Joseph A. *The Letter to Philemon: A New Translation with Introduction and Commentary*. Anchor Bible 32C. New York: Doubleday, 2000.

Glancy, J. A. *Slavery in Early Christianity*. Oxford: Oxford University Press, 2002.

Hawthorne, G. F. *Philippians*. WBC 43. Waco, TX: Word Books, 1983.

Knox, J. "Introduction and Exegesis of Philemon." In *The Interpreter's Bible*, edited by George Arthur Buttrick, 11:555–61. Nashville: Abingdon Press, 1957.

37. So, e.g., Balch and Osiek, *Families*, 178.

38. Paul calls himself πρεσβύτης (*presbutēs*, old man), but the word may also be equivalent to πρεσβεύτης (*presbeutēs*, ambassador), the representative of Christ, cf. 2 Cor. 5:20; Eph. 6:20.

———. *Philemon among the Letters of Paul: A New View of Its Place and Importance*. Rev. ed. New York: Abingdon Press, 1935, 1959.

Malherbe, A. J. *The Letters to the Thessalonians: A New Translation with Introduction and Commentary*. Anchor Bible 32B. New York: Doubleday, 2000.

Osiek, C. *Philippians, Philemon*. ANTC. Nashville: Abingdon Press, 2000.

Petersen, N. R. *Rediscovering Paul: Philemon and the Sociology of Paul's Narrative World*. Philadelphia: Fortress Press, 1985.

Reumann, J. *Philippians: A New Translation with Introduction and Commentary*. Anchor Bible 33b. New Haven, CT: Yale University Press, 2008.

Richard, E. J. *First and Second Thessalonians*. Sacra pagina. Collegeville, MN: Liturgical Press, 1995.

Wanamaker, C. A. *The Epistles to the Thessalonians: A Commentary on the Greek Text*. New International Commentary on the New Testament. Grand Rapids: Eerdmans, 1990.

12

Paul and the Corinthians

12.1 Interpreting 1 Corinthians

12.1.1 Corinth: City and Church

A two-hour visit as a tourist, or a quick glance at a map of the Mediterranean, immediately reveals why Corinth became an important city politically, religiously, and commercially. The city sits astride the narrow isthmus separating the Aegean and the Adriatic, the ancient counterpart of the Panama Canal;[1] its strategic location as a crossroads of East and West generated a large, prosperous, and sophisticated city.

The Romans destroyed the city in 146 BCE, when Corinth joined a coalition that attacked Sparta, an ally of Rome. Corinth continued to exist as a Greek city until refounded as a Roman colony by Julius Caesar in 44 BCE; in Paul's time it was more Roman than Greek. In Paul's day the city of about 200,000 was the capital of the Roman province of Achaia, both a thoroughly Roman urban center promoting the Caesar cult and a melting pot of Mediterranean culture. The broad spectrum of Hellenistic religion found expression in numerous temples and cults (see fig. 35).

Archaeological evidence for synagogues in Corinth is later than New Testament times, but Acts and other contemporary literary evidence indicates a flourishing Jewish community in the Corinth of Paul's time. The Isthmian Games, second only to the Olympics, were located in Corinth, held every other year, the second and fourth year of each Olympiad; there were also contests in oratory, drama, and music. Corinth was attractive to philosophers and their schools but, along with sophisticated intellectual currents, also had uneducated, if prosperous, masses who disdained culture. The city's bad reputation for sexual debauchery was proverbial, but also exaggerated by other cities competing with Corinth commercially. The widespread description of "a thousand priestess-prostitutes" available in local temples has been shown to be false.[2] The city was no better or worse than other large seaports. In short, Corinth was the kind of place Paul would choose for a mission center, and he did so.

The pluralism of the city's population was reflected in the group of new converts. Most of the Corinthian church members were poor and without status, but the congregation included a few of the wealthy and powerful (see 1 Cor 1:26—"not many," but some). Among these were the synagogue leader Crispus (see 1 Cor 1:14; Acts 18:8); Gaius, whose house was large enough to provide a meeting place for the whole

1. Ancient attempts at building a canal failed; the present canal was completed in 1883.

2. Hans Conzelmann, *Korinth und die Mädchen der Aphrodite: Zur Religionsgeschichte der Stadt Korinth* (Göttingen: Vandenhoeck & Ruprecht, 1967), 247–61.

FIGURE 35: Corinth Temple, Acropolis. PHOTO CREDIT: M. EUGENE BORING.

FIGURE 36: Corinthian Bema. PHOTO CREDIT: M. EUGENE BORING.

church; and Erastus, a prominent city official (see Rom 16:23, written later from Corinth.)

The church was primarily of Gentile background, which would have included previous experiences of extraordinary spiritual phenomena (see the tactful reference in 1 Cor 12:2). The church also included a minority of Jewish Christians and probably several God-fearers, who would have followed their synagogue leader into the new community.

12.1.2 Historical Setting of 1 Corinthians

A full discussion of Paul's relationships and communications with the Corinthian church must await our study of 2 Corinthians. Here we briefly sketch the events that lead up to the writing of 1 Corinthians. After an effective ministry of at least eighteen months (Acts 18:11), Paul leaves Corinth. We next hear from him in Ephesus (1 Cor 16:8; Acts 18:18–19:40). In the meantime, Corinth is visited by other Christian teachers, including Apollos and advocates of Petrine Christianity (1 Cor 1:12; 3:4–6, 11, 22; 4:6), and Apollos has joined Paul in Ephesus (1 Cor 16:12). Apollos presumably has brought news of the Corinthian church to Ephesus. Responding to these reports, Paul writes a letter to the Corinthians (1 Cor 5:9). This letter is now lost, unless a fragment of it is preserved in 2 Corinthians. The Corinthians send a letter to Paul, also lost, which includes a list of questions (1 Cor 7:1), and Paul hears further oral reports about matters they have not reported in their letter (1 Cor 1:11; 16:17). Paul sends Timothy to Corinth (1 Cor 4:17) and composes a second letter to Corinth, our 1 Corinthians, in response to their letter and the other issues of which he has heard.

12.1.3 Literary Integrity

Certain phenomena in the text of 1 Corinthians have given rise to theories that the canonical document is an editorial combination of more than one letter. There seem to be tensions, for example, in the differing responses Paul gives to the issue of eating meat sacrificed to idols in chapters 8 and 10 (see below). Most scholars now regard 1 Corinthians as a unity, explaining the tensions as the result of the compositional strategy of the letter. The matter is different, however, with 2 Corinthians (see below).

12.1.4 Structure and Outline

The typical structure of the Pauline letter is bipartite: a theological section explicating God's saving act, followed by a paraenetic section calling for human response (see above §10.2.3). The body of 1 Corinthians is also bipartite, yet the structure of the letter is determined not by the indicative/imperative structure of Paul's thought, but by the circumstances that led to his writing the letter. In Part I, Paul gives his own instructions regarding four situations in the church of which he had heard, but about which they had not asked him. Part II of the letter is structured by Paul's response to matters about which they have written, with each such topic beginning with the formula περὶ δέ (*peri de*, "now concerning").

Epistolary Introduction

1:1–3	Greeting
1:4–9	Thanksgiving

Letter Body, Part 1: Paul Responds to Issues He Has Heard About

1:10—4:21	"Wisdom" and "Signs" vs. the Scandal of the Cross
1:10–17	Factions
1:18–2:5	The message of the cross demolishes all pretensions of human wisdom
2:6–16	True wisdom for the mature
3:1–22	Divisions and leaders
4:1–21	Apostolic mission
5:1–13	Immorality—A Man Living with His Stepmother
6:1–11	Lawsuits
6:12–20	Christian Freedom and Casual Sex

Letter Body, Part 2: Paul Responds to Issues Raised by the Corinthians' Letter

7:1–40	περὶ δέ (*peri de* now concerning) Marriage, Divorce, Sex, and the Single Life
7:1–16	Counsel for those who are or have been married
7:17–24	General principle: Remain as God called you
7:25–40	περὶ δέ (*peri de* now concerning) Counsel for the unmarried
8:1–11:1	περὶ δέ (*peri de* now concerning) Food Laws and Participation in Pagan Society

8:1–13	Food, knowledge, and love
9:1–27	Having rights, insisting on them, and giving them up
10:1–22	The biblical example of Israel
10:23–11:1	Do all for the glory of God and the sake of the Christian mission
11:2–34	Further Questions about Worship
11:2–16	Proper attire in Christian worship
11:17–34	Correcting abuses at the Lord's Supper
12:1–14:40	περὶ δέ (*peri de* now concerning) Spiritual Gifts
12:1–11	One Spirit, many gifts
12:12–30	One body, many members
12:31–13:13	The still more excellent way
14:1–40	Prophecy and tongues
15:1–58	The Resurrection
15:1–11	The resurrection of Jesus as the foundation and core of Christian faith
15:12–34	The future resurrection of all
15:35–58	The resurrection of the body
16:1–24	Concluding Instructions and Greetings
16:1–4	περὶ δέ (*peri de* now concerning) The offering
16:5–11	Travel plans
16:12	περὶ δέ (*peri de* now concerning) Possible visit of Apollos
16:13–24	Final messages and greetings

12.1.5 Exegetical-Theological Précis

1:1–9 Epistolary Introduction

1:1–3 Greeting In contrast to the situation reflected in his previous letters, Paul's apostleship is an issue in his letter to Corinth, where leadership in the congregation has become a disputed point. For the first time in his extant correspondence, Paul expands the conventional greeting by designating himself as *apostle*, that is, "authorized representative," one who has been *called* by the risen Jesus (see §§10.1.3, 13.3.2). He was not called "to be" an apostle, but he is a called apostle—an apostle because he has been called. Paul did not volunteer; he was a draftee. This does not distinguish Paul from the Corinthian Christians, however—they too are called (same Greek word). He is an apostle because he was called; they are saints because they are called. They are addressed not as a collection of individuals, nor even as an independent congregation, for their call has joined them to the whole church, all those in every place who invoke the name of Jesus Christ.

1:4–9 Thanksgiving Again, the conventional brief thanksgiving section is expanded, but not so elaborately as in 1 Thessalonians. The thanksgiving typically anticipates major themes of the letter. Paul will call for critical discernment with regard to spiritual gifts, but can give thanks that the Corinthians are already enriched in speech (λόγος, *logos*) and knowledge (γνῶσις, *gnōsis*)—though in view of, for example, 1 Corinthians 4:8, there may be some irony in Paul's tone of voice. Despite the faults and foibles of the new converts—which Paul will severely criticize—he regards them as called into the Christian community by the risen Christ, who will sustain them until their final salvation on the imminent day of the Lord. As in 1 Thessalonians, Christian life is described as living in the interim between Jesus' resurrection and the parousia. Eschatology is not reserved for the final section of the letter, but permeates it throughout. Just as eschatology is not a matter of the end of the world or of the Christian's life, so God's plan culminating at the eschaton forms the framework for the whole of life.

Letter Body, Part 1: Paul Responds to Issues He Has Heard About

1:10—4:21 "Wisdom" and "Signs" vs. the Scandal of the Cross

1:10–17 Factions Since the founding of the church by Paul, three or four competitive groups have emerged, each perhaps related to a particular house church. (1) Some identify themselves with Paul and his theology. (2) Some are attracted to a gifted Christian teacher named *Apollos* who has visited Corinth. We know nothing directly about Apollos, but in Acts he is reliably pictured as a Jewish Christian from Alexandria, intellectual center of Platonic philosophy. He is a teacher "mighty in the Scriptures," who had been instructed more accurately in the "way of the Lord" as expounded by Prisca, Aquila, and Paul (Acts 18:24–28). (3) Followers of *Peter* (Aramaic *Cephas*), or perhaps Peter himself, have also come to Corinth. The Petrine version of the faith is presumably more closely related to the life and teaching of the pre-Easter Jesus and to the Jewish Christianity of Jerusalem than is the case in Paul's theology. The Petrine group may emphasize stories of the miraculous signs performed by the earthly Jesus—entirely absent from Paul's theology—and perhaps are already quoting a saying in which Jesus has made Peter the rock on which the church is built (Matt 16:16–19). Those Christian leaders in Jerusalem and Antioch who oppose Paul's Gentile mission may have adopted Peter—a *real* apostle—as their patron, with or without Peter's knowledge or approval. In the light of the Corinthians' response to the Petrine apostolic claims and their admiration for Apollos as biblical interpreter, Paul begins for the first time to emphasize his own apostleship and the biblical foundations of his own gospel (see §11.2.2). (4) There was probably a fourth group designating itself "*we are of Christ*." The Christ group is the most difficult to identify. Apparently they claimed a direct relationship to the exalted Christ, not mediated by any human figure.

Paul declares the redemptive significance of Jesus' death and reminds them that their baptism did not divide them into different groups but united them with Christ and each other (cf. 12:13).

1:18–2:5 The message of the cross demolishes all pretensions of human wisdom. Why does Paul go from the problem of factions to the scandalous message of the cross? The factions were only the surface expression of a deeper problem. The underlying issue is the Corinthians' fascination with "eloquent wisdom" (σοφία λόγου *sophia logou*), literally "logos wisdom," that is, wisdom that fits the Christian faith into a persuasive comprehensive logical or mythological system. Paul does not begin with a philosophical idea and fit the Christ event into it, but with the shameful event of the cross itself as God's wisdom that overturns all human pretensions. Paul's opponents and detractors at Corinth may have included a proto-Gnostic faction that considered Paul's gospel too simple (see above under [Proto-]Gnosticism, §9.2.2).

2:6–16 True wisdom for the mature This section seems at first to be a reversal of what Paul has just said, but he is probably taking up the language of the Corinthian advocates of "wisdom" and using it against them, with a heavy dose of irony. The Corinthians suppose that Paul has only given them preliminary and elementary instruction intended for beginners, and their later teachers have supplemented this with advanced teaching appropriate for sophisticated believers, which some of them have become. Paul responds that he does in fact proclaim wisdom for the mature, but that they cannot receive it because they remain in the babyhood stage (3:1). This wisdom is not for a sophisticated elite, but is given by the Spirit to all: all baptized Christians, not a select spiritual group, receive this wisdom.

3:1–22 Divisions and leaders Paul here resumes his argument that the divisions in the Corinthian church should not be applauded as a wholesome variety or healthy competition that is good for church business, but are a manifestation of the false claims of human wisdom—not an expression of advanced spirituality but of this-worldly "fleshly" would-be wisdom. Surprisingly, he does not adopt their standards and argue against Peter and Apollos (nor does he ever directly address the "Christ" group) by pressing the claims of the Pauline group; rather, he embraces Peter and Apollos as fellow ministers, brothers and colleagues in ministry. Paul sees himself as the irreplaceable founder and father because of his apostolic role. At Corinth, they are supplementary fellow workers, building on the foundation he has laid. Christ himself is the foundation (an indirect critique of the Petrine group's claims that Jesus had made Peter the rock the "foundation" (see Matt 16:17–18). Their work, like his, will be evaluated in the Last Judgment. Like the Qumran community, Paul considers the community of faith itself to be the true and holy temple of God. The Spirit of God dwells in the temple-community as a whole, not in individual charismatic leaders.

4:1–21 Apostolic mission In Paul's view, the Corinthians have an exaggeratedly realized eschatology, celebrating the "already" dimension of the Christian faith, which tends to evaluate Christian ministry by this-worldly standards of honor and success. Paul aligns authentic ministry, his and that of the other apostles, with the cross of Christ, with the "not yet" eschatological dimension. By the standards of the present age, it comes off poorly (4:8–13), but just as the future parousia of Christ will vindicate the ministry of the weak and crucified one, so Paul's own future appearance in Corinth will manifest God's power (4:14–21).

5:1–13 Immorality—A Man Living with His Stepmother

Paul introduces a new topic—again, one they have not regarded as a problem and have not asked about. In Paul's view, there is continuity with the preceding in that the problem is not merely the individual conduct of the couple involved, but the arrogant attitude of the church, based on a theological misunderstanding of the gospel and the church's mission.

"Living with" indicates a long-term sexual relationship. The exact situation, though clear to the Corinthians, is no longer apparent to us. The allusion to Leviticus 18:7–8, which stands in the background, makes it obvious that the woman is not the man's biological mother. The relationship is not incest in the sense of cohabiting with a blood relative. Apparently the father has died, leaving behind a younger wife; son and stepmother are living together as man and wife. This relationship is a violation of community standards, as a breach of both the Jewish Torah and Gentile law.

Paul does not address the couple, but the church as a whole. This decision is not merely their own private business. The congregation's problem is its smugness in considering itself free from such considerations of "what people think." This attitude is probably a combination of their "human wisdom," involving proto-Gnostic "spiritual" superiority to conventional "worldly standards," and their understanding of Paul's own preaching of Christian freedom.[3] For Paul, however, it represents a gross misunderstanding that does not take into account their responsibility to represent the church's mission to the world at large.

Paul commands that the man be expelled from the community (nothing is said of the woman, who may not be a member of the church), that he be turned over to Satan, that is, that he be placed back in the situation to which he belonged before entering the church. Though the expulsion of the man is necessary so as not to impede the mission of the church, so far as the man himself is concerned, it is remedial and disciplinary, the ultimate goal being his salvation at the parousia (see 3:10–15). The church itself is not to "go out of the world" (5:10) in reclusive or monastic fashion, but is to carry on its mission in the midst of a sinful society. This requires that it discipline its own members.

6:1–11 Lawsuits

The Corinthians have continued their normal preconversion practice of settling disputed

3. The phrase "in the name of the Lord Jesus" (1 Cor. 5:4) probably belongs with "the man who has done such a thing," as in the NRSV margin. The man claimed that he was acting in the name of the Lord, in view of the new creation proclaimed by Paul.

legal issues by taking each other to court. Here again Paul illustrates that apocalyptic eschatology is not merely a concluding appendage to his theology but permeates it, not as a matter of speculation but as the basis for concrete decisions. Believers will participate in the final judgment as judges themselves, sharing the role of God and Christ. They will even help preside over the judgment of the fallen angels (see 2 Pet 2:4). Paul introduces these apocalyptic images not as an element in his "teaching about the end of the world," but to make the practical point that Corinthian Christians are capable of handling their own internal disputes without going to court before pagan judges. Paul's ecclesiology is also brought to bear on the concrete issue: believers may need to suppress their individual rights for the sake of the mission of the church (to be elaborated in chaps. 8–11). Here too, Paul's apocalypticism and his theology of the cross are combined as the basis for the distinctive Christian ethic.

6:12–20 *Christian Freedom and Casual Sex*

Except for Judaism, there was little connection in the Hellenistic world between religion and ethics. There were many varieties of ethical teaching, some with high standards of morality, but ethics generally had a philosophical or commonsense foundation, not a religious one. It was an unfamiliar idea to most of the Corinthian converts that their new Christian faith meant a transformation of their previous ethical understandings, and Paul found it necessary to instruct them in "my ways in Christ" (4:17). Appealing to both the Scripture and his understanding of the church as the body of Christ, Paul explains that Christians cannot continue their previous practice of casual sex. Some Corinthians apparently appeal to Paul's own doctrine of Christian freedom as the rationale for their practice. Since quotation marks or their equivalent were not used in the ancient world, it is sometimes difficult to recognize quoted material. There is good evidence, however, that here and elsewhere Paul cites Corinthian slogans that were distortions of his own teaching. Thus "All things are lawful for me" and "Food is meant for the stomach and the stomach for food" are probably such slogans (so, e.g., NRSV), as well as "Every sin that a person commits is outside the body" (6:18). The latter slogan may represent a proto-Gnostic understanding of sin, that is, that a person's acts do not affect the true spiritual self, but only the external bodily shell. Though Paul can use language expressing the Greek dualistic distinction between body and spirit radicalized and exploited by Gnostic thought, his own sex ethic affirms the unity of the whole person as the creation of God. As such, and as part of God's temple, the community of faith in which God's Spirit lives, each believer is a temple of the Spirit. Such an understanding must inform one's sexual ethics.

Letter Body, Part 2: Paul Responds to Issues Raised by the Corinthians' Letter

7:1–40 περὶ δέ (peri de *now concerning*) *Marriage, Divorce, Sex, and the Single Life*

The formula περὶ δέ (*peri de*, now concerning) often marks a new beginning point; it is repeated at 7:25, 8:1, 12:1, 16:1, 16:12, each time marking a new subsection dealing with an issue raised by the Corinthians' letter. This paraphernalia associated with letters is a good reminder that Paul is here not attempting an essay on "The Christian View of Sex and Marriage," but is responding to specific questions put to him.

7:1–16 ***Counsel for those who are or have been married*** "It is well for a man not to touch a woman" is almost certainly a Corinthian slogan quoted by Paul, either as a current maxim of Hellenistic or proto-Gnostic philosophy, or a gnosticizing misinterpretation of Paul's own teaching. The slogan represents a point of view that misunderstood Paul as discouraging sex as belonging to the fleshly, material world. This view prohibited sex even for married couples

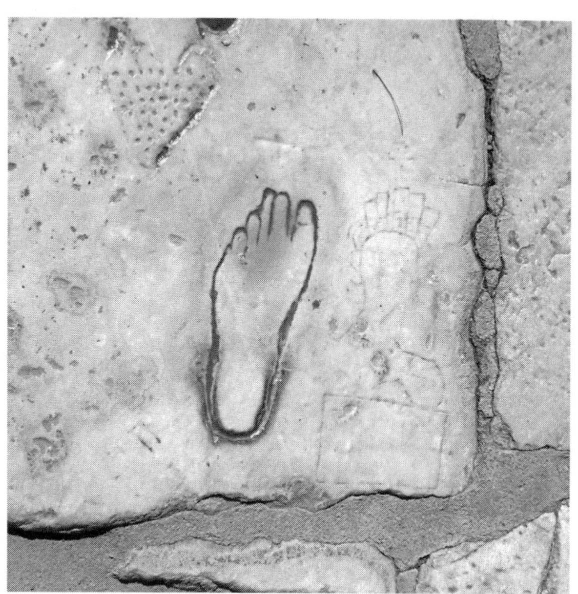

FIGURE 37: This carved footprint in a sidewalk in Ephesus was formerly thought to be a sign pointing to the local brothel; the footprint is now regarded as part of a cluster of signs of unknown meaning. PHOTO CREDIT: M. EUGENE BORING.

who were truly "spiritual." Paul rejects this. "Have" in 7:2 is meant in the sexual sense, as in 5:1. Paul does not here give grudging permission for engaged couples to get married as a second-best status, but precisely the opposite (his address to those who have never been married does not begin until 7:25).

Married couples are to have a normal sex life, neither partner subordinate to the other, but being mutually concerned for the other. Paul's own unmarried status is not the norm, but a particular gift. But neither is married status the norm. The dignity and value of the single life is affirmed as one of the ways of living one's life in the service of God. In this context, "the unmarried" (v. 8) probably refers to widowers, and the following instructions are directed to the issue of the remarriage of widowers and widows.

Paul not only provides his own instruction, but appeals to "commands of the Lord." This apparent distinction between his own teaching and sayings of the Lord should not be pressed. On the one hand, "words of the Lord" refers not only to sayings of the historical Jesus but includes sayings of the risen Jesus delivered by Christian prophets (including Paul himself). On the other hand, Paul considers his own apostolic teaching the command of the Lord, given through the Spirit (see 7:6, 10, 12, 25, 40; 14:37).

7:17–24 General principle: Remain as God called you Marriages should not be dissolved on the basis of the "spirituality" of the one partner; slaves should not assume that their conversion has lifted them out of the given structures of society. The relationship of slaves and masters within the Christian community is transformed "in Christ," but Paul does not address the issue of slavery as a social institution. Paul insists that the call of God and service to God are independent of social status (see Philemon!).

7:25–40 περὶ δέ **(peri de *now concerning*)** ***Counsel for the unmarried*** As is the case with married couples and slaves, so also for the unmarried: it is better to remain as they are. Here Paul's point is supported primarily by his apocalypticism. In view of the nearness of the

FIGURE 38: Relief of a couple, second century, Beroea. USED BY PERMISSION OF DAVID PADFIELD.

parousia and the breakdown of societal and biological structures as the end approaches,[4] it is not a good time to be getting married and starting a family—though Paul does not forbid it. His particular instruction is thoroughly conditioned by his apocalyptic eschatology, as is the matter of going to court discussed above. The more comprehensive perspective within which the life of faith is to be lived is presented in 7:29–31. Believers do not flee into interior subjectivity, nor do they conceive the church to be a monastic community separated from worldly concerns. Firmly rooted in the everyday life of this world, they live their lives in a way not dominated and ultimately controlled by worldly circumstances.

4. Some streams of apocalyptic thought understood the normal processes of nature to break down as the end approaches. A heifer brought to the temple to be sacrificed brought forth a lamb in the temple court (Josephus, *War* 6.289–92); just before the end, "menstruous women shall bring forth monsters. . . . children a year old shall speak with their voices. . . . pregnant women shall give birth to premature children at three and four months, and these shall live and leap about" (2 Esd. 5:8; 6:20–21).

8:1–11:1 περὶ δέ (peri de *now concerning) Food Laws and Participation in Pagan Society*

8:1–13 Food, knowledge, and love The Corinthians had asked Paul about the problem of eating meat sacrificed to idols. The complex, many-layered issue was posed by the fact that meat sold in the marketplace had generally been sacrificed to pagan gods in the temples, and by the fact that the biblical food laws prohibited the eating of certain kinds of meat, such as pork, and of any meat that had not been properly slaughtered (Lev 7:26–27; 17:10–16). These biblical prescriptions would have been important not only to the minority of Jewish Christians that may have belonged to the Corinthian church, but to Gentile Christians who found these regulations in what was now the authoritative Scriptures of early Christianity. Did eating such food violate the will of God revealed in Scripture? Did eating meat ritually dedicated to some idol involve recognizing pagan religion? Was it somehow participating in devotion to pagan gods?

The question was not only religious but social and economic. Much social and business life revolved around the guilds, including dinners at which eating such meat and perfunctory acknowledgment of pagan gods was part of the program. Was there any difference between going to private dinner parties where such meat might be served and participating in business, professional, and public gatherings involving idol meat? Were Christians expected to withdraw from all such associations, which would not only have severe economic and social consequences, but would damage the Christian mission? This was not a trivial matter or a simple one.

Some in the Corinthian church argued that their newfound faith taught them there is only one God, that the pagan idols are really nothing, that Paul himself had taught them that they were free from the biblical food laws; so they were free to eat whatever they wanted. "All of us possess knowledge" and "No idol in the world really exists" seem to represent the slogans of this group, cited by Paul in 8:1, 4. Others in the church had deep religious scruples about participation in such activities and regarded the eating of meat sacrificed to idols as both dangerous to one's own faith and sending the wrong message to the community.

In principle, Paul agrees with the "liberated" group, but argues that the driving force of the Christian life is not knowledge but love. To proceed only on the basis of one's own conscience, without regard to the effect on one's "weaker," unliberated brother or sister, is a sin against one's fellow church members, an impediment to the church's mission, and a sin against Christ himself.

9:1–27 Having rights, insisting on them, and giving them up It is in this context that Paul brings up his own role as an apostle. He is not here concerned about his personal status, but wants to instruct the church about the proper function of one's "rights" within the Christian community. The individual Christian has every right to eat idol-meat, but may be called on to give up this right for the sake of the Christian sister or brother and the Christian mission as a whole. So also, as an apostle, Paul has a right to support from the congregation, but in Corinth he has voluntarily given up this right and supported himself by manual labor, in order to advance the Christian mission.

It is likely that advocates of both the "weak" and the "liberated" views invoked Scripture texts to support their case. Paul in turn established his own point by appeal to the Bible, giving an allegorical interpretation of the instruction in Deuteronomy 25:4 about the care and feeding of oxen so that it applies to the issue of supporting Christian missionaries.[5] The key point, however, is 9:12b: "*Nevertheless*, we have not made use of this right." Paul has knowledge, Paul is free; but true freedom means being freed from worrying about one's rights and one's image, and adapting one's life to various situations for the sake of the Christian mission (9:19–23; see 10:31–33).

10:1–22 The biblical example of Israel The ancient Israelites, freed from their previous slavery, in their newfound freedom too quickly adapted themselves to pagan ways, eating and drinking like the Gentiles—and received God's judgment (Exod 32). In 1 Corinthians 10 Paul's instructions seem more restrictive than in chapter 8. There, eating idol-meat is not wrong in principle but should be avoided for the sake of the weak brother or sister; here, eating at the Lord's Table and participation in pagan cultic meals seem to be mutually exclusive. There, an idol was nothing; here, pagan gods represent demonic powers. Such discrepancies have sometimes been regarded as evidence that 1 Corinthians is composite. It is more likely, however, that Paul is here drawing the line against actual involvement in pagan worship. Eating idol-meat at a private dinner party or guild

5. On Christian reinterpretation of the Old Testament, see above, §9.2.2. Here, Paul's interpretation is purely allegorical. Contrast Jesus' use of the *qal wahomer* hermeneutic (e.g., Matt 6:30; 12:11–12).

banquet is not the same as such overt participation in the pagan cults.

10:23–11:1 Do all for the glory of God and the sake of the Christian mission. The letter character of Paul's communication is apparent in his allusion to additional slogans of some of the Corinthians. "All things are lawful" (10:23) represents a distortion and inappropriate application of Paul's own teaching. "Why should my liberty be subject to the judgment of someone else's conscience? If I partake with thankfulness, why should I be denounced because of that for which I give thanks?" (10:29b–30). This rhetorical question does not represent Paul's own view but the protest of those who feel their liberty encroached upon by Paul's instructions. In concluding this subsection by appeal to himself and Christ as examples (11:1), Paul presents self-giving for the sake of others as the driving force in Christian discipleship.

11:2–34 Further Questions about Worship

The next topic beginning with a περὶ δέ (*peri de*, now concerning), signaling a question in the Corinthians' letter to which Paul responds, is not found until 12:1. This is preceded by two more items they had not asked about, but about which he had heard (11:18). The concern for what is appropriate in worship seems to be the connecting thread. Paul thus discusses proper attire and conduct for women and abuses of the Lord's Supper in this context.

11:2–16 Proper attire in Christian worship If we assume that the passage was written by Paul, it illustrates his conviction that the Corinthian church needs traditions that will guide them in their struggle to evaluate their new situation. The powerful manifestation of the Holy Spirit in their midst had broken through many of the cultural conventions, some of which were oppressive. When Paul was with them, he had delivered traditions, instructions handed along (horizontally) from the earlier and wider church, to guide the Corinthians in their newfound freedom and enthusiasm for the direct (vertical) experience of the Spirit. They seem to be convinced that the "new age" has already arrived (see 4:8–9), that they are already "equal to angels," that the conventional gender distinctions of "this age" no longer apply to them. It is not clear whether the issue was hairstyle or the wearing of veils on the head, just as we cannot be sure of the cultural significance of veils or hairstyles in the Corinth of Paul's day.

It is clear that women played leadership roles in congregational worship, leading in prayer and preaching in the power of the Spirit ("prophesying"). Since women wore their hair differently in the privacy of their own home than in public, it may be that the small congregations meeting in private homes, where everyone was "brother" and "sister," invited a relaxing of conventions. Also, some of the Corinthians seem to have been infatuated with ideas of "angels" and "authority," which probably played a role in the discussion, and Paul is here reflecting a vocabulary they had introduced into the debate. Again, it is important to keep the letter character of the text in mind. Paul is not writing an essay on "Women's Role in Worship" or "Appropriate Headgear in Church," but responding to a specific situation. The original readers knew the specifics of that situation. Modern readers do not, and should resist the impulse to read in their own agenda. The original reference is no longer clear to us.

What is clear is that they are to judge for themselves (11:13; cf. 10:15), but their decision must also accord with the tradition of the larger church to which they belong (11:2, 16). Here again, their primary responsibility is not to their individualistic sense of freedom, real and true as it is, but to the mission of the church in the world; they decide for themselves, but not by themselves. Christians should make decisions about dress and hairstyle in such a way that outsiders are not put off by the peculiarity of Christians in such matters, judged by conventional standards. Paul wants outsiders to ask about the gospel, not about whether Christians wear unconventional hats or hairstyles—even if in principle they are free to do so.

11:17–34 Correcting abuses at the Lord's Supper The eucharistic meals of the Corinthian church had degenerated to the point that they do "more harm than good" (CEB). The problem was not with bad eucharistic theology per se, but in allowing the table fellowship of the church to continue to represent the kind of social distinctions that were normal in the Hellenistic world.[6] The central act of worship was the Eucharist, celebrated in the context of a real meal, the congregation meeting in private homes of those wealthy enough to provide for such meetings. The setting of the church service somewhat resembled a dinner party, with ten to twelve guests reclining in the dining room, the rest spilling over into the atrium. It was entirely normal on such occasions that those of higher status received better food in the dining room, while those down the social ladder, including household slaves, received lesser portions in the atrium (cf. first-class and coach seating on a modern jetliner). When Paul charges them with not discerning the body of Christ, this does not mean that they thought of the eucharistic bread and wine as merely normal food; they in fact seem to have had a "high" sacramental theology. What they failed to discern was the nature of the church as the body of Christ; as a result, they allowed conventional social patterns to prevail in the Christian community where all things had been made new (2 Cor 5:17). This problem of elitism carries over into the following discussion of spiritual gifts.

12:1–14:40 περὶ δέ (peri de *now concerning*) *Spiritual Gifts*

12:1–11 One Spirit, many gifts Paul addresses the Corinthian Christians as Gentiles who had been acquainted with spiritual phenomena prior to their conversion. Inspired speech, both intelligible (prophecy) and unintelligible (glossolalia) is a common denominator of all religion; such phenomena occur wherever people are intensely religious. The Corinthians' question concerned the relative value of such speech, directly inspired by the Spirit, compared with other gifts. Perhaps the question arose from an actual incident in Corinthian worship in which someone declared, "A curse on Jesus." Some understand this as the expression of hyperspiritual Christians who disdained the earthly Jesus in contrast to the exalted spiritual Christ.[7] Others consider it Paul's own hypothetical exaggeration illustrating what can and cannot be done in the name of the Spirit. *No one* who says, "A curse on Jesus," speaks by the Spirit; *everyone* who says the fundamental Christian confession, "Jesus is Lord," speaks by the Spirit, which does not belong to a spiritual elite but to the body of Christ as such. Not only those who have the sensational gifts of glossolalia and prophecy are inspired by the Spirit, but every baptized believer is energized by the Spirit for the common good by the Creator, whose Spirit energizes the universe (v. 6).

12:12–30 One body, many members Πνεῦμα (*pneuma*) means "wind," "breath," or "spirit," and is here incorporated into the metaphor of the body. Σῶμα (*sōma*, body) was a common metaphor in the Roman world for the body politic, sometimes used to encourage people in the lower strata of society to be content with their status, since this was necessary for the smooth functioning of society as a whole. In adopting and adapting this metaphor, Paul emphasizes equality, not privileged stratification. Moreover, Paul refers to the body of *Christ*, not the body of Christians; the church represents the continuing presence of Christ in

6. Cf. Gerd Theissen, *The Social Setting of Pauline Christianity: Essays on Corinth* (Philadelphia: Fortress Press, 1982).

7. See summary and bibliography of various options for interpreting this difficult text in Jouette M. Bassler, "1 Cor 12:3—Curse and Confession in Context," *JBL* 101, no. 3 (1982): 415–18.

the world. It is a living body, animated by the breath/Spirit. Just as each member of a human body participates in the life-giving breath because it is incorporated into the body, so individual Christians participate in the life of the Spirit by being incorporated into the body at baptism (12:13). "Member" thus means a functioning organ in a living body, not "membership" in the sense of having one's name on a list and paying one's dues.

In a human body, variety is not merely tolerated, but is necessary. Each member needs the others, and the body needs them all. In declaring the church to be the body of Christ, Paul states a fact; he does not urge an ideal. The Corinthians are to recognize what has already happened to them and to act accordingly. This includes affirming and valuing the contribution of those members who do not have the more spectacular gifts. Paul's list of spiritual gifts is not definitive or exhaustive. He does not catalogue "the" gifts of the Spirit, but gives illustrative lists that are not entirely consistent (12:8–11; 12:28–31; Rom 12:6–9). By here listing these gifts ranked in a certain order, Paul is not violating his affirmation of equality, but responding to the Corinthian situation. They had placed a priority on tongues; it is last on Paul's list.

12:31–13:13 The still more excellent way This famous passage is not an independent poem idealizing love in general. It is not a poem at all, but lyrical prose, praising love as the concrete expression of the Christian life in the midst of the conflicts of a first-century church that was fascinated with "spirituality" and "spiritual gifts."[8] The "more excellent way" does not denote a single gift that tops them all, but the all-embracing gift that is manifest in them all, transcending any of the particular gifts the Corinthians valued so highly. Without love, any other spiritual gift amounts to nothing (13:1–3). Such love acts in distinctive ways (13:4–7). Paul delineates the nature of Christian love by what it does and does not do, with fifteen action verbs—often obscured by English translations as a list of adjectives representing qualities or attitudes.[9] Such love is the ultimate gift, God's own love working its way through human lives. Unlike other gifts, which are temporary and provisional, such love lasts into the new age that is already dawning (13:8–13).

Paul also contrasts love with γνῶσις (*gnōsis*, knowledge), another gift valued by the Corinthians. He too claims to know, but only partially, ἐκ μέρους (*ek merous*, in fragments). Paul emphasizes that present knowledge of God and God's works, though real, inspired, and revealed, is nonetheless fragmentary and indirect, to be complete only at the eschaton.

14:1–40 Prophecy and tongues Paul's main point in this extended section is that, of the charismatic-speech gifts, prophecy is more valuable than tongues—thereby reversing the Corinthian evaluation. Paul emphasizes the corporate dimension of Christian existence and Christian worship. Tongues are not understood by the congregation; they edify the individual and should therefore be practiced in private. Prophecy, which is neither ordinary Christian preaching nor prediction of the future, but direct inspired speech, is more valuable than tongues because it is understandable by the congregation and thus strengthens and encourages

8. Some Corinthian Christians were especially enthralled by unintelligible glossolalia, which they understood not as other human languages but as the heavenly language of the angels—they already participated in the worship of the heavenly world (see 7:1; 11:2–6; 10). The *Testament of Job* (ca. 100 BCE–100 CE) refers to such ecstatic speech as "the language of angels."

9. Paul's elaboration of this point was necessary. Contrary to a popular tradition of interpretation, such love cannot be delineated merely by designating it as ἀγάπη (*agapē*) rather than some other Greek word for love. Ἀγάπη is used interchangeably with other Greek words for love (e.g., Wis. 8:2; John 5:20; 16:27; 21:15–17). It is found often in the Song of Solomon for sexual love. Ἀγάπη (*agapē*) and the cognate verb ἀγαπάω (*agapaō*) can be used in the "bad" sense (e.g., John 3:19; 2 Tim. 4:10; 2 Pet. 2:15). Christian love as active, unselfish care for others is a distinctive kind of love, but the distinction is not a matter of vocabulary.

the church. Though worship is directed to God, Paul is also concerned with the impression it leaves on visitors and outsiders: tongues will give the wrong impression and confirm outsiders in their unbelief, while prophecy may lead to their conversion (14:13–25). Thus here too, as in 5:1–13 and chapters 8–10, Paul is concerned to subordinate individual enjoyment of Christian freedom and "spiritual experiences" to the mission of the church.

The injunction that women keep silence in church (14:34–36) is now generally (but not universally) considered not to be Paul's own. He may be quoting the argument of male leaders in the Corinthian congregation, so that the words should be placed in quotation marks, as in 8:1, 4, 8 and 10:23. On this view, Paul quotes this view only to offer his rebuttal.[10] More likely, the words are a post-Pauline interpolation, added by later scribes to bring Paul's teaching into line with instructions later developed in the Pauline school, such as 1 Timothy 2:11–12.[11] Such considerations do not affect the status of these words as part of Holy Scripture for the Christian community but do affect how they are interpreted—not as Paul's own teaching, but the efforts of later Pauline teachers to adapt his instruction to later situations (see on Ephesians and the Pastorals).

When Paul concludes his discussion of charismatic speech with the solemn and emphatic command that the Corinthians acknowledge what he is writing to them as the Lord's command (14:37), this is not personal authoritarianism, but Paul's effort to help the church sort out the variety of claims to inspired speech. Paul believes that the risen Christ still directly addresses the church through inspired spokespersons, but warns against uncritical acceptance of prophetic messages delivered in worship, unless they are evaluated and received by the whole congregation (see on 1 John 4:1–3). The universal Christian confession (12:3) is one criterion by which such new revelations are to be tested; apostolic writings are another criterion. By making his own letters a norm by which the church may discern where the word of God is heard and where not, Paul here takes a decisive step in the formation of the canon, the Christian Bible.

15:1–58 The Resurrection

Here begins a new topic, introduced on Paul's own initiative, not one of their questions (see on 7:1). For Paul, the resurrection is not one topic among others but is foundational for Christian faith as such. While eschatology permeates his theology and his letters, he characteristically saves eschatological instruction for the final part of the body of his letters.

15:1–11 The resurrection of Jesus as the foundation and core of Christian faith As in 11:23, "handed on" and "received" are technical words adopted from the Jewish community for the transmission of sacred tradition. To those who doubt the resurrection (see v. 12), Paul reminds them that the original gospel he had proclaimed to them centered on Jesus' death and resurrection, and that he had taught them the early Christian creedal formulation he himself had been taught (15:3–5), presumably at his conversion. This early Christian creed thus goes back to the earliest days of Christianity, prior to 35 CE, and probably derives from the church at Jerusalem or Antioch (see §9.2.2). The list of appearances is not evidence Paul offers to convince unbelievers—neither here nor elsewhere does Paul attempt to prove the resurrection by

10. So, e.g., Paul J. Achtemeier, Joel B. Green, and Marianne Meye Thompson, *Introducing the New Testament: Its Literature and Theology* (Grand Rapids: Eerdmans, 2001), 346.
11. For evidence and arguments for this view, now widely accepted across the theological spectrum, see, e.g., Bart D. Ehrman, *Misquoting Jesus: The Story Behind Who Changed the Bible and Why* (San Francisco: HarperSanFrancisco, 2005); James D. G. Dunn, *Jesus and the Spirit* (Philadelphia: Westminster Press, 1975), 435; Gordon D. Fee, *The First Epistle to the Corinthians*, NICNT (Grand Rapids: Eerdmans, 1987), 699–708. Dunn, *Beginning from Jerusalem*, 824, now considers the passage to be original, Paul's instructions to wives of prophets not to participate in the congregational evaluation of prophecy.

evidence—but is intended to clarify for believers the nature of resurrection faith. In this paragraph, Paul is concerned to remind them that the resurrection of Jesus was fundamental to their own conversion, that it is traditional Christian faith, and that Paul's proclamation is in agreement with that of the other apostles and the church at large.

15:12–34 The future resurrection of all For Paul and the first generation of Christians, the resurrection was not a peculiar event that happened only to Jesus. The coming of the Christ and the resurrection were part of the eschatological events. Jesus' resurrection was the initial instance of the general resurrection, the first sheaf of the full harvest soon to come (15:20). Those in Corinth who denied the resurrection were not necessarily denying the general idea of life after death. What they rejected was the idea that God raises dead *bodies*, which sounded crude within the framework of sophisticated pagan philosophy. The standard Greek view was dualistic—the mortal body dies, but the inner spirit, the real person, does not die, but leaves the mortal shell in which it is encased and is released to eternal life in the spiritual world.

The standard Jewish view, taken over by Christianity, was not dualistic, but saw the human person in holistic terms. The whole person, the unity of body and soul, was the creation of God but was not immortal. When the person died, there was no immortal "part" that survived. The person's hope was not in a theory of the immortality of the soul, but in the act of God who raises the dead. Paul regards the whole matter from his Jewish Christian perspective, in which to deny the resurrection meant to deny the reality of hope beyond the grave. Paul's argument weaves back and forth between Jesus' past resurrection and the believer's future resurrection. In each case, there is a real death, beyond which the only hope is in the act of God, who raises the dead. That Jesus really died is necessary for the truth of gospel; Jesus' death on the cross was not a sham death in which Jesus' immortal soul was released, but the death of *Jesus*. God's act in raising up Jesus involved both Jesus and "all." The Adam/Christ typology in 15:22 begins in the exclusive sense of "all in Christ," not "all humans"; but the comparison with Adam is already moving from the exclusive sense "all in Christ" to the inclusive sense "in Christ all," which Paul will elaborate in Romans 5:12–21.

15:35–58 The resurrection of the body The point of this whole section is that future existence of resurrected believers in the transcendent world of God will be neither the continuation of the flesh-and-blood existence of this world nor the ghostly "spiritual" existence of disembodied spirits, but will involve an *unimaginable* transformation. Christian hope involves the "redemption *of* our bodies" along with the whole creation (Rom 8:23), not escape *from* them. In the whole discussion, "body" means something like "person," the whole self, as in "somebody," "anybody," and the colloquial American "what's a body to do?"

The Corinthian "spiritualists" issued the challenge: "How are the dead raised?" This was not a request for information, but the rhetorical question of those who see the body as the barrier that stood between them and their entering into the purely spiritual existence they already experienced. Paul's response, "Fool!" is not mere frustration, nor intended to indicate the intellectual level of the questioner. In biblical parlance, the fool is the arrogant one, the one who fails to take God into account, the one who lives as though all issues must be settled in terms of his or her own intelligence—which may, in fact, be quite high (Pss 14:1; 92:6). In the science of Paul's time, his analogy of the seed that becomes a flower (15:36–38) is not a matter of "natural" transformation, but of God's act in giving the seed a new "body," a new form of existence. In his worldview, act of God, not natural process, is the point. Looking at a seed, one could never imagine a flower.

Thus for Paul the gap between life in this world and the form of life in the age to come is beyond our power to imagine. The resurrected person ("body") is not flesh and blood (15:50), but a "spiritual body." This does not mean a body composed of spirit instead of flesh, but something like "a self constituted by God's transcendent power, the Spirit," a "self" that we have no way of imagining. Paul's point is that human minds cannot grasp the nature of transcendent reality into which we are taken by God's act at the resurrection; nonetheless the resurrected person shares in the power of God's transcendent world, just as the present earthly body shares in the weakness of this world.

When he wrote 1 Corinthians, Paul still expected to be alive at the parousia (15:51; cf. 1 Thess 4:15–17). The whole discussion focuses not on the fate of individuals, but on the final triumphal coming of God's kingdom, when all the powers that enslave human life will be destroyed (sin, law, death). The section concludes in thanksgiving and worship, grateful praise to the God of hope who makes it possible to live in hope and confidence, knowing that service to such a God is not in vain (15:56–58).

16:1–24 Concluding Instructions and Greetings

16:1–4 **περὶ δέ (peri de *now concerning*) *The offering*** Paul was engaged in gathering a substantial offering from the predominately Gentile churches of Galatia, Asia Minor, Macedonia, and Greece for the poor among the Jerusalem Christians. The offering was intended not only to relieve the poverty of needy people, but to serve as a symbol of unity between Jewish and Gentile Christians (Rom 15:25–32; 2 Cor 8–9; Gal 2:10) and to represent the eschatological pilgrimage of the nations to Zion, who would bring gifts to the holy city as part of the eschatological drama (see Isa 2:2–3; 45:14; 60:5–7, 10–14). It was Paul's part of the arrangement made at the Jerusalem Council that represented the endorsement of his Gentile mission by the Jerusalem church (Gal 2:10); he was passionately devoted to fulfilling this act as the climax and validation of his mission and the unity of the church.

Paul's reference to the first day of the week (Sunday) as the regular meeting day of Christians is the earliest such reference. The seventh day (Saturday) was the Jewish Sabbath. Sunday did not become a holiday for the culture at large until after Constantine, in the fourth century. The first Christians met on a "workday," before or after their work.

16:5–11 Travel plans Paul writes from Ephesus, in the spring of 54 CE, prior to Pentecost (see "Chronology," §13.3.3). He plans to arrive in Corinth late the next fall, spending some months en route through Macedonia, and then winter in Corinth. Paul is worried that Timothy, his representative, might not be well received (16:10). Paul's own next visit, which he does not here envisage, turned out to be a disaster (2 Cor 1:1–11; 7:12).

16:12 **περὶ δέ (peri de *now concerning*) *Possible visit of Apollo*** Apollos is a respected colleague, but not a subordinate who acts at Paul's behest.

16:13–24 Final messages and greetings In these closing comments, Paul incidentally mentions churches in Jerusalem, Galatia, Macedonia, Asia, and Ephesus, another reminder that the Corinthians are not an independent congregation, but are part of a network of churches that is becoming worldwide. The letter concludes with five elements that later became standard items in the liturgy, indicating that Paul anticipated the letter being read in worship, probably just prior to the celebration of the Eucharist: (1) the *holy kiss*, (2) the *anathema* (the solemn ritual pronouncement against those who pervert the life and message of the church), (3) the *Maranatha* invocation, praying for the Lord's presence at the Eucharist and for his final parousia, (4) the *blessing* "grace and peace be with you," and (5) the final *amen*.

12.2 Interpreting 2 Corinthians

THE PLACE OF 1 CORINTHIANS WITHIN THE narrative framework of Paul's Aegean ministry is relatively clear. This is not the case for 2 Corinthians, since our perception of the sequence of events in Paul's interaction with the Corinthian Christians after he left Corinth depends on judgments regarding the literary unity of 2 Corinthians. Before continuing the story, we must first discuss whether 2 Corinthians is a single letter or an editorial combination of more than one letter.

EXCURSUS 1

The Unity of 2 Corinthians and Partition Theories of the Pauline Letters

THERE IS NO DOUBT THAT THE EXTANT PAULINE CORPUS is the product of editorial work after the individual letters left Paul's hands (see above §2.3). This fact has generated various hypotheses as to the nature and extent of this editing. It certainly included adding titles to the documents and arranging them in some order, just as it included combining the individual letters into a single corpus. Did this editorial process also include combining more than one of Paul's letters or surviving fragments into a single letter? Such partition theories have been proposed in regard to almost all the Pauline letters. The most persistent and important questions have revolved around 1 and 2 Corinthians, Philippians, and 1 Thessalonians. Since the strongest case for partition theories has been made in regard to 2 Corinthians, we here explore the evidence and arguments for and against the original unity of the letter in some detail. If the case for partition can be sustained here, the possibility for editorial combination in other letters is enhanced. If 2 Corinthians is judged to be an original unity, it is likely that this is the case for the other letters as well.

This excursus has multiple purposes.

1. This will enable the student to appreciate the complexity of the issue and see the relative strength and weaknesses of the various proposals, without supposing that they can be quickly summarized or dismissed.

2. This will help to see something of the history of the problem, which has been studied and discussed in laborious detail by numerous scholars in broad streams of scholarship. Partition theories are not merely idiosyncratic proposals of a particular recent scholar.

3. By focusing on the details of one historical issue, the student has the opportunity to reflect on the nature of the Christian faith as the revelation of God in history, and on the related theological implications of studying the Bible historically. The issue might be stated as follows: Does the nature of the Christian faith itself constitute a call to study the Bible historically, and to accept the resultant relative certainty and ambiguity? Or can responsible study of the Bible ignore such issues as irrelevant, or claim to settle them dogmatically, in terms of what one's theology or ideology requires? A grasp of the issue requires some painstaking study. Since we cannot go into such detail on the literary unity of every New Testament book, we here provide a fairly extensive sample of this type of study by examining 2 Corinthians, and will then make only brief references to similar issues in other letters.

4. The question of the literary unity of 2 Corinthians not only has historical and literary dimensions, but poses a significant theological issue, in that it presses the question of whether we suppose we receive the New Testament documents directly from their presumed authors or from the hands of the church through the transmission of Christian tradition.

Is 2 Corinthians an original unity?

What at first may appear to be a yes-or-no issue turns out to be more complex. Neither the affirmation nor the denial of the "unity" of 2 Corinthians is meaningful without a clarification of terms, since "unity" in such cases is not a univocal term. The claim that 2 Corinthians is a single letter cannot mean that it was written all at one sitting. The length alone and the manner of ancient letter writing (see §10.2.2) exclude that. It must, in any case, have been written over a period of some days. When considered from the perspective of the writing of the letter, the issue is then whether the author saw the document as a single letter, composed according to a single plan. *The issue is clarified by regarding it from the viewpoint of the recipients: even if 2 Corinthians were written over a period of some days or even weeks, was it received by the Corinthian readers on one occasion as a single letter in its present form, or did they receive a series of letters that were later combined into a single document?*

Chapters 10–13

Since the issue of the unity of 2 Corinthians has most often focused on whether 10:1–13:13 was originally part of the same letter as chapters 1–9, we begin with the arguments that have been given for regarding chapters 10–13 as part of a separate letter:

1. *Different tone.* Chapters 10–13 have such a different tone from that of the preceding chapters that it is difficult to regard them as part of the same letter. Chapters 1–9 express the joy and relief of the apostle who is now back on good terms with the congregation he has founded, and speaks repeatedly of their comfort (7:4, 6–7, 13), joy (7:4, 7, 9, 13b), earnestness (7:7, 11, 12), and obedience (7:15), and his confidence (7:16) and pride (7:4) in them. Chapters 10–13, on the other hand, are filled with recrimination and sarcasm, repeatedly expressing Paul's frustration and anger. Their obedience is not complete (10:6); they do not love him adequately (12:15b), and they suspect that he does not love them (11:11; cf. 12:13). They are turning toward a different gospel (11:2–4). In 7:8–12, they have repented, and their repentance is copiously analyzed; in 12:20 they still need to repent. The numerous contrasts between chapters 10–13 and the rest of 2 Corinthians can best be appreciated by the reader's making a two-column chart comparing the details of these two sections. The following samples could be multiplied:

1:24 you stand firm in the faith.	13:5 Examine yourselves to see whether you are living in the faith.
7:4 I often boast about you; I have great pride in you; I am filled with consolation; I am overjoyed in all our affliction.	10:2 I ask that when I am present I need not show boldness by daring to oppose those who think we are acting according to human standards.
7:16 I rejoice, because I have complete confidence in you.	11:3 But I am afraid that as the serpent deceived Eve by its cunning, your thoughts will be led astray from a sincere and pure devotion to Christ.
8:7 Now as you excel in everything—in faith, in speech, in knowledge, in utmost eagerness, and in our love for you—so we want you to excel also in this generous undertaking.	12:20 For I fear that when I come, I may find you not as I wish, and that you may find me not as you wish; I fear that there may perhaps be quarreling, jealousy, anger, selfishness, slander, gossip, conceit, and disorder.

2. The same vocabulary is used differently in the two major sections. For instance, in chapters 1–9 Paul repeatedly uses the καυχάομαι word group (*kauchaomai*, boast, have confidence in, be proud of) in a positive sense of his relation to the Corinthians: he has confidence in them and they in him, he is proud of them (2 Cor 1:12, 14; 5:12; 7:4, 14; 8:24; 9:2–3). In chapters 10–13, the same set of words is used consistently in a negative, sarcastic, and ironic manner (2 Cor 10:8, 13, 15, 16, 17; 11:10, 12, 16–18, 30; 12:1, 5–6, 9). This suggests that the later letter (2 Cor 1–9) attempts to

remove some of the sting from the harsh use of these words in the earlier letter (2 Cor 10–13).

3. There are key syntactical differences between the two sections. In chapters 1–9, the first person plural predominates, while chapters 10–13 are written primarily in the first person singular mode. This shift is not found in any other Pauline letter.

4. The two major sections of the letter reflect two different situations in Corinth.

   — In 7:7–16 the Corinthian Christians support the Pauline gospel. In 10:1–11 they support Paul's rivals.

   — In chapter 8, the delegation from Ephesus has not yet arrived. In chapter 12, Paul's coworkers from Ephesus are already at work in Corinth.

5. There are other major discontinuities between chapters 1–9 and chapters 10–13:

   — Chapters 8–9, if part of the same letter, encourage the Corinthians to give generously to the offering for Jerusalem Paul is administering. The sarcasm and bitterness of chapters 10–13 would nullify this appeal. Titus's task would hardly have been possible if he were supposed to organize and promote a collection while bearing a letter that included chapters 10–13.

   — In 8:11 and 9:2, 12–15, Paul praises them and gives thanks for their response; in 12:16–18 they accuse him of taking advantage of them.

   — In 8:16–17, the Corinthians consider Titus reliable; in 12:17–18, both Titus and Paul are suspect.

6. The two sections project different narrative worlds. The references to Titus's visit(s) to Corinth do not all seem to fit into one letter. In chapters 1–9, Titus has previously made only one trip to Corinth, alone; in 12:18a, there is a reference to a second trip by Titus, with a famous brother.

Considerations such as these have convinced most scholars that chapters 10–13 of 2 Corinthians were not written at the same time as the preceding chapters. This means, of course, that our present New Testament document is the product of an editorial process that joined parts of letters written by Paul at different times; this immediately raises the question: if the original unity of 2 Corinthians is no longer assumed, are there parts of other letters that can be recognized, in addition to the separation of chapters 10–13? Chapters 10–13 is itself a unity, and there have been no proposals to find elements of more than one letter in this section (with the possible exception of the concluding 13:11–13; see below). But are chapters 1–9 an original unity?

Chapters 8–9

Critical scholarship has long noted that chapters 8 and 9 stand out from their context: 8:1 does not follow naturally from 7:16, and there is a sharp break between 9:15 and 10:1. If chapter 8 had been written to follow chapter 7, it is difficult to understand, for example, why there is no mention in chapter 7 of Titus's willingness to return to Corinth, and why chapter 8 gives no indication that he has just arrived from there. Likewise, different pictures of the situation among the Macedonian churches are given in chapters 7 and 8. In the former, Paul is concerned about the disputes (see μάχαι, *machai*, 7:5), but 8:1–5 portrays a much more positive scene, suggesting that some time intervened between the composition of the two chapters. Furthermore, 9:1 seems to be a fresh beginning, introducing the topic of the collection as though it had not been the subject of the whole preceding section. Even a superficial reading with the question in mind indicates that chapter 9 is *parallel* to chapter 8, rather than *following* it logically—we have an item by item duplication of the preceding chapter, not a development from it. Detailed syntactical and rhetorical analysis seems to confirm that each chapter manifests the rhetorical structure of an independent letter, complete in itself.[12] That chapters 8 and 9 represent two

12. Cf. esp. Hans Dieter Betz, *2 Corinthians 8 and 9: A Commentary on Two Administrative Letters of the Apostle Paul*, Hermeneia (Philadelphia: Fortress Press, 1985), and the extensive bibliography he provides. The rhetorical

different letters is also suggested by the tensions between them: in chapter 9, the Corinthians are eagerly participating in the collection, so that Paul can boast about them to the Macedonians; in chapter 8, their interest seems to have lagged and needs to be rekindled. Such evidence has convinced several scholars that chapters 8 and 9 were originally composed as brief, separate letters written to facilitate the collection of the offering for Jerusalem among the churches of Achaia, of which the Corinthian church was the principal congregation.

2:14–7:4

A clear break in the line of thought occurs at 2:14. Paul has been describing his deep distress at what had happened to him in Ephesus, and his anxiety about what was happening in the Corinthian church. He goes to meet Titus as he returns from Corinth with the report; not finding him in Troas, he proceeds into Macedonia, looking for Titus on the route he will surely take. Then the narrative is abruptly dropped, and we find an extensive, profoundly theological defense of Paul's apostleship, which continues until 7:4. At this point, the happy reunion with Titus in Macedonia is finally recounted. Many readers have noticed how well 7:5 connects with 2:13; if one skips the intervening material, not only is it not missed, but the letter now makes better sense. Furthermore, the thanksgiving and description of Paul as a condemned prisoner being led along in a triumphal procession of 2:14–17 is a mind-wrenching picture that is very difficult to understand as related to the preceding paragraph, and the transition from 7:4 to 7:5 is equally problematic.

Most importantly, the situation presupposed in 2:14–7:4 and Paul's relation to the Corinthian community are in conflict with the rest of 1:1–7:16, so that 2:14–7:4 appears as a discrete section, the "First Apology." In this section, Paul is passionately defending his understanding of apostleship and contrasting it with that of his rivals, trying to convince the Corinthian church of his view. There are several allusions to conflicts (2:17; 3:1; 4:2–3; 5:12), reflecting the discord between Paul (and his followers within the congregation) and those who understand church and apostleship differently. Unlike the sarcastic anger of chapters 10–13, in 2:14–7:4 Paul is still trying to reason with the Corinthians, attempting to provide a positive theological argument that will convince them to remain with or return to his understanding of the gospel. In 5:20, "be reconciled to God" is addressed to the Corinthians. This challenge is difficult to understand in any place in the chronology, but can hardly have been in his final letter to them. Already in the First Apology, Paul pleads for them to be reconciled to God, to each other, and to himself.

All this, however, is also in contrast with the section that frames 2:14–7:4, in which the conflict is over, the church has rejected the rival leadership, and is so firmly back on Paul's side that it is in danger of overreacting and punishing the opposition too severely (1:3–7; 2:5–11; 7:5–16). The framework is a joyful letter of reconciliation; in the inserted section, the battle is still underway and seems inappropriate in a letter of reconciliation. In addition, the image of Paul in 2:14 is that of the conquered victim at the end of the triumphal parade, who will be executed at its conclusion. This is Paul's own ironic cruciform theology of Christian ministry. The present context and meaning in 2 Corinthians, however, reflects the post-Pauline editor's view that the life and mission of Paul were a triumphal march of the gospel from east to west, a view also found in *1 Clement* and Acts.[13] Thus, to many scholars, 2:14–7:4 appears to be part of a different letter that has been secondarily inserted into its present framework.

6:14–7:1

Like the First Apology (2:14–7:4), of which it is a part in the present form of the text, this brief

argument is double-edged, however. J. D. H. Amador, "Revisiting 2 Corinthians: Rhetoric and the Case for Unity," *NTS* 46 (2000): 92–111 argues for unity of the whole letter on the basis of its rhetorical structure.

13. Cf. further in Richard I. Pervo, *Dating Acts: Between the Evangelists and the Apologists* (Santa Rosa, CA: Polebridge Press, 2006), 319–21.

polemical paragraph is inappropriate in the larger context of a letter of reconciliation. It also stands out from its immediate context, interrupting the train of thought, so that 6:13 is followed naturally by 7:2. This paragraph represents a different critical issue than the preceding discussions, however. Here scholarly questions have been raised, concerning not only whether it originally was a part of the letter, but whether Paul wrote it at all. There is a density of non-Pauline vocabulary—nine words in this brief section not found elsewhere in any Pauline writing,[14] including a different word for Satan. There are also phrases that contrast with Paul's customary usage, such as καθὼς εἶπεν ὁ θεός (*kathōs eipen ho theos*, as God said). Some of Paul's theological vocabulary, reflecting his own deep-seated theological conceptuality, is used in a non-Pauline (or even anti-Pauline) way. When referring to Christian believers, Paul always uses πιστεύων (*pisteuōn*), the participle of the word for faith. In 6:15, however, he uses the adjective πιστός (*pistos*), which he elsewhere only uses in the sense of "faithful, trustworthy."

The imperative of 7:1 presents two further examples: (1) Paul never elsewhere indicates that believers have it in their own power to "cleanse themselves from defilement," or to "perfect themselves in holiness," which might easily be understood as the kind of works righteousness Paul opposed. (2) Likewise, "flesh and spirit" (σάρχ, *sarx,* body, NRSV) is used in a non-Pauline way. For Paul, flesh and spirit are opposing realities of the transcendent world, force fields in which the Christian life is lived. The flesh is the suprapersonal power of sin, as the Spirit is the suprapersonal power of God that delivers from sin. It is difficult to see Paul as calling for Christians to "cleanse" flesh and spirit; the flesh cannot be "cleansed," and the spirit has no need of cleansing. In any case, the general tenor of the passage seems to be fundamentally un-Pauline, for Paul does not call for Christians to separate themselves from unbelievers, but to live responsibly among them. The passage manifests several other un-Pauline features, and in some ways is closer to the vocabulary and conceptuality of the Qumran community than to Paul's own letters (see the technical commentaries for details). Thus, while many have explained the textual data as the insertion by a post-Pauline editor of a non-Pauline fragment, others have seen Paul himself as incorporating at this point a traditional unit he did not himself compose but found helpful for his argument. However the phenomena are explained, the text does not seem to fit well into this context in 2 Corinthians.

1:1–2:13; 7:5–16; 13:11–13

Finally, it has been argued that when all the inserted materials have been removed, we have a coherent letter of reconciliation, Paul's letter to Corinth after receiving the good news from Titus that the church had repented and returned to the Pauline gospel, his last writing to them prior to his final visit. In the various partition theories, this letter provided the framework into which a later editor inserted elements from other Pauline letters (and the un-Pauline fragment 6:14–7:1) to produce our present canonical 2 Corinthians.

Can a probable historical order be established?

We now can see that establishing a chronology for the Corinthian correspondence depends on one's judgment as to how many letters are involved. If 2 Corinthians is a unity, then Paul wrote four letters to Corinth, and 2 Corinthians in its entirety is the last letter Paul wrote to Corinth:

First, founding visit to Corinth

- Letter A, mentioned in 1 Cor 5:9 (lost)
- Letter B, our 1 Corinthians

Second visit to Corinth (2 Cor 2:1; 13:2)

- Letter C, the Severe Letter mentioned in 2 Cor 2:2–4; 7:8 (lost)

14. "Mismatched" (ἑτεροζυγοῦντες, *heterozygountes*); "partnership" (μετοχή, *metochē*); "agreement" (συμφώνησις, *sumphōnēsis*); "Beliar" (Βελιάρ, *Beliar*); "agreement" (συγκατάθεσις, *sygkatathesis*); "walk" (ἐμπεριπατέω, *emperipateō*); "welcome" (εἰσδέχομαι, *eisdechomai*); "Almighty" (παντοκράτωρ, *pantokratōr*). It should be noted that three of the nine words are from a Scripture citation, which does not agree with the LXX.

Letter D, our 2 Corinthians

A number of scholars defend the unity of 2 Corinthians, and therefore the traditional chronology, on critical grounds,[15] with the following arguments:

1. The burden of proof is on those who affirm partition theories, and they have not proven their case. In all historical study, the traditional view should be affirmed unless there is proof to the contrary. Second Corinthians appears in the New Testament and in all manuscripts as a single document. This principle was already enunciated by Johannes Weiss in 1917: "In spite of everything, however, we should at least have got to the point that it should be considered an axiom that a document must be read in the sense and in the form in which it stands until *proof* is brought forward that this is *impossible*" (my emphasis).[16]

   This approach, however, inherently has a double problem: (1) Defenders of any traditional view will always win the argument on this basis, for it can always be claimed that positive proof has not been presented to the contrary. (2) What can be considered "absolute proof" remains a subjective judgment, as is clear from the opposite conclusions of Weiss and Schnelle: Weiss considered 2 Corinthians an editorial composition of four different letters; Schnelle makes a strong argument for its unity.

2. The jeopardy of the slippery slope is sometimes offered as an argument for unity; that is, once the unity of the document is surrendered, partition theories open the door to all sorts of excesses. Schmithals, for example, has found a total of thirteen letters in the Corinthian correspondence.[17] Practically all scholars consider this excessive, far exceeding the evidence, but the slippery-slope principle argues that the only sure protection against such excesses is never to venture onto the slope in the first place. Historical method, however, must take the risk and attempt to avoid extreme theories that exceed the evidence. This is best done by critical discussion of proposed results, not by a priori prohibitions. The basic issue in such studies is whether one examines the evidence and then postulates the most plausible theory to account for the data.

3. The difficulty in regarding 2 Corinthians as a unified composition has been exaggerated. More careful historical exegesis is able to show continuities of thought where partition theories have seen only disjunctions.

4. Some differences and tensions within 2 Corinthians are obvious, but these can better be understood as Paul's addressing more than one situation in the letter. Thus Matera argues (reflecting Bieringer, et al.) that in chapter 7

   > Paul is dealing with two crises, one that has already been resolved (the crisis of the painful visit and the offender) and another that has not yet been resolved (the crisis occasioned by the presence of intruding apostles and the continuing problem of immorality) but that Paul hopes to settle by appealing to the goodwill generated by the repentance of the Corinthians for their role in the first crisis.[18]

   Analogously, Schnelle can argue that the differences between chapters 8 and 9 are due to Paul's addressing the Corinthians proper in chapter 8, but the other churches in Achaia in chapter 9. (This, however, is also used as an argument for regarding chapters 8 and 9 as originally separate letters.)

5. The alleged editorial process for producing 2 Corinthians is too speculative and difficult to imagine. There are indeed difficulties here, for

15. The most helpful, fair, and thorough case for the unity of 2 Corinthians is the collection of essays by Reimund Bieringer and Jan Lambrecht, eds., *Studies on 2 Corinthians*, BETL 112 (Louvain: University Press, 1994).

16. Weiss, *Earliest Christianity*, 153. This line of argument is affirmed most recently by Schnelle, *Paul*, 237–45.

17. Walter Schmithals, *Die Briefe des Paulus in ihrer ursprünglichen Form*, Zürcher Werkkommentare zur Bibel (Zürich: Theologischer Verlag, 1984), 19–85.

18. Frank J. Matera, *II Corinthians: A Commentary*, NTL (Louisville, KY: Westminster John Knox Press, 2003), 30.

the redactor must be imagined as eliminating the beginnings and conclusions of all but one letter, and of making insertions at points in the text for which there seems to be no clear reason. The First Apology (2:14–7:4) is inserted into the middle of Paul's report of his meeting with Titus, and then *it* receives an insertion (6:14–7:1) that is difficult to explain.

Advocates of partition theories respond that the same difficulties apply if one affirms a unified composition, but then Paul himself must be responsible for the awkward transitions. The logical disjunctions are then explained as Pauline digressions rather than editorial insertions, or as responding to new reports from Corinth after part of the letter had already been written. Recent advocates of the unity of 2 Corinthians have taken up this challenge, and have presented various scenarios that allow Paul to have composed 2 Corinthians as a single document. The grandfather of such theories is Lietzmann's famous comment that the change in tone between chapters 1–9 and chapters 10–13 is the result of a "sleepless night" after Paul's having already dictated chapters 1–9. Recent explanations are more elaborate, portraying the composition of 2 Corinthians as an incremental process that lasts some weeks as Paul journeys through Macedonia after meeting Titus. He is interrupted, goes off on tangents, begins afresh, and both repeats himself and gives new versions of what he has already said. He then receives new information from Corinth: the reconciliation reported by Titus that evoked the beginning of the letter has turned out to be premature, and the church is following the rival missionaries. This stirs up Paul to write the angry and sarcastic concluding chapters.[19]

A major difficulty with this scenario is that it is Paul himself who sends off the letter with the harsh conclusion appended to the tender letter of reconciliation, which now no longer applies. How should we imagine the Corinthian readers as having understood this letter, supposedly composed over an extended time by Paul in varying moods, but which they received as a single communication that addresses them in conflicting ways? A further difficulty is that on this hypothesis, the last picture we receive from Paul's letter is that of an alienated church in rebellion, while the next picture we have from Paul's letters is that he is comfortably at home in Corinth as he makes his future plans and composes the letter to the Romans (Rom 15:19–16:27). Regarding the letter as a unity thus makes difficulties for understanding the chronology of Paul's relation with the Corinthian church. The following proposed chronology, based on one variation of the partition hypothesis, provides a more plausible construction of this history. To the extent that it is persuasive, the chronology constructed on this basis is itself an argument for the partition theory.

Chronology of Paul's Corinthian Correspondence: A Proposal

In 1 Thessalonians, our earliest New Testament document, Paul and his coworkers are in Corinth, writing to the new congregation in Thessalonica. If we restrict ourselves to the information in Paul's letters, when we next catch sight of Paul's contact with the Corinthians, he is in Ephesus, writing back to the Corinthian church some three years after writing 1 Thessalonians, about two years after leaving Corinth (1 Cor 16:8).

Paul refers to four different letters he wrote to the Corinthians during this period. Two letters are thus either lost or partially incorporated in extant letters. The possibility that 2 Corinthians is composite then opens the door to postulating even more than four letters from Paul to Corinth. This possibility, in turn, opens the door to several different constructions of the events between 1 Corinthians and the final form of 2 Corinthians. The following chronology of Paul's relations with the Corinthian church seems to the present writer to be the most plausible construction:

1. The founding of the church by Paul (and Timothy and Silvanus?) (1 Cor 1:14, 2:1, see Acts 18:1–17)

19. For more detailed versions of this scenario, which the authors acknowledge to be speculative, see, e.g., Schnelle, *New Testament Writings*, 79–90; Dunn, *Beginning from Jerusalem*, 842–57.

Paul becomes closely acquainted with Prisca and Aquila, and they become his coworkers in Corinth (Acts 18:2–3). Paul considers himself the sole "father" of the church (1 Cor 4:14–16).

Paul has an effective ministry in Corinth for at least a year and a half (Acts 18:11).

Paul leaves Corinth and (after a trip to Jerusalem and Antioch?) works in Ephesus (1 Cor 16:8; Acts 18:18–19:40).

2. Apollos and advocates of Petrine Christianity visit Corinth (1 Cor 1:12, 3:4–6, 11, 22, 4:6; cf. Acts 18:24-19:1).

   These visits occur while Paul is in Ephesus, or en route from Syria back to Ephesus.

   Does the Petrine group already introduce the issue of authentic apostleship, advocating a more official apostolic office, already representing the countermission, or perhaps just a more Antioch/Petrine understanding of apostleship in continuity with Jerusalem-Antioch? Do these visits result in some suspicion of Paul?

   Henceforth, Paul will be struggling on two related fronts: locally, to help the church to be an authentic church, understanding its faith and living a life appropriate to the gospel; and ecumenically, to understand its relation to the apostolic faith, to the wider church and its mission.

3. Apollos joins Paul in Ephesus (1 Cor 16:12).

   Apollos presumably brought news to Ephesus from Corinth, a factor in Paul's letters to them.

4. Paul writes LETTER A (1 Cor 5:9).

   This letter was presumably written from Ephesus (1 Cor 16:8).

   Unless a fragment of it in is preserved in 2 Corinthians 6:14–7:1, this letter is now lost.

5. The Corinthians send a letter to Paul, which included a list of questions (1 Cor 7:1), and Paul hears oral reports from Corinth about matters they had not reported in their letter (1 Cor 1:11, 16:17).

   Their questions are not merely from curiosity, nor are the Corinthians simply asking for instruction. There is already some conflict at Corinth, and, in the earliest extant correspondence with Corinth, Paul himself is already suspect there.

   Paul receives reports from "Chloe's people" (slaves, business associates, or employees), and from the bearers of the letter, Stephanas, Fortunatus, Achaicus.

   Paul urges Apollos to visit Corinth, but he is unwilling (1 Cor 16:12).

6. Paul writes LETTER B—our 1 Corinthians (54 or 55 CE, from Ephesus, 16:8)

7. Timothy visits Corinth and returns to Paul.

   Timothy and 1 Corinthians seem to have been well received (1 Cor 4:17, 16:10; 2 Cor 1:1; cf. Acts 19:22).

   Timothy may have been sent in advance of Paul's letter, or 1 Corinthians 4:17 may be an epistolary aorist, with Timothy as the bearer of the letter.

8. Fresh difficulties arise at Corinth: suspicions of Paul's apostolate become more open and problematical.

   It is not clear whether this occurs as the internal tensions within the church heat up, or whether there are rival missionaries already visiting Corinth.

9. Paul sends Titus back to Corinth instead of coming himself.

   For some reason(s) Paul changed his original plans to come to Corinth from Ephesus shortly after Pentecost (1 Cor 16:5–7), and sent Titus instead, with instructions about the collection (2 Cor 2:13–17; 8:6–23). (This visit of Titus is different and earlier than the one mentioned in 2 Cor 7:6.) Paul learns from Timothy and/or Titus of the new difficulties in Corinth.

10. Paul sends a letter dealing with the offering, and sensitive to the issue of apostleship (LETTER C, 2 Cor 8, our earliest fragment of 2 Corinthians).

The similar vocabulary, imagery, and concerns to that of 1 Corinthians suggest that this letter was written as a follow-up to 1 Corinthians (this is not the case for the rest of 2 Corinthians, which makes little reference to 1 Corinthians and uses new vocabulary and imagery). First Corinthians, written from Ephesus, had already dealt with both offering and apostleship.

The Corinthians had begun the collection the previous year, and now need to complete it.

This letter is not only about the offering, but manifests some sensitivity on the issue of apostleship, though this is not yet a critical issue, and Paul addresses the congregation in a cooperative spirit.

Paul is sending Titus, the famous brother, and another brother.

11. The challenge to Paul's apostleship intensifies; Paul becomes increasingly aware of the problem and responds with LETTER D (2 Cor 2:14-7:4, the First Apology).

Paul does not yet perceive the situation as critical and tries to persuade the Corinthians by explaining the nature of true apostleship that corresponds to the cross.

Already 1 Corinthians had indicated some suspicion against Paul's apostleship in Corinth, perhaps related to the Petrine group, and offers a mild defense of Paul's apostleship. Now, in the First Apology, the questions are sharper and are more persistent, and there is a sense of some alienation. Paul writes passionately about God's reconciliation of the world in Christ and pleads with the Corinthians to be reconciled. Paul makes a full defense of the nature of true apostleship. Already, "letters of recommendation," "death," and "life" are buzz words. This probably means that the false apostles with their letters have already arrived, but Paul does not yet realize how polarized the situation has become.

The first reference to the rivals is the τινες (*tines* =some; certain people) 3:1, who have letters of recommendation. In 2 Corinthians 5:12, "those who boast in outward appearance and not in heart" are already present, the same as "some" who have letters of recommendation.

The First Apology is more a defense of his own apostleship than an attack on the new "apostles." Paul does not perceive the seriousness of the new situation until his visit.

12. Paul makes the painful visit—not in Acts (2 Cor 2:1, 5–8; 7:12; 12:14; 13:1).

Paul makes a trip to Corinth to try to bring the church back into the orbit of the Pauline mission. He is grossly wronged, insulted, and humiliated by someone (local? visiting missionary?) and leaves Corinth in defeat. We do not know the nature of this event, but it hurt Paul deeply. Only during the painful visit does the situation explode, and Paul responds explosively in 2 Corinthians 10–13. The incident included a controversy with/about the newly arrived "apostles," but may not have been limited to this issue. The one who wronged Paul was apparently aligned with the rival apostles/missionaries, but the confrontation may have involved more than claims to apostolic authority.[20]

Paul finally perceives the claims and nature of the new "apostles." These newcomers are not differing colleagues, like Apollos and Peter, but "false apostles" who "make slaves" of them (2 Cor 11:4, 12–15, 20–23), ministers of Satan (11:15). They are Jewish Christian missionaries who regard Paul's missionary churches as defective and in need of correction. There had been

20. Margaret Thrall discusses the several possibilities and suggests that there was a theft of some of the offering money, that the purported thief denied the charge, that it was Paul's word against his, and that the church did not stand by Paul. Unable to take action against the man he suspected, Paul returned to Ephesus and wrote the angry letter, now lost (Margaret E. Thrall, *A Critical and Exegetical Commentary on the Second Epistle to the Corinthians*, 2 vols., ICC [Edinburgh: T. & T. Clark, 1994], 68–69). This, of course, is at least as speculative as the theories she rejects. Dunn, *Beginning from Jerusalem*, 831, likewise lists several possibilities and says we are "in the dark," "hopelessly unclear."

internal suspicions of the legitimacy of Paul's apostolate; these are now fanned into a flame by the newcomers. The (majority of the) Corinthian Christians respond favorably to the new teachers.

13. Paul writes LETTER E—the Severe Letter (2 Cor 10–13; see 2:1–4, 9; 7:8–12).

After Paul's painful visit to Corinth, he returned to Ephesus and wrote an angry letter, which he sent back to Corinth with Titus (or perhaps ahead of him). While we know that Paul sent this letter, we cannot be certain that any of it has been preserved. It is either lost or partially preserved in 2 Corinthians 10–13. A number of scholars who have written major works on 2 Corinthians argue that chapters 10–13 cannot have belonged to the same letter as chapters 1–9, but also that it cannot be the severe letter referred to in 2:1–4 and 7:8–12;[21] they are united on the latter point with those who argue for the unity of the letter.

Among the arguments that chapters 10–13 precedes Letter F, and is therefore to be identified with the Severe Letter:

— We know there was such a letter, so the proposal is not pure speculation.

— The discussion of the offering in chapter 8 reflects no suspicion of Paul's integrity with regard to the offering, but this situation has changed in chapters 10–13 (see 12:16–18).

— Chapters 10–13 presuppose the present reality of a severe crisis between Paul and the Corinthian church, while the final letter of reconciliation in chapters 1–7 looks back on the resolution of this crisis. This is perhaps the strongest evidence for the identification, for if chapters 10–13 were written after the letter of reconciliation, then the worst crisis comes after the reconciliation, not before it, and chapters 10–13 represent Paul's last word on the situation.

— In 12:14 and 13:1 Paul gives the impression that he is coming to Corinth immediately, so that when he did not, he was charged with failing to keep his word—a charge to which he responds in 1:15–17, which must then be later than chapters 10–13.

— In 10:16, Paul speaks of Rome as lying "beyond" Corinth. This is more plausible if he had not yet left Ephesus than if he was writing from Macedonia. It is thereforefore more likely that Paul wrote 2 Corinthians 10–13 from Ephesus, prior to the letter of reconciliation written from Macedonia.

— Statements in chapters 10–13 referring to the future are spoken of as already past in Letter F, for example, 13:10/2:3; 13:2/1:23; 10:6/2:9.

— In the letter of reconciliation Paul seems intentionally to use some words in a positive sense that he had used in a sharply negative sense in chapters 10–13, thereby removing some of their sting (e.g., see above on "boasting").

— Positing chapters 10–13 as the Severe Letter fits the progressive intensification of the conflict over apostleship that we observe beginning in 1 Corinthians and continuing in letters C through E as here outlined, reaching its climax in the Severe Letter, before being resolved in Paul's favor as reflected in Letter F, the letter of reconciliation.

— The primary and strongest argument, however, is that Paul says he has written, "out of much distress and anguish of heart and with many tears" (2:4), a letter that caused them grief and led to their repentance, a letter so strong that he had regretted having written it, but no longer regrets it, since it led to their repentance. To many scholars, 2 Corinthians 10–13 seems to be part of just such a letter. If the Severe Letter is not represented by chapters 10–13, then we must posit a later outbreak of trouble in Corinth, after the letter

21. C. K. Barrett, *A Commentary on the Second Epistle to the Corinthians*, HNTC (New York: Harper & Row, 1973); Furnish, *II Corinthians*; Thrall, *Second Epistle to the Corinthians*, who details the arguments for and against (1:13–20).

of reconciliation, which is addressed by chapters 10–13, and which is Paul's last word on the subject before we see him happily settled in Corinth again.

This seems implausible to many scholars, but by no means to all: In addition to challenging each of the arguments given above, those who understand chapters 10–13 to be part of a separate letter written *after* chapters 1–9 consider it decisive that the painful visit and related troubles are unrelated to the primary issue of chapters 10–13. They argue that the painful visit, and thus the Severe Letter, focused on Paul's being offended by a member of the Corinthian church, while chapters 10–13 focus on the problem of rival missionaries from outside. The Severe Letter as described in chapters 2 and 7 knows nothing of rival apostles/missionaries, and chapters 10–13 know nothing of the individual who wronged Paul. Thus the letter of reconciliation found in chapters 1–2 and 7 makes no reference to the false apostles who are the subject of chapters 10–13. Advocates of the identification of chapters 10–13 with the Severe Letter consider it likely that these are two sides of the same coin, that the rival apostles/missionaries from outside found followers among the resident Corinthian Christians, including one key member who terribly offended Paul during the painful visit.

14. The church repents, reaffirms its loyalty to the Pauline gospel, and punishes the offender (2 Cor 2:6; 7:9–11).

    The crisis in Galatia occurred about this time, and Paul writes the letter to the Galatians.

15. Paul, who has already been endangered and imprisoned in Ephesus earlier in his work there, now leaves for Macedonia and Achaia, meeting Titus en route (2 Cor 1:8–9, 2:12–13; 7:6–16; Acts 19 uproar).

    Paul goes to Troas and has a great missionary opportunity, but pushes on to rendezvous with Titus somewhere in Macedonia.[22]

16. Paul writes LETTER F—the Letter of Reconciliation (1:3–2:13 + 7:5–16 + 13:11–13).

    This letter was sent by Titus and possibly the "two brothers" of 8:16–24.

    This letter became the framework for our present 2 Corinthians. It was written ten or eleven months after Letter B, canonical 1 Corinthians.

17. LETTER G, our 2 Corinthians 9, is sent to make further arrangements for the collection.

    This brief letter is an addendum to the Letter of Reconciliation, providing final instructions for the offering, which is again underway and proceeding apace.

18. Paul makes his final visit to Corinth.

    Paul has a positive relationship to the church, stays three months, receives the collection, prepares to take it to Jerusalem, and writes Romans from there (Rom 15:25–29, cf. Acts 20:2–3), about 55 or 56 CE.

19. *First Clement* 3.2–3 portrays the situation in Corinth prior to the editing and circulation of Paul's remaining correspondence that became canonical 2 Corinthians.

    Around the end of the first century CE, the Corinthian church had another crisis of leadership, in which the established leaders were ejected. Clement writes from Rome to encourage the church to reinstate its leaders. In the course of his letter, he refers to the letter (singular) Paul

22. Two different efforts to maintain the unity of the letter focus on this segment of the story. (1) In the one view, Titus brings "mixed news": the Corinthians had obeyed Paul and punished the offender; Paul's shifting travel plans led to charges of insincerity, and a group of Jewish Christian intruders had arrived. "Paul's response to this mixture of issues is our 2 Corinthians" (Philip Towner, "Corinthians, Second Letter to," in *New Interpreter's Dictionary of the Bible*, 748). This "mixed news," however, is a necessary postulate for maintaining the unity of 2 Corinthians, but the letter itself says nothing about mixed news, only the good news of the Corinthians' repentance. (2) In a variation of this hypothesis, Titus brings good news, Paul composes 2 Cor 1–9; but before he sends it he receives news of a fresh rebellion in Corinth, dictates chaps. 10–13, adds them to the previous composition and sends it as our 2 Corinthians (Schnelle, *New Testament Writings*, 86–87; Dunn, *Beginning from Jerusalem*, 834–57).

had written them (47.1 "take up the letter of the blessed Apostle Paul"), quoting several times from 1 Corinthians, but is unaware of 2 Corinthians, though it would be the most appropriate for the occasion. Most scholars doubt that Clement knew 2 Corinthians, which means it was not yet circulated in Rome—though several other Pauline letters were available to the Roman church (cf. §17.2.4).

Summary: Theories, Methods, Theology

Since the issue first emerged at the beginning of critical study of the Bible, with Semler's 1776 theory initiating the discussion, scholarly analysis has generated a mind-numbing number of hypotheses and their variations, with detailed arguments for and against each point.[23] The results can be summarized as follows, with representative advocates of each view:

— One letter: Chapters 1–13 were composed by Paul in their present order and delivered to the Corinthians as one coherent letter.[24]

— *Two letters*: Chapters 10–13 are part of a separate letter prior to chapters 1–9, and are to be identified as part of the Severe Letter,[25] or are part of a separate letter written after chapters 1–9, with the Severe Letter having been lost.[26]

— *Three or More Letters*: When chapters 1–9 was no longer regarded as a unity, theories began to multiply and become more divergent. R. H. Strachan classically argued for a combination of three letters, abstracting the First Apology (2:14–7:4) as the earliest letter, then the Severe Letter of chapters 10–13, then the letter of reconciliation from Macedonia, chapters 1-9 (less 6:14–7:1).[27] The most popular recent theory has argued for five letters (plus the interpolated 6:14–7:1), separating chapters 8 and 9 as individual letters written after the crisis had been resolved, especially as argued by Günther Bornkamm.[28] The chronology argued above affirms the five-letter hypothesis, but with chapter 8 as the earliest of the five.

12.2.1 Structure and Outline

The major structural elements are clear, even from a superficial reading: Chapters 1–7 deal with Paul's ministry among the Corinthians, chapters 8 and 9 with the offering, and chapters 10–13 with Paul's struggle with the rival apostles/missionaries in Corinth. The secondary divisions are not so clear and may well reflect the compositional or redactional history of the present form of the letter rather than a single integrated outline.

1:1–2	Greeting
1:3–2:13 (+7:5–16; 13:11–13)	Reconciliation and Eschatological Shalom
1:3–11	Blessing and Thanksgiving
1:12–2:13; 7:5–16	Recent Relations with the Church: Alienation and Reconciliation

23. See the surveys and bibliographies in Betz, *2 Corinthians 8 and 9*; Thrall, *Second Epistle to the Corinthians*; and Bieringer and Lambrecht, eds., *Studies on 2 Corinthians*.

24. R. Bieringer, "Plädoyer für die Einheitlichkeit des 2. Korintherbriefes," in *Studies on 2 Corinthians*, ed. R. Bieringer and Jan Lambrecht, BETL (Louvain: University Press, 1994); Schnelle, *New Testament Writings*, 79–88. Some recent commentaries argue this view, e.g., Matera, *II Corinthians*; Jan Lambrecht, SJ, *Second Corinthians*, SP (Collegeville, MN: Liturgical Press, 1999).

25. This position was classically argued by Alfred Plummer, *Second Epistle of St. Paul to the Corinthians*, ICC (Edinburgh: T. & T. Clark, 1966; first edition 1915), was advocated in the standard critical New Testament introductions for a generation (e.g., James Moffatt, *An Introduction to the Literature of the New Testament*, 3rd ed., International Theological Library [Edinburgh: T. & T. Clark, 1949]), and has recently been argued by, e.g., Hans-Josef Klauck, *2. Korintherbrief*, 3rd ed., Neue Echter Bibel 8 (Würzburg: Echter Verlag, 1994).

26. Barrett, *Second Epistle to the Corinthians*; Furnish, *II Corinthians*; Thrall, *Second Epistle to the Corinthians*.

27. R. H. Strachan, *The Second Epistle of Paul to the Corinthians*, Moffatt New Testament Commentary (London: Hodder & Stoughton, 1965).

28. Bieringer's table, current to 1994, lists thirty-one scholars supporting this view, more than for any other position. Additional recent works could be added to the list. Of course, scholarly opinions must be weighed and not merely counted, so it is important to note that the advocates for this view include several scholars who have written major and influential works on 2 Corinthians.

2:14–7:16	Paul's "First Apology": The Nature of Authentic Ministry
2:14–17	God's Triumphal Procession, Paul's Humiliation
3:1–4:6	Two Kinds of Ministry, Two Covenants
4:7–15	Ministry: Treasure in Clay Jars
4:16–5:10	Ministry: Visible and Invisible
5:11–21	The Ministry of Reconciliation, God's and Paul's
6:1–7:4	Reconciliation in and through the Church
7:5–16	The Church's Repentance, Paul's Joy
8:1–24	The Offering, Note #1
9:1–15	The Offering, Note #2
10:1–13:10 (–13)	True and False Apostles
10:1–11	Response to the Painful Visit
10:12–18	Boasting and Boundaries
11:1–6	"Another Jesus, a Different Gospel"
11:7–33	The "Fool's Speech"
12:1–13	Visions, Revelations, and the "Thorn in the Flesh"
12:14–13:13	Final Appeal and Warnings

12.2.2 Exegetical-Theological Précis

The major units of the letter that constitute the outline may well be the result of its compositional history: each major section may originally have been a separate letter, or part of one. Whether written as one letter or edited from more than one, we receive the letter as a unity from the hands of the church. The present form of the letter made some kind of theological sense in its canonical form, and we will look at its theological message from the point of view of its final form, noting that it may have been composed from previous elements.

1:1–2 Greeting

Paul's theological version of the conventional greeting (see §10.2.3) here emphasizes that the Corinthian congregation is part of the larger church. It does not mean that 2 Corinthians is a circular letter addressed to all the other churches in Achaia, or that part of it is addressed to the Corinthians proper and other parts to other churches in Achaia (see 6:11, where the addressees are all "Corinthians").

1:3–2:13 (+7:5–16; 13:11–13) Reconciliation and Eschatological Shalom

1:3–11 Blessing and Thanksgiving

The standard thanksgiving (see §10.2.3) here takes the form of a blessing, praise to God for the comfort and encouragement generated by the good news brought by Titus, that the Corinthian church had regained its confidence in Paul's mission and apostleship. Here as elsewhere, the thanksgiving signals the major themes of the letter to follow. In the NRSV, God is called "the God of all consolation." The noun παράκλησις (*paraklēsis*) and its cognate verb παρακαλέω (*parakaleō*, often translated "consolation" and "comfort" in the NRSV) is deeply embedded in biblical faith and vocabulary. There is no single English word that serves as an adequate translation. It is sometimes rendered "comfort" or "encouragement," but all these English words have unsuitable connotations. The word is used to express the ultimate salvation promised by God to Israel, the "hope of Israel," the final act of God that will bring the divine peace and justice, the fulfillment of God's promises, the ultimate coming of the kingdom of God. Those who lament the present situation of God's world and long for the future redemption will be "comforted" (Matt 5:4). In Luke 2:22–32 the aged Simeon's longing for the promised future salvation for Israel and all peoples is called "looking forward to the consolation [παράκλησις *paraklēsis*] of Israel." When Paul goes on and on about the "comfort" or "consolation" he receives at Titus's report,[29] his earthly and human joy is in continuity with God's messianic act that ultimately means the reconciliation of the world, a foretaste of which is the reconciliation that has occurred between the Corinthians and Paul. After Paul's humiliating rejection by the supporters of the intrusive new teachers in Corinth, he had gone back to Ephesus, where he had faced a life-threatening situation and despaired of surviving, probably an imprisonment in which he expected to be sentenced to death (1:8–9).

1:12–2:13; 7:5–16 Recent Relations with the Church: Alienation and Reconciliation

Paul was delivered from this crisis, composed the Severe Letter responding to his ill-treatment in Corinth (2:3–4, 9), and sent it back to Corinth with Titus, planning to meet him in Troas and learn of the situation in Corinth. At Troas, Paul had an opportunity for fruitful mission work, but could not endure the suspense, so set out to meet Titus en route through Macedonia (2:12–13). In the present form of the letter, the intense train of thought is interrupted by an extended defense of Paul's ministry (2:14–7:5). Paul describes his inner turmoil in Macedonia as he sought for Titus, and his great relief and joy to learn that the Corinthians had renewed their support of the Pauline mission and disciplined the ringleader of the opposition (7:5–16).

These are the important theological aspects of this letter/section:

— Here as elsewhere, Paul interprets the this-worldly events of his life and mission in the light of God's saving act in Jesus Christ. Paul believes something has actually happened that makes everything different. If this event happened, the world and life is different, and Paul strives to see his life and mission in the light of this event that makes all the difference.

— Paul had changed his travel plans announced to the Corinthians, giving rise to the suspicion that he was untrustworthy, talking out of both sides of his mouth, saying both "Yes" and "No" (1:15–17). His response is not only on the level of his own sincerity and trustworthiness (1:12); he affirms his own dependability within the framework of God's faithfulness made known in the Christ event. While the human rejection represented in the crucifixion made it appear that Jesus had also been rejected by God, that he was the divine "No," the resurrection revealed that the Christ event was God's overruling, eternal "Yes," not only to the promises made to Israel, but to all human hopes based on the faithfulness of the Creator (1:18–20).

— When the Corinthian church regained its confidence in Paul's apostolic mission through the Severe Letter and the pastoral work of Titus, they severely disciplined the leader of the opposition who had supported the rival apostles/missionaries. Paul does not gloat over this "victory," but expresses forgiveness and pastoral concern for the erstwhile antagonist (7:8–13). His letter not only affirms God's reconciling act in the cross and resurrection of Jesus (5:11–21), but manifests the reality of this reconciliation in the way he treats other people who have wronged him.

2:14–7:16 Paul's First Apology: The Nature of Authentic Ministry

This letter/section includes Paul's affirmations and imagery that deal with the most profound dimensions of his theology: the old and new covenants (chapter 3); Christ as the

29. Forms of παρακαλέω, παράκλησις (*parakaleō*, *paraklēsis*, comfort, console, encourage) occur twenty-nine times in 2 Cor, six times in the blessing of 1:3–11, continued with four times in 7:6–13 (additional evidence that 7:5–16 is the continuation of 2:13).

image of God (4:5); believers' transformation into the image of Christ (3:18); human destiny as the replacement of the earthly tent with the heavenly dwelling (5:1–10), the evaluation of human works as we stand before the eschatological judgment seat of Christ (5:10), being "in Christ" and the "new creation" (5:17), God's reconciliation of the world through the death of Christ (5:19–21). As always, Paul speaks from the depths of his theological conviction, yet he is not here "teaching theology," but responding to specific charges made by people he cares about, whom, he fears, are being misled by their new teachers. The charges have to do with Paul as minister and the character of his ministry. This letter/section 2:14–7:4 is a defense of authentic ministry.

2:14–17 *God's Triumphant Procession, Paul's Humiliation*

The note of thanksgiving originally may have been the customary beginning of a letter. It pictures the progress of Paul's life in the imagery of a triumphal procession, a Roman victory parade in which prisoners were forced to march. Paul himself is not pictured triumphantly, but as a prisoner in the procession led by God. His ministry is stamped not with the glory of the triumphant Christ, but with the shame of the crucified Jesus. The comment "like so many" (2:17; see 3:1; Phil 3:18) is the first indication of the presence of rival missionaries in Corinth.

3:1–4:6 *Two Kinds of Ministry, Two Covenants*

The new teachers come from elsewhere with impressive letters of recommendation (3:1). They present themselves as models of authentic ministry who manifest, in their appearance, speech, and demeanor, the triumph of Christ, and have raised questions about Paul's competency. Ἱκανός (*hikanos*, competence; sufficiency) was a key word in their vocabulary (four times in this brief section). Unlike his rivals, Paul points to nothing about himself; he has no observable competence, which belongs to and is validated by the unseen world of God. His only "letter of recommendation" is the Corinthian church itself, written not on stone tablets but on the hearts of Paul and his coworkers (or the Corinthians' hearts; see NRSV footnote). If people want evidence of the validity of Paul's mission, let them look at the Corinthian church, founded by Paul and his coworkers—into which the interloper teachers have now intruded.

At 3:7, the contrast between the opponents' letters of recommendation and Paul's writing on people's hearts takes an unexpected turn. The rival apostles/missionaries' letters were written on papyrus, in contrast to Paul's "letter" written on the Corinthian hearts. The modern reader thus expects hearts-vs.-papyrus, but Paul writes hearts-vs.-stone tablets. How did "stone tablets" get into the picture? The reference, of course, is to the stone tablets of the law of Moses (Exod 34). It seems that the new teachers in Corinth emphasized the law of Moses in a way that contrasted with Paul's teaching, and that Paul contrasts his own ministry of the new covenant prophesied by Jeremiah (Jer 31:31–33) with the old covenant represented by Moses.

It may be that the opposing teachers challenged Paul's claim to be an apostle who had encountered and been commissioned by the risen Lord, for the bodily presence of such an apostle should manifest the glory of the Lord, just as Moses' own face reflected his encounter with God (Exod 34:27–35). Paul interweaves allusions to Exodus 34 and Jeremiah 31. Both are covenant texts—one written on stone, the other on human hearts—and God is the writer in *both* instances. Paul uses such allusive language in a way that presupposes his Gentile Christian readers are familiar with the Old Testament, the Jewish Scriptures now part of the Christian Bible (as in, e.g., 1 Cor 5:6–8). The language of the new covenant was a regular part of the church's eucharistic liturgy (1 Cor 11:23–26), so Paul may be appealing to an element of their common tradition to oppose the new teachers' emphasis on the old covenant. It may be that the contrast between the externally visible letters and the letters Paul writes on human hearts, visible only to faith, suggested the contrast found in Jeremiah 31:31–33. A combination of these factors may have generated Paul's shift to the language and imagery of the new covenant as the validation of his ministry.

In any case, Paul does not here launch into an abstract and anachronistic discussion of whether the new covenant supersedes the old, or the relation of the Old Testament part of the Christian Bible to the New Testament section. Nonetheless, since 2 Corinthians 3 often emerges in modern discussions of the relation of Christianity to Judaism and the relation of the New Testament to the Old Testament, the contemporary reader needs to remember how the language of newness is used in the Bible. For Paul, in such contexts "new" refers to God's eschatological new creation, which is already begun and anticipated in the Christ event but is not yet fulfilled (see §§1.2, 1.3).

Covenant was not a major category of Paul's own theology. Paul uses covenant terminology only in 2 Corinthians and Galatians, written about the same time in his mission, both reflecting a crisis situation and the views of his opponents. Paul's response may be outlined in five statements:

1. God made a covenant with Israel to be a special elect people among all the peoples of the world (who are also God's people by creation). Israel's election and covenant was not to privilege but to mission.

2. Israel did not live up to the responsibilities of the covenant, and in this sense broke the covenant, but God did not revoke it. Israel's unfaithfulness did not nullify God's faithfulness (Rom 3:2).

3. The old covenant was associated with external, written laws that spelled out Israel's responsibility.

4. The law itself was holy and good, but was commandeered by the evil power of sin that perverted it from its original good purpose and function (Rom 3:31; 7:7–25).

5. By the Christ event God overthrows the power of sin and renews the covenant in such a way that God's law is no longer an external constraint that rules and condemns but an internal power that accomplishes God's will in the believer by the power of the Spirit. This Spirit is not just an internal attitude (as in the phrase "the spirit of the law, not the letter of the law"), but the eschatological gift of the Holy Spirit at work in the life of the church. The new covenant is distinguished by a series of contrasts based on Jeremiah 31:31–33 and Ezekiel 16:59–62; 34:25–26. Paul emphasizes these contrasts as letter vs. Spirit, death vs. life, glory vs. more glorious, condemnation vs. justification, temporary vs. permanent.

Paul responds to his challengers' charges that his unimpressive appearance corresponds to the nature of God's surprising eschatological act in the cross of Christ, which overturns all human expectations, frames of reference, and this-worldly criteria. Paul validates his ministry by seeing his own little, unimpressive story as inserted into the cosmic story line of God's plan from creation (4:6) through the covenant with Israel and God's decisive reconciling event in Christ, the eschatological renewal of the covenant (3:7–14) to the consummation, the new creation already dawning with the coming of Christ and gift of the Spirit (3:18; 5:17–21).

4:7–15 *Ministry: Treasure in Clay Jars*

Paul's rivals had apparently insinuated that the grand eschatological drama of salvation he proclaimed was belied by his bodily appearance. Paul's response: the priceless treasure of the gospel is indeed held in a fragile—and already somewhat broken—clay vessel. Paul's body bore the scars of numerous beatings. These were not the proud battle scars on the face, arms, and chest, but the shameful marks on the back. Paul validates his ministry as authentic service of the gospel, not by external signs to which he can point, but by inserting his story into the story of God, of which the Jesus story is the defining center (4:10–12, 14) and by his appeal to this story as represented in Scripture (4:13=Ps 115:1 LXX; NRSV Ps 116:10, translated differently).

4:16–5:10 *Ministry: Visible and Invisible*

This contrast between the externally visible and the invisible but real continues. The imagery of putting off the temporary earthly tent and receiving an eternal, heavenly building from God is in tension with the resurrection imagery of 1 Corinthians 15, and indeed with the preceding paragraph of this letter (2 Cor 4:14). The contrast here is a continuation of the main topic, a defense of his ministry. Paul's scarred body, his working for a living, his unimpressive weakness and "groaning" (5:2) are not indications that his ministry is invalid, for all authentic ministry is validated from the point of view of the heavenly world, which Paul longs for but does not yet belong to. Likewise, the statement about the final judgment in which all stand before the judgment seat of Christ (5:10) insists that the validation of one's ministry cannot yet be seen (on the opponents' terms) but awaits final validation by God.

5:11–21 *The Ministry of Reconciliation, God's and Paul's*

Paul's ministry is not validated or characterized by demonstrable "success;" it is an extension of God's act in reconciling the world through the Christ event. It is no surprise that "from a human point of view" Paul does not look like a successful minister. Jesus died a shameful death on the cross, but just as the truth of what happened there cannot be known "from a human point of view" (κατὰ σάρκα, *kata sarka*, 5:16), so Christ's authentic ministers cannot "boast in outward appearance" (5:12). God was acting in Jesus' death for the reconciliation of the world. With Jesus' resurrection, the eschatological new creation breaks into this world. Individuals are transformed by faith in the resurrection and the power of the Holy Spirit, but the "new creation" is not merely personal.[30]

Something happens to the *world* at Jesus' resurrection, not only to the subjectivity of believers. Paul thinks in cosmic and apocalyptic terms: like the resurrection, the new creation was to occur at the end. But in the Christ event this eschatological power already breaks into the present. Jesus is the leading edge of God's new world. Those "in Christ" already participate in this new reality but continue to live their lives in a world still dominated by the lingering powers of sin and death, though the days of these powers are numbered (see Rom 6 and 8 and the overlapping of the "ends of the ages" in which Christians presently live [1 Cor 10:11]). God's reconciling act in Jesus continues in Paul's ministry and bears the same character, announcing and mediating God's reconciling love in the most unexpected ways.

As elsewhere in Paul, "practical" dimensions of ministry evoke and are based on profound theological reflection. The offering in 8:9–10, the appeal for the Corinthians to be reconciled to each other, to him, and to God are all based on, and are extensions of, God's act in Christ for the reconciliation of the world. This is a two-way street: theology is not abstract, doctrinal, speculative, but works itself out in the world; practical teaching on this-worldly issues in the world is both based on profound theology and shapes the way this theology is formulated. Paul is here urging reconciliation between the Corinthians and himself on the basis of the universal reconciliation that God has already accomplished in the Christ event.

30. Contrast, e.g., RSV, NIV, "Therefore, if anyone is in Christ, he is a new creation; the old has gone, the new has come!" and the NRSV, "So if anyone is in Christ, there is a new creation: everything old has passed away; see, everything has become new!" and TNIV, "Therefore, if anyone is in Christ, the new creation has come: The old has gone, the new is here!" (2 Cor. 5:17).

6:1–7:4 Reconciliation in and through the Church

This reconciling act of God continues not only in Paul's ministry, but extends itself into the life of the Corinthian church. "Working together" (6:1) means not only "with God" but "with Paul and each other." The church is the community of reconciliation, bearing witness to God's reconciling act for the world and manifesting this reconciliation in its own life. Thus the Corinthian Christians, though suspicious of Paul and misled by their new leaders, are never addressed as the enemy, but are seen as Paul's partners in the ministry of reconciliation. After once again cataloguing his paradoxical "qualifications" by which he "commends himself," qualifications that reflect the cross/resurrection reality of the reconciling event (6:4–10), Paul concludes this letter/section with his openhearted declaration of love and confidence in those who, like himself, have been reconciled to God through God's own loving act. Paul has shown that the recent relations between himself and the Corinthians—good and problematic alike—are part of a grand story. It is not just the story of Paul and Corinth—though it is that. It is part of a cosmic/historical story of God's reconciliation of the world in Jesus Christ.

The entire section 2:14–7:4, though rightly considered Paul's defense of his ministry, is thus not about *Paul*. Here we are at the furthest pole from egocentric insecurity that must convince others of its own importance. The whole section might better be called "The Ministry of Reconciliation," based on a profound understanding of God's reconciling act in Jesus, which creates a reconciled and reconciling community with a mission to the world.

7:5–16 The Church's Repentance, Paul's Joy

In the present form of the letter, Paul's joy at the Corinthians' repentance and his reconciliation with them is the framework that encloses the defense of authentic ministry.

8:1–24 The Offering, Note #1

Paul had begun organizing the offering during his founding visit to Corinth, and had given instructions for it in 1 Corinthians 16:1–4. Difficulties between Paul and the Corinthians, and their suspicion of him, seem to have caused enthusiasm for the offering to lag. This note seeks to give the project renewed momentum by sending Titus (8:6) along with the brother "famous among all the churches for his proclaiming the good news" who had been chosen by the Macedonian congregations (8:18), and by another of Paul's assistants chosen and appointed by himself. This taking care to have representative supervision of the offering (a large sum of money) is not only ordinary prudence, but suggests the Corinthians may already be developing suspicions that Paul may be lining his own pockets under the pretext of helping the poor Jerusalem saints.

Paul characteristically invites participation not only on humanitarian grounds and the example of the Macedonian Christians (8:1–5), but by an allegorizing use of Scripture and especially by appealing to a profound christological image: the preexistent Christ "became poor," so that by his self-emptying act the Corinthians might "become rich" (8:9; see Phil 2:6–8, written previously). Here too, Paul bases the practical dimensions of church life on the fundamental convictions of the gospel. As his and the church's proclamation of reconciliation is based on God's reconciling act in Christ, so Christian generosity is an extension of Christ's own self-giving. The Christology of preexistence and incarnation is not abstract speculation but eventuates in this-worldly self-giving love among Christians; Christian service to others is not moralizing "good works," but the continuation of Jesus' own self-giving.

The modern reader's judgment as to whether this mission of Titus and his colleagues succeeded depends on how one understands the literary unity of 2 Corinthians and the chronology of events between 1 and 2 Corinthians (see above).

9:1–15 Offering, Note #2

Chapter 9 seems to be a self-contained unit giving further instructions about the offering. It has been understood as a (fragment of a) separate letter, as addressing a different readership from the rest of 2 Corinthians (all the churches in Achaia, in distinction from Corinth), or merely a renewed discussion to the same readers, perhaps after a pause in dictation. As Paul writes, he is en route through Macedonia, where he is encouraged by the generous response of the Macedonian churches. The troubled relationship between the Corinthians and Paul has caused the collection to lag. Paul sends "the brothers" ahead to facilitate the completion of the offering before he arrives with the delegation from Macedonia. While 8:1–6 indicates Paul praised the Macedonian generosity as a model for the Corinthians,[31] here he reports that he had used the Corinthians as a model to encourage the Macedonians—and in turn now points to the Macedonian expectation of the Corinthians' gift as a further spur to the Corinthians to make good on Paul's boasting about them. The final picture transcends the Achaia/Macedonia relationships, as Paul's mind leaps ahead to the reception of the offering in Jerusalem, where the Jewish Christians of the mother church will thank God not only for the offering they have received, but for the grace of God that has been poured out on the Gentile churches.

10:1–13:10 (–13) True and False Apostles

10:1–11 Response to the Painful Visit

In these chapters Paul responds to the terribly painful incident that had occurred on his recent visit to Corinth, with deep sarcasm reflecting what was said about him there: he writes powerful letters from a distance, but his personal presence is contemptible and his speech does not manifest the power of the Spirit. The singular pronouns of 10:7, 11 and the singular verb of 10:10 (in the Greek text) may refer to the particular individual who had ridiculed Paul and led the church to reject him during the painful visit (see 2:1; 7:12).[32] Paul threatens them with apocalyptic judgment on his next visit if they do not repent (see 1 Cor 5:3–5).

10:12–18 Boasting and Boundaries

Paul understands himself to have been commissioned by the risen Christ as apostle to the Gentiles and Christ's spokesperson to the churches he has founded, a commission acknowledged by the Jewish Christian leaders in Jerusalem (Gal 2; Acts 15). This authority has been challenged by the new teachers in Corinth. Paul considers them interlopers, trespassers into churches they did not found, who disdain and challenge Paul's legitimate authority, and finds himself having to defend himself against outsiders in the churches he has founded and nurtured. The issue is not Paul's ego and wounded pride, or a dispute over turf, but the nature and legitimacy of apostleship. The language of "boasting" had become prominent in the dispute. Paul's point is that legitimate "boasting" is not a matter of one's personal accomplishments, but can only be "in the Lord" (10:17, citing Jer 9:23–24; see 1 Cor 1:31). His opponents agree with this but think in terms of the powerful Lord of glory. Paul thinks in terms of the crucified Jesus.

11:1–6 "Another Jesus, a Different Gospel"

Paul sets his opponents' Christology in contrast to his own, which emphasizes the vulnerability and weakness of the crucified Jesus, whose earthly life was devoid of divine power

31. Whether this is earlier, later, or in the same letter as the communication on chap. 9 depends on one's understanding of the unity of the letter, and (if it is composed of more than one part) the relative chronology of the various parts.

32. In each case the NRSV changes this to the plural in the interest of gender-inclusive language, but misses the pointedness of Paul's reference to a particular person (cf. RSV, REB, NJB).

(see 1 Cor 1:18–2:5; 2 Cor 13:4; Phil 2:5–11). The false apostles thus seem to have emphasized the power of the miracle-working Jesus, whose earthly life was filled with divine power—a view that had no place in Paul's understanding. His rivals performed miracles themselves, spoke in the power of the Spirit, and may have used miracle stories about Jesus as a means of communicating their "different gospel." Since Christology and discipleship are always correlative concepts, their view of a powerful Jesus meant that his earthly representatives should likewise manifest this triumphant divine power, and this is what they claimed to do.

They rejected Paul as an authentic apostle, since his appearance, demeanor, and speech clearly did not demonstrate such power. He proclaimed the Jesus "crucified in weakness" (13:4) and believed that authentic discipleship and apostleship was marked by the sign of the cross. Neither Paul nor his opponents had a theological means of combining these images of the power-filled life of Jesus with the weakness of his death on the cross, and these two christological paradigms could only appear as alternatives between which one must choose. Paul's rivals advocated a powerful Jesus and minimized his sufferings and death; Paul proclaimed Jesus "crucified in weakness" (13:4) and has nothing to say about Jesus' miracles. Prior to the Gospel of Mark, these two Christologies and views of discipleship struggled against each other (see §20.1.2). In 2 Corinthians 10–13, we hear one side of a christological debate within the church.

11:7–33 *The "Fool's Speech"*

Paul's strong language ("false apostles," "deceitful workers," "ministers of Satan") expresses his conviction that a decisive line had been crossed. Paul was tolerant and open to other versions of the Christian faith than his own, and had expressed this to the Corinthians (1 Cor 3:21–23). But, while there is more than one way to affirm the authentic faith, not just any way is acceptable. In Paul's view, the new teachers in Corinth were not just representing a different version of the common faith; they were in fact denying its very basis in the crucified Jesus.

Thus Paul responds to their impressive credentials, not by attempting to present even more impressive credentials of his own in the same frame of reference ("this worldly," "according to the flesh"), but by cataloguing his experiences that correspond to the scandal of the cross. They "boasted," and he will "boast" too—in the literary form of the "fool's speech," which parodies their own list of achievements. While he has the same Jewish credentials as his challengers (11:22), his "achievements" are a list of beatings, imprisonments, and disasters that manifest not his strength but his weakness. In an honor/shame culture in which honor was as significant as money is in our own, this reversal of values was as upsetting as the idea of a crucified Messiah, and is its correlative.

12:1–13 *Visions, Revelations, and the "Thorn in the Flesh"*

Paul is always reluctant to bring up his personal spiritual experiences and never does so except under the pressure of circumstances. Apparently his opponents displayed their charismatic gifts of speaking and healing, and related experiences in which they, like the biblical prophets, had received visions and revelations that validated their apostolic claims. Paul too has had such experiences, though rarely, and he speaks of them reluctantly (cf. his similar approach to charismatic phenomena in the discussion of 1 Cor 12–14). He had indeed experienced such phenomena, but they were not the proof of his apostleship. He had also received a "thorn in the flesh"—some sort of physical affliction we can no longer identify—as a reminder that God's power is made perfect in weakness.

12:14–13:13 *Final Appeal and Warnings*

Among the Corinthians' objections and suspicions was the way Paul had handled his finances. He refused to take pay from them for his preaching and teaching but accepted money from the Macedonians. This was an offensive rebuff in a world in which honor/shame and patron/client relationships were driving forces that made society work. The new apostles in Corinth exploited Paul's refusal, insinuating that if he were really an authentic apostle, he would accept the expected pay for his missionary work, and that his supporting himself by manual labor was demeaning to the church and its ministry. The offering Paul was promoting (chaps. 8–9) also raised the question of whether he was refusing a regular salary but augmenting his own income under the pretext of an offering for the poor saints in Jerusalem.

As Paul writes 2 Corinthians 10–12, he is preparing for a final showdown with the recalcitrant Corinthians (13:1), but it is the kind of reckoning a loving parent must sometimes have with disobedient children. He sees himself as their "father" in the sense that he brought the church into being and is responsible for it (1 Cor 4:15; 2 Cor 11:2–3; see Phlm 10). He loves the church and wants to protect it, so that as the "father of the bride" he can present it to Christ as a holy and pure church at the parousia (11:2). He knows that the power of God that effects God's judgment does in fact work through his ministry, and he hopes that he will not have to be the instrument of this power in his next meeting with the church.

12.3 For Further Reading

Barrett, C. K. *A Commentary on the First Epistle to the Corinthians*. HNTC. New York and Evanston: Harper & Row, 1968.

———. *A Commentary on the Second Epistle to the Corinthians*. HNTC. New York: Harper & Row, 1973.

Betz, H. D. *2 Corinthians 8 and 9: A Commentary on Two Administrative Letters of the Apostle Paul*. Hermeneia. Philadelphia: Fortress Press, 1985.

Bieringer, R., and J. Lambrecht, eds. *Studies on 2 Corinthians*. BETL 112. Leuven: Leuven University Press, 1994.

Fee, G. D. *The First Epistle to the Corinthians*. NICNT. Grand Rapids: Eerdmans, 1987.

Furnish, Victor Paul. *II Corinthians*. Anchor Bible 32A. Garden City, NY: Doubleday, 1984.

———. *The Theology of First Corinthians*. New Testament Theology. Cambridge: Cambridge University Press, 1999.

Hays, Richard. *First Corinthians*. Interpretation series. Louisville, KY: John Knox Press, 1997.

Lambrecht, J., SJ. *Second Corinthians*. Sacra pagina. Collegeville, MN: Liturgical Press, 1999.

Matera, F. J. *II Corinthians: A Commentary*. NTL. Louisville, KY: Westminster John Knox Press, 2003.

Strachan, R. H. *The Second Epistle of Paul to the Corinthians*. London: Hodder & Stoughton, 1965.

Thrall, M. E. *A Critical and Exegetical Commentary on the Second Epistle to the Corinthians*. ICC. 2 vols. Edinburgh: T. & T. Clark, 1994.

13
Paul's Last Letters

13.1 Interpreting Galatians

NO ONE TODAY DOUBTS THAT PAUL WROTE Galatians; if Paul wrote anything in the New Testament, he wrote Galatians. Nor is there any problem with the unity of the letter or with its text. The copy of Galatians in our New Testament is virtually identical to the original Paul sent to the churches of Galatia.

The problems are with the letter's *addressees* (their identity and location: who and where were the Galatians?), its relative *date* (how does it fit into Paul's life and mission?), the problem posed by the *rival missionaries* to which the letter responds (who were they and what was their message?), and its literary *type* (it is a letter, but what kind of letter is it?).

13.1.1 Who and Where Were the Galatians?

In the early third century BCE, warlike tribes of Celtic origin from central Europe spread both westward into Gaul (modern France and Belgium) and as far as Britain, and south and east into Asia Minor (modern Turkey), where they established themselves in the central highlands around present-day Ankara. The region settled by these "Gauls" was known as Galatia. In the course of generations of political and military struggles, they finally lost their independence and in 25 BCE were incorporated, along with several neighboring regions, into the extensive Roman province of Galatia. In Paul's day, "Galatia" could thus refer to either the original region dominated by ethnic Gauls or the large Roman province including ethnic Galatia and several other regions (parts of Phrygia, Lycaonia, and Pisidia).

When Paul addresses the "foolish Galatians" (Gal 3:1), the original readers of course knew their identity, location, and history. Several scholars argue persuasively that only ethnic Galatians can be addressed in 3:1. However, the letter gives no explicit indication to later readers whether Paul writes to ethnic Galatians residing in the traditional region of Galatia (the North Galatian theory) and/or to churches in the ancient regions of Pisidia and Lycaonia that had been incorporated into the Roman province of Galatia (the South Galatian theory). The letter provides only indirect and ambiguous clues as to when it was written relative to the other Pauline letters. These issues are more important than they may seem at first, both for interpreting the letter and for constructing the chronology of Paul's mission.

Where were the Galatian churches? If *Paul's letters* referred to churches in specific cities of either south Galatia (the province) or north Galatia (the region), this would settle the issue. Unfortunately, he never does this. From Paul's letters, we would never know he had been in the "south Galatian" churches. Acts 13–14 refers to the founding of churches in Pisidian Antioch, Iconium, Lystra and Derbe in

Lycaonia, but never refers to these cities as in Galatia. *Acts* has only two references to Galatia. In Acts 16:6, Paul, Silas, and Timothy pass through the region of Phrygia and Galatia on the "second missionary journey," but nothing is said of founding churches; in Acts 18:23, however, on the "third missionary journey," Paul passes through the same region "strengthening the disciples"—which, of course, indicates Paul had previously founded churches there. This suggests the churches of Galatia were in northern, ethnic Galatia.[1]

The addressees belonged to the urban, Hellenized, Greek-speaking population, not to the rural population, who mostly still spoke the ancestral Celtic language. They were Gentile converts from paganism (see Gal 4:8–9). There is no evidence that there were any Jews in north Galatia until much later.[2] This is crucial for understanding the letter.

1. This was the uniform view of ancient and modern interpreters until 1748, when Joh. Joachim Schmidt first proposed that the churches of Acts 13–14 were the Galatian churches (Werner Georg Kümmel, *Introduction to the New Testament*, trans. Howard Clark Kee, 2nd ed. [Nashville: Abingdon Press, 1975], 296). This theory has since been adopted by numerous interpreters, often (but not always) in the interests of harmonizing Acts with the Pauline letters. If Paul's account of his meeting with the Jerusalem leaders in Gal. 2:1–10 can be identified with the "famine visit" to Jerusalem of Acts 11:29–30, and the addressees identified with the churches founded on the "first missionary journey" of Acts 13–14, then Galatians can be dated before the Jerusalem Council of Acts 15, and the conflicts between Galatians and Acts are reduced. On this view, Galatians could be the earliest of Paul's letters, ca. 48 CE.
2. See evidence and bibliography in J. Louis Martyn, *Galatians: A New Translation with Introduction and Commentary*, AB 33A (New York: Doubleday, 1997), 16. That Galatians was written to churches in an area with no Jews can only be true on the basis of the North Galatian hypothesis. Thus Galatians must be read entirely differently if it is directed to the churches founded in Acts 13–14, which do have Jewish Christians in them and Jews in neighboring synagogues. Paul takes a different approach in Romans, where the church had many Jewish Christians, and where there was a large Jewish element in the Roman population.

13.1.2 Date and Provenance: How Does It Fit into Paul's Life and Mission?

When were the Galatian churches established? Galatians has been regarded as *earliest* and *latest* of Paul's extant writings, as well as everywhere in between.[3] The South Galatian theory makes possible, but does not require, an early date for both the beginning of the churches and the writing of the letter, at any time from 48 CE on. On the North Galatian theory, the churches could not have been established until after the Jerusalem Council and the beginning of the Aegean mission. This makes it possible to date the letter any time from about 51 to about 57, from before 1 Corinthians to after 2 Corinthians. Paul's letters and other NT references provide the following data:

— 1 Corinthians 16:1. Paul indicates to the Corinthians, about 55, that he has given the Galatian churches instructions about the offering (presumably in a letter now lost). This is the earliest reference to the Galatian churches in Paul's letters, indicating that by the time he writes 1 Corinthians the churches are in existence, are participating in the offering for Jerusalem, and with no indication of difficulties between the Galatians and Paul.

— Galatians 1:6. The Galatians have "quickly" deserted the Pauline gospel for the teaching of the rival missionaries. This may represent actual chronology or may have only rhetorical force, and thus it provides little information on the time lapse between establishing the churches, the Galatians' defection, and Paul's writing the letter.

3. Earliest: F. F. Bruce, *The Epistle to the Galatians. A Commentary on the Greek Text*, NIGTC (Grand Rapids: Eerdmans, 1982), 55; latest: John Knox ("Galatians, Letter to the," in *Interpreter's Dictionary of the Bible*, 2:342–43) suggests Galatians was written from the Roman imprisonment, though elsewhere he favors a date shortly prior to Romans (John Knox, *Chapters in a Life of Paul* [London: Adam & Charles Black, 1950], 85, 88).

— Galatians 1:11–2:21. The Galatian churches were established after all the events described in Paul's "autobiographical" section, that is, after the Jerusalem Council, the subsequent encounter with Peter at Antioch, and the launching of Paul's Aegean mission—in Acts terms, during or after the "second missionary journey" (see above §10.1.9). Galatians 2:5 indicates Paul remained steadfast in defense of the Gentile mission so that the truth of the gospel could (then) extend to the Galatians; if he had yielded to the advocates of circumcision at the Jerusalem Council, the Galatians would never have heard the Christian message.

— Galatians 4:13. Paul originally preached to them not as part of his missionary plan, but because of ἀσθένειαν τῆς σαρκός (*astheneian tēs sarkos*, literally "weakness of the flesh"), usually understood as an illness or chronic physical condition (cf. English translations), but may refer to wounds Paul had received from beatings or accidents (see Gal 6:17; 2 Cor 11:24–26). The Greek expression τὸ πρότερον (*to proteron*, before, previously) does not indicate that Paul had preached in Galatia more than once prior to writing the letter.

— Galatians 1–6. The presence of the letter in the New Testament indicates that it was preserved by the Galatian Christians, whether or not they were immediately won back to Paul's gospel by the letter.

— 1 Peter 1:1. Near the end of the first century CE, the author of 1 Peter addresses churches in Galatia, along with other areas of Asia Minor.

— 2 Timothy 4:10. A generation or two after Paul's time, the author of the Pastorals portrays Crescens, one of Paul's coworkers, as having left (abandoned?) Paul and gone to Galatia. Does this indicate there was a continuing church in Galatia, but that it was no longer Pauline? Or is it a fictive reflection of the letter to the Galatians itself, showing that in Paul's time the Galatians were alienated from Paul, and those who deserted Paul might go to Galatia. In 2 Timothy 1:15, "all Asia" has turned away from Paul, which indicates the fictive world projected on Paul's time by the Pastor. It does not mean that the church in Asia of the Pastor's time was no longer Pauline.

The letters thus do not provide clear data that allow Galatians to be dated relative to the other Pauline letters, except to indicate that the Galatian churches were founded and the letter was written after the Jerusalem Council. Scholars have attempted to date the letter more precisely within the Aegean mission by locating it on a line of development of events or ideas: (1) the offering, (2) opposition to Paul, and (3) the doctrine of justification by faith apart from works of the law.

1. *The offering*. J. Louis Martyn presents what appears at first to be a clear and cogent argument for the date of Galatians relative to the other letters:[4] the letters that do not mention the collection (1 Thessalonians, Galatians, Philippians) are relatively early; letters that deal with the collection (1 and 2 Corinthians, Romans) are relatively late. Philemon, which does not mention the offering, is too short and too different to be taken into account. Thus Galatians comes early in the Aegean mission, prior to 1 Corinthians. Three problems are present in this procedure. (a) It assumes that any letter written during the period while the offering project was underway must discuss the offering. This is inherently improbable, since a letter written to address some particular crisis need not mention the offering, even if the project had already been begun. (b) The argument assumes the unity of 2 Corinthians. But if 2 Corinthians is composite, then more than one of Paul's letters to Corinth do not mention the offering, though the project was already in progress. (c) Martyn's argument

4. Martyn, *Galatians*, "Comment #24 The Collection for the Jerusalem Church and the Chronological Place of Galatians," 222–27.

also assumes his view that Paul accepted responsibility for the offering at the Jerusalem Council (Gal 2:10), that he abandoned the project for a while during the beginning of his own Aegean mission, and that only late in this mission, after writing Galatians, he decided to initiate a new offering project on his own. In Martyn's view, this idea had not yet occurred to Paul when he wrote Galatians, so the letter must be early. It is better to see Paul's interest in the offering as his continuation of the original project, even after he began the Aegean mission, as a symbol of continuity and solidarity with the Jerusalem church (see above on 2 Cor 8–9). Thus references to the offering do not provide a sure means of fixing the relative date of Galatians.[5]

2. *Opposition to Paul from rival apostles/missionaries*. It is possible to arrange the undisputed letters of Paul on a scale of intensifying opposition to his mission and/or his increasing awareness of this opposition. On this grid, the letter to the Galatians comes at the climax of the development, and would place Galatians late in the Aegean mission, just prior to Romans.

3. *The explicit, exclusive doctrine of justification by faith apart from works of the law*. This is the most significant, and in some ways, the most controversial, of the arguments for a relatively late date for Galatians. All agree that Paul's most developed explication of this doctrine is found in Romans, his last letter before the end of the Aegean mission and trip to Jerusalem that led to his arrest and imprisonment. It is important to note the similarity between Galatians and Romans, not only in their general structure and themes, and even in their vocabulary, but also in their *train of thought*. The first two-thirds of each letter is a dense theological argument, with the last third devoted to parenesis, in each case connected by the key term οὖν (*oun*, therefore) playing the same structural role that bases the Christian life on the preceding theological argument:

Gal 1:1–4:31 theology	5:1 "therefore"	5:2–6:18 parenesis
Rom 1:1–11:36 theology	12:1 "therefore"	12:2–16:27 parenesis[6]

Udo Schnelle spells this out in detail (see Box 10):[7]

BOX 10: Schnelle's Comparison of the Structure of Galatians and Romans

Gal 1:15–16	Rom 1:1–5	Set apart as an apostle
Gal 2:15–21	Rom 3:19–28	Righteousness through faith
Gal 3:6–25, 29	Rom 4:1–25	Abraham
Gal 3:26–28	Rom 6:3–5	Baptism
Gal 4:1–7	Rom 8:12–17	Slavery and freedom
Gal 4:21–31	Rom 9:6–13	Law and promise
Gal 5:13–15	Rom 13:8–10	Set free to love
Gal 5:17	Rom 7:13–15	Conflict between willing and doing
Gal 5:16–26	Rom 8:12–27	Life in the Spirit

As Schnelle elaborates,

> Only here do we find the alternative "by faith, not by works of the law;" only here do we find a reflective and thought-through understanding of the law. The differences in the way the law is understood in Galatians and Romans derive from the fact that Galatians is more conditioned by its particular situation. It is precisely the development of *these particular ideas that first emerge in Galatians* that are further developed in Romans (emphasis mine).[8]

5. How the absence of references to the offering in Galatians is to be explained remains unclear, but the early dating of Galatians is by no means the only possibility. Paul had already given the Galatians instructions regarding the offering (1 Cor 16:1). They may have already completed the offering and/or delivered it to Jerusalem, or their defection from Paul may have meant that their participation in the offering would not be via Paul's project but directly through the rival apostles/missionaries. In any case, Paul's heated argument in response to the later crisis represented by Galatians was not the appropriate context for discussing the offering (cf. 2 Cor 10–13 understood as the Severe Letter, which does not mention the offering, though it is already underway).

6. See above on the structure of the Pauline letters, subsection "Body," §10.2.3.

7. Schnelle, *New Testament Writings*, 94; Schnelle, *Apostle Paul*, 270.

8. Schnelle, *Apostle Paul*, 270.

It becomes clear that the dating of Galatians relative to the other Pauline letters is important for understanding both the letter in particular and Pauline theology as a whole. If Galatians is early, this means that the explicit doctrine of justification was an integral element of Paul's theology from early in his career, that it lay dormant as he wrote to the Thessalonians, Corinthians, and Philippians, and then reemerged in Romans. In this view, the central elements of Pauline theology were always explicitly present in his theology, with various components making their way into particular letters as the occasion called for it.

The alternative view, based on the late date for Galatians, is that Paul's theology is essentially occasional. While the fundamental, life- and world-changing reality of the Christ event was basic to his theology from the time of his conversion on, what this meant theologically did not become evident until Paul thought it through in terms of particular situations. While preliminary traces of what became his doctrine of justification by faith apart from works of the law are present in earlier letters, in the letter to the Galatians it emerges for the first time as a coherent structure in response to the crisis generated by the rival missionaries, and is then refined in a more reflective mode for a different readership in the letter to the Romans.

While none of the arguments are absolutely compelling, the weight of the evidence suggests that Galatians was written relatively late in Paul's Aegean mission, around the same time as 2 Corinthians 10–13, and shortly before Romans, that is, from Ephesus or in Macedonia en route to Corinth.

13.1.3 Results: The Story to Which the Letter Belongs

J. Louis Martyn has compared reading Galatians to coming into a play at the third act. Much has already transpired of which the actors on the stage are aware, but the viewer must piece together what has already happened by references in the scenes he sees. The following story emerges:

Founding of the church by Paul. The church was founded by Paul and his fellow missionaries near the beginning of the Aegean mission, on the basis of the apostolic message of "Jesus Christ crucified" (3:1). They did not consider themselves to be "daughter churches" of the "mother church" represented by Jerusalem and the Antioch mission of Paul's early period. They knew their churches had been founded during the Aegean mission, in which Paul operated in the conviction that he was sent directly by the risen Christ, without appealing to any authorization from Antioch or Jerusalem. Although, as always, Paul was assisted by his coworkers, he considered himself the founding apostolic figure, the "apostle to the Gentiles," and the churches began as congregations of former pagans (4:8–9) converted directly to the Pauline understanding of the faith.

Like his other congregations, the Galatians were taught to understand themselves as incorporated into God's ongoing plan in history, incorporated into the story of Israel, and adopting the Jewish Scriptures as their authoritative sacred texts. There were no cultic requirements; from the beginning, the Galatian churches understood themselves as accepted by God into the holy people of the covenant, apart from circumcision and the adoption of other identity markers that distinguished Jews from Gentiles (food laws, observance of the Sabbath and other Jewish holy days). During this initial period of ministry among the Galatians, Paul trained several teachers who continued to instruct the churches in the Pauline understanding of the faith after his departure (6:6).

A period in which they were "running well" (5:7). At the beginning they treated Paul well (4:13–14), and there were warm, cordial relations between Paul and the Galatians. They experienced the power of the Holy Spirit (3:1–5) and for a while continued to "run well" along the path of Christian service and discipleship (5:7a), under the leadership of the teachers Paul had trained and appointed. They agreed to participate in the offering for Jerusalem (1 Cor 16:1).

The arrival of rival missionaries and Paul's response. New missionaries arrive representing themselves as authorized by the "mother church" in Jerusalem (see Gal 4:26), claiming to supplement Paul's incomplete gospel. They saw themselves as preachers of the gospel and advocates of the biblical faith, instructing the new Galatian Christians in their responsibilities to keep the biblical laws as interpreted by Jesus and the authentic Jewish apostles in Jerusalem, including James the brother of Jesus.[9] They displaced Paul's teachers with themselves and their own followers (Gal 6:6 is probably a plea to reinstate the teachers Paul had installed). Paul hears of the defection of the Galatians and writes the present letter. What sort of letter is it?

13.1.4 Letter Type

Galatians is a letter. It is not an essay on "justification by faith" or "faith vs. works." What *kind* of letter is it? How Paul's letters fit into the known types of Hellenistic letter writing remains a disputed point (see above §10.2.2). Since the 1979 publication of Hans-Dieter Betz's commentary on Galatians, the debate has often focused on whether Betz was right in arguing that Paul followed the standard rhetorical pattern of the apologetic letter. Betz's detailed analysis[10] is summarized as follows:

I.	Epistolary Prescript	1:1–5
II.	Exordium	1:6–11
III.	Narratio	1:12–2:14
IV.	Propositio	2:15–21
V.	Probatio	3:1–4:31
VI.	Exhortatio	5:1–6:10
VII.	Epistolary Postscript (Conclusio)	6:11–18

Numerous objections and counterproposals have been made, and the matter is still under discussion.[11] The outline below is indebted to Betz's analysis, but without assuming or arguing that Paul is consciously following a strict rhetorical model.

13.1.5 Structure and Outline

In general, the body of the letter follows the Pauline bipartite schema (see above §10.2.3), roughly divided into theological argument (chaps. 1–4) and parenesis (chaps. 5–6).

1:1–10	Epistolary Introduction
1:1–5	Greeting
1:6–10	Thesis statement: No Other Gospel
1:11–5:1a	Part 1: Theological Argument—Paul's Defense of His Mission and Apostleship
1:11–2:21	Autobiographical argument: Paul's minimal and independent relation to the Jerusalem apostles
3:1–4:31	Seven theological arguments against the rival missionaries and for Paul's Gospel
3:1–5	The Galatians have already experienced the power of the Spirit.
3:6–9	Abraham was justified by trust in God before being circumcised.

9. N.B.: Though Paul's opponents in the churches have previously often been labeled "Judaizers," this designation properly refers only to those Gentile Christians who have adopted Jewish customs, not to Jewish Christian leaders who are insisting that Gentile Christians adopt Jewish practices. The term means "live like a Jew," not "persuade other people to live like Jews." It is also important to remember that no New Testament evidence presents James as insisting on circumcision for *Gentile* Christians.

10. See Hans Dieter Betz, *Galatians: A Commentary on Paul's Letter to the Churches in Galatia*, Hermeneia (Philadelphia: Fortress Press, 1979), esp. 16–23

11. See Philip H. Kern, *Rhetoric and Galatians: Assessing an Approach to Paul's Epistle*, SNTSMS 101 (Cambridge: Cambridge University Press, 1998); and the various essays in Mark D. Nanos, ed., *The Galatians Debate: Contemporary Issues in Rhetorical and Historical Interpretation* (Peabody, MA: Hendrickson, 2002), and the bibliography they provide.

3:10–14	The law does not add something positive to what you already have, but brings a curse.
3:15–29	The law came 430 years after the covenant and could add nothing to what Abraham and his offspring and heirs had already received by faith.
4:1–11	You have already been freed from slavery to the elemental spirits of the universe to become children of God.
4:12–20	You have already accepted me and my message as an angel of God; how could I now have become your enemy (as the rival missionaries claim)?
4:21–31	The rival missionaries' appeal to Abraham misunderstands the Scripture.
5:1a	Conclusion: Christ has set you free.
5:1b–6:10	Part 2: Parenesis—Christian Freedom: Faith Working through Love
5:1b–12	You are already free; therefore do not return to slavery.
5:13–15	Freedom and love
5:16–21	Works of the flesh, fruit of the Spirit
6:1–10	Life in the Spirit-filled community
6:11–18	Conclusion in Paul's own hand

13.1.6 Exegetical-Theological Précis

1:1–10 Epistolary Introduction

1:1–5 Greeting

Paul expands the typical Hellenistic greeting formula (see on §10.2.3) with an insistent, almost shrill, declaration that he is an apostle called directly by God, not secondarily by human commission or human authority. The apparent egocentricity is not Paul's doing. As in 2 Corinthians 10–13, it is the rival missionaries that have made Paul the agenda. The validity of Paul's apostleship is the disputed point.

While Paul usually expands the greeting formula with warmly affectionate words about the addressees, here he uncharacteristically greets them brusquely as the "churches of Galatia." The trademark pronouncement of "grace and peace" is expanded into a liturgical doxology praising God as the one who through the Lord Jesus Christ has set us free from the enslaving powers of the present evil age—thus setting the tone for the body of the letter.

1:6–10 Thesis Statement: No Other Gospel

Between the greeting and the letter body, the conventional letter form usually included a proem. In all his other extant letters, Paul makes it into an elaborate thanksgiving to God for the letter's recipients. Here, the thanksgiving is conspicuously replaced by Paul's shock that the Galatians are (on the verge of) being converted to a different gospel than the message Paul had originally proclaimed to them. Paul poses the issue in terms of the gospel, not as rival apostolates. The apostle is validated by the gospel, not vice versa. The gospel is the saving, liberating power of God unleashed in the world by the Christ event. The authority of the apostle is only as agent and interpreter of the gospel. The possibility of an angel from heaven preaching a different gospel is rhetorical—neither Paul nor angel is likely to do this—but the radicality of the image demonstrates the priority of message over messenger. Though Paul aggressively defends his mission and apostleship, it's not about Paul.

1:11–5:1a Part 1: Theological Argument—Paul's Defense of his Mission and Apostleship

Paul's theological argument rests on two pillars, oriented respectively to Paul himself and to the Galatians: (1) *I* am an authentic apostle, so what you received from me is all you need to belong to the people of God (1:11–2:21). (2) *You* already have what the rival missionaries claim to be offering you, as proven by your own experience and by Scripture (3:1–5:1a).

1:11–2:21 Autobiographical Argument: Paul's Minimal and Independent Relation to the Jerusalem Apostles

This is the most extensive and organized section in all Paul's letters that deals with his own life. He is forced into recounting the chronology of his life story relevant to his mission by the crisis precipitated by the new teachers in Galatia, who claim that Paul derived his missionary authority from the Jerusalem apostles and that he had not been faithful even to this; he had not told the whole story to the Galatians when he founded the churches in Galatia. In particular, in contrast to the real apostles, he had not told them of the rigid demands the new Christian faith made upon them. Paul's narrative of his life is a fourfold refutation of this charge.

1. *1:11–20*. Paul was an authentic apostle and missionary *before* he ever met any of the Jerusalem apostles. The ultimate source of Paul's authority is from God, manifest in his encounter with the risen Christ. Throughout, Paul's focus is on authority, not content. His denial that he received his gospel from human beings does not contradict his statements elsewhere that the contents of his gospel message were common apostolic tradition, mediated by church instruction, as pictured in 1 Corinthians 11:23–26; 15:3–5; 1 Thessalonians 1:5; 2:12–13; 4:1–2; see Acts 9:1–19, which combines divine call and human instruction.

Paul emphasizes that his present stance toward the law is not the result of ignorance or indifference. He was thoroughly schooled in the law and a dedicated defender of the traditions of Judaism (1:11–14; cf. his self-designation as a Pharisee, Phil 3:5). Then, in the encounter with the risen Christ, God revealed to him the true identity of the crucified Jesus (1:15–16). The "revelation of Jesus Christ" (1:12) has both subjective and objective dimensions; the revelation is both from Jesus Christ and about him. Since in 1:15–16 God is the subject who reveals Jesus Christ to Paul, the genitive is primarily an objective genitive: God revealed the identity of Jesus Christ to Paul. Paul's point here has to do with chronology: after this revelation, he did *not* go immediately to Jerusalem but carried on a mission in Arabia, and did not go to Jerusalem to visit Peter until three years later. During this visit, which lasted only fifteen days, he saw none of the other apostles and was unknown to the churches in Judea—though he did see James the brother of Jesus. Paul swears before God that this is the whole truth (1:20).

2. *1:21–24*. Paul had only *minimal* contact with the Jerusalem leaders during his missionary career. After the visit with Peter, Paul went to Syria and Cilicia for fourteen years. Antioch was located in Syria, and Tarsus, Paul's hometown according to Acts (9:11, 30; 11:25; 21:39; 22:3), was the capital of Cilicia. Galatia is not mentioned. It would have served his purposes well if he could have claimed that he established the Galatian churches during this time, as required by the South Galatian theory. But Paul had not yet been to Galatia, and the churches do not yet exist. During this period, Paul was a missionary under the auspices of the Antioch church, but he understandably does not make this explicit. His point is that during all these years of mission work, he was in Jerusalem only once—hardly an appointee of the Jerusalem leaders. His report of the second Jerusalem visit that immediately follows does not alter this picture.

3. *2:1–10*. Paul's mission and message, though not derived or authorized by the Jerusalem leaders, accord with that of the Jerusalem apostles and are acknowledged by them. Paul's account of the Jerusalem Council emphasizes that he did not go as a delegate of the Antioch church, nor was he summoned by the Jerusalem apostles, but he went on the basis of divine revelation. Titus, an uncircumcised Gentile Christian, was accepted by the Jerusalem leaders as an authentic Christian and missionary. Paul's mission was acknowledged, and an agreement was made

that Paul would go to the Gentiles and Peter to the Jews. James, Peter, and John gave Paul the right hand of fellowship (κοινωνία, *koinōnia*), not just friendly feelings but full communion in the unity of the one church. He received the *handshake* of collegiality and equality, not the *laying on of hands*, which would have meant he was commissioned by them. The legitimacy of Paul's mission was acknowledged. Paul was glad to accept or continue the responsibility of gathering an offering from the Gentile churches for the poor Christians in Judea.

4. *2:11–21*. Paul challenged Peter, the leading Jerusalem apostle, when Peter deviated from the truth of the gospel. This is the meaning of the scene usually called the "Antioch incident." Setting this scene with "when Cephas came to Antioch" indicates that Paul is located in Antioch. This accords with information we have from elsewhere that during this period Paul is serving, along with Barnabas, as a missionary commissioned by the Antioch church. In this context, however, Paul is hesitant to picture his situation in these terms (see Acts 11:20–26; 13:1–4; 14:26–28). Peter comes to Antioch from Jerusalem. We do not know the purpose of his visit, but he stayed some time, and adopted the practice of the Antioch church in which Jewish and Gentile Christians ate together at common meals, including eucharistic celebrations. Then "certain people came from James," who apparently objected that such conduct by Jews was a hindrance to the mission to observant Jews, of which Peter was supposed to be the leader and model (2:9). The Jerusalem Council had apparently envisioned two separate but equal missions to Jews and Gentiles, but did not address the issue of how mixed congregations would conduct their common life.[12] Paul understands that accepting the Gentile mission means accepting Gentile Christians into the one church of Jews and Gentiles, that such a church must be united in table fellowship, that Peter, leader of the Jewish mission, had agreed to this by his joining with Gentile Christians around the common table, and that Peter had now played the hypocrite by backing away from his former conduct.

Paul's whole purpose in recounting this incident in which Peter's conduct "compels the Gentiles [Gentile Christians] to live like Jews," is to address the Galatian crisis generated by the rival missionaries, for this is precisely what they are attempting to do in the Gentile churches of Galatia. Paul speaks over the head of Peter in the Antioch scene to address the Galatian scene directly. His voice modulates from address-to-Peter-back-then to address-to-Galatians-now. It is difficult to determine where in Galatians 2:14–16 Paul is still reporting what he said to Peter in Antioch, but in the following verses he directly addresses the Galatian churches.

For Paul, the "truth of the gospel" is at stake, not his personal status or authority (2:5, 14). Acceptance with God (that allows mutual acceptance of Christians around a common table) is not a matter of any sort of human achievement, including "works of the law," but is the result of the "faithfulness of Jesus Christ."[13] The proclamation of the death and resurrection of Christ with which Paul began this letter (Gal 1:1–5) is the world-changing act of God on which everything depends. Paul's description of himself as being crucified with Christ, and the resurrected Christ continuing to live in him, is a matter not of Paul's own "spirituality" or personal "mystical" piety, but of acknowledging God's act in Christ as all-sufficient, which needs no supplement. To add on rigorous religious rituals, as the new teachers in Galatia are attempting, is to "nullify the grace of God." Paul's point throughout this heated section is not a general discussion of the value of personal

12. The Apostolic Decree of Acts 15:29 is apparently later than the Jerusalem Council. Paul shows no awareness of it in his letters, and explicitly states that no extra requirements were imposed on his churches (Gal. 2:6, 10; see above, §10.1.7).

13. On the discussion of whether such texts refer to the believer's faith and/or to the faithfulness of Christ, see below on Rom 3:21–25.

religious experience vs. religious law and ritual, not a general liberal polemic against "legalism"—and certainly not against Judaism—but an affirmation of the gospel, the good news of what God has done in Christ, which needs no human supplement.

3:1–4:31 Seven Theological Arguments against the Rival Missionaries and for Paul's Gospel

The general line of argument of chapter 3 begins with the promise God made to Abraham and to his offspring. The rival teachers argued that those who wanted to belong to the covenant people of God must belong to the group established through Abraham; that is, they must be born Jews or must convert to Judaism by being circumcised and keeping the law. Paul argues that Christ is the fulfillment of the promise made to Abraham. Those who are in Christ are the true children of Abraham, those who receive the promise. *All* who are baptized receive this promise; the distinction between Jew and Gentile is abolished, as is the distinction between male and female, slave and free. The ἔργα νόμου (*erga nomou*, works of the law) no longer exist as the boundary marker that defines the identity of the covenant people of God. This is not a matter of general human openness and tolerance, "liberal" vs. "conservative," "inclusive" vs. "exclusive." The question is how the purpose of God, embodied in the covenant people of Israel, continues in history. The Jew/Gentile distinction was the obvious boundary marker necessary for the existence of the covenant people of God. To be in the "Israel of God," one had to be or become a Jew. It is not so often noticed that the male/female and slave/free distinction were likewise part of the "people of God" concept. Previously, women and slaves were in Israel by virtue of their relation to Israelite men, that is, by incorporation into the patriarchal Israelite family. For Paul, it is being in Christ that matters for being in the Israel of God, for the promise was to Christ. While Galatians 3:27–28 has been central in modern arguments for Christian inclusiveness, for Paul *the punch line of this argument is Galatians 3:29: "If you belong to Christ, then you are Abraham's offspring, heirs according to the promise."*

This argument is developed in seven steps.

3:1–5 The Galatians have already experienced the power of the Spirit. The Galatians have already experienced the reality of the power of the Holy Spirit among them on the basis of Paul's preaching of the crucified Christ. They know from their own experience they have already received the Holy Spirit, are already "in." They did not have to wait for the supplement to their "incomplete" faith offered by the rival missionaries. This argument from the church's experience of the Spirit is the same argument as Acts 10–11: the Spirit acts without waiting for doctrine and theology to keep up.

3:6–9 Abraham was justified by trust in God before being circumcised. It is striking that Paul here appeals to the Old Testament in his argument against the law. He does not appeal to sayings or example of Jesus, words of the heavenly Lord, or to his own experience. Although he argues against the understanding of the law as a necessary supplement to faith in Christ, this by no means suggests that Paul rejects the law as such. The Jewish Scripture, the later Christian Old Testament, continued to be authoritative Scripture for Paul. The issue was how to understand it.

The relation of law to Christ event, law to gospel, law to faith, continued to perplex Paul. It appears that Paul never developed a consistent, systematic "doctrine of the law," but responded situationally, as a dimension of his missions strategy of being "all things to all people" (1 Cor 9:22). It seems that his thinking changed as he encountered various situations, and that this accounts for some of the differences. It may be that he struggled with the issue and never resolved it abstractly, but was convinced he knew what to do in each situation.

In Galatians, Paul responds to the rival missionaries' appeal to Abraham by arguing from the Torah itself that Abraham was justified by trust in God (Gen 15:6), so that it is those who believe as Abraham did who are blessed along with Abraham.

3:10–14 The law does not add something positive to what you already have, but brings a curse, from which Christ has already delivered believers. Paul's argument, supported by Scripture texts from the Torah itself:

— The law does not rest on faith, but requires doing the commands of the law in order to receive the promised blessing of life (Lev 18:5).

— The law pronounces a curse, not a blessing, on those who do not measure up to its requirements by performing what is required. Here as elsewhere, Paul may be citing a text used by the rival missionaries (Deut 27:26). They used it to incite obedience to the law; Paul cites it to show that those who enter the realm of the law are subject to its curse.

— Christ redeemed us from this curse by receiving this curse in our behalf, since the law pronounces a curse on everyone hanged (Deut 21:23).

— Thus no one is justified before God by doing the works of the law, for the one who is righteous will live by faith in Christ/the faithfulness of Christ (Gen 15:6; see on Rom 3:21–31).

3:15–29 The law came 430 years after the covenant, and could add nothing to what Abraham and his offspring and heirs had already received by faith. Just as the rival missionaries have come to Galatia after the believers there had already experienced the new life in Christ and the power of the Spirit through Paul's original preaching, and could add nothing to what the Galatians already had, so in the history of salvation the law came 430 years after the promise to Abraham that he had already received by his trust in God. Paul plays on the double meaning of διαθήκη (*diathēkē*, covenant; will; see §1.1, Heb 9:15–17), arguing that once a will is established, it cannot be modified by the later addition of someone else.

In response to the rival missionaries' advocacy of the law, Paul's presents an entirely negative view. The law arrived late on the scene and adds nothing to the original promise (3:15–18). It was added, not as a means of salvation, but "because of transgressions" (3:19). This difficult phrase has been interpreted in a variety of ways, but probably means God gave the law to identify innate human sinfulness as the violation of God's will, and that the law was given to restrain this inherent human sinfulness, as a curb on the evil in the world. The law was not, in fact, given directly by God, but "through angels," which in Paul's view is a minus (3:20; on Paul's view of angels, see Rom 8:38; 1 Cor 6:3; 2 Cor 11:14; Gal 1:8). The law was our guardian or disciplinarian (παιδαγωγός, *paidagōgos*, mistranslated "schoolmaster" in earlier English translations), that is, the slave charged with taking the child to school, responsible for his or her security until they were mature. This is a negative role, inhibiting the child's freedom, until the child is able to make responsible decisions and no longer needs such protection.

Paul does not argue that baptism replaces circumcision. His argument does contend that what the rival missionaries claim the Galatians do not yet have, because they need to be circumcised and keep the law, they in fact already have, because they have been baptized into Christ: they are full members of the holy people of God, in which there is no longer any distinction between Jew and Greek, male and female, slave and free. Since they already belong to Christ, they are already children of Abraham and heirs of the promise made to him.

4:1–11 You have already been freed from slavery to the elemental spirits of the universe to become children of God. The στοιχεῖα τοῦ κόσμου (*stoicheia tou kosmou*) are the elemental spirits of the universe that oppress all humanity, the enslaving conditions of human existence as such (see on Rom 8:38–39; 1 Cor 15:20; Phil 2:5–11). By saying "we" (4:3), Paul includes himself. The evil powers had commandeered God's good law, just as they had taken control of God's good creation. All human beings, whether Jew or Gentile, were under the same oppressive slavery. God's sending forth Christ "in the fullness of time" is a matter of God's apocalyptic timetable, set by God himself in the divine plan for salvation history. It is not a matter of God waiting for, or preparing, good historical conditions (Roman roads, widespread Greek language, etc.) as preparation for the Christian mission. The saving event is thought of in apocalyptic terms: enslaved humanity, God's liberating act in the Christ event. As in Philippians 2:5–11 the preexistent Christ enters into the limitations of human existence in order to allow the divine act of liberation, so here Christ enters into the human situation by being born under the law. The divine invasion from the transcendent world is an act of apocalyptic liberation. Former slaves are now free; no longer slaves, they are adopted as sons (υἱοί, *huioi*, "children" in the NRSV's gender-inclusive language). In the power of the Spirit, they address God with the intimate, family language of "Abba." As in 3:1–5, Paul appeals to the Galatians' corporate experience of the Spirit as proof that they already fully belong to God's people without complying with the additional prescriptions of biblical law made by the rival missionaries. The new missionaries urged the Galatians to advance beyond the incomplete beginnings given them in Paul's gospel, and to become full members of the people of God by adding on the full requirements of God's law. For Paul, this is not an advance but a return to their previous slavery.

4:12–20 You have already accepted me and my message as an angel of God; how could I now have become your enemy (as the rival missionaries claim)? Paul again appeals to the undeniable close personal relationship he had enjoyed with the new Galatian converts. In saying, "I have become as you are" (4:12), Paul indicates that even though he knew the rigorous discipline of Jewish law and tradition, he lives in freedom from the law among the Gentile churches (see 1 Cor 9:21–22). In his unplanned original visit to them because of an injury or health problems that resulted in their conversion, they had received *him* as an angel of God. Now they seem to be impressed by the new teachers' talk of angels. The rival missionaries "want to exclude you," that is, *they* do not become like the Galatians, but maintain their "professional distance," impressing the Galatians with their credentials, while Paul numbered himself among his converts as a brother and fellow disciple within the community of faith where such distinctions have been abolished (3:27–28). "I am again in the pain of childbirth" (4:19) reveals Paul's pastoral heart. He is not the self-centered, authoritarian, distant figure he is sometimes made out to be. Despite his sharp critique of them, he loves them with a mother's heart. As he once labored to give them birth, the present crisis is a renewal of labor pains, and he must now "reconvert" them, with all the pain and labor involved.

4:21–5:1a The rival missionaries' appeal to Abraham misunderstands the Scripture. The rival missionaries had appealed to the biblical covenant with Abraham, had argued that Abraham not only believed but obeyed God's command to be circumcised, an essential requirement of belonging to God's covenant people. The modern interpreter might read Genesis 17:1–14 and ponder the way the new Galatian missionaries understood it: circumcision was not optional, circumcision was not temporary, but an "everlasting covenant" (Gen 17:13; see the repeated "forever" in, e.g., Lev 16:29–31; 17:7; 23:14, 21, 31, 41; Deut 5:29).

The Scripture repeatedly emphasized these requirements as valid "throughout the generations" for those who want to be included in God's people. The rival missionaries have set the agenda, and Paul must respond with a different reading of the Abraham story in the light of Christian faith.

Utilizing the allegorical method common among various Jewish interpreters of his time (see above, §§5.1.3, 7.4), Paul argues we must understand the story in terms of *two* covenants. Paul is not discussing the Old Testament and New Testament as parts of the Christian Bible, nor is he speaking about Judaism and Christianity. Both the covenants of which he speaks are Old Testament in that sense, that is, from the time of Abraham. "According to the flesh . . . through the promise" refers to two realms of existence. "Flesh" does not refer to a person's "lower," physical nature, in contrast to a "higher," spiritual nature, but to the world as determined by human abilities, resources, and values (see 1 Cor 3:1; 2 Cor 5:16; 10:2; Rom 8:5–13). "Promise" (identified with "Spirit" in v. 29) refers to the world as determined by God. Paul's symbolic interpretation of Hagar and Sarah as representing two covenants can be outlined as follows:[14]

Hagar	**Sarah**
Slave child born from slave mother	Free child born of free mother
"According to the flesh"	"According to the promise/Spirit"
Present Jerusalem church our "mother"	Heavenly Jerusalem our "mother"
Children of the flesh like Ishmael	Children of the promise like Isaac
Persecutes other group	Is persecuted by other group
Cast out and does not inherit	Receives the inheritance

Paul concludes with an appeal to Scripture, citing Sarah's command to cast out Hagar and Ishmael from the family as the word of "Scripture." Paul understands it as authorizing the Galatians to throw their new teachers out of the church (see 1 Cor 5:1–13, especially the concluding command). Paul had considerable tolerance for a broad range of understandings of the Christian faith. He also recognized a line at which it was not only a different perspective, but a different gospel that was being proclaimed (see 1 Cor 3:21–23; 2 Cor 10–13).

Paul's conclusion for the whole theological argument, made in the indicative mode, declares God's apocalyptic act of liberation: "Christ has set us free" (5:1a).

5:1b–6:10 Part 2: Parenesis—Christian Freedom: Faith Working through Love

5:1b–12 *You are already free; therefore do not return to slavery.*

The indicative, "Christ has set us free," is followed by the imperative, "Stand firm in this freedom. Do not voluntarily return to a state of

14. It has not often been noticed that covenant theology is infrequent in the New Testament and that Paul uses this terminology only in 2 Corinthians and Galatians, written during the same period of his mission, both reflecting a crisis situation. He then backs away from covenant vocabulary in the more reflective Romans, written shortly thereafter, which no longer reflects the crisis situations in Corinth and Galatia. Though he heard or recited the words in every eucharistic celebration (1 Cor 11:23–24), Paul seems to have made covenant terminology a part of his own theological vocabulary only as a polemical response to his opponents' use of the word. "Covenant" is a problematical concept for explicating God's relation to Jews and Gentiles, Jews and Christians, God's comprehensive plan for history. Covenant language and conceptuality raise the question: in the present, is there one covenant or two? Covenant language is in danger of either becoming supersessionism (which Paul rejected) or picturing God as making two distinct covenants, one with Israel and one with the church (which Paul also rejected). Shortly after Galatians (in Romans), Paul will formulate his understanding in categories that avoids the use of covenant terminology.

slavery." Here Paul sees grace and law as two incompatible realms; one cannot be in both at the same time. One's status before God, one's place in the holy people of the covenant, cannot be a combination of what God does and what we do, "God's part" and "our part." Law and grace are two mutually exclusive ways of relating to God.

This does not mean, however, that *refusing* to be circumcised qualifies one as acceptable to God. "For in Christ Jesus neither circumcision nor uncircumcision counts for anything; the only thing that counts is faith working through love" (5:6). The claim to be "free from the law" can become the same kind of claim for status as doing "works of the law." Paul's point is that neither doing nor not doing the law can be a matter of human achievement. Paul sums up the essence of the Christian life as "faith energized by love." This is not a bland general principle but requires the scandal of the cross, which cannot be given up. What Paul is talking about is not just general human niceness vs. "legalism," but a life shaped and energized by God's own love revealed in the scandalous act of crucifixion (see 2:20–21).

5:13–15 *Freedom and Love*

Freedom is not only freedom *from*, but freedom *for*. It is likely that the rival missionaries argued the need for the law both as moral guidance and as a curb on human inclinations to evil. "If we are free from the law, what is to guide us in knowing God's will, and what is to prevent us from being overcome by evil?" Paul's response: believers are indeed free, but freedom must not become a supply base from which the "flesh"—the sinful power resident in human life and culture—can operate. God's act of deliverance not only set believers free from oppressive powers, but set them free for a life of service to each other and to others. Paul uses the daring and paradoxical metaphor of slavery. In this context, in which he has insisted that Christians are set free from bondage, he then directs them to become slaves of each other. The "to one another" is crucial; the service of which he speaks is not hierarchical, in which some are slaves and others are masters, but all are slaves, all are masters.[15]

Christian freedom from the law does not mean that believers are set adrift without a moral compass. In a surprising move, Paul cites the law itself (Lev 19:18) as providing its own summary and fulfillment. When read in the defining light of the Christ event, the love of God revealed in Jesus' death on the cross provides both guide and power to live the life of freedom to which God has called his people.

5:16–21 *Works of the Flesh, Fruit of the Spirit*

The rival missionaries in Galatia were morally serious people. They were not merely the stodgy, rigid, legalistic types that liberals love to caricature. They recognized the power of evil in the world, represented in Jewish tradition by the "evil desire," the "desire of the flesh," which was not thought of, as in the Greek style, as the individual's "lower nature" manifest mostly in sexual sins. They saw the power of evil in the world and believed that God had given the Torah as the means of combating it. The halakah (הלכה, derived from the verb "to walk") was the positive gift of God, the body of legal material placed in the world as the means of resisting the power of evil. To be "free from the law" was morally dangerous, in that it removed the protective shield against the power of evil.

Paul's response is this: God's incursion into the world in the Christ event had not only delivered believers from the slavery to which they had been subject—including the law, which had been commandeered by the powers of evil—but had provided the dynamism of God's own Holy Spirit as guide and power to the believing community.

15. Cf. the opening words of Martin Luther's 1520 *On the Freedom of a Christian*: "A Christian is a free lord, subject to none. A Christian is a perfectly dutiful servant, subject to all."

Over against the "works of the flesh" Paul places the "fruit of the Spirit." Flesh and Spirit are not internal "parts" or "aspects" of the individual's life, but the force fields in which all human life is lived. At baptism, the believer is indeed delivered from the law, but is not left without moral guidance and power. At baptism, the believer is placed within the community of faith where God's Spirit prevails. Two contrasts are important: (1) the "works of the flesh" are plural, the manifestations of the power of evil; the "fruit of the Spirit" is singular, the love of God in its various manifestations. (2) The contrast is not between two kinds of works, flesh and Spirit, but between works and fruit. Works can be done, and the challenge is to be more disciplined and work harder. Fruit is a matter of organic, spontaneous growth, the result of the nature of the tree. Paul does not challenge the Galatians to try harder to live up to Christian ideals; he speaks in the indicative, declaring what happens in the community empowered by the Spirit. Something has happened that has defeated the powers of the old way of life. A real death stands between Christians and the old world. Christ's crucifixion was the price of deliverance; Christians are united with Christ in that death.

6:1–10 *Life in the Spirit-Filled Community*

Paul's profile of the "works of the flesh" in 5:19–21 had not emphasized sexual irregularities in an individualistic sense, but as sins that destroy community. Life subject to the force field flesh is individualistic seeking after this-worldly "success"; life in the Spirit creates community. Paul now gives concluding instructions on the meaning of such a life.

In addressing "you who have received the Spirit," Paul speaks to the whole body of believers. Erring members are to be restored; no Christian can live his or her own "spiritual life," disregarding others in the community as "not my business." Bearing one another's burdens is not only the responsibility of the strong, but a promise to the weak. They are not in this alone, but are supported by a compassionate, caring community, members of a family in which there is mutual care. *This* is the "law of Christ." This phrase may reflect a motto of the rival teachers, who pointed out the need for Christians to continue to obey the law, with Christ the ultimate interpreter of its meaning. Paul takes up this phrase, asserting that the mutual love of the community guided by the Spirit *is* living by the "law of Christ"—love as the summary of the law (5:14=Lev 19:18). The declaration that "all must carry their own loads" is not a contradiction to "bear one another's burdens," for here Paul is pointing to the eschatological future judgment, in which each one will be held personally accountable to God for what they have done—including whether or not they have shared the burdens of their fellow Christians.

Paul thus makes it clear in his closing instructions that his opposition to "works of the law" is not a call to irresponsibility or sloth, that trust in the faithfulness of God for salvation does not mean believers have nothing to do. They are to "work for the good of all": the doctrine of salvation by grace without meritorious works does not cut the nerve of social action for the good of the human community. The church is in the world to represent God's care for the whole world, whether or not the world responds.

6:11–18 Conclusion in Paul's Own Hand

Paul has been dictating to a scribe. At 6:11 he takes the pen in his own hand to write a concluding word that sums up the contrasts he has drawn in the letter, the choice confronting the Galatians. On the one side he lumps together the conventional world of human norms ("the flesh"), the world of human striving and ambition ("boasting"), focused in the rival missionaries' demand for circumcision. On the other side Paul places the cross and the new creation. Here the cross is not only the event that mediates God's forgiveness, but the world-shattering apocalyptic incursion of God into the cosmos that brings the old world to a close and inaugurates the promised eschatological new creation (see Isa 65:17–25; 2 Cor 5:17; Rom 8:19–23; Rev 21:1–5). Especially to be noted is that in his concluding words on the key issue of the letter, Paul does not place "circumcision" in the old world and "uncircumcision" in the new. In the old world, religious distinctions such as circumcision and uncircumcision count for something; in the new creation that is already dawning, *neither circumcision nor uncircumcision* matters.

Equally striking is the concluding declaration that those who live by this rule—those baptized into Christ, for whom such old-worldly human distinctions no longer matter (3:27–28)—receive the blessing that belongs to the "Israel of God." Over against the teaching of the rival missionaries, the Gentile Christians of Galatia already belong to God's people Israel, without circumcision and observance of the law. The final contrast: if one still wants to speak of bodily marks that identify one as belonging to Israel, Paul the Jewish Christian apostle to the Gentiles points not to his circumcision, but to the scars received in the service of the crucified Christ.

For Further Reading, see 13.4

13.2 Interpreting Romans

THE APOSTLE TO THE GENTILES WRITES HIS longest and most thoroughly thought-through letter to the Christian congregations in the capital city of the empire. As it has turned out, Romans was also his most influential letter, "perhaps the most important single expression of gospel and theology every penned."[16]

13.2.1 The Church in Rome: The First Generation

We do not know when, how, or by whom the church in Rome was begun. When Paul writes, it had been in existence for "many years" (1:13; 15:22–23), at least since the 40s. The later tradition that it was founded by Peter has no historical foundation. Though Peter will later come to Rome and will die there (see introduction to 1 Peter, §17.2), he has not been to Rome when Paul writes. Neither has Paul himself been there; of all the undisputed Pauline letters, only Romans is written to a church he has not founded. When Paul writes, he greets by name twenty-six people he has met elsewhere who are now in Rome (Rom 16:3–20), and refers to five different house churches, suggesting a relative large number of Christians. A few years later, at the time of Nero's persecution, there were many hundreds.

We do know something of the composition and history of the Roman congregations. The Christian community began as messianic believers within the synagogues.[17] They would have been both ethnic Jews and proselytes, but also would have included God-fearers who identified with the Jewish community and attended the synagogue. For generations, there had been a large Jewish community in Rome, which sometimes lived a precarious existence. They mostly belonged to the lower social classes, lived and worked in the poorer sections of the capital; more than once they had been forced to leave the city. They had made strenuous efforts, typical of Diaspora Judaism in urban centers, to adjust to their social and political environment—in particular to demonstrate that they were loyal subjects of Rome—without compromising their faith or their identity. Most striking in this regard is that some synagogues that can be dated to the first century are named after

16. Dunn, *Beginning from Jerusalem*, 932. Histories of theology and biblical interpretation regularly point out the rediscovery of the message of Romans at decisive turning points in Christian history, especially its influence on Augustine, Aquinas, Luther, Wesley, and Barth.

17. See especially Brown and Meier, *Antioch and Rome*, section "The Beginnings of Christianity in Rome," 92–104, and Lampe, *Paul to Valentinus*, 7–16, 69–84, 153–83.

leading Romans, including the emperor himself. There are synagogues named after Augustus, Marcus Agrippa, Herod the Great, and Volumnius. This could not have been done without official approval and demonstrates the exertions of the Jewish community to integrate itself into Roman society and secure their legal status.[18]

Despite these efforts, once again Jews were forced to leave the city under the emperor Claudius, in 49 CE (cf. the case of Prisca and Aquila, Acts 18:2). This would mean that the Jewish Christian element in the leadership of the churches, presumably a sizable contingent, was forced to leave and that the Christian congregations would be composed primarily of Gentile Christians—many of whom had presumably been God-fearers before becoming Christians. In the meantime, the membership of the Roman churches would be augmented by Gentile Christians from elsewhere who had moved to the capital, as evidenced by the list of names in Romans 16. When Claudius's decree was rescinded after his death in 54 CE, many of these Jewish Christians (including Prisca and Aquila) returned to Rome, finding that the congregations to which they belonged now had a predominately Gentile Christian character.

Even so, the Roman congregations remained rooted in the Jewish traditions of their origins. A generation or more after Paul's time, the Gentile Christian author of *1 Clement*, writing as a representative of the Roman church, shows that Roman Christianity remained oriented to the Jewish Scripture and postcanonical Jewish traditions, which continued to be important to the Roman congregations. Tacitus seems to think that Roman Christianity derived from Judea (*Annals* 15.44.2–5). This history and these tensions are reflected in Paul's letter. In Rome, the relation of Jews and Christians, Jewish Christians and Gentile Christians, is not only a profound and complex theological issue but a practical issue of church life.

13.2.2 Literary Integrity

Previous generations of critics have sometimes argued that Romans 16 did not belong to the original text of Romans, but was part of a letter to Ephesus added to Romans during the editorial process that produced the Pauline corpus. This conclusion was supported by two primary arguments: (1) The chapter is appropriate to Ephesus, but not to Rome. In Ephesus, Paul has many friends and contacts, but he has never been to Rome. Romans 16 contains greetings to twenty-eight individuals, twenty-six by name, sixteen of these with an additional note. How could he greet so many people in the Roman church? In particular, some of the people greeted were last located in Ephesus (see 1 Cor 16:19; Acts 18:18–19, 24–28; 2 Tim 4:19 [Aquila and Prisca]; Rom 16:5 [Epaenetus]). The polemic against false teaching in Romans 16:17–20 fits Ephesus, where Paul had lived and worked, but not Rome, where he was personally unacquainted, and does not fit the tone of the rest of Romans. (2) The manuscript tradition of Romans manifests great variety regarding the way the document ends:[19]

a. 1:1–16:23 + 16:25–27: $\mathfrak{P}^{61vid}$ ℵ B C

b. 1:1–14:23 : Marcion (according to Origen)

c. 1:1–15:33 + 16:25–27 + 16:1–23: $\mathfrak{P}^{46}$

d. 1:1–16:23 + 16:24: D 06 (Greek original) F 010gr G

e. 1:1–16:23 + 16:24 + 16:25–27: D 06 F 0101 at Pel

f. 1:1–14:23 + 16:25–27 + 15:1–16:23 + 16:24: n l sy^{h}

g. 1:1–14:23 + 16:25–27 + 15:1–16:23 + 16:25–27: A

18. See Dunn, *Beginning from Jerusalem*, who cites Karl P. Donfried and Peter Richardson, eds., *Judaism and Christianity in First-Century Rome* (Grand Rapids: Eerdmans, 1998), 17–29.

19. The table is taken from Schnelle, *New Testament Writings*, 116.

This data was taken as evidence that Romans originally circulated without the final chapter, which was added secondarily in a variety of constellations, with the concluding doxology and the blessing of 16:24 occurring in a number of different locations and combinations. Textual analysis has revealed fifteen different textual forms of the concluding section of Romans.[20] Romans 16:17–20 and 16:25–27 are now often considered post-Pauline interpolations.

The majority opinion now, however, is that Romans 16, with or without the interpolations, belongs to the original letter to Rome. (1) In regard to the first category of evidence: Paul's greeting so many people in a church to which he has never been is best explained by the history of the church and by one of Paul's motives in writing the letter. Jewish Christians earlier banished from Rome whom Paul had met elsewhere, such as Prisca and Aquila, had now returned. In the course of his widespread mission work, Paul had met many Christians, and he now greets as many of them as possible in order to cement relations between himself and this church, to which he is otherwise personally unknown, since he is asking them to support his future mission. (2) The complex manuscript tradition of the ending of Romans is the result of the ripple effect of Marcion's editing the Pauline corpus. Marcion excised all the sections of Paul's letters that sounded pro-Jewish or reflected the Jewish Scriptures, considering them to be later non-Pauline additions (see above §2.2.1). This meant that a truncated edition of Romans circulated, without the concluding section with its Jewish-sounding elements, including the specific designation of Jesus as "servant of the circumcised" (15:8). In the process of transmission and editing, the shorter Marcionite version apparently interacted with the original longer edition, generating the variety of endings. Most scholars now see Romans 16 not only as part of the original letter but as important in understanding the letter as a whole.[21]

20. Jewett, *Romans*, 4.

13.2.3 Letter Type, Occasion, Purpose

Romans is the most systematic and clearly organized of Paul's letters, but it is not Paul's systematic theology, not a "compendium of Christian doctrine," in Melanchthon's famous phrase.[22] It is not a complete statement of Paul's faith. While the letter discusses one of the meanings of Christian baptism, for instance, it does not mention the Eucharist. If we had only Romans, we would not know that the Pauline churches had a eucharistic tradition and practice. While Romans considers the death of Jesus theologically important, the letter never explicitly mentions the cross or crucifixion—though it is presupposed in 6:6, "our old self was crucified with him." If we had only Romans, we might not grasp the crucial role the cross plays in Paul's theology. Romans is a letter, which means it too must be understood as a document composed for a particular occasion and readership, within a particular chronology and projecting a particular narrative world. A helpful way to approach the letter is to view it in the light of the key locations in Paul's life and mission that illuminate the purpose(s) and influence the content of the letter.

Galatia. Sometime in the recent past, probably while in Macedonia and only a short while before arriving in Corinth where he is writing Romans, Paul had written the fiery letter to the Galatian churches. The issues of that letter are still much on his mind: the role of the law of Moses in the Christian life; circumcision as

21. See practically all recent commentaries on Romans, as well as the thorough treatments in Lampe, *Paul to Valentinus*, 153–64, and in D. C. Parker, *An Introduction to the New Testament Manuscripts and Their Texts* (Cambridge: Cambridge University Press, 2008), 270–74.

22. *Christianae religionis compendium*, Philipp Melanchthon, *The Loci Communes of Philip Melanchthon*, trans. Charles Leander Hill (Boston: Meador, 1944), 69, from 2.1.7 of Melanchthon's collected works, *Melanchtons Werke in Auswahl.*

the mark of the covenant; Christian believers, including Gentiles, as "children of Abraham." As Paul writes to Rome, he has the opportunity to think through these issues in a more reflective mood. Rome itself is not threatened by these teachers, so Paul is not writing to confront directly an actual situation. But the Roman Christians have probably heard bad reports about Paul and his gospel, including his sarcastic references to the Jerusalem leaders ("so-called 'Pillars'"; see Gal 2:2, 6, 9). There were close connections between the Jerusalem church and the Roman church, which may have been to some extent a product of the Jerusalem mission. In the letter to the Romans, Paul can write about the same issues he had dealt with in Galatians, but with less heat and more light. He does not merely reaffirm his earlier position in a softer tone of voice; he rethinks it and adjusts it. There is a sense in which Romans is the first commentary on Galatians, and by the original author.

Corinth. As Paul writes to Rome, he is in Corinth, where the Aegean mission has come full circle. Near the beginning of the Aegean mission, Paul writes from Corinth to the new church in Thessalonica, his first extant letter and our earliest New Testament document. As he now brings the Aegean mission to a close (Rom 15:19), he writes from Corinth what is probably his last extant letter, which was to become his testament—though not written specifically as such.

Paul has come to Corinth from Ephesus, where he had suffered life-threatening persecution and imprisonment, through Macedonia, where he learned from Titus that the troubles between him and the Corinthian church had been resolved (Acts 19:23–20:3). He is now settled in Corinth for a relatively comfortable three-month stay, presumably provided by his well-to-do hosts (Phoebe, Gaius, Erastus, Rom 16:2, 23), who also seem to have provided the services of a professional scribe (Tertius, Rom 16:22). There is no reference in Romans, as in previous letters, to his working at his own trade to support himself (1 Thess 2:9; 1 Cor 4:12; 9:3–18; 2 Cor 11:7–11), a "boast" in regard to his mission strategy on which he had apparently backed down as part of his reconciliation with Corinth.

Corinth was also the setting of Paul's previous debate concerning spiritual gifts and charismatic phenomena (see 1 Cor 12–14; 2 Cor 11:16–12:10). These experiences are still present in his mind as he writes to Rome. The similarities between Romans and 1 Corinthians in Paul's instructions about charismatic gifts, using the metaphor of the body of Christ animated by the *pneuma*/breath/Spirit, may be at least as much the result of the setting in which he writes the letter as the situation to which he writes (cf., e.g., 1 Cor 12–13 and Rom 12:3–21). There is a sense in which Romans is the first commentary on 1 Corinthians, and by the original author.

Jerusalem. During his three months in Corinth, Paul is also occupied with making the final arrangements to deliver the offering to Jerusalem. Several people will accompany him, the delegates from the churches, and Paul's own coworkers (Acts 20:4; 1 Cor 16:3; 2 Cor 8:23). Before coming to Rome, he will go to Jerusalem. The leaders of the Jerusalem church are suspicious of him and his Gentile gospel to Gentile churches. He wants to reassure them that he has not abandoned the ancestral faith in which God's promise to Israel is irrevocable, that the Gentile churches fit into and do not violate this plan of God worked out through history. He wants the offering to be a tangible symbol of the unity of Jews and Gentiles in the one church. He fears that he, his message, and his offering may not be acceptable (Rom 15:25–32). The argument of Romans is a dress rehearsal for Jerusalem.

Spain. Paul's plans are to take the offering to Jerusalem and then to come to Rome. But the capital city is not his final goal. He wants to spend some time there, strengthening the church, and—he is careful to say to this church that he did not found and does not belong to "his" missionary orbit—being strengthened by *them* (Rom 1:11–12). But his final goal is Spain, the western limit of the world he knows.

One of the reasons for writing Romans is to set before the Roman church the nature of the gospel he preaches, for he is clear in advance that he wants them to support his Spanish mission (Rom 15:24, 28).

Rome. Though what he has to say is influenced by these other settings in Paul's life and mission, the content of Paul's letter to the Romans is primarily influenced by Rome itself. It may be the case that, though Paul has not been there, he is well-informed about the particular issues and difficulties the Roman church is dealing with and directs his apostolic instruction to the particulars of the Roman situation. It is certainly the case that Paul has in view the general Roman situation: a Christian community meeting in distinct house congregations, probably of Jewish origin and heritage, that now, because of the history outlined above, is struggling with the relation of a Jewish Christian minority to a Gentile Christian majority. Jewish and Gentile Christians are having difficulties with each other, and both are struggling with the nature of their relationship to the parent body of Roman Judaism.

As the Jewish Christian apostle to the Gentiles preparing for a crucial meeting in Jerusalem, the world capital of Judaism, before he visits the capital of the Gentile world, he feels a special responsibility toward this church that he did not found, but that he knows plays a key role in the worldwide church—though he could not know what a crucial role this church and this letter was to play in Christian generations to come. With forebodings that he may not survive the fateful encounter in Jerusalem, he wants to leave a statement of the Pauline gospel on file in the capital city of the Gentile world—just in case he is not able to preach there in person. This is Paul's letter to the Romans.

13.2.4 Structure and Outline

The macrostructure of the letter is clear, arranged in the bipartite structure corresponding to Paul's theology, with an extensive doctrinal argument (chaps. 1–11) followed by a predominately paraenetic section of instructions (chaps. 12–16; see above, §10.2.3). Within the first part, a clear division comes at 9:1, with chapters 9–11 comprising a discrete section on the role of Israel in God's plan for history. The first eight chapters are further bifurcated by a distinct turning point in the argumentation at 3:21, as Paul turns from the human plight of universal sinfulness to the saving act of God. Within chapters 5–8, the phrase "in/through Jesus Christ our Lord" occurs at regular intervals, marking off distinct units (5:1, 11, 21; 6:23; 7:25; 8:39). The whole is framed by the opening greeting, thanksgiving, and thesis statement and the concluding section of travel plans, greetings, and benediction.

1:1–17	Epistolary Introduction
1:1–7	Greeting
1:8–15	Thanksgiving
1:16–17	Thesis of the Letter
1:18–11:36	Part 1: God's Righteousness in History
1:18–8:39	The Revelation of God's Righteousness
1:18–3:20	The necessity of God's righteousness: *Universal human sin.*
1:18–32	The revelation of the wrath of God
2:1–16	Judge others . . . condemn yourself.
2:17–3:8	The Jews and the law
3:9–20	All . . . are under the power of sin.
3:21–5:21	The reality of God's righteousness: *Universal divine grace*
3:21–31	God's saving act in Christ
4:1–25	The human response of faith
5:1–11	Salvation as past, present, future
5:12–21	Christ and Adam
6:1–7:6	Objection and response
6:1–14	You are baptized.

6:15–23	You are a freed slave with a new master.
7:1–6	You are freed from the law through participating in the death of Christ.
7:7–25	The law is not sin, but (like us) is the victim of sin.
8:1–39	Freedom in the Spirit
8:1–17	The power of the Spirit
8:18–39	Vivid expectation of redemption along with the cosmos
9:1–11:36	God's Righteousness and the Role of Israel in God's Plan for History
9:1–29	God's freedom
9:30–10:21	Christ the *telos* of the law
11:1–36	God the source and goal of all
12:1–15:33	Part 2: God's Righteousness Lived Out in Christian Lives as Response to God's Grace
12:1–2	From Indicative to Imperative
12:3–8	Life Together
12:9–13:14	Love in Practice
14:1–15:33	The Inclusive Church as Prolepsis of the Present-and-Coming Kingdom of God
14:1–15:13	The inclusive church
15:14–33	Apostle to the Gentiles and mission strategy
16:1–27	Greetings, Warnings, Doxology

13.2.5 Exegetical-Theological Précis

1:1–17 Epistolary Introduction

1:1–7 Greeting

Though missionary colleagues are with him as he writes (16:21–23), only here in the undisputed Pauline letters does Paul's name stand alone as the sender. To this church that he did not found, that he has never visited, and where he is relatively unknown, these opening words twice refer to his apostolic office (vv. 1, 5). Yet, in this most extensive of all the Pauline letter salutations, Paul does not expand on his own role but elaborates the nature of the gospel. In the opening words, he thus signals the major theme and purpose of the letter: to set forth the Pauline gospel to a church that does not know him.

This gospel is not merely Paul's personal message, but is the gospel promised by Israel's prophets in the Scripture and summarized in a traditional creedal statement. This creed (vss. 3–4) represents Christ in a twofold affirmation as the legitimate Messiah of Israel, the human Son of David born "according to the flesh," who "according to the Spirit of holiness" was designated (by God) as Son of God in power by the resurrection from the dead. This two-stage christological affirmation apparently derives from the tradition of Jewish Christianity, was recognizable by the Roman church, and may indeed have been a common element in their liturgy. Though it does not represent the three-stage Christology Paul affirms when articulating his own understanding of the Christ event (see on Phil 2:5–11), he shows in the opening lines that he can affirm the common faith of the church expressed in other ways. He is sincere in this, but also diplomatically laying the groundwork for the argument of the letter affirming the one church of Jewish and Gentile Christians.

1:8–15 Thanksgiving

Paul's thanksgiving is likewise sincere and more than the customary formality. He wants to come to Rome to preach the gospel to them and impart some spiritual gift (χάρισμα, *charisma*, see on 1 Cor 12), and he somewhat defensively explains why he has not been there already. Yet he acknowledges their independence from him, is grateful that quite apart from him their faith is already known throughout the world and that when he comes he will not only give to them but receive from them, in a mutual exchange of spiritual gifts and encouragement. It is not until the conclusion of the letter that it becomes clear that he wants financial support from them for his proposed mission to Spain (15:22–24).

1:16–17 *Thesis of the Letter*

— What is Romans *about*? Paul answers this question in advance in this tightly packed propositional statement that anticipates and summarizes the argument of the letter. He here follows the form of classical rhetoric, in which the argument of the discourse is preceded by a short statement of the thesis to be developed, the *propositio* that precedes the *probatio*.[23]

— The gospel is God's saving power for *all* who believe, whether Jew or Gentile.

— This gospel is God's saving power because it is the revelation of the *righteousness of* God (δικαιοσύνη θεοῦ, *dikaiosynē theou*). This complex phrase[24] can refer to (1) a *quality of* God, an aspect of God's eternal nature (see 3:26, where the opposite would be an unrighteous God); (2) the *act of* God, present and future, in establishing justice in the world (Matt 5:6, 6:33, where it is identified with God's kingdom, God's eschatological act in establishing justice) (3) the *status from* God for the individual, the not-guilty status of one who has been charged before the court. This status can be (a) *declared, imputed*, a declaration of amnesty or not guilty that makes one's legal status real, and/or (b) *enacted*, more than a declaration of status, a transformation of one's being in which an unrighteous life is regenerated to become a righteous life, and an unjust world is transformed to become a just world.

— This gospel is not a new reality, discontinuous from what has gone before, but is in continuity with, and the fulfillment of, the Scriptures of Israel. Habakkuk 2:4 is here cited as the biblical basis for his theology, with much more Scripture to come (Romans cites the Bible more than any other Pauline letter).

— The Pauline gospel is not a continuation of the proclamation of Jesus. It rests on God's act in the Christ event as such, not on the content of Jesus' life and teachings.

— The contrast is between the righteousness of God and human righteousness, not between two kinds of human righteousness (by works of the law, by faith). The key text in Romans does not deal with the justification of sinners, but with justifying God, especially if its context and meaning in Habakkuk is taken into account. Habakkuk's basic concern is with theodicy.

Each of these initial declarations is unpacked in the argument that follows.

1:18–11:36 Part 1: God's Righteousness in History

1:18–8:39 *The Revelation of God's Righteousness*

1:18–3:20 The necessity of God's righteousness: Universal human sin The overall purpose this section and its place in the argument of the letter as a whole is clear: all people, irreligious and religious, Gentiles and Jews, have rebelled against their Creator, spread

23. See Jewett, *Romans*, 29–30 and passim, who sees Paul structuring Romans throughout according to the classical rhetorical pattern: *exordium* (1:1–12); *narratio* (1:13–15); *propositio* (1:16–17); *probatio*, a proof divided into four discrete arguments consisting of ten pericopae each (1:18–4:25; 5:1–8:39; 9:1–11:36; 12:1–15:13) and a *peroration* (15:14–16:16, 21–23, with 16:17–20 and 25-27 regarded as later interpolations).

24. In interpreting this central phrase in Pauline theology, it must be kept in mind that English has no single set of terms that corresponds to the adjective δίκαιος (*dikaios*, righteous, just), δικαιόω (*dikaioō*, justify), and δικαιοσύνη (*dikaiosunē*, righteousness, justice). Cf. "rightwising," used by Kendrick Grobel in Bultmann, *Theology of the New Testament*, 1:253 note, and "rectitude," "rectify," used by Leander Keck, *Romans*, ANTC (Nashville: Abingdon Press, 2005), 52 and passim.

injustice in the world, and stand under the wrath of God, with no hope of justifying themselves. Paul first elaborates the sinfulness of Gentiles, who do not have the written Law of God given through Moses (1:18–32), then the sinfulness of religious people who condemn the immorality of others (2:1–16), including especially Jews who pride themselves on possessing the Law of God (2:17–3:7). He concludes with a medley of Scripture texts that declare all human beings without distinction to be guilty sinners in need of God's grace. The law is not a means of salvation, but only brings the knowledge of sin, "so that every mouth may be silenced, and the whole world may be held accountable to God" (3:19–20). Though the main line of the argument is unmistakable, it takes some turns and contains some expressions not immediately transparent to the modern reader.

1:18–32 The revelation of the wrath of God

The *wrath of God* does not refer to emotional outbursts, but is the biblical expression for the impartial and just response of God's holiness to human sin (153 times in LXX, including the Wisdom tradition, e.g., Sir 5:7; 48:10). The gospel of God's act in the Christ event makes real both God's judging act (*wrath*) and God's justifying act (*righteousness*). *Revealed* does not refer to the disclosure of information, but in each case means *put into effect*. This revelation is both present and future; both judgment and salvation are put into effect as the already/not-yet reality of God's act in Christ.

Paul illustrates the nature of sin with a traditional vice catalogue. Such lists were a common technique of ancient moralists (cf. 1 Cor 5:10–11; 6:9–10; Gal 5:19–21; Eph 4:31; 5:3–5; Col 3:5, 8; 1 Tim 1:9–10; 6:4–5; 2 Tim 3:2–4; Titus 3:3). They are not definitive catalogues but illustrative samples of the nature of sin, representing immorality as conventionally regarded in the author's context. Paul speaks from within his background in Diaspora Judaism, where Gentile idolatry was regarded as inevitably leading to immorality. In contrast to the Gentile context, homosexual acts were regarded as particularly sinful, since they represented the intentional perversion of the will of the Creator and "the exchange of natural sexual roles," an argument explicitly developed in Wisdom of Solomon (11:15–16; 12:24–27; 14:12, 26).

Paul stands in this tradition that regards homosexual acts as willful choices made by heterosexual persons who have intentionally perverted the way God created them—a sin against the Creator. The concept of homosexuality as a sexual orientation not chosen by the person, but received as part of God's creation, was unknown to Paul. Given such a cultural context, it is understandable that Paul regards homosexual acts as illustrating the primal sin, the rejection of the Creator and the perversion of God's good creation (1:20–21). For Paul, sin is not the transgression of a list of rules, but the refusal of the creature to have God as Creator, the refusal to honor God as God, the will to power that places human will and understanding in the place of God.

2:1–16 Judge others . . . condemn yourself.

At 2:1 the argument turns from the condemnation of flagrant Gentile sins to those moral and religious types who join Paul in condemning the blatant evils of society, assuming that their judgment of others makes them immune from God's own judgment. Paul is not here addressing a "judgmental attitude," the opposite of which would be the liberal enlightened virtue of "tolerance." Paul has in view the more fundamental sin that supposes the condemnation of social wrongs exempts one from accountability before God. Though details of the argument are ambiguous or unconvincing, Paul relentlessly pursues his main point: God's ultimate judgment is universal and impartial (2:11). But if all human beings are ultimately judged by the same divine standard, what is the role of the law in God's plan, and what is the meaning of God's choice of Israel to be a special people called by God and given the law? This profound problem troubled both Paul and his readers, and he will return to it as a main focus of the letter. Here, Paul only makes a two-fold point: (1) All human beings live under the law of God, whether it be the law of the Creator revealed in nature (1:18–32) the effects of which are written on the hearts of all people (2:14–15) or the law of Moses revealed on Mount Sinai (2:17–29). (2) What counts, however, is not merely having the law, but living by it, for this is the basis of God's judgment—and no one can claim to have done *that*.

2:17–3:8 The Jews and the law
It is sometimes assumed that the argument shifts from Gentiles to Jews at 2:1, but Paul does not explicitly address Jews until 2:17. The point is underscored: not merely having the law, but doing it, is what counts. Even circumcision, the sign of belonging to God's covenant people, does not deliver from God's judgment unless one keeps the law (2:25). Uncircumcised people who keep God's law are accepted by God; circumcised people who transgress God's law are subject to God's judgment. Adopting the diatribe style, in which protests are placed in the mouth of the presupposed objector, Paul asks, "Then what advantage has the Jew? Or what is the value of circumcision?" One expects the assumed logic of the argument to call forth the response "None at all!" but Paul surprisingly responds, "Much in every way!" He shifts the argument to another level. Rather than remaining at the level of human acts of faith and asking how human beings can be justified, he responds in terms of the faithfulness of God (ἡ πί στις τοῦ θεοῦ *hē pistis tou theou*) and God's being justified (δικαιωθῇς *dikaiōthēs*).[25] Paul's gospel of the unconditional grace of God—yet to be spelled out in this letter—likewise generates the objection that if Paul's version of the Christian gospel is true, "Let us do evil that good may come." Paul will give a full response (6:1–23) after he has given a more complete statement of his understanding of grace. Here, he dismissively rejects such a willful misunderstanding: "Their condemnation is deserved" (3:8).

3:9–20 All . . . are under the power of sin.
The noun "sin" occurs here for the first time in Romans. Though the Greek text says simply "under sin" (so KJV, NIV), the NRSV, TNIV, REB, and other translations are correct in translating "under the power" or "dominion" of sin. Except when citing tradition, Paul never refers to "sins" as individual transgressions, but always refers to "sin" in the singular as a personified, enslaving power. Human sinfulness is here thought of, not as an accumulation of mistakes, but as being subject to a power that sweeps all human beings before it like an irresistible flood (Paul elaborates in 6:15–7:25). The Jew/Gentile distinction, like the righteous/unrighteous distinction, disappears into the common situation of all humanity in bondage to the power of sin.

Paul recites a collection of biblical passages he has assembled to show that the understanding of universal human sinfulness he advocates is not a new Christian doctrine, but is repeatedly documented in the Jewish Scriptures. Nor is his view of human sinfulness an inference from observing the human scene (which always appears to us as a mixture of good and evil). This perspective on the human situation is a matter of revelation, derived from Scripture and the Christ event. While the revelation was given in Israel's Scripture, it reveals the situation of humanity as a whole: No one is righteous (Eccl 7:20). For Paul, all human beings, even with the law of God and our own good intentions, left to ourselves, are doomed.

3:21–5:21 The reality of God's righteousness: Universal divine grace A major turn in the argument occurs at 3:21, νυνὶ δέ (*nuni de*, But now), as Paul contrasts human acts (both irreligious and religious efforts to keep the

25. These are not yet full or satisfactory responses to the legitimate, troubling questions Paul has raised, which he will deal with later (3:1=9:1–5; 3:3=9:6; 3:5=9:14; 3:7=9:19; 3:9=9:30–10:21). See elaboration by N. T. Wright, "The Letter to the Romans," in *The New Interpreter's Bible*, ed. Leander Keck (Nashville: Abingdon Press, 2002), 10:454.

divine law) that lead to condemnation, with God's own act that leads to salvation. The contrast is not between two theories, "law" and "grace," but between the human situation seen on its own and the human situation seen in the light of God's saving act in Christ. Likewise, the contrast is not merely chronological, "before Christ" and "after Christ," as though with the advent of Christ God had changed the divine plan of salvation; for Paul will immediately show that trust in God's faithfulness has always been the way of salvation (4:1–25). So also Paul does not present a chronology in which human beings vainly sought to secure their own acceptance before God, only to end in despair that prepared them for the coming of Christ. The situation described in the preceding section, in which all humanity is under the wrath of God, is seen only retrospectively from the viewpoint of Christian faith.

3:21–31 God's saving act in Christ

The righteousness of God, that is, God's justifying act that both *declares* human beings to be in right relation with God and *effects* righteousness in them, is revealed on another basis than law. This righteousness comes διὰ πίστεως Ἰησοῦ Χριστοῦ, *dia pisteōs Iēsou Christou*, an ambiguous phrase that may legitimately be translated either as "faith in Jesus Christ" or "the faithfulness of Jesus Christ."[26] The phrase has been intensively discussed in recent scholarship,[27] with a growing number of interpreters arguing that, at least in some texts, the right understanding and translation is the subjective genitive "faith(fulness) of Jesus Christ" rather than the objective genitive "faith in Jesus Christ." The decision need not be global, as though the word πίστις (*pistis* faith/faithfulness) and its relation to a following noun in the genitive (God, Christ) must always have the same meaning. The phrase can well be understood as "the faithfulness of" (Christ or God) in some contexts; in other contexts, the objective genitive *must* be the meaning ("faith in . . ."). In the latter case, however, this does not mean that God went looking for human righteousness and, not finding it, was willing to take the human act of faith as a substitute.

The modern discussion tends to conceive the subjective genitive/objective genitive distinction too rigidly and to pose a false alternative, the either/or of human faith or divine faithfulness. Rather, both are embraced in the saving event of the faithfulness of God enacted in the faithfulness of Jesus, to which the human response is human trust in God's saving act. Paul surely intends throughout that salvation is not a matter of human attainment, whether this be conceived as "works of the law" or by making a "decision of faith," but as a matter of God's faithfulness to the covenant promises in sending the Messiah, and the faithfulness of Jesus in obedience to God. The faithfulness of Jesus in going to the cross is perceived and made real as God's saving act only to those who have faith.

This saving act of God can be apprehended and expressed only in terms of metaphors. No single metaphor is adequate. The plurality of metaphors keeps the soteriological language from being understood literally or in an objectifying sense. Such metaphors are expressed in referential but nonobjectifying language; the language refers to something beyond its own linguistic world, but this "something" cannot be conceived in an objectifying manner, as an event in space/time reality observable by a neutral spectator from which logical inferences could be made. Interpreters generally agree

26. The phrase πίστις [Ἰησοῦ] Χριστοῦ (*pistis [Iēsou] Christou*) occurs five times in Paul, with the analogous πίστις τοῦ υἱοῦ τοῦ θεου (*pistis tou huiou tou theou*, faith in / faithfulness of the Son of God) in Gal. 2:20. Cf. πίστις θεοῦ (*pistis theou*) of Rom 3:3, which must be subjective genitive, "the faithfulness of God," and is so rendered by all modern translations.

27. For summaries of the discussion, and bibliography listing advocates of each side of the issue, see Richard B. Hays, "PISTIS and Pauline Christology," in *Looking Back, Pressing On*, ed. E. Elizabeth Johnson and David M. Hay, *Pauline Theology* (Atlanta: Scholars Press, 1997), 35–60; James D. G. Dunn, "Once More, PISTIS CHRISTOU," in *Looking Back, Pressing On*, 61–91; Jewett, *Romans*, 277–78.

that Paul here takes up a traditional creedal or hymnic affirmation affirming God's saving act, which portrays God's act in a variety of metaphors, including the law court (*justification*; the sinful person is acquitted by the judge), the slave market (*redemption;* the slave is purchased and set free), and the sacrificial cult (*sacrifice of atonement*; the estranged person is reconciled to God by the act of sacrifice).

4:1–25 The human response of faith
In 1:2 and 3:21 Paul had declared that the gospel of justification by faith was not a Christian innovation but was witnessed to by the "law and the prophets" of Jewish Scripture, the Christian Old Testament. He now illustrates this by the examples of Abraham and David.

4:1–12 The examples of Abraham and David Abraham is not introduced as a random example, but as the patriarch who stands at the head of the covenant community. The importance of being somehow a participant in this Abrahamic community had already become a key issue in the dispute with the rival Jewish Christian teachers in the Galatian churches (see above on Gal 1:7; 3:6–18) and was no doubt prominent among the Jewish Christian segment of the Roman church. How did Abraham become acceptable to God? During the dispute with the Galatian false teachers, Paul had reread the Abraham story through his Christian eyes and focused on a text (Gen 15:6) that presents Abraham as already declared righteous by God on the basis of his faith, not on the basis of his own achievement.[28] This declaration was made before he was circumcised, before he had kept the law. So also David, assumed to be the author of Psalm 32:1–2, speaks not of human righteousness but of God's forgiveness.

4:13–25 God's promise realized through faith *Promise* and *law* are here presented as two fundamentally different and mutually exclusive ways of relating to God. Promise is a matter of God's initiative and act; law is a matter of human beings meeting certain requirements. The promise is not exacted but is God's free choice; it does not exclude human response and responsible action, but it does exclude making a legal claim on God by human action, whether this be the human action of keeping the law or the human action of believing in Christ. *Faith* in Paul's sense cannot be understood as a *work*, a human achievement substituted for keeping the law (see on 3:21–31). Paul's gospel of salvation is oriented to God's promise, not to human acts, whether these be works or faith.

Abraham illustrates the meaning of faith as radical trust in God's power to give life. The promise is radical. God is not merely the one who supplements our lack after we have done our best and still not measured up ("nobody's perfect"), but the Creator who initiates and takes responsibility for the whole, the God who *justifies the ungodly, creates out of nothing, and raises the dead* (4:5, 17). This is the *one* God (3:30), the God of all peoples, the God who promised Abraham that he would be father of *many* nations (including the Gentile Christian readers), and who fulfills this promise in the event of Christ's death and resurrection (4:25).

5:1–11 Salvation as past, present, future
In 5:1–8:39 Paul presents God's righteousness as made real in human life. God's saving act is a reality in the past, present, and future. While Paul's theology is not structured by his use of Greek tenses, it is striking that four times in this brief section the past/present/future model is used to portray God's saving act (5:2, 8–9, 10). The "when" of salvation is located in the *past*

28. Genesis 15:6 had already been interpreted in some streams of first-century Jewish tradition in a way that combined Abraham, faith, and righteousness in a manner similar to Paul (cf. 1 Macc 2:52; Philo; Dead Sea Scrolls). It is this stream of Jewish interpretation that Paul develops in the light of God's saving act in the cross of Jesus. Thus Judaism should not be stereotyped as uniformly advocating "works righteousness." The new element in Paul and early Christianity is not an *idea*, an argument about "faith versus works," but an *event* in which this theology had been enacted by God's saving act in Christ.

as something that has already happened: salvation occurred in the event in the common past of humanity, when Christ died for us, and in the event of each person's history when he or she came to faith. Salvation is something that is *presently underway* (we are in the process of being saved, a process that includes suffering). And salvation is a reality *yet to be realized* (we will be saved at the parousia). Here too salvation is thought of in the already/not-yet dialectic. The metaphors modulate from the legal picture of justification taken from the law court into the image of reconciliation taken from the world of personal relations and of social conflict. Paul's Christology and soteriology are summarized in verse 8: *Christ's* death represents *God's* love for us. Even here, Paul does not spell out a theory of the atonement; Paul believes it is the fact of Christ's death for sinners that mediates the saving grace of God, without explicating a theory of how this is so.

5:12–21 Christ and Adam

For Paul, both sin and salvation are corporate realities. Human beings are not lone individuals who may or may not strike up relations with others; to be human means our lives are already bound up in the network of humanity before we ever make individual decisions. Paul represents this as our corporate life in Adam. The story of the "fall" in Genesis 3—Adam's rebellion against God and expulsion from paradise—plays no role in Old Testament theology, but in Paul's context in first-century Judaism, Adam's sin was sometimes seen as bringing sin and death into the world (e.g., 2 Esdras, *2 Baruch*, *Apocalypse of Moses*, rabbinic texts). Paul is not constructing an original argument that sin and death were released into the world through Adam, but presupposes that this understanding of sin is known to his readers in the Roman church.

Paul does not think of "original sin" in the sense of a biologically transmitted disease or as later generations being held accountable for the deed of a remote ancestor. Adam's act released a power into the world to which all human beings are subject; to be human is to be subject to sin and death. Paul does not understand death to be the natural end of human life. Rather, like sin, death is a transcendent power that overcomes and enslaves human life. Modern (and postmodern) readers can think of something like "systemic evil," an overwhelming network of sin and death in which we are already involved before we ever make conscious decisions and from which we cannot extricate ourselves. The meaning is not that God punishes all later generations for what Adam did, but that Adam's story is the representative story of everyone.

So also with Christ's story. Adam was a "type," a prototype and paradigm, of the one to come (Christ) in that the act of each, both Adam and Christ, was representative of humanity as a whole. (The Hebrew word אָדָם *adam* means "humanity," "humankind"; it is not merely the name of an individual, but the representative of the human race.) Over against the picture of universal human disobedience represented by Adam, Paul presents Jesus as the one person in human history who realized in his own existence what it means to be a truly human being. He was truly obedient to God. Here, rare in Paul's theology, it is not only Jesus' death but also how he lived his life that is the saving event (see Phil 2:8, where Jesus' whole life is characterized as "obedience"). Jesus' obedience was God's saving act that reversed previous human history and created a new humanity. Jesus is not merely paralleled to Adam; the consequences for humanity resulting from Adam's disobedience to the will of God are *more than* counterbalanced by Christ's obedience to the will of God; note the repeated "not" in verses 15–16. Where sin abounded, grace superabounded, hyperabounded (v. 20).

6:1–7:6 Objection and response Paul has made his case. He again adopts the diatribe style, posing a real objection to the argument he has just made, the classical protest to the claim that salvation is by grace: if salvation is an unconditional gift from God's side, if sinners are freely accepted by God's grace, then why not continue in sin, so that grace may abound (cf. 3:5–8)? Paul does not retract or dilute his radical affirmation, but in a threefold response shows that the response to God's grace cannot be do-as-you-please libertinism. Paul regards the objection itself as a kind of legalism in which grace is understood as indulgence to sin. Such a view looks for sanctions to keep this from happening—but this misunderstands the character of grace.

6:1–14 You are baptized.
Paul's initial response is surprising to the modern reader: he responds not with a theoretical argument but by pointing to an event. Something has happened that makes it impossible for the believer to continue in sin. This liberating event of the death and resurrection of Christ did not happen only to Jesus. Christians are incorporated into this new reality by baptism, so that their lives are no longer determined by the old Adamic reality. Death frees from sin. The story of believers is fused with the story of Christ; they are "in Christ," and his death is theirs.[29] Believers are dead to sin (indicative, 6:2, 7); they must therefore consider themselves to be dead and not allow sin to continue to rule over them (imperative, 6:11, 12).

The language throughout is reminiscent of the exodus event. As Israel was in Egyptian slavery, had been delivered by God's act, passed through the waters, and was en route to the promised inheritance, so Christians have been redeemed from slavery, have passed through the waters of baptism, and are en route to the promised eschatological inheritance (see 1 Cor 10:1–14, where this is made explicit).

In baptism, believers are dead and buried with Christ, but Paul stops just short of clearly affirming that we are also risen with him. The resurrection of *Jesus* is in the past, but that of *believers* still in the future (note future tense of 6:5). This is Paul's "eschatological reservation," the dialectic of his already/not-yet understanding of Christian existence (see 1 Cor 6:14; 2 Cor 4:10, 14; Phil 3:8–12; Gal 5:5; Rom 8:17–18, 23). Believers are already united with the death of Christ, are buried with him, and rise to walk in a new life—but they still live in a world of death, and their resurrection is yet to come.[30]

6:15–23 You are a freed slave with a new master.
Paul restates the objection of 6:1, and again responds with an absolute μὴ γένοιτο (*mē genoito*, absolutely not).[31] Again, he responds not with a theoretical argument but by pointing to an event: God's act in Christ has overcome the enslaving power of sin, and believers have been set free from the old master in order to serve a new one. For Paul, as for Jesus (Matt 6:24; Luke 16:13), human existence as such can never be autonomous. Human beings are not independent, but always find themselves as subordinate to a higher power. The question is not *whether* human beings will be slaves, but *to whom?* Paul reminds his readers that for them the question is already decided. God's act in Christ has set them free from the dominating power of sin so that they may serve their true Lord, "whose service is perfect freedom."[32] Again, the indicative "you have been set free"

29. On the Pauline formula ἐν Χριστῷ see §13.3.2. See Gal. 2:20, cocrucifixion with Christ, where the "I" is not only Paul, but all who are in Christ.

30. One wing of the later Pauline school relaxed this dialectic and clearly claimed that believers are already risen with him (see Col 3:3) or even ascended with him (Eph 2:6). This interpretation of Paul appeared too gnosticizing to others of Paul's followers, who regarded the view that the believer's resurrection has already occurred as dangerous false teaching (see 2 Tim. 2:18).

31. This strong negation is found fourteen times in Paul (Rom 3:4, 6, 31; 6:2, 15; 7:7, 13; 9:14; 11:1, 11; 1 Cor. 6:15; Gal. 2:17; 3:21; 6:14; elsewhere in the New Testament only Luke 20:16). Translated "God forbid!" by the KJV, it has been variously rendered in modern translations as "by no means!" "certainly not!" "absolutely not!" "out of the question!" and the like.

32. This phrase from the Anglican *Book of Common Prayer* translates a phrase from the Latin patristic prayer adapted by Augustine, *cui servire, regnare est*, literally, "to whom to be in subjection is to reign," i.e., to share the reign of Christ.

(6:18, 22) must become the imperative. The gift becomes an assignment.

7:1–6 You are freed from the law through participating in the death of Christ.
As death frees from sin, so death frees from law. This is illustrated in 7:1–3 by the marriage relationship: the death of one partner ends the legal claim. This is only an illustration; in the reality presupposed by Paul, it is not the law that dies, but, as in 6:1–11, the believer dies by being united with the death of Christ.

The law is understood as a power that "lords it over" human life; the good life intended by the Creator cannot be established as a legal relation between Creator and creature. Conclusion: Christian life is guided not by law but by the Spirit.

7:7–25 The law is not sin, but (like us) is the victim of sin. In all this, a disturbing thread woven into the argument has occasionally surfaced, and, before proceeding, Paul now deals with it specifically: is the law itself an evil power from which believers are delivered by God's saving act? In the exodus paradigm, never far beneath the surface of Paul's thought, after deliverance from slavery and passing through the waters that separate them from the old life, Israel is brought to Sinai, where they receive the law as a blessing from God. Here, however, the law is presented along with sin and death as partners that together dominate this world, the old age that has come to an end by God's act in Christ. Paul regards sin, law, and death as quasi-personal powers that have usurped God's creation and hold it in slavery, preventing the world and human life from being what God created them to be. He thus uses the terms interchangeably: to be under sin, or law, or death, is to be under the power of this enslaving triumvirate. Sin and death are clearly the evil challengers of God's good rule. But the law? Is it also evil? In his heated dispute with the Galatians, Paul had come close to regarding the law as an evil, enslaving power. The discussion that follows is not a digression or parenthesis, but is required by his argument.

7:7–13 The law as victim
Paul is emphatic: the law is not sin, but as the law of God, is holy, just, good, spiritual. The law serves God's purpose by making known God's will and revealing sin for what it is (7:7–8). Yet the law, though God's good creation, has been commandeered by the evil power of sin and has been used to bring about alienation from God and leads to death (7:9–13).

7:14–25 The problem is not with the law, but with "me." Like the law, "I" am sold under sin. Both the law and "I" stand on the same side, as God's creatures that as unwilling accomplices have been perverted by the power of sin. Sin commandeered the law and used it for its evil purpose, so that it does not function according to its true nature (7:7–13). So also, sin has taken "me" captive (7:23). "Not I" but "sin in me" is analogous to "not the law" but "sin that took over law" (7–13). Just as sin uses the law, so sin uses me, but neither the law nor the "I" is inherently evil.

In the context of Paul's line of thought, the struggle described in 7:14–25 is thus not a digression on the internal struggle common to all conscientious human beings between good intentions and actual performance. So also, the continuing debate about whether Paul is describing a preconversion or postconversion experience is misplaced. Nor is it autobiographical. He is not describing his personal spiritual journey. Paul's discussion is not about "me," but about the law. In the course of explaining that the law is not sin, Paul describes the nature of human life as the sin-commandeered self caught between the sin-commandeered law and the law as God intended it. If the issue is nevertheless posed as to whether Paul is describing the nature of pre-Christian existence or the postconversion struggle of the believer to do God's will, it is best to regard 7:14–25 as the nature of preconversion human life under the power of sin and the law, but this situation can be seen in its true reality only from the postconversion perspective of life in the Spirit.

8:1–39 *Freedom in the Spirit* Here Paul returns to the main line of his argument and brings to its climax the line of reasoning begun at 5:1. The first section, 8:1–17, speaks of the present life of the believer as empowered by the Spirit (used fifteen times). The second section, 8:18–39, repeatedly uses the terminology of "wait" and "hope." Both sections conclude on the same note: "glorified." The first section thus emphasizes the "already" of the Pauline dialectic of salvation, with the second section accenting the "not yet" dimension.

8:1–17 The power of the Spirit
The law continues to be the primary subject, now seen in the light of Christ. The Spirit-law, equated with "life in Christ Jesus" (see on §13.3.2 for Paul's understanding of life "in Christ"), represents the true law of God (v. 7), which is spiritual (7:14). The Spirit-law prevails over the sin-death-law, the law commandeered by the transcendent power of evil. Since God's intent in giving the law was frustrated by the weakness of sinful flesh, that is, human life as dominated by the transcendent power of evil, God intervened by sending his Son into the world of sinful flesh and condemned Sin on its own turf. Thus those who are in Christ are rescued from the legal threat of the law's domain, are no longer condemned by the law, but by the power of the Spirit live according to God's will.

8:18–39 Vivid expectation of redemption along with the cosmos
Just as the law was not inherently evil, but victimized by the power of sin, so the world itself (including the "flesh") is God's good creation, and—though now under the domination of sin—will be ultimately redeemed. Paul does not picture individual souls being saved out of the world, but the world itself being redeemed from its current slavery. As part of creation as a whole, believers "wait" and "groan" (8:19, 23, 25) in anticipation, as in their present sufferings they wait for the final renewal, already underway and partially experienced in the power of the Spirit, which is both foretaste and guarantee of God's final act. "Hope" for Paul does not mean "maybe" but "sure confidence." The object of hope is real, but not yet. This certainty is expressed in terms of God's sovereign unilateral action, as foreknowledge, election, and predestination. Salvation is God's act, and nothing can frustrate it.

9:1–11:36 God's Righteousness and the Role of Israel in God's Plan for History
If Paul's argument had been about the standing of the individual before God, his discourse could have gone directly from 8:39 to 12:1, along the lines of "human sin" (chaps. 1–3) "but the grace of God" (chaps. 4–8), "therefore the Christian way" (chaps. 12–16). In this individualistic schema, chapters 9–11 are seen as a complex digression on election and predestination that may be skipped. This is a mistaken reading of Romans, based on modern individualistic views of salvation. "Justification by faith" is not the result of speculating on the universal, abstract problem of how people are saved, but pondering the place of Israel in God's plan, despite the present refusal of most Jews to accept Jesus as the Messiah, a result of reflection on the missionary task of the church and God's plan for universal history. The main theme of Romans is not the individual's standing before God, but God's plan for history, which includes both Jews and Gentiles; chapters 9–11 are integral to and the climax of the argument that runs from 1:16 through 11:36. The section 9:1–11:36 may be outlined in three parts: God's freedom (9:1–29); Christ the end of the law (9:30–10:21); God the source and goal of all (11:1–36).

9:1–29 *God's freedom* Paul is not writing a philosophical essay on divine sovereignty vs. individual freedom; he writes a letter addressing a particular issue. He begins not with an abstract problem but the concrete issue, the given historical reality of his own time: Israel, God's covenant people, had for the most part not accepted the promised Messiah. Does this mean that God has changed the divine plan for history or gone back on the promises made to Abraham and Israel? Paul's argument is aimed at refuting this objection. Just as the law is not sin (7:7–25), so Israel is not rejected. Just as the law is to be seen in two perspectives (sin-law and Spirit-law), so Israel is to be seen as flesh-Israel (empirical Israel) and promise-Israel (Israel constituted by God's choice and promise, not by genetics, nationalism, or culture). Paul argues that it has always been the case that Israel was called into being by the freedom of God's word rather than as a matter of birth and heredity. God's word, God's promise has not failed (9:6). Throughout the discussion, Paul deals not with individual predestination, but with God's choice of a covenant people.

Paul is intent on establishing God's ἐξουσία (9:21, *exousia*, right, authority, freedom). God chooses, and has a right to choose, because God is God, the Creator. If God can be called to account by some external standard superior to God—even if this standard be the creature's own ideas of justice and fairness—then God is no longer God. Paul does not "answer" or "explain" that God is just and fair after all. Paul does not allow the question, does not allow the creature to call the Creator to account (9:20–21). Because God is God, God has the "right" to do as he wills; if God "must" or "should" do something else, then God is something less than the Creator. For God to show mercy, God must be free. Paul establishes this freedom, beyond which there is no appeal. Grace cannot be extracted or compelled; otherwise, it is no longer grace. But while God *could* do whatever God pleases, God *has in fact* put up with disobedient creatures in order to show mercy on all, Jews and Gentiles (9:22–24).

The use of the first-person plural (9:24, "we," "us") shows that Paul's whole discussion is in the mode of the confessional language of the insider, not the speculative language of the spectator, who coolly examines the issue at some distance. He confesses the faith of those in the Christian community, does not attempt to assume the "objective" stance of one who is neither Jew nor Gentile, neither believer nor unbeliever. This confessional language assumes that the Scriptures are to be read from the point of view of Christian faith. There Paul finds, in Hosea (1:10; 2:23) and Isaiah (1:9; 10:22–23) that God's plan for history, the merciful inclusion of Jews and Gentiles in the one covenant community, was already promised in the prophets (see Paul's initial declaration in 1:2).

9:30–10:21 Christ the* telos *of the law The thesis of this complex and problematic section is that Christ is the end and/or goal of the law (τέλος can be translated either way). Paul is still thinking about the concrete issue of the law and Israel, the covenant people, in God's plan for history. The topic is not Israel's unbelief as such, but differing perceptions of the role of the law in God's plan. By declaring that Christ is the end of the law, Paul does not mean that the law is now terminated and has no validity or standing. Paul will in fact make his point by quoting from the law (10:6–8 cites Deut 30:11–14). Nor does he mean that Jesus perfectly performed the law, or that Jesus' teaching explained the real meaning of the law, or that the law's purpose was to predict the coming of Christ. Rather, Paul begins with the conviction of Christian faith in the reality of the Christ event as the goal of God's plan witnessed to by the law (1:2; 3:21). Likewise, "righteousness of God" here means neither a quality of God nor the forensic, justifying righteousness God confers (as in Phil 3:9), but God's justifying act in the Christ event as a whole.

From Paul's perspective, then, Israel's problem, for which Israel is responsible, is their rejection of the message of this saving event. Israel's problem is not that they didn't try (9:31; 10:3). Nor is it that they *did* try, in some "legalistic" way, to justify themselves by their own works, as though all along they should simply have trusted in God. Paul is not contrasting two human approaches to God, "works" and "faith," but contrasting two responses to God's saving act in Christ: belief and unbelief.

Nor is the problem that they have not heard, have not had the opportunity to respond. Paul's argument in 10:14–21 is that, as in the case of biblical Israel, God has sent messengers to them, but they have not responded in faith. Israel's present rejection is thus not that God has been unfaithful, but that Israel has not believed God's definitive revelation. This sets the stage for the final phase of Paul's argument: God has not rejected his people, and Israel's present rejection is not final.

11:1–36 God the source and goal of all Again, the writing is not an abstract discussion of "the role of Israel in God's plan," but a letter addressing a concrete situation in the church of Rome, addressing Christian Gentiles who are misinterpreting the widespread Jewish rejection of the Christian message and recent events in Rome, as meaning God had now nullified the promise to Israel and rejected the covenant people. Paul responds that (1) he himself is living proof to the contrary; (2) just as in the time of Elijah, when it seemed that the whole people had apostatized, God had in fact preserved a remnant of seven thousand (see 1 Kgs. 18:20–19:18). "Remnant" here does not mean "leftover" or "residue," but has its biblical reference to those who survive as a witness to God's grace and guarantee of the future. Israel has stumbled, but not fallen.

The stumbling has caused others, the Gentile Christians, to overtake and pass Israel, but the stumbling runner has not been ejected from the race, nor has his place been taken by others. Rather, seeing their lead, the runner recovers and is spurred on by their apparent victory. At the finish line, everybody wins! To be sure, the imagery does not work in an actual race, in which there must be winners and losers, but Paul's meaning is clear: the successful spread of the gospel among Gentiles will make Israel "jealous" and enable them to continue the race and join with Gentiles in God's eschatological victory—the reconciliation of the world and life from the dead.

The imagery shifts to the olive tree, symbol of Israel, rooted in God's ancient covenant. Jewish "branches" who did not accept Jesus as the Messiah were broken off, and Gentiles believers were grafted in. They are grafted in "among them," not "in their place" (as translated in NRSV). But God can and will regraft the presently unbelieving Jews into their own olive tree. The present disobedience of Israel does not finally frustrate God's purpose. Both Jews and Gentiles will be included. The "all" of universal sin and disobedience is matched by the grace of God for "all" (3:21; 5:12, 18; 11:32). In Paul's view, God is finally in charge; God can remove and add at will. When God finally (eschatologically) acts (v. 26), it is a matter of God's unilateral faithfulness to the covenant (11:26); it is God's choice, which is irrevocable. Gentile Christians do not come into God's people as a separate, parallel, community, nor do they replace Israel. Jews and Gentiles together constitute the one people of God, the wholeness of the new humanity (5:12–21). Since the sovereign God can incorporate the present rejection and disobedience of Israel into the ultimate divine purpose—the same God who incorporated humanity's rejection of God expressed in the crucifixion of Jesus into the ultimate expression of God's own love and grace—there is literally nothing that can prevent the triumph of God's purpose for his creation.

From our centuries-later perspective we can see that Paul was mistaken in both the "how" and "when" of the ultimate fulfillment of God's purpose. The expansion of Gentile Christianity did not make Jews "jealous" and cause them to accept the gospel. Contrary to his expectations, the program Paul projected did not happen in his own time. Yet, for those who share Paul's faith (not necessarily the details of his theology), the fundamental affirmation expressed in this theology remains valid: the sovereign Lord of creation is not ultimately frustrated by human disobedience, and finally turns even this to the achievement of his will.

Here, at the end of this torturous and profound chain of theological thought, Paul acknowledges that the ways of God are beyond human understanding, that there is no "explaining" the mystery of God's plan. Any attempt to express it, even on the basis of revealed mystery (11:25–32), inevitably results in fractured logic and the juxtaposition of contrasting, irreconcilable statements: all are saved/only some are saved; salvation is unconditional, a matter of God's unconditional love/only believers are saved, a matter of human decision and responsibility. In making such grand declarations, Paul illustrates the openness that is typical of this theology. He acknowledges that he is theologically in over his head, that believers now know only in fragments (see 1 Cor 13:12). This awareness that all human theologies are finally unable to grasp the divine mystery does not paralyze Paul into silence, but frees him to do hard thinking about the meaning of his faith and to express it in conflicting, fragmentary form. The inability of human minds to grasp God's purposes leads not to despair, but to praise. The long theological section begun at 1:17 does not conclude with a crisp analytical summary, but modulates into worship before the Creator from whom, through whom, and to whom are all things.

12:1–15:33 Part 2: God's Righteousness Lived Out in Christian Lives as Response to God's Grace

12:1–2 From Indicative to Imperative

This key paragraph makes the transition from the indicative exposition of God's saving acts in chapters 1–11 to the imperative of the Christian life in chapters 12–16. The believer's response is not to offer God things or particular actions, but to offer the self as a *living sacrifice*, to make one's life a continuous act of worship. Christian ethics is not a matter of obeying rules, but of doing the *will of God*. This is a matter of ongoing discernment from case to case, not prescriptions that can be known in advance. It is a matter of "Daybreak Ethos,"[33] of conforming one's life to the dawning new age, rather than to the darkness that is already passing away (12:2 forms a bracket with 13:11–14).

12:3–8 Life Together

Such ethical decisions are not merely a matter of individual discernment, but of participation in the body of Christ to which the Christian was added at baptism. This body is enlivened by the breath/Spirit of Christ; the Spirit both guides and empowers the individual Christian within the corporate reality (see on 1 Cor 12; Paul writes this from *Corinth*, where he has worked through these issues with the Corinthian congregations).

12:9–21. . .(13:1–7). . .13:8–14 Love in Practice

As in 1 Corinthians 12–13, Paul concludes his discussion of life in the Spirit by pointing to ἀγάπη (*agapē*, love) as the supreme gift of the Spirit. The parenesis of 12:9–21 consists of twenty-one items, all expressions of Christian love (so 13:8–10), which Paul declares to be the "fulfillment of the law." Even in the "practical" section of Romans, Paul does not forget that the Roman congregation is suspicious of his teaching about the role of the law, and makes clear that the Christian ethic is not an alternative to fulfilling God's law, but its mode.

13:1–7 Christian Life as Subordination to the Governing Authorities

Embedded within this paraenetic section is a paragraph on the Christian responsibility to be obedient to governing authorities, which stands out clearly from its context. The reader can proceed directly from 12:21 to 13:8 with no sense that anything is missing. Thus some interpreters have regarded this paragraph as

33. Keck, *Romans*, 289.

a later interpolation or as Paul's own citation of a fragment of tradition from the Hellenistic synagogue.[34] If, as is likely, the passage is from Paul, it is not an abstract discussion of "church and state," but a concrete example of Christian responsibility to "live peaceably with *all*" (12:18), including pagan rulers, who, even though they do not realize it, are servants of the Creator, who establishes government and orderly society as the precondition of human life. The instruction does not establish the divine right of particular governments, but of government as such. It does not oppose revolution, but anarchy. Paul did not foresee a generations-long future in which the church must work out its relation to the state. Christians may still engage in civil disobedience for conscience' sake, but must be willing to accept the legal consequences.

14:1–15:33 The Inclusive Church as Prolepsis of the Present-and-Coming Kingdom of God

This concluding section is often divided into two parts, Paul's instructions to the "weak" and "strong" groups (14:1–15:13) and his concluding travel plans (15:14–33). These are better understood as one interrelated unit, with Paul's vision of the nature of the church and his own mission strategy calling for a particular kind of life together in the Christian community.

14:1–15:13 The inclusive church God's purpose is to reunite fragmented humanity in the eschatological kingdom of God. The church is foretaste and model of this. It is within this grand vision of the nature of the church that Paul addresses the differing groups of Christian believers in the capital city. How is it possible for people with profoundly different religious convictions to live together as one community of faith?

Paul designates the groups as "strong" and "weak," making it clear that he takes his stance among the "strong" (14:14; 15:1). The "strong" eat meat, drink wine, and do not observe special holy days, while the "weak"—not their self-description; they surely considered themselves the "strong"—did not eat meat or drink wine, and were strict in their observance of holy days. These convictions are surely related to the differences of religious observance that would create tensions between Jewish Christians and Gentile Christians, and Paul's response is an aspect of his theology of the one church of Jews and Gentiles.

Yet his discussion indicates that the problems in Rome cannot be reduced to Jew-Gentile issues. Abstinence from wine, for instance, was no part of Jewish religious practice, but the issue did play a role in the tensions within the Roman church (14:21). A variety of religious traditions and taboos, Jewish and Gentile, are represented. Each group is charged by Paul to *receive* (=welcome, affirm) the other as authentic members of the one body of Christ. His appeal is christologically grounded, not merely a request to be individualistically "tolerant," which can be mere indifference. Each person is to be fully persuaded in his or her own mind (14:5, 22), yet no one of them lives to himself or herself, and the matter cannot be resolved in terms of "live and let live." But how can a church with fundamental differences on such issues live together as one community of faith? Paul addresses each group in turn.

The "strong" are not to *disdain* the "weak." The term is sometimes translated "despise" (so KJV, RSV, NRSV), but ἐξουθενέω (*exoutheneō*) does not mean "despise" in the sense of dislike or detest, and the temptation of liberal Christians is not to despise their more conservative brothers and sisters, but to condescendingly disdain them as still unenlightened.

The "weak" are not to *judge* the "strong." Again, the conservatives are not warned against criticizing the liberals, but are instructed not to evaluate them in terms of their own theological

34. E.g., Walker, *Interpolations*, 221–31; Wayne A. Meeks, *The First Urban Christians: The Social World of the Apostle Paul* (New Haven, CT: Yale University Press, 1983), 208.

convictions. Conservatives tend to pronounce the beliefs and practices of liberals to be unacceptable to God because they cannot understand how, in terms of their own theology, God *can* accept people who believe and practice in such unbiblical and nontraditional ways. Paul's response: you do not have to understand how God can accept them; God *has* accepted them, so you cannot pronounce judgments on someone else's servant. God is the judge of all, God decides who will stand in the judgment, and God is able to make them stand, whether or not the conservatives can fit it into their theology.

Each group is called to welcome the other, for God has welcomed both. The burden, however, is on the "strong" (15:1). Precisely because they are the "liberal," they are free to adjust to the more conservative faith and practice in a way that the conservative cannot, in good conscience, reciprocate. Liberals are free not to insist on their own way (1 Cor 13:5!) in a way their conservative brothers and sisters cannot. For such liberals, authentic freedom means willingness to be misunderstood as more conservative than they actually are, for the sake of the unity of the church and its mission.

15:14–33 Apostle to the Gentiles and mission strategy Paul writes from Corinth, is on his way to Jerusalem with the offering from the Gentile churches in Macedonia and Achaia, then plans to come to Rome as the launching pad for his mission to Spain. He claims already to have "fully preached" from Jerusalem to Illyricum, so there is "no longer any room" for his mission in the whole eastern Mediterranean. This cannot mean, of course, that Paul had preached to every individual. As the apostle to the Gentiles, he thought of his mission in terms not of individuals, but of Gentile nations, and developed a master plan for his missionary enterprise. Such phrases as the salvation of "the fullness of the Gentiles" and "all Israel" (Rom 11:25–26) did not mean that he expected all individuals in each group to be converted before the parousia.

What he did commit himself to was a mission that would generate an inclusive community, representative of the eschatological kingdom of God. As Christ was not merely an individual, but the firstfruits of the resurrection, so the church is the firstfruits of the eschatological reality, and must model in this world, before the parousia, the comprehensive reality that is to come. At the parousia, Paul wanted to be able to present, as a priestly offering, the gift of one church that represented all nations, a sample of the work of salvation God had already achieved on earth, a prolepsis of the grand unification of all peoples to be accomplished in the coming kingdom of God.

16:1–27 Greetings, Warnings, Doxology
Paul surprisingly draws the deep theology of chapters 1–11 and the related ethics of chapters 12–15 to a close with an extensive list of greetings. Twenty-six members of the Roman church are greeted by name, not counting the house churches greeted as groups. Phoebe, the bearer of the letter, is commended, and greetings are sent from eight of Paul's coworkers who are with him in Corinth, for a total of thirty-five names in Romans 16. The theology that spans the cosmos and all history, creation to eschaton, is not therefore less personal, but corresponds to the people-oriented narrative theology of the New Testament itself—which in fact refers to 423 different individuals by name!

13.3 Comprehensive and Continuing Issues

HERE WE WILL NOT ATTEMPT A COMPREHENSIVE or systematic presentation of Paul's theology, and not only because of space limitations.[35] Paul himself never offered a comprehensive and systematic statement of his

35. Two excellent systematic treatments of Paul's theology, with different emphases and perspectives, are James D. G. Dunn, *The Theology of Paul the Apostle* (Grand Rapids: Eerdmans, 1998), and Schnelle, *Apostle Paul.*

theology, but expressed his theological convictions in connection with the situations that occasioned each letter. His theology is thus best studied as constituent elements of each letter, in the unfolding narrative of the Pauline mission. I have attempted to facilitate such a grasp of Paul's basic theological convictions in the *Exegetical-Theological Précis* for each Pauline letter. There are also, however, some key, disputed, or problematic aspects of Paul's theology that cut across the letter corpus as a whole, and thus are better treated in a single discussion.

13.3.1 The "New Perspective" on Paul

Since the Reformation, Christian interpreters of Paul have often understood Judaism as the foil of Christianity, the "narrow legalism" of "works righteousness" that served as the dark backdrop for Paul's gospel of salvation by grace. Paul was cast in the role of Luther; Roman Catholics represented the continuation of the presumed Jewish understanding of salvation by works. Two sea-change events made it impossible for these stereotypes of either Judaism or Roman Catholicism to persist. The Holocaust made New Testament scholars much more sensitive to the anti-Judaism of their interpretations, and Vatican II revealed that Roman Catholicism could no longer serve as the foil for a Protestant reading of Paul. Developing earlier leads, the author principally responsible for this "new perspective on Paul" was E. P. Sanders.[36] Based on detailed examination of the texts representing first-century Judaism, Sanders argues that the Jewish context for both Jesus and Paul was a religion of "covenantal nomism," a religion of grace and forgiveness that called for repentance and ethical living on the basis of God's gracious covenant-making act, not a religion attempting to win God's favor by "works of the law." While the old stereotypes have been definitively shattered, other issues generated by the "new perspective" continue to be vigorously discussed by Pauline scholars.

13.3.2 The Centrality of Participation "in Christ"

God acted in Christ to deliver human beings from all the enemies that threaten authentic life, in this world and the world to come. Human salvation is in relation to this saving event. Paul's most frequent and distinctive expression for this relationship is ἐν Χριστῷ, (*en Christō*, in Christ).[37]

Data: The phrase "in Christ" or some variation thereof ("in the Lord," "in Jesus," "in the beloved," "in him," "in whom") is found in the New Testament 170 times, only in Paul and in the literature influenced by him:

Comments and interpretation (see Box 11). "In Christ" is a strange phrase. While Paul did not create the expression—it seems to have been a constituent element in some pre-Pauline baptismal traditions (1 Cor 1:30; 2 Cor 5:17, Gal 3:27–28)—it was Paul who injected it into the mainstream of early Christian conceptuality and vocabulary. The roots of the concept appear to be in some streams of theology represented in the Jewish Scriptures. In Hebrew thinking,

36. E. P. Sanders, *Paul and Palestinian Judaism: A Comparison of Patterns of Religion* (Philadelphia: Fortress Press, 1977). The issue of the "new perspective"—a designation coined by James D. G. Dunn—has generated a heated discussion. See, e.g., James D. G. Dunn, ed., *The New Perspective on Paul: Collected Essays*, WUNT 195 (Tübingen: Mohr Siebeck, 2005). Some of the insights of the new perspective were anticipated by Krister Stendahl's famous essay, "The Apostle Paul and the Introspective Conscience of the West," in *Paul among Jews and Gentiles* (Philadelphia: Fortress Press, 1976). Critical perspectives on the "new perspective" are found in, e.g., Francis Watson, *Paul, Judaism, and the Gentiles: Beyond the New Perspective*, rev. ed. (Grand Rapids: Eerdmans, 2007), and rigorously by R. Barry Matlock, "Sins of the Flesh and Suspicious Minds: Dunn's New Theology of Paul," *Journal for the Study of the New Testament* (1998): 67–90.

37. The key figure in the modern interpretation of "participation in Christ" as central to Paul's theology is Albert Schweitzer (Albert Schweitzer, *The Mysticism of Paul the Apostle*, trans. William Montgomery [London: A. & C. Black, 1931]). For a recent exposition of Paul from this point of view, see Schnelle, *Theology of the New Testament*, 204–5; 276–78, and passim.

there is no firm line between the individual and the community of which he or she is a constituent element. A clue to Paul's usage is that Paul himself can speak of human beings as being "in Adam" (1 Cor 15:22), with "Adam" being not only the individual of the Genesis story but the humanity constituted by him (see on Rom 5:12–21). Individual persons are not human beings by virtue of their individual qualities, but by belonging to the human race, with its sin and mortality. At baptism believers are incorporated into the new humanity constituted by Jesus Christ; they are no longer, or not only, "in Adam," but "in Christ."

Paul himself never uses the explicit phrase "in Jesus" (though see Eph 4:21; Rev 1:9). It is clear, however, from his "in Christ Jesus" (e.g., Rom 6:11; 8:1; 1 Cor 1:2; Gal 5:6; Phil 1:1) that the expression points both to the historical individual Jesus of Nazareth, crucified and risen, and the transcendent Christ. Paul uses the phrase to point to an experienced and transcendent reality inseparably linked to the person of the crucified and risen Jesus, a reality that resists conceptual and linguistic clarity. Paul thus uses several overlapping and equivalent expressions. He and all Christians are in Christ (Rom 16:9; 2 Cor 1:21, and often), and Christ is in them (Rom 8:10). To be "in Christ" is to be "in the Spirit" (Phil 2:1), which is the same as "the Spirit in you" (Rom 8:9–10). The parallel and related expression "with Christ" points to the same reality. Beyond this life, the believer will share the full and constant communion with Christ (Phil 1:23, "to depart and be with Christ"), but this reality is not merely future and transcendent: it penetrates the life of the believer in the present, who is crucified, dead, and buried with Christ (Rom 6:4–8; Gal 2:19), and whose life is already determined by the power of the resurrection (Rom 6:8–11; Phil 3:10). While Paul's eschatological reservation made him hesitant to say clearly that believers are already "risen with him," it is clear that for

BOX 11: Paul's Use of "in Christ"

1 Thessalonians	7	(0 pronominal)
1 Corinthians	23	(1 pronominal)
2 Corinthians	13	(4 pronominal, 3 in 1:19-20)
Philippians	20	(1 pronominal)
Philemon	5	(0 pronominal)
Galatians	9	(0 pronominal)
Romans	21	(0 pronominal)
	98	occurrences in the undisputed Pauline letters (6 pronominal = 6%)
***		
2 Thessalonians	4	(0 pronominal)
***		
Colossians	19	(12 pronominal)
Ephesians	35	(13 pronominal)
***		
1 Timothy	6	(0 pronominal; all "in Christ Jesus")
2 Timothy	3	(0 pronominal; all "in Christ Jesus")
Titus	0	(0 pronominal)
	165	occurrences in the Pauline and deuteropauline tradition
1 Peter	3	(all "in Christ")
Revelation	2	(0 pronominal)
	170	occurrences in the New Testament

Paul the event of Jesus' death and resurrection was not something that happened only to Jesus, but the crucial event of all human history, an event in which believers participate. For those "in Christ," the story of Jesus has been made their own story.

While the phrase is multidimensional and many-faceted, the fundamental reality to which the metaphor points is spatial: to be "in Christ" is to be located in a new sphere of being. In this sense it is "mystical"—the believer does not simply admire Christ or follow him, but is united with him. At baptism (Gal 3:27–28) outsiders become insiders, nonmembers of the body of Christ are incorporated into a transcendent body of believers, the Christian community animated by the Spirit/breath of Christ that is still very much a this-worldly reality. Thus Paul's "in Christ" language is parallel to his "new creation" language (2 Cor 5:17; Gal 6:15). This is analogous to the way in which the created world is the sphere of being in which all humans live their lives, with the resurrection of Jesus the leading edge of God's new creation is already present, already impinging on the present world. It is this world made new in which believers already live, though the old world is still very much present with them.

13.3.3 Apostolicity and the Challengers to Paul's Apostleship: Paul's Detractors, Rivals, and Opponents

Apostle, Apostleship, Apostolicity

Like Jesus, Paul was a controversial figure.[38] Whether one loved or hated him, supported or opposed his mission, one could not ignore him. The controversies in which Paul was involved were not one-dimensional; theological issues were mixed in with a variety of personal, social, and cultural issues. Yet theology was the major issue, and Paul's understanding of his own apostleship was an important point of difference between Paul and his rivals.

There was no preformed office of apostle into which early Christian apostles could be fitted. The English word "apostle" is simply the transliteration of the Greek ἀπόστολος (*apostolos*), which basically means "one sent" and was used in a variety of senses in the pre-Christian first-century Hellenistic world.[39] New Testament authors adopted the term to designate one sent as a commissioned representative, whether of a congregation (2 Cor 8:23; Phil 2:25), or as an authorized representative of the risen Christ. The former sense is best translated by "delegate" or "missionary," with "apostle" being reserved for the latter sense of authorized representatives of the risen Christ. Even so, in the earliest times there were numerous individuals who claimed to be apostles, with the Twelve as a distinct group (see the distinction between the Twelve and "all the apostles" in 1 Cor 15:5–7).

By the middle of the fourth century, apostolicity was an essential mark of the true church, expressed in the Nicene-Constantinopolitan creed (325 CE, revised 381) as "I believe in one holy catholic and apostolic church." By the end of the first century, a clear, hierarchical understanding of the church was already advocated by Clement of Rome: God sent Christ, Christ sent the apostles, the apostles appointed bishops and deacons (*1 Clement* 42). Even in *Clement*, the apparent straight-line chain of command, in which the authority of God is represented in the church by the apostolic bishops and deacons, is more complex than it at

38. For comprehensive and detailed studies pursued with methodological rigor, and with full bibliography, see esp. Gerd Lüdemann, *Opposition to Paul in Jewish Christianity*, trans. M. Eugene Boring (Minneapolis: Fortress Press, 1989), and Jerry L. Sumney, *Identifying Paul's Opponents: The Question of Method in 2 Corinthians*, JSNTSup 40 (Sheffield: JSOT Press, 1990). See also the essays in Stanley E. Porter, ed., *Paul and His Opponents*, Pauline Studies 2 (Leiden: Brill, 2005).

39. Cf. Karl Heinrich Rengstorf, "ἀποστέλλω κτλ.," in *TDNT*, 1:398–447; J.-A. Bühner, "Ἀπόστολος," in *EDNT*, 1:142–46.

first appears, since God's authority is mediated not merely by the transmission of authority from Christ through the apostles, but is bound up with the gospel, the Holy Spirit, and the proclamation of the coming kingdom of God. "Authority is the interpretation of power," and power resides in the gospel, not merely in the office of the apostle.[40] Nonetheless, the chain-of-command paradigm manifest in *Clement* is vitally important in Paul and in the New Testament generally. For all, God is the ultimate authority—but *which* God? Who is God, and how does one know the character and will of this God? Throughout the New Testament, the identity and character of God are not matters of human discovery, but divine revelation. For Christians, Jesus is the definitive self-revelation and authorized representative of God. Though the early Christians rarely thought of the key role of Jesus in the plan of God in specifically apostolic terms, all Christians assigned Jesus the role of God's apostle—the one authorized and sent by God, the one who represents God. To deal with Jesus is to deal with God.[41] The next issue that inevitably follows: *which* Jesus? Jesus is the authorized representative of God, but who represents Jesus?

Since the authority of the risen Christ was mediated to the churches through the apostles, the identification of authorized apostles became a major issue in the formation of early Christian theology. Paul claimed to be an apostle commissioned directly by the risen Lord. This claim was disputed.

Challengers to Paul's Apostleship

For about the first sixteen years of his mission, that is, from his conversion/call to the break with the Antioch-Jerusalem missions program and the launching of the Aegean mission, all the active opposition to Paul reflected in his letters was from outside the Christian community. If there was opposition to Paul from other Christian leaders or groups, the extant letters make no reference to it. Like other early Christians, Paul frequently suffered at the hands of the political authorities (see 1 Thess 2:2, 14–16 and the tantalizing glimpse of 2 Cor 11:32–33, mentioned only incidentally as an illustration of another point). As a Jewish Christian, Paul continued to subject himself to the discipline of the synagogue authorities and suffered at their hands (2 Cor 11:24).

We first perceive opposition to Paul from within the Christian community after the beginning of the Aegean mission. From 1 Corinthians on, we see a growing opposition to Paul's apostleship and/or Paul's increasing awareness and acknowledgment of a rival apostate that challenges the legitimacy of his own apostolic ministry and seeks to "correct" the deficiencies of the Pauline version of the Christian faith. Paul never mentions Jerusalem or Antioch as the source of the opposing missionaries. The reason may well be that he wishes to keep lines of communication open between his mission and the Jerusalem church, does not want to condemn Jerusalem or hold the Jerusalem leadership responsible for the actions of the missionaries that are troubling his churches. Indeed, Paul avoids describing any configuration that would align the rival apostles/missionaries with the Jerusalem leaders and the Jerusalem church. Throughout, he contends that he, his gospel, and the churches he had founded belong to the larger church, in *koinonia* with the Jerusalem

40. Cf. John Howard Schütz, *Paul and the Anatomy of Apostolic Authority*, introduction by Wayne Meeks, 2007 ed., NTL (Louisville, KY: Westminster John Knox Press, 1975), 4 and passim.

41. Only Heb. 3:1 explicitly calls Jesus *apostle*, but the Fourth Gospel repeatedly speaks of Jesus as having been sent, and the Johannine Jesus speaks of God as "the one who sent me" as almost a divine title (e.g., John 3:17; 4:34; 5:23, 30, 36, 37; 6:29, 38, 39, 44; 7:18; 8:16, 42; 12:44, 45, 49, 57; 17:3, 18). Note that the Johannine Jesus several times links his being sent from the Father to his own sending of the Spirit or the disciples, i.e., the Johannine model of apostolic authority is the same as that of *1 Clement*, though with a different vocabulary. Cf. also Matt 10:40; 18:5–6; Luke 10:16; John 12:44.

church and the Twelve, and that if this were not the case, he would have "run in vain" (see 1 Cor 15:1–11; Gal 2:2).

13.3.4 The "Life of Paul": Chronological Issues[42]

Sources and Method

All agree that the major methodological question in constructing the Pauline chronology is whether and how to combine the two major sources, the undisputed letters of Paul and the book of Acts. The issue is not so simple as it first appears. On the one hand, critical judgments must be made on the historical accuracy of Acts in such matters; on the other hand, the present form of some of Paul's letters may be the editorial combination of more than one letter, which obviously complicates issues of chronology.

Efforts to construct Paul's life story on the basis of the undisputed letters alone have proven to be unsatisfactory to most scholars. While it is possible to comb through Paul's letters with biographical and chronological questions in mind, note all data, and arrange them chronologically without appealing to Acts,[43] very few scholars have been satisfied with this minimalist approach. In particular, Paul's letters themselves provide almost no information indicating their location in world history.[44] When Acts is incorporated in the construction, the question remains of how and to what extent the Acts material not found in the letters is to be used. The older, uncritical approach attempted to use Acts as the primary source, adopting the Acts narrative as straightforward history and inserting the letters at what appeared to be the appropriate points, attempting to harmonize "apparent" conflicts between Acts and the letters into one congruent narrative. The majority approach today is to use the letters as the primary source, supplemented by material from Acts that survives critical historical examination.

There are, in fact, numerous places where the letters and the Acts narrative provide complementary materials that fit quite well into a single picture. There is no doubt that some reliable historical information about Paul comes from Acts, information Paul himself does not happen to mention in the extant undisputed letters. Only Paul, for instance, tells us that he was from the tribe of Benjamin (Rom 11:1; Phil 3:5), and only Acts indicates that he was also known as Saul (Acts 13:9). Since the first Israelite king, Saul, was from the tribe of Benjamin, the patronymic name would have been very appropriate. In all probability, the historical Paul bore both the Greek name Paul and the Jewish name Saul—a biographical datum obtained only by combining material from the letters and Acts. On other biographical and historical issues, how or whether to combine the two sources is not so clear.

A major and complex issue is the relation of Paul's travels as indicated in his letters to the "three missionary journeys" as delineated in the Acts arrangement (see map 2 above, §10.1.9). This issue comes sharply into focus when one attempts to correlate Paul's visits to Jerusalem mentioned in his letters with those portrayed in

42. For outlines and brief discussions of Pauline chronology, see Knox, *Chapters in a Life of Paul*, 47–110; Soards, *Apostle Paul*, 10–11, 34–35; Hans Dieter Betz, "Paul," in *Anchor Bible Dictionary* 5:186–201; Martyn, *Galatians*, "Comment #17—Chronology and Geography," 180–86; Schnelle, *Apostle Paul*, 47–56; Dunn, *Beginning from Jerusalem*, 497–518; Jürgen Becker, *Paul: Apostle to the Gentiles*, trans. O. C. Dean (Louisville, KY: Westminster John Knox Press, 1993), 17–32; Wayne A. Meeks and John T. Fitzgerald, eds., *The Writings of St. Paul*, 2nd ed. (New York: Norton, 2007), xix–xxvii; John A. Darr, "Chronologies of Paul," in Russell Pregeant, *Encounter with the New Testament* (Minneapolis: Fortress Press, 2009), 205–14. Thorough discussions of the issues and methods involved, with reconstructions, are found in Robert Jewett, *A Chronology of Paul's life* (Philadelphia: Fortress Press, 1979), Gerd Lüdemann, *Paul, Apostle to the Gentiles: Studies in Chronology*, trans. F. Stanley Jones (Philadelphia: Fortress Press, 1984), and Riesner, *Paul's Early Period*, 1–228.

43. Cf. Knox, *Chapters*; Lüdemann, *Chronology*.

44. The only datable contact with external history in all his letters is the reference to Paul's escape from Damascus during the reign of Aretas IV (d. 40–41 CE), but even here the data is ambiguous (2 Cor 11:32).

Acts. Paul is explicit that he visited Jerusalem only three times; his (minimal) relationship to the Jerusalem leadership was important to him theologically, so he is emphatic and clear. For the same period, the Acts narrative depicts Paul as making five visits to Jerusalem (see Box 12).[45]

In each case, the first and last visits correspond. P1/A1 is Paul's initial visit to Jerusalem after his conversion, when he gets acquainted with Peter (and, according to Acts, the other apostles). P3/A5 is the trip to Jerusalem to deliver the offering, during which Paul is arrested and finally sent to Rome. The key question is determining which of the Acts visits corresponds to P2, the "conference visit" described in Gal 2. Differing decisions on this issue, and similar judgment calls on other ambiguities, result in some variety in the way Pauline chronology is understood.

A second important factor is the way the relative chronology of Paul's letters is understood. If one begins with the seven undisputed letters and attempts to arrange them in chronological order, four fall into a clear progression, from 1 Thessalonians through 1 and 2 Corinthians to Romans. The relative location of Galatians, Philippians, and Philemon is not so clear, appearing at different points in the variety of constructions (see introductions to each book).

A third variable in such discussions is the ambiguity of some time expressions in the relevant sources. For instance, the key passage Galatians 1:13–2:10 contains a double ambiguity. (1) It is not entirely clear whether the expressions "then after three years" (1:18) and "then after fourteen years" are consecutive or cumulative; does the second mean "fourteen years after my conversion" or "fourteen years after the first visit," a total of seventeen years? (2) In the Hellenistic world, parts of years were often counted as years, so that "three years" could mean from a year and a half to three years

BOX 12: Jerusalem Visits

Jerusalem Visits in Paul's Letters	*Jerusalem Visits in Acts*
P1 = Gal 1:18–24	A1 = 9:26–30
P2 = Gal 2:1–10	A2 = 11:27–30
	A3 = 15:1–29
	A4 = 18:22
P3 = Rom 15:25–32	A5 = 21:17–23:30

depending on the context, and likewise "fourteen years" could mean from twelve to fourteen years. Theoretically, the period here described could thus be from a little over thirteen to more than seventeen years, so that other factors must be introduced to determine the exact length of time Paul intends.

A fourth important factor is the correlation of the relative chronology with datable events external to early Christian history to establish an absolute chronology. The key relevant events:

— Aretas IV's rule in Nabatea and Damascus. The Nabatean king Aretas apparently had control over Damascus from 37 CE until his death in 40–41 CE, so Paul's reference to his flight from Damascus must have occurred during this period.[46]

— Gallio's proconsulship in Corinth. Fragments of an inscription discovered at Delphi in 1905 indicate that Gallio was proconsul in Corinth in 51–52 CE. In Acts 18:12–17, Paul is brought before Gallio. Acts 18:11 states that Paul spent eighteen months in Corinth. Assuming the relative accuracy of Acts on both points, the date of some events in Paul's Aegean mission

45. The helpful chart is from David J. Downs, "Chronology of the NT," in *New Interpreter's Dictionary of the Bible*, 1:634.

46. Martyn, *Galatians*, 182: "If one is concerned to fix absolute dates, the safest point from which to take one's bearings may be Gal. 1:18. Assuming that the trip to Jerusalem mentioned there was taken from Damascus, as seems almost certain, we can reasonably equate it with the reference to a departure from Damascus mentioned in 2 Cor. 11:32–33. And since the latter reference includes the notice that this departure happened when Aretas was king in Damascus, we can place Paul's first trip to Jerusalem between A.D. 37 and 39."

prior to and after this relatively fixed point can be calculated with some confidence.

— Claudius's expulsion of Jews from Rome. Suetonius (*Divus Claudius* 25.4) briefly mentions that Claudius expelled the Jews from Rome, apparently in 49 CE—though this date, too, is not entirely undisputed. This was the occasion of Prisca and Aquila's coming to Corinth, where they meet Paul (Acts 18:2).

Results

Since these variables can be evaluated and combined in different ways, differing outlines of Paul's life and ministry have been constructed. While the general outline of Paul's life is clear, the detailed chronology, sometimes important for interpreting the letters, is a complex matter upon which scholars are not united. Some major and representative constructions are presented in Box 13.[47]

13.4 For Further Reading

Interpreting Galatians

Betz, H. D. *Galatians: A Commentary on Paul's Letter to the Churches in Galatia*. Hermeneia. Philadelphia: Fortress Press, 1979.

Bruce, F. F. *The Epistle to the Galatians*. A *Commentary on the Greek Text*. NIGTC. Grand Rapids: Eerdmans, 1982.

Hays, Richard. "The Letter to the Galatians." In *The New Interpreter's Bible*, edited by Leander Keck, 11:181–348. Nashville: Abingdon Press, 2000.

Martyn, J. L. *Galatians: A New Translation with Introduction and Commentary*. Anchor Bible 33A. New York: Doubleday, 1997.

Interpreting Romans

Barth, K. *The Epistle to the Romans*. Translated by Edwyn C. Hoskyns. London: Oxford University Press, 1953.

Dunn, James D. G. *Romans*. WBC 38A-B. 2 vols. Dallas: Word, 1998.

Jewett, R. *Romans: A Commentary*. Hermeneia. Minneapolis: Fortress Press, 2007.

Käsemann, Ernst. *Commentary on Romans*. Translated by Geoffrey W. Bromiley. Grand Rapids: Eerdmans, 1980.

Keck, L. *Romans*. ANTC. Nashville: Abingdon Press, 2005.

Wright, N. T. "The Letter to the Romans." In *The New Interpreter's Bible*, edited by Leander Keck, 10:393–770. Nashville: Abingdon Press, 2002.

47. Only the undisputed Pauline letters are listed. Scholars who affirm Paul's authorship of 2 Thessalonians uniformly locate the letter in proximity to 1 Thessalonians. Scholars who affirm Pauline authorship of Colossians, Ephesians, and the Pastorals generally locate them all in the 60s, after Paul's arrival in Rome. Bruce represents scholars who have great confidence in the accuracy of Acts, harmonizing Acts and Galatians on the basis of the "South Galatian Theory" and by identifying the Jerusalem conference of Gal 2 with the "famine visit" of Acts 11:30. See F. F. Bruce, *Apostle of the Heart Set Free* (Grand Rapids: Eerdmans, 1977), 475.

Schnelle, *New Testament Writings*, 15–28; Schnelle, *Apostle Paul*, 47–56, represents the mainstream rigorously critical approach, affirming only the seven undisputed letters as written by Paul, the late date of Galatians and the "North Galatian" theory, but fairly often defending traditional positions. He identifies the conference of Gal 2 with that of Acts 15, argues for the literary unity of each the Pauline letters, and locates Philippians and Philemon in the Roman imprisonment.

Dunn, *Beginning from Jerusalem*, 497–518, argues for the "South Galatian Theory" and for the early date for Galatians, but not that Galatians was written before Jerusalem Council. He does not harmonize Paul and Acts by equating the "famine visit" of Acts 11:29 with the Jerusalem visit of Gal 2.

Jewett identifies the conference visit of Gal 2 with the visit of Acts 18:22. Cf. Jewett, *Chronology*.

Lüdemann, *Chronology*, 262–63, develops the views of Knox, *Chapters*, 47–110, with slight variations. Paul's "first mission journey" extended into Macedonia, so that 1 Thessalonians was written early, in advance of the Jerusalem conference; the conference visit of Gal 2 is identified with the visit of Acts 18:22. The numbers given assume the death of Jesus in 30 CE; Lüdemann thinks it could have occurred in 27 CE, in which case some dates are three years earlier.

Fitzmyer's view is cited from Joseph A. Fitzmyer, SJ, "Paul," in *The New Jerome Biblical Commentary*, ed. Raymond E. Brown, Joseph A. Fitzmyer, SJ, and Roland E. Murphy (Englewood Cliffs, NJ: Prentice-Hall, 1990), 1333–37. Betz's view is from Betz, "Paul," 186–201. Martyn's view is from Martyn, *Galatians*, 182–83.

Boring's view is documented in this book.

BOX 13: Suggested Outlines of Paul's Life and Ministry

	Bruce	*Schnelle*	*Dunn*	*Jewett*	*Lüdemann*	*Fitzmyer*	*Betz*	*Martyn*	*Boring*
Death of Jesus	30	30	30	30	30		27		30
Conversion	33	33	32	34	33	36	28	35	33
Jerusalem Visit Acts 9	35	35	34/35	37	36	39	31	38	35
In Cilicia & Syria Gal 1:21; Acts 9:30	35–46	36–42	34/35–47	37–46	37	40–44	31-43	38–48	36–
Jerusalem Visit Acts 11	46								
1st Mission Journey	47–48	45–47	ca. 45–47	43–45	37	46–49			–47
(Galatians)	48?								
Jerusalem Visit Acts 15	49= Council	48= Council	47/48= Council			49= Council	43/44= Council	48	48
Early Aegean Mission	49–52	48–52	50–55	46–57	39	50–58	After 44	48-?	48–52
Paul in Corinth	50–52	50/51	50–52	50–51	41	51–52	51–53		50–52
1 Thess	50	50	50	50	41	51	51		50
(Galatians)			51				52–55		
Jerusalem-Antioch Visit Acts 18	52	51/52	51/52	51= Council	50= Council	52–54			51/52
Paul in Ephesus	52–55	52–55	52/53–55	52–57	51–53	54–58	52–54/55		52–56
(Galatians)				53		54			
1 (–2) Cor	55	55	52–55	55	52	57	54/55		54/55
(Philippians)	?			55	?	56–57	55/56?		52/53
(Philemon)	?			55	?	56–57	55/56?		52/53
Paul in Macedonia, Corinth	55–57	55–56	56/57	56	53–54	57	56		56
2 Corinthians	56	55		56	53	57	55–56		56
(Galatians)		55			53				56
Romans	57	56	56/57	56–57	54–55	58	56		57
Jerusalem Visit Acts 21	57	56		57	55	58	59		57
Arrival in Rome	60	59	60	60–61		61	61		60
(Philippians)	?	60	61–62						
(Philemon)	?	61	61–62						
Death of Paul	65?	64	62–64	62			63–64		63/64

Comprehensive Studies and Continuing Issues

Becker, J. *Paul: Apostle to the Gentiles*. Translated by O. C. Dean. Louisville, KY: Westminster John Knox Press, 1993.

Betz, H. D. "Paul." In *The Anchor Bible Dictionary*, edited by David Noel Freedman, 5:186–201. New York: Doubleday, 1992.

Bruce, F. F. *Apostle of the Heart Set Free*. Grand Rapids: Eerdmans, 1977.

Bultmann, R. *Theology of the New Testament*. Translated by Kendrick Grobel. 2 vols. New York: Scribner, 1951.

Dunn, J. D. G. *The Theology of Paul the Apostle*. Grand Rapids: Eerdmans, 1998.

Hay, David, Elizabeth Johnson, Jouette Bassler, et al., eds. *Pauline Theology*. 4 vols. Minneapolis: Fortress Press, 1991–1997 (vols. 1–3 Fortress Press; vol. 4 Atlanta: Scholars Press).

Jewett, Robert. *A Chronology of Paul's Life*. Philadelphia: Fortress Press, 1979.

Knox, J. *Chapters in a Life of Paul*. London: Adam & Charles Black, 1950.

Lüdemann, G. *Opposition to Paul in Jewish Christianity*. Translated by M. Eugene Boring. Minneapolis: Fortress Press, 1989.

———. *Paul, Apostle to the Gentiles: Studies in Chronology*. Translated by F. Stanley Jones. Philadelphia: Fortress Press, 1984.

Meeks, W. A. *The First Urban Christians: The Social World of the Apostle Paul*. New Haven, CT: Yale University Press, 1983.

Meeks, W. A., and J. T. Fitzgerald, eds. *The Writings of St. Paul*. 2nd ed., Norton Critical Edition. New York: Norton, 2007.

Porter, S. E., ed. *Paul and His Opponents*. Pauline Studies 2. Leiden: Brill, 2005.

Sanders, E. P. *Paul and Palestinian Judaism: A Comparison of Patterns of Religion*. Philadelphia: Fortress Press, 1977.

Schnelle, U. *Apostle Paul: His Life and Thought*. Translated by M. Eugene Boring. Grand Rapids: Baker Academic, 2005.

Schütz, J. H. *Paul and the Anatomy of Apostolic Authority*. NTL. Introduction by Wayne Meeks, 2007 ed. Louisville, KY: Westminster John Knox Press, 1975.

Schweitzer, A. *The Mysticism of Paul the Apostle*. Translated by William Montgomery. London: A. & C. Black, 1931.

Sumney, J. L. *Identifying Paul's Opponents: The Question of Method in 2 Corinthians*. JSNTSup 40, Sheffield: JSOT Press, 1990.

14

Ephesus and the Pauline School

14.1 What Happened after Romans?

THE MAIN OUTLINES OF THE END OF PAUL'S life are virtually certain: Paul goes to Jerusalem, is arrested and sent to Rome, where he is finally executed by the Romans in the early 60s CE. A more detailed construction of the last years of Paul's life depends on how one regards the results of critical study of the relevant New Testament documents.

The traditional construction, as represented, for example, in the *NIV Study Bible*,[1] is based on the presuppositions that (1) Acts is entirely accurate history; (2) all thirteen letters attributed to Paul were in fact written by him, and none are composite; (3) there are no historical conflicts between Acts and the Pauline letters; (4) Acts, the secondary source, is basic to the construction. Letters and events that can be fitted into the Acts framework are inserted at the relevant points. Events and letters that cannot be inserted into Acts are considered to have occurred after the Acts story concludes.

The result of these presuppositions produces the following chronology for the end of Paul's life:

— Romans written at Acts 20:3, from Greece (Corinth).

— As recounted in Acts 20–28, Paul goes to Jerusalem, is arrested and detained for two years, then sent to Rome, where he spends two years in imprisonment awaiting trial.

— During this "first Roman imprisonment," Paul writes Philippians, Philemon, Colossians, and Ephesians.

— After the story of Acts concludes, Paul is released about 62 CE and carries on further mission work for about five years, possibly including a mission to Spain. During this period, he writes 1 Timothy and Titus.[2]

— Paul is arrested and imprisoned again in Rome about 67 CE. During this "second Roman imprisonment," he writes 2 Timothy, his last letter.

— Paul is martyred in Rome about 68 CE.

The construction of the end of Paul's life based on critical study argues that (1) Acts

1. Kenneth L. Barker and Donald W. Burdick, eds., *The NIV Study Bible*, 10th anniv. ed. (Grand Rapids: Zondervan, 1995), 1664, "Timeline of Paul's Life" and Introductions to Acts, Philippians, Philemon, Colossians, Ephesians, and the Pastoral Letters. Some elements of the traditional view are supported by some critical scholars, e.g., those who argue for the Roman provenance of Philippians and/or the Pauline authorship of Colossians, Ephesians, or the Pastorals.

2. Some scholars attempt to find a place for 1 Timothy and Titus during Paul's Aegean mission, and then place 2 Timothy during Paul's only Roman imprisonment (see Luke Timothy Johnson, *The First and Second Letters to Timothy*, AB 35A [New York: Doubleday, 2001], 136–37).

has some historical traditions, but reflects the author's theological purpose, and may not be used uncritically to construct the actual history; (2) a distinction must be made in the way undisputed Pauline letters are used and the way those probably not written directly by Paul are used; (3) there are unresolvable conflicts between the undisputed letters and Acts; (4) the undisputed letters are primary sources and are basic to the construction. Material in Acts that appears to be historical on the basis of critical sifting may be used to supplement the picture from the undisputed letters; (5) possibly relevant information from noncanonical sources is to be used with the same critical caution as the canonical sources.

These presuppositions produce the following chronology for the end of Paul's life:

— After writing Romans, Paul went from Corinth to Jerusalem to deliver the offering, accompanied by the delegation from the churches of the Aegean mission.

— Whether and how the offering was received by the Jerusalem church is unclear. Acts is reluctant to mention the offering; the only reference is the incidental comment in 24:17, in Paul's defense before Felix. The Jerusalem church kept its distance from Paul. If they accepted the offering at all, it was apparently done on the side, out of public view. More likely, they declined to accept the offering and what it symbolized, the unity of Gentile and Jewish Christians.

— Paul was arrested in Jerusalem by the Roman authorities as a troublemaker. There is no indication in Acts or the letters possibly from Rome that the Jerusalem church supported Paul or came to his defense during his extended incarceration in Jerusalem and Caesarea.

— Paul was sent to Rome in a prisoner transport, where he continued to be incarcerated in moderate conditions. During this time, the Roman church, which had close connections with Jerusalem, likewise kept its distance. We probably have no letters from this period, so that Romans is our last document from Paul's hand—though some scholars place Philemon, Philippians, and Colossians in the Roman imprisonment (see introductions to the individual books).

— After a period of Roman imprisonment, Paul was executed about 62–64 CE, possibly in connection with Nero's persecution of Roman Christians.

14.2 The Pauline School Tradition Continues

AFTER PAUL'S DEATH, AN INFORMAL NETwork of Christian teachers looked back to Paul as the primary (or exclusive) apostolic leader of the church and attempted to interpret and adapt his message for later contexts. The following factors are important:

1. Paul himself had been no individualist but the primary leader of a Pauline mission team. His education as a Pharisee (Phil 3:5; Gal 1:14) prepared him to think in terms of a continuing school tradition. Although he had an intensely personal conversion experience, he always understood this as his call to be an apostle in a churchly context. Paul did not work alone but had numerous coworkers.[3] One can enumerate about forty; the brief letter to Philemon alone mentions nine such, six of whom are with him as he writes, three among the addressees. He often used the term "coworkers" or "fellow workers," in a quasi-technical sense (Rom 16:3, 9, 21; 1 Cor 3:9; 2 Cor 1:24; 8:23; Phil 2:25; 4:3; 1 Thess 3:2; Phlm 1, 24). He sometimes authorized his coworkers to remind his churches of his teaching, to continue it, and he charged the churches to attend to his teaching given through his colleagues (see 1 Cor 4:17; Rom 6:17; 16:17).

3. See especially E. Earle Ellis, *The Making of the New Testament Documents* (Leiden: Brill, 2002), 36–42.

2. Within the Pauline congregations, the *teachers* formed an identifiable group (1 Cor 12:28–29; see the later Eph 4:11). Their task would have been to inculcate and elaborate the traditions Paul had communicated during the founding of the churches (1 Cor 11:2, 23; 12:28; Gal 6:6; Rom 12:7; see 2 Thess 2:15; 3:6).

3. In his letters to churches Paul characteristically joined his name with others. This was extremely unusual. Of the hundreds of extant ancient letters, the only other known instance is Cicero, *Epistulae ad Atticum* 11.5.1. All Paul's letters except Romans include cosenders in the initial greetings.[4] When Paul says "we," he does not always mean it in the sense of "editorial we" or "the whole church, all Christians," but refers to the group of evangelists and teachers around him. This frequent use of the first-person plural is to be taken seriously as an indication of Paul and his coworkers.

4. The contents of Paul's letters reflect his belonging to a school that passed on traditions.[5] The numerous adoptions and interpretations of traditions are not merely incidental items he had picked up while "attending church" or that he happened to think of as he composed his letters. Certain texts stand out from their context, not as inherited from pre-Pauline tradition, but as preletter formulations within the Pauline school. First Corinthians 13 is an example (see also 1 Cor 7:12, 25; 9:14; 11:23–26; 15:3–5; 1 Thess 4:15–17). Some of these texts appear to be midrashic arguments not composed ad hoc, and not composed by an isolated individual (e.g. 1 Cor 10:1–13; Gal 4:21–31). When Paul became a Christian, he was taught a tradition; as missionary and evangelist he was engaged in passing on and interpreting a tradition. Thus something like a "Pauline school" already existed during Paul's lifetime.

5. Strands of the Pauline tradition struggled or flourished in various locations, but Ephesus seems to have become the primary center of the Pauline school. According to Acts, Ephesus became a center of Paul's missionary efforts, where he spent more time than in any other mission station. From 52 to 55 CE he and several associates established churches not only in Ephesus but in the surrounding regions of Asia Minor. By the end of the first century, there were several strands of the Christian movement present in Ephesus. In the years after Paul's death, the developing Pauline school thus encountered not only the vital Greco-Roman religions of Ephesus, but other versions of Christianity and dissenting subgroups within its own ranks.

6. The Pauline school continued and developed Paul's practice that had made the letter form a means of apostolic instruction and direction. When the Pauline school issued documents in Paul's name intended to continue his apostolic teaching, they continued to use the letter form that Paul himself had made his primary mode of teaching and communication with the churches under his care.[6] It is not the case that a number of Christian communities independently adopted the letter form in preference to other possibilities. It was Paul who had made the letter form the exclusive medium of communication of the apostolic faith; this practice was continued and developed by Paul's disciples after his death. It is not merely that Paul's reputation as a letter writer survived; the letter form itself was seen to be an appropriate form for communicating the Christian faith.

7. The Pauline school adopted not only the letter genre as such, but particular features of

4. Gal 1:2 mentions no names, but includes "all the members of God's family who are with me" as cosenders. Reference to cosenders was continued in the Pauline school by Colossians and 2 Thessalonians, but not in Ephesians and the Pastorals.

5. Ellis, *Documents*, 53–142, identifies many such preformed traditions and the criteria for identifying them.

6. This was not only, or mainly, "for purposes of authority" (so Johnson, *Timothy*, 139), as often assumed by both advocates and opponents of pseudonymity. The point was not to claim Paul's authority for *their* opinions, but to extend *Paul's* teaching into a new time and place, and to do this not in the form of composing church orders such as the *Didache*, but to continue the occasional narrative form and function of the Pauline letter.

Paul's distinctive epistolary form, including the basic structure of the Pauline letter form, its unique greeting form, and much of Paul's theological vocabulary and conceptuality. So also people, places, incidents and details from Paul's letters and the oral legendary tradition that was already developing about him were worked into the deuteropauline letters as a means of projecting the fictive narrative world represented by the letters of the Pauline school. Colossians is the first of these, and closest to Paul's own writings.

8. Paul's letters were collected and combined into a single corpus (see above §2.3). Paul did not do this himself. Even if he retained copies of his correspondence, it is difficult to imagine his carrying them all with him during his travels and imprisonments, and that they would have survived the shipwrecks he experienced (not only Acts 27–28, but the several implied in 2 Cor 11:25). While originally each letter had been sent individually to a single congregation or cluster of churches, after Paul's death they were circulated only as a corpus. No single letter of Paul comes to us in isolation. In our earliest manuscripts, the letters have already been combined into a collection, the Pauline Corpus. We do not know when, how, or by whom Paul's letters were collected, edited, and "published" (circulated to the church at large). Theoretically, this could have been a random and informal process, as letters were copied and exchanged among the churches, and various collections emerged here and there. We should not suppose that the collection was made all at once, that there was a single collection, or that all the collections included the same documents. The uniform titles and other features of all extant manuscripts, however, indicate that at some stage a single collection was produced that became the definitive edition for all later copies.[7] A seven-letter collection, formulated on the model that Paul wrote to seven churches, seems to have existed before the end of the first century and formed the pattern for the sevenfold corpus in Revelation 2–3 and for the collection of the letters of Ignatius.[8]

9. One purpose of collecting the letters was to make them available to the larger church. Paul always wrote to particular congregations or clusters of congregations in a particular area. He wrote neither to individuals nor to the whole church, and never expected that his occasional writings focused on a particular situation would be read in the church at large. After he died and his letters were circulated, the form was extended to address the church as such. This involved a reinterpretation of his letters as no longer addressing only a particular congregation, but addressing the wider church.

10. The letters were not only collected; they were edited (see above, §2.3). An isolated letter needs no title. When several letters were combined into a corpus, titles had to be given to each document. Paul himself had not written "1 Corinthians" as the heading of any letter he composed. Likewise, the letters had to be placed in some order. The most common arrangement in the extant manuscripts is based on length, from longest to shortest. Some letters may have been edited in the churches to which they were addressed, and/or particular letters may have been edited by teachers in the Pauline school in the process of forming the Pauline corpus (see the introductions to the individual books, especially Philippians, 2 Corinthians, and Romans).

7. G. Zuntz argues the Pauline corpus came into being ca. 100 CE, on the grounds that a collection is known to Ignatius, but not to Clement of Rome. Kurt and Barbara Aland, on the other hand, argue the references in *1 Clement* to Romans, 1 Corinthians, and Hebrews point to a collection of Paul's letters in Rome prior to 100 CE (see data in Parker, *New Testament Manuscripts*, 250). David Trobisch, *Paul's Letter Collection: Tracing the Origins* (Minneapolis: Fortress Press, 1994), 17–18, argues Paul himself assembled and disseminated a collection of his own writings, but the theory has not convinced most scholars.

8. For details and bibliography, see Gamble, *Books and Readers*, 58–63, who argues that the codex was introduced into Christian usage in order to contain this collection, which was far longer than the normal papyrus scroll could contain.

11. New letters were composed in Paul's name. The existence of the Pauline school seems to be confirmed by the existence of the deuteropauline writings, representing four different authors or groups. Just as Paul's own writings should not be regarded as individualistic productions, so the deuteropauline documents are not the products of enterprising individuals who privately decided to attempt to foist something "Pauline" on the rest of the church. They represent the group of Pauline teachers committed to representing the continuing voice of Paul. This is analogous to the speeches of Paul in Acts, though presented in a different literary genre (see below §23.3.1). During his lifetime Paul not only had sent his letters in his own name, but had included the names of his associates Timothy, Titus, and Silvanus as senders of the letters, even though he was the principal author (see above). As there was a sense in which he had written in their names, so they continued to write in his name (see the introductions to Colossians, Ephesians, 2 Thessalonians, and the Pastorals, and the Excursus on Pseudepigraphy below §14.2).

12. The teachers and authors of the later Pauline school do not merely repeat Paul, just as Paul did not simply repeat himself. The deuteropauline authors both respect Paul's apostolic mission and message and creatively transform it to speak to later situations. Paul's letters to the Corinthians deal with the same issues in different ways; Romans is a slightly later and more reflective restatement of the same themes dealt with in Galatians, adjusting the earlier message to a later and different situation. So also Paul's later followers interpreted him afresh in new situations, in continuity with what he had done. The roots and foundation of their work were in the authentic Paul, which they had from Pauline letters and church tradition—and in the decades after Paul's death, from his personal associates and disciples.

13. The literary products of the Pauline school represent interchange, discussion, and debate among the teachers who continue the Pauline tradition, working with shared texts and materials. The obvious overlappings and parallels between Colossians and Ephesians, for example, should not be explained on the cut-and-paste desktop model of one author merely using or copying from the other; questions of literary relationships are more complex and nuanced than usually represented in the mode of "who used whom?"[9]

14. Paul's followers did not always agree about the proper interpretation of Paul (then and now). There was no monolithic post-Pauline tradition, but disputes emerged within the Pauline school as to who were his legitimate heirs and how he should be best represented in the later situation. The New Testament includes *more than one* post-Pauline development, but not all the writings later written in his name were accepted as representing the apostolic faith. As in the formation of the New Testament canon in general, the rule was *more than one thing but not just anything*. Already 2 Thessalonians 2:2 shows that there was a dispute about which letters authentically represented Paul.

15. The deuteropauline letters thus continue the biblical model of reinterpretation: 1 and 2 Chronicles reinterpret 1 Samuel–2 Kings; Daniel reinterprets Jeremiah; the continuing Isaiah tradition of Deutero- and Trito-Isaiah reinterpret the eighth-century Isaiah of Jerusalem; Matthew and Luke reinterpret Mark and Q.

16. We know little concerning the personnel of the group's leadership. These will originally have been Paul's personal associates, then their associates who had not known Paul personally. We know nothing about how one became

9. For a detailed discussion of this issue, see Ernest Best, "Who Used Whom? The Relationship of Ephesians and Colossians," *NTS* 43, no. 1 (1997), who considers all the logical possibilities, investigates the parallels in great detail, concludes that the phenomena of the text are not best explained on a consistent diachronic model of one author using the text of the other. "This paper would favor the view that the similarities and dissimilarities of the two letters can be explained most easily on the assumption of distinct authors who were members of the same Pauline school and had discussed together the Pauline theology they had inherited" (96).

a member of this group, how it was structured, what sort of lines of authority developed, what networks of communication existed among various congregations and their leaders. Though the second-generation bearers of the Pauline tradition were probably not formally organized, informal associations can still be tight and rigid, as illustrated by modern sects and denominations that have no central, top-down organization but are still closely knit, aware of the line that separates insiders from outsiders, and sensitive to deviations and conflicts within the group.

17. The canonical documents that emanated from the Pauline school, as well as those that claimed to represent Paul but were not included in the canon, indicate a number of issues that continued to be disputed within the Pauline school, including:

— *The language and theology of the Holy Spirit*. This had been important to Paul, but could lead to excesses and misunderstandings. Some later Pauline authors continued and elaborated Paul's Spirit terminology (e.g., Ephesians); others were hesitant, and minimized it (Colossians, the Pastorals).

— *Structure and church leadership*. The charismatic leadership of the first generation of the Pauline churches (1 Cor 12) could not continue indefinitely after the death of Paul and the delay of the parousia, but Paul's followers were not of one mind on the role of emerging church offices.

— *Biblical interpretation*. Paul had appropriated the Jewish Scriptures and reinterpreted them christologically, but second-generation Paulinism was divided on whether and how to understand the Jewish Scriptures as the Christian Bible.

— *Relation to gnosticizing thought*. The proto-Gnostic philosophical and religious currents abroad in Asia Minor seemed to some Paulinists an appropriate vehicle of Christian faith. Others saw the danger of this and rejected such "speculative" approaches to reconfiguring theology.

— *Eschatology*. Paul had formulated his theology in view of the nearness of the parousia. How should his followers rethink eschatology in view of the continuing delay of Christ's return?

— *Ecumenism and apostolicity*. Paul had struggled against some other versions of the Christian faith represented by "false apostles" (2 Corinthians, Galatians). How should the continuing Pauline school relate to other streams of early Christianity? Were all non-Pauline Christians and their theology to be considered opponents, or as brothers and sisters in the one church? If the latter, were they to be regarded as in need of correction and further instruction, or as complementary versions of the one faith? How broad was the ecumenical net to be cast?

EXCURSUS 2

Pseudepigraphy[10]

TERMINOLOGY. WHILE OUR CULTURE CONDITIONS us to devalue and be suspicious of anything with the prefix "pseudo-," no value judgment is implied in the technical terms *pseudonym* and *pseudepigraphy*. To refer to a document as pseudonymous or as pseudepigraphical simply means it was not written by the person represented by the document itself to be its author. This is different from anonymity, in which an author's name is secondarily attributed to a document that makes no claims to specific authorship. For instance, 1 Timothy represents itself as written by Paul. If Paul did not write it, the document is pseudonymous. The Gospel of Matthew, on the other hand, makes no claim to have been written by Matthew. If Matthew did not write it, an anonymous document has been given a title designating Matthew as the author, but it is not a matter of pseudonymity. Likewise, *authentic* in such

10. An extensive literature has developed on the subject. For a selection representing the whole range of opinion, and further bibliography, see Ernest Best, *A Critical and Exegetical Commentary on Ephesians*, ICC (Edinburgh: T. & T. Clark, 1998), 10n7.

contexts is not a value judgment, but merely means a particular document was written by the author to whom it is ascribed. In regard to the Pauline letters, *deuteropauline* is used as a synonym for *pseudepigraphical,* that is, not written by Paul himself but belonging to the Pauline tradition. *Fictive* refers to the world projected by the document itself, the imaginary world represented by the text of the document. A parable of Jesus, for instance, projects a fictive world in which there are particular characters and events, but *fictive* in such contexts is a technical literary term that makes no claim that what the document has to say, in its own terms, is true or untrue. In any case, to discuss authorship issues of New Testament books using such terms as "deceit," "lie," and "forgery" is inappropriate and does not advance the cause of understanding.[11]

Approach. Alongside the use of inflammatory language, a typical approach of defenders of the traditional view of authorship has been to affirm the tradition and declare that the burden of proof is on those who challenge it.[12] The arguments against the tradition are then examined piecemeal, and the conclusion is drawn that the case has not been proven. Since in the nature of the case, historical judgments are matters of probability and not of absolute proof, this line of argument will always lead to victory for whatever is declared to be the traditional view. A more neutral starting point is necessary, one that offers evidence and arguments for each side and then asks which seems to be most probable.

Importance. It is certain that after Paul's death disciples and advocates of Paul wrote letters in his name and circulated them among the churches (*3 Corinthians, Epistle to the Laodiceans, Epistles of Paul and Seneca*). The question is whether any such letters are in the New Testament. This is not a marginal issue. Of the fourteen New Testament letters traditionally attributed to Paul, many critical scholars consider seven to have been written by Paul himself, six to be pseudepigraphical (deuteropauline), and one, Hebrews, to be anonymous but later attributed to Paul. The issue is, of course, important for the New Testament as a whole. Of the twenty-seven New Testament books, eighteen claim specific authorship, the others being anonymous. Of these eighteen, most critical scholars regard only the seven undisputed letters of Paul as written by the traditional author; all the others are pseudonymous.[13] A careful evaluation of pseudonymity both historically and theologically is thus mandatory for anyone who takes the New Testament seriously. The starting point for such an evaluation is important.

Modern and Ancient Perspectives. If we start in our world, we know of several genres of pseudonymous writings. Even in our modern Western setting, we do not pose the issue simply as "truth or lie," but have a somewhat nuanced spectrum of how we view authorship: forged checks, plagiarism, literary forgeries such as the Hitler diaries, ghost writing of books and speeches for celebrities and political figures, academic publications mostly

11. This view, advocated here and by many critical scholars, is opposed from both left and right, e.g., Bart D. Ehrman, *Jesus Interrupted: Revealing the Hidden Contradictions in the Bible (and Why We Don't Know about Them)* (New York: HarperOne, 2009), 112–37, on New Testament pseudepigraphy. "That's why people wrote forgeries—to fool people" (115). Carson and Moo argue that if letters that claim apostolic authorship were not in fact written by their purported authors, they are liars, and, since they condemn lying, they are also hypocrites. D. A. Carson and Douglas J. Moo, *An Introduction to the New Testament*, 2nd ed. (Grand Rapids: Zondervan, 2005), 346, 349.

A few authors have suggested an alternative vocabulary to *pseudepigraphical* that is not so prone to abuse and misunderstanding. I. Howard Marshall, for example, an evangelical scholar who concluded that the Pastorals were not written by Paul, has proposed that we substitute "allograph" and "allonymous" for "pseudepigraphy" and "pseudonymous." His suggestion is based on the Greek word ἄλλος (*allos*, other) and means the actual author is other than the purported author. The suggestion has not caught on, and we seem to be stuck with a terminology that will continue to need explanation. See I. Howard Marshall, *The Pastoral Epistles*, ICC (Edinburgh: T. & T. Clark, 1999), 57–92.

12. So, e.g., Harold W. Hoehner, *Ephesians: An Exegetical Commentary* (Grand Rapids: Baker Academic, 2002), 2–61.

13. Thus for the New Testament as a whole:

Authentic (=written by the author claimed by the document itself): Romans, 1–2 Corinthians, Galatians, Philippians, 1 Thessalonians, Philemon, Revelation (by "John," not the apostle).

Anonymous: Matthew, Mark, Luke, John, Acts, Hebrews, 1–3 John (2 and 3 John by unnamed "elder").

Pseudonymous: Ephesians, Colossians, 2 Thessalonians, 1–2 Timothy, Titus, James, 1–2 Peter, Jude.

written by anonymous assistants, pen names (Mark Twain=Samuel Clemens, George Eliot=Mary Ann Evans), executive letters written by a secretary "over my signature," published letters written as a transparent literary device.[14] Some of these examples involve legal rights, copyright laws, and ethical issues, while others are an accepted part of our culture. They have differing perspectives on the nature of the truth they express; we recognize this and do not lump them all together. How was it in the ancient world?

The Bible of the early church, the Christian Old Testament, offers numerous examples of both anonymous and pseudonymous writings.[15] In the process of collection, psalms that were originally written anonymously were attracted to the name of David and assembled under his name for the whole collection. Anonymous wisdom materials were attracted to the name of Solomon and later regarded as written by him (Proverbs). Then pseudonymous works were written in Solomon's name (e.g., Wisdom of Solomon). Apocalyptic texts provide clear examples: texts were written in the name of Adam, Enoch, Abraham, Elijah, and others. In Hellenistic and Diaspora Judaism, pseudepigraphy was the *rule*, so that those who wrote in their own name may be easily named as exceptions (e.g., Jesus ben Sirach, Josephus, Philo).

In the Hellenistic world of the New Testament, revered authorities of previous generations were kept current *not* by publishing commentaries on their writings, in which "then" and "now" were clearly distinguished, but by composing new documents in their name—not what they once *said* to past generations, but what they *say* to the present. Most educated people would have had practice in school of slipping into the role of a famous author and writing in his style, including the creation of "realistic" details to show that they were writing "in character."[16] In Paul's time collections of Plato's letters circulated, containing both authentic and inauthentic texts. Likewise, of the 280 works attributed to Pythagoras, only about 80 were written by Pythagoras himself. The collection of Cynic epistles was mostly composed of letters written in the name of famous Cynic teachers of the past. After Paul's time, but contemporary with the later Pauline tradition, the seven authentic letters of Ignatius to the churches of the Aegean and Rome were supplemented by others written in the name of the revered martyr bishop, and all circulated together as Ignatius's writings until modern times.[17] Pseudepigraphy was sometimes explicitly affirmed in the early Christian tradition. For example, both the Muratorian Canon and Augustine included the Wisdom of Solomon in their Bible, while denying that it was written by Solomon.

14. In the "Letters to the Editor" section of a newspaper or magazine, a piece entitled "From George Washington to the American People" attempting to reinterpret the contemporary relevance of the first president's original advice for the new nation to "avoid entangling alliances" might include: "As I was walking down by the Potomac picking my wooden teeth, I was reflecting on the increasing isolationism in American politics. I was just saying to Martha the other day, isolationism is a good political philosophy for the Thirteen States, but if there is ever a day when one can travel from Europe to America in half a day, and there is instant electronic global communication, we may need to reconsider isolationism." Anachronisms and other features would make it clear that the letter is a contemporary political statement in the name of George Washington.

15. Full documentation is provided in D. G. Meade, *Pseudonymity and Canon: An Investigation into the Relationship of Authorship and Authority in Jewish and Earliest Christian Tradition*, WUNT 39 (Tübingen: Mohr, 1986), 17–102. Meade argues that pseudonymity in the Bible is a claim to actualize authoritative tradition, not a claim about literary origins.

16. Lewis R. Donelson, *Pseudepigraphy and Ethical Argument in the Pastoral Epistles*, HUT (Tübingen: Mohr, 1986), 64–65, has good examples of such details used to convey the realistic presence of the sender to the recipients. Abraham J. Malherbe, *The Cynic Epistles: A Study Edition*, SBLSBS 12 (Missoula, MT: Scholars Press, 1977), allows the modern reader to see many detailed examples of "realistic" details included in letters that were obviously pseudepigraphical, and known to be so.

17. Those written by Ignatius himself were not disentangled from the deutero-Ignatian letters until the latter part of the nineteenth century, by the work of Theodor Zahn (1873) and Adolf Harnack (1878) in Germany, and esp. by J. B. Lightfoot (1885) in England (see Michael W. Holmes, *The Apostolic Fathers: Greek Texts and English Translations*, 3rd ed. [Grand Rapids: Baker Academic, 2007], 171–81).

In the earliest days of the church, Christian tradition was passed along anonymously, in the name of the Lord rather than being ascribed to particular Christian teachers.[18] Collections of Jesus' sayings and stories from his life circulated without the name of any "author" or "editor" attached. Paul delivers anonymous Christian tradition to his churches in the name of the Lord, without giving the name of the Christian teachers from whom he had received it (e.g., 1 Cor 11:23–32; 1 Thess 4:15–17). In such cases, the line is vague between what he had received and his own contemporizing additions. Not only was there no *concept* of copyright, "intellectual property," and such; there were no *mechanics* for citation (quotation marks, parentheses, footnotes, and such). This is not because they were "primitive" and couldn't distinguish quoted material from updated additions and later compositions, but because they had a different perspective on the whole process.

A new development occurred about 50 CE, when Paul began to write letters to churches in his own name as a form of apostolic instruction. Because they were *letters,* they bore his name. As the Pauline letters circulated in the churches, they formed a separate genre alongside the varieties of oral and written anonymous tradition. Paul's letters typically presented themselves as written not only by Paul; they included his coworkers in the opening line and continued in the first-person plural that is more than an "editorial we." Though this "we" style does not indicate coauthorship, it indicates that already in Paul's lifetime his letters were associated with and sent forth under the names of his disciples and colleagues.

With the death of the first generation of apostolic leaders, the devastating war in Palestine that destroyed the setting of the earliest church and scattered its leaders, and the delay of the expected parousia, a new generation was faced with new issues: how does it pass on the apostolic faith, how does the later generation assure itself it is the apostolic faith they are passing on? The Pauline churches adopted the dual procedure of collecting, editing, and circulating Paul's letters, and composing new letters in his name. Anonymous writing continued, represented in the New Testament by the Gospels and Acts. Except for Paul's letters, no extant Christian literature was written under the name of its real author until near the end of the first century CE. Then, in and after the third Christian generation, some church leaders begin to write in their own names (e.g., *1 Clement*, Revelation, Ignatius), while others continued to promote their understanding of the apostolic faith by writing in the name of the revered figures of the first generation (e.g., Barnabas, Paul, James, Thomas).

Thus the production of pseudepigraphical documents was not merely a matter of enterprising individuals who wanted to foist their own opinions on the church by attributing them to some famous author of the past. New Testament pseudepigraphy was bound to a particular transitional historical situation between the presence of apostles in the church of the first generation and the presence of authoritative ministry and documents in the second century.[19] The authors saw it as important that the church of each generation understand itself as part of the ongoing community of faith in history, not the spontaneously generated group of believers and seekers in any given time and place (cf. Deut 5:1–5; 26:5–9; 29:13–14, and pseudepigraphical texts such as 2 Pet 1:12–21), but continuing to be addressed by its apostolic leaders.

Pseudepigraphy made Paul's writings available to the larger church. All Paul's letters had originally

18. See Oscar Cullmann, "The Tradition," in *The Early Church*, ed. A. J. B. Higgins (London: SCM Press, 1956), 59–104.

19. David A. deSilva, *An Introduction to the New Testament: Contexts, Methods, & Ministry Formation* (Downers Grove, IL: InterVarsity Press, 2004), 685–89, is cautiously positive on pseudonymity, making the valid point that the first (and second) generations after the death of the apostles were in a different situation than later. By Tertullian's time at the beginning of the third century CE, new compositions claiming to be from Paul were rightly rejected as forgeries (de Baptismo 17), as they would be today—unless transparently a literary device. The Tertullian instance fits the later situation, as it would fit today's. The incident cannot be used to prove all early Christians of the second and third generation rejected pseudonymity in principle. To be seen aright, we must not start from the later situation and work backward, but from the problem of the immediate post-apostolic situation.

been written to particular congregations and situations. Some modern scholars who affirm pseudonymous authorship for particular letters still write as though the deuteropauline letters were directed to the single congregation in the address. But letters such as 2 Thessalonians and Colossians, if not written by Paul, were written after Paul's letters were being circulated and, like the post-Pauline letter collection, were directed to the larger church. They imitated both the authorship and destination of the original letters, including their particularity and local color. Not only the pseudonymous author but the implied readers belong to the fictive world projected by the letter. If the Pastorals were not written by Paul, neither were they written to Timothy and Titus. Colossians and 2 Thessalonians, if not by Paul, were not written to Colossae or Thessaloniki, but to the larger church. They were intended to be read as, for example, 1 Corinthians was read in the 80s and 90s: once written by Paul to a particular situation, but now appropriated as having a message to the whole Christian community. Ephesians, if not by Paul, is an exception in this regard, lacking the details that associate it with a particular address, either historical or fictive.

The deuteropauline letters reflect a struggle for the Pauline heritage. The specific claim that Paul is writing it, and warnings against letters written in his name, do not occur in the undisputed letters, but only in pseudonymous ones (2 Thess 2:2, 15; 3:17). This reflects a post-Pauline time, when various letters were circulating in his name. Only then was this a danger. Then, and not before, authors would need to claim, "This, not the other letters, is the real Paul."

For the some modern readers, the primary issue is theological. Can pseudepigraphical documents be Holy Scripture, legitimate vehicles of the word of God? *For some*, this is a matter of conflict with their church tradition, which, officially or unofficially, regards affirming traditional views of authorship as theologically important and necessary. Prior to 1962, this was the stance of the Roman Catholic Church, but responsible historical criticism is now not only affirmed, but mandated in the Roman Catholic community. Most Roman Catholic scholars now argue that the Pastoral Letters, for example, are pseudonymous.[20] For *others*, the idea of pseudepigraphical documents in the canon conflicts with their personal ideas of how God works: "God would not let forgeries become part of the Bible." Quite apart from the appropriateness of "forgery" language in this regard (see above), Christians who believe the definitive revelation of God happened in the life, death, and resurrection of a crucified carpenter turned itinerant preacher might be cautious in asserting that we know in advance how God works and what God would do and would not do.

Such general discussions, of course, do not settle anything about whether or not particular New Testament books were written directly by Paul or by his disciples after his death. These decisions must be made from case to case, by examining each book. In each of the New Testament books whose authorship is disputed, I will give a brief summary of the arguments pro and con, with a full treatment in the discussion of the Pastorals.

14.3 For Further Reading

Beker, J. C. *Heirs of Paul: Paul's Legacy in the New Testament and in the Church Today*. Minneapolis: Fortress Press, 1991.

Donelson, Lewis R. *Pseudepigraphy and Ethical Argument in the Pastoral Epistles*. HUT. Tübingen: Mohr, 1986.

Meade, D. G., *Pseudonymity and Canon: An Investigation into the Relationship of Authorship and Authority in Jewish and Earliest Christian Tradition*. WUNT 39. Tübingen: Mohr, 1986.

Trebilco, P. R. *The Early Christians in Ephesus from Paul to Ignatius*. WUNT 166. Tübingen: Mohr Siebeck, 2004.

20. Cf. the essays in Raymond E. Brown, *The Critical Meaning of the Bible* (New York: Paulist Press, 1981), and the thoroughly critical Brown, Fitzmyer, and Murphy, eds., *New Jerome Biblical Commentary*, which provides the history of the appropriation of historical criticism in the Roman Catholic Church, and illustrates throughout how Christian believers in biblical authority, who affirm the Bible as Word of God, can utilize the insights and methods of critical biblical study.

15

Colossians, Ephesians, 2 Thessalonians

15.1 Interpreting Colossians

THE MOST DISPUTED ISSUE IN INTERPRETing Colossians is that of *authorship*. If written by Paul, the letter is probably from his latest, Roman imprisonment. If not by Paul, it is the earliest extant product of the Pauline school, the closest to Paul's own writings in both substance and date. While the majority of critical scholars at present regard Colossians as deuteropauline, a significant minority continue to argue for some version of Pauline authorship. It is better not to ask simplistically, "Did Paul write Colossians or not?" but to explore the different possible scenarios for the composition of the letter. There are five of these.

15.1.1 Five Scenarios for the Origin and Interpretation of Colossians

1. Paul to Colossae

Paul wrote to the Colossians, a church that he had not founded directly, but that had been begun by the missionary work of Epaphras, a coworker (1:7, reading "our behalf"; 2:1). Paul wrote as a prisoner (4:3, 10), but it is not clear whether the prison is in Rome, Ephesus, or elsewhere. The letter may have been written at the same time as Philemon (see the traditional construction, §11.3.3). Yet in this scenario the differences between Philemon and Colossians may be better explained if Colossians is written later than Philemon: Onesimus has been freed, has now returned to Paul's prison location and is working with him, and now revisits the Lycus Valley churches at Paul's behest, this time with Tychicus (not mentioned in Philemon). The differences between the lists in Box 14 below would then be explained by changes in the situation between the writing of Philemon and the writing of Colossians. We thus see that even "the" traditional view resolves itself into numerous variations: Paul wrote to Colossae from Rome, Ephesus, Caesarea, or some unknown prison, either at the same time as Philemon or somewhat later. Those scholars who regard the letter as written by Paul do not agree on which of these options is correct.

2. Timothy to Colossae

Some scholars are convinced that Colossians cannot have been written directly by Paul himself, but regard the letter as reflecting Paul's own situation so closely that it must have been written during Paul's lifetime. In this view, the actual author of the letter was most likely Timothy—his name in 1:1 is taken with utmost seriousness—at a time when the imprisoned Paul could not write it himself. Paul hears of the difficulties caused by the attractiveness of the heretical "philosophy" in the Lycus Valley churches, and commissions Timothy to compose a response over the signature of the two of them. A few influential

FIGURE 39: Hierapolis, showing the calcified cliffs formed by the hot springs. PHOTO CREDIT: M. EUGENE BORING.

scholars have adopted and elaborated this view, which attempts to do justice both to the concrete situation addressed and to the personal details included in the letter.[1] It should be noted that this argument does not really affirm Pauline authorship, but attributes the letter to a disciple of Paul—as in the deuteropauline hypothesis—but regards the letter as written during Paul's lifetime. The real Paul saw and approved the letter, though he did not write it.

3. A Paulinist to Colossae

In this scenario, this deuteropauline letter is still seen as a real letter by a teacher in the Pauline school to a concrete situation in Colossae (and neighboring churches in Laodicea and Hierapolis).

If not by Paul, however, there are difficulties in seeing the letter as addressing a particular situation in Colossae and environs soon after Paul's death. Did the Pauline school in Ephesus issue authentic-sounding directives in Paul's name to particular churches, as though he were still alive, even though both author and readers surely knew of his death? The modern reader must ask, if the author is not the historical Paul, should the readership be considered the historical Colossians? Do they not both belong to the same fictive world projected by the letter?

4. A Paulinist to the Church Universal

If Colossians is not written to the particular situation of Colossae and its neighboring churches, is it then addressed to the church at large—the first "catholic" letter? Colossians does in fact manifest a certain "catholicity": it is addressed not only to Colossae but to the other churches in the Lycus valley, and beyond that to

1. E.g., Eduard Schweizer, "Der Kolosserbrief–weder paulinisch noch nachpaulinisch?" in *Neues Testament und Christologie im Werden. Aufsätze*, ed. Eduard Schweizer (Göttingen: Vandenhoeck & Ruprecht, 1982), 150–63. So also Carl R. Holladay, *A Critical Introduction to the New Testament* (Nashville: Abingdon Press, 2005), 394; Dunn, *Beginning from Jerusalem*, 1038–1104; Ulrich Luz, "Der Brief an die Kolosser," in *Die Briefe an die Galater, Epheser und Kolosser*, ed. Jürgen Becker and Ulrich Luz, *Das Neue Testament deutsch* (Göttingen: Vandenhoeck & Ruprecht, 1998), 185–190.

all who have not known Paul personally (2:1). This would fit second-generation Christianity in general, not just the Colossians. Some passages particularly emphasize the universal nature of the church (1:6, 23, 28; 3:11). However, the chief difficulty with regarding Colossians as a "Catholic Letter" is that it appears to address a concrete, somewhat local situation. While this could be an aspect of the fictive literary world projected by the letter, it would mean that many readers not in the situation threatened by the "Colossian heresy" would find much of the letter both difficult to understand and irrelevant to their own time and place.

5. A Paulinist to the Pauline Churches in Asia Minor

The final scenario, and the one favored in this book, is that this earliest of the deuteropauline letters is written in Paul's name ten or fifteen years after his death, ostensibly to address a particular threatening situation in Colossae, Hierapolis, and Laodicea. The threat actually exists in the author's own time, and in an area larger than the Lycus valley, namely, in the sphere for which the Pauline school feels itself responsible: Ephesus, the surrounding regions of Asia Minor, and other churches in the orbit of the Pauline mission. The author writes in Paul's name to a congregation that probably no longer exists (see below), but the letter itself indicates it is written for a larger readership and is to be circulated (2:2; 4:13, 16). The letter is heard in the Pauline churches of Asia Minor in the late 70s or 80s as authoritative Pauline instruction on a current issue in their own time and place. Both Paul and Colossae are now gone, but the voice of Paul continues to be heard, instructing the Pauline churches throughout the area in which he had centered his mission.

15.1.2 Authorship

The strongest historical argument for Pauline authorship is the relation of Colossians to the undoubtedly authentic letter to Philemon. Eight (possibly nine) of the ten people mentioned in Colossians are also mentioned in Philemon. Box 14 delineates the similarities and differences.

Some discrepancies between the two lists may be noted: Epaphras is a prisoner in Philemon, not in Colossians; Aristarchus is a prisoner in Colossians, not in Philemon; Jesus Justus is mentioned as with Paul in Colossians, is absent

BOX 14: Names Mentioned in Both Philemon and Colossians

Philemon	*Colossians*
Timothy, v. 1	1:1 ("from" him too, in both letters)
Epaphras, v. 23, "fellow *prisoner*," knows the readers; "home church" not indicated	1:7, 4:12; a resident of Colossae who has come to Paul; *not* a prisoner
Mark, v. 24	4:10, the cousin of Barnabas, a Jewish Christian ("one of the circumcision group")
Luke, v. 24	4:14, the beloved physician, a Gentile
Aristarchus, v. 24	4:10, a *prisoner* in Col, *not* in Phlm
Demas, v. 24	4:14
	4:11, **Jesus Justus**
Addressed to **Archippus**, **Philemon**, and **Apphia**, v. 1	4:17, Archippus told to complete his ministry. No reference to Philemon, Apphia
Onesimus, v. 10	4:9, bearer of the letter ("one of you")
(Tychicus—not mentioned in Philemon or the other undisputed Pauline letters)	4:7, **Tychicus** is bearer of the letter (cf. Acts 20:4; Eph 6:21; Titus 3:12; 2 Tim 4:12)

from Philemon (unless the conjectural emendation be accepted); Archippus is *addressed* in Philemon, but in Colossians is spoken of in the third person as though absent; Philemon and Apphia are not mentioned in Colossians; Tychicus is not mentioned in Philemon, but is introduced as the bearer of the letter in Colossians (and Ephesians; he is mentioned only in Acts 20:4 and the disputed letters of the later Pauline tradition, Eph 6:21–22; 2 Tim 4:12; Titus 3:12). In addition, Colossians is consistently more full in its descriptions: Mark is one about whom they have received instructions, the cousin of Barnabas, and will pay them a visit; Luke is the beloved physician.

Thus while there are similarities that seem to bind the two letters together, there are also differences that distance the letters from each other. In every case, the Colossians list is more detailed, *providing information unnecessary if the letter were written for the historical Colossian Christians*. There is a connection between Philemon and Colossians, but it seems to be a literary connection rather than a historical one. (1) The two letters were not written at the same time, even if both are by Paul. In Philemon 22, Paul expects to visit Philemon's church soon, but there is no suggestion of this in Colossians. (2) "If *Mark* comes, welcome him" (Col 4:10) reflects what is said of *Timothy* in 1 Corinthians 4:17; 16:10, that is, it reflects data from the Pauline corpus. The author of the letter cannot refer to Timothy in this way here, since the letter pictures him as with Paul when he writes (Col 1:1). (3) Although the two letters cannot have been written at the same time, the same list of persons around Paul is presented. While this is not impossible, it is not likely. (4) The list in Colossians appears to be an elaboration of the list in Philemon; the author seems to know the persons mentioned only from the text of Philemon. He then expands this list with traditional elements. There is an ecumenical slant to this elaboration, as the Pauline school expands its horizons. The connections with the Jewish Christians Barnabas and Mark show that the Pauline churches are not discontinuous with the earliest churches founded by Jewish Christians, yet the emphasis on Epaphras as "one of your own" shows that the churches of Asia were not founded by the Jerusalem mission that opposed Paul, and that Paul himself, unlike the rival Jewish Christian missionaries, is not an outsider but has local connections in Asia.

On all these counts, the most plausible explanation is that Colossians was composed by an author in the Pauline school who adopted, adapted, and elaborated material from Philemon and the Pauline tradition.

Language

As is to be expected in a document emanating from the Pauline school, Colossians has numerous reflections of the vocabulary and phraseology typical of the authentic Pauline letters.[2] These include Paul's characteristic greeting χάρις ὑμῖν καὶ εἰρήνη (grace to you and peace), the ἐν Χριστῷ (in Christ) formula and its variations, and minor terminological similarities such as ἐν μέρει (in regard to). Eleven words appear in the New Testament only in Colossians and the Pauline letters. Some passages are verbally identical with the authentic letters (e.g., the first twelve Greek words of Colossians 1:1 are identical with 2 Corinthians 1:1 (cf. 1 Cor 1:1); the list of those with Paul in Colossians 4:11–14 is identical with Philemon 23–24; the triad faith/hope/love of Colossians 1:4–5 is found in 1 Thessalonians 1:3; 5:8; 1 Corinthians 13:13). If not by Paul, the letter seems to have been composed by someone who had carefully studied a collection of Paul's letters, and was influenced by Paul's vocabulary.

More striking to the careful reader, however, are the differences between Paul's language and that of Colossians. This brief document contains eighty-six words not found in the undisputed letters of Paul: thirty-four words unique to

2. For a detailed analysis, see Lohse, *Colossians and Philemon*, 84–91. On style, see the detailed analysis of Walter Bujard, *Stilanalytische Untersuchungen zum Kolosserbrief als Beitrag zur Methodik von Sprachvergleichen*, Studien zur Umwelt des Neuen Testaments 11 (Göttingen: Vandenhoeck und Ruprecht, 1973).

Colossians (*hapax legomena* NT), twenty-eight words found elsewhere in the New Testament but not in the undisputed Pauline letters, and an additional twenty-five words found only in Colossians and Ephesians. Some of this distinctive vocabulary can be explained by the author's response to the unique situation to which Colossians is addressed (the "Colossian heresy"). The vast majority of this list, however, cannot be explained in relation to the particular situation addressed by Colossians, and represent the author's own vocabulary and traditional material not found in the undisputed Paulines.

An extensive list of specifically Pauline words, especially those used in expressing his distinctive theological position over against opposing views, is *missing* from Colossians. These include ἁμαρτία (*hamartia*, sin) in the singular, δικαιοσύνη (*dikaiosunē*, righteousness, justification), ἐλευθερία (*eleutheria*, freedom), νόμος (*nomos*, law), πιστεύω (*pisteuō*, believe), σώζω, σωτηρία (*sōzō*, *sōtēria*, save, salvation). Although Paul directly addresses his readers in the undisputed letters with the familiar "brethren" (ἀδελφοί *adelphoi*, brothers and sisters), he never does so in Colossians (or Ephesians). It is true that some undisputed Pauline letters also lack some key words of Paul's theology (e.g., 1 Thess lacks the terminology of "justification"; "cross" does not occur in Romans). Neither Paul nor anyone else is required to use his whole theological vocabulary in every letter. Yet it is striking that, in opposing the false teaching at Colossae, the author refrains from using a whole cluster of words that elsewhere represent the fundamentals of Pauline thought.

Furthermore, the list of typical Pauline words missing from Colossians includes a large cluster of words without substantial content and unimportant theologically, such as conjunctions and particles—the kind of words an author uses unconsciously to construct clauses and sentences. There are at least seventeen such words and phrases, including ἄρα (*ara*, so, then twenty-five times Paul), διό (*dio*, therefore, twenty-two times Paul), διότι (*dioti*, for, nine times Paul), εἴ τις (*ei tis*, if anyone . . . , thirty-one times Paul), ἔτι (*eti*, still, yet, fifteen times Paul), οὐδέ (*oude*, neither, thirty-one times Paul), οὔτε (*oute*, neither, thirty-three times Paul), οὐκέτι (*ouketi*, no longer, fourteen times Paul). While it is true that authors may intentionally alter their vocabulary and style from one situation to another, this list of words, totaling scores of occurrences in the undisputed letters of Paul but totally absent from Colossians, cannot be explained on this basis, and points to a different author.

Style

The letters of Paul were a substitute for his personal presence and reflect the direct address of the preacher to the congregation (see §10.2.2). This is true even of Romans, Paul's most reflective letter, written to a church he had never visited personally. The undisputed letters thus contain anacolutha, broken syntactical constructions, frequent in oral discourse but rare in written communication. Paul's letters were enlivened with real and rhetorical questions, dialogues with an imaginary partner (diatribes), and direct address to the hearers with the term ἀδελφοί (*adelphoi*, brothers and sisters). None of these traits is found in Colossians. There is, for instance, only one question in the letter (2:20–21). Though the author uses ἀδελφοί as a term for "Christians" (1:2; 4:15), he never speaks directly to the hearer/readers with this address. In contrast to the lively style of Paul, sentences go on and on, loosely held together by conjunctions and relative pronouns. These are broken up in English translations for the sake of readability; in the Greek text 1:1–8 constitutes one sentence, as does 1:9–20 (into which the hymn of vv. 15–20 is inserted bodily). So also 1:21–23 and 1:24–29 each comprise a single sentence. Thus after the standard greeting of 1:1–2, all of chapter 1 consists of but four sentences. There is nothing like this in the undisputed letters of Paul.

The letter as a whole is characterized by a solemn liturgical-hymnic style, infused with much traditional language. Another distinctive stylistic element of Colossians is expressions using more than one word from the same stem. English translations usually vary these for the sake of English style. A few samples, translated somewhat literally, illustrate the style: "empowered with power," 1:11; "his energy being energized," 1:29; "grows the growth," 2:19. Likewise, the multiplication of synonyms is found often, for example, "praying and asking," 1:9; "endurance and patience," 1:11; "holy, blameless, and irreproachable," 1:22; "from the ages and from the generations," 1:26. This full, somewhat flowery style is particularly manifest in the heaping up of series of independent genitive expressions, the following samples again represented somewhat literally to represent the Greek style: "in the word of the truth of the gospel," 1:5; "into the kingdom of the son of his love," 1:13; "the riches of the glory of this mystery," 1:27. Some constructions typical of Colossians are not found at all in the unquestionably authentic letters, for example, ὅ ἐστιν (*ho estin* which is), used idiomatically by the Colossian writer so that the "which" need not match the gender of its antecedent.

Some Pauline words and phrases are used differently from the undisputed letters, such as the distinctive Pauline phrase "in Christ" or some variation thereof ("in the Lord," "in the beloved"; see Box 11, §13.3.2).

The English reader who has worked carefully through the undisputed letters of Paul and has become familiar with their vocabulary and style recognizes that he or she is in a different linguistic world when starting to translate Colossians (or the other deuteropaulines). For the sake of readability, these peculiarities are inevitably smoothed out in English translations and must be examined in detail in the Greek text.

Distinctive Elements of the Theology of Colossians

Of course the theology of Colossians is not absolutely discontinuous with that of Paul. The whole point of the Pauline school's program was to continue to advocate *Paul's* theology in their new situation. As a member of the Pauline school, the author adopts and adapts several of the major theological themes and perspectives of the school's apostolic founder. For instance, the characteristic dialectic of indicative/imperative is thoroughly Pauline (e.g., 3:3 "you died"/3:5 "therefore put to death"; 3:10 "you have clothed yourselves"/3:12 "clothe yourselves"). As in Paul's own writings, the letter as a whole is structured according to this dialectic: chapters 1–2 are the indicative "doctrinal" section, which forms the basis for chapters 3–4, the imperative paraenetic section (cf. Gal 1–4/5–6 and Rom 1–11/12–16). However, the author adopts and adapts Pauline theology in a manner that distinguishes Colossians from the undisputed letters, as illustrated in the following examples.

Paul's Apostolic Role

Paul had fierce debates concerning the validity of his apostleship (1 Cor 9; Galatians; 2 Cor 10–13), but Paul never insinuated that he was the only legitimate apostle. Apostleship for him meant that he belonged to the group of authentic representatives commissioned personally by the risen Christ, including Peter, James, and others (1 Cor 15:1–11). This group contained some variety, and Paul never insisted that his way was the only way.

In Colossians these debates of the first generation are past. Paul is the only apostle mentioned in Colossians. In the circles for which this letter is written, Paul is the sole apostle and exclusive authority. The understanding of Paul's apostleship in Colossians differs from that of the undisputed letters (see further in the *Exegetical-Theological Précis* below).

Tradition, Scripture, and "Orthodoxy"

In opposing false teaching or expounding his own doctrinal points, Paul often appealed to Scripture, understood in the light of the Christ event.[3] Although Colossians is directed against

3. The later letters Galatians, 1 Corinthians, 2 Corinthians, Romans fall in this category. The earlier 1 Thessalonians, Philippians, Philemon do not oppose false doctrine and do not contain biblical arguments.

the false teaching of the "philosophy," the author never quotes or alludes to Scripture, just as he never makes explicit that the church is incorporated into the continuing history of Israel as the people of God. Instead, the author appeals to recognized elements of Christian tradition as the basis for establishing sound teaching and confuting heresy.

Paul himself had used traditional material taken over from pre- and para-Pauline Christianity, utilizing such materials for paraenetic, polemical, and edifying purposes. The author of Colossians, however, uses traditional elements as the very basis of the Christian life, in a way uncharacteristic of Paul (see further in the *Exegetical-Theological Précis* below). Colossians reflects direct literary contact with Philemon (see, e.g., Box 14 above), but is indirectly influenced in both form and content by other Pauline letters as well. We cannot say how many letters had already been collected in Ephesus at the time Colossians was composed, but, in addition to Philemon, the influence of Romans, 1–2 Corinthians, Galatians, and Philippians seems likely. Yet the letter is not merely a patchwork of phrases from the Pauline letters, as in the later apocryphal letters to the Laodiceans, but is a creative reinterpretation of the Pauline tradition.

Christology and Ecclesiology

In Colossians as in Paul, ecclesiology is a function of Christology. The church is constituted by the cosmic victory of Christ, and itself already participates in this cosmic sphere. Thus the Pauline image of the church as Christ's body (1 Cor 12, Rom 12) takes on a new meaning in Colossians. In the undisputed letters, Paul uses "church" to refer primarily to the congregation, not the universal church;[4] the diversity of the members of the Christian congregation is compared to the whole body of Christ; Christ is identified with the whole body, and believers are particular members (eye, ear, nose, hand, foot, 1 Cor 12:14–30). In Colossians, the church is identified with the cosmic body of Christ, of which Christ himself is the head; Christ is identified as the head of the body (1:18), not with the whole body as in Paul. The sphere of Christ's rule extends throughout the universe, and the church as Christ's body already participates in this rule (1:13, 18). Just as the body of Christ is both the cosmic reality and the flesh-and-blood body of Jesus, so the church is the Christian community composed of ordinary human beings and yet is a divine cosmic reality.

Eschatology

Paul affirmed the already/not yet dialectic inherent in the Christian confession that Jesus is the Christ (see on Rom 5:1–11). The Christ has come, but the world continues in its unredeemed state, looking forward to the final victory of God at the parousia—which Paul, from his earliest to his latest letter, expected to occur soon. The believer is identified with the Christ event at the point of the cross. Paul maintained the "eschatological reservation" (Rom 6:1–4; Phil 3:7–16; Gal 2:19–20, opposing the "already" of the Corinthians' realized eschatology reflected in 1 Cor 4:8–13). For Paul, the believer is *already* "crucified with him," but *not yet* "risen with him."

Colossians maintains this dialectic, but dramatically shifts the center of gravity. The cosmic Lord is already ruler of the universe (1:15–20; 2:9–10; 3:1–2, 11) and does not have to await the final apocalyptic victory (vs., e.g., 1 Cor 15:20–28). There will be a future consummation—Colossians decidedly does not reduce everything to the present or to the interiority of the believer's own existence—but the eschaton does not bring the resurrection of the dead and the redemption of the cosmos. This has already happened in the Christ event centered in Jesus' death, resurrection, and defeat/reconciliation

4. Ἐκκλησία (*ekklēsia*, church), forty-four times in the undisputed letters; nineteen times in plural. In the comprehensive sense only 1 Cor. 10:32; 12:28; 15:9; Gal. 1:13; Phil 3:6. Colossians uses ἐκκλησία only in the singular, twice for the universal church identified with the body of Christ (1:18, 24), and twice for the local congregation (4:15–16).

of the cosmic powers. The eschaton brings the revelation of the hidden, present reality. Thus Colossians goes beyond Paul's theology in which the believer's life is joined to Christ's at the point of the crucifixion, tones down Paul's eschatological reservation, and presents Christians as *already* "risen with him" (3:1–4). The expectation of the nearness of the parousia has completely disappeared, and Christian life is focused on the believer's present union with Christ.

The Holy Spirit

For Paul, to be a Christian is to participate in the life of the Holy Spirit, the divine breath that enlivens the body of Christ (e.g., 1 Cor 12:13). To be "in Christ" is to be in the sphere of the Spirit (Rom 8:8–10). No one can make the Christian confession unless empowered by the Spirit (1 Cor 12:3); no one who does not have the Spirit belongs to Christ (Rom 8:9). The undisputed letters of Paul refer to the Holy Spirit more than ninety times. This is in sharp contrast to Colossians, which has only two references to "spirit," both of which probably refer to the human rather than the divine spirit (1:8; 2:5; there are two additional references to "spiritual," 1:9; 3:16). For the author of Colossians, to be a Christian is to live in the sphere of Christ, empowered by him (1:11, 29; 2:12), but this is not expressed, as in Paul, in terms of the Holy Spirit.

Conclusion

The evidence of language, style, and theology has convinced many scholars that the letter is deuteropauline. Considerations of date, situation, addressees, the occasion and source of the letter, and the sources used by the author tend to confirm this judgment. The point is further strengthened when one studies the relation of Colossians and Ephesians.[5]

15.1.3 Date

If Colossians is written by Paul, the latest possible date (*terminus ante quem*) would be the date of Paul's death in the early to mid-60s (see Pauline Chronology above, §13.3.4); if not by Paul, this same period constitutes the earliest possible date (*terminus a quo*). The earliest attestation of Colossians outside the New Testament is in Irenaeus's *Against Heresies* 3.14.1, about 185 CE. To say that the letter must have been written by 185 is not helpful, however, in determining the date when Colossians was written, since no scholar now dates Colossians as late as the second century. The letter does not contain any references or allusions to contemporary political or secular events that would help to establish its date.

If, as argued here, the letter is deuteropauline, the letter is before Ephesians, which uses it as a major source and may be considered its first commentary. It is also earlier than the Pastorals, which represent the Pauline school at a considerably later and more developed date. While we may adopt the relative dating Colossians ⇒ Ephesians ⇒ Pastorals with some confidence, this does little to establish an absolute date. If Colossians reflects awareness of a collection of Pauline letters (see above), it should not be dated too soon after Paul's death.

There is one datable event that may shed light on the date (and interpretation) of Colossians. According to Tacitus (*Annals* 14.27.1), Laodicea was demolished by an earthquake in 60/61 CE, apparently the same event referred to by the fifth-century historian Orosius, who claims Laodicea, Hierapolis, and Colossae were all destroyed by an earthquake. Laodicea was quickly rebuilt by the inhabitants without aid from the empire. The fate of Colossae is not clear—whether it was in fact destroyed and, if so, whether it was rebuilt. The city had been historically prominent for centuries before but seems to have disappeared from history after

5. If Paul wrote either Colossians or Ephesians, he must have written them both at the same time. But the kinds of changes between Colossians and Ephesians make it very difficult to imagine a plausible historical situation in which Colossians and Ephesians were both written at the same time. See Andrew T. Lincoln, *Ephesians*, WBC 42 (Dallas: Word, 1990), xlvii–lviii; lvi–lxviii.

61 CE, and the Colossian church plays no further role in early Christian history. The site has never been excavated (though the Turkish government is presently making plans to begin excavation at Colossae). The most likely hypothesis thus seems to be that a teacher in the Pauline school in Ephesus composed a letter in the 70s or 80s CE, ostensibly directed to "Colossae," which all the readers knew no longer existed. They could read the letter as actually addressing a church and its problems that once did exist, or, and perhaps more likely, they would perceive the address to "Colossae" as part of the fictive framework, and read the letter as a message from their beloved martyr apostle to the contemporary churches of Asia Minor.

15.1.4 Structure and Outline

Colossians manifests the basic bipartite outline that had become traditional in Pauline circles (see above §10.2.3). The first two chapters constitute the indicative, theological section that provides the basis for the imperative, ethical section of the final two chapters.

1:1–11	Epistolary Introduction
1:1–2	Greeting
1:3–11	Thanksgiving
1:12–2:23	Part 1: Theological Instruction—The Universal Christ
1:12–23	Theological Foundation: Redemption and Reconciliation in Christ
1:12–14	Redemption
1:15–20	*The Christ hymn*
1:21–23	Reconciliation
1:24–2:5	The Apostolic Office and Mission
2:6–23	The "Colossian Heresy"
3:1–4:6	Part 2: Ethical Instruction—Living as Christians
3:1–4	The Basis: Risen with Him
3:5–17	The Old Life and the New
3:18–4:1	Life in the Orderly Christian Household
4:2–6	Mission and Prayer
4:7–18	Epistolary Conclusion
4:7–9	Concerning the Apostle
4:10–17	Greetings
4:18	Farewell

15.1.5 Exegetical-Theological Précis[6]

1:1–11 Epistolary Introduction

1:1–2 Greeting

The first verse is exactly the same as 2 Corinthians 1:1. The formula in which Paul conspicuously introduces himself as *apostle* reflects earlier disputes and has become traditional in the opening line (see above, §11.2.2). Timothy does not represent apostolic authority to the church, but is a *brother*, like the recipients.

1:3–11 Thanksgiving

The conventional epistolary thanksgiving section had already been modified by Paul to become a substantial element of the letter (see above §10.2.3). Here, the thanksgiving is further developed into a series of three lengthy and complex sentences (vv. 3–8; 9–20; 21–23). The thanksgiving modulates into the body of the letter, incorporating the fundamental confession expressed in the Christ hymn incorporated at 1:15–20.

The faith/hope/love triad also represents Pauline tradition (1:4; cf. 1 Cor 13:13; 1 Thess 1:3; 5:8). For the author, hope is not a subjective attitude but an objective reality already laid up in the heavenly world; its focus is the present rather than the eschatological future. This

6. The following summary represents a reading of the letter as a deuteropauline document. For interpretations based on Pauline authorship, see Peter Thomas O'Brien, *Colossians, Philemon*, WBC 44 (Waco, TX: Word Books, 1982).

corresponds to the spatial images for salvation dominant in the Colossian-Ephesian branch of the Pauline school, in contrast to Paul's temporal imagery (Rom 5:2; 8:18–24).

Paul did not found the readers' congregation. They do not know him and he does not know them (1:8–9). Apostolic authority is represented among them by Pauline disciples and teachers such as Epaphras (1:7; see 4:12) and by the Pauline letters being circulated after Paul's death (4:15–16). So also the church to which they belong is not merely their local congregation but is part of the worldwide church (1:6; see 1:23). The author wants to cultivate the awareness among the readers that they belong to a worldwide community of faith, guided by leaders and by Pauline letters that represent Paul's own apostolic authority.

1:12–2:23 Part 1: Theological Instruction—The Universal Christ

1:12–23 Theological Foundation: Redemption and Reconciliation in Christ

The author declares the theological foundation for the new life to which the readers are called, and the basis for resisting the false teaching that threatens their understanding of the faith. This foundation is God's all-sufficient act in Christ, expressed as redemption and reconciliation. The centerpiece of this affirmation is the Christ hymn, but it is framed by soteriological affirmations of redemption and reconciliation.

1:12–14 Redemption

The readers once shared the fate of all human beings living in their natural state, subject to the powers of the darkness that rule this present world (v. 16). Then God's act in the Christ event defeated these evil powers and transferred the Colossian believers into the kingdom of the beloved Son. "Sin" for Paul was an enslaving power; he did not speak of the plural "sins" except when citing traditional material. Paul always associated redemption with God's act of liberation from bondage to sin or the law, associating it with the saving act of God in the past and the ultimate liberation of the eschatological future (Rom 3:24; 8:23; 1 Cor 1:30; Gal 3:13). Here, a theologian of the Pauline school reinterprets Paul so that the gift of redemption is already experienced as the forgiveness of sins.

For theologians in the Pauline tradition, baptism was the point at which redemption was experienced and the forgiveness of sins was made real. This forgiveness of sins is not merely a legal transaction but is the result of the reconciliation Christ accomplished in his body of flesh; Christ is now enthroned as heavenly Lord, but his body is represented by the church that extends throughout the world, and believers are already incorporated into this body. This is a development from Paul's own use of the body imagery, in which the body, head and all, is the local congregation (1 Cor 12; Rom 12). The Christ hymn that follows may have been part of the baptismal liturgy sung or recited when believers were incorporated into the universal body of Christ at baptism. The hymn is thus not only about Christ but about the nature of the church to which they belong, made specific in verse 18b.

1:15–20 The Christ hymn Although there is some difference in detail in various reconstructions, the basic bipartite structure is clear. Christ is the one through whom God created the universe; Christ is the one through whom God has reconciled the universe. Just as there is nothing independent of God's creation, so nothing stands outside God's reconciling act.

I. Creation

He is the image of the invisible God,
  the firstborn before all creation.
For in him all things were created
  in the heavens and on the earth,
  the visible and the invisible,
    whether thrones
    or dominions
    or principalities
    or powers.
All things were created through him and for him.

Interlude

And he is before all things.
And all things cohere in him.
And he is the head of the body,
that is, the church.

II. Reconciliation

He is the beginning,
the firstborn from the dead,
in order that he might be first in all things.
For in him all the fullness was pleased to dwell
and through him to reconcile all things to him,
making peace through the blood of his cross through him,
whether on earth
or in the heavens.

The author is clearly not composing these verses ad hoc but citing a traditional hymn, creed, or liturgy. This corresponds to the nature of the readers' conversion to the Christian faith, which was a matter of being taught the message that had been reliably handed on as tradition (2:6–7). As the author prepares to oppose the false teaching, he does not appeal to his own teaching, to reason, or even to Scripture, but to the authentic tradition handed on in the Pauline communities, the tradition they had been taught and identified with Christ himself. The verb used in Colossians for "receiving" Christ (παραλαμβάνω *paralambanō*, 2:6) means "receiving that which is handed on in tradition," as in 1 Corinthians 11:23 and 15:3. This is the primary reason Colossians is permeated with traditional elements (not only the obvious citations such as 1:15–20 and 3:18–4:1, but numerous other echoes of traditional church teaching and liturgy). Over against "human tradition" the author places not "divine tradition" but Christ himself, indicating that receiving Christ as Lord means learning and responding to the authentic tradition handed on in the Pauline community. This corresponds to Paul's own view that the risen Lord is encountered in the tradition (see on 1 Cor 11:23). Thus the key term πίστις (*pistis*, faith) that in Paul had meant "obedience in personal trust," the life-changing gift that changed one's self-understanding and relation to God, has come to mean in Colossians primarily "*the* faith," the body of material that represents the authentic Christian teaching, in which the readers are exhorted to "stand firm" over against false teaching (1:23; 2:5, 7). Colossians' understanding of Christ present in the tradition is authentically Pauline, but its emphasis and preponderance in Colossians is more appropriate to second-generation Christianity that had learned the tradition not directly from Paul but from his authorized disciples, who continue to represent his teaching as the guard against heresy (1:7).

The hymn represents the cosmic Christ as supreme over all cosmic powers. It is not mere speculative interest that generates such affirmations; the author responds to the "philosophy" attractive to the readers by affirming that faith in Christ need not be supplemented by placating other cosmic powers—they have all been created, sustained, vanquished, and reconciled "in him." The whole fullness of God dwells in him. That the cosmos itself is "in" him is a distinct emphasis of Colossians; he is not pantheistically "in all things," but as the one "in" whom all things are created and sustained, "all things" are "in" him. It is this cosmic Christ, the functional equivalent of God, who is incarnate and whose blood shed on the cross becomes the divine act that mediates forgiveness and reconciles the universe to God (1:20).

1:21–23 Reconciliation The cosmic reconciliation became personal when the readers believed and were baptized. As the readers were once in the world of darkness, they were estranged from God. Though they did not realize it, their evil works had separated them from God. These "evil works" were not the shocking deeds of criminals or social misfits, but the ordinary lives of ordinary people who did not realize they had been alienated until they were reconciled, did not know they were in darkness until they had been transferred into the kingdom of light (1:12–13).

1:24–2:5 The Apostolic Office and Mission

Paul's apostleship and its role in God's plan has itself become a matter of theological reflection in the Pauline school. Paul's sufferings complete "what is lacking in Christ's afflictions for the sake of his body, the church" (1:24). This difficult phrase apparently represents a reinterpretation of the "messianic woes." In some apocalyptic schemes, the world and the people of God must undergo a period of intense suffering just before the final triumph of God. Here the sufferings of Paul are interpreted as substituting for the suffering of the church as a whole. This is another aspect of the deapocalypticizing of Pauline theology (see below): the *not-yet* messianic woes expected for the future have *already* taken place in the suffering of Paul. In the retrospective view of the second generation, Paul suffered for those he had not seen, represented in the letter's fictive world by the Colossian Christians.

The apostle became the church's servant "according to God's οἰκονομία (*oikonomia*)" (1:25), a word that can be translated as "commission," "plan," or "stewardship" (and other ways; see the variety of renderings in English translations). While the meaning of 1:24–25 is not entirely clear, the most likely interpretation seems to indicate that Paul's work as the suffering apostle has been incorporated into the pattern of God's saving work in history; Paul's apostleship is a part of the Christ event itself. Paul's own sufferings are integral to the salvific suffering of Christ and complete it. This cannot mean that Christ's own suffering and death were inadequate in themselves, which would contradict the argument of the whole letter, especially 1:15–20. Nevertheless, Paul's role in suffering for the whole church, while not detracting from the exclusive and sufficient saving act of God in Christ, is part of God's saving plan. Looking back on Paul's martyr death, the author of Colossians perceives that his life was given for the whole church. Here Paul is not only apostle to the Gentiles, but *the* apostle for *all*, as he was regarded in some streams of second-generation Pauline Christianity. Paul himself never regarded his ministry in this way; this view appears to express the theological reflection of a later generation that considered Paul's work as a constituent element in God's saving act in Christ.

As in Colossians Paul is the only apostle, so apostolic ministry is the only ministerial "office" mentioned in Colossians. Some words used of Paul's associates and representatives seem to be becoming quasi-technical terms for ministry: διάκονος (*diakonos*, deacon, servant, minister) is used of Paul (1:23, 25), Epaphras (1:7), and Tychicus (4:7), and Archippus is said to have a διακονία (4:17, *diakonia*, service, ministry), but there is no order of deacons, just as there are no bishops or elders. Συνεργός (*sunergos*, coworker), σύνδουλος (*sundoulos*, fellow slave/servant), and perhaps ἀδελφός (*adelphos*, brother/sister) are used in a quasi-official sense of Paul's fellow missionaries, but do not refer to church offices. Teaching plays a key role in the life of the church, but there is no class of official teachers, and teaching is the responsibility of the congregation as a whole (3:16).

This appears to reflect a similar situation as in Paul's own time (cf. 1 Cor 14:26–33), yet the charismatic enthusiasm has receded. There is minimal or no reference to the Holy Spirit (see above), no reference to prophecy or glossolalia. The responsibility of leadership and teaching seems to rest on particular members who continue to represent Paul's own teaching, though this arrangement has not yet been formalized into specific offices. Paul himself, the primary or exclusive apostle, continues to be the church's teacher; his apostolic word is represented in the documents of the Pauline school such as the letter of Colossians itself.

2:6–23 The "Colossian Heresy"

One factor in the composition of Colossians was the emergence of the "philosophy" (2:8) that the author saw as a threat to the faith and life of the Christian community, sometimes called the "Colossian heresy." The original readers knew the nature of this teaching from their own experience and thus recognized that the letter addressed it from the very beginning. The Christological hymn of 1:15–20 would be perceived as a challenge to the "philosophy" that called the readers back to the faith expressed in the apostolic tradition.

The modern reader can perceive the contours of the "philosophy"[7] only indirectly, as it is refracted through the lens of the author's characterization, objections, and warnings. Thus the author's warning against "human tradition" (2:8) is not a general admonition, but an indication that the advocates of the "philosophy" represented their doctrine as ancient tradition, not as an innovation. It claimed to impart wisdom, insight, and knowledge (1:9, 28; 2:3; 3:16; 4:5). This "deeper wisdom" involved knowledge of the "elements of the universe" (στοιχεῖα τοῦ κόσμου, *stoicheia tou kosmou*), which were conceived not as abstract principles but personal beings—angelic powers and cosmic rulers who must be worshiped and placated by rigorous discipline and obedience, which allowed the devotee to participate in the divine "fullness" (2:8–10, 18–20).[8] Proper observance included ascetic practices, withdrawal from the world and severe discipline of the "body of flesh," and the observance of special days and dietary regulations (2:11, 16, 21, 23).

While the "philosophy" involved Jewish elements (2:16, "sabbaths"; 2:11, "circumcision"; cf. 3:11), it is clearly not a recurrence of the controversy met in Galatians. The issue of whether Gentile Christians should keep the law plays no role in Colossians; the word "law" is entirely absent from Colossians. There is no demand by the rival philosophy that Gentile Christians be circumcised in order to belong to God's people.[9] There is no reference to Jerusalem, already destroyed in the author's time. In contrast to Paul's own time, Jerusalem Christianity and its apostles are no threat to Pauline Christianity. The "philosophy" seems to be the residue effect, from a generation earlier, of the Jewish Christian opponents of Paul, whose doctrine has now been combined with general Hellenistic religiosity of a gnosticizing bent. The adherents of the "philosophy" probably had initiation rites that involved visionary spiritual experiences. The difficult Greek phrase in 2:18, ἃ ἑόρακεν ἐμβατεύων (*ha heoraken embateuōn*), literally, "what he saw when he entered," reflects the terminology used in the initiation rites to the mystery cults.[10] The author of Colossians insists that the traditional Christian faith is the authentic "mystery" (1:26–27; 2:2; 4:3), which is identified with Christ, not the esoteric teachings of the "philosophy."

Current research indicates that the Colossian "philosophy" was a syncretistic combination of authentic Christian tradition and Jewish, proto-Gnostic, and native popular religions and philosophies of Asia Minor. Its advocates did not understand themselves to be presenting an alternative to the Christian faith, but an older, deeper, and more comprehensive religious and philosophical system into which the gospel should be fitted. Jesus Christ is not replaced, but

7. "Philosophy" here does not denote an abstract conceptual system, but a religious cult. Cf. Josephus's use of φιλοσοφία, *philosophia* as a designation for the branches and sectarian movements of Judaism.

8. The "worship of angels" in 2:18 can be understood as an objective genitive in which believers are called to worship angelic beings, or as a subjective genitive in which the angels worship God and believers are encouraged to participate in visionary experiences in which they see this and worship along with the angels.

9. In Colossians, circumcision is not a loaded or dangerous word. The author himself seems to introduce the theme of circumcision as the mark of the covenant, understood in the symbolic sense as baptism. Circumcision had already been understood in nonliteral senses in the Old Testament and Jewish tradition (Deut 10:16; 30:6; Jer 4:4; Ezek 44:7; 1QS 5.5) and by Paul himself (Rom 2:29). The readers had been estranged from God and in the realm of death, living in "trespasses and the uncircumcision of your flesh," i.e., as Gentile sinners. Then they had heard the Christian message, and had been baptized into the realm of salvation. The author's point: you are already baptized into Christ, and do not need supplementary religious rituals to become more "spiritual."

10. Lohse, *Colossians and Philemon*, 130, translates it specifically "as he had visions of them [the angelic cosmic powers] during the mystery rites."

supplemented and understood as a significant figure within an impressive religious structure. The false teachers and their followers appeared to be more, not less, religious than those who adhered to the Pauline tradition. Thus the letter's emphasis that faith in Christ needs no religious supplements: the whole "fullness" of God resides in Christ, and believers already have "fullness" of life (1:19; 2:9–10). Christ himself is the mystery of God (1:26–27; 2:2; 4:3), and must not be incorporated as one element among others into an impressive network of religious thought and observance.

3:1–4:6 Part 2: Ethical Instruction—Living as Christians

3:1–4 The Basis: Risen with Him

The brief section 3:1–4 is transitional, restating the principal affirmation of the preceding section, the all-sufficiency of the Christ event, and incorporating the believers' lives into it. Christ has already died and been raised; the believer is incorporated into Christ at baptism (2:12). While Paul hesitates to follow the logic that declares believers are already risen with Christ (the famous "eschatological reservation"; see on Rom 6:1–11), the author of Colossians takes this bold step: believers are *already* risen with him. The point here is that the advocates of the new "philosophy," with their heavenly visions and powerful experiences of spirituality, can add nothing to what baptized believers already have.

The contrast between "things that are above" and "things that are on the earth" perhaps takes up some of the language of the new teachers, but does not use it in a dualistic manner that disdains "earthly things." This earth is not evil matter, in contrast to divine spirit, but is God's creation through Christ and is not to be disdained by rigorous, spiritual-sounding rules; such religion is actually too earthbound (see 2:20–21). This contrast is not merely a matter of subjective attitude, but expresses an ontological reality: in baptism believers' lives are actually relocated "in Christ" and "in God." At the present, however, this is a hidden reality, which will be manifest at the eschaton, when Christ appears in glory. While the author has shifted Paul's eschatological emphasis, he has not completely reduced eschatology to present experience. There is still a future eschatological climax to God's saving act (3:4; see 1:27; 3:6).

3:5–17 The Old Life and the New

The indicative "you have died" becomes the imperative "put to death." A traditional vice list of what was once acceptable social behavior has now become unacceptable for those who have been united with Christ (3:5–9). The old self has died, the old garments have been put aside, and the new self is clothed with the Christian virtues as understood in the Pauline tradition (3:10–14). These characteristics of the new life did not correspond to the virtues of Greco-Roman culture. It is not the case that the Pauline school simply baptized traditional "middle class" values as the Christian way of life. As in Jesus and Paul, love for God and others has the priority in all ethical conduct (3:14). The new way of life is not merely individualistic spirituality, but is expressed in the new Christian community, in which the old cultural and social distinctions that had been taken for granted no longer apply (3:10). It is a community that lives not merely in the Pax Romana, but in the *Pax Christi* brought about by Christ's victory over all the cosmic powers threatening the authentic life God intends for his creatures, and that worships together in grateful praise (3:15; see 1:2, 20).[11] It is a community in which the voice of the living Christ continues to be heard, as believers teach and admonish one another, using such traditions as those cited in 1:15–20

11. This peace of Christ includes the inner peace of confident trust in God, but it is more than that. As pointed out by Jerry L. Sumney, *Colossians: A Commentary*, NTL (Louisville, KY: Westminster John Knox Press, 2008), 220, this peace is a realm into which readers have been called, a realm established by God's victory in Christ, and *it* is to rule in their hearts.

in their worship and instruction (3:16–17). The final exhortation to do *everything* in the name of the Lord dissolves all boundaries between a sacred, "religious" realm of life and ordinary, "secular" concerns. Everything in life is to be brought under the lordship of Christ. This leads directly to the household code.

3:18–4:1 *Life in the Orderly Christian Household*

At least from the fourth century BCE on, when Aristotle listed the duties of members of the household, tables of such duties had formed part of the moral code of the Hellenistic world. Prior to early Christianity, Hellenistic Judaism had adopted and adapted such codes. Paul himself did not utilize them. Beginning with Colossians, the Pauline school and the later epistolary tradition in the New Testament adapted such codes to Christian moral instruction (Eph 5:21–6:9; 1 Tim 2:1–15; 3:1–15; 5:1–21; 6:1–2; Titus 2:1–10; 1 Pet 2:13–3:7).

The presence in the Christian Bible of household codes calling for the subordination of wives, children, and slaves to their husbands, fathers, and masters—often the same person, the paterfamilias—has proven to be a problem for interpreters of these texts in later generations where differing social mores prevail. On the one hand, these texts have been cited as divine approval of patriarchy and slavery, while other readers have found them to be an embarrassment, scandal, or evidence of the repressive nature of biblical faith. From the modern perspective, these criticisms are sometimes justified, but often one-sided. The following general considerations are important for interpreting such texts:[12]

12. A helpful discussion on interpreting the household codes in general and Colossians in particular is provided by Sumney, *Colossians*, 230–55; see also "Christian Existence and Conduct in the Given Structures of Society," in M. Eugene Boring, *1 Peter*, ANTC (Nashville: Abingdon Press, 1999), 102–28. Some of the above discussion is adapted from M. Eugene Boring, "Household Codes," in *New Interpreter's Dictionary of the Bible*, 2:905–6.

1. The household codes are a reminder that faith does not lift believers out of the givenness of their historical situation, and that the life of faith must always come to terms with the realities of society and history, rather than fleeing into internal individualism, monastic withdrawal, or eschatological extremism. The historical structures themselves are neither justified nor condemned, but accepted as the given historical reality of their time and place. The household codes—and the deuteropauline letters in general—should not be interpreted merely as a step backward from the eschatological freedom of the first generation as represented by Paul. They are the price the early church paid for its willingness to engage the world rather than withdrawing from society into sectarian communities such as those of the Essenes.

2. The household codes do, however, represent an adjustment of the first generation's eschatological fervor, which saw the present structures of this world passing away (1 Cor 7:31). Later generations needed direction for coming to terms with a world that they saw was going to endure for some time.

3. The kind of religious enthusiasm that threatened to break down all social conventions in the name of the new life of the Spirit was sometimes regarded as a danger, to both personal morality and the mission of the church. Early Christian communities needed patterns and models for ethical conduct that both manifested the newness of the Christian life to which they had been called and exhibited to the world that their manner of life was not a scandalous breach of generally accepted social norms. The formulation and adoption of such models had both the internal purpose of providing needed ethical norms and the missionary purpose, both evangelistic and apologetic, of showing to the world that the Christian faith did not undermine family and society but affirmed its highest values. The household codes taught insiders and reassured outsiders that Christians did not flee from the world but assumed a responsible place within it.

4. Commands to be subordinate affirm the order God the Creator has established in the world, which is always better than chaos. The commands do not establish any particular social order as given by God.

5. The New Testament codes are always presented in the context of letters addressed to a particular situation, do not purport to give valid rules for every time and place, and must be reinterpreted anew in every situation. The household code of 3:18–4:1 emphasizes (among other things) that the setting for Christian faith is not ascetic rigor, advocated by the rival "philosophy," but the normal life of the household in the Hellenistic world.

6. While the specific instruction of the household codes cannot be directly applied to later and different situations, the modern church has much to learn from "overhearing" these directions given to early Christians who struggled to live out their Christian faith within the confines of a society oriented to a different understanding of what life is for and about.

7. In the New Testament codes, especially in Colossians, Ephesians, and 1 Peter, instruction is given in terms of mutuality, not merely in terms of hierarchy. The New Testament household codes address women, children, and slaves directly, as persons who can make responsible decisions themselves—a radical move in first-century society.

8. On the lengthy instructions to slaves, see above §11.3.5. These instructions are not only directed to literal slaves but serve as a model for the community as a whole.

9. All members of the Christian community, whether master or slave, male or female, old or young, are called to live their lives aware that they have a higher Lord than those masters present in the society of which they are a part. The heavenly Lord calls those in positions of authority to act with a sense of justice and equality (4:1). The mission assigned by the heavenly Lord to Christians of every social status has a higher priority than individualistic rights. Mission, not sub-mission, is the focus of New Testament household codes. They represent the radicality of Christian faith, not its dilution or surrender.

4:2–6 Mission and Prayer

The request for prayer continues the missionary thrust of household code. The apostolic hero who is in prison and suffers for the sake of the church (1:24) is pictured as asking for the prayers of the church. Paul and the church can be faithful in proclaiming the gospel in word and deed, but only God can open a door for the word, and God's help is needed to make the message clear. Even the apostle cannot do this on his own. Paul's mission, continued in the Pauline community after his death, is dependent on God. The people in the churches are aware that they need God's wisdom in order to know how to live and speak to those outside the Christian community, those who are unaware that they already reconciled to God and are destined finally to become insiders, included in God's cosmic act of reconciliation (1:18–20).

4:7–18 Epistolary Conclusion

The personal details and greetings in this section of a pseudepigraphical letter emphasize the epistolary nature of the communication—a particular letter to particular people, rather than a general essay on ethics. The list of names emphasizes the network of teachers and missionaries of the Pauline school as the authentic heirs of Paul's message.

4:7–9 Concerning the Apostle

The function of this section is to claim that Paul is in fact represented by his authorized coworkers, who accompany his letters and provide continuing authentic interpretation in the absence of Paul himself.

4:10–17 Greetings

For notes and further discussion of the individuals here mentioned, see above, §15.1.2. The reference to exchanging letters with the church in Laodicea indicates that Paul's letters are now understood to address a wider circle than their original addressees.

4:18 *Farewell*

That the concluding words are written in the apostle's own hand represents the claim of the letter to represent the apostolic faith and is not evidence of actual authorship (see on 2 Thess 3:17).

15.2 Interpreting Ephesians

IN THE TRADITIONAL VIEW, PAUL WROTE four letters from his "first Roman imprisonment" about 62 CE (see introductions to each book, and §14.1). Philemon, Colossians, and Ephesians were all composed about the same time and sent together, delivered by Tychicus and Onesimus. Colossians and Philemon were sent to the churches in the Lycus valley, and Ephesians to the church in Ephesus.[13] The letter to the Philippians was written about the same time.

15.2.1 Ephesians: A Didactic Text of the Pauline School

Most scholars now regard Ephesians as a teaching document interpreting key elements in Paul's theology for the generation after Paul's death, composed by a teacher in the Pauline school in the form of a Pauline letter and circulated among the churches of the Pauline mission for their instruction and edification. This view is argued by all scholars who regard Colossians as deuteropauline, and by some scholars who affirm the Pauline authorship of Colossians.[14] The main arguments for this view are as follows:

The document was not written to the church at Ephesus.

The words ἐν Ἐφέσῳ (in Ephesus) are missing from all the oldest manuscripts (𝔓[46], ℵ, B), which read, "to the saints who are also faithful in Christ Jesus." The original document apparently did not specify a particular church as addressees. In the second century, the document circulated under more than one name, with Marcion's text giving it the title "To the Laodiceans," presumably on the basis of Colossians 4:16. We do not know when it was first called "Ephesians." The first author to cite the letter explicitly as to the Ephesians was Irenaeus, about 180 CE.

Apart from the 1:1 reference to Ephesus in later manuscripts, the letter gives no indication that it was addressed to Ephesus. Paul had spent considerable time in Ephesus and was well known to the congregation there. Yet Ephesians contains no greetings, has no personal references to Paul's time among the readership, indicates that the author knows the readers only by hearsay and that they know him only by his reputation and writings (1:15; 3:2–4). Efforts to explain this in terms of the traditional view of Pauline authorship sometimes argue that it had been some years since Paul had been in Ephesus and that he addresses mainly the newcomers who had joined the church in his absence and did not know him personally. This does not fit Paul's modus operandi in other letters, however. On the traditional view, Ephesians was written about the same time as Philippians, from the Roman prison in the early 60s. On this view, Paul had also not visited the church in Philippi for some years, yet Philippians is filled with personal references and warm greetings, contrasting with the impersonal tone of Ephesians. It

13. Defenders of Pauline authorship represent a broad theological spectrum, including Markus Barth, *Ephesians*, 2 vols., AB 34–34A (New York: Doubleday, 1974); Heinrich Schlier, *Der Brief an die Epheser: Ein Kommentar*, 6th ed. (Düsseldorf: Patmos, 1968); Johnson, *Writings*; Max Turner, "Ephesians, Letter to the," in *New Interpreter's Dictionary of the Bible*, 2:269–76; Hoehner, *Ephesians*.

14. E.g., Ralph P. Martin, *Ephesians, Colossians, and Philemon*, Interpretation (Atlanta: John Knox, 1991); Holladay, *Critical Introduction*, 394, 413.

appears that, whether written by Paul or not, the letter was not written to Ephesus or any other specific church.

A profile of the intended readership can be gained from the letter itself (see the *Exegetical-Theological Précis* below). The letter presupposes its addressees are members of the church and stand in the Pauline tradition. It is addressed neither to all Christians everywhere nor to people in general. The readers are not all members of the same local congregation but of the one church throughout the Pauline mission territory—identified with the cosmic reality of the one universal church. They are addressed as Gentiles, who are not now and were not previously members of a synagogue. They are not persecuted or facing any particular crisis. Though they are warned against being tossed about by various doctrines, they are not threatened by a specific heresy.

The Relation of Ephesians to Colossians

Ephesians shares with Colossians many features that set these two letters apart from the rest of the Pauline corpus. Many of the arguments that Colossians is pseudonymous also apply to Ephesians, and these will not be repeated here (see above on Colossians, §15.1.2). Analyzing and evaluating the specific relation of Ephesians and Colossians is crucial in coming to a decision on the authorship of Ephesians and its place in the emerging literature of early Christianity. The literary contacts—both similarities and differences—must first be brought into sharper focus, and then an effort made to provide a plausible explanation.

Similarities

The common structure of Colossians and Ephesians is evident:

Although Ephesians (2,423 words of Greek text) is half again as long as Colossians (1,582 words), the macrostructure of the two letters exhibits much similar content, and the blocks of material they share are in precisely the same order (see Box 15). Colossians carefully follows the Pauline bipartite structure apparent in the undisputed letters; Ephesians adopts and expands this outline (see §§10.2.3 and 15.1.4), omitting only the hymn of 1:15–20 (though utilizing some of its material elsewhere), the instructions against the false "philosophy" of 2:6–23, and the list of personal greetings in 4:10–17. The two letters have the same structure, with Ephesians filling in the outline of Colossians with additional material. This general picture could be explained on the basis of common authorship, whether by Paul or by a later teacher in the Pauline school. The author composed Colossians for one church, then expanded it for a different or broader audience. This explanation becomes more difficult, however, when the similarities are examined in more detail and the differences, both major and minor, are taken into account.

Microstructure. Within the main blocks of material, the individual elements are often arranged in the same order. Thus, for example, the parenesis of Colossians 3:5–17 is expanded in Ephesians 4:17–5:20 by the insertion of other material, but the Colossian order is maintained exactly:

Strip off the old self	Col 3:9	Eph 4:22
Clothe with new self	Col 3:10	Eph 4:24
Image of God the creator	Col 3:10	Eph 4:24
Chosen/marked out by God	Col 3:12	Eph 4:30
Forgive one another	Col 3:13	Eph 4:32
Clothe yourselves/live in love	Col 3:14	Eph 5:2
Songs, hymns, spiritual songs	Col 3:16	Eph 5:19
Always give thanks	Col 3:17	Eph 5:20

So also, while the Ephesian *Haustafel* (5:21–6:9) has much material not found in Colossians 3:18–4:1, and has a different orientation, the order—wives/husbands, children/parents, slaves/masters—is followed exactly. Of the several household codes, only Colossians and Ephesians have precisely this common order.

Vocabulary and style. We have already noted the conspicuous differences in vocabulary and style between Colossians and the undisputed Pauline letters (see above §15.1.2). Ephesians shares several of these features: (1) Sentences of extraordinary length, complexity, and redundancy (e.g., 1:3–14 is one sentence in Greek, as is 4:11–16). (2) Colossians and Ephesians share a preference for long genitive chains and for constructions that employ participles or relative pronouns to join together long series of clauses. (3) About half of Ephesians has verbal contacts with Colossians; about a third of the words in Colossians are found in Ephesians; about a quarter of the words in Ephesians are found in Colossians. (4) Ephesians shares twenty-eight words with Colossians not found in the undisputed letters, including ἄφεσις (*aphesis*, forgiveness, release, remission), συζωοποιέω (*suzōopoieō*, to make alive together with), and συνεγείρω (*sunegeirō*, to help raise up; to raise together with). (5) Significant theological terms and usages are shared by Colossians and Ephesians that distinguish them from the undisputed Paulines, for example, Christ is the head of the church, which is his body (Col 1:18; 2:19; Eph 1:22; 4:15–16; 5:23); a divine fullness in which the church shares (Col 1:19; 2:9; Eph 1:10, 23; 3:19; 4:13); the essence of Christian faith as a profound mystery (Col 1:26–27; 2:2; 4:3; Eph 1:9; 3:3, 4, 9; 5:32; 6:19). (6) A comparison of corresponding paragraphs on similar themes

BOX 15: **Comparison of Colossians and Ephesians**

Colossians

1:1–11 Epistolary Introduction
- 1:1–2 Greeting
- ——————
- 1:3–11 Thanksgiving

1:12–2:23 Part One: Theological Instruction—The Universal Christ
- 1:12–23 Theological Foundation: Redemption and Reconciliation in Christ
  - 1:12–14 Redemption
    - *1:15–20 The Christ-Hymn*
  - 1:21–23 Reconciliation
- 1:24–2:5 The Apostolic Office and Mission
- 2:6–23 The "Colossian Heresy"
- ——————

3:1–4:6 Part Two: Ethical Instruction—Living as Christians
- 3:1–4 The Basis: Risen with Him
- 3:5–17 The Old Life and the New
- 3:18–4:1 Life in the Orderly Christian Household
- ——————
- 4:2–6 Prayer and Conduct

4:7–18 Epistolary Conclusion
- 4:7–9 Concerning the Apostle
- 4:10–17 Greetings
- 4:18 Farewell

Ephesians

1:1–11 Epistolary Introduction
- 1:1–2 Greeting
- 1:3–14 Blessing
- 1:15–23 Thanksgiving

2:1–3:21 Part One: Theological Instruction—The Universal Church
- 2:1–22 Theological Foundation: Salvation and Reconciliation in Christ
  - 2:1–10 Salvation
  - ——————
  - 2:11–22 Reconciliation
- 3:1–13 The Apostolic Office and Mission
- ——————
- 3:14–21 Prayer: Intercession and Doxology

4:1–6:20 Part Two: Ethical Instruction—Living as Christians
- 4:1–16 The Basis: Called into the One Church
- 4:17–5:20 The Old Life and the New
- 5:21–6:9 The Christian Household, Christ, and the Church
- 6:10–20 Armed Conflict with the Powers
- 6:18–20 Prayer

6:21–23 Epistolary Conclusion
- 6:21–22 Concerning the Apostle
- ——————
- 6:23 Farewell

reveals striking verbal connections. For example, Ephesians 3:1–13 on apostolic suffering has much common vocabulary with Colossians 1:24–29. (7) Although Paul directly addresses his readers in the undisputed letters with the familiar "brethren" (ἀδελφοί, *adelphoi*, brothers and sisters), he never does so in Ephesians (or Colossians).

Differences between Colossians and Ephesians

Although Ephesians agrees with Colossians in many respects in which both differ from the undisputed Pauline letters, there are also striking differences.

Pneumatology. Colossians is very reserved in regard to Paul's own use of πνεῦμα (*pneuma*, Spirit) terminology (see above). Ephesians returns to Paul's own enthusiastic expression of the Spirit as the manifestation of the presence and power of God in the life of the church (Eph 1:3, 13, 17; 2:18, 22; 3:5, 16; 4:3, 30; 5:18; 6:17). There was apparently some tension within the Pauline school on the value of *pneuma* language. Such terminology could be misunderstood in terms of the common Hellenistic body/spirit dualism in which bodily existence is denigrated, or in the sense of spirit possession and ecstasy as the expression of authentic religion—views foreign to biblical thought. Thus Colossians (and the Pastorals) avoided such terminology. Ephesians recovers or maintains Paul's own view, in distinct contrast to Colossians.

Ecclesiology, church offices. Ephesians extends the Pauline theology of the church especially in four directions: (1) *Catholicity*. Paul had used the term "church" (ἐκκλησία, *ekklēsia*) mainly for the local congregation and had no developed ecclesiological concepts for the church as a whole. For Colossians, the church is a cosmic reality, but "church" can still be used for the house church, the local congregation (Col 4:15–16). In Ephesians, however, the nine instances of "church" all refer to the cosmic and ecumenical body of Christ, never to the local congregation. (2) *Ecclesiology as Christology:* In Ephesians as in Colossians (but in contrast to Paul), the body metaphor for the church does not include the head; Christ is the head of the body, the church. (3) *Ecclesiology and cosmology, present and future*. This image of Christ as head modulates from ecclesiological to cosmological imagery: as head of the cosmic church, Christ is the head of all creation as such, τὰ πάντα (*ta panta*, the All, the Universe, Col 1:16–17, 20; Eph 1:10, 23; 3:9; 4:10). An integral connection exists between the ecclesiological and cosmological use of τὰ πάντα; the lordship of Christ, already recognized by the church, and the salvation, already experienced there, are an anticipation of the destiny of the whole universe. Christ is already head of the universe, though unknown and unacknowledged by the world, but the church already illustrates what the universe will become. (4) *Church offices*. In Colossians, Paul is the sole apostle, but revelation is received by the whole church (Col 1:26). In Ephesians, Paul is a key figure, but revelation is received by a distinct, quasi-official group, the apostles and prophets, of which Paul is one (Eph 2:20, 3:3–5). In Colossians, there is no reference to any church leadership except Paul himself. The author could have sorely used official representatives in the church he addresses to help quell the heretical movement he opposes. In Ephesians, not only did the first generation have a plurality of apostles and prophets; the church of the readers' own time is blessed with evangelists and pastor-teachers to keep it stable rather than being tossed about by every wind of doctrine (Eph 4:11–16). On this issue, Ephesians stands between Colossians and the later Pastorals.

Church and Israel. Except for the echo of the circumcision debate in Colossians 2:11, one could read Colossians without ever realizing that for Paul, the church belongs to the history of Israel, shares Israel's Scripture as its own, and expresses its own faith in concepts derived from the history and religion of Judaism. The Paul of Colossians never makes or supports his point by citing the Scripture; there are minimal allusions or echoes.[15] For Ephesians, on the other hand, being included in God's covenant with Israel and belonging to the ongoing people of God is a central element of the church's identity (Eph 2:11–22). Accordingly, the author repeatedly adds references and quotations from the Scripture to the Colossian contexts he is adopting and expanding (e.g., Eph 1:22 citing Ps 8:6, cf. Col 1:18; Eph 4:8 citing Ps 68:18, cf. Col 3:12–15; the Colossian *Haustafel*, 3:18–4:1, is expanded with citation from Gen 2:24 at Eph 5:31 and Exod 20:12 at Eph 6:2).

Vocabulary and usage. Ephesians differs from Colossians numerous times in using different vocabulary for the same reality, or using the same vocabulary in a different sense. Among the instances that could be cited:

The vocabulary, style, and syntax of Ephesians are more Semitic than that of Colossians or any of the other letters attributed to Paul. Only Ephesians, for example, refers to human beings with the thoroughly Semitic phrase τοῖς υἱοῖς τῶν ἀνθρώπων (*tois huiois tōn anthrōpōn*, literally "sons of men," 3:5; the only other New Testament instance is Mark 3:28). Qumran research has revealed numerous points of contact between the Dead Sea Scrolls and Ephesians; this is not the case with the language of Colossians (or for other letters in the Pauline tradition, whether by Paul or his disciples).[16] While Paul's Jewish background is the protorabbinic theology of the Pharisees, the author of Ephesians is influenced by the kind of eschatological sectarian Judaism documented in the Qumran texts.

Colossians refers to the transcendent realm of God, where Christ is enthroned, three times, using the noun ἐν τοῖς οὐρανοῖς (*en tois ouranois*, in heaven). Ephesians uses the same phrase five times in the same significant sense, but each time uses a slightly different word, the adjective ἐπουρανίοις (*epouraniois*, for "the heavenly [places]"), a phrase found only in Ephesians.

Paul, Colossians, and Ephesians all refer to the transcendent powers of evil. In the undisputed letters, Paul consistently uses "Satan," while Ephesians always uses "the devil." Neither designation is found in Colossians. Paul's term for the evil spiritual powers of the universe στοιχεῖα τοῦ κόσμου (*stoicheia tou kosmou*) is adapted by Colossians (Col 2:8, 20; cf. Gal 4:3, 9), but the phrase is not found in Ephesians.

Both Colossians and Ephesians use μυστήριον (*mustērion*, mystery) as a key theological term, but in different senses: for Colossians, the mystery is Christ himself (Col 1:26–29; 2:2–3), while for Ephesians the mystery is the revealed purpose of God to unite Jews and Gentiles in the one church (Eph 3:3–6). Likewise, both authors make significant theological use of πλήρωμα (*plērōma*, fullness), but Colossians uses the term christologically (the fullness of God dwells in Christ, Col 1:19; 2:9), while Ephesians uses it ecclesiologically (Eph 1:23, the church is the fullness of the one who is filling the universe; cf. 3:19; 4:13).

Though Colossians is also represented as being written from prison, and at the same time as Philemon, only Ephesians represents Paul as distinctively ὁ δέσμιος (*ho desmios*), *the* prisoner of the Lord (3:1; 4:1), each time with the article as though it has become a traditional title.

Paul characteristically addressed his readers, including those to whom he was personally unknown, with the familiar term ἀδελφοί (*adelphoi*, brothers and sisters). The term is found 133 times in the whole Pauline corpus; nineteen times in Romans, to a church he had never visited; nine times in the shorter Philippians, written according to the traditional view about the same time as Ephesians, five times

15. For a generous assessment of the number and extent of such allusions, see G. K. Beale, "Colossians," in *Commentary on the New Testament Use of the Old Testament*, ed. G. K. Beale and D. A. Carson (Grand Rapids: Baker Academic, 2007), 841–70.

16. Cf., e.g., "Semitic syntactical occurrences appear four times more frequently in the Epistle to the Ephesians than in all the remaining letters of the corpus Paulinum" (K. G. Kuhn, "The Epistle to the Ephesians in the Light of the Qumran Texts," in *Paul and Qumran: Studies in New Testament Exegesis*, ed. Jerome Murphy-O'Connor [London: Chapman, 1968], 115–31).

in the shorter Colossians, written according to the traditional view at the same time as Ephesians, and to a church where he is not personally acquainted. Yet ἀδελφοί does not occur at all in the body of Ephesians, appearing only twice in the conventional concluding greetings.

Both Colossians and Ephesians use the non-Pauline *Haustafel.* For Colossians it functions primarily as instruction on rules for the Christian household, while in Ephesians the *Haustafel* has become a traditional text interpreted midrashically as a sermon on the church (Col 3:18–4:1; Eph 5:21–6:9). In Colossians it is the slaves who get the most instruction; in Ephesians the longest section is directed to husbands, for it is they whose social role allows them to imitate Christ.

Colossians uses no *salvation* terminology for the Christ event; the entire vocabulary related to the verb σῴζω (*sōzō,* to save) is missing. However, it is common in Ephesians: the gospel of salvation (1:13); believers have been saved (2:5, 8) and don the helmet of salvation (6:17); Christ is the Savior (5:23) and the model for Christian husbands.

The Paul of Colossians asked the readers to pray that a door for the word will be opened (Col 4:3); the Paul of Ephesians, in the corresponding passage, asks the readers to pray that Paul's mouth will be opened to proclaim the gospel clearly (Eph 6:19).

Even in such seemingly minor stylistic variations as the usage of the common "in Christ" vocabulary, there is a distinction between Ephesians and Colossians. Ephesians uses the phrases "in the Lord Jesus," "in Christ Jesus," or "in Jesus" six times, but these phrases are never found in the numerous Colossians parallels.

Each of these points—and this is only a sample—seems rather minor taken by itself. The cumulative weight, however, is considerable. It is the total pattern of agreement and disagreement that must be explained—crucial differences on important topics combined with numerous stylistic differences on unimportant topics. This is difficult to do on the assumption that Colossians and Ephesians were written by the same author at about the same time, as posited by the traditional view. The *similarities* point to a close relationship of some kind between Colossians and Ephesians; the *differences* indicate a different author at a later time.

The evidence seems to point to Ephesians as having been composed by a later author who was very familiar with Colossians and adopted it as the basic structure of his own composition, augmented with material from the other Pauline letters and oral tradition that circulated in the Pauline school. We should not, however, imagine an "editor" with Pauline texts before him, composing Ephesians in a cut-and-paste manner, but a teacher in the Pauline school who composes a new manifesto of Pauline theology for use in the churches of the Pauline mission, selecting, combining, and reinterpreting from the Pauline material in which his mind was steeped. Ephesians probably reflects personal contact between such teachers, discussion and exchange of traditions among them. The author is not trying to imitate Paul, but to rethink him—as did Deutero-Isaiah for Isaiah of Jerusalem. Thus the objection that only a foolish plagiarist or editor would have made such obvious changes to Paul is beside the point. The author is not trying to fool readers into thinking they have a previously unknown letter written by Paul, but to re-present Paul, to think Paul's thoughts *after* him.

Type, Date, Provenance

Except for the introductory and concluding greetings and the second-person form of address, Ephesians does not read like a letter. It has been called a tractate, manifesto, meditation, wisdom speech, and homily in the form of a letter. Ephesians does read like a teaching document written in the epistolary form that had become normative in the Pauline school, expressing a summary statement of Paul's theology that advances beyond previous statements in the Pauline school, reinterpreting Paul's statement of the faith and the life to which it calls the church.

The literary dependence on Paul's letters and especially on Colossians indicates it was written after the Pauline corpus had begun to be circulated and after the composition of Colossians. The earliest references to Ephesians that may be positively identified are in Polycarp's letter to the Philippians (ca. 120 CE); Ignatius to Polycarp (ca. 110 CE) probably alludes to Ephesians 5:25, 29. Clement of Rome and 1 Peter (ca. 95) may have known Ephesians, which would mean it was already circulating in Rome in the 90s.[17] All this suggests a date in the late 80s or early 90s for the composition of Ephesians.

There are no clear indications of the letter's provenance. The associations with Ephesus and the second-generation Christianity of Asia Minor suggest Ephesus as a plausible place of origin.

15.2.2 Structure and Outline

The letter is structured according to the dialectical bipartite structure that had become traditional in the Pauline school (§§10.2.3, 15.1.4). The letter falls clearly into two parts, chapters 1–3 and chapters 4–6. Part 1, chapters 1–3, ends with a doxology/benediction and amen. Part 2, chapters 4–6, begins with οὖν (*oun* therefore), corresponding to Romans 12:1 and Colossians 3:1.

1:1–23	Epistolary Introduction
1:1–2	Greeting
1:3–14	Blessing
1:15–23	Thanksgiving
2:1–3:21	Part 1: Theological Instruction—The Universal Church
2:1–22	Theological Foundation: Salvation and Reconciliation in Christ
2:1–10	Salvation
2:11–22	Reconciliation
3:1–13	The Apostolic Office and Mission
3:14–21	Prayer: Intercession and Doxology
4:1–6:20	Part 2: Ethical Instruction—Living as Christians
4:1–16	The Basis: Called into the One Church
4:17–5:20	The Old Life and the New
5:21–6:9	The Christian Household, Christ, and the Church
6:10–20	Armed Conflict with the Powers
6:18–20	Prayer
6:21–23	Epistolary Conclusion
6:21–22	Concerning the Apostle
6:23	Farewell

15.2.3 Exegetical-Theological Précis

1:1–23 Epistolary Introduction

1:1–2 Greeting

Writing in the persona of Paul and using the epistolary greeting formula that had already become traditional in the Pauline school, the author greets the ecumenical church. In contrast to all the undisputed letters except Romans, no associates are included as cosenders; the focus is entirely on Paul himself, and his authority is claimed for the teaching document that follows.

After the greeting, Paul typically included an extensive thanksgiving anticipating the theological body of the letter to follow, regularly introduced with εὐχαριστῶ (*eucharistō*, I give thanks), though in 2 Corinthians 1:2

17. Pol. *Phil* 1.3=Eph 2:5, 8, 9; Pol. *Phil* 12.1=Eph 4:26; Pol. *Phil* 4.1 possibly reflects Eph 6:11. Ign. *Pol.* 5.1=5:26, 29. Some scholars find allusions to Ephesians in *1 Clement* (*1 Clem.* 46.6/Eph 4:4–6; *1 Clem.* 59.3/Eph 1:17–18) may represent common traditions rather than Clement's knowledge of Ephesians. On possible connections between Ephesians and 1 Peter, see the introduction to 1 Peter below.

he uses the common Jewish prayer formula εὐλογητός (*eulogētos*, Blessed be). The author of Ephesians combines both forms: 1:3–14 is the blessing, 1:15–23 the thanksgiving. The introductory blessing/thanksgiving of chapter 1 is then bracketed with an extended prayer of 3:14–21, so that the entire theological body of the letter is essentially a prayer.[18] The section is laced with liturgical elements, probably reflecting the worship of the Pauline churches in Asia.

1:3–14 Blessing

These verses are one sentence in Greek: ponderous, solemn, liturgical, joyful. Though going on and on, with the clauses and phrases connected by conjunctions, relative pronouns, and participles, the author does not just ramble; the unit is carefully structured, setting forth the reasons why God is to be blessed and praised. This opening outburst of praise can no more be "summarized" than can Handel's "Hallelujah Chorus." Some key points can be identified:

By a dense use of the Pauline phrase "in Christ" and its equivalents,[19] the author praises God for what God has done in Christ. The readers are in Christ, so God's saving action is at one and the same time what God has done through Christ and for believers. The lives of believers are embedded in the life of Christ, and this life spans the universe and the aeons. The saving event is thought of as both spatial and temporal, both vertical and horizontal, both "in the heavenly places" (1:3) and chosen "before the foundation of the world" (1:4).[20] These spatial and temporal axes, both transcendent, intersect in the Christ event. As in Colossians, Christ is the Preexistent One who has come into history as the saving act of God.

Believers are earthly, mortal beings, are not preexistent (as in earlier Platonism and later Gnosticism), but their mortal lives are joined to that of Christ. As Christ is risen and enthroned in the transcendent world, so are believers (1:3–4). There is a contrast with Paul's eschatological reservation in which the emphasis is on the believer's identification with the cross, and the resurrection is still in the "not yet" category (see on Rom 6:1–11). The author even goes beyond Colossians' affirmation that believers are already risen with him (Col 3:1), and represents Christians as already ascended and enthroned with Christ "in the heavenly places." Yet Ephesians does not believe that Christians have been mystically lifted out of history; they still live their lives in this world, and must represent the reality of their call by living lives that are different from the surrounding culture (chaps. 4–6). They still look forward to the consummation, just as they look backward to the creation, the covenant with Israel, the Christ event, and their own initial call to be Christians. But the essential reality of their life is already joined to Christ's, and Christ is already crucified, risen, and ascended. This is an explication and advancement of Colossians' declaration that the lives of believers are "hidden with Christ in God" (Col 3:3).[21]

18. Cf. Karl Barth: "The first and basic act of theological work is prayer" (Karl Barth, *Evangelical Theology: An Introduction*, trans. Grover Foley [New York: Holt, Rinehart, and Winston, 1963], 160), reflecting the dictum of the fourth-century monk Evagrius Ponticus.

19. See above, §13.3.2. Eph 1:3–14 uses the phrase eleven times in twelve verses. Ephesians as a whole uses the phrase twice as often as in the undisputed letters of Paul.

20. This is the earliest temporal horizon of Ephesians and the only reference to precreation reality. It is in striking contrast to the precreation Gnostic myths (see §9.2.2).

21. Such variations probably represent discussions and debates within the Pauline school and with other Christian streams in Asia. The Johannine community, also located in Ephesus, is also in the process of reinterpreting first-generation apocalyptic eschatology, with a shift toward present reality without giving up the future hope (see below, §27.5.4, on John 13:31–17:26). It appears that sometimes the debate revolved around the same imagery. Cf. Rev 3:21, where the promise that faithful Christians will be enthroned with the risen Christ is an image of future consummation. Such imagery is being reinterpreted in both the Pauline and Johannine schools, in the same geographical region; their discussions may well have influenced each other. In Ephesians, we overhear one side of a dialogue/debate on how Pauline apocalypticism should be reinterpreted in the generation after Paul's death, in dialogue with other Paulinists and Johannine and other teachers, sometimes using the

Though Ephesians may be in a positive dialogue with gnosticizing ways of thought, exploring them as a vehicle of Christian theology,[22] the theology of Ephesians is in fundamental contrast with emerging Gnosticism, conceiving the saving event within a horizontal metanarrative that affirms history and this world, locating the believer's life within this grand historical narrative that stretches from creation to eschaton. Christ existed before creation, and believers were chosen "in him" before the foundation of the world (1:4); but, in contrast to Gnosticism, there is no mythological explanation of evil in terms of what happened before the creation. All history proceeds under the sovereign plan of the Creator from creation to eschaton, with the coming of Christ into the world as the defining midpoint.

In concord with much of early Christian theology, the overarching metanarrative presupposed by Ephesians is composed of five acts: creation, covenant, Christ, church, consummation (see above §1.5.3). Within this common framework, the distinctive perspective of Ephesians is represented in the following aspects:

— The covenant with Israel is retained as a constituent element of God's all-embracing plan, but the promise/fulfillment scheme is not used to explicate this. Nor are specific figures and details of Israel's history important—there is no reference to Abraham, Moses, David, or the prophets of Israel.

— The Christ event is almost identified with the event that calls the church into being. The author cannot think "Christ" apart from "church," nor "church" apart from "Christ," so that Christology and ecclesiology are practically fused. The church is part of the Christ event and is defined by it.

— Though the defining center has already occurred, the consummation of God's plan is still to come. The center of gravity has shifted from the "not yet" to the "already," but the Pauline tension is maintained. There is still a future consummation, and the "one hope" (4:4) is still an indispensable element of Christian existence. Ephesians, in fact, is the only Pauline document to retain the common Jewish apocalyptic terminology of the two ages (1:21).

— In this grand view, the particulars of Israel's history in the past and the church's history in the eschatological future are submerged in the grand vision. So far as Ephesians is concerned, the creation may have been millennia ago, and the consummation millennia in the future. The Pauline expectation of the near parousia has clearly disappeared, but not the overarching historical and eschatological framework of his theology.

— The consummation of this plan will be the "summing up" of all things in Christ (1:10). The destiny of the universe, which is God's creation but presently fractured, is to be restored and brought under one heading. Christian believers are those who already know this mystery of God's plan for the universe. They are already participants, in a preliminary but real way, in the destiny of the cosmos as a whole (1:12–13). The Christ event will lead to the wholeness of a fragmented universe, in which not only divided humanity will be reconciled to itself and to God, but the universe itself will be made whole. In contrast to Gnosticism but in agreement with Paul (e.g., Rom 8:18–24), God's saving act is not concerned with saving individual souls out of the mess of this world and history, but with bringing the whole creation to its original and intended goodness.

This breathtaking plan of God for the creation is not a matter of speculative philosophy. God's plan, this comprehensive mystery, is revealed "in Christ" (1:9–10). Human intellect could never have arrived at this truth, which is a matter of revelation "in Jesus" (4:21).

same themes and texts. In Revelation and the Fourth Gospel, we hear variations on the same theme within the contemporary and neighbor Johannine school.

22. Cf. especially Schlier, *Epheser*.

1:15–23 Thanksgiving

This paragraph is another single sentence in the Greek text, corresponding to the thanksgiving section typically introducing Paul's letters. Though shifting from the initial blessing format of the preceding paragraph, the theme of *revelation* continues. The author pictures Paul giving thanks for the readers and praying that they will receive the wisdom and insight that come from the Spirit. The definitive revelation has already been made in the Christ event as interpreted by apostles and Christian prophets (1:8–9; 2:20; 3:3–5). The second generation does not merely receive this revelation indirectly as handed on from the past, however. The Spirit was not only at work in the first Christian generation, but continues in the life of the church (1:17). Each generation's appropriation of the past revelation is itself a Spirit-given revelation, and the continuing activity of the Spirit gives new insights into the present meaning of the faith.

The Spirit will open the readers' "eyes of the heart" to perceive the Christian hope, to recognize where the universe is finally going under the sovereignty of God (1:18). They will come to understand that they are part of "God's inheritance," that is, that they belong to Israel, God's people. Their eyes will be opened to the power of God at work among them. The author is not oblivious to the human imperfections of the church, but prays that his readers will see the church as more than a community that functions by the good intentions of its members. Just as the universe is not an independent entity but is driven by "the one who energizes all things" (1:11), so the church exists and carries out its mission by the power of God, and the author prays that his readers will see this (1:19).

This power has already raised Christ from the dead and enthroned him above all cosmic powers. Verses 22–23 have several exegetical problems, but the general thrust is clear: the Christ who is already head of the universe is also head of his body, the church. Christ fills the church with his presence and power. The church is a prolepsis of what the universe will be. The church as that reconciled, believing, loving community that worships the creator is portrayed as a preliminary installment of what the whole creation is to become. While this can be pictured as Christian triumphalism—the universe is to become one big church—it need not be. The author of Ephesians claims that the love of God already manifest in the Christ event and the church will finally prevail as the true reality of the whole creation.

2:1–3:21 Part 1: Theological Instruction—The Universal Church

2:1–22 Theological Foundation: Salvation and Reconciliation in Christ

Worship in Israel and Judaism often included the recitation of God's mighty acts of salvation (e.g., Pss 105, 106). The author of Ephesians here expounds the saving acts of God in the sending of Christ and the formation of the Christian community, corresponding to Colossians 1:12–23 in the template he is following (see above). In his own reconfigured outline, it is difficult to separate this grand liturgical thanksgiving from the body of the letter.

2:1–10 Salvation Like Paul, the author expounds the drama of salvation in three acts: *the way we were* (2:1–3; cf. Rom 1–3); *the saving act of God* (2:4–8; cf. Rom 4–11); *the good works of the Christian community* (2:9–10; cf. Rom 12–16).

The way we were. The Jewish Christian author does not distinguish his own past from that of his Gentile Christian readership. As in Paul's climactic "there is no difference" regarding human sin of Romans 3:22, so the author of Ephesians includes all human beings in their pre-Christian state as "by nature children of wrath, like everyone else" (2:3). He has no mind-body dualism in which the flesh is evil but the mind has good intentions that it cannot carry out because it is drawn down by fleshly desires. The whole person, body and mind, is enmeshed in the network of evil controlled by the demonic rulers of this world that control its value system and modus operandi. This is the state of *death*.

The saving act of God. Dead people cannot extricate themselves from the enslaving power of death. God's act in raising Christ from the dead included the giving of new life to believers, who are raised and enthroned with him (see above). The resurrection was not merely a spectacular divine event of the past; it embraces believers because it happened not only to Jesus, but to them.

The good works of the Christian community. These are not attributed only to their own increased resolve; they too are the result of God's initiative. Here, as elsewhere in Ephesians, the dialectic of divine sovereignty and human freedom is fully operative, neither compromising the other. Just as in their pre-Christian state humans were both responsible for their own decisions and under the power of evil, so in the present Christians must make responsible decisions (see the exhortations in chaps. 4–6), but when they do, they are performing the good works that God had already prepared for them (2:10). Human beings are not robots, either prior to faith or as believers, but neither are they independent of the sovereign God. As was true for Paul, all this was not seen at the time, but only in retrospect, through eyes of faith.

While the author here affirms the fundamental underlying structure of Paul's theology, he does so with differing conceptuality, vocabulary, and emphases. The Pauline emphasis on the cross and Jesus' death is replaced by the resurrection and exaltation. The believer does not die with Jesus but is raised with him. The progression can be sketched:

— *Paul*: Believers die with Christ and are buried with him and receive new life, but resurrection is in the future (Rom 6:1–11; Phil 3:7–12).

— *Colossians*: The believer dies, is buried, and is raised with Christ, the reality of which will be revealed in the ultimate future revelation of Christ's glory (Col 3:1–4).

— *Ephesians*: Believers are already risen and ascended with Christ, with no reference to dying with him or a future resurrection.

In all this, the struggle of Paul's day with Judaizing Christians about the necessity of keeping the Jewish law no longer plays a role. The issue is not whether "works of the *law*" are necessary for salvation, but whether human works as such play a role. Here, salvation as God's gracious gift is contrasted with human striving for salvation. The issue in the 80s and 90s in the Pauline churches of Asia is not opposition to a Judaizing interpretation of Christian faith, but its incorporation into a general concretizing religiosity in which salvation is still a matter of human activity.[23] In Colossians, there were still Judaizing elements in the opposing views combated by the author. This is no longer the case for the Jewish Christian author of Ephesians, who is in fact concerned to help the church recover its Jewish heritage, as we see in the next section.

2:11–22 Reconciliation These verses project another view of the three-act drama, this time from the perspective of divided humanity and the divine act of reconciliation. The Gentile readers had previously been outsiders to the divine plan for the world embodied in the covenant history of Israel, symbolized by circumcision and the law that set Israel apart from the rest of humanity. The Christ event had reconciled all people, Jews and Gentiles, to God, and consequently reconciled them to each other.[24]

23. Cf. Lincoln, *Ephesians*, 120.

24. Some interpreters have seen in the broken wall of 2:14 a specific reference to the wall that separated Jews from Gentiles in the Jerusalem temple. This wall that prohibited Gentiles from entering the sacred confines had in fact been broken down by the Roman armies that destroyed Jerusalem in the 66–70 CE war. Other scholars have seen a proto-Gnostic background for this imagery, in which the wall was a barrier that separated the heavenly world from the earthly. Either or both of these images may be in the background of the author's thought, but they are not necessary to it. The fundamental point is that, for Christian faith, the barrier separating Jew and Gentile has been abolished.

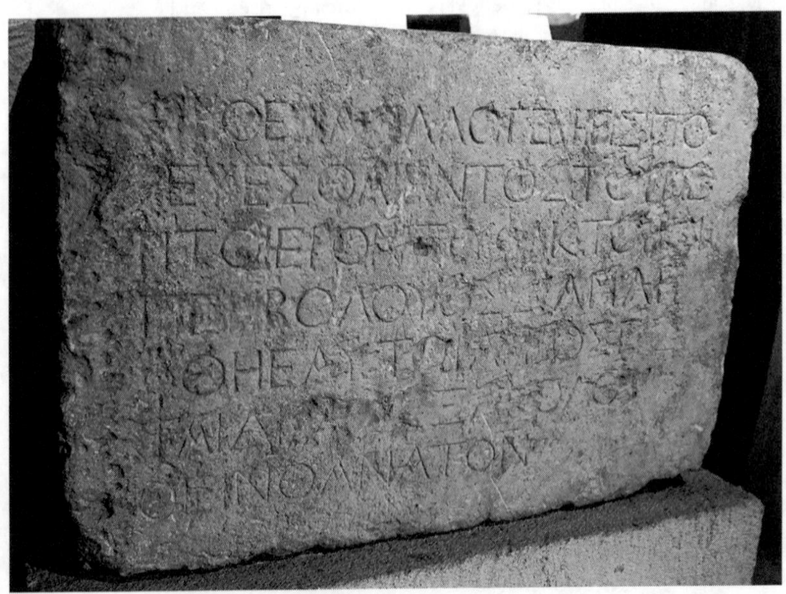

FIGURE 40: Temple warning inscription: "No outsider shall enter the protective enclosure around the sanctuary. Whoever is caught will only have himself to blame for his death." USED BY PERMISSION OF DAVID PADFIELD.

The Jew/Gentile division represents fragmented humanity as such. Since it has been abolished in the one church of Jews and Gentiles, all national, racial, and cultural barriers that separate people no longer exist. The reuniting of fragmented humanity within the church is another instance of how the author sees the church as a foretaste of God's plan for bringing the whole universe together under its rightful head. Within this comprehensive affirmation, the following distinctive points may be noted about the way the author develops his theology.

The *blood of Christ* (2:13) and the *cross* play a decisive role in the saving event, but the focus is not, as in Paul, on Christ's death as the means of salvation, but on the function of Christ's death in bringing the Gentiles into God's covenant. Paul, in a complex and nuanced argument on the relation of Jew and Gentile in God's plan for the ages, had insisted that his understanding of the faith did not abolish the law (Rom 3:31). A generation later, Ephesians declares, in the only reference to νόμος (*nomos*, law) in the whole letter, that the law, which was the wall that had separated Jew and Gentile, was abolished by the death of Christ (2:15). This does not mean that the author rejects the Jewish law as such. On the contrary, the Gentile Christians to whom he writes are already too prone to ignore or reject their Jewish heritage, including the Jewish Scriptures now appropriated as the church's Bible.

The author wants to help his readers appropriate their Jewish inheritance. He wants them to see that the history of salvation did not begin with them, but that they have been incorporated into God's ongoing plan, to which they were previously outsiders. Gentile Christians may even have begun to look down on their Jewish, and Jewish Christian, forebears, and the author—himself a Jewish Christian disciple of the Jewish Christian Paul—wants to correct that.

Nonetheless, there is a contrast with Paul a generation earlier, who in the heat of debate was accused of abolishing the law by accepting Gentiles into the church without circumcision (see Galatians, Romans, Acts 9–15). Paul had furiously denied that charge. Those days are over, and a generation later a teacher in the Pauline school writing to Gentile Christians can declare without debate that the law, as the means of separating Jews and Gentiles, has in that sense been abolished. Its continuing validity as Scripture is apparent for the author, who alludes to and quotes from it as an assumed authority (e.g., 4:8, 25–26; 5:31; 6:2), and who assumes the outline of the biblical narrative as the framework for his own theology.

3:1–13 ***The Apostolic Office and Mission***

This section corresponds to Colossians 1:24–2:5 in the template the author is following, elaborating on the role of the first-generation apostles and prophets in the formation of the church and the revelation of God's plan for history. In the view of Ephesians, this plan was not revealed to the Old Testament prophets, nor was it included in the ministry of the historical Jesus,[25] but was first revealed through the Holy Spirit in the life of the church, through apostles and Christian prophets. This had already happened in the foundational first generation, to which the readers of Ephesians look back (2:20). It is not a matter of controversy, as during Paul's time.

The revelatory gestalt has three elements. First, there is an event in history—the revelation does not come out of the blue, but in relation to something that has happened or is happening: some churches begin to accept Gentiles into the people of God without circumcision and the pledge to keep the Torah. But the event in itself is ambiguous: it could be a new and definitive phase in God's plan for history, or it could be due to yet another failure of God's people to maintain the divinely given standards. In this ambiguous situation, a prophet or prophetic group gives the interpreting word. Yet even this does not settle the issue, for there are varying prophetic claims. It is the whole community of faith that must discern when the Spirit is speaking. This was already Paul's understanding (see 1 Thess 5:20–21; 1 Cor 12:4–11, 27–31; 14:1–40) and was still a live issue in the churches of Asia to which Ephesians is directed (cf. Rev 2:20). This fusion of event + prophetic interpretation + discernment by the Spirit-guided community had resulted in the one body of Christ composed of Jews and Gentiles. The community as a whole is able to discern that the revelation had in fact been given, not necessarily because they had direct experience of divine revelations, but by reading what Paul had written (3:3). In context, this probably refers to the text of Ephesians itself, but also points to the corpus of Pauline writings being assembled and circulated in the churches of Asia as the normative guide to their faith.

In the theology of Ephesians, there is both a narrowing and a broadening of previous understandings of how the revelation functions. On the one hand, the idea that the revelatory Spirit works through the church as a whole is focused on a smaller group: the apostles and prophets, who are regarded as "holy" and "the foundation" (3:5; cf. 2:20). New insights and revelations must now correspond to this standard. On the other hand, the focus on Paul as the sole apostle prevalent in other streams of the Pauline school (see Colossians and the Pastorals) is now broadened in an ecumenical direction.[26] Paul is still a key figure, but he is one of a number of authoritative apostles,

25. That Christ "preached peace" (2:17) does not refer to the preaching of the historical Jesus, which plays no role in Ephesians. It was not the example of the historical Jesus that caused the first-generation churches of the Hellenistic mission to admit Gentiles without the requirement of circumcision and keeping the Torah (see above §9.2.2); there was no such example (cf. Mark 7:27; Matt 10:5–6; 15:24, and the struggles of the church to admit Gentiles recorded in Acts 10–15). It was the person of Christ and his cross, the Christ event as such, that after Easter brought about the unity of Jew and Gentile in the one church. Like Paul, the author of Ephesians regards the church's preaching of the Christian message to be Christ's own preaching through the Spirit at work in the church (see Rom 10:14b, 17).

26. Cf. the contrast between Ephesians' view of Paul's universal apostolic office and 1 Cor 9:2, "If I am not an apostle to others, at least I am to you; for you are the seal of my apostleship in the Lord." In contrast to Ephesians' identification of the church's one foundation as the apostles and prophets, cf. Paul's insistence in 1 Cor 3:11, "For no one can lay any foundation other than the one that has been laid; that foundation is Jesus Christ."

one of the foundation stones of which Christ is the keystone. This is one aspect of coming to terms with his death and the loss of Paul as the unifying center of the church. There is no hint of tension or conflict between Paul and the other apostles, or that he had had to struggle for a slot in the apostolic college. The theology of Ephesians is not yet that of the protocatholic church of the second century, but it is definitely en route to the One Holy Catholic Apostolic church.

3:14–21 Prayer: Intercession and Doxology

This section is an insertion into the outline of Colossians the author has been following, replacing the section on the "Colossian heresy" as no longer necessary or relevant. As the letter body had begun with an extended prayer and thanksgiving (1:3–23), so the first part concludes with this magnificent prayer and doxology, expressing the writer's faith that the living Christ continues to work powerfully by the Spirit in the community as a whole, not only in its increasingly official leadership.

4:1–6:20 Part 2: Ethical Instruction—Living as Christians

The two parts are bound together by *calling*: 1:18, 4:1. In Part 1, the author expounded the theological meaning of God's calling the church into being; Part 2 sets forth the obligation to live in a way appropriate to this calling. The theology of Part 1 did not have in view opposing theologies it intended to correct or displace, but the *holiness* of the people of God. Theology is for the support of the ethical practice of the Christian community, not for a theoretical debate with competing theologies.

4:1–16 The Basis: Called into the One Church

A major dimension of the new Christian responsibility is to live in such a way that the unity of God's people given by the Spirit is not destroyed. Maintaining the unity of the church, living together in a community that exhibits to the world that the walls that separate people have in fact been abolished (2:11–21), is a part of the church's mission. This unity is the expression and continuation of Jewish monotheism, manifest in one God, one Lord, one Spirit, one baptism, one church (the body), one faith, one hope. The "one loaf," the Pauline eucharistic theology that all Christians gather about the one table, is missing here and elsewhere in the deuteropauline letters—though there may be an allusion to it in the "one body" (cf. the identification of "bread" and "body" in 1 Cor 10:17; 11:23–24).

The Pauline idea that every member of the body receives a gift is reaffirmed, though without Paul's specific vocabulary. Psalm 68:18 is interpreted to mean that the risen Christ gives gifts to his church. These gifts are now understood in a semiofficial sense as the church's ministry. In Paul's time, the apostles, prophets, and teachers were all contemporaries. The author of Ephesians looks back on apostles and prophets as belonging to the first generation, while contemporary church leadership is represented by evangelists and pastor-teachers. Evangelists were apparently traveling missionaries who founded new congregations, while pastor-teachers were a distinct group charged with teaching and pastoral care of congregations (it is not clear whether pastors and teachers were separate categories of ministers, or a single ministry of pastor-teacher). In contrast to later developments within some streams of the Pauline churches, church leadership is not yet a matter of ordination, nor are there presbyters, bishops, and deacons within the purview of the author of Ephesians (cf. 1 Tim 3; Titus 1). There is already an identifiable group of ministers, but no firm process of selection and ordination. The ministries of evangelists and pastor-teachers, though distinct, were probably overlapping.

4:17–5:20 The Old Life and the New

In this section the author adopts and amplifies the parallel section in Colossians 3:5–17 (which see). Some distinctive elements in Ephesians:

— Though themselves ethnically Gentiles (2:11; 3:1), they are no longer to live "as the Gentiles." The readers belong to the new Christian community that transcends the Jew/Gentile split. Though not ethnically Jews, they can regard themselves as citizens of Israel and look on the unbelieving world and their own unbelieving past as a "Gentile" way of life that must not continue (cf. 1 Cor 12:2; 1 Pet 2:12; 3 John 7).

— Paul's emphasis on the power of the Spirit in the life of the church as the driving force of ethical behavior (4:23, 30; 5:18) had been practically eliminated in Colossians. Ephesians recovers the distinctive Pauline view.

— For the first time in the Pauline tradition, the exalted place of Christ in the divine plan is expressed in the phrase "the kingdom of Christ and God" (5:5). Jesus had proclaimed the kingdom of God, as had the earliest church and Paul. Colossians refers separately to the "kingdom of the Son" (Col 1:13) and the "kingdom of God" (Col 4:11). Ephesians combines them. While this phrase is unique to the whole Pauline corpus, 2 Timothy 4:1 and Revelation 11:15 indicate that in the second and third generation the figures of Christ and God were being merged in the thinking of the churches of Asia.

— Ephesians expands the parenesis of Colossians by adding the image of the church as the bearer of light to a dark world (5:7–14 is unique to Ephesians). This light of the gospel is not only to expose and reprove, but to allow the darkness itself to become light, to allow unbelievers to see their situation in the light of Christ and become believers themselves. This light that radiates from the church will finally transform the whole creation (see on 1:10, 23). As the readers themselves have been transformed from darkness to light, they may have hope for the whole universe.

5:21–6:9 The Christian Household, Christ, and the Church

The author's appropriation and expansion of the Colossian household code is marked by two distinctive emphases (see above at Col 3:18–4:1 for general discussion of interpreting New Testament household codes):

Mutuality. The Colossian *Haustafel* begins with "Wives, be subject. . ."; Ephesians 5:21 begins with words addressed to the whole church: "Be subject to one another." Unlike Colossians, Ephesians addresses a situation in which all concerned belong to the church (wives and husbands, children and parents, slaves and masters) and has no instructions for subordinate members who have unbelieving husbands, parents, or masters. There are, in fact, more instructions to husbands on loving their wives than to wives on being subordinate to their husbands (5:25–33 vs. 5:22–24). The reminder that God shows no partiality is shifted from the address to slaves in Colossians 3:25 to that to masters in Ephesians 6:9.

Christological paradigm for family life. Within the given social structures, the Christian family is to be modeled on the relation of Christ to the church. The author adopts the image of the church as bride of Christ, itself adapted from the biblical imagery in which Israel was the bride of God (Hos 1–3, Ezek 16:8–14). Weaving back and forth between this christological image and earthly family life has the effect of lifting the marriage relationship to a sacred level (in the Hellenistic world it was a secular contract without religious associations). While for Paul the present is the time of engagement, with the wedding to be celebrated in the eschatological future, the author of Ephesians characteristically shifts the emphasis to the present: the church is already the bride of Christ, and Christian marriage should reflect this. The imagery remains androcentric, reflecting the male-dominated culture of the times.

In this paradigm, the priority is christological, not sociocultural. The author does not argue, "Just as the husband is head of the wife, so Christ is head of the church," but from the prior christological reality to life in the Christian community: "Just as Christ loves the church and nourishes it, so husbands must love their wives." While modern family life should not and cannot replicate the situation of the first-century church, the fundamental challenge for modern interpreters who want to take such texts with theological and ethical seriousness may be Ephesians' insistence that personal, family, and civic life be shaped by the Christ event, rather than the expectations of modern culture.

6:10–20 ***Armed Conflict with the Powers***
This section has no parallel in Colossians. The theological presuppositions that stand behind and inform the exhortation for Christians to arm themselves with the "whole armor of God" begin with the awareness of biblical imagery of God as the divine warrior who defeats his enemies with great power and violence (e.g., Exod 15:1–21; Judg 5). This imagery had already been applied to the hoped-for eschatological deliverer (e.g., Isa 11:4–5; 49:2; 59:17). The author is aware of the transformation brought about by the Christian affirmation that the hoped-for Messiah is Jesus, that this deliverance was brought about by the cross and resurrection, and of Paul's specific claim that "God's power is made perfect in weakness" in the Jesus who was "crucified in weakness" (2 Cor 12:9; 13:4).

Paul had specifically included elements of the armor of the divine warrior in his own exhortation, but with his characteristic emphasis on salvation as future—the breastplate is faith and love, and the helmet is the *hope* of salvation (1 Thess 5:8). Paul's future hope typically becomes present reality for the author of Ephesians, and Christians are urged to put on the helmet of salvation (6:17). For this author, God's cosmic opponents are already defeated and will finally be included in the reconciliation of the cosmos at the consummation of history, but they are at present still hostile and active enemies of God's universal purpose for the creation. Thus believers cannot be passive, but are called to be active participants in the struggle, with both defensive and offensive weapons that come from God and represent God's power. This image of participating in a war that is in principle already won, but still calls for steadfast resistance, was abroad in other Christian circles in Asia near the end of the first century (see below on Revelation, esp. Rev 5, 12). Ephesians, here and elsewhere, may represent some theological cross-fertilization with these contemporary streams of Christian faith.

6:18–20 ***Prayer*** The final exhortation to prayer, adapted from Colossians 4:2–4, here becomes the final aspect of the believer's equipment. Prayer is not a specific piece of offensive or defensive equipment, but characterizes the whole course of action by which believers are equipped for mission. As theology is worked out before God in prayer (cf. above), so the Christian life as a whole is lived before and from God, permeated by prayer.

6:21–23 ***Epistolary Conclusion***
Much of this is reproduced verbatim from Colossians 4:7–8, a clear indication of literary dependence. Unlike Colossians 4:18, there is no claim here that the final greeting was written in the apostle's own hand (cf. on 2 Thess 3:17). At the end of his composition, the author reverts specifically to the letter framework with which he began, inserting his text into the fictive literary world of Paul addressing his churches. The author does not send his text forth as an essay or list of instructions, but as a letter from Paul, projecting the Pauline narrative world that is the framework for the readers' Christian faith.

15.3 Interpreting 2 Thessalonians

15.3.1 Authorship and Historical Context

Second Thessalonians is a brief document; among the Pauline writings, only Philemon is smaller. The letter is composed of only three interrelated themes: persecution, eschatology, and the "idlers." In the traditional historical construction, Paul writes another letter to the new congregation of Christians in Thessalonica shortly after writing 1 Thessalonians, mainly in order to correct the readers' misunderstanding of his earlier eschatological teaching. It was supposed that their intense expectation of the nearness of the parousia, occasioned in part by Paul's earlier letter, had caused some in the congregation to quit their jobs. They had become a problem to the other members, and Paul writes to explain that the second coming is not going to be all *that* soon, so they should get back to work. In the process, he reaffirms his earlier encouragement about enduring persecution.

More careful study made this interpretation problematic: 2 Thessalonians has a different, more official tone than 1 Thessalonians, with no personal words or greetings. The two documents manifest a close literary relationship unparalleled among the undisputed Pauline letters, with many similarities of structure and wording, but also significant differences (see selection of details below). The two letters cover much the same ground, the most obvious difference being the eschatological section of 2 Thessalonians 2:1–12. Especially, the eschatological program of 2:1–12 seems difficult to reconcile with that of a letter by the same author to the same church on the same subject written only a short time earlier. Coming to terms with the data revealed by intensive study of 1 and 2 Thessalonians has produced the following positions:

1. Both letters were written by Paul, in the present order. The similarities are explained by their proximity in time: the structure and wording of 1 Thessalonians were still fresh in Paul's mind when he wrote 2 Thessalonians. The differences are due to the changed situation of the Thessalonians in the interval.[27]

2. Both letters were written by Paul, but 2 Thessalonians was written first (the present order and titles are editorial, based on their length). It is very difficult to understand 2 Thessalonians as written by the same author, shortly after he had written 1 Thessalonians to the same church. The problems are supposedly minimized if 1 Thessalonians is seen as an elaboration and expansion of the earlier 2 Thessalonians.[28]

3. Both letters were written by Paul, but not to the same addressees. The similarities are explained as above, while differences are explained in terms of the different readerships for which they were intended. There are variations of this view:

— First Thessalonians was addressed to the Gentile Christian majority, 2 Thessalonians to the Jewish Christian minority;[29]

— First Thessalonians was addressed to a limited segment of the church, but 2 Thessalonians to the entire community;[30]

— First Thessalonians was written to Thessalonica, but 2 Thessalonians to a different church in another city.[31]

— A further variation: both letters were written by Paul to the church at Thessalonica, but each letter had a different "primary group" within the church as its primary focus.[32]

27. Cf., e.g., Ernest Best, *A Commentary on the First and Second Epistles to the Thessalonians*, Black's New Testament Commentaries (London: Adam & Charles Black, 1972), 37–59, who opts for this solution after pondering all the alternatives.

28. The argument was first made in 1642 by Hugo Grotius (*Annotationes in Novum Testamentum*, 1641–50). In more recent times, the classic statement is T. W. Manson, "St. Paul in Greece: The Letters to the Thessalonians," *BJRL* 35 (1952–53); cf. now a commentary based on this order: Charles A. Wanamaker, *The Epistles to the Thessalonians: A Commentary on the Greek Text*, NIGTC (Grand Rapids: Eerdmans, 1990).

29. So Adolf von Harnack, "Das Problem des 2. Thessalonicherbriefes," *SPAW.PH* 31 (1910): 560–78, followed by only a few scholars.

30. So Martin Dibelius, *An die Thessalonicher I, II*, 3rd ed. (Tübingen: Mohr, 1937), 57–58.

31. To Philippi, argued by Eduard Schweizer, "Der zweite Thessalonicherbrief ein Philipperbrief?" *Theologische Zeitschrift* 1 (1945): 90–105; to Beroea, argued by Maurice Goguel, "L' Enigme de la seconde épître aux Thessaloniciens," *Revue de l'histoire des religions* 71 (1915): 248–72. Neither suggestion has found an echo in the discussion.

32. First Thessalonians was written to those Paul had converted and knew personally; Second Thessalonians, a bit later, was primarily to those converted in the meantime,

4. All the above theories assumed Pauline authorship of both letters. All critical scholars are now confident that Paul did in fact write 1 Thessalonians, but since the 1801 work of J. E. C. Schmidt, the problems have often been resolved by arguing that 2 Thessalonians is pseudepigraphical.[33] In recent decades, a growing number of scholars have become convinced that the difficulties of regarding 2 Thessalonians as written by Paul himself are overwhelming, and that there is compelling evidence the letter is pseudepigraphical. This is now probably the majority view among critical scholars. There are variations of this view as well:

— The letter was written by Timothy and/or Silvanus to the church in Thessalonica, but in Paul's time and with his approval, correcting a misunderstanding of Paul's eschatological teaching prevalent in the church in Thessalonica.[34]

— The letter was written by a Paulinist to the church at large, opposing the growing Gnostic interpretation of Pauline theology.[35]

— The letter was written by a member of the Pauline school in the 80s or 90s of the first century CE, to the churches of the Pauline mission, reinterpreting the eschatology of the first generation and objecting to theological and ecclesiological developments in the Pauline churches. Interpreting the letter within this presupposed context provides the most plausible reading of the letter, is advocated by numerous scholars,[36] and will be developed in the following paragraphs.

15.3.2 2 Thessalonians as a Product of the Pauline School

The authorship of 2 Thessalonians continues to be debated, along with the interrelated issues of date and setting. A selection of the reasons 2 Thessalonians is here considered pseudepigraphical follows.

Literary Relationship

Second Thessalonians closely follows 1 Thessalonians in both structure and content, as evident in the following parallel outlines:[37]

2 Thessalonians	1 Thessalonians
1:1–2 Greeting	1:1
1:3–2:17 Thanksgiving/ Letter Body	1:2–3:13
2:13–15 Second Thanksgiving	2:13–3:10
2:16–17 Benediction	3:11–13
3:1–15 Parenesis: The Life to Which Christians are called	4:1–5:22
3:16–18 Letter close	5:22–28
3:16 Peace wish	5:23–24
3:17 Greetings	5:26
3:18 Second Benediction	5:28

The peculiar structure of 1 Thessalonians, with two thanksgivings and two benedictions,

who had appropriated a distorted understanding of 1 Thessalonians. So Malherbe, *Thessalonians*, 350–53, 364.

33. J. E. C. Schmidt, *Vermutungen über die beiden Briefe an die Thessalonicher* (BKENT; Hadamar1801).

34. Karl P. Donfried, "2 Thessalonians and the Church of Thessalonica," in *Paul, Thessalonica, and Early Christianity*, ed. Karl P. Donfried (Grand Rapids: Eerdmans, 2002), 49–68.

35. So William Wrede, *Die Echtheit des zweiten Thessalonicherbriefs*, TUGAL 24 (Leipzig: J.C. Hinrichs, 1903), 3–36 (ca. 100–110 CE); Willi Marxsen, *Introduction to the New Testament: An Approach to Its Problems*, trans. G. Buswell (Philadelphia: Fortress Press, 1970), 38–39 (soon after 70 CE).

36. E.g., Frank Witt Hughes, *Early Christian Rhetoric and 2 Thessalonians* (Sheffield: Journal for the Study of the New Testament Press, 1989); Georg Strecker, *Theology of the New Testament*, trans. M. Eugene Boring (New York: De Gruyter, 2000), 594–604; Edgar Krentz, "Second Thessalonians," in *Anchor Bible Dictionary*, 517–23; Wolfgang Trilling, *Der Zweite Brief an die Thessalonicher*, EKKNT 14 (Neukirchen-Vluyn: Neukirchener Verlag, 1980), 26–28.

37. Adapted from J. A. Bailey, "Who Wrote II Thessalonians?" *NTS* 25 (1978): 133. In the Pauline tradition, such parallel structure is found only in Colossians/Ephesians, also probably pseudepigraphical.

is precisely followed. Second Thessalonians introduces no topics or themes, but is devoted entirely to three themes taken from 1 Thessalonians: persecution, eschatology, and the "idlers." The greeting in 1 Thessalonians 1:1, unique among the undisputed Pauline letters, is reproduced verbatim in 2 Thessalonians 1:1–2, and there are numerous other close echoes of the vocabulary and wording, for example, "with toil and labor we worked night and day, so that we might not burden any of you" (1 Thess 2:9/2 Thess 3:8). Some incidental vocabulary of 1 Thessalonians is found elsewhere in the Pauline tradition only in 2 Thessalonians (e.g., καὶ διὰ τοῦτο, *kai dia touto*, also for this reason [1 Thess 2:13/2 Thess 2:11]); the emphatic pronoun ἡμεῖς (*hēmeis*, we), seems to occur in 2 Thess 2:13 only because it is found in precisely the same setting in 1 Thess 2:13, though it now has a different function; the combination στηρίξαι καὶ παρακαλέσαι [*stērixai kai parakalesai*, strengthen and encourage], using precisely the same verbal forms [1 Thess 3:2/2 Thess 2:17]). Of course, it is conceivable that a few such instances could be coincidental; the large number of such incidental agreements requires explanation.

There are also striking differences between 2 Thessalonians and 1 Thessalonians.

Style

Second Thessalonians differs from 1 Thessalonians (and the other undisputed Pauline letters) in significant matters of style. The lengthy sentences (1:3–12; 2:5–12; 3:7–9), repetitions of words and phrases, and frequency of synonymous parallelism all contrast with Paul but are reminiscent of Colossians and Ephesians. The Pauline parenthetic expressions, play on prepositions, use of triads, pictorial manner of expression, and short staccato imperatives in the paraenetic section are all missing or minimized. In 1 Thessalonians, the authorial "we" is sometimes the equivalent of Paul's "I" (1 Thess 2:18; 3:2, 5), but in 2 Thessalonians the "we" is intended more literally: it is the network of some teachers in the Pauline school that speaks (2 Thess 2:15).[38] The characteristic Pauline "in Christ" is missing (§13.3.2, though see 2 Thess 3:4, 12), as in the Pastorals. This is in contrast to the undisputed letters and especially to Colossians and Ephesians, where this terminology is multiplied.

Tone

Second Thessalonians contains no greetings to the congregation, no personal data whatever about Paul or his readers, and has a somewhat official, impersonal, and authoritarian tone. It is the didactic tone of the teacher addressing a general readership personally unknown to him, rather than the warm tone of 1 Thessalonians addressing fellow believers he has recently converted and whose sufferings he shares. In this regard, the tone of 2 Thessalonians is analogous to that of Ephesians (see above), as in general the relation of 2 Thessalonians to 1 Thessalonians is analogous to the relation of Ephesians to Colossians. In each case, the author has adopted a letter from the Pauline corpus as model and template for his own composition, but has transformed the personal tone of the template into the more general tone of the general letter addressing a wider readership.

Implied Situation and Date

1. *Second Thessalonians was written after Paul's letters and other letters attributed to him had begun to be circulated.* The author of 2 Thessalonians not only knows 1 Thessalonians well, and adopts it as the template for his updated version of some aspects of Paul's theology (see

---

38. J. Christaan Beker, *Heirs of Paul: Paul's Legacy in the New Testament and in the Church Today* (Minneapolis: Fortress, 1991). See also Hans-Martin Schenke, "Das Weiterwirken des Paulus und die Pflege seines Erbes durch die Paulusschule," *NTS* 21 (1975): 505–18; and Paul K. Jewett, "The Redaction of I Corinthians and the Trajectory of the Pauline School," *Journal of the American Academy of Religion* 46, no. 4 (1978): 389–44.

above), but is familiar with other Pauline letters as well. The author is not attempting to compose a summary of Paul's theology, but only to address three particular, interrelated issues. In the process, he echoes statements and phraseology of several of Paul's letters. These allusions are not the product of a cut-and-paste editorial process, as though the author had Paul's letters before him and cites words and phrases from them, but the kind of echoes that one who is familiar with the Pauline corpus works in to his own composition. Among such allusions: 2 Thessalonians 3:9 is a clear reflection of Paul's argument in 1 Corinthians 9:6 that he had an apostolic right to be supported by the churches instead of working for a living with his own hands, but had declined to make use of this right. Samples of other, less distinct, echoes of Pauline letters: 2 Thessalonians 1:4 (=2 Cor 1:24; 7:4, 14; 8:24; 9:3, on boasting to the other churches about the readers); 2 Thessalonians 1:5 (=Phil 1:28, evidence of the righteous judgment of God); 2 Thessalonians 1:12 (=Rom 1:18, 32, God's judgment means they reject the truth, believe the lie, and practice unrighteousness); 2 Thessalonians 2:10 (=1 Cor 1:18, unbelievers are οἱ ἀπολλύμενοι, *oi apollumenoi*, those who are perishing); 2 Thessalonians 3:2 (=Rom 15:31, request for prayer that Paul will be delivered from his opponents); 2 Thessalonians 3:13 (=Gal 6:9, do not grow weary in well doing). Second Thessalonians seems to reflect the theological developments present in Colossians and Ephesians, while these letters betray no awareness of 2 Thessalonians. In particular, Ephesians shows familiarity with virtually all the undisputed letters of Paul and with Colossians, but not with 2 Thessalonians. If 2 Thessalonians had been written by Paul, immediately after he wrote 1 Thessalonians, some of the echoes from 1 Thessalonians could be explained by claiming that the first letter was still fresh in his mind. But the phraseology of letters written years later should not appear in 2 Thessalonians if it were written by Paul.

2. Second Thessalonians was written at a time when discussions and disputes were current in the Pauline churches about continuity with Paul himself and which traditions represented the authentic Pauline gospel. Paul himself had debated with other, non-Pauline versions of the early Christian faith (e.g., esp. 2 Corinthians, Galatians, Romans). First Thessalonians reflects none of this debate. In 2 Thessalonians, there is an insistence that the churches adhere to the original message as taught by Paul, that is, that the understanding of the faith represented in the letter was the same that Paul had originally taught and that had been handed on by reliable tradition (2 Thess 2:5, 15; 3:6). The readers are warned against other traditions claiming to be from Paul or new prophetic revelations through the Spirit (2 Thess 2:2). This hardly fits Paul's own time, but accords with the situation near the end of the century in Asia Minor, when new and disputed prophetic insights were promulgated (e.g., Revelation and its prophetic rivals, see §26.1.8, on Rev 2–3 below).

3. Second Thessalonians was written at a time when Pauline churches were beginning to distinguish "heretical" from "orthodox" interpretations of the Pauline gospel. In contrast to Paul a generation or two before, the author of 2 Thessalonians uses the language of developing orthodoxy. For Paul, πίστις (faith) was the key word denoting the believer's relation to God, obedience-in-personal-trust. Faith for Paul is primarily *fides qua creditur*, the faith with which one believes. While he could also use the term in the sense of *fides quae creditur*, the faith that one believes, the body of material that constitutes the contents of one's faith (e.g., Gal 1:23), in the vast majority of cases, by "faith" Paul means the believer's commitment to and trust in God. Second Thessalonians uses this key term only twice, once in the Pauline sense, in the conventional thanksgiving of 1:3, copied from 1 Thessalonians 1:3. The second instance, 2 Thessalonians 3:2, is entirely the author's own composition, and includes the rationale οὐ γὰρ πάντων ἡ πίστις (*ou gar pantōn hē pistis*, "not

everyone has the faith."[39] Here "faith" is the content of orthodox belief, the correct interpretation of Paul for a later generation, in opposition to interpretations of Pauline theology the author considers to be false. This is not quite yet the perspective of the author of the letter of Jude, who instructs his readers to "contend for the faith that was once for all entrusted to the saints" (Jude 3), but it is on the way to that understanding of faith. It resembles the use of "the faith" in the later Pauline tradition represented by the Pastorals (e.g., 1 Tim 1:19; 3:9; 5:8; 6:10, 12, 21; 2 Tim 3:8; 4:7; Titus 1:13; 2:2). Likewise, the author's understanding of orthodox Pauline faith as "belief of the truth" over against the demonic "lie" advocated by his opponents (2 Thess 2:10, 12, 13) is uncharacteristic of Paul, but in line with the developing orthodoxy and its vocabulary at the end of the first century CE in Asia Minor.[40]

4. Second Thessalonians was written after pseudepigraphical letters had been written and churches had to discern which of those represented Paul and which did not. The author warns against "letters as though from us" (2 Thess 2:2) that advocate a realized or imminent eschatology. This reflects second-generation Pauline Christianity in which various streams of the Pauline tradition were advocating their reinterpretations of Paul's eschatology by writing letters in his name. It is very difficult to believe that in the early 50s, shortly after writing 1 Thessalonians, Paul had to warn his new churches against letters circulating in his name, but this fits second- and third-generation Pauline Christianity in Asia Minor very well. More specifically, the author may well have in view the realized eschatology of Colossians and Ephesians.[41] While there are no specific textual allusions to Colossians and Ephesians, the author of 2 Thessalonians seems to have in view the reinterpretation of Paul's eschatology represented by the traditions and positions found in them. The author is in dialogue and debate with other Pauline teachers and warns his readers against letters written in Paul's name representing this point of view. The author insists that his own writing represents the "real" Paul.

This is the meaning of the claim in 3:17 that Paul has signed 2 Thessalonians in his own hand and that this is the mark of every authentic Pauline letter. It was conventional to dictate the letter to a trained scribe, then, if the author could indeed write, to add a brief note in the author's own hand. Two of Paul's own letters reflect this convention (1 Cor 16:21; Gal 6:11), as does the probably pseudepigraphical Col 4:18. Since Paul's letters were heard in the congregation as they were read forth by the lector, this practice could hardly serve as a means of authenticating the letter for the hearers, unless they examined the original copy themselves. Once a letter was copied, the distinctive handwriting of the author would become the same as the rest of the letter. Thus in second-generation Pauline Christianity, such concluding notes served to claim that the letter authentically represented Paul, not necessarily that he had directly written it. In any case, the claim could not have been taken literally, since it would have disqualified every Pauline letter except 1 Corinthians and Galatians—even 1 Thessalonians—and would have authenticated the deuteropauline Colossians opposed by the author. The question the early Christians had to face was not authorship literally understood, but what the claim to authorship signified: whether the document represented the apostolic faith. That

39. This is routinely missed in English translations (though cf. the NASB note), but preserved, e.g., in the 1978 French *Nouvelle Version Second Révisé*, and the 1979 *La Sainte Bible, Nouvelle Edition de Genève*.

40. Among all the New Testament documents, by far the greatest preponderance of "truth" vocabulary is found in the Johannine writings, especially the polemical 2 and 3 John. This reflects the disputes among Johannine Christians in Asia Minor at the turn of the century (see below, §§26.2–4). The Johannine school was in contact with Pauline Christians in the same province; there is some cross-fertilization between the Johannine developments and 2 Thessalonians. The "truth" vocabulary of 2 Thessalonians seems to reflect this development.

41. So, e.g., Hughes, *Early Christian Rhetoric*, 86–91.

2 Thessalonians is included in the canon indicates their positive decision.

15.3.3 Conclusion

The combination of *similarities* in structure, content, and vocabulary and *differences* in style, tone, implied situation, and theology, indicates 1 and 2 Thessalonians were written by different authors and that 2 Thessalonians was written considerably later than 1 Thessalonians. Second Thessalonians was written at a time when three interrelated theological issues had become critical in the churches of the extensive Aegean mission: the persecution of Christians, the delay of the parousia, and changes in church leadership and structure. All three of these issues, along with others, had been dealt with in 1 Thessalonians, which served as model and point of contact for updating Paul's theology in the situation of the author of 2 Thessalonians. All three issues point to a time near the end of the first century CE.

15.3.4 Structure and Outline

On the similarities to the structure of 1 Thessalonians, see above §15.3.2.

1:1–2	Greeting
1:3–2:17	Thanksgiving/Body
(1:5–10	*First Insertion: Persecution, Reversal at Christ's Coming)*
1:11–12	Thanksgiving Continued
(2:1–12	*Second Insertion: The Day of the Lord)*
2:13–17	Second Thanksgiving and Benediction
3:1–15	Parenesis: The Life to Which Christians Are Called
3:1–5	Prayer for the Missionaries
3:6–13	Warning the "Idle"
3:14–15	Warning the Disobedient
3:16–18	Second Benediction

15.3.5 Exegetical-Theological Précis

1:1–2 Greeting

The greeting is verbally identical with that of 1 Thessalonians 1:1 (see comments there), to which the Pauline "from God our Father and the Lord Jesus Christ" is added. Here the plural authorship reflects the network of teachers in the Pauline school.

1:3–2:17 Thanksgiving/Body

The cool "we are obligated to give thanks" (1:3, repeated 2:13) is a bit more officious than Paul's customary warm "we give thanks." The way in which the conventional Pauline thanksgiving section modulates into the body of the letter is based on the similar structure of 1 Thessalonians 1:2–3:13, reflecting the intended use of the letter in the worship assemblies of the Pauline churches: doctrine is communicated within the framework of worship and praise. The faith/love/hope triad of 1 Thessalonians is reduced to faith and love—it is in the matter of the Christian hope, the readers' eschatological understanding, that the author finds them in need of correction and further instruction.

(1:5–10 First Insertion: Persecution, Reversal at Christ's Coming)

The author omits all the autobiographical particulars of 1 Thessalonians and goes directly to the first theme related to his own agenda, the persecution threatening the readers. Paul had dwelt on the steadfastness in persecution manifest in the life of the new converts in Thessalonica, which they had endured with joy inspired by the Holy Spirit (1 Thess 1:6). The experience of persecution bound them together not only with himself, but with Jesus and with the earliest churches in Judea (1 Thess 1:6,

2:14), placing them in the succession of the suffering people of God. The author of 2 Thessalonians has a different perspective on the topos of persecution: now it is not merely the local persecution in Thessalonica, but an aspect of the general persecution suffered by all believers. Persecution is cast in an apocalyptic and universal light. At the parousia, the tables will be turned by the returning Lord Jesus; those now afflicted will be comforted, and the persecutors will be punished with everlasting destruction. Paul himself did not dwell on the fate of unbelievers; 2 Thessalonians 1:9 is the only reference to "eternal punishment" in the Pauline corpus. The indications of general persecution, apocalyptic reversal, and eternal punishment are reminiscent of the imagery of Revelation, and suggest some interaction between the Pauline and Johannine traditions circulating in the environs of Ephesus at the end of the first century.

1:11–12 Thanksgiving Continued

The author resumes following the outline of 1 Thessalonians, with the themes of Paul's prayer for them and their being counted worthy of their calling (cf. 1 Thess 2:12).

(2:1–12 Second Insertion: The Day of the Lord)

The author has already prepared for this section by placing the persecution in the framework of apocalyptic theology. This is the most distinctive section in 2 Thessalonians. The topic is "the parousia of our Lord Jesus Christ and our being gathered together to him," and the issue is the time of the Lord's return. Has it already occurred in some spiritual sense? Is it about to occur in a literal sense, as signaled by the persecution some Christians are experiencing? Or is it not yet on the horizon, though still to be awaited in the future? The author opposes a misunderstanding about the "day of the Lord," but the false claim he opposes is not clear. The verb used, ἐνέστηκεν, *enestēken*, can be translated "has come" (so RSV; cf. NRSV, REB "is already here," NIV, TNIV "has already come") or "is at hand" (so KJV, NAB).

Most translations and interpreters understand the error as a realized eschatology that no longer looks forward to a future fulfillment. Colossians and Ephesians were tending in this direction, and it may be that the author of 2 Thessalonians understood them or their tradition to have completely collapsed the future hope into present experience. This was one way of coming to terms with Paul's expectation of the near parousia. Paul was not mistaken, the expected eschatological events had indeed taken place, and they were realized as the presence of the Lord in the experience of the faithful community. We know that such interpretations were advocated in the Johannine school contemporary with 2 Thessalonians (see below on John 13–17). The errorists he opposes were within the Pauline tradition; the false interpretation of the eschatological events come from prophetic revelations, oral traditions, and/or letters "as though from us" (2 Thess 2:2); that is, they are propagated in the name of Paul. The Paulinist author wants to reassert the original Pauline teaching as found in 1 Thessalonians. Just as the author of Revelation reasserts apocalyptic against developing realized eschatology in the contemporary Johannine school, so the author of 2 Thessalonians considers this "progressive" step in the Pauline school a step in the wrong direction for the reinterpretation of Christian faith in the generation after Paul, and reasserts futurist apocalyptic eschatology.

On the other hand, if the verb ἐνέστηκεν (*enestēken*) is understood to mean "is at hand," the error opposed is a superheated near expectation of the parousia.[42] Paul's original expectation was not fulfilled in the first generation but is now about to be fulfilled, and the persecution the church is enduring is a sign of the nearness of the end. This was the reinterpretation of

42. A significant minority argues this view, e.g., Traugott Holtz, *Der erste Brief an die Thessalonicher*, EKKNT 13 (Neukirchen-Vluyn: Neukirchener Verlag, 1986); Richard, *Thessalonians*.

eschatology affirmed by Revelation. In this case, the author of 2 Thessalonians would oppose the view that the church's present troubles are a sign of the immediate end. However ἐνέστηκεν (*enestēken*) is understood, it is clear that the author reaffirms the apocalyptic hope—the Lord has neither already returned in the experience of believers, nor is he about to come in the near future. *This* is the point of the apocalyptic scenario he depicts. His interest is not in drawing up an apocalyptic calendar as such, but in refuting false expectations about the present. His argument, based on his combination of traditional apocalyptic imagery that was again becoming current in Christian circles in Asia in the 90s (see Revelation), is that certain signs must precede the end. Since these have not happened yet, the end cannot have already come in some spiritual sense, nor can it be imminent in a literal sense.

Before the parousia can occur, there must come the ἀποστασία (*apostasia,* rebellion, apostasy), a time of general falling away from God. This will be followed by the appearance of the "lawless one," the "son of perdition" ("the one destined for destruction"), who will enter the temple and claim to be God.[43] This figure is clearly not merely an ordinary human being claiming divine powers but resembles the eschatological opponent of God portrayed in the contemporary document Revelation. He will operate by the power of Satan, be accompanied by deceitful signs and wonders, and will be destroyed by the returning Lord Jesus.

The power that is presently holding back these apocalyptic events must be taken away (2 Thess 2:6–7). Some power or person, divine or human, is restraining the advent of the final events that will lead to the apostasy and the coming of the Lawless One.[44] God will remove this restraining power in due time, but the readers' present is distinguished from that future eschatological time. The "mystery of lawlessness" is already at work, but the readers do not live in the end time or its immediate prelude. The false eschatology being promulgated in the author's time is a lie and delusion sent by God; all who believe it will be condemned when Christ appears at the parousia (2 Thess 2:11). Second Thessalonians calls the churches to believe the saving truth of the tradition as taught by Paul—while he was with the readers, in 1 Thessalonians, and now in 2 Thessalonians (2:10–12).

2:13–17 Second Thanksgiving and Benediction

Following the corrective insertion on eschatology, the author returns to the template provided by 1 Thessalonians, with a second thanksgiving section that concludes with a second benediction (see pattern displayed above).

3:1–15 Parenesis: The Life to Which Christians Are Called

3:1–5 Prayer for the Missionaries

The parenesis section follows the normal Pauline pattern. The distinctive prayer request for deliverance from evil and ἄτοποι people (*atopoi,* out of place, disorderly) probably refers to the same group that does not have "the faith," that is, those who in the author's view have departed from the developing "orthodox" interpretation of Paul. This prayer request reflects the later experience of Paul and his appeal in Romans 15:31. The confidence that they will do

43. The reference to the temple is sometimes claimed as evidence that 2 Thessalonians was written before the temple's destruction in 70 CE, but the imagery is inherent in generic apocalypticism. In any case, in the fictive world of the letter written by Paul, the temple was in fact still standing, but not in time of the real author and readers.

44. The author refers to the restraining power both impersonally (neuter τὸ κατέχον, *to katechon,* 2:6) and as a person (masculine ὁ κατέχων, *ho katechōn*). He is not interested in a more precise identification (cf. the analogous Mark 13:9, where "abomination" is neuter, but the corresponding pronoun is the masculine "he"). The point is that the restraining power is still in place; therefore the eschatological events have not happened or begun to happen—the end is still some time in the future.

what he commands prepares the way for the following paragraph, in which "command" occurs three times.

3:6–13 Warning the "Idle"

The "idle" (those who live ἀτάκτως, *ataktōs*, "in defiance of good order"[45]) are internal to the church, a different group from the opponents of the previous paragraph who do not have "the faith." The author here takes up the admonition to the ἄτακτοι (*ataktoi*, "disorderly" of 1 Thess 5:14, where it is often translated "idlers"). In 1 Thessalonians, it is usually understood as a warning against members of the congregation who had stopped working and had become dependent on the church. However, the context there has to do with church leadership. The author of 2 Thessalonians may interpret the earlier text to refer to those in his own time who do not respect the kind of lay charismatic leadership instituted by Paul. In the situation of 2 Thessalonians near the end of the first century CE, the author seems to have in view not only local members of the congregation taking advantage of the church's welfare program, but a general issue affecting the wider Pauline church: those emerging leaders within the congregations who were claiming or accepting financial support for their work, and Christian missionaries of the late first century who went from church to church designating themselves as "apostles" (=missionaries) and "prophets" (=spokespersons for the risen Christ), teaching and preaching and expecting the churches to support them. The situation is portrayed in another document of the late first or early second century responding to this situation:

> Concerning the apostles and prophets, conduct yourselves according to the ordinance of the Gospel. [4]Let every apostle who comes to you be received as the Lord; [5]but he shall not abide more than a single day, or if necessary, a second day; but if he stays three days, he is a false prophet. [6]And when he departs, he is to receive nothing except bread to supply him until his next station; but if he asks for money, he is a false prophet. . . . The false prophet can be distinguished from the true prophet on this basis. [9]No prophet ordering a table in the Spirit shall eat of it; otherwise he is a false prophet. [10]And every prophet teaching the truth, but not living according to his own teaching, is a false prophet. . . . [12]And do not listen to anyone who says in the Spirit, "Give me silver" (or anything else); but if he tells you to give on behalf of others that are in want, then he is not to be judged . . . . [12:2]If the new arrival is a traveling missionary, assist him, so far as you are able; but he shall not stay with you more than two or three days, and then only if it be necessary. [3]But if he has his own trade and wishes to settle with you, let him work for and eat his bread. [4]But if he has no craft, according to your wisdom provide how he shall live as a Christian among you, but not in idleness. [5]If he is not willing to do this, he is making Christ into a cheap way of making a living. Beware of such people. (Didache *11:3–12:5, trans. M. Eugene Boring*)

The two generations after Paul saw the development of a resident "clergy," ordained bishops, elders, and deacons, some of whom were apparently salaried and devoted their full time to the work of the church. The Pastoral Letters represent this development within the Pauline school (see below §§16.1.2, 16.1.5). Second Thessalonians opposes this developing separate class of ministers supported by the churches by appealing to the example of Paul himself. Second Thessalonians 3:9 reflects 1 Corinthians 9:6, appealing to Paul's example of earning his own living, refusing to take pay from the church. The author of 2 Thessalonians considers such paid ministers to be "disorderly" and "disruptive" (a better translation of ἄτακτοι

45. Walter Bauer, Frederick William Danker, *A Greek-English Lexicon of the New Testament and Other Early Christian Literature*, 3rd ed. (Chicago: University of Chicago Press, 2000), 148.

than "idlers"), though they probably thought of themselves as advocates of the new structures and orders of Christian ministry. The author represents the point of view that ministry in the church cannot be relegated to a particular group but is always "lay" ministry.

In the author's view, the new developments in the direction of an ordered clergy paid by the local congregation violate both the example of Paul himself and his instructions in his letters. The author gives no indication of how he thinks church leadership should function. He does not repeat or reaffirm the admonition of 1 Thessalonians 5:12–13. He affirms the work of the Spirit in the life of the church, but is suspicious of purported new revelations (2 Thess 2:2); otherwise, there is no reference to charismatic gifts or prophetic revelations.

The church is to be guided by Paul's own example and instruction, continued into the present by Paul's letters (especially 1 Thessalonians as here updated) and the Pauline tradition, but the author gives no hint as to how this is actually implemented, or by whom. Another member of the Pauline school presents a mediating view in which God gives specialized ministries to the church, but the special vocation of pastor-teachers is to equip the whole church for its mission in the world (Eph 4:7–13). In 2 Thessalonians, Ephesians, and the Pastorals the modern reader can overhear an ongoing debate among the followers of Paul on the development of new forms of ministry.

3:14–15 *Warning the Disobedient*

It may be that some members of local congregations were following the example and taking up the claims of the traveling missionaries, so that those who claimed church support were both internal to the local congregation—local church leaders who wanted to give their full time to church leadership (see Acts 6:1–6)—and visitors from outside. The author does not consider them heretics to be rejected, but brothers and sisters to be cordially and sternly warned.

3:16–18 Second Benediction

The letter concludes with a second benediction (cf. 1 Thess 3:11–13 and the chart above), insisting that there be no confusion about which letters represent the authentic Paul. Amid the conflicting claims to Paul's authority in the second generation, *this* letter represents Paul's authentic message for the readers' own time. The later church affirmed this claim by including 2 Thessalonians in the New Testament canon—but without excluding the alternatives represented by Colossians, Ephesians, and the Pastorals.

15.4 For Further Reading

Barth, M. *Ephesians*. Anchor Bible 34, 34A. 2 vols. New York: Doubleday, 1974.

Best, E. *A Critical and Exegetical Commentary on Ephesians*. ICC. Edinburgh: T. & T. Clark, 1998.

Brown, Raymond E. *The Churches the Apostles Left Behind*. New York: Paulist Press, 1984.

Hoehner, H. W. *Ephesians: An Exegetical Commentary*. Grand Rapids: Baker Academic, 2002.

Krentz, E. "Second Thessalonians." In *The Anchor Bible Dictionary*, edited by David Noel Freedman, 517–23. New York: Doubleday, 1992.

Lincoln, A. T. *Ephesians*. WBC 42. Dallas: Word, 1990.

Lohse, E. *Colossians and Philemon: A Commentary on the Epistles to the Colossians and to Philemon*. Translated by William R. Poehlmann and Robert J. Karris. Hermeneia. Philadelphia: Fortress Press, 1971.

MacDonald, M. Y. *The Pauline Churches: A Socio-historical Study of Institutionalization in the Pauline and Deutero-Pauline Writings*. SNTSMS 60. Cambridge: Cambridge University Press, 1988.

Martin, R. P. *Ephesians, Colossians, and Philemon*. Interpretation. Atlanta: John Knox Press, 1991.

O'Brien, P. T. *Colossians, Philemon*. WBC 44. Waco, TX: Word Books, 1982.

Sumney, J. L. *Colossians: A Commentary*. NTL. Louisville, KY: Westminster John Knox Press, 2008.

16
The Pastorals and the Struggle for Paul

16.1 Interpreting the Pastorals

THE KEY PROBLEMS FOR INTERPRETATION of the Pastorals are directly related to the question of authorship. The issues of date, historical setting, occasion and purpose, and major theological themes are interwoven with each other; all are inseparable from the issue of authorship and will be woven into this discussion. The extensive listing of data and arguments on the authorship issue here provided is not only part of an introduction to the Pastoral Letters in particular, but an example of how arguments for and against pseudepigraphy function, how much persuasive power they may contain, and how much they may lack. Of the disputed letters, the universal opinion is that the Pastorals are the least likely to have been written by Paul.[1] If Paul did not write the Pastorals, their presence in the New Testament poses the issue of whether other documents attributed to Paul may be pseudepigraphical (Colossians, Ephesians, 2 Thessalonians). On the other hand, scholars who believe Paul wrote the Pastorals tend to believe he wrote all the other books that claim Pauline authorship. The issue is thus a watershed for the critical approach to the New Testament, should not be resolved on the basis of dogma from right, left, or center, and calls for thorough discussion.

16.1.1 The Pastorals as Real Letters from Paul to Timothy and Titus

Some scholars continue to interpret the Pastoral Letters as real letters from Paul to Timothy and Titus.[2] Their arguments are as follows:

1. The biblical texts themselves claim Pauline authorship. In this regard, the Pastorals are not like the Gospels, Acts, Hebrews, and 1 John, for which the tradition later provided author's names in their respective titles for documents that are themselves anonymous. Not only does the first word of each of the Pastoral Letters explicitly claim that the letter was written by Paul; each represents itself throughout as from Paul himself, including narrative references to personal history and incidental details (1 Tim 1:3; 3:14; 4:13; 5:23; 2 Tim 1:4–6, 15–18; 2:2; 3:10–11; 4:9–21; Titus 1:5; 3:12–13).

2. The canonical status of the Pastorals argues for their authenticity. This is argued both historically and theologically. It is claimed that, as a matter of history, the early church would not have accepted the Pastorals into the canon

1. See all recent critical commentaries. The classic work of P. N. Harrison, *The Problem of the Pastoral Epistles* (London: Oxford University Press, 1921), has recently been reprinted. A judicious treatment by a leading evangelical scholar concludes that the Pastorals are post-Paul pseudepigraphical texts: Marshall, *Pastoral Epistles*, 57–92.

2. Recently argued, e.g., by E. Earle Ellis, "Pastoral Letters," 658–66, Johnson, *Timothy*, and Ben Witherington, *Letters and Homilies for Hellenized Christians*, vol. 1, *A Socio-Rhetorical Commentary on Titus, 1–2 Timothy and 1–3 John*, 2 vols. (Downers Grove, IL: IVP Academic, 2006).

if they had not believed they were actually written by Paul. Theologically, some modern authors argue that the doctrine of the inspiration of the Bible and the reality of the Bible as word of God are incompatible with pseudonymous authorship. Unless Paul wrote them, they are not the inspired word of God. Thus the important commentary of Ceslas Spicq,[3] despite its erudition, makes essentially a theological argument: if not by Paul, the Pastorals are forgeries and cannot be canonical. But they are canonical. Therefore, they must be by Paul.

3. Tradition supports Pauline authorship. From the time of Irenaeus (ca. 180 CE) until the early nineteenth century, no one in mainstream Christianity questioned Pauline authorship. The works of J. E. C. Schmidt (1804) and Friedrich Schleiermacher (1807) challenged 1 Timothy, arguing it could not be fitted into the life of Paul. In 1812 the *Einleitung in das Neue Testament* of J. G. Eichhorn was the first introduction to the New Testament to argue that all three of the Pastorals were pseudonymous.

4. Opposing arguments are inconclusive. Defenders of Pauline authorship begin with the tradition, examine the arguments for pseudonymity one by one, and do not find them compelling: it has not been proven that Paul could not have written them.

16.1.2 The Pastorals as Pseudepigraphical Documents by a Teacher in the Pauline School

Those who interpret the Pastoral Letters as having been written by someone other than Paul himself base their view on the following arguments:

1. The documents' claim to Pauline authorship can be explained historically and theologically and is thus not compelling evidence for Pauline authorship. For Christian teachers in the second and third generations of the church, the apostolic *faith* was important, but not necessarily apostolic *authorship* of normative texts. The Gospels of Mark and Luke, for example, were accepted as representing the apostolic faith, though it was never claimed that they were written by apostles. Many versions of Christianity were beginning to compete, each representing itself as the valid legacy of the first generation. In such a situation, the claim to represent the apostolic faith was sometimes expressed in the form of a document purportedly written by an apostle or apostles (e.g., the *Didache* [*Teaching of the Twelve Apostles*], the *Didascalia Apostolorum*, the *Apostolic Tradition* of Hippolytus, and the *Apostolic Constitutions*). All these are, of course, pseudepigraphical. The question for the ancient church, however, was not the historical issue of who actually composed them, but the theological issue of whether or not they represented the apostolic faith. Paul had not composed theological essays or manuals of church order, but letters. For the Pauline school, Paul was *the* apostle. The appropriate way for his students to update and continue his teaching was to compose letters in his name, in which his voice continued to address the church.

2. The reasons for the early church's *acceptance* of the claim of the letters to represent Paul can be explained historically and theologically (see §14.2). The argument that all the church fathers accepted the claim of Pauline authorship at face value seems strong at first, especially since several of them were astute scholars sensitive to the finer points of language, theology, and style, since their mother tongue was the language of the New Testament, and since they were centuries closer to the events than modern critics. This is a deceptive argument, however (see Exc. 3.1 on the use of patristic data in New

3. Ceslas Spicq, *Saint Paul: Les Épîtres Pastorales*, 4th ed. (Paris: Gabalda, 1969). A helpful English summary of Spicq's two French volumes is provided in Mark Harding, *What Are They Saying about the Pastoral Epistles?* (New York: Paulist Press, 2001), 19–21. Similar theological arguments are offered by E. Earle Ellis, "Pseudonymity and Canonicity of New Testament Documents," in *Worship, Theology and Ministry in the Early Church: Essays in Honor of Ralph P. Martin*, ed. Michael J. Wilkins and Terence Paige (Sheffield: JSOT Press, 1992), 212–24; Stanley E. Porter, "Pauline Authorship and the Pastoral Epistles: Implications for the Canon," *Bulletin for Biblical Research* 5 (1995), 105–123, and Carson and Moo, *Introduction*, 337–353.

Testament research). The church fathers were theologians first and historians second. They did not first examine the historical evidence and then decide whether the document represented authentic theology, but quite the reverse (see above §2.2.2 for Bishop Serapion's evaluation of the *Gospel of Peter*). A document that represented the apostolic faith was apostolic, regardless of authorship. Furthermore, the bishops and teachers of the second and third centuries were not isolated individuals who made their personal theological-historical judgments that they then handed down to the church. They represented the whole body of believers, and it was the use of various documents in the church as a whole, and whether they found resonance within the wider community of faith, that determined whether they were accepted or rejected (see above on canon, §2.2.2, especially Luther's key statement). The acceptance or rejection of apostolic authorship was a consequence, not the cause, of such acceptance or rejection. What became the mainstream of early Christianity uniformly accepted the Pastorals as representing the apostolic faith. On this basis, their apostolic authorship was accepted, just as they had been composed to make this claim.

3. The chronology and personal allusions presupposed by the Pastorals do not fit into the lifetime of Paul as otherwise attested:

— 1 Timothy 1:3 "Remain in Ephesus." Paul is portrayed as having left Ephesus for Macedonia, leaving Timothy in charge. The apostle intends to return to Ephesus soon (1 Tim 3:14; 4:13). When was this? According to Acts 19:22 it was not Paul who traveled to Macedonia while Timothy remained in Ephesus, but the opposite: Timothy is sent ahead to Macedonia while the apostle remained in Ephesus.

— Titus 1:5 "I left you behind in Crete." It is presupposed that Paul and Titus had conducted an extensive mission in Crete, during which several congregations had been established, but appropriate leaders had not been installed. Paul has gone to Nicopolis (and other places? cf. Titus 3:12). No place can be found in Acts or the other Pauline letters for a Pauline mission on Crete and related travels.

— 2 Timothy 1:8 ". . . me his prisoner." Paul is in prison, but the situation described fits none of the possibilities presupposed in Acts or the letters, including the final Roman imprisonment of Acts 28 (on Paul's imprisonment and death, see §14.1).

— 2 Timothy 3:10–11 This indicates that Timothy "observed" Paul's sufferings at Antioch, Iconium, and Lystra, that is, that he was personally present. But in Acts, these troubles are reported in chapters 13–14, on the "first missionary journey," while Timothy is not converted until 16:1–3, on the "second journey."

Most scholars consider it impossible to fit these and other events presupposed in the Pastorals into the framework of Paul's life as presented in Acts and the undisputed letters. The Pastorals are our only source for the extensive mission work they portray. If Paul is their author, he must have been released from the "first" Roman imprisonment and then carried on huge mission projects not otherwise attested, during which time he wrote 1 Timothy and Titus. He was then arrested again and brought to Rome, where he wrote 2 Timothy just before his execution.[4]

4. The Pastorals manifest their own internal inconsistencies that make them difficult to regard as historically accurate on these points. According to 2 Timothy 1:15; 4:10–11, 16, all Paul's coworkers except Luke have abandoned him, while in the same letter Paul sends greetings from four coworkers and "all the brothers" (2 Tim 4:21). In 2 Timothy, Paul is facing death and expects his martyrdom to come soon, yet he

4. A few scholars, of whom L. T. Johnson is a recent example, argue that the gaps in the chronology of Acts and Paul's letters make it possible to fit 1 Timothy and Titus into Paul's Aegean mission in the 50s. Second Timothy was written from the imprisonment of Acts 28 (see Johnson, *Timothy*, 55–102; 135–37; 319–30). On this hypothesis, the Pastorals then clash with the style, tone, and theology of the undisputed letters written during this period.

asks Timothy to bring books and a cloak (a trip of several weeks from the Aegean to Rome) and to come before the winter storms make travel on the Mediterranean impossible. This plea sounds as though Paul still foresaw an extended time in prison. In Titus 3:12, Titus is to come as quickly as possible; in 1:5 he is to travel through cities of Crete and appoint elder-bishops in every church. As conventional in pseudepigraphical letters, such incidental comments contribute "realism" to the document, but do not fit into the framework of factual history.

5. There are tensions between Paul's self-understanding as presented in the Pastorals and the undisputed letters. The Pastorals portray Paul's pre-Christian life differently than did Paul himself: Titus 3:3 reports, "At one time we too were foolish, disobedient, deceived and enslaved by all kinds of passions and pleasures." Contrast, for example, 1 Corinthians 6:9–11, where Paul provides a vice catalogue, concluding "such were some of *you*." The Pastor's use of Paul as a model for the readers' own conversion (1 Tim 1:16) includes portraying Paul as though he used himself as an example of pre-Christian sin. This "before and after" pattern became a typical scheme of preaching in the Hellenistic churches after Paul's time. But Paul himself saw his pre-Christian life as "righteous" and "blameless," entirely different from that of Gentiles who had been converted from paganism (see Phil 3:4–11; Acts 23:1).

Paul himself did not distinguish between his call to be a Christian and appointment as apostle. However, 1 Timothy 1:12–17 counts these as two separate events. Since the Pastor considered Paul the model par excellence for Christian ministry, it was necessary to separate Paul's call to be a minister from his conversion, because new converts are not eligible to be ministers until they demonstrate that they are faithful.

Paul insisted that he was an authentic apostle alongside other apostles who differed from him but whose mission and theology he affirmed. He did not claim to be the only apostle or to have a monopoly on authentic Christian faith and theology (e.g., 1 Cor 3:21–23; 15:3–11, esp. "whether it was I or they, so we proclaim and so you have come to believe"). So also, in Philippians 1:15–18 (in the traditional view, written about the same time as 1 Timothy and Titus), Paul celebrates that the gospel is proclaimed by others, both colleagues and rivals. The Paul of the Pastorals, however, represents a later Pauline tradition that knows Paul as *the* apostle, who does not acknowledge a variety of several forms of the apostolic faith, and who rejects all non-Pauline forms of the tradition.

6. The letters are inappropriate as letters to Timothy and Titus from Paul. If Paul is the author writing actual letters to Timothy and Titus, these would be the only extant personal letters to an individual from Paul. All Paul's letters are to churches. Philemon is no exception; it too is a church letter (see above §11.3.1).

But can the Pastorals be understood as personal letters? It is a good exercise for the modern student to read through the Pastorals with this question in mind. Can the Paul who had known and worked with these men for many years write to them like this? The most recent defense of Pauline authorship attempts to overcome this by arguing that 1 Timothy and Titus represent the literary type of "royal correspondence" in which a ruler writes to subordinates, authorizing them and giving them directions. Such letters, documented in inscriptions and papyri fragments, supposedly "provide an analogy to the social relationship in 1 Timothy: a superior writes to a representative or delegate with instructions concerning the delegate's mission."[5] But this is a far cry from what we have in the Pastorals. Paul is not a royal figure issuing mandates, and Timothy and Titus are beloved brothers and veteran missionaries who have endured hardship with Paul for many years. The content and tone of the Pastorals are simply not appropriate to such a relationship. Some examples:

5. Ibid., 139; cf. 137–42.

— The greetings are highly formal and liturgical: 1 Timothy 1:1–2; 2 Timothy 1:1–2; and especially the lengthy, solemn, and ornate Titus 1:3.

— First Timothy 1:3 begins abruptly with a command, without the conventional thanksgiving.

— In 1 Timothy 1:3, the opening command instructs a veteran missionary to instruct "certain people" not to teach any different doctrine from the Pauline tradition (see 3:14; 4:13–15). One must ask what function such instructions would have in a real letter, in view of the brief absence of Paul. Likewise, the directions on selecting bishops and deacons in 3:1–14 indicate that Paul hopes to rejoin Timothy soon, but in the meantime gives instructions "on how one ought to behave in the household of God." These are not interim, short-term instructions. In any case, one wonders why Timothy did not know these things already, and, if not, why did not Paul tell him what to do before leaving him in charge? The teacherly tone is hardly appropriate; by 65 CE, Timothy would have more than fifteen years' experience as a trusted lieutenant of Paul's. Paul had sent him to Thessalonica and Corinth to settle problems, and then sent Titus to Corinth, who did resolve the problem. The Pastorals throughout contain elementary instruction appropriate as a manual for training new ministers, authoritative guidelines for ministers as a class, and directions to the church about their qualifications and duties. Such instruction is not appropriate in real letters between colleagues.

— First Timothy 4:12 addresses Timothy as a young man, though he would have been a seasoned, mature adult in the purported situation in the 60s, who had already proven himself by weathering many crises with Paul (Acts 18:5; 19:22; 20:4; Rom 16:21; 1 Cor 4:17; 16:10; 2 Cor 1:1, 19; Phil 1:1; 2:19; 1 Thess 3:2, 6). "Let no one despise your youth" is appropriate as pastoral counseling from an older minister to novice. It is not appropriate to the real Paul and Timothy; nor is "my child" of 2 Timothy 1:2 and 1:5; or "shun youthful passions" of 2 Timothy 2:22.

— In 1 Timothy 1:12–17 the extensive depiction of Paul's conversion and (as a separate event) his appointment to be an apostle is understandable as instruction for the Pauline churches of the third generation. But why would the real Paul be telling the real Timothy the meaning of his conversion, in a letter written during a brief absence, after they had worked together for several years?

— First Timothy 2:7, "I am an apostle, I am telling the truth, I am not lying," echoes Paul's passion as he appeals to his churches against false accusations (Rom 9:1; 2 Cor 11:31; Gal 1:20). It is appropriate to congregations in the third generation in that it maintains the apostolic claim made by Paul in continuity with the other letters in the Pauline corpus. It is hardly appropriate as part of a personal letter to an old friend and coworker.

— First Timothy and Titus contain no news from Paul's own situation. First Timothy closes abruptly, with "Grace be with you [pl.]," with no greetings to those Paul knows in Ephesus, where he had spent more time than in any other church. The "you" in the closing greetings is consistently in the plural. The opening greetings studiously avoid the singular pronoun "you" (σοι, *soi*), and purported letters to individuals cannot have the plural (ὑμῖν, *humin*); this makes them the only letters in the Pauline tradition that do not have a pronoun of direct address in the greeting. Thus, the letters were written to a collective, to the ministry and the church at large, intended not for private reading by Timothy and Titus, but for public reading in the church, along with the other letters of the Pauline corpus. The author uses the literary technique of an open letter, for a church that admires Paul and his colleagues, and looks back upon him and them as heroes of the faith, a church that wants to follow their instructions for their later situation. The letters have the appropriate tone for the purpose for which they were composed, but are inappropriate as personal letters.

7. The letters are appropriate to the third generation of Christian leaders, where there is a struggle for the true succession of Paul's leadership. That Timothy represents the third generation is clear from 2 Timothy 1:5. The church situation presupposed is different from that of Paul's day, and more akin to the world reflected in Christian writings after Paul's time: Revelation, the Gospels and Letters of John, Ignatius, Polycarp (see below on date). Within the Pauline churches of the third generation, there is dissension concerning what it means to continue the Pauline mission after the death of their charismatic leader. Who are the legitimate heirs and interpreters of the Pauline tradition? This is the point of the opening line in each of the letters, specifying that Timothy and Titus are γνήσιος (*gnēsios*, legitimate) and ἀγαπητός (*agapētos*, beloved in the sense of chosen, authorized).[6] What Paul began in the first generation, represented by the letters of the Pauline corpus, is now continued by his authorized representatives in the Pastoral Letters. This is the claim of each of them in their opening words.

8. The Pastorals refer to heretical opponents. The Pastor portrays the Spirit in Paul's time as predicting the troubles of the church in the time of the Pastor, a time when there would be various claims to be led by the Spirit, and a spectrum of teachings claiming Paul's authority (1 Tim 4:1), a time when the church would need the discernment of faithful teachers in the Pauline tradition to guard the community from the errors of well-meaning insiders. The Pastor faces opponents who are not outsiders, but teachers in the church or former teachers who have left. It is difficult to characterize these opponents, since the Pastor does not enter into debate with them, but simply dismisses what they teach as "profane myths and old wives' tales" (1 Tim 4:7; see 4:1–2; 6:3–5, 20; 2 Tim 3:1–5; 4:3–4).

This itself is, of course, different from Paul. The few direct statements about the opposition indicate that they teach differently from Paul and are interested in speculative interpretations of myths and genealogies (1 Tim 1:4; 2 Tim 4:4; cf. Titus 1:14 "Jewish myths"; 3:9 "stupid controversies, genealogies, dissensions, and quarrels about the law"). At least some of them represent themselves as impressive teachers of the law (1 Tim 1:7). They advocate an ascetic understanding of Christian faith and life, "forbidding marriage and demanding abstinence from certain foods" (1 Tim 4:2–3). Some of them, at least, reject future eschatology, claiming that the resurrection is past already (2 Tim 2:18).

Some are "idle talkers and deceivers" who must be opposed, "especially those of the circumcision" (Titus 1:10). It is not clear whether Jews, Jewish Christians, or Gentile Christians infatuated with Jewish Scripture are here opposed. Since the internal debate over the admission of uncircumcised Gentiles to the church is not mentioned, this is apparently an issue of the past. Indirect inferences from the Pastor's own affirmations suggest that the opponents disdained the world, not acknowledging it as God's good creation (1 Tim 4:4), and rejected the drinking of wine (1 Tim 5:23). They persuaded women to embrace an ascetic life that rejected marriage and family and encouraged them to teach and preach, all in violation of respectable community standards (1 Tim 2:11–15).

The insistence on faith in the one God, and that there is only one mediator between God and humanity and that this mediator is Jesus, the truly human being, seems to point to the

6. "Beloved son/child" are found in the New Testament only in reference to God's commissioning of Jesus (Matt 3:17 and par.; 17:5 and par.), the authorized and commissioned "beloved son" in Jesus' parable (Mark 12:6 and par.), and in 1 Cor. 4:17, the Pastor's model for his address to Timothy and Titus. Speaking to the Corinthians, Paul writes, "For this reason I sent you Timothy, who is my beloved and faithful child in the Lord, to remind you of my ways in Christ Jesus, as I teach them everywhere in every church."

Gnostic systems involving complex series of mediators between the divine world and the human world. This might then mean that the rival teachers' "genealogies" refer to allegorical interpretations that point to the transcendent world, rather than the biblical figures represented by Old Testament genealogical tables. We do not know whether all these traits characterize a single group of opponents, or whether more than one group is intended. In any case, the opposition seems to reflect a later time than Paul and to have a different agenda.

9. Since F. C. Baur in 1835, a few scholars have seen 1 Timothy 6:20 as a direct reference to Marcion; "what is falsely called 'knowledge'" is Gnosticism; "contradictions" alludes to the title of Marcion's publication *Antitheses*. This is possible, but problematic for two reasons: (1) It would require a date for the Pastorals about the middle of the second century, which most scholars regard as too late (see below). (2) Marcion rejected the Jewish Bible, but (at least some of) the teachers the Pastor opposes claim to be teachers of the law and major in "genealogies" and "Jewish myths." It may be that some of the rival teachers developed speculative allegorical interpretations of the Old Testament (as did some Gnostics), while others rejected it altogether (as did Marcion). That the Pastor insists on the divine inspiration of the Old Testament and champions its continuing authority and importance in the church suggests that at least some of his opponents did not do so, and could point to Marcionite tendencies the Pastor opposes.

10. The Pastorals include references to church order and ecclesiastical offices. For Paul, the church is guided by the Holy Spirit resident in the body of Christ as a whole. The Pastor has only minimal reference to the Spirit (see below). Only once does the Holy Spirit play a role in the ministry of the church, and there the Spirit serves to keep the church on track by preserving the tradition that has been handed on through the church's ministers (2 Tim 1:14). Likewise, the charismatic gift of prophecy that generated and empowered ministry in Paul's day is still present, but related to the process of ordination. The Pastor sees the Spirit as working through channels, at work in the selection of candidates for ministry, conferred by the laying on of hands at ordination, and helping authentic ministers maintain the tradition they have received (1 Tim 1:18; 2 Tim 1:6, 14; cf. Acts 13:1–3).

The Pastorals thus presuppose both a different vision of church leadership and a different church structure than existed in Paul's day. Paul's own churches were not devoid of leaders and did not depend on purely spontaneous Spirit-led leadership (see 1 Thess 5:12–13; Phil 1:1; 1 Cor 12:28; 16:16; Rom 12:8; 16:1). Yet the understanding of church order in the Pastorals is consistently different from that of the undisputed letters. The prescriptions for ministers are not mandated in the form of a church manual (as, e.g., the *Didache* and *Apostolic Constitutions*), but in the letter form appropriate to the Pauline school tradition. The Pastor is not instituting a new structure, but seeking to regulate an existing structure, a structure that may not be accepted by all his readers. The duties and functions of elders and deacons are assumed as familiar; instructions regarding these offices deal only with the kind of persons Timothy and Titus should seek for them and have nothing to say about their responsibilities, functions, and relation to each other.

The letters reflect a period of transition, which is not taking place in all areas at the same pace. In 1 Timothy (Ephesus), the presbytery and diaconate are assumed, as offices that have been in place for some time. In the letter to Titus (Crete), elders do not yet exist in all churches but are to be appointed in every town. The Pastor lends the support of Paul's voice for the continued development of one kind of structure that was becoming dominant in at least one stream of the Pauline tradition. The designations of the offices themselves are not yet firmly fixed: "elder" can be interchangeable with "bishop/supervisor" and can refer to a specific office to which one can be appointed, as well as continuing to be used in its normal sense of an older person. At least some official elders are salaried; the Pastor argues for the financial support of local elders, using the same imagery and Scripture texts Paul had used to argue for the support of apostles and missionaries (cf. 1 Cor 9:7–14; 1 Tim 3:8; 5:17–18; 2 Tim 2:2–4; 1 Pet 5:2; Pol. *Phil.* 11.1).

The membership of the church can be described as consisting of "older" and "younger" (1 Tim 5:1–2), which can be understood in terms of age groups or/and official leaders and laypeople.[7] Likewise "deacon" can be used in both an official sense of a class of Christian ministers and in its generic sense of "servant, helper."[8] "Widow" refers not only to women whose husbands have died and who are dependent on the church for financial support, but a specific group of unmarried women who are "enrolled," who take a pledge not to (re)marry, who devote themselves to continual prayer and good works, and who are financially supported by the church treasury (1 Tim 5:3–16). This seems to be a preliminary stage of what became the later orders of nuns and religious sisters. All this represents a degree of institutionalization of church leadership we do not yet find in the undisputed letters of Paul.

Since the precise structure of church leadership is assumed rather than explicated, there is some variation in constructions of "the" church order presupposed by the Pastorals. Some constructions set forth a clear hierarchical order of the threefold ministry found in the letters of Ignatius and the later church, in which a local monarchial bishop presides over a council of presbyters (elders) and deacons, with an auxiliary order of widows and younger single women who have committed themselves to a celibate life in the service of the church. In this construction, there is a firm distinction between clergy and laity; church funds support the order of widows and the bishop and presbyters charged with teaching, preaching, and administration; and there is a single bishop who presides over presbyters and deacons in a particular city or area.[9] Other constructions point to the apparent interchangeability between the terms "elder" and "bishop" (Titus 1:5, 7; see Acts 20:17, 28) and the slight differences between 1 Timothy 3 and Titus 1, arguing that there was some variety, and that the system of having a single bishop in charge of the congregations in a city or district was not yet (fully) established.

Modern interpreters should be wary of supposing that the churches in the Pastor's time had developed a single structure that was entirely uniform and rigid. Likewise, a consistently diachronic approach is questionable, as though the Pastorals, *1 Clement*, and Ignatius could be located at various points along a single developmental line between Paul and the emerging catholic church of the late second century.

The role of Timothy and Titus in this developing structure is also unclear. Since they choose and ordain bishops, presbyters, and deacons, and can hear charges against them (1 Tim 5:19–25; Titus 1:5), they seem to represent an office higher even than the bishop. This line of thinking would make Timothy and Titus archbishops, with the Pastor himself the "Pope" of the Pauline churches. This undoubtedly takes the imagery too far. In the fictive world projected by the letters, Timothy and Titus, like

7. So also in 1 Pet 5:1–5; 1 John 2:1–12; Luke 22:26. This reflects the LXX's embracing the whole community in the two groups/classes of πρεσβύτεροι/νεανίσκοι (*presbuteroi/neaniskoi*, elders/younger; cf. Gen 19:4; Exod 10:9; 2 Chr 36:17; Jdt 6:16; 1 Macc 1:26; Joel 2:28; Ezek 9:6). See Paul R. Trebilco, *The Early Christians in Ephesus from Paul to Ignatius*, WUNT 166 (Tübingen: Mohr Siebeck, 2004), 530. Or: two groups of leaders, "senior" (elders) and "junior" (deacons, etc.). Cf. current American use of "senior minister" of a young person, "associate minister" even if older. Cf. Pervo, *Dating* 211: ὁ νεώτερος, *ho neōteros* refers to "junior functionaries; its antonym is presbyter," referring to Heb 13:7, 17; *1 Clem.* 1.3.

8. See the clearly documented explication in Trebilco, *Ephesus*, 447–73.

9. Cf., among others, Fred D. Gealy, "Introduction to 1 and 2 Timothy and Titus," in *The Interpreter's Bible*, ed. George Arthur Buttrick (Nashville: Abingdon Press, 1957), 345–50; 407–18; Schnelle, *Theology of the New Testament*, 597–600.

Paul himself, are prototypes for ministers at all levels, as they are models for believers and do not correspond to any superior office in the real world of the churches to which the Pastorals are addressed. The role of Paul is filled by the author of the Pastorals, representing one stream of the Pauline school tradition that is the real authority mediating (its understanding of) the apostolic faith to the third generation Pauline churches of Asia.

Whatever the exact structure of the congregations addressed by the Pastoral Letters was (and there was apparently still some variety), it was different from that of Paul's day. Paul depended on charismatic leadership in his churches, with informal rather than institutionalized leadership. Paul has no firm structure or officers in the Corinthian church to which to appeal during the troubles he is dealing with in 1 and 2 Corinthians. The church is guided by the Spirit, who works through a variety of gifts; prophets and teachers are inspired by the Spirit, and the congregation as a whole must discern the will of God (1 Cor 12–14). Paul's letters indicate no awareness of ordination or the office of πρεσβύτερος (*presbyteros*, presbyter/elder) that is central in the Pastorals. In Paul, the term διάκονος (*diakonos*, deacon/servant/minister) is a generic term for service used in a variety of senses, and is beginning to be used in a specific sense of people who have a ministerial role, but is not yet used for a particular office. In Philippians 1:1 Paul refers to "overseers" and "helpers," with no indication that they represent specific ministerial offices present in the church as a whole. The Pastorals thus fit best into the third phase of the movement begun during Paul's Aegean mission in the first third of the second century CE (see below §16.1.3).

11. The Pastor's perspective on women's role in the church reflects the period after Paul. Paul had taught the essential equality of women and men in the community of faith (Gal 3:27–28), had women coworkers and partners in ministry who were leaders in the church (Rom 16:1, 3, 7; Phil 4:2–3), and affirmed their liturgical, preaching and teaching activities (1 Cor 11:5; 16:19). The one text in the undisputed letters that restricts women's leadership roles is probably an interpolation (see above on 1 Cor 14:34–35). The Pastor, however, has a very different view—and a reactionary one—apparently in response to what he regarded as unwholesome and dangerous developments in the Pauline churches of his own time. He presupposes that presbyter/bishops will be married men who are the heads of households (1 Tim 3:1–7; Titus 1:5–9). He gives instructions for the worship service, in which men are to pray and women are to keep silent, with a theological rationale based on the order of creation and the differing roles of Adam and Eve in their response to Satan the deceiver (1 Tim 2:1–15).

In particular, women are forbidden to teach. These instructions would hardly have been given unless women were in fact participating in worship and teaching in some capacity. The Pastor instructs male teachers to pass on the tradition to other men (the NRSV's interest in inclusive language at 2 Tim 2:2 is misleading; the author intends the church's teachers to be "men," not "people"). The group of widows has grown too large and influential, and the Pastor seeks both to reduce the number of women enrolled and to minimize their influence (1 Tim 5:3–16).

All this seems to reflect a situation in which women are already teaching, already serving as deacons (1 Tim 3:11),[10] and have been attracted to the false doctrine opposed by the Pastor. The heretical group who "forbid marriage" (1 Tim 4:3) may have seen themselves standing in the authentic Pauline tradition, and offered widows and unmarried women the opportunity to devote themselves to preaching and teaching in

10. The meaning of the reference to "the women" in 1 Tim 3:11 is disputed (see NRSV footnote), but in this context it seems clearly to refer to an office, which has qualifications comparable to that of men deacons. Paul already knew of women deacons (Rom 16:1), and the Pastor's contemporary, Pliny, the governor of Bithynia, referred to two Christian slave women "whom they call deacons" he had arrested and tortured in order to gain information about the Christians (*Epistle* 10.96).

a way that seemed dangerous to the Pastor. They did not (re)marry, were not under the authority of a husband or paterfamilias, were supported by the church treasury (like the presbyters engaged in preaching and teaching, 1 Tim 5:17–18), and in their teaching in the various house churches seemed to the Pastor to be both spreading false doctrine and bringing the church into social disrepute. The Pastor considers their "teaching" to be only "gadding about from house to house," a matter of "gossip" and "saying what they should not say," of a piece with the "profane myths," and "old wives' tales" of the false teachers who have been deceived and have deceived these women (1 Tim 4:7; 5:13). Part of his strategy to curtail the heretical teaching is to restrict the role of women to that of wives and homemakers. Both the situation presupposed and the Pastor's response to it represent a different time, theology, and voice than Paul's own.[11]

12. The pseudepigraphical stance of the letters is seen in their dual temporal perspective. On the one hand, the letters represent themselves as from the time of Paul, reflecting his own circumstances, associates, and concerns. Paul refers incidentally to events and persons that are part of the fictive world of the letters but in the past of the actual readers. This is a conventional feature of the pseudepigraphical genre and is not the "clumsy" efforts of a "forger" to "imitate" Paul's own time and to "deceive" the readership.

On the other hand, from within this fictive framework, Paul is pictured as predicting a later time, which is the present time of the actual readership (1 Tim 4:1–5; 2 Tim 3:1–6; 4:3–4). These predictions of "later" heresy are analogous to the scene of Acts 20:29–35, in which Paul's own time was free of false teaching within the church, with opposition only from outsiders, but after his death false teachers are predicted to appear even within the church and its presbytery. This stance of predicting the readers' present from the assumed past standpoint modulates into present address, as the fictive wall separating Paul's time from that of the readers evaporates, and the voice of Paul from the past speaks directly to the readers' concerns of the present. This is in fact the stance assumed in most of the content of the letters, as, for example, Paul gives directions for the appointment of elders, deacons, and widows (1 Tim 3:1–13; 5:3–16) and encouragement for a church under stress (2 Tim 1:8–14; 3:10–12).

13. The Pastorals understand themselves to supplement Pauline letters already in circulation. They do not make this explicit, as in 2 Thess 3:17, but the author knows the Pauline corpus and assumes his readers know it and will recognize allusions to it (e.g., 1 Tim 2:7 echoes Gal 1:20).[12]

14. The assumed original setting of the letters and the process by which they were collected and included in the canon point to a pseudepigraphical origin. The letters presuppose that they will be read aloud to the churches, who are to hear them and take them seriously. How did this happen? On the traditional view, one must imagine that personal letters were received by Timothy and Titus, on separate occasions. They presumably received them and kept them in their personal belongings, until they finally made their way into the general life of the church and then into the New Testament canon—the only personal letters to do so. The pseudepigraphical explanation is more natural. It argues they are in the *form* of personal letters but were written from the beginning to be circulated along with the growing corpus of Pauline letters, and were

11. In the Pastor's time, it was presupposed as a matter of general decorum that women should be silent in public assemblies, a cultural norm supported by statements of philosophers such as Democritus, Sophocles, and Aristotle (*Pol.* 1.13 [1260a.30]). The Pastor reasserts the conventions of contemporary society that had been challenged by Paul and his coworkers, but which he now regards as being abused and subjecting the church to the inroads of heresy.

12. Cf. further data in Andreas Lindemann, *Paulus im ältesten Christentum: Das Bild des Apostels und die Rezeption der paulinischen Theologie in der frühchristlichen Literatur bis Marcion*, Beiträge zur historischen Theologie 58 (Tübingen: Mohr, 1979), 134–49.

directed to the churches, not just the individuals Timothy and Titus. The third-generation readers are accustomed to reading *all* the Pauline letters as "not written to us" but hearing them as communicating a normative message "to us." They were never private letters that had to find their way into the church's public reading of Scripture, but were written to be read that way from the beginning.

15. The Pastorals reflect and interact with later New Testament movements and literature current after Paul's time. After the war of 66–70 CE, the Johannine stream of tradition was centered in Ephesus (see below §25.3.2). There were personal and literary interactions between the two traditions. The Pastorals were influenced by the issues, concerns, and conflicts alive in the Johannine traditions, reflecting and adopting some of their vocabulary and conceptuality. Such phrases as ἦλθεν εἰς τὸν κόσμον (*ēlthen eis ton kosmon*, he came into the world, 1 Tim 1:15) are not found in Paul but occur nine times in the Fourth Gospel and once in 2 John 10. The combination of water, Spirit, and new birth in Titus 3:5 is not found in Paul but has its closest parallel in John 3:3–5. The doxology of 1 Timothy 6:15 is closer to the hymns of Revelation than to the doxologies in Paul.[13]

16. The style and vocabulary of the Pastorals point to a post-Pauline setting. College and seminary students learning to read the New Testament in Greek can confirm that after one has become quite proficient at reading the letters of Paul, reading the Pastorals presents an entirely new challenge, because of their different vocabulary and style. Paul's is an oral style, lively, with anacolutha, digressions, and parentheses. The Pastorals represent a composed, written style which flows smoothly, with longer sentences than the Paul of the undisputed letters. Paul *argues*, using diatribe, deduction, interpretation of biblical texts, entering into a dialogue with his readers, debating and pleading with them. The Pastor has a somewhat ponderous, lecturing style that tends toward pronouncements, not only different from the Paul of the undisputed letters but particularly problematic in purported letters to close colleagues.

Some typical grammatical and syntactical features of Paul's style are missing from the Pastorals. For example, Paul uses the editorial "we" fairly often, saying "we" and using the first-person plural form of the verb, when he clearly means "I" (e.g., Rom 1:5; 1 Cor 9:11–12; 2 Cor 10:11, 13). This usage is never found in the Pastorals, though the plurality of the Pauline school stands behind them.

The Pastor's vocabulary is strikingly different from Paul's. This contrast is not merely a matter of impression but has been worked out precisely.[14] The Pastorals contain a total of 3,484 words, composed of a vocabulary of 902 different words, 54 of which are proper names. Of these 902 words, 175 do not occur elsewhere in the New Testament. More importantly, 335 are not found in the undisputed Pauline letters. If Colossians, Ephesians, and 2 Thessalonians are regarded as Pauline, the Pastorals still contain 306 distinctive words. Thus about one-third of the vocabulary of the Pastorals is composed of words Paul never used in any of the other letters in the Pauline tradition. On the other hand, only 50 words are shared exclusively by the undisputed letters and the Pastorals—a very small number, considering that the author was an admirer and exponent of Paul who knew and had internalized much of the Pauline corpus.

Some of the words peculiar to the Pastorals are central to his thought, illustrating the differences between them and the undisputed letters:

— "Sound" (describing doctrine, words, or faith; ὑγιαίνω, *hygiainō* or ὑγιής, *hygiēs* [healthy; the Greek word is related to English "hygiene"])

13. For an extensive discussion of such literary contacts, see Trebilco, *Ephesus*, 351–627. The numerous contacts with Paul's letters, but lack of contacts with Hebrews, suggests that Hebrews was not circulating in the circles in which the Pastorals originated.

14. The classic work is that of Harrison, *Problem*, recently reprinted.

occurs nine times in the Pastorals as a fundamental concept, never in the undisputed letters.

— The "deposit" of faith that is to be preserved is likewise fundamental to the Pastor's thought. Παραθήκη (*parathēkē, depositum* in the Vulgate) occurs three times, each time in combination with φυλάσσω (*phylassō,* guard, keep). The term is never used by Paul. On the other hand, Paul's own words for tradition and its transmission are not found in the Pastorals (παραδίδωμι, *paradidōmi*; παράδοσις, *paradōsis*). The author defines the meaning in 2 Timothy 2:2: "what you have heard from me in the presence of many witnesses entrust to reliable men who will be qualified to teach others as well" (my trans.).

— Διδασκαλία (*didaskalia,* teaching) is one of the author's favorite terms, occurring fifteen times. The rest of the New Testament has only six occurrences, only two of which are in Paul.

— Σωτήρ (*sōtēr,* savior) is used by Paul only once (Phil 3:20), contextually appropriate as he addresses the church in a Roman colony where the title was often applied to Caesar. "Savior" has become a standard title in the Pastorals, where it is found ten times. Six of these are in the phrase "God our Savior," never found in Paul.

— Ἐπιφανεία (*epiphaneia,* epiphany), absent from the undisputed letters of Paul, occurs six times in the Pastorals as the key summary term for the Christ event, denoting both the incarnation and parousia.

— Εὐσέβεια (*eusebeia,* piety, godliness, authentic religion) was widely used in the Hellenistic world to express the virtue of respect for the gods and their gift of an orderly world, including "law and order" and "family values." Εὐσέβεια and its cognate εὐσεβής (*eusebēs,* devout, pious) are found thirteen times in the Pastorals expressing the core meaning of the Christian life. They occur nine times in the later New Testament literature (four times in Acts; five times in 2 Peter) but not at all in the undisputed letters of Paul.

— Εὐαγγελιστής (*euangelistēs,* evangelist) and πρεσβύτερος (*presbyteros,* presbyter; elder) are terms for church leaders not used by Paul, but used in the later Pauline tradition, and found as key terms six times in the Pastorals.

— Πιστὸς ὁ λόγος (*pistos ho logos,* the saying is sure) is found five times in the Pastorals as a key concept, but never in Paul.

On the other hand, some typical Pauline words are rare, entirely missing, or used in a different sense in the Pastorals:

— Πνεῦμα (*pneuma,* spirit) is used eighty times in Paul, but only three times of the Holy Spirit in the Pastorals, each time in quotations or traditional material. There were tensions within the Pauline school about the value of the continued use of Paul's language of the Spirit, which was subject to misunderstanding in the Gentile churches. The Pastor sides with the author of Colossians in minimizing this language that had been important to Paul, while other teachers in the Pauline school (e.g., the author of Ephesians) amplified Spirit terminology (see above, §15.2.1).

— Ἐν Χριστῷ (*en Christō,* in Christ) is absent in Paul's sense (ninety-eight times in the undisputed letters of Paul, including "in him," etc.; repeatedly in every letter, including six times in Philemon; see above, §13.3.2). Paul's exact phrase "in Christ" is never found in the Pastorals, nor is "in whom" or "in him." "In Christ Jesus" is found six times in 1 Timothy and three times in 2 Timothy, but never in the Pauline sense of incorporation in the body of Christ, and not at all in Titus.

— Σῶμα Χριστοῦ (*sōma Christou,* body of Christ) concept and terminology is completely absent from the Pastorals.

— Ἀδελφός, ἀδελφή (*adelphos, adelphē,* brother, sister) is used 112 times by Paul as an insider term for fellow believers, many of them as direct address to his readers, five times in the one-page letter to Philemon. The Pastor uses the term only five times in three letters, never in direct address, though the letters are purportedly written to close friends and coworkers.

— Δικαιοσύνη θεοῦ (*dikaiosunē theou*, righteousness of/from God), nine times in Paul as a fundamental concept, is completely absent from the Pastorals.

— Υἱός (*huios*, son) is found eighty times in the undisputed letters of Paul, mostly in a theological sense as a christological title or as a designation for Israel or Christians. The Pastor never uses "son," even in the nontheological sense, but always τέκνον (*teknon*, child).

— Ἐν ἐσχάταις ἡμέραις (*en eschatais hēmerais*, in the last days, 2 Tim 3:1) is a phrase never used in the undisputed letters, even though Paul believed he was living in the eschatological times. Similar phrases are found in the later New Testament literature (e.g., Jas 5:3; 1 Pet 1:5; 2 Pet 2:20; 3:3; 1 John 2:18; Jude 18). Such vocabulary links the Pastorals more closely to the literature of the third generation than to Paul.

— After 1 Thessalonians, Paul's earliest extant letter, his standard greeting is χάρις ὑμῖν καὶ εἰρήνη ἀπὸ θεοῦ πατρὸς ἡμῶν καὶ κυρίου Ἰησοῦ Χριστοῦ (*charis humin kai eirēnē apo theou patros hēmōn kai kyriou Iēsou Christou*, Grace to you and peace from God our Father and the Lord Jesus Christ). This greeting became Paul's trademark, unvarying in all his letters, not found anywhere except in Paul and authors dependent on him (see §10.2.3). In each of his letters, the Pastor adopts this greeting, but consistently with minor changes: "Grace, mercy, and peace from God the Father and Christ Jesus our Lord/Savior." He makes three modifications not found in any of the undisputed letters: he omits "to you" (which would have to be either singular or plural, and neither fits his purpose), he adds ἔλεος (*eleos*, mercy), in line with more Hellenistic-Jewish letter greetings, and he changes "the Lord Jesus Christ" to "Christ Jesus our Lord/Savior." This combination is consistently found in all three Pastorals, never in the undisputed letters.

— Paul's standard εὐχαριστέω (*eucharisteō*, I give thanks) is missing, replaced by χάριν ἔχω (*charin echo*, literally "I have gratitude"="I am grateful"; elsewhere in the New Testament only Luke 17:9; Heb 12:28).

— The contrast between Paul and the Pastor includes not only substantial theological terms and phrases but the way they use common *particles*, words that have no substance but function merely to connect elements in the sentence. A number of such particles found in Paul—ἄρα (*ara* twenty-seven times), διό (*dio* twenty-two times), ἐπεί (*epei*, ten times), ὅπως (*hopōs*, eight times), πάλιν (*palin* twenty-eight times), τε (*te* twenty-four times) and the *prepositions* ἀντί (*anti* three times) ἔμπροσθεν (*emprosthen* seven times), σύν (*sun* thirty times) are *absent* from the Pastorals. Paul's word for "with" (σύν *sun*) regularly becomes μετά (*meta*); there is no difference in meaning, only in vocabulary. Some of Paul's commonly used connectives are *rare* in the Pastorals: μέν (*men* 55/3), δέ (*de* 538/62), οὖν (*oun* 91/7).

These considerations provide substantial reasons for the view that the Pastorals are post-Paul compositions emanating from the Pauline school. This view finds incidental support from the date, attestation, canonicity, text, structure, and especially from the theology of the Pastoral Letters.

16.1.3 Date, Attestation, Canonicity

None of the Pastorals is reflected in any other New Testament books.[15] This is particularly

15. The usage of "God and Savior Jesus Christ" in 2 Pet. 1:1 may reflect Titus 2:13; 2 Tim. 1:10. If so, the Pastorals are reflected in the latest New Testament writing, perhaps as late as the middle of the second century CE. Or both the Pastorals and 2 Peter may independently reflect that such christological language was beginning to be used in the third Christian generation.

striking in the case of Ephesians, which reflects virtually all the other Pauline letters. Likewise, the reflections of Paul's writings in 1 Peter and *1 Clement* document that a collection of Paul's writings was circulating in Rome around the end of the first century CE, a collection that did not include the Pastorals. The first positive allusions to and citations of the Pastorals are in the writings of Athenagoras, Theophilus, and Irenaeus (ca. 180 CE). There are possible, but disputed allusions to the Pastorals in Polycarp's *Letter to the Philippians* (ca. 120–135 CE; Pol. *Phil.* 4.1, 9.2=1 Tim 6:7, 10; Pol. *Phil.* 9.2=2 Tim 4:10). If Polycarp knew the Pastorals, this would mean they were circulating in at least one collection of Paul's letters in Asia Minor about 130. The Pastorals are absent from Marcion's canon, formulated about the middle of second century. Since later Marcionites accepted the Pastorals, there was no explicit prohibition from Marcion against accepting them. This would mean that Marcion did not know them, rather than that he knew them but did not consider them Pauline—but the issue is debated. According to Jerome, Tatian (d. ca. 170 CE) accepted Titus, but rejected 1 and 2 Timothy. The Pastorals are included in the Muratorian Canon (probably ca. 200 in Rome, see above §2.2.1). In a list otherwise arranged from longest to shortest, the Pastorals follow Philemon, which may indicate they were added to a list already complete. These data mean the Pastorals must have been written by 170 CE at the latest, by 130 if Polycarp knew them. The earliest physical evidence of their existence is provided by papyrus fragments from about 200 CE. Other manuscripts from the same period do not contain them.

The problems the author deals with seem to be characteristic of third-generation Christianity. The Pastor's response to these problems likewise presupposes that not only is Paul no longer present; his direct associates are also gone, and the church is dependent on Pauline traditions that can no longer be validated by people who had known Paul personally—hence the dispute about who is the heir of the authentic tradition. The third generation would also fit the description of Timothy as a third-generation believer (2 Tim 1:5), and the chain of tradition presupposed in 2 Timothy 2:2. The Pastor lives in the third phase after Paul and Timothy, representing those Christian teachers who received the deposit of faith from the "Timothies" of the second generation. The beginning of the third generation could be thought of as about 100 CE. If the Pastorals are regarded as opposing Marcionism, even in its earlier phases, prior to the actual publication of Marcion's work, they must be dated at least twenty-five years later. This is not impossible, but most scholars consider it unlikely. The most popular date among critical scholars is about 100 CE.

16.1.4 Provenance

The Pastorals are saturated with place names of Asia Minor, reflect the geography accurately, and have little to say about any other region. Two letters are addressed to Timothy, who came from Lystra, was acquainted with Iconium, and worked with Paul in Phrygia, Galatia, and provincial Asia (Acts 16:1–11). First Timothy 1:3 portrays Paul as leaving Timothy temporarily in charge of the church at Ephesus, which is also referred to in 2 Timothy 1:18. There are further references to Pisidian Antioch, Iconium, and Lystra (2 Tim 3:11), to Galatia, Ephesus, Troas, and Miletus (2 Tim 4:10–13, 20). Noticeable similarities exist between the Pastorals and the letter of Polycarp, bishop of Smyrna, to the Philippians, which at least suggest a common milieu. In the post-Pauline period, Ephesus would be the most likely candidate as the location where the Pauline tradition was nourished and the Pastoral letters were composed.

16.1.5 Theology of the Pastoral Letters: Continuity and Change

The Pastorals are not a new beginning or an alternative to Paul—this is what they *oppose*. Many items in the Pastorals are in continuity with Paul.[16] The letter form encourages a reading of the Pastorals in continuity with the authentic letters, with which they circulated. They were not intended to displace the "real" Paul, but to let him speak in a new situation. The Pastorals were composed by Paul's disciples, who *also* gathered, edited, and circulated the authentic letters, by Christian teachers who wanted to preserve Paul and present him as teacher to the whole church (see 1 Cor 4:16–17).

Nonetheless, the Pastorals do not simply repeat Paul but present him as adapting his theology to the post-Pauline situation. In addition to themes mentioned incidentally above, some other theological aspects of the Pastorals distinguish them from Paul's own theology.

Shift of Emphasis from Faith to "the" Faith

The Pastor reaffirms and continues the main lines of Paul's theology, familiar to him from tradition and the corpus of Pauline writings that is already in circulation. In the Pastor's setting, the essential elements of Paul's theology are being congealed into a compact body of material, the "mystery of our religion" (1 Tim 3:16) or the "plan of God" (1 Tim 1:4 NAB; cf. "God's plan," REB, NJB). Paul had indicated he had been entrusted with a commission from God (1 Cor 9:17, οἰκονομία, *oikonomia*). On this basis, the Pauline school formulated the phrase "plan of God" as a summary term for the essential elements of Pauline theology. The phrase is found only in the deuteropauline letters (Col 1:25; Eph 1:10; 3:1–3, 9 [equated with μυστήριον, mystery]; 1 Tim 1:4; cf. Ign. *Eph* 20.1). This summary had not yet become a firm list of the items of the faith, as in the later creeds, but was beginning to serve the same purpose: a concise statement to guide the faithful in the battle against perversions of the faith. The summary statements in the Pastorals make its outline clear (Titus 1:1–4; 2:11–15; 3:4–7; see Eph 1:9–10):

- There is one God, the Creator. The world is God's good creation.
- All humanity is sinful and in need of salvation, as illustrated in the story of Adam and Eve.
- God's saving history continued through the biblical people of God (Moses, David, inspiring all Scripture).
- Human beings cannot save themselves by doing good works.
- God sent Jesus Christ as the Savior from sin. The appearance of Jesus Christ in history is the center and core of the Pastor's theology.
- God established the church as the community of the saved, who are to manifest the saving act of God before the world by teaching and living in such a way that the faith is not brought into disrepute. Love is the goal of authentic faith (1 Tim 1:5).
- Christ will appear at the end of history to complete God's saving work for all people.

Over against the "speculations" of his opponents who are taking Pauline theology in a different direction, the Pastor solidifies Pauline traditions around this sound core, and urges that it be maintained and handed on. This involves a particular hierarchical "chain of command" in which Paul himself plays a crucial role. The sound doctrine originates with God/Jesus Christ our Savior.[17] This core teaching is revealed to Paul and entrusted to him; Paul then transmits these faithful words about the Christ event to Timothy and Titus, who are to pass it on to

16. See the impressive list in Johnson, *Timothy*, 81.

17. The Pastor uses "Savior" of both God and Christ. The images of God and the transcendent Christ tend to blend into each other, so that even God-language can be used of Christ (1 Tim. 1:1; Titus 1:4; 2:13). This was also happening in the contemporary and neighboring Johannine school in Asia (John 1:1; 20:28; 1 John 5:20–21), and in Ignatius's letters to the Asian churches.

faithful teachers in the Pauline schools who will teach others (2 Tim 2:2; Titus 1:1–4). In this revelatory chain, Paul plays an indispensable role; his apostolic mission is incorporated into the Christ event as part of God's saving act. The Pastor's theological perspective here continues Paul's own emphasis on the legitimacy of his apostleship, but narrows the focus such that the apostolic function is exercised by Paul alone. In so doing, the Pastor maintains the Pauline paradigm of salvation history in which the content of the earthly life and teaching of Jesus plays a minimal role.

That Jesus Christ appeared in history, and will appear again at the end of history as savior, is central to his Christology. Both appearances are embraced in the key word ἐπιφανεία (*epiphaneia*, epiphany, see above). The Christ event is this divine epiphany in the human Jesus who has appeared in history, who died as a ransom for all, who was raised from the dead by God, and who will complete his saving work at the end of history. The Pastor is aware of sayings of Jesus, which he may even cite as "Scripture," but, like Paul, bases his theology on the cosmic narrative rather than telling stories about the earthly Jesus.[18]

The Pastor agrees with Paul that the goal of all theological instruction is not pure doctrine itself, but love (1 Tim 1:5); he does not ground this in the Scripture or sayings of Jesus, but in the Christ event as such. The ethic generated by this faith is elaborated not by examples or sayings from the life of Jesus, but in terms of the moral ideals of the Hellenistic world. Like Paul, it is crucial for him that there was an actual incarnation, but he provides no content to the "life and teaching of Jesus." As in other branches of the Pauline school (see, e.g., on Col 1:24 above), it is in fact the life and death of Paul that exemplifies the meaning of the Christian faith and provides the model for the Christian life.

Faith and the *faith.* The Pastor repeatedly refers to this core teaching as *the* faith, in the sense of *fides quae creditur,* the content of faith that is believed (see above on 2 Thess, §15.3.2). "Faith" is "the truth," what the faithful are to believe. Paul too had occasionally used "faith" in this sense (2 Cor 1:24; 13:5; Gal 1:23; Phil 1:27). For Paul too faith had content, but the overwhelming majority of Paul's ninety-one instances of πίστις (*pistis* faith) refer to *fides qua creditur,* the personal faith with which one believes, one's obedient trust in God. This is true even of the forty-one instances where Paul uses πίστις with the article. For the Pastor, a major shift of emphasis has taken place. Paul's statements about faith were in the context of debates about the role of the law in the saving event. For the Pastor, these debates are in the distant past, so that his contrast is not between "faith" and "works of the law" but between "the faith" and "false doctrine." Thus virtually all of the thirteen instances of "the faith" refer to the body of orthodox doctrine (e.g., 1 Tim 1:19; 4:1, 6; 6:10; 2 Tim 2:18; Titus 1:13).

James Denney's often-cited quip has become proverbial: "Paul was inspired; the writer of these epistles is sometimes only orthodox."[19] The proverb is only partially true. To be sure, the Pastor is not the creative genius of Christian theology in the first generation, but neither is he merely the conservative institutionalizer in the second or third. His reinterpretation of the Pauline gospel for a later time required a depth of theological thinking that cannot be easily

18. There are indications that by the Pastor's time there are Christian groups that cite sayings and stories from the life of Jesus as authority (1 Tim. 5:18 cites a saying of Jesus found in Luke 10:7/Matt 10:10). The contemporary Johannine community in Asia Minor, with whom the Pastor has contacts, is using the Jesus tradition in this way (cf. Trebilco, *Ephesus*, 351–403). But the Pastor does not see the Christian faith as essentially a matter of following the teaching of the historical Jesus. The "sound words of our Lord Jesus Christ" (1 Tim. 6:3) is equated with "the teaching that is in accordance with godliness," i.e., the "sound words" are the church's traditional kerygma about the Christ event, not the sayings of the historical Jesus (see 93–99; 154–55).

19. James Denney, *The Death of Christ: Its Place and Interpretation in the New Testament* (London: Hodder & Stoughton, 1909), 203.

dismissed. Even his conservative moves, rightly problematic and objectionable to modern sensibilities, can be seen in positive terms in his own situation. The Pastor protects the developing Christian community from radical distortions, but does not present merely the domesticated or diluted too-radical Paul. Seen against the background of the second-century heresies, the Pastorals cease to be prosaic orthodoxy and become a dynamic reassertion of the Christian faith, rescuing Paul from abuse at the hands of the heretics and allowing the church to carry out its mission in an ongoing hostile world.

In preserving the essential core of Pauline theology and reinterpreting it for a later generation, the Pastor develops several points that are distinctly different from Paul's own theology, including the following examples.

Spirits, Angels, and the Holy Spirit

For Paul, the Holy Spirit was the divine reality that guided and enlivened the church, and a key term in his theology and vocabulary. The Pastor too affirms the Spirit of God as empowering the church and guiding its life, but expresses this differently than Paul. He is speaks of the Spirit cautiously, referring to the Holy Spirit only five times in three letters (vs. more than ninety times in Paul's seven letters). The Spirit was at work in the time of Israel, inspiring the Scriptures (2 Tim 3:16), in the incarnation and exaltation of Jesus (1 Tim 3:16), in the life and work of Paul (predicting the "later times" in which the Pastor lives, 1 Tim 4:1), and in the lives of all believers (2 Tim 2:14; Titus 3:5). Yet the Pastor is wary of claims of direct prophetic inspiration and special charismatic gifts in his own time, and tends to bind the working of the Spirit in the life of the church closely to the ministerial office (see above and 1 Tim 4:14; 2 Tim 1:6–7, 14). This difference from Paul appears incidentally even in relatively minor points. For some early Christian teachers, "Spirit" and "angel" were related or identical figures (e.g., Acts 7:51–53; 8:26–29; 10:7, 19; 23:8; Heb 1:7, 13–14; Rev 1:1, 4; 2:7, 11, 17, 29; 3:1, 6, 13, 22). Paul, however, never had a good word to say about angels. He thought of them only in negative terms, as those intermediate beings between heaven and earth who were hostile to God's purposes and who could appear as demonic spirits leading the church astray (Rom 8:38; 1 Cor 4:9; 6:3; 11:10; 2 Cor 11:14; 12:7; Gal 1:8). In contrast to Paul, the Pastor speaks easily and positively of angels (1 Tim 3:16; 5:21), as did some other members of the Pauline school (2 Thess 1:7).

How Does the Holy Spirit Guide the Church?

Paul's metaphor of the church as the body of Christ enlivened by the divine *pneuma* is replaced with the image of the "household of God," understood in terms of the Greco-Roman family in which women, children, and slaves have their appointed place, governed by the paterfamilias. As such, the church is the "pillar and ground of the truth" (1 Tim 3:15). In equipping the church for its struggle with false teaching, the Pastor sees the church as grounded in three interrelated foundational elements: canon, clergy, and creed.[20]

Canon. Paul had assumed that the Jewish Scriptures continued in the church as divine authority, with the Christ event as the hermeneutical key to their meaning (see above §§9.2.2, 11.1.1). In this regard, the Pastor finds that he must fight on two fronts. On the one hand, the false teachers want to be "teachers of the Law," apparently basing their doctrine on allegorizing interpretations that support their speculative mythologies. On the other hand, some apparently want to discard the Jewish Scriptures

20. It is, of course, anachronistic to use these later terms for the Pastor's own time. They are used here to symbolically indicate that these standard aspects of later church life in maintaining itself in its journey through history are developments from the strategy delineated by the Pastor. I am not suggesting that a rigid canon, a firmly institutionalized order of ministry, and uniform, verbally fixed creeds existed in the Pastor's time.

altogether.[21] Over against both views, the Pastor develops a doctrine of Scripture, (re)claiming the Jewish Scriptures as Christian canon. While Paul had simply assumed biblical authority, the Pastor insists on it, cites from it and alludes to it as authority, and instructs Christian teachers to occupy themselves with it (e.g., 1 Tim 2:13–15; 5:18–19; 2 Tim 2:15; 3:14–17; Titus 2:14). When the Pastor pictures Paul, in the waning moments of his life, asking Timothy to bring "the books, and above all the parchments" (2 Tim 4:13), he is not referring to Homer or Plato. The Pastor makes explicit that the Christian faith cannot be understood by beginning with Jesus and ignoring the Jewish Scriptures, but only within a community that includes the Jewish Scriptures in the Christian Bible.

Clergy. The Pastor is interested in promoting and furthering the development of established orders of ministry as a means of guaranteeing the transmission of the core Pauline tradition (see above).

Creed. Firm traditional summary statements of the faith circulated in the Pauline churches. This is indicated not only by the five "Faithful Sayings" (1 Tim 1:15; 3:1; 4:9; 2 Tim 2:11; Titus 3:8) but by the emphasis on handing on the "deposit of faith" (1 Tim 1:18; 6:20; 2 Tim 1:12, 14; 2:2) and by elements of several fixed traditional units (1 Tim 1:5–6; 3:16; 6:7–8; 6:11–12, 15–16; 2 Tim 1:9–10; 2:11–13; Titus 3:4–7).

The Pastor thus has a threefold arsenal in his fight against heresy. These three components work interactively. The authentic faith cannot be identified or defended by appealing to the Bible alone, or to tradition alone, or to the church hierarchy. The Bible and the creeds must be interpreted by authorized teachers; the teachers cannot merely speak on their own but must interpret Bible and tradition. Neither Bible nor tradition exists independently of each other. This dynamic, three-sided dialectic of canon, creed, and clergy cannot be reduced to a single, once-and-for-all source of authority, but as the church moves through history, the Holy Spirit works within the church through Scripture, tradition, and authorized ministry to keep the church on course. This is the Pastor's faith and his contribution to the later church.

Eschatology

As in other branches of the post-Pauline tradition, Paul's expectation of the imminent parousia is abandoned by the Pastor. Eschatology no longer determines crucial decisions about lifestyle, such as engagement, marriage, and family (cf. 1 Cor 7:25–29, 32–34 with 1 Tim 5:11, 14). There is no indication, however, that the delay of the parousia had become a theological problem for him or his readers. Belief in the future parousia itself is not discarded. The final epiphany of Christ is affirmed, but postponed to the indefinite future, to a time that God has predetermined but not revealed (1 Tim 6:14–15). On the other hand, spiritualizing the future hope and reducing it to the idea that "the resurrection has already occurred" is to be rejected as false teaching (2 Tim 2:18). The Pastor disagrees with other teachers in the Pauline school who are more favorably inclined toward realized eschatology, including the authors of Colossians and Ephesians—though neither of them completely abandons the future hope.

Ethics and the Christian Life

The Pastor's understanding of ethics, Christian freedom and responsibility has a different emphasis and perspective from that of Paul. In 1 Corinthians 8–10 and Romans 14, for example, Paul had dealt with the scruples of "weak" Christians in a pastoral manner that encouraged the "strong" Christians to adjust their behavior to the convictions of their "weak" brothers and sisters. The "strong" are encouraged to give up meat and wine if their freedom becomes a stumbling block to those with a different conscience. So also Paul, who affirmed marriage and family as such, had recommended against marriage

21. If the Pastorals were written near the middle of the second century, this would be in direct opposition to Marcionite views. See on the concluding words of 1 Tim. 6:20–21.

in view of the eschatological crisis he believed was present (1 Cor 7:1–40). In the Pastor's later situation, he regards the contemporary development, such tendencies as expressions of the false doctrine threatening the churches (1 Tim 4:1–5), and takes a firm stand against them. While some streams of the post-Pauline tradition developed the image of Paul as the "model ascetic,"[22] the Pastor is closer to Colossians and Ephesians, and reasserts the goodness of creation and the obligation to enjoy it as essential to the believer's outlook on life (1 Tim 4:3; 6:17). It is part of Timothy's responsibility as Christian leader *not* to be a teetotaler (1 Tim 5:23).

Like Colossians and Ephesians, but unlike Paul, the ethic of the pastorals is concerned with tables of household duties for members of the family (Col 3:18–4:1, Eph 5:22–6:9, 1 Tim 2:8–15, 5:1–16, Titus 2:1–10). The Pastor's ethic is concerned with, but not controlled by, "what people think," that is, he does not want outsiders to have the wrong impression of the church as a disruptive sect encouraging a kind of life that violates conventional community standards.

"Protocatholicism"

In this book, I am using "protocatholic" as a neutral term referring to the postapostolic developments toward what became mainstream Christianity, the catholic church of the Apostolic Fathers as represented especially by Irenaeus. Earlier studies, especially in the German Lutheran context, sometimes spoke of the developments of postapostolic Christianity tending toward institutionalism and sacramentalism as *Frühkatholizismus* (early catholicism). The term sometimes carried a disparaging tone, suggesting a decline, away from the earlier existential concern for personal faith lived in the eschatological community awaiting the return of Christ, and moving toward a concentration on correct doctrine, accommodation to an ongoing world, and development of canon, creed, and clergy. This terminology and perspective is not now widely used. The post-Pauline developments in the deuteropauline and Catholic letters are increasingly seen as having their own validity when interpreted in their own terms and not merely as a decline from a first-generation golden age.

16.1.6 Order, Structure, and Outline

The Pastorals are always attested as a unity; most scholars regard them as having been composed together, intended to circulate and be read together, to complement each other.[23] How one perceives the structure of each of the Pastoral Letters depends in part on how one views their origin. If each letter is regarded as a distinct composition from a particular situation within the lifetime of Paul, they must be analyzed independently and in their presumed chronological order. On the other hand, if (as here) the Pastorals are thought of as emanating from the Pauline school, together or about the same time, then they represent a single (complex) situation, and, since they were read together as a single communication by the first readers, they should be studied as a single composition by a single author, in the context of the Pauline school.

Assuming the Pastorals always circulated together, we still do not know in what order they were arranged. The canonical titles are, of course, secondary and are based on the relative length of the documents. In the fictive world of the letters, 2 Timothy was obviously written last, as Paul's final testament. Since Titus presupposes congregations that are just beginning to have elders appointed in them, while 1 Timothy assumes a more developed situation regarding church leadership, it may have been that the letters were composed to be read in this

22. Cf. Roetzel, *Paul: The Man and the Myth*, 135–51; Meeks and Fitzgerald, eds., *Writings of St. Paul*, 291–95, and the literature to which they refer.

23. So, e.g., Jouette M. Bassler, *1 Timothy, 2 Timothy, Titus*, ANTC (Nashville: Abingdon Press, 1996), 22–23. Johnson, *Timothy*, considers this a serious mistake that has contributed to their misinterpretation and their being considered pseudonymous.

order: Titus, 1 Timothy, 2 Timothy. The letter to Titus is the frontispiece of the Pastor's three-document corpus. Titus introduces the corpus and prepares the reader for the whole; the reader of 1 Timothy already knows the letter to Titus, and 2 Timothy is written to readers who look back not only on the life and letters of Paul, but on the preceding Pastoral letters as well.

Outline of Titus

1:1–4	Salutation
1:5–3:11	Body of the Letter
1:5–9	Elders
1:10–16	Warnings
2:1–10	Instructions for the Christian household
2:11–15	Theological basis: The appearance of Christ
3:1–2	Instructions to the whole church
3:3–8a	Theological basis: Conversion and baptism
3:8b–11	Final warning
3:12–15	Travel Plans, Greetings, Benediction

Outline of 1 Timothy

1:1–2	Salutation
1:3–20	Introduction
1:3–7	False teachers
1:8–11	Right and wrong interpretation of the law
1:12–17	The (delayed) thanksgiving
1:18–20	Charge to Timothy
2:1–6:19	Body of the Letter
2:1–15	Instructions concerning proper worship
3:1–13	Instructions concerning church leadership
3:14–16	The church's great confession
4:1–5	The "later times" predicted
4:6–6:2	Instructions for ministers
4:6–16	Characteristics and character of the good minister
5:1–6:2	The minister in the household of God
6:3–10	False teaching
6:11–19	Final exhortation to Timothy
6:20–21	Epistolary Conclusion

Outline of 2 Timothy

1:1–2	Salutation
1:3–4:8	Body of the Letter
1:3–2:26	Thanksgiving, encouragement, instructions
3:1–9	False teachers and the last days
3:10–4:8	Paul's charge to Timothy
4:9–18	Personal Instructions and Final Greetings

16.1.7 Exegetical-Theological Précis

Much of the theological substance of the letters has already been dealt with in the discussion of authorship and setting above. Here, we will concentrate on the flow of the argument and particular features of each document.

Titus

1:1–4 Salutation

If Titus originally began the corpus of Pastoral letters, this lengthy and solemn introduction sets the tone for the three letters read as a unit. The whole scheme of Pauline theology, as understood by the Pastor, is compressed into these opening words. The plan of God that began before history was revealed by God/Christ in the kerygma, was entrusted to Paul, who commissions his legitimate son and heir to appoint authorized teachers and leaders who will maintain the tradition. Paul is *the* apostle to whom the kerygma was entrusted; Titus is the *legitimate* heir, so that those claiming to follow the Pauline gospel who operate contrary to this tradition are "illegitimate children."

1:5–3:11 ***Body of the Letter***
After the greeting, the author immediately launches into the body of the letter, without the thanksgiving typical of Paul (missing only in the polemical Galatians). Such abruptness is unusual in actual personal letters.

1:5–9 Elders The chain of tradition is to be continued by the appointment, on Paul's authority, of responsible presbyters in every city. The catalogue of qualifications is more than a characterization of the kind of persons the Christian community needs for its leadership in order to meet the expectations of society and minimize criticisms of the church (though it is also that). The list is an inherent critique of and guard against the false teaching the Pastor opposes. On the one hand, the list is antiascetic: elders are to be married men with families, who may indulge in wine if they don't overdo it. At the same time, the requirements are antilibertine: no debauchery or rebelliousness is allowed in the household of God, led by a presbyter who is himself disciplined and self-controlled. The primary qualification is that the presbyter have a firm grasp of the "word of faith," the sound doctrine that he is to teach (1:9, echoing the "faithful sayings" of 1 Tim 1:15; 3:1; 4:9; 2 Tim 2:11; Titus 3:8). He is to be able to refute those who contradict it. That he is "God's steward" (οἰκονόμος θεοῦ, *oikonomos theou*, 1:7) echoes the saving plan of God (οἰκονομία θεοῦ, *oikonomia theou*, God's economy, plan, 1 Tim 1:4) with which he has been entrusted.

1:10–16 Warnings The Pastor does not engage the false teachers in dialogue but dismisses them with defamatory epithets. The Cretans, among whom the addressees live in the fictive world of the Pastorals, are called "greedy liars." They must simply be rebuked and silenced. The description of the opponents as "those of the circumcision" who advocate "Jewish myths" likewise is merely disdainful. Such comments may represent the Pastor's effort to reflect the controversies with Jews and Jewish Christians of Paul's own day (cf. Romans, Galatians), a part of the "realism" of the fictive world he wants to create. More likely, the false teaching the Pastor opposes probably had Jewish elements mixed with proto-Gnostic and other ingredients. Labeling the false teachers as "Jewish" is guilt by association, part of the Pastor's antiheresy arsenal. It is a far cry from the real, heart-wrenching struggles of Paul the Jewish Christian as he engages real opponents within the church who believed they must insist on circumcision as the entrance requirement to the people of God (see Rom 9:1–5). These debates have receded into the past, and "Jewish" has regrettably become an epithet with which to condemn one's opponents.

2:1–10 Instructions for the Christian household For other examples of the Pauline school's adoption and adaption of the Hellenistic tradition of the *Haustafel* (household code), see on Colossians 3:18–4:1 and Ephesians 5:21–6:9. Analogous to his instructions for elders above, the Pastor here both commends a particular lifestyle for various groups of believers and implicitly rejects the deviant teaching of his opponents. Women may teach—as they probably are continuing to do in some in some circles addressed by the Pastor—but they are to teach only younger women, not the congregation at large, and their curriculum is to be restricted to domestic tranquility, not the content of the faith (see above on the Pastor's wariness about women teachers, §16.1.2).

2:11–15 Theological basis: The appearance of Christ The good order of the household, maintaining a respectable, inoffensive lifestyle as urged by the Pastor is part of the mission of the church, the people God has chosen and redeemed to witness to God's saving act in Christ, which is for all people. The church lives between the two epiphanies of Christ's first and second coming, and must not impede the message that "the grace of God has appeared, bringing salvation to all." Outsiders must not be put off by a false stumbling block, occasioned by the unconventional family life of the Christian household, so that they can be confronted by the saving message of the Christian kerygma.

3:1–2 Instructions to the whole church The Pastor returns to instructions that were already current tradition circulating in the Pauline churches (cf. Rom 13:1–7; 1 Pet 2:13–17; 1 Tim 2:1–2). Even in a pagan society, Christians are not to withdraw from the world but to conduct themselves as good citizens. All people are to be treated with respect and more—with love, as God's beloved creatures whom God wills to save, whether they realize it or not (2:11).

3:3–8a Theological basis: Conversion and baptism In the third theological summary statement (1:1–4; 2:11–14), the Pastor joins himself and other insiders to the masses of unbelievers loved and redeemed by God. Speaking in the persona of Paul, the Pastor outlines the history of salvation in terms of Paul's own biography. This schema requires that he make Paul's pre-Christian experience the same as that of unbelieving Gentiles (see above). The pattern is:

A. sinful humanity

B. God's initiative and grace in Jesus Christ, who does not save on the basis of good works

C. The believer's response in baptism and receiving the Holy Spirit

D. Living in the sure hope of eternal life.

This traditional unit is designated as one of the "faithful sayings" (3:8a), representing the core of Pauline faith as transmitted in the second and third generation.

3:8b–11 Final warning This traditional core of the Pauline gospel is to be taught and lived out, in contrast to the "foolish controversies . . . and quarrels about the law" disdained by the Pastor.

3:12–15 Travel Plans, Greetings, Benediction

The people, places, and events belong to the fictive world of the pseudepigraphical letter, and cannot be fitted into what we otherwise know about Paul's life and mission. The names and tasks are not merely random, however. They portray Paul as in charge, delegating responsibility and arranging for the continuation of the apostolic mission after he is gone, and in the absence of his contemporaries such as Titus—who is authorized to send delegates of his own.

1 Timothy

The reading of the letter to Titus has already prepared the Pastor's audience for 1 Timothy.

1:1–2 Salutation (see above on Titus 1:1–4)

God and Christ Jesus modulate into one transcendent figure who gives the apostolic gospel to Paul. Timothy, like Titus, is declared to be a "legitimate son," authentic heir of the Pauline tradition. "Christ Jesus our hope" reaffirms the future eschatology of the authentic Paul, over against the realized eschatology of the false teachers.

1:3–20 Introduction

1:3–7 False teachers The conventional thanksgiving is deferred to verse 12, and the Pastor goes immediately to the business at hand: correcting unidentified rival teachers who are replacing the traditional Pauline theology of the "plan of God" (see above) with impressive, speculative myths. After the death of Paul, who is in charge, to whom should they look in order to understand their faith? The Pastoral letters represent the response of one wing of the Pauline school, "left behind" in Ephesus, the center of the Pauline school, addressing this need in opposition to rival claims.

1:8–11 Right and wrong interpretation of the law Paul's debates on the role of the law now lie in the distant past. Only here does the Pastor refer to the law. For him, the danger represented by the law is not that it is a condition of salvation, but that it might become the basis of speculative theology. The Pastor warns against this as a misuse of the law, which was intended only for the insubordinate and rebellious, to curb their lawlessness. The aim of sound Christian teaching is a life oriented to love, a pure heart, and sincere faith, not the mastery of a complex system of biblical interpretation.

1:12–17 The (delayed) thanksgiving The author now turns to the conventional thanksgiving section, transforming it into Paul's thanksgiving for the grace of God in his own conversion, which is to be seen as a model for Christian conversion generally (see above on Titus 3:3–8). Paul's biography, now regarded in legendary and paradigmatic terms, is seen as the prototype of the then/now schema of Gentile conversion: from sin, ignorance, blasphemy, and unbelief to salvation in the people of God. Despite his emphasis on conventional morality and values, the Pastor affirms and understands Paul's radical doctrine of grace, which has "superabounded," as in Romans 5:20—more than enough.

1:18–20 Charge to Timothy What about prophecy? Members of post-Pauline churches in Asia were asking how this gift of direct speaking the word of God by the Spirit's inspiration is related to the emerging claims of a more institutional ministry. The charismatic gift of prophecy, important in Paul's time (see 1 Cor 12–14), was alive and well in the contemporary and neighboring Johannine community, though here too it was not undisputed. Within the Pauline school it was often regarded as problematic or dangerous. Prophets spoke by direct authority from God, outside the developing official structures of church leadership (see the tensions in *Didache* 11.3–12.5 and the discussion at 2 Thess 3:6–13 above).

The Pastor does not reject the prophetic gift, but uses Timothy as an illustration of the relation of charisma and church structure: authentic prophecy is not a competitive, independent phenomenon within the church, for authentic charismatic utterances point to legitimate, authorized teachers who stand in the Pauline tradition (see 1 Tim 4:14, the only other reference to prophecy in the Pastoral letters, and the relation of charisma and ordination in 2 Tim 1:6). Paul himself then becomes the model for excommunicating deviant teachers such as Hymenaeus and Alexander.

2:1–6:19 Body of the Letter

2:1–15 Instructions concerning proper worship The modern reader should again be reminded that we are not reading a church manual, but directions for a concrete situation expressed in the form of a Pauline letter. When so read, Paul's instructions take on a particular nuance in which his instructions can be overheard by later readers in an edifying manner that does not claim to give universal instructions for all time.

The instructions to pray for all people, the vast numbers of pagan people (including pagan rulers) beyond the boundaries of the small Christian community, is based on the will of God, the creator of all people, who wills the salvation of all (see on Titus 2:11–14). The Synoptic saying of Mark 10:45 ("for many") is rephrased so that Christ explicitly died "for all." In the Pastor's situation, such declarations have a double edge. On the one hand, they show that the church is not to be understood as a sectarian community over against the world—in contrast to a tendency of the Johannine community contemporary with the Pastor, which tended to draw firm lines between church and world. For the Pastor, Christians are to take their place as responsible citizens within the world, for which it prays (cf. John 17:9).

On the other hand, the affirmation that there is one God, and one mediator, the man Christ Jesus, rejects the claims that the emperor is the divine/human mediator, God, and savior. Christians will pray *for* him, but not *to* him. Likewise, that there is one mediator, the human being Jesus Christ, opposes the Gnostic and docetic claims that there is a great chain of transcendent mediators between God and humanity, to which the divine Christ belongs as one link among others.

Men are instructed to pray; women are to remain silent, to be dressed modestly, and to be good homemakers. They must not presume to be teachers, as encouraged by the rival faction that the Pastor opposes. The Pastor emphasizes that only Eve was deceived (in contrast to Gen 3 and Rom 5; but cf. Paul in 2 Cor 11:3), because it was particularly the women in his congregations who were being deceived by the rival teachers (2 Tim 3:5–7). With Genesis 3 still in mind, the Pastor insists against the ascetic teachers that marriage and childbirth are not a curse from God, but that normal family life is the model of the saved, redeemed life.

3:1–13 Instructions concerning church leadership Just as women in the church are to represent the ideal cultural image of their role in society, so also with the male leadership of the church. The Pastor represents Paul as assuming that church leaders will be male heads of families who take care of the church, the household of God, in the same way they administer their household—which is a responsibility shared with women (3:11–12).

3:14–16 The church's great confession These instructions about how believers are to conduct themselves in the "household of God" during the indefinite interim between the death of Paul and the return of Jesus are founded on the common faith of the whole Christian community, expressed in a liturgical tradition, a creed or hymn with which the readers are already familiar.

He was revealed in flesh,	a
vindicated in spirit,	b
seen by angels,	b
proclaimed among Gentiles,	a
believed in throughout the world,	a
taken up in glory.	b

The formula consists of a relative pronoun "who" that refers to God/Christ, followed by six lines, each of which begins with a passive verb in the past tense. The formula is constructed on the pattern a-b/b-a/a-b. Each of the "a" lines refers to this historical, temporal, material world ("flesh," "nations;" "world"); each of the "b" lines refers to the divine, transcendent world ("spirit," "angels," "glory"). In the incarnation and resurrection, the act of God in Christ bridges this chasm. The entire creed/hymn affirms that it is in this world that the transcendent God has acted in the Christ event, and that this is the message proclaimed and believed throughout the world.

4:1–5 The "later times" predicted This section describes the false teachers of the author's time. As in Acts 20:28–30, Paul's own time is portrayed as a golden age that maintained the purity of the faith, with destructive heresies emerging only after Paul's death. Paul is portrayed as reporting the prediction of a Christian prophet about the last days, the time of trouble preceding the end. The Pastor's rivals also appeal to guidance by the Spirit, but he regards their teaching as inspired by Satan (see 2 Cor 11:13–15). The Pastor does not question the reality of spiritual phenomena; the issue is whether it is the Holy Spirit or other spiritual powers at work.

As in the case of the Colossian false teaching (see on Col 2:8–23 above), the author's opponents advocate an otherworldly asceticism; the marks of an authentic Christian life include renouncing marriage and family and rejecting certain foods and drinks. The Pastor's own views on women, marriage, and the family may be seen as an (over?)reaction to the teaching of his opponents, which was attractive to many, especially the women of his churches, giving them freedom from the patriarchal family and the opportunity to serve as teachers in the church (see 2:9–15; 3:11; 5:2–16; 2 Tim 3:6; Titus 2:3–4).

4:6–6:2 *Instructions for ministers*

4:6–16 *Characteristics and character of the good minister*
Here "servant" (διάκονος *diakonos*, deacon) is used in the generic sense, "minister," which can include both the developing official ministerial office and the lay ministry of all Christians. Teaching is a central responsibility of the minister's role (vv. 6, 11, 13, 16). The rival teachers—some of whom were women—and their disciples considered their doctrine to be deeply theological interpretations of the Bible and philosophy. The derogatory description of the Pastor puts their teaching in the category of gossip exchanged by elderly housewives.

Timothy is portrayed as youthful and inexperienced, in need of elementary instruction. This corresponds to the need for pastoral instruction in the church of the author's time, but not to that of the historical Paul and Timothy. The young ministers of the Pastor's church, however, who were sometimes called on to teach and even reprove church members older than themselves, needed to be instructed to conduct their ministry in such a way that it could not be disdained or dismissed because of their relative youth. The Pastor charges these young "Timothies" to equip themselves and their congregations by devotion to the Scripture and the tradition.

In 4:14 the charisma of ministry is conveyed through ordination by the presbytery, the council of elders. In 2 Timothy 1:6 this gift of ministry is conferred by Paul's hands. The point is that *Paul's* apostolic authorization continues in the regular ordination process conducted by the elders. This is not yet "apostolic succession" in the sense of an unbroken chain of ordained clergy that extends back to the apostles, but it does claim that the regular ordination by elders represents an apostolic ministry. In the laying on of the presbytery's hands, Paul's hands are laid on the ordinand; that is, he is affirmed as a legitimate representative of the apostolic faith.

5:1–6:2 *The minister in the household of God*
This section loosely follows the general pattern of the household code that was being adopted and adapted in the Pauline churches (see on Col 3:18–4:1), but with extensive digressions and gaps. While Timothy is addressed in the second person singular, the Pastor speaks over his head to the congregations on how life in the Christian community should be conducted. Instructions are given regarding constituent elements of the congregation, corresponding to the members of a large household: older men, older women, younger men, younger women, widows, and slaves.

In two cases, groups included in this list are singled out and receive extensive instruction: the widows and ordained elders. In these cases, the natural group has modulated into a (semi) official group. Who qualifies as a "real" widow to be on the church's list occupies more of the Pastor's attention than any other issue, indicating it was a pressing problem (see above). The group of elders modulates from "older men" of 5:1 to a quasi-official group of presbyters (same word as 5:1) who rule, teach, and are to be paid for their work, and against whom charges can be brought. Here we have more than the household codes in Colossians and Ephesians, but not yet a firm church order that distinguishes "clergy" and "laity." In all this, Timothy represents the role of those who ordain (v. 22) and hear complaints against elders; the office he represents is superior to theirs, corresponding to that of the later bishop.

6:3–10 *False teaching* The Pastor returns to the theme with which the letter began, opposing the sound doctrine about Jesus Christ to the sickly, puffy teachings of the opponents. Their bad theology and numbed conscience results in their living only by the profit motive, using their religious teaching as a means of making money.

6:11–19 *Final exhortation to Timothy* In contrast to religion for profit, Timothy and those he represents are to flee the love of money and cultural success. They are to "keep the commandment." "Keep" here means "preserve intact." The "commandment" is the charge received by ministers to preserve the deposit of faith entrusted to them by faithfully teaching it to their contemporaries and handing it on to future generations until Christ returns (see on 6:20, 2 Tim 1:14; 2:2). This means going against, not with, the grain of the culture. Like Jesus when he stood before Pilate, they are to make the countercultural good confession. Though the Pastor is sometimes accused of being too accommodating to pagan culture, here he insists that Christian ministers and all believers hold fast to the confession that Jesus is "King of kings and Lord of lords"—like "God and Savior" a title claimed by the Roman emperors.[24]

6:20–21 *Epistolary Conclusion*

The "contradictions of what is falsely called 'knowledge'" use two terms that became common in Marcion's heresy. "Contradictions" can also be translated "Antitheses," the title of the appendix to Marcion's "New Testament" published about 140 CE in Rome. Marcion's *Antitheses* listed a large number of contradictions (hence the title of his book) between the second-rate Creator god of the Old Testament and the true God of the New Testament revealed in Jesus. The Pastor's final admonition can thus be read as meaning, "Avoid Marcion's book called *Antitheses*, related to that movement falsely called 'knowledge,' 'science,' or 'Gnosticism.'" If this is a direct reference to Marcion, either the Pastorals were written as late as the mid-second century, or Marcion's terminology was current earlier.

24. Such titles are documented by numerous inscriptions. Particularly relevant to the Pastorals is an inscription from Ephesus praising Julius Caesar as "God manifest, the common Savior of human life" (*SIG* 347; see above, §9.2.2).

2 Timothy

1:1–2 *Salutation*

The salutations of 1 and 2 Timothy are very similar to each other, but somewhat different from those of the undisputed letters of Paul. Likewise, the brief closing greetings (1 Tim 6:21; 2 Tim 4:22; Titus 3:15) are practically identical, though different from Paul, suggesting the Pastoral letters were written at about the same time, as a single collection to be circulated together.

1:3—4:8 *Body of the Letter*

1:3—2:26 Thanksgiving, encouragement, instructions Second Timothy is essentially a characterization of authentic ministry as represented by Paul and how this ministry is to be continued after his death. The Pastor emphasizes continuity in the lives of both Paul and Timothy: Paul is faithful to the tradition of his Jewish ancestors. Timothy is a third-generation believer who has been taught by his grandmother and mother. The Pastor emphasizes that both Paul and Timothy are rooted in their ancestral faith and the Jewish Scriptures. The church is not an innovation but is in continuity with the people of God throughout the ages. Especially, as Paul's "beloved son," Timothy is his heir who continues Paul's own ministry. Second Timothy has several characteristics of the testament genre in which an aged patriarch says farewell and commissions his successors. Such testaments, uniformly pseudepigraphical, are found in the Bible and in extracanonical Jewish literature (e.g., Jacob in Gen 49; Moses in Deut 33; the *Testaments of the Twelve Patriarchs*) and represented in the Pauline tradition by Paul's farewell to the Ephesian elders (Acts 20:18–38).

Timothy's "tears" (v. 4) are not a psychological characteristic of the individual Timothy but reflect the tearful farewell of Acts (20:37–38).

In the charge to Timothy the readers of the Pastoral letters hear themselves called to endure suffering for the sake of the gospel (1:8). While the Pastor is interested in the church's fitting into respectable pagan society, this is not his first priority. When necessary, Christians must suffer and even die for being true to their faith. Again, Paul himself has already become the model of such faithful suffering (2:10, "for the sake of the elect"). Suffering and endurance is a central dimension of the believer's life (1 Tim 6:11; 2 Tim 1:8, 12; 2:3, 8–10, 12; 3:11–12; 4:5; Titus 2:2), not only "living a quiet and peaceable life" in society (1 Tim 2:2).

Paul also presents himself as *teacher* (1 Tim 2:7; 2 Tim 1:11; 3:10). In the undisputed letters, Paul claims various charismatic gifts and ministerial roles (apostle, prophet, speaker in tongues, slave) but never refers to himself as teacher. In the post-Pauline period, it is important for the readers to know that as they receive the tradition of "sound doctrine" they are being taught by Paul himself, who is the paradigmatic model of the minister as teacher. Once again, the chain of tradition (Paul ⇒ Timothy ⇒ faithful teachers) is emphasized as the means by which the faith is handed on (2 Tim 2:2).

The Christian leaders actually addressed in the Pastorals belong to this chain themselves and know from whom (plural, 3:14) they have received this instruction. Timothy is to be the model for teachers who are capable of "rightly explaining the word [λόγος, *logos*] of truth," the Pauline gospel,[25] which as "sound doctrine" is contrasted with "*their* talk [λόγος] that will spread like gangrene." The Pastor always speaks of Paul's teaching in the singular, in contrast to the "teachings" (plural) of his opponents. Catechetical instruction that passes along the substantial content of the faith requires a single-minded kind of ministry that is not a sideline. Like soldiers and farmers, such ministers must devote their whole lives to this service (2 Tim 2:3–6), and thus must be paid for it (1 Tim 5:17–18).

Paul's personal faith in God is represented by his confidence that God will preserve the gospel represented by the deposit of tradition with which Paul has been entrusted (understanding παραθήκη, *parathēkē* in the sense of the NRSV footnote, "what has been entrusted to me"). Though ministers are themselves responsible for faithful preservation and proclamation of the Christian faith, they are not alone, but conduct their ministry by faith in the power of God who works in and with them (cf. Phil 2:12–13), and "with the help of the Holy Spirit," 1:14.

That "all in Asia" have turned away from Paul (1:15) may be a rhetorical appeal for the readers to remember the historical Paul, who resolutely went to his death despite being deserted by friends and colleagues, as encouragement for the readers to be willing to do the same. More pointedly, these words reflect the struggles in the Pastor's own situation, when many would-be followers of Paul are actually turning away from him—the rival teachers who are enjoying some success in the Pauline churches. Readers are encouraged not to "turn away" but to stand by their man, as had Onesiphorus (1:16–18; 4:3–4).

For the most part, the Pastor merely disdainfully dismisses his opponents without indicating the content of their false teaching. In 2:18 we see (his understanding of) their realized eschatology, which he summarizes as "the resurrection has already taken place." This may be illuminated by later texts of Gnostic Christianity:

> The disciples ask Jesus, "When will the resurrection of the dead occur, and when will the new world come?" He said to them, "What you expect has already come, but you do not recognize it." (*Gospel of Thomas* 51)

25. The "word of truth" of 2 Tim. 2:15 is often understood to refer to Scripture. While Paul expects Christian teachers to study the Bible and be proficient in interpreting it to the church (1 Tim. 4:13; 2 Tim. 3:16), this text refers to the core tradition of the Pauline gospel.

> If one does not receive the resurrection while still alive, one will receive nothing at death. (*Gospel of Philip* 73.1–5)

> You already have the resurrection. (*De Resurrectione*, as cited in Hippolytus, Fragment 1)

Like his fellow teacher in the Pauline school who wrote 2 Thessalonians (see 2 Thess 2:2) and an out-of-step prophet within the Johannine community (see Rev 20:5), the Pastor rejects this hyperrealized eschatology and reasserts the Christian hope of the triumph of God in the ultimate future, including the parousia, the resurrection of the dead, the judgment of living and dead, the final coming of the kingdom of God, and eternal life (4:1, 18).

3:1–9 False teachers and the last days Although the Pastor had encouraged Timothy to teach in a pastoral style, "not to be quarrelsome but kindly to everyone, . . . correcting opponents with gentleness . . . so that they may repent and come to know the truth" (2:24–26), he also has the view that "in the last days" there will be deceitful teachers interested only in money, who are incorrigible, and who are to be avoided. The Pastor dismisses them with a long list of insulting terms—a list of eighteen vices.

3:10—4:8 Paul's charge to Timothy As Paul faces his imminent death, he declares that he has "kept the faith," which in this context means not only that Paul has maintained his personal faith in Christ, but that he has kept the content of the faith intact, maintaining the sound doctrine that was entrusted to him. He charges Timothy to do the same. Paul has guarded the faith; a changing of the guard is taking place. Timothy and his hearers are now responsible.

4:9–18 Personal Instructions and Final Greetings

The Pastor pictures Paul's life as ending on a very personal note. The warrior for the faith and teacher of the church had been concerned not only with right doctrine, but with people. After his death, the large group of coworkers continues his message and mission. Second Timothy mentions twenty-three names, more than any other letter in the Pauline tradition. Of these, only eight appear in the undisputed letters (Timothy, Titus, Prisca, Aquila, Mark, Luke, Demas, Erastus). A few others appear in Acts or the other deuteropauline letters. Some of the rest appear in the apocryphal *Acts of Paul and Thecla*, sometimes in different roles and relationships. This does not indicate literary dependence, but that both draw on the growing legendary material about Paul circulating in Asia in the second century. This large number of names points to the teachers and missionaries of the generations after Paul, and the struggle of the Pauline school to find faithful transmitters of its tradition.

16.2 Retrospect: The Struggle for Paul

AFTER THE DEATH OF PAUL, THE FORMATION of the later Pauline churches was a matter not only of religion and theology, but of politics and sociology. While these aspects are inseparable historically, the whole history can be analyzed from one or the other perspective. From a sociological point of view, the development from Paul to the Pastorals can be seen in terms of three stages:[26]

I. *Paul*: Community building

II. *Colossians and Ephesians*: Community stabilizing

III. *The Pastorals*: Community-protecting institutionalization

26. Margaret Y. MacDonald, *The Pauline Churches: A Socio-historical Study of Institutionalization in the Pauline and Deutero-Pauline Writings*, SNTSMS 60 (Cambridge: Cambridge University Press, 1988).

The churches begun by Paul and his colleagues around the Aegean represent the first generation of the church's mission. In the second and third generations, several groups struggled with each other for the authentic interpretation of Paul for their own time. Each claimed to be the main stream, but from our perspective they can be roughly sorted out into the (1) "radical left," composed of various types of gnosticizing interpretations; (2) the "left wing" interpreters represented in various ways by Colossians and Ephesians; (3) a "centrist" stream of Pauline tradition represented by 2 Thessalonians; (4) the "right wing" interpreters represented by the Pastorals; and (5) the "radical right" represented by the *Pseudo-Clementines*. The later church would include in the canon not only Paul's own letters, but more than one type of his later interpreters—though not all of them. Along with Paul's own letters, the "left," "centrist," and "right" wings were included, though they would have been uncomfortable with each other, and even with the Paul they claimed to represent. Both the "radical left" and "radical right" were excluded. The church's process of discernment, which it claims is guided by the Holy Spirit, did not result in a neat single form of the faith, indebted to a single apostle, but in a limited plurality. More than one version of the Pauline gospel was acceptable—but not just any version. Here we have an anticipation of the nature of the New Testament canon.

16.3 For Further Reading

Bassler, J. M. *1 Timothy, 2 Timothy, Titus*. ANTC. Nashville: Abingdon Press, 1996.

Collins, R. F. *I and II Timothy and Titus: A Commentary*. NTL. Louisville, KY: Westminster John Knox Press, 2002.

Johnson, L. T. *The First and Second Letters to Timothy*. Anchor Bible 35A. New York: Doubleday, 2001.

Marshall, I. H. *The Pastoral Epistles*. ICC. Edinburgh: T. & T. Clark, 1999.

17

Rome and the Consolidation of Traditions

IT WAS BECAUSE PAUL AND THE PAULINE tradition had made the letter form the primary vehicle of Christian instruction that early Christian teachers continued to use this form. The letters of the Pauline tradition placed their stamp on Christian instruction to such an extent that later documents that were not letters in the usual sense, but were intended for reading aloud before the whole congregation, tended to assume some features of the letter form and to be classified as such. We can see the influence of this tradition most clearly in 1 Peter, and also the emerging influence of Rome as a center for the cultivation and dissemination of such didactic letters.

17.1 Roman Consolidation of Pauline and Petrine Traditions

IN THE LATE 50s AND EARLY 60s BOTH PAUL and Peter came to Rome. Paul came as a Roman citizen in protective custody awaiting trial (Acts 21:27–28:31). We do not know how Peter came. Paul's associates and fellow missionaries accompanied him and after his death continued to propagate the Pauline understanding of the faith, in Rome and elsewhere. Although we have no details, something analogous seems to have been true of Peter. After both Paul and Peter had sealed their testimony with their own deaths, the Roman church became heir to the traditions of both the great apostles.

While the traditions represented by Paul and Peter were different, they were not mutually exclusive alternatives, and were not seen as such by the Roman church, which in the latter part of the first century began to see itself as supporter of and teacher to other struggling churches outside Rome. The *Pseudo-Clementines* represent a Petrine tradition that took Peter's side against Paul. Marcion was a Roman Christian leader who took Paul's side against Peter. But the mainstream Roman church held Peter and Paul together. *First Clement* is the clearest testimony that the Roman church adopted both Peter and Paul as patron saints and saw itself as the world leader of both Jewish and Gentile Christianity within the one church. That this development need not be seen in a sinister perspective as a power grab is apparent from Ignatius, who already in 110 CE, from his Antiochene perspective, considers "Peter and Paul" simply as *the* apostles (Ign., *Rom* 4.1). Both Clement and Ignatius always cite the apostolic pair in this order; Peter has become the major figure, who incorporates Paul. Ignatius congratulates the Roman church as having "taught others" (Ign. *Rom.* 3.1). Twenty years later Hermas, *Vision* 2.4.3 refers to the Roman church as having previously sent writings to other churches. Thus by the end of the first century, there had been an amalgamation of Pauline and Petrine traditions in Rome, which is acknowledged in the next generation by 2 Peter's claiming Paul as a brother apostle whose teaching, however, must be understood within the perspective of the Petrine tradition (2 Pet 3:14–16). The consolidation of Pauline and Petrine traditions into one whole is represented in another way by the author of Luke–Acts, who in the first part of the second century CE (also in Rome?) retold the story of the early church in such a way that Peter and Paul are dual representatives of the one apostolic tradition. Acts is clear documentation that in the third generation in some circles of early Christianity there was deep interest in presenting the Christian message on the dual pillars of Petrine and Pauline tradition. First Peter also fits into this trajectory of developing Petrine tradition.

17.1.1 The (Pauline) letter form of expressing the faith becomes common beyond the Pauline circle.

It is not to be taken for granted that secondary Christian literature would assume the letter form. There were other forms of literature in the wake of Paul (novels, apocalypses, canonical Acts, and later non-canonical variations of the genre). It was Paul who established the letter form as the primary means of Christian instruction. Here we may anticipate the conclusions suggested below regarding the later New Testament epistles. As it turned out, Paul influenced not only the Pauline school, but early Christian literature in general. This was obviously the case with the deuteropaulines (Colossians, Ephesians, Pastorals). Hebrews is a marginal example of the Pauline letter form, but was finally accepted into the Pauline corpus as a letter.

The tradition that letters were an appropriate form of Christian instruction to be read alongside the Scripture in congregational worship was a formative influence on the non-Pauline documents that later were assembled as the Catholic Epistles. James and Jude reflect the circulation of Paul's letters and imitate them with epistolary openings but no further epistolary forms in the body and conclusion of their respective documents. First Peter is very Pauline; 2 Peter knows Jude and both 1 and 2 Peter, and writes under their influence. The Johannine school knew both Gospels and letters; 1, 2, and 3 John were written in Ephesus, where Pauline letters were circulated and Pauline tradition was cultivated. Revelation directly reflects the Pauline letter form. We can see the influence of this tradition most clearly in 1 Peter, and also the emerging influence of Rome as a center for the cultivation and dissemination of such didactic letters.

17.2 Interpreting 1 Peter

17.2.1 Peter and Petrine Tradition in the Early Church

After Jesus and Paul, Simon Peter is the best-known figure in early Christianity. He is referred to in Paul's letters, all four Gospels and Acts, the two canonical letters attributed to him, and a large body of noncanonical literature associated with his name, much of it claiming his authorship: *The Gospel of Peter, The Letter of Peter to James, The Kerygma Petrou, The Kerygmata Petrou, The Acts of Peter, The Pseudo-Clementines, The Apocalypse of Peter, The Passion of Peter and Paul, The Acts of Peter and the Twelve Apostles, The Acts of Peter, The Martyrdom of Peter, The Passion of Peter.*[1] Much of this material is generations or even centuries later than the historical Simon Peter, with whom it has only a nominal connection. After the church became a worldwide institution within which Peter was an accepted authority figure, material was associated with him or even attributed to him that had no connection with the life and mission of Simon Peter. Nonetheless, there is solid canonical and patristic evidence that the

1. For texts and introductory material, see especially Edgar Hennecke and Wilhelm Schneemelcher, eds., *New Testament Apocrypha*, 2 vols. (Philadelphia: Westminster Press, 1963, 1964) and individual articles in *Anchor Bible Dictionary*.

ministry of the apostle Peter continued among disciples influenced by him and in a stream of tradition emanating from him, somewhat analogous to the Pauline school that continued to reinterpret Paul's message after his death.[2] As in the case of Paul, details of Peter's life and work are disputed, but there is widespread agreement on the following outline.

Simon before Jesus

There was, of course a real person named Simon, renamed "Peter" (Matt 16:16–18; John 1:41–42; Aramaic *Kepha* [כֵּיפָא], Greek transliteration *Cephas* [Κηφᾶς], translated *Petros*, English "Rock"). Simon's father's name was Jonah (Matt 16:17) or John (John 1:42; 21:15)—two different names are represented in Aramaic and Greek, as in English. His mother's name is unknown. As a contemporary of Jesus, Simon was presumably born sometime in the period 10 BCE–10 CE, perhaps in the bilingual and multicultural Bethsaida (see John 1:44; 12:21). Peter's native language was Aramaic, but it is probable that, like many people in Galilee, Peter could also speak and understand Greek to some extent. Simon was married (Mark 1:30–31) and was accompanied by his wife on later mission trips (1 Cor 9:5). He, along with his brother Andrew, was in the fishing business, belonging to the lower-middle social class of small businessmen and craftsmen. The tradition preserved in John 1:35–42 suggests that both Andrew and Simon may have been disciples of John the Baptist prior to the call to follow Jesus, that is, that they already were oriented to the apocalyptic stream of Judaism.

Simon with Jesus

Sometime during his mission, Jesus of Nazareth called Simon to be his disciple, and Simon responded. The three versions of this encounter in the New Testament (Mark 1:16–20=Matt 4:18–22; Luke 5:1–11; John 1:35–42) vary in details, in major elements of chronology, and in their understanding of the significance of the event (e.g., was Simon called first, as in Mark and Matthew, or not, as pointedly in John?). Further, the similarities between Luke 5:1–11 and John 21:1–19 show that the post-Easter perspective of the church influenced the retelling of all the stories.

When Simon became a disciple of Jesus, his life was completely reoriented. He left home, family, and business and became a participant in the Jesus movement and its mission. Not only so, it is clear that he became the leading member of the group of disciples. He is pictured as belonging to the inner circle (e.g., Mark 9:2; 13:3; 14:33), as being the spokesperson for the other disciples (e.g., Mark 8:29; 9:5), as being the disciples' representative to whom Jesus speaks and with whom he deals (e.g., Mark 8:33), and as the representative member of the group whom others approach (e.g., Matt 17:24). While later interpretations are at work in these stories, it is also clear that already during Jesus' mission Simon was the leader of the Twelve and is always named first in the various lists (Matt 10:2; Mark 3:16; Luke 6:14; Acts 1:13).

Peter in the Early Church

The encounter with the risen Lord enabled Peter to become the principal leader in regathering the disciples and in the formation of what was to become the church. The risen Jesus appeared to Simon and (re)constituted him to be the "Rock" on which the new Christian community is established (1 Cor 1–5; Luke

2. Cf. Oscar Cullmann, *Peter: Disciple, Apostle, Martyr*, rev. ed. (Cleveland: World, 1958), 70–154; Brown and Meier, *Antioch and Rome*; Pheme Perkins, *Peter: Apostle for the Whole Church* (Columbia: University of South Carolina Press, 1994); Raymond E. Brown, Karl P. Donfried, and John Reumann, eds., *Peter in the New Testament* (Minneapolis: Augsburg Press, 1973). On the existence of a Petrine "school," "circle," or "group," see Lutz Doering, "First Peter as an Early Christian Diaspora Letter," in *The Catholic Epistles and Apostolic Tradition*, ed. Karl-Wilhelm Niebuhr and Robert W. Wall (Waco, TX: Baylor University Press, 2009), 233, 455 n117, and the bibliography there given.

24:34; Mark 16:7). By the time of Paul's first letter to the Corinthians, Peter is already a well-known figure in Gentile Christianity far beyond Palestine (1 Cor 9:5). Whether or not Peter had personally visited Corinth, a group appealing strictly to Petrine authority existed within the Corinthian congregation (1 Cor 1:12). Paul may have already found it necessary to polemicize subtly against what he considers a misunderstanding of Peter's role as the rock on which the church is founded (1 Cor 3:11; cf. Matt 16:18). In writing to the Galatians, even while emphasizing the minimal contacts he had had with the original apostles, Paul nevertheless indicates that he went up to Jerusalem "to visit Cephas" (Gal 1:18) and that fourteen years later Peter (along with James and John) was still one of the three "Pillars" of the Jerusalem church (Gal 2:7–8).

Peter was clearly the principal leader of the earliest Christian community in Jerusalem, which was composed of both "Hebrews" and "Hellenists," that is, Christians of Aramaic-speaking Palestinian culture and Christians of Greek-speaking Hellenistic culture (see §§7.4.2; 9.2.2; Acts 6:1–6). Acts 2–6 pictures Peter as bridge between the two groups, not just as leader of one. Early in the church's development, Peter's influence extended into Gentile Christianity. The later picture of Acts 2–12 and Acts 15, though written from Luke's perspective, is still essentially correct in its broad outline: Peter was from the beginning both a principal leader and agent of unity in what was already becoming a church containing internal tensions. Peter's leadership of the Jerusalem church receded in favor of the more strict James, brother of Jesus, but this need not be attributed to theological conflict. Peter advocated a more moderate position, closer to Paul than to James. Even so, Peter was clearly the proponent of a Christianity oriented more to the law and the theology and practice of the new faith's roots in Judaism than was Paul.

In Paul's letters, Peter appears at first as the leading figure in the Jerusalem church (Gal 1:18), then several years later as one of the three "Pillars" (Gal 2:9), then as an influential leader in the Antioch church (Gal 2:11–14). We lose sight of Peter after the Antioch incident (ca. 50 CE), though he apparently continued various missionary journeys (1 Cor 9:5)—which, however, did not include the provinces to which 1 Peter is addressed (1 Pet 1:1). In Acts, Peter disappears abruptly from the narrative at 12:17 (mid-40s CE) and departs Jerusalem for "another place," to reappear only once at the Jerusalem Conference (ca. 48 CE). Although in some older interpretations the "other place" was Rome, it appears that Peter did not arrive in Rome until after Paul had written Romans (ca. 56 CE). According to reliable early Christian tradition, Peter died as a martyr in the mid-60s.

17.2.2 Authorship

The spectrum of possibilities may be delineated as follows:

1. Peter wrote the letter personally, from Rome in the 60s. His thorough Greek education and experience made him fully capable of doing this without help from Silvanus or anyone else.[3]
2. Peter supplied the ideas but the vocabulary, syntax, and style belong to Silvanus, who did the actual writing at Peter's behest. Peter then approved and authorized it. This view usually dates 1 Peter in the 60s as above, but J. Ramsey Michaels has revived the older view of A. M. Ramsey that Peter lived into the 80s when the letter was written by Peter with secretarial help from Silvanus.[4]
3. Silvanus wrote representing Peter, who commissioned the letter. Peter is the authority that stands behind the letter, but Silvanus is its actual composer, who made his "own

3. This position is argued by, e.g., Wayne Grudem, *1 Peter*, TNTC (Grand Rapids: Eerdmans, 1988), 21–32.
4. J. Ramsey Michaels, *1 Peter*, WBC 49 (Waco, TX: Word, 1988), lxii.

contribution to the substance no less than to the language" of the letter.[5]

4. Silvanus wrote in Peter's name after Peter's death, using Petrine tradition. Silvanus is the actual author of the letter.[6]

5. An anonymous member of the "Petrine circle" in Rome wrote in Peter's name after his death. "Peter" is fictive, but "Silvanus," "Mark," and the "elect sister" are real people who are members of the Petrine group.[7]

6. An anonymous Roman Christian wrote on the basis of Petrine tradition.[8]

7. A *Paulinist* wrote in Peter's name, primarily on the basis of *Pauline* tradition.[9]

Considerations discussed below indicate #5 or #6 to be the most likely solution. The authorship question for 1 Peter is a different kind of question than, for example, the authorship of the Pastorals, where we have several undisputed letters of Paul and do not have to speculate as to what Paul would have written. But 1 Peter is the only possibility that we have something in the New Testament written by Peter himself, or by any of the original disciples of Jesus. The following reasons are convincing to most contemporary scholars that 1 Peter was not written by Peter himself but by an anonymous disciple in Peter's name.

1. Except for the first word, the letter itself makes no claim, direct or indirect, to authorship by an apostle, but specifically indicates that the letter was written by an elder who is a coelder with other leaders in the churches of Asia (5:1).

2. Perhaps the most compelling reason to attribute 1 Peter to a second-generation disciple rather than to Simon Peter himself is the lack of the kind of material one would anticipate from a personal companion of Jesus and eyewitness of his ministry. Except for the name in 1:1, the letter makes no claim to be from an eyewitness of Jesus' words and deeds. The contrast in 1:8 is not between the author, who has seen Jesus, and the readers, who have not, but is a statement about the Christian life as such. Christians, including the author, love, trust, and obey Christ, whom they have not seen, on the basis of the faith that has come to them by Christian preaching and the power of the Holy Spirit (1:12). The author's claim to be a witness to the sufferings of Christ (5:1) is not a claim to have been present at the crucifixion—which in any case would not apply to Simon Peter (Mark 14:50–72)—but that he, along with his fellow elders, bears witness to the salvific meaning of Jesus' suffering for others. The author refers to no sayings of Jesus or stories about him, even when these would suit his purpose admirably. Thus, for example, the saying cited in Mark 12:17 would support the point made in 1 Peter 2:13–17. At 1 Peter 3:9, where Jesus' saying against retaliation would be most appropriate (Matt 5:38–42), the author cites Psalm 34:13–17. Such Jesus traditions as the letter includes are not cited as sayings of Jesus, but as Christian parenesis that has already been affected by the Jesus traditions circulating in early Christianity.

3. Even more importantly, the Christology of 1 Peter is not expressed or illustrated by stories from the life of the historical Jesus, but by incorporating the life of Jesus within a cosmic framework in which the weakness of the earthly Jesus

5. So Edward Gordon Selwyn, *The First Epistle of St. Peter: The Greek Text with Introduction, Notes and Essays* (London: Macmillan, 1964), 11, and Peter H. Davids, *The First Epistle of Peter*, NICNT (Grand Rapids: Eerdmans, 1990), 30.

6. J. N. D. Kelly, *A Commentary on the Epistles of Peter and of Jude*, HNTC (New York: Harper & Row, 1969), 33, accepts it with reservations.

7. John H. Elliott, *1 Peter: A New Translation with Introduction and Commentary*, AB 37B (New York: Doubleday, 2000), 270–80.

8. Leonhard Goppelt, *A Commentary on 1 Peter*, trans. John E. Alsup (Grand Rapids: Eerdmans, 1993), 51–52, though also having sympathies for #4 above; Paul J. Achtemeier, *1 Peter: A Commentary on First Peter*, Hermeneia (Minneapolis: Fortress Press, 1996), 199.

9. Francis Wright Beare, *The First Epistle of Peter: The Greek Text with Introduction and Notes*, 2nd rev. ed. (Oxford: Blackwell, 1961), 24–30; Helmut Koester, *Introduction to the New Testament*, vol. 2, *History and Literature of Early Christianity*, Foundations and Facets (Philadelphia: Fortress Press, 1982), 2:292–95.

becomes part of the saving act of God. God's victory over the demonic powers that threaten human life is not thought of in terms of the exorcisms of the earthly Jesus as in the Gospel of Mark (also associated with Peter in early Christian tradition). Rather, the saving act of God in the Christ event is portrayed as the cosmic victory accomplished by the resurrection/ascension, as in the Pauline kenosis Christology that portrays the earthly Jesus in the weakness of a truly human life (e.g., Phil 2:5–11; 2 Cor 13:4). One would anticipate that a letter from an eyewitness to the life of Jesus would at least make contact with the kind of Christology found in the Gospels, but it functions altogether within the framework of the epistolary christological tradition oriented to Paul.

4. The letter reflects knowledge and appropriation of the Pauline tradition in a way difficult to imagine for the historical Peter, Paul's contemporary who sometimes opposed Paul (Gal 2:11–21; see below).

5. First Peter is written with a high level of literary and rhetorical competence by someone thoroughly at home in the Greek language and culture, and who was intimately familiar with the LXX. First Peter exhibits a better level of Greek than does Paul, a well-educated Hellenistic Jew who grew up in Tarsus, and better than 2 Peter, which was most probably not written by the same person who wrote 1 Peter.[10] This argument does not presuppose that the historical Peter was an illiterate fisherman who knew no Greek, for this was probably not the case. Peter may well have been literate and may have known enough Greek to function in a multilingual society. The difficulty, however, is in believing that a Palestinian fisherman would be able to write the sophisticated and elegant Greek of 1 Peter, with its numerous allusions to classical and Hellenistic culture, and that a Palestinian Jew would not only cite the LXX—this is credible enough in a missionary situation—but betray no knowledge of the original Hebrew texts and allude almost unconsciously to LXX phraseology. This indicates that the author's own world of thought is represented by Greek literature and the LXX. First Peter sometimes even improves the rough grammar and syntax when he cites the LXX (as in 3:10–12).

Petrine authorship cannot be salvaged by the secretary theory, as though the basic ideas go back to Peter, but the sophisticated language, rhetorical skill, and particular theology are from Silvanus. Such a theory fails to understand the relationship between thought and language. The letter is composed by, and represents the thought of, the one who put it into language. The "basic thoughts" of 1 Peter do not exist in abstraction from their particular linguistic expression. If Silvanus had in fact played such a role in the composition of the letter, his name should appear as at least coauthor in 1:1, where it is conspicuously absent (cf. 1 Cor 1:1; 2 Cor 1:1; Phil 1:1; 1 Thess 1:1; Phlm 1). In any case, the phrase in 5:12 (διὰ Σιλουανοῦ, *dia Silouanou*, usually translated "through Silvanus") does not refer to the writing of the letter but to its delivery (cf. Acts 15:27; Ign. *Rom.* 10.1, Ign. *Phld.* 11.2; Ign. *Smyrn.* 12.1; Pol. *Phil.* 14.1). Even if, nonetheless, the secretary hypothesis is still maintained, the result is still that the letter is composed not by Peter himself but by a faithful disciple, and that the authority of Peter stands somehow behind it—which is precisely what the theory of pseudonymous authorship claims!

6. All the evidence that the letter was written near the end of the first century CE (see below) means it could not have been written by Peter, who almost certainly perished about 64 CE in connection with the arrest of Roman Christians under Nero.

It is thus best to interpret 1 Peter as not written by Simon Peter, but written in his name as an expression of the apostolic authority of its

10. Details and lists in Achtemeier, *1 Peter*, 3–9; Marion L. Soards, "1 Peter, 2 Peter, and Jude as Evidence for a Petrine School," in *Aufstieg und Niedergang der römischen Welt*, ed. Joseph Vogt, Hildegard Temporini, and Wolfgang Haase (Berlin: de Gruyter, 1988), 3833; Selwyn, *First Epistle of St. Peter*, 489–501.

message and the continuation of Roman Petrine tradition by his disciples. This conclusion is strengthened by considerations of the situation of the implied readers, date and occasion of the letter, the author's provenance, sources, and the genre of his composition.

17.2.3 Readers and Their Situation

First Peter is addressed to Christians in a broad geographical area, the five Roman provinces comprising virtually all of Asia Minor north of the Taurus Mountains, whose combined territory was over 200,000 square miles, larger than the combined area of Ohio, Pennsylvania, New York, and the six New England states. Since Bithynia and Pontus had been combined into a double province, it is peculiar that Pontus, the easternmost of the two, is mentioned first, with Bithynia separated and mentioned last. This is probably best explained as reflecting the route to be taken by the messenger who delivered the letter to the scattered churches, who on coming from Rome would have landed in Pontus, then made his way through Galatia and Cappadocia, then back through Asia, ending in Bithynia. This is further evidence that we are dealing with a real letter (see below). This broad area represents a combination of Pauline mission territory (Galatia and Asia) and areas that by the end of the first century were associated with Petrine preaching (see Acts 2:9). The letter does not suggest that Peter or the pseudonymous author had himself evangelized the area or was known personally to the churches there. While there were likely some Jewish Christians among the addressees, the letter indicates that the readers were primarily Gentiles who had formerly not known the true God and who had lived the sinful, idolatrous life of pagans (1:14, 18, 21; 2:1, 9–11, 25; 4:3). In fact, the principal reason for their social marginalization and distress that occasioned the letter was due to their having withdrawn from participation in aspects of their former life they now considered to be sinful (4:4).

The address to the readers as "exiles of the Dispersion" (1:1) and "aliens" who "live in exile" (1:1, 17; 2:11) is not intended literally. Although the readers may include some Jewish Christian refugees who resettled in Asia Minor during and after the 66–70 CE war in Palestine, they are not literally foreigners. They are mainly Gentiles who previously participated in the society that now rejects them. The author applies to the Christian community the biblical imagery of the patriarchs and Israel as the wandering people of God who live as sojourners without rights in lands ruled by others.[11]

It was formerly often thought that the distress the readers were suffering (1:6; 2:12; 3:8–17; 4:12–19; 5:8–10) reflected a period of official Roman persecution, whether under Nero in the mid-60s, Domitian in the mid-90s, or Trajan in the second decade of the second century. More recent study has convinced most scholars that 1 Peter reflects a time of distress and social harassment, but not an official persecution initiated by the government. In any case there was no empirewide Roman persecution until the time of Decian in the third century. Nonetheless, the readers suffer for wearing the name Christian (4:16), and the kind of social rejection and harassment they experienced could easily bring them before unsympathetic local magistrates and governors, where they might even face life-or-death decisions. The letter of Pliny, governor of Pontus, to the emperor Trajan (ca. 112 CE) not only details the perilous situation of Christians in his time and place but indicates that in previous incidents twenty years earlier some Christians were harassed to the point that they repudiated their new religion.

11. Cf. the similar theme in Hebrews and *1 Clement*, also from the Roman church of the same period. On 1 Peter's use of the biblical patriarchs as models for the church as foreigners in their own country, see esp. Reinhard Feldmeier, *Die Christen als Fremde*, WUNT 64 (Tübingen: Mohr, 1992), and Reinhard Feldmeier, *The First Letter of Peter: A Commentary on the Greek Text*, trans. Peter H. Davids (Waco, TX: Baylor University Press, 2008), 53 and passim.

This would be the time of 1 Peter (Pliny *Letters* 10.97; see text at §26.1.4 below).

17.2.4 Date and Occasion

The earliest allusion to 1 Peter is probably 2 Peter 3:1, but the date of 2 Peter is not clear. There seem to be clear allusions in Polycarp's *To the Philippians* (ca. 135 CE; 1.3=1 Pet 1:8; 2.1=1 Pet 1:13, 21, 4:5; 2.2 =1 Pet 3:9; 10.1= 1 Pet 3:8; 10.2=1 Pet 2:12, 5:5; 14.1=1 Pet 5:12). According to Eusebius's *Ecclesiastical History* 3.39.17, Papias (early 2nd cent.) quoted from 1 Peter. Irenaeus (ca. 185 CE) is the first Christian author to quote 1 Peter directly and to designate Peter as the author (*Against Heresies* 4.9.2, 16.5; 5.7.2). The *terminus a quo* is provided by references or clear allusions within the letter itself. The metaphorical reference to Rome as "Babylon" in 5:13, a usage that did not originate until after the destruction of Jerusalem in 70 CE, seems to locate the letter after 70. Within the range 70–135 CE, the most likely date for 1 Peter is about 90 CE. This is the majority opinion of critical scholars, based on the following evidence:

— First Peter presupposes that the Christian faith has spread throughout the vast territory of the five provinces. There is no evidence for Christian congregations in Pontus, Bithynia, and Cappadocia in the first generation. An early tradition indicates Paul was explicitly forbidden by the Holy Spirit to preach in Bithynia (Acts 16:7). But Pliny indicates Christians were numerous in Pontus by about 92 CE.

— The abundant similarities in vocabulary and thought world shared by 1 Peter and *1 Clement* (written from Rome around the end of the first century CE), while they do not point to literary dependence in either direction, do indicate that both derive from the same situation, making use of a common tradition.

— The combination of Pauline and Petrine traditions suggests a period of several years after the death of the two great apostles (ca. 64 CE), during which time their traditions were amalgamated.

— Although the readers, and perhaps the author, are Gentile Christians, the relation of the church to Judaism, the role of the law in salvation, and the status of Israel in salvation history are unproblematic. The Jewish Scriptures are appropriated as belonging to and speaking directly to the church. Such features point to a time when these theological battles of the first generation were now past.

— While there is no direct literary dependence on the undisputed Pauline letters, the author has been extensively influenced by them, and probably by Ephesians as well (but not by the Pastorals). This points to a time when Paul's letters had been collected and circulated as a corpus.

— Elders as church leaders (5:1) are unknown to the undisputed letters of Paul, but are the standard form of congregational church leadership that appeared in the Pauline/Petrine tradition in second-generation Christianity and are documented in Acts in the third generation (Acts 11:30; 14:23; 15:2, 4, 6, 22; 16:4; 20:17, 18; see on the Pastorals above, §§16.1.2; 16.1.5).

The letter thus seems to fit best into the situation of the Roman church near the end of the first century. Having suffered persecution under Nero, understanding itself to be the custodian of the two pillar apostles, Peter and Paul, and responding to the challenge of Hebrews 5:12 that it should be teaching others in behalf of the Roman church, a congregational leader writes with apostolic authority to encourage the harassed sister congregations of Asia Minor.

17.2.5 Provenance

The letter claims to have been written from "Babylon" (5:13). This cannot be meant literally. There is no evidence that Peter was ever in Babylon or that Petrine tradition was located there. The once-great city that had included a significant Jewish population was by the middle of the first century an insignificant small town that the Jewish community had left, and was practically uninhabited by the time 1 Peter was written (Diodorus *Sic.* 2.9.9; Strabo *Geog.* 16.1.5). Thus "Babylon" must be understood as a cryptogram for Rome. After 70 CE this became fairly common in Jewish apocalyptic documents (*2 Apoc. Bar* 11.1–2; 67.7; 2 Esd 3:1–2, 28; *Sib. Or.* 5.143, 155–161, 434, 440), and is adopted by the Christian author of Revelation in the 90s (Rev 14:8; 16:19; 17:5; 18:2, 10, 21). Our choices are thus that 1 Peter was actually written from Rome, or that Rome=Babylon is part of the fictive literary world projected by the pseudonymous style.

If the figures of Mark and Silvanus (5:12–13) are taken to be fictive elements belonging to the pseudepigraphical framework, then the purported setting in Rome could itself be a part of this same fictive world.[12] However, it may well be that both Mark and Silvanus are real persons who had worked with both Paul and Peter, and who continued to be active in the Roman church after the two apostles had been killed. The numerous points of contact between 1 Peter, Hebrews, and *1 Clement* seem to locate 1 Peter in Rome, as does the earliest tradition.

17.2.6 Sources

First Peter is not an artificial patchwork of sources but a real letter (see below). This does not mean, however, that it was composed ad hoc. The author drew from a deep well of traditional materials composed of Jewish Scripture and Christian tradition.

12. So, e.g., Schnelle, *New Testament Writings*, who locates 1 Peter in Asia Minor. Doering ("Diaspora Letter," 233) and Hunzinger (C. H. Hunzinger, "Babylon als Deckname für Rom und die Datierung des 1Petrusbriefes," in *Gottes Wort und Gottes Land*, ed. Henning Reventlow [Göttingen: Vandenhoeck & Ruprecht, 1965]), 77, suggest the letter originated in Syria or Asia Minor.

Jewish Scripture. The author uses the Old Testament as a Christian book in which what was once said to and about Israel passes seamlessly and unpolemically into address to the church. The Spirit that inspired the biblical prophets was the Spirit of the preexistent Christ (1:11), the same Spirit that inspired Christian preaching (1:12). When the relative size of the documents is considered, 1 Peter makes more extensive use of the Old Testament than any other New Testament author except Revelation. His thought world is the LXX, from which the only direct quotations or allusions from any source are taken. The montage of biblical imagery in 2:1–10 is one of the densest in the New Testament, though only 2:6 is a direct quotation. While the author knows the Old Testament thoroughly himself, the choice and combination of citations is not made independently, but reflects church tradition. He quotes some of the same obscure texts as other New Testament authors (e.g., Prov 3:34 in 5:5; see Jas 4:6) and the same combinations of texts (e.g., Isa 28:16 and 8:14 in 2:6–8; see Rom 9:33). This must be more than coincidence but need not be direct literary dependence. A tradition of textual selection and interpretation had developed that emerges in Paul, James, 1 Peter, and others. The Roman provenance of this hermeneutical tradition is suggested by the common use of Psalm 34 (LXX Ps 33) in Hebrews, 1 Peter, and *1 Clement*. The contacts between 1 Peter and James (using some of the same obscure Scripture texts) may suggest their dependence on common tradition with roots in Jerusalem Christianity. This probability is enhanced by the general Jewish character of first- and second-generation Roman Christianity.[13]

Christian tradition. First Peter is a distinctively Petrine formulation of a stream of Christian tradition that was widely influential in early Christianity. This steam of tradition included hymnic, creedal, liturgical, and catechetical

13. Brown and Meier, *Antioch and Rome*, 92–158. See below, §18.4.

materials (e.g.. 1:18–20; 2:13–17, 18–25; 3:1–7, 18–19). The existence and contents of this stream of tradition has been persuasively documented by the detailed charts cataloguing identical and similar content, form, wording, and patterns, representing the results of comparative analyses of 1 Peter and other New Testament documents.[14] A comparison of 1 Peter 5:5–9 with James 4:6–10 indicates numerous contacts in which even the casual reader can detect an underlying common tradition.

Pauline letters. Not only does the author adopt the letter form itself under the influence of the Pauline tradition; the utilization of several particular features of the Pauline letter form comes directly or indirectly from Paul. This is illustrated by the trademark salutation χάρις ὑμῖν καὶ εἰρήνη (*charis humin kai eirēnē*, grace to you and peace, 1:2), and by distinctive Pauline vocabulary such as χάρισμα (*charisma*, gift, 4:10) and ἐν Χριστῷ (*en Christō*, in Christ, 3:16; 5:10, 14). Paul's peculiar word for "fleshly" sinful desires (σαρκικός, *sarkikos*) is not found in the LXX or elsewhere in the New Testament except the Pauline letters (five times) and 1 Peter 2:11. The terminology of "angels, principalities, and powers" is found outside the Pauline corpus only in 1 Peter 3:22. The author derives from Paul the view that the believer's life "in Christ" means participation (κοινωνία, *koinōnia*) in Christ's sufferings in a way that goes beyond imitation of Christ as a model (see, e.g., Phil 2:1; 3:10; 2 Cor 1:5; 1 Pet 1:11; 5:1). Scholars have compiled extensive lists of linguistic, stylistic, formal, and theological features distinctive of Paul and found in 1 Peter (sometimes only in Paul and 1 Peter).

The older view that regarded 1 Peter as merely a Paulinist has properly been rejected, but interpreters should guard against an overreaction that minimizes the influence of the Pauline letters on 1 Peter. Such data do not necessarily indicate a direct literary connection between 1 Peter and the Pauline letters, in the sense that the author of 1 Peter had Pauline letters open before him as he wrote. He has heard them read often as part of the worship and instruction of the church in Rome, where he is probably a teaching elder, assumes that these letters have circulated in the churches of Asia Minor to which he writes, and thus presupposes his readers are also familiar with them. So also the incorporation of Paul's associates Mark and Silvanus (Silas) into the fictive literary world projected by the document (5:12–13) illustrates the author's co-option of the Pauline tradition. This represents a secondary amalgamation of Pauline and Petrine traditions, not a strategy of the historical Simon Peter. It is hardly conceivable that the historical Peter in Rome would, in a letter to the Pauline mission territory of Asia and Galatia, allude to Mark and Silas, but not to Paul himself (cf. 2 Pet 3:14–16, where even the pseudepigraphical 2 Pet is constrained to do this). The author takes over the Pauline letter form, much Pauline content and theology, and even Paul's relationships and associates—but presents them all under the name of *Peter*.

Distinctive Petrine tradition. The primary source from which 1 Peter draws its materials, concepts, and language is a stream of Christian tradition, elements of which are ultimately rooted in early Palestinian Christianity. First Peter's tradition is often Jewish Christian tradition associated with Jerusalem, as documented by the contacts with James. This stream of tradition has been reinterpreted and augmented by intense engagement with the world of Hellenistic religions, and received a stable form in the Roman church during the generation 60–90 CE. Although this tradition has deep Jewish roots, there is no indication that the author had imbibed the kind of Jewish traditions cultivated in the rabbinic academies that later received written deposit in the Mishnah, midrashim, and the Talmud. There is no direct literary contact between 1 Peter and the Dead Sea Scrolls, but the combination of thematic similarities such as election, purification by a

14. Selwyn, *First Epistle of St. Peter*, 365–466. Cf. also Elliott, *1 Peter*, 20–40.

water ritual, the community as eschatological house of God, eschatological interpretation of Scripture, the identification of the community itself as the people of God, and the call to holiness may well point to the earliest stage of the tradition now found in 1 Peter as having originated in the same thought world as that of Qumran, namely, on the margins of Palestinian Judaism, in tension with the dominant religious authorities.

Included as part of the deposit of early Palestinian Christian tradition is the early kerygma of the saving event of Jesus' death and resurrection, and some reflection of the sayings of Jesus. There are no direct quotations from Jesus' teaching in 1 Peter. The extent of allusions to sayings of Jesus is disputed, but attempts to detect large numbers of them has not been convincing to most scholars.[15] Whatever reflections of Jesus' sayings there may be in 1 Peter, they bear the features not of personal memory but of having already been incorporated into paraenetic church tradition.

17.2.7 Genre

In the late nineteenth and first half of the twentieth century, numerous scholars argued that the bulk of 1 Peter was not originally composed as a letter. Already in 1887 Adolf Harnack confidently declared that 1 Peter was "a sermon not a letter," that a baptismal homily (1:3–5:11) had later been inserted into a letter framework.[16] In 1911 E. R. Perdelwitz refined the theory to argue that 1:3–4:11 was a baptismal sermon to new converts, later incorporated into a letter that added exhortations to a new situation of persecution. This view of the document's composition was widely adopted. However, further research has shown the unity of the letter, of which practically all scholars are now convinced.[17] First Peter was written all at once as a real letter, but does include a large proportion of traditional paraenetic materials, including baptismal imagery and allusions, that have provided the occasion for other hypotheses.

The letter form is not part of the fictive literary world projected by the pseudonymous document; 1 Peter is a real letter to real churches. First Peter is not a letter to individual churches, but neither is it a catholic letter addressed to the church as a whole; it is a circular letter to all the Christians in a wide area, corresponding to the distinct literary type of the "diaspora letter."[18] It is thus a transitional form, from the particularity of Paul's letters addressing a specific situation to the later Catholic Letters addressed to the church universal. Unlike the authentic Pauline letters, it does not reflect any awareness of particular events in the life of specific congregations. The Petrine author knows of the addressees' situation only what he knows theologically of Christians as such (see 2 Tim 3:12). Like the Pauline letters, it was intended for reading in the worship services of the congregations, not for private study. It thus contains preaching and teaching material appropriate to congregational instruction and edification. It is not essentially a catechetical letter concerned with Christian doctrine, but a paraenetical letter designed to encourage a certain kind of conduct in a situation of testing and adversity (5:12).

15. Cf. Robert H. Gundry, "'Verba Christi' in I Peter: Their Implications Concerning the Authorship of I Peter and the Authenticity of the Gospels Tradition," *NTS* 13 (1967): 336–50, and the response by Ernest Best, "I Peter and the Gospel Tradition," *NTS* 16, no. 2 (1970): 95–113.

16. Adolf von Harnack, *Die Geschichte der altchristlichen Literatur bis Eusebius*, 2 vols. (Leipzig: Hinrichs, 1897, 1904), 451–65.

17. William Joseph Dalton, *Christ's Proclamation to the Spirits: A Study of 1 Peter 3:18–4:6* (Rome: Pontifical Biblical Institute, 1965), 62–87; several commentaries and studies give the history of the rise and fall of such hypotheses (e.g., Achtemeier, *1 Peter*, 58–64; Soards, "Petrine School," 3834).

18. So, e.g., Feldmeier, *Peter*, 30–33. Cf. Jer 29:4–23; 2 *Bar* 78–87; 2 Macc 1:1–2:18. Cf. Doering, "Diaspora Letter," 215–37.

17.2.8 Structure and Outline

1:1–2	Greeting
1:3–12	Thanksgiving
1:13–5:11	Body of the Letter
1:13–2:10	The New Identity as the Elect and Holy People of God
2:11–3:12	Christian Existence and Conduct in the Given Structures of Society
3:13–5:11	Responsible Suffering in the Face of Hostility
5:12–14	Epistolary Conclusion

17.2.9 Exegetical-Theological Précis

1:1–2 Greeting

The prescript adopts and adapts the greeting formula that had become standard in the Pauline letters, but presents the author as the apostle Peter. The letter addresses its readers as "exiles of the Dispersion," applying biblical and Jewish imagery for the people of God to its Christian readers. The author writes from the sister church in "Babylon" (5:13), that is, is himself a part of the Diaspora, awaiting the final restoration and homecoming of God's people (see on Jas 1:1). To be exiles, foreigners, not at home, belongs to the essential character of Christian existence. To be Diaspora is to belong to the ongoing people of God, to be set apart and sprinkled with the blood of the covenant. They are not volunteers but have been chosen and destined by God, portrayed in proto-Trinitarian terms ("chosen . . . by God, sanctified by the Spirit . . . , obedient to Jesus Christ").

1:3–12 Thanksgiving

The thanksgiving section that normally follows is present here in the form of an extended blessing (as in 2 Cor 1:3–11 and Eph 1:3–14), typically signaling the themes to be developed in the letter: the new life and hope that has come through the resurrection of Jesus Christ, the severe trials the readers are facing because of their newfound faith, and their place as God's people within the comprehensive plan of God announced by the biblical prophets. The Christ in whom they believe is not merely the crucified man of Nazareth, but the one destined before the foundation of the world (1:20), who spoke through the prophets (1:11), who appeared at the end of the ages, dividing all history into "then" (ποτέ, *pote*, 2:10; 3:5, 20) and "now" (νῦν *nun*, 1:12, 2:10, 25, 3:21). This "now" spans the appearance of Christ in history, where he suffered, died, and was raised, until his final manifestation at the end of history, which is soon to occur.

The "first" and "second" comings of Christ are seen as comprising one event, the "end of all things" (τέλος πάντων, *telos pantōn*, 4:7). The author and his readers live in this "now," the time of the revelation of Christ between his appearance in history and his final advent. The readers have been integrated into this ongoing history of the mighty acts of God by God's initiative. They are elected, called, reborn, and kept by the power of God. None of these grand affirmations is mere speculative theology; they function to encourage the readers to hold fast to their faith despite the difficult test they are enduring.

1:13–5:11 Body of the Letter

The body of the letter concerns the readers' new identity as the elect and holy people of God (1:13–2:10), how they are to conduct themselves within the given structures of society (2:11–3:12), and a call to follow the model of Christ by enduring the unjust suffering to which they are being subjected (3:13–5:11).

1:13–2:10 The New Identity of the Elect and Holy People of God

The readers' new identity is explicated with biblical language and imagery originally referring to Israel, with numerous echoes of the language of the exodus. Jesus is their unblemished Passover lamb (1:19). The readers are to "gird up the loins of their minds," that is, roll up their mental sleeves to engage in the hard thinking to follow, in imitation of the original Hebrews of the exodus who were to "gird up their loins" in preparation for their departure from the slavery of Egypt (Exod 12:11). As Israel pledged their obedience to God by accepting God's covenant at Sinai, so Peter's Christian readers have become obedient and had the covenant blood applied to them (Exod 24:7–8; 1 Pet 1:2). The displaced wanderers of the exodus were tempted to look back to their former life, as are the distressed Christians of Asia Minor (e.g., Exod 16:2–3; 1 Pet 4:3–4). At Sinai, Israel was called by God, with the command "Be holy because I am holy" (Lev 11:44), words the author applies directly to his Christian readers.

This first section is climaxed by addressing his readers in terms of seven biblical images for the people of God:[19]

1. The church is pictured as the *temple of God*, built of Christians as "living stones" (2:5). The "stone" imagery is applied to Christ and Christians (not to Peter), and "rock" is used as a synonym of "stone" in 2:8, with no hint of a Petrine ecclesiological role indicated by his name. The readers' experience of social rejection is interpreted christologically. Being rejected and crucified was not an episode in the career of Jesus that was put behind him by the resurrection. Christ continues through history as the Rejected One, modeling the present status of his disciples, who await future vindication.

2. Like Israel at Sinai, the readers are addressed as a *holy priesthood* or royal priesthood (2:5, 9). The image of Exodus 19:6, used for Israel, is here applied to the church. Just as Israel as a whole was a priestly community, mediating between the one God and the whole of humanity, so the church is the community that mediates God's grace and purpose to all people. The later issue of the priesthood of all believers, understood individualistically, is not here in view. The point is that the Christian community as a whole plays the role of the continuing people of God in history, which includes being a priestly community on behalf of the world.

3. As heirs of Israel, the readers are addressed as a *chosen race* (2:9).

4. As heirs of Israel, the readers are addressed as a *holy nation* (2:9; cf. Exod 19:6; Wis 17:2).

5. As heirs of Israel, the readers are addressed as *God's own people* (2:9). The list of honorary titles is summed up and concluded by applying two designations taken from Hosea 1:6, 9–10; 2:23 (also used in a similar context by Paul in Rom 9:25).

6 and 7. As heirs of Israel, the readers are addressed as the *people of God* and as *those who have received mercy* (2:10). Although the readers are mostly or entirely ethnic Gentiles (see 1:14, 18), as the holy people of God they are contrasted with Gentiles (2:12).

2:11–3:12 Christian Existence and Conduct in the Given Structures of Society

The preceding section has dealt with the self-understanding of the Christian community. On this theological foundation, the next part of the letter turns outward to the church's relation to the world, presenting specific instruction on how the community is to conduct itself within the given structures of society. It was a world in which imperial rule, institutionalized slavery, and the patriarchal family were not only assumed as "the way things are," but were considered essential for an ordered society legitimized by the gods and maintained by loyal adherence to the cultural religion. Those who had committed themselves to the new faith could not

19. Though 1 Peter never uses the term "church," the letter has at least forty-six images of the community of faith. This section comprises one of the most dense constellations of ecclesiological imagery in the New Testament.

participate in much of the normal community life involving the mixture of traditional (i.e., pagan) religion and patriotism. They were thus seen as adherents of a new and dangerous cult, a threat to the values of an orderly world. How should they respond? Withdraw? Resist?

The author's response includes traditions from Hellenistic and Christian household codes (see on Col 3:18–4:1), but is not merely a reversion from Christian freedom and equality to compliance with more conventional standards. Government is to be respected as the guarantor of order, but is not legitimized in religious terms. Emperor and governors are part of God's world, but they are "human institutions" (2:13). Caesar is to receive the same respect that all people receive—but only God is to be worshiped (2:17). The basic mandate is to live among the "Gentiles"[20] in such a manner that Christians are seen to be not evildoers and troublemakers, as their compatriots suppose, so that their suspicious neighbors will see their good works and finally come to glorify God (2:11–12, 15).

In such a situation, in which Christians are suspected of destructive and criminal activity, doing good means to accept the authority of every human institution, including the emperor and his officials (2:13–17). Two classes of people are then singled out as examples for the whole community: Christian slaves in non-Christian households (2:18–25) and Christian wives of non-Christian husbands (3:1–7). Such slaves and wives are a microcosm of the situation of the church as a whole, an island of faithfulness to God in a sea of unbelief. They, like the community as a whole, are called to fit into the social hierarchy as part of their Christian mission, which has a higher priority than their individual rights (see on Col 3:18–4:1).

20. The readers are themselves ethnic Gentiles, but here the word is used to mean "those who do not belong to the covenant people of God," another instance of author and readers unselfconsciously assuming the identity of biblical Israel. Such language can be heard as commandeering the Scriptures and identity of ethnic, empirical Israel, but this issue seems not to arise for the author himself.

3:13–5:11 Responsible Suffering in the Face of Hostility

Living in this manner may result in unjust suffering; if so, it is to be borne patiently. Christ is the example. He suffered unjustly but was vindicated by God; this is the pattern for Christians as well. Christ's suffering and death appeared to mean defeat. This is how the readers' neighbors interpreted the death of Jesus, who was executed by the government as an enemy of society. But this defeat was only apparent; in reality, God raised Jesus, who effected God's victory not only over earthly powers but throughout the cosmos. This affirmation is developed by citing a fragment of a tradition that is no longer clear to us (3:18–22). This lack of clarity allowed it to become part of the later interpretation found in the *Gospel of Peter* and finally embodied in the "descended into hell" clause of Apostles' Creed. This explanation is now generally abandoned.

5:12–14 Epistolary Conclusion

More than a formality, this brief conclusion gives its own summary of the message of the letter. Readers are called to endure unjust suffering for the sake of Christ and as testimony to others to the truth of the gospel. The suffering involved in the Christian life is not merely a passing burden that must be endured in order to receive later salvation, but is to be received as a gift, the grace of God in which they are to stand fast.

17.3 Interpreting Hebrews

"MUCH TO SAY THAT IS HARD TO explain"—these friendly words of warning are from the author himself, after luring readers well into the document (5:11). "Beautifully written, powerfully argued, and theologically profound. . . . Its anonymous author summons readers to a vision of reality and a commitment of faith that is at once distinctive, attractive, and disturbing." These are the opening words of a helpful and detailed recent commentary.[21] Hebrews is indeed a *historical* challenge to the modern reader, because this text continues to resist the methods by which we have become accustomed to approach (and domesticate) ancient texts. The main issues of historical criticism continue to resist definite answers—who wrote it, when, where, to whom, and why. Hebrews is *theologically* challenging to modern readers, not only because its confession of faith is written from within a worldview very different from our own, but because it projects a vision of reality, centered in God's act in Christ, that is both intellectually demanding and existentially disturbing to our comfortable common sense.

Hebrews first appears on our historical screen in 𝔓[46], our oldest extant collection of Pauline letters, where it is found immediately after Romans and before 1 Corinthians. This means that at least by about 200 CE a major stream of Eastern Christianity considered Hebrews to be (1) a letter (2) by Paul (3) to the "Hebrews." This identification of literary type, author, and intended readership, crucial to grasping the meaning of the document, was already challenged in the ancient world. Modern scholarship is virtually unanimous that (1) Hebrews is not a letter, (2) Paul is not the author, and (3) the document was not addressed to "Hebrews." These conclusions may seem negative at first, but they turn out to be a positive foundation for apprehending the message of the book.

17.3.1 Hebrews is not a letter.

Hebrews is included in 𝔓[46], as in all later collections, as a letter. Yet Hebrews does not read like a letter. It does not begin with the conventional letter opening and manifests no epistolary characteristics until the very end, when, *after* the concluding benediction, an epistolary conclusion in the Pauline style is appended (13:22–25).[22] Thus a few scholars have argued that Hebrews was originally composed as a treatise, and that the epistolary ending is an addition intended to make Hebrews appear as a Pauline letter and thus fit in to the developing tradition of authoritative documents.[23] In this case, Hebrews would be considered quasi-pseudepigraphical, adopting minor features of the Pauline letter and the fictive Pauline world, borrowing the figure of Timothy known from the Pauline letters, with an indication that he is going to visit the addressees as in 1 Corinthians 4:17; 16:10, Philippians 2:19; 1 Thessalonians 3:2. However, recent analyses have shown that the epistolary conclusion is integral to its context and was most likely composed by the original author.[24]

The composition itself, however, is clearly not a letter and has been adapted to the letter format by the epistolary ending. But neither is Hebrews a treatise, essay, or tract. It directly addresses the audience in the second person (fifty-one times, plus ten first-person-plural hortatory subjunctives), as the communication of one who knows their history and concrete circumstances and is known by them (e.g., 5:12; 6:9–10; 12:4–13:25). The author refers to his composition as a λόγος τῆς παρακλήσεως (*logos tēs paraclēseōs*, word of exhortation, 13:22), the same phrase used in Acts 13:15 for a sermon preached in the context of worship. The author seems to be a preacher with some status

21. Luke Timothy Johnson, *Hebrews: A Commentary*, NTL (Louisville, KY: Westminster John Knox Press, 2006), 1.

22. Cf. James, which begins like a letter but continues as an oration with no further epistolary characteristics. The "letter" of 1 John neither begins nor ends as a letter, but does manifest letterlike qualities (second person direct address; dealing with a specific situation known to the readers).

23. William Wrede, *Das literarische Rätsel des Hebräerbriefs: mit einem Anhang über den literarischen Charakter des Barnabasbriefes*, FRLANT 8 (Göttingen: Vandenhoeck & Ruprecht, 1906), 39, followed by a few recent scholars, including the important work of Erich Grässer, *An die Hebräer*, 3 vols., EKKNT 17 (Neukirchen-Vluyn: Neukirchener Verlag, 1990–1997), 1:22; 3:413–16.

24. E.g., Harold W. Attridge, *The Epistle to the Hebrews*, Hermeneia (Philadelphia: Fortress Press, 1989), 404–5; Craig R. Koester, *Hebrews*, AB 36 (New York: Doubleday, 2001), 580–84.

in the community he addresses, who is absent and detained in some situation that prohibits him from directly preaching to the assembled congregation. He composes his sermon to be read in his absence, appends a brief epistolary conclusion, sends the document by an associate to the congregation, where it is read forth en toto to the assembled congregation(s) in his absence. Modern specialists in homiletics and rhetoric consider it to be a masterpiece of early Christian preaching.[25]

To call Hebrews a sermon raises interesting questions for the modern reader: How typical of first-century preaching is this sermon? Were the house churches to which it was presumably addressed accustomed to such length, theological depth, and presuppositions about their own biblical and theological knowledge and interest, or were they staggered by its expectations? Did preachers, including the author, regularly compose such a sermon, or is Hebrews a special case? Did the congregation "get it" in their first and only hearing, or was it intended for repeated reading and reflection? It is clearly not "catholic" in the sense that it was intended for the church universal; but was it intended for only one congregation, or for several in the same general area and situation?

Hebrews is a sermon with an epistolary ending. However, the ending was not appended merely because the author happened to be absent. Hebrews, like the deuteropauline and Catholic Epistles, are what they are by virtue of the Pauline letter tradition. The author thinks in terms of a worship service in which the Scripture is read. By his time this sometimes included the reading of Pauline letters in the same liturgical setting. This tended to give them the same normative status as Scripture (see the later 2 Pet 3:15–16). Such letters do not circulate privately and individually as written documents, but within the worship life of the community. They are teaching documents, not merely dealing with particular local issues, but interpreting the Scripture and Christian tradition in the ongoing life of the church.

17.3.2 Paul is not the author.

In 𝔓[46] Hebrews is assumed to be a Pauline letter, and it was often so considered in the Eastern churches (e.g., Clement of Alexandria). This assumption was already widely challenged in the ancient church, and was not generally accepted by Western churches until late in the fourth century. In the early third century, Tertullian of Carthage acknowledged the authority of Hebrews and cited it against Hermas of Rome (*On Modesty* 20), but attributed it to Barnabas—a reasonable guess, since Barnabas was a Levite and companion of Paul. Origen also accepted the document as canonical, sometimes cited it as "Paul" and "Scripture," but finally concluded that the author is unknown. Other candidates for author have been proposed, including Apollos, Priscilla, Luke, Epaphras, and Mary the mother of Jesus. The historical probability that any of these proposals is correct ranges from minimal to zero, so that most scholars affirm Origen's concluding judgment, which has become part of the tradition universally cited in discussion of the authorship of Hebrews: "God only knows" (first cited by Eusebius, *Hist. eccl.* 6.25.11–14).

While we do not know who wrote Hebrews, the virtually unanimous opinion of contemporary scholarship is that it was not written by Paul and in fact could hardly have been written by him.[26] Not only do the linguistic, rhetorical, historical, and theological factors detailed below make this next to impossible; it is difficult to imagine the author of Galatians, who

25. Cf. Fred B. Craddock, "The Letter to the Hebrews: Introduction, Commentary, Reflections," in *The New Interpreter's Bible*, ed. Leander Keck (Nashville: Abingdon Press, 1998), 4, 21 and passim; Thomas G. Long, *Hebrews*, Interpretation (Louisville, KY: John Knox Press, 1997), x and passim.

26. The few remaining advocates of Pauline authorship are reviewed and rejected by David Lewis Allen, *Lukan Authorship of Hebrews*, NACSBT 8 (Nashville: B&H Academic, 2010), 46–77.

insists that his gospel and apostleship came directly from the risen Lord, calmly placing himself in the same category as his addressees, who received the faith as Christian tradition from earlier believers who had heard the Lord himself (2:3).[27]

What we can know about the author of Hebrews is limited to what we can learn from the document itself. Thus turns out to be quite a bit.

1. The author (and his addressees) have substantial contact with the Pauline tradition. This is indicated in the first place by the general "epistolary pressure" that caused the sermon to be adapted to the Pauline letter form (see above §§1.4; 10.2.1; 10.2.4). The early reception of the letter into a collection of Paul's letters (𝔓[46]) shows it was perceived to stand in the Pauline tradition. Although "Timothy" was a common name, the Timothy of 13:23 probably refers to the companion of Paul. While there are striking theological differences between Paul's letters and Hebrews, the broad outlines of the author's Christology, which he assumes his readers share, represent the Pauline tradition. The focus is almost exclusively on the death and resurrection of the earthly Jesus, but not his life, miraculous deeds, and teaching represented by his sayings. Some themes that first emerge only briefly in Paul are extensively developed in Hebrews. Among these we may mention that "access to God" is given through Christ (Rom 5:1; cf. Heb 4:16; 10:19–22), the image of Christ as "firstborn among many brothers and sisters" (Rom 8:29; cf. Heb 2:10–12), the interpretation of the death of Jesus in sacrificial terms, using imagery associated with the sprinkling of blood on the mercy seat on the day of atonement (Rom 3:21–26; cf. Heb 7:1–10:18), the new covenant (2 Cor 3:1–11; Heb 7:22–10:16), and, especially, the heavenly Christ as intercessor and the extensive elaboration of the image of Christ as heavenly high priest (Rom 8:34; Heb 6:19–10:22). Scholars have catalogued numerous detailed points of contact with Paul's letters.[28] While some of these represent common Christian tradition, others are distinctive Pauline features reflected in Hebrews. Both author and readers seem to belong to a community in which Paul's letters are read and Pauline traditions are alive. The circulation of Paul's letters here presupposed points to the time after Paul's death.

Such points of contact do not mean that Hebrews belongs to a "Pauline School" tradition in the sense of Ephesians, Colossians, and the Pastorals. The author is influenced by Paul, but is not his student, and for him Paul is not *the* apostle. So also, Hebrews is a different voice in the Roman context from that of 1 Peter, with which it has many points of contact. The author is not attempting to fuse divergent streams of tradition or harmonize conflicting apostolic claims. He does not adopt the name of an apostle of the previous generation, but writes in his own voice, so familiar to his audience that he does not name himself (13:22–25). Hebrews is distinctive in the New Testament, but not isolated or independent. It is neither an interpretation of Pauline tradition nor a theological development independent of Paul, but represents a Roman theologian in the latter part of the first century incorporating Pauline and other traditions current in his setting, interpreting them all in an independent, creative manner.

2. The author and his readers are acquainted with earlier Christian writings/traditions. The author manifests no awareness of any Gospel, canonical or extracanonical, nor is there any indication that he or his readers are acquainted with sayings of Jesus or stories about him. The

27. It must be remembered, of course, that in the author's own theology these earlier witnesses proclaimed to them the word of God, so that it was God himself who called them to faith (13:7; cf. the similar theology in 1 Pet 1:12, 25).

28. See esp. Ceslas Spicq, *L' Épître aux Hébreux*, 2 vols., Etudes bibliques 8 (Paris: Gabalda, 1952), 155–56; Koester, *Hebrews*, 54–56. Contacts with particular letters are explored in such essays as Ben Witherington, "The Influence of Galatians on Hebrews," *NTS* 37, no. 1 (1991): 258–66. There are no indications of influence from the Pastoral Letters, another indication of their late date.

Jesus who is quoted is the transcendent Christ who speaks through the words of Scripture (2:11–13; 10:5–7). There is an allusion to the Jesus whose tearful prayer in the face of death was heard even though he died (5:7), but no explicit reflection of the Gethsemane scene in the Synoptics (Mark 14:32–36 and par.). Author and readers have experienced the miraculous power of God in their own history, as the Holy Spirit worked signs and wonders to confirm the Christian message (2:4), but they do not know stories of Jesus' own miraculous power (2:1–9). The author thus writes to a Christian community that does not know, or does not accept, the Gospel mode of communicating the faith. Yet he and his readers are influenced by other traditions and texts. We have noted the connections with *1 Clement*. Hebrews' closest contacts are with 1 Peter.[29] Each document describes itself as an "exhortation" (Heb 13:22; 1 Pet 5:12). Each relates itself self-consciously to Pauline traditions (see above). Both focus on the saving event of Christ's death, relating it to the "sprinkling of blood" (Heb 10:22; 12:24; 1 Pet 1:2), "washing" and baptism (Heb 6:2–4; 10:22; 1 Pet 3:20–21), "conscience" (Heb 9:9, 14; 10:2, 22; 1 Pet 2:19; 3:16, 21), and "holiness/sanctification" (Heb 10:10, 29; 1 Pet 1:2; 2:22). Both Hebrews and 1 Peter portray Christians as "strangers and sojourners" of the exodus, the Christian life as a pilgrimage (Heb 11:8–16; 12:22; 13:14; 1 Pet 1:1; 2:11) and Christ as the "chief shepherd" (1 Pet 5:4; cf. Heb 13:20).[30] Thus, while the author's approach to Christian faith is independent in the sense that he is not merely the interpreter of one stream of prior traditions, he is not idiosyncratic, but launches his "word of exhortation" into a setting where there is a fraternal and energetic interchange of Christian traditions.

3. The author is a master of Greek language and rhetoric. It is generally agreed that Hebrews is the best Greek in the New Testament. The writer has a large and sophisticated vocabulary. His thirteen chapters contain 150 words not found elsewhere in the New Testament, not counting proper names. Ten of these occur nowhere else in extant Greek literature. The author composes for the ear, with great rhetorical skill. He begins with a lengthy and elegant periodic sentence (1:1–4) that sets the tone for the whole, and utilizes a variety of rhetorical devices throughout the document to maintain the hearers' engagement and persuade them to action. One example of many: in 5:8, the author makes effective use of the wordplay common in Hellenistic moral discourse, μαθεῖν παθεῖν (*mathein pathein*), "to learn is to suffer; to suffer is to learn" (cf. the English "no pain, no gain" from the athletic training field).

4. The author is well educated in Greco-Roman culture, especially in the Middle Platonism popular in the first century. The writer's Bible is the LXX. Sometimes the key point is absent from the Hebrew text and is dependent on Greek translation (see below on, e.g., 2:5–9). The author seems to be especially adept at relating the vertical understanding of faith that thinks in Platonic categories to the horizontal, historical understanding of faith fundamental to the Hebrew Scriptures and Jewish tradition. In this he is like the Alexandrian Jewish philosopher Philo (see above, §§5.1.3; 9.2.2) and utterly unlike Paul. Though he drinks from the same philosophical spring as Philo, the author of Hebrews is not directly influenced by him, and does not adopt his allegorical method of biblical interpretation.[31]

5. The author seems to write for a situation after the destruction of the temple. The author of *1 Clement*, writing around the end of the first century CE, clearly makes use of Hebrews (e.g.,

29. See analysis in Allen, *Authorship*, 82.

30. For further parallels and points of contact, see Spicq, *Hébreux*, 139–44; Attridge, *Hebrews*, 30–31.

31. On Hebrews and Philo, see especially James Thompson, *Hebrews*, Paideia (Grand Rapids: Baker Academic, 2008), 23–25 and passim, and his earlier *The Beginnings of Christian Philosophy: The Epistle to the Hebrews*, CBQMS 13 (Washington, DC: Catholic Biblical Association of America, 1982).

1 Clem. 36.1–4 unmistakably reflects Heb 1:1–7, 13; 2:18), so Hebrews must have been written some time before 100 CE. How much earlier continues to be a disputed point. A principal argument for a pre-70 date has been the lack of any reference to the destruction of the temple, and the use of the present tense for the priesthood and sacrificial cultus, as though the Jerusalem priesthood were still functioning at the time of writing (8:4; 9:25; 10:1, 11).[32] It is claimed that if the temple's destruction had already occurred, pointing this out would clinch the author's argument that the priesthood and sacrifices of the old covenant are no longer valid. However, Josephus, *1 Clement*, and others writing some decades after the destruction of the temple continue to use the present tense in regard to the temple's functions. Moreover, the author of Hebrews does not refer to the *temple* at all, but to the *tabernacle*, the sacred tent portrayed in the exodus narrative. Why is this? Some scholars have conjectured that the author was influenced by that stream of Hellenistic Judaism that was antitemple, represented by the "Hellenists" of Acts 6 (see above, §7.4.2). The temple was, in fact, subjected to considerable critique by the Old Testament prophets, who tended to idealize the time of Israel in the wilderness. Moreover, Exodus reports, and Hebrews emphasizes, that God instructed Moses on how to build the tabernacle and revealed to him the divine heavenly archetype (Exod 25–26; Heb 8:5). But the Old Testament has nothing to say about God providing instructions for the construction of the temple.

Hebrews' whole discussion of priesthood and sacrifice is carried on within the framework of the biblical world of the Pentateuch, not the empirical world of the history of his own time. The readers know the tabernacle because they know the Bible, but they do not know the temple from their own experience. The way in which he discusses such matters fits the time after the destruction of the temple (see below). A post-70 date is also supported by the reflections of Pauline corpus and other later Christian traditions such as 1 Peter, which relate Hebrews more closely to the post-70 period than earlier. The author looks back to an earlier period for the beginnings of the Christian tradition (2:3), and presupposes the death of the first generation of Christian leaders (13:7).

17.3.3 The addressees were not "Hebrews."

The editor of 𝔓[46] (or someone prior to him) attached the title "To the Hebrews" to an anonymous document when it became part of a collection of Pauline letters, bringing it into line with the titles assigned to other such letters: "To the Romans," "To the Galatians," and so on. Presumably the title "Hebrews," which does not occur in the document itself, was suggested by its content, which has much to say about covenant, priesthood, and sacrifice. On the basis of such Jewish imagery, it was supposed that the document was directed to Jews or Jewish Christians. While it is clear that the addressees are Greek-speaking Christians at home in the Hellenistic world, not Jews who do not make the Christian confession, some scholars continue to regard the document as addressed to Hellenistic Jewish Christians.[33]

We have already seen, however, that presupposing thorough acquaintance with the Jewish Scriptures and institutions does not automatically signal that the readers are Jewish Christians. For example, the predominately Gentile Christian congregations addressed by

32. L. T. Johnson argues any date between 45 and 70 is possible, assumes a pre-50 date in his exegesis, and declares "Hebrews may well be among our earliest extant Christian writings" (Johnson, *Hebrews*, 38, 50, 68). Yet Johnson occasionally forgets his claim, e.g., finding "echoes of Paul's language in 1 Cor. 12:11" in Heb 2:1–4 [p. 89]).

33. Thus, e.g., Craddock, "Hebrews," 10, assumes unproblematically that the readers are "Hellenistic Jewish Christians," and Hagner describes them as "Jewish Christians who seem to have been attracted *back* to Judaism" (Donald A. Hagner, *Encountering the Book of Hebrews: An Exposition*, Encountering Biblical Studies [Grand Rapids: Baker Academic, 2002], 23, 87, emphasis mine).

the Corinthian letters, Romans, and 1 Peter are assumed to know biblical and Jewish traditions that form the basis of the argument and the symbolic universe in which the communication takes place. We have also seen that the neat distinction between "Jewish Christians" and "Gentile Christians" is not helpful (see above §10.1.8). Hebrews seems to be addressed to one or more congregations in the same general setting that contain Christians of both Jewish and Gentile backgrounds, in a context heavily influenced by Jewish history and traditions.

A traditional view, still maintained by some scholars, is that Hebrews was written to Christian converts from Judaism who are tempted to lapse back into the Judaism from which they came. Hebrews was understood to stress the superiority of Christianity to Judaism in order to discourage their return to Judaism. The advances in our understanding of Hebrews' argument that the readers already have a better covenant, and the lack of supersessionism in Hebrews, have made this understanding very questionable (see below on 1:1–2:18; 4:1–13; 8:1–10:18).

Rather, the textual data suggests a harassed community living with the threat of suffering and imprisonment because of their faith. False teaching is only a minimal problem (barely mentioned in 13:9); relapsing into Judaism is not mentioned at all. The temptation is not to accept false theology or to return to Judaism, but to keep a low profile, avoiding the shame and abuse involved in the Christian profession. The textual data seem to converge on congregations in Rome in the 80s, in the aftermath of Nero's persecution of Christians in 64 and the Roman destruction of Jerusalem and the temple cultus in 66–70 CE.

Hebrews clearly has a Roman (Italian) connection. The epistolary conclusion includes greetings from "those from Italy," one of the few specific indications of the provenance of the document. Even this phrase is ambiguous. It could refer either to Italian Christians sending greetings from Italy to other churches elsewhere (cf. Rom 16:16), or to church members from Italy who have emigrated or who are temporarily absent and are sending greetings back home. That the latter is the more likely situation is indicated by the use of the same or similar phraseology for people from Rome temporarily living abroad (Acts 2:5, 10; 6:9; 18:2). It is difficult to read Hebrews as a general letter sent from Italy to Christians abroad. The more natural understanding is that of a letter addressed *to* congregations of Christians in Rome and its environs, from a Roman teacher who is temporarily absent, perhaps detained or incarcerated, who is in touch with Italian Christians in his setting who send their greetings (13:22–25). The author is from Rome and knows the situation there; he writes from elsewhere, so that Hebrews has a Roman provenance in a double sense, being both "from" and "to" Rome.

There are particular indications of a Roman provenance:

— The Jewishness of Hebrews is particularly appropriate to Roman Christianity, which had a Jewish origin and maintained its Jewish Christian ethos and its relationships with Jerusalem and the mother church there, even after it had become a predominately Gentile church (see above §13.2.1).

— Paul's last and longest letter was written to Rome. He died there as a martyr and was revered by the Roman church, including those who did not stand directly in the Pauline tradition. Not only Romans, but Paul's other letters and traditions associated with him were circulated in Rome in the decades after his death. Romans is the Pauline letter most like Hebrews in vocabulary, style, and theology. Hebrews is best understood as written from a context in which Romans and other Pauline letters were regularly read.

— The literary and material connections with 1 Peter, *1 Clement*, and Hermas, all of Roman provenance, connect Hebrews to Rome (see above §17.3.2).

— The generic term for "leaders" in 13:7, 17, 24 (participle of ἡγέομαι, *hēgeomai* lead) is particularly appropriate to the Roman church, which did not develop a firm and uniform leadership structure in the first generation after Paul's death. This terminology is also used in *1 Clement* and Hermas.

— The imagery of 12:21–22 contrasts Mount Zion with Sinai. On their journey from Sinai to the city of God, Christians have not come to the earthly Zion/Jerusalem but to the heavenly one. This contrast is particularly appropriate to Rome in the 80s. The Bible, some Jewish traditions, and some Jews contemporary with the author hoped for a restoration of the earthly city, but Hebrews no longer looks for a temple or city of God in this world, but focuses on the heavenly one, the "city with foundations" (Gal 4:26; *2 Bar.* 4:2–6; 2 Esd 7:26).

— Many of the Roman Christians would be immigrants from other parts of the empire. They were not welcomed, either as Christians or as immigrants, and would be subject to abuse and harassment. "Many in the first century sought opportunities in Rome, a city with ancient foundations. For the crowd of newcomers 'there is hardly sufficient housing accommodation; the majority of them are aliens' who have 'flooded in from the country towns of Italy, in fact from all over the world. . . . Rome, the greatest and loveliest city in the world—but not theirs'" (Seneca, *Helv.* 6.2–3). Thus "those from Italy" of 13:24, though "Roman," were also "sojourners, not at home, looking for a city that has foundations."[34]

— The reference to a time of past persecution, which the present generation remembers but has not personally endured (10:32–34), would be especially appropriate for Rome in the generation after Paul's death.

— It may be that the location of Hebrews immediately after Romans in $\mathfrak{P}^{46}$ is analogous to 1 and 2 Corinthians and 1 and 2 Thessalonians, that is, Romans and Hebrews were placed together because they were both written to Rome.

— Only Hebrews and Hermas (of Roman provenance) are concerned with the issue of whether a second repentance is possible.

— Hebrews addresses its readers as members of one or more Christian communities in the same locale, but is hesitant to use the term *church* (ἐκκλησία, *ekklēsia*) of them. Ἐκκλησία occurs only twice (2:12; 12:23), in neither case as a designation of the Christian community in Rome. Likewise, Paul's letter to the Roman Christians does not refer to them as a church or churches. Even 1 Peter, despite the tradition of Matthew 16:16–18 and its massive ecclesiological imagery and vocabulary, does not use the term "church."

— There is inscriptional evidence of a "synagogue of the Hebrews" in Rome, whose members may have come from Palestine or from conservative Jewish Diaspora families who cultivated Hebrew or Aramaic at home, or who designated their synagogue as a place where Hebrew was the liturgical language (instead of the Greek of other Diaspora synagogues; cf. the "Hellenists" and "Hebrews" of Acts 6).

— The solitary warning against dangerous doctrine of 13:9–10 could well be read in the context of the Roman church of the 80s: don't be carried away by strange doctrines that have to do with regulations about food. This is plausibly read in the context of Roman Christians with a Jewish background, disputing the continuing validity of food laws in the wake of the temple's destruction.

The date and provenance of Hebrews is still far from certain. However, reading the document with the hypothesis of a Roman origin in the 80s illuminates some problematic issues and particular texts (see below, the

34. Cf. Koester, *Hebrews*, 496–97, who describes the respective status of citizen, resident alien, transient foreigner.

Exegetical-Theological Précis). On this hypothesis, a loose cluster of Roman house churches without strong central leadership had by the 80s experienced a varied and turbulent history. Christian groups had developed within the synagogues, from which they had been separated by the decree of Claudius in 49 CE and especially by the terrible events of Nero's persecution in 64 CE (see above §§6.2.6; 9.2.2). Ethnically, the congregations were primarily Gentiles, many of whom had been God-fearers before becoming Christians, and with a significant element of ethnically Jewish Christians.

The pervasive thought world for the whole community was that of the Jewish Scriptures and the Jewish tradition from which their congregations had come. The Roman congregations had looked to Jerusalem as the home of the mother church, with much respect for the kind of Christianity represented by James (see below §§18.1, 18.4). Thus the war in Judea that destroyed the holy city and its temple was yet another devastating blow. While the community faced the major issues of how to respond to the social pressures while remaining true to its faith and its mission, a key theological issue was concerned with rethinking the faith in the light of the destruction of the temple. Diaspora Judaism throughout the Hellenistic world was discussing and debating the way forward without temple or priesthood. "Now that the temple, sacrifices, and the high priest are gone, what does this mean for faith?" This was not an abstract question to faithful Jews, including Jewish Christians of various stripes and Gentile Christians who took seriously their status as children of Abraham incorporated into Israel.

Christian teachers such as the author of Hebrews turned to the Scriptures, which they reread with the conviction that God had raised the crucified Jesus and exalted him to the heavenly world, where he has been installed as the ultimate high priest that makes all this-worldly priesthood unnecessary. The "Jewishness" of Hebrews is *biblical*, not ethnic or empirical. The author draws on the biblical world of the exodus and the tabernacle, of Moses and the Sinai covenant, not on the empirical world of Jerusalem and temple. He understands the life of faith to be a journey that culminates in the eschatological fulfillment of God's purpose. Christian believers are like the Israelites in the wilderness, en route to the fulfillment of God's promises. This symbolic universe fits the tabernacle imagery of the wandering people of God still looking for a city that has foundations, not the time of the Jerusalem temple after Israel had "arrived."

The imagery of being on the way between Egypt and the promised rest, looking for a city, going outside the camp, projects the biblical narrative world of which the readers are a part. The author enters with his readers into the narrative world of the text, where priests offer sacrifices, and finds there a superior priesthood exercised by Jesus in a sanctuary that can never be destroyed. This high priest has already finished his earthly course and is enthroned in God's eternal world. Readers are to follow the course marked out by Jesus.

17.3.4 Structure and Outline

All agree that Hebrews is not a rambling composition but one sustained argument from beginning to end—the longest such argument in the New Testament. All agree that Hebrews is carefully structured, but there is little agreement on how best to represent the author's structure. The author makes use of chiastic and rhetorical structures, the alternation of didactic and paraenetic sections, and a linear, cumulative argument that leads to his conclusion. A good rhetorician does not make his outline obvious but subordinates it to the flow of the argument. Topics are not neatly segmented, but overlapping and interwoven. Unlike Paul, with his typical bipartite arrangement of the body of his letters, the author of Hebrews does not wait until the end of the theological section to give his paraenetic instructions, but inserts several hortatory sections into the theological argument en route. As an aid to the modern reader's grasping the content of the document as a whole, the following outline attempts to represent the main sections of the text and turns of the argument.

1:1–4	Introductory Statement of Faith and Preview of the Argument
1:5–2:18	Christ Superior to Angels
2:1–4	*Exhortation*: Do not drift away, do not neglect.
2:5–9	The Cosmic Christological Drama as Model
2:10–18	"Perfection"
3:1–6	Christ Superior to Moses
3:7–19	*Exhortation*: Do not harden your hearts in unbelief.
4:1–13	"A sabbath rest still remains for the people of God."
4:14–16	*Exhortation*: Hold fast the confession.
5:1–10	The Main Topic Introduced: Christ the Superior High Priest
5:11–6:20	A Digression in Preparation for the "Difficult Discussion"
6:1–12	*Exhortation:* Do not become sluggish, but go on to complete the course to the very end.
6:13–20	The Christian Hope Anchored in Christ
7:1–10:18	The Main Topic Developed: Christ the Superior High Priest Who Mediates a Superior Covenant
7:1–28	Melchizedek
8:1–10:18	The New Covenant
10:19–39	*Exhortation*: Hold fast the confession without wavering.
11:1–40	The Endurance by Faith of the People of God
12:1–17	*Exhortation*: Run with endurance the race set before us.
12:18–24	The Superiority of the Believer's Present Status
12:25–13:17	*Concluding Exhortations*
13:20–21	Benediction
13:22–25	Epistolary Conclusion

17.3.5 Exegetical-Theological Précis

1:1–4 Introductory Statement of Faith and Preview of the Argument

Hebrews begins with a magnificently elegant and compact declaration of the identity of Jesus Christ that anticipates the main points of the book and serves as the basis for the "word of exhortation." Though profoundly christological, the introduction is in the service of the hortatory aim of the book as a whole: to strengthen believers who are tempted to relax or quit the race they have begun. The encompassing metaphor of the journey or race becomes explicit only later, but is always assumed. God's goal for humanity and the world has *already* been definitively revealed and realized in Jesus, but this goal ("perfection," "completion") has *not yet* been reached by humanity and the world. The central issue for the author of Hebrews is what God is finally "up to" in history, and whether God will be able to "pull it off" (bring it to "perfection"). The answer is clear in regard to *Jesus*, who is both archetype and example. The one through whom the worlds were made and maintained came into this world, finished his course by dying in a way that effected purification for sins, and is now enthroned at the right hand of God. The question is whether *the Christian readers* to whom this book is addressed will follow him and complete their own course. Four features of these majestic opening words are to be emphasized, all elaborated in the dense argument of the book itself:

1. *God is the subject.* The barebones substructure of this complex opening sentence is utterly simple: "God" is the subject, "has spoken" is the verb: "God has spoken to us by a Son." Just as God is the subject of this opening sentence, so the acting subject in this christological drama, from creation to eschaton, is God.

2. *Continuity and discontinuity.* Though there are tensions and discontinuities between the old revelation and the new, it is the same God who spoke to Israel through the prophets who has now spoken definitively through the Son. Previous revelation is affirmed, not repudiated, not superseded.

3. *Jesus as ultimate priest.* That Jesus "sat down at the right hand of the Majesty on high" signals Jesus' function as the heavenly high priest, on which the author will elaborate at length on the basis of Psalm 110:1–4. Interpreting the biblical texts christologically, he discovers the meaning of the Christ event in Jesus' high priestly ministry, which binds together Jesus' earthly life, present heavenly ministry, and the believers' relation to him.

4. *"Better" as relative language for an absolute claim.* The author concludes his introductory paean with a claim that modulates into the opening section that follows: Jesus has inherited a more excellent name than the angels. This initial claim that Christ has effected something "better" pervades the book of Hebrews:[35] Jesus is worthy of more glory than Moses (3:3). Christ mediates a better hope than what the law provided (7:19). Jesus provides a better covenant, with better promises (7:22; 8:6). Jesus ministers in a better tabernacle than the this-worldly tent of the earthly priesthood (9:11), which is purified by a better sacrifice (9:23). Christian believers have a better and more lasting possession than the this-worldly things they have lost (10:34), just as they desire a heavenly country that is better than either the earthly promised land or the treasures of Egypt (11:26). This language of being "better" must not be misunderstood as claims to the relative superiority of the Christian religion in comparison with other religions. The distinction is not in degree, but in kind. The author necessarily uses the language of relativity, but is aware that the Christ event mediates a reality that is not merely relatively better on the same ontological plane, but belongs to another, ultimate order of reality. He will make use of the language and conceptuality of Middle Platonism current in his time to communicate the ultimacy of God's revelatory act in Christ (see further on 8:1 below).

1:5–2:18 Christ Superior to Angels

That the author's use of "better" in an absolute, rather than relative, sense is immediately seen in his declaration that Christ is superior to angels. The author, like his readers, has a high regard for angels. They were God's agents in the giving of the Old Testament revelation (2:2), have a continuing validity and ministry in serving God's people (1:14), and will be part of the eschatological celebration in the heavenly city (12:22). Unlike Paul, the author feels no need to denigrate angels or cast them in a negative role, in order to make Jesus and the Christian faith shine the brighter. Christ does not "supersede" angels, as though he were a superior figure in the same series. Christ's superiority is that he belongs to another category altogether. He is God's Son, they are God's servants. This superiority is demonstrated by a sevenfold citation of christologically interpreted Scripture, in which Christ is contrasted with the angels not only as the unique Son, but as one who is addressed as "God" and "Lord." Here we find some of the raw materials to be formulated at Nicaea.

Why this initial insistence on Jesus' superiority to angels? It has sometimes been thought that the author is combating an "angel Christology" or the "veneration of angels" (cf. on Col

35. Of the nineteen occurrences of the comparative κρείττων (*kreittōn*, better) in the New Testament, thirteen are found in Hebrews, which manifests a similar preponderance of other comparatives (greater, more).

2:18; Rev 19:10; 22:8–9). The rank of "angel," whether explicitly so labeled or not, has indeed from earliest times been a tempting category by which believers might interpret the person and function of Jesus. Angels are more than human, but less than divine. Jesus could be affirmed as belonging to this category of heavenly beings without compromising monotheism. An "angel Christology" thus seems to offer a way of thinking about Jesus in which he is not "just a man," but is still not "God," *neither* "truly human" nor "truly divine." The later church (Chalcedon) rejected such a Christology. The author of Hebrews, though not thinking in these terms, would certainly have rejected it as well. Yet there is no evidence that he is combating an explicit "angel Christology" among his readers. He uses angels in a positive manner, as he will later use Moses, Aaron, the covenant with Israel, and the tabernacle. Yet all these are ultimately transcended by Jesus Christ, who represents a different realm of being than any of them.

2:1–4 Exhortation: Do not drift away, do not neglect.

Into this heady Christology, the author interposes a reminder that his primary purpose is not to teach doctrine but to motivate his hearers to hold fast to the faith they were in danger of neglecting.

2:5–9 The Cosmic Christological Drama as Model Interpreters who see the author structuring his discourse by a rhetorical template regularly identify this paragraph as the *proposition*. Psalm 8:4–6 is cited, which contrasts the angels and the "son of man." The psalm originally compared human beings as God's creatures with heavenly beings in the divine court. Humanity is glorified as the crown and heir of God's creation. The author of Hebrews reads the psalm christologically as portraying the cosmic course of Jesus Christ. The Hebrew text had declared that humans were only a "little bit" lower than the heavenly beings. The LXX had been so translated that this phrase could be understood temporally ("little while" instead of "little bit"). The "son of man," in Hebrew parallelism a synonym for "human being," can be read in terms of the earthly life of Jesus. In the author's christological reading, the divine Christ becomes a truly human being, for a "little while" lower than the angels, suffers and dies, and is exalted to the heavenly world, where he is crowned with glory and honor and becomes heir of all creation. In later Chalcedonian terms, the author presents Christ as "truly divine," addressed as God and participating in the creation of the universe, then divesting himself of deity and becoming "truly human," for a "little while," then being exalted to his divine status once again and forever. During his earthly life, while he was "lower than the angels," Jesus is unable to accomplish the miraculous deeds appropriate to deity. There no suggestion, here or elsewhere in the New Testament epistles, that the earthly life of Jesus was characterized by divine power. The pattern, but not the language and conceptuality, is similar to Paul's kenosis Christology of Philippians 2:5–11.

2:10–18 "Perfection" The point of portraying this cosmic drama is not to explain something about Jesus, but to explicate God's purpose in history. "God, for whom and through whom all things exist," is "bringing many children to glory." Jesus is the forerunner and exemplar of God's purpose for humanity. He has already been "made perfect," which refers not to moral perfection but to his having finished the course, so that the completion of God's intention for humanity is already manifest and realized in Christ. In the vocabulary of Psalm 8 co-opted by the author, God's intention for ἄνθρωπος (*anthrōpos*, man, humanity) is already completed in the exemplar, the υἱὸς τοῦ ἀνθρώπου (*huios tou anthrōpou*, Son of Man, exemplar of humanity). The Son of Man is the prolepsis of what humanity is to become. Jesus has completed the course; Christians are urged to stay the course.

The author of Hebrews uses the word group derived from τέλος (*telos*, complete, perfect) to express this key pattern of his theology.[36] This vocabulary is not univocal, but has a broad range of related meanings. The author uses it in a complex and subtle manner. The basic and encompassing image is the completion of God's purpose for the world and humanity in the transcendent future eschatological realm. This is the completion of something already underway, already achieved in the course completed by Jesus Christ, something in which Christian believers *already* participate, but which they have *not yet* completed. "Perfection" does not refer to moral perfection in the case of either Jesus or his followers, though ethical seriousness and moral growth is an indispensable aspect of inclusion in God's program for the world and history. It calls believers to present commitment and endurance, but it is not only individual or even communal, but transcendent and cosmic. Jesus did not "become perfect" by increasing levels of internal, individual moral excellence, but by completing his course—which includes "learning obedience by the things he suffered." In this he is example and paradigm for his followers, who are addressed in this document.

3:1–6 Christ Superior to Moses

Like the angels, Moses was a faithful servant of God, but Jesus is superior to Moses just as he is superior to the angels, and for the same reason: he is Son, they (angels and Moses) are servants.

3:7–19 Exhortation: Do not harden your hearts in unbelief.

For the author's purpose, the Israelites of the wilderness generation provide the key negative example. They too were on a journey to the "rest" of the promised land, but they did not hold their "first confidence firm to the end," and so "were unable to enter because of their unbelief."

4:1–13 "A sabbath rest still remains for the people of God."

The author includes "us" (Christian believers) and "them" (the Israelites in the wilderness journey) in the one people of God. It is the word of God that calls the people of God into being, then and now. God's good news came to them on their journey, just as it comes to us (4:2). The discussion presupposes the richness of Jewish Sabbath tradition, where Sabbath can be the sign and symbol of ultimate salvation.[37] The complex combination of Scripture and logic demonstrates, from the author's perspective, that the promise of "rest" was never ultimately the this-worldly promised land, but God's own state of being, God's own "sabbath rest" after creating the universe (4:4; Gen 2:3). Although Joshua/Jesus[38] did finally bring Israel to Canaan, this was not the ultimate goal of the people of God. The author illustrates this by pointing to the fact that much later than Joshua's time, David still urges the people of God to enter into that rest "today" (Ps 95:7–11). The biblical "today" of David's time collapses into the "today" of the author's own time; if David was still making the appeal to enter God's rest generations after Israel's arrival in Canaan, this

36. Words from this cluster are found twenty-one times in Hebrews, far more than in any other New Testament book: τελειόω, *teleioō*, to finish, to make perfect = 9; τέλειος, *teleios*, complete, perfect = 2; τέλος, *telos*, end, goal = 4; ἐπιτελέω, *epiteleō*, to complete, to perform = 2; συντέλεια, *sunteleia*, consummation, completion, perfection, end = 1; συντελέω, *sunteleō*, to finish, to end = 1; τελειότης, *teleiotēs*, completeness = 1; τελείωσις, *teleiōsis*, completion, fulfillment = 1.

37. The Sabbath had been instituted by God at creation, and God himself had observed it (Gen 2:2), as had the angels in heaven and the patriarchs even before the law was given (*Jub.* 2:18–23; *Gen. Rab.* 11 [8c]). The Sabbath is thus on earth a foretaste of the eschatological joy, pictured as a perpetual Sabbath celebration (2 Esd. 7:31; *2 En.* 33.1–2), and even now the Sabbath is observed in heaven, while the unrighteous tormented in Gehenna are granted a reprieve from their sufferings every Sabbath.

38. The Hebrew name Joshua (יְהוֹשֻׁעַ *Yehoshua*) was transliterated in the LXX as Jesus (Ἰησοῦς) so that Christian readers of the LXX found numerous references to "Jesus."

sabbath rest must refer to something beyond Canaan, namely, God's transcendent world into which Jesus brings his people; and "a sabbath rest still remains for the people of God" (4:9).

4:14–16 *Exhortation: Hold fast the confession.*

The Christian's "Joshua" has already entered the heavenly "rest." Believers are again urged to hold fast their confession and follow him on this way he has prepared. The imagery now morphs from Joshua/Jesus leading his people to the true "rest" to Jesus the true high priest entering into the heavenly sanctuary on behalf of his people. This central priestly role of Jesus alluded to in the preceding (1:3; 2:17; 3:1) is now fully developed.

5:1–10 The Main Topic Introduced: Christ the Superior High Priest

The author introduces the topic with a series of affirmations: (1) Our high priest became as we are, sharing our human weakness, tempted and tested as we are, like us in every respect but one: he was without sin, totally obedient to God (2:17; 4:14–15). This obedience included loud cries, tears, and death, from which his prayers did not deliver him. (2) Christ did not "aspire" to this role or "attain" to it, but was appointed to it by God. As in the fundamental Christian confession that Jesus is the Christ, so with the confession that Jesus is our great high priest: God is the actor, and the affirmation confesses something about who God is and what God has done. (3) Christ's priesthood is "according to the order of Melchizedek." The author acknowledges that this claim, so arcane to the modern reader and apparently unfamiliar to the original readers, is difficult to understand and will require lengthy explanation. Before launching into the meaning of this deep subject, the author inserts a lengthy warning.

5:11–6:20 *A Digression in Preparation for the "Difficult Discussion"*

The author blames the readers' lack of understanding on their own immaturity. They have been Christians long enough to be teachers themselves, but are still in need of basic instruction.

6:1–12 *Exhortation: Do not become sluggish, but go on to complete the course to the very end.*

The readers' lack of spiritual insight is no small matter. Their passive "drifting" (cf. 2:1) is not benign, but can reach a point of no return in which the faith has been abandoned and there is no way back. The words about the impossibility of repentance after apostasy are not a theoretical dogma about an "unpardonable sin," but a practical warning that they must forge ahead on the path of discipleship rather than passively drifting. The author assures them that they are not already in this hopeless situation, but that he has held up this frightful prospect as a warning.

6:13–20 The Christian Hope Anchored in Christ

The metaphor is mixed, but the point is clear. The reality that God has sworn by himself that the promise would be fulfilled, and that it is in fact already fulfilled in the person of Christ, is the ground of Christian hope. Jesus' procession into the heavenly sanctuary is like an anchor cast into the transcendent future that steadies the believers' course as they follow him into the heavenly world. Their hope is not in a theory about the afterlife, but is based on something that has happened: God has raised Jesus from the dead.

7:1–10:18 The Main Topic Developed: Christ the Superior High Priest Who Mediates a Superior Covenant

The author wants to use the priestly model as the comprehensive metaphor for God's saving work in the Christ event. The human problem is sin/impurity. God has acted in Christ to overcome this problem. Jesus' death was the sacrifice that takes away sin and restores human beings to an acceptable status before God. While Jesus' death was a once-for-all, unrepeatable event, his human followers continue to be sinful beings who need forgiveness. As the great high priest, Jesus continues to make intercession in the heavenly world for his imperfect followers and to maintain them in communion with God. This transcendent Christ is the perfect priest, for he has shared our human existence and knows our needs, and he now shares the very being of God, so he is not a third party interceding between sinful humanity and the holy God. Jesus represents God himself, who bridges this gap.[39] This, and not philosophical speculation, is the reason for the author's interest in the "deity of Christ."

7:1–28 Melchizedek We have seen that the whole line of argument of Hebrews is very appropriate to the situation in Rome in the decades immediately after the destruction of the temple, when the question "What now?" was in the air. How can the priestly functions continue if the priesthood is gone? Answer: there were two priesthoods in the Old Testament, the temporal and the eternal. The author thinks in terms of the cultic framework of altar, sacrifice, and priest as the way God relates to the world. Yet he cannot use the Levitical priesthood of the Old Testament as the category for interpreting the person and work of Jesus, for two reasons: (1) the old priesthood was inevitably this-worldly. Though ordained by God, it was a human institution staffed by imperfect human beings themselves in need of purification, and could only mediate incomplete, this-worldly salvation. (2) According to the Scriptures themselves, Jesus was not qualified for this priesthood. He was a descendant of David of the tribe of Judah; priests must be from the tribe of Levi.

The author (or a predecessor) searches the Scripture and finds another priest, superior to the Levitical priesthood in each of these two ways. Melchizedek appears in only two Old Testament texts. In Genesis 14, he suddenly materializes, interrupting the context, blesses Abraham, and receives tithes from him—clearly showing, to the author's mind, that he was superior to Abraham. Melchizedek is the first priest mentioned in the Bible; he is prior to the Levitical priesthood. The priests descended from Abraham were thus already subordinate to the priesthood of Melchizedek. In Psalm 110:4 the one who is installed at God's right hand is declared to be "a priest forever according to the order of Melchizedek." He does not belong to the tribe of Levi; the cultus over which he presides is not a this-worldly affair. He appears in this world without human genealogy and is installed in the heavenly world as a priest forever. He is not only priest, but king—indeed, king of Jerusalem ("Salem," interpreted both as the name of a city and as the essence of salvation: "peace"). He is the perfect model for Jesus the royal high priest.

8:1–10:18 The new covenant The following points are important in order to grasp the author's meaning:

The language of "new covenant" was not devised by the early Christians, but was taken from Jewish Scriptures and Jewish history. The author of Hebrews brackets this section with citations from Jeremiah 31:31–34—the longest citation of the Old Testament in the New Testament (8:8–12; 10:16–17). Jeremiah promised that God himself would finally take responsibility for renewing the covenant in such a way that the relationship of God and people would be what God always intended. This hope for the new, eschatological covenant was alive in the Judaism of New Testament times. The Jewish community at Qumran believed that they were living in the time of the fulfillment of this eschatological promise, that they were the people of the new covenant. The early Christian community, believing that the Messiah had come, sometimes expressed their faith in "new covenant" language, which may indeed go back to Jesus himself (Mark 14:24 and par.; Luke 1:72; Rom 11:27; 1 Cor 11:25; 2 Cor 3:6, 14). Hebrews gives the most extensive theological

39. Note that *pontifex*, the Latin word for "priest," is related to *pons*, *pontis*, bridge.

elaboration of "covenant" as a key term of New Testament theology.

"New" is an absolute, categorical, eschatological term. In this context, "new" does not mean relatively new, but absolutely so, the promised eschatological renewal of the one covenant God has made with Israel (see above, §1.2 and on 2 Cor 3). Thus the language of a "first" and "second" covenant (8:7; 9:15; 10:9) does not denote instances of a series on the same plane, in which one might be relatively better than the other, and then be superseded by a still better (see on 1 Cor 15:47 and Rom 5:12–21). The "first" covenant is God's historical, this-worldly covenant with Israel. The "second" is not a successor or replacement for this covenant, but its fulfillment in the transcendent world of God's own reality (see the discussion of "rest" in Heb 4 above). It is not a newer version of the first covenant, the best of a series, but is unique, belonging to a category of one. In the language of Søren Kierkegaard and the early Karl Barth, the difference between the old and the new covenant represents the *infinite qualitative distinction* between time and eternity.[40]

So also, "better" is here a relative term with an absolute claim (see above on 1:4). The comparative "better," like the superlative "best," ordinarily claims that one item in a given category is better than another, or better than any (=best). The author of Hebrews, however, is clear that he (and all of us) must use the this-worldly language of relativity to express the absolute claims of the transcendent world of God and divine reality. Again, the teachers in the Jewish Scripture and tradition had already made use of the language of relativity—the only language we have—to express absolute claims. Such affirmations as "the LORD is greater than all gods" (Exod 18:11) and "God is greater than any mortal" (Job 33:12), though expressed as comparisons, are categorical statements, not relative ones. The monotheistic faith of Israel and the church does not consider YHWH, the God of Abraham, Isaac, Jacob, and Jesus, to be the best example of deity in a series of other deities, but in a different category altogether. Israel's apologists do not defend Jewish faith as relatively better than other religions, or YHWH as relatively better than Zeus. On this basis, it is difficult to make a case that the God of Deuteronomy and Joshua is a "better" god than the gods of the Greeks and Romans. Rather, the difference is categorical, not relative. Though the language of comparison is used, the claim is that the one, unique God of Israel is the only *real* God (cf. also Exod 15:11; 1 Chr 16:26; 2 Chr 2:5; 32:19; Pss 86:8; 95:3; 135:5).[41]

The author of Hebrews stands in this tradition when he claims that the "new" covenant is "better," and repeatedly uses "better" to describe the realities of Christian faith. He is not making a case that shoppers in the religious marketplace should compare religions, then choose Christianity because it is "better" than others, but that God's eschatological act in Christ transcends all human religions.

The author combines the approaches of Platonic ontology and biblical history to communicate this point. A popularized form of Plato's philosophy, now called Middle Platonism, was widespread in the first-century Hellenistic world. It is represented, for example, by Philo, the prolific Jewish philosopher who interpreted traditional Jewish faith in terms of Middle Platonism (see above §§5.1.3; 9.2.2). As is well known, this Platonic view conceptualizes reality on a vertical scale, regarding the real world of ideas as above the material world. The objects of the material world have only a secondary reality derived from their ideal prototypes in the transcendent world.

The author of Hebrews uses this conceptuality and language to communicate his point.

40. Karl Barth, *The Epistle to the Romans*, trans. Edwyn C. Hoskyns (London: Oxford University Press, 1933), 10.

41. Even if, as is likely, some such Old Testament statements originally assumed the existence of other gods, by the time Hebrews was written, they were all understood in terms of the absolute monotheism of Israel's faith.

Thus the true tabernacle is in the transcendent world (Heb 8:2); the earthly tabernacle is only a sketch and shadow of the heavenly one (Heb 8:5). On Mount Sinai God let Moses see the heavenly archetype, and the earthly tabernacle served by the Levitical priesthood was necessarily only a copy, an imitation. This is also related to the philosophic categories of being and becoming, the one and the many, the transient and the eternal, the invisible and the visible, the type and the antitype, the substance and the shadow. In this frame of reference, the true tabernacle is the one set up by God, and its opposite is not a false tabernacle, but the one set up by mortals in this world (8:2). Hebrews' point is that the new covenant belongs to this transcendent world, in which the true tabernacle and true priesthood of Christ represents the true, divine reality. In this frame of reference, faith is the apprehension of the reality of this eternal world, which allows one to endure the troubles of temporal existence.

None of this means that the author of Hebrews reduces the biblical understanding of the God who acts on the horizontal plane of history (diachronic time) to a timeless, vertical Platonic understanding of eternal ideals (synchronic space). The author of Hebrews combines these two conceptualities, so that God's transcendent world is both synchronic and diachronic, both spatially "up there" in the heavenly world and temporally "out there" ahead of us in history. He looks not only up to the reality of the present transcendent world; he looks ahead to the future consummation of God's plan for history. This is described by the author's vocabulary of "perfection," that is, the eschatological completion of God's plan in the transcendent future world at the end of this-worldly history. This does not mean that the author is merely interested in abstract hermeneutics. Like the prophetic author of Revelation, the author sees a great crisis in the near future that the Christian community must face (12:4; 13:3). Although the community has suffered persecution in the past, the present generation has not, and had grown lax (5:11; 12:12–13; 10:25). They need a vision of the future that lies before them, πίστις (*pistis*, faith that lays hold of the transcendent world and makes it real in the present) and ὑπομονή (*hupomonē*, steadfast endurance, see on Jas 5:7–11; Rev 2; §26.1.4) to endure until the appearance of God's new world shortly to come. The author of Hebrews is unique in the New Testament in his expression of the Christian faith through this fusion of the Platonic/Greek and apocalyptic/Hebrew understanding of reality, and does this for an altogether practical purpose: to strengthen the community's faith expressed in love and good works (10:24; 13:1).

Hebrews' understanding of the new covenant shares the already/not yet tension of New Testament theology in general. The new covenant already exists and believers participate in it. But the old covenant also continues to exist, and believers participate in it as well. The new age has come with the coming of Christ, and believers have already tasted its powers (6:5); indeed they have been "perfected for all time" by the perfect sacrifice of Christ (10:14). Christ has already completed the course and has been "made perfect forever" (5:9; 7:28), but believers must "go on toward perfection" that lies in the future consummation (6:1). Though already participants in the eternal covenant, they still live in time. Actual perfection, the completion of God's plan, still belongs to the future. Believers' present participation in the new covenant still has the eschatological reservation. They do not yet experience the full reality of the new covenant, when no one shall need to teach another, because all know God directly (8:11), as evidenced by this didactic document itself.

Do we find supersessionism or anti-Judaism in Hebrews? Several elements in New Testament theology, but especially Hebrews' language of a new covenant that made the old covenant "obsolete" (8:13; 10:9 NRSV), have encouraged some Christians throughout history to claim that the new covenant supersedes the old.[42] This has sometimes been understood to mean that Christianity supersedes Judaism. Especially after the Holocaust, many Christians have become aware of the role of a kind of Christian theology that, intentionally or not, supported the oppression of Jews in many countries throughout history, tragically climaxed in the movement that led to the mass murder of European Jews. Such increased sensitivity has rightly caused many Christian theologians to attempt to discern whatever elements of anti-Judaism or supersessionism there may be in the New Testament itself. While this can sometimes lead to retrojecting contemporary views and issues into the first century and defensive overreaction, study of the New Testament from this perspective is needed, and Hebrews, with its language of a "better covenant," seems to offer a prime example. If supersessionism is to be found anywhere in the New Testament, then surely here.

The above considerations, however, show that Hebrews, understood in its own context, offers no support for the view that God has replaced Israel with the church. The claim of Hebrews is more like that of the covenanters of Qumran, who also saw themselves as the people of the new covenant. They were a sectarian group within Israel, and of course could not claim that God had replaced Israel with their group. While their claim was sectarian and exclusive, it was not supersessionism. Supersessionism can exist only after Christianity considers itself to be a separate religion. The author of Hebrews continues to understand the new covenant of Jeremiah 31:31 as "with the house of Israel and the house of Judah" (Heb 8:8). He is misunderstood when interpreted to mean something like "the first covenant was with Judaism, but the new covenant is with the church." So long as Christians were one group within the broad Jewish tradition, they may have been exclusive and sectarian, but they did not claim that their religion has superseded Judaism.

For the author of Hebrews, the issue is not whether Christianity is better than Judaism, but whether his Christian hearers will maintain their faith that the Messiah has come and has inaugurated God's rule, and whether they will persevere in following him into God's new world they have already come to experience in part.[43] The first covenant and all its institutions will not endure into the coming age; that is, it will endure in the age to come as the promised eschatologically renewed covenant. This new covenant has erupted into this world with the coming of Christ. The two ages and the two covenants overlap. They do not exist side by side, as though one could compare them and choose between them. Neither do they exist in a series, as though the second replaces the first.[44]

10:19–39 Exhortation: Hold fast the confession without wavering.

The "difficult discussion" concluded, the author once again appeals to his readers to remain steadfast. This unwavering hanging in there is not merely personal and individualistic. Believers are to provoke each other to good works, and to resist the temptation to keep a low profile by neglecting attendance at the

42. Thus, e.g., B. F. Westcott, *Commentary*: "The New Covenant is not only better, and founded on better promises than the Old; yet more, it supersedes the Old." More recently, F. F. Bruce: Hebrews "proclaims the supersession of the earlier covenant, and Christ's priesthood is exercised under this new and better covenant" (F. F. Bruce, "'To the Hebrews': A Document of Roman Christianity?" in *Aufstieg und Niedergang der römischen Welt*, ed. Joseph Vogt, Hildegard Temporini, and Wolfgang Haase [Berlin: De Gruyter, 1987], 3503). Richard B. Hays, *Echoes of Scripture in the Letters of Paul* (New Haven, CT: Yale University Press, 1989), 98: "Indeed, the typological strategy in the Letter to the Hebrews is relentlessly christocentric and relentlessly supersessionist."

43. Thus a Jewish New Testament scholar concludes her discussion of this point with, "In short, the author does not engage in any anti-Jewish polemics" (Pamela Michelle Eisenbaum, *The Jewish Heroes of Christian History*, SBLDS 156 [Atlanta: Scholars Press, 1997], 8).

44. For further discussion along this line, see Johnson, *Hebrews*, 33–34 and the literature he gives, esp. Clark M. Williamson, "Anti-Judaism in Hebrews?" *Interpretation* 57, no. 3 (2003): 266–79.

regular assembly with fellow Christians for worship, instruction, mutual support, and mission that might attract the attention of a hostile culture. Paul had made the text from Habakkuk 2:4 current in the author's circle. He now interprets this text in a different sense than Paul, contrasting "living by faith" not with "works of the law," but with "shrinking back."

11:1–40 The Endurance by Faith of the People of God

The author of Hebrews defines faith not as the acceptance of something as true, but as experiencing the reality of something unseen, and living one's life on this basis. Faith sees the invisible and perseveres. This invisible world is both the transcendent world of God ("things not seen") and the future invisible world to come ("things hoped for"). The comprehensive metaphor of being in a race is continued and embraces both the upward and forward perspectives. The race believers are running turns out to be not a marathon, but a relay. The readers are themselves in the last lap of a race they are urged to complete, but they were not there at the beginning of the race. They have been handed the torch of faith by their predecessors of the past—with no hint that the heroes of Israel's faith belonged to a second-rate religion that has now been "superseded."

The author himself sets the agenda for his roll call of the faithful. He does not go looking in his Bible for all the occurrences of words such as "faith" or "believe." Of his eighteen named examples, "faith" terminology is mentioned only with reference to Abraham, and even here the author does not cite texts that refer to Abraham's faith. Rather, the author has a particular understanding of faith and gathers up biblical illustrations to represent it. Faith is not mentioned at all in the accounts of Noah or Moses, for example, but their stories serve as illustrations for the understanding of faith the author of Hebrews wants to convey. The heroes of faith endure "as seeing the invisible" (11:27). Moses is a prime example of such faith because he did not make his decisions based on empirical observation; he had been adopted into the Pharaoh's household and was living his life in the context of wealth and power. Yet he abandoned all this and chose to suffer ill-treatment with the people of God rather than enjoy the fleeting pleasures of palace life. He did this both because he "saw him who is invisible" (the synchronic upward dimension of faith) and because he was "looking ahead to the reward" (the diachronic forward-looking dimension of faith). Faith makes real both the transcendent world above and the eschatological world to come, and empowers believers to live against the grain of the dominant culture, which is based on the way things appear to superficial observation. These present and future dimensions of faith are intertwined throughout the catalogue of the faithful people of Israel's past, who become transparent to the demands of Christian faith in the present.

Just as Christian believers are challenged to have the same faith found in the biblical heroes of the Bible, so these ancient heroes are assumed to have the same faith as the Christian believers of the present. Moses already endured abuse "for the sake of Christ" (11:26). There is an unbroken continuity of faith from the pages of the Bible into the believer's own time. Just as ancient heroes could be portrayed as pre-Jesus Christians, so the ancient words of Scripture can be heard by Christians of the author's own time as the voice of Christ (e.g., 10:5–9, where Ps 40:6–8 is cited as words of Christ).

12:1–17 Exhortation: Run with endurance the race set before us.

The "therefore" of 12:1 introduces another hortatory section based on the preceding teaching. The hearers are portrayed as still in the race, but in danger of dropping out. They are urged to endure to the finish line, not only by the examples of the faithful endurance of those figures from the past. Previous believers who remained faithful and finished the course are now in the grandstands, the "cloud of witnesses" who are now cheering on the contestants to make it to the finish line. Once again, the exalted Jesus Christ is the supreme example of such endurance. For the third time, the utter seriousness of dropping out is emphasized. Esau is the example of those people without faith, who judged life only by what they could see, and whose rejection was final (see 6:4–6; 10:26–31).

12:18–24 The Superiority of the Believer's Present Status

This paragraph contrasts the experience of biblical Israel at Sinai with the present experience of the readers. Biblical Sinai was a matter of this-worldly sensory experience, something frightfully real because it could be seen, touched, and heard. The hearers have come to a different mountain—Mount Zion, but not the this-worldly mountain in Judea. Zion refers to Jerusalem, the city of the living God, the city with foundations that the ancestors longed for, with innumerable angels in festal gathering, the assembly of the firstborn enrolled as citizens in the heavenly city, into the very presence of God and the risen and exalted Jesus. This city, though it cannot be touched, is the true city of God, real to those who have eyes of faith. Here the already/not yet tension reaches its most intense point. This city, the goal of the Christian pilgrimage, is not yet manifest to all, though its reality already pervades and shapes the lives of believers.

There is a triple contrast here. Not only is transcendent Mount Zion utterly superior to this-worldly Mount Sinai; the readers' citizenship is in God's Ultimate City, which is far better than belonging to either the "eternal city" of Rome or the earthly Jerusalem. If, as suggested here, Hebrews is addressed to Roman Christians in the 80s CE, this is a particularly meaningful concluding vision. In Rome, the readers are outcasts and cannot participate in the assembly as citizens, and there are judges who condemn them. Nonetheless, they already belong to the assembly of the heavenly city, where God the judge of all has vindicated them. In the 80s, the earthly Jerusalem lies in ruins, but the true high priest presides in the heavenly sanctuary, and the saints of all the ages, the "spirits of the righteous made perfect," have completed their course and await the arrival of the harassed Christian community to which Hebrews is addressed.

12:25–13:17 *Concluding Exhortations*

On the basis of this grand vision, the readers are called to hear not just the instruction of this document, but the one who speaks to them from heaven. Hebrews begins with the affirmation of the God who speaks, who has spoken his definitive word in Jesus, and concludes with the call to hear the word of God that still speaks to them. Harkening to this voice means mutual love and hospitality within the community, remembering and helping those imprisoned and tortured members of the church (rather than trying to avoid attention from the authorities by not identifying oneself as a member of the Christian group), responsible sex ethics, obedience to leaders of the church, and continuing the sacrificial cult by their worship that confesses the name of Christ.

13:20–21 Benediction

The liturgical benediction ends the sermon, and is also appropriate to the ending of a letter in the Pauline tradition composed to be read in the regular worship service of the church.

13:22–25 Epistolary Conclusion

This could have been added later to conform the sermon to the epistolary style that had become traditional, but more likely is an authentic note appended by the original author. The Timothy here mentioned could be the companion of Paul who had come to Rome and was known there, or some other person by that common name.

17.4 For Further Reading

Achtemeier, P. J. *1 Peter: A Commentary on First Peter*. Hermeneia. Minneapolis: Fortress Press, 1996.

Attridge, H. W. *The Epistle to the Hebrews*. Hermeneia. Philadelphia: Fortress Press, 1989.

Bauer, W., G. Strecker, R. A. Kraft, and G. Krodel, eds. *Orthodoxy and Heresy in Earliest Christianity*. 2nd ed. Philadelphia: Fortress Press, 1971.

Boring, M. Eugene. *1 Peter*. ANTC. Nashville: Abingdon Press, 1999.

Craddock, Fred B. "The Letter to the Hebrews: Introduction, Commentary, Reflections." In *The New Interpreter's Bible*, edited by Leander Keck, 12:3–173. Nashville: Abingdon Press, 1998.

Donfried, K. P., and P. Richardson, eds. *Judaism and Christianity in First-Century Rome*. Grand Rapids: Eerdmans, 1998.

Elliott, J. H. *1 Peter: A New Translation with Introduction and Commentary*. Anchor Bible 37B. New York: Doubleday, 2000.

Feldmeier, R. *The First Letter of Peter: A Commentary on the Greek Text*. Translated by Peter H. Davids. Waco, TX: Baylor University Press, 2008.

Goppelt, L. *A Commentary on 1 Peter*. Translated by John E. Alsup. Grand Rapids: Eerdmans, 1993.

Johnson, L. T. *Hebrews: A Commentary*. NTL. Louisville, KY: Westminster John Knox Press, 2006.

Koester, C. R. *Hebrews*. Anchor Bible 36. New York: Doubleday, 2001.

Lampe, P. *From Paul to Valentinus: Christians at Rome in the First Two Centuries*. Translated by Michael Steinhauser; edited by Marshall D. Johnson. Minneapolis: Fortress Press, 2003.

Long, T. G. *Hebrews*. Interpretation series. Louisville, KY: John Knox Press, 1997.

Michaels, J. R. *1 Peter*. WBC 49. Waco, TX: Word, 1988.

Niebuhr, K.-W., and R. W. Wall, eds. *The Catholic Epistles and Apostolic Tradition*. Waco, TX: Baylor University Press, 2009.

Thompson, James. *Hebrews*. Paideia. Grand Rapids: Baker Academic, 2008.

18

James, Jude, 2 Peter

18.1 Interpreting James

18.1.1 The Implied Author: James the Just, the Brother of Jesus

The English name James is the Anglicization of the Hebrew יַעֲקוֹב (*Ya'aqob*, Jacob), which came into the LXX as Ἰακώβ and the Greek New Testament as Ἰάκωβος (*Iakob*, Jacob). The New Testament name James is thus the same as the Old Testament and Jewish Jacob. Jacob was the father of twelve sons whose descendants became the twelve tribes of Israel (Gen 25–50). His name became a favorite in Second Temple Judaism, so that there are several instances of Jacob/James in the New Testament. Two of the twelve disciples called by Jesus bore this name: James the brother of John, the son of Zebedee (Mark 1:19), and James the son of Alphaeus, traditionally "James the Less" (Mark 3:18). One of Jesus' four brothers was named James (Mark 6:3). Though there was some confusion already in the early church as to the identity of the various Jameses, the only figure to come into serious consideration as the implied author of the letter is James the brother of Jesus. Later theological interests have obscured aspects of the historical James, but the following sketch represents a view widely accepted.

Birth. In the New Testament, James appears unproblematically as the son of Mary and brother of Jesus (Matt 13:55 [27:56?]; Mark 6:3 [15:40?], 16:1; [Luke 24:10?]; Gal 1:19; 1 Cor 9:5; Acts 1:14). If we had only the New Testament, we would assume that James was the son of Joseph and Mary, born after Jesus, a view acknowledged by leading Roman Catholic scholars.[1] The New Testament stories of the virginal conception of Jesus would thus mean that James was the biological half brother of Jesus. The dogma of the perpetual virginity of Mary appears in later traditions promoting ascetic understandings of the Christian life. The brothers of Jesus were then understood to be stepbrothers, the children of Joseph by a former marriage, as in the second-century *Protevangelium of James*. Still later, it was argued that the biblical term brother has a broader meaning that includes the extended family, so that Jesus' "brothers" were really cousins, the sons of Mary's sister (so Jerome, ca. 400 CE).

Early life and education. James presumably experienced the same kind of boyhood and family life as did Jesus (see above §8.3), growing up in the village of Nazareth, perhaps attending a local school, learning a trade from his father, who also taught him the Scripture and traditions of Judaism.

Pre-Easter disciple of Jesus? When Jesus left Nazareth to be baptized by John the Baptist, then to begin his own itinerant ministry of preaching, teaching, and healing, James remained at

1. E.g., Raymond E. Brown, *An Introduction to the New Testament*, ABRL (New York: Doubleday, 1997), 725.

home. He became neither a disciple of John nor a disciple of Jesus. He was not among the Twelve Jesus called to leave home and family and follow him. There is no indication that James heard Jesus' preaching and teaching, or that he was an eyewitness of Jesus' extraordinary deeds of healing and exorcism. He did not follow Jesus to Jerusalem on the journey that resulted in his execution, was not present at Jesus' death, did not attempt to claim the body for burial. The Gospels preserve only two incidental vignettes in which James appears. In Mark 3:20–34, people were saying Jesus was deranged, and his family, presumably including James, came to take him back home. Jesus does not receive them or go with them, but declares that his real brothers and sisters are those who do God's will. So also in John 7:2–5, Jesus' brothers are contrasted with his disciples, and are said not to believe in him. The Gospels, however, are concerned to make clear that no one can come to authentic faith in Jesus until after the fundamental events of the crucifixion and resurrection, so that the family of Jesus is portrayed in the same terms as others—including his disciples. It is not necessary to understand the historical James (and Jesus' family in general) as disappointed, embarrassed, or actively hostile to Jesus during his ministry; but for them, like others, the decisive event in their becoming Jesus' followers was not their family connection but their coming to faith in Jesus as the risen Lord.

The resurrection appearance to James. The earliest extant document that refers to James is Paul's first letter to the Corinthians. In 1 Corinthians 15:3–7 Paul quotes tradition that lists an appearance of the risen Jesus to James that establishes him as one of the founders of the Christian movement. As was the case for Peter and Paul, so also for James, his place as an authorized leader in the early church was guaranteed directly by the risen Lord. Reference to this appearance is not incidental; its inclusion in early tradition that was widely circulated among the churches is a claim to parity, or sometimes primacy, among the founding leadership.

James as leader of the Jerusalem church. The earliest history of Jerusalem Christianity is obscured by our lack of sources (see above, §9.2.1). After the report of the resurrection appearance to James, he next appears in Galatians 1:19, written about 56, but referring to Paul's first visit to Jerusalem after his call, about 35. Paul went to Jerusalem to visit Peter; the only other church leader he mentions seeing is James the Lord's brother. In Paul's eyes, at least, Peter seems to have been the primary leader in Jerusalem, but James was not to be ignored. Although the "brothers of the Lord" are reported to have traveled on mission trips (1 Cor 9:5), this seems not to have included James, who remained in Jerusalem—not his hometown Nazareth.

When Paul made his second visit to Jerusalem fourteen years later, he reports that he consulted with the acknowledged Pillars: James, Cephas, and John (at the Jerusalem Council, see Gal 2:1–10; Acts 15:1–29, and §10.1.7 above). James is mentioned first and now seems to be the primary leader. The Pillars all agree that Gentiles may be accepted into the church without circumcision. The status of Gentile Christians vis-à-vis the people of Israel, and table fellowship between Jewish Christians and Gentile Christians in the same congregation, were issues not clarified by the Council, or at least understood in different ways by the parties involved.

James seems to have been more conservative than either Peter or Paul on this issue. Sometime after the Council, "certain people from James" came to Antioch insisting that Jewish Christians withdraw from table fellowship with Gentile Christians. Peter yielded to the people claiming to represent James, resulting in a sharp dispute between Paul and Peter, whereupon Paul left to found an independent mission, and the Antioch church continued under the direction of Peter, apparently acknowledging the authority of James in Jerusalem. It is not clear whether or to what extent "those from James" accurately represented James's own position.

In all this, James appears as the defender of traditional Jewish faith, upholder of the Torah, willing to accept Gentiles into the Christian community, but insisting that Jewish Christians continue to abide by the Jewish law and tradition. (It must be kept in mind that James is never pictured in the New Testament as advocating that *Gentile* Christians be circumcised in order to be fully accepted in the people of God.) This picture is sustained by Acts' final portrayal of him (Acts 21:17–26). James is now clearly the leader of the Jerusalem church. Paul reports to him in the presence of the elders, and they urge Paul to perform a temple ritual to illustrate his own fidelity to the law and allay the suspicions of Jewish Christians about him.

The death of James. The stature and reputation of James among both Jews and Jewish Christians is apparent in Josephus's report of his death. The Jewish high priest Ananus took advantage of the interim between the death of one Roman governor and the arrival of another to dispose of some of his enemies (62 CE):

> Ananus thought that he had a favorable opportunity because Festus was dead and Albinus was still on the way. And so he convened the judges of the Sanhedrin and brought before them a man named James, the brother of Jesus who was called the Christ, and certain others. He accused them of having transgressed the law and delivered them up to be stoned. Those of the inhabitants of the city who were considered the most fair-minded and who were strict in observance of the law were offended at this. They therefore secretly sent to King Agrippa urging him, for Ananus had not even been correct in his first step, to order him to desist from any further such actions. Certain of them even went to meet Albinus, who was on his way from Alexandria, and informed him that Ananus had no authority to convene the Sanhedrin without his consent. Convinced by these words, Albinus angrily wrote to Ananus threatening to take vengeance upon him. King Agrippa, because of Ananus' action, deposed him from the high priesthood which he had held for three months and replaced him with Jesus the son of Damneus. (*Josephus*, Ant. *20.200–203*)

To be noted is that James is not charged with being a Christian or with false faith, but with "breaking the law." Josephus's declaration that those who were "most fair-minded" and "strict in observance of the law" were offended by the high priest's action suggests that the Sadducean high priests regarded James as allied with the Pharisees, who protested his action against James and the others. James is portrayed as a martyr for his strict Jewish faith and practice, not his confession of Jesus as the Messiah.

The growth of the James legend. The strict and much-admired piety James had practiced during his life was confirmed and sealed by his death. Nothing about his death or his later veneration in some Christian and Jewish circles is found in the New Testament, which is primarily shaped by the broad spectrum of Gentile Christianity. If we had only the canonical documents, James would appear as the representative of marginalized Jewish Christianity, quickly surpassed by the growth of Gentile Christianity under the united leadership of Paul and Peter. Historically, however, it is clear that James was not a minor figure in earliest Christianity. He not only played a leading role in the mother church in Jerusalem, but was a figure to be reckoned with throughout the early church.

In the decades after his death, James became the legendary hero of strict Jewish Christianity, the primary founder and leader of the church. Various elements of this considerable body of Christians believed that James had been with Jesus at the Last Supper, and that he was the first person to whom the risen Lord appeared on the first Easter Sunday. He was appointed by the risen Christ (or by the apostles) as the first bishop of Jerusalem. He came to be called "James the Just," that is, "The Righteous One," because of his strict observance of the Torah, and because of his constant prayer in the temple for the Jewish people. He spent so much time on his knees that they became calloused and hard like the knees of a camel. He is pictured as a strictly ascetic Nazirite who had taken a lifelong vow, so that he never bathed, anointed his body with oil, cut his hair, drank wine, or ate meat. He was so admired by the people that the Jewish leaders persuaded him to speak to the multitudes from the parapet of the temple and warn them against becoming disciples of Jesus and straying from the law. In this legendary account, James ascended the temple steps to the highest point and proclaimed to the crowds that Jesus is the heavenly Son of Man who will come as judge. This so angered the scribes and Pharisees that they threw James down from the parapet. He survived the fall, but was killed by a laundry worker with the club he used in his job.

After the destruction of Jerusalem and the temple in the 66–70 CE war, the decimation of the population of Judea, and the migration of many Jewish Christians to Pella, Asia Minor, and elsewhere, Jewish Christianity played only a marginal role in developing mainstream Gentile Christianity that became the protocatholic church of the second century. Shunned and out of touch with what was to become the catholic mainstream, some elements of Jacobite Christianity were influenced by emerging Gnosticism. In some of these streams, James assumed the role of Gnostic revealer whose asceticism, originally a matter of strict Torah purity, was reinterpreted in terms of Gnostic antiworld dualism. He receives the authentic secret tradition from the risen Lord, which is unknown to emerging catholic Christianity. The Paul who had become the hero of mainstream Christianity becomes the villain; the image of James is magnified and embellished not only against Paul, but even Peter plays a secondary role to James:

> The disciples said to Jesus, "We know that you will depart from us. Who is to be our leader?"
>
> Jesus said to them, "Wherever you are, you are to go to James the Righteous, for whose sake heaven and earth came into being." (Gospel of Thomas *12*)

This sample from the *Gospel of Thomas* is the tip of a large iceberg. The Nag Hammadi discoveries have confirmed that there were large segments of early Christianity that looked back to James—not Paul or Peter and the Twelve—as their founder, model, and authority, and that they produced an extensive literature expressing their faith.[2]

18.1.2 The Letter

How does the New Testament *Letter of James* fit into this extensive scenario? The first word of the text unquestionably intends to attribute the document to James the brother of Jesus, not to any other James. The author addresses "the twelve tribes of the Dispersion," implying that he writes from Judea or Jerusalem. The document itself gives no further direct information about either writer or readers. The letter is deeply rooted in Jewish Scripture and tradition, including the teaching of Jesus, but written in the language and style of sophisticated Hellenistic Greek. The fact that the letter is not addressed to a specific congregation and is composed mainly of aphoristic and wisdom materials that could fit a variety of historical settings has given rise to a number of theories as to its real author, date, provenance, genre, and purpose.

1. A Christianized Jewish Document

The name of Jesus or the title Christ occurs only twice (1:1; 2:1). The document never refers to Jesus' death or resurrection, the Holy Spirit, or to specifically Christian leaders or events. Most of the content fits unproblematically

2. This literature includes not only the *Gospel of Thomas*, but the *Apocryphon of James*, the *First Apocalypse of James*, the *Second Apocalypse of James*, the *Apocryphal Epistle of James*, the *Gospel of the Egyptians*, and elements of the *Pseudo-Clementine Homilies* and *Pseudo-Clementine Recognitions*.

within the framework of Hellenized Judaism. A few scholars in the early days of critical New Testament study thus regarded James as a document of Jewish wisdom instruction similar to Ben Sira, adopted by a Christian teacher who inserted the two references to Jesus and perhaps a few other Christian touches to make it into a text for Christian moral instruction. While it is true that James is heavily indebted to Jewish tradition, the substantial Christian elements and perspective (see below) have convinced most scholars that the document was originally composed by a Christian teacher.

2. James the Brother of Jesus to Jewish Christians outside Jerusalem

From the fourth century through the Middle Ages, the Letter of James was regarded as having been written by the brother of Jesus and was unproblematically combined with the teaching of Paul. This changed at the Reformation. In the preface to his 1522 translation of the New Testament, Luther objected that James does not understand the Christian gospel centered in Paul's doctrine of justification by faith. Compared to Paul and John, it is a "right strawy epistle" that could not have been written by the brother of Jesus, and it belongs to the New Testament only in a marginal sense. Luther printed it only as an appendix to the truly canonical books, analogous to his reducing the deuterocanonical books of the Old Testament to the status of Apocrypha. In contrast to the fate of the Apocrypha in Protestant tradition, James continued to be included in the canon—but was marginalized in actual practice. James was weighed in the Pauline balances and found wanting.

This dogmatic perspective on the content of James as theologically off-center and lightweight, combined with the view that it is almost entirely composed of disconnected aphoristic wisdom sayings, led to the relegation of James to the margins of New Testament scholarship and the almost unanimous view that it is a late pseudepigraphical document. More recent scholarship, however, has rejected the traditional approach that reads James only through Pauline spectacles, and has insisted that James be read in its own terms, with positive and enlightening results.[3] For a few scholars, this reaction has included a reassertion of the claim that the letter was actually written by the brother of Jesus to Jewish Christians outside Jerusalem, addressing a real situation of conflict between rich and poor.[4] In this view, James the Just wrote the letter prior to the time that Pauline theology became a problem for him, or even before he had met Paul.[5]

3. James as Post-70 Pseudepigraphy

For the following reasons, most scholars continue to regard the Letter of James as a document written to the wider church after 70 CE, in the name of the revered leader of Jewish Christians.

Attestation. The earliest positive evidence for the existence of the Letter of James is its citation by Origen about 227 CE. There are similarities between James and earlier literature (Matthew, 1 Peter, *1 Clement*, Shepherd of Hermas) that could be considered echoes of James, but even in such cases there is no clear literary dependence. In the few cases that could be considered

3. See especially the collection of essays on James in Robert L. Webb and John S. Kloppenborg, eds., *Reading James with New Eyes: Methodological Reassessments of the Letter of James*, Library of New Testament Studies 342 (Edinburgh: T & T Clark, 2007), and Karl-Wilhelm Niebuhr and Robert W. Wall, eds., *The Catholic Epistles and Apostolic Tradition* (Waco, TX: Baylor University Press, 2009), 43–202.

4. Leading contemporary advocates: Luke Timothy Johnson, *The Letter of James*, AB 37A (New York: Doubleday, 1995); Richard Bauckham, *James: Wisdom of James, Disciple of Jesus the Sage* (London: Routledge, 1999); Douglas J. Moo, *The Letter of James*, Pillar New Testament Commentary (Grand Rapids: Eerdmans, 2000).

5. So Moo, who argues James wrote prior to the Jerusalem Council he dates in 48 CE, when James first became acquainted with Paul's preaching. "Had he known what Paul truly preached (as he would have after A. D. 48), he would have put matters differently than he did" (Moo, *Letter of James*, 26).

literary contacts prior to Origen, the direction of dependence would still be ambiguous. The points of contact with Paul and the Pauline school, for instance, are clearly James's reflection of earlier Christian writings, not the other way around. Most second-century patristic writers give no indication at all that the Letter of James existed. The second century gives ample evidence of literary interest in James (*Protevangelium of James*, *Gospel of Thomas*, *Memoirs* of Hegesippus, elements of the Clementine *Recognitions*), but little or no awareness of the canonical Letter of James. The shadowy existence, or nonexistence, of James until the third century is difficult to explain if it had been written by the brother of Jesus of Nazareth.

Canon history. Likewise, the canonical history of James is difficult to explain if written in the first century by James the Just. During the first three centuries of the church's life, no list of canonical books includes the Letter of James, and no Christian writer quotes or clearly alludes to it. Eusebius's *Ecclesiastical History* (*Hist. eccl.* 3.25, ca. 325 CE) places James in the "still disputed" category. Even Jude, shorter and more obscure than James, and presenting itself as written by the "brother of James," was generally accepted earlier than James; Jude, but not James, is mentioned in the Muratorian Canon (see above, §2.2.1). About 350 CE, James is included in Codex Sinaiticus (along with the *Epistle of Barnabas* and the Shepherd of Hermas) with the twenty-seven books that finally became canonical. The first complete list of the canonical New Testament books is that of Athanasius's Thirty-Ninth Festal Letter in 367 CE. If written by the brother of Jesus and leader of the Jerusalem church in the first century, one must ask why much of the church was not only unaware of its existence for so long, but hesitant to accept it as authoritative teaching until the fourth century.

Language and culture. James is composed in a higher level of Greek than that of Paul, who grew up in the Diaspora with Greek as his mother tongue. When James cites the Bible, he quotes the text of the LXX, even when this differs from the Hebrew (Prov 3:34/Jas 4:6.) The brief text contains sixty-five words unique to the New Testament, forty-five of which are found in the LXX. James manifests familiarity with Greek culture and forms of argument. He alludes to scientific terminology that would have been familiar and attractive to people with a Greek education (e.g., Jas 3:6). Jesus and his family, including James, spoke Aramaic as their native tongue. To be sure, Palestine, including Galilee and Jerusalem, was thoroughly Hellenized, and it is likely that Jesus and James could speak and understand some Greek. This is an entirely different matter, however, from claiming that someone with the educational background of James could compose the kind of sophisticated Greek represented by the Letter of James.

18.1.3 Place in Early Christianity

Relation to Jacobite Christianity

That James is a *Christian* document is clear not only from the references to Jesus as the risen Christ and Lord in 1:1 and 2:1, but by the following features: the address to readers as brothers and sisters (1:2; 2:1; and often) who have been reborn by the word of truth (1:18), the expectation of the parousia (5:7–9), the basing of faith on the Christ event (1:12–25), the "good name that is called over you" (2:7), the engagement with (and misunderstanding of) the Pauline doctrine of justification by faith (2:14–26), the references to Christian teachers (3:1) and elders of the church (5:14), the echoes of the sayings of Jesus and other Christian traditions and documents (see below).

James represents a *particular* stream of *Jewish* Christianity. While it represents Christian faith, it is theocentric rather than Christocentric, representing now as it did originally a bridge between Christians and all who believe in the one God, such as Jews and Muslims. When James summarizes the content of faith, it is the Jewish Shema "God is one," rather than "Jesus is the Christ" (2:19). That James is written from and to a context of Jewish Christians is clear from the address to "the twelve tribes of the Dispersion" (1:1), its similarities to Hellenistic Jewish Wisdom literature, its assumption that the law is a continuing authority for Christians (1:25; 2:8–13; 4:11), and its presentation of James as normative teacher of the community (1:1). Yet the letter does not fit the James who appears elsewhere in the New Testament as the champion of the continuing validity of circumcision and the ritual laws for Jewish Christians (Gal 2:1–14; Acts 15:1–29; 21:17–26). There is no reference to the ritual law, nor any indication that circumcision, Sabbath, or the food laws had been a problem for the churches. There is no hint that Jews and Gentiles had engaged or were engaging in disputes about the role of the law in Christian communities. Purity is necessary to approach God, but it is purity expressed by faith in action, not ritual purity (1:27; 4:8). As in Jesus and Paul, the law is summed up in the command to love the neighbor as oneself, affirmed as the "law of liberty," the "royal law" (1:25; 2:8). Nor does James appear either as the Gnostic revealer of secret wisdom or the advocate of rigid asceticism, as in some later Jacobite literature. The inclusion of James in the canon, at the head of the Catholic Epistles (see below), indicates that it was not understood as representing a different church, but as a complement and supplement to the dominant Pauline Christianity of developing catholic Christianity, and so the author seems to have understood himself.

Relation to Jesus and the Jesus Tradition

Even though not written by the brother of Jesus, or by one who had known Jesus personally and heard him preach, the Letter of James does have a distinctive relation to the developing tradition from and about Jesus. On the one hand, there are no reports or even allusions to the events of Jesus' life. The references to healing practices implemented in the life of the church (5:14–15) have no point of contact with the healing stories of the Gospels. The promise of forgiveness is related neither to the death of Jesus (which is not mentioned at all) nor to incidents in Jesus' life in which he pronounced forgiveness for sinners.

On the other hand, James is closely related to the developing tradition of Jesus' sayings. Although the author never quotes Jesus directly or attributes any of the content of his letter to him, there are a few obvious reflections of sayings of Jesus; for example, see a comparison of James 5:12 and Matthew 5:34–37 in Box 16.

Most of the points of contact with the tradition of Jesus' sayings, however, are elusive and evocative rather than explicit citations; there is thus a wide spectrum of opinion on their identification and number. Most scholars regard at least the following as reflecting the tradition of Jesus' sayings: James 1:1–2, 12 (Q 6:22–23); James 1:5 (Q 11:9); James 1:6 (Matt 21:21, Mark 11:23); James 1:22–25 (Q 6:47–49); James 2:5 (Q 6:20); James 2:8 (Matt 22:39; Mark 12:31; Luke 10:27); James 3:12 (Q 6:44); James 4:9 (Luke 6:21, 25b); James 4:10 (Q 14:11; 18:14);

BOX 16: James and the Jesus Tradition

Matthew 5:34–37 "But I say to you, Do not swear at all, either by heaven, for it is the throne of God, or by the earth, for it is his footstool, or by Jerusalem, for it is the city of the great King. And do not swear by your head, for you cannot make one hair white or black. Let your word be 'Yes, Yes' or 'No, No'; anything more than this comes from the evil one."

James 5:12 Above all, my beloved, do not swear, either by heaven or by earth or by any other oath, but let your "Yes" be yes and your "No" be no, so that you may not fall under condemnation.

James 4:11–12 (Q 6:37); James 5:2 (Q 12:33b).[6] It is clear that James is rooted in and draws from the teaching of Jesus, especially that stream of tradition of Jesus' sayings that was deposited in Q's Great Sermon now found in Matthew 5–7 and Luke 6:20–49, and in Matthew's special traditions (on Q, see below Exc. 3.5). The conjunction of wisdom, prophecy, and eschatology in both Q and James is particularly striking. Does it reflect the setting in which James was composed, or somewhere along the line in the tradition that came to James? In any case, the ethic of James is rooted in the sayings of Jesus, understood as the definitive interpretation of God's law, rather than in the indicative/imperative schema of the cosmic drama found in the Pauline tradition.

Relation to Paul, His Letters and Theology

The "letter" of James does not fit the letter genre; it is not a letter in any real sense. Then how and why did it receive the epistolary prescript, and why was it received into the canon as a letter? Like 1 John, Hebrews, and Revelation, James is shaped by the tradition established by the Pauline letter (see §§10.2.4; 17.1.1). Although James can no longer be interpreted as merely a response to Paul (see above), it would be a serious mistake to suppose the letter can be understood apart from the Pauline tradition. The letter appears to have been composed with Paul in view, and with the expectation that its readers would view it in relation to the Pauline tradition, that is, after the Pauline corpus had been widely circulated. The section 2:14–26 not only seems to address those who have, in the author's understanding, misread Paul, but there are direct points of contact. The subject matter of "faith and works," the justification terminology, the use of Abraham as the key example, and the citation of Genesis 15:6 all point to James's awareness of the text of Romans. The verbal agreements would appear to put this point beyond dispute (see Box 17).

The citation from Genesis 15:6 is precisely according to the text of Romans, which has slight variations from the LXX text itself. These are not mere coincidental agreements, for the sequence of the argument is precisely the same in Romans and James:[7]

BOX 17: Comparison of Romans and James

Underline = exact or almost exact parallel wording   Dotted underline = similar wording

Romans 3:28–4:3	James 2:20–23
For we hold that a person is justified by faith apart from works prescribed by the law. . . . What then are we to say was gained by Abraham, our ancestor according to the flesh? For if Abraham was justified by works, he has something to boast about, but not before God. For what does the scripture say? "Abraham believed God, and it was reckoned to him as righteousness."	Do you want to be shown, you senseless person, that faith apart from works is barren? Was not our ancestor Abraham justified by works when he offered his son Isaac on the altar? . . . Thus the scripture was fulfilled that says, "Abraham believed God, and it was reckoned to him as righteousness," and he was called the friend of God.

6. Cf. Patrick J. Hartin, "James and the Jesus Tradition," and especially John S. Kloppenborg, "The Reception of the Jesus Tradition in James," in Niebuhr and Wall, eds., *Catholic Epistles*, 55–70, 71–100, who provide detailed analyses of the issue, survey the types of solutions, and give extensive bibliography.

7. These data are taken from David R. Nienhuis, "The Letter of James as Canon-Conscious Pseudepigraph," in *The Catholic Epistles and Apostolic Tradition*, ed. Karl-Wilhelm Niebuhr and Robert W. Wall (Waco, TX: Baylor University Press, 2009), 186–89, who gives more details.

a. Issue posed in terms of faith and works	Rom 3:27–28/ Jas 2:14–18
b. Significance of claiming "God is one"	Rom 3:29–30/ Jas 2:19
c. Appeal to father Abraham as test case	Rom 4:1–2/ Jas 2:20–22
d. Citation of proof text, Gen 15:6	Rom 4:3/ Jas 2:20–22
e. Conflicting interpretations of the proof text	Rom 4:4–21/ Jas 2:23
f. Conclusion of the argument	Rom 4:22/ Jas 2:24

Nor are the parallels between Paul and James limited to the "faith and works" section of James 2:14–26, or between James and Romans. There are relatively large areas of formal agreement in subject matter and topic that range over the whole of James, as well as verbal points of contact between James, 1 and 2 Corinthians, and Galatians (e.g., Rom 2:11/Jas 2:1; Rom 2:13/ Jas 1:22–25; Jas 1:8; 3:8, 16/1 Cor 14:33; 2 Cor 6:5; 12:20). "Romans 3:28, Galatians 2:16, and James 2:24 are the only verses in all of Christian Scripture where πίστις (*pistis*, faith) and ἔργον (*ergon*, work) are paired with the verb δικαιόω (*dikaioō*, justify)."[8] James's argument reflects the structure of Paul's sentences (see Box 18).

The author does not write explicitly in opposition to Paul, whom he never mentions. He knows the Pauline letters, assumes his readers know them, and wants to be sure they do not misunderstand Paul's teaching.

BOX 18: Faith and Works

Galatians 2:16 We know that a person is justified not by the works of the law but through faith in Jesus Christ.	James 2:24 You see that a person is justified by works and not by faith alone.

8. Ibid., 186.

Relation to Other Christian Literature

The author of James seems to have known a collection of Pauline letters, and manifests points of contact with the sayings tradition of the Synoptic Gospels. There are, however, no reflections of the final form of the Gospels themselves. By far the closest and most numerous contacts are with 1 Peter, *1 Clement*, Hebrews, and the *Mandates* of Hermas—all of which have a Roman provenance around the end of the first and beginning of the second century CE.[9] Illustrative examples of dozens of such contacts: only James, 1 Peter, and *1 Clement* use the "diaspora" vocabulary for the early church; the rare word δίψυχος (*dipsychos*, double-minded) is found only in James and Hermas's *Mandates*; the vocabulary and imagery of James 1:2–3 and 1 Peter 1:6–7 are strikingly similar; Rahab is used as an example in Hebrews 11:31 (of faith) and in James 2:25 (of works), and nowhere else in the New Testament. The whole discussion understands faith in the same way as Hebrews. Just as James 2:21–24 takes up the Pauline example of Abraham as example of faith and makes him an example of works, so James 2:25 takes up Hebrews' example of Rahab as a model of faith and makes her a paradigm of works. The combination Abraham/ Rahab is also found in Hebrews and *1 Clement*, both of Roman provenance. The concluding citation of Proverbs 10:12, "Love covers a multitude of sins," unites James 5:20, 1 Peter 4:8, and *1 Clement* 49.5.

18.1.4 Date and Provenance

The letter contains no direct internal indications of its time of writing, and its external

9. These points of contact have been analyzed and tabulated very carefully. For details and charts, see Matthias Konradt, "The Historical Context of the Letter of James in Light of Its Traditio-Historical Relations with First Peter," in Niebuhr and Wall, eds., *Catholic Epistles*, 101–26; C. Freeman Sleeper, *James*, ANTC (Nashville: Abingdon Press, 1998), 27–28.

attestation is unclear until the third century (see above). This ambiguity has made it possible to consider James the earliest New Testament writing as well as the latest.[10] The considerations discussed above argue the letter was composed after the corpus of Pauline letters was in circulation. The contacts of James with 1 Peter, Hebrews, *1 Clement*, and Hermas (see above) suggest they all derive from the same milieu. For instance, James's use of the same obscure texts as other Roman documents suggests a Roman provenance (e.g. Prov 3:34 is found in both 1 Pet 5:5 and Jas 4:6). First Peter 5:5–9 is very like James 4:6–10. The roots of the Roman church in Jerusalem Christianity seem to be reflected in both 1 Peter and James. That the readers might be dragged into court for "the name" probably points to a time when being a Christian was itself considered a crime, which did not happen until the latter part of the first century CE (see on 1 Pet 4:14). A number of locations have been suggested (Jerusalem, Alexandria, Syria, Asia, Rome). The contacts with other literature of Roman provenance, as well as the Jewish roots and orientation of Roman Christianity, indicate Rome as the most likely location. That James is relatively late, but knows only elders as church leaders, with no reference to the developing episcopal office, also argues for Rome—where the church continued to be administered by elders long after the bishop's office was accepted elsewhere. This possibility of a Roman origin for James is strengthened if the corpus of Catholic Epistles was later assembled in Rome, and/or if Acts was composed in Rome (see below, §§18.4.1; 24.2).

10. Earliest: Theodor Zahn, *Introduction to the New Testament*, trans. John Moore Trout, et al., 3 vols. (Edinburgh: T. &T. Clark, 1909), 91–93, who dates the letter in the 40s, prior to Paul's Gentile mission work. So also, e.g., Moo, *Letter of James*, 25–26. Latest: Nienhuis, "Pseudepigraph," 183–202, who argues the letter was composed to introduce the collection of Catholic Epistles in the late second century CE.

Summary and Conclusion

The Letter of James seems to have been composed in the name of James the Just, the brother of Jesus, in a setting in which he was the recognized and esteemed authority of the mother church in Jerusalem, probably in Rome around the end of the first century CE. In the letter we see interaction with the tradition of Jesus' sayings, but without incorporating them in a narrative framework. We see influence of the Pauline letter form, though James is not written as a continuation or extension of either the Pauline or deuteropauline letters. Thus both the developing Gospel and Epistle modes of Christian confession influence the composition of James. The letter is in the dominant epistolary tradition, but aware of and influenced by the tradition of Jesus' sayings.

18.1.5 Structure and Outline

The influential commentary of Martin Dibelius interpreted James as the parade example of parenesis, which he understood as the collection and stringing together of originally unrelated aphorisms. The "one consistent feature of James" is that "the entire document lacks continuity in thought."[11] In this view, each saying should be interpreted in and of itself, without attention to its present literary context. Recent study of James has tended to reject this view, and has perhaps overreacted in pronouncing that "far from being a haphazard agglomeration of wisdom motifs, James is a carefully crafted composition."[12] It does seem to have become clear that James is not a random collection of unrelated proverbial maxims, that the author has creatively composed his materials into a meaningful arrangement, and that the first section 1:2–27 provides an "overture," "epitome,"

11. Martin Dibelius and Heinrich Greeven, *A Commentary on the Epistle of James*, trans. Michael Williams, Hermeneia (Philadelphia: Fortress Press, 1976), 2.
12. Johnson, *James*, 80.

or "table of contents" for the remainder of the document, resulting in the following outline.

1:1	Greeting
1:2–27	The Exhortation in Outline
1:2–4	Enduring testing (cf. 1:12; 5:7–11)
1:5–8	The prayer of faith (cf. 4:3; 5:13–18)
1:9–11	Reversal of rich and poor (cf. 2:1–7; 4:13–5:6)
1:12–18	Evil desire vs. God's gift (cf. 3:13–4:10)
1:19–20	Controlling the tongue (cf. 3:1–12)
1:21–27	Words and deeds (cf. 2:14–26)
2:1–27	The Deeds of Faith
2:1–13	Christian morals and the law
2:14–26	Faith and works
3:1–12	Responsible Speech
3:13–4:12	Conversion and Conflict
3:13–18	Wisdom and conduct
4:1–12	Conflict among believers
4:13–5:6	Wealth and Arrogance
5:7–20	Life within the Faith Community
5:7–11	On patience and endurance
5:12–20	Speech in the assembly of faith

18.1.6 Exegetical-Theological Précis

1:1 Greeting

The epistolary greeting is the standard Hellenistic form (Acts 15:23; 23:26). The author's instruction is thus initially cast in letter form, but (perhaps pointedly) without the Pauline elaboration. The author's identity as James the Just, brother of Jesus, is assumed. The "twelve tribes of the Dispersion" could theoretically refer to all Jews outside Palestine, symbolically to all Christians, or—as here taken to be the more probable—to Jewish Christians throughout the Mediterranean world. "Diaspora" is here a theologically loaded term. It was a reminder, common in Second Temple Judaism, that the scattering of the people of God was divine punishment for violation of the covenant, but was not the ultimate identity and situation for God's people. A major feature of Israel's eschatological hope was the restoration and return, the regathering of Israel as part of God's plan for the consummation of history. Though uninterested in speculative eschatological schemes, James shares and communicates this between-the-times existence of believers who are convinced that the Messiah has come, but who still await the consummation of God's purpose. The letter as a whole is not practical, proverbial advice for individuals, but a letter to the scattered Jewish Christian communities, to be read in their congregational worship alongside the Scriptures and other Christian texts.

1:2–27 The Exhortation in Outline

After 1:1, the letter form is abandoned, and the document assumes the mode of Hellenistic Jewish wisdom instruction, which begins immediately without the customary thanksgiving.

1:2–4 Enduring Testing (cf. 1:12; 5:7–11)

Faith is central in the letter's first sentence, remains so throughout, and is dealt with in James's own terms, not merely in response to Paulinism. Enduring temptations or testings (πειρασμός, *peirasmos* can mean either or both) was a standard topic of wisdom instruction. The larger context of James places such testing in an eschatological perspective, so that it can refer to the personal struggle against evil and/or the time of trial that immediately precedes the end.

1:5–8 The prayer of faith (cf. 4:3; 5:13–18)

Faith is expressed in prayer for divine wisdom. James makes no reference to the Holy Spirit; the role in the Pauline tradition played by the

Spirit, or the presence of Christ in the believer, is assumed by wisdom as the gift of God that guides and empowers the believer's life. The opposite of faith is to be δίψυχος, *dipsychos*, double-minded (literally "two-souled), that is, without a personal center but wavering between God and the world.

1:9–11 Reversal of rich and poor (cf. 2:1–7; 4:13–5:6) James regards the Christian community as a fellowship of equals, in which the high and mighty are brought down and the lowly and weak are raised up. Both are to celebrate their new status, their common denominator being their love for God and neighbor (1:12; 2:8).

1:12–18 Evil desire vs. God's gift (cf. 3:13–4:10) The struggle against evil is not a matter of being tested by God or of being in the grip of the overwhelming power of sin. In line with good biblical and Jewish tradition, evil originates in the human will, and human beings are able to overcome it. The human self includes both good and evil impulses, and believers are able to choose the good and to do it. This is different from the Pauline understanding of sin as a transcendent power overcome by God's act in the cross of Jesus, the resurrection, and the gift of the Spirit. Though Paul's view is not directly confronted and resisted, there is nothing here like Paul's cry of desperation, "Wretched man that I am! Who will rescue me from this body of death?" (Rom 7:24). For James, God's grace and faithfulness in creation imply an optimistic view of human potential, an innate ability to live according to God's revealed will. Nonetheless, James does not view the Christian community as those who have simply tried hard to do what is right, and have succeeded. Their existence as believers is the result of rebirth, being begotten and born by the gospel, the word of truth (1:18).

1:19–20 Controlling the tongue (cf. 3:1–12) Reflecting the tradition of Jesus' sayings also used by Matthew (Matt 5:22, 37; 12:32–37), James relates speech to anger, and signals the theme of the importance and power of words he will develop later. James addresses believers who owe their salvific status to the saving power of God's word they have received. They are to be careful with their own words, which can disrupt and spoil the life of the community of faith.

1:21–27 Words and deeds (cf. 2:14–26) The evil words the author warns against are not words that spread false teaching, but words that are unrelated to action. The widows and orphans are the vulnerable ones in society, those without the normal protection of belonging to a close family unit. The word translated "visit" in the KJV and still preserved in some modern translations (RSV, NASV, ESV) is better translated "care for" (NRSV) or "look after" (NIV). It does not refer to paying social calls, but to providing for social needs. This is true religious observance, true purity.

2:1–27 The Deeds of Faith

This section has a common theme, divided into two sections by the address of 2:1, "my brothers and sisters," renewed at 2:14.

2:1–13 Christian morals and the law The preceding emphasis on how faith is expressed in the fellowship of equals is illustrated in the warning against partiality. The Christian community, those who wear "the name" (2:7), must express their faith and their love for neighbor—both rich and poor—by the impartial way they greet people in their assemblies. The phrase νόμος βασιλικός (*nomos basilikos*, NRSV "royal law;" REB "sovereign law"; NJB "supreme law") refers to Leviticus 19:18, "You shall love your neighbor as yourself," which Jesus had designated (along with the command to love God) as the greatest commandment (see Mark 12:31), and Paul had called the summary of the law (Gal 5:14). James refers to neither Jesus nor Paul, however, but assumes that both he and his readers acknowledge the continuing validity and authority of the law itself. He takes for granted that believers look carefully and persistently into the law for direction and empowerment in doing God's will, referring to such engagement with the law six times in this context (1:25; 2:8, 9, 10, 11, 12). The bad thing is not that one looks into the law for direction, but that one looks only superficially, and quickly forgets the image of oneself that one sees there (1:23–25).

The law itself, as interpreted by Jesus, is considered the good gift of God as the guide to doing the will of God. In all this, no mention is made of the key boundary markers commanded by the law for the people of God: circumcision, Sabbath, food laws, observance of the festivals. It is not clear whether these are simply presupposed as having continuing validity for Jewish Christians, or whether the controversies surrounding them belonged to an earlier generation and are no longer relevant. In any case, the issue for James is not the theological understanding of the law, but the law's revelation of justice and mercy as God's will to be *done*. This theme continues in the following section.

2:14–26 Faith and works These verses do not represent a new section in which the author now turns to address a fresh topic, for he has been speaking of faith from the beginning, and has repeatedly stressed that faith must be a matter of what one does, not merely what one says. Nor is this section merely a response to Paul's doctrine of justification by faith. James is pursuing his own agenda, not reacting to Paul's. Yet the manner in which he does this, reflecting Paul's categories, vocabulary, and choice of illustrations, indicates that he is aware of Paul's writings and does not want his own readers to be misled by a superficial understanding of a Pauline doctrine of salvation by "faith alone" (a phrase that does not occur in Paul). *Paul's* point was soteriological and ecclesiological: human beings cannot be justified before God by performing "works of the law" (a phrase that does not occur in James), that is, the ritual requirements of the Torah that identified Israelites as the true and faithful people of God. *James's* point is not soteriological but ethical: faith must be supplemented by good works. For *James*, faith without works is incomplete. For *Paul*, faith without works is inconceivable. Both would agree that God calls for the response of the whole person in trust, love, and obedience, and that mere intellectual assent to the conventional monotheistic creed is inadequate. But they express this differently, and Paul's way of affirming salvation by grace through faith was subject to misunderstanding, as attested in his own letters (Rom 3:1–8; 6:1–23). Paul and James are indeed different and should not be harmonized too quickly. Nonetheless, Paul too can speak positively of Christian good works (e.g., 2 Cor 9:8), and his later disciples had no hesitation in using the language of "good works" to characterize the Christian life (Col 1:10; 2 Thess 2:17; 2 Tim 3:17; 1 Pet 3:11, 13, 16; 4:19).

James expresses the continuing validity of the demand of God for justice and mercy expressed in one's deeds, as found in the Law and Prophets of Israel, culminating in the proclamation of Jesus (especially as represented in the Gospel of Matthew). James makes clear what he is *against* (2:14–17), and it is not a faulty doctrine of justification. It is the kind of religious life that has the correct creed and pronounces words of blessing on needy people who lack food and clothing without doing anything to help them.

3:1–12 Responsible Speech

Readers might expect that James's "practical" perspective, interested in deeds, not mere words, would lead to exhortations along the line of "less talk and more action." But James, like the wisdom tradition in general and the Bible as a whole, considers words themselves as powerful acts. The discussion of disciplined speech begins with those for whom speaking is a vocation: the teachers, among whom the author numbers himself (see the "we" of 3:1). If the author is the brother of Jesus or the first bishop of Jerusalem, he here modestly misses a good opportunity to say so. Teachers are no longer a spontaneous, inspired group informally generated by the work of the Spirit in the life of the church, as in Paul (Rom 12:7; 1 Cor 12:28–29), but a somewhat official group with status, to which one can aspire (cf. the elders of 1 Tim 3:1). The author warns them against superficial aspirations, for teaching is a responsible task not to be entered into lightly or unadvisedly. In all this, the author seems unconcerned about false teaching in the sense of faulty doctrine. The author's concern is the danger inherent in words, in the power of the tongue to damage people's lives and disrupt the community. Thus the exhortation that begins with an address to teachers modulates into a challenge to the whole community. Here too James stands in the tradition of the Matthean Jesus (Matt 5:33–37; 12:32–37). Despite his disclaimers, the author believes that people can be justified or condemned not only by their works, but by their words.

3:13–4:12 *Conversion and Conflict*

3:13–18 *Wisdom and conduct* The wisdom that comes from above provides an entirely different orientation to life than the wisdom of the world. (This is comparable to the guidance of the Spirit given to the community of faith in Paul's theology.) In the conventional human way of looking at things, there is a limited supply of goods, so that the more one person has, the less the other has. Competition is thus the law of life, and one person benefits only at the expense of others. In James's wisdom-given perspective, such viewing of the world in terms of itself is replaced with the view of the world in terms of God the faithful Creator, the God who gives all gifts generously and ungrudgingly to all people (1:5). Faith in such a God means believers are freed from the natural competitive mentality, so that they love and care for others. Party spirit and conflict recede. The "dualism" of James's ethic is not the Greek mind/body or spirit/matter dualism, in which body and world are inherently evil. James advocates the alternative presented by the Hebrew Bible and by Jesus: faith in the Creator and covenant God of Israel opposes the value system of the world as it sees itself apart from God. Thus James's perspective, expressed in a different conceptuality and vocabulary, is close to Paul's "according to the flesh"/"according to the Spirit" (see above on Gal 4:21–5:1a).

4:1–12 *Conflict among believers* The party spirit, based on insecure competitive selfishness that assumes assertiveness is the norm, also invades the community of faith. When this happens, members of the community are being unfaithful to the covenant in which God has embraced them as his own people, and are in effect worshiping other gods. This was the constant temptation of biblical Israel and was constantly challenged by the prophets. They called such unfaithfulness "adultery," violation of their covenant with God (see Hos 2; Jer 3:20; Ezek 16:15–52). James not only stands in the wisdom tradition, but shares the heritage of the prophets and their concern for social justice. This is probably the meaning of addressing his readers as "adulteresses" (fem. pl., 4:4), portraying them as the unfaithful wife of the one God of the covenant. Like both the prophets and sages of Israel, James declares that "clean hands and pure hearts," originally a matter of cultic ritual purity, must be manifested in repentance, conversion, humility, and authentic words and deeds of love for the neighbor (see Job 17:9; Isa 1:16; Pss 24:4; 73:13; Sir 38:10). So also the extreme language of war and murder is not here meant literally, though such language may be rooted in earlier struggles, when the first followers of Jesus had to decide whether or not to get involved in the Zealot movement against Rome. The "wisdom from above" delivers believers from the temptation to think that what they desire can be obtained by violence, whether in the Christian community or the larger society.

4:13–5:6 *Wealth and Arrogance*

The tirade against the rich reflects both the tradition of the Hebrew prophets (e.g., Amos 2:6–8; 8:4) and the social situation of the churches James addresses, in which most of the members were poor and saw themselves as victimized by the wealthy. James thus shares a common perspective with the beatitudes and woes of Luke 6:20–26 (Q), which also sees itself in the succession of the biblical prophets. This is not merely a convenient lambasting of absent opponents, however; the letter addresses insiders to the Christian community, who are themselves tempted to envy the wealth of the rich and to adopt their perspective on the world and life. Here the main problem is not wealth itself but the arrogance that supposes that, with adequate money, life is under one's own control, and insensitivity to the fact that one's wealth is based on the hard work of others. It should not be forgotten that, from James's perspective, the withholding of wages from the laborers is a violation of Torah (cf. Lev 19:13, from a chapter James has already cited; Deut 24:15; Jer 22:13; Mal 3:5).

5:7–20 *Life within the Faith Community*

5:7–11 *On patience and endurance* Unlike most wisdom instruction, James's teaching reflects a strong apocalyptic flavoring. James clearly affirms the "soon coming of the Lord" and that his readers are living "in the last days." This is not superficial repetition of what has become empty theological slogans. He takes his eschatology with ethical seriousness. Yet he shows no interest in apocalyptic timetables, does not relate current events to an eschatological program or elaborate his apocalyptic perspective in specific imagery. James shows that the social-justice ethic of the Old Testament prophets can continue in the ethics of the church, and is not an alternative to an eschatological perspective on God's action in history. Thus he laments that even in the last days, the arrogant rich store up their treasure produced by the hard labor of the workers.

But the day of reckoning and reversal is fast approaching. Readers are called to patient endurance (verb ὑπομένω, *hupomonē*; cognate noun ὑπομονή, *hupomonē*), a virtue prominent in the Christian literature near the end of the first century CE, especially in Hebrews, the Catholic Letters, and Revelation (six times Hebrews; five times James; twice 1 Peter; twice 2 Peter; seven times Revelation). Such "patience" is not passivity or resignation, but a life oriented to the tough-minded confidence that the present order of things is not ultimate, lived in the sure hope of the ultimate coming of God's kingdom. James takes his key example from the Scripture; Job, not Jesus, represents faithful endurance in suffering. Once again, this is surprising if written by James the brother of Jesus, but accords with the theological orientation of the author we have observed all along.

5:12–20 *Speech in the assembly of faith* It should not be surprising that James, who has emphasized authentic speech throughout, concludes his instruction with directives on the right use of language. "Above all . . . do not swear" is not the pious horror of "swearing" in the sense of profanity and crude language, but the priority of one who, in the biblical tradition, respects the validity and power of language. Thus a simple "yes" should be a real "yes" and a "no" a real "no," with no need of confirmation by oaths. Thus prayer, language spoken before God and to God, is charged with the power to heal and forgive.

James's closing illustration of the powerful prayer of Elijah is another example of that kind of confessional language that focuses on the one point it is making, in contrast to objectifying language from which further inferences can be made. That God responded to Elijah's prayer with a drought for three and a half years affirms the power of prayer, but the reader should not inquire about the devastating effect of the drought on hungry farmers and their families, who were praying for rain to no avail.

18.2 Interpreting Jude

18.2.1 Jude and James

Name and identity. In the Jewish Scriptures, Judah was the fourth son of Jacob and the ancestor of the tribe of Judah, for which Judea, Judeans, Judaism, and Jews are named. In Greek, Judah (יְהוּדָה *yehudah*) became Judas or Jude (Ἰούδας), analogous to the way Jacob became James. From the time of the Maccabees on, *Jude/Judas* was a very common Jewish name. Although *Jude* and *Judas* are the same in Greek, English translations of the Bible have often distinguished the two in order to differentiate the Judas who betrayed Jesus from other persons of the same name. In addition to one of the ancestors of Jesus (Luke 3:30), the New Testament knows of six persons with this name: (1) Judas Iscariot; (2) another apostle named Judas (Luke 6:16; John 14:22, Acts 1:13); (3) a Galilean who led a rebellion against Rome (Acts 5:37); (4) a Christian in Damascus with whom Paul lodged (Acts 9:11); (5) Judas Barsabbas, a prophetic leader in early Palestinian Christianity (Acts 15:22, 27, 32); (6) a brother of Jesus (Matt 13:55; Mark 6:3). There can be no doubt that the author intends to represent the letter as written by the brother of Jesus.

Representative of Jewish Christianity. The author's primary identity is his relation to James. Like the author of James, the author of Jude identifies himself not as a brother of Jesus, but as a slave/servant/representative (δοῦλος *doulos*) of the Lord Jesus Christ—with the further identification that he is "brother of James" (v. 1). It is unusual to identify oneself by one's *brother*. The point here is to associate the author with *the* James, the leader of Jewish Christianity (see introduction to James). It is important for the writer to identify himself with the acknowledged leader of Palestinian Jewish Christianity, James the brother of Jesus. *This* is why he does not refer to himself as "brother of *Jesus*." It is not a matter of humility, as though the author modestly declines to mention that he is the brother of Jesus himself, but a matter of authority: the author intends to speak with authority derived from the leader of the mother church in Jerusalem.

Like James, Jude thus represents Jewish Christianity, as is also made clear by his massive use of Jewish Scripture and tradition. The author writes with authority, but it is a derived authority: he cites authoritative texts and traditions, interpreted for their present meaning by one who is related to James. He cites the Jewish Scriptures, but not as one who only has the LXX. He knows both the original texts and Jewish traditions that supplement the scriptural texts. Genesis 6 is elaborated on the basis of *1 Enoch*, and Cain, Korah, Balaam, and Michael's dispute with the devil represent a broad stream of Jewish tradition beyond the Scripture (Jude 5–11). The author is situated in a context where Jewish tradition, and not the Scripture alone, is assumed by both author and readers. This Jewish Christianity is not, however, that of the strict advocates of the Torah who opposed Paul in the first generation. As in the Letter of James, those debates have long since been resolved, and there is no reference to Sabbath, circumcision, or the food laws. Νόμος (*nomos*, law) is entirely missing from Jude.

Pseudonymous? As is the case with James, early Christian tradition correctly saw that the letter makes no claim to have been written by an apostle; the author speaks of "the apostles" as an earlier group to which he does not belong (v. 17). Even though the Letter of Jude played a minimal role in the history and theology of the later church, the traditional view that it, like James, is an actual writing of one of Jesus' brothers prevailed until the rise of modern critical study of the Bible. The prevailing view of historical criticism came to be that Jude was a pseudepigraphical writing from the emerging protocatholic church in the late first or early second century. The standard reasons were that the level of language and culture represented by Jude is beyond that of a Galilean peasant, that the letter reflects the postapostolic period, and that it was accepted into the canon only late and with hesitation, which would not have been the case if it had been written by a brother of Jesus.

Reassertion of the tradition. Some scholars have recently argued that the early tradition was correct in attributing the document to Jude the brother of Jesus. This revival of the traditional view is not merely dogmatically based, but is supported with critical arguments. A leading exponent of this view does not oppose pseudonymity as such, or on theological grounds, and regards 2 Peter as pseudepigraphical, but argues critical evidence is best understood as supporting the traditional view: Jude the brother of Jesus wrote to a group of Palestinian churches in the 50s who were threatened with a perversion of Paul's teaching.[13]

Current majority view. Most critical scholars remain unconvinced by the resurgence of support for the traditional view. There is widespread, but not unanimous, support for the view that the Letter of Jude, analogous to the Letter of James, is a pseudepigraphical tract in epistolary form written in the name of a brother of Jesus, representing Jewish Christianity in the latter part of the first or early part of the second century CE, opposing misunderstandings of the dominant Pauline teaching that were a threat to developing catholic Christianity. This view is supported and illuminated by examining the relation of Jude to the Pauline tradition.

18.2.2 Jude and Paul

There is solid evidence that Jude is post-Pauline. First is the somewhat forced letter form adopted by the author for his composition. In terms of genre, the document is a sermonic tract with an epistolary introduction. It resembles Hebrews, James, and 1 John in being an essentially nonepistolary form on which the epistolary form has been imposed (see §§10.2.4; 17.1.1).

Not only the general epistolary form, but particular items of the content and vocabulary of Paul's letters, are reflected in Jude. If one reads carefully through Jude on the hypothesis that the author and intended readers are familiar with the Pauline letters, numerous items emerge that support the hypothesis. Some samples:

13. Richard Bauckham, *Jude, 2 Peter*, WBC (Waco, TX: Word, 1983), 3–127. More hesitantly, Duane F. Watson, "The Letter of Jude," in *The New Interpreter's Bible*, ed. Leander Keck (Nashville: Abingdon Press, 1998), 12:471–500.

— Jude 1 The binitarian greeting from God and Christ is from the Pauline tradition. Ἐν θεῷ πατρί (*en theō patri*, in God the Father) is found in the New Testament only here and 1–2 Thessalonians 1:1.

— Jude 1 Addressing the hearers as "the called" (κλητοῖς, *klētois*) is found only here and in the Pauline tradition. "Called" is used in the effective sense as in Paul, not in the sense of "invited, whether one responds or not" as in, for example, Matthew 22:14.

— Jude 3 The plural ἅγιοι (*hagioi*, saints) is used for Christians only here and in texts exhibiting contact with the Pauline tradition (not in James, 1–3 John, or the Gospels).

— Jude 4, 15, 18 Jude's favorite word, ἀσεβής (*asebēs*, ungodly), and related forms, which he uses five times in this brief letter, is found eleven times in the New Testament outside Jude, always in Paul or Pauline tradition.

— Jude 4 Παρεισέδυσαν (*pareisedysan*, intruders have "stolen in among you") is reminiscent of the similar situation and vocabulary of Galatians 2:4 παρεισάκτους (*pareisaktous*, false brothers "secretly brought in"), each unique in the New Testament. In general, Jude is like Galatians in opposing those who claim spiritual experiences and distort the law. Though representing a different theology from Paul's, Jude is modeled on Galatians and reflects some of its vocabulary (cf. also reference to "angels" below).

— Jude 5 "I want to remind you" is like Romans 1:3; 1 Corinthians 10:1; 1 Thessalonians 4:3, though the vocabulary is not identical.

— Jude 6 Ἀΐδιος (*aïdios*, eternal) is found only here and Romans 1:20; οἰκητήριον (*oikētērion*, dwelling) is found only here and 2 Corinthians 5:2.

— Jude 20–21 The faith/ hope/ love triad is found often in Pauline tradition, and nowhere else (1 Cor 13:4–7, 13; Eph 1:15–19; 4:1–6; Col 1:3–8; 1 Thess 1:2–10; Heb 10:19–25). This and several other similarities, such as the greeting, are often attributed to "common New Testament tradition," without noting that it is specifically Pauline.[14]

— Jude's characterization of the intruders appears to be influenced by their own self-understanding as charismatics in the Pauline tradition. They apparently understand themselves to speak by the power of the Spirit, and consider themselves to be πνευματικοί (*pneumatikoi*, spiritual; cf. 1 Cor 2:12, 15; 12:1; 14:37; Gal 6:1) and prophets. Jude considers them to be "dreamers" rather than prophets (Jude 8), and ψυχικοί (*psychikoi*, unspiritual, merely psychical/physical, Jude 19), rather than spiritual.

— Likewise, the intruders' scorn for angels (Jude 8–11) probably represents the extension of Paul's own disdain for hostile transcendent beings (see above on Rom 8:38–39; 1 Cor 6:3; 11:10; Gal 4:1–11; Phil 2:5–11). In Galatians, Paul borders on claiming that the law was not given directly by God, but by angels (Gal 1:8, 3:19). The opponents' rejection of authority (Jude 8) is to be understood in this context, rather than their charismatic objection to the emerging structures of protocatholicism. Jude seems to understand the intruders to claim that they rejected the law, as Paul did, because it was given by angels, and need not be obeyed. They disdain both angels and law. Jude respects both and charges the intruders with blaspheming things they do not understand.

All this is not to suggest that Jude uses the Pauline letters as a "source," but that Jude is written in a context in which both author and readers are aware that Paul's letters are often read as authoritative documents in the context of Christian worship and instruction, and where the Pauline tradition is being understood in a way that Jude considers a grave distortion. The opponents of Jude seem to appeal to Paul and consider themselves his heirs. Jude does not reject Paul, but he appeals to *James*.

18.2.3 Relation to Other Early Christian Documents

Analyses similar to the above indicate a variety of kinds of contacts between Jude and other early Christian literature. Details cannot be given here, but the results may be summarized:

— Literary points of contact with Hebrews, 1 Peter, and Acts include formal, material, and theological similarities, and suggest some sort of interrelation among the documents. Jude does not use any of these documents as a source, nor are they reflected in the same way as the Pauline tradition is echoed. Jude looks back at Paul and reflects Pauline texts circulating in his own context. The contacts with Hebrews, 1 Peter, and Acts seem to indicate they were composed in the same general milieu.

— There are numerous obvious points of contact between Jude and 2 Peter, but this is because 2 Peter uses Jude as a source, making copious use of the text of Jude in 2 Peter 2:1–3:4 (see below).

— There is no clear indication the author of Jude knew or utilized the New Testament letter of James. He reveres the figure of James as an authority, but apparently does not know the canonical book of James, which may not have been written yet (see above, introduction to James).

— The (probably) late-second-century Muratorian Canon lists Jude (but not James) as an authoritative document. Jude is still considered to be among the disputed books in Clement of Alexandria, Origin, and Eusebius, even though they are later than the Muratorian Canon.

18.2.4 Date and Provenance

In Jude 17–18, the "apostles" are represented as having predicted the scoffers of the last days,

14. E.g., Steven J. Kraftchick, *Jude and 2 Peter*, ANTC (Nashville: Abingdon Press, 2002), 63. Bauckham, *Jude, 2 Peter*, 33–34, 50, cites Jude as dependent on "general Christian tradition," but the only examples he gives are from Paul.

that is, Jude's own time. As in 1 Timothy 4:1; 2 Timothy 3:1, 6; and Acts 20:29–30, the apostolic age is seen as a heresy-free golden age in which the apostles predicted the heresies of later times. Not only are the apostles regarded as a body and viewed from some distance (analogous to the Old Testament prophets), they are no longer present to speak directly. Jude could be dated any time after the first generation and prior to its use by 2 Peter (ca. 125–150).

There are no external data directly helpful for locating the setting in which Jude was written. The interconnections among other writings of likely Roman provenance (1 and 2 Peter, Hebrews [Acts?]) suggest that Jude too was composed within the orbit of the Roman church. Jude can plausibly be located within the Jewish Christian stream of second- or third-generation Christianity in Rome, where he opposes a radical turn in the Pauline tradition and invokes James as a counterpoint to Paul within the limited pluralism of the emerging protocatholic church. If not originally composed in this setting, the Letter of Jude later found a congenial setting within the corpus of Catholic Letters representing Roman Christianity.

18.2.5 Structure and Outline

After the initial greeting, the body of the letter is arranged chiastically:

3	Charge: Contend for the faith	A
4	Identification of the intruders	B
5–19	Elaborate warning against intruders	B′
20–23	Charge: Church responsibility	A′

This arrangement is framed by the greeting of verses 1–2 and the benediction of verses 24–25. The central section begun by verse 5, the lynchpin of the letter's rhetorical structure, is elaborated by two sets of three warning examples from the Scripture, by the prophecy of Enoch, and by the prediction of the apostles, in each case applied to the intruders, resulting in the following outline:

1–2	Greeting	
3–4	Occasion and Theme	
3	Church responsibility: Contend for the faith	A
4	Identification of the intruders	B
5–23	Body of the Letter	
5–19	Elaborate warning against the intruders	B′
5–13	Prefigured in the Scriptures	
5–7	Three examples: Israel, angels, Sodom	
8–10	Applied to intruders	
11	Three examples: Cain, Balaam, Korah	
12–13	Applied to intruders	
14–16	Prophesied by Enoch	
14–15	Enoch's prophecy	
16	Applied to intruders	
17–19	Predicted by the Apostles	
17–18	Apostles' prediction	
19	Applied to intruders	
20–23	Church responsibility	A′
24–25	Doxology	

18.2.6 Exegetical-Theological Précis

1–2 Greeting

The author adopts and only slightly adapts the standard Pauline greeting that had become conventional, identifying himself not as an apostle or brother of Jesus, but as Jude, servant of Jesus Christ and brother of James. The greeting continues in the Pauline style by addressing the readers as called (by God), beloved in God, and kept safe for Jesus Christ, that is, kept in God's care until the parousia. Where Paul has "grace and peace," Jude has "mercy, peace, and love," in the prayer form "may it be multiplied" (πληθυνθείη, *plēthuntheiē*), found elsewhere only in 1 Peter 1:2 and 2 Peter 1:2.

3–4 *Occasion and Theme*

As in Galatians (and only there in the Pauline corpus), the conventional thanksgiving section that normally follows the greeting is missing. In Galatians, the abrupt transition to the body of the letter reflects Paul's exasperation and anger that the Galatian churches he had founded are beginning to follow new teachers regarded by Paul as perverting the gospel. Although Jude gives no indication that the author is personally known to the recipients, the same urgent situation shapes his letter. Jude had intended to write a more expansive letter on the topic of the salvation shared by all Christians—the reader might think of something like Paul's letter to the Romans. This project, which so far as we know was never carried out, was deferred because of the urgency of the situation, resulting in the present brief letter. Intruders have crept into the church, but this should not surprise the readers, for they were predicted (literally, "programmed for this") long ago. The intruders pervert the grace of God into licentiousness; that is, the good news of salvation by grace as proclaimed by Paul in Romans has been understood as a license for immoral living. The readers are challenged to reject the intruders' doctrine and to contend for the faith once for all entrusted to the saints.

5–23 *Body of the Letter*

What appears at first to be a somewhat bombastic and rambling blast against the intruders turns out on closer examination to be a well-structured argument. The opening paragraph, verses 3–4, is composed of two elements: (a) a charge, "contend for the faith," and (b) an identification of the intruders. The body of the letter expands each of these, in reverse order, giving a chiastic structure to the whole. The description of the false teachers is elaborated (B′, vv. 5–19); then Jude concludes with an elaboration of the responsibility with which the readers are charged (A′, vv. 20–23).

5–19 *Elaborate warning against the intruders* The readers should be neither dismayed nor surprised by the intrusion of the false teachers, for they have been prefigured in the Scriptures (vv. 5–13), prophesied by Enoch (vv. 14–16), and predicted by the apostles (vv. 17–19).

5–13 Prefigured in the Scriptures
Reading his Scripture typologically, the author sees the troublemakers of his own day typified in the unfaithful Israelites, who, though they had been delivered from Egypt, failed to continue their faith in the wilderness, and were destroyed. Likewise the "angels" did not keep their proper place, but joined themselves to earthly women, and have been arrested and confined by God until the great day of judgment. Here Jude adopts the elaboration of the myth of Genesis 6:1–4 found in *1 Enoch* 6–19. The "sons of God" (divine beings, members of the heavenly court) of the Jewish Scriptures often were understood as "angels" in the LXX and later Judaism. They had left their proper heavenly dwelling and lusted after human women, thereby violating the divine order of creation. God did not punish them immediately, but imprisoned them beneath the earth, awaiting their final eschatological judgment.

Jude's point is not to teach speculative doctrines about the angels, which he assumes, but to use the story of the angels as an illustration of those who violate the divine order of things and receive God's judgment. They thus become a prefiguration of the intruders into the churches of Jude's time, and of their sure and certain future judgment. So also Sodom and Gomorrah are illustrations of those who violate the divine order (Gen 19:4–11). As the angels had lusted after human flesh, so the humans of Sodom had lusted after angelic "flesh," in each case stepping outside the boundaries appointed by God. While this way of thinking may seem strange to the modern reader, Jude's point is not to teach anything about homosexuality, but to use two stories of angel/human interaction to drive home his point that those who violate these orders of creation will receive God's judgment.

The intruders are guilty of precisely this sin. They revile the angels (the "glorious ones," v. 8) and reject authority. Jude cites another pseudepigraphical Jewish writing, the *Assumption of Moses* or the *Testament of Moses*,[15] in which Satan, the heavenly prosecuting attorney (cf. Job 1), who is now functioning as the demonic prince of this world, claims the body of Moses. The story of Moses' death in Deuteronomy 34 had been elaborated in Jewish apocryphal works. In the story here referred to, the archangel Michael is about to take Moses' body to heaven, but Satan intervenes, claiming that he owns the body, since Moses was a murderer, and because as Satan he is "lord of matter," that is, the material body of Moses. Michael does not presume to condemn Satan himself, but cites the Scripture "The Lord rebuke you." This reflects Zechariah 3:2, from a section of Zechariah that provides several motifs for Jude's letter, which throughout focuses biblical texts on the threat of the intruders in his own situation. His point is that the intruders insolently slander the angelic world, which they do not in fact understand.

The first triad of examples is followed by a second: Cain, Balaam, and Korah, all of whom are understood in first-century Judaism as rebels and heretics condemned by God. So it is with the intruders: they make great claims, participate in the eucharistic fellowship dinners (ἀγάπαι, *agapai*, lovefeasts) of the church, where they are blemishes (or dangerous submerged reefs; σπιλάδες, *spilades* can be translated either way).

15. The uncertainty is due to the fact that this episode is lost from the extant manuscripts of these documents, and is known to us only from patristic citations.

14–16 Prophesied by Enoch

As Jude had indicated knowledge and respect for *1 Enoch* in the preceding, he then explicitly quotes *1 Enoch* 1.9, which he understands as a prophecy of the intruders of his own time. This is a common part of the apocalyptic scenario. If written by the brother of Jesus, the author here misses a good opportunity to quote Jesus himself (e.g., Mark 13:5–6, 21–23) and cites a pseudepigraphical Jewish apocalyptic writing instead.

17–19 Predicted by the apostles

Just as the Scripture and *Enoch* had predicted the present troubles, so also the Christian apostles who had founded the church and taught them the original core of the faith had also predicted the evil, divisive false teachers plaguing the readers' congregations.

20–23 Church responsibility Jude is not only a condemnation of the false teachers, but a call to responsibility. Readers are both to continue in the faith handed on to them and respond with pastoral care to those who are wavering under the influence of the intruders. The final exhortation includes a brief summary of Christian theology, expressed in proto-Trinitarian terms, and an outline of Christian living as embracing faith, prayer, love, and hope (vv. 20–21). Those members of the church who are tempted to follow the new teachers, or have already done so, are to be ministered to with both mercy and urgency (vv. 22–23).

24–25 Doxology

Although the letter calls its readers to critical alertness and responsibility, it concludes with a blessing directed to the God who is able to bring them finally into his presence. This beautiful benediction, the best-known verses in the book, was probably not composed ad hoc just for this letter, but was adopted from the rich liturgical life of the church. Jude was composed to be read in church. It begins as letter, continues as monitory sermon, and concludes as liturgy.

18.3 Interpreting 2 Peter

UNLIKE 1 PETER, WHICH IMMEDIATELY relaxes the claim to apostolic authorship after 1:1 and specifically identifies itself as written by an elder in the Roman church (5:1, 13), 2 Peter maintains the fictive authorship of Simon Peter throughout. In 1:16–18 the author represents himself as, along with the other apostles, recipients of a heavenly revelation of Jesus' sonship; Jesus personally revealed the apostle's imminent death to him (1:14); the present author has already written one letter to the readers (3:1, referring to 1 Peter); he speaks of "our beloved brother Paul" as a personal acquaintance, and places himself on the same level (at least) as Paul. The letter presents itself as written by the apostle Peter in earlier history to warn the present leaders of false teachers to come, so that they would not be surprised when they actually appear—as they now have—but regard them as a sign of the coming end (2:1–3), and thus learn how they should lead their lives (3:11, 14, 17). Is this really Simon Peter?

The sixteenth-century reformer John Calvin, competent classics scholar, reviewed the doubts of the fourth-century Eusebius and the conclusion of fifth-century Jerome that the apostle Peter could not have written this book, so different in language and style from what one would anticipate from a Galilean fisherman. On the basis of the evidence, Calvin was inclined to agree with Jerome, but finally decided that

> If it be received as canonical, we must allow Peter to be the author, since it has his name inscribed, and he also testifies that he had lived with Christ: and it would have been a fiction unworthy of a minister of Christ, to have personated another individual.[16]

Calvin was able to maintain both his scholarly integrity and his theory of biblical inspiration and authority (God would not allow pseudepigraphical writings in the canon) by attributing the actual composition of the letter to a skilled secretary. While Calvin believed that 2 Peter is truly from the apostle Peter, this means "not that he himself wrote it, but that some one of his disciples set forth in writing, by his command, those things which the necessity of the times required."[17] Today, virtually all scholars regard 2 Peter as pseudepigraphical, probably the latest New Testament document to be written, except those whose theology requires apostolic authorship as prerequisite to canonicity.

We now consider the key features of 2 Peter in deciding about authorship, date, historical setting—and thus meaning and significance.

18.3.1 Language and Culture

This was the chief problem for Calvin and remains a principal obstacle to all attempts to attribute the letter to Simon Peter. The book was obviously written by a different author from the composer of 1 Peter, as indicated by the contrasting vocabulary, style, and content. The author is thoroughly at home in Greek, which is his mother tongue. There are no Semitisms. The LXX is his Bible. His Greek is in the same general bracket as James, 1 Peter, Hebrews, and the Pastorals, superior not only to Revelation and Mark, but even to Paul. His composition has the highest proportion of *hapax legomena* in the New Testament. Many of the fifty-seven words unique to him in the New Testament are found in the Apostolic Fathers, Philo, Josephus, and other Hellenistic Jewish authors. His linguistic proficiency includes rhetorical skills (alliteration, assonance, chiastic structures) and a knowledge of the Greek classics. He appears, in fact, to presuppose the Greek classical narratives and fit his biblical knowledge into them, rather than vice versa. Like the Titans in Greek

16. Jean Calvin, David W. Torrance, and Thomas Forsyth Torrance, *Calvin's Commentaries*, 12 vols. (Grand Rapids: Eerdmans, 1959), 12:228.

17. Ibid.

mythology, the evil angels of Genesis 6 are thrown into Tartarus (2:4).[18] Here and elsewhere, 2 Peter is more Hellenistic than Jude, one of his principal sources. Thus the author knew the Greek stories from his childhood education and understood the biblical stories in these categories when he became a Christian.

18.3.2 Genre

Second Peter combines two literary genres, the testament and the letter. The testament was a familiar genre: in view of his impending death, the patriarch or leader is granted a vision of the future that he shares with his followers, warning them of things to come and encouraging them to be faithful (e.g., Gen 47:29–49:28; Deut 28–31; Josh 23–24; John 13–16; Acts 20:18–35; 2 Tim 3–4; TOB 14:3–11; 2 Esd 14:28–36; *Jubilees* 21–22, 35.1–36.18; *Testament of Moses*, *Testament of Job*, the *Testaments of the Twelve Patriarchs*). Second Peter has the character of such a testament (1:12–15), but it is fitted within the epistolary framework that, in the wake of Paul, had become the normative genre of Christian instruction (see §§10.2.4; 17.1.1).

18.3.3 Temporal Perspective

The testamentary framework requires the future perspective from the point of view of the purported author, who looks ahead to the time of the readers he addresses. For the most part, 2 Peter in fact exhibits this temporal perspective (note the future tenses of 1:12, 15; 2:1–3; 3:3). But in 2:14–19 and 3:5, the predicted false teachers are already present, and "Peter" speaks directly to the hearer-readers of the letter. As in the Pastorals (1 Tim 4:1–5; 2 Tim 3:1–9) and Acts 20:29–30, the future perspective of the testamentary fictive world modulates into the present real world of the reader (which is also, of course, the real world of the author).

18.3.4 Relation to the Jesus Tradition

As in the case of 1 Peter and Jude, if 2 Peter were written by one who had been an eyewitness and companion of the earthly Jesus, one would expect some indication of this in the text itself. Second Peter, however, gives no indication of knowledge of sayings and events from the life of the historical Jesus. The supposed reference to the transfiguration is not an exception to this (see on 1:17–18 below). The authorities on which Christian faith and life are based are the biblical prophets and the command of Jesus Christ spoken through the apostles, not the teaching and example of Jesus (3:2). In this, 2 Peter follows the pattern established by the Pauline letters and continued by every New Testament letter.

18.3.5 Use of Jude

The modern reader who comes to 2 Peter from a careful reading of Jude is immediately struck by the numerous obvious and close connections between Jude and 2 Peter (cf. Box 19). Clearly Jude and 2 Peter have some sort of literary connection. There are four theoretical possibilities, each of which has had its defenders:[19] (1) The two documents were written by the same author; (2) they have a common source, either literary or oral; (3) 2 Peter was written first and utilized by the author of Jude; (4) Jude was written first, and is utilized by the author of 2 Peter. The consensus of current scholarship is that 2 Peter utilizes Jude.

Not only are there striking verbal similarities as indicated in Box 19, there are instances where the text of 2 Peter is not understood unless the reader is aware of the underlying text

18. For further examples, see, e.g., Earl Richard, "Peter, Second Letter of," in *New Interpreter's Dictionary of the Bible*, 4:471.

19. For details, see Lauri Thurén, "The Relationship between 2 Peter and Jude: A Classical Problem Resolved?" in *The Catholic Epistles and the Tradition*, ed. Jacques Schlosser, BETL (Leuven: Leuven University Press, 2004), 451–60.

BOX 19: Jude – 2 Peter Parallels

Bold = common to Jude and 2 Peter. Underline = exact or almost exact parallel wording. Dotted underline = similar wording. *Italics* = clear allusions to and quotations of noncanonical Jewish documents in Jude, omitted in 2 Peter.

JUDE

4. For **certain** intruders have **stolen in** among you, people who long ago were designated for this condemnation as ungodly, who pervert the grace of our God into **licentiousness and deny** our only **Master** and Lord, Jesus Christ.

5. Now I desire to remind you, though you are fully informed, that the Lord, who once for all saved a people out of the land of Egypt, afterward **destroyed** those who did not believe. 6. And **the angels** who did not keep their own position, but left their proper dwelling, he has **kept** in eternal chains in **deepest darkness for the judgment** of the great **Day**. 7. Likewise, **Sodom and Gomorrah** and the surrounding cities, which, in the same manner as they, **indulged** in sexual immorality and **pursued unnatural lust**, serve as **an example** by undergoing a **punishment** of eternal fire.

8. Yet in the same way these dreamers also defile the flesh, reject **authority**, and **slander the glorious ones**. 9. But when the **archangel** *Michael contended with the devil and disputed about the body of Moses,* [*Testament of Moses*] **he did not dare to bring a condemnation of slander against him**, but said, "The Lord rebuke you!" 10. **But these people slander whatever they do not understand, and they are destroyed** by those things that, **like irrational animals**, they know **by instinct**. 11. Woe to them! For they go **the way of** Cain, and abandon themselves to **Balaam's error** for the sake of **gain**, and perish in Korah's rebellion. 12. These are **blemishes** on your **love**-feasts, **while they feast with you** without fear, feeding themselves. **They are waterless** clouds **carried along by the winds**; autumn trees without fruit, twice dead, uprooted; 13. wild waves of the sea, casting up the foam of their own shame; *wandering stars,* [*1 Enoch* 18.15–16; 21.5–6] **for whom the deepest darkness has been reserved** forever.

14. It was also about these that Enoch, in the seventh generation from Adam, prophesied, saying, *"See, the Lord is coming with ten thousands of his holy ones, 15. to execute judgment on all, and to convict everyone of all the deeds of ungodliness that they have committed in such an ungodly way, and of all the harsh things that ungodly sinners have spoken against him."* [*1 Enoch* 1.9–10]

16. These are grumblers and malcontents; they **indulge** their own **lusts**; they are **bombastic** in speech, flattering people to their own advantage.

17. But you, beloved, must **remember the predictions of the apostles of our Lord** Jesus Christ; 18. for they **said** to you, **"In the last** time there will be **scoffers, indulging their own** ungodly **lusts**."

2 PETER

2:1 . . . , **who will secretly bring in** destructive opinions. They will **even deny** the **Master** who bought them —bringing swift destruction on themselves. 2 Even so, many will follow their **licentious ways**, and because of these teachers the way of truth will be maligned. 3 . . . Their condemnation, pronounced against them long ago, has not been idle, and their **destruction** is not asleep.

2:4 For if God did not spare **the angels** when they sinned, **but** cast them into hell and committed them to chains of **deepest darkness** to be **kept** until **the judgment**; 5 and if he did not spare the ancient world, even though he saved Noah, a herald of righteousness, with seven others, when he brought a flood on a world of the ungodly; 6 and if by turning the cities of **Sodom and Gomorrah** to ashes he **condemned** them to extinction and made them **an example** of what is coming to the ungodly; . . . 9 then the Lord knows how to rescue the godly from trial, and to **keep** the unrighteous under punishment **until the day of judgment** 10 —especially those who **indulge their flesh** in **depraved lust**, and who despise **authority**.

Bold and willful, they are not afraid to **slander the glorious ones**, 11 whereas **angels**, though greater in might and power, **do not bring against them a slanderous judgment** from the Lord. 12 **These people, however, are like irrational animals**, mere creatures **of instinct**, born to be caught and killed. They **slander what they do not understand, and** when those creatures are destroyed, **they also will be destroyed**, 13 suffering the penalty for doing wrong. They count it a pleasure to revel in the daytime. They are **blots** and blemishes, reveling in their dissipation **while they feast with you**. 14 They have eyes full of adultery, insatiable for sin. They entice unsteady souls. They have hearts trained in greed. Accursed children! 15 They have left the straight road and have **gone astray**, following **the road of Balaam** son of Bosor, who **loved** the **wages** of doing wrong, . . .

2:17 **These are waterless** springs and mists **driven by a storm**; **for them the deepest darkness has been reserved**. 18 For they speak **bombastic** nonsense, and with licentious **desires** of the flesh . . . 21 . . . turn back from **the holy** commandment **that was passed on** to them.

3:2 . . . you should **remember the words spoken in the past by the** holy prophets, and the commandment **of the Lord** and Savior spoken through your **apostles**. 3 First of all you must understand this, **that in the last** days **scoffers will come**, scoffing and **indulging their own lusts** 4 and **saying**, "Where is the promise of his coming? For ever since our ancestors died, all things continue as they were from the beginning of creation!"

of Jude. For example, one must know the story of the confrontation between the archangel Michael and the devil alluded to in Jude 9 to get the point of 2 Peter 2:11. The author writes for a readership already thoroughly aware of Jude. (See below for instances of his reinterpretation of Jude.) Like Jude, 2 Peter does not conclude like a letter, but with a doxology appropriate for instructional texts to be read in the setting of congregational worship.

18.3.6 Relation to Paul and the "Other Scriptures"

Both author and readers are aware that Paul's letters have been collected, circulated, and are read in Christian worship alongside the Scripture, that is, that they themselves are beginning to be considered Scripture (3:15–16; cf. also the Roman *2 Clem.* 14.2, where the authoritative documents are "the books [of Scripture] and the apostles"). The false teachers also acknowledge Paul's letters as authority for the Christian community, but from the author's point of view they willfully misinterpret Paul, who is in any case difficult to understand. This does not cause the author to reject Paul, surrendering him to the false teachers. "Our beloved brother Paul" wrote by wisdom given him from God (3:15).

As is the case with the Jewish Scriptures that have become the Christian Bible, the issue is not authority, but interpretation. As the false teachers misinterpret Paul, so they misinterpret the Scripture generally. The issue is who is authorized to interpret them. The prophecies of Scripture are not of private interpretation, but are rightly understood only by those who have been given the apostolic key by the risen Christ (1:20). Both Paul and the Scriptures are to be interpreted only in terms of authentic apostolic tradition as represented by Peter.

18.3.7 Relation to Other Early Christian Documents of Roman Provenance

The author of 2 Peter intentionally takes his stand in the tradition of 1 Peter (3:1) and assumes that his readers know that letter. There is thus a connection between 1 and 2 Peter, but it is not the same kind of connection as that between, for example, 1 and 2 Corinthians. In 2 Peter we have a different author, a different generation, a different situation. Language, style, and content are all different. Second Peter does not represent a Petrine school in the sense of a group of students of the same teacher who continue and develop his thought along similar theological lines, for 1 and 2 Peter are quite different theologically. There was no Petrine school that collected and edited Petrine materials, as the Pauline school did for Pauline traditions. But if "school" is defined more generally, as in the discussion of a "Pauline school" above, 1 and 2 Peter could be seen as belonging to the same school tradition (in the same sense that Ephesians and the Pastorals, different as they are, both represent the "Pauline school"). Some prefer not to speak of a "school" but a Petrine "circle" or "group," an unofficial association of Christian teachers who look back to Peter as their common authority.[20] First Peter is dependent on the Pauline tradition, but 2 Peter is dependent on Jude, and exhibits hardly any contact with other canonical documents. There are, however, close contacts between 2 Peter and *1 Clement*, *2 Clement*, and the *Shepherd* of Hermas. "These three works are 2 Peter's closest relatives in the early church," whose similarities "probably indicate their common indebtedness to a tradition of Roman Christianity."[21] Especially significant is the close relationship between the apocalyptic ideas of 2 Peter 3:4 and those of *1 Clement* 23.3 and *2 Clement* 11.2.

20. On a Petrine "school," "circle," or "group," see Doering, "Diaspora Letter," 233 and n117; Bauckham, *Jude, 2 Peter*, 146, and Soards, "Petrine School," 3828–49 for further discussion and bibliography.

21. Bauckham, *Jude, 2 Peter*, 150–51, 284, 304, who provides details on a "common language milieu" and "shared traditions." So also Kraftchick, *Jude and 2 Peter*, 76. If, as is likely, Hebrews and Acts are from Rome, the points of contact with these two documents further strengthen the probability of a Roman provenance for 2 Peter.

18.3.8 Attestation, Canonicity, Date

In the considered opinion of most scholars, 2 Peter is the latest writing included in the New Testament. There may be echoes of it in the second-century *Apocalypse of Peter* of uncertain date, but the first author specifically to mention Peter as author was Origen, about 225 CE—who does not consider it authentic (Eusebius, *Hist. eccl.* 6.27.1). It was still listed among the disputed books by Eusebius about 325 CE (*Hist. eccl.* 3.1–4; cf. 25.3) and not generally included in canonical lists until the end of the fourth century. When finally accepted by most churches into the canon, it was on the basis of its apostolic content, not on any reliable evidence of apostolic authorship. The letter itself indicates it was composed in a situation long past the lifetime of Simon Peter. The author looks back on the time of the early prophets and apostles (3:2), the time of the "fathers" (οἱ πατέρες, *hoi pateres*, NRSV "ancestors," 3:4), the leaders of the first Christian generation. The reference to the author's previous letter indicates that 1 Peter also was assumed to be generally known. Second Peter is thus after the collection and circulation of Paul's letters, and after they had come to be regarded as Scripture (3:15–16), after the composition and circulation of 1 Peter (3:1), after the composition and circulation of Jude (2:1–3:4), some time after the generation of the founding fathers was dead and the world was still continuing its normal course (3:4), after the delay of the parousia could be used as evidence against traditional eschatological expectations (3:3–4), after a tradition in which Jesus predicted Peter's death was in circulation (1:14; first attested in the latest stratum of the Gospel of John, 21:18–19), after the inclusion of citing noncanonical texts as authority (as in Jude 9, 14–16) had become problematical. The evidence seems to converge on the period 120–150 CE as the setting for the composition of 2 Peter.

18.3.9 Heresy and Orthodoxy

The opponents seem to represent an extreme form of the later developments in the Pauline school represented by Colossians and Ephesians. From the perspective of 2 Peter (and Jude), the heretics have perverted Paul's doctrine of grace into licentiousness, and their emphasis on experience of the Spirit and the present reality of salvation makes futuristic eschatology unnecessary. The emphasis on "already" cultivated in Colossians and Ephesians led to a rejection of the "not yet" dimension of salvation.

Summary and Transition

Second Peter comes at the climax of an extended development of ecumenical Christianity in Rome that looked back to Peter as its guide and model. Writing sometime in the first half of the second century, the author wants to avoid the dangers of the more radical elements in Pauline Christianity, not by rejecting Paul but by incorporating him. The church is not to be divided between Paulinists and Jewish Christians. Paul is to be included in a broad developing mainstream that includes the Jewish Christianity of Jude (and hence James), but Paulinism is not the norm to which all else must conform. As 1 Peter had included Paul by adopting the Pauline letter form, elements of Pauline tradition and theology, and even Paul's companions Mark and Silvanus, so the author of 2 Peter incorporates Paul (and James and Jude) under the unifying figure of Peter, and indicates Paul is to be valued and interpreted within *this* (Petrine) frame of reference. The core elements of what is to become the biblical canon are already affirmed as a defense against heresy:

1. The Jewish Scriptures are adopted and affirmed, but (in contrast to Jude) "purified" of books that came to be considered noncanonical. The insistence that the writers of the Bible were inspired by the Holy Spirit (1:21) is not in the interest of a doctrine of biblical inspiration per se, but is set over against the claims of the opponents, who claim to speak by divine inspiration. Over against these claims of present revelation, the author sets the divinely inspired Scripture. The church is indeed guided by the Holy Spirit, but the Spirit guides the church

through the Scriptures, not through contemporary revelations.

2. The Scriptures include the writings of Paul (3:16). The writings of Paul and of Peter are (both!) affirmed as authorities, but both must be interpreted within the guidelines of church tradition.

3. There is no reference to written Gospels, although the Synoptics had been circulating in some circles of the church for decades. While the Gospels are not yet affirmed as sacred texts, the reference to the scene in which the heavenly voice came on the mountain represents Gospel tradition (1:16–18). The Old Testament, Letters, and Gospels were to become the canon of mainstream Christianity. These are already deployed in 2 Peter in the church's struggle to guard the faith from heretical perversions. In this sense, 2 Peter is indeed a representative of protocatholic Christianity. But 2 Peter is an extension of the epistolary tradition begun by Paul, with only minimal contact with the life-of-Jesus tradition represented by the Gospels. In the next section of this book, we will turn to the other major stream of New Testament theology that generated the Gospels.

18.3.10 Structure and Outline

1:1–2	Greeting
1:3–11	Thematic Summary: God's Acts and the Believers' Response
1:12–3:13	Body of the Letter: Peter's Testament, Responding in Advance to the False Teachers
1:12–2:22	True and false prophecy
1:12–21	Peter, the apostles, and true prophecy
2:1–22	False prophets, then and now
3:1–13	Eschatological existence
3:14–18	Concluding Exhortation and Doxology

18.3.11 Exegetical-Theological Précis

1:1–2 Greeting

The opening words signal the ecumenical, inclusive perspective of the letter, combining the purported author's Jewish and Greek names, just as they combine the self-designations "servant" from Jude and "apostle" from 1 Peter. Using the Jewish form of his name (cf. Acts 15:14), *Simeon the servant* speaks as one who was companion of Jesus and rooted in the earliest church, declaring that the readers of a later generation share the same faith. *Peter the apostle* likewise guarantees the validity of the tradition as apostolic. An authoritative apostolic voice from the past addresses readers of a later generation. The letter is not addressed to a specific congregation or congregations, but specifically to all who share the common faith. Here, as in Jude 2, *faith* refers not only to the personal trust with which one believes, but to the content of the faith itself. Those who come after the first generation do not have a hand-me-down, secondhand faith, but one that is equal to that of the first generation. "Our God and Savior Jesus Christ" is already tending toward the later use of God-language for Christ. In contrast to the Pastorals, where γνῶσις (*gnōsis*, knowledge) is used only in a bad sense, here Christian faith gives the believer true knowledge.

1:3–11 Thematic Summary: God's Acts and the Believers' Response

1:3–4 Ernst Käsemann's influential essay made popular the view that 2 Peter is mainly a defense of primitive Christian eschatology.[22] He was wrong, however, in supposing this was only an indication of the decline of Christian faith from its early existential vitality into an insipid

22. Ernst Käsemann, "An Apologia for Primitive Christian Eschatology," in *Essays on New Testament Themes*, Studies in Biblical Theology 41 (London: SCM Press, 1964), 169–95.

"early catholicism" (see above §16.1.5). The author of 2 Peter is not concerned with eschatology as a dogma, but with the Christian life as eschatological existence—living "between the times" of God's definitive act in Christ and the future consummation of the kingdom of God at the parousia. God has acted in the past not only in the saving Christ event, but by calling the readers into the community of faith. God will act in the future—this is the implication of "his precious and very great promises" that are denied by the false teachers. Living one's life on the line between God's act in Christ and the final coming of God's kingdom has ethical consequences. For the author, this weaving together of faith and life is crucial. Bad ethics results from bad theology; good theology must produce ethical living.

1:5–11 This combination of faith and ethics is immediately illustrated by adapting a list of virtues to represent the distinctive substance of the Christian life. There are numerous such catalogues in Hellenistic and rabbinic literature. Typically, such lists began with *knowledge*, and right understanding was considered the basis for the good life. In contrast, Peter begins with *faith*, which in this text refers not to the content of what is believed, but to personal trust in the God revealed in Christ. The conventional Hellenistic virtues follow, but the whole is flavored by Christian content.

Characteristic is the use of the εὐσέβεια word group (*eusebeia*, godly, godliness, piety), found only in later New Testament writings (four times Acts, thirteen times Pastorals, five times 2 Peter). The list is not a catalogue of ideals to be striven for, but profiles the life of those who see their lives as determined by God's act in Christ—past, present, and future. Eschatological existence, not idealistic virtues, is the motor that drives the believers' life. The list that begins with faith concludes with love, expressed by the word ἀγάπη (*agapē*). Love is here not one virtue among others, but the sum and goal of all ethics.

1:12–3:13 Body of the Letter: Peter's Testament, Responding in Advance to the False Teachers

1:12–2:22 True and false prophecy

1:12–21 Peter, the apostles, and true prophecy

1:12–15 Here the author makes the testamentary character of his writing explicit. The tradition that Jesus informed Simon Peter of his impending martyr's death is also found in John 21:18–19. Although the author himself is reinterpreting the traditional faith into new categories, he presents his interpretation as only reminding the readers of what they already know, that is, their inherited, traditional faith, which does not become something new by being reinterpreted in new language and concepts.

1:16–21 The author does not charge his opponents with propagating "cleverly devised myths" (cf. 1 Tim 1:4; 4:7; 2 Tim 4:4; Titus 1:14). Rather, the false teachers charge traditional Christians who affirm the eschatological parousia with believing myths, fabricated to manipulate immature people. The author responds that the basis of faith is not mythology spun out of speculative imagination, but authentic apostolic testimony of actual events (1:16–18) and the prophetic word of Scripture (1:19–21). Since the event described "on the holy mountain" is similar to the transfiguration scene portrayed in the Synoptic Gospels (Mark 9:2–8; Matt 17:1–8; Luke 9:28–36), this text has traditionally been understood as "Peter's" claim to have been present at the transfiguration. So understood, it is difficult to see the connection between this claim and the following references to the prophetic word of Scripture being confirmed. It is likewise difficult to understand why the author appeals to an event in Jesus' life rather than to his exaltation at the resurrection.

It is likely, however, that the author does in fact intend to refer to the revelation of the glory of the risen Christ. The reference is not to the transfiguration story in the pre-Easter framework of the Synoptic Gospels. The words from heaven in 2 Peter do not verbally correspond to any of the accounts in the Synoptic Gospels; there is no indication that the author is acquainted with any of the Gospels, or that he sees the scene "on the holy mountain" as the pre-Easter transfiguration scene of the Gospel narrative. It was Mark who first located the story there, where the earthly Jesus became transparent to his future heavenly glory, that is, a *transfiguration* of his human appearance that quickly faded away. Matthew and Luke follow Mark in this (the story does not appear in John).

As in the case of James, the author is aware of traditions from and about Jesus, but does not incorporate them within the framework of the earthly life of Jesus; the Gospel narrative mode of confessing the faith seems to be unknown or rejected (see §18.4.1 below). The "holy mountain" does not refer to an unnamed mountain in Galilee; the term is used twenty times in the LXX, always with reference to Jerusalem, Mount Zion, the scene of Christ's resurrection appearances in Luke and John. This is what it would mean in Roman Christianity, with its Jewish Christian background and history. The author of 2 Peter thus appears to appeal to the revelation of Christ's post-Easter glory granted to the apostles in *Jerusalem* (not just the three disciples in Galilee, as in the Synoptics).[23]

This corresponds to the only other reference to narrative material now included in the Gospels, Jesus' prediction of Simon's death, which is clearly a post-Easter scene (John 21:18–19). The author's line of thought seems to be as follows. He and other Christian teachers appealed to the Scriptures to support their view of the eschatological parousia of Christ. The false teachers dispute this interpretation of Scripture, claiming that the Petrine group follow "cleverly devised myths." The author responds that this interpretation is not merely a matter of private, idiosyncratic interpretation, but is confirmed by a revelatory experience that revealed Jesus as God's Son enthroned in heavenly glory, the one who will come as eschatological judge and savior. The church may be assured of seeing the glory of Christ in the future, because the glory of the exalted Christ has already been seen in the past. In this reading, "Peter" is not appealing to a pre-Easter transfiguration, but to a post-Easter prophetic revelation that confirms his reading of the prophetic Scriptures (see Matt 28:18–20; 1 Thess 4:15–17). Neither Scripture nor interpretation is a matter of arbitrary human will, but divine prophetic revelation.

2:1–22 False prophets, then and now

Alongside the authentic prophets there were false prophets. This too corresponds to the situation of the readers. This extensive central section is an attack on the false teachers, responding to their objections and charging them with defective theology, rejection of divine authority, and personal immorality. The author relies heavily on Jude, adapting the earlier material by making some significant changes: (1) Whereas Jude simply condemns the intruders, 2 Peter specifies and refutes their beliefs. (2) He adjusts the chronology to conform to that of biblical narrative. Jude's triad *Israel/sinful angels/Sodom and Gomorrah* becomes *sinful angels/Noah/Lot*, in the order found in Genesis 6–9. (3) He includes positive examples of God's deliverance (Noah, Lot) contrasting with the negative examples of God's judgment. Noah's role is extended so that he becomes a preacher of righteousness, and Lot, whose tender soul is irked by the conduct of his pagan neighbors, is painted in more pious colors than in Genesis. (4) He omits Jude's citations from noncanonical literature (*1 Enoch*, *Testament of Moses*), basing his argument entirely on material considered biblical. The point of all this is not to convert the false teachers, who

23. The later *Apocalypse of Peter* also understands this scene to be post-Easter, suggesting that this was the common view of some streams of Petrine tradition. It is difficult for the modern reader to hear these words in the framework given by 2 Peter without interjecting the perspective of the narrative framework of the Gospels, but this is not the way 2 Peter intends the scene to be understood.

are not addressed, but to warn the unsuspecting churches of the dire threat in their midst.

3:1–13 Eschatological existence Broad streams of first-generation Christianity had expected Christ to return soon to complete his saving work by establishing God's justice and bringing in the kingdom of God (see Mark 9:1; Matt 10:23; 16:28). The false teachers of the author's own time argue that the whole idea of Christ's second coming was false and should be abandoned, adducing three main arguments: (1) Since Jesus did not return within the expected time, history has shown it to be a false expectation. (2) The constancy and consistency of the world order, which continues to function as it always had done, shows that history will continue without divine intervention—hence there is no final judgment to be feared. (3) In any case, Christ has set us free from the law; we will not be called to account, so judgment is unnecessary.

The author is not responding to a crisis of faith caused by the delay of the parousia. His concern is not only to refute the false teachers, but to point out the importance of an eschatological understanding of history for Christian life. The author of 2 Peter understands the false teachers' rejection of eschatology as an excuse for promoting moral laxity; his interest in eschatology is not speculative, but ethical. The climax of his eschatological discussion is not a correct eschatological calendar, but a declaration of "what sort of people we then ought to be" (3:11–12).

The author opposes the false teaching by appealing to the constancy of God's act as seen in Scripture. The biblical pattern of creation, judgment, and re-creation will be repeated at the end. The delay of the parousia does not mean it will not happen. Appealing to Psalm 90:4, the author argues that as a (human) day is a thousand years for God, and a thousand (human) years is one day for God, so God's promises are not constrained by human conceptions of time. There are several parallels to this idea in Jewish literature. For the author of 2 Peter, the "delay" from the human perspective is in reality an expression of the patience of God, who wants all people to repent, and gives them time to do so. The author's ultimate conviction is that the parousia is certain, whenever it may come, because it is not a matter of human speculation but of God's promise.

3:14–18 Concluding Exhortation and Doxology

The writings of Paul had apparently been exploited by the false teachers, who interpreted Paul's emphasis on Christian freedom and the presence of salvation to mean there would be no future judgment. The author (re)claims Paul for emerging mainstream catholic Christianity. This affirmation of *Pauline* Christianity by "Peter" is an extension of the unifying theology of 1 Peter (see introduction to 1 Peter).

The brief concluding doxology emphasizes remaining steadfast in the traditional faith until the return of Christ, the day of eternity.

18.4 The Church in Rome: the Second and Third Generations

THE DISCUSSION OF THE INDIVIDUAL books above suggests that Rome was the setting where *differing epistolary traditions* were merged, under the dominant influence of the Pauline letter form. Hebrews, 1 and 2 Peter, James, and Jude all seem to have Roman connections (see the introductions to the individual books above). In the second century, Rome also seems to have been the place where the *Gospel* and *Epistle* categories formed the basis of what was to become the New Testament, after that model had emerged in the Johannine community.

For the origins of the Roman church and first-generation Roman Christianity, see above under *Romans*. For the second generation, *1 Clement* is our clearest evidence, since it was certainly written from Rome around the turn of the century. Using *1 Clement* as the basis, supplemented by New Testament and other documents that seem to have a Roman connection from this period, we may construct the following sketch:[24]

Roman Christians assume some teaching responsibility for the larger church. *First Clement* is clearly an expression of this ecumenical responsibility, writing in the name of the Roman church to assist the troubled church in Corinth. A little earlier, as the first Christian writing from West to East, 1 Peter is the first evidence that Rome is becoming a center or the center for Christian faith. First Peter simply assumes that the fusion of Pauline/Petrine faith it represents is shared by and is normative for the churches in the wide-ranging provinces of Asia Minor.

Roman Christianity of this period represented an ecumenical expression of a limited variety, a unity without uniformity. Reflecting the loose structure of Roman Judaism that formed its background, Roman Christianity shows that Pauline, Jacobite, Petrine (including Jude) traditions could all fit under one ecumenical umbrella, with a core tradition but without a central authority. Even the 144 CE expulsion of Marcion (see above, §2.2.1) was done by representative "elders and teachers."

The Roman Christians of this period were mostly poor Gentiles with strong Jewish roots without Roman citizenship. After the turn of the century, Hermas indicates that there were numerous wealthy members of the Christian community. Though predominately Gentile, their Christianity cultivated awareness of and appreciation for its Jewish origin and tradition. While Nero's persecution in 64 CE was able to identify Christians as a distinct group, the Jewish roots and orientation of the Christian community in Rome continued to characterize the church there. Not only or even primarily Paul, but Peter and James were the symbolic founding figures of Roman Christianity. James, 1 Peter, Jude, and to some extent 2 Peter all represent Jerusalem-centered Jewish Christianity, speaking to people whose symbolic universe is seen from within the Old Testament story line as the people of God, still the Diaspora of the exile.

Roman Christianity represented the kerygma of God's act in the Christ event, with minimal attention to the "life and teaching of Jesus" as the content of the Christian faith. None of the Roman documents of this period reflect the Gospel mode of confessing the faith by narrating the words and deeds of Jesus. The epistolary tradition that was focused in Rome became the basis for Apostles' Creed, which goes directly from "born of the Virgin Mary" to "crucified under Pontius Pilate." The structure of this creedal tradition is already found in 1 Peter, which has almost all the elements of the Apostles' Creed, gathered more compactly than any other New Testament document. Individual elements of Jesus tradition circulated in Rome in this period. The contacts between James, 1 Peter, and the sayings tradition (perhaps Q or a Q-like collection; see below) indicate a common source/milieu for their allusions to Jesus' sayings, but there is no indication of a connected narrative of Jesus' life until later.

18.4.1 Summary: The Epistles and the Formation of Early Christianity

Before we turn to a study of the Gospels and Acts, we may draw together two important facets of the crucial role of letters in the formation of early Christianity.

Preliminary Canonical Letter Collections and the "Catholic Epistles"

We have already discussed (1) the preliminary collections that were later combined into the New Testament canon (see above, §§2.2.1; 2.3).[25] Here it is important to note that (2) the Catholic Letters were not a miscellaneous or random collection of all available non-Pauline letters, but had a specific focus on the Pillars of

24. See details in Lampe, *Paul to Valentinus*, 67–152.

25. See the important collection of essays in Niebuhr and Wall, eds., *Catholic Epistles*.

the Jerusalem church and the family of Jesus. (3) The collection of seven letters (symbolic number!) represents a response and complement to (not an alternative to) the authoritative collection of fourteen Pauline letters. (4) They are directed not to specific individuals or congregations, as Paul had done, but to the larger church. (5) James introduces the collection and Jude concludes it—the brothers of Jesus frame the letters, indicating continuity with the life of Jesus and stressing the role of the Jerusalem church in a way that is lacking in Paul's letters. (6) In some streams of tradition, Acts was placed before the letters as the narrative framework for interpreting them. This combination of Acts and the Catholic Letters became a common arrangement, circulating as a separate collection in numerous New Testament manuscripts. (7) By about 225 CE Origen could designate 1 Peter and 1 John as "catholic letters." A century later, Eusebius (*Hist. eccl.* 2.23.24–25) speaks of the "so-called Catholic letters," including James and the "so called" Jude. In the East, "catholic" in this connection was usually understood in terms of the addressees. In contrast to the Pauline letters addressed to particular congregations, the "catholic letters" were addressed to the universal church. So understood, this designation is only partially appropriate, since 1 Peter and 1 John address a particular group of churches, 2 John is to a single congregation, and 3 John is to an individual in a church context. In the West, the phrase "Catholic Epistles" was understood not in terms of addressees, but general acceptance: the Catholic Epistles were those generally accepted by the universal church. (8) We ought not to assume that either the Pauline or Catholic letter collections were always used alongside a collection of Gospels. For major streams of Christianity, for several generations, the authoritative texts read in church alongside the (Old Testament) Scripture were these normative documents of the Christian faith in epistolary form. Before turning to the Gospel mode of confessing the faith, we might summarize this epistolary form.

The Epistolary Mode of Confession of the Christian Faith

The story of God's saving act in Jesus is a cosmic story. The epistles are representatives of a narrative form that presupposes this story. The saving act transpires on a cosmic stage. The enemies overcome by the saving act are cosmic enemies. Salvation takes place by the reality of God's act in the man Jesus, and is not explicated by particular stories and sayings from his life.

This kerygmatic theology about Jesus includes minimal data from Jesus' life. Except for Jesus' birth, true humanity, and shameful death, the earthly career is barely mentioned. No letter quotes a saying of Jesus or tells a miracle story about him. Paul refers four times to a "command" or "word" of the Lord (1 Thess 4:15–17; 1 Cor 7:10, 25; 9:14). In none of them does he make it clear that he refers to a saying from the pre-Easter historical Jesus; all are probably understood by him to be commands of the risen Lord Jesus, even if they contain elements of pre-Easter tradition. Paul can also refer to his own instruction as "command of the Lord" (1 Cor 14:37). Even if all four are taken to be sayings of the historical Jesus, or intended by Paul to be understood as such, this is still a very small number. The only actual citation of an event from the pre-Easter life of Jesus is the eucharistic "words of institution" in 1 Corinthians 11:23–25. Even this is not cited as a biographical datum from the life of Jesus, but as part of the liturgy of the church.

The issue is not whether Paul and the other epistolary authors "could" have known the tradition from and about Jesus. Certainly Paul, though he was converted after the death of Jesus, had opportunity to learn stories about Jesus and sayings from him. He spent fifteen days with Peter (Gal 1:18), met and talked with James the Lord's brother (Gal 1:19; 2:9), and spent some years as a missionary of the Antioch church, which cultivated the tradition from and about Jesus (see below on the Gospels of Mark and Matthew). Yet his letters reflect almost nothing of the details of Jesus' life and teaching.

Scholars who insist that Paul "must" have known a good bit about Jesus' life and teaching can document only a few such items reflected in his letters, even on a generous interpretation of the evidence.[26] The same is even more true of the deuteropauline and Catholic letters. Even if they were written by the authors assigned to them in tradition, the letters themselves never quote Jesus directly or tell a story from his life.

The Christian ethic of the epistles is not an ethic of following the example or teaching of the historical Jesus. For Paul, the Christian life is based on the believer's being incorporated into the Christ event, receiving the Holy Spirit, and discerning the will of God as taught within the community of faith. It is the cosmic drama, not the stories of Jesus in Galilee and Judea, that provides the guideline for the Christian life. When appeal is made to the example of Jesus, it is to his weakness, suffering, and death, not miracles, his teaching about the law, or his conduct in particular situations (see, e.g., Phil 2:5–11, the paradigmatic example; 1 Pet 2:21–25; Heb 2:5–11; 12:1–3). Thus such texts as 1 Thessalonians 4:1–2 do not mean that Paul taught his new converts the elements of the "life and teaching of Jesus" as part of basic Christian instruction. Except for the foundational kerygma of Jesus' death and resurrection, there is nothing of this in 1 Thessalonians. We should also note that Paul indicates his previous directions about the Christian life consisted of instructions *in* and *through* the Lord Jesus (4:1, 2), that is, how they should live in the light of God's act in Christ and the soon coming of the Lord, given in the power and Spirit of the risen Christ. Likewise, the statement that the Thessalonian Christians became "imitators of the Lord" does not mean that Paul held up incidents from the life of Jesus as an ethical model to be imitated; he refers specifically to Jesus' suffering, along with that of the apostle himself, as the model of the Christian life.

26. A. M. Hunter, *Paul and His Predecessors* (Philadelphia: Westminster Press, 1961), 10–11, eager to trace the maximum amount of Jesus tradition in Paul, lists the following as the sum total of Paul's knowledge of the earthly Jesus that can be gleaned from his letters: Jesus was a man (Rom 5:15), a Jew (Rom 9:5), born of a woman and under the law (Gal 4:4), a descendant of Abraham and in the line of David (Gal 3:16; Rom 1:3). He had brothers (1 Cor 9:5), one of whom was called James (Gal 1:19). He ministered among Jews (Rom 15:8). He had a band of twelve disciples (1 Cor 15:5). He was meek and gentle (2 Cor 10:1), obedient to God (2 Cor 5:19), possessed endurance (2 Thess 3:5) and grace (2 Cor 8:9). He was delivered up (which Hunter takes to be a reference to the betrayal by Judas). He celebrated a last supper with his disciples. He was crucified and buried. Hunter is able to list only the four sayings mentioned above, and no specific incidents from the life of Jesus. Dunn, though sharing Hunter's optimism about how much Paul knew about the historical Jesus, properly concedes, "In short, Paul tells us next to nothing about the life and ministry of Jesus. Had we possessed only Paul's letters, it would be impossible to say much about Jesus of Nazareth" (Dunn, *Theology of Paul*, 184).

18.5 For Further Reading

Bauckham, R. *James: Wisdom of James, Disciple of Jesus the Sage*. London: Routledge, 1999.

———. *Jude, 2 Peter*. WBC. Waco, TX: Word, 1983.

Dibelius, M., and H. Greeven. *A Commentary on the Epistle of James*. Translated by Michael Williams. Hermeneia. Philadelphia: Fortress Press, 1976.

Johnson, L. T. *The Letter of James*. Anchor Bible 37A. New York: Doubleday, 1995.

Kelly, J. N. D. *A Commentary on the Epistles of Peter and of Jude*. HNTC. New York: Harper & Row, 1969.

Kraftchick, S. J. *Jude and 2 Peter*. ANTC. Nashville: Abingdon Press, 2002.

Moo, D. J. *The Letter of James*. Pillar New Testament Commentary. Grand Rapids: Eerdmans, 2000.

Painter, J. *Just James: The Brothers of Jesus in History and Tradition*. Minneapolis: Fortress Press, 1997/1999.

Sleeper, C. F. *James*. ANTC. Nashville: Abingdon Press, 1998.

Webb, R. L., and J. S. Kloppenborg, eds. *Reading James with New Eyes: Methodological Reassessments of the Letter of James*. Library of New Testament Studies 342. Edinburgh: T. & T. Clark, 2007.

19

From Jesus to the Gospels

WHAT IS THE LINK BETWEEN THE EVENTS of the life of Jesus and the written texts of the Gospels? Basically three answers have been given in Christian history to this question: (1) divine inspiration; (2) individual memory; (3) community tradition. These are not necessarily mutually exclusive.

19.1 Divine Inspiration

ESPECIALLY IN THE EARLY CENTURIES OF the church's history and in some streams of modern fundamentalism, interpreters have appealed to the miracle of verbal inspiration as the source of the materials in the Gospels: the Holy Spirit miraculously directed the minds or pens of the evangelists. This was not the view of the Gospel writers themselves[1] or of early Christianity that accepted them as canonical (see above, §2.2.2). While the church has always believed that the Spirit of God was at work in the process of the formation of the Bible, the appeal to a particular theory of inspiration has not proven to be a satisfactory means of explaining the phenomena of the text.

19.2 Individual Memory

THE MATERIALS FROM AND ABOUT JESUS were handed on orally for about a generation between the death of Jesus and the first written Gospel. The ancient world from which the Bible emerged was primarily an oral culture. It was possible then, as it is still possible, for human beings to memorize and transmit book-length stories orally. For example, Greek epics such as Homer's *Iliad* and *Odyssey* and extensive collections of Jewish tradition (the Mishnah) were handed on orally for generations before being written down.

A few scholars have argued for a particular kind of oral transmission as the key to the formation of the Gospels.[2] Jesus is pictured as a rabbi and his disciples as rabbinic students. In this view, Jesus compelled his disciples to

1. Luke is the only Gospel writer to say anything about his compositional procedure, referring to original events, church tradition, and written sources (Luke 1:1–4). Some later scribes considered this inadequate, and added to Luke's "it seemed good to me" the phrase "and to the Holy Spirit" at Luke 1:3 (the Old Latin manuscripts b, q, and some manuscripts of the Vulgate).

2. Cf. esp. Harald Riesenfeld, *The Gospel Tradition and Its Beginnings: A Study in the Limits of 'Formgeschichte'* (London: Mowbray, 1961); *The Gospel Tradition: Essays*, trans. Margaret E. Rowley and Robert A. Kraft (Philadelphia: Fortress Press, 1970); Birger Gerhardsson, *Memory and Manuscript: Oral Tradition and Written Transmission in Rabbinic Judaism and Early Christianity*, trans. Eric J. Sharpe, ASNU 22 (Uppsala: Uppsala University Press, 1961); Rainer Riesner, *Jesus als Lehrer*, 3rd ed. (Tübingen: Mohr, 1988).

memorize his sayings, and this memorized tradition is now contained in the Gospels. Few scholars have accepted this view, which has been sharply criticized for the following reasons: (1) The picture is anachronistic, derived from later Jewish materials and imposed on the first-century Judaism that was the setting for Jesus' mission. (2) Jesus was not a rabbi in the later Talmudic sense, and his disciples were not rabbinic students. (3) The rabbinic model is more appropriate to legal and sayings materials, but hardly fits the Gospels' narrative materials. Rabbis trained their students to memorize legal materials, not stories about themselves. (4) The extant form of the texts do not represent the product of this kind of transmission process, which cannot account for the extent and kind of variations found in the Gospels.

Jesus had disciples who heard and saw what he said and did. There can be no reasonable doubt that some of their memories have been included in the present form of the Gospels.[3] But the textual phenomena of selection, order, and verbal agreement presented below cannot be accounted for merely on the basis of individual memory.

19.3 Community Tradition

THE FOLLOWING SKETCH REPRESENTS THE way much of mainstream contemporary New Testament scholarship has understood oral tradition as the bridge between Jesus and the earliest New Testament documents. The Gospels represent a selection from the materials handed on in the church in its preaching, teaching, worship, and mission. This view does not deny that the Gospels contain materials that ultimately derive from eyewitnesses (a judgment to be made on historical grounds) or that the Holy Spirit was active in the process of Gospel formation (a matter of faith and theology). This view does not begin with a theory and attempt to conform the texts to it, but is based on an inductive study of the Gospels themselves, asking what kind of process would have resulted in the extant biblical texts. The link between Jesus and the Gospels is the Christian community that collected, preserved, and interpreted these materials as the expression of a vital faith.

The discipline of *form criticism* has enabled us to see the various settings in which the oral tradition of the early Christians functioned in worship, instruction, and conflicts. Particular forms developed to preserve, interpret, and transmit each form of the tradition in its life setting (*Sitz im Leben*) in the church's mission. The community that transmitted this tradition did not view Jesus as merely a great individual whose words and deeds should be carefully preserved as a model for future generations, but as the one in and through whom God had definitively acted for the salvation of the world. This revelatory act called into being a new community. It was to this community, guided by the Holy Spirit, that God entrusted the transmission and interpretation of this saving and revelatory act. This was the theological understanding at work in early Christianity's preservation and transmission of the materials from and about Jesus.

This is in contrast to the way the life and teaching of various pagan teachers was preserved. Thus Clyde Votaw points out how this resulted in our knowing more about Epictetus (50–130 CE) and Apollonius (10–97 CE) than we do about Jesus. Arian, a pupil of Epictetus, took verbatim notes and published them about five years after the death of his teacher. Damis, Apollonius's traveling companion and pupil for forty years, kept a journal carefully recording his teacher's sayings and deeds. The preserved teaching of Epictetus is more than twice the size of all four Gospels. Philostratus's *Life of Apollonius* is many times the size of the

3. For a vigorous reassertion of the importance of this, see now Richard Bauckham, *Jesus and the Eyewitnesses: The Gospels as Eyewitness Testimony* (Grand Rapids: Eerdmans, 2006).

Gospels.[4] So also, biographically speaking, we know more about Paul than we do about Jesus. Historians may regret that we have no comparable records of Jesus' life and teaching, but the early Christians saw the matter differently.

19.3.1 Types of Material from and about Jesus

A study of the outlines of the Gospels reveals that the same stories and sayings appear at different points in the Gospels and that the connecting links were not original, but supplied by the tradition and the Gospel redactors. At first, individual stories and sayings circulated as separate units, which were then combined in various ways in the process of tradition and redaction. The process has been likened to stringing beads: the beads are the individual units of tradition, the strings were provided by later collectors, editors, and the Gospel writers. This need not imply random stringing together; it can be done with intention and artistry. Perhaps weaving a tapestry is a more appropriate analogy.

Identification of pre-Gospel units of tradition In our discussion of traditional elements included in the Pauline and other letters, we have already explored how such units can sometimes be identified by their formal structure (see above, §9.2.2). Analogous methods are utilized, with more or less probability, to identify the shape, function, and *Sitz im Leben* of pre-Gospel units of tradition incorporated, adapted, and interpreted by the evangelists.[5] Although modern Western society is much more a text-oriented culture than the first-century Mediterranean world, we can still identity some fixed formulae of oral tradition and their *Sitz im Leben* in our own culture. Thus, when one hears or reads, "Dearly beloved, we are gathered here in the sight of God . . . ," "The story is told of a man who . . . ," or "The great state of X proudly nominates Y as the next president of the United States," one immediately knows the speaker or writer is not composing ad hoc but is utilizing a fixed formula at home in a particular social location in our culture. We immediately identify the genre and function of a unit that begins "Once upon a time" and ends "they lived happily ever after." We know that the speaker or writer is not devising this phraseology on the spot but is utilizing a traditional form, and knows that it functions only in specific settings—not, for instance, in court records or business contracts.

Although the distinction is not absolute, for purposes of analysis, form critics of the Gospels have divided the tradition into two main categories: *sayings* and *narratives*. Each includes a variety of types and subtypes. Within the narrative tradition, the following main types have been identified, each of which has its subtypes (all illustrations are from the earliest Gospel, Mark, but examples are found in all the Gospels):

Narrative traditions *Miracle stories*. Some examples: Mark 2:1–28; 4:37–41; 7:31–37. Stereotyped forms already existed in the Hellenistic world for telling stories about the wondrous deeds of miracle workers.[6] Some early Christians adopted and adapted this form to communicate the good news of what God had done in the Christ event. The typical form (which may be elaborated with stereotypical details) portrays some life-threatening human situation

4. Clyde Weber Votaw, *The Gospels and Contemporary Biographies in the Greco-Roman World*, Facet Books, Biblical Series 27 (Philadelphia: Fortress Press, 1970), 13–14.

5. The pioneering works in this field are still valuable: Rudolf Bultmann, *The History of the Synoptic Tradition*, trans. John Marsh (New York: Harper & Row, 1963, originally pub. 1921; latest rev, and updated English trans. 1976); Karl Ludwig Schmidt, *Der Rahmen Der Geschichte Jesu. Literarkritische Untersuchungen zur ältesten Jesusüberlieferung* (Darmstadt: Wissenschaftliche Buchgesellschaft, 1969); Martin Dibelius, *From Tradition to Gospel* (New York: Scribner, 1935); Vincent Taylor, *The Formation of the Gospel Tradition* (London: Macmillan, 1953). Helpful, more recent treatments include Edgar V. McKnight, "Form and Redaction Criticism," in *The New Testament and its Modern Interpreters*, ed. Eldon J. Epp and George W. MacRae (Atlanta: Scholars Press, 1989), 149–74.

6. See the numerous examples in Boring, Berger, and Colpe, eds., *Hellenistic Commentary*.

from which ordinary human beings are not able to deliver themselves: sickness, demon possession, hunger, death. The miracle worker steps in and resolves the problem by supernatural power. The amazement of the spectators validates the miracle, which often concludes with a "choral response." Much of the Gospel tradition is in the form of such stories.

Historical stories and legends. Some examples: Mark 1:16–20; 2:13–14; 8:27–30; 14:1–2, 10–11; 14:3–9. The birth stories in Matthew 1–2 and Luke 1–2 can be included in this category. These portray significant events in the story of Jesus important for the later Christian community's understanding of their faith, with or without legendary accretions.

The passion story. In each Gospel, the longest connected narrative is the story of Jesus' arrest, suffering, and death (Mark 14:26–15:47; Matt 26:30–27:66; Luke 22:39–23:56; John 18:1–19:42). The common core of this narrative seems to have been composed very early and may have been regularly recited during the eucharistic worship of the early Jerusalem church.

Sayings traditions *Pronouncement stories, also called apophthegms; paradigms, chreiai.* The form is a brief narrative setting that climaxes in a "punch line" from Jesus, which makes the saying of Jesus the point of the story. Some examples: Mark 2:1–12; 2:15–17; 2:18–22; 2:23–28; 3:1–6. Since these sayings involve a brief narrative setting, some form critics classify them as narratives.

Logia, wisdom sayings, proverbs; maxims, chreiai. Some examples: Mark 2:19b–22; 4:21–25; 10:31. Both Jesus and the early church created and adapted wisdom sayings from tradition and the wider cultural context, filling them with new eschatological content.

Prophetic and apocalyptic sayings. Some examples: Mark 1:15; 3:28–29; 10:29–30; 13:4–31. Jesus himself functioned as a prophet and sometimes expressed his message in typical prophetic forms. Christian prophets also appeared in the early church, speaking in the name of the exalted Lord. Just as Israel's prophets used identifiable prophetic forms of speech (e.g., "Thus says the Lord"), so did Jesus and the early Christian prophets.

Legal sayings and church rules. Some examples: Mark 3:28; 7:15; 11:25. The earliest Christians sought guidance in making decisions about their common life in the Christian community, and preserved, interpreted, and amplified sayings of Jesus to meet this need.

Similitudes and parables. Some examples: Mark 4:3–8; 12:1–9. The historical Jesus certainly communicated much of his message in parabolic form. The earliest church preserved these striking and troubling stories, sometimes contemporizing them to address the post-Easter situation.

I–Sayings. Some examples: Mark 2:17; 10:45. Some sayings serve as the self-identification of Jesus. Since Christian prophets spoke in the name *and person* of the risen Lord, just as Israel's prophets had spoken in the first person as YHWH, some "I am" sayings may have been generated or reformulated by prophetic spokespersons for the risen Jesus.

19.3.2 A Faithful and Creative Community: Preservation, Expansion, and Interpretation of the Tradition

On the basis of critical study of the Gospels themselves, no scholar doubts that the Gospels contain stories and sayings from the original disciples of Jesus who saw and heard him. On the basis of the same kind of study, no critical scholar believes that any of the Gospels is merely a transcript of such eyewitness testimony. All the materials, even if transmitted with verbatim accuracy, were transmitted within the community of faith, and seen in the perspective of the resurrected Lord. In the course of transmission and interpretation, this tradition was modified and expanded. Since our modern culture conditions us to think of the truth of the Gospels in terms of accurate reporting that frowns upon editorializing, expanding, or otherwise interpreting the material, it may be helpful for the modern reader to consider the factors at work in the literary creativity apparent in the study of Gospel texts.[7]

— *Lack of quotation paraphernalia in the ancient world.* Ancient documents made no use of quotation marks, parentheses, or footnotes. In the Greek text, it is often difficult to distinguish direct from indirect quotation, or to tell where direct quotation ends and the author himself begins to speak. A clear example is provided by 1 Corinthians 15:3–8. Paul begins by citing verbatim an early Christian creed. The quotation clearly begins at 15:3b, and by 15:8 Paul himself is speaking, but where does the quotation end? So also, in John 3:10–21, Jesus begins to speak to Nicodemus, but where does the character Jesus cease speaking to Nicodemus, and the narrator himself begin to speak to the reader? If one is making a red-letter edition of the New Testament, or placing direct speech in quotation marks, as in the NRSV, does the direct citation of Jesus' words end at verse 13, verse 15, or verse 21? All this, of course, is not due to the inability of ancient writers to make such things clear. Rather, such phenomena illustrate their different perspective and mindset. If they had been interested in reporter-like truth, they could easily have devised the means to express this. Modern Greek, influenced by the modern Western idea of truth as factual reporting, has adopted quotation marks.

— *Historical and biographical writing in the ancient world.* Neither biographers nor historians in the ancient world hesitated to create speeches and place them in the mouths of their heroes. This is different, of course, from modern biographical and historical method, but was widely practiced and accepted as normal among ancient writers (see §23.3.1).

— *Literary creativity of the storyteller.* The author of a narrative must choose what kind of narrator he or she will have tell the story. The Gospel writers—and presumably their predecessors, the preachers and tellers of Jesus stories in the pre-Gospel period of oral tradition—all chose the "omniscient narrator." Such a narrator can be everywhere, knows everything, is the silent observer and listener to every conversation—and lets the reader do the same. Thus, for example, the narrator lets the reader overhear the private conversation between the magi and King Herod (Matt 2:7–12) and Jesus' prayer in Gethsemane when the disciples were asleep (Mark 14:32–42). On the reporter model, the reader must ask where the Gospel authors got the information for these verbatim "reports." The same question arises with regard to the interchange between Jesus and the devil (Matt 4:1–11) and numerous other places, but it is an issue only for the reporter mentality. For the ancient writer and reader, the conventions of the storyteller made the question unnecessary.

— *Midrash and Jewish tradition.* The teachers of Israel who handed on the tradition amplified and interpreted it to facilitate its speaking to later generations. For example, in the Qumran *Genesis Apocryphon*, the book of *Jubilees* from the Pseudepigrapha, and in rabbinic midrashim such as the *Exodus Rabbah*, the Old Testament stories were retold and amplified, including the addition of legendary events and extensive conversations and speeches not found in the original biblical texts. The story of Moses' bringing water from the rock for the thirsty Israelites was expanded by relating that the rock followed them from place to place and repeatedly provided water for them (Palestinian Targum of Num 20:7–13; 21:16–18). This midrashic expansion is accepted by Paul and included in his exhortation to the Corinthians (1 Cor 10:4). The Jewish Scriptures

7. Here, the use of a synopsis that facilitates the comparison of parallel accounts is indispensable. One might begin by comparing the differing forms of familiar texts such as the Beatitudes, Lord's Prayer, Peter's Confession, and the Eschatological Discourse, §§51, 62, 158, 287–95 (paragraph nos. are from Barbara Aland, Kurt Aland, J. Karavidopoulos et al., *Novum Testamentum Graece*, 27th rev. ed. [Stuttgart: Deutsche Bibelgesellschaft, 2001]).

had already affirmed and incorporated such midrashic elaborations of the original texts. The author of 1 and 2 Chronicles, writing centuries after Samuel–Kings, presents numerous speeches, conversations, and events not narrated in the original texts and explicitly refers to such midrashic expansions as among his sources (2 Chr 13:22).

— *Faith in Jesus as the risen and living one who is present in the church's life and ministry*. Most importantly, for the early Christians and the authors of the Gospels, Jesus was not only a teacher who had lived and died "back there" in history, whose sayings might be remembered and passed on, like Socrates, Plato, Gamaliel, or Akiba. He was the living Lord, both "up there" in the transcendent world and "out there" in the church and the world, the present and active Lord whose own voice was heard in the tradition of the church and in the proclamation of Christian evangelists and teachers (see, e.g., 1 Cor 11:23–26; Matt 10:40; 28:16–20; Luke 10:16).

— *Charismatic Christian prophets*. The general phenomenon of the presence of the risen Christ in the life of the church was focused in a particular way in the figures of Christian prophets, who continued to speak "the word of the Lord," which was not always distinguished from the sayings of the historical Jesus.[8] Since there were both male and female prophets in the early church (see, e.g., 1 Cor 11:5; Acts 21:9), this means that some sayings preserved in the Gospels as words of Jesus may represent oracles of prophetic women who spoke in Jesus' name.

While most of the traditional materials came into being as individual sayings or stories that were handed on and around orally, early Christian teachers and scribes assembled some of them into thematic collections for catechetical, liturgical, and other uses. Some of these were written. For example, some scholars have seen collections of *parables* reflected in Mark 4:1–33, collections of *pronouncement stories* reflected in Mark 2:1–3:6 and 11:27–12:37, and collections of *miracle stories* reflected in Mark 4:34–6:56 and John 2–11. A pre-Gospel collection of miracle stories has sometimes been regarded as a kind of proto-Gospel, picturing Jesus as a θεῖος ἀνήρ (*theios anēr*, divine man). By far the most convincing of such arguments is that some teachers in the Palestinian community of Jesus' disciples composed a collection of Jesus' sayings now lost, but visible as a common source (Q, *Quelle*) later used by Matthew and Luke in the composition of their Gospels.

8. Cf. Boring, *Sayings of the Risen Jesus*; and *The Continuing Voice of Jesus*.

19.4 Which Was the First Gospel?

THE MOST WIDELY ACCEPTED VIEW IS THAT Mark is the earliest extant comprehensive narrative of Jesus' life, death, and resurrection. This theologically innovative and creative work was known and interpreted by Matthew and Luke, and perhaps by John as well. A significant minority argues that Matthew was the first Gospel, and only an occasional scholar that Luke or John was first.

Does the issue really matter? Yes. Any historical understanding of the biblical text requires location of the documents in their particular setting in time and space. Can one be absolutely sure one has the right answer? No. All historical study is a matter of probability, involving the risk that the interpreter may turn out to be wrong. Does this uncertainty mean the effort should be abandoned? No. The alternative is flight into subjectivism or an unhistorical faith. The gospel, and the Gospels, are matters of history. Some such matters can be settled with a high degree of confidence, and some are virtually certain, but historical truth is in another realm than absolute certainty. Such issues, however, are not matters of biblical authority. Matthew is just as authoritative, whether written before or after Mark, and whether or not either author used a lost document now called Q. John is just as much Holy Scripture, whether written in dependence on the Synoptics or in ignorance of them, and whether written first or last. But each of the Gospels will be *understood* differently, depending on the decisions made on these historical issues, and so will the development of early Christian history.

To be sure, when the Bible is read devotionally and for personal edification, the issues of source analysis do not and should not occupy the foreground of attention. Each Gospel is rightly read within the framework of the imaginative narrative world it creates for the reader. Detailed comparison with the other Gospels is not necessary and may even be a hindrance in such reading. However, if one is interested in historical understanding of the Gospels, which means understanding them in their own terms and their own contexts, the question of which is prior and which is secondary is an important hermeneutical issue. Only a non- or antihistorical approach to the New Testament can be disinterested in the question of who first devised the Gospel form.

Of the four canonical Gospels, the first three are related to each other in a way that is different from the relation of any of them to the Gospel of John. Even a casual reading of the Gospels makes this clear, but it is best seen by comparing the four Gospels in a synopsis. Much of the material in the first three Gospels can be arranged in parallel columns on the same page so that they can be "seen together" and compared (*syn-* = "together" + *optic* = "seen"). A book that prints them in such columns to facilitate comparison is thus called a synopsis; and the Gospels that can be so printed are called the Synoptic Gospels. The Gospel of John overlaps the Synoptics at only a relatively few points. The first three Gospels resemble each other quite closely, while the Fourth Gospel is distinctive in both content and form. It is generally agreed that the Fourth Gospel is later than the Synoptics; there is no consensus as to whether the Fourth Gospel knows and/or uses the Synoptics (see §27.3).

The question of the literary relationships among the Synoptic Gospels, especially the issue of which was the earliest and whether they are dependent on a hypothetical lost source now traditionally called Q, is one of the most thoroughly researched and debated topics in the study of the New Testament. The conclusion held by the majority of scholars and the presupposition of many books and articles is that Mark was the earliest Gospel, that neither Matthew nor Luke knew the other, but that each independently used Mark as a source, and independently used the lost source Q for non-Markan material they share. Each Gospel includes materials peculiar to itself. This is now the "standard" view, widely but not universally accepted.

Many students simply accept this theory as the consensus or "assured results" of historical criticism without thinking through the problem and proposed solutions for themselves. It is valuable, however, for serious students to work through the following section on the Synoptic Problem, not only because of the importance of the issue for understanding the Gospels and for insight on numerous Gospel texts and themes, but also as an exercise in critical methodology. By exploring in depth one critical issue, students can both hone their own skills at interpretation involving such issues, and attain a better sense of how confident—and how hesitant—one may be concerning the majority results of critical scholarship.

EXCURSUS 3

The Synoptic Problem

UNDERSTANDING THE NATURE OF ANY ANCIENT document, including the Gospels, is based on two kinds of evidence, data external to the writing, and the phenomena internal to the document itself.

Exc. 3.1 External Data: Church Tradition

The external data relevant to understanding the authorship of the Gospels, their relative order, and their possible literary relation to each other is provided by the citations from the church fathers. Space prohibits the citation and discussion of each of the texts themselves. The original Greek and Latin of all relevant texts can be found in the appendix to the Aland *Synopsis*; English translations are readily available.[9]

The beginning student might naturally suppose that, since the church fathers were so much closer to the time of the composition of the Gospels, they would have more reliable information than what can be gleaned from the texts themselves by scholars working centuries later. The following summary observations give one pause:

1. The relevant patristic data is *minimal.* The Fathers were not interested in the Synoptic Problem in the modern sense. Their concern is to link each canonical Gospel to apostolic authority and to show that, despite their chronological and other discrepancies, each canonical Gospel was an authentic witness to the truth of the Christian faith.

2. The patristic testimony does not represent a series of independent historical witnesses. The church fathers had no firsthand information on the writing of the Gospels. From the early second century on, their testimony is itself *interdependent reinterpretation of earlier tradition.* Eusebius in the fourth century and Augustine and Jerome in the fifth century did not have independent early traditions, but only what had been handed along in previous church tradition. Even Irenaeus and Clement of Alexandria in the late second century are no longer in direct contact with the earliest witnesses, but are themselves dependent on the chain of tradition. Papias in particular cast a long shadow.

3. The content and significance of Papias's testimony is *already disputed when it first emerges.* Irenaeus in the late second century already uses the Papias testimony from a generation earlier uncritically, stating that Papias claimed to have talked with the apostle John. Eusebius in the fourth century rightly rejects this as Papias's view.

4. The patristic testimony is *inconsistent.* Some texts portray Mark as getting his material directly from the oral preaching of Peter (Papias, Irenaeus, Clement of Alexandria, Jerome), while Augustine understands Mark to be the abbreviator of the written text of Matthew. Some Fathers state Mark was written while Peter was still living, others that he wrote after Peter's death. Some state that Peter saw and approved Mark's Gospel, others that Mark wrote and circulated it without Peter's knowledge. When chronological priority is explicitly mentioned or can be inferred (Irenaeus, Clement of Alexandria, Augustine), Matthew is considered the first Gospel. It was assumed that the nonapostles Mark and Luke could not have priority over the apostle Matthew. Of ancient authors who regard Matthew as the first Gospel, only Augustine thinks of Mark as dependent on Matthew. Augustine's point, however, is not literary dependence but apostolic authority. So also Clement of Alexandria, who seems to consider both Matthew and Luke as earlier than Mark, regards Mark as deriving his material directly from Peter, not from Matthew. The interpretation of several patristics texts is disputed.

5. In the second century, as numerous gospels were circulated throughout the church, points of contact with eyewitness tradition were sought for the anonymous gospels by the emerging stream of Christian tradition that would become the protocatholic mainstream orthodoxy, partly as a defense against developing Gnosticism and other Christian movements later deemed heretical. We observe this interest in legitimization by

9. Kurt Aland, ed., *Synopsis Quattuor Evangeliorum: Locis parallelis evangeliorum apocryphorum et patrum adhibitis*, 15th rev. ed. (Stuttgart: Württembergische Bibelanstalt, 1997), 531–48; Eusebius, *The Ecclesiastical History*, trans. Kirsopp Lake, 2 vols., LCL (Cambridge: Harvard University Press, 1973); Bart D. Ehrman, *The Apostolic Fathers*, trans. Bart D. Ehrman, LCL 24–25 (Cambridge: Harvard University Press, 2003); Holmes, *Apostolic Fathers*; Alexander Roberts, James Donaldson, and A. Cleveland Coxe, eds., *The Ante-Nicene Fathers; Translations of the Writings of the Fathers down to A.D. 325*, 10 vols. (Grand Rapids: Eerdmans, 1950; American reprint of the Edinburgh ed.).

eyewitnesses in other Christian documents at the turn of the century and later (e.g., 1 John 1:1–3; Luke 1:1–4; Acts 1:1–2, 21–22). In all this it is clear that the church's interest was in theological legitimization of the Gospels as representing the apostolic faith, not the historical accuracy of traditions about authorship, though the first generations of the church did not distinguish these two aspects: the claim to apostolic authorship represented the claim to theological legitimacy.

The external data turns out to be minimally helpful in illuminating the authorship and relative order of the Gospels; the interpreter must rely on the internal data of the texts themselves.

Exc. 3.2 Internal Data: The Phenomena of the Text

Careful comparison of the Synoptic Gospels reveals three patterns of phenomena that call for explanation: (1) *selection* of materials, (2) *order* of pericopes, and (3) verbatim or near-verbatim *parallels in wording*.

Selection and Proportion

Jesus lived for about thirty years (see Luke 3:23). His public mission occupied several months according to the Synoptics, about two and a half years according to John. Only a relatively small number of incidents and days are selected by the Gospel writers, (ca. sixty-five separate days, combining their chronological segmentation). Yet the Synoptics agree in selecting essentially the same elements from this sea of material.

In all three Synoptics, the incidents of the last five days of Jesus' life are narrated much more fully than any previous segment. In the standard Greek text, the Gospel of Mark occupies sixty-one pages. The last week of Jesus' life requires twenty-three pages, 38 percent of the narrative. Mark 11:20–13:37 narrates the events of Tuesday of "Holy Week." This one day requires one-seventh, 14 percent of Mark's text. Both Matthew and Luke include every incident in Mark's account of this day, in mostly the same wording (Luke omits the problematic cursing of the fig tree), with the events of Tuesday occupying the same disproportionate amount of space in each Gospel's structure. In their selection of material, the Synoptics are strikingly similar to each other, and all are strikingly different from John.

The phenomenon of selection can be focused even more sharply, as illustrated in the case of the material about John the Baptist. His preaching mission extended some months or years (again the Synoptics and John disagree). Yet the Gospels agree in selecting a tiny fraction of his preaching. John's preaching is recorded in Matthew 3:7–12/Mark 1:7–8/Luke 3:7–17/John 1:26–27. Mark reports two sentences of John's message, in the same wording as Matthew (some manuscripts have one word not found in Matthew); Matthew's expansion devotes 122 words to present John's message, which takes about a minute to read aloud. Luke is identical in selection and wording, with the addition of the dialogue in 3:10–14. In other words, Matthew and Luke agree in selecting from John's ministry the same one minute of his total proclamation and report it in identical Greek words.

These are not isolated samples. Almost all of Mark is paralleled in either Matthew or Luke, with most of it being found in both (the triple tradition).[10] Of Mark's 661 verses, at least 80 percent are found in Matthew and at least 65 percent in Luke. Every pericope of Mark has parallels in Matthew and/or Luke except §§116, 152, and 156 (Mark 3:20–21; 7:31–37; and 8:22–26).[11] When scattered individual verses not paralleled in either Matthew or Luke are added to the tabulation, the result is that of Mark's

10. Material found in all three Synoptics is customarily designated triple tradition, that found in Matthew and Luke but not in Mark as the double tradition, and material found in only one Gospel as Special Material (*Sondergut*). Of Mark's 11,242 words, ca. 94 percent are found in either Matthew or Luke, ca. 72 percent in both. For detailed analysis, see Bruno de Solages, *La Composition des Évangiles de Luc et de Matthieu et leurs Sources* (Leiden: Brill, 1973) and Robert Morgenthaler, *Statistik des Neutestamentlichen Wortschatzes* (Stuttgart: Gotthelf-Verlag, 1958).

11. The pericope numbers of Aland, ed., *Synopsis Quattuor Evangeliorum* are used throughout. §126 (Mark 4:26–29), often listed in this category, actually has verbal parallels with Matt 13:24–30 in every verse.

661 verses, all but 45 have parallels in Matthew and/or Luke (93.2 percent).[12] In addition, Matthew and Luke share about 235 verses not found in Mark (the double tradition, the basis for the Q hypothesis). Both Matthew and Luke have a substantial element of special material unique to each Gospel.

Order

The Synoptic Gospels have the same general order: the baptism and temptation of Jesus; his Galilean mission; his journey to Jerusalem; his mission in Jerusalem; his arrest, trial, death, and resurrection. It may seem self-evident that all the Gospels should follow this general chronological outline as simply "reporting the way it happened," until one reflects on the facts that (1) John has quite a different order and (2) one can readily imagine a number of other ways of narrating the same story—for instance, involving flashbacks, a literary technique known to the evangelists (Mark 6:14–29/Matt 14:1–12). That Matthew has exactly the same kind of flashback, at the same location in the narrative, and that the technique occurs only here in the two Gospels, is itself a striking phenomenon of order that calls for an explanation.

This general agreement in order extends to detailed agreement in order. Consulting the conspectus of the Gospel parallels in the standard Synopsis[13] is a convenient way to observe the structure of each Gospel as a whole and to see the agreements and variations in the order of pericopes at a glance. Some striking features that call for explanation: All three Synoptics mostly have the same order, but whenever Matthew has a different order from Mark's, Luke almost always agrees with Mark; whenever Luke has a different order from Mark's, Matthew almost always agrees with Markan order. There are virtually no disagreements between the order of pericopes in Matthew and Luke when they have Markan parallels, but they often disagree with each other in non-Markan passages.[14] Of the 115 pericopes in Mark (as arranged in the Aland *Synopsis*), though each of the evangelists has occasionally varied the order for his own theological purpose, only Mark 3:31–35 and parallels occurs in a different chronological location in each of the Synoptics. Matthew's order varies considerably from Mark's in Matthew 4:23–11, but never deviates from the Markan order of pericopes from Matthew 12:22/Mark 3:22 to the end of the Gospel.

Wording

Perhaps the most noticeable literary similarity among the Synoptic Gospels is their verbal agreement in narrating the same events or reporting the same sayings. The similarity in wording is striking even to the casual reader, but the full impact of similarities and differences cannot be experienced until one carefully marks the verbal parallels for the whole text of the Gospels in a synopsis.[15] A few samples of various types and degrees of agreement are here provided (see Boxes 20 and 21).

One first notes the common sequence. There are two independent stories, the healing of the paralyzed man and the call of a tax collector to be a

---

12. Mark 1:33; 2:2, 19, 27; **3:20–21;** 5:5; 6:22, 27, 31; 5:5; 6:22, 27, 31, 52; 7:3–5, 9, 24–26, **33–36; 8:22–26;** 9:10, 15–16, 21, 23–24; 10:10, 24, 50; 11:16; 12:29, 32–34; 14:51–52; 15:8, 44–45. Those in **bold** represent whole pericopes.
13. Aland, ed., *Synopsis Quattuor Evangeliorum*, 551–75 and corresponding pages in the English and Greek-English editions. This same arrangement, without the Aland numbers, can also be found in *The HarperCollins Study Bible* (San Francisco: HarperSanFrancisco, 2006), 1653–63. See also the helpful chart of Alan Barr, *A Diagram of Synoptic Relationships* (Edinburgh: T. & T. Clark, 1938, repr. 2000).
14. The possible exceptions to this generalization (7 of 367 pericopes!) are discussed by Joseph A. Fitzmyer, SJ, *The Gospel According to Luke (I–IX)*, AB 28 (Garden City, NY: Doubleday, 1981), 1:68–69. For more detailed discussion of the phenomenon of order, see Frans Neirynck, "Synoptic Problem," in *The New Jerome Biblical Commentary*, ed. Raymond E. Brown, Joseph A. Fitzmyer, SJ, and Roland E. Murphy (Englewood Cliffs, NJ: Prentice-Hall, 1990), 588–90; John S. Kloppenborg Verbin, *Excavating Q: The Historical Setting of the Sayings Gospel* (Minneapolis: Fortress Press, 2000), 18–32.
15. The analyses here presented are made on the basis of the Greek text, the details of which are not always rendered with literal precision in English translations, but the NRSV translation here used for convenience renders the parallels in the Greek text quite closely. For suggestions in marking your *Synopsis* to make your own analysis, see Exc. 3.6, pages 504–5.

BOX 20: Verbal Parallels (Aland *Synopsis* §43)

Underline = exact or almost exact parallel wording   Dotted underline = similar wording
Bold underline = identical Markan parallels in both Matthew and Luke

Matthew 9:1–8

1 And after getting into a boat he crossed the sea and came to his own town.

2 ¶ And *just* then some people were carrying a paralyzed man lying *on a bed*.*

When Jesus saw their faith, he said to the paralytic,

"Take heart, son;
your sins are forgiven."

3 *Then* some of the scribes said to themselves,

"This man is blaspheming."

4 But Jesus, perceiving *their* thoughts,

said,
"Why do you think evil in your hearts?

5 For which is easier, to say,
'Your sins are forgiven,' or to say, 'Stand up and walk'?

6 But so that you may know that the Son of Man has authority on earth to forgive sins"—he then said to the paralytic—

"Stand up, take your *bed* and go to your home."

7 And he stood up and *went to his home*.

8 When the crowds saw it, they were filled with *awe*, and they glorified God, who had given such authority to human beings.

Mark 2:1–12

2:1 ¶ When he returned to Capernaum after some days, it was reported that he was at home.

2 So many gathered around that there was no longer room for them, not even in front of the door; and he was speaking the word to them.

3 Then some people came, bringing to him a paralyzed man, carried by four of them.

4 And when they could not bring him to Jesus because of the crowd, they removed the roof above him; and after having dug through it, they let down the mat on which the paralytic lay.

5 When Jesus saw their faith, he said to the paralytic,

"Son,
your sins are forgiven."

6 Now some of the scribes were sitting there, questioning in their hearts,

7 "Why does this fellow speak in this way? It is blasphemy!

Who can forgive sins but God alone?"

8 At once Jesus perceived in his spirit that they were discussing these questions among themselves; and he said to them, "Why do you raise such questions in your hearts?

9 Which is easier, to say to the paralytic,

'Your sins are forgiven,' or to say, 'Stand up and take your mat and walk'?

10 But so that you may know that the Son of Man has authority on earth to forgive sins"—he said to the paralytic—

11 "I say to you, stand up, take your mat and go to your home."

12 And he stood up, and immediately took the mat and went out before all of them; so that they were all amazed and glorified God, saying, "We have never seen anything like this!"

Luke 5:17–26

17 ¶ One day, while he was teaching, Pharisees and teachers of the law were sitting near by (they had come from every village of Galilee and Judea and from Jerusalem); and the power of the Lord was with him to heal.

18 *Just* then some men came, carrying a paralyzed man *on a bed*. They were trying to bring him in and lay him before Jesus;

19 but finding no way to bring him in because of the crowd, they went up on the roof and let him down with his bed through the tiles into the middle of the crowd in front of Jesus.

20 When he saw their faith, he *said*,

"Friend,
your sins are forgiven you."

21 *Then* the scribes and the Pharisees began to question,

"Who is this who is speaking blasphemies?

Who can forgive sins but God alone?"

22 When Jesus perceived *their* questionings, he *answered* them,
"Why do you raise such questions in your hearts?

23 Which is easier, to say,
'Your sins are forgiven you,' or to say, 'Stand up and walk'?

24 But so that you may know that the Son of Man has authority on earth to forgive sins"—he said to the one who was paralyzed—

"I say to you, stand up and take your *bed* and go to your home."

25 Immediately he stood up before them, took what he had been lying on, and *went to his home*, glorifying God.

26 Amazement seized all of them, and they glorified God and were filled with *awe*, saying, "We have seen strange things today."

---

* I have noted a few places in this pericope where Matthew and Luke agree *against* Mark, printing them in italics. A careful analysis will also note instances where Matthew and Luke agree in "omitting," i.e., in not having, Markan words and phrases, such as "and take your mat" in Mark 2:9. These are examples of "Minor Agreements" (see Exc. 3.5).

BOX 21: Verbal Parallels (Aland *Synopsis* §44)

Matthew 9:9	Mark 2:13–14	Luke 5:27–28
9 ¶ As Jesus was walking along, he saw a man called Matthew sitting at the tax booth; and he said to him, "Follow me." And he got up and followed him.	13 ¶ Jesus went out again beside the sea; the whole crowd gathered around him, and he taught them. 14 As he was walking along, he saw Levi son of Alphaeus sitting at the tax booth, and he said to him, "Follow me." And he got up and followed him.	27 ¶ After this he went out and saw a tax collector named Levi, sitting at the tax booth; and he said to him, "Follow me." 28 And he got up, left everything, and followed him.

disciple ("Levi" in Mark and Luke, "Matthew" in Matthew). The two incidents are not directly linked in Mark or Matthew (only Luke has "after this"). There is no particular logical or historical reason why they should be connected in this order, with nothing in between, yet all three have the same sequence. Instances are abundant.

As to wording: Matthew has 147 words; Mark has 233 words; Luke has 238 words (see Box 22; statistics based on the Greek text).

In addition, several strings of identical words in identical order are shared by each pair of Gospels and by all three. The striking parenthetical aside in which the narrator interrupts Jesus' words is found in the identical location in all three Gospels (Matt 9:6/Mark 2:10/Luke 5:24).[16]

In the comparison in Box 23, Matthew has seventy-six words; Luke has seventy-two words. The pericope is not in Mark.

Matthew and Luke have 86 percent verbal agreement. Most of the variations occur in the introductory lines. The speech of John the Baptist itself is verbally identical for sixty-four Greek words, except for the singular "fruit" (Matthew) and plural "fruits" (Luke) and the auxiliary verb "presume" (Matthew) and "begin" (Luke). *The agreements are in the Greek text, though John preached in Aramaic.* Anyone who has translated from one language to another knows that it is virtually impossible for any two translators independently to have chosen exactly the same Greek words in exactly the same order. This is possible for a few phrases, but not for a sentence or an extended passage.

In §43 above (Box 20), the agreements are shared by Matthew and Luke with Mark (triple tradition); in §14 below (Box 23), Matthew and Luke agree on the wording of a text not in Mark (double tradition).

BOX 22: Synoptic Verbal Agreement Statistics

Matthew and Mark 69 percent verbal agreement:	
Exact agreement	91 = 62 percent
Same word with variations*	10 = 7 percent
Luke and Mark 53 percent verbal agreement:	
Exact agreement	99 = 42 percent
Same word with variations	25 = 11 percent
Matthew, Mark, and Luke 38 percent verbal agreement:	
Exact agreement	68 = 30 percent
Same word with variations	18 = 8 percent

* Nouns, pronouns, adjectives, and articles that are the same lexical word but with variations in case or number; verbs that are the same lexical word with variations in tense, mood, voice, person, or number. Nominal and verbal cognates are also counted in this category.

16. Additional examples of parenthetical comments, narrator to the reader: Mark 13:14/Matt 24:15 "let the reader understand"; Mark 5:8/Luke 8:29 "for he had said to him"; Matt 27:18/Mark 15:10 "For he knew it was out of envy"; Robert Stein, *The Synoptic Problem: An Introduction* (Grand Rapids: Baker, 1987), 37–42, gives other examples.

BOX 23: Verbal Parallels (Aland *Synopsis* §14)

Matt 3:7–10	(Mark)	Luke 3:7–9
7 But when he saw many Pharisees and Sadducees coming for baptism, he said to them, "You brood of vipers! Who warned you to flee from the wrath to come?		7 John said to the crowds that came out to be baptized by him, "You brood of vipers! Who warned you to flee from the wrath to come?
8 Bear fruit worthy of repentance.		8 Bear fruits worthy of repentance.
9 Do not presume to say to yourselves, 'We have Abraham as our ancestor'; for I tell you, God is able from these stones to raise up children to Abraham.		Do not begin to say to yourselves, 'We have Abraham as our ancestor'; for I tell you, God is able from these stones to raise up children to Abraham.
10 Even now the ax is lying at the root of the trees; every tree therefore that does not bear good fruit is cut down and thrown into the fire."		9 Even now the ax is lying at the root of the trees; every tree therefore that does not bear good fruit is cut down and thrown into the fire."

For examples of more complex patterns of agreement and disagreement, see §13 (Matt 3:1–6/Mark 1:2–6/Luke 3:1–6); §§117–118 (Matt 12:22–37/Mark 3:22–30/Luke 11:14–23; 12:10; 6:43–45), in which there is a mixture of Matthew/Mark, Luke/Mark, and Matthew/Luke agreements. See also §279 (Matt 22:1–14/Luke 14:15–24) as an example of parallel pericopes that seem to have some relationship, but with a minimum of verbal agreement.

The three pericopes displayed above are only a tiny fraction of the phenomena exhibited by the Gospel texts, but illustrate the typical phenomena of verbal agreement that pervade the Synoptics as a whole.

Exc. 3.3 Possible Explanations

How are these phenomena of selection, order, and verbal agreement presented above to be explained?[17] A number of different explanations have been proposed, not all of them mutually exclusive, so that some interpreters have combined aspects of more than one approach.

Oral Tradition

While hardly anyone doubts the importance of oral tradition as forming a link between the earliest period and written documents, some scholars have attempted to explain the similarities and differences in the Gospels themselves entirely or mainly on the basis of their independent use of oral tradition, without any of the evangelists having used the other as a source.[18] To be sure, a living oral tradition

17. Only an outline of an extensive and complex debate can be presented here. For more details, see William R. Farmer, *The Synoptic Problem: A Critical Analysis* (New York: Macmillan, 1964), 1–198 (from the perspective of the 2GH) and Kloppenborg Verbin, *Excavating Q*, 11–54 (from the perspective of the 2DH).

18. J. G. Herder (1797) initiated this approach, which was soon seen to be unsatisfactory and gave way to various theories of written sources. The continuing importance of oral tradition is seen, however, in the fact that a few modern scholars have continued to argue for oral tradition as the principal solution to the Synoptic Problem. See John M. Rist, *On the Independence of Matthew and Mark*, SNTSMS 32 (Cambridge: Cambridge University Press, 1978); Bo Ivar Reicke, *The Roots of the Synoptic Gospels* (Philadelphia: Fortress Press, 1986).

influenced the developing Gospel tradition, and it continued alongside the Gospels after they were written. However, the authors of the Gospels themselves are not reciters or mere transcribers of the oral tradition, but writers, composers who indicate that they are utilizing written sources and expect their compositions to be read aloud from their written text (Mark 13:14; Luke 1:1–4; John 20:30–31; 21:24–25). The texts of the Gospels manifest characteristics of oral transmission at a stage behind the written texts, but the phenomena of the texts themselves (selection, sequence, wording) cannot be explained only in terms of popular oral tradition. After more than a century of concentrated study, the virtual consensus of scholarship is that the phenomena of the text discussed above cannot be explained apart from interrelations among written texts.

Written Fragments

In 1832 Friedrich Schleiermacher argued, primarily on the basis of patristic testimony and Luke 1:1–4, that soon after the beginning of the church, written collections of Jesus' sayings and deeds were circulated (the passion story, collections of Jesus' miracles, parables, etc.), and that the evangelists independently used these collections to compose the later written Gospels. In this view, none of the evangelists was aware of the work of the others, but all were dependent on the same collections of overlapping written sources. This view was a step toward the literary interdependence of the Gospels, but by itself could not account for the phenomena of the text, especially the complex phenomenon of selection, order, and the overlapping and intertwined order of each of the Synoptics.

Literary Interdependence

Interpreters were driven to the inevitable conclusion: the phenomena of selection, proportion, order, and wording described above are remarkable, cannot be coincidental, cannot be explained on the basis of individual memory or oral tradition, and call for some kind of literary interrelationship.

This is not merely a modern solution; in the fifth century Augustine argued that each of the later Gospels used the earlier Gospels as sources.[19] The phenomena cannot be explained as merely the coincidental agreement in wording or order by authors who are independently writing about the same subject matter. For example, in the case of multiple biographies of the same figure, the phenomena of selection, order, and wording manifest in the Gospels are not present except when they are clearly quoting the same sources.

It was common in the ancient world for writers to incorporate wholesale large blocks of material from other writers. For his history of Roman times, Josephus adopted and rewrote much of the account of Nicholas of Damascus, court historian and friend of Herod the Great.[20] The author of 2 Maccabees indicates in his preface that his book is a rewriting of the five-volume history of Jason of Cyrene (2 Macc 2:23), but in the document itself there is no indication of which material and wording come from his source and which belong to the anonymous author himself. The author of 1 and 2 Chronicles incorporates and modifies several sources, some of which later became canonical, some of which he specifies and others of which he does not .[21] Isaiah 2:2–4 is

19. Augustine believed the Gospels were composed in their canonical order, and consequently that Matthew was first, Mark abbreviated Matthew, and Luke used both Matthew and Mark as sources. See Augustine, "Harmony of the Gospels," in *Saint Augustine: Sermon on the Mount, Harmony of the Gospels, and Homilies on the Gospels*, ed. Philip Schaff, *A Select Library of the Nicene and Post-Nicene Fathers of The Christian Church* (Grand Rapids: Eerdmans, 1888, 1979), 1.2. Although this was the standard view of Synoptic relations until the nineteenth century, it has since been almost completely abandoned, its most recent major defender being Basil Christopher Butler, *The Originality of St. Matthew: A Critique of the Two-document Hypothesis* (Cambridge: Cambridge University Press, 1951).

20. E.g., Josephus, *Ant.* 15–17, is taken from Nicholas's work without documenting his copying or being worried that anyone would notice or care about such standard procedure.

21. 1 Chr 29:29 mentions "the records of the seer Samuel, . . . the records of the prophet Nathan, and . . . the records of the seer Gad," and 2 Chr 9:29 lists as sources "the acts of Solomon . . . written in the history of the prophet Nathan, and in the prophecy of Ahijah . . . and the visions of the seer Iddo," but the narrative itself does not indicate what elements were derived from which source. The genealogical lists of 1 Chr 1–9 are derived from the genealogies of Genesis, Exodus, Numbers, Joshua, Samuel, and Ruth, and/or from the sources used

identical with Micah 4:1–3, with no indication by either writer that he is using the other as a source (or that they are using a common source). The editorial process by which the Psalter was formed resulted in the duplication of several psalms (e.g., Pss 14 and 53), indicating that some psalms were in more than one of the final editor's source documents. Psalm 18 is identical with 2 Samuel 22, indicating that one has used the other as a source, or that both used a common source.

Illustrations could be multiplied, but these are adequate to indicate that when the evangelists made use of written sources, including other documents that later became canonical, they were in step with the literary practice of their time as well as with their Bible. Thus practically all contemporary scholars from almost the whole theological spectrum approach the task of interpretation convinced that source analysis is a legitimate and valuable element in the hermeneutical enterprise.

The acknowledgment of the value and legitimacy of source analysis, however, does not in itself illuminate the actual literary interrelationship that may have existed among the Synoptic Gospels. How are they in fact related? Which was the first Gospel, and which are later interpretations?

Number of possibilities

If three documents are literarily interdependent, there are eighteen possible ways in which they may be related. If two or more used a common lost source or sources, the number of possibilities is increased by a staggering amount. In fact, however, only a small number of possibilities has been proposed and defended as viable options. A sketch of their history is illuminating for the present discussion.

Augustine

The overlapping of the Gospels in terms of parallel material and wording was recognized early. Ammonius, a third-century teacher, published an edition of the Gospel of Matthew with parallel sections of the other Gospels alongside the Matthean text. Eusebius, fourth-century bishop of Caesarea and leading figure in the Council of Nicaea, developed tables of cross-references that facilitated comparison of any paragraph in the Gospels with its parallels in the other Gospels. These are still useful and are printed in the introductory matter and margins of the Nestle-Aland editions of the Greek New Testament. Augustine saw that the textual phenomena of the Gospels required some sort of literary dependence, and argued that the Gospels were written in canonical order, with each of the later evangelists aware of and utilizing his predecessors. In this view, Mark is seen as the "abbreviator of Matthew," and Luke as using both Matthew and Mark.

This solution to the Synoptic Problem was refuted by J. B. Koppe, a Göttingen New Testament scholar, in his 1782 *Marcus non epitomator Matthaei* (Mark No Abbreviator of Matthew). Augustine had not had a synopsis that allowed him to compare the Gospels in parallel columns. Koppe, using Griesbach's new synopsis for Gospel studies, saw immediately that, while Mark is shorter than Matthew overall, from pericope to pericope Mark is often longer. See, for example, Aland *Synopsis* §137 (Mark 5:1–20/Matt 8:28–34), in which Matthew uses only 134 words to tell the same story for which Mark uses 325.

J. J. Griesbach 1774, 1776, 1783

In 1774 J. J. Griesbach published the first edition of his *Synopsis,* bound with his new edition of the Greek New Testament. In 1776 his *Synopsis* was published separately, followed in 1783 by his own solution to the Synoptic Problem. Griesbach retained the priority of Matthew, but argued Mark was the last of the Synoptics to be written, using both Matthew and Luke as sources. This proposal, which was not absolutely original, became quite popular and was adopted by leading New Testament scholars of Europe. By the middle of the nineteenth century it was the leading theory. F. C. Baur and the circle of scholars known as the Tübingen school advocated this view, which was especially congenial to their dialectical understanding of the course of early Christian history (see above, §9.2.2). In this view, the original conservative Jewish Christianity (thesis = Matthew)

by those books. The chapter 1 Chr 16 is composed of a combination of Pss 105, 95, 106, with no indication that the author is using the written Psalter as a source.

generated a liberal Gentile Christianity as its reaction (antithesis = Luke); the common elements of these two were then combined in the protocatholic church of the second century (synthesis = Mark).

An "Original Gospel"? Lessing 1778

A new era was opened up in New Testament studies by G. E. Lessing, a German philosopher who, along with Griesbach, brought the end to harmonization as the scholarly way of dealing with discrepancies in the Gospels. His 1778 composition introduced the "Original Gospel" theory of Gospel origins, according to which our three Synoptics all used an original Gospel called the "Gospel of the Nazarenes." This document is now lost, but was known to the Church Fathers as the "Gospel of the Apostles," the "Gospel of the Hebrews," the "Gospel of the Nazarenes," or the "Gospel of Matthew." This theory was elaborated in the next century by the Göttingen scholar J. G. Eichhorn, but the hypothesis of a lost Original Gospel could not establish itself by explaining the data, and was abandoned.

The Priority of Mark: C. H. Weisse, 1838

A few scholars had previously proposed Mark as the earliest Gospel, but the first to argue a systematic case for this view is generally considered to be the Leipzig philosopher C. H. Weisse. Once the priority of Mark is accepted, the common material in Matthew and Luke not found in Mark must be explained. The three possibilities are obviously (1) Matthew used Luke as a source, (2) Luke used Matthew as a source, or (3) they both used a common source or sources now lost. That Matthew and Luke independently used both Mark and Q came to be called the Two-Source Hypothesis (2SH) or Two-Document Hypothesis (2DH). The Göttingen Orientalist H. G. A. Ewald was the first scholar to make this view the exegetical basis for a commentary. His 1850 study of the Synoptics printed the sources in different fonts.

The Two-Document Hypothesis: Holtzmann (1863) and Streeter (1924)

The late nineteenth and early twentieth century was a period of vigorous and thorough debate on the Synoptic Problem. At first, the view that Matthew was the first Gospel continued to hold the field. This view was supported both by the official teaching of the Roman Catholic Church (in the form of the Augustinian solution: Matthew → Mark → Luke) and by the influential group of left-wing Protestants of the Tübingen School (in the form of the Griesbach solution: Matthew → Luke → Mark).

The 2DH continued to gain ground, however. The 1863 publication of *Die synoptischen Evangelien* (The Synoptic Gospels) by Heinrich Julius Holtzmann of Heidelberg summarized scholarship up to that time, and set forth the 2DH in a way that became convincing to most scholars. The results of a continuing seminar at Oxford, 1894–1909, were published in a significant volume in 1911.[22] By 1924, when B. H. Streeter's *The Four Gospels* became the classic English-language statement for this view, the 2DH was already the dominant paradigm for Gospel studies, often considered the "assured results" of biblical criticism. The 2DH, which had never been unanimously accepted, received serious challenges in the latter part of the twentieth century that forced its advocates to reexamine the whole issue. The 2DH continues as the dominant theory, with the Farrer-Goulder Hypothesis (FGH) and the Two-Gospel Hypothesis (2GH, also still known as the Griesbach Hypothesis) the other major candidates.[23]

Exc. 3.4 The Priority of Mark

A combination of types of evidence has convinced most scholars that Mark was the earliest Gospel. Though the categories are overlapping, for purposes of discussion the evidence may be classified as follows:

Orality

The earliest written Gospel, whichever it was, will necessarily have primarily used oral sources. It is widely recognized that, of all the Gospels, Mark

22. William Sanday, ed., *Studies in the Synoptic Problem: By Members of the University of Oxford* (Oxford: Clarendon Press, 1911).
23. FGH = priority of Mark, Luke used Matthew, no Q. 2GH = priority of Matthew, Luke used Matthew, Mark used both Matthew and Luke, no Q.

is closest to the oral style. Mark seems to be only one step removed from oral tradition, preserving many of the features of oral style, including Aramaisms and parataxis (see below), frequent use of the historical present, the lively pace of the narrative (εὐθύς, *euthus*, immediately, directly, next, forty-two times, vs. three times Luke, six times Matthew, three times John), vivid details ("in the stern, asleep on the cushion," 4:38; "green grass," 6:39; the extended story with its gory details of the death of John, 6:14–29), the tantalizingly abrupt and thought-provoking ending, 16:8. Mark does not appear to be a literary conflation of Matthew and Luke, the end result of a tedious literary process of combining texts, but an original composition directly related to the oral tradition.

Content: Mark's Omissions or Matthean/Lukan Additions?

Mark is significantly shorter overall than Matthew and Luke, which are approximately the same length (Mark: 115 pericopes, 11,242 words; Matthew: 178 pericopes, 18,305 words; Luke: 185 pericopes, 19,228 words). Did Matthew and Luke expand Mark, or did Mark abbreviate one (Augustine) or both (Griesbach) of the other Gospels? Most scholars consider the relative brevity of Mark to be evidence for Mark's originality. This is not because of a general presumption that the shorter account is always earlier. In particular stories in triple-tradition passages, Mark is in fact typically longer. The argument is rather that it seems more convincing that Matthew and Luke would expand Mark by adding birth and resurrection stories and additional sayings material rather than that Mark would omit them. After their different and independent birth stories (wealthy magi in Matthew, poor shepherds in Luke), Matthew and Luke begin to agree with each other at Matthew 3:1 and Luke 3:1, that is, at the point where they become parallel with Mark. They follow Mark until Mark 16:8, then cease to agree with each other in their independent and different resurrection stories. Mark has no appearance stories; Matthew has Jesus appear to the disciples only in Galilee, while Luke has only Judean appearances. Likewise, difficult Markan stories such as Jesus' family considering him mentally unbalanced (Mark 3:30–31) and Jesus requiring two attempts to heal a blind man (Mark 8:22–26) can understandably have been omitted by Matthew and Luke, but it is difficult to think of Mark making difficulties for himself and his readers by adding these stories after omitting so much else that Matthew and Luke have in common.

Mark pictures Jesus as a teacher, referring to his teaching activity thirty-four times. The 2GH is particularly hard pressed to explain why Mark gives only a small sample of Jesus' teaching, omitting, for example, the material in Matthew's Sermon on the Mount (Matt 5–7), and Luke's Sermon on the Plain (Luke 6:20–49). It seems comprehensible to most interpreters that Matthew and Luke would expand Jesus' teaching in Mark by adding Q and other materials, but hard to understand why Mark, after emphasizing the role of Jesus as teacher, would systematically reduce Jesus' teaching available to him in Matthew and Luke. On the other hand, a more satisfactory explanation can be given for Matthew and Luke's relatively few omissions from Mark (see data above).

Order

The phenomena of order described above clearly indicate some kind of literary relationship among the Synoptic Gospels. The phenomenon itself is striking, but does it prove Mark's priority? Whenever Matthew's order differs from Mark's, Mark's order agrees with Luke's; and whenever Luke's order differs from Mark's, Matthew agrees with Mark.

When stated abstractly, the argument seems to prove only that Mark is the "middle term" between Matthew and Luke, that is, that Mark stands between Matthew and Luke and is related to both, whether first (as in the 2DH) or last (as in the 2GH). How one sees the phenomenon of order depends to a great extent on how the pericopes are divided and arranged in a synopsis.

However, what is required is an examination of each case when all three do not have the same order, to determine how and why each evangelist has changed the order of his presumed source (see below). Sometimes, for example, Matthew has located an incident at a different chronological place than in the Markan order but has incidentally left hints that it is Matthew who is altering Mark, rather than vice versa. Thus in Matthew 8:16 the phrase "evening having come" agrees verbatim with Mark 1:32. In the Markan context, the function of the phrase is to indicate that people came for healing only after the Sabbath was over (see Mark 1:21; in Mark all the incidents 1:21–34 occur on the same Sabbath day). In Matthew, the scene has been relocated in another context, no longer on a Sabbath; yet the Markan phrase is retained, though no longer serving any purpose. Such data indicate it is Matthew who is rearranging his Markan source, rather than vice versa. So also Luke 4:23 would make chronological sense in Mark 6:1–6, where Jesus has already worked miracles in Capernaum, but not in Luke 4, where Jesus does not visit Capernaum until after this episode at Nazareth (Luke 4:31 is the first reference to Capernaum in the Gospel of Luke). Here Luke seems to presuppose Mark. Another example: Luke mentions Simon in 4:38, but his call is not narrated until 5:1–11. In Mark, Simon's call had already occurred in 1:16–20; when Luke moved this story to a later setting in order to provide a basis for it in Jesus' miracles, this resulted in a premature reference to Simon in the narrative as though he were already known. Such data indicate that it is Luke who has rearranged the Markan order, not vice versa. An examination of all such instances where Matthew or Luke have a Markan incident in a different location from Mark has convinced most scholars that more plausible explanations can be given on the basis of the priority of Mark.

Language and Style

Another category of material in which it appears that Matthew and Luke have edited Mark, rather than vice versa, is provided by examining their respective use of the Greek language. The following types of phenomena indicate Markan priority:

General Level of Mark's Greek

Numerous studies have shown in detail that Mark's text, in terms of the level of Greek in which it is written, reflects the unsophisticated composition of a person without higher education.[24] Mark is a profound theologian and gifted writer, but his story is composed in simple, awkward, and sometimes incorrect Greek. Matthew is more skilled in Greek than Mark, and Luke even more so. A few examples (much of this does not, of course, come through in English translations, which necessarily smooth out the differences):

The historical present. Mark has 151 examples. While not incorrect, use of the historical present was considered vernacular, not literary style. Matthew's longer text has only 78 instances, changing most of the occurrences in the Markan narrative—though retaining and even increasing those with the formula "Jesus says . . ." Luke eliminates all but one of Mark's historical presents (Mark 5:35=Luke 8:39).

Parataxis. Mark tends to string together his sentences with the coordinating conjunction καί (*kai,* and). Of Mark's 115 paragraphs, 92 begin with "and." While this may reflect the Aramaic background of Mark's tradition (see below), which was poor in conjunctions and regularly used paratactic style as in the Old Testament, it also reflects the uncultured vernacular style. In any case, both Matthew and Luke typically join their clauses with a variety of conjunctions and participles. It is unlikely that this more elegant use of the Greek language was intentionally deconstructed by Mark.

Repetitive "immediately" and "for". Mark uses the adverb εὐθύς (*euthus,* immediately, next) forty-two times. When understood to mean "immediately," it has sometimes been used as evidence for Mark's "dynamic" Jesus, who acts without hesitation and seems to hurry from one thing to the next, but the word in Mark's usage often

24. See the survey in E. J. Pryke, *Redactional Style in the Marcan Gospel: A Study of Syntax and Vocabulary as Guides to Redaction in Mark*, SNTSMS 33 (Cambridge: Cambridge University Press, 1978), 25–31: "Markan linguistic studies since Hawkins and Turner" (with annotated bibliography). For a convenient survey of Markan linguistic features, see Vincent Taylor, *The Gospel according to St. Mark* (New York: Macmillan, 1959), 44–54.

has its weakened meaning of "next" and serves to relieve the monotony of καί (and) discussed above, serving only as a colorless conjunction to link actions together. Matthew retains the word only five times, never outside Markan parallels, and Luke eliminates the word altogether. Not only does it seem more likely that Matthew and Luke have eliminated or drastically reduced an unrefined Markan expression (rather than Mark having sprinkled their narratives with the word); the five instances in Matthew offer further evidence of Markan priority: the word, obviously not one of Matthew's favorites, occurs in Matthew only in passages parallel to Mark. If Matthew were first, some "invisible hand" must have guided him to use it only in passages Mark would later choose to incorporate.[25]

Coarse vocabulary. Mark sometimes uses uncouth terminology that is altered by Matthew and/or Luke. For example, in Mark 2:11 the word for "mat" (κράβαττος, *krabbaton,* like "bunk" or "pad," a somewhat slangy word for "bed") is replaced by a more elegant word by both Matthew and Luke, who differ not only from Mark but from each other.

Pleonistic ἄρχομαι (*archomai,* begin). The Greek word for "begin" is used twenty-six times by Mark, not as a real verb meaning to initiate something, but as an auxiliary verb—as in colloquial "he went and did it" for "he did it" in sections of the southern United States, where "went" does not describe an action but serves as an idiomatic auxiliary. Matthew and Luke are clearly nervous about this usage, Matthew adopting only six and Luke only two of Mark's twenty-six occurrences.

Colloquial use of diminutives. Mark is particularly fond of words with the diminutive ending –ιον. This is the rough equivalent of the English diminutive ending "-ie" or "-y," which may be used in colloquial speech without referring to something literally small (e.g., "doggie," "sweetie," "hubby"). Since in Greek such words are used as an element of colloquial speech in ways differently than English (where they are predominately children's words), they are not always rendered by diminutives in English translations. Mark does not indulge in baby talk, but in using the following words he is more colloquial than literary writers: θυγάτριον (*thugatrion,* 5:23; 7:25, little daughter, "girlie"); κοράσιον (*korasion,* 5:41; 6:22, 28, little girl); ἰχθύδιον (*ichthudion,* 8:7, small fish); κυνάριον (*kunarion,* 7:27, 28 little dog, puppy); σανδάλιον (*sandalion,* 6:9, "sandie" for sandal; cf. English "jammies" for pajamas); ψιχίον (*psichion,* 7:28, "crumbs"); ὠτάριον (*ōtarion,* 14:47, "earie" for ear; cf. English "footsie," "chinny chin chin"). None of these words is found in Luke; Matthew never has them except in passages parallel to Mark, and even there eliminates or changes most of them. Both Matthew and Luke seem to have recognized such expressions as colloquialisms, not true diminutives, and upgraded Mark's Greek.

Aramaic and Hebrew

Aramaic, which belongs to the same linguistic family as biblical Hebrew, was the mother tongue of Jesus and the earliest church. Mark contains seven direct Aramaic expressions from Jesus: *Boanerges* (3:17, Sons of Thunder); *Talitha cum* (5:41, Little girl, get up); *Corban* (7:11, an offering for God); *Ephphatha* (7:34, be opened); *Abba* (14:36 father); *Golgotha* (15:22, Golgotha); *Eloi, Eloi, lema sabachthani* (Mark 15:34, My God, my God, why have you forsaken me?).

Luke has parallels to five of these seven texts, but the Aramaic is missing in each case. Matthew has parallels to all seven Markan passages, but has none

25. See Stein, *Synoptic Problem,* 82, who elaborates the argument, and points out an analogous phenomenon. Mark has 66 γάρ (*gar,* for) clauses, 34 of which are not part of the internal dialogue of the narrative but are editorial comments directed to the reader. Matthew has 123 γάρ clauses, but only 11 are explanatory notes to the reader. Of these 11, all but one are paralleled in Markan material. Again, if Matthew were first, he must have known the 10 sections that Mark would incorporate and used this construction only there, whereas on the hypothesis of Markan priority, a favorite construction of Mark's is included by Matthew when following Mark, but hardly used by him at all elsewhere.

of the Aramaic words except "Golgotha" in Matthew 27:33 (=Mark 15:22). The Aramaic form of Jesus' cry of dereliction in Mark 15:34 had already been accommodated to the text of the Hebrew Bible (Ps 22:1); Matthew carries this further, giving the cry a more Hebrew form than in Mark.

In addition, Mark has the common Hebrew word "Amen," but used in an unusual way at the beginning of a statement, rather than at the end (Mark fourteen times; Luke six times; Matthew thirty-one times). The striking manner in which Jesus introduced sayings with "Amen I say to you" (usually translated as "truly" or "verily") was adopted in early Christianity and made a feature of Jesus sayings, being added to traditional sayings where it had not been originally. The Markan usage is increased in Matthew, corresponding to the general development of the tradition, but decreased by Luke, who found the expression ill-fitting for his more cultured Gentile readers.

In all these cases the flow is more readily understood as from Mark to Matthew and Luke, rather than in the other direction. The alternative would mean that Mark, writing for a Gentile church, had inserted Aramaic words into his text. The same is true of Mark's language in general, which reflects more Aramaic influence in vocabulary, grammar, and syntax than either Matthew or Luke.

Intercalations

In at least six passages, Mark has a combination of two stories in which one has been inserted into the other, producing the form $A_1/B/A_2$: 3:20–30; 5:21–43; 6:7–30; 11:12–25; 14:1–11; 14:53–72.[26] This appears to be a Markan redactional formulation; these six stories did not travel in the oral tradition already combined in this way. Matthew retains three (Mark 5:21–43 par.; 14:1–11 par.; 14:53–72) and Luke retains two (Mark 5:21–43 par.; 6:7–30 par.). Neither author seems to appreciate the subtlety, irony, and dramatic literary power with which Mark has endowed the form; neither Matthew nor Luke uses it except in the Markan passages cited. Matthew once loses the thread, forgets that the inserted story is a flashback, and continues the middle element without returning to the framework in which it had been enclosed (Matt 14:1–13; cf. Mark 6:1–32). It is difficult to understand the process as having gone the reverse direction.

Doublets

Doublets are repetitions of the same or similar stories or sayings in the same Gospel. Box 24, adapted from Joel Marcus,[27] clearly presents the data.

While it is possible for an author to use a story or saying he has found in oral tradition or in a single written source more than once (as Mark seems to have done in 9:35/10:43–44 and Matthew in 9:27–31/20:29–34 = Mark 10:46–52), the pattern of doublets strongly suggests that both Matthew and Luke had Mark as a source, and then also included a variation of the saying or story found in another, non-Markan source they have in common. Mark has only one doublet, but Matthew has ten and Luke has eight, in every case taking one from Mark and the other from their common source. Other source theories have difficulty accounting for this phenomenon.

Redundancy ("Dualistic Expressions")

Mark repeatedly uses wordy, double expressions; sometimes part of the expression is found in Matthew and part in Luke. A clear example is provided by Mark 1:32 and parallels (see Box 25).

Since this pattern is found frequently, and since it has been claimed as evidence that Mark is the latest

26. Other examples often mentioned: 1:21–28; 2:1–12; 13:5–27. By including texts where the form is not so complete, as many as twenty-six passages have been identified as Markan intercalations. See Tom Shepherd, *Markan Sandwich Stories: Narration, Definition, and Function*, Andrews Universtiy Seminary Doctoral Dissertation Series 18 (Berrien Springs, MI: Andrews University, 1993); Tom Shepherd, "The Narrative Function of Markan Intercalation," *NTS* 41 (1995): 522–40.

27. Joel Marcus, *Mark: A New Translation with Introduction and Commentary*, 2 vols., AB 27–27A (New York: Doubleday, 2000). The listing is conservative. Twenty-two doublets and double traditions are listed in John C. Hawkins, *Horae Synopticae: Contributions to the Study of the Synoptic Problem*, 2nd ed. (Oxford: Clarendon Press, 1968). The list could be expanded by including, e.g., the various versions of the feeding stories and the passion predictions.

BOX 24: Doublets

	Item	*Mark*	*Matthew*	*Luke*
	In Mark and Luke			
1.	First become last	9:35		9:38b
		10:43–44	20:26–27	18:26
	In Matthew and Luke			
2.	To the one who has	4:25	13:12	8:18
			25:29	19:26
3.	Taking up cross	8:34	16:24 10:38	9:23 14:27
4.	Losing one's life	8:35	16:25	9:24
			10:39	17:33
5.	Receiving Jesus as a child	9:37	18:5	9:48
			10:40	10:16
	In Matthew			
6.	Beelzebul accusation	3:22	9:34	
		12:24	11:15	
7.	Sign of Jonah	8:11–12	16:1–2a	
		12:38–42	11:29–32	
8.	Divorce	10:11–12	19:9	
			5:32	16:18
9.	First shall be last	10:31	19:30	
			20:16	13:30
10.	Faith moves mountains	11:22–32	21:21	
			17:19–20	17:5–6
	In Luke			
11.	The lamp	4:21		8:16
			5:15	11:33
12.	Hidden and revealed	4:22		8:17
			10:26	12:2
13.	Ashamed of Jesus	8:38		9:26
		10:32–33		12:9
14.	The Spirit's help	13:9–11		21:12–15
			10:19	12:11–12

BOX 25: Redundancy

Matt 8:16
That evening they brought to him many who were possessed with demons

Mark 1:32
That evening, *at sundown*, they brought to him all who were sick or possessed with demons

Luke 4:40
As the sun was setting, all those who had any who were sick with various kinds of diseases brought them to him

Gospel, conflating Matthew and Luke, it has been studied very carefully.[28] There are 213 examples of such dualistic expressions, but the vast majority do not appear to be a Markan combination of Matthew and Luke. Of the 213 instances:

— Matthew has one half, Luke the other half seventeen times.

— Matthew has one half, Luke has both halves eleven times.

— Matthew has one half, Luke has no parallel forty-six times.

— Luke has one half, Matthew has both halves seventeen times.

— Luke has one half, Matthew has no parallel twenty-five times.

— Both omit the same half thirty-nine times.

— Both have Mark's duplicate expression six times.

— Matthew has both halves, Luke has no parallel fourteen times.

— Luke has both halves, Matthew has no parallel once.

— Matthew and Luke both have no parallel thirty-seven times.[29]

The evidence turns out to support Markan priority. Such double expressions are not evidence of conflation, but a feature of Markan style, somewhat like the parallelism often found in the Old Testament. But neither Matthew nor Luke had much appreciation for this stylistic feature, and dealt with it in the variety of ways shown above.

28. Thomas R. W. Longstaff, *Evidence of Conflation in Mark? A Study in the Synoptic Problem*, SBLDS (Missoula, MT: Scholars Press, 1977); Frans Neirynck, *Duality in Mark: Contributions to the Study of the Markan Redaction* (Leuven: Leuven University Press, 1988); C. M. Tuckett, *The Revival of the Griesbach Hypothesis: An Analysis and Appraisal*, SNTSMS 44 (Cambridge: Cambridge University Press, 1983), 1621.

29. Tuckett, *Griesbach Hypothesis*, 20.

Mark's Harder Readings

There are numerous texts in which Matthew and/or Luke has eliminated or changed objectionable features within the Markan text:

— Matthew 8:16/Mark 1:32–34/Luke 4:40. In Mark, people bring all the sick and Jesus heals many. In both Matthew and Luke, people bring many and Jesus heals all.

— Matthew 4:24/Mark 3:9–10/Luke 6:17–19. Again, Mark's many becomes all in Matthew and Luke.

— Matthew 13:58/Mark 6:5–6/Luke 4:16–30. In Mark, Jesus could not do miracles in his hometown (with a few exceptions); in Matthew, Jesus did not do (many) miracles, and the fault lies with the unbelief of the people. Luke eliminates the whole reference.

— Matthew 19:16–17/Mark 10:17–18. In Mark, Jesus refuses to be called "good," for only God is good, but Matthew removes the problem: Jesus is not addressed as "good," and his response does not deny that he is good (though the Matthean text continues presupposing the text as in Mark).

— Matthew 3:1, 15–16/Mark 1:4, 9. Similarly in Mark 1:4 John baptizes for the forgiveness of sins, and in Mark 1:9 Jesus is baptized by John without objection or explanation. In Matthew, however, "forgiveness of sins" is removed from John's preaching, and in 3:14–15 an explanation is given for Jesus' being baptized by John. Luke 3:3 retains forgiveness as ingredient to John's baptism, but Luke never narrates Jesus' baptism, getting John off the narrative stage before Jesus comes on (see Luke 3:19–20).

— Mark 1:2. The quotation is incorrectly attributed to Isaiah. This mistake is omitted by Matthew and Luke.

— Mark 2:26. Abiathar is high priest, but in 1 Samuel 21 the high priest is Ahimelech. This mistake is omitted by Matthew and Luke.

To most scholars it makes more sense to understand these and similar texts as Matthean and Lukan interpretation and smoothing out of Markan difficulties, rather than seeing Mark as having introduced difficulties into the texts of Matthew and Luke.

Markan Text Presupposed by Matthew and Luke

Another category of phenomena indicating Markan priority is provided by numerous texts in which Matthew and/or Luke has inadvertently incorporated Markan elements into his texts that made sense in their Markan setting, but no longer fit their new context. A selection:[30]

— Matthew 9:2/Mark 2:1–5. In Mark, "When Jesus saw their faith" refers to the dramatic evidence of their faith in making an opening in the roof and letting the paralyzed man they were carrying down through it, so he could be healed by Jesus. Matthew's abbreviation of the story has eliminated this colorful incident, but nevertheless retains the Markan "When he saw their faith."

— Matthew 9:18–26/Mark 5:21–43. In Mark, Jairus comes to request healing for his sick daughter, who dies while Jesus is en route to heal her, but contrary to all hopes Jesus restores her to life. In Matthew, the little girl is dead at the beginning of the story, and Jairus comes to Jesus asking him to raise her. At the beginning of the story, the Matthean Jairus already has the faith for which the Markan story calls at the end. Nonetheless, remnants of the Markan story remain in Matthew. In Mark, the intercalation of the woman with the hemorrhage interrupts the story and builds suspense, for Jesus is urgently needed before the girl dies. So also, when Jesus and Jairus arrive at the house, the funeral is already underway, as in Mark, though this no longer fits the Matthean story.

— Mark 15:6–13/Luke 23:18–21. Luke has the crowd cry out for the release of the prisoner Barabbas, though he has omitted the Markan explanation that provides the basis for their cry.

— Matthew 20:20–23/Mark 10:35–40. Mark has James and John make a request of Jesus, illustrating their misunderstanding of his teaching about the kingdom of God. Matthew removes the embarrassment by having their mother make the request, but then continues by having Jesus respond not to the mother, but to the disciples, as in Mark.

The cumulative weight of such instances is important for the issue of source analysis. This category of evidence points to the priority of Mark.

Historical Situation Presupposed

In some cases, the historical situation presupposed in Matthew and/or Luke is later than that of Mark. In the apocalyptic discourse Mark 13:5–37, the destruction of Jerusalem and the temple seems to be imminent, to be in progress, or to have just occurred. Both Matthew and Luke seem to look back on the destruction of Jerusalem from some distance, and to rewrite their sources from this perspective (Matt 22:4–8; Luke 21:20–24).

The conflicts between Jesus and the Pharisees in Matthew, especially Jesus' denunciations of the Pharisees, reflect a historical setting some decades later than is the case in Mark (see introduction to Matthew).

Redaction Criticism and Theology

There has been an enormous amount of study of the Gospels relevant to the redaction-critical approach.[31] A few samples, all related to christological issues, will illustrate the explanatory power of the

30. For others, see, e.g., Kümmel, *Introduction*, 61; Stein, *Synoptic Problem*, 70–76. Mark Goodacre, *The Synoptic Problem: A Way through the Maze* (London: Sheffield Academic Press, 2001), 71–76, calls these "editorial fatigue" or "continuity errors" and regards them as the "most decisive indicator" of Markan priority (76), giving several examples.

31. See the bibliographies in Sherman E. Johnson, *The Griesbach Hypothesis and Redaction Criticism* (Atlanta: Scholars Press, 1991) and Peter M. Head, *Christology and the Synoptic Problem: An Argument for Markan Priority*, SNTSMS 94 (Cambridge: Cambridge University Press, 1997).

hypothesis of the priority of Mark. It is instructive to work through a synopsis noting the christological statements, direct and indirect, in each of the Gospels, in each case asking which seems to be primary and which secondary, which direction the current of christological interpretation seems to flow. This is not merely a matter of "simple" to "advanced." Specifically, it is not a matter of an "adoptionist" Christology "developing" to a "higher" Christology. The issue is, which is the more likely to be the basis of the other, which is more likely to be the interpretation of the other, which presupposes which?

"This was to fulfill." A basic conviction of Mark's is that the Christ event is the fulfillment of God's plan as revealed in the Scriptures (e.g., 1:1–4, 15; 4:12; 7:6–7; 8:18; 11:9–10, 17; 12:10–11, 36; 13:24–25; 14:27). On one occasion he has the rudiments of a quotation formula, "let the Scriptures be fulfilled" (14:49). Matthew and Luke also have this conviction that the life and mission of Jesus is the fulfillment of Scripture, which Matthew expresses in a more developed form, including ten "formula quotations" (1:22–23; 2:15; 2:17–18; 2:23; 4:14b–16; 8:17; 12:18–21; 13:35; 21:4–5; 27:9–10). On the 2DH, Matthew has developed the Markan beginnings in a more elaborate and systematic manner, elaborating the single Markan quotation in a programmatic tenfold manner. On the 2GH, Matthew began with this elaborate scheme, which Luke has systematically eliminated, though he agrees with the theology, and Mark has followed Luke, except for preserving an echo of Matthew in Mark 14:49. To most interpreters, it is more plausible that Matthew and Luke elaborated Markan beginnings.[32]

The secrecy motif. In Mark, Jesus' identity is not recognized by the characters in the narrative until the story is over. This is a key element in Mark's narrative strategy, a way of preserving conflicting christological images of Jesus in one story (see §20.1.2). Minimal elements of the secrecy motif are also found in Matthew and Luke, but these are in tension with their respective ways of telling the story, in which Jesus' parents, disciples, and enemies all recognize who he claims to be. The secrecy elements included in Matthew and Luke are difficult to explain except as remnants of Markan theology taken over from their source (e.g., Matt 16:13–20 vs. Mark 8:27–30). Likewise, the places where the secrecy motif is present in Mark but absent in Matthean or Lukan parallels are difficult to explain as Markan insertions (e.g., Mark 6:51–52 vs. Matt 14:32–33; Mark 5:43 vs. Matt 9:26).

The disciples' misunderstanding. It was important to Mark that not even the disciples understand Jesus' true identity before his death, for authentic Christian faith must include the cross and resurrection. Matthew and Luke have other theological and narrative means of expressing this, which allows a more positive picture of the disciples and their understanding to be included in their narratives. Matthew omits, modifies, or offers a supplemental correction for every passage in Mark that pictures the disciples as misunderstanding or failing to understand (e.g., Matt 13:10, 18, 51–52/Mark 4:10, 13; Matt 16:12/Mark 8:21).[33] What is true of the disciples' misunderstanding is also true of the generally negative descriptions of Peter and the disciples in Mark, which are improved in Matthew and Luke (e.g., Mark 8:27–33/Matt 16:13–23/Luke 9:18–22; Mark 10:35–37/Matt 20:20–21). The view that Mark

32. Krister Stendahl's detailed analysis of Matthew's interpretation of the Old Testament concludes that he follows Mark and Q in using the LXX in passages he takes over from them, but Matthew and his school have made their own translation for the formula quotations. This means Matthew must come after Mark and that Matthew and Luke must be independent. The quotation phenomenon "corroborates what has for long been the most generally accepted view [the 2DH]" (Krister Stendahl, *The School of St. Matthew and Its Use of the Old Testament* [Philadelphia: Fortress Press, 1968], 151). See also Robert Horton Gundry, *The Use of the Old Testament in St. Matthew's Gospel: With Special Reference to the Messianic Hope*, NovTSup 18 (Leiden: Brill, 1967), who argues convincingly that Mark does not go through Matthew and select only those quotations with LXX text types, but that the dependence goes the other way. Gundry began his study accepting the priority of Matthew and became convinced of the 2DH in the course of his study.

33. Cf. Gerhard Barth, "Matthew's Understanding of the Law," in *Tradition and Interpretation in Matthew*, ed. Günther Bornkamm, Gerhard Barth, and Heinz Joachim Held, New Testament Library (Philadelphia: Westminster Press, 1963), 105–12.

first developed the motifs of the messianic secret and the misunderstanding of the disciples, which were later interpreted by Matthew and Luke, seems more plausible to most scholars than Mark's imposition of these motifs on the earlier narratives of Matthew and/or Luke.

"Lord" as a christological title. While the title "Lord" (κύριος, *kurios*) was sometimes used simply as an honorary form of address corresponding to English "Sir" (as in Matt 27:63, Jewish address to Pilate; cf. German *Herr,* Spanish *Señor,* French *Seigneur*), in both Judaism and the Gentile religious world it was used as a term for deity. Jews adopted it as a term for God in place of the sacred Tetragrammaton YHWH; Greeks and Romans used it for their gods, including in the emperor cult as a title for the divine Caesar. At a very early period, at least some streams of Christian tradition adopted the word as a christological title for Jesus (e.g., Acts 2:36; Rom 1:7; 10:9; Phil 2:9–11). The Synoptic Gospels manifest the following usage of "Lord" as a title for Jesus: Mark uses the term six times, but never unambiguously for the earthly Jesus (1:3; 5:19; 7:28; 11:3; 12:36–37; [2:28]). The author clearly understands "Lord" as an appropriate title for the exalted Christ (the offstage voice of God so addresses him in 1:3, and see 12:36–37). Yet no one in the narrative calls Jesus "Lord,"[34] nor does the narrator ever refer to him in this manner. Matthew applies this term to Jesus thirty-four times, both in his own compositions and inserting it into Q and Markan contexts. In Mark, the disciples never use "Lord" when they speak to Jesus (e.g., cf. Mark 9:5/Matt 17:4), but in Matthew disciples regularly address Jesus as "Lord" and only unbelievers use "teacher." So also Luke uses "Lord" very often (104 times, in a variety of contexts), referring both to God (e.g., 1:68) and to Jesus (e.g., 2:11). The narrator uses the term of Jesus (e.g., 7:13), and people in the narrative, both disciples and nondisciples, address Jesus as "Lord" (e.g., 9:59; 10:17). To most interpreters, it makes more sense to see Matthew and Luke increasing the use of this christological title and retrojecting the post-Easter insight of the church into their narrative of the life of Jesus, than to claim that Mark later virtually eliminated this usage.

"Son of David" as a christological title. Similarly, Mark appears to have deep reservations about "Son of David" as a christological title, using it only twice, never in a clearly positive sense. He apparently rejected its violent and militaristic overtones. In 12:35 the Markan Jesus uses the Scripture against the scribes to show the problem with this title, and in 10:47 a blind person addresses Jesus with this title—but only before his blindness is healed. The crowds, who, as it turns out, misunderstand Jesus and his mission, refer to the coming kingdom of David that he brings (11:10). This is different in both Matthew and Luke, who use Davidic language of Jesus often and positively (Matthew fifteen times, Luke eleven times), including the insertion of the title into Markan contexts (e.g., Matt 21:9, 15/Mark 11:9–11; Luke 1:27, 32, 69; 2:4, 11). Again, most interpreters find it easier to understand Matthew and Luke as amplifying and reinterpreting Markan usage than Mark filtering out Matthew's and Luke's use of the term, and reinterpreting in a negative sense the few references he retains.

"Son of God" as a christological title. "Son of God" is a key christological title for Mark (1:1, 11; 3:11; 5:7; 9:7; [13:32], 14:62, 15:39 [cf. 12:6]). Yet during the course of the narrative this title is known only to Jesus himself, to God, and to the demons (and to the post-Easter reader), with the characters in the story never recognizing Jesus as Son of God. It is only at the end of the story, in the shadow of the cross, that Jesus acknowledges himself to be Son of God (14:62). Then the crucified Jesus is confessed by a Gentile to be Son of God (15:39). That Jesus' true identity is known only in retrospect, in the light of the crucifixion and resurrection, is a central element of Markan Christology (see on §20.1.2 below). Again, Matthew and Luke reinterpret Mark by retelling the story in such a way that Jesus is known as Son of God to the characters in the story during his earthly life (e.g., Matt 1:18–15; 3:17 [cf. Matthew's "this is" with Mark 1:11 "you are"]; 14:33 [cf. Mark 6:52]; Luke 1:35).

34. The Gentile woman's address in 7:28 is probably to be understood at the narrative level as "Sir," though the post-Easter reader knows to understand it at a more profound level.

Distribution of christological titles. The pattern of how christological titles are distributed within the first three Gospels is also evidence of the priority of Mark and the 2DH. This can be seen by noting the distribution of the variety of titles in the triple tradition, the double tradition, and in each of the categories of Mark's and Luke's special materials. Two examples from the double tradition are evident in Box 26:

1. "Son of Man" is virtually the only christological title in the double tradition (see below). This means that of the numerous christological titles in the Synoptics as a whole, the material common to Matthew and Luke but not in Mark expresses its Christology exclusively in terms of one title. This is readily explainable if the Q materials used only "Son of Man" and retained this characteristic when Matthew and Luke added them to their Markan outline. It is difficult to explain if Matthew had the whole spectrum of christological titles (but with sections totaling about 230 verses in which Son of Man was used exclusively), and Luke adopted them all without mixing other titles into the double tradition sections, and Mark finally excluded only those sections in which "Son of Man" was the exclusive title. Proponents of Matthean or Lukan priority must claim that something like an "invisible hand" guided the evangelists' use of such materials. Unless a cogent explanation is given for this phenomenon, the distribution of "Son of Man"

BOX 26: Son of Man in the Synoptic Gospels

p = present s = suffering, dying, rising c = coming

			Matt	Mark	Luke
1.	Q	p	8:20		9:58
2.	Mk	p	9:6	2:10	5:24
3.	M	c	10:23		
4.	L	p, c?			6:22
5.	Q	p	11:19		7:34
6.	Mk	p	12:8	2:28	6:5
7.	Q	p	12:32	[3:28]	12:10
8.	Q	c	12:40		11:30
9.	M	p	13:37		
10.	M	c	13:41		
11.	M	p	16:13		
12.	Mk	s		8:31	9:22
13.	Q, Mk	c	16:27	8:38	9:2612:8
14.	M	c	16:28		
15.	L	p			[9:56]p v. l.
16.	Mk	s	17:9	9:9	
17.	Mk	s	17:12	9:12	
18.	Mk	s	17:22	9:31	9:44
19.	L	p	[18:11]		
20.	M	c	19:28		

			Matt	Mark	Luke
21.	L	c			18:8
22.	Mk	s	20:18	10:33	18:31
23.	Mk	p	20:28	10:45	
24.	Q	c	24:27		17:24
25.	M	c	24:30a		
26.	Mk	c	24:30b	13:26	21:27
27.	L	c			17:22
28.	Q	c	24:37		17:26
29.	Q	c	24:39		17:30
30.	Q	c	24:44		12:40
31.	M	c	25:31		
32.	M	s	26:2		
33.	L	c			21:36
34.	Mk	s	26:24a	14:21a	22:22a
35.	Mk	s	26:24b	14:21b	22:22b
36.	Mk	s	26:45	14:41	
37.	L	s			22:48 (cf. 14:45)
38.	Mk	c	26:64	14:62	22:69
39.	L	s			24:7

terminology appears to be strong evidence for the 2DH.

2. There are three categories of Son of Man sayings: those that speak of the present life and authority of the Son of Man during the time of Jesus, those that speak of the future parousia of the Son of Man in glory, and those that speak of the suffering, dying, and rising of the Son of Man.

These categories do not mix; for example, of the thirty-nine Son of Man sayings in the Synoptics, not counting parallels, there are none that speak of both his present authority and the suffering, dying, and rising, or of both the suffering, dying, and rising and the future parousia. The sayings appear to have traveled in separate traditional channels. It is noteworthy that the double tradition has only present and future, but no suffering sayings. Neither do the "M" or "L" materials have independent suffering sayings. It thus appears that all the suffering sayings are in Mark or in Matthean or Lukan passages parallel to or derived from Mark. The double tradition has "Son of Man" as virtually the only christological title, yet none of the suffering Son of Man sayings appear in the double tradition. This can be explained on the basis that Matthew and Luke combined Mark and Q and their respective types of sayings, but not on either of the other major theories of Synoptic interdependence.

Exc. 3.5 The Sayings Source Q

The hypothesis that both Matthew and Luke used a second source, now lost, in addition to Mark, is a byproduct of accepting the priority of Mark. On this hypothesis, when Matthew and/or Luke agree with Mark, this is a result of using Mark as one of their sources. When the Markan parallels to Matthew and Luke are thus accounted for, there remains a substantial body of material (ca. 235 verses, about the size of 2 Corinthians) in which Matthew and Luke are parallel in non-Markan passages (=the double tradition). Most scholars are convinced that the most adequate explanation of the data is that Matthew and Luke used, in addition to Mark, a source consisting primarily of sayings of Jesus, thus sometimes called the "Logia" or "Sayings Source."[35] Since the nineteenth century, this lost source has been called "Q" (the abbreviation of the German word for "source," *Quelle*).

The Extent of Q

It is relatively easy to construct a rough-and-ready approximation of this lost source by leafing through a synopsis and collecting those texts in which Matthew and Luke are parallel in non-Markan contexts. This procedure then needs to be refined by

— Eliminating a few passages printed as parallel in some synopses for the sake of convenience of comparison, although there is obviously no literary dependence (e.g., §19, Matt 1:2–17/Luke 3:23–28, "The Genealogy of Jesus").

— Adding pericopes in which Matthew and Luke agree in having the same additional material in Markan pericopes, the "Mark/Q overlaps" (e.g., §191, 8:11–12/Matt 12:38–42/Luke 11:29–32, "The Sign of Jonah").

— Noting that some Q material was inserted by Matthew *or* Luke within a Markan context, which the other has located in a different context. For example, in Matthew 13:16–18, Matthew has inserted material in the Markan parables discourse, which Luke has located in a different context, 10:23–24.[36]

— Assuming that some passages may have been in Q, but either Matthew or Luke omitted them, so they show up as only as Matthean or Lukan special material, not as Matthew/Luke parallels.

Since there is a degree of subjectivity with regard to these four categories, which affects a relatively small percentage of the material, the

35. Some scholars have recently promoted the practice of calling this source the "Sayings *Gospel*," but in terms of literary genre the document was not a Gospel.

36. That Matthew and Luke never insert Q materials into the *same* Markan context is part of the argument for the existence of Q; see below.

reconstruction of Q is not a mechanical process. There is substantial agreement, however, on the contents of Q listed below (see Box 27), though the wording of particular passages must be reconstructed from the differing redactions of Matthew and Luke. The reconstruction is "minimal Q" in terms of pericopes, with questionable passages highlighted in gray.

The Existence of Q

The agreements between Matthew and Luke in non-Markan passages could theoretically be explained in three ways: (1) Matthew knew and used Luke; (2) Luke knew and used Matthew; (3) both used a common source.

Did Matthew Know and Use Luke?

This hypothesis has the advantage that it does not call for Luke's having dismantled the long and carefully composed Matthean speeches and scattered the materials in a variety of contexts (e.g., examine the parallels to Matthew's Sermon on the Mount, Matt 5–7, in a synopsis, and note in how many different Lukan contexts these materials appear). If either Matthew or Luke knew the other, it seems a priori more likely that Matthew would have gathered up scattered sayings than that Luke would have deconstructed Matthew's speeches. Moreover, Matthew sometimes seems to have a later interpretation of an earlier form found in Luke (e.g. Luke 6:20 "poor" vs. Matt 5:3 "poor in spirit"; Luke 6:21 "hunger" vs. Matt 5:6 "hunger and thirst for righteousness"; the short form of the Lord's Prayer in Luke 11:2–4, seemingly elaborated in Matt 6:9–13). The major objection to this view, considered compelling by most scholars, is that the general flow of the tradition is from an earlier Jewish form to a later Gentile form. Since Luke is typically more Gentile than Matthew, if Matthew used Luke as a source, he would have "re-Judaized" materials from the Gentile Luke. As illustrated by the technical commentaries, there are also numerous details in individual texts that pose difficulties for the view that Luke used Matthew as a source. Thus few scholars have ever advocated that Matthew used Luke, and the view has no major advocates today.[37]

Did Luke Know and Use Matthew?

That Luke knew and used Matthew, on the other hand, has been repeatedly argued and is the leading contender against the 2DH.[38] The principal arguments for the view that Luke used Matthew are as follows:

1. *Economy.* A well-known law of logic seems to oppose the Q hypothesis. "Occam's Razor," named after the fourteenth-century scholastic philosopher, is the label popularly given to the "law of economy" or "law of parsimony," that hypotheses are not to be multiplied beyond necessity. Applied to the issue of the existence of Q, the question becomes, "Is Q a *necessary* hypothesis?" This was Farrer's approach, continued by Goulder and others: if the data *can* be explained without resorting to Q, they *should* be. "It [the Q hypothesis] needs no refutation except the demonstration that its alternative

37. Though see Martin Hengel, *The Four Gospels and the One Gospel of Jesus Christ: An Investigation of the Collection and Origin of the Canonical Gospels* (Harrisburg, PA: Trinity Press Int., 2000), 169–85, who argues Matthew used Q *and* Luke, but primarily on the basis of his theory of Gospel titles and chronology, and without offering a detailed analysis of the texts.

38. Recent opposition to the Q hypothesis often cites the classic essay of Austin Farrer, "On Dispensing with Q," in *Studies in the Gospels: Essays in Memory of R. H. Lightfoot*, ed. D. E. Nineham (Oxford: Blackwell, 1955), reprinted in Arthur Bellinzoni, Joseph B. Tyson, and William O. Walker Jr., eds., *The Two-Source Hypothesis: A Critical Appraisal* (Macon, GA: Mercer University Press, 1985), 321–56. The cause was taken up by his student Michael D. Goulder and is argued with precision and vigor in Michael D. Goulder, *Luke: A New Paradigm*, JSNTSup 20 (Sheffield: Sheffield Academic, 1989) and other publications. In turn, Goulder's perspectives are reviewed sympathetically (with some criticisms), developed, and advocated by Mark Goodacre, *Goulder and the Gospels: An Examination of a New Paradigm*, JSNTSup 133 (Sheffield: Sheffield Academic, 1996); *Synoptic Problem*; and *The Case against Q: Studies in Markan Priority and the Synoptic Problem* (Harrisburg, PA: Trinity Press Int., 2002).

BOX 27: Reconstruction of "Minimal Q" Pericopes (with questionable passages highlighted in gray)

Aland§§	*Luke*	*Matthew*	*Pericope Title*
14	3:3, 7–9	3:7–10	John's Preaching of Repentance
16	3:16–17	3:11–12	John's Messianic Preaching
18	3:21–22	3:13–17	The Baptism of Jesus
20	4:1–13	4:1–11	The Temptation
78	6:20–23	5:3, 4, 6, 11, 12	The Beatitudes
79	6:24–26	5:4, 6, 11	The Woes
80	6:27–36	5:39–42, 44–48, 7:12	On Love of One's Enemies
81	6:37–42	7:1–5; 15:14; 10:24	On Judging
82	6:43–45	7:16–20; 12:33–35	"By Their Fruits. . ."
83	6:46–49	7:21, 24–27	The House Built on the Rock
85	7:1–10	8:5–10	The Centurion of Capernaum
106	7:18–23	11:2–6	John the Baptist's Question and Jesus' Answer
107a	7:24–28	11:7–11	Jesus' Witness concerning John
107b	7:31–35	11:16–19	Analogy of Children Playing
176	9:57–60 (61–62)	8:19–22	On Following Jesus
177–179	10:2–16	9:37–38; 10:7–16; 11:21–24	Commissioning the Seventy(-two)
181a	10:21–22	11:25–27	Jesus' Thanksgiving to the Father
181b	10:23–24	13:16–17	The Blindness of the Disciples
182	10:25–28	22:34–40	The Lawyer's Question (The Great Commandment)
185	11:2–4	6:9–13	The Lord's Prayer
187	11:9–13	7:7–11	Encouragement to Pray
188	11:14–23	12:22–30	The Beelzebub Controversy
189	11:24–26	12:43–45	The Return of the Evil Spirit
191	11:29–32	12:38–42	The Sign of Jonah
192–193	11:33–36	5:15, 6:22–23	Concerning Light; the Sound Eye
194	11:39–52	23 passim	Against the Pharisees and Lawyers
196–198	12:2–12	10:26–33, 12:32	Exhortation to Fearless Confession
201–202	12:22–34	6:25–33, 6:19–21	Anxieties about Earthly Things
203a	12:39–40	24:43–44	Watchfulness and Faithfulness: the Thief
203b	12:42–46	24:45–51	Watchfulness and Faithfulness: the Returning Lord
204–205	12:51–56	10:34–36; 16:2–3	Division in Households
206	12:57–59	5:25–26	Agreement with One's Accuser
209–210	13:18–21	13:31–33	Parables of Mustard Seed and Leaven
211	13:23–30	7:13–14, 22–23; 8:11–12; 19:30; 20:16; 25:10–12	Exclusion from the Kingdom
213	13:34–35	23:37–39	The Lament over Jerusalem
215	14:11, 18:14	23:12, 18:4	Teaching on Humility
216	14:16–24	22:2–10	Parable of the Great Supper
217	14:25–27	10:37–38	The Conditions of Discipleship
218	14:34–35	5:13	Parable of Salt
219	15:4–7	18:12–14	Parable of the Lost Sheep
224	16:13	6:24	On Serving Two Masters
226a	16:16	11:12	The Kingdom Suffers Violence
226b	16:17	5:18	Concerning the Law
227	16:18	5:32	Concerning Divorce
229	17:1–2	18:6–7	Warning against Offenses
230	17:3–4	18:15, 21–22	On Forgiveness
231	17:5–6	17:20	On Faith
235	17:22–37	24:23, 26–28, 37–41, 10:39	The Day of the Son of Man
266	19:12–27	25:14–30	The Parable of the Pounds
313	22:28–30	19:28	Precedence among the Disciples and the Reward of Discipleship (=12 Thrones)

[Luke used Matthew] is *possible*."[39] While it is true that hypotheses should not be invented arbitrarily and needlessly, and that every proposed solution should make logical sense, the Synoptic Problem is not a problem of logic but of history. The issue is not what is logically possible, but the most probable explanation of the data.[40] Still, "dispensing with Q" has been attractive because it seems to avoid hypothetical documents. Yet all history is a matter of constructing hypotheses (see above, §9.2.1). All theories of the formation of the Gospels (and other New Testament writings) posit source materials we no longer have. Whichever Gospel was written first depended on lost sources. Much of the early Christian writing referred to or assumed in our extant literature has been lost (see, e.g., 1 Cor 5:9; Col 4:16, and, until recently, the *Gospel of Thomas*). The strength of the argument from economy is only apparent, for the price of dispensing with Q is either the postulation of a number of other lost sources to account for Matthean and Lukan material not in Mark or (as in the case of Goulder) arguing that all the non-Markan material in Matthew and Luke was invented by the final authors themselves.

2. *The Minor Agreements.* If Matthew and Luke independently used Mark and Q, they should often agree with each other in both Mark and Q passages, but should only rarely agree with each other *against Mark in passages in which they are parallel to Mark.* Both used Mark, but neither knew what the other was doing with Mark, so agreements against Mark should be only rare and coincidental. In fact, however, there is a relatively large number of such "Minor Agreements" (MAs).[41] Examples are the numerous instances where Matthew and Luke agree in having δέ (*de*, but) or another conjunction for Mark's repeated καί (*kai*, and), and more substantial (but less numerous) MAs such as πᾶσαν τὴν περίχωρον τοῦ Ἰορδάνου (*pasan tēn perichōron tou Iordanou,* all the region about the Jordan, Matt 3:5/ Luke 3:3; missing from Mark 1:5), and most famous of all, τίς ἐστιν ὁ παίσας σε (*tis estin ho paisas se,* who is it that struck you? Matt 26:68/ Luke 22:64; missing from Mark 14:65).

The MAs constitute the strongest objection to the simple version of the 2DH, whose defenders have labored mightily to explain them without modifying the theory.[42] Within the framework of the 2DH, proposals to account for the MAs have appealed to (1) independent redaction of Mark by Matthew and Luke (e.g., the many changes of Mark's "and" to some other conjunction), (2) textual assimilation of Luke to Matthew or vice versa, (3) the continuing influence of the pre-Gospel oral tradition, (4) Luke's use of Matthew in addition to Mark

39. Farrer, "Dispensing with Q," 62, emphasis mine.

40. When the issue is transferred from the classroom to the courtroom, which deals in historical events, not logical neatness, the issue is not "*Could* the accused have done it," but the entirely different question, "What is the evidence that he in fact *did* it?" If the evidence is compelling that the accused could have done it, the question of whether he actually did it remains to be answered on the basis of historical evidence, not logical possibility. More apropos the Synoptic Problem: when looking at a completed house (or document), the question is not whether one carpenter (or author) *could* have constructed/composed it, but in fact how many did. The Synoptic problem is not an abstract puzzle to be attacked with neat logic, but a messy concrete problem of dealing with a concrete historical phenomenon.

41. One often reads "about 1,000" in the literature on the problem, but the number depends on how they are defined, and on which Greek manuscripts constitute the basis of the analysis. The most detailed analysis is given by Frans Neirynck, *The Minor Agreements of Matthew and Luke against Mark with a Cumulative List* (Leuven: Leuven University Press, 1974). On the problems of the issue in general, with detailed examination of a test case (concluding that the 2DH offers the best explanation of the data), see M. Eugene Boring, "The Synoptic Problem, 'Minor' Agreements and the Beelzebul Pericope," in *The Four Gospels 1992-Festschrift Frans Neirynck*, ed. Frans van Segbroeck et al., BETL (Leuven: Leuven University Press, 1992), 1:586–620 and M. Eugene Boring, "The 'Minor Agreements' and the Synoptic Problem," in *New Oxford Studies in the Synoptic Problem*, ed. Andrew Gregory et al. (Oxford: Oxford University Press, 2010), 227–52.

42. E.g., Burnett Hillman Streeter, *The Four Gospels: A Study of Origins*, rev. ed. (London: Macmillan, 1930), 293–331, and the essays by Tuckett and Neirynck in Georg Strecker, ed., *Minor Agreements: Symposium Göttingen 1991*, GTA 50 (Göttingen: Vandenhoeck & Ruprecht, 1993).

and Q, and/or (5) Matthew and Luke having used an edition of Mark slightly earlier (Ur-Markus) or later (Deutero-Markus) than the canonical edition.[43] Most scholars are convinced that a combination of these reasons offers a satisfactory solution to the MAs on the basis of the 2DH, but the problem has not been completely resolved.

The arguments for Luke's use of Matthew are not persuasive to most scholars, who also find the arguments against it to be compelling:

1. *Lukan omissions.* If Luke knew Matthew, explanations must be given for the Lukan omission of the huge amount of Matthean material he does not take over, or for which he substitutes other accounts (e.g., Matt 1–2: genealogy, birth story, flight to Egypt and return; various Matthean stories and teachings one would think congenial to Luke, such as 25:31–46; Matt 28:8b–10 resurrection appearances prior to Galilee). In particular, *the absence in Luke of Matthew's modifications of Mark* must be accounted for. Matthew repeatedly edits Mark by modifying the Markan text (e.g., the heavenly voice at Jesus' baptism: Mark 1:11, "You are my beloved Son" addressed to Jesus becomes "This is my beloved Son," addressed to John and/or the crowds in Matt 3:17). There are dozens of such redactional modifications in Matthew, but Luke always has the Markan form, without the Matthean alterations (apart from the Minor Agreements). So also, Matthew frequently adds material to his Markan text, as Jesus' blessing to Peter in Matthew 16:17–19 (cf. Mark 8:29–30) and the series of "fulfillment quotations" added to Markan contexts such as Matthew 4:14; 8:17; 12:17–21; 13:35; 21:4–5; 26:56. Luke never incorporates or reflects any knowledge of these Matthean additions. When incorporating Markan texts into his Gospel, Luke seems to have known only Mark, not Matthew's revisions of Mark.

   Likewise, on the FGH, Luke's omissions of distinctively Matthean elements in his non-Markan materials is difficult to explain. One example: δίκαιος (*dikaios*, righteous) and related words (righteousness, justice, justify, right, rightly) are important and common words in both Matthew (twenty-six times) and Luke (nineteen times Luke and twelve times Acts). Luke takes over this word when it occurs in Mark, as did Matthew (Mark 2:17/Matt 9:13/Luke 5:32). Yet in the non-Markan passages in Matthew containing the δίκαιος word group, the word is almost always absent from the Lukan parallel, including all the six instances in Matthew's Sermon on the Mount. Furthermore, Luke omits the δίκαιος terminology from the double-tradition texts Matthew 13:17 and 23:35. Even in such a triple tradition text as Matthew 27:19, where Matthew's addition to Mark includes his favorite word δίκαιος as a characterization of Jesus, the word is absent from Luke, though δίκαιος is Luke's favorite expression for Jesus as the suffering righteous one, especially in the passion narrative. Luke has added δίκαιος to Markan or Matthean contexts in Luke 10:29; 12:57; 14:14; 15:7; 16:15; 18:20, and three times in the crucifixion scene (23:41, 47, 50). These purported omissions of a favorite Lukan word found in Matthew are readily explicable on the view that Matthew has added the word to Q or Mark and Luke, who had not seen Matthew, has not; they are difficult to explain as Luke's omissions from Matthew.

2. *Lukan modifications.* If Luke knew Matthew, explanations must be given for Luke's industrious rearrangement, that is, deconstruction, of the grand compositions of Matthew such as the Sermon on the Mount. The materials in Matthew 5–7 appear in the following locations and order in Luke: 6:20–23; 14:34–35; 8:16; 16:16–17; 12:57–59; 16:18; 6:29–30; 6:27–28; 11:1–4; 12:33–34; 11:34–36, 16:13; 12:22–32; 6:37–42; 11:9–13; 6:31; 13:23–24; 6:43–49. Similar scattering of Matthew's extended coherent

43. For discussion and evaluation of Deutero-Markus as a significant factor in explaining the MAs, see Folkert Fendler, *Studien zum Markusevangelium* (Göttingen: Vandenhoeck & Ruprecht, 1991), "Deuteromarkus—die erste Bearbeitung des Markusevangeliums? Eine Analyse der minor agreements in den synoptischen Evangelien," 147–94.

collections into a variety of contexts would have to be posited for Matthew's mission discourse (9:36–10:42), parable discourse (13:1–58), discourse on church order (18:3–35), and eschatological discourse (23:1–25:46). The editorial and compositional procedure that Luke would have used in omitting and modifying Matthean material has seemed incomprehensible to most scholars.[44]

Evidence for the Existence of Q

The strength of the Q hypothesis is partially a matter of negative evidence, that is, the difficulties involved in seeing either Matthew or Luke having used the other as a source. There is also positive evidence that Matthew and Luke used a second common source in addition to Mark:

1. *Arguments from order and coherence.* The non-Markan material in Matthew and Luke is presented above in the Lukan order. Q researchers agree that, in general, Luke has preserved the original order of Q more closely than Matthew, who has rearranged it considerably. Thus Q texts are now commonly designated by their Lukan location, for example, Q 11:2–4 = Luke 11:2–4/Matt 6:9–13. This does not mean that the materials as presented in Box 27 represent the original structure of Q, but only a rough approximation. Even so, a coherent document emerges that begins with the preaching of John and the baptism and temptation of Jesus, is followed by the Great Sermon of Q 6:20–49, then by other clusters of sayings, and concludes appropriately with an eschatological discourse. Cogent arguments have been made that other, more subtle and precise substructures can be detected within the overall outline.[45] Yet even the rough outline still present in the Lukan order shows that the Q materials were not a random collection of sayings, but a coherent composition—more so than the somewhat analogous collection in the *Gospel of Thomas*, which we now know to have existed.

   Two other phenomena of order also point to the existence of Q. Matthew and Luke naturally agree on the initial placement of the Q materials regarding the preaching of John and the baptism and temptation of Jesus. But after the temptation story Matthew and Luke never agree in placing a section of Q material into the same Markan context. This is an astonishing fact on any theory, and strong support for the view that Matthew and Luke make independent use of the Q materials. It is difficult to explain on either the 2GH or the FGH, both of which must account for Luke's having gone through Matthew and extracted every Q section from its Matthean context, where it often fits very well, and placed it in a different context relative to Mark, where its appropriateness is not so apparent. Good explanations can be given, however, for the editorial procedure of both Matthew and Luke if they were independently using Mark and Q (see introductions to Matthew and Luke, respectively).

2. *The older form.* A hard-line application of the 2GH or FGH would mean that in the double tradition Matthew should always have the earlier form, and that the interpreter should be able to give redactional reasons for Luke's changing Matthew. In practice, the 2GH often argues that in some places Luke appears to have the earlier form, and thus "must have" had another source alongside Matthew, that is, something very like the Q hypothesis the theory supposedly

44. To be sure, if one is already convinced that Luke used Matthew, then explanations can be given for why he might have done so, as in the extensive arguments of Allan J. McNicol, David L. Dungan, and David Peabody, *Beyond the Q Impasse: Luke's Use of Matthew; A Demonstration by the Research Team of the International Institute for Gospel Studies* (Valley Forge, PA: Trinity Press Int., 1996); Goodacre, *Case against Q*, 81–104; Goodacre, *Synoptic Problem*, 123–28. Such discussions do not constitute arguments that Luke actually used Matthew.

45. See, e.g., Arland D. Jacobson, *The First Gospel: An Introduction to Q* (Sonoma, CA: Polebridge, 1992), chap. 4, "The Literary Unity of Q: Form Critical and Thematic Coherence."

rejects.[46] Goulder's defense of Luke's use of Matthew argues Luke had only Mark and Matthew, so the Lukan form must necessarily always be the later form. To most scholars, it appears that in the double tradition it is sometimes Matthew and sometimes Luke who has the earlier form—which calls for their independent redaction of a common source. Some texts where Luke seems to have the earlier form: the Beatitudes, Luke 6:20–23/Matthew 5:3–12; the Lord's Prayer, Luke 11:2–4/Matthew 6:9–13; the eschatological sayings, Luke 17:26–30/Matthew 24:37–39.

3. *Doublets.* See above, Exc. 3.4. The existence of doublets, and their distribution (at least 9 in Matthew, at least 8 in Luke, only 1 in Mark) is not only an argument for the priority of Mark, but evidence of the existence of Q. On the 2DH, Mark and Q sometimes had varying versions of the same saying or incident, called "Mark/Q overlaps." Matthew and Luke each made various choices or combinations of these two documents, resulting in the complex textual phenomena of our present texts. The most familiar examples are the accounts of *John the Baptist and Jesus' baptism* (§13, Matt 3:1–6/Mark 1:2–6/Luke 3:1–6 and Matt 11:10/Luke 7:27) and the *Beelzebul controversy* (§§117–18, Matt 12:22–37/Mark 3:22–30/Luke 11:14–15, 17–23; 12:10; 6:43–45).[47]

4. *Analogous genres: wisdom and prophecy.* It was once thought strange to posit as circulating in early Christianity a document such as Q is supposed to have been. It was deemed particularly difficult to think of a document composed primarily of sayings of Jesus and a minimum of narrative. Yet after the rediscovery of the *Gospel of Thomas* among the Nag Hammadi codices in 1945, we have solid evidence of such sayings collections. The similarity is real but should not be exaggerated, for there are also important differences. Both *Thomas* and Q are primarily sayings material, yet Q, unlike *Thomas*, is not a random collection of individual sayings. The Q material is arranged into larger complexes of speeches and has a modicum of narrative, with the whole arranged into a coherent composition. Some scholars see Q as analogous to collections of Jewish wisdom sayings.[48] Others see an even closer parallel to the Old Testament prophetic books: a document that begins with a brief narrative of the prophet's call and testing and continues with eschatological oracle-like sayings, with a small amount of narrative.[49] We know that early Christianity experienced a rebirth of prophecy. Prophetic figures, inspired by the Spirit, spoke in the name of the risen Lord, both creating new sayings of the risen Jesus and re-presenting and modifying traditional sayings as the contemporary address of Jesus to his church (e.g., Matt 23:34; 28:16–20; Mark 13:11; John 16:12–15; Acts 11:27; 13:1; 15:32; 21:9–10; Rom 12:6; 1 Cor 11:4–5; 12:28–29; 14:1–39; 1 Tim 1:18; 4:14; Rev 2–3 and passim). Q may well represent the deposit of such a stream of early Christianity. In any case, it is no longer problematic to locate a document such as Q is supposed to have been within the life of the early followers of Jesus, or to imagine a document that combined wisdom and prophecy.

46. See, e.g., William R. Farmer, "Reply to Michael Goulder," in *Synoptic Studies: The Ampleforth Conferences of 1982 and 1983*, ed. Christopher Tuckett, JSNTSup (Sheffield: Sheffield Academic, 1984), 107

47. For an analysis of this text as evidence for Mark/Q overlaps, see M. Eugene Boring, "The Unforgivable Sin Logion Mark 3:28–29/Matt 12:31–32/Luke 12:10: Formal Analysis and History of the Tradition," *Novum Testamentum* 17 (1976): 258–79.

48. So especially James M. Robinson, "LOGOI SOPHON: On the Gattung of Q," in *Trajectories through Early Christianity*, ed. James M. Robinson and Helmut Koester (Philadelphia: Fortress Press, 1971), 71–113 and John S. Kloppenborg, *The Formation of Q: Trajectories in Ancient Wisdom Collections*, Studies in Antiquity and Christianity (Philadelphia: Fortress Press, 1987).

49. Streeter, *Four Gospels*, 291–92; Richard A. Edwards, *A Theology of Q: Eschatology, Prophecy, and Wisdom* (Philadelphia: Fortress Press, 1976); Boring, *Sayings of the Risen Jesus*, 137–82; Migaku Sato, *Q und Prophetie* (Tübingen: Mohr, 1988); Richard A. Horsley and Jonathan A. Draper, *Whoever Hears You Hears Me: Prophets, Performance, and Tradition in Q* (Harrisburg, PA: Trinity Press Int., 1999).

Q and Early Palestinian Christianity

Despite the uncertainties and ambiguities related to using Q as a source for early Christianity, the following may be said with a reasonable degree of confidence:

— The existence of Q as a structured literary composition shows that early Palestinian Christianity already had prophetic teachers who preserved, reformulated, and expanded the message of Jesus as the word of the exalted Lord to the new situation after Jesus' death.

— Q seems to have been composed in *Greek*, showing that some streams of Palestinian Christianity used the Greek language as their primary medium of communication (see on the Hellenists, §7.4.2).

— The Q disciples understood themselves in continuity with both John the Baptist and Jesus (see Q 7:27).[50] While they had a high regard for John as the last and greatest prophet of the old era, they understood Jesus as the exalted, transcendent Son of Man, virtually the only christological title in Q (ten times).[51] As Son of Man, Jesus had been on earth as God's representative, teaching and living out the true will of God, had suffered and died, had been taken to the heavenly world, and would soon come in glory as the eschatological judge. Jesus' death is seen as integral to his mission, as in the Deuteronomistic view of the prophets, but is not given soteriological importance. While resurrection terminology is not specifically used, God vindicated Jesus after his death, taking him into the heavenly world, perhaps on the model of Enoch, Elijah, or the suffering righteous man of Wisdom 5:1–8.

— The Q community understood itself as called to confess their faith in Jesus as Son of Man, and as persecuted because of this confession (Q 6:22; 12:8).

— The Q disciples affirmed the Torah as God's revelation, considered tithing and ritual purification to be valid expressions of the faith when not done superficially (Q 11:39–42; 13:34–35), but understood Jesus to be the sovereign interpreter of the Torah. The Q tradents were thus in tension and conflict with the understanding of the Law advocated by the Jewish leaders and teachers (Q 16:16, a new era in relation to the Torah began with Jesus). Purity was a matter of inner disposition, not externals (Q 10:41). The temple had been abandoned, was no longer the place of divine presence and atonement (Q 13:34–35).

— The Q disciples understood themselves as sent by God, like the prophets of Israel, John the Baptist, and Jesus himself (Q 6:23; 10:2; 12:2–9), and, like them, as empowered by the eschatological Holy Spirit (Q 12:10–12). As Jesus had worked miracles and performed exorcisms, so did his disciples, working in his power and authority. As Jesus had spoken by the power of the Holy Spirit, so his prophetic disciples continued to speak his word in the power of the Spirit.

— Like John and Jesus, the Q disciples had carried on a mission to Israel, proclaiming its understanding of Jesus, Law, and temple, and like them, had been rejected. Their opponents regarded their claims to empowerment by the Holy Spirit as blasphemous, an expression of satanic power (Q 11:14–23 [reading Luke's Spirit as in Q]). They pronounced woes on the Galilean cities that had rejected them (Q 10:12–15).

50. I use "Q disciples" to represent the group that composed and utilized Q, without prejudice to whether or not it was a distinct "Q Community" within, alienated from, or even opposed to what became mainstream Christianity. The prophetic and scribal teachers who composed Q used μαθηταί (*mathētai*, disciples) as their self-designation (see Q 6:20, 40; 10:2 [Matt]; 11:39 [Matt]; 14:26, 27).

51. "Christ" and "Lord" are not used at all of Jesus. Only the devil calls Jesus "Son of God" (Q 4:3). "Son" in the absolute sense is used by the heavenly voice in Q 3:21 at Jesus' baptism, and by Jesus himself in Q 10:21–22. In Q 7:19–23 Jesus is implicitly identified with "the one who is to come."

— The rejection by "this generation" of Israel, the new interpretation of Law and Temple, and the use of the Greek language all indicate a radical openness to Gentiles. Jewish leaders are criticized (Q 11:37–54); the faith of the centurion is praised as surpassing anyone in Israel (Q 7:1–9; 13:23–29).

— The faith of the Q disciples in Jesus as the Son of Man had caused divisions within families (Q 12:49–53; 14:26–27) and had generated conflicts, not only between them and the Jewish religious leaders, that led to indictment and condemnation before the courts, leading to suffering and even death (Q 11:47–51; 12:11–12; cf. John 9:1–41). Q gives us a window into the opposition and conflicts faced by some of Jesus' disciples in the first decades after his death and resurrection.

Current Issues in the Study of Q

The great majority of scholars believe that Matthew and Luke used Q in the composition of their respective Gospels, but once the existence of Q is posited, it is subject to the same critical questions as other early Christian documents. An introductory book such as this cannot discuss all the issues, but only list them. Among the questions that continue to be disputed are these:[52]

Written? Was Q a single coherent document, or does it represent a stratum of oral tradition? Majority opinion: Written.

One document, or several? Was there a single coherent Q, or only a number of smaller q's? Majority opinion: Single document, though Matthew and Luke probably had slightly different recensions.

Original language? Majority opinion: Greek.

Contents? There are relatively minor differences among the numerous reconstructions of Q (see Box 27, representing the majority opinion), but substantial agreement on its main content.

Singly attested? Are there materials found only in Matthew or Luke that should also be ascribed to Q? Majority opinion: Yes, but not often.

Sequence and wording? When Matthew and Luke disagree in the wording or sequence of Q texts, which should be preferred? Majority opinion: The original order of Q is typically better preserved in Luke, the original wording often better preserved in Matthew, but the content, order, and wording of Q must be decided from case to case, on the basis of several criteria.

Markan overlap? Did Q overlap Mark at points? Majority opinion: Yes, but not often.

Genre? Assuming Q was a document, to which literary genre did it belong? Majority opinion in North America: "Sayings of the Wise," or "Sayings Gospel," that is, collection of wisdom sayings; majority opinion in Europe: prophetic-apocalyptic text, though the distinction between wisdom and prophecy is not absolute.

"Gospel"? Was Q a "Gospel"? This depends on definition; in terms of literary genre, Q belongs to a different genre than the canonical Gospels.

Authorship? Majority opinion: Not by a single author, but represents the work of Christian scribes/prophets.

Date? Majority opinion: Sometime prior to Matthew and Luke, that is, 50–70 CE. Since Q was apparently not a stable document, but an expanding collection of materials, it may have had pre-50 and post-70 versions.

Provenance? Majority opinion: Galilee or southern Syria, though some see it as representing Jerusalem Christianity or elsewhere.

52. For detailed discussions, see Kloppenborg Verbin, *Excavating Q*, presenting not only his own views but surveying the debate and providing extensive bibliography. By risking to designate "majority" views, I am merely providing my own impression, giving more weight to the dominant voices in the discussion, not tabulating a numerical majority, and without any presumption that the majority is always right.

Stratification? Majority opinion: There are earlier and later layers of tradition in Q, but it is questionable whether they can be identified with any confidence.[53] Positing the existence of Q does not necessarily represent a claim to chart the prehistory of the document. Efforts to identify the composition history of the Gospel of John provide a cautionary note on attempts to delineate the earlier strata of Q (see below, §27.3). In the Fourth Gospel, we have a finished text. While there is widespread agreement that the present text of John developed in redactional stages, there is little agreement in identifying them. The problem is compounded with Q, where the text itself must first be reconstructed.

Social setting? Can the Q disciples (Q community/Q group) be constructed from the Q text? Majority opinion: Q represents a particular tradition or group within the variegated history of first-generation Palestinian Christianity (see above, §9.2.2). The relation of this group to what became mainstream Christianity is unclear. For some scholars, Q represents the original Jesus movement that continued Jesus' lifestyle and social critique after his death, by disciples of Jesus who did not affirm the resurrection and saw no salvific significance in his death, and who were alienated from what became the Christian church. Other scholars regard Q as one expression of Christian faith within the emerging early church that had other, kerygmatic and more christological and ecclesiological documents, so that it is historically adventurous to construct a Q community on the basis of one hypothetical document. Some argue that the history and character of the Q community can be correlated to the presumed layers in Q, so that the history of the community that produced it can be constructed in some detail. Other scholars agree that the group or groups behind Q were likely a developing, changing community, but that the details of this history cannot be constructed. Thus, while most agree that Q sheds light on pre-70 Palestinian Christianity/ Jesus movement, methodology and results are very disputed.

Theology? Can we speak of a "theology of Q"? Majority opinion: We can, but the numerous studies have come to differing conclusions, especially as to whether Q presupposed the kerygmatic theology of Jesus' death/resurrection that becomes dominant, or represents an alternative to this theology. It seems to be clear, however, that the teachers who compiled/composed Q regarded Jesus as the Son of Man who had exercised divine authority during his time on earth, who had presented the definitive interpretation of the will of God by his exposition of the Torah, who had been exalted to heaven, and who would return shortly to judge the world by this standard.

Literary contacts? What is the relation of Q to other literature, in and out of the canon? Majority view: Q was known to Matthew and Luke, but not to Mark (otherwise, it is argued, Mark would have included more of it). For an alternative view, see introduction to Mark below (§21.3). Were the Q sayings known in the Pauline and other Gentile churches outside Palestine? Majority opinion: No.

Historical value? How historically accurate are the materials Q transmits? What is the relation of Q to the historical Jesus? Majority view: The earliest layer of Q preserves elements of Jesus' own preaching, but it is difficult to construct.

53. Kloppenborg, Robinson, and others speak of two main redactional layers, the earlier primarily Cynic-like wisdom and the later prophetic and eschatological, with a final small layer composed of the (baptism and) temptation story. Other scholars, such as Athanasius Polag, *Die Christologie der Logienquelle*, 1. Aufl., WUNT 45 (Neukirchen-Vluyn: Neukirchener Verlag, 1977), likewise sees two main stages in the redactional development of Q, but reverse the order: the prophetic, apocalyptic stratum was earlier, with the scribal, wisdom layer coming at the end. Heinrich Schürmann, "Zur Kompositionsgeschichte der Redenquelle: Beobachtungen an der lukanischen Q-Vorlage," in *Der treue Gottes trauen: Beiträge zum Werk des Lukas; Für Gerhard Schneider*, ed. Claus Bussmann and Walter Radl (Freiburg: Herder, 1991), 325–42, has a four-stage process in the composition of Q; Burton L. Mack, *The Lost Gospel: The Book of Q & Christian Origins* (San Francisco: HarperSanFrancisco, 1993), 203–4, lists five stages.

Fate? What happened to Q? Majority opinion: "Lost," that is, dropped out of use after being incorporated in Matthew and Luke. Perhaps more likely "suppressed," that is, deemed dangerous and/or inadequate by developing mainstream Christianity (like the *Gospel of Thomas*).

Importance? Does positing the existence of Q matter? Majority opinion: Yes. Whether or not Q existed matters for constructing the original message of Jesus, for insight into the development of early Christianity, and for interpretation of the Gospels.

Is the Synoptic Problem Solved?

Every proposed solution to the Synoptic Problem falls short (and always will fall short) of absolute certainty. Here are some historical factors that keep equally competent, open-minded scholars of good will from coming to the same results:

1. We do not have absolutely precise texts to work with. Our texts of the Synoptic Gospels are reconstructions from the ancient manuscripts, no two of which are alike. Such reconstruction is inevitably theory-laden. It is thus true we do not have Q, but only our best efforts at reconstructing it. It is also the case that we do not have Matthew, Mark, or Luke, in any absolute sense, but only our reconstructions of their text from the plethora of available manuscripts (cf. above, §3). There is no one text of Matthew, Mark, or Luke to work with, and the (relatively slight) differences between the available manuscripts of each of the Gospels become important when comparing minute similarities and differences (see the "Minor Agreements" discussion earlier in this section).

   In the ancient world, the texts of the Gospels were basically stable, but not absolutely so. It is certain, for example, that the Gospel of Luke and the book of Acts went through at least one minor revision, for we have two distinct forms attested in our manuscripts (see introduction to Luke–Acts). This means that the copy of Mark used by Matthew was not exactly the same as that used by Luke, and that neither was exactly the same as our (reconstructed) text of Mark. To be sure, there is a vast difference between the task of reconstructing the lost document Q from Matthew and Luke and the task of reconstructing the lost original text of Matthew and Luke from the large number of differing manuscripts, but there is a significant analogy between the two projects.

2. The oral tradition, and its variations, did not evaporate when the tradition was written down by the evangelists and their sources, but continued to interact with the written texts. In any given pericope contained in their sources, both Matthew and Luke may have had one or more versions of the oral tradition that influenced one or both of them more than the written forms of Mark and Q available to them.[54]

3. All this means that the complex historical process must be taken into consideration in discussing the Synoptic Problem (and all other problems of New Testament introduction). Our Gospels are the product of a community, not only of a few individual authors/editors working with precisely defined texts.

Thus the view accepted and represented in this book is that the 2DH is our best working hypothesis, but should be seen in a context where documents and authors/editors were utilizing somewhat unstable versions and editions of both Mark and Q, while interacting with continuing oral tradition. Some documents may not have been composed in their present form all at once but may have gone through more than one edition. Such a view makes the most sense of the data and

54. Although no modern text of the English Bible has "forgive us our trespasses as we forgive those who trespass against us," many people have this traditional wording in their memory as a result of the oral tradition passed along in the liturgy, and if asked to copy Matt 6 or Luke 11, might well—intentionally or unintentionally—insert the oral form into their copy although all their written texts had another form.

is the most helpful approach in grasping the theological meaning of the texts themselves, but it will always be open to both objection and refinement. The standard diagram often presented in introductory textbooks is thus helpful in representing the main lines of the formation of the Gospels, but it is too neat, should not be thought of in a scissors-and-paste manner.

This is the typical diagram, with all its clarity and rigidity:

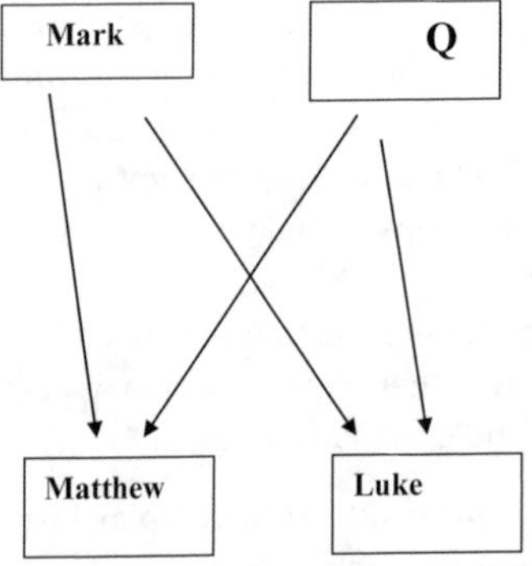

One should rather think of a flexible and dynamic diagram with curved and interwoven connecting lines, all floating in a sea of oral tradition:

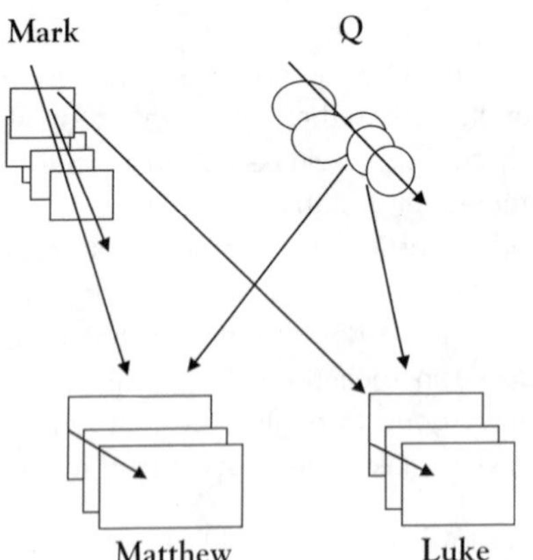

Such a perspective would envision the formation of the Gospels not as scissors-and-paste desk work, but the continuing reinterpretation of the gospel in the life of the church.

Exc. 3.6 A Suggested Procedure for Marking Synoptic Gospel Parallels In *Synopsis of the Four Gospels*[55]

The basic tricolor scheme: Mark/Matthew = blue; Mark/Luke = black; Matthew/Luke = red

1. Underline in blue the parallels between Matthew and Mark. Underline in both Matthew and Mark. Use solid, unbroken lines where the parallels are exact, word for word, and the words are in identical order.

2. Where the same word is used in both Gospels, but in different forms (e.g., one has present tense, other has past; or, one has singular, other has plural; or one has noun, other has verb of same word), underline in broken lines.

3. When the same words are used, but not in the same order, underline the relevant words, but do not connect the lines, leaving spaces between the words not in the same order.

4. Be careful to note transpositions of material. That is, Matthew may have some of the same words as Mark, but not in exactly the same place within the pericope. These too should be marked and noted.

5. When you have finished marking all the Matthew/Mark parallels, do exactly the same with the Luke/Mark parallels, using black. This will mean that some places in Mark will be underlined twice, once in blue for Matthew/Mark parallels, once in black for Matthew/Luke parallels.

55. See also Mark Goodacre's six-color method, which is more complex but also more objective (Goodacre, *Synoptic Problem*, 33–34). His suggested scheme: Matt: *blue*; Mark: *red*; Luke: *yellow*; Matt Mark: *purple*; Matt+Luke: *green*; Mark+Luke: *orange*. For students who wish mainly to study the Synoptic Problem and who want the maximal clarity in visualizing the phenomena of the text, not seen through the lens of a particular theory, Goodacre's is a helpful procedure. The simpler tricolor scheme suggested above allows the interpreter to see all the data of the text in the light of the dominant theory, without excluding the visibility of data that challenge the theory.

Those with double underlining in Mark will represent the *triple tradition*.

6. In non-Markan pericopes, for example, Aland § 14, mark all Matthew/Luke parallels in red, the *double tradition*.
7. After you have marked all the Matthew/Mark and Luke/Mark parallels, go back over the pericope and see if there are any agreements of Matthew and Luke that do not come from Mark (the Minor Agreements). Mark these Matthew/Luke agreement in red. Note common additions and places where both Matthew and Luke have a different form of the same word as in Mark, Matthew and Luke having the same form. These could be noted with red parentheses around the words concerned, since they will already have been underlined in steps 1–5 above.

When completed, you should be able to read down the Matthew column and see exactly where Matthew is identical with Mark (blue underlining) and where it is identical with Luke (red underlining).

You should be able to read down the Luke column and tell exactly where Luke is identical with Mark (black) and where with Matthew (red, *double tradition*).

You can also tell, by reading down the Mark column, what material is used by Matthew (blue), what by Luke (black), what by both (both blue and black=*triple tradition*).

In each case, material peculiar to each Gospel remains without underlining.

The analysis could now be transferred to an English Bible or Greek New Testament, making clear at a glance the literary connections of every word in the Gospels.

19.5 For Further Reading

General Studies of the Gospels

Boring, M. Eugene. *The Continuing Voice of Jesus: Christian Prophecy and the Gospel Tradition*. Louisville, KY: Westminster John Knox Press, 1991.

———. *Sayings of the Risen Jesus: Christian Prophecy in the Synoptic Tradition*. SNTSMS 46. Cambridge: Cambridge University Press, 1982.

Bultmann, Rudolf. *The History of the Synoptic Tradition*. Translated by John Marsh. New York: Harper & Row, 1963.

Dibelius, Martin. *From Tradition to Gospel*. New York: Scribner, 1935.

Gerhardsson, Birger. *Memory and Manuscript: Oral Tradition and Written Transmission in Rabbinic Judaism and Early Christianity*. Translated by Eric J. Sharpe. ASNU 22. Uppsala: Uppsala University Press, 1961.

Koester, Helmut. *Ancient Christian Gospels: Their History and Development*. Philadelphia: Trinity Press Int., 1990.

———. *From Jesus to the Gospels: Interpreting the New Testament in Its Context*. Minneapolis: Fortress Press, 2007.

Stuhlmacher, Peter. *The Gospel and the Gospels*. Grand Rapids: Eerdmans, 1991.

The Synoptic Problem and Q

Bellinzoni, A., J. B. Tyson, and W. O. J. Walker, eds. *The Two-Source Hypothesis: A Critical Appraisal*. Macon, GA: Mercer University Press, 1985.

Farmer, W. R. *The Synoptic Problem: A Critical Analysis*. New York: Macmillan, 1964.

Goodacre, M. *The Case against Q: Studies in Markan Priority and the Synoptic Problem*. Harrisburg, PA: Trinity Press Int., 2002.

———. *The Synoptic Problem: A Way through the Maze*. London: Sheffield Academic Press, 2001.

Gregory, A., D. A. Foster, J. S. Kloppenborg, and J. Verheyden, eds. *New Oxford Studies in the Synoptic Problem*. Oxford: Oxford University Press, 2010.

Kloppenborg, J. S. *Q Parallels: Synopsis, Critical Notes, and Concordance*. Sonoma, CA: Polebridge, 1988.

Kloppenborg Verbin, J. S. *Excavating Q: The Historical Setting of the Sayings Gospel*. Minneapolis: Fortress Press, 2000.

Neirynck, F. "Synoptic Problem." In *The New Jerome Biblical Commentary*, edited by Raymond E. Brown, Joseph A. Fitzmyer, SJ, and Roland E.

Murphy, 587–95. Englewood Cliffs, NJ: Prentice-Hall, 1990.

Robinson, J. M., P. Hoffmann, and J. S. Kloppenborg, eds. *The Critical Edition of Q: Synopsis including the Gospels of Matthew and Luke, Mark and Thomas with English, German, and French Translations of Q and Thomas*. Hermeneia. Minneapolis: Fortress Press, 2000.

Stein, Robert. *The Synoptic Problem: An Introduction*. Grand Rapids: Baker, 1987.

Streeter, B. H. *The Four Gospels: A Study of Origins*. Rev. ed. London: Macmillan, 1930.

Tuckett, C. M. *The Revival of the Griesbach Hypothesis: An Analysis and Appraisal*. SNTSMS. Cambridge: Cambridge University Press, 1983.

Tuckett, C. M., ed. *Synoptic Studies: The Ampleforth Conferences of 1982 and 1983*. JSNTSup 7. Sheffield: Sheffield Academic, 1984.

20
Mark and the Origin of the Gospel Form

THE CREATION OF THE GOSPEL GENRE AND the formation of the Gospels was the most important turning point in the history of early Christian literature.[1] It is not obvious or inevitable that the Gospel form should have developed at all. The composition of the first Gospel was an innovation only gradually accepted by what became mainstream Christianity. There is no indication that the Christian community in Rome, during the period when it was becoming the leading church in the empire, accepted Gospels into their collection of normative Christian documents until well into the second century. One reason for the hesitant reception of the Gospels is that the reading of narratives of Jesus' life and teaching did not already have the accepted slot in Christian worship that had become standard by virtue of reading the Pauline letters and other letters in the Pauline tradition alongside the Scriptures. It is likely that another, theological reason played a role as well: narratives focused on a miracle-working, divine man Jesus were too easily misunderstood in docetic terms, and difficult to reconcile with the epistolary focus on the cross and resurrection.

1. Some of the following is dependent on M. Eugene Boring, "The Birth of Narrative Theology: The Gospel of Mark," in *Chalice Introduction to the New Testament*, ed. Dennis E. Smith (St. Louis: Chalice Press, 2004), 136–51, and M. Eugene Boring, *Mark: A Commentary*, NTL (Louisville, KY: Westminster John Knox Press, 2006), 1–25, where it is explicated in more detail.

20.1 What Is a Gospel? The Problem of Genre

WHEN READERS OR HEARERS OF THE FIRST century heard the Gospel of Mark (which was not yet called a "Gospel" or attributed to "Mark"), what set of expectations did they bring with them? What did they suppose they were reading? The options would have included myth, history, biography, memoirs, and romance (fiction, novel).

Students of the New Testament have not reached a consensus on the question of the Gospel genre. Numerous conflicting and overlapping designations have been made, several of which seem to have grasped some distinctive or essential element of the nature of the genre, but none has won a majority vote from exegetes, historians, or scholars of ancient or modern literature.[2] The debate is many-sided, but the issue may be helpfully focused by posing the issue as

2. I have catalogued thirty-seven different designations of the Gospel genre in the academic discussion of the last century, several of which I will simply list here for effect, without documentation or elaboration: history, myth, prophecy, parable, parable-myth, apocalypse, aretalogy, Christian Passover Haggadah, lectionary, tragedy, tragicomedy, passion narrative with extended introduction, Socratic dialogue, extended apophthegm, political apologetic, eschatological memorabilia, story of the suffering righteous man of the Wisdom literature, commentary on the kerygma, parabalized biography, midrash, apocalyptic history, clumsy construction, Hellenistic novel, encomium, theodicy about creation and recreation, Hellenistic biography (*bios*).

a choice between the two most prominent candidates: *Hellenistic biography* (*bios*) or *new literary genre*. Assuming Mark to be the earliest Gospel, the question may be posed by asking whether Mark adopted an existing genre or created a new one.

20.1.1 Was Mark a Biography of Jesus?

It is now everywhere acknowledged that the Gospels are not biographies in the modern sense. The Gospels do not give us a description of Jesus' appearance or his psychological development, nor do they relate the events of his life in accurate chronological order. However, recent decades have seen a resurgence of the view that the Gospels were biographies in the ancient Hellenistic sense, belonging within the genre of βίοι (*bioi*, lives).[3] An early advocate of this point of view was Clyde Votaw, who saw striking parallels between the first-century career of Jesus as presented in the Gospels and the career of Socrates four centuries earlier, as presented by the writings of his disciples:[4]

1. Each was representative of the highest conscientiousness, intelligence, aspiration, and purpose of his nation.
2. Each regarded himself as appointed by God to a special mission for the uplift of his people and as continually guided by God to its performance.
3. Their public careers had a common function—to inaugurate a new standard of conduct, to replace the current morality with a superior type of moral thought and practice.
4. Both pointed out the defects of the commonly accepted standard and the un-ideal conduct of the national teachers and leaders.
5. Both held aloof from the institutions and classes of the social order, working in an unattached and single-handed way, reaching the public through a direct personal relationship and appeal.
6. Their ministry was without charge. Neither was a paid professional.
7. Each attached to himself a number of close followers, who absorbed his message and exhibited its proper influence.
8. In due time, they found themselves in open conflict with the public authorities and met violent death at their hands.
9. Each came to be viewed as the founder of a movement, which their disciples carried forward, organized, and expanded.
10. Successive generations revered them, made use of their messages, and perpetuated their memory.

When said like this—I have mostly quoted Votaw verbatim in these ten points—Jesus and Socrates do look a lot alike, and the Gospels do resemble Hellenistic *bioi*.

Not only did the careers and deaths of Jesus and Socrates have striking parallels; the writings of their disciples after their deaths had striking parallels. Here is my summary of his points:

1. In each case, the master had not written out his teaching or biography, but had taught orally.
2. In each case, disciples sought to carry on the teaching of their martyred teacher and to tell his story in writing.
3. In each case more than one disciple did this. The leading authors who sought to continue Socrates' story and teaching were Plato and Xenophon.
4. Their biographers were similar in the motives that inspired them: to restore and refurbish the reputation of their teacher, who had been put to death by the state as a dangerous person, but

3. Among the influential books advocating this point of view are Charles H. Talbert, *What Is a Gospel? The Genre of the Canonical Gospels* (Philadelphia: Fortress Press, 1977); Richard A. Burridge, *What Are the Gospels? A Comparison with Graeco-Roman Biography*, SNTSMS 70 (Cambridge: Cambridge University Press, 1992).

4. Votaw, *Biographies*, 30–62.

whose contribution to human welfare must be preserved.

5. Their respective writings were similar in their contents: memorabilia of their respective teacher's significant sayings, deeds, and personal traits.

There are thus significant features of the Hellenistic *bios* important for interpreting the Gospels. The Gospel of Mark and later Christian Gospels were probably more like the *bios* than any other available genre, so that many of their first readers may well have begun their reading or hearing of Mark with the supposition that they were reading a Christian example of this genre devoted to Jesus.

Distinctive Elements in the Gospel Genre

In the ancient world no one ever referred to the Gospels as "biographies." In terms of literary genre, the Gospels do not fit easily within any category already known to the Hellenistic world. This does not mean that they were absolutely unique. Communication requires some recognition in terms of known genres. However, to communicate, what is expressed need not be expressed *within* known genres, but only expressed *in relation to* them. Thus to claim that the Gospel was a new Christian creation does not mean that it had no relation to previous genres. Even when it is argued that Mark created a new genre, no one claims that it was a *creatio ex nihilo*. Perhaps the most fruitful approach is not to ask, in yes-or-no categories, whether the Gospel is a *bios*, but to note the distinctive features that distinguish it from other contemporary narrative literature.

Kerygma. Mark and his successors are kerygmatic compositions, centered on the act of God in the Christ event, not—in contrast to the *bioi*—on the "essence" or "character" of Jesus. Mark is not mainly concerned with presenting a series of anecdotes that communicate "what sort of person" Jesus is, but telling the story of *Jesus* in a way that communicates the saving act of *God*. Jesus appears in almost every scene in the Gospels. Yet the story is not about Jesus per se, but about Jesus-as-the-Christ, the one in and through whom God acts. There is a real sense in which the Gospels are not about Jesus, but about God. The cultic act of proclamation of the gospel in the context of the Christian worship service distinguishes it from the *bioi*, which were not composed for this setting and function.

Composed of kerygmatic units of tradition. The sayings and stories of which the Gospels are composed have not been gathered from random sources and memories, but have been filtered through the life of the community. Each unit of tradition had already functioned with its own kerygmatic and didactic purpose to proclaim and instruct. Before being placed in the narrative literary context of the Gospel, each little story or saying had functioned as something of a mini-Gospel that made its own theological statement, which would often include a perspective on Christology and the meaning of discipleship. The Gospel form is a combination of small traditional units, so that the Gospel as a whole appears to be somewhat episodic, but not merely anecdotal. The episodes are not strung together piecemeal, but in terms of overarching themes.

Anonymous, community production. Hellenistic *bioi* were published under the name of the author; all the Gospels were originally anonymous. Though composed by authors with specific theological perspectives and didactic intentions, they were not literary creations in the Hellenistic sense, by individuals who could be cited by name. The form critics referred to them as *Kleinliteratur* ("small-caliber writing") as opposed to *Hochliteratur* (high-class literature, *belles lettres*), literature considered as a fine art. That the Gospels were folk literature does not mean that they grew naturally out of the oral tradition. The Gospels, beginning with Mark, were written as intentional, creative acts by theological authors drawing from the tradition of the Christian community, not by writers interested in selling books or in their own literary reputation. Yet they did not begin their work on the basis of generally available folk traditions or investigation into public archives or private letters and diaries, but with the kerygmatic tradition of the Christian community.

Definitive segment of universal salvation history. The Gospels do not tell the story of Jesus as the account of a great individual. The Gospel of Mark is a narrative intercalated into a larger story, the macronarrative from creation to consummation, with the Christ event as the defining center. The Gospel narrates a segment of a comprehensive line that extends from creation to eschaton. This is different from a biography. Jesus is not pictured as a "great man," but as the Christ. The Christ is the one sent by God at the climax of history to establish God's kingdom. History is seen in eschatological perspective, with the Messiah sent as the fulfiller and redeemer of history. Since the "life of Jesus" is portrayed as the definitive segment of the line of redemptive history, the story of Jesus is not related as complete in itself. Within history, within one life, the meaning of the whole of history is disclosed, an advance picture of the eschatological victory of the kingdom of God. This is fundamental to the confession "Jesus is the Christ." The kind of narrative appropriate to this confession is the Gospel.

This is in sharp contrast, for example, to the understanding of the life of Socrates in the Greek *bioi*. The Socrates event was not seen and could not have been seen as the ultimate event of universal history ruled by one sovereign God; there is not and could not be any soteriological, kerygmatic use of the Socrates story. The plot line of the Gospel is eschatological and christological, which is necessarily lacking in the Greek biographies. Thus the structuring principle of the Gospel is not the "life of Jesus," but "who Jesus is in the plan of God." The Gospel narrative insists that it cannot be understood in and of itself. Its meaning depends on the events and expectations that precede it and on the history that follows it.

Simultaneity, fusion of horizons. The figure of Jesus in the Gospels is portrayed simultaneously as a historical figure of the past and a transcendent figure of the present, both "back there" in history and "up there" in the heavenly world, as well as "out there" in the church and the world. This is the literary consequence of faith in God's act of raising up Jesus, so that the past events of Jesus' life and teaching are all seen and heard in the perspective of the resurrection faith. This, too, contrasts with Hellenistic *bioi* such as the lives of Socrates. While Socrates was thought to be an immortal who survived death, who lived on in the other world after death, and whose memory continued to serve as a guide to his disciples, this was an entirely different thing from the early Christians' faith in the resurrection of Jesus. Jesus' disciples believe not merely that Jesus has survived death, but that he has been *resurrected*, that is, that he has been exalted to a new order of being, that he has been made Lord of the universe, that he is the beginning and guarantee of the eschatological event, and that his life continues in a real sense as the presence of God, the presence of the Holy Spirit active in the community of Christian believers. In the *bioi*, the story of the hero is told in order to keep his memory alive. In the Gospels, Jesus is alive independently of the story, and continues to act and speak in the world of the reader. Thus the Jesus of the Gospels speaks past the stipulated audience in the narrative, speaking over their heads to the implied reader in such a way that the there-and-then story recounted in the pre-Easter framework becomes contemporary with the here-and-now experience of the post-Easter reader. Such a way of composing a story depends on the resurrection faith of the early Christians, and has no parallel in the Hellenistic *bioi*.

This fusion of temporal horizons also reflects the biblical perspective on history. Early Christian teachers such as Mark are acquainted with biblical narratives in which the past becomes contemporary. As in the Pentateuch Moses speaks from within the narrative but from a postexodus perspective, so in the Gospels Jesus speaks from within the pre-Easter narrative with a post-Easter perspective (see explicitly Deut 5:1–5; 9:1–29, and the modulation from past report to present address and confession in Deut 26:5–11). In the Gospels, the story is told in such a way that the Jesus of the narrative always tends to become contemporary with the reader.[5]

20.1.2 The Gospels as Narrative Christology

All the distinctive features discussed above are aspects of a single category: Christology. The Gospels are essentially christological texts, expressing in narrative form the themes that had already become important in authentic Christian confession, and that would later be elaborated in the classical creeds and confessions: the true deity and humanity of the Christ, the Christ event as the definitive act of God in universal history, the historical figure who is at the same time the resurrected Lord. Without claiming that "narrative Christology" is a literary genre, it has become common to use this term to characterize the essential features of the Gospels.[6] In particular, two features of Gospel narrative Christology are expressed in Mark's creative composition: (1) God's saving act in the Christ event is communicated by the tensive juxtaposition of two conflicting portrayals of the figure of Jesus. (2) These two images of the life of Jesus are combined in one narrative by means of the secrecy motif.

5. Cf. the concepts of "contemporaneity" and "the disciple at second hand" developed by Søren Kierkegaard, *Philosophical Fragments or A Fragment of Philosophy* (Princeton, NJ: Princeton University Press, 1962), 68–142.

6. E.g., Robert C. Tannehill, "The Gospel of Mark as Narrative Christology," *Semeia* 16 (1980): 57–96; Helmut Koester, *Ancient Christian Gospels: Their History and Development* (Philadelphia: Trinity Press Int., 1990), 292; Brown, *Introduction to the New Testament*, 103. The concept is splendidly fine-tuned in Elizabeth Struthers Malbon, *Mark's Jesus: Characterization as Narrative Christology* (Waco, TX: Baylor University Press, 2009), 1 and passim.

Tensive Juxtaposition of Two Contrasting Views of Jesus

Adopting the pattern established by Mark, the Gospels combine two prior modes of thinking and speaking about the Christ event. On the one hand, Jesus is presented as a human being who suffers and dies a truly human death at the hands of his oppressors. In this, he is like Socrates. On the other hand, Jesus is also presented as a divine being, the Son of God filled with miraculous power, able to overcome all human problems, including death. This is in contrast to Socrates, who works no miracles, just as it is in contrast to Apollonius of Tyana, who works miracles but is not a truly human being (see above, §9.2.2). A distinctive characteristic of the Gospel genre is that it juxtaposes these two modes of christological confession, uniting the vulnerable human Jesus and the powerful Son of God in one tensive narrative.[7]

Kenosis Christology: The Weakness and True Humanity of Jesus

A major stream of early Christian theology presented Jesus as a truly human being who shared human weakness, who truly suffered and died a human death. We have seen that Paul insists on the reality of Jesus' death as essential to the saving event, and does not hesitate to speak of Jesus' "weakness" (2 Cor 13:4). This does not mean, of course, that by human standards Jesus was a weakling, but that he fully participated in the weakness of humanity as such (see, e.g., on the classical passage Phil 2:5–11 above). The deity of Christ was seen as belonging to his transcendent life in the heavenly world before or after his earthly life, which was empty of divine power and was not characterized by miracles. This emptying is represented by the Greek term κένωσις (*kenōsis*, see Phil 2:7).

7. For elaboration, see M. Eugene Boring, *Truly Human/Truly Divine: Christological Language and the Gospel Form* (St. Louis: CBP Press, 1984); Boring, *Mark*, 248–58 and passim.

Prior to Mark, some of the stories and sayings attributed to Jesus portrayed the life of Jesus in nonmiraculous ways.

— *Epistolary literature*. All the epistolary literature accepted into the New Testament followed this Pauline pattern of kenosis Christology (e.g., Heb 2:5–18).

— *The birth and boyhood stories of Matthew 1–2 and Luke 1–2*. The attention of modern readers is so quickly drawn to the miraculous phenomena surrounding Jesus' birth that they may fail to notice the shocking character of telling of the *birth* of a divine being. Babies are weak, helpless, and vulnerable. In contrast to the novelistic stories of the superboy Jesus later found, for instance in the *Infancy Gospel of Thomas*, the miraculous power displayed in the birth stories of the Gospels is not the superhuman power of Jesus, but the power of *God*; the infancy and boyhood of Jesus are devoid of miracle stories. (see below on Luke 2:41–52).

— *The Q temptation story of Matthew 4:1–11/Luke 4:1–13*. In its present contexts in Matthew and Luke, this story is included in a narrative with many of Jesus' miraculous deeds. But in the oral, pre-Gospel period when this story circulated as a separate unit of tradition, the story assumes that Jesus did not do miraculous deeds such as changing stones to bread or defying the law of gravity by leaping from the temple. Taken by itself, the story may assume that Jesus *could* have done these things, but insists that he *did* not do them, and that choosing the option to do them was a demonic temptation.

— *Mark 8:11–13, Matthew 12:38–42, Luke 11:29–32*. Again, these stories and sayings are presently included in the framework of the Gospel narrative along with numerous miracle stories. But taken by themselves, as they circulated in the pre-Markan tradition, they picture a nonmiraculous life of Jesus. In Mark 8:11–13, Jesus categorically refuses to do any sign. In Luke 11:29–32, Jesus declares that the only sign to be given is the sign of Jonah, who preached God's message, but worked no miracles. Matthew or the form of tradition used by him interprets the sign of Jonah to refer to the resurrection as the only sign. In either case, the life of Jesus was empty of the powerful deeds of divinity, and the only sign would be the act of God in raising him from the dead.

The kenosis Christology affirmed that God acted in Christ for human salvation, but pictured the life of Jesus as truly human, with God's saving act occurring at its extremities of Jesus' life, at the incarnation and the resurrection. This christological pattern became the basis of the classical creeds, which proceed from "born of the Virgin Mary" to "crucified under Pontius Pilate," with no intervening picture of a powerful, miracle-working Son of God. Such a Christology can picture the life of Jesus as fully sharing the human situation and dying a truly human death, but cannot portray the saving act of God by recounting incidents in the life of Jesus. This is the Christology assumed by all the New Testament letters.

Epiphany Christology: The Life of Jesus as a Manifestation of the Saving Power of God

"Epiphany" means "manifestation," a revelation or making obvious. In the Hellenistic world, "epiphany" was commonly used for the manifestation of the power of a god. Thus the Hellenistic king Antiochus Epiphanes, for example, was so called because he claimed, as did many Oriental rulers, to be a manifestation of the deity. "Epiphany Christology" is thus a term used to describe that kind of thinking about Jesus that interpreted his ministry as filled with manifestations of divine power. During the period of oral tradition between Jesus and the Gospels, each miracle story was an expression of epiphany Christology. In this Christology, the basic Christian affirmation that God has acted in Christ for our salvation was pictured in such a way that each miracle story became a miniature

Gospel that portrayed the saving act of God in the Christ event as a whole.

In the pre-Markan tradition, one way the church confessed its faith in God's saving act was to tell a story in which some fundamental human need is pictured, a story in which life is threatened or already lost. Into this situation strides Jesus, the mighty Son of God, who is not helpless in the face of human need. He acts, by his divine power, to deliver us from that which is robbing us of life. The situation of need and the deliverance are pictured in this-worldly terms, since they are portrayed as scenes from the earthly ministry of Jesus, but each story points beyond the particular situation of a few people in Galilee in 30 CE to the human situation generally, and to God's act in Jesus to deliver human beings from the tyranny of that situation. Although the stories deal with ordinary needs, it is humanity's ultimate salvation that is pictured, and ultimate deliverance to eternal life of the kingdom of God that is proclaimed.

Mark, and the pre-Markan tradition, identified "salvation" with "life." In Jesus' encounter with the rich young man in 10:17–31, for instance, the terms "be saved" (10:26), "enter the kingdom of God" (10:25), and "eternal life" (10:17) are all used to mean the same thing: the goal of all humanity's searching and striving, fulfillment of life. In such expressions, the adjective "eternal" is not simply a quantitative term when it modifies "life," to mean "live forever and ever," but is a qualitative modifier: "eternal life" is life as it was meant to be, the life of the age to come when God has destroyed all the threats to genuine living, life that is "really living." Thus Mark can sometimes simply equate "enter the kingdom of God" with "enter life" (9:43, 45, 47). To receive salvation, to "be saved," is to receive the gift of life from God, to have all the threats to life overcome, to be saved from the enemies of life that rob it of being really life:

Deliverance from the enemies of life: hunger (Mark 6:30–44; 8:1–10). Modern Western well-fed folk, who are calorie-conscious and worry about obesity as a social problem, may have to work at remembering that for most human beings for most of human history, hunger has been the constant threat that keeps life from being what it should be. Hunger is a monster that, even when it does not succeed in literally destroying life physically (which has happened and is happening to more humans than most of us can imagine), perverts life into a subhuman scratching about for the next meal. Hunger transforms human beings who were created to love and be loved into creatures competing with each other for bare existence that is not life. In the stories of Jesus miraculously feeding the multitudes, Jesus overcomes this enemy; people sit down to eat with each other in the presence of plenty, give thanks for it, and share food and fellowship. Thus some of Israel's pictures of ultimate salvation portrayed the messianic banquet (Isa 25:6–8), a great feast at the end of history when all God's people sit down together around a great table at which there is food and fellowship for all—life indeed!

Deliverance from the enemies of life: demonic power (Mark 5:1–20). Even modern folk with a scientific mentality are often aware that our lives are lived in a larger context sometimes dominated by forces hostile to human life that we are powerless to resist. When a fragile human life is up against it, the cosmos takes on a demonic aspect. To many modern people, it is the very impersonality of the universe that is threatening. There is no use pleading with the flood, there is no bargaining with the storm, no rituals affect the path of the tornado. In the ancient world, this feeling was very personal, and people felt they were in the grip of an evil something more powerful than they were. In the exorcism stories, Christian preachers told of God's act in Christ as delivering life from this oppressive demonic reality.

Deliverance from the enemies of life: sickness (Mark 1:29–34, 40–45; 2:1–12; 3:1–6, 7–12; 7:31–37; 8:22–26; 10:46–52). The many healing stories in the Gospel tradition portray the saving event as the restoration of health. Sick people experience sickness as robbing them of life as it was meant to be. Just as salvation, *salus*, means health or wholeness, so sickness is the representative of death, death's leading edge. In the miracle stories Jesus steps into this situation, usually at his own initiative, and performs the healing act of God. It would be a mistake to understand the healing stories as allegories of the ultimate human situation, as though the persons in the stories were not sick people but only ciphers for sick humanity. But it would also be a mistake to hear the stories as mere reports of what the individual faith healer Jesus once did for some sick Palestinians who were fortunate enough to be sick in his geographical and temporal vicinity. The early church preserved and retold these stories because they pointed beyond themselves. They somehow pictured that saving event that has been accomplished by God for humanity as a whole. According to the Christian gospel, God overcame the enemies of life by acting for us in Christ, an act that gives us life, even if we are sick our whole life long.

Deliverance from the enemies of life: death (Mark 5:21–43). Death is the enemy of life, the ultimate enemy (1 Cor 15:26). This is seen clearly in the death of a twelve-year-old. To impress this upon us with poignant clarity, Mark has taken two miracle stories and inserted one into the other.

A little girl lies dying. It is the death of hope, the death of joy. Her father, a religious man, a man of faith, believes that Jesus can heal her. Good news! He finds Jesus, who agrees to come. Shattered hope is reborn. If only they can get there in time! While there is life, there is hope.

They are stopped! No, worse than that. Jesus has stopped voluntarily for a sick woman. But there is no need to stop, actually; she has already been healed, just by the surreptitious touch of his garment as he went by. But why is there delay now, with the mother of the little girl looking down the road, wondering if he will get there in time? Anyway, this woman has put up with her malady for years and could come and be healed on any other day. Why this palaver? Jesus must get there before it is too late. Then comes the message from back home: "Your daughter is dead. Why trouble the teacher any further?" Why indeed?

There is no way to express the tragedy of the death of a twelve-year-old girl. But what is already infinite is magnified in this case by the realization that it could have been prevented. If not by us, by God, if there is a God who hears the prayers of twelve-year-old dying girls. "Your daughter is dead; why trouble the teacher any further?" But whether said with anger or resignation, it is logical and reality-accepting. However, Jesus ignores it (5:36) and leads the way to the girl's house. Amid the jeers of those mourners who easily switch from wailing to heckling, he pronounces those words that only God can pronounce at the last day: "Little girl, I say to you, arise." Even when it's too late, it's not too late.

Even if the preachers of such stories, and their hearers, believed that they literally happened, the issue is not whether or not Jesus raised a little girl from the dead once upon a time in Galilee, but whether God raised Jesus from the dead once for all time in Jerusalem. The individual miracle story was told as a way of communicating the good news of God's act in the grand miracle of the Christ event. Thus stories of Jesus' forgiveness of individuals (Mark 2:5–7) proclaimed God's forgiveness in the event of Jesus Christ. Stories of calming storms (Mark 4:35–41) and walking on the water (Mark 6:45–50) proclaimed the God who had acted in the Christ event as Lord over all natural phenomena, another way of proclaiming Paul's message that there is nothing that can separate us from the love of Christ, even if we must go down with the ship (cf. Rom 8:37–39).

The Conflict of Christologies

The faith of Paul, who focused on the suffering and death of Jesus, and the faith of those who told miracle stories about Jesus was the same faith that God had acted in Christ for our salvation. There was a deep-seated conflict, however, between the ways they expressed this faith, that is, in the respective Christologies involved, the way they each portrayed the earthly life of Jesus. Same faith, different theologies; the theologies clash. The weak human Jesus and the powerful divine Jesus seemed mutually exclusive, and indeed they were if each supposed it was speaking about the literal reality of the life of Jesus of Nazareth. He could not have *been* both ways (history). But he could be legitimately thought of and spoken of in both ways (theology). There is no perfect theology. Each Christology had its advantages and disadvantages.

The *kenosis Christology* is able to portray the life of Jesus as an utterly human identification with the weakness of humanity and to present his suffering and death as real and salvific. It insisted that no one can come to authentic faith apart from the cross and resurrection. So kenosis Christology could not tell stories of people who became Christian believers during Jesus' earthly life. It cannot portray the saving power of God as effective in the life of Jesus, must wait until the story is over, and must present the Christ event in mythological terms on a cosmic stage in order to proclaim that God was active in the life and death of Jesus. If the story is not narrated in cosmic terms, the significance of Jesus is reduced to that of a prophet or martyr like other "great men," but such a Jesus cannot be the definitive revelation of God. Some early Christians continued to tell the Jesus story only in this way. The later church rejected this approach, labeling it the heresy of Ebionism: Jesus was a great human being, but not the Son of God.

The *epiphany Christology*, on the other hand, can tell powerful stories from the life of Jesus that communicate God's saving act. Such stories were told as events within the pre-Easter framework of Jesus' life but were told in the light of the Easter faith, by and for post-Easter believers. The cosmic powers that threaten human life are presented as the concrete realities of everyday existence, in a way recognizable in our common life: sickness, hunger, natural disasters, death. In the kenosis Christology of Paul and his successors, there was hardly any reason to narrate the words and deeds of the earthly Jesus, but in the epiphany Christology, the story of Jesus' life on earth can be told in such a way that God's saving power is manifest. However, there is a problem: the Jesus of such miracle stories could not be presented as sharing the frailty of human existence. It is difficult to imagine the Jesus who heals the sick as himself being sick. Can the Jesus who raises the dead really die? This became the crucial question. A Son-of-God Jesus who walks on the water could come down from the cross if he wanted to (Mark 15:29–32). This is the commonsense logic of the miracle stories, and the options seemed to be that he was not the Son of God or that he did not really suffer and die. Ebionism chose the former option; Docetism chose the latter. In the docetic Christology represented by several of the Christian texts not accepted into the New Testament canon, Jesus was Son of God and so must have only appeared to die.

As the later church rejected Ebionism as heretical, so it rejected Docetism. In the pre-Gospel period, advocates of each Christology considered the other to be the enemy. Though each Christology had advantages and disadvantages, each way of thinking about the Christ event rejected the other as inadequate and distorting the meaning of the Christ event. In the latter half of the first century CE, teachers of the Christian faith were faced with the issue of whether these two Christologies were simply alternatives between which Jesus' followers must choose. Or was there a way to preserve the theological values of each approach?

The Markan Affirmation of Both Christologies

The author of the Gospel of Mark saw the values of each of these theological approaches and included both of them in his narrative. The first half of his narrative represents primarily the powerful divine Jesus of the epiphany Christology, the second half primarily the vulnerable human Jesus of the kenosis Christology.

On the one hand, the Markan Jesus shares the weakness and true humanity represented by the kenosis Christology. A few sample texts:

— 1:9; 10:18. Jesus is in solidarity with sinful human beings. Our first glimpse of Jesus in the Gospel of Mark is of one who has come from Nazareth in Galilee to stand in the same line with sinful human beings who are waiting to be baptized by John "for the forgiveness of sins" (1:4). In 10:18 the Markan Jesus responds to the flattering accolade "Good Teacher" with "Why do you call me good? No one is good but God alone" (10:18). The later Gospels rewrite these texts to make it clear that Jesus himself was not involved in human sin (see, e.g., Matt 3:13–17; 19:17). Mark has no such compulsion.

— 1:35; 6:46; 14:32–42. Jesus prays. Human beings pray to God in praise and gratitude, but especially in acknowledgment that they cannot live out of their own resources, that they are dependent on God's power to sustain their lives. Divine beings do not pray. Especially the Gethsemane scene portrays Jesus' human weakness (Mark 14:32–42). Barely in control, on the verge of panic, reflecting not only the depth of suffering of a human being who shudders on the threshold of torture and death, but also the numinous terror of the eschatological, transcendent nature of what is about to transpire, a sorrow and anguish so intense it already threatens his life, desiring human companionship in his time of need (vv. 34, 37), Jesus fell to the ground and cried out to God in prayer (v. 35).

— 2:16; 3:21; 4:38; 5:30; 9:16, 21; 11:12–14; 13:32; 14:44. Jesus gets hungry, eats, gets tired, sleeps, asks questions, is surprised, is considered deranged by his family. He doesn't look like a god. At his arrest, Judas must point him out.

— 3:6; 8:31; 9:31; 10:33–34; chaps. 14–15. Jesus dies. Death is the common denominator of all human existence. The Markan Jesus shares with all other human beings this defining characteristic of human life. More: not only does he die, he is killed. He goes willingly to his death, but he is passive, not in control. He is betrayed, denied, questioned, tried, convicted, abused, and killed, but others are the actors. Like ourselves, he is the victim, engulfed by the circumstances.

If we had only this collection of texts from Mark, it would never enter our minds to think of the earthly life of Jesus in any other way than as a thoroughly human person, differing from ourselves only in the quality of his obedience to God and in his love for his fellow human beings. This is the kenosis Christology of the epistles, and it is indispensable to Mark. But alongside of and interwoven with these images, Mark also affirms stories of Jesus in which, with divine power, he overcomes all the enemies that threaten human life. He miraculously feeds the hungry, casts out demons, heals the sick, calms the storm, walks on the water, raises the dead.

Mark sees the values of each way of proclaiming the act of God in the human being Jesus and is thus confronted by a problem not faced by any author of Hellenistic *bioi.* How can the portrayal of the powerful Son of God be combined in one narrative with the humanly weak Jesus of Nazareth? How could the Messiah accomplish divinely powerful deeds and not be recognized as the Son of God until after the cross and resurrection?

Mark's response to this problem was to take the elements of secrecy and misunderstanding that were already resident in various elements of the stories about Jesus and to develop them into a comprehensive means of presenting the whole story of the Christ event: Jesus had done the miraculous saving acts during his earthly life as pictured in the epiphany Christology, *and* God's saving act in him had not been recognized until after the story was over, as called for by the kenosis Christology. Mark constructs the paradoxical narrative of "secret epiphanies" that allows him to tell the story of Jesus in such a way that the saving power of God is already manifest in his earthly life, but that his true identity could not be grasped until after the cross and resurrection.[8]

The secrecy motif is woven into the narrative throughout. Here are some examples:

— 1:1. From the very first line, Mark's audience knows who Jesus really is. They know something the participants in the story do not know. It is a device for explaining why the characters in the pre-Easter story did not recognize Jesus for what he really was, and it presupposes that this recognition came only after the resurrection.

— 1:9–11. When Jesus appears for the first time in the narrative, there has been no birth story or supernatural phenomena by which his identity is disclosed to his parents, the magi, or shepherds, nothing by which the characters in the story might recognize him. Thus John the Baptist does not identify him as the Mighty One he has predicted, and baptizes him without a word. In Mark, the address of the heavenly voice is only to Jesus: "You are," not "This is." The readers overhear the declaration from heaven that Jesus is the divine Son, but no one in the story does (cf. Matt 3:17).

— 1:24, 34; 5:7, 9. The demons, by supernatural knowledge, know who Jesus is, so he commands silence. Too late! They have already disclosed the secret. But in 1:27 this disclosure seems to have had no effect at all. The crowd is still ignorant of Jesus' true identity and asks, "What is this?" This tension in the narrative is our first hint that the secrecy motif may be a later overlay on the original story. So again, the disclosure is to the audience, not the persons in the story.

— 1:44. After healing the leper, Jesus insists that he tell no one.

— 2:12. After Jesus claims to have the divine power to forgive sins, demonstrated by his healing the paralyzed man, the crowds, still in ignorant mystification, do not identify Jesus.

— 3:7–12. In 2:1–3:6, Mark takes over and reworks a cluster of materials that have apparently already congealed in the pre-Markan tradition. In this cluster of traditions, Jesus functions publicly with an authority that he claims to be divine. Mark edits this cluster of traditions, imposing his own editorial patterns upon it, but the publicity motif of 2:10; 2:28; and 3:3 is in the pre-Markan tradition. When Mark begins to compose freely again in 3:7, he has Jesus withdraw from the publicity given him in 2:1–3:6, and in 3:12 his characteristic command to silence reappears.

— 3:21, 31–35. Jesus' identity is concealed even from his family members, who think he is out of his mind. In Mark, they never penetrate his secret. This is the only picture Mark gives us of Mary and Jesus' brothers and sisters: they stand outside with those who do not understand (cf. 4:11!).

— 4:10–12, 34. In Mark, the crowd does not understand Jesus' parables, and he does not intend for them to understand. Jesus privately explains the parables to his disciples, but the crowds do not get the explanation. This description of a teacher who conceals what he is teaching from his hearers seems so strange to Matthew that he again rewrites it to place the responsibility for the crowds' lack of understanding on their own dullness, not on the intention of Jesus (Matt 13:10–17).

— 4:22. A traditional saying is used by Mark to assert that though the secret is to be kept for the time being, there will come a time when it will be revealed to all.

— 4:41. Unlike the crowds, the disciples have had the opportunity to perceive Jesus' message and identity—but they clearly have not done so. Even though Jesus displays his power over the demon storm, the disciples can only rub their eyes and ask, "Who is this?"

8. The phrase "secret epiphany," as well as the key function of the messianic secret in facilitating the creation of the Gospel form, was popularized by Dibelius, *Tradition to Gospel*, 297 and passim.

— 5:43. After Jesus has brought the funeral to an end and dramatically presented the girl alive and instructed her to be fed, there follows the command that no one is to know about this! Here the incongruity of this as an actual event in the 30-CE life of Jesus is most clear. Again, the messianic secret motif seems to be a later overlay, not part of the original story, and it seems to serve a different function from the story itself (again, Matthew omits this aspect of the story).

— 6:2–3. The hometown folk acknowledge Jesus' mighty works but do not penetrate the secret of his person, and in the end they chase him out.

— 6:48–52. Though Jesus walks on the sea, the disciples respond in awe and terror (but not with perception). In verse 52, they do not understand because of the (divine?) hardening of their hearts. Mark indicates not only that they do not understand but that they cannot understand. Not *yet*. Something is yet lacking before perceiving Jesus' true identity can occur. Once again, Matthew finds this impossible, and has the disciples praise Jesus as the Son of God (Matt 14:33).

— 7:17–23. As in 4:10–12 and 4:34, Jesus' teaching is explained only in private, and its meaning is withheld from the crowds.

— 7:31–37. Jesus performs the miracle privately, and when it is completed he commands silence—to a man to whom he has just given the gift of speech!

— 8:17–21. The disciples, supposedly initiated into the secret of Jesus' teaching about the kingdom of God, and having seen both the miraculous feedings, here have the same words applied to them as are applied to the "outsiders" in 4:11–12. Mark, in contrast to the tradition he had received, emphasizes that during Jesus' ministry not even the disciples understand who Jesus is or the significance of his mighty acts.

— 8:26. As usual, the healing of the blind man is to be kept secret.

— 8:27–30. In the context of several inadequate answers concerning Jesus' identity, Peter gives the right answer. Jesus is the Christ, as Mark had already told the reader (1:1). But it turns out that Jesus' response to Peter's confession is ambiguous in the extreme, neither accepting it nor rejecting it, and that in any case the disciples are commanded not to say that Jesus is the Christ to anyone else.

— 9:2–10. The transfiguration is a secret epiphany of Christ's glory. Three chosen disciples see it and hear the heavenly voice that acknowledges Jesus to be the divine Son. It is not clear that they understand the significance of what they have seen, but in any case they are commanded to be quiet about it until the resurrection. This is the first time that the terminus of the secret is disclosed. This disclosure had to wait until Jesus had announced his coming suffering and death (8:31), and this announcement had to wait until he was confessed as the Christ. At this point the reader sees for the first time that the messianic secret is to be dissolved at, and by, the crucifixion and resurrection event. At that point, and not before, Jesus will be disclosed for what he really is, which has already been disclosed to the (postresurrection) audience.

The Messianic Secret thus appears to be the literary strategy of the 70-CE author of the Gospel of Mark to accommodate both christological views of Jesus within one narrative. In Hans Conzelmann's famous succinct formula, "the secrecy theory is the hermeneutical presupposition of the genre, 'gospel.'"[9]

20.2 For Further Reading

Black, C. C. *Mark: Images of an Apostolic Interpreter*. Columbia: University of South Carolina Press, 1994.

9. Hans Conzelmann, "Present and Future in the Synoptic Tradition," *Journal for Theology and the Church* 5 (1968): 43.

Boring, M. Eugene. *Truly Human/Truly Divine: Christological Language and the Gospel Form*. St. Louis: CBP Press, 1984.

Burridge, R. A. *What Are the Gospels? A Comparison with Graeco-Roman Biography*. SNTSMS 70. Cambridge: Cambridge University Press, 1992.

Koester, Helmut. *Ancient Christian Gospels: Their History and Development*. Philadelphia: Trinity Press Int., 1990.

———. *From Jesus to the Gospels: Interpreting the New Testament in Its Context*. Minneapolis: Fortress Press, 2007.

Stuhlmacher, Peter. *The Gospel and the Gospels*. Grand Rapids: Eerdmans, 1991.

Wrede, W. *The Messianic Secret*. Translated by James C. G. Greig. Library of Theological Translations. London: James Clarke, 1971.

21
Interpreting Mark

21.1 A Literary Approach to Mark

THE GOSPEL OF MARK IS NOT A RECORD made by a reporter or a collection assembled by an editor, but a narrative composed by an author. Literary criticism in biblical studies today connotes something more comprehensive than analysis of language and style, namely, the study of the rhetorical techniques used by the author in composing the narrative.[1]

Mark did not compose ex nihilo, but certainly used sources and traditions grounded in the actual events of the life of Jesus and the early Christian movement. Yet the final composition is the literary creation of an author, who made authorial decisions about (1) whether and how to adopt or adapt available literary genres for his composition; (2) where and how to begin and end the story; (3) how to structure the narrative so that its movement communicated the meaning he wanted to evoke in the hearer/readers; (4) what kind of narrator would tell this story to the hearer/readers;[2] (5) from what point of view the story would be told;[3] (6) how the narrative was to be plotted; (7) who the characters would be and how they would be characterized; and (8) the implied reader, that is, the ideal reader presupposed by the way the document is written, the intended readers in Mark's church, who may or may not correspond to actual readers.

Just as source criticism dominated Gospel studies of the late nineteenth and early twentieth centuries, form criticism prevailed in the period between the two world wars, and redaction criticism became foremost during the generation after World War II, so in the last generation literary criticism, without replacing the other approaches, became a prominent and indispensable method of Gospel interpretation. Instead of attempting to reconstruct sources and earlier forms of the text in order to look *through* it as a window to the events that lay behind it, literary criticism strives to look *at* the final

1. From the recent bibliographical explosion on this subject, the following provide readable introductions to literary criticism of the Gospels, and further bibliography: Norman R. Petersen, *Literary Criticism for New Testament Critics* (Philadelphia: Fortress Press, 1978)); Mark Allen Powell, *What Is Narrative Criticism?* (Minneapolis: Fortress Press, 1990); David Rhoads, Joanna Dewey, and Donald Michie, *Mark as Story: An Introduction to the Narrative of a Gospel*, 2nd ed. (Minneapolis: Fortress Press, 1999).

2. The Markan narrator is omnipresent and omniscient in relation to the world of the story, allowing the reader to stand with the narrator as the silent observer of every scene. Temporally, the narrator is located after the resurrection but prior to the parousia, during the time of the church's duress in this world. The story world constructed by the author and communicated by the narrator is limited in time and space, however, not extending to the transcendent world of God or the demons, nor to precreation or post-parousia time.

3. The narrator's point of view is related to, but not entirely identical with, that of the main character Jesus, creating a certain tension for the implied audience. For elaboration of this recent insight, see Malbon, *Mark's Jesus*.

form of the text as a whole, to enter into the story world it creates, and to be addressed by the message of the story itself. While the redaction-critical approach permitted the interpreter to state the message of the Gospel in a series of abstract statements summarizing the main points of the "theology of the evangelist," illustrated by the redactional changes he had made, literary criticism insisted on the inseparability of the message and the story form in which it is embodied, which is not a disposable container for the "message" or "theology" of the evangelist. Literary criticism reminds us that the Gospel form, the story about Jesus, is in continuity with the form of communication used by Jesus himself, the parable. In the Gospel, the teller of stories becomes himself the principal character in a story; the parabler becomes the parabled.

21.2 Authorship

WHO WAS THE PERSON WHO CREATED THIS powerful theological narrative? The question of authorship could not be discussed intelligently as the first issue; one must first get an idea of the nature of the document before asking the question of authorship. The preceding discussion has already made clear that, while it contains materials that go back to the time of Jesus, the materials available to Mark come through the experienced faith of the Christian community in its teaching, preaching, worship, and debates, not via a chain of individual eyewitnesses. It represents the work of an early Christian teacher and theologian who intended to combine previous ways of confessing faith in Jesus into a profound and provocative presentation that functions at a different level and in a different manner than mere report.

Like the other Gospels, Mark is anonymous. The name "Mark" later attached to it could represent the name of the actual author—it was the most common masculine name in the Hellenistic world. More likely, however, in the process of canonization of the Gospels, Mark's name was attached to it as a way of affirming it as a representative of the apostolic faith. Who was this Mark, why did the church attribute the Gospel to him, and was the church historically correct in doing so?

A certain "Mark" first appears in the New Testament in Philemon 24 as among those with Paul who send greetings from his imprisonment. The letter to Philemon has traditionally been regarded as written from Rome in the early 60s, but both location and date are disputed; many scholars regard the letter as having been written from Ephesus in the 50s (see above, §11.3). A similar, but elaborated, list of greetings appears in Colossians 4:10–14, adding the additional information that Mark is the "cousin of Barnabas." Colossians is probably not written directly by Paul (see §15.1.2) but takes up the tradition from Philemon that Paul had a coworker named Mark. The same is true of the only other reference to Mark in the Pauline tradition, 2 Timothy 4:11, which pictures Paul as (again) in prison, this time in Rome, asking Timothy to come to him and bring Mark. Near the end of the first century, a member of the Petrine stream of tradition in Rome ("Babylon") wrote 1 Peter, indicating that Mark is now Peter's "son" (1 Pet 5:13).[4] The author of Acts later refers three times to a John Mark who was a member of the Jerusalem church who had contacts with both Peter and Paul (Acts 12:12, 25; 13:5, 13; 15:37, 39). The only one of these references that is historically certain is Philemon 24: there was a historical figure named Mark who was Paul's coworker in the mid-50s. The other references point to a developing picture of "Mark" in early Christianity as one who first worked with Paul, and later was Peter's coworker in Rome.[5] Unless Philemon was written in Rome, the earliest

4. For the trajectory that led to the combination of Petrine and Pauline traditions in Rome at the end of the first century, see above, §17.2.1, and Boring, *1 Peter*, 19–27.

5. For a thorough treatment of this tradition, see C. Clifton Black, *Mark: Images of an Apostolic Interpreter* (Columbia: University of South Carolina Press, 1994).

connection between Mark and Rome—and thus with Peter—is in 1 Peter, about 95 CE.

Beginning with Papias in the second century, a tradition developed in various forms that attributed the authorship of the Gospel of Mark to this John Mark, who had been the companion of both Paul and Peter (Eusebius, *Hist. eccl.* 3.39.15). In all its variations, the ancient tradition makes clear that Mark's Gospel was accepted and valued in the church, not because of its historical accuracy, but because it represented Peter's apostolic authority. The Gospel of Mark itself makes no claim to have been written by an eyewitness and gives no evidence of such authorship. While most critical scholars consider the actual author's name to be unknown, the traditional view that Mark was written in Rome by a companion of Peter is still defended by some scholars who begin with the church tradition cited above and do not find convincing historical evidence to disprove it.[6] For convenience, in this book we continue to refer to the Gospels by the names of their traditional authors.

21.3 Sources

WE HAVE SEEN THAT MARK WAS NOT AN eyewitness or in direct communication with eyewitnesses and that the living oral tradition of the Christian community was his principal source. Some elements of this tradition seem to have already been arranged in topical clusters, for example, the conflict stories of 2:1–3:6, the parables of 4:1–32, and the passion narrative of 14:1–15:47. This does not necessarily mean that when Mark begins to write he has only the materials transmitted and edited by others. We do not know what Mark had been doing prior to the time of composing the Gospel, but presumably he was himself a Christian teacher who collected, arranged, interpreted, and transmitted sayings and stories about Jesus. When he begins to write, it is not the first time he has seen or interpreted these materials; he may well have been teaching these materials for some years, and previously composed some written texts he incorporated in the Gospel.

Was Q among Mark's sources? The issues of whether Mark knew Q, and whether he used Q as one of his sources, are two separate issues. The Q materials were probably already collected, edited, and in circulation by Mark's time, and in his locale. Mark's own material overlaps the Q material (see Exc. 3.5 on the "Mark/Q overlaps"), but this need not mean that he knows Q directly; they both may well have used the same or similar traditions. The primary argument usually given against Mark's knowledge of Q is that, if he had known it, he surely would have used it. This is not necessarily the case. Mark may have been suspicious of a genre of sayings material too closely associated with Christian prophets who continued to proclaim new sayings of the risen Jesus, and may have kept his distance from a body of Jesus material that had minimal or no kerygma of the cross. Scholars continue to be divided on whether Mark used, or even knew, the Q materials.[7]

21.4 Date, Occasion

ON THE ONE HAND, THE GOSPEL MUST have been written late enough to allow for the development of the oral tradition on which it is based, that is, about a generation, and, on the

6. Thus Vincent Taylor, *The Gospel according to St. Mark: The Greek Text with Introduction, Notes, and Indexes* (London: Macmillan, 1950), 26: "There can be no doubt that the author of the Gospel was Mark, the attendant of Peter." The most thorough recent defense of the Papias tradition is the 1,051-page commentary by Robert H. Gundry, *Mark: A Commentary on His Apology for the Cross* (Grand Rapids: Eerdmans, 1993), esp. 1026–45.

7. For arguments and bibliography that Mark knew and used Q, see Harry T. Fleddermann, *Mark and Q: A Study of the Overlap Texts* (Louvain: University Press, 1995), and *Q: A Reconstruction and Commentary*, Biblical Tools and Studies 1 (Louvain: Peeters, 2005); for the contrary view, see Christopher M. Tuckett, *Q and the History of Early Christianity* (Edinburgh: T. & T. Clark, 1996) and Neirynck's "Assessment" as part of the Fleddermann 1995 volume.

other hand, early enough to have been used by Matthew and Luke around the turn of the century. These general considerations would locate Mark roughly between 60 and 80 CE. This period is narrowed somewhat by the apocalyptic discourse of chapter 13, with its prediction of the temple's destruction, which seems to reflect the tumultuous times of the war in Judea 66–70, but it is not clear whether Mark was written during, just before, or just after the war. The reference to the death of James and John in 10:39 is also relevant. In the story line all these events are still in the future and predicted by Jesus; the question is whether the narrative itself reflects that they have already happened. Thus practically all scholars date Mark in the period 65–75, with the major issue being whether or not Mark 13 is understood to reflect the destruction of Jerusalem as something that has already occurred.

21.5 Provenance

WE HAVE SEEN THAT A TRADITION DEVELoped that the Gospel of Mark was composed in Rome. This tradition is first attested in the anti-Marcionite prologues of the late second century. Although there were other traditions (e.g., Alexandria), the Roman provenance became the dominant tradition. This tradition is not based on data from the Gospel itself, although some data internal to the Gospel is consistent with a Roman provenance. The allusions to suffering and persecution (e.g., 8:34–38; 13:9–13) may well reflect Nero's persecution of Roman Christians in 64 CE, but this would have affected Christian self-understanding throughout the Roman world, and while it is compatible with a Roman location, is not evidence for composition in Rome. Likewise, the number of Latinized words is sometimes taken as evidence of a Roman origin, but the influence of the language of the Romans was not restricted to the city of Rome or to Italy, but pervaded the empire (as English became a world language after WWII).

Against the tradition of Roman provenance is the fact that Mark does not reflect Paul's letter to the Romans written about fourteen years previously, that is, does not appear to emerge from a church where *Romans* was regularly read. Not only are key words of Pauline theology in general and Romans in particular (e.g., "law," "the righteousness of God") missing from Mark, the general christological perspective of the Gospel is different from Paul's, who never communicated his Christology by telling stories of the earthly Jesus, but concentrated everything on the death and resurrection. Neither is there any internal evidence that links the contents of Mark to the preaching of Peter. The Markan negative picture of Peter and the Twelve argues against this connection. Likewise, the Gospel of Mark is not reflected in any of the earliest Christian writings emanating from Rome. First Peter and *1 Clement* both come from Rome near the end of the first century; neither indicates directly or indirectly any awareness of the Gospel of Mark, and neither has the Gospel type of narrative Christology that includes stories of Jesus' life, but only the Pauline cosmic Christology. So also the Old Roman Creed, ancestor of the Apostles' Creed, represents the confession of the Roman church at the end of the second century CE, and has the Pauline Christology that goes directly from the birth of Jesus to "crucified under Pontius Pilate," with no place for the kind of Markan narrative Christology portraying the ministry of Jesus. Though the Gospel of Mark was certainly accepted and current in Rome at the end of the *second* century, the creed was apparently formulated in Rome before narrative Christology represented by the Gospels became the accepted norm. This creed is compatible with 1 Peter and *1 Clement*, but not with Mark, which suggests that the Gospel of Mark came to Rome from someplace else, some time near the end of the first century CE, and was not immediately or generally accepted.[8]

8. The strongest defense of the traditional view of the Roman origin of Mark is still probably B. W. Bacon, *Is*

Some implications for the social and religious setting of Mark may be inferred from the text itself. The debate with Jewish scribes and traditions (e.g., 7:1–23; 11:27–12:40) points to a community that is seriously engaged with Jewish tradition and synagogue leadership. The lack of reference to large cities (except Jerusalem), the primarily agrarian imagery, the lack of urban metaphors, the preponderance of situations in which poor people play leading roles, and the limitation of reference to monetary units to small-denomination coins suggest that the community from which Mark came belonged to the lower socioeconomic strata. The community is not undergoing direct persecution, yet stands in tension with its environment and may be harassed by both Jewish and Gentile authorities (13:9). The community knows the phenomena of charismatic gifts of the Spirit in its midst (13:10; cf. 1:8, 3:28–29), including prophets who speak in the name of the risen Lord (13:6), as in the Pauline churches (e.g., 1 Cor 14) and those pictured in Acts (e.g., Acts 11:27–29), but Mark is suspicious of them (13:22). The Markan church was an apocalyptic community that expected the end to come soon (9:1; 13:28–30).

That Aramaic terms and Jewish customs are translated or explained (e.g., 5:41; 7:1–4, 11, 34; 14:36; 15:34) indicates that it was directed to a Greek-speaking church composed primarily of Gentiles. The indications in Mark 13 of the proximity of the author and his community to the war of 66–70 suggest Syria or Palestine. The author's imprecise knowledge of Palestinian geography points to a setting outside Palestine proper (for example, compare 7:31 with the map!). On the 2DH, awareness of Mark first surfaces when Matthew uses Mark as a source. Since Matthew was probably written in or near Antioch, this suggests a Syrian provenance for Mark as well. Someplace in Syria, not too far from Galilee, seems to be the most likely provenance.[9]

21.6 Structure and Outline

MARK STRUCTURES HIS NARRATIVE according to his theology and rhetorical strategy. The opening line declares Jesus to be the Christ. The first half of the narrative recounts many mighty works of Jesus, but no human being recognizes his true identity. About halfway through the narrative, Peter confesses Jesus to be the Christ—clearly a turning point in the story (8:27–29). From 8:30 to the end, Jesus reveals his own identity as the Son of Man who will suffer, die, be raised by God, and return in glory at the end of history. Thus the narrative can be thought of as bipartite, 1:1–8:29/8:30–16:8. Yet the carefully structured 8:22–10:52 is clearly a unit that would be divided by such a bipartite structure. Topographical and other considerations point to Part 1 as comprising 1:1–8:21 and Part 2 as 11:1–16:8, joined by the transitional section 8:22–10:52, which overlaps and unites the bipartite structure (see Box 28).

The two major parts correspond to the emphases of Mark's Christology. Neither "Galilee" nor "Jerusalem" is merely a topographical indication; both have symbolic overtones. Part 1 begins with Jesus' call of the disciples to become "fishermen who fish for people" (1:16–20) and concludes with Jesus' challenge to them, "Do you not yet understand?" (8:21). Part 2 begins with Jesus' welcome by the crowds in Jerusalem, who end up joining those who crucify Jesus, and concludes with the postresurrection command

Mark a Roman Gospel? Harvard Theological Studies 7 (Cambridge: Harvard University Press, 1919). More recently, Gundry, *Mark*, gives a detailed exposition presupposing Roman provenance.

9. E.g., Gerd Theissen, *The Gospels in Context: Social and Political History in the Synoptic Tradition*, trans. Linda M. Maloney (Minneapolis: Fortress Press, 1991). For a solid defense of Syrian provenance, see Marcus, *Mark*, 25–37, in the context of other possibilities.

to return to Galilee to follow Jesus, who "goes before" them. The two parts are joined by the important transitional section 8:22–10:52, which both separates and joins Part 1 and Part 2 by representing the "the Way" of Jesus from Galilee to Jerusalem (and back, 16:7!) and the transition from blindness to sight.

The transitional section, "The Way," is bracketed by two stories in which Jesus heals a blind person, the only two such stories in Mark. The internal structure of the section is provided by the three passion predictions (8:31; 9:31; 10:33–34). The recurring pattern is (1) affirmation about Jesus; (2) passion prediction; (3) failure of the disciples to understand; (4) Jesus renewing his call and continuing to teach them (see Box 29).

Mark has two, and only two, extended discourses of Jesus. The parables discourse (4:1–34) is inserted in the middle of Part 1, the apocalyptic discourse (13:5–37) in the middle of Part 2, each providing interpretation of its major

Box 28: Structure of Transitional Section

Part One 1:1–8:21	Overlapping Transitional Section 8:22–10:52	Part Two 11:1–16:8

Part 1 — 1:1–8:21	**Part 2 — 11:1–16:8**
Galilee	Jerusalem
Calling, sending disciples	No calling or sending disciples
Miraculous ministry	No miraculous ministry
Exorcisms	No exorcisms
Success	Rejection
Major central discourse: parables	Major central discourse: apocalyptic
Kingdom parables	No kingdom parables
Mystery of the kingdom	Jesus the king
Kingdom hidden in present	Kingdom manifest in future
Purity, Sabbath, synagogue	Temple
Jesus' message to Israel	Jesus' message to his disciples
Secrecy commands	No secrecy commands
Disciples don't understand	Disciples misunderstand
Unhealed blindness	Blindness healed
No valid confession	Valid confession: by Jesus, the centurion
Key symbols: bread, sea, boat	Key symbols: cup, way, cross

Box 29: Transitional Section

Gradual, secret healing of blind man		8:22–26	
Affirmation about Jesus	8:27–30	9:2–29	[9:37; 10:18, 27]
Passion prediction	8:31	9:31	10:33–34
Disciples fail to understand	8:32	9:32	10:35–40
Renewed call and instruction	8:33–9:1	9:33–50	10:41–45
Full, public healing of blind man		10:46–52	

narrative unit. The major structural elements can be represented as follows:

1:1–15 Title and Prologue: Judea and Galilee

Part 1: Galilee 1:16–8:21
- 1:16–3:35 Authority, Rejection, and the New Community
- *4:1–34 Central Discourse: Parables and the Mystery of the Kingdom of God*
- 4:35–8:21 Crossing Borders

"The Way": Galilee to Jerusalem 8:22–10:52

Part 2: Jerusalem 11:1–15:47
- 11:1–13:4 Public Demonstration and Conflict
- *13:5–37 Central Discourse: Historical Troubles and the Coming of the Son of Man*
- 14:1–15:47 Trials and Death

16:1–8 Epilogue: Resurrection and Mission: Back to Galilee

21.7 Exegetical-Theological Précis

1:1–15 Title and Prologue: Judea and Galilee

1:1 Title

The first verse functions as a title for the whole narrative. The first word ἀρχή (*archē*) means both *beginning* and *norm*. The title declares that the whole narrative that follows is the beginning of the story that continues into the time of the author and audience, and the norm for the gospel as proclaimed by the Christian community of their own time.

1:2–15 Prologue

Before the action on the historical stage begins, the audience hears the offstage transcendent voice of God speaking to "the Lord" in the words of Scripture, declaring that he has a "way." In the opening scene of the this-worldly story, John the Baptist proclaims a baptism for forgiveness of sins and calls for repentance, and announces the coming of a Mighty One who will baptize in the Spirit. All Jerusalem and Judea respond, but only Jesus comes from Galilee. When Jesus is baptized, the Holy Spirit descends into him; he is led into the wilderness to be tested by Satan and is with the wild animals and served by angels. The prologue thus moves on another level than the narrative that follows, with an extraordinary cast: God, Isaiah, "the Lord," John the Baptizer, Holy Spirit, Satan, wild animals, and angels. The figure of the Lord Jesus himself is the point of intersection and line of continuity between these two worlds: he is addressed by God in the metahistorical world (1:2–3), and he is the this-worldly figure addressed by the heavenly voice and into whom the divine Spirit descends (1:10–11). The 70-CE audience of Mark's story, but not the participants in the body of the narrative, is party to these extraordinary scenes, events, and voices, and is prepared to understand the story in a way that the characters in the story cannot—until after the cross and resurrection.

Part 1: Galilee 1:16–8:21

Part 1 of Mark is mainly a narrative explication of epiphany Christology. Jesus appears as the promised Mighty One who vanquishes the enemies that are a threat to the life God intended for humanity.

1:16–3:35 Authority, Rejection, and the New Community

Authority. In this opening section of Jesus' ministry, he acts with divine authority. Just as the God of Israel had called prophets, Jesus calls disciples by his powerful word (1:1–16; 2:14). The first words the reader hears Jesus speak are "Follow me," addressed to the fishermen whom he calls to be his disciples (1:17; the author's summary of Jesus' preaching in 1:15 is indirect speech). Jesus teaches with authority (1:22, 27). He encounters demonic powers and defeats them (1:23–26, 39; 3:11). He heals sick people, even curing and cleansing untouchable lepers (1:29–34, 40–45; 2:1–11; 3:1–6, 10). In veiled, parabolic language, he indicates that he is the "Mighty One" promised by John and that the eschatological promise of the "binding of Satan" is already being fulfilled in his ministry of exorcism and healing (3:25–27; cf. Rev 20:2). He speaks with divine authority to forgive sins (2:5). He teaches and acts with a sovereign authority that transcends all rules about fasting, Sabbath, and ritual purity (1:41; 2:16, 23–28; 3:1–6).

Jesus' advent generates a conflict between the present evil age and the coming rule of God; the issue is a matter of jurisdiction, of realms of authority. Jesus is not reactive but takes the initiative as the leading edge of the coming kingdom of God. The demonic world is on the defensive, and is overwhelmed by the onslaught of the promised Mighty One. The "newness" Jesus brings (1:27; 2:21–22) is the eschatological renewal of creation. In all this, Mark narrates with a knowing look to his post-Easter audience, but the full meaning of the events is lost to the characters in the story.

Rejection. The crowds acknowledge that he speaks and acts with authority, but in befuddled amazement do not perceive his true identity (1:22, 27; 3:7–8). Those who are skilled in religious matters do not recognize him, accuse him of blasphemy, and reject him (2:6–7; 3:22–30). Even his close associates and his family fail to recognize him, think he is deranged, and attempt to get him out of the public eye.

New community. Jesus calls to himself a new community of disciples and followers (1:16–20; 2:14–15, 18, 23; 3:7, 9). Jesus' first deed of power is to call disciples, making clear from the beginning that the Jesus story is not the story of a great individual, but the founder of a new community—the renewed Israel, the people of God. It is not said that the disciples recognize his true identity or understand him, but they follow nonetheless. He identifies them as "those who do the will of God," and his true family (3:34–35). From within this large following, he chooses twelve, symbolic of renewed Israel, to share his ministry of preaching, healing, and casting out demons (3:13–19). Here and elsewhere, this portrayal of the pre-Easter life of Jesus is transparent to the life-situation of the Markan audience. In Mark's situation, about 70 CE, the risen Jesus continues to speak and call disciples; most who hear the Christian message misunderstand and reject it, but some respond even if their understanding is incomplete.

4:1–34 *Central Discourse: Parables and the Mystery of the Kingdom of God*

The fast-paced narrative now pauses, and for the first time Jesus makes an extended speech, bisecting and interpreting Part 1 of Mark's comprehensive story. The three seed parables Mark has included (4:3–9, 26–29, 30–32) preserve the impact of Jesus' own explosive and disorienting parabolic language, and the interpretation of the Sower parable (4:13–20) exhibits one way Jesus' parables were interpreted in the post-Easter church. It is as the redactional construction of Mark himself, however, that the speech addresses the audience of Mark's own time. Like the similar discourse in the middle of Part 2 (13:5–37), Jesus' speech serves to interpret the action—but to Mark's readers, not to the characters in the story, who do not understand it and are not intended to do so (4:10–12). The present form of the discourse interprets to Mark's readers how it could be that the hope of Judaism, the Messiah who brings God's kingdom, had been rejected by the Jewish people during Jesus' lifetime and how his own disciples had not understood him. After the cross and resurrection, in the time of Mark's readers, believers had recognized Jesus as the Messiah, but the messianic community was becoming mostly a Gentile church. Those who had not recognized Jesus, and who continued to be blind, were "hardened," like the pharaoh of the exodus. Analogous to Paul's dealing with the same issue in Rom 9–11 (see above, §13.2.5), Mark presents the hardening of the hearts and blinding of the eyes of those who heard the original message as part of the mystery of God's plan. The mystery remains, but three statements of Mark's "parable theory" woven into the discourse (4:10–12, 21–25, 33–34) show that the hiddenness of the revelation could not be manifest until it was complete (in the death and resurrection of Jesus, as is later made clear; see on 9:9–10). The word of Jesus was meant to be understood, and finally will be; what is hidden is destined to be finally revealed. On the one hand, the hidden revelation of Jesus' time in the pre-Easter narrative framework will become manifest after the resurrection. On the other hand, Mark does not think that he and his readers simply live in the time of full revelation; they too still live in a time of ambiguity, awaiting the full revelation at the Parousia (13:5–37).

4:35–8:21 ***Crossing Borders***

Two themes are interwoven in this section: (1) the revelation of God's saving power in Jesus and (2) the extension of the gospel of Jesus to the Gentiles. In terms of both history and Mark's theology, neither of these occurred, or could occur, until after the cross and resurrection.

1. The disciples and others see the epiphany of God's power in Jesus, but do not understand, that is, not *yet*. This section is framed with a key Markan term, οὔπω (*oupō*, not *yet*, 4:40) as the punch line of the opening scene, and twice in the closing scene (8:17, 21) as Jesus' poignant final question: "Do you not yet understand?"

2. The historical Jesus probably never entered Gentile territory (cf. Matt 10:5–6, 23). But after the resurrection the new Christian community gradually, guided by the Holy Spirit, the presence of the risen Christ, and with some conflict and distress, learned to cross geographical, cultural, and religious boundaries (see Acts 2–15). Mark assembles and retells stories of Jesus in such a way that his audience recognizes their own experience and struggles in the narrative of Jesus and the disciples.

4:35–41 Stilling the storm Jesus calls his disciples to follow him to the "other side," the eastern, non-Jewish bank of the Sea of Galilee. It is a stormy passage, the disciples are afraid, but Jesus is with them and calms the storm. They do not yet understand who he is or the mission that calls them to other peoples.

5:1–20 The Gerasene demoniac Just as the Jewish mission began in a synagogue by exorcising a demon, so in Jesus' first step on Gentile soil he encounters and overcomes demonic powers. The healed man, though he does not yet understand Jesus' identity, proclaims the message in the Gentile area of the Decapolis, an anticipation of the Markan church's later Gentile mission.

5:21–6:44 Mission and feeding Jesus and his disciples return to the Jewish west bank of the Jordan, where Jesus continues his mighty acts of salvation. Extending the message to Gentiles does not mean abandoning the Jewish people. Jesus responds to the plea of the ruler of a synagogue and restores his daughter to life; he heals a Jewish woman of her physical and ritual impurity (5:21–43). He is misunderstood and rejected in his hometown (6:1–6), but nonetheless continues his mission and extends it by sending out his disciples (6:7–13). Crowds flock to him, and he is admired as Elijah, one of the ancient prophets, or even John the Baptist risen from the dead; but no one penetrates the secret of his identity (6:14–31). He miraculously feeds the hungry multitudes, with twelve baskets of food left over—Messianic abundance, but unrecognized (6:32–44).

6:45–7:23 Expanded and frustrated mission After the feeding, Jesus forces his disciples into the boat and they depart for the eastern Gentile shore, while he stays behind in the Jewish west; the post-Easter Gentile mission had been launched "without" the presence of Jesus, who had been "left behind" in the Jewish past. The disciples do not make it to the other side on their own, and the impossible happens: Jesus comes to them walking on the water, and

Mark points out in the closing line: they do not understand the miracle of the loaves. They believe it happened, but do not grasp its meaning (6:45–52). They end up back on the western Jewish bank (6:53). Jesus continues his ministry of healing, which generates a conflict with authorities from Jerusalem (6:54–7:23).

In post-Reformation times, the dispute has often been cast in terms of Scripture vs. tradition, but in Mark's situation the primary issue had to do with ritual purity. How could the people of God include Gentiles who were ritually unclean? The debate was not only between Jews and Christians, but was an inner-Christian debate: "some" of Jesus' disciples ate with ritually unclean hands (7:2), which means that others followed the prescribed rules. Jesus' response is not a pronouncement on hand washing, but on clean and unclean foods as such (7:17–23). This issue of table fellowship had to be resolved before the Gentile mission could continue. The letters of Paul and Acts 10–15 let the modern reader see something of the soul-searching, inner-church struggle generated among Jesus' disciples by the Gentile mission. Mark retells the story of Jesus from this perspective. As Jesus had proleptically cleansed Gentile lands (not just the individual demonized person; see 5:10) from demonic power, so he proleptically declares all foods clean (7:19). Mark's point: there is no ritual or biblical reason for objecting to the Gentile mission.

7:24–8:21 Jesus guides the slow disciples to broader horizons. Once again Jesus leads into Gentile territory, on a trip that heads north through Tyre and Sidon, then by a very circuitous route back to Galilee "by way of Sidon towards the Sea of Galilee, in the region of the Decapolis" (NRSV). The route is difficult to imagine historically; see the map and the various English translations that attempt to make geographical sense of the route. Mark, however, is more interested in theology than geography, and may not have been familiar with the area in any case. His point is that the present Gentile mission of the church was already anticipated in the mission of Jesus, though the disciples could not yet understand this. In Gentile Tyre, a woman beseeches Jesus' help for her afflicted daughter, and Jesus himself rebuffs her with the standard theological chronology of the priority of Israel in salvation history. "First to the Jew, then to the Gentile" (Rom 1:16 TNIV). "The children [Israel] must first be *fed*." The woman persists with a sharp rejoinder, causing Jesus to adjust the chronology of God's saving plan. He not only heals the woman's daughter, but *feeds* Gentile multitudes on the eastern shore, just as he had fed Jewish multitudes on the western shore (8:1–9). Better said, on the eastern shore he feeds a multitude that is neither exclusively Jewish nor Gentile, but universal, a prolepsis of the Markan church. A quick trip back to the western shore generates another controversy with the Pharisees (8:10–12). In the boat heading once again to the eastern Gentile shore, the obtuse disciples demonstrate that, despite everything, they do not understand (8:13–21). Not *yet*.

"The Way": Galilee to Jerusalem 8:22–10:52

In Mark—and following him, Matthew and Luke—Jesus makes one trip from Galilee, the scene of his ministry, to Jerusalem, the scene of his death. This pattern is a Markan construction. In addition to (1) the symbolic geographical shift from Galilee to Jerusalem, there is (2) a transition in the image of Jesus from miracle worker to one who is going the way of the cross. In Galilee Jesus works many miracles, in Jerusalem none, on the transitional journey only one exorcism and the concluding restoration of sight to Bartimaeus (9:14–27; 10:46–52). A further transition is (3) from teaching the crowds to private instruction to his disciples, which also involves (4) a shift from veiled, parabolic speech to clear and explicit revelation about his coming death. A structural element in this section is the thrice-repeated passion predictions, spoken clearly and nonparabolically (8:31; 9:31; 10:33–34). A final transition in this section is that (5) as the meaning of Jesus' identity as suffering Son of Man comes more sharply into focus, the inseparable bond between Christology and discipleship becomes more clear. A suffering Messiah calls for disciples to take up their own cross (8:34).

In the pre-Easter portrayal of the disciples, they continue to be blind to this double reality of the nature of Christ and the meaning of discipleship, but there is hope that their blindness will be healed. This is represented by the two different stories of healing blind men, which frame this section. The first (8:22–26) is from Bethsaida, the traditional home of Peter and other disciples (John 1:44, 12:21—though this is not mentioned in Mark). Jesus' effort to heal his blindness does not succeed at first, but after a second attempt the man sees clearly. This seems to be analogous to the experience of Peter and the disciples, who come to believe in Jesus as the Messiah (8:27–30), but are still blind as to what this means. At the conclusion of this section, a blind man who had been beside the road (literally, "alongside the way," 10:46) confesses Jesus to be the "Son of David" (a misunderstanding, as it turns out), has his blindness healed, and follows Jesus "on the way" (10:52). The "way" is the original way announced in 1:3, the "way of the Lord" that leads to the cross. This transition, from being off-track to on-the-way, from being blind to seeing, is the key to this section of the narrative.

Part 2: Jerusalem 11:1–15:47

The second major part of Mark is primarily a narrative explication of kenosis Christology. Miracles virtually disappear. Jesus performs no healings, exorcisms, or other miracles that manifest the saving power of God. He becomes more and more passive. Jesus suffers as the victim of the actions of others, but he is not an unwilling victim. Though he struggles with human weakness and fear of death (14:32–42), he goes willingly and resolutely to meet his suffering and death in full awareness of what lies ahead.

11:1–13:4 Public Demonstration and Conflict

Like the prophets of Israel, Jesus engages in radical symbolic acts. With his followers, he makes a veiled messianic procession into the holy city, is hailed with the acclamation that he is restoring the kingdom of David—a profound misunderstanding of the nature of the kingdom of God (11:1–11). The symbolic act of closing down the temple is framed by the strange story of cursing the barren fig tree (11:12–25). The historical Jesus and the characters in Mark's narrative looked at the reality of the temple as present and asked how it should function. Mark and his readers live in the time when the temple is already under siege and soon to be destroyed, or is already gone. They look on the temple retrospectively and ask how the people of God could continue after the temple's demise. Quoting Isaiah, the Markan Jesus pronounces the temple to be a "house of prayer for all the nations" (Mark 11:17=Isa 56:7). Just as Judaism was replacing the role of the destroyed temple with the synagogue as the house of prayer, Mark may be pointing to the international Christian community as the locus of God's presence in the renewed people of God. Jesus disputes in the temple with various groups of the Jewish leadership, then definitively leaves the temple (11:15–13:1).

After fielding all their questions and avoiding all their traps, Jesus poses a question to them on whether the Christ is "Son of David." For the readers of Mark's time, the issue was whether God's deliverance would come through the military violence of the Davidic-like leaders of those leading the war against Rome. The blind Bartimaeus had addressed Jesus, before his blindness was healed, as Son of David (10:47–48), and the crowds had greeted Jesus as the bringer of the Davidic kingdom (11:10). At the conclusion of the day in the temple, Jesus declares that the equation of the Messiah with the Son of David is a profound mistake (12:35–37). He and his disciples leave the temple, never to return.

13:5–37 Central Discourse: Historical Troubles and the Coming of the Son of Man

In this private speech to the original four disciples (1:16–20), Jesus interprets the events the disciples are living through—the event of his own suffering and death, and the troubles experienced by the readers in their own time. The interpretation is given from the apocalyptic perspective, and manifests many (but not all) of the features of apocalyptic thought (see §7.7). Mark 13 is thus often called the "Little Apocalypse."

Although at the narrative level the speech is given prospectively, from within the framework of the life of Jesus, the death of Jesus is viewed and interpreted retrospectively. It was a part of the plan of God that spans the ages. God has vindicated Jesus as the apocalyptic Son of Man, who will soon return in power and glory (13:26). *How soon?* This was not a theoretical question for Mark and his audience. Some early Christian prophets saw in the terrors of Nero's persecution (64 CE) and the unthinkable catastrophe of the destruction of the temple and the holy city in 66–70 CE that these must be the signs that the end was to come immediately. Mark shares the view that Christ will come within a generation of Jesus' death (9:1; 13:30). Yet the wars and natural catastrophes he and his church are living through are not signs of the immediate end, but only the first beginnings of the final period (13:8). In response to Jesus' prediction of the destruction of the temple, the disciples had asked about the *timetable* ("when?" 13:4a) and about the *signs* that would identify it (13:4b).

I. *The end is not yet* (13:5b–23). Current events are not the signs of the imminent end. "Labor pains" (13:8) was a standard technical term of apocalypticism, reflecting the apocalyptic view that the world must go through a time of terrible suffering, the labor pains of the world that brings forth the Messiah before the end comes (see on Rom 8:18–39). Mark's point is that the labor pains have begun, and the disciples of Jesus will suffer. But they are not on their own; God's Spirit is with them. The Spirit belongs not just to the charismatic prophets who predict the future, but to every believer under duress, and gives them what they need to say (13:11). And though the end is near, it is not immediate—there is time for the worldwide mission of the church (13:10). Mark opposes the false prophets who announce that the end is near, and calls the church to mission and service.

II. *The end will come* (13:24–27). At verse 24 Mark begins to speak of events in his own future, the parousia of the Son of Man that will be signaled by heavenly disturbances visible to all. Mark's rejection of the interpretation of current events by those he considers false prophets does not mean he discards the early Christian eschatological viewpoint. Jesus will return as Son of Man. But when the end comes, it will not be preceded by signs that only a few prophets can interpret. The parousia will be signaled by cosmic signs that all can see. The audience is enjoined to recognize that they live their lives between the death of Jesus and his return in power; their own struggles are given meaning as part of that divinely plotted time line.

III. *When?* (13:28–37). The discourse concludes with two parables that express this dialectic of knowing and not knowing. Twice in the parable of the Fig Tree the hearers are warned, "You know" (13:28–29). Twice in the concluding parable of the Returning Householder (13:33, 35) the Markan Jesus insists "You do not know." *No one knows*, not the Son of God or the angels of heaven (13:32). This statement, which would trouble later Christian thinkers who struggled with the christological issues it raised, was directed to a problem current in Mark's church. Christian prophets spoke with the voice of the risen Lord, claiming revelations from angels (13:6; cf. Rev 1:1–2) and claiming that the events of their own time were the promised signs of the end. Mark's response: the events of 66–70 are not the end, not even its prelude. Even if the church prophets speak as authorized by the Son and the angels, they still do not know the time of the end, which only God knows. Mark's point is thus not addressed to speculative apocalyptic questions ("When will the end come?") but to the business of Jesus' disciples in the worldwide Christian mission, for which God provides time (v. 10).

There is thus a sense in which the "Little Apocalypse" is *anti*-apocalyptic. It is not a vision report, but a narrative speech inserted into a lengthy narrative, which it interprets and which also interprets it. The speech is placed prior to the crucifixion and resurrection, within the framework of the life of Jesus that leads to the cross, rather than at its conventional place as the post-Easter revelation of the risen Lord. In Mark, the risen Jesus speaks only within the narrative framework of the story of the crucified Jesus (see on 16:1–8).

14:1–15:47 Trials and Death

Jesus is anointed by an anonymous woman; he interprets her act as preparation for his burial. He celebrates a last meal with his disciples, interpreting the bread and wine as his body and blood given for others. From 14:1 on, Jesus is almost entirely passive, and others are the actors. Mark uses the term παραδίδωμι (*paradidōmi*, hand over, deliver up) twenty times, more frequently than any other New Testament author. Jesus is "handed over" by Judas, by the chief priests, scribes, and elders, and by Pilate. Six times the word has no explicit subject, five of these are in the passive voice, presumably a "divine passive," often used in Judaism and the New Testament as a way of expressing the hidden action of God (e.g., 4:11). The term *paradidōmi* had been used by 2 Isaiah of the Suffering Servant who is delivered up by God for the sins of others. Mark has only a minimum of explicit atonement theology (10:45; 14:24), and makes no effort to explain how it is that the death of Jesus is God's saving act. Likewise, he does not excuse the human actors in the drama in which Jesus is delivered up. But neither does he reduce it to the decisions of human actors. Yet, in and through the human actors responsible for Jesus' death, Mark traces the hand of God (14:27).[10]

When efforts to convict Jesus on the testimony of false witnesses fail, Jesus confesses that he is the Messiah and Son of God, who will be enthroned at God's right hand and will return in power and glory as the Son of Man (14:55–64). He is then condemned on the charge of blasphemy. For the first and only time in the Gospel, Jesus declares his true identity, and it costs him his life. He is brought before Pilate, the Roman governor, and condemned to death on the charge of claiming to be a king (15:1–27). He is mocked by Jewish leaders, Roman soldiers, and passersby (14:65; 15:16–20). The Roman officer in charge of the crucifixion watches him die and becomes the only human being in the story to confess Jesus to be the Son of God (15:39). Unknown to the centurion or others at the crucifixion scene, the reader knows that the confession is divinely confirmed by the supernatural darkness and the tearing of the temple veil, torn from top to bottom (15:38).

In Mark, Jesus dies forsaken and alone. He had been betrayed by Judas, publicly denied by Simon Peter, and abandoned by all his disciples (14:10–11, 43–46; 50–52, 66–72). His only word from the cross was the cry of abandonment by God, the prayer of Psalm 22:1. He is buried by a friendly member of the Sanhedrin, observed by the women who had followed him from Galilee.

10. Without minimizing human responsibility, Mark has told his story throughout with God as the hidden actor, often signaled by the passive voice. When God strikes the shepherd, the sheep do not scatter, but are scatter*ed* (14:27). Their hearts are not hard, but harden*ed* (6:52; 8:17). In Gethsemane, the disciples' eyes are weigh*ed* down, not just heavy; they are blind*ed*, not just blind (14:40).

16:1–8 Epilogue: Resurrection and Mission: Back to Galilee

The women come to the tomb belatedly to anoint the body and are startled to find that Jesus' body is not there. A young man in angelic attire and authority interprets the event: God has raised Jesus, and he goes before the disciples to Galilee. The audience is directed back to Galilee, back to the beginning of the Gospel, which can now be reread with new eyes. The risen Jesus is already out there in the world ahead of them, continuing to lead them in the mission he began in chapter 1. The women are directed to go and tell, but they are overcome by fear and say nothing to anyone.

Mark apparently intended to end his story without closure, in the middle of a sentence, with open tomb and open ending. All in the narrative have failed and abandoned Jesus. The women have stayed with him until the end and beyond. Will they turn out to be the only faithful witnesses? When they too fail, the reader, who may have thought the story about other people, is left with a decision to make.

21.8 For Further Reading

Black, C. Clifton. *Mark*. ANTC. Nashville: Abingdon Press, 2011.

Boring, M. Eugene. *Mark: A Commentary*. NTL. Louisville, KY: Westminster John Knox Press, 2006.

Broadhead, Edwin K. *Mark: Readings; A New Biblical Commentary*. Sheffield: Sheffield Academic Press, 2001.

Collins, Adela Yarbro, *Mark: A Commentary*. Hermeneia. Minneapolis: Fortress Press, 2007.

Donahue, John R., and Daniel J. Harrington. *The Gospel of Mark*. Sacra pagina. Collegeville, MN: Liturgical Press, 2002.

Malbon, E. S. *Mark's Jesus: Characterization as Narrative Christology*. Waco, TX: Baylor University Press, 2009.

Marcus, J. *Mark: A New Translation with Introduction and Commentary*. Anchor Bible 27 and 27A. New York: Doubleday, 2000.

Moloney, Francis J. *The Gospel of Mark: A Commentary*. Peabody, MA: Hendrickson, 2002.

———. *Mark: Storyteller, Interpreter, Evangelist*. Peabody, MA: Hendrickson, 2004.

Rhoads, D. *Reading Mark, Engaging the Gospel*. Minneapolis: Fortress Press, 2004.

Rhoads, D., J. Dewey, and D. Michie. *Mark as Story: An Introduction to the Narrative of a Gospel*. 2nd ed. Minneapolis: Fortress Press, 1999.

Telford, W. R. *The Theology of the Gospel of Mark*. Oxford: Oxford University Press, 1999.

Telford, William, ed. *The Interpretation of Mark*. Issues in Religion and Theology 7. Philadelphia: Fortress Press/London: SPCK, 1985.

van Iersel, Bas M. F. *Mark: A Reader-Response Commentary*. Translated by W. H. Bisscheroux. JSNTSup 164. Sheffield: Sheffield Academic Press, 1998.

22
Interpreting Matthew

22.1 Authorship

THE GOSPEL WAS ATTRIBUTED TO THE apostle Matthew in the second century as a way of affirming its authentic witness to the apostolic faith. Today, practically all critical scholars consider the evidence against apostolic authorship to be overwhelming: (1) Apostolic authorship is a claim made for the book, not a claim made by the book itself, which is anonymous. It makes no claim to eyewitness testimony, nor gives any evidence that the author was present at the scenes he narrates. (2) The use of Mark and Q and the apparent second- or third-generation date undercut the later claim to eyewitness testimony. (3) The Greek language in which the Gospel was composed was the native language of the author, and represents greater linguistic skill than the relatively unpolished Greek of Mark. The LXX is his Bible. (4) Arguments sometimes introduced to support authorship by the tax collector Matthew, for example, that the numerical patterns of the narrative supposedly point to a tax collector's handiness with figures, are fanciful and unconvincing.

Though we do not know his name, from the document he has given us we can surmise that the author was of Jewish background, a Diaspora Jew who had grown up in a Hellenistic city (presumably Antioch) speaking Greek and reading the LXX.[1] He may have been able to handle Hebrew well enough to facilitate biblical study, and he knew enough Aramaic for informal communication. He knew the traditions and methods of the synagogue, but had never received the formal scribal training that was becoming standard for scribes in formative Judaism. He was likely a teacher within his community, though it is difficult to describe this in official terms. He may have drawn a cameo self-portrait in 13:52 as the "scribe trained for the kingdom of heaven," but "scribe" is not intended in the technical sense.

22.2 Sources, Influences, and Traditions

PAGAN SOURCES? ALTHOUGH MATTHEW IS influenced by and makes use of religious ideas that were in the air in the Hellenistic world, he reflects no direct literary influence from pagan writings.

1. A significant minority of scholars understand the strong Gentile orientation of the Gospel to mean the author himself must have been a Gentile, attributing the Jewish elements in the Gospel to the evangelist's tradition rather than his redaction (Georg Strecker, *Der Weg der Gerechtigkeit: Untersuchung zur Theologie des Matthäus*, 3rd ed., FRLANT 82 [Göttingen: Vandenhoeck & Ruprecht, 1971]; John P. Meier, *Matthew*, New Testament Message 3 [Collegeville, MN: Liturgical Press, 1980]).

The Jewish Scriptures. The one set of documents that we may be certain were present in Matthew's community and exercised a profound influence on the composition of his Gospel is his Bible. Matthew's tensions with the Jewish community did not result in any lessening of his interest in the Jewish Scriptures. On the contrary, he was concerned to show that the Jewish Scriptures find their fulfillment in Jesus and the church (see below, §22.7.3).

Other Jewish literature. Matthew contains no direct quotations from the deuterocanonical/apocryphal books or any other literature outside the Hebrew canon. That Matthew was acquainted with ideas and phraseology used in both the deuterocanonical books and the Pseudepigrapha seems to be clear, however, from the fact that there are seventy-eight allusions to them (fifty-eight to the deuterocanonical/apocryphal books, twenty to other extracanonical texts such as *4 Maccabees* and *1 Enoch*).[2]

Paul? The Matthean stream of Christianity, which presumably was located in or near Antioch, was not directly influenced by Paul's letters or tradition, but does probably reflect a moderate reaction to Paul's theology as it was understood near the end of the first century (see also the Letter of James). Matthew emphasizes the Petrine roots of the church, which probably also reflects its Antiochene location or connections, since Peter continued to be revered in Antioch.

The Q collection of sayings of Jesus. From the early history of the Matthean church, probably from the time of its founding, Q had been a revered document. It was presumably often read in the worship and/or instruction of the Matthean congregation(s), and shaped and expressed the ethos of Matthean Christianity.

The Gospel of Mark. The Gospel of Mark, probably in an edition slightly revised from the form preserved in the canon (see above, Exc. 3.4) provided the basic framework and content of Matthew's Gospel, which could be seen as a revised and expanded version of Mark. Matthew incorporated the Q materials within the narrative structure of the Gospel of Mark. In its original form, Q tended to be a growing, unstable document, too readily amenable to expansion by new "sayings of the risen Jesus" spoken by Christian prophets. By inserting it into the preresurrection framework of Mark's narrative, Matthew was able both to preserve the continuing address of Jesus to his church present in Q and to prohibit its continued expansion by grounding it in the history of the pre-Easter Jesus.[3]

The "M" materials. In addition to Q and Mark, Matthew had traditions and materials peculiar to his own community. "M" was not a separate document, but represents this body of peculiarly Matthean traditions. Since these traditions were formed and/or handed down by the local churches that also helped form Matthew's own theological perspective, it is at times difficult to distinguish M tradition from Matthew's redaction. The author of Matthew seems to have been a Jewish Christian scribal teacher for some time prior to his composition of the Gospel. He had presumably worked with, edited, and interpreted such materials for an extended period before incorporating them in the Gospel. Matthew or teachers like him had adapted, modified, and expanded such materials to address new situations, but also had sometimes preserved earlier forms of the tradition with remarkable fidelity, especially traditions affirming earlier Jewish Christianity's adherence to the Torah. M may have contained collections of Scripture quotations particularly relevant to Matthean theology ("testimonia"), Christian scribal interpretations of such quotations, midrashic comments and developments of Q and Markan texts and other items of Christian

2. These figures are derived from the indexes of Aland, Aland, Karavidopoulos, et al., *Nestle-Aland*, 27th ed., 800–806.

3. For elaboration of this point and evidence for it, see Boring, *Continuing Voice of Jesus*, 191–234, 242–46, 255–56.

tradition, as well as sayings and stories from and about Jesus unique to the Matthean tradition. Though a few of the M materials could have been written down prior to Matthew, most if not all were handed on orally.

The sacred tradition of Matthew's community. Matthew was steeped in all his sacred texts and traditions. He treated them all with great seriousness and respect without being slavishly bound to any of them. Just as Matthew was familiar enough with his Bible to make scores of allusions to the Scripture without specifically calling attention to it (see below), so Q, Mark, and M texts formed part of the warp and woof of his mind for some time before he composed the Gospel. His use of Q and Mark is at the furthest pole from "cut and paste" use of them as "sources." Matthew's mind is so saturated with Q and Mark that he can make allusions to them even in sections where he is not directly using them as sources. Markan phrases creep into a Q passage and vice versa.

22.3 Date

MATTHEW'S COMMUNITY STRETCHES over an extended period, developing and changing as it confronted and adapted to new situations (see below). But the Gospel itself represents a cross-section of this growing tradition at a particular time, a "freezing" of it in the theological composition of one particular scribal leader of the community at a specific moment in its history. Since there are no explicit chronological data in the Gospel that identify its time of composition, this date cannot be pinpointed, but there are indications of a general period.

1. On the Two-Document Hypothesis, Matthew must have been written after Q and Mark. There are good reasons for dating Mark a few years either side of 70 CE, so Matthew must be enough later for Mark to have become the sacred tradition of a community.

2. The war of 66–70 CE and the destruction of Jerusalem are almost certainly reflected in 22:7; see also 21:41; 23:38. Yet Matthew does not seem to be overwhelmed by the catastrophe, which seems some distance away in both space and time.

3. Matthew seems to be engaged with the developments in formative Judaism in the generation after 70 CE.

4. Matthew, and not merely Matthean tradition, seems to have been used by both the *Didache* and Ignatius (see above). The *Didache* probably comes from the period around 100 CE; Ignatius writes about 110 CE.

It thus seems that Matthew was composed in the period 80–100, for which 90 may serve as a good symbolic figure.

22.4 Provenance

SEVERAL LOCATIONS FOR THE MATTHEAN community have been argued: Palestine (Galilee, Caesarea, Jerusalem), Syria (Tyre, Sidon, Antioch), Egypt (Alexandria), Trans-Jordan (Pella). The majority of scholars favor Antioch, for the following reasons: (1) Internal evidence of the Gospel points to some Greek-speaking urban area where Jews and Christians were in intense interaction. Greek was the dominant language of Antioch, which probably had the largest Jewish population in Syria. Matthew seems to breathe a more urbane air than either Q or Mark. Whereas Mark refers to cities eight times and villages seven times, Matthew has twenty-six references to cities and only four references to villages. (2) Peter is prominent in both Matthew and in Antiochene tradition, which made him the first bishop of Antioch. (3) Jerusalem seems out of the question, since James plays no role. (4) Matthew introduces "Syria" into his sources (4:24), perhaps as a pointer to his own church and to ground it in saving history. (5) The designation of Jesus as a Nazorean (2:23) speaks for Syria, where Christians were known as "Nazoreans." (6) The contacts with Ignatius, the *Didache*, and the *Gospel of the Nazarenes*, all related to the region of Syria or Antioch in particular, point to this area as the origin of the Gospel of Matthew. (7) The equation of a stater with two didrachmas (17:24–27) fits Antioch, the only location where this equation is documented. (8) Situating Matthew in Antioch fits the situation described in Acts, where Palestinian Christians started the Antiochene church, which then developed a Gentile mission and the resulting tensions. (9) The respect in which Matthew and his readership held the Q materials suggests an area in which the Q missionaries were active. Upper Galilee and Syria corresponds to the area of influence of the Q community.

22.5 The Gospel of Matthew: Reinterpretation for Changing Times

THE GOSPEL OF MATTHEW IS NOT THE product of an isolated individual author, but reflects the life and concerns of a particular Christian community. Matthew has long been known as the most ecclesiastical Gospel, the only Gospel to use the word "church" (16:18; 18:17). Matthew's church has obviously been involved in an intense relationship with the surrounding dominant Jewish community and cannot be defined, as it did not define itself, apart from that relationship. Matthew's composition includes voices and interpretations from earlier times the author wants to preserve from the community's past history, even though they clash with what he regards as necessary to be said for his own present situation.

22.5.1 Matthew the Jew

We may picture Matthew himself and some members of his community as Jews who had grown up in the period before the 66–70 war, with the synagogue as their spiritual home. Matthew has interests that are distinctively Jewish: his fundamental affirmation not only of the Law but of Jewish tradition (5:17–20; 23:3), of the importance of the Sabbath (24:20), the holy city (5:35; 4:5; 27:53), the validity of temple and Jewish festivals (5:23–24; 26:17–30). Prior to Easter, the Matthean Jesus limits the mission to Israel (10:5–6; 15:24). He feels no need to explain Jewish customs, as did his Markan source (15:1 vs. Mark 7:1–4). His Gospel contains texts that suggest his community had been—and perhaps still was in his own time—subject to the disciplinary measures of the synagogue authorities (10:17–23; 23:2). "Gentiles" can be used as synonymous with "pagan" (5:47; 6:7, 32; 18:17; 20:25).

22.5.2 The Q Missionaries: "Messianic Jews" at Home in the Synagogue

Prior to the destruction of the temple, early missionaries of the Jesus movement evangelized Matthew's Jewish community in Syria. These missionaries were probably related to or identical with the missionary-prophets of the Q community with their eschatological message of Jesus' return as Son of Man. They presented Jesus as the ultimate interpreter of the Torah, God's last word before the final judgment. Most Jews rejected this preaching, but those who were convinced by the message of the Q missionary-prophets also adopted the document that preserved Jesus' teaching. Careful study of the Gospel of Matthew indicates that the author, and presumably the earlier members of the group that became the Matthean church, had treasured the Q document for some years before the Gospel of Matthew was written. It formed the earliest core of what was to become their authoritative Christian tradition, and they continued to prefer its version of some of Jesus' sayings and teachings after they had received the Gospel of Mark and later interpretations. They became believers in Jesus as the Son of Man, the fulfillment of their hopes for the coming Messiah, without ever dreaming that this would eventually alienate them from their religious and cultural home in Judaism. They believed that Jesus was the Messiah and would soon return in power, but neither for themselves nor for their fellow Jews did this mean a separation from Judaism.

22.5.3 "Messianic Jews" as a Distinct Group within the Synagogue

Tensions developed. We do not know the details or the issues, but they probably involved disputed interpretations of the Law according to the teaching and example of Jesus, and whether one who had been crucified could be the Messiah. Those who had become disciples of Jesus found themselves becoming an isolated group within the synagogue. Matthew's group may have eventually formed one or more separate synagogues; if so, they were still synagogues of Jews within the orbit of Judaism, somewhat analogous to the synagogue of the Hellenists in Jerusalem (Acts 6:1; 9:29; 11:20, and §§7.4.2; 9.2.2 above).

22.5.4 The War, Jamnia, Self-Definition, and Polarization

In the generation following the 66–70 war, the destruction of the temple, and the beginnings of reformation of Judaism at Jamnia, Matthew's group found not only itself, but the synagogue(s) to which they were related, in the process of change, and tensions increased. By the time Matthew writes, he and his community are alienated from these developing structures. They refer to their own gathering as the "church" (ἐκκλησία, *ekklēsia*; the word is found only in Matthew in the Gospels, 16:16; 18:17).[4] The Matthean Jesus refers to "my church," but "their synagogues" (16:18; 10:17; cf. the narrator's voice in 4:23; 9:35; 12:9; 13:54). The restructuring of post–70 Judaism under the leadership of the Pharisees generated mutual suspicion and hostility between the Matthean community and the Pharisees, against whom Matthew carries on a vigorous polemic (e.g., 5:20; 6:1–18; 15:1–20; 23:1–36).

22.5.5 Gentiles

The Antioch church was the first Christian center in which the Jewish Christian mission openly appealed to Gentiles and accepted them without requiring that they become Jews first (see above, §9.2.2). After Paul lost his struggle with the more conservative faction in Antioch and left to begin his Aegean mission (see above, §10.1.9), Antiochene Christianity would have become more interested in preserving its Jewish traditions and connections with Jerusalem, without surrendering its Gentile mission. Within this complex matrix, as Matthew's group became increasingly distant from the traditional synagogue, they became more open to the reception of Gentiles, who may have been attracted to their preaching of Jesus as the Messiah, and who may have joined the Jewish Christian group without their status as Jews being entirely clarified. Peter and Petrine tradition seemed to have played a moderating role, continuing the Gentile mission but preserving the Jewish legacy. By the author's time, his church is carrying on a full-scale mission to Gentiles. In some ways they now find themselves more oriented to the Gentile world than to the emerging shape of Judaism, while continuing to affirm their Jewish past, of which they consider themselves the legitimate heirs.

22.5.6 Reception of Mark

Some time after 70 CE the Gospel of Mark arrived in the Matthean community, was accepted as part of the community's own sacred tradition, and was used in its life and worship. Mark had been written in and for a Gentile Christian community no longer living under the rule of Torah (Mark 7:1–23). While toning

4. The two additional instances found in the NRSV of Matt 18:15, 21 are translations of ἀδελφοί, *adelphoi*, usually translated "brothers and sisters."

down Mark's critique of Torah observance (cf. Matt 15 with Mark 7), the Markan narrative became a fundamental part of the Matthean church's way of telling the Jesus story, along with its characteristic emphases: Jesus the miracle worker, Jesus the crucified and risen one, Jesus the inaugurator of the Gentile mission. If the Gospel of Mark was already associated with Peter, this strengthened the emphasis on Peter as the leading apostle, an emphasis already present in the Matthean stream of tradition, and facilitated the Gospel's acceptance as a normative Christian text for Matthew's church. Matthew did not merely "combine" Q and Mark. He made the Markan narrative basic, inserting his Q and M materials into the Markan story line, to which they were subordinated. Generically, Matthew is an elaboration and new interpretation of the Markan narrative, not a continuation of the Q sayings collection.

22.6 Matthew's Christian Community

22.6.1 Relation to Formative Judaism

Matthew's church sees itself as the messianic community, the eschatological people of God, distinct from all who do not believe in Jesus as the Messiah, whether Jews or Gentiles. Matthew continued the Jewish practice of using "Gentile" in the sense of "outsider." Thus both Matthew's "anti-Jewishness" and his "anti-Gentile" bias are in effect an expression of his sense of belonging to the Christian community distinct from the non-Christian world, both Jewish and Gentile.

The traditional way of posing the question—whether Matthew's church was still Jewish and still in the synagogue, or Gentile and already out of the synagogue—is no longer adequate.[5] Rather than representing Judaism and synagogue as static entities, with a post-70 council of Jamnia making decrees for an established Judaism, we should think rather of an extended period after the 66–70 war, stretching to the time of the codification of the Mishnah about 200 CE, as the period of formative Judaism. During this time the pre-70 Pharisaic party competed with other Jewish groups that had survived the war (priestly, scribal, apocalyptic, Christian, to some minor extent even Sadducean and Zealot) and finally established itself as the definitive element in that kind of rabbinic Judaism that became "normative." Within this mix, the Matthean community was apparently a movement still related to formative Judaism in both positive and negative ways, a group that regarded itself as the authentic people of God, experiencing itself as a persecuted minority at the hands of the dominant Pharisaic leadership (see, e.g., 5:13–16; 10:23, 32–33, 40–42; 25:31–46).

Matthew is in some kind of continuity, intense dialogue, and debate with formative Judaism. Developments in contemporary Judaism, including especially what is going on at Jamnia and its effects in the synagogues in his own environs, are of deep concern to him. He regards the developing Pharisaic leadership and its program for all Judaism as the chief opponents and alternatives to his own understanding of the way forward for the people of God. His Gospel includes traditional Jewish Christian materials that were important enough for him to include, and that he still in some sense affirms (5:17–20; 10:5–6; 23:1–3). While such texts as 10:16–25 express alienation from "their" synagogues, yet the fact that Christians could be beaten in them and brought before local Jewish courts ("sanhedrins") shows the victims of such abuse are still in some sense interior to the Jewish community. Likewise, the debate within Jerusalem Judaism provoked by the execution of James (62 CE) shows that Christian leaders could still be regarded as internal to Judaism a generation after Jesus' death. In this sense, Matthew's church is "Jewish."

5. So also, the inadequacy of speaking of "Jewish Christianity" or "Gentile Christianity" in either/or categories must be avoided. See above, §10.1.8, for Raymond Brown's four categories.

Though Matthew's church and/or the Q community from which it sprang had previously carried on an unsuccessful mission to the Jewish people, it has now abandoned a specifically Jewish mission, no longer sees itself as a renewal movement in Judaism, and is now engaged in a mission to the Gentiles, that is, the "nations," of which Israel is now one (28:18–20). Matthew understands the present and future of his church to be oriented to the Gentiles and regards developing non-Christian Judaism only as competitor and opponent. In this sense, Matthew's church is "Gentile."[6]

Is Matthew "anti-Semitic"? Or anti-Jewish? Since through the centuries texts from Matthew have been cited in support of racism and anti-Semitic statements and actions (especially 21:43 and 27:25), this issue must be honestly faced by Christians who wish to take Matthew seriously as canonical Scripture. To pose the question in terms of "anti-Semitism," however, is anachronistic, for the issue in Matthew is not racial prejudice, but religious conflict.[7] The historical situation from which the Gospel of Matthew emerged was filled not only with tensions between Jews and Gentiles, but with internal strife among various Jewish groups (of which the Matthean church was one). The Matthean Christian community, itself partly or even predominantly Jewish, felt itself to be persecuted by the Jewish leadership. In the conflict, sharp words were exchanged, so that from Matthew's side negative caricatures of Jewish leadership and religious practice were presented as a part of the polemic (e.g., 21:43; 23:1–36; 27:24–26).[8]

While it is false and anachronistic to accuse Matthew of anti-Semitism—he pictures Jesus and the disciples as Jewish, is himself a Jew, and writes for a church with a Jewish tradition and membership—it is lamentably true that the sayings and imagery deriving from the conflict of Matthew's church and the Jewish leadership have been used to fuel the fires of anti-Semitism. Just as modern interpreters must be on guard that Matthean texts not be used to encourage anti-Semitism, so legitimate modern sensitivities about anti-Semitism must not be allowed to obscure a historical understanding of Matthew's negative and polemical stance toward formative Judaism of his own time.

22.6.2 Structure and Leadership

Since Matthew reflects the situation of the addressees only indirectly, it is difficult to determine the details of the structure and life of the churches to which the Gospel is addressed.

Peter, Apostles, Disciples

The disciples in Matthew's narrative often transparently represent the post-Easter Christian community (e.g., 10:17–42; 18:15–20). Though Matthew uses the phrase "the twelve disciples" (10:1; 11:1; 20:17) or simply "the twelve" (10:5; 26:14, 20, 47), he thinks of the disciples as the whole group of those who have committed themselves to follow Jesus, not just the twelve (8:21; 9:14; 10:25, 42; 12:49; 27:57; 28:19). Within this group there is a central, symbolic core of twelve who represent the present leaders and future judges of the renewed, twelve-tribe people of God (19:28).

Within this group of twelve, Peter plays a distinct, symbolic role. Matthew modifies and adds to his tradition to emphasize the special role of Peter (10:2; 14:22–33; 15:15; 16:16–19; 17:24–27). Peter's significance in Matthew cannot be reduced to that of representative or typical disciple, a cipher for the Twelve or for the church as a whole. He is called first (4:18–19) and is designated as the "first" (10:2, added to Mark). He plays a singular role in the founding and maintenance of the Christian community and receives a special christological revelation

6. For an informative, balanced, and insightful study, see the 1988 presidential address to the Catholic Biblical Association of America, Donald P. Senior, "Between Two Worlds: Gentile and Jewish Christians in Matthew's Gospel," *Catholic Biblical Quarterly* 61, no. 1 (1999): 1–23.
7. Cf. Cohen, *Maccabees to the Mishnah*, 46–49.
8. Cf. Johnson, "Anti-Jewish Slander," 419–41.

from God, a unique pronouncement of blessing by Jesus, and a specific (and unrepeatable) responsibility in the founding of the church (16:17–19). Peter had spent some time in Antioch (Gal 2:11), the probable provenance of the Gospel, and in later tradition was considered the patron apostle of the church in that city and then its first bishop (Pseudo-Clementine, *Homilies* 20.23; *Recognitions* 10.68–71; Origen, "Homily on Luke 6" [GCS Origen IX, 32]). Petrine traditions and Petrine Christians may have played a role early in the history of Matthew's community, which may have regarded some of the M traditions as deriving from Peter or being especially associated with him. In Matthew's stream of tradition, Peter was looked upon as *the* representative apostolic figure, corresponding to Paul in the deuteropauline stream, James in the Jacobite stream, and the Beloved Disciple in the Johannine stream. Unlike his contemporaries Luke and the author of 1 Peter, who honor both Peter and Paul as legendary coleaders of the first generation of Christians, Matthew does not consolidate Petrine and Pauline traditions. The Matthean church was Petrine rather than Pauline, Jacobite, or Johannine. Matthew understands Peter to be significant for the church as a whole, not just his own community.

Charismatic and Ordered Ministry

It may seem surprising that the most ecclesiastical Gospel has no references, direct or indirect, to formal ministerial structures. There is no mention of bishop or deacons. This is particularly surprising if Matthew was written in Antioch or its environs, since only a few years later Ignatius of Antioch was making a strong case for the monarchial episcopate as the normal form of church government. Ignatius apparently stood in the Matthean tradition and used the Gospel of Matthew (*Eph.* 19.1–3; *Smyrn.* 1.1 = Matt 3:15; *Phld.* 3.1 = Matt 15:13; *Pol.* 2.2). Likewise the *Didache*, also in the Matthean tradition, reflects the transition from earlier charismatic ministry to the formal structures of bishops and deacons. Matthew seems to be in the same historical trajectory that led to Ignatius and the *Didache*, but unenthusiastic about the development of formal ecclesiastical offices. Some members of his community seem to have been interested in adopting the offices and titles that formative Judaism was beginning to use and invest with more formal authority than before ("rabbi," "father," "instructor"; see 23:8–12). Matthew resists this tendency.

The Matthean community seems to have had *prophets* among its leadership, probably as its principle leaders, as in the earlier days of the community reflected in the *Didache* and Q (Matt 5:12 compared to Luke 6:23; Matt 10:41; 23:34; even 7:21–22 presupposes there were "good" prophets in the community). These prophets were charismatic figures who received and transmitted revelations from the exalted Lord and who led the community in other ways. They were at home in the settled life of the community, but some of them also made missionary journeys (10:41). Matthew valued such prophets and saw them as a model for all church leadership and the Christian life as such (5:12), but also saw the danger of such charismatic leadership (7:15, 21–22; 24:11, 24). In contrast to Mark, for whom the problem was false interpretation of current events as the prelude to the eschaton, Matthew sees the danger of such "false prophets" to be their lax attitude toward ethics, including strict observation of the Torah (ἀνομία, *anomia*, lawlessness, understood in terms of the Torah, "Torahlessness").

Matthew also understood the risen Lord to have sent *sages* and *scribes* to function as leaders in the church (13:52; 23:34). The exact functions of these ministers is not clear, but they apparently served in roles analogous to roles in surrounding Judaism. Sages would have transmitted and interpreted the wisdom traditions of the community, but differently than in Judaism, since Matthew not only understood Jesus to be the messenger of wisdom, but utilized the figure of transcendent Wisdom as a christological category for understanding the status of the risen and exalted Christ.[9] Scribes not only would have worked over and transmitted biblical materials and provided midrashic interpretations and fulfillment quotations, but presumably would have done the same with the other sacred traditions of the community, namely, Q, Mark, and some of Matthew's special materials. This means that Matthew already has some Q and Markan traditions that have been interpreted by Christian scribes. Matthew himself is probably such a Christian scribe who brings out of his accumulated traditional treasure both old and new things for the edification of the community (13:52). Sages and scribes (like prophets) seem to have participated in the teaching ministry within the community, but the exact roles and how they were related to each other can no longer be determined.

22.6.3 Social Status

That Matthew appears to represent an urban community is illustrated by the above evidence for Antioch. Additional data suggest a community that had at least some relatively wealthy members. The Q beatitudes to the "poor" and "hungry" become in Matthew "poor in spirit" and "hunger and thirst for righteousness" (Matt 5:3, 6//Luke 6:20–21). References to small-denomination copper coins are replaced by references to gold and larger-denomination coins (Mark 6:8//Matt 10:9; Luke 19:11–27//Matt 25:14–30), and stories are told of high finance (e.g., 18:23–35) and lavish dinner parties (22:1–14). Matthew specifically adds to Mark that the Joseph of Arimathea who buried Jesus was both a disciple and a wealthy man (27:57).

9. Cf. 11:18–19, 25–30; 23:34 vs. Luke 11:49; M. Jack Suggs, *Wisdom, Christology, and Law in Matthew's Gospel* (Cambridge: Harvard University Press, 1970); Russell Pregeant, "The Wisdom Passages in Matthew's Story," in *Treasures New and Old: Recent Contributions to Matthean Studies*, ed. David R. Bauer and Mark Allen Powell (Atlanta: Scholars Press, 1996), 197–232.

22.7 Theological Issues and Themes

22.7.1 Conflict of Kingdoms

Matthew's story of Jesus is told within the overarching apocalyptic framework of cosmic conflict (see above, §7.6.1). The plot is dominated by the conflict of kingdoms. The reader should note that the conflict is not ultimately between Jesus and the Jewish leaders, or between the Roman Empire and the kingdom of God, but that the narrative unfolds as the earthly, historical segment of a cosmic story (see on 4:1–11; 12:22–32; 13:36–39). The this-worldly conflict with which the narrative is concerned has a cosmic, mythological backdrop and points beyond itself. Thus God is the hidden actor in the story throughout, and Satan is the hidden opponent (see above, §7.6.2).

22.7.2 Ethics: Doing the Will of God

Matthew is supremely interested in ethics, by which he means *the will of God* (6:10; 7:21; 12:50; 18:14; 21:31; 26:42), summed up as δικαιοσύνη (*dikaiosunē*, righteousness, justice, 3:15; 5:6, 10, 20; 6:1, 33; 21:32). To do right is to do the will of God. Although the Matthean Jesus speaks with the authority of God, giving specific instructions for doing the will of God, Matthew's ethic is not expressed in a list of rules, but in the Matthean story as a whole. This story is not only the story of Jesus that provides the substance and plot of Matthew's narrative, but the metanarrative of which it is a part, the story of God from creation to eschaton, of which the Jesus story is the defining center.[10] Although Matthew insists that the Law and the Prophets, as interpreted by Jesus, represent God's will and must be done, the will of God is finally revealed in a life of discipleship to Jesus,

10. On both points, see Russell Pregeant, *Knowing Truth, Doing Good: Engaging New Testament Ethics* (Minneapolis: Fortress Press, 2008), 123–44.

with the command to love God and neighbor as its essential norm.

22.7.3 Fulfillment of Scripture

Matthew directly quotes the Scripture forty times with an explicit indication such as "it is written" (e.g., Matt 4:4 = Deut 8:3). Matthew also contains several other direct citations not explicitly so identified (e.g., Matt 27:46 = Ps 22:1; their exact number depends on how strictly one distinguishes between quotation and allusion), making a total of sixty-one direct quotations in twenty-eight chapters, plus a plethora of biblical paraphrases, allusions, and imagery. The Nestle-Aland Greek New Testament lists 294 allusions, more than ten per chapter.

A special category is formed by ten "formula quotations," sometimes called "reflection citations" (*Reflexionszitaten*) or "fulfillment quotations":[11]

— 1:22–23 = Isaiah 7:14 "Behold, a virgin shall conceive and bear a son, and his name shall be called Emmanuel" (which means, God with us)."

— 2:15 = Hosea 11:1 "Out of Egypt have I called my son."

— 2:17–18 = Jeremiah 31:15 "A voice was heard in Ramah, wailing and loud lamentation, Rachel weeping for her children; she refused to be consoled, because they were no more."

— 2:23 (= Isaiah 11:1?) "He shall be called a Nazarene."

— 4:14b–16 = Isaiah 9:1–2 "The land of Zebulun and the land of Naphtali, toward the sea, across the Jordan, Galilee of the Gentiles — the people who sat in darkness have seen a great light, and for those who sat in the region and shadow of death light has dawned."

— 8:17 = Isaiah 53:4 "He took our infirmities and bore our diseases."

— 12:18–21 = Isaiah 42:1–4 "Behold, my servant whom I have chosen, my beloved with whom my soul is well pleased. I will put my Spirit upon him, and he shall proclaim justice to the Gentiles. He will not wrangle or cry aloud, nor will anyone hear his voice in the streets; he will not break a bruised reed or quench a smoldering wick, till he brings justice to victory; and in his name will the Gentiles hope."

— 13:35 = Psalm 78:2 "I will open my mouth in parables, I will utter what has been hidden since the foundation of the world."

— 21:4–5 = Isaiah 62:11; Zechariah 9:9 "Tell the daughter of Zion, Look, your king is coming to you, humble, and mounted on a donkey, and on a colt, the foal of a donkey."

— 27:9–10 = Zechariah 11:13, attributed to "Jeremiah" "And they took the thirty pieces of silver, the price of him on whom a price had been set by some of the sons of Israel, and they gave them for the potter's field, as the Lord directed me."

All are introduced by Matthew into their contexts. Except for the four formula quotations in the birth narrative, all are triggered by a Markan context. Except for Zechariah 9:9 cited in Matthew 21:4–5, none is cited elsewhere in the New Testament. They thus seem to belong exclusively to Matthew and/or his own tradition. They are distinguished from the other quotations, including the others peculiar to Matthew (1) by their introductory formula identifying an event in Jesus' life as the fulfillment of Scripture, (2) by the fact that all are spoken by the narrator to the reader, not by a character in the story to other characters, and (3) by their text type. While Matthew generally follows the LXX, these ten are distinctive in diverging from the LXX and from all other known text types.

11. Four additional citations are sometimes included in this group (2:6; 3:3; 13:14–15; 26:56). Although fourteen is a significant number for Matthew (1:2–17), the additional four do not meet the criteria cited here, and are all of a different text type—and ten is also a significant number for Matthew.

The full introductory formula is found in the first quotation—"All this took place to fulfill what had been spoken by the Lord through the prophet (saying)" (1:22)—and is repeated with minor variations in all the others.

22.7.4 Moses Typology

From the beginning of his composition, Matthew has narrated the story of Jesus so as to evoke the images of Moses from both the Scripture and Jewish tradition.[12]

— 1:18–21 In a dream an angel announces Moses' birth and that he will work miracles and save his people (cf. Exod 2:1–10; Ps Philo, *Bib. Ant.* 9.10).

— 1:18–25 Moses is conceived in a miraculous way. The biblical story was expanded in Hellenistic Jewish tradition to give Moses a miraculous birth (not in the Old Testament, but cf. Philo, *Cherubim* 40–52; *Contempl. Life* 25; *Dreams* 1.200; *Moses* 1.279; *2 Enoch* 71.1–23).

— 2:1–15 At his birth he is threatened by the wicked king (Exod 1:8–22).

— 12:14 (see also 13:54–58; 21:33–40; 27:15–26) He is initially rejected by his own people (Exod 2:11–14 [Acts 7:27–35]).

— 2:1–4:11 He comes out of Egypt; passes through the water, and is tested in the wilderness (Exod 12–Deut 34).

— 5:1–7:27 He ascends the mountain and gives authoritative commands (Exod 19–23). The phrase "went up the mountain" (Matt 5:1), common in the OT, is almost exclusively associated with Moses. Even the note that Jesus "sat down" while teaching may also reflect Moses on the mountain, since in some Jewish interpretations Deuteronomy 9:9 was understood to portray Moses as specifically sitting on Mount Sinai; this became a topic of rabbinic discussion.[13]

— 8:1–9:34 He does ten great deeds of power in liberating the people of God (Exod 7–12). But Jesus' mighty deeds are all acts of mercy and deliverance—even for the Romans—rather than judgment on the oppressor. As Matthew has transformed the violent, conquering "Son of David" into the healing king who does not retaliate but withdraws (see on 12:9–21), he has transformed the violent acts of deliverance into acts of compassion.

— 17:1–9 A number of Mosaic traits were already in the pre-Markan form of the transfiguration story (cf. Exod 24:1–18; 34:29–35; Deut 18:15–18): "six days" (Exod 24:26); "high mountain" (Exod 24:12); a bright cloud overshadows the mountain; a select group of three (Aaron, Nadab, Abihu = Peter, James, John); a voice from the cloud; the response of fear; the command "hear him" (Deut 18:15). Matthew preserves these traits and focuses his attention on Jesus in the role of Moses, developing this typology by mentioning Moses first, by adding the description of Jesus' face shining like the sun (Exod 34:29–35), by describing the cloud as "bright," making the cloud more like the Shekinah that rested on the tabernacle and temple, and by having Jesus echo Moses' words about this "perverse and crooked generation" (Matt 17:17 = Deut 32:5). The heavenly cloud of God's presence appears on the mount of transfiguration, as on the tabernacle of Moses' day (Exod 40:34–35). As of old, the heavenly voice comes from the cloud, and the God who had previously spoken on Mount Sinai only to Moses speaks directly to Jesus' disciples.

— Chapters 5–7, 10, 13, 18, 23–25 Given the other evidence, the five great discourses of the teacher Jesus in Matthew probably also have a parallel in the five books of Moses.

12. For a more detailed and nuanced discussion, see Dale C. Allison, *The New Moses: A Matthean Typology* (Minneapolis: Fortress Press, 1993).

13. W. D. Davies and Dale C. Allison, *The Gospel according to Saint Matthew*, 3 vols., ICC (Edinburgh: T. & T. Clark, 1988–1997), 1:424.

Moses imagery looms in the background, and the Gospel can hardly be read without reflecting on how Jesus' life and authoritative teaching relates to Moses and the Torah given on Sinai—a live issue in the Matthean community.

22.7.5 Jesus the Teacher; No Messianic Secret

We have seen the role of the theme of the messianic secret in the formation of Mark, the first Gospel (§20.1.2), and that the secrecy theory required that Jesus be portrayed as an enigmatic teacher whose message could not be understood until after the resurrection. The disciples then had to be portrayed as failing to understand Jesus' teaching. For Matthew, the conditions that generated the Gospel of Mark no longer obtain; Matthew accepts Mark's resolution of the christological issues that generated the Gospel form, and does not need to reinvent the wheel. Probably like most Christians since, Matthew accepts Mark's juxtaposition of the divine Son of God and the truly human Jesus who suffers and dies, without reflecting on how this could be so. Matthew has other concerns, one of which is to present Jesus as authoritative teacher for the community, a teacher who wants to be understood, and who is understood. Matthew thus dismantles and/or reinterprets the Markan texts that express the messianic secret (his Q and M materials do not have this distinctively Markan literary device). Some examples:

— 1:18–2:12 Jesus' birth as Messiah and Son of God is a revelation of his identity. Astral phenomena indicate his significance and guide the magi. Herod, the chief priests, and scribes are aware of Jesus' identity. Mary and Joseph know he has no earthly father but is born as Son of God.

— 3:13–15 John the Baptist recognizes Jesus and is hesitant to baptize him until Jesus authoritatively commands him. John and the others present hear the voice from heaven, "This is my beloved Son" (Mark 1:11, "You are my beloved Son," to Jesus; the others, including John, do not hear).

— 9:25–26 Matthew omits the command of Mark 5:43 not to tell anyone of the miracle of raising the little girl from the dead (difficult to imagine historically in any case). In some places, Matthew retains the Markan command to secrecy, but they either play a different role in Matthew than in Mark or are simply vestigial.

— 13:10–17 Matthew greatly expands and rewrites the difficult Markan "explanation" of why Jesus taught in parables, eliminating the idea of Mark 4:10–12 that the parables were intended to keep people from understanding.

— 13:51 passim Matthew omits, modifies, or offers a supplemental correction for every passage in Mark that pictures the disciples as misunderstanding or failing to understand.[14]

The modification of the secrecy theory allows Matthew to present Jesus as an authoritative teacher whose interpretations of the Torah and directives about the will of God are understood and practiced by the disciples. This image then becomes a central aspect of the church's continuing mission: to make disciples of all nations, teaching them to obey all that Jesus, the supreme teacher, has commanded (28:16–18; see 23:8).

22.7.6 Emmanuel and the Continuing Presence of Christ

Like the other Synoptics (in contrast to John), Matthew has little to say about the presence of the Holy Spirit in the life of the post-Easter community of faith. His way of doing this is to speak of the continuing presence of Christ, equated with the presence of God, the presence of the Holy Spirit.

14. Cf. details in Barth, "Law," 105–12.

— 1:23 Matthew quotes the promise of Isaiah in relation to Jesus' birth: "they shall name him Emmanuel, which means 'God-with-us.'" This is not literally Jesus' name, of course. As often in the Bible, "name" is not a matter of label, but of essential being. "They" in this text is an indirect way of speaking of God. Thus this key text at the beginning of the Gospel means "God will constitute Jesus as God-with-us." The story of Jesus is a way of talking about God. In Jesus and his story, God is with us.

— 28:20 The last words of the risen Jesus are "Remember, I am with you always, to the end of the age." There is no ascension in Matthew; the risen Christ remains with his disciples. With 1:23, this text forms a bracket for the whole Gospel, affirming the continuing presence of God.

— 10:40 Jesus sends out his disciples, authorizing and empowering them to continue his own work (10:1–5). Those who receive Jesus' disciples receive Jesus himself, and those who receive him, receive God.

— 13:37 Jesus himself, the exalted Son of Man, accompanies his church through history as the one active in preaching the gospel throughout the world.

— 16:18 It is the transcendent Christ who continues to build the church.

— 18:20 Christ is present when the church convenes "in his name."

— 18:5, 25:40 Christ is met in the encounter with little children and needy human beings.

22.8 Structure: Matthew as Composer

MATTHEW ADOPTS THE BASIC MARKAN outline, restructuring it as follows:

— Matthew prefixes the genealogy and birth story at the beginning.

— Matthew adds resurrection appearances at the end. These two changes smooth out the abruptness of Mark's beginning and ending, and shift the narrative more in the direction of a Hellenistic *bios*.

— Matthew inserts the Q material into the narrative framework. Mark had been wary of floating collections of sayings of Jesus that were not grounded in the narrative that leads to the cross. By including them within the Markan outline, the sayings material is subordinated to the kerygma of the cross and resurrection.

After Matthew's creative editing, the basic Markan outline remains: Jesus' ministry unfolds in Galilee, after which he makes one trip to Jerusalem, where he is killed. Various proposals have been made to locate key turning points in Matthew's elaboration of Mark's outline.

Speeches. Five times Matthew concludes a major speech of Jesus with an almost identical formula, "Now when Jesus had finished saying these things" (7:28; 11:1; 13:53; 19:1; 26:1). The formula is not merely concluding, but transitional, pointing back to the completed speech and forward to the continuing narrative, relating Jesus' words to his deeds, and binding speech and narrative together.

1. The *Sermon on the Mount*, 5:3–7:29, presents the authoritative teaching of the Messiah who has come not to destroy the Law but to fulfill it.

2. The *Missionary Discourse*, 10:5b–42, is the address of Christ to his disciples, who are sent forth in mission as representatives of Christ and with his authority.

3. The *parable collection*, 13:1–52, portrays the hiddenness of the kingdom of God in the present, in conflict with the evil kingdom of this age, but ultimately triumphing over it.

4. *Directions for the internal life of the church*. This discourse, 18:1–35, addresses the church's need of both rigorous discipline and profound forgiveness if it is to live together as Christ's disciples.

5. The concluding *Judgment Discourse*, 23:1–25:46. This corresponds to the initial paradigmatic Sermon on the Mount, placing the life called for there in a specific eschatological context of universal judgment and the triumph of God's kingdom.

The speeches are an important structuring device, but Matthew should not be regarded as a structure of five speeches held together by narrative connections. The speeches are inserted into the narrative, which is primary.

Matthew's sacred traditions (Mark and Q) as the key to his structure. Matthew was deeply influenced by the structure of both his major sources, which had long been familiar to both him and his readers. In Part 1 of his composition, Matthew basically follows the order of Q, inserting material from Mark mainly in the collection of miracle stories in chapters 8–9, and arranging the whole section in a chiastic pattern. Matthew's Part 2 begins at 12:22 (=Mark 3:22). From this point on, he never deviates from the Markan order.

Matthew's church, already acquainted with Mark's Gospel and Q, has now been given a new framework for interpreting their sacred tradition. From 12:22 on, the narrative sections simply follow the Markan outline and order. Matthew imposes his stamp on it by inserting his own traditions and compositions into the narrative sections and by developing the Markan speeches into major compositional units to correspond to the Sermon on the Mount and the Missionary Discourse in Part 1. The resulting series of five speeches thus form the interlocking structure between Parts 1 and 2.

22.8.1 Outline

PART 1: The Conflict of Kingdoms Initiated and Defined	1:1–12:21
A. Jesus as Messianic King, Son of David and Son of God	1:2–25
B. Conflict with the Kingdom of This Age	2:1–23
C. Jesus and John: Baptism, Temptation, Beginnings	3:1–4:17
D. The Disciples Called	4:18–22
E. The Authority of the Messiah in Word and Deed	4:23–9:35
1. Messiah in word: Sermon on the Mount	*(Discourse 1) 5:1–7:29*
2. Messiah in deed: Ten mighty acts of deliverance	8:1–9:35
D′. The Disciples Authorized and Sent	*(Discourse 2) 9:36–11:1*
C′. Jesus and John: Identity and Response	11:2–19
B′. Conflict with the Kingdom of This Age	11:20–12:14
A′. The Servant King	12:15–21
PART 2: The Conflict of Kingdoms Developed and Resolved	12:22–28:20
Conflict, Decision, and Gathering the True Community	12:22–50
Parables and the Kingdom	*(Discourse 3) 13:1–52*
The Formation of the New Community amid Continuing Conflict	13:53–17:27
The opposition of the old community	13:53–16:12
The disciple's confession and the new community	16:13–28
God's confession and the new community	17:1–27

Life Together in the Community of Faith	*(Discourse 4) 18:1–35*
Conflict and Ultimate Polarization	19:1–22:46
Instructing the disciples en route to the passion	19:1–20:34
Jerusalem: The final confrontation	21:1–22:46
The Judgment Discourse	*(Discourse 5) 23:1–25:46*
Passion Narrative	26:1–28:20
Plot against Jesus, extravagant devotion to him	26:1–16
Passover/Last Supper	26:17–30a
Abandonment, betrayal, arrest	26:30b–56
Jewish trial: Jesus' confession and Peter's denial	26:57–27:1
Roman trial: Jesus condemned and mocked	27:2–31a
Crucifixion and burial	27:31b–66
Resurrection	28:1–28

22.9 Exegetical-Theological Précis

MATTHEW'S POINT OF DEPARTURE FOR HIS story of Jesus is Jesus' message of the present and coming kingdom of God. (Matthew often uses "kingdom of heaven" due to his reverence for the word "God"; the two phrases mean the same.) The cosmic conflict between God's kingdom and Satan's kingdom (12:22–30) is the background for the foreground conflicts between Jesus and his opponents that lead to his death.

Part 1: The Conflict of Kingdoms Initiated and Defined (1:1–12:21)

A. Jesus as Messianic King, Son of David, and Son of God (1:2–25)

The title of 1:1 introduces Jesus as Messiah, the hoped-for Son of David (see above, §7.6) and son of Abraham, in whom all nations will be blessed (Gen 12:1–3). The genealogy (1:2–17) is not a list, as in Luke 3:23–38, but is already a narrative that summarizes the history of the people of God from Abraham to Jesus. It presents Jesus as the fulfiller of Jewish hopes, descended through the royal line of David, who is mentioned five times. Jesus' ancestors also include those outside the mainstream people of God who were incorporated into the covenant people (Tamar, Rahab, Ruth, Bathsheba). The genealogy is unrelated to Luke's, with which it cannot be harmonized (see notes there).

In the opening scene, Joseph discovers that his fiancée is pregnant, and not by him. The Torah prescribes the punishment in such cases (Deut 22:23–27). Joseph had already decided not to do what the law commanded, even before he learned from the angel that the child had no earthly father. Yet Joseph is called a "righteous man" (1:19) and addressed as "Son of David" (1:20). But how can one who does not strictly keep the law be considered righteous? This will be a subplot of the Gospel throughout, for it is a question with which Matthew's own community is deeply concerned. They too reverence the Torah as the Law of God, but do not observe it in the traditional manner.

B. Conflict with the Kingdom of This Age (2:1–23)

The birth of Jesus is the birth of a king (2:2). Though welcomed by distinguished Gentile visitors from afar, there is already a "king of the Jews" in place, and there is room for only one king. Herod tries to destroy the newborn king. The earthly, evil ruler is not destroyed by divine violence. The newborn king "withdraws" (ἀναχωρέω, *anachōreō*), first to Egypt and then to Nazareth (2:14, 22). Moses, when threatened by Pharaoh, had also "withdrawn" to another country (Exod 2:15 ἀναχωρέω), but finally prevailed. Matthew uses this verb four times in this section (2:12, 13, 14, 22), anticipating the character of Jesus' kingship. He will use this key term six other times, almost exclusively for Jesus' response to threat and aggression (4:12; 10:23; 12:14–21; 14:13; 15:21). This "withdrawal" is not cowardice, self-preservation, or strategy, but represents Jesus' alternate vision of kingship, which is nonviolent and nonretaliatory. Jesus is the "Son of Man who has nowhere to lay his head" (8:20). Though he is the messianic king, Jesus is a displaced person in this world. This portrayal reflects both the post-Easter experience of his disciples and the Matthean picture of Jesus who responds to aggression in a nonretaliatory withdrawal (5:38–42; 26:53–56). Matthew has adopted it from Exodus 2:15 and its only use in Mark (3:7), where this was Jesus' response to the threat of 3:6, and made it into a leitmotiv of his Gospel. Moses had resisted Pharaoh with divine power, and so will Jesus, but the power of God as manifest in Jesus will be an essentially different kind of power.

C. *Jesus and John: Baptism, Temptation, Beginnings (3:1–4:17)*

At this point Matthew begins to follow his two major sources. Both Q and Mark began with John the Baptist. In contrast to the Markan John, the Matthean John recognizes Jesus and considers himself unworthy to baptize him. Jesus is in charge, speaks his first words in Matthew, which include the Matthean key terms "righteousness" and "fulfill." The heavenly voice declares Jesus to be God's Son and servant, combining texts from Psalm 2:7 and Isaiah 42:1. John and Jesus are united in their common commission to "fulfill all righteousness"; Jesus is declared Son of God precisely as one obedient to God's will (in contrast to the violent king Herod).

The temptation of 4:1–10 is no longer the power struggle, as in Mark, but a debate between Jesus and the devil on how the Son of God should exercise his ministry. It is related to the testing of Israel in the wilderness (Deut 6–8) and resembles the debates between Jesus and the Jewish leaders (cf. 21:23–27; 22:15–23:36). Satan too has a kingdom (12:26). The cosmic clash of God's and Satan's kingdoms is expressed in the debates between Jesus and his opponents, and can even come to expression in the well-intentioned protest of a disciple (16:23).

The news that John the Baptist had been arrested triggers Jesus' withdrawal to Galilee and the beginning of his own preaching ministry, fulfilling the Scripture's promise to "Galilee of the Gentiles" (4:12). Each term is theologically significant for Matthew. "Arrested" is παραδίδωμι (*paradidōmi,* hand over, deliver up), the same term used for the Suffering Servant of Isaiah 53:6 and for Jesus' betrayal, arrest, and being "delivered up" by God for human sins—which will happen to Jesus' own disciples (10:4, 19, 21; 17:22; 20:18; 24:9; 26:2, 15, 21, 23, 48; 27:3, 18, 26). On "withdrew," see above on 2:1–23. "Galilee" represents the later spread of the gospel to Gentiles (28:16–18).

D. *Disciples Called (4:18–22)*

This brief passage is structurally significant in Matthew's story, the calling of the disciples corresponding to their being sent in 9:36–11:1 (see outline above, §22.8.1). As in Mark, Jesus takes the initiative. They respond to his authoritative word. Their discipleship is not the fulfillment of their own religious quest, or based on their seeing his miracles or hearing his teaching, but the result of Jesus' effective call. They do not yet know where they are going but must learn along the way.

E. *The Authority of the Messiah in Word and Deed (4:23–9:35)*

The central core of Matthew's Part 1 is his presentation of Jesus' authority in word (the Sermon on the Mount) and deed (a collection of ten miracles), framed by the almost identical summary statements 4:23/9:35. The Messiah in word precedes the Messiah in deed. For Matthew, Jesus is supremely the Teacher (23:10). It is his teaching that validates his miracles, not the other way round.

Both teaching and actions are reminiscent of Moses. From a mountain, Jesus delivers instructions on how to live. Jesus performs ten acts of power, delivering his people and forming a new community. The relation of Jesus and Moses was a live issue in Matthew's Jewish Christian community.

1. Messiah in word: Sermon on the Mount (5:1–7:29) The Sermon on the Mount is not a report of a particular 30-CE speech on a Galilean hillside. While some of its materials go back to the 30-CE Jesus, the Sermon is Matthew's composition. It is the most carefully structured speech in the Gospel. Matthew takes over the Great Sermon of Q and follows its order almost exactly, amplifying it with other material from elsewhere in Q, his own special materials, and a few sayings from Mark (see Luke 6:20–49, and Box 30 below).

Here we find Matthew's response to the question raised in the opening scene of the Gospel (Matt 1:18–19), a question that profoundly troubled the Matthean church: how is it that people who do not obey the letter of the divine Law can still be "righteous" in God's eyes? The Matthean Jesus makes it clear that he has not come to destroy the Law (5:17–20). His life and teaching are a fulfillment of the Law. The central requirement of the Law is love for others (5:43–48; 7:12; see 22:34–40). Whoever loves God and neighbor is in fact fulfilling the Law and the Prophets. This demand does not remain abstract and general. Six focal instances ("Antitheses") illustrate what this means in practice (5:21–40). Each follows the same pattern: reaffirmation of the Law, radicalization of the Law, situational application of the Law. The first three illustrate the situational application; the last three are open-ended, leaving the disciple to discern from situation to situation what love for God and the neighbor requires, on the basis of the examples given and the character of God as revealed in Jesus.

When Jesus concludes his challenge to live by the love command by appealing to God's own perfection, he makes clear this most radical form of the love command: "in view of God's 'Yes' to us, a 'No' to our fellow human beings can no longer be our final word. Not 'as you have done to me, so I will do to you,' but 'as God has done for me, so I will do for you'—that is the 'perfection' to which the disciple of Jesus Christ is called."[15]

2. Messiah in deed: Ten mighty acts of deliverance (8:1–9:35) In this section, the Messianic authority and power of Jesus is portrayed by assembling nine miracle stories relating ten mighty acts of salvation (9:18–26 combines healing the woman with the hemorrhage and raising the ruler's daughter). The nine stories are clustered in three groups of three; the ten mighty acts are reminiscent of the ten Egyptian plagues. Matthew has used each of two stories twice to get this pattern, using the story of healing the blind man in Mark 10:46–52 in both 9:27–31 and 20:29–34, and the Q story of healing the mute demonized man (Luke 11:14–15) in both 9:32–34 and 12:22–24. Jesus is like Moses, but his mighty deeds express God's compassion rather than judgment.

The twin summaries that bracket this section emphasize healing, not exorcisms or nature miracles (4:23/9:35). While in Mark Jesus' mighty deeds all tended to have exorcistic traits, portraying Jesus as victor over the demonic powers, in Matthew they all tend to take on the character of healing stories. Thus for Matthew the expected "Son of David" (ten times in Matthew) is transformed from the military victor who operates with divine violence into the compassionate healer. Despite Jesus' compassionate, nonaggressive behavior, rejection and

15. Reinhard Feldmeier, *"Salz der Erde": Zugänge zur Bergpredigt*, Biblisch-theologische Schwerpunkte 14 (Göttingen: Vandenhoeck & Ruprecht, 1998), 442.

Box 30: The Sermon on the Mount

Section	Matthew	Parallels
Introduction: Setting of the Sermon	4:23–5:2	Mark 1:39, 3:7–13, Luke 6:12, 17–20a
I. Triadic pronouncements that constitute the disciples as the eschatological community, 5:3–16		
A. The Beatitudes: Character and destiny of the disciples	5:3–12	Luke 6:20b–23
B. The disciples as salt	5:13	Luke 14:34–35 Mark 9:49–50
C. The disciples as light	5:14–16	Luke 8:16; 11:33 Mark 4:21
II. Tripartite instructions on the way of life in the eschatological community, 5:17–7:12		
A. Part 1: "The Law"	5:17–48	
1. The Law and the "greater righteousness"	5:17–20	Luke 16:16–17
2. Three antitheses modeling the greater righteousness, 5:21–32		
a. Anger	5:21–26	Luke 12:57–59 Mark 11:25
b. Lust	5:27–30	Mark 9:43
c. Divorce	5:31–32	Luke 16:18 Mark 10:3–4, 11:12
3. Three antitheses for the disciples' application, 5:33–48		
a. Oaths	5:33–37	M
b. Retaliation	5:38–42	Luke 6:29–30
c. Love	5:43–48	Luke 6:27–28, 32–36
B. Part 2: "The temple service": Three acts of righteousness before God, 6:1–18		
1. Giving to charity	6:1–4	M
2. Prayer, 6:5–15		
a. Not like the hypocrites or the Gentiles	6:5–8	M
b. The Lord's Prayer	6:9–13	Luke 11:2–4
c. The condition of forgiveness	6:14–15	Mark 11:25(–26)
3. Fasting	6:16–18	M
C. Part 3: "Deeds of loving kindness": Additional instruction in authentic righteousness, 6:19–7:12		
1. Serving God or mammon	6:19–24	Luke 12:33–34 11:34–36 16:13
2. Anxiety	6:25–34	Luke 12:22–32
3. Judging	7:1–5	Luke 6:37–42 Mark 4:24–25
4. Pearls before swine	7:6	M
5. Asking and receiving	7:7–11	Luke 11:9–13
6. Concluding summary: The Golden Rule	7:12	Luke 6:31
III. Three eschatological warnings, 7:13–27		
A. Two ways	7:13–14	Luke 13:23–24
B. Two harvests (false prophets)	7:15–23	Luke 6:43–46 13:25–27
C. Two builders	7:24–27	Luke 6:47–49
Conclusion of the sermon	7:28–29	Mark 1:22

conflict emerge in this section for the first time in the Gospel (9:3).

D′. Disciples Authorized and Sent (9:36–11:1)

This is the second of Jesus' five great discourses in Matthew (see above on structure). In both Q and Mark, Jesus gives a commissioning speech as he sends forth his disciples. Matthew typically combines these into one speech, in contrast to Luke, who preserves each speech separately (Luke 9:3–5 as "Sending the Twelve," Luke 10:2–20 as "Sending the Seventy[-two]"). Jesus' mission is only to Israel (10:5–6; cf. 15:24). After Easter, the mission is to all nations (28:16–20). Yet, here as elsewhere, Jesus' discourse collapses the post-Easter perspective into the pre-Easter narrative framework, speaking over the heads of the disciples at the story level to address the Gospel's audience of Matthew's time at the discourse level. Matthew takes material from Mark's apocalyptic discourse, in which Jesus gives directions for the later time of discipleship after the resurrection, depicting the troubles and terrors of the church's own time, and inserts it into the mission discourse (Mark 13:9–13 = Matt 10:17–25). Thus Matthew both separates the life of Jesus from the time of the church, and compresses these into a single perspective. He both prohibits the disciples from going to the Gentiles *and* warns them that they will testify to the Gentiles when put on trial by Gentile rulers (10:5–6; 18). The reference to Jesus' crucifixion and the disciples' cross (10:38) cannot yet make any sense at the story level, but Matthew's readers look back on the whole story of Jesus and know the Gospel of Mark quite well, and it speaks to them and their situation.

C′. Jesus and John: Identity and Response (11:2–19)

This section is the counterpart of John's initial appearance and preaching in 3:1–4:17 (see outline above, §22.8.1), the Q materials about John to compare John and Jesus and assign each his role in salvation history. John is a borderline figure, last and greatest of the biblical prophets, and though he proclaims the kingdom, he does not yet belong to it. Jesus and his disciples proclaim and live out the reality of the kingdom that has appeared in Jesus. Yet neither John nor Jesus fits the expected criteria of God's messengers. Both become stumbling blocks for those who suppose they already know how God acts, and both are rejected (11:11–19). Knowing the true God is a matter of God's own revelation, not of measuring God by human criteria (11:25–27).

B′. Conflict with the Kingdom of This Age (11:20–12:14)

All three units of this section deal with the increasing conflict that results from Jesus' call to repentance, and correspond in Matthew's outline to the clash of kingdoms begun in 2:1–23. The surface conflict expresses the fundamental opposition between the kingdom of God represented by Jesus and the demonic kingdom represented by his opponents. The section concludes with the Pharisees' decision to destroy Jesus (12:14).

A′. The Servant King (12:15–21)

Jesus responds to the plot by "withdrawing" (ἀναχωρέω, *anachōreō*, see above) and by healing. This section is the closing bracket, which corresponds to the opening scene presenting Jesus as messianic king, and echoes the divine words from heaven proclaiming him to be Son and servant of God, endowed with God's powerful Spirit, the king who exercises his imperial power with gentleness and mercy.

Part 2: The Conflict of Kingdoms Developed and Resolved (12:22–28:20)

Matthew's extensive Part 1 has now given his readers a new context in which to hear the story of Jesus with which they had become familiar from Q and Mark. From this point on (Mark 3:22 = Matt 12:22), Matthew retains practically everything in Mark and never departs from the

Markan order. The following summary will only point out Matthew's key additions to Mark and reinterpretations of Mark.

Conflict, Decision, and Gathering the True Community (12:22–50)

Matthew has been building to the key scene in which the kingdom of God confronts the kingdom of Satan. He makes the polarizing distinction between those who regard Jesus as working by Satan's power and those who see him as representing the (transformed, compassionate) Son of David (12:23–24) and adds Q material illustrating that the conflict is between the Spirit of God and the demons.

Parables and the Kingdom (13:1–52)

Matthew extends Mark's parable collection by adding additional parables from Q and M and by rewriting and amplifying Jesus' explanation for why he teaches in parables. Thus Matthew no longer presents Jesus as intending to conceal his teaching from the crowds, as in the Markan story line controlled by the messianic secret. He concludes by assuring the readers that the disciples understood (13:51), presenting a parabolic portrait of the skillful Jewish Christian teacher who brings *both* old and new teaching from his treasure (13:52)—probably something of a self-portrait of the author.

The Formation of the New Community amid Continuing Conflict 13:53–17:27

The opposition of the old community (13:53–16:12) The focus is increasingly on the Pharisees and Sadducees as representatives of those who oppose the kingdom of God (Matthew adds 15:12–13; 16:11–12).

The disciple's confession and the new community (16:13–28) The scene of Peter's confession is still a dramatic focus of the action in Matthew, as it had been in Mark, but in a different way. In Mark, it had been an extraordinary breakthrough, in which Jesus' messiahship was confessed for the first time, though tragically misunderstood. In Matthew, Jesus' identity has been known from the beginning, and the disciples have already worshiped him as Son of God (14:33). In Matthew, Peter receives Jesus' blessing for making the confession, and the focus is shifted from Christology to ecclesiology: Christ will build his church, it will endure till the end of history, and Peter will be the foundational figure. Matthew had already added a paragraph in which not only Jesus, but Peter, walks on the water (then Peter almost sinks; 14:28–32). Here Matthew reverses Mark by adding Jesus' blessing to Peter's confession, and announces that Peter is the rock on which Jesus will build the church (then Peter misunderstands and becomes the stumbling block). The additional material Matthew inserts here (16:17–19) does not seem to have been created by Matthew but to represent an older tradition, post-Easter but pre-Matthean, that magnified Peter's role in the formation and guidance of the church.

God's confession and the new community 17:1–27 In the transfiguration scene, Peter's prior confession on earth is confirmed by the divine confession from heaven. Peter, guided by Jesus, leads the new community to see that, although they are free from the obligation to pay the temple tax, they should pay it so as not to give offense to others who otherwise might misunderstand. This is analogous to the obligation of conducting one's life in the church so as not to hinder its mission, as argued by Paul (1 Cor 8–10; Rom 14). As promised in 16:18–19, Peter speaks in Jesus' behalf on disputed issues, and Jesus confirms Peter's answer as his own (17:24–27).

Life Together in the Community of Faith (18:1–35)

By adding sayings and parables from Q and M, Matthew amplifies Mark's brief section (Mark 9:33–47) into a full-blown discourse on church discipline, with an emphasis on forgiveness within the Christian community.

Conflict and Ultimate Polarization (19:1–22:46)

Instructing the disciples en route to the passion (19:1–20:34) Matthew basically reproduces Mark, his only major additions being the paragraph on those who renounce marriage for the sake of the kingdom of God (19:10–12) and the parable of the Laborers in the Vineyard (20:1–16).

Jerusalem: The final confrontation (21:1–22:46) Matthew follows Mark closely, only adjusting the chronology so that the "triumphal entry" and "cleansing the temple" come on the same day, which is now Monday of Jesus' last week (in the parallel Mark 11:1–19, the entry was on Sunday, the cleansing on Monday). Again Matthew emphasizes that Jesus is Son of David, but as nonviolent healer (21:4–17). In Mark, Jesus performs no healings in Jerusalem and rejects the title Son of David. Matthew's major addition to Mark in this section is his reworked version of the Q parable of the Wedding Banquet (cf. Luke 14:16–24), now transparent to the subsequent history in which Jews mostly reject Christian preaching, Jerusalem is destroyed, and Gentiles are brought into the people of God.

The Judgment Discourse (23:1–25:46)

Jesus' fifth and final discourse is often divided into two, the speech against the scribes and Pharisees of chapter 23 and the eschatological discourse of chapters 24–25. Matthew probably intended these as one discourse, not only to correspond to his five-speech schema with five similar concluding formulae, but to comprehend the whole section under the rubric of the coming judgment at the return of the Son of Man. The declarations against scribes and Pharisees reflect the polemics of Matthew's own time and use the conventional polemical language. Mark had a speech against the scribes, Q a speech against the Pharisees. Each had an eschatological discourse. Matthew typically combines these into one comprehensive discourse, while Luke preserves them as separate speeches (cf. Mark 12:37b–40; 13:5–37; Luke 11:37–54; 17:20–37; 21:8–36).

Passion Narrative (26:1–28:20)

Matthew's additions and modifications of Mark are basically of three types.

1. Mark had divided his story so that virtually all Jesus' mighty deeds as Son of God were performed in the first, Galilean section, so that the passion story in Jerusalem portrays only the weak and vulnerable human being Jesus. Matthew adjusts Mark's perspective, extending some of the traits of the powerful Jesus into the passion story. He is less the victim, more the sovereign Son of God firmly in control. Matthew adds an additional passion prediction to Mark's three, showing that, while the opponents are still trying to find a way to destroy him, he already knows what is to happen (26:2–5). Just as Jesus has healed people after his entrance into Jerusalem (21:14, contrary to the Markan view), so in Gethsemane he *could* call for help from the angelic armies, but *does* not (26:52–54).

2. In Mark, the passion story for the first time reveals the true identity of Jesus as Son of God (Mark 14:61–62; 15:39). For Matthew, this identity has been revealed since the first chapter, and the emphasis shifts from secrecy to the rejection of the Messiah by his own people.

3. Matthew adds legendary elements that manifest the significance of the events, especially their eschatological dimension and the more specific pictures of Jewish guilt for Jesus' death: Judas's suicide (27:3–10), Pilate's wife's dream (27:19), Pilate's hand-washing (27:24–25); the earthquake at Jesus' death and the emergence of past saints from the tombs (27:51–53); the guarding and sealing of the tomb, and the bribing of the guard by the Jewish leaders (27:62–66; 28:11–15).

Most significant is the addition of appearance stories to Mark's narrative of the discovery of the empty tomb and the commissioning of the disciples for mission to the whole world.

In 28:16–20, the climactic scene of the narrative, Matthew emphasizes that the Risen One is the same Jesus who has lived, taught, and died. The risen Jesus gives no new, secret instruction to the disciples but charges them to teach what he has already taught during his earthly life. The message of the risen Jesus is inseparable from the life and teaching of the earthly Jesus.

22.10 For Further Reading

Allison, D. C. *The New Moses: A Matthean Typology*. Minneapolis: Fortress Press, 1993.

Balch, D. L., ed. *Social History of the Matthean Community: Cross-Disciplinary Approaches*. Minneapolis: Fortress Press, 1991.

Boring, M. Eugene. "Introduction, Commentary, and Reflections: Matthew." In Leander E. Keck, ed. *The New Interpreter's Bible*, 8:87–505. Nashville: Abingdon Press, 1995.

Bornkamm, Günther, Gerhard Barth, and Heinz Joachim Held. *Tradition and Interpretation in Matthew*. NTL. Philadelphia: Westminster Press, 1963.

Carter, W. *Matthew and Empire: Initial Explorations*. Harrisburg, PA: Trinity Press Int., 2001.

Davies, W. D. *The Setting of the Sermon on the Mount*. Cambridge: Cambridge University Press, 1966.

Davies, W. D., and Dale C. Allison. *The Gospel according to Saint Matthew*. ICC. 3 vols. Edinburgh: T. & T. Clark, 1988–1997.

Hagner, Donald A. *Matthew*. WBC. 2 vols. Dallas: Word Books, 1993–1995.

Luz, Ulrich, *Matthew*. Translated by James E. Crouch. Hermeneia. 3 vols. Minneapolis: Fortress Press, 2001–2007.

Meier, John P. *Matthew*. New Testament Message 3. Collegeville, MN: Liturgical Press, 1980.

Overman, J. A. *Matthew's Gospel and Formative Judaism: The Social World of the Matthean Community*. Minneapolis: Fortress Press, 1990.

Stendahl, K. *The School of St. Matthew and Its Use of the Old Testament*. Philadelphia: Fortress Press, 1968.

23
Luke: Theologian, Composer, Historian

BY FAR THE LONGEST COMPOSITION IN THE New Testament is the two-volume narrative now called the Gospel of Luke and the Acts of the Apostles—137,490 words of Greek text, 27.5 percent of the New Testament. "Luke," as we shall continue to call the author for convenience (on authorship, see below) dominates the New Testament, not only in terms of sheer size, but in other significant ways as well. Luke–Acts has provided the framework for the church's liturgical calendar and the comprehensive historical outline within which later generations would tend to fit material from the rest of the New Testament. Only Luke gives the sequence Birth/Baptism/Triumphal Entry/Good Friday/Easter/Ascension/Pentecost that forms the basis for the liturgical year and for much traditional Christian thinking about the story of Jesus and the church. Many stories, sayings, and images found only in Luke have become an indispensable part of Christian consciousness. The *Prodigal Son*, the *Good Samaritan*, the *Rich Man and Lazarus*, the *Pharisee and the Publican*, the encounter with the Risen One on the *Road to Emmaus*, the *Magnificat*, the angel's song *Peace on Earth* are only in Luke, but it is difficult to imagine the Christian tradition without them.

23.1 Luke the Theologian: The Reconfiguration of Salvation History

LUKE INTEGRATED THE SAVING ACTS OF God into universal history, with the Christ event as the defining center. Luke himself would probably have said it otherwise: the history of the world and its empires is integrated into the universal history of God's saving acts. God the Creator is the Lord of all history, beginning to end. History is filled with evil, but Israel's faith was that the God of the covenant would not let the present evil of the world be the last word about creation. At the end of history God will establish justice. One of the ways this hope was expressed was to look forward to the coming of the Messiah, the anointed one sent by God who would (re-)establish God's just rule over creation (see above, §7.6.3). *The Christ comes at the end of history.*

The earliest Christians believed that God had indeed sent his Messiah, Jesus of Nazareth, that he had been rejected and killed by the collaboration of religious and political leaders, but that God had vindicated him by raising him from the dead and made him Lord and Christ (Acts 2:36). The resurrection meant not only that God had sent the promised deliverer, but that the end of history had come. *The resurrection comes at the end of history.* The earliest Christians saw themselves living in the eschatological times of fulfillment, between the resurrection of Jesus, the firstfruits of the universal resurrection, and the final triumph of God that would occur before very long, in their own lifetimes. They lived in a joyful, tension-filled between-the-times existence: the Christ had come, but the end had not. Yet those who had experienced the advent of the Messiah would themselves also experience the ultimate coming of the kingdom of God, which would occur in their own lifetimes. They did not waver in their faith, expressed in the secure terms of traditional theology: the Christ comes at the end of history; the Christ has come; we are living in the last days of history.

History moved on. Climactic events occurred that seemed to some, Jews and Christians alike, to signal the end of history. In 39 CE, the emperor Caligula attempted the ultimate profanation of the temple, intending to place his own image in the Jewish temple. In 64 CE, the emperor Nero blamed the Christians in Rome for the fire that destroyed part of the city, and he subjected them to cruel persecution. In 66–70 CE, the Roman army besieged and destroyed the Holy City, and the temple went up in flames. In 79 CE, Vesuvius erupted, changing the climate of the whole Mediterranean basin for more than a year. In the mid-90s, the emperor Domitian insisted that he be worshiped as God, and some Christians who resisted were arrested or killed. During each of these tragic events, apocalyptic hope flamed anew within the Christian community: this *must* be the sign of the end, Jesus is coming back soon to establish God's ultimate reign. Yet Jesus did not come back. History moved on. What had been thought to be eschatological events turned out to be historical events—tragic, but not the end of the world.

The hopes that were fanned to renewed life by such events were disappointed, but we should not think that they precipitated a sharp experiential crisis for Christian believers. Modern millennial movements typically do not experience an existential crisis of faith when their predictions about the end of the world turn out to be wrong. But theological and calendrical adjustments must be made. For Luke, as history moved on and Christ did not return, this meant that a radical rethinking of the meaning of the Christ event was called for. *The Christ comes into the midst of ongoing history, not at its end*. This is Luke's achievement, one of the major reconfigurations of Christian theology in the history of the church. All the Gospels project a narrative world of which the Christ event is the defining center. Luke is the most reflective and the most explicit. The major convictions represented by his rethinking the meaning of the Christ event are as follows:

1. *God the Creator has a plan for universal history*. This is expressed in one of Luke's favorite terms, βουλή (*boulē*, often translated *plan of God*; of the twelve occurrences in the New Testament, nine are in Luke–Acts). It is thus Luke's equivalent for the οἰκονομία (*oikonomia*, plan, economy) of Ephesians 1:9 (see notes there). Although the characters in the story are mostly unaware of the metanarrative in which they are playing a role, the narrator shares with the reader that the story is unfolding according to the plan of God. The individual incidents take on their real meaning only in the light of this overarching purpose. So also, Luke uses many compounds with πρό– (*pro-*, before), emphasizing that God has foreseen and predestined the course of history. God's lordship over history is also expressed in Luke's frequent use of δεῖ (*dei*, "it is necessary," "what must be," forty times Luke–Acts, e.g., Luke 2:49; 4:43; 9:22; 17:25; 21:9; 22:37; 24:26, 44; Acts 3:21; 4:12; 17:3; 19:21; 23:11; 27:24, 26). This δεῖ is not impersonal fate, operating in a mechanical way, but the expression of God's plan.

Luke does not affirm the sovereignty of God over universal history in a way that diminishes human freedom and responsibility (see Luke 17:1–3; 22:22). History is not a monologue but a dialogue between divine and human actors; but history is a dialogue in which the Creator, taking human response and responsibility fully into account, has the last word. Like other New Testament writers, and like Jewish thinkers of his own time, Luke does not explain how these two convictions are to be reconciled.[1] Casting

1. See, e.g., Luke 22:22—the Son of Man goes to his death in accord with the plan of God, but Jesus makes his own decision, and those who betrayed and killed him are nonetheless guilty. In this, Luke is like his contemporary Josephus, who describes the Pharisees as believing in both the sovereign providence of God and in human freedom, without explaining how this is so (Jos. *Ant.* 13.171–72; *War* 162–63).

his story in the form of this comprehensive plan for history ruled by the sovereign God allows Luke to show how the resistance, rejection, and disappointments of human beings within the story are incorporated into the larger purpose of God. Human beings have power and make decisions for which they are held responsible; God not only rules, but overrules.

2. *This "plan of God" is set forth in Scripture*; this is the importance of "according to Scripture" in Luke–Acts. Luke's interest in Scripture is an aspect of his doctrine of God, the God of universal history whose plan is set forth in Scripture. This perspective is not limited to a Jewish context and presuppositions, however, but makes contact with Hellenistic understandings of universal history. Thus in Athens, within a context of philosophical discussion, Luke can present the Christian missionary Paul as representing the God of the whole world and all history (Acts 17:22–31) and, with powerful understatement, can remind a Roman governor and Hellenistic king that "this thing was not done in a corner" (Acts 26:25–26).

3. Within universal history, God's saving plan unfolds in three epochs between creation and consummation:[2] There are thus three distinct periods of salvation history:

I. The time of Israel—the kingdom of God *promised*

II. The time of Jesus—the kingdom of God *present* in the life of Jesus

III. The time of the church—the kingdom of God *proclaimed*

2. The view here presented generally follows the main outlines of Luke's theology as represented by Hans Conzelmann, *The Theology of St. Luke*, trans. Geoffrey Buswell (New York: Harper & Row, 1961). Conzelmann's view, very influential for a generation, has rightly been subjected to severe criticism in its details, but its general outline continues to be important for both those who adapt it and those who dispute it. A detailed summary of the responses and alternatives to Conzelmann's book is found in François Bovon, *Luke the Theologian: Fifty-five Years of Research (1950–2005)* (Waco, TX: Baylor, 2006), 1–86.

The result is that the Christ event occurs not at the end of history but within the ongoing course of history. There is now a theologically significant time between the Christ event and the end. The church is itself an integral part of the plan of God, in and through which God continues to act.

I. The Time of Israel—the Kingdom of God Promised

This period begins with the promise to Abraham and extends through the ministry of John the Baptist. In Luke's composition, it is represented by the extensive narrative of the birth and childhood of John and Jesus (Luke 1–2), with 3:1–4:13 being a transitional section that concludes John's work and begins the ministry of Jesus. These initial stories are written in the style of the Jewish Scriptures, the "conclusion of the Old Testament," in which John the Baptist is the last and greatest prophet. The Law and the Prophets were in effect up to and including John, but he did not proclaim the kingdom of God (Luke 16:16). John is a hinge figure who stands in the time of Israel and points ahead to the Coming One.

II. The Time of Jesus—the Kingdom of God Present in the Life of Jesus

The period of Jesus does not begin with his birth and childhood, which belongs to the time of Israel. The time of Jesus begins with his ministry, in which the kingdom of God is both proclaimed and enacted. Where Jesus is present, the kingdom is not only announced, but is present (Luke 4:43; 6:20; 7:28; 8:1; 10:9–11; 11:20; 16:16; 17:20). The eschatological blessings expected at the consummation of history are already present in the life of Jesus; what he says and does is already a foretaste of the future kingdom (Luke 7:18–28).

The "time of Jesus" was a special one-year time, in which the kingdom was present and Satan was absent. The specific year is identified in a sixfold synchronization, Luke 3:1–2. Citing the promised "year of the Lord's favor" of Isaiah 61:2, Jesus announces that it is fulfilled "today." The year of jubilee (Lev 25:8–12) represented the time of restoration of property that had been lost through debt, a time of celebration in which "liberty is proclaimed throughout the land" (the inscription on the Liberty Bell of American history). The jubilee was to occur every fifty years, but there is no evidence that it was ever put into practice. Jubilee imagery was transferred to the eschatological future. Jesus' initial proclamation echoes the hopes associated with the year of jubilee: now it will happen, and it is happening.

In the strand of apocalyptic theology that forms the framework for Luke's understanding, Satan is the demonic prince of evil who delegates the power by which the world operates (Luke 4:6). During the ministry of Jesus, the unique year in human history, this power is broken. After his initial defeat, Satan leaves Jesus *for an appointed time*; only Luke adds this limitation (Luke 4:13). During Jesus' ministry, wherever Jesus goes, demonic power is overcome, and Satan himself is never mentioned (thus Luke 9:22–23 omits the reference to Satan in Luke's source at Mark 8:33). Luke has so portrayed the ministry of Jesus that "kingdom of God" is no longer only a vague future hope, but has actually been realized in the life and work of one human being, Jesus the Messiah. If one asks Luke "what is the kingdom of God like" (Luke 13:18), Luke himself responds by telling the whole story of Jesus: in this life we see what the world is like when God's kingdom is present.

III. The Time of the Church—the Kingdom of God Proclaimed

The church begins at Pentecost in Acts 2, as the Spirit descends on the disciples to guide and empower them to continue Jesus' mission. The passion, resurrection, forty-day period of teaching, and the ascension form the transition from the time of Jesus to the time of the church. Thus the unique one-year period when the kingdom of God was on earth, manifest in the life and work of Jesus, comes to an end at the Last Supper. At 22:3 Satan returns, enters into Judas, and sets in motion the events of the passion. At this supper the Lukan Jesus himself announces that the special time is over, that his disciples must now live out their lives in an ongoing world in which they must think about this-worldly realities of economics and self-defense (Luke 22:35–38). They will still look forward to the final coming of the kingdom of God—though it is a mistake to suppose it will "appear immediately" (Luke 19:11)—but they will also look back on a time in which it was a reality on this earth.

The time of the church, like the time of Israel, is an extensive time, from the first Pentecost until the parousia. The opening scene in the book of Acts makes clear that the time of the church is not an afterthought to the story of Jesus, nor a time when Jesus' disciples are to be scanning the heavens looking for his return (Acts 1:11). From the first scenes of his story onward, Luke has a generations-long perspective (see Mary's song in Luke 1:48—"all generations will call me blessed"). Logically, this could lead to the assurance that the end will not come in the readers' own time, and they can relax and go about their business. Luke does not draw this conclusion (e.g., Luke 12:22–53). Luke's understanding of history is less pedestrian and more dialectic than sometimes thought.

Like the time of Israel, the time of the church is an integral part of God's plan, the time when the Spirit-empowered community of disciples carries the Christian message to the ends of the earth. During the time of Jesus, the Spirit had rested on one person only. Jesus received the Spirit, but does not confer the Spirit on others until Pentecost. Thereafter, Jesus' disciples are empowered by the Spirit and confer it on others. Though in a different way from Paul's kenosis Christology, Luke too has a way of showing the time of the church is even more filled with powerful deeds than was the life of Jesus.

In the time of Jesus, the Spirit was present in him, and Satan is vanquished for the year of the Lord's favor. In the time of the church, Christians have the Spirit, but temptation and Satan have returned. The time of the church is thus a dialectically "mixed" time—not the same as the time before the coming of Christ, but also not yet really fulfilled, and a time when Jesus' disciples pray for the full advent of the kingdom of God at the parousia. Most New Testament authors recognize this "between the times" character of Christian existence, but Luke gives it the most explicit narrative representation. Thus Luke's own present as the time of the church is anything but a sighing after the past of the earthly Jesus or a longing for the parousia. It is the time of God's continuing activity, a time of joy and fulfillment, also a time of salvation—though in a different sense from the time of Jesus or the coming consummation of the kingdom.

Luke–Acts: Jesus' Disciples in Caesar's World—The church assumes a place in continuing history alongside other historical institutions.

A major aspect of Luke's purpose is to provide his Christian readership with resources for thinking through their situation in a world that is not about to go away. How should believers committed to the lordship of Jesus relate to the political claims of the lordship of Caesar? How should Christians understand themselves in relation to their parent/sibling Jewish community? What is the right stance of believers in the one God toward the polytheistic religious society in which they are immersed? In short, how do believers in Jesus as the Messiah understand themselves in relation to Rome, to Judaism, and to pagan religions? On each of these crucial questions, Luke offers a dialectical on-the-one-hand/on-the-other-hand response. Texts can be cited on both sides of each issue. Modern readers should be wary of imposing either a simplistic either/or or a facile both/and perspective on Luke–Acts, should neither attempt to get Luke on their side nor to accuse him of waffling on each crucial issue. The narrative mode does not offer simple, direct answers to any of these questions, but provides resources and guidance for readers of Luke–Acts to work out responsible adjustments to a variety of situations, without being merely reactionary or compromising.

1. The Roman Empire: Political Apology?

Luke is more explicitly concerned with the relation of the church to the political world and social structures than any of the other Gospels. Only he mentions the name of any Caesar. Luke's stance to the political structures of his day cannot be conducted along the lines of "church and state." It was impossible in Luke's world to conceive of these as two separate realities that need to be "related." All government rested on religious sanctions, and would continue to do so until the eighteenth century in North America and Europe. The political reality of the Roman Empire constituted a religious claim. The issue must not be posed too simply, as though biblical authors and modern readers can choose either to "support" or "oppose" imperialism.

On the one hand . . . Luke is keenly aware that the founder of his religious movement had announced an alternative kingdom (βασιλεία, *basileia*, also means empire), was executed as a political rebel against authorized government, and that its leading missionary was executed in Rome as a criminal against Roman law. Luke thus wants to assure all potential readers, insiders and outsiders to the Christian community, that Christians are not out to overthrow the government, that there are ways they can be faithful Christians and still fit in as good subjects and members of Roman society. In this he is like other Christian theologians of the second and third generations, such as the authors of 1 Peter and the Pastorals. Even a cursory skimming of Luke–Acts reveals a series of texts that show Christians are no political threat to Roman law and order (on all points, see further in the Exegetical-Theological Précis below):

Luke 1:1–4. The initial address/dedication to "Your Excellency Theophilus" suggests a person of high rank in society (elsewhere in the New Testament only of the governors Felix and Festus, Acts 23:26; 24:2; 26:25). This does not mean that Luke–Acts is in fact addressed to a Roman governor, analogous to the later Apologists. The author does not write directly to or for outsiders to the Christian community. Luke–Acts contains too much material presupposing the implied readers' interest, knowledge, and commitments, which would have been irrelevant or counterproductive if it had been written as an evangelistic tract or apologetic argument for interested or concerned outsiders. A Roman governor Theophilus such as imagined by Streeter[3] would never have waded through reams of sayings and stories about Jesus and the early Christians, permeated with the LXX that is part of the implied readers' equipment, in order to filter out some information that supposedly would give him a favorable impression of the Christian group. This opening paragraph does, however, set the tone for the whole two volumes: Christians are to think of how their religious commitments are viewed by the Roman authorities. "Theophilus" may represent both Christians of high status in official circles who are struggling to adjudicate their conflicting commitments, and outsiders who are wondering whether the Christian group is dangerous.

Luke 2:1–7. The unborn Jesus is obedient to the Roman emperor, as are his parents. Luke knows the census was problematic and caused some to rebel, Acts 5:37. The response of Jesus the Galilean is contrasted with that of Judas the Galilean (cf. §§6.2.4; 7.4.5).

Luke 3:10–14, 19. John the Baptist has a real concern for the poor and oppressed, but does not call for dismantling the Roman tax and military system. His prophetic message calls for ethical responsibility *within* the given social structures (again, cf. 1 Peter). In this, John is precursor of the Lukan Jesus and follower of the prophets of Israel. They called for social justice but did not advocate political revolution (the *false* prophets did *that*; see Jeremiah). John's apocalypticism gives visions of the ultimate justice of God's coming kingdom that God will bring about at the end, but John does not call for revolutionary violence. When John is arrested, a nonpolitical explanation is given (Luke 3:19). The church is called to follow the pattern set by both John and Jesus, but without explicit instructions on concrete problems. Tax collectors have bosses who insist on profits. Soldiers have generals who give orders about vandalizing villages and extorting monies. The narrative mode leaves decisions about how to cope with these realities in the hands of the reader.

Luke 4:18–27. The messianic program announced in Jesus' keynote address presents his career as revolutionary, but without violence and in nonpolitical terms. Thus in 9:7–9, Herod's interest in seeing Jesus is not political; he is curious about Jesus' ability to work miracles but has no interest in him as a rival king.

Luke 7:1–10. One of Jesus' first miracles is for a wealthy Gentile military officer, who is presented positively as a supporter of Jesus' own religious community.

Luke 22:35–38. The special time of Jesus' ministry is over, and his disciples must come to terms with the economics and power structures of the world as it is, carrying out their mission within it. But Jesus' followers have a different understanding of rulership and the uses of power, so that the reference to "sword" still does not mean revolution.

Luke 23–24. Jesus is charged with a crime against Rome, but Romans consistently declare him "not guilty." This is finally reaffirmed in the centurion's declaration at the cross, where Luke changes Mark's "Truly this man was the Son of God" to "Certainly this man was innocent" (Mark 15:39/Luke 23:47). To anticipate: this does not mean that Luke's understanding is reduced to

3. Streeter, *Four Gospels*, 529–39. "Acts is 'the first of the Apologies,' i.e., of defenses of Christianity addressed to the educated Roman world" (529).

"Rome made an honest mistake, under pressure from the Jewish leaders." Even though Rome is clear that Jesus is no terrorist, empire cannot tolerate people like Jesus and instinctively knows it must try to eliminate them.[4]

Acts 10–11. The first official Gentile convert is a Roman military officer, pious and righteous (cf. Luke 7:1–10).

Acts 16–26. In Luke–Acts the Romans never move against Jesus or his followers unilaterally. It is always the Jews who take initiative; there is no instance of Roman intervention without previous agitation by the Jews. The Romans, in fact, become the protectors of Christians from mob violence. In the ten trial scenes, Christian missionaries are always cleared of violating Roman laws. Especially the policy of "hands off—this is an internal Jewish problem, not a matter of Roman law" illustrates the Roman attitude Luke seeks to cultivate (Acts 16:35–39; 18:12–17).

Acts 19:31. Some of the Asiarchs (Ἀσιαρχῶν; NRSV "officials of the province of Asia") protect Paul during the riot in Ephesus. These were responsible for promoting the Caesar cult in the province. Neither here nor elsewhere does Luke suggest any difficulty for Christians living in a society where the emperor is worshiped as divine.

Acts 28:31. It is no accident that the final word of Luke's lengthy narrative is the adverb ἀκωλύτως (*akōlutōs*, without hindrance). Luke and his readers know that, as the story ends, Paul is in Roman custody and was finally executed. Yet Luke succeeds in leaving this final impression on the reader's mind: in the capital city of the world, the leading missionary, himself a Roman citizen enjoying Rome's protection, proclaims the gospel without interference from the government.

While Luke–Acts is not a political apology directed to outsiders, his narrative wants to make clear that Christians are no overt threat to Rome, and can be good citizens. Both Christians and authorities should know this. Nonetheless, when push comes to shove, Luke is clear that the ultimate loyalty of Christian believers is to God rather than any human authority (Acts 5:29). Thus:

On the other hand . . . Luke has some statements, stories, and images that explicitly resist the empire, or offer an alternative to it.

Luke 1:4. The ἀσφάλεια (*asphaleia*, security, confidence; NRSV "truth") promised by Luke's narrative echoes the slogan of the *Pax Romana*, "peace and security" (εἰρήνη καὶ ἀσφάλεια, *eirēnē kai asphaleia*; cf. 1 Thess 5:3). What Caesar promised, only the God of Jesus Christ can deliver.

Luke 1:32. God will give Jesus the throne of David, and he shall rule.

Luke 1:52. The advent of the Savior will bring down the mighty from their thrones, and exalt the lowly.

Luke 4:6. In Luke, the devil gets one additional line in the temptation story. Worldly power over the nations of the civilized world (οἰκουμένη *oikoumenē*, used of the Roman Empire) has been given to him, and he gives this authority to whomever he will. This reflects the apocalyptic theology sketched above, in which God is pictured as temporarily granting power over the world to angelic or demonic beings (§§7.6.1–2). This is a miniature version of the apocalyptic scheme pictured on a grand scale in Revelation, where the Roman Empire is seen as an expression of demonic power. Here it means concretely that the present rulers of the world have received their power and authority from Satan. Jesus resists the offer to rule the world by this kind of power. He offers an alternative, and it will prevail. God will rule.

Luke 4:43; 8:1; 9:2; and others. "Kingdom of God" is found thirty-seven times in Luke–Acts. This is the central message of Jesus, the reason for which he is sent by God, the commission he gives his disciples. Jesus is explicitly called

4. Cf. C. Kavin Rowe, *World Upside Down: Reading Acts in the Graeco-Roman Age* (Oxford: Oxford University Press, 2009).

"king" four times, and hearers of the Christian message rightly recognize that the missionaries announce "another king named Jesus" (Acts 17:7). Jesus tells stories that transparently refer to himself as king (Luke 19:11–27). Jesus is explicitly hailed as king at his triumphal entrance into Jerusalem (19:38, added to Mark 11:10). He acknowledges before Pilate that he claims to be king, and does not reassure him, as in John 18:33–38, that the kingdom is otherworldly and spiritual. Like Pilate, the reader perceives that Jesus represents an alternative kingship to Roman rule.

Acts 14:22. "It is through many persecutions that we must enter the kingdom of God." God's kingdom and Caesar's do not fit amicably together.

Acts 17:6–7. Though Jesus' followers are misunderstood as "acting contrary to the decrees of Caesar" (just as Jesus was falsely accused of forbidding people to pay taxes to Caesar, Luke 23:2, cf. 20:25), their message and practice nonetheless means turning the world upside down.

2. *Judaism*

Judaism continues. Relatively few Jewish people are converted to faith in Jesus as the Messiah. Judaism does not become Christianity, but continues as the vast majority, with the Christians a small community, partly within but mostly alongside Judaism. The Hellenistic world has long since been aware of Jews, but how is this new group to be understood in relation to them? And how are Christians to understand themselves vis-à-vis Judaism?

Luke does not give a single clear answer to this question.[5] *On the one hand*, he can be understood as portraying the church as a group within Judaism, akin to the Pharisees, entitled to the protection the empire extends to Jews as a recognized, legal religion. *On the other hand*, some scholars have understood Luke as intending to distance the church from Judaism. The closing scene of Acts is amenable to various interpretations, leaving the modern reader still pondering the future God intends for Jews and Christians. The ambiguity is not the product of confusion, but is inherent in the subject matter, involving the convictions concerning the faithfulness of God's irrevocable covenantal promises to Israel, that God has sent the Messiah, and that Israel has for the present, for the most part, rejected Jesus as the Messiah.

Some general points to be kept in mind:

- Luke emphasizes, celebrates, and elaborates the facts that Jesus himself and all his earliest followers were faithful Jews. But by Luke's time, the Christian community had become predominately Gentile.
- Luke and his readers look back on the catastrophic event of the Jewish revolt against Rome in Palestine and the ensuing destruction of Jerusalem and the temple by the Romans. If Luke–Acts was written as late as the second decade of the second century, a second Jewish revolt had by then soured much public opinion against Jews, and this may have influenced both Luke and his readers.[6]
- During Luke's time, he and his readers are looking back on the mostly failed mission of Jesus' disciples to the Jews, a time in which Christians had sometimes been persecuted by Jews.
- Luke distinguishes between the Jewish leaders (Pharisees, scribes, Sadducees, elders, "rulers of the synagogue"), on the one hand, and the Jewish people as a whole (the crowds, the people), on the other, and makes the former primarily responsible for Jesus' death and the persecution of Christians. This distinction is not absolute; there are exceptions within both groups, and

5. For an insightful survey with further bibliography, see Joseph B. Tyson, *Luke, Judaism, and the Scholars: Critical Approaches to Luke–Acts* (Columbia: University of South Carolina Press, 1999).

6. So Pervo, *Dating Acts*, 311, 369–72: Luke does not want to see the church as a subheading under Judaism. The events of the Second Revolt had generated much cultural anti-Jewish sentiment. Luke wanted to show that the church was not part of this group that was causing disturbances. See his appendix, 369ff.

loyalties shift in the course of the narrative (except for the Sadducees and high priests, who are uniformly hostile to Jesus and the church). The people as a whole respond positively to Jesus at first (Luke 3–9), begin to shift their allegiance during the journey to Jerusalem (Luke 9:51–19:44), finally join with the Sanhedrin in asking for Jesus' death (23:13–25), but even during the course of the crucifixion many repented (23:27, 39–43, 48). After the resurrection, the people as a whole are charged with the guilt of Jesus' death, while Pilate, Herod, and the centurion all declare him innocent—though Luke does not attempt to conceal that they too are responsible for Jesus' death (23:15, 22–24, 41, 47; Acts 2:23; 3:13–17).

— Luke condemns especially the Sadducees and priestly leaders, who no longer exist as a power group in his own time. On the other hand, Luke spares the Pharisees, often presenting them in a positive light. Like the Christians and in contrast to the Sadducees, the Pharisees believe in the resurrection; the early Christians were aligned with the Pharisees in that they proclaimed the general resurrection of the dead, of which Jesus was the first example (see Luke 20:27–38; Acts 4:2; 23:8; 24:15, 21; 26:8, 23). Sometimes Pharisees responded positively and helpfully to Jesus and his disciples (Luke 13:31; Acts 5:33–39; 23:6–10). Some Pharisees become Christians, without ceasing to be Pharisees (Acts 15:5; 23:6), with Paul himself as the chief example.

— Despite the seemingly pessimistic final scene in Acts, Luke goes out of his way to show how *many* Jews had in fact come to faith in Jesus as the Messiah. The promises of Luke 1:16, 68 are fulfilled as thousands of Jews become Christians without ceasing to be Jews (Acts 2:41; 4:4; 5:12–16; 21:20).

3. *Pagan Religion*

The early church did not find itself in a situation of bringing religion to irreligious people, but of bearing witness to God's saving act in Christ in a world already permeated by religious faith and institutions (see above, §9.2.2).

The Christian community for which Luke writes lives in a polytheistic society in which religion is interwoven with every aspect of economics and politics. This includes the Caesar cult, in which all decent religious and patriotic persons are expected to participate. Yet this community lives by its faith that there is only one God, who has acted definitively in Jesus Christ, affirming that "There is salvation in no one else, for there is no other name under heaven given among mortals by which we must be saved" (Acts 4:12). As the church settles in for the long pull, it must reflect on its relationship to other religious communities, among which it is a new and disdained tiny minority. It is not merely a matter of survival—though Christians must learn how to be true to their faith while making a living and being responsible members of society. They are also charged with a mission to bear witness to the gospel to the whole world (Luke 24:46–48; Acts 1:7–8). The church is essentially a missionary community, with a message that belongs to the whole world. In its pluralistic religious context, it cannot adopt a stance of live-and-let-live, to-each-his-or-her-own. Luke wants to help the church think through its theology of mission and does so by interweaving a variety of perspectives into his narrative.

On the one hand, if the God of Jesus Christ is the only God and salvation is available only through him, does this mean that only Christians have an authentic relationship to God and only Christians are saved or will be saved? Is *this* the basis of the Christian missionary imperative? Does it represent a kind of Christian arrogance, imperialism, and exclusiveness?

On the other hand, if pagans already experience the one true God in their own religion, why should Christian missionaries preach to them?

Luke is aware of this dilemma. He does not address it directly or claim to resolve it conceptually. The following points, though they do not fit together into a logical system, represent important dimensions of his missionary theology:

— There is one God, creator of all. The whole world, all people and all history already belong to God (Acts 17:24–27). Christian missionaries do not first bring God to the pagans. God is already there.

— God is already revealed in the natural world, so that the regularity of the seasons, the gifts of rain and food, and the everyday experiences of enjoying life testify to the reality and goodness of God (Acts 14:16–17). Luke does not develop this into an abstract natural theology and does not reflect on how such general revelation relates to the special revelation of biblical prophets and the Christ event. But he does not want his readers to suppose that, prior to the arrival of Christian missionaries, the world was without God.

— Pagan religions also represent worship of the one true God, who is present in them, though pagan worshipers do not have an authentic knowledge of God's identity. Luke's view is that they have a real experience of God, but a bad theology: "The one you [already] worship in ignorance, I proclaim to you" (Acts 17:23). It is the one God of Jesus Christ who is already present and worshiped in pagan religion and all authentic religious experience, though pagans do not know this, and need to learn the identity of the God they already worship, "groping for and finding him, though he is not far from each one of us" (Acts 17:27).

— Christians and Christian missionaries are to respect other religions and not allow themselves to be thought of as defamers and blasphemers of the religious institutions of the people to whom they are missionaries. Christian leaders can be friends with leaders of pagan cults and respected by them without compromising their faith, even as they make clear the difference between statues of the gods and the one living God (Acts 14:11–18; 17:22; 19:31, 37)

— The problem of religious ignorance is not resolved by knowledge, but by repentance. Luke does not understand the missionary situation as merely supplementing the defective religious knowledge pagans already have, as though they could strike out "Unknown God" from the altar inscription and write in "The God of Jesus Christ." The problem is ignorance, for both Jews and pagans (Acts 3:17; 17:30), but it is the kind of ignorance that is not cured by knowledge, but by repentance. Thus all people are called to repentance. Christian mission is not a matter of those who know sharing their knowledge with those who don't, but of announcing the definitive act of the God already known in both Judaism and paganism, the God who now calls all people to reorient their lives in the light of this ultimate revelation.

In Luke's view, none of these issues—relation to the ongoing political, cultural, and religious life of the Hellenistic world—was faced by Jesus' disciples during his ministry, when the kingdom was present in a special way in the life of Jesus. It is only in the third period, after the ascension, in the time of the church and the proclamation of the kingdom in the Christian mission, that Jesus' disciples must rethink their relation to the ongoing world. Luke the composer responds to this need with his extensive narrative.

23.2 Luke the Composer: Literary Character and Style

LUKE IS NOT A REPORTER WHO ATTEMPTS merely to recount "just the facts." Neither is he just an editor who arranges his sources and traditions into a coherent whole. Luke is a composer, an author who creatively constructs a narrative to inform and persuade. As an author, he makes choices regarding *genre*, *language and style*, and *structure*.

23.2.1 Genre

The attempt to locate a first- or second-century genre that included both the Gospel and Acts has been unsuccessful. Of course, Luke had models for some of the elements of his two-volume work, but, taken as a whole, there was nothing like it in his context. Luke began with the Gospel, adopting, adapting, and expanding Mark. After composing the stories of the resurrection and ascension, as he began volume two, he did not ponder the generic issue—"let's see, what shall I do now?"—but continued to tell the story of Jesus and his disciples. Acts is the continuation of the Gospel, sharing its deficiency and awkwardness in regard to fitting into available genres.

Luke is unique; he had no predecessors, and no successors. None of the apocryphal Acts has a Gospel as its first part; they take Acts as an independent work and elaborate it in the direction of Hellenistic novels. None of the noncanonical Gospels has a corresponding Acts. For Acts, Luke's models are not the Hellenistic historians, but the narrative sections of the LXX. Acts is thus not a separate "history of the early church," but the continuation of the Gospel story of Jesus, continuing to follow the models of "biblical history." While biblical history is not itself a specific genre, Luke's Bible, especially the Samuel-Saul-David stories of 1–2 Samuel, provided models he adopted and adapted in both the Gospel and Acts.

23.2.2 Language and Style

Most of pre-Lukan Christian writing, including Paul's letters and the Gospel of Mark, were in-house writings for Christian congregations, with no aspirations to be accepted in the wider literary world. With Luke–Acts, Christian literature moves into a new league, as indicated by the preface (Luke 1:1–4) and by Luke's revisions of Mark. This point should not be exaggerated, however, as though Luke were a master of Greek language and style. He writes a midlevel Greek, without literary pretensions, more in the style of the LXX than of Thucydides or Dionysius of Halicarnassus. Most of Luke's vocabulary is found in the LXX (90 percent), and he is an able imitator of the style of its narrative sections such as 1–2 Samuel. Thus Luke's literary world is composed of neither other New Testament documents nor the top-level Hellenistic literature of his time, but the Bible and middlebrow Hellenistic literature.[7]

23.2.3 Structure

Unity: Luke–Acts a Single Composition

In the present shape of the New Testament canon, Luke is read as one of the four Gospels, while Acts functions as a narrative bridge connecting the Gospels to the Letters, and serving as the framework for interpreting the Letters. A historical understanding, however, requires that Luke and Acts be read together.[8]

Were they written to be read as one literary unit? Virtually all scholars consider Luke and Acts to have the same author. This is a different question, however, from the issue of their literary unity, which means they were composed as two parts of a single work. The traditional scholarly view, which continues to be the majority opinion, is stated by W. C. van Unnik: "Acts was not an afterthought or a second, independent work

7. See Henry J. Cadbury, *The Book of Acts in History* (New York: Harper, 1955), 34; Martin Dibelius and Heinrich Greeven, eds., *Studies in the Acts of the Apostles* (London: SCM Press, 1956), 2, 88–89, 132; Pervo, *Acts: A Commentary*, 7–8; Gamble, *Books and Readers*, 35.

8. This is analogous to the canonical history of the Johannine writings, in which the Gospel became part of the four-Gospel canon, and the Letters were included with the Catholic Epistles. On the distinction between historical and canonical perspectives, see above, §5.1.4, and the argument of Brevard S. Childs, *The New Testament as Canon: An Introduction* (Philadelphia: Fortress Press, 1984).

on another topic; Luke–Acts was well planned as one work in two volumes."[9]

This presumed unity was quickly obscured in the early church. The author himself contributed to this, by dividing his work into two volumes, each of which would fit into the maximum length of a standard papyrus roll, thus making it possible to read each document as an independent work. Even if intended to circulate and be read together, Luke and Acts were separated in their transmission and canonical history, with Luke being joined to the four-Gospel canon, and Acts becoming the introductory narrative to the Catholic Epistles (*not* the Pauline corpus!). Thus, in liturgical reading and academic study, for centuries Luke and Acts were read separately. Most introductions to the New Testament still treat them as discrete works. Beginning in the early twentieth century, Luke and Acts began to be treated as a single work, especially in the wake of Henry J. Cadbury, whose term "Luke–Acts" has become standard, and has been especially developed by scholars who have applied literary methods.[10]

A strong challenge has recently been presented to this assumed literary unity.[11] Parsons and Pervo point out numerous differences between Luke and Acts in terms of genre, narrative unity, theology, and general tone, indicating that the author changed some of his views and emphases in the interval between writing the Gospel and Acts. Only one example: the Gospel is heavily permeated with an eschatological view that sees the approaching eschaton as a great divine reversal of the present structures of society, in which the poor will be blessed and the rich receive God's wrath. In Acts, eschatology all but disappears, and the church seems to celebrate its newfound status in which prestigious people of wealth become disciples.

One could also point to the role that the miracles of the pre-Easter Jesus play in the kerygma of the Gospel, and their virtual absence from Acts, where the emphasis is almost exclusively on God's act in the resurrection. The "life and teaching of Jesus" hardly plays a role in Acts. Yet the *reader* in fact already has from the Gospel the picture of Jesus as exorcist and miracle worker and knows that there is no polemic against or playing down of the Jesus of the miracle stories. Thus, reading Luke's two volumes in sequence is like reading the later New Testament in its canonical form. Just as most readers of the Epistles continue to think of the Christ of the Gospels and are hardly aware that it is the New Testament canon that holds the different representations of Jesus together, so also in reading Luke–Acts. Acts *presupposes* the Gospel and its Christology, but is not the *same*. Luke–Acts is a first consolidation of the Gospel and Letters of the New Testament canon, a juxtaposition, not a harmonization. Thus the Gospel and Acts are something of a prolepsis of what the New Testament canon would become.

On the Structure of the Gospel of Luke

The preceding considerations impact the way in which one perceives the structure and outline of Luke–Acts. Is there an overarching literary structure for the whole work, or separate, independent outlines for the Gospel and Acts? The following considerations are based on the literary unity of the two documents.

The core and anchor point of his narrative is the account of the one-year ministry of Jesus taken from the Gospel of Mark. Mark began with the baptism of Jesus and concluded with the crucifixion and discovery of the empty tomb; his story included only one Passover, and one visit of Jesus to Jerusalem, giving the impression that all Jesus' public activity transpired within one

9. W. C. van Unnik, "Luke–Acts, a Storm Center in Contemporary Scholarship," in *Studies in Luke–Acts*, ed. Leander Keck and J. Louis Martyn (Nashville: Abingdon Press, 1966), 22.

10. Henry J. Cadbury, *The Making of Luke–Acts* (London: SPCK, 1927, 1968). For more recent arguments, see esp. Robert C. Tannehill, *The Narrative Unity of Luke–Acts: A Literary Interpretation*, 2 vols. (Philadelphia: Fortress Press, 1986, 1990).

11. Mikeal Carl Parsons and Richard I. Pervo, *Rethinking the Unity of Luke and Acts* (Minneapolis: Fortress Press, 1993).

year. Luke understands this year as the defining *center* of universal history (see above, §23.1). His own narrative is composed by expanding the Markan account in three directions: (1) Using some traditional materials, Luke composes an extensive narrative of the birth and childhood of John and Jesus, representing the concluding phase of the story of Israel. (2) Mark's narrative had been basically bipartite, Galilee/Jerusalem, with a brief transitional section (see above, §21.6). Luke expands Mark's brief middle section into an extensive *travel narrative*, incorporating much of his non-Markan Q and L materials into this section. (3) Using traditional material and probably some written sources, Luke composes an extensive account of the mission of Jesus' disciples after the resurrection and ascension. This has the effect of placing Mark's story of Jesus as the defining segment of universal history.

The Gospel of Mark formed the basis and framework for Luke's volume 1. Luke uses his sources in blocks, alternating between sections of Mark and sections of Q + L:

— 1:1–2:52 (L) Preface, birth stories of John and Jesus

— 3:1–6:19 (Mark [with brief Q elements])

— 6:20 (or 7:1)–8:3 (Q + L) "Lesser Insertion"

— 8:4–9:50 (Mark)

At 9:18—Luke's "Great Omission" of Mark 6:45–8:26

At 9:51—Luke's "Lesser Omission" of Mark 9:42–10:12

— 9:51–18:14 (Q + L) "Greater Insertion"

— 18:15–24:11 (Mark)

— 24:12–53 (L)

Mark's polarized bipartite structure has become in Luke three distinctive periods of Jesus' one-year ministry:

I. Touring *Galilee/Judea*, preaching and embodying the kingdom of God (3:1–9:50)

II. The *journey* to Jesus' destiny in Jerusalem (9:51–19:44)

III. Jesus' ministry in *Jerusalem* (19:45–24:53)

On the Structure of Acts

Whatever sources for Acts he may have had, Luke has neither a comprehensive narrative from the beginnings of the church to the death of Paul comparable to Mark, nor a collection of speeches of the apostles analogous to Q. While Mark, Q, and some Pauline letters had already assumed authoritative status in some streams of early Christianity, so that some Christians were accustomed to hearing Gospels and Epistles read during their worship, no similar authoritative role was played by traditions about the early Christian missionaries. While Luke had already used his Gospel sources with considerable freedom, he *is much more free in Acts to structure the narrative in terms of his own priorities and goals*.

Discerning Luke's own structure means that some ways of outlining Acts that have become traditional need to be rethought. The traditional outlines of Acts based on Paul's "missionary journeys," typically found in biblical maps (first, second, and third missionary journeys and journey to Rome) do not represent Luke's own structure. The concept of "missionary journeys" reflects the nineteenth-century understanding of Christian mission as based in the Christian West, from which missionaries traveled to pagan lands for missionary tours and returned to their home base. The concept does not fit the historical Paul, the chronology derived from the Pauline letters, or Luke's own theology of mission and literary structure of Acts. Luke does not understand mission as the expansion of Christendom in terms of discrete missionary journeys. It is not as though Paul was settled in Antioch, from which he makes missionary journeys to the west, returning to report his home base. Nor are there three journeys. The second and third actually collapse into one; note the artificiality of the division at Acts 18:22, and how quickly Paul travels from the Aegean to Antioch and back to his mission work in Ephesus. The mission base and point of orientation moves from east to west, from Jerusalem to Rome.

The structure of Luke–Acts is influenced by Luke's theological convictions that influence the whole of his two-volume work. We have already discussed the dominant structuring element, Luke's conception of the history of salvation in which the Christ event is the "midst of time." Three additional Lukan theological themes influence the structure of Luke's composition.

Jerusalem and Rome, Peter and Paul, Jews and Gentiles

How the locus of God's mission moves from Jerusalem, the religious center of the covenant people Israel, to Rome, capital of the Gentile world, is a key principle in Luke's compositional structure. The particular place of Jerusalem in salvation history is emphasized in the way Luke has structured his two volumes. "Jerusalem" occurs far more in Luke–Acts, and with far greater frequency, than in any other New Testament document (139 times New Testament; 91 times in Luke–Acts). The narrative begins in the Jerusalem temple, and the boy Jesus appears there in a significant scene at the end of Part 1 (Luke 1:5–23; 2:41–52). After a period of touring Galilee and Jerusalem, Jesus "steadfastly sets his face" to go to Jerusalem, to accomplish the "exodus" that will deliver his people by his suffering and death (9:51). In the course of the *travel narrative* (9:51–19:44), Jerusalem is mentioned thirteen times (three times Matthew; three times Mark). Jesus' extended ministry in Jerusalem at the end of the Gospel is continued by the church's ministry in Jerusalem in the first twelve chapters of Acts. From Luke 20 through Acts 7, all the action takes place in Jerusalem. During his missionary career, the Paul of Acts repeatedly visits the mother church in Jerusalem. His final journey to Jerusalem is a parallel to Jesus' own last journey.

Yet Jesus dies in Jerusalem, and Paul dies in Rome. The story of Paul has key scenes in which the Jerusalem→Rome shift takes place. Paul's utterance in Acts 19:21 is parallel to Jesus' in Luke 9:51, but the destination is Rome instead of Jerusalem. In Acts 23:11, God confirms Paul's resolute determination to see Rome, just as in the Gospel, the transfiguration is divine confirmation of Jesus' resolute determination to go to Jerusalem and death (Luke 9:22–35; 51). The story of Jesus in the Gospel is oriented *toward* Jerusalem; the story of the church in Acts begins in Jerusalem (Luke 24:47), but is oriented *away from* Jerusalem, to Judea, Samaria, and "the ends of the earth," with Rome as the last station mentioned (Acts 1:8).

This expansion of the church geographically and theologically is the key to the literary structure of Acts. At the same time, it is the story of the two leading missionaries, the symbolic heads of two major streams of Christian mission. *Peter* represents the Jewish Christianity that has been integrated into the ecumenical mission of the church, and continuity from the beginning of Jesus' mission to the time when the church became the inclusive people of God embracing both Jews and Gentiles. Chapters 1–12 (Peter) move the story from Jerusalem to Antioch, which becomes the center of the Gentile mission. Chapters 13–28 (Paul) then portray the story of the Gentile mission, in which the story moves from Antioch to Rome. The first half of Acts is dominated by the figure of Peter, the second half by Paul (see list of parallels below). This intention to consolidate these two streams of tradition influenced the structure of Acts. Within the first half, the key scene is the "conversion of Cornelius" in chapters 10–11, in which full Gentiles are integrated into the church under the leadership of *Peter*. The focal scene of the second half is the Jerusalem Council, in which the Gentile mission is "officially" confirmed and becomes the basis for the rest of the narrative, which will bring Paul and the readers to Rome.

Conflict

This move does not occur without conflict. The story of the church in Acts mirrors the story of Jesus in the Gospel. Both the Gospel and Acts begin in the heart of Judaism, in the temple. Jesus' story begins in the heart of a faithful Jewish family attending synagogue and temple, celebrating the Jewish festivals, with the advent of Jesus affirmed by pious representatives of Judaism. Opposition begins in Luke 4, as Jesus proclaims that the promises of Jewish Scripture are fulfilled in him. The conflict mounts, and Jesus' life becomes one long journey to passion and death in Jerusalem. So also in Acts: in the opening scenes of the story, there is no opposition to the new group, which could be seen as a renewal movement within Judaism. The church experiences great numerical success and the approval of "all the people" (2:47). Beginning in chapter 3, the Jewish leaders oppose the new group, and its leaders are arrested and beaten. As the church continues to expand in numbers, opposition mounts, and in 6:12 for the first time "the people" appear hostile to Christians. From chapter 8 on, "the Jews" tend to become a hostile bloc opposing the "Christians," a role they play, with few exceptions, through the final scene of the book. One factor in the way the story is structured is to reveal the "parting of the ways" between Jews and Christians that in Luke's understanding had become a reality in the time of Luke and his readers, and to do this while continuing to encourage the church to hold on to its Jewish heritage and Jewish Scripture.

These considerations result in the following outline of Luke's two-volume narrative:

Preface	(Luke 1:1–4)
Part 1: The Time of Israel Reaches Its Climax	(Luke 1:5–2:52)
Part 2: The Time of Jesus	(Luke 3:1–Acts 1:26)
The Mission of Jesus and His Disciples in Galilee and Judea—Gathering the Witnesses	(Luke 3:1–9:50)
The Journey to Jesus' Destiny in Jerusalem—Preparing the Disciples	(Luke 9:51–19:44)
The Ministry, Martyrdom, and Vindication of the Messiah in Jerusalem	(Luke 19:45–24:53)
Transition	(Acts 1:1–26)
Part 3: The Time of the Church (=The Continuation of God's Act in Jesus)	(Acts 2:1–28:31)
Petrine Christianity: The Jewish Mission from Jerusalem to Antioch	(Acts 2:1–12:25)
Christian beginnings in Jerusalem	(Acts 2:1–8:1)
The church expands to Samaria and beyond	(Acts 8:2–40)
Conversion of Paul	(Acts 9:1–31)
Key scenes: Peter, the conversion of Cornelius, and formation of the Antioch church	(Acts 9:32–12:25)
Pauline Christianity: The Gentile Mission from Antioch to Rome	(Acts 13:1–28:31)
Gentile mission promoted from Antioch	(Acts 13:1–14:28)
Gentile mission confirmed in Jerusalem	(Acts 15:1–35)
Gentile mission climaxed in Rome, incorporating "Paul's passion narrative"	(Acts 15:36–28:31)
Paul's passion story	(Acts 21:17–28:31)

23.3 Luke the Historian: Luke–Acts and History

HOW DOES LUKE MEASURE UP AS A HISTOrian? In pondering this question, we need to consider (1) Luke and the Hellenistic historians; (2) Luke's sources, traditions, and influences; (3) controls for assessing Luke's "historical accuracy"; (4) particular features of Lukan composition.

23.3.1 Luke and Hellenistic Historians

A comparison on several points will help to locate Luke–Acts with reference to Hellenistic historiography.

Variety

"Hellenistic history" is not a monolithic term. As used here, it includes not only historians contemporary with the author of Luke–Acts (e.g., Lucian, Plutarch, Tacitus, Suetonius) but classical historians that were read in the Hellenistic world and were factors in shaping expectations of what good history writing should be (Herodotus, Thucydides). Luke can hardly be compared to "Hellenistic historians" in general, but specific points of comparison with specific historians can be made.

Truth Claims, Fiction, Rhetoric, Entertainment

The ancient world certainly knew the difference between history and fiction. It was a commonplace of historians to claim that "the one task of the historian is to describe things exactly as they happened," that "this is the one thing essential in history, to sacrifice to truth alone" (Lucian, *How to Write History*, 39). Lucian's treatise, however, proceeds to show that historians mingle enjoyment and amusement with their narrative: they write history not merely to report facts, but to be useful, to edify, to entertain. History was understood to be a branch of rhetoric; good history writing was the art of persuasion. Nonetheless, they did not understand themselves to be writing fiction. They and their readers understood that their recounting of the facts was in the service of a higher cause, to which such facts as they had should be adjusted. The sense of "objective, scientific" history, as the discipline is often popularly understood in the modern world, would have been alien to them.[12] Richard Pervo has pointed out that this is summed up in Horace's motto "Profit with delight"[13]—profiting from reading history need not exclude the delight of a story well told, including entertaining action scenes in which the hero escapes from prison, endures shipwreck, and deals heroically with riot, stoning, murder plots, and snakebite.

Chronology

In contrast to his sixfold synchronism in dating the one-year ministry of Jesus, Luke is sparing, vague, and confused in the chronological data offered by Acts. Correlations with known events and persons in Roman history are either chronologically vague ("during the reign of Claudius," Acts 11:28) or nonexistent: dates for Herod, Gallio, Felix, Festus, Agrippa are not given. Thus there is no chronological data from the beginning of the church (30 CE) to the Jerusalem Council, and the reader has only

12. This understanding of the nature of history still found in popular discourse is no longer dominant in modern historiography. History is not and cannot be a matter of "reconstructing what actually happened." For a helpful discussion of this issue from the point of view of biblical theology and the truth of the Christian faith, see Schnelle, *Theology of the New Testament*, 27–35, "How History is Made and Written" and "History as Meaning-Formation."

13. Richard I. Pervo, *Profit with Delight: The Literary Genre of the Acts of the Apostles* (Philadelphia: Fortress Press, 1987). Some historians of the Roman era have pointed out that even ancient historians such as Herodotus can combine reliable information with novelistic features and a strong ideological framework (so, e.g., Irina Levinskaya, *The Book of Acts in Its Diaspora Setting*, The Book of Acts in Its First Century Setting 5 [Grand Rapids: Eerdmans, 1996]), viii.

the vaguest impression of whether, for example, Paul's conversion was months or years after the crucifixion. During the "second" and "third" mission trips, Paul and company stay in Corinth eighteen months and in Ephesus three years, with two years in prison in Caesarea followed by two years of waiting in custody in Rome, but Luke provides no fixed chronological peg on which to hang this data. When Luke looks back over past history, he locates the revolutionary Theudas "some time ago," and then mistakenly places Judas "after him . . . in the days of the census" (5:36–37). To us, this may appear to be sloppy historical writing, but it does not disqualify him as a "Hellenistic historian." Writers in the Hellenistic era tended to see the past not as a connected chronological series of events, but a vast reservoir of past events floating at various depths in an amorphous sea, from which they could be fished and arranged as necessary for the present narrative.

Selection, Proportion

Acts is so well written that the reader is carried along with the story and hardly notices the selective hand of the author. The death of Stephen, newcomer to the faith, is reported at length, and he is given an extensive speech, the longest in Acts. The death of James, eyewitness of Jesus' ministry, one of the inner group of three, one of the first four called, is noted only incidentally (12:2). Peter's activities at the time, including his entertaining encounter with the maid Rhoda, is extensively reported. The mission in Ephesus, important center of Christianity from Paul's day on, is recounted in a few verses, but Paul's last days occupy a third of the narrative, including detailed conversations between Paul and his captors unrelated to the Christian mission and the meaning of the Christian faith. They make for good reading and serve Luke's purpose, but have more in common with the stories of 1 Samuel, on the one hand, and tales of Hellenistic novels, on the other, than they do with Hellenistic history writing.

Narrator

The narrator of Luke–Acts is omniscient and omnipresent, able to report what people think and what happens in private, such as the executive session of the Sanhedrin, including Gamaliel's speech, and the private conversations of the governor Festus and King Agrippa (Acts 5:34–39; see, e.g., Luke 5:22; Acts 10:19; 21:29; 25:13–22). All is reported verbatim, properly placed in quotation marks in modern translations. Luke's modus operandi is showing rather than telling, a lively, engaging manner of telling a story, the regular mode of novelists—and biblical authors. Luke does not qualify himself as historian in this regard, but follows the biblical model of refusing to interject a summarizer or interpreter between the action and the reader.

Speeches

About a third of Acts is in the form of speeches, reported as direct discourse. When smaller conversations are included, 51 percent of Acts is presented as verbatim quotation. This is a far higher ratio of speech to narrative than in the Hellenistic historians, though the composition of speeches by the author and attribution to leading persons in the narrative was common practice.[14]

Thucydides was and is considered a model historian, but he viewed literary creativity differently than in modern historiography:

14. On the speeches in Acts, see the variety of perspectives in Henry J. Cadbury, "The Speeches in Acts," in *The Beginnings of Christianity, Part I: The Acts of the Apostles, Additional Notes and Commentary*, ed. F. J. Foakes Jackson and Kirsopp Lake (Grand Rapids: Baker, 1979), 402–7; Marion L. Soards, *The Speeches in Acts* (Louisville, KY: Westminster John Knox Press, 1994); Conrad H. Gempf, "Public Speaking and Published Accounts," in *The Book of Acts in Its Ancient Literary Setting*, ed. Bruce W. Winter and Andrew D. Clarke, The Book of Acts in Its First-Century Setting 1 (Grand Rapids: Eerdmans, 1993), 259–303. Even the most rigorous defenders of "historical reliability" acknowledge a considerable Lukan element in the speeches.

> As for the speeches which were made by different men either when they were about to begin the war or when they were already engaged therein, it has been difficult to recall the words actually spoken with strict accuracy, both for me about what I myself heard and for those who from various other sources have brought me reports. So the speeches are given in the language in which, as it seemed to me, the several speakers would express, on the subjects under consideration, the sentiments most befitting the occasion, though at the same time I have adhered as closely as possible to the general sense of what was actually said. *(Thucydides,* Hist. *1.22)*

Another example is from Tacitus (*Annals* 11.24), who includes a speech of the emperor Claudius to the Senate. His report differs widely from the inscription of the original, which is extant and which Tacitus and his readers must have known. Josephus, *War* 6.34–53, 7.124–28, gives the moving speech of Eleazar urging suicide to the defenders of Masada, a speech obviously created by Josephus himself. Like the Old Testament, he repeatedly gives verbatim accounts of speeches and conversations of people in situations from which he could have had no information.

The same creativity is seen in biographical and similar writings. There are numerous examples: In Plato's *Protagoras*, Socrates is the narrator, who speaks in the first person at length. Plato knew Socrates very well personally, studied at length with him, and yet does not hesitate to compose long speeches and place them in the mouth of Socrates and the other participants in the dialogue. In the ten books of the *Republic*, 148 pages of small print, the dialogue is narrated by Socrates the next day after the speeches took place. On the first page of the *Theaetetus*, Euclid speaks of writing up a long conversation of many pages "as soon as I got home," then later inquiring of Socrates concerning points he had forgotten, rewriting it, then having a slave read it to him and his guests for discussion.[15] None of this was understood to be fiction, but neither was its truth judged by accuracy of the "reports." All understood they were hearing and responding to the authors Thucydides, Tacitus, and Plato, not to Socrates and the other characters who speak in their narratives.

23.3.2 Sources, Traditions, Influences

One's reading of Luke–Acts is heavily dependent on how one views the sources at the author's disposal. Three types of resources were available to him:[16] (1) direct personal memory and experiences, (2) general personal experiences and influences, and (3) particular written documents.

1. Personal Memory and Experiences—The We-Passages

The author makes no claim to have been present at the scenes he recounts in the Gospel of Luke. In the standard text of Acts, however, a series of passages is abruptly narrated in the first-person plural: 16:10–17; 20:5–15; 21:1–18; 27:1–28:16.[17] The reader gets the impression that the author joined Paul, Silas, and Timothy at Troas and accompanied them to Philippi, where he remained until Paul's last trip to Jerusalem. The author then rejoined the group and accompanied Paul to Jerusalem and the meeting with James and the elders of the Jerusalem church. He drops out of the story during Paul's arrest and trials in Jerusalem and Caesarea,

15. Plato, *Plato*, trans. J. Harward, Great Books of the Western World 7 (Chicago: Encyclopedia Britannica, 1952), 38, 512.

16. The self-referential masculine participle at Luke 1:3 indicates the author was male. Cf. Heb. 11:32.

17. The manuscript tradition is not univocal in delineating the we-passages. Irenaeus, *Against Heresies* 3.14.1, reflects a text in which Acts 16:8 was a we-passage, indicating the author was already with Paul when the missionary party came to Troas. The Western text documented in D, some Old Latin manuscripts, and citations in Augustine begin the we-passages at 11:28, thus locating the author of Acts at Antioch. In the vast majority of manuscripts, the we-passages begin at 16:10, as above.

which are recounted in the third person, then rejoins him for the transport to Rome. The events in Rome and the end of the narrative are then concluded in the third person. The phenomenon of the we-passages has been thoroughly examined in dissertations, monographs, and detailed analytical commentaries, without unanimous results. Three theories are on the current scene:

1. Luke, companion of Paul and author of Luke–Acts, here draws on his own memory or/and personal travel diary. Several critical scholars continue to support this traditional view.[18] However, in addition to the difficulties involved in regard to authorship and date (see below), this view is faced with the problem of explaining why the author shifts into the first person to narrate minor details, while leaving major items of early Christian missionary history undocumented, though he presumably was present.[19] The first-person passages begin and end without transition or explanation.

2. The author was not himself present at the we-passage scenes, but has somehow come into possession of the travel diary of a companion of Paul, or fragments thereof, which he has introduced verbatim into his account. This was a popular view during the nineteenth century, when scholars industriously tried to discover a core of historical sources embedded in the later text. Thus, though not an eyewitness himself, the author of Acts has substantial material from a companion of Paul. A recent monograph claims to have identified the author of this diary: Silas.[20]

3. One of the difficulties with the second theory is that the language and style of the we-passages are virtually identical with that of the author himself. It seems that the author of an actual diary is also the author of Acts, or that the otherwise-unknown author of Acts composed the diary, that is, that it is not a real diary but a literary device of the author. The latter view has become common in recent scholarship.[21] The author occasionally shifts into the

18. E.g., Joseph A. Fitzmyer, SJ, *Luke the Theologian* (New York: Paulist Press, 1989), 1–26, "The Authorship of Luke–Acts Reconsidered," has the most cogent defense of Luke as author of the we-source. Luke stayed in Philippi on the second journey and did not rejoin Paul until the last journey back to Jerusalem, so was not present during the intense period of letter writing and formation of Paul's theology. Fitzmyer discusses whether he then had heard Philippians while in Philippi or Romans while in Rome, and decides he did not. The author of Luke–Acts is thus distant from both Paul and his theology. He thus used other sources and considerable literary imagination in composing Acts (see in detail Joseph A. Fitzmyer, SJ, *The Acts of the Apostles*, AB 31 [New York: Doubleday, 1998]). Ben Witherington, *The Acts of the Apostles: A Socio-rhetorical Commentary* (Grand Rapids: Eerdmans, 1998), 165–73, and Colin J. Hemer and Conrad H. Gempf, *The Book of Acts in the Setting of Hellenistic History* (Tübingen: Mohr, 1989) represent those scholars who, persuaded that Luke the companion of Paul wrote Acts, argue he hardly needed any other sources. According to Witherington, Luke experienced part of the story himself and learned the rest from interviewing Paul and other eyewitnesses. The two-year enforced stay during Paul's incarceration in Jerusalem and Caesarea provided the opportunity to interview Jesus' family (James, Mary), the mother of John Mark, Philip, Mary Magdalene, Joanna of the Herodian court, and, e.g., to get the story of Cornelius's conversion from the centurion himself. "Indeed, he could even have traveled on to Damascus and Antioch during this time" (169).

19. One example: on this view, the author of Acts was resident in Philippi for a number of years, yet shares nothing from the life and mission of the church at Philippi, information that would be of great interest to readers both ancient and modern. Paul had an enduring, close relationship with this church, which supported him financially and received letters from him. What was its worship like? How was its leadership structured? How large was it and where did it meet? One house church or several? What problems did it face? Acts provides some vivid pictures of some of Paul's initial experiences in Philippi, but these are not included in the we-passages.

20. Jürgen Wehnert, *Die Wir-Passagen der Apostelgeschichte*, GTA 40 (Göttingen: Vandenhoeck & Ruprecht, 1989).

21. E.g., Ernst Haenchen, "'We' in Acts and the Itinerary," in *Journal for Theology and the Church*, vol. 1: *The Bultmann School of Biblical Interpretation: New Directions?* (1965), 65–99; Ernst Haenchen, *The Acts of the Apostles: A Commentary* (Philadelphia: Westminster Press, 1971); Haenchen regards the we-passages as the creation of the author, but on the basis of a traditional annotated itinerary. Beverly R. Gaventa, *The Acts of the Apostles*, ANTC (Nashville: Abingdon Press, 2003), see 57; Pervo, *Acts: A Commentary*; Jürgen Roloff, *Die Apostelgeschichte*, Das Neue Testament Deutsch 5 (Göttingen: Vandenhoeck & Ruprecht, 1981); Tannehill, *Narrative Unity*. This view has recently been further undergirded by narrative theory by William S. Campbell, *The "We" Passages in the Acts of*

first person as a literary means of making the narrative more vivid. This technique was found among ancient writers, including historians.[22]

Two important theological points are to be added to this literary convention: (a) Luke has adopted the biblical style and perspective of the Jewish Scriptures, which insist that the events they recount were not merely there-and-then, but that, as the Scripture is read, the boundaries between past and present are dissolved, involving the readers directly in the events narrated (see, e.g., Deut 5:1–5). The author's preface at Luke 1:1–4 is important here. It applies to the whole work, to both volumes. He does not claim to be an eyewitness of the events in either the Gospel or Acts, but to be a third-generation believer who receives traditions and utilizes sources from his predecessors. The author of Acts has no personal memories of events in the earliest church and mission journeys with Paul on which to draw. His own experience does not seem to relate him directly to the events of the first generation, but is nonetheless important: the issues and categories that drive his narrative are shaped by the concerns of his own time. (b) Like the authors of the deuteropauline letters, the author of Acts wants to represent Paul to a later generation, but he does not write letters in Paul's name. The "we" of Acts expresses the author's claim to speak as an authentic representative of Paul.

2. General Personal Experience and Influences

The author is, of course, no outsider to the Christian community. He participates in worship, engages a variety of Christian congregations and individuals, encounters a number of Christian traditions. He has heard Jewish Scriptures read in worship and interpreted in Christian sermons and instruction. He has heard stories and sayings of Jesus and the oracles of Christian prophets. He has heard hymns sung, and the prayers of individuals and the congregations. This variegated body of Christian tradition doubtless contributed to the story of the church as narrated by Luke and influenced the manner in which the author portrayed the church and its mission. That Luke knew and used such traditions can hardly be doubted, though for the most part they cannot now be identified. At two points where the traditions received by Luke overlapped those of other Christian communities, we can see various points of contact.

3. Traditions of the Johannine and Pauline Communities

Among these are traditions of the Johannine school that eventually became part of the Gospel of John. At some point or points in the tradition prior to the composition of either Luke or John, their respective authors were acquainted with some elements of the same body of tradition.[23] Some examples:

— Luke and John are both concerned with the role of John the Baptist and his disciples, and their relation to the ongoing life of the church (Luke 1:5–80; 3:1–20; 7:18–35; Acts 19:1–7; John 1:19–35; 3:22–36; 5:31–38).

— All careful readers have noticed that the story of the call of the four fishermen (Luke 5:1–11)

the Apostles: The Narrator as Narrative Character, SBLSBL 14 (Atlanta: Society of Biblical Literature, 2007).

22. E.g., Achilles Tatius, *Leucippe and Clitophon* 1.3.1. Other examples in Eckhard Plümacher, "Wirklichkeitserfahrung und Geschichtsschreibung bei Lukas," *ZNW* 68 (1974): 2–22.

23. It is possible that the author of John was familiar with the Gospel of Luke (see below, §27.3). Whether "possible" can be elevated to "plausible" or "probable" depends not only on analysis of their parallel passages, but on the probable date assigned to each. Mark A. Matson, *In Dialogue with Another Gospel? The Influence of the Fourth Gospel on the Passion Narrative of the Gospel of Luke*, SBLDS 178 (Atlanta: Society of Biblical Literature, 2001), argues the converse option: Luke used some version of John. This may have been an early form of the present Gospel, or traditions of the Johannine school also known to Luke.

is quite different from Luke's Markan source (Mark 1:16–20), but has numerous points of contact with the Johannine story in John 21:1–11.

— The Lukan use of "Jews" and "Israelites" is unlike Mark, but similar to that of the Fourth Gospel.[24]

— Both Luke and John place Peter's confession immediately after the feeding of the five thousand and in connection with it (Luke 9:18–20; John 6:1–69).

— Jesus issues the commands to silence, not because they have the wrong idea of Messiah, as in the other Synoptics, but because the time has *not yet come*, as in the Fourth Gospel. Contrast Luke 9:21 and 19:39–40.

— The sisters Mary and Martha are only in Luke and John, as is Lazarus. In John, Lazarus is their brother who dies and is raised by Jesus. In Jesus' parable in Luke, Lazarus dies, and after his death it is said that even if someone were raised from the dead, people would not believe (Luke 10, 16; John 11–12).

— "*Hour*," "*darkness*" (Luke 22:53, etc.) are reminiscent of the imagery of the Fourth Gospel, not of the other Synoptics (John 1:5; 2:4; 7:30; 12:27, 35, 46).

— The Last Supper begins with the comment that Satan has entered into Judas (Luke 22:3; John 13:2).

— The radical image of the master serving slaves (Luke 12:37; see 22:27) is not found elsewhere in the Synoptics, but see John 13:4.

— Only Luke and John know of Annas as high priest alongside Caiaphas (Luke 3:2; Acts 4:6; John 18:13, 24).

— At the scene of Jesus' arrest, only Luke and John state that it was the servant's *right* ear that was cut off (Luke 22:50–51; John 18:10). There are numerous such small details common only to Luke and John.[25]

— Luke, like the other Synoptics, has no reference to nails or nailing in the crucifixion account (victims were often tied); nails are mentioned only in John 20:25. Yet Luke 24:39 seems to presuppose that Jesus' hands and feet were nailed at the crucifixion. Here the Johannine tradition seems to be presupposed, though not plotted. Has the author (and readers?) heard the story told this way?

— Luke 24:26 does not speak of the Son of Man who will be raised, as in the Markan passion predictions Luke has adopted, but of the Messiah who enters into his *glory*. The resurrected Jesus speaks with the accents of the Johannine tradition (John 7:39; 12:23; 17:1, 4).

The situation vis-à-vis Luke and the Johannine materials is similar to that with regard to some of the traditions of the Pauline school. He may well have known some of the written texts collected and composed by this group of Paulinists, including Colossians and Ephesians (see above §§15.1–2). It is not likely that he knew the Pastorals, however, which were probably written about the same time as Luke–Acts. Yet there seems to be some use of common traditions. The sequence of mission stations Antioch-Iconium-Lystra of Acts 13–14 correlates well with 2 Timothy 3:10–11. There are so many points of correspondence in vocabulary and general ethos between Acts and the Pastorals that a few scholars have argued they have the same author.[26] While Luke does not use the

24. Cf. Pervo, *Acts: A Commentary*, 343.

25. E. Osty, "'Les points de contact entre le récit de la passion dans saint Luc et dans saint Jean', *Mélanges Jules Lebreton*," *Recherches de science religieuse* 39, no. 12 (1951): 146–54 points out more than forty instances of something in the passion narrative common to Luke and John alone. Cf. also Matson, *Dialogue*, passim.

26. E.g., S. G. Wilson, *Luke and the Pastoral Epistles* (London: SPCK, 1979). Few have been convinced the same

Pastorals as a source, he operates in the same linguistic and theological milieu.

There are thus numerous points of contact between the traditions inscribed in Luke–Acts and in other New Testament documents. However, such traditions are difficult to identify with even a minimum degree of confidence, except in the case of written documents that have been preserved. Fortunately for the historian, there are several such cases.

4. Particular Written Documents

We know, of course, that Luke used written sources, not only from his own preface (Luke 1:1–4) but from comparing his text with surviving sources he (must/may have) used. We discuss them on a scale of descending probability.

The Septuagint; Lukan Reinterpretation of Scripture

Luke's Bible, the LXX, is one of the powerful generative influences that provided both form and content for his composition. The beautiful stories of Zechariah, Elizabeth, and their baby John; of Mary, Joseph, and their baby Jesus; of Simeon and Anna in the temple, interwoven with their songs, prayers, and blessings, are heavily dependent on similar stories in the Jewish Scriptures. We would not know this if we did not have these texts ourselves (see below, Exegetical-Theological Précis, on Luke 1–2). The stories of Jesus restoring the widow of Nain's son to life (Luke 7:11–17) and of Paul's restoration of the sleepy Eutychus from death (Acts 20:9–12) resemble, in form and content, the stories of Elijah and Elisha in 1 Kings 17:17–24 and 2 Kings 4:32–37. Examples could be multiplied. Luke sees the story of Jesus and the church as the continuation of the story of Israel. In the conviction that this story prefigures and points to its climax and fulfillment in his own time, in good conscience he adopts and adapts material from his Bible with which to tell the Christian story.

author composed both, but detailing the similarities indicates some sort of indirect relationship.

The Gospel of Mark and Q

Most scholars are convinced that Luke's primary sources for the Gospel were the Gospel of Mark and Q (see Excursus 3, §19.4); his two-volume work is basically a comprehensive expansion of Mark. A few scholars have argued for a *Proto-Luke*, according to which Luke had already combined his Q and L materials into a coherent text before he became aware of Mark. Luke then inserted blocks of Mark into his previously composed text to produce the present Gospel of Luke.[27] It should be remembered that Luke also had Mark and Q as sources for Acts, not only for the Gospel.

Paul's Letters?

Luke certainly did not use Paul's letters as a source in the same way he sometimes specifically cited the LXX and incorporated blocks of material from Mark and Q. This, however, is not the real issue. The question is whether Paul's letters were available to the author of Luke–Acts and whether he was influenced by them and even drew material from them, selecting, rewriting, and adapting in the ways that he utilized his other sources—including the ways he sometimes drew on LXX, Mark, and Q without actually citing them. The extant Pauline letters were written in the 50s. Luke–Acts was written in the 60s at the earliest, more likely at least a generation later. Paul is his hero. Luke

27. So Streeter, *Four Gospels*, 199–222. Joachim Jeremias and Friedrich Rehkopf were among those who advocated a modified form of this theory (Joachim Jeremias, *The Eucharistic Words of Jesus*, trans. Norman Perrin [New York: Scribner, 1966]), 96–100; Friedrich Rehkopf, *Die lukanische Sonderquelle: Ihr Umfang und Sprachgebrauch*, WUNT 5 [Tübingen: Mohr, 1959], but it has not survived more critical examination. See now J. Verheyden, "Proto-Luke, and What Can Possibly Be Made of It," in *Studies in the Synoptic Problem: Oxford Conference, April 2008: Essays in Honour of Christopher M. Tuckett*, ed. Paul Foster et al., BETL (Louvain: Peeters, 2011), 617–56.

can hardly have been unaware that Paul wrote letters, whether or not he was the companion of Paul on mission trips, for Paul's letters began to be circulated, singly and as an edited corpus, within a generation of Paul's death. As an enthusiastic participant in the Pauline stream of Christian tradition, Luke must have often been present when Pauline letters were read in Christian worship and instruction. On the traditional view, Luke had resided at Philippi and was present with Paul at Rome, and Paul had written letters to both these churches. On the traditional view of authorship, Luke was with Paul when he wrote Colossians, Philemon, and 2 Timothy, and sends greetings in two of these letters (Col 4:14; Phlm 24, 2 Tim 4:11). Without any examination of the texts themselves, there would seem to be a strong a priori likelihood that Luke not only knew of Paul as a writer of letters, but knew at least some of them. Thus the staunch defender of traditional authorship and dates for New Testament texts, William Ramsay, assumed and often stated that Luke knew Paul's letters.[28]

Strangely enough, the majority of scholars of all theological and critical persuasions have continued to resist the idea that Luke knew Paul's letters—though there are major exceptions.[29] Most scholars have apparently assumed that if Luke had known the letters, he would have made more specific use of them and would have portrayed Paul as writer of important church documents. Luke knew that letters from Christian leaders were sent to groups of congregations as a means of Christian instruction, and provides explicit quotations (Acts 15:22–29). He cites a letter from James and the Jerusalem apostles and elders, a letter *delivered* by Paul and Barnabas to churches throughout a wide region (16:1–4); so surely he would have cited his hero Paul if he had known his letters—so the argument runs.

Among the responses to this objection, I mention three: (1) Paul's letters were being used in a way considered objectionable by Luke. To some extent, this may have been the case in the contemporary Pauline school, which had edited and circulated the Pauline corpus as the major authority. In this school, Paul was the only apostle, and all church life was oriented to Pauline authority. Luke wanted to combine the Pauline stream with others, particularly the Petrine stream. This would be a motive for suppressing the image of Paul the letter writer while upholding Paul as authoritative church leader. (2) The letters were occasional pieces, often directed to damage control within the church, making it painfully clear that the first generation of churches did not always accept Paul's authority. Paul was opposed within his own churches by rival groups and leaders. Paul's letters contributed to these conflicts as well as sometimes resolving them. This is a picture Luke wishes to replace; only after Paul's death did destructive heresies emerge within the church (see on Acts 20:30). (3) Acts may well have been written late enough (see below) to oppose Marcion or a brand of proto-Marcionism. Having rejected the Jewish Scriptures as authoritative for the church, Marcion's collection of authoritative Christian Scriptures consisted of *Gospel* (an early, truncated version of Luke's own Gospel?) and *Apostle* (a collection of ten truncated Pauline letters). To this Luke opposes his own Gospel and Apostle, but the second volume is a continuation of the Gospel's narrative into apostolic times, not a collection of Paul's letters. His *Acts* serves a similar function as the Pauline letter collection, without playing into the hands of his opponents (Marcionites) or alternatives (the Pauline school). This is, to be sure, speculation, but any explanation of the absence of Paul's letters from Acts is speculative. The view suggested here is well-grounded speculation.

28. William M. Ramsay, *St. Paul the Traveller and the Roman Citizen* (Grand Rapids: Baker, 1895), 16 and passim.

29. Modern study of the issue is surveyed in William O. Walker, "Acts and the Pauline Corpus Reconsidered," *Journal for the Study of the New Testament* 24 (1985): 3–23; the most thorough documentation of the evidence that Luke used Paul's letters is Pervo, *Dating Acts*, 51–147.

Other Christian Texts?

Acts manifests a long list of contacts with 1 Peter, Hebrews, and *1 Clement* (see the critical commentaries). If he knew them, rather than the traditions and general ethos they shared, he did not make direct use of them as sources.

Josephus?

There are important points of contact between Luke–Acts and the writings of Josephus. These include the census at the time of Jesus' birth (Luke 2:1–3), the sixfold synchronism at the beginning of Jesus' ministry (Luke 3:1–2), the grotesque account of the death of Agrippa I (called "Herod" by Luke, Acts 12:20–23), the references to three Jewish leaders of revolts against Rome (Theudas, Judas, and "the Egyptian"), as well as general references to Sicarii, deceivers, and imposters reminiscent of Josephus's descriptions and vocabulary (Acts 5:35–39; 21:37–38). In addition, there are numerous similarities in the ways Acts and Josephus describe various scenes, so that, for example, the riot in the temple narrated in Acts 21:30–33 has some resemblance to similar scenes in Josephus. Several scholars have considered the evidence to require the conclusion that the author of Luke–Acts knew Josephus's writings, including his *Antiquities*.[30] The evidence seems to require Luke's knowledge of Josephus and therefore a date after 93 CE.

Other Identifiable Sources for Acts?

Especially during the nineteenth century, biblical scholarship attempted with great rigor to locate other sources of Acts (as with other biblical texts). The goal was to get behind the biblical text, as close to the events themselves as possible. Otherwise, our knowledge of the period 30–50 CE, for example, is severely limited. The work of Adolf Harnack represents the apex of this effort. He claimed to identify three sources for Acts: *Source* A from Jerusalem or Caesarea (3:1–5:16; 8:5–40; 9:31–11:18; 12:1–23) and, of less historical value, *Source* B (2:1–47; 5:17–42). Most valuable, he thought, was *Source* C, the *Antioch Source* (6:1–8:4; 11:19–30; 12:25–15:35). Then the *we-source* kicked in at 16:10, supplying reliable information for much of the rest of the book. Taken together, these sources put the modern historian in touch with much of the actual history. Especially the *Antioch Source* found resonance with later scholarship, but further research has eroded confidence in the results of the quest for sources. By the mid-twentieth century it had virtually been abandoned.

23.3.3 Controls for Assessing Luke's "Historical Accuracy"

In the case of Luke–Acts, and only here in the New Testament, we are in the fortunate situation of being able to assess his "historical accuracy" by comparing his work with some of his sources, with actual letters from one of the main characters in the story, and with archaeological and textual data from his contemporary world.

Extracanonical: Archaeology, Roman History

In reaction to the excessive skepticism of the nineteenth-century Tübingen critics, some scholars intensively investigated the historical allusions in Acts. William Ramsay is the pioneer and legendary hero in this regard.[31] A

30. E.g., F. Crawford Burkitt, *The Gospel History and Its Transmission* (Edinburgh: T. & T. Clark, 1906), 105–10; Morton Scott Enslin, *Christian Beginnings* (New York: Harper & Bros., 1938), 422–24; and Streeter, *Four Gospels*, 557–58. The most recent thorough study is Pervo, *Dating Acts*, 149–200. On the other side, see F. F. Bruce, *Commentary on the Book of the Acts: The English Text with Introduction, Exposition and Notes* (Grand Rapids: Eerdmans, 1955), 125.

31. Ramsay published numerous scholarly tomes on Roman history, widely respected among classicists, for which he was knighted (frequently cited as *Sir* William Ramsay). His readable works summarizing the relevance of his studies for New Testament interpretation are William Mitchell Ramsay, *The Church in the Roman Empire before A.D. 170* (New York: G.P. Putnam's Sons, 1893); *Paul the Traveller; Cities of St. Paul; Luke the Physician: And*

classical scholar of the highest reputation, who was himself somewhat skeptical of the accuracy of the biblical record, Ramsay entered the world of New Testament studies in search of historical data to illuminate the Hellenistic world of Asia Minor. To his surprise, his geographical and archaeological studies repeatedly demonstrated the historical accuracy of items mentioned only incidentally in Acts, such as geographical locations and the titles of Roman administrators. Incidental references in Roman historians and contemporary works—material with which many New Testament scholars are often unfamiliar—seemed to confirm the accuracy of the details of Luke's account. Ramsay experienced something of an intellectual and religious conversion, came to believe that "Luke's history is unsurpassed in respect of its trustworthiness,"[32] and continues to be regarded as patron saint and hero whose conversion story is legendary in the struggle for the "historical reliability" of Acts.[33]

Ramsay's work made a valuable contribution. No one can now claim, as did his opponents of the Tübingen school, that Luke and Acts reflects the political and cultural situation in the middle of the second century or that the author is entirely uninformed about the early decades of the Christian movement. However, establishing the historical accuracy of some details does not prove, nor provide evidence, that the story as a whole is historical fact. Establishing that Luke is quite accurate on matters of Hellenistic geography and the terminology for provincial officers does not establish the factuality of his account of Paul's missions, but only of their setting. A film director who makes a movie about the U.S. Civil War, or a novelist whose story is set in the United States in the 1860s, may have very good information on the historical background of the story, from research, personal experience, or both. But this does not establish the facticity of the scenes, events, and speeches in the novel or movie.

Mark and Q

Assuming the Two-Document Hypothesis, we can tell with considerable precision how Luke used Mark and, with less accuracy, his use of Q. He sometimes reproduces both Mark and Q verbatim, or virtually so (e.g., Mark 1:23–31/Luke 4:33–39; for Q, see Matt 3:7–10/Luke 3:7–9 [see Box 23, p. 479]). On the other hand, in numerous places we can observe Luke rearranging, rewriting, and expanding Mark. He moves the story of Jesus' rejection at Nazareth from its midpoint in Mark to the beginning of Jesus' ministry and elaborates it to become the opening keynote scene in Luke (Mark 6:1–6a/Luke 4:16–30). Mark's laconic story of finding the empty tomb becomes in Luke an elaborate resurrection-and-ascension story filled with symbolic meaning. Of course, the best way for students to gain an impression of Luke's use of his sources is to work through a synopsis. Observing the ways in which Luke rearranges, expands, deletes, and interprets Mark and Q does not generate confidence that he was interested in the modern ideal of "objective reporting" or that he shared the modern equation of truth and "historical accuracy."

Paul's Letters

Among the New Testament documents, only in Acts do we have both primary sources and a secondary narrative covering the same period. Acts and Paul's letters agree, of course, on the major outline: Saul the persecutor is converted, becomes Paul the Christian apostle/missionary, and succeeds both in establishing new congregations in the Asia-Aegean area and in his struggle for a Gentile Christianity free from the law. There are also numerous places where details in the letters mesh well with the story in Acts, such as the order persecuted-in-Philippi/

Other Studies in the History of Religion (London: Hodder & Stoughton, 1908).

32. Ramsay, *Luke the Physician*, 179.

33. See the admiring summaries of his work in F. F. Bruce, *The New Testament Documents: Are They Reliable?* (London: Inter-Varsity Fellowship, 1960) 90–91; W. Ward Gasque, *A History of the Criticism of the Acts of the Apostles* (Grand Rapids: Eerdmans, 1975), 136–42.

evangelizing-in-Thessalonica (Acts 16:20–24/1 Thess 2:2), and Paul's adventurous escape from Damascus by being lowered over or through the wall in a basket (Acts 9:24/2 Cor 11:33). If Luke is not dependent on the letters, such "undesigned coincidences" indicate that he is aware of and utilizes some reliable details about Paul's mission work in composing Acts. If Luke draws from Paul's letters, he seems to use them with even more freedom than is the case with Mark and Q.

Whether or not he knew the letters, Acts' portrayal of events often differs from that in the letters, revealing Luke's editorial interest. For example, even though the famous escape from Damascus is independently attested, in 2 Corinthians 11:33 it is the pagan king who tries to apprehend Paul, but in Acts it is characteristically the Jews (Acts 9:24). Acts calls the followers of Jesus "Christians" and regularly refers to church members as "disciples"; Paul never uses either term. Acts speaks of elders as congregational leaders in every church, a designation never used by Paul. The most striking difference is the chronology and perspective on Paul's relation to the Jerusalem church and its leaders as detailed in Acts 9–15/Galatians 1–2. See above, §10.1, especially the discussion of "Jerusalem #2—The Council (Gal 2:1–10; Acts 15:1–29)," §10.1.7.

The careful reader of Paul's letters notices how much is omitted from the Acts account. There are large gaps in the author's story of Paul. There is little in Acts that corresponds to Paul's list of sufferings in 2 Corinthians 11:23–29. The author of Luke–Acts relates nothing from Paul's early missionary period in Tarsus, a period of at least ten years (Acts 9:30–11:25). Paul claims to have done mission work as far west as Illyricum, which is not in Acts and can hardly find a place in the Acts outline. Titus, who plays a major role in Paul's letters, is never mentioned in Acts. Such omissions are difficult to reconcile with one who knew Paul personally or placed a premium on historical accuracy. We note two major omissions:

1. In Acts, Paul has no internal problems with his congregations. Difficulties are caused by outsiders, principally the Jews. If we did not possess the epistles, we would never suppose that the Gentile Pauline churches were ever disturbed by theological quarrels and divisions. There is no indication in Acts, for instance, of the problems among the Corinthian Christians and between them and Paul, and of the repeated trips across the Aegean by Paul and his coworkers struggling to bring the church back into line. Luke reduces the quarrel between Barnabas and Paul to a personal matter, not an issue of theology or missionary policy. It is only after Paul's death that serious theological problems will arise (Acts 20).

2. The offering was a major part of the final phase of Paul's mission. Though Luke here goes into greater detail than any other part of the story, only once does he refer to Paul's bringing money to Jerusalem (Acts 24:17). Even there, the matter is referred to so obliquely that, apart from the letters, the reader would never suspect what was involved. Luke is either ignorant of the offering or intentionally suppresses the outcome: the Jerusalem church did not accept it or Paul. Instead of this final offering that was apparently rejected, in Acts 11:27–30 Luke has Paul and Barnabas deliver an offering from Antioch that was accepted in Jerusalem, a trip that has no place in Paul's letters. This leaves no explanation for the large entourage that accompanies Paul on his last trip to Jerusalem (Acts 20:1–5).

So also the major differences between Paul's letters and the picture of Paul in Acts on eschatology, Christology, and apostleship are problematic for Acts' "historical accuracy" (see below, §24.1.2).

23.3.4 Particular Features of Lukan Composition

Evaluating the "historical accuracy" of Luke must take into account some particular features of his compositional method.

Luke's Tendency to Collapse a Theological Point into One Scene

Here are only two examples:

1. Historically speaking, there can hardly be any doubt that the early church, in the light of its resurrection faith, discovered a new perspective on reading the Scripture and, guided by its teachers, gradually accumulated a tradition of christological biblical interpretation and a stock of key texts (see above, §9.2.2). The risen Christ, at work in the ongoing life of the church through the Holy Spirit, guided the disciples into a new apprehension of the Scriptures. Instead of writing an essay on "Christological Reinterpretation of the Bible as Guided by the Spirit in the Life of the Church," Luke presents a memorable and dramatic scene on the first Easter Sunday, in which the risen Jesus teaches the disciples how to understand their Bible christologically, all in one afternoon (Luke 24:13–27, 44–47). This new approach to Scripture in the early church is historically true in the sense that it *happened*, but this extended process is not portrayed in Luke 24 in terms that are "historically accurate."

2. So also Acts 1–15 portrays the slow and painful struggle of the disciples, as they gradually came to realize, under the guidance of the Spirit, that the church is to be an inclusive community accepting Gentiles without the requirement of circumcision and observance of the biblical Law. Again Luke compresses this into one scene on the evening of the first Easter Sunday, in which the risen Christ commissions his followers to proclaim the gospel of forgiveness to all nations (Luke 24:46–49).

Luke's Imposition of His Own Patterns on the History

The modern reader does not expect to find subtle literary patterns in straightforward, accurate reporting or in history books devoted to factual accuracy. Numerous literary patterns have been noted in Luke–Acts.[34] We will note only two:

Pairing of male and female figures Luke repeatedly pictures the divine mission in the world unfolding with stories and imagery of female and male pairs:

— Zechariah and Elizabeth (Luke 1:5)

— Mary and Joseph (Luke 1:27)

— Simeon and Anna (Luke 2:25, 36)

— Man who plants mustard seed and the woman who takes leaven (Luke 13:18–21)

— Man who searches for the lost sheep and woman who searches for the lost coin (Luke 15:4–10)

— Jesus' raising a widow's only son and Jairus's only daughter (Luke 7:12; 8:42).

— Sabbath healings of the crippled woman and the man with dropsy (Luke 13:10–17; 14:1–6)

— List of male apostles (Luke 6:12–16) and female followers (Luke 8:1–3).

— The Good Samaritan, praising activity (Luke 10:29–37), followed by Mary and Martha, (Luke 10:38–42), in which reflective receptivity of Jesus' teaching is even more important than action

— Both men and women active in the beginning of the church (Acts 1:13–14)

— Christian congregations in Acts composed of "men and women" (Acts 5:14; 8:12; 17:12; 21:5)

34. Several authors have discovered and analyzed literary patterns in Luke's composition. An example, which may be too enthusiastic about a valid point, is Charles H. Talbert, *Literary Patterns, Theological Themes and the Genre of Luke–Acts*, SBLDS 20 (Missoula, MT: Scholars Press, 1974). If Talbert is correct in even half his proposals, Luke was not an "objective reporter" and was not trying to be. He was a skilled author creatively imposing his own patterns on his sources to communicate his theology.

— Ananias and Sapphira showing that the Christian mission can be impeded by defective disciples, both male and female (Acts 5:1–11)

— Both women and men persecuted and suffering for the faith (Acts 8:3; 9:2; 22:4)

— Both a woman and a man raised from the dead (Tabitha, Acts 9:36; Eutychus, Acts 20:9)

— At Philippi, Paul helped by both Lydia and the jailer (Acts 16:14–40)

— Response to the Christian message in Athens by specifically Dionysius (m.) and Damaris (f.) (Acts 17:34)

— Priscilla and Aquila mission partners with Paul (Acts 18:2, 18, 26)

This list represents Luke's editing material from Mark, Q, and his special materials, but this paired format appears in none of them. Luke himself has created this arrangement. Luke has a particular emphasis on the role of women among Jesus' followers and in the early church. This has sometimes been seen as advocating leadership roles for women, against the cultural stream, or—since Luke never portrays women as congregational leaders in Acts, but always in a subordinate role—as a means of continuing to affirm their cultural role. Perhaps Luke's presentation represents his interest in integrating the Pauline model, in which women functioned as church leaders on a par with men (thus resisting the stream of later Pauline tradition represented by the deuteropauline letters), with the Jewish Christian Petrine stream, in which the subordinate role of women continued. He handles it with narratives, not rules. Each tradition finds itself both affirmed and challenged in Luke–Acts.

Parallels between Peter and Paul in Luke–Acts Among Luke's interests is to consolidate the conflicting streams of Petrine and Pauline Christianity, portraying the church's story as unified and harmonious. One way Luke does this is to balance his presentation of Peter and Paul so that they appear as coleaders in the development of the church's worldwide mission. Though Paul is his hero, Luke is not just a Paulinist. He does not magnify Paul at Peter's expense. Like 1 Peter, Luke (also probably in Rome, see below) combines Peter and Paul. Peter is the first called, the first commissioned, the first to confess Jesus as the Christ, the first to receive a resurrection appearance, the first preacher of the gospel of the risen Lord, and the first missionary to the Gentiles. In the outline of Acts, Peter is the main character in chapters 1–12; then the narrative becomes almost exclusively the story of Paul. Note the following parallels:

— Each has a double name: Simon/Peter; Saul/Paul.

— The risen Jesus appears to both (to Peter, Acts 1 [cf. Luke 24:34]; to Paul, Acts 9, 22, 26).

— Peter and Paul both begin their ministry by healing a lame man (Peter, Acts 3; Paul, Acts 14).

— Both not only work miracles—many people in early Christianity do that—but do so in ways that surpass other miracle workers (Peter, with his shadow, Acts 5; Paul, with cloths that have touched him, Acts 19).

— Demons flee before both (Peter, Acts 5; Paul, Acts 19).

— Each meets and vanquishes a magician (Simon Magus, by Peter, Acts 8; Elymas bar-Jesus, by Paul, Acts 13).

— Each raises the dead (Peter Dorcas, Acts 9; Paul Eutychus, Acts 20).

— Both at first oppose preaching the gospel to Gentiles but are "converted," and the conversion is narrated three times in each case. Each "conversion" involves a vision, a voice, and a call to the Gentiles (Peter, Acts 10, 11, 15; Paul, Acts 9, 22, 26).

— While praying, each falls into a trance and receives a vision sending him to the Gentiles (Peter, Acts 10:10–15; Paul, Acts 22:17–21). In each case, the vision is at noon (Peter, Acts 10:9; Paul, Acts 26:13; cf. 22:17, verbal parallels to 10:10). In each case, the vision does not tell Peter or Paul specifically what to do; each must go to another town where he learns what the vision requires of him (Peter, Acts 10–11; Paul, Acts 9, 22, 26).

— Both are presented as initiators of major new evangelistic developments in the life of the church, although they in fact had predecessors (Peter, Acts 10:1–11:18; 11:19–21; Paul, Acts 18:1–4; 18:18–19:10).

— The first Gentile convert of each is a prominent Roman (Peter, Cornelius, Acts 10:1–48; Paul, Sergius Paulus, Acts 13:6–12).

— Both are worshiped as divine but reject the divine honors (Peter by Cornelius, Acts 10:25; Paul by people at Lystra, Acts 14:11–13).

— Both accept the hospitality of a Gentile God-fearer who has become a Christian (Peter, Acts 10:48; Paul, Acts 16:15).

— Both are supported by Pharisees in the Sanhedrin against Sadducees. (Peter [by Gamaliel, *Paul's* teacher], Acts 5; Paul, Acts 23).

— Both are imprisoned, bound with two chains, and miraculously delivered (Peter, Acts 12:11; Paul, Acts 16:19–28; cf. 12:6, 21:11).

— The Spirit initiates a mission after previous unfaithfulness (Peter, Acts 2:1–4; Paul, Acts 13:1–4).

— Both champion the Gentiles against more narrow Jewish Christians (Paul does this throughout, esp. Acts 11–15; but *Peter* is the one who *initiates* and struggles for the Gentile mission, Acts 10–11).

— Both Peter and Paul remain loyal to Jewish traditions, even though their Gentile converts are not required to "Judaize" (Peter, Acts 3:1; 10:1–11:30; 15:1–29; Paul, Acts 21:17–26; 15:1–29).

— Each goes to a spiritually deficient Christian group and gives the Spirit by the laying on of hands (Peter, Acts 8:14–17; Paul, Acts 19:1–6).

— Each appoints leaders in the churches by prayer and laying on of hands (Peter, Acts 6:1–6; Paul, Acts 14:23).

— Each experiences an earthquake in response to prayer (Peter, Acts 4:31; Paul, Acts 16:25–26).

— Both strengthen their fellow disciples (Peter, Luke 22:32; Paul, Acts 14:22).

— Neither is greedy; each refuses money in payment for services rendered (Peter, Acts 3:6; 8:18–20; Paul, Acts 20:33–34).

— Each announces he is ready to suffer and die for Jesus (Peter, Luke 22:33; Paul, Acts 21:13–14). Only Paul carries through on this in the narrative. By Luke's time, both had done so.

— Both are helped by an angel during their imprisonment (Peter, Acts 12:7; Paul, Acts 27:23).

— Jerusalem Jews reject both (Peter, Acts 3–12; Paul, Acts 9:28–30; 21:27–24:9)

— Their speeches are parallel:

- The word "gospel" occurs only twice in Luke–Acts: Acts 15:7 (Peter); Acts 20:24 (Paul), in each case identified with "grace."

- Each quotes Psalm 16 in his first speech, interpreting Psalm 16:10 by making the point that David's body suffered corruption, so the words of Scripture must refer to Christ and not to David (Acts 2:27; 13:35).

- Each refers to Galilean witnesses of the resurrection (Peter, Luke 23:35; Acts 1:11, 22; Paul, Acts 13:31; this excludes Paul from being such a witness [see on Acts 1:21–22]).

- Each kerygmatic message has the same structure, from Israel to John the Baptist to cross and resurrection, without reference to Jesus' pre-Easter ministry (Peter, 1:22; Paul, 13:24–27).
- Each refers to the death of Jesus as human evil corrected by God, not as saving event (Peter, Acts 10:39–40; Paul, Acts 13:28–30).
- Each announces forgiveness of sins as the content of salvation (absent from Paul's undisputed letters) (Peter, Acts 2:38; Paul, Acts 13:38).

The Extravagant Numbers in Acts Represent the Church in Epic, Biblical Terms

The author of Luke–Acts is very interested in numbers. Should they be taken as an example of his "historical accuracy"? His use of round numbers, rounded off to the nearest thousand, is not the issue, for all historians do this. The question has to do with the large number of converts and the size of the congregations portrayed in his narrative: 3,000 converts on the first day (2:41), later 5,000 men (4:4), then many tens of thousands (21:20). As the population of Jerusalem was about 20,000 at the time, these numbers are difficult to accept historically; they seem to be examples of Lukan rhetoric and theology. As in the case of the astounding number of Israelites delivered at the exodus, these "statistics" communicate Luke's faith that God himself was at work.[35] The thousands converted on Pentecost and the "myriads of believers" in the relatively small town of Jerusalem, where Christians remained a minority (Acts 21:20), are like the epic numbers in the exodus story. The church is portrayed as the (somewhat triumphalistic) continuation of biblical history. The point is not accurate history, but church-as-continuation-of-Israel.[36]

23.3.5 Summary: "Creative Theologian" or "Reliable Historian"?

Like authors of the Jewish Scriptures and like Jesus, Luke embodies his theology in a story. Luke expresses his theology not by writing philosophical essays, but by composing a narrative that he intends to be read as the continuation of the biblical story. His model is not Josephus or Thucydides, but the episodic stories of the LXX. He does not write fiction, but about real people. Jesus did not die in a story, but on a real Roman cross; Paul died in a real Roman prison. But neither does Luke write "the history of the early church," and the truth of his narrative is not to be judged by its "historical reliability." Luke's testimony of the continuing act of God in the Christ event is expressed in categories he has learned from his Bible.

23.4 For Further Reading

Bovon, F. *Luke the Theologian: Fifty-five Years of Research (1950–2005)*. Waco, TX: Baylor, 2006.

Cadbury, H. J. *The Book of Acts in History*. New York: Harper, 1955.

35. The difficulty in accepting the numbers of Numbers has often been pointed out, e.g., the total of 603,550 fighting men, not counting women, children, men too old to do military service, the infirm, or the tribe of Levi (Num. 1:46). This would mean a grand total of at least three million Israelites on the wilderness wanderings for forty years. The figure itself is inherently very difficult to accept historically; the difficulties increase when examined more carefully. The number of firstborn was 22,273 (3:43), which would be an average of 27.1 sons per mother. Nor did three million people get water for themselves and their animals from twelve springs in a single evening (Exod 15:27; Num. 33:9). Examples can be multiplied.

36. The large numbers of the Acts story are defended as historical by Wolfgang Reinhardt, "The Population Size of Jerusalem and the Numerical Growth of the Jerusalem Church," in *The Book of Acts in Its Palestinian Setting*, ed. Richard Bauckham, The Book of Acts in Its First Century Setting 4 (Grand Rapids: Eerdmans, 1995), 237–65.

———. *The Making of Luke–Acts*. London: SPCK, 1927, 1968.

Conzelmann, H. *The Theology of St. Luke*. Translated by Geoffrey Buswell. New York: Harper & Row, 1961.

Dibelius, M., and H. Greeven, eds. *Studies in the Acts of the Apostles*. London: SCM Press, 1956.

Fitzmyer, J. A., SJ. *Luke the Theologian*. New York: Paulist Press, 1989.

Foakes Jackson, F. J., and K. Lake. *The Beginnings of Christianity, Part I: The Acts of the Apostles*. 5 vols. New York: Macmillan, 1920–1933; reprinted Grand Rapids: Baker, 1979.

Gasque, W. W. *A History of the Criticism of the Acts of the Apostles*. Grand Rapids: Eerdmans, 1975.

Keck, L., and J. L. Martyn, eds. *Studies in Luke–Acts*. Nashville: Abingdon Press, 1966.

Pervo, R. I. *Dating Acts: Between the Evangelists and the Apologists*. Santa Rosa, CA: Polebridge Press, 2006.

Winter, B. W., David W. J. Gill, Howard Marshall, et al., eds. *The Book of Acts in Its First-Century Setting*. 5 vols. Grand Rapids: Eerdmans, 1993–1996.

24
Interpreting Luke–Acts

24.1 Authorship and Date

THE ISSUES OF AUTHORSHIP, SOURCES, and date are inseparably interwoven. We have discussed the author's sources above. Before examining the issue of authorship, some considerations of the date of Luke–Acts are in order.

24.1.1 The Date of Luke–Acts

The earliest possible date (*terminus a quo*) is set by the latest event plotted in Acts, Paul's two years in Roman imprisonment, about 62 (Acts 28:30–31). The latest possible date (*terminus ante quem*) is set by the earliest certain citation of the book. This is disputed, with some scholars finding echoes of Acts as early as *1 Clement* (ca. 95 CE) and others not finding indisputable evidence of the use of Acts until after the middle of the second century (Justin, Irenaeus). A full discussion, with citation of the primary sources so readers can decide for themselves, is provided by Haenchen.[1] Within this range of 62–150 CE, the issue of sources becomes crucial. If Luke used Josephus, a date after 93 CE is mandatory. An additional important factor is the setting in church and world history reflected in the work's contacts with the vocabulary, ethos, and issues reflected in other literature. Since some subjectivity is involved in determining both sources and presupposed context, some contemporary scholars despair of locating the book historically and settle for "between the early sixties and the early second century" as the best we can do.[2]

Assuming that Luke–Acts uses Mark and looks back on the destruction of Jerusalem, and is therefore post-70, but does not reflect a knowledge of the Pauline letter collection, the majority of scholars continue to date Luke–Acts about 80–90 CE. If, as here, one is persuaded that the author was aware of the Pauline corpus and the writings of Josephus, the Lukan double work fits best into the early second century. Not only does this cohere best with other writings of the 90–120 era, but the widespread anti-Judaism that erupted as a backlash to the Jewish revolts in the Diaspora (115–17) helps account for the author's stance toward Judaism. This is the same period as the Pastorals, in which the church is threatened by heretical "wolves" and needs protective shepherds.[3] The author sees the church as facing the threat of Marcion or proto-Marcionite teachers. The church reflected in Luke–Acts is on uneasy terms with the empire,

1. Haenchen, *Acts*, 3–9.

2. So, e.g., Charles H. Talbert, *Reading Acts: A Literary and Theological Commentary on the Acts of the Apostles*, rev. ed., RNT (Macon, GA: Smyth & Helwys, 2005), 2. When pressed, he inclines toward a date of ca. 100 CE.

3. The wolf/shepherd imagery is pervasive in this period (Revelation, Ignatius, Matthew, John, 1 Peter, *1 Clement*, Polycarp, and especially the Pastorals). This is the third period of the building/stabilizing/protecting periods outlined by Margaret MacDonald (see §16.2 above).

but is not facing the persecution of either the Neronian or Domitian periods.

24.1.2 Companion of Paul?

Luke–Acts is anonymous, like the other Gospels and like the biblical narratives that served as his model. This is in contrast to the Hellenistic historians, including Josephus, who signed their names in the preface of their works. The earliest extant attribution of Luke–Acts to Luke the companion of Paul is from Irenaeus and the Muratorian Canon in the latter part of the second century, followed by Clement of Alexandria, Tertullian, Origen, and Eusebius.[4] This attribution could represent historical memory. It could also have been deduced from the narrative itself. The "we" that appears intermittently in Acts 16:10–28:16 suggests a companion of Paul. Those mentioned in the third person in the narrative can be eliminated (Timothy, Barnabas, Silas, John Mark, etc.). The Luke of Philemon 24, Colossians 4:14, 2 Timothy 4:11 remains.

The argument that Luke–Acts was written by a companion of Paul consists of (1) the title, (2) the second-century church tradition, (3) a particular understanding of the "we" passages, and (4) the purported "medical language."

1. The title ΚΑΤΑ ΛΟΥΚΟΝ (According to Luke) attributes the Gospel to Luke, presumably the companion of Paul. Scholars such as Dibelius have argued that the title must be original, for it is inconceivable that it appeared "in the bookshops" without an author's name appended, so attribution to Luke goes back to the initial "publication" of the work.[5] This view of authorship is a byproduct of Dibelius's view of Luke as a literary author who for the first time brings Christian literature into the "book market." But Luke is not writing for this market. He is following the church and biblical model, in which texts appear anonymously in the community and are accepted or rejected on the basis of their content, not their authorship. In any case, if the title were original, it would only establish the claim to Lukan authorship, not that the author was actually a companion of Paul (see the deuteropauline letters). On the origin and historical reliability of the Gospel titles, see above, §2.1.

2. It is argued that the tradition of Lukan authorship was universally accepted by the ancient church and unquestioned until modern times and the rise of historical criticism, and thus should be considered correct unless proof to the contrary is presented. However, the problematic historical value of patristic data regarding authorship of New Testament documents (see above, Exc. 3.1) means the burden of proof is on advocates of its reliability.

3. It is argued that the we-passages indicate the author was a companion of Paul. This is the strongest argument for Lukan authorship. However, there are other, more likely interpretations of the we-passages (see above, §23.3.2).

4. It is argued that the "medical language" of Luke–Acts suggests the author was a medical doctor, which would fit the "beloved physician" of Colossians 4:14. This view was popularized by the 1882 publication of W. K. Hobart, and accepted by several scholars, including Adolf Harnack. The theory was carefully examined and demolished in the Harvard doctoral dissertation of H. J. Cadbury,[6] who demonstrated that the supposed technical language was common among educated people of all walks of life, as, for example, "cardiovascular" and "oral hygiene" are widely used today.

These arguments have convinced several modern critical scholars of the validity of traditional authorship,[7] but most contemporary

4. Original texts and English translations are found in Cadbury, "Tradition," 5:209–61. See, more recently, C. K. Barrett, *The Acts of the Apostles*, 2 vols., ICC (Edinburgh: T. & T. Clark, 1998), 1:30–48.

5. Dibelius and Greeven, eds., *Studies in Acts*, 104.

6. Henry J. Cadbury, *The Style and Literary Method of Luke*, HTS 6 (Cambridge: Harvard University Press, 1920), esp. 50–51. This book gave rise to the quip that Cadbury earned his doctorate by depriving Luke of his.

7. E.g., Dibelius and Greeven, eds., *Studies in Acts*; Bruce, Acts, 17–24; I. Howard Marshall, *The Acts of the Apostles:*

critical scholars remain unconvinced that Luke–Acts was written by a companion of Paul, for the following reasons:

1. The preface of Luke 1:1–4 applies to both the Gospel and Acts, distinguishes the author from the eyewitnesses, so that the author of Acts makes no claim to have been present at the events he narrates, and thus did not write the we-passages.

2. There are significant conflicts between events as reported in Acts and as we otherwise know them from Paul's letters and other sources (see above on Luke the historian).

3. Since Vielhauer's classic 1950 essay, the primary focus has been on the theological differences between Paul's letters and Acts.[8] The lengthy list of such differences includes:

Law. The Paul of the letters is adamant that the Law must not be imposed on Gentile churches. The Paul of Acts delivers the compromise worked out at the Jerusalem Council, in which Gentile churches accept a minimum of Law observance for the sake of the church's unity. Particular noteworthy is the contrast between Galatians 3:19 and Acts 7:38, 53. For both Paul and Acts, the Law of Moses was not given directly by God, but mediated by an angel. For Paul this shows the second-rate nature of the Law, for Acts its validity.

Angels. The undisputed letters of Paul and Luke–Acts have opposing perspectives on angels. Paul views angels in a uniformly negative light, as beings in the transcendent world who are emissaries of Satan and obstruct the human approach to God (Rom 8:38; 1 Cor 6:3; 2 Cor 12:7 [NRSV "messenger"], Gal 1:8; 3:19). For Luke–Acts, angels are always servants in the heavenly court, messengers from God who confer blessing and assist in the Christian mission (Luke 1:11–13, 30–38; 2:9; 9:26; 12:8; 15:10; 16:22; Acts 5:19; 8:26; 10:3; 27:23).

Eschatology. Paul's understanding of Christian life and mission was fundamentally shaped by his conviction of living in the brief interim before the parousia. The Gospel of Luke sometimes reaffirms the eschatology of its sources Mark and Q, reaffirming the imminence of the parousia, but often adjusts the eschatological expectation in prospect of an extended period before the end (see above, §§23.1; 24.5). In Acts, where Luke is more free to compose on his own, eschatology as such recedes, and the expectation of the near parousia plays no role at all in the church's missionary message.

Christology. (a) Preexistence. Luke does not share Paul's understanding of Christ as a preexistent divine being. There is nothing in Luke–Acts that indicates his awareness of or sympathy with the kind of Christology expressed in Philippians 2:5b–11. For Luke, the story of Jesus begins at Bethlehem; Jesus is Son of God by virtue of his birth (Luke 1:35). Neither Luke nor anyone in the New Testament combines the idea of preexistence and birth stories. The preexistent Son of God did not enter Mary's womb to be born as a baby who must then "increase in wisdom," learning as other children do (Luke 2:46, 52; contrast the stories of the superboy Jesus in the *Infancy Gospel of Thomas*). (b) Life of Jesus as kerygma. Paul does not, and cannot, affirm the epiphany Christology in which the saving power of God is manifest in the life of Jesus, especially in the miracle stories (see above, §20.1.2). Since the Gospel of Mark had already combined the epiphany Christology with the kenosis Christology represented by Paul, Luke can unproblematically adopt the miracle stories as vehicles of Christian faith, which Paul could never have done, and did not do. (c) Meaning of the death of Jesus. Luke sees the death of Jesus as part of the plan of God, but in strong contrast to Paul does not attribute soteriological value to it as such (see below on Luke 23 in the Exegetical–Theological Précis). "Christ died for our sins,"

An Introduction and Commentary, TNTC (Grand Rapids: Eerdmans, 1980), 44–46; Fitzmyer, *Acts*; Witherington, *Acts*; Jacob Jervell, *Die Apostelgeschichte*, 17 ed.; 2 vols., KEK (Göttingen: Vandenhoeck & Ruprecht, 1998).

8. Philipp Vielhauer, "On the 'Paulinism' of Acts," in *Studies in Luke–Acts*, ed. Leander Keck and J. Louis Martyn (Nashville: Abingdon Press, 1966), 33–50.

crucial and central for Paul's gospel, is missing from the theology of Luke–Acts.

Ecclesiology. (a) Church structure. Paul's churches had little official leadership, were guided by the free flow of the Spirit, and knew nothing of presbyters/elders. The churches in Acts are also guided by the Spirit but have presbyters appointed by Paul, and the power of the Spirit is correlated with structured leadership (see on Acts 15 and the Pastorals). (b) Apostleship. Paul passionately insisted that he had been directly called to be an apostle by the risen Christ, and was an apostle of the same status as the Twelve (1 Cor 9:1–2; 15:8–11; Gal 1:1, 17, 19). In the interests of Christian unity, Luke considered it necessary to have an apostolic college to guide the church through the changes necessary for its expanding mission and to authorize such changes. It is Peter, leader of the Twelve, who makes the dramatic step of officially initiating the Gentile mission, and who leads the other apostles to accept this momentous decision (Acts 10–11). This group of authentic apostles had to be in continuity with the life of Jesus; Paul did not qualify (Acts 1:21–22). The Paul of Acts reports to the apostles in Jerusalem, supports the Jerusalem church where they are in charge and from which they authorize the church's wider mission, and delivers their decisions to other churches (Acts 9:26–30; 11:27–30; 15:1–35; 18:21–23; 19:21). The Paul of Acts affirms this view of apostleship; it is "those who came up with him [Jesus] from Galilee to Jerusalem, who are now his witnesses to the people" (Acts 13:31).[9] It is very doubtful that one who knew Paul personally, had traveled with him, and admired him as a missionary hero could have been unaware of or misunderstood Paul's fundamental apostolic self-understanding.

9. Acts uses "apostle" of Paul only in 14:4, 14, but in the nontechnical sense of "missionary," as in Phil 2:25, where the NRSV rightly translates ἀπόστολος *apostolos* as "messenger." This is clearly Luke's understanding in Acts 14, where both Paul and Barnabas are called ἀπόστολοι, but not in the sense of apostles.

Summary: We know a good bit about the author of Luke–Acts, but all that we know for sure is derived from the text itself. The book was composed by a well-educated, well-traveled man with a good command of Greek, at home in the upper-middle class of the Hellenistic world. The author was not an eyewitness of the things he recounts. He is an admirer of Paul, but does not share Paul's own view of himself as an apostle; his own theology is considerably different from Paul's on key points and does not represent Paul's own views accurately.

24.2 Provenance

THERE IS NO SCHOLARLY CONSENSUS ON where Luke–Acts was composed and the identity of its initial readership. Some would accept Barrett's despairing conclusion, "As to the place of writing almost any guess will do."[10] Some familiarity with a wide range of locations is reflected in the narrative itself. The narrator of the we-passages knows the Aegean, Jerusalem, Caesarea, and Rome. The implied author seems familiar with Ephesus. Where did the actual author compose his work?

Antioch? A fairly widespread ancient tradition identifies Luke as a physician from Antioch,[11] but even if correct, it tells us nothing as to where the document itself was composed or for whom. The labors to identify an "Antioch source" for Acts are no longer considered convincing to most scholars, but the data they point to does strongly suggest that Luke has materials from Antioch and the surrounding area. A onetime residence in, or contact with, the Antioch church(es), where both Peter and Paul had been active and had also experienced a parting of the ways, would help explain Luke's

10. Barrett, *Acts*, 2:xliii.

11. Jerome, *Commentary on Matthew*, preface, 26–39; Anti-Marcionite Prologue to Luke; Eusebius, *Hist. eccl.* 3.4.

materials from, and interest in, Antioch. This is not evidence that Luke–Acts was written there.

The Aegean area in the context of the Pauline school? There is a relationship between Luke–Acts and the traditions of the Pauline school centered in Ephesus. But the author does not belong to the Pauline school in the sense of the deuteropauline epistles. Well-traveled person that he is, he may well have been around the province of Asia; he has Ephesian traditions, as he has Antiochene traditions. But, unlike the deuteropaulines, he doesn't merely reinterpret *Paul,* as much as he admires him, but brings together *Paul* and *Peter*. For the deuteropauline texts of the Pauline school, Paul is the sole link in the chain of tradition between Jesus and the church. For them, "apostolic" means "Pauline." In Luke–Acts, Paul does not belong to the apostolic circle, and is necessarily no higher than the second link in the authoritative chain that binds the risen Jesus and the church. In this consolidation of Pauline and Petrine traditions, Luke is no exclusive Paulinist but is an ecumenist. Like the author of 1 Peter and probably in the same location, he is interested in consolidating the Pauline and Petrine traditions. There is nothing in the Acts 19 story of Paul in Ephesus that suggests Acts was written for residents of the Ephesian area.

Rome? Ancient traditions connected Luke-Acts with Rome. Even ancient authors such as Jerome, who accepted the tradition that Luke came from Antioch and was a personal companion of Paul on his journeys, regarded Luke–Acts as having been written in Rome (his understanding, bringing together previous patristic traditions, is summarized in *De Viris Illustribus* 7). This tradition may have originated on the basis of Acts itself, which begins in the east and traces the missionary course of Christianity to Rome, where the story ends. However, strands of evidence support the view that the author did in fact come from the east, collected traditions from Antioch through Asia and the Aegean mission, and finally composed his two-volume work to address the situation of the third-generation church in Rome. The Roman church began with a strong orientation toward the Jewish Christianity sponsored by Jerusalem, with Peter and especially James as its heroes. The Roman Christians had received a major letter from Paul, and then Paul himself, as apostle to the Gentiles. The relation of Jewish and Gentile versions of an increasingly Gentile Christianity was a major issue in Rome. For some time, its normative Christian documents had been in the epistolary form, following the model of the Pauline letters. Luke–Acts can be best understood as addressing this situation in a manner that attempts to consolidate the varying traditions of the Roman church and solidify its own self-understanding as a united church with the heritage of the two major Christian missionaries, in full communion with the Jacobite mother church in Jerusalem.

This general view of a Roman provenance is supported by incidental observations:

- — Luke's emphasis on the large numbers of Jewish Christians in Palestine/Jerusalem (Acts 2:41; 4:4; 21:20, "myriads" there when Paul arrives) would be particularly encouraging to a church in Rome that understood itself as heirs of the Jewish Christian tradition, but where local Jews had mostly rejected Christian preaching.[12]
- — Luke–Acts seems unconsciously to presuppose the geography and weather of the western Mediterranean. It is the south wind that brings heat, not the east wind off the desert, as in Syria and Palestine (see Luke 8:22–23, 33; 12:54–55). Houses have tile roofs in which individual tiles can be removed, not the mud and straw mixture that must be "dug through" (Luke 5:19; cf. Mark 2:4). Luke's consistent designation of the "sea" of Galilee as a lake (Mark's θάλασσα, *thalassa* replaced with λίμνη, *limnē*) suggests a cosmopolitan perspective.

12. See Nils A. Dahl, "The Story of Abraham in Luke–Acts," in *Studies in Luke–Acts*, ed. Leander Keck and J. Louis Martyn (Nashville: Abingdon Pess, 1966), 151.

— The farewell scene in Acts 20 brings Paul's work in the east to a close. The narrative has constantly looked toward Rome as its divinely directed goal (19:21; 23:11!). Wherever it was actually composed, Luke–Acts seems to be oriented to Rome, seeing the whole history from the perspective of this final goal.

— The Lukan Paul seems to be influenced by Romans. It is not the radical Paul of Galatians, but the diplomatic Paul of Romans that is reflected in Acts. The Davidic-Jewish perspective of the christological creed quoted in Roman 1:3–4 fits a congregation with Jewish Christian traditions, but does not represent Paul's own preexistence Christology, and suggests Paul's interest in establishing common ground with a church with such views. Luke–Acts has more references to this Davidic christological perspective than any other New Testament document.

These general indications of a Roman provenance are strengthened by literary and theological contacts between Luke–Acts and Christian texts known to be, or very likely to be, of Roman provenance.

Contacts with Hebrews. Numerous scholars have carefully documented the phenomenon that the linguistic contacts between Luke–Acts and Hebrews are numerous and striking, closer and more numerous than the contacts between either and the Pauline letters. A few samples, from scores of examples:[13]

— Both Hebrews and Acts focus on angels as God's servants sent forth to assist in the Christian mission, to help prisoners, and to give directives (e.g., Acts 5:19; 8:26–28; 10:3, 22; 27:23; 12:6–11; Heb 1:14). Both identify ἄγγελος (*angelos*, angel) and πνεῦμα (*pneuma*, spirit).

— Hebrews and Luke–Acts rely heavily on citations from the same psalms in their proof-from-prophecy scheme. In the New Testament, Psalm 2:7 is cited explicitly only in Acts 13:33 and Hebrew 1:5; 5:5.

— Only Luke–Acts (five times) and Hebrews 6:17 speak of the βουλὴ θεοῦ (*boulē theou*, counsel/plan of God).

— The term for "leader, author, pioneer" (ἀρχηγός, *archēgos*) is found only four times in the New Testament, twice in Acts and twice in Hebrews, in each case as a christological term (Acts 3:15; 5:31; Heb 2:10, 12:2).

Such similarities are so numerous and so close that a few authors have argued that Luke–Acts and Hebrews are by the same author. Common authorship has seemed virtually impossible to most modern scholars, nor is it likely that either is directly dependent on the other or that they share common sources. Thus the striking linguistic phenomena are weighty evidence that the two authors are from the same literary milieu, namely, Rome.

Contacts with 1 Peter. Numerous linguistic points of contact also link Luke–Acts and 1 Peter.[14] Here is a brief sampling:

— The term Χριστιανός (*Christianos*, Christian) is found in the New Testament only in Acts 11:26; 26:28 and 1 Peter 4:16.

— The term ἀγαθοποιέω (*agathopoieō*, doing good) is found only nine times in New Testament; of these, four are in Luke and four in 1 Peter.

— That Christ was not abandoned to Hades is found only in Acts 2:24–32; 1 Peter 3:19–22.

— Christ crucified on a "tree" (Acts 5:30; 10:39; 1 Pet 2:24; both likely dependent on Gal 3:13).

All such contacts associate Luke–Acts with the same literary orbit as 1 Peter, namely, Rome.

13. See, e.g., the data detailed in W. K. L. Clarke, "The Use of the Septuagint in Acts," in *The Beginnings of Christianity, Part I: Prolegomena, Part II: Criticism*, ed. F. J. Foakes Jackson and Kirsopp Lake (Grand Rapids: Baker, 1925, 1979), 66–75; and Allen, *Authorship*, 83–174.

14. Detailed and analyzed in Elliott, *1 Peter*, 25–27.

Contacts with 1 Clement. The author of *1 Clement* was certainly a teacher in the Roman church. Here too there are numerous points of contact with Luke–Acts.[15] A brief sample:

— Compare the numerous references to "repentance" in *1 Clement*, for example, chapters 7–8, where "repentance" is a summary of conversion (as, e.g.. Acts 11:18).

— Both Acts and *1 Clement* see church leadership in the hands of presbyters appointed by the apostles, while neither affirms the threefold hierarchical pattern of a monarchial bishop to whom presbyters and deacons are subordinate. Each uses ἐπίσκοπος (*episkopos*, overseer, bishop) only in the plural, and as a synonym for πρεσβύτερος (*presbyteros*, presbyter, elder).

— In the New Testament, the phrase from *Clement* "remember the words of the Lord Jesus" (*1 Clem*. 13.1; 46.7) is found only at Acts 20:35, echoed also in Luke 22:61 and Acts 11:16. See also 2 Peter 3:2, also with Roman connections.

We cannot be sure where Luke–Acts was written. Perhaps the most we can say is that numerous and substantial features relate Luke–Acts to Rome and make it appropriate there, and nothing prohibits this identification of its provenance. As in the epistolary tradition, the center of gravity moves from the variety of Christian streams in the eastern Mediterranean toward consolidation in Rome.

24.3 Summary: The Origin of Luke–Acts "And so we came to Rome" (Acts 28:14)

THERE IS NO CERTAINTY OR SCHOLARLY consensus as to when, where, by whom, and for what purpose Luke–Acts was written. Several items in the above discussion, however, seem to converge on the following scenario.

1. Somewhere in the eastern Mediterranean, probably in Syria, a second- or (more likely) third-generation Christian teacher with an ecumenical vision had become acquainted with a variety of Christian traditions, including the collection of Jesus' sayings now known as Q. He did not come across these texts while browsing in a bookshop, but in the only settings for which they were composed and in which they functioned—the worship and instruction of early Christian congregations. He had come to appreciate both Peter and Paul as founding leaders of the first generation and had developed an appreciation for the narrative mode of communicating the Christian faith represented by Mark. Luke then moved to Rome, bringing this new form with him. The Gospels of Mark and Matthew may already have had a limited circulation in Rome before Luke's arrival there, but the Roman Christians had not accepted the Gospel genre as a normative form for Christian teaching. It was Luke's updating Mark and issuing it in combination with Acts that finally made the Gospel form current among Roman Christians.

2. Somewhere along the line, perhaps during a period in Ephesus or its environs, this well-traveled author becomes a member of a Pauline congregation, and thinks of himself as a Pauline Christian.

3. The author lives in Rome for some time, participating in its church life, is shaped by its ethos, and sees the need for rethinking the self-understanding of the Christian community. He does this not by lecturing or writing essays, but by composing a grand narrative, a foundation document not for the Roman church alone, but for the whole Christian movement, which he now sees as centered in Rome. His story is "From Jerusalem to Rome." The church began in Jerusalem and was initially directed from the holy city. Luke respects the mother church, but as he writes, Jerusalem lies in ruins. Without rejecting Jerusalem, the center of gravity in God's plan

15. Pervo, *Dating Acts*, 201–342, provides full listing and charts of parallels between Acts and the Apostolic Fathers, often indicating that Luke–Acts is the later writing.

for history has now shifted from the capital of Israel to the capital of the world, from Israel to all nations, including Israel. Luke wants to provide a comprehensive, normative account of the Christian movement and how it came to Rome. Luke–Acts is a legitimating narrative—"how we got to be who we are"—that seeks to bring into being the church as he describes it in Luke–Acts.

4. Luke–Acts is written for insiders. Luke knows of several influential and wealthy Romans who are in a position to help the church, including insiders to the Christian community (who still need further clarification and instruction). They will be edified and encouraged by reading of the centurions of Luke 7 and Acts 10–11 (both of whom have a number of slaves; the first had enough money to build a synagogue for the local Jews); King Agrippa of Acts 26; Felix and Festus, Sergius Paulus of Acts 13:6–13; and the men and women of high standing of Acts 17:12, people who had churches in their houses.

5. For the first time in the development of Christian literature and theology, a Christian author composing instruction primarily for the Christian community *also* explicitly looks beyond the church to the interested outsider. Although the author does not write directly to outsiders, he has them in mind, in a double sense: (1) He writes the kind of literary work that could circulate in sophisticated circles as an example of who the Christians are and what they believe, showing they are not an ignorant, fanatical, dangerous sect of whom decent Romans should be wary. (2) He models for insiders the kind of lives they might live to represent the faith to outsiders and to equip them to represent the church to the wider world. In both regards, he is somewhat like 1 Peter, written in Rome about the same time or somewhat earlier than Luke–Acts. (Cf. 1 Pet 3:15, "Always be ready to make your defense to anyone who demands from you an accounting for the hope that is in you.")

6. Luke has outsiders in the corner of his eye, but he does not directly address Roman leaders, neither does he write for the general public. There was no "general reading public" in modern terms. Luke does not write for the "book market."[16] There was no "publishing company" to advertise, market, and distribute the book. Publication was by means of an informal network of wealthy friends or sponsors. In the case of Luke–Acts, the text was probably first read out at an informal gathering of church people. It is the church, represented by people like Theophilus (whether a real or fictive character), that publishes and circulates it, and when it is read, it represents the church, not just the individual author.

7. A Christian teacher sympathetic to tensions in the church's past traditions and to current issues in the Roman church composes a narrative in which both sides of important tensive issues, while not conceptually resolved, are held together in one story, just as Luke thinks they should continue to live together in one community. For the first time, he brings together the Gospel that affirmed the story of the life of Jesus as the normative expression of the Christian faith and the explicitly post-Easter testimony of the church's leading apostles into one literary collection. "Gospel" and "Apostle" as distinct-but-inseparable units were a new way of thinking about the texts by which the church should communicate, solidify, and defend its faith.

This may well have happened in Rome. But even if not (e.g., if actually composed in Ephesus or Antioch), the story line brings the reader to Rome as the culmination of the chain of events directed by God. Rome is now the point of departure for the continuation of the church's story.

24.4 Text and Transmission History

IN ADDITION TO THE USUAL ACCUMULATION of textual variations that accrue in the process of transmission, Luke–Acts manifests

16. The point is elaborated and documented in Gamble, *Books and Readers*, 40, 133, and passim, and Haenchen, *Acts*, 136.

two interrelated constellations of textual phenomena that call for particular attention, both related to the Western text (see above, §3.1).

1. *The Gospel of Luke and "Western non-interpolations."* The Western text is usually longer (see below on Acts), generally considered to be a later expansion of the more original Alexandrian text, represented by B, ℵ, $\mathfrak{P}^{66}$, $\mathfrak{P}^{75}$. In a few places in Luke, however, the Alexandrian text and the great majority of other witnesses have the longer text. Westcott and Hort, loathe to acknowledge that their favored Alexandrian text (which they dubbed the "Neutral" text) had been interpolated, coined the phrase "Western non-interpolations" for the readings where they considered the shorter Western reading to be original. Though both inelegant and inaccurate, the label stuck and has become traditional nomenclature. The nine "interpolations" are the longer form of the Last Supper and eight expansions of the resurrection narrative:[17]

— 22:19 Then he took a loaf of bread, and when he had given thanks, he broke it and gave it to them, saying, "This is my body, which is given for you. Do this in remembrance of me." 20 And he did the same with the cup after supper, saying, "This cup that is poured out for you is the new covenant in my blood.

— 24:3 but when they went in, they did not find the body of the Lord Jesus.

— 24:5–6 He is not here, but has risen. Remember how he told you, while he was still in Galilee,

— 24:9 and returning from the tomb, they told all this to the eleven and to all the rest.

— 24:12 But Peter got up and ran to the tomb; stooping and looking in, he saw the linen cloths by themselves; then he went home, amazed at what had happened.

— 24:36 While they were talking about this, Jesus himself stood among them and said to them, "Peace be with you."

— 24:40 And when he had said this, he showed them his hands and his feet.

— 24:51 While he was blessing them, he withdrew from them and was carried up into heaven.

— 24:52 And they worshiped him, and returned to Jerusalem with great joy;

The Last Supper pericope 22:19b–20 is particularly important for interpretation, since it is the only clear reference to the salvific effect of the death of Jesus in the Gospel.

The older critical view, following Westcott and Hort and expressed in editions of the Greek New Testament and English translations, tended to treat this cluster of readings as a unit, to regard the longer readings as interpolations, and to prefer the shorter versions as the more original. The more recent approach of "reasoned eclecticism" judges each reading separately, and is inclined to adopt several of the readings into the reconstructed text. The RSV favored the Western text and thus omitted most of them, while the NRSV tends to follow the Alexandrian readings (see their respective marginal notes).

2. *The expansive Western text of Acts.* The textual phenomena of Acts are more complex. The Western text, represented especially by D (Bezae Cantabrigiensis), is almost 10 percent longer than the Alexandrian text represented by B (Codex Vaticanus). Many of the variations seem trivial to the casual reader—and numerous remain so after more careful study—but several present interesting and substantial differences from the "standard" Alexandrian text. For the most part, the D text is smoother, clarifying difficulties that could arise from the earlier text, sometimes with obvious theological intent. A few samples of this variety:[18]

17. Westcott and Hort's list included Matt 27:49 but not Luke 24:9. The list printed above has become more or less standard.

18. The full text of Acts in the Alexandrian (B) and Western (D) versions is printed side by side in James H. Ropes, *The Text of Acts*, The Beginnings of Christianity, Part I:

— 1:1 D omits the article before the name "Jesus." This may be a matter of copying carelessness (whether the Alexandrian or Western is considered original) or may have a minor significance. Proper names rarely have the article in English, but often do in Greek, to connect the person mentioned in the narrative with a previous reference. The article in the Alexandrian text could point back to the Jesus of the Gospel, thus connecting the two books; its omission in Acts could signal the beginning of a new work. I mention this minute variation (one letter in Greek) as an illustration of hundreds of such in Acts, each of which could have some significance, major or minor, but most of which do not.

— 2:1 D adds "all the apostles," resolving the problem of who received the baptism of the Holy Spirit.

— 2:47 D substitutes "to the church" for the unclear phrase translated "to their number."

— 3:8 D has the apostles leave "the temple" with the healed person, while the people stand in the portico of Solomon. This is a more precise description of the temple layout, evidencing later and better knowledge of the temple complex than the description given by the original author.

— 5:29 D reads, "Whom must we obey? God or mortals?" replied Peter. He [the high priest] said, "God." Peter said to him, . . .

— 15:20, 29; 21:25 The "Apostolic Decree" occurs three times in Acts, in prospect (15:20), the "official text" (15:29), and in retrospect (21:25). For the first two of these, the Alexandrian text has four prohibitions, all cultic: "abstain from what has been sacrificed to idols and from blood and from what is strangled and from fornication" (understanding "fornication" to refer to marriage within forbidden degrees of kinship). The Western text understands the initial prohibition to refer to idolatry, omits "what is strangled," understands "fornication" as sexual immorality, and adds a negative form of the Golden Rule, "and do not do to others what you would not want them to do to you." In the Western text, the Apostolic Decree has thus been completely transformed from a minimal set of ritual laws that permit Jewish and Gentile Christians to live and worship together into a general set of ethical maxims.

Some scholars have argued that this proliferation of expansive, often periphrastic readings is only the effect of the random accumulation of variations in the course of transmission. This is certainly true in part, as it is true of all other New Testament manuscripts. The dominant view, however, is that the Western text represents some sort of intentional revision. The large number of variations from the Alexandrian text often seem not to be random, but to cohere into particular patterns. A small number of scholars have contended that the Western text is the more original, and the Alexandrian text derived from it. A few others have argued that Luke himself composed both versions of the text.

It is necessary to study the textual phenomena of Luke–Acts in conjunction with the transmission history of the two volumes. In the nature of the case, this cannot be confidently traced in detail. After a century and a half of careful study, the formation of the distinctive Western text remains something of a historical mystery. Without claiming to solve this mystery, a plausible rough outline might be:

a. Luke writes a single work in two discrete volumes. Though planned and executed as a literary unity, we do not know how much time intervened between their composition.

b. The Gospel of Luke was early separated from Acts and joined to what became the fourfold Gospel canon.[19] Acts appears to have

the Acts of the Apostles 3 (Grand Rapids: Baker, 1979; orig. pub, 1925]. Relevant sections of the two texts are printed in parallel in Pervo, *Acts: A Commentary*.

19. In no extant manuscript does Acts follow directly after Luke. In 𝔓[45] Acts is included with the Gospels, but still separated from Luke, added after John.

circulated independently for a while, then was joined to the Catholic Letters. After the Gospel and Acts were separated, the two volumes had separate textual histories.

c. The two main streams of transmission affected both the Gospel and Acts. Each document is represented by manuscripts of both Alexandrian and Western types.

d. In one stream of textual transmission, as Acts circulated independently of the Gospel, the Western text of Acts developed its own expanded version of the text. Being part of the fourfold Gospel that was read in the churches exercised some influence on the Gospel of Luke. On the one hand, such wide exposure in a somewhat controlled context and alongside the other Gospels provided a deterrent from casual and wholesale expansion. Acts, on the other hand, at first had no such controls, and invited paraphrasing and novelistic elaboration.

Despite the labors of textual critics, uncertainty about numerous texts remains (see NRSV footnotes). Did Jesus send out seventy or seventy-two disciples? (Luke 10:1–2; good arguments and symbolic meaning for each option can be given.) Did the words of institution at the Last Supper include a saying about the cup and the redemptive meaning of Jesus' death, or is the short text original (Luke 22:19b–20)? During his suffering on the cross, did Jesus pray for the forgiveness of those who were killing him (Luke 23:34)? In Acts, not only the differences between the Alexandrian and Western texts continue to be discussed, but at several points the text seems so confused or corrupt as to defy confident judgments on what the author originally wrote, for example, 1:2; 2:43; 3:16; 4:25; 5:13; 6:9; 7:46; 9:25; 10:11, 30, 36; 12:25; 13:27–29, 32, 34, 43; 14:8; 15:21; 16:12, 13; 19:13–14, 25, 40; 20:6, 24, 28; 21:15–16; 22:30; 24:19; 25:13; 26:16; and 26:20.[20]

24.5 Exegetical-Theological Précis

Preface (Luke 1:1–4)

Of the four canonical Gospels, only Luke begins with a formal preface, one complex sentence in which the author directly addresses the readers, introducing the audience to the narrative that follows. The following points are important:

— The summary repetition of this preface at Acts 1:1–2 establishes the author's intent that the two volumes be seen as two parts of a single work. Thus "the events that have been fulfilled among us" include both the life of Jesus and the story of the early church.

— The author claims to have done his homework, but does not claim to be an eyewitness of the events he narrates. This already raises a question as to whether the we-passages of Acts intend to claim that the author was eyewitness to some of the events he reports. What he has to say is communicated reliably, but indirectly; his message is dependent on a trustworthy chain of tradition that extends back to the revelatory and salvific events themselves.

— These events are described not as merely "happening," but as "having been fulfilled," that is, by God. They represent the fulfillment of God's promises to Israel, God's purposes for the world. From the very beginning, Luke indicates that his narrative, while based on historical events, is no mere chronicle, but theologically interpreted history.

— These redemptive events are perceived and communicated by "eyewitnesses and ministers of the word." Grammatically, this phrase could refer to two separate groups, but more likely it refers to a single group who both saw the original events and perceived them to be the work

20. The list is from Pervo, *Acts: A Commentary*, 2. See Hans Conzelmann, *Acts of the Apostles: A Commentary on the Acts of the Apostles*, trans. James Limburg, Thomas A. Kraabel, and Donald Juel, Hermeneia (Philadelphia: Fortress Press, 1987), ad loc.

of God. It is not a matter of "bare facts" seen by eyewitnesses that were later interpreted by others as acts of God. Interpretation is inevitably already involved in the act of perception. Such discernment is not merely a matter of objective observation, but is the gift of God. In Luke's view, some of those who had been eyewitnesses of the events of the life of Jesus and the early church were, after Easter, enabled by the Holy Spirit to recognize the hand of God in these events.

— Luke is not the first to write such a narrative. The "many" predecessors of 1:1 is part of the conventional rhetoric of such prefaces, and does not necessarily imply a large number. The "many" here refers to Mark, Q, L, and the oral and written traditions Luke used in the composition of Acts (see above on sources).

— We know from Luke's rearrangement of his sources (see, e.g., on 4:16–44 below) that his claim to write "accurately" and "in order" does not mean he professes to give a chronologically correct account, accurate in every detail. He works as a creative interpreter of his sources and traditions, and intends that his book represent a comprehensive, coherent, well-organized literary and theological presentation of the truth of the Christian faith.

— Luke attributes the decision to write his two-volume work to his own volition ("it seemed good to me also"). Some later scribes perceived this to be a defect, so that a few manuscripts add "and to the Holy Spirit" at this point (cf. Acts 15:28). The author believes that the Holy Spirit is operative in the life of the church as a whole but claims no particular inspiration for himself.

— The narrative is intended for believers within the Christian community, to strengthen their faith and to deepen their understanding, but also looks beyond them to interested outsiders who may have received misleading impressions about the new Christian movement.

Part 1: The Time of Israel Reaches Its Climax (Luke 1:5–2:52)

A dramatic stylistic shift occurs at 1:5, obvious even in English translations. Whereas 1:1–4 is composed in the high-level, complex, somewhat grandiloquent Greek customary in such prefaces, the reader enters a different linguistic and cultural world at 1:5. This lengthy section is written in the style of Israel's narrative literature and breathes the atmosphere and piety of biblical history. Grammar, style, vocabulary, and characterization echo the stories of the Old Testament. Luke obviously intends Part 1 of his composition to sound like the continuation (and conclusive climax) of the biblical story of Israel. Here Luke imitates the style of the LXX, as a modern author wanting to give his or her composition a biblical flavor might imitate King James English ("and it came to pass," "he said unto her," and the like). As in the Old Testament, participants burst into songs that interpret the narrative (Mary's Magnificat, Zechariah's Nunc Dimittis, the angels' Gloria), which does not happen in Parts 2 and 3 of Luke–Acts. Readers immediately sense that they have entered into an ongoing story, the story of Israel looking back to the promises made to Abraham and David, looking forward to the time of fulfillment guaranteed by the faithfulness of God. The devotion and piety of the characters invite the reader to take a positive attitude toward Torah obedience and the Jewish hope.

Luke works important theological themes into Part 1, which set the tone and agenda for much of the following narrative:

— *Continuity between the story of Israel, the story of Jesus, and the story of the church.* The major figures are all devout, observant Jews. The story begins with the pious priest Zechariah offering incense in the temple while the people pray (Luke 1:9–10), includes the purification of Mary and dedication of Jesus in the temple, attended by the saintly Jewish prophetic figures

Simeon and Anna (2:22–38), and ends in the temple, which the boy Jesus calls "my Father's house" (2:41–52). Both John and Jesus are circumcised, incorporated into the covenant people of Israel (1:59; 2:21). Zechariah and Elizabeth live "blamelessly according to all the commandments and regulations of the Lord" (1:6). The "law of Moses" or "law of the Lord" is mentioned five times in the brief account of the holy family's temple visit (2:22–39). The (future) inclusion of Gentiles is announced (2:32), but when it happens later in Luke's story—not without soul searching and struggle on the part of Jesus' followers—the people of God continues to be rooted in Jewish Scripture, tradition, and practice.

— *John and Jesus are both eschatological figures, but in different ways*. John is the last and greatest of the Old Testament prophets, who stands at the turn of the ages. Jesus is the proclaimer and embodiment of the kingdom of God, whose life and work constitutes the reality and presence of the kingdom to which John still looked forward.

— *Especially the inspired canticles interpret the saving significance of the events narrated*. Mary's Magnificat (Luke 1:46–55), Zechariah's Benedictus (1:67–79), and Simeon's Nunc Dimittis (2:29–32) celebrate the themes of eschatological reversal that are becoming reality in the events they are experiencing. The poor and powerless are exalted, and the high and mighty are brought down from their thrones. The faithfulness of God to the promises made to Israel is now being fulfilled. People are being converted and experiencing the joy and reality of God's mighty acts of salvation.

— *Luke expresses the dialectic of accommodation and obedience to the imperial power while offering an alternative kingdom that will finally displace human empire*. It is in obedience to Caesar that Mary, Joseph, and the unborn Jesus travel to Bethlehem to register. There is no overt opposition to Rome. Yet the story represents the birth of Jesus as the event that truly brings the good news claimed by the emperor (see above, §9.2.2), and the baby in the manger is proclaimed "Savior" and "Son of God" (1:35; 2:11), standard titles of the Caesar. In contrast to the *Pax Romana* and *Pax Augustana*, it is Jesus who brings ultimate peace, the *shalom* of God's rule (1:79; 2:14).

Part 2: The Time of Jesus (Luke 3:1–Acts 1:26)

The Mission of Jesus and His Disciples in Galilee and Judea—Gathering the Witnesses (3:1–9:50)

3:1–2

The sixfold chronological synchronization locates the Jesus story within universal world history, and marks the special one-year ministry of Jesus. Although John the Baptist appears in this transitional scene, he is clearly identified as belonging to the period of Israel. "*The word of God came to* . . ." is the revelatory formula used of Old Testament prophets (Jer 1:4 and often). It is used of John, but not of Jesus. While John is the last and greatest of the prophets of Israel, the narrative specifically rejects the view that Jesus is "one of the old prophets" (7:26–28; 9:19; see 16:16).

3:10–14

John is given a message of social justice reminiscent of Israel's prophets (3:10–14, only in Luke), further characterizing him as belonging to the period of Israel. He preaches like the Old Testament prophets, but not like Jesus, who proclaims the kingdom of God (John does not, in Luke—contrast Matt 3:2).

3:19–22

Although Luke knows Jesus was baptized by John, he transfers the note about John's arrest to this point from its later place in Mark, getting

John off the stage before Jesus comes on, thus emphasizing the new stage of salvation history that begins with Jesus' ministry. Jesus' baptism is not related backward to the work of John, but forward to the life of the church. The Holy Spirit does not descend directly on Jesus at his baptism, but as Jesus is praying. So also, in Acts 2, Jesus' disciples are praying when they receive the Spirit that equips them for mission.

4:1–13

Luke's seemingly minor changes and additions to the temptation story register distinctively Lukan points: The devil claims that authority over the nations of the civilized world (οἰκουμένη, *oikoumenē*, used of the Roman Empire) has been given to him, and he gives this authority to whomever he will. The temptation here is not a one-time-only kneeling before the devil, but "serving him" (4:8), that is, adopting the values and methods of the devil-dominated world in order to gain control over it. This was a real temptation to Jesus, pictured here in dramatic imagery. When the temptation is over, the devil leaves "until an opportune time" (4:13). He will be vanquished during the ministry of Jesus, while the kingdom of God is manifest on the earth (see above for Jesus' ministry as the "Midst of Time," §23.1), but will return at the end of Jesus' ministry (22:3). Though already defeated, Satan will continue to harass the church and the world until the parousia (Luke 8:12; Acts 5:3; 13:10; 26:18).

4:16–30

Luke moves this scene forward from its location in the Markan outline (Mark 6:1–6) to become the opening scene and keynote address in Jesus' public ministry. Luke's expansions and modifications of Mark highlight characteristic Lukan themes that set the tone for Jesus' ministry as a whole:

— Jesus is God's anointed prophet for the climax of history as prophesied in Isaiah. The text cited in Luke is actually a combination from Isaiah 61:1–2 and Isaiah 58:6; that is, it is not a literal report of the text Jesus read in the synagogue, but Luke's theological combination.

— "Good news to the poor and oppressed" is the theme of both the biblical text and Jesus' ministry (1:52–53; 3:10–11; 6:20–21; 7:21–22; 14:13, 21).

— "The year of the Lord's favor" is the year of Jesus' ministry (3:1–2), in which the kingdom of God is present in the life and ministry of Jesus, with overtones of the idyllic year of jubilee (Lev 25:10). This is why Luke works the words from Isaiah 58 into his citation of Isaiah 61.

— God's astonishing acceptance of Gentiles in the time of Luke was actually already anticipated in the time of Elijah and Elisha, when a Lebanese widow and Syrian army officer were recipients of the grace of God.

— When Jews reject, the acceptance of Gentiles is emphasized. This anticipates the later history of "to the Jew first" reflected in Acts and Paul.

— God's saving offer is made in Nazareth among Jesus' own people, but it is rejected. The rejection of God's anointed prophet corresponds to that of the prophets of Israel (Luke 4:24; 6:22–23; 11:49–51; 13:33–34; Acts 7:52). This is a theme throughout Luke, from "no room in the inn," through rejection in his hometown, in Samaria (9:52–56), and ultimately in Jerusalem (19:41–44; 22:39–23:25).

Luke 5:1–11

The Lukan version of the call of the disciples seems to be a variation of the story in John 21:1–11. Yet one is set in the pre-Easter framework of the life of Jesus, and the other in the context of the appearance and call of the risen Lord. Here is a key example of the flexibility and fluidity of such traditions in the early days of the church, in which firm lines were not drawn between "pre-Easter" and "post-Easter," and all sayings and stories of the pre-Easter life of Jesus could be told as expressions of faith in the risen Jesus, and vice versa.

6:20–49

The "Sermon on the Plain": Here begins the "Lesser Insertion" of Q and L materials into the Markan framework (6:20–8:3 inserted at Mark 3:19, with some rearrangement of Mark). Luke begins the inserted section with the Great Sermon that was the opening discourse of Q (see above, Exc. 3.5); Matthew has combined this same Q sermon with his M materials to construct the Sermon on the Mount of Matthew 5–7. Both this sermon and the traditional materials about John the Baptist (7:18–35) emphasize the recurring themes of Jesus' ministry: the reality of the kingdom of God experienced as good news to the poor, love of enemies, deliverance to the oppressed, healing to the sick, recovery of sight to the blind, life to the dead.

8:1–3

Luke concludes this inserted section with the note that several women accompanied Jesus and the Twelve during their Galilean mission tour. It is important to Luke that women be registered among the Galilean witnesses "from the beginning." They are present at the passion and in the early days of the church. They are wealthy and of high social standing, and support Jesus and the disciples financially. Women play a prominent role in the Gospel (though they are not sent out to preach, teach, and heal); in Acts, though they are present, they hardly play a role in the church's leadership (Priscilla is an outstanding exception).

Luke is sensitive to cultural realities, and does not portray women disciples in Acts as challenging these. Nonetheless, he retains the Gospel's images of Jesus' acceptance and affirmation of women as a challenge to the church of his own time, which the church must implement in appropriate ways that do not damage the mission of the church. In this, Luke is like the deuteropauline letters and 1 Peter, with which he is contemporary. This accommodation is one aspect of the church's coming to terms with its existence in history for the long term, a reality that Paul and the first generation of Christians was not forced to deal with.

8:19–21

The scene in which Jesus' mother and brothers come to hear him preach illustrates Luke's handling of the important theme of the relation of Jesus to his family.[21] Mary and Jesus' brothers do not appear in Q. In Mark (in which there is no birth story) they fail to recognize him and consider him deranged (Mark 3:20–35; cf. John 7:5, "not even his brothers believed in him"). Luke has made the following editorial-hermeneutical moves: (1) He omits Mark 3:20–21, in which Mary and Jesus' brothers and sisters think he is mentally disturbed. (2) He moves the conclusion of that section referring to Mary and Jesus' family to this context, where it is the conclusion of Jesus' explanation of the parable of the Sower. They are now shining examples of "good soil" who receive the word and believe, just as Mary had been pictured as the model believer in 1:26–56. (3) Luke slightly adjusts the syntax, so that the offensive sentence in Mark 3:34–35 should be translated in Luke 8:21 as "My mother and my brothers, they are the ones who listen to the Word of God and act on it."[22] (4) Luke omits the insider/outsider language in which the family had been outsiders. (5) In 4:24, Luke omits "family" and "house" from Mark 6:4. (6) Thus in Acts 1:14 Mary and Jesus' brothers are in the core group that will become the church, of which James the brother of Jesus will become the leader (Acts 12:17; 15:1–29; 21:17–26).

---

21. For a helpful treatment of the various ways New Testament authors present the role of Mary, see the study sponsored by the United States Lutheran–Roman Catholic Dialogue and written jointly by Catholic and Protestant scholars, Raymond E. Brown, Joseph A. Fitzmyer, SJ, and John Reumann, eds., *Mary in the New Testament* (Philadelphia: Fortress Press, 1978).
22. So, e.g., Fitzmyer, *Luke the Theologian*, 76.

9:1–6

Jesus sends out the Twelve on a mission in which they are not to take staff, knapsack, money, or even a change of clothes, since they need not worry about food, shelter, or self-defense—it is the "midst of time," the special time of the presence of the kingdom, the time of celebration and joy, when the evil powers are vanquished (10:17–24; see above, §23.1). At the Last Supper, Jesus will rescind these commands as directly applicable to the time of Luke's readers (22:35–38, combined with the instructions to the seventy in 10:4). This does not mean the instructions for the idyllic *time of Jesus* are no longer relevant for the *time of the church* in which Luke's readers live. Such historicization of the radical discipleship called for in the Gospel does not neutralize or domesticate this image of what it means to be a follower of Jesus.

The church still has this set of images of the way it was during the presence of the kingdom in the life of Jesus, is still challenged to live by them. But the church no longer has direct instruction on how this is to be done, as it comes to terms with Christian mission in an ongoing world. Led by the Spirit, the post-Easter church must interpret, from case to case, what such instruction means; it can no longer hear it as a direct command of Jesus, but neither can it ignore it as though it only applied to a time now past.[23]

9:18–22

Luke has omitted all of Mark 6:45–8:26 (see above, §23.2.3, on the structure of the Gospel). This omission means that the following scene no longer takes place outside Galilee at Caesarea Philippi, as in Mark, but at the same location as the feeding the five thousand. As in the Gospel of John, Peter's confession follows immediately on the feeding story (cf. John 6:1–65, 66–69).

9:23

With one deft stroke, Luke illustrates how Jesus' sayings to the first generation as presented in Mark can and should be reinterpreted for a later generation. Jesus' challenge to take up the cross and follow him (Mark 8:34) needed no interpretation in Mark's time in the late 60s or early 70s, when Christians had been literally crucified in Rome. In Luke's time, a generation or more later, the saying could no longer be understood literally. With the insertion of the two Greek words καθ᾿ ἡμέραν (*kath' hēmeran*, daily), Luke reaffirms Jesus' challenge in a way that it can be taken seriously in his own time. In each case, Jesus called for the life of his disciples: in Mark, by giving it once for all in martyrdom; in Luke, by unspectacularly giving it away one day at a time in the way one lives. The same saying in a different situation is not the same saying; to merely repeat Mark is to be unfaithful to him. Luke can only preserve Jesus' meaning in Mark by changing the Markan saying. In contrast to his earlier contemporary John of the Apocalypse, who sees God's destruction of Rome looming on the immediate horizon, Luke does not see his task as equipping the church for martyrdom in view of the impending end, but as preparing the church to live as faithful witnesses within the ongoing Roman Empire.

The Journey to Jesus' Destiny in Jerusalem—Preparing the Disciples (9:51–19:44)

This lengthy section—the longest unit in Luke's outline—is oriented to the "exodus" that Jesus will accomplish in Jerusalem (see 9:31). During this *travel narrative*, as it is traditionally called, Jesus seems to wander, hardly making progress, though Jerusalem is repeatedly mentioned as the projected goal (9:51, 53; 13:22, 33–34; 17:11; 18:31; 19:11, 28). This is due partly to the author's lack of a clear idea of Palestinian geography—he had no maps in the back of his Bible and seems never to have lived or traveled in the area—and partly because he

23. See Friedrich Wilhelm Horn, *Glaube und Handeln in der Theologie des Lukas*, GTA 26 (Göttingen: Vandenhoeck & Ruprecht, 1983), 197 and passim.

has used this section to incorporate much of the Q and M materials not found in the Gospel of Mark, which forms the basic structure of his narrative.

This does not mean that the *travel narrative* has become merely a receptacle into which Luke randomly inserts his other materials; it has its own purpose in Luke's narrative design. Just as the preceding section (3:1–9:50) was the period of mission to the people of Galilee and Judea as a whole, during which Jesus called disciples who would later be his witnesses in the time of the church after Easter, so 9:51–19:44 is the time of instructing the disciples and preparing them for the days ahead. Jesus' teaching is not always addressed directly to the disciples. However, like the readers, they are always present and overhear Jesus' dialogues with the crowds and his opponents. Nor is this a time of private instruction. In contrast to Mark, this mode of private teaching almost disappears in Luke. The disciples learn as they overhear Jesus' dialogues with crowds and opponents (e.g., 14:25–35; 16:14). This section contains some of Jesus' most well-known stories and sayings, found only in Luke: the Good Samaritan (10:29–37); the Prodigal Son (15:11–32); the Rich Man and Lazarus (16:19–31); the Pharisee and the Publican (18:9–14).

9:51–56

Corresponding to the preceding section, which began with Jesus' rejection in his hometown of Nazareth (4:16–30), this section begins with Jesus' rejection by the Samaritans. This rejection is not merely an example of the Samaritan/Jewish antipathy, but is specifically because Jesus has "set his face to go to Jerusalem." The Samaritan response is in explicit (though unintended and unconscious) opposition to the divine plan that is to reach its definitive climax in Jerusalem. In contrast to Elijah, who has just been mentioned, Jesus does not retaliate by bringing down fire from heaven (Luke 9:51–56; cf. 2 Kgs 1:2–10). Like the God he represents, Jesus is kind to the ungrateful and wicked (6:35–36).

9:57–62

In the preceding section, Jesus' powerful word had called people into the life of discipleship. At the beginning of this section, three would-be disciples are warned about the rigors involved in the decision to follow Jesus, and he gains no new disciples. This sets the tone for the instructions in the *travel narrative*, which emphasize the cost of discipleship (10:3–12; 12:4–12, 41–53; 13:22–35; 14:25–35; 17:33). In Luke, a major aspect of the call to discipleship is the renunciation of money and property. Emphasis is often placed in this section on good news to the poor, the call to share one's goods with others, the value of the life of poverty, and the dangers of wealth (9:58; 10:4; 12:13–34; 14:12–14, 15–24; 16:1–31; 18:18–30; 19:1–10). Early in the story, the crowds and people as a whole were positive in their response to Jesus, and it was only their leaders who opposed him. During the *travel narrative*, as the nature of Jesus' messiahship and the meaning of being his disciple became clearer, the crowds begin to shift their loyalty, so that by the time Jesus and his disciples reach Jerusalem the crowds have virtually joined the opposition of the religious leaders.

10:1–23

In Luke Jesus not only sends out the Twelve (9:1–6) but seventy (or seventy-two; the manuscripts evidence is divided). Both seventy and seventy-two have symbolic significance. There were several significant groups of seventy leaders in Israel's history, from the seventy appointed by Moses (Exod 24; Num 11:24–25) to the Sanhedrin of Jesus' time and the seventy elders Josephus appointed over Galilee during the revolt against Rome (*War* 2.570). Seventy-two, though less frequent, was also symbolic: according to the LXX table of nations in Genesis 10, the world was composed of seventy-two nations; there were seventy-two elders appointed to translate the Jewish Scriptures into Greek, the language of the Gentile world, and various Jewish traditions indicated the world had seventy-two rulers and seventy-two languages (*3 Enoch* 17.8; 18.2–3; 30.2).

As the mission of the Twelve corresponds to the people of Israel, the mission of the seventy (-two) prefigures the wider mission to the whole world. Luke knows, of course, that it was after Easter, and only gradually and with much soul-searching and struggle, that Jesus' followers came to the realization that the plan of God enacted in Jesus includes all people, as documented in Acts 1–15. Yet he can portray this as already anticipated during the life of Jesus by the mission of the seventy(-two).

10:30–37

Jesus' parable of the Good Samaritan tells of a traveler, presumably Jewish, who was robbed, beaten, and left for dead. Two Jewish religious officials from whom help could be expected pretended not to notice and passed by without helping. The original hearers would now expect the hero of the story to be one of their own group, a Jewish layman if the hearer was anticlerical, a Pharisee if one was antipriesthood. In the disturbing, disorienting conclusion of the story, an outsider of another religion turns out to be the one who follows the greatest commandment of love to God and neighbor.

The upsetting cutting edge of this story has been neutralized in modern times by making it a moralizing example story of "openness" and "tolerance": instead of being prejudiced against minorities, we should help everyone, regardless of color, creed, or sexual orientation. Such a reconfiguration of the story places the Samaritan in the ditch, with modern liberal Westerners encouraged to overcome their prejudice and help everyone. This is not the original parable: the Samaritan was the helper, not the needy victim. The mental framework of Jesus' hearers was shaken by such stories, which did not merely give them new bits of information to fit into their old conceptual structures of how things are, but shook the frameworks themselves. In Luke's narrative, Jesus' parable has become an example story, "Go and do likewise." Nonetheless, it still retains something of the original shock treatment, for the example of the love of God and neighbor comes from an inconceivable source, and Luke's readers are challenged to examine not just the items of their own thought world, but its foundation.

14:25–27

The scandalous, undomesticated provocation of Jesus' original parables is a challenge to the conventional reading that wants to preserve the traditional way of looking at the world, even if it is willing to add on the values of Jesus' teachings. Jesus' call to discipleship repeatedly rejects the bland, tolerant both/and and calls for a radical either/or. Following Jesus, living according to the kingdom of God he teaches and embodies, can only be the top priority that relativizes *everything* else. The claim that following him means "hating" father and mother, spouse and children must be heard in this context. "Hate" in Semitic idiom in the background of this saying does not connote hostility, but choice. When faced with two options, to choose one is necessarily to reject, that is, "hate" the other.

The Jesus of the Gospels confronts his hearers with only two choices. There is no middle ground, no way not to decide. In this paradigm, God cannot play second fiddle to money and property, not even to home and family, and still be God. Thus, in 6:6–11 one must either do good or do harm, save life or destroy it—there is no holy both/and or neither/nor. In 6:46–49 there are only two kinds of builders. In 9:50 and 11:23 there are only those for and those against Jesus, gatherers and scatterers, According to Jesus' statement in 12:51–53, he has come not to bring peace but to divide families, and in 16:13 one serves either God or money. This corresponds to the scene in Jesus' parable where the self-righteous Pharisee and the excluded tax collector both pray, but, contrary to all proper religion and theology, the tax collector is justified before God and the Pharisee is not

(18:14).[24] The eschatological scenario of 17:34–35 confirms this radical either/or dualism: on the last day, one is taken and the other is left.

Luke repeatedly claims that this radical call to discipleship as the renunciation of money and property is the necessary choice if one is to follow Jesus on the way to the cross, memorably expressed in the story of the rich ruler (18:18–30). To become Jesus' disciple, the man must sell all he has and give it to the poor; this should not be relativized by making him into a special case that does not apply to others. In 14:33 this demand had already been made of all disciples.

Luke's theology of history, in which the time of Jesus was a special time in which the reality of the kingdom of God was on earth, frees him from having to portray discipleship during the life of Jesus in terms of the realities of his own times (see above, §23.1). This is analogous to the way the historical Jesus' own eschatological perspective functioned in facilitating the proclamation of his call to radical obedience (see above, §8.3). In the Gospel, in the narrative between Jesus' baptism and the Last Supper, Luke is free to picture the authentic life to which believers are called without relativizing it in advance by the realities of later church life. He can point back to a time when there was an actual person, a truly human being, in whom God's rulership was actualized: "It happened. If you want to know what the kingdom of God is like, read the story of Jesus in this Gospel."

He writes for readers who did not live in that time, yet who can see what the kingdom of God is, and what it means to put God's kingdom first in the way one lives one's life. But that was then, and this is now; how should later believers live? Luke does not believe that Jesus' teaching during the special one year of the presence of the kingdom of God on earth can be directly applied to his own time. But neither are Jesus' teaching, example, and call to radical discipleship only a matter of history, receding ever farther into the past. Luke and his contemporaries (and modern believers) are members of the Spirit-led community who can and must decide from case to case how this call of Jesus is to be lived out in their own time. For Luke, Jesus' teaching cannot mean for his own time that all disciples must necessarily sell all they have, give it to the poor in order to be Jesus' disciples. Yet this cannot be heard with a sigh of relief. In Acts, Luke provides instructive examples of this continuing process of reinterpretation of the radical ethic of Jesus (see above, on Luke 9:23).

15:1–32

The famous story of the Prodigal Son is the final parable of a trilogy that continues the radical either/or dualism of Jesus' call to discipleship. There are only the lost and the found, no limbo group of spectators. Those who suppose they are already insiders and object to God's radical grace that accepts the outsider turn out to be outsiders themselves—but with the continuing invitation to become insiders.

17:20–37

Luke adopts and adapts the Q eschatological discourse to make three points important to his own theology of the coming of the kingdom.

1. The kingdom is present in the ministry of Jesus. The rare phrase ἐντὸς ὑμῶν (*entos humōn*), only here in the New Testament, not in the LXX at all, was translated "within you" in the KJV and Douay versions, followed among contemporary versions only by the NIV. The phrase was then misunderstood to refer to the kingdom of God as an internal reality, "in your heart," in contrast to the external political/military/social reality supposedly anticipated by the Pharisees. So understood, the text became a central proof text in the old liberalism that

24. This story illustrates the difficulty for modern readers familiar with the Bible and Christian tradition to experience the story's original impact. The modern reader knows in advance that the humble, self-effacing tax collector is the good guy, and the smug self-righteous Pharisee is already condemned in the modern mind before he opens his mouth. Since modern readers already expect the tax collector to be acceptable and the Pharisee to be rejected, the story would have its original effect for us if its polarities were reversed.

contrasted the supposed external legalism of the Pharisees with the interior religion of the heart advocated by Jesus.

This translation is almost certainly a mistake; most modern translations correctly render the phrase as "among you" or "in your midst" (e.g., NRSV, TNIV, NIV2011, REB, CEB). Luke's point is not that the kingdom is a matter of the heart rather than externals—the kingdom is never in anyone's heart in the New Testament—but that, in the words and deeds of Jesus the kingdom of God expected for the future is in fact already a present reality among them. This corresponds to Luke's theology, in which the time of Jesus is the time of the presence of the kingdom on earth. But when Jesus departs, the kingdom is no longer present in this way, and continues to be a hope for the future, identified with the Parousia of Jesus as the Son of Man.

2. There are no historical signs that signal the nearness of the kingdom of God, no portents of where contemporary history is to be located on the divine timetable. "When is the kingdom of God coming?" is not a question that can be answered by providing historical signs that show that the kingdom is near. In particular, Luke wants to emphasize that the dramatic historical events experienced by his own generation are not signs of the end. The destruction of Jerusalem, Nero's persecution, the explosion of Vesuvius (and the Diaspora revolts of 115–17, if Luke is that late) are all a part of ongoing history, not eschatological signs of the approaching end.

3. When the end does come—and come it will, in Luke's theology—it will happen suddenly, without warning, as sudden as a flash of lightning across the sky. In the days of Noah just before the flood (Gen 6), and in the time just before the destruction of Sodom and Gomorrah (Gen 18), there was no warning, but when the catastrophe came it was visible to all. This is Luke's theology of the kingdom: once truly present in Jesus, the kingdom will reappear in power at the close of the age. There will be no warning, but when it comes, there will be no question that the end is here. Luke and his readers live between these times, both looking back to the reality of the kingdom in the life of Jesus and looking forward to his reappearance at the end of history: Jesus, the once and future king.

19:37–44

In this scene the long *travel narrative* reaches its goal, which has throughout been oriented to Jerusalem. Jesus will confront the center of Jewish national and religious life with his message of peace. Luke writes many decades later, knowing that in 66–70 CE the city did not follow the way of peace, but that the revolt incited by the militaristic rebels brought the catastrophic destruction of city and temple. Thus in Luke it is his disciples—not the residents of Jerusalem—who celebrate his entrance into the city as the king who comes in the name of the Lord. Jesus weeps because the city was blind to the reality of God's kingdom and did not recognize the time of God's visitation and the things that make for peace (13:34–35; 19:42).

The Ministry, Martyrdom, and Vindication of the Messiah in Jerusalem (19:45–24:53)

While still following the basic outline of Mark and incorporating much of his material, Luke rewrites and amplifies Mark to express his own theology. The following distinctive elements characterize the Lukan passion story:

Jesus conducts a prolonged teaching ministry in Jerusalem. The Markan Holy Week, Sunday–Sunday, which included only one day of teaching in the temple, becomes in Luke an indefinite period of teaching that extends over many days, a third period in the ministry of Jesus corresponding to the two earlier ones and of equal importance (19:47; 20:1, 37; 22:39, 53–54). Although Jesus is pictured as teaching daily, Luke provides no additional content to the material he has derived from Mark.

The miraculous element in the portrayal of Jesus is reduced to a bare minimum. The time in Jerusalem is primarily a time of teaching; no exorcisms or nature miracles are reported; the only healing is at the time of his arrest (22:51). Luke thus basically adopts the Markan model of the powerful divine Jesus in the early part of the story replaced by the weak human Jesus of the passion story, but this paradigm is no longer his overruling christological consideration. Jesus still exercises his divine power, and in general acts with sovereign authority throughout (e.g., 22:39–53).

The responsibility for Jesus' death is shifted, so that the Jerusalem priests, scribes, and elders are primarily to blame (Luke 20:1–2; 22:52, 66; 23:4, 10; 24:20). The Pharisees, often Jesus' opponents in Galilee and during the travel narrative, disappear from the Jerusalem passion story. They occur twenty-seven times in the earlier narrative and reappear in Acts 5:34, but their last appearance in the Gospel is at 19:39. Luke does this intentionally, changing the Pharisees of Mark 12:13 to the people in general. Pilate and Rome are practically exonerated. In passages added to the Markan source, Pilate three times pronounces Jesus innocent, as does the Roman centurion in charge of the crucifixion (23:4, 14–15, 22, 47). One could even read 23:25 to mean that Pilate turned Jesus over to the Jews, as though Jesus had actually been crucified by Jews, though Luke later indicates that Jesus died at the hands of the Romans (23:47, 52). During the trial, it becomes clear that the crowds, representing the Jewish people as a whole, who had previously been supportive of Jesus, now switch sides and also share the guilt for Jesus' death (23:13). In Acts, Christian preachers not only will place the blame for Jesus' death on the Jewish leaders but will hold the people as a whole responsible (Acts 2:22–23, 36; 3:11–13, 17).

The death of Jesus produces a division among the Jewish people. Although the people as a whole were responsible for Jesus' death, even as it takes place there is a twofold response to the actual event. Some continue to reject and mock, while others lament and repent (Luke 23:26–30, 35, 39–43, 48). Powerfully represented in the scene of the two Jewish criminals crucified with Jesus (23:39–43), this prefigures the divided response to the apostolic preaching in Acts. Thus Jesus' death, though not presented in sacrificial imagery as having atoning power or functioning to reconcile humanity to God, is nonetheless the crucial event that affects how people respond to God.

The Last Supper becomes the time of final instruction and reorientation of the apostles. Luke expands the Markan account of the Last Supper so it becomes an extensive period of instruction, moving in the direction of the Johannine Farewell Discourse (see below, John 13–17). The devil, absent from the ministry of Jesus, returns to plague the disciples (22:3, 31). The special time of Jesus' ministry is now over, and they must live within the compromising conditions of ongoing history (22:35–38). Luke moves the disciples' dispute about who will be greatest in the coming kingdom to this setting. With heavy irony, he presents Jesus as indeed having royal power (22:29; cf.19:11–27, 37–40), but it is expressed in service and dishonor, not in being served and receiving honor (22:24–27). The disciples will indeed share in the royal power of this kingdom and will "sit on thrones, judging the twelve tribes of Israel," but this means they will share Jesus' rule expressed in suffering and shame (22:29–30). The disciples will share Jesus' kingship but have not yet learned how Jesus' rule in the kingdom of God works. The disciples are not pictured as abandoning Jesus, as in Mark (Mark 14:50–52 omitted; Luke 22:28 added; cf. 23:49), but still lack understanding and will do so until the Holy Spirit comes upon them in Acts 2. Though his denial of Jesus is predicted, Peter is addressed as the one who then will turn back and strengthen the other disciples as their leader.

Luke presents no explicit interpretation of the death of Jesus as salvific. Luke has virtually no clear statement of the atoning death of Jesus, no imagery of Jesus' death as a sacrifice that brings forgiveness, nothing comparable to the "Christ died for our sins" of the Pauline tradition (1 Cor 15:3). In the Gospel, the textually uncertain 22:19b–20 is the only such indication; in Acts, 20:28 is the only text that can be so interpreted. Luke never portrays the early Christian preachers in Acts as proclaiming the redemptive death of Jesus, and omits or alters the references to the atoning death of Jesus in his sources (Mark 10:45 becomes Luke 22:25–27). Thus some critics are insistent that Luke's theology has no place for the salvific death of Jesus.

However, Luke does repeatedly affirm that the death of Jesus is integrated into the overarching plan of God from the very beginning. Luke's repeated δεῖ (*dei*, it is necessary) in this connection represents his insistence on the death of Jesus as fulfillment of Scripture, and means that it was not meaningless, did not catch God by surprise or cause a change in the divine plans. Luke fits the death of Jesus into the pattern of the rejection of the prophets and the death of the martyrs. This was John's destiny, it was Jesus', it is the way his prophetic followers are treated. Fundamental to it all is that Luke, like the early Christian community in general, begins with the death of Jesus as a given historical reality he interprets in retrospect, though the narrative is told in prospect. Thus, for Luke too, Jesus' death was not merely a human tragedy corrected by God at the resurrection. For Luke, "Jesus gave his life for us" means he gave it by living in a way that brought him to his death. This is analogous to Luke's reinterpretation of Mark 8:34 in Luke 9:23; as "dying for Jesus" becomes "living for Jesus," so "Christ died for us" becomes "Christ lived for us"—the whole life of Jesus, the whole Christ event was for us.

24:1–53

In his Markan source, the three women come to the tomb on Easter morning, find the tomb empty, are charged by the young man (angel) to "go and tell," but remain silent; the Gospel ends without closure in midsentence. In Luke, the larger group of women who have been Jesus' witnesses since Galilee also become witnesses of the crucifixion and the empty tomb. Luke expands the Markan story by adding four scenes in 24:12–52—Luke's own resurrection narrative:

1. The women do go to tell the disciples, but the disciples do not believe them.
2. The risen Jesus encounters two disciples, not members of the Twelve, on the road to Emmaus, but they do not recognize him until the "breaking of bread" at the evening meal.
3. They return to Jerusalem to tell the eleven, and learn that Jesus has already appeared to Peter, in an offstage event not plotted in the narrative. Jesus appears to them all and commissions them to preach the gospel to all nations.
4. Jesus leads them out to Bethany, blesses them, and ascends to heaven.

These are the distinctive elements in Luke's resurrection account:

— The locale is confined to Jerusalem or its environs (road to Emmaus, Bethany). The apostles are commanded to remain in Jerusalem (Acts 1:4), and they do remain there. There are no Galilean appearances, and no room for them.

— The corporeality of the resurrection is emphasized. The risen Jesus is not a ghost but has flesh and bones. He invites the disciples to touch him and eats a piece of fish to convince them of the reality of the resurrection.

— The exaltation of Jesus from human existence to lordship at the right hand of God is pictured as a two-stage event. Resurrection and ascension are discrete events. In Luke 24, both events occur on the first Easter Sunday; in Acts 1, there is a forty-day interval. The traditional church year has followed the expanded calendar of Acts, separating Easter and ascension. That Luke has it both ways shows he is not attempting to establish an objectively real chronology. On the one hand, he wants to complete the story of Jesus in the Gospel as volume 1 of his two-volume work, which will fit into one papyrus roll, so that it can be read as a somewhat complete work in itself. On the other hand, he wants to rehearse part of the story at the beginning of volume 2, linking the church's story to the continuing story of Jesus. The time of the church is distinct from the time of Jesus, but there is overlap, vital connection, with both continuity and discontinuity.

— Luke's theology of the resurrection comes through the narrative, as he illustrates that empty tomb, visions of angels, even touching the risen Christ is not adequate to establish authentic faith. The resurrection of Jesus is disclosed as more than an isolated event. Along with Jesus' life and death, the resurrection is integral to God's plan for universal history, which is revealed in christologically interpreted Scripture and made real in the common life of the church as it breaks bread and engages in mission together.

Transition (Acts 1:1–26)

1:1–5

The preface presents the narrative to follow as the continuation of the Gospel of Luke. The first sentence of Acts binds the work of the Holy Spirit to the work of Jesus (1:1); God is the one at work in both Jesus and the Spirit.

1:6–11

Eschatology is revised. The ascension is narrated for the second time (see on Luke 24), in Acts depicted as occurring forty days after the resurrection. During this period of instruction regarding the kingdom of God, the apostles are given the insight now communicated to the readers of Acts. Nonetheless, even after the intensive seminar of almost six weeks, the disciples are still unclear about the *time* of the eschaton. However, their perception of the *nature* of the eschatological fulfillment is valid. "Restoring the kingdom to Israel" is for Luke a valid image of the final consummation, when the promises made to David will be fulfilled and the twelve-tribe wholeness of the people of God will be restored (see Luke 1:32; 22:29–30; Acts 13:34; 15:16). The "time of universal restoration that God announced long ago through his holy prophets" is a valid expression of the Christian hope (Acts 3:21). But the final consummation will not be soon. Jesus' followers are not to be continually peering upward into the heavens awaiting his return. The gaze of Jesus' followers is shifted 90°, reeoriented outward to "the ends of the earth," where they have a job to do.

1:12–26

The group of the Twelve Apostles is restored to its full complement after the defection and death of Judas. Jesus himself called the original Twelve. The vacancy was not filled by the risen Jesus during the forty days, but entrusted to the apostles, who now function under divine guidance. Later, when James is killed, he will not be replaced (12:2). Luke thus does not consider the Twelve a continuing institution, but does consider it essential that the church begin on the foundation of the Twelve, reflecting the views of other Christian teachers around the turn of the second century (see Eph 2:20; Rev 21:14). The new appointee, Matthias, is never heard from again in Acts; of the original Twelve, only Peter continues to play a role. For Luke, it is the symbolic number of the Twelve Apostles, not the feats of individual apostles, that is important in order to validate the authenticity of the new beginning, not the feats of individual apostles.

Part 3: The Time of the Church (=The Continuation of God's Act in Jesus) (Acts 2:1–28:31)

For a discussion of the actual history of the period covered by Acts (ca. 30–62 CE), see §9.2

above. Here, we shall consider the literary and theological aspects of Luke's narrative addressed to his readers in the early second century, the story world of the text and its meaning, rather than the history behind the text.

Petrine Christianity: The Jewish Mission from Jerusalem to Antioch (Acts 2:1–12:25)

Christian Beginnings in Jerusalem (Acts 2:1–8:1)

2:1–47

Here is the story of Pentecost and the beginning of the church. Luke's main point: the church begins as the act of God. The disciples are not pictured as followers of Jesus who resolutely decide to start putting the teachings of Jesus into practice. They are told to wait, and they do wait. Then "the Lord"[25] acts by sending the Spirit, multitudes respond to the preaching of the apostles, and the church is born. Other key features of Luke's presentation:

The universality of the church is proleptically portrayed. Luke knows, of course, that the earliest church was a movement within Judaism. Yet he wants to portray its beginnings in such a way that its universal, inclusive nature is already evident. He does this with two dramatic moves: (1) Although the hearers of the first Christian sermon are all Jews residing in Jerusalem, they already represent "every nation under heaven" (2:5), and the initial promise is made to "all who are far away, everyone whom the Lord our God calls to him" (2:39). (2) Only here in the New Testament is the phenomenon of glossolalia interpreted as the God-given ability to speak powerfully and intelligibly in other languages that the speaker has not learned.[26]

The beginning of the church is pictured as the reversal of Babel (Gen 11:1–9). The divine judgment on human arrogance that resulted in misunderstanding among the nations of the world begins to be healed. The people of God is renewed as a community in which Spirit-given mutual understanding is created, a community in which national and linguistic barriers are overcome. This ideal is present in the imagery of the church's beginnings; the narrative of Acts will show that the church must struggle to realize its true identity as this universal community.

In the Christian proclamation, Jesus the proclaimer becomes the proclaimed. Peter's message, the first Christian sermon, does not repeat the preaching of Jesus. The substance of the church's proclamation is not the "life and teaching of Jesus," which are barely mentioned, and represented as God's act (2:22). The essence of the Christian message is that the Scripture is fulfilled, that God has acted in the Christ event by raising the rejected Jesus from the dead. In Acts, it is the epistolary kerygma, not the Gospel life of Jesus, that forms the core of the church's mission preaching. This does not mean, of course, that Luke rejects the Gospel mode of narrating the life of Jesus as essential Christian teaching. He has made it clear that authentic apostles must be witnesses of the entire ministry of Jesus from baptism onward, not just of the cross and resurrection (Acts 1:21–22; 10:39–41). And he has provided the readers with the extensive and irreplaceable Gospel of Luke! But it is the readers, not Peter's hearers in the Acts narrative in Jerusalem, who have this story.

25. "The Lord" (κύριος, *kurios*) appears ten times in the opening paragraphs of Acts (1:6, 21, 24; 2:20, 21, 25, 34, 36, 39, 47), in such a way that the figure of the Lord Jesus modulates inseparably into that of the Lord God of Israel. To ask which one is intended in each case is to pose the question contrary to Luke's own usage (this point of Lukan usage is documented and elaborated by Christopher Kavin Rowe, *Early Narrative Christology: The Lord in the Gospel of Luke*, BZNW 139 [Berlin: Walter de Gruyter, 2006], passim).

26. See 1 Cor 12–14 and elsewhere in Acts (10:46; 19:6), where glossolalia is not a matter of human languages, but spiritual experiences expressed in unintelligible speech.

Recurring question, different answer In each of the two preceding periods of salvation history, some of those addressed by God's appointed messenger have responded with the same question: "What should we do?" John the Baptist, the final prophet of the time of Israel, responded with an Amos-like summary, the divine command to live one's life in justice and compassion, responding to the needs of others (Luke 3:10–14). During the time of Jesus, the defining center of salvation history, Jesus responded to the "What must I do?" question twice: once with the summary of divine law, love for God and neighbor, illustrated in the story of the Good Samaritan (10:25–37), and once with a summary of the summary, "Follow me" (18:18–22).

Luke's understanding of the periodization of salvation history does not mean for him that in his own time, the time of the church, these previous answers are now "no longer in force," "null and void," as though the divine administration of the world were a succession of different constitutions. John the Baptist's demand expressing the call for justice is still "in force," and the teaching and example of Jesus as God's revelation of what God requires have not been superseded. Luke has taken care that his readers have, and continue to have, both the prophetic revelation in the Jewish Scriptures and the definitive revelation of the way of life in the words and example of Jesus.

Yet Peter in the first Christian sermon does not repeat either the Jewish prophets or the teaching of Jesus in response to the "What must I do?" question. Now that the definitive saving event has happened in the life, death, and resurrection of Jesus, all people everywhere are called to respond to this revelation by believing in Jesus as Lord and Christ (2:36), by reorienting their thinking and living in the light of this decisive act of God ("repentance"), by being baptized into the renewed people of God, where God's forgiveness and the power of God's Spirit are operative (2:37–38; see 8:4–8, 34–40; 9:1–19; 16:25–34; 22:6–16).

The life of the new community A large church came into being, almost instantly—three thousand the first day (2:41), by 4:4 five thousand, by 21:20 tens of thousands. The historical accuracy of such enormous figures is not at issue here (see above, §23.3.4). Luke tells the story of the renewed people of God in terms of the narratives in Exodus and Numbers, in which God called into being a whole nation with huge numbers and miraculously sustained them in their wilderness wanderings. Luke never calls the church the "New Israel," but tells the story of Christian beginnings as the continuing story of Israel, in terms of biblical models.

This community lives by the divine call to justice and compassion and by the teaching and example of Jesus, at the same time realizing the Hellenistic ideal of friendship: true friends have all things in common. Luke's picture shows that the remarkable deeds of sharing by the earliest church demonstrate that they took seriously Jesus' teaching about wealth, which the reader knows from the Gospel. Yet they did not follow them literally. The special one year of the presence of the kingdom of God on earth is over, the King has been exalted to his heavenly throne, and his disciples on earth must decide how to negotiate their life and mission in the continuing realities of the real world. For Luke, the earliest church provides an example that his readers must, in turn, take seriously and adapt to their own times, without necessarily repeating it (though they cannot ignore it either).

3:1–8:1 Conflicts and Problems

Peter continues to preach, and to manifest the healing power that had been present in Jesus (3:1–26), and thousands respond (4:4). Yet the idyllic scene of chapter 2 is now over, and the new church faces both external opposition and internal tensions. As was the case with Jesus, the opposition comes from the Jewish leaders (not the people as a whole), principally the Sadducees. Luke makes the proclamation of the resurrection the initial bone of contention and the grounds for the disciples' arrest (4:2–3). The

Sadducees deny the late, apocalyptic doctrine of the resurrection, which is affirmed by the Pharisees (see above, §§7.5–7). The Christians are pictured as Jews who believe in the resurrection, like the Pharisees, and are defended by the revered Pharisaic teacher Gamaliel (5:33–39).

This, of course, is a much oversimplified and inadequate portrayal of the issues that divided Jews and Christians, and Luke will later acknowledge that Christology, criticism of the temple, rejection of the Torah, and the Christians' numerical success were among the intolerable aspects of the new movement (4:18; 5:17, 40; 6:13). Yet Luke is interested in showing that Jesus' disciples are not a deviant new religion the Romans should be worried about politically, but are an internal movement within Judaism, holding different views than other Jews, siding with the Pharisees—dominant in Luke's own time—on the important issue of the resurrection (23:6, 8; 24:15, 21). The point of view that Luke wishes to inculcate among the Roman leadership is expressed in 25:19.

The apostles, represented by Peter and John, courageously resist their oppressors, and the church continues to flourish. Yet, just as Israel in its formative days was plagued not only by external foes but by internal problems, so also with the new church. Using his biblical models, Luke shows that, to be sure, the early church had in-house difficulties but, like Israel of old, dealt with them constructively under the guidance of its Spirit-endowed leadership. Just as greed and deceit had emerged among the holy people of God in the time of Joshua and had been divinely punished, lest the people as a whole be defiled and defeated (Josh 7), so Ananias and Sapphira attempted to keep for themselves monies they claimed had been given to God's work, and promptly became subject to the divine wrath (5:1–11). This story, of course, is filled with historical and ethical difficulties when taken as literal history (entrapment, divinely sanctioned sting operation, lack of forgiveness or compassion among church folk). For Luke, writing in the confessional language of faith, the point is that the church is the continuing holy people of God where honesty before God and one's fellow believers must prevail for the sake of the church's mission.

Problems emerge between "Hellenists" and "Hebrews" within the church. The issue is how the life of the large and complex Christian community in Jerusalem is to be administered. Again, this is nothing new to the people of God. Just as Moses had dealt with such a situation in the life of biblical Israel, so the apostles make administrative arrangements that continue to get the benevolence work of the church done, and without a severe riff emerging in the united people of God. Here Luke has apparently papered over serious historical difficulties, but again his point is clear: the early church to which he wants his own community to look back as an instructive model met and resolved emerging difficulties under the guidance of their Spirit-led leaders. It is to be noted in all this that Luke does not see either the Scripture in the period of Israel or Jesus during his ministry as having given instructions in advance that need only to be looked up and followed. As the church meets new situations, in the power of the Spirit it is both authorized and competent to make new decisions about its ongoing life. The third period of salvation history, the time of the church, is also—like the time of Israel and the time of Jesus—a time in which God continues to be active.

The first Christian martyr (Stephen, 7:1–60) was not one of the apostles, not a "Hebrew," but a "Hellenist." The reason given for his arrest was that he spoke against Moses, the Law, the holy place, and God—not that he proclaimed the resurrection. Luke places in his mouth the longest speech in Acts, rehearsing the history of Israel as the history of rejecting God's prophets.

Jesus is pictured as a prophet like Moses. Luke is impressed by the biblical promise that the ultimate deliverer will be the eschatological prophet, the prophet like Moses (Deut 18:15–18; Acts 3:22; 7:37). Moses was sent *twice* to Israel. The first time, he was not recognized as the savior sent by God and was rejected by his own people (Exod 2:11–15; Acts 7:23–29). God overlooked this ignorance and sent Moses a second time, endowed with God's own power, and with signs and wonders he brought the people out of bondage (Exod 3–15). Likewise, the Jesus who was not recognized as God's deliverer at his first coming and was rejected—not only by outsiders but by his own people—returns in power. This return of Jesus is in two stages, represented by two sets of images.

In a sense, Jesus "returns" on Pentecost, when the Spirit comes upon his disciples and Jesus is present among his disciples as they continue his work. Thus volume 2, the story of the mission of Jesus' disciples guided and empowered by the "Spirit of Jesus" (Acts 16:7), is the continuation of what Jesus began to do and teach in volume 1 (Acts 1:1). Jesus speaks in the apostles' preaching, and those who receive the apostles' message receive Jesus (Luke 10:16). Thus, to persecute the church is to persecute Jesus (Acts 9:4). During this period, those who did not recognize Jesus during his earthly life are given a second chance, to respond to God's act in Christ now made present in the Holy Spirit (see Luke 12:10; Acts 7:30–51; 17:30–31). This represents Luke's own time, the time of the church between Pentecost and the parousia. During this time, some of those who previously rejected Jesus now accept him. Yet this is not the final word. Jesus will appear at the end of history as Lord of all, to deal with those who have rejected him.

Stephen's death introduces Saul, on the side of the persecutors, and unleashes a persecution in which the Jerusalem church is scattered into Judea and Samaria, thus contributing to the preordained spread of the church (cf. 1:8).

"Except for the apostles" (8:1): this briefly noted exception to the scattering of the church makes a Lukan point, that the growth and development of the early church did not take place haphazardly and without supervision. In Luke's view, the original Twelve, authorized by the risen Lord for the task of supervising the formation of the church, remained in the city of the mother church as a central authority, to which appeals could be made on disputed points as the church expanded geographically and crossed new theological boundaries (see 8:14–25; 9:26–28; 11:1–18; especially 15:1–33).

This portrayal also raises historical questions as to whether the earliest church was as united as Luke represents it. It is the liberal "Hellenists," who relax the law and are critical of the temple, who are persecuted, while the observant "Hebrew" apostles remain in Jerusalem unmolested. Stephen and the Seven, though chosen to handle administrative tasks while the apostles preach and pray, are never pictured doing the job for which they were chosen, but appear as preachers and evangelists. Beneath the surface of Luke's narrative, the reader can detect two streams of Christianity, Hellenist and Hebrew, that emerged early in the church's history, only later amalgamated into what became the emerging protocatholic church of Luke's own time.

The Church Expands to Samaria and Beyond (Acts 8:2–40)

Persecution does not cause the church to shift into a survival mode and turn inward, but results in the expansion of the mission with which it had been charged (cf. 1:8). The Samaritans were a kind of Judaism not recognized by mainstream Judean Jews centered in the Jerusalem temple. The Samaritan mission is thus something of a halfway house between Jews and Gentiles. Its leader is Philip, one of the seven chosen to administer the welfare program of the Jerusalem church, but—like Stephen—functioning as evangelist and missionary. Many Samaritans believe the Christian message and are baptized. The Jerusalem apostles hear of the missionary success and send Peter and John to investigate. They approve, pray for them, and confer the Holy Spirit through the laying on of their hands. The new Samaritan Christians are incorporated into the expanding apostolic church with the approval of the Jerusalem church.

With the conversion of the Ethiopian government official, a eunuch, the expansion of the gospel takes another giant step forward—again through the ministry of the Hellenist Christian evangelist, Philip. In paganism eunuchs were valued as palace officials, but they were forbidden to participate directly in Israelite worship and could not become proselytes (Deut 23:1; Josephus, *Ant.* 4.290–91). The Ethiopian had been to Jerusalem to worship, although he could not enter the temple court restricted to Jews. He was reading the Jewish Scriptures but could not understand their central content.

According to the book of Isaiah, eunuchs would be admitted to the renewed people of God at the eschaton (Isa 56:3–5). The conversion of the Ethiopian eunuch shows that God is already leading the church to include such Gentiles in the church. It happens off to the side of the main stream of the story, on a deserted road, without the knowledge or approval of the Jerusalem church authorities. Luke, who is very concerned that the church expand in an orderly fashion, under apostolic direction and approval, also wants his readers to know that the Holy Spirit does not always work through channels or wait for official approval. This approval will be given—not without struggle and soul-searching—but it is not given in advance. Although the Holy Spirit does not wait for Jerusalem's approval, the mission directed by the Holy Spirit does not proceed without it, as will be dramatically granted in the events of chapters 10–11. But first, the hero of the second half of the story must be introduced.

Conversion of Paul (Acts 9:1–31)

The importance of this event for Luke is apparent in that he recounts it three times: once by the narrator (chap. 9), twice in the speeches of Paul (chaps. 22, 26). The three accounts do not reflect different sources. In each case, the variations are tailored to the author's literary and theological purpose in the context.[27] The zealous, sincere persecutor is transformed by his encounter with the risen Christ. Paul himself is not the hero of the story. He is almost entirely passive. God, the director and driving force behind the expansion of the Christian mission, chooses Paul to be missionary to all people, including Gentiles. The story begins and ends in Jerusalem. As persecution had proceeded from authorized leaders in Jerusalem, so does the mission to the Gentiles. The first Gentile has already been converted, from the exotic land of Ethiopia, representing the "ends of the earth." The one who will be the primary missionary to all people, Jew and Gentile, has now been converted. But in Luke's view, before the universal mission led by Paul is narrated (Acts 13–14), the Jerusalem apostles must be brought back into the story.

Key Scenes: Peter, the Conversion of Cornelius, and Formation of the Antioch Church (Acts 9:32–12:25)

10:1–11:18 Conversion: of Cornelius or Peter? This section is traditionally labeled the conversion of Cornelius, as part of a series of other conversion stories in Acts. More recently, some scholars designate the story the conversion of Peter. There is some truth here, for it is indeed Peter who undergoes a fundamental transformation. Yet the story should not be seen as merely an illustration of the modern ideology of toleration, the story of a prejudiced person who learns to be more open and accepting. From Luke's perspective, the fundamental issue is not racial prejudice or religious dogmatism, but the will of God as set forth in Scripture. How could the renewed people of God that is extending the mission of Jesus include Gentiles, when God had clearly established rules of ritual purity to mark off the holy people of God as part of their mission and witness to the world?

It must be remembered that in Luke–Acts, Jesus has not abolished the food laws (Mark 7 is omitted from the Gospel), and Jesus and the

27. For full discussion, see Gaventa, *Darkness to Light*, 52–95. On the actual history that lies behind Luke's story, see above, §10.1.3.

disciples have lived according to the Torah. Peter, who has traveled about with Jesus and been instructed by the risen Christ, has always observed the Jewish purity laws. When Peter protests to the visionary messenger that nothing unclean had ever entered his mouth (Acts 10:14), he is only doing what the other apostles and Jesus himself had always done. To do otherwise now is not merely to abandon human prejudices, but to begin to live in a way radically different from that commanded in the Bible, honored by the martyrs, and practiced by Jesus and the earliest church. More is at stake here than becoming less prejudiced and more tolerant.

As elsewhere throughout the program of saving history manifest in Acts, God is directing the action from behind the scenes. As God had given the purity laws to mark off the people of God from the idolatrous world, as part of the divine mission to the world, so God now removes the purity laws as a barrier to the continuing divine mission to the world. Luke's point is that it was not an individualistic freelancer who began the mission to the Gentiles on a deserted road (8:26–40), or anonymous Hellenistic missionaries operating independently (11:19–21); rather, this momentous step was taken by the legitimate, apostolic church under the leadership of Peter.

The revelation of God's will does not come as a bolt from the blue. Both Peter and Cornelius receive divine revelations—incomplete promptings that must be pondered, followed up, shared with and evaluated by others, both those who had revelations and those who did not. It is not a picture of Peter the missionary bringing light to those who wait in darkness. Cornelius, the Gentile non-Christian, also has a vision; the Spirit of God is already at work in Caesarea before Peter arrives with the Christian message. Cornelius has God-given clarity about why missionaries should come before things become clear to Peter. In the *missio Dei*—the mission of God—all concerned are both subjects and objects of mission. The missionized have something to share with the missionaries (see on Acts 27 below). Luke believes God is directing the mission, but not without human discernment, struggle, response, and ambiguity.

Antiochene Christianity, Peter's exit (Acts 11:27–12:25) In the process of telling the preceding story, Luke has once again integrated diverse theologies and practices under the umbrella of emerging mainstream Christianity. As the baptism of the Samaritans means that they must then receive the Holy Spirit and be incorporated into the one church under the leadership of Jerusalem, so the reception of the Holy Spirit by the Gentile Cornelius and his household and friends in Caesarea means that they must be baptized. The meaning of the events of Samaria and Caesarea is thus made fully explicit in Luke's portrayal of the church in Antioch, the first integrated church of Jews and Gentiles, now for the first time called *Christians*.

The Jerusalem church sends Barnabas to investigate the new developments in Antioch. He approves, conveys Jerusalem's approval, fetches Paul from Tarsus, reintroduces him into the story, and they work together in the new church. When the Antioch church sends financial help to the Jerusalem church, the narrative camera moves back to Jerusalem. The apostle James is killed, but not replaced; the role of the founding apostles is completed. So also Peter's leadership role now comes to a close. After his miraculous release from prison, he reports to the assembled disciples, points to James the brother of Jesus as the church's leader, and quietly exits. He will appear only once more in Acts, at the Jerusalem Council. The future of the church belongs to the Gentile mission; Paul will be the leading character.

Pauline Christianity: The Gentile Mission from Antioch to Rome (Acts 13:1–28:31)

The remainder of Acts is the story of the Gentile mission, traditionally structured as

Paul's three "missionary journeys" and his final journey to Rome as a prisoner. Luke's own perspective is better portrayed as follows: As the first half of Acts had shown the growth of Christianity in numbers and scope under the leadership of Peter until this growth was embodied in the Antioch church, so the second half shows the expansion of Christianity from Antioch to Rome under the leadership of Paul (for summary comments on the history involved, see above, §10.1.9.).

Acts 13–14	Gentile mission begun from *Antioch* (traditional first missionary journey)
Acts 15	Gentile mission confirmed in *Jerusalem* (Jerusalem Council)
Acts 16–28	Gentile mission climaxed in *Rome*, incorporating Paul's passion narrative (traditional second and third missionary journeys, Journey to Rome)

Gentile Mission Promoted from Antioch (Acts 13:1–14:28)

Barnabas, Saul, and John Mark sail to Cyprus, traverse the whole island, preaching in synagogues. They convert the Roman governor, meet and vanquish a Jewish magician; but there are no reports of founding new churches. They sail to the mainland of Asia Minor. John Mark returns to Antioch. Barnabas and Paul (after 13:9 his Jewish name Saul is no longer used) proceed to the interior. Amid many troubles they establish churches in Pisidian Antioch, Iconium, Lystra, and Derbe; then they also return to the home base in Antioch. Luke's first comprehensive picture of the Pauline Gentile mission focuses on the following features:

— *God the initiator.* The opening and closing scenes of this "first mission journey" picture the beginning of the Gentile mission as the work of God, who is active throughout. The mission is under the auspices of the Antioch church, but the scenes of 13:1–4 and 14:27 form a bracket showing it is the Spirit at work within the church that sends the missionaries forth.

— *To the Jews first.* From his own perspective, Luke could look back over two or three generations of early Christian history and see that the Christian mission began in a Jewish context, where relatively few responded, and then was extended to Gentiles, who were more receptive. By Luke's time the church had become predominately Gentile. Neither Paul nor Luke wanted their respective readers to forget the priority of the Jewish people in the plan of God (Rom 1:16, chaps. 9–11). Luke encapsulates this pattern of the history of the whole church to his time in the particular stories of the founding of churches in Acts. The missionaries consistently begin their mission in the synagogue (see 17:2, Paul's "custom"), at first receive a positive response, then rejection and persecution, then turn to the Gentiles (13:5, 42–48; 14:1–7; see 18:5–6).

— *Samples of mission preaching.* Luke frequently reports Paul as preaching and teaching, but only three times does he give a major sample of his sermons: once to Jews (13:16b–47), once to Gentiles (17:16–31), and once to Christian leaders (20:17–35). Each is carefully composed to be appropriate to the audience envisioned in the narrative world, but really, of course, directed to the readers of Acts.

— *Community, order, and "hierarchy."* In some conversion stories (e.g., the Ethiopian eunuch, 8:26–40; Sergius Paulus, governor of Cyprus, 13:7, 12), one could get the impression that conversion was only an individual matter (see fig. 41).

This would be a mistaken impression of Luke's intention. He regularly shows the missionaries not merely converting individuals, but establishing churches. To become a follower of Jesus is to be added by God to the church (2:41–42, 44; 4:32; 9:1–20; 10:34–48; 11:19–26). Thus Luke concludes the picture of the initial model

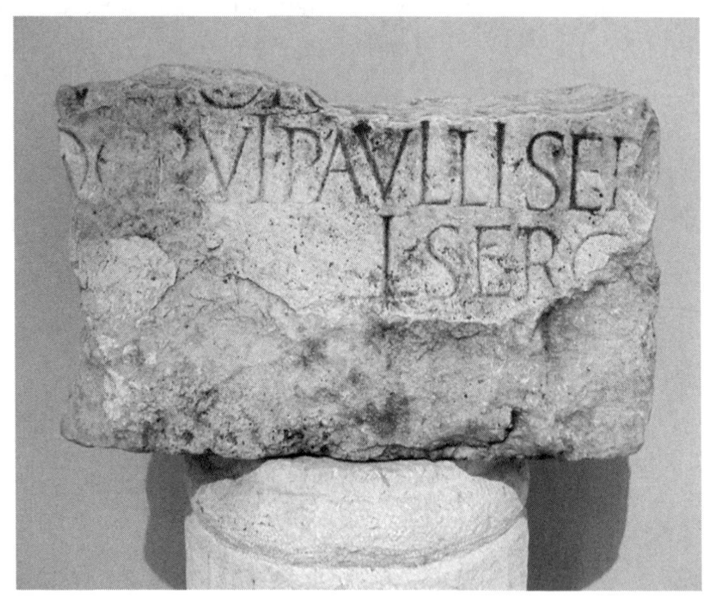

FIGURE 41: An inscription documenting Sergius Paulus as governor of Cyprus. PHOTO CREDIT: M. EUGENE BORING.

Pauline mission enterprise with the missionaries returning through the cities where they had established churches, and appointing presbyters (elders) as leaders in each church (14:21–23). Just as those who "turn to the Lord" are not simply individual believers but are incorporated into churches, so the churches are not, in Luke's understanding, independent congregations but are related to the whole church. There is as yet no firm hierarchy, but the connectional lines are clear: the Antioch church was approved and authorized by the mother church in Jerusalem (11:19–26). In turn, the mission of Barnabas and Saul was not conducted on their own authority but was commissioned by the church in Antioch. The new mission churches have leaders appointed by representatives of the Antioch church. The chain of command is loose, not as tight as in the Pastorals written about the same time (see above, §16.1.5), but the line from Jerusalem through Antioch and Paul to the mission churches governed by presbyters he has appointed is clear, and will be illustrated in the next scenes. This is Luke's view of ideal church structure.

Gentile Mission Confirmed in Jerusalem (Acts 15:1–35)

The success of the Pauline Gentile mission in Asia Minor generated problems. Some individuals from the Jerusalem church come to Antioch, objecting that the new missionary enterprise is rejecting God's law, which must be observed by all who will be members of the people of God, the community of the saved (15:1; cf. 15:5). Luke is at pains to show that these individuals were not authorized by the mother church in Jerusalem (15:24), yet the problem was a real one. Will the church split into a Jewish church and a Gentile church? How can Jewish Christians and Gentile Christians live together in one Christian community? The Antioch church does not see itself as having the authority to proceed on its own, and authorized delegates are sent to Jerusalem to discuss the issue. Apostles and elders ponder the matter (15:6). Peter, in his last appearance in Acts, declares that God had already decided the issue by choosing him, Peter, as the agent through whom Gentiles were brought into the church, that circumcision and keeping the Torah was not necessary for Gentile Christians, that "we believe that we will be saved through the grace of the Lord Jesus, just as they will." The Pauline message of salvation by grace is here placed in Peter's mouth; "Paul himself could not have said it better."[28] With these words, Peter disappears from the Acts narrative, having pointedly illustrated Luke's view that there is no fundamental conflict between the Petrine and Pauline versions of the Christian faith. Peter, however, does not play the decisive role in Jerusalem. James (Jesus' brother, not the apostle, who was killed at 12:2) is presiding. He announces his decision—a compromise, but one that clearly comes down on the side of the Pauline Gentile mission. Gentile Christians need not be circumcised and keep the law in order to be saved or to be part of the church. They should, however, observe the kind of minimal rules required of Gentiles sojourning among Israelites (see Lev 17:10–14; 18:6–18, 26). All agree this is a splendid solution, and it is conveyed to the church at Antioch as the decision of "the apostles and elders, with the consent of the whole church" in Jerusalem (15:22). The Gentile mission, as conducted by Paul, has the approval of the apostles in Jerusalem, with relatively minor regulations that will facilitate fellowship among Jewish and Gentile Christians.[29]

The leaders of the church in Acts make pragmatic decisions for new situations guided by the Spirit (Acts 6, 15): "it has seemed good to the Holy Spirit and to us" (15:28).

Gentile Mission Climaxed in Rome, Incorporating "Paul's Passion Narrative" (Acts 15:36–28:31)

15:36–16:5 The mission continues. With Jerusalem's stamp of approval, the mission continues. The Jerusalem agreement had made a unified mission possible. Paul, now the leader, proposes that he and Barnabas visit the churches they established on their first mission trip. A sharp disagreement over whether to take John Mark with them results in Paul and Barnabas going their separate ways. We know from Paul's letters that the actual issue was theological and deeper (see on Gal 2:11–14), and resulted in a breach that affected not only his partnership with Barnabas, but his relationship with the Antioch church. Luke is intent on showing that the earliest church was united theologically and worked out all such differences amicably, and that divisive theological disputes did not emerge until after the apostolic age (see on 20:29–30). Barnabas takes John Mark with him to Cyprus and disappears from the story line. Paul takes Silas from Jerusalem as his new coworker, maintaining his continuity with Jerusalem and exhibiting the support of the Jerusalem church for the Pauline mission. They visit the new churches, delivering the decisions made in Jerusalem. Luke indicates that this strengthens the churches, enabling Jewish and Gentile Christians to work together in the same congregations.

16:6–17:15 The Spirit guides the mission to Europe. Paul's efforts to extend the mission into new territory are thwarted by the Holy Spirit. At Troas on the western coast of Asia Minor, they respond to a vision to evangelize in Macedonia, and the mission moves from Asia to Europe. Despite many troubles and persecutions (including beatings, imprisonment, and an earthquake), churches are successfully founded in the Macedonian cities of Philippi, Thessalonica, and Beroea. At Philippi, a Roman colony proud of its Roman connections and status, the reader learns for the first time that Paul and Silas are themselves Roman citizens (16:35–40), not disclosed until after they had been illegally beaten and jailed. Paul is accused before the courts—not just within the synagogues—four times: twice by Jews (17:5–7;

28. So Alfred Loisy, *Les Actes des apôtres* (Paris: Rieder, 1925), ad loc.: "Paul n'aurait pas mieux dit."

29. The reader is reminded that what is pictured here is the Lukan understanding of how things were and ought to be, as represented in his narrative. For a discussion of the history behind the narrative, see above, §9.2.2.

18:12–13) and twice by Gentiles (16:19–21; 19:24–27). Paul is not a problem only for Jews; the Gentile cultural and political world also resists the Christian message. This sets the stage for Paul's speech in Athens, the traditional center of Gentile culture.

17:16–34 Paul in Athens This is a key scene in Acts, in which Luke portrays Paul as setting forth the Christian gospel to the intelligentsia of his age. While Paul himself disdained the attempt to express the scandalous message of the cross in terms of the wisdom of this world (1 Cor 1:18–2:5) and was not known for his rhetorical abilities (2 Cor 10:10), Luke is concerned to show that the Christian message can hold its own in the intellectual center of the world. He presents Paul as a commanding speaker, at home with philosophers, one who can quote the pagan poets to clinch his point (17:28). Taken with the first brief address to Gentiles in 14:15–17, the story of Paul in Athens represents Luke's view of what the church's evangelistic message to the Gentile world outside the synagogue and the Jewish tradition should be, the best of Christian missionary preaching in his own time.

18:1–19:41 The mission in Corinth and Ephesus After leaving Athens, Paul goes to Corinth, where he settles in and engages in evangelistic work for more than a year and a half (18:11), then moves the center of his mission activity to Ephesus, where he works for about three years (19:10; 20:31), not including the time involved in a fleeting trip back to Jerusalem, Antioch, and visiting churches previously founded in Galatia and Phrygia (18:21–23). In this section his story is focused almost entirely on the church's external relations, illustrated by scenes from Corinth and Ephesus.

— *The Pauline mission generates a stable network of congregations aware that they belong to an ecumenical community transcending ethnic and cultural boundaries.* Luke points out that Paul settles down in a particular location for an extended period. Christian missionaries are not fly-by-night transients; the congregations they found are not fleeting interest groups. Nor are they local. The travels and connections of people like Aquila, Priscilla, and Apollos manifest the connections of the new church in Ephesus, for instance, with Pontus, Rome, Corinth, and Alexandria; and Paul's trip during this period to Jerusalem and Antioch, making contact with churches in Galatia and Phrygia on his return trip, shows that the new churches are integrally related to the whole church—and with Rome, already mentioned in 18:2, in view from 19:21 on.

— *The mission churches pose no direct threat to the orderly political, religious, or social life of the community.* In Corinth, when Paul is hauled before Gallio's Roman court (18:12–17), the governor dismisses the case. The missionaries are not guilty of any crime against Roman law; the dispute is only an internal matter involving differing views of Jewish law, which are to be handled internally. This is the view Luke wants to promote among government officials. In Ephesus, the near-riot fomented by silversmiths, who are worried about decreasing sales of religious objects, is calmed down by the local city manager, who urges people to bring their complaints, if they are legitimate, to the appointed courts (19:23–41). This is the attitude Luke wants to promote among local city leaders. In the process, he indicates that Paul has friends among the higher-ups, the Asiarchs (19:31). Rome is on the side of law and order. The Christians are not violating this.

— *The mission churches generate ambiguous relations between Christians and Jews.* Both Corinth and Ephesus illustrate that Paul continues to begin his work in the synagogue, continues to find opposition there, and continues to work with Gentiles when rejected by Jews (18:4–11, 19–21; 19:8–10). He does not make a clean break. In Corinth, even after his dramatic declaration, "From now on I will go to the Gentiles" (18:6), he does not leave town, but only moves his operation next door to the synagogue, continues to include Jews in those to whom he preaches, and makes some converts even among Jewish leaders (18:8). In Ephesus, after leaving the synagogue under duress, "taking the disciples with him," he continues to preach successfully to "both Jews and Greeks" (19:9–10).

— *Irregular disciples are incorporated into the emerging protocatholic church.* Luke has already narrated two scenes in which irregular developments in evangelism and conversion are standardized within what he sees as formative mainline Christianity (see on the Samaritan Christians at 8:14–17; the household and friends of Cornelius at 10:34–11:18). In connection with the Ephesian church, Luke tells of two cases related to John the Baptist. (1) Apollos, a brilliant and effective biblical preacher with roots in Alexandria, becomes a member and coworker in the church in Ephesus. He knows the Bible (i.e., the Scriptures of Israel) and accurately knows "the things concerning Jesus," is already gifted with the Holy Spirit, but is unacquainted with Christian baptism—he knows only John's baptism. Priscilla and Aquila bring him up to speed on Christian doctrine, in Luke's terms moving him theologically from stage 2, the "time of Jesus" represented by the Gospel of Luke, to stage 3, the "time of the church" represented by the book of Acts (see above, §23.1). (2) Then Paul finds twelve disciples of John the Baptist in Ephesus who represent a more severe theological lack. In Luke's scheme of salvation history, they are only at stage 1, still in the "period of Israel," as was John himself. In contrast to Apollos, they are inadequately informed about Jesus and have never heard of the Holy Spirit. They are (re)baptized with Christian baptism, Paul ritually lays his hands on them, and they manifest the full power of the Spirit as had the apostles on Pentecost and the Gentile converts of Cornelius's household. It is not necessary to fetch the apostles from Jerusalem to make this happen; here Paul operates with the authority of the Jerusalem apostles. In all this, the details of theology and practice are not to be pressed, and cannot serve as a model for presumably analogous modern situations. Luke's point is again that, as the church expands and encounters disciples of Jesus whose theology or practice is defective, they can be incorporated into the emerging one holy catholic church.

20:1–21:16 Paul's last journey to Jerusalem At 19:21, Paul had "resolved in the Spirit" to go through Macedonia and Greece en route to Jerusalem, with Rome as his final goal. As Jesus, at a decisive moment in the Gospel, had "steadfastly set his face" toward Jerusalem (Luke 9:51), where he would suffer and die, so Paul, at a decisive moment in Acts, turns toward Jerusalem, and "Paul's passion story" begins. The same key word δεῖ (*dei,* it is necessary) is used as in the passion predictions in the Gospel, indicating that the suffering and death of Paul is part of the same divine plan as the suffering and death of Jesus.

Acts 20:18–35 is the final sample of Paul's speeches delivered during his active mission (see above on 13:16–47; 17:16–31). Paul's address to the Ephesian elders reflects the themes of Jesus' instruction to the twelve apostles and the seventy(-two) missionaries in the Gospel (Luke 9:1–6; 10:1–16). Paul is presented as the ideal church leader. Even though Paul and his hearers had never heard Jesus, Luke's readers have heard Jesus' instruction to the Twelve and the seventy(-two) and recognize that Paul is the kind of leader Jesus intended and an example to others. Paul had supported himself, giving an example to later church leaders (20:33–35).

Luke also makes a conscious effort to reflect Paul's own theology, emphasizing "the message of his [God's] grace" (20:32), "repentance toward God and faith toward our Lord Jesus" (20:21), and for the only time suggesting that Jesus' death had redemptive value (20:28). Paul declares that he has not withheld anything from those who are now to be the church's leaders after he is gone. He has declared the "whole purpose of God" (20:27), which was done both publicly and from house to house, and to both Jews and Greeks; there is no esoteric Pauline doctrine known only to the few, no purely Gentile gospel that abandons God's purpose for the Jewish people. Luke portrays the churches as working through theological problems and maintaining their unity during the apostolic generation. During this theological golden age the churches continued resolutely in the apostles' teaching (2:42). Paul and the church suffered from Jews and polytheists, but divisive theological disputes from within the church itself came only later (20:29–30).

Luke is quiet about theological controversies during Paul's own time, never suggests Paul himself was a controversial figure within the churches and that he was sometimes on the losing side. The Lukan Paul knows that after his death such destructive heresies will come. Like the Pastor (see above, §16.1.5), Luke portrays Paul as preparing faithful leaders for the following generations—Luke's own time. Luke has no doctrine of apostolic succession, but nonetheless regards those presbyters Paul has appointed as having been installed by the Holy Spirit as supervisors (ἐπίσκοποι, *episkopoi*, bishops), charged to protect the flock from the false teaching of the savage wolves to come. The tender farewell scenes and warm hospitality represent Paul as beloved brother and trusted friend, not only as authorized church leader and teacher (20:36–38; see 21:4–16).

Paul's Passion Story (Acts 21:17–28:31)

21:17–26 Reception in Jerusalem

Luke has worked throughout to present the tensions between Jerusalem Christianity and the Pauline Gentile mission in a positive light. Paul and his colleagues receive a warm welcome in Jerusalem (21:17). He is greeted by James and the elders—the apostles have long since disappeared from the story, and Jerusalem Christianity is directed by James. They reaffirm Paul's Gentile mission and the conditions worked out in the "Apostolic Decree"—though Paul seems to be informed of them here for the first time. Paul is to defend himself against the false charges that he teaches Jews and Jewish Christians to abandon the Torah and circumcision by publicly demonstrating his loyalty to the Torah, temple, and tradition. Paul agrees to pay the expenses for the purification rites of some Jewish Christians in Jerusalem.

James and the Jerusalem church drop out of the story at 21:26. During Paul's troubles and trials that follow, they never lift a hand in Paul's defense or attempt to contact or support him. The historical reality was apparently that the Jerusalem church could not in good conscience accept money from one they considered a traitor to both Judaism and the church, and declined to accept the offering.[30] Luke does his best to minimize this reality, and to portray Paul as both loyal Jew supported by Pharisees and Christian leader in full communion with James and Jerusalem Christianity.

21:27–23:11 Paul's Arrest and Initial Defense

A tragic misunderstanding leads to Paul's arrest. While Paul goes out of his way not to offend Jewish sensitivities and to lay to rest the suspicions against him, some Jewish visitors mistakenly think he has profaned the temple by bringing Gentiles into its sacred space reserved for Jews (see on Eph 2:14). In the ensuing riot they attempt to kill Paul. He is rescued by the Roman tribune and his soldiers, who are charged with maintaining law and order, and from 21:33 to the end of Acts, Paul is in Roman custody. There are to be no more miraculous prison releases. Luke knows that Paul was eventually executed in Rome, even though—precisely like Jesus—he was innocent of violation of Roman

30. The reader of Paul's letters knows that delivering the offering was the major reason for his final trip to Jerusalem (see Rom 15:25–29 and §12.2.3 above). The Acts narrative struggles to supply a reason for Paul's trip and provides only vague indications that Paul brings a considerable sum of money with him. In 24:17 Paul incidentally mentions that he brings offerings "to his nation," and the governor Felix supposes he might receive a substantial bribe from Paul (24:26).

law. How to explain this is the burden of the remainder of the book, expressed in both the narrative and Paul's several speeches.

In the course of this dramatic narration, Luke incidentally makes or reemphasizes several points significant to his overall purpose:

— *Christian faith and the hope of Israel.* The Lukan Paul repeatedly asserts that he is on trial for the "hope of Israel" (23:6; 24:15; 26:6–7; 28:20). This is not primarily an attempt to get Roman authorities to regard Christians as included within the boundaries of Judaism, a religion recognized by Roman law—though it is also that. Luke wants his Christian readers to see that the Christian faith is inseparable from Judaism. The coming of the kingdom of God, the resurrection, even the eschatological restoration of the twelve tribes (Acts 26:7, see Luke 22:30), are all constituent elements of the Jewish hope, documented in the Scriptures and experience of Judaism, and indispensable for understanding what the Christian faith is all about. Faith in Jesus as the Messiah is integral to *this* hope for the kingdom of God realized in the Messiah's reign that fulfills his promises to Israel.

— *Paul and the movement in which he is a leader are no threat to the domestic tranquility established by Rome.* The specific charge of profaning the temple is neglected by his accusers, and Paul is portrayed more generally as "an agitator," a "pestilent fellow" who is a "ringleader in the sect of the Nazarenes" who is disturbing the *Pax Romana* "throughout the world." While Luke has been concerned to argue that the Romans need not interfere with problems internal to Judaism, these are charges they cannot ignore. Luke wants the Roman authorities to recognize that these are false charges. He portrays Paul as a gentleman prisoner (24:23), a commanding figure who speaks eloquently in his own defense, is treated with dignity and respect, is the leader in a movement that does not operate "in a corner" (26:26), has no secrets to hide, is not interested in overthrowing the government, is no direct political threat.

— *At another level, the faith Paul represents is a fundamental threat to Rome.* To read Luke–Acts one-sidedly as though Luke is intent only on reassuring Rome that they need not worry about the Christians is an oversimplification. Alongside Luke's argument that the church has no directly political designs, he shows that the message and way of life advocated by the followers of Jesus does indeed challenge the Roman ethos, as it does all human efforts to structure the world according to its own priorities. Early on, he had indicated that the powers that rule this world are ultimately demonic (see on Luke 4:6), that the community of Jesus' followers understands rulership and authority differently from the practice of worldly sovereignty (Luke 22:24–27). The Christian mission has rightly been recognized as a threat to business as usual in the social and political structures of this world, for they turn the world upside down and, over against the lordship of Caesar, proclaim another king, named Jesus (Acts 17:6–7). Though addressed by a missionary in chains who is himself a Roman citizen, Roman governors rightly recognize that they are confronted by an ultimate threat, and they tremble at Christian preaching centered on faith in Christ Jesus, justice, self-control, and the coming judgment (Acts 24:24–25). Christians join in the Jewish confession that there is only one Lord; they confess that God's lordship is manifested in Jesus; this confession is ultimately incompatible with the lordship of Caesar. Rome recognizes that Paul (like Jesus) is innocent of political crime. Rome recognizes the threat and knows that Paul (like Jesus) must be killed.[31]

— *Paul's destiny and the plan of God.* Luke looks back on the death of Paul. For Luke, the death of Paul, like the death of Jesus, is simply a

31. This point is compellingly elaborated in Rowe, *Early Narrative Christology*; Rowe, *World Upside Down*.

given, a reality of past history. He knows that Paul's appeal to Caesar did not turn out to be the means of his escape from death. He does not absolve the human actors of guilt, but portrays the weakness and selfishness of Felix, Festus, and Agrippa as contributing to the death of an innocent man.[32] Again, the pattern of Jesus' death is repeated. Luke does not see this as merely a human tragedy or a meaningless surd. In retrospect he sees it as part of God's plan, as human foibles—personal, political, religious—are taken up into the overarching divine sovereignty. As in the case of Jesus, this is seen through eyes of faith in retrospect, but the story is told in prospect: as Jesus must die in Jerusalem, Paul must die in Rome.

27:1–28:31 To Rome

This action-packed account, in which Paul not only survives storm, shipwreck, and snakebite, but is the leading character in heroically saving all 276 crew, passengers, and prisoners, concludes calmly with Paul in his own hired house in Rome, boldly preaching and teaching the Christian faith to all comers, *without hindrance*. This final word of Luke–Acts (ἀκωλύτως, *akōlutōs*) sums up one of the author's main purposes, to portray the leading missionary of the Christian faith in the capital city of the world, proclaiming the gospel without interference from the Roman authorities—though he is in their custody. Along the way, Luke leaves some significant final impressions:

A wholesome picture of "barbarians." The centurion Julius is pictured as a good and decent man. The Maltese natives are, to be sure, "barbarians"—they do not speak Greek and do not belong to the wider Greco-Roman world—but they manifest great human kindness, caring for the wet and shivering survivors of the shipwreck over an extended period. They also manifest the superficial fickleness of pagan religion, at first judging the snake-bitten Paul to be an escaped murderer finally overtaken by justice, then, since he survived both shipwreck and serpent, "they changed their minds and began to say that he was a god" (28:6). Through all this, Paul calmly goes about his business, including a Eucharist-like meal (27:35), healing the host's father and many others (28:8–10), generating respect and affection from the island's inhabitants.

The "barbarians" were not waiting in darkness for the missionaries to come. When they do come, the missionized have something to share with the missionaries, not merely something to receive from them. Malta and the barbarians are already children of the one God, living in God's world. Not a word is said about Paul preaching to them. There is no condemnation of their pagan ways. No converts are won, no churches established, though Paul is with them three months. In fact, during the several months from the time Paul leaves Caesarea until his arrival in Rome, there is no reference to Jesus, Christ, preaching, repentance, believing the gospel, kingdom of God. Luke has made it clear that the Christian mission extends to all, that God calls all people everywhere to believe the gospel and repent, that "there is no other name under heaven given among mortals by which we must be saved" (Acts 4:12). Yet Luke is not compulsive about this certainty.

Alongside this conviction is another picture. Woven unobtrusively into this quaintly entertaining narrative is an impression of Christian believers living in the midst of the pagan world, giving and receiving the milk of human kindness. These are the kind of Christians to whom the world might eventually decide to listen.

The final scene in Rome. No reference is made to Roman Christians. Roman Jews are invited to Paul's apartment. They accept his invitation and report that they have received no bad reports from Jerusalem about Paul, but they know that people everywhere speak against "this sect," using the term elsewhere applied in Acts only to particular groups within Judaism (Sadducees, 5:17; Pharisees, 15:5; 26:5;

32. See the literary analysis of Tannehill, *Narrative Unity*, 2:297–329.

Nazarenes, 24:5; "the Way," 24:14). Once again and finally, the Lukan Paul declares that "it is for the sake of the hope of Israel that I am bound with this chain" (28:20). Some, apparently only a few, accept Paul's message. Most refuse. Although there are significant exceptions, the Jewish community rejects the Christian faith. In the words of Isaiah 6, Paul pronounces God's judgment on them and declares that henceforth God's salvation is being sent to the Gentiles, who will be more receptive.

This closing scene has been variously interpreted. Some have seen it as Luke's final rejection of Judaism, as the church turns to the Gentile mission. Others see the conclusion as more open-ended, with neither Paul, Luke, nor God giving up on the Jews. The ending of Acts can be read as an open-ended, hopeful conclusion, reminiscent of the end of 2 Chronicles.

Why does Acts end where it does? The abrupt/open ending of Acts has been explained three ways:

1. The author is a companion of Paul who completed the composition of his narrative during Paul's Roman imprisonment and before his trial. The author has brought the story up to date and there is nothing more to write. The author's work is complete as he planned it.[33]

2. The author knew that Paul was tried, acquitted, and released, and planned a third volume in which the further history of the church's mission would be recounted. The author was not able to carry through on this plan, so his work remains incomplete.[34]

3. The two preceding views find little support among contemporary scholars. Most are convinced that the author writes some time after Paul's death. After arguing throughout that Rome considers Paul innocent and portraying the Roman justice system as Paul's protector, it would be anticlimactic to have the hero killed in the plotted narrative. Both author and readers know that Paul was condemned and executed. In any case, the narrative itself gives clear signals. The divinely given promise of Acts 27:24 that Paul would stand before the emperor must have been fulfilled. The absence of any reference to Paul's hope of doing mission work in Spain after his visit to Rome (Rom 15:24, 28) indicates it never happened. Paul's statement in Acts 20:25 that he would never see his Ephesian friends again, emphasized by their lamentation in Acts 20:38, is a sure indication that Paul's trip to Rome ended in his martyrdom.

A biography of Martin Luther King Jr. could end powerfully with a confident scene with his friends the day before he leaves for a speech in Memphis. Luke ended where he intended. Luke–Acts is a unity and is complete. Readers understand.

It is from Rome that this double-edged sword of the Word will continue to spread throughout the world. In his own way, Luke has combined Gospel and Epistle, affirming that both Gospel and Apostle, the story of God's act in Jesus continued in the story of the apostles, are valid and necessary expressions of the Christian faith. It was a right instinct that led the church to combine the Gospel of Luke with the other Gospels, and to make Acts the frontispiece for the Epistles. Luke stands at the end of a development in which these two kinds of tradition had been flowing in separate channels; he brings Gospel and Apostle together into a coherent whole, without explicitly including Epistles in the combination. Another group of Christian teachers, dealing with some of the same issues but with different traditions and a different history, will make the combination of Gospel and Epistle explicit.

24.6 For Further Reading

Barrett, C. K. *The Acts of the Apostles*. ICC. 2 vols. Edinburgh: T. & T. Clark, 1998.

33. In later life, this was the view of Adolf von Harnack, *The Date of the Acts and of the Synoptic Gospels*, trans. J. L. Wilkinson, New Testament Studies 4 (London: Williams and Norgate, 1911), 90–116.

34. So Zahn, *Introduction*, 2:58–59.

Bovon, François *Luke 1: A Commentary on the Gospel of Luke 1:1-9:50*. Hermeneia. Minneapolis: Fortress Press, 2002.

Bruce, F. F. *Commentary on the Book of the Acts: The English Text with Introduction, Exposition, and Notes*. Grand Rapids: Eerdmans, 1955.

Carroll, John T. *Luke: A Commentary*. NTL. Louisville: Westminster John Knox, 2012.

Conzelmann, H. *Acts of the Apostles: A Commentary on the Acts of the Apostles*. Translated by James Limburg, Thomas A. Kraabel, and Donald Juel. Hermeneia. Philadelphia: Fortress Press, 1987.

Craddock, Fred B. *Luke*. Interpretation: A Bible Commentary for Teaching and Preaching. Louisville, KY: John Knox Press, 1990.

Fitzmyer, J. A., SJ. *The Gospel according to Luke*. Anchor Bible. 2 vols. Garden City, NY: Doubleday, 1981–1985.

———. *The Acts of the Apostles*. Anchor Bible 31. New York: Doubleday, 1998.

Gaventa, B. R. *The Acts of the Apostles*. ANTC. Nashville: Abingdon Press, 2003.

Haenchen, E. *The Acts of the Apostles: A Commentary*. Philadelphia: Westminster Press, 1971.

Marshall, I. H. *The Acts of the Apostles: An Introduction and Commentary*. TNTC. Grand Rapids: Eerdmans, 1980.

Pervo, R. I. *Acts: A Commentary*. Hermeneia. Minneapolis: Fortress Press, 2009.

Rowe, C. K. *World Upside Down: Reading Acts in the Graeco-Roman Age*. Oxford: Oxford University Press, 2009.

Talbert, C. H. *Reading Acts: A Literary and Theological Commentary on the Acts of the Apostles*. Reading the New Testament. Rev. ed. Macon, GA: Smyth & Helwys, 2005.

Tannehill, R. C. *The Narrative Unity of Luke–Acts: A Literary Interpretation*. 2 vols. Philadelphia: Fortress Press, 1986, 1990.

25
Johannine Community and Johannine School

25.1 Inclusiveness of the Johannine Community and Its Writings: An Advance Summary

FIVE WRITINGS IN OUR NEW TESTAMENT traditionally bear the name "John": the *Gospel of John*, the three *Letters of John*, and the *Revelation to John (Apocalypse)*. The particulars of authorship, date, and setting of each of the writings will be explored below. To anticipate, we may say that this cluster of documents seems to have emerged in the generation that spans the turn from the first to the second century CE, from a network of churches in Asia that we may call the *Johannine community*. The Gospel and letters appear to represent a smaller circle of teachers and tradition bearers within this community, now often known as the *Johannine school*.

As an exploratory template we can project the following scenario: Around the end of the first and beginning of the second century CE, several streams of tradition coalesced in the Roman province of Asia to form a distinctive Christian community alongside the Pauline churches and other Christian groups. The community itself had a changing and volatile history as it interacted with other streams of Christian tradition and with its Jewish and pagan context. It experienced severe internal tensions. At the end of the New Testament period, this community and its literature emerged as an inclusive circle that accepted and was accepted by the emerging main stream that became the early catholic church of the late second century. The Johannine community thus became a microcosm of the whole church, and its literature an anticipation of the bipartite Epistle/Gospel canonical New Testament. The Johannine community had gone through a sectarian phase, but resisted sectarian dynamics, and became broadly ecumenical. Its own capacity for inclusion and integration is a prototype of the later church and its canon and involves the following interrelated elements:

1. *Palestine and the wider Hellenistic world.* Johannine writings represent the whole New Testament: geographical expansion from Palestine to the wider world, theological expansion, sociological and cultural expansion. The traditions incorporated in both Revelation and the Gospel of John made the transition from Judea to Ephesus.

2. *Jewish and Gentile Christianity.* The Johannine community included both Jewish Christians and new converts from the Gentile world with no Jewish heritage, and their respective traditions. This situation posed both an internal hermeneutical challenge and the task of interpreting the faith in non-Jewish categories to outsiders.

3. *"Old Testament" and "New Testament."* Revelation and the Gospel of John are thoroughly steeped in the Jewish Scriptures now adopted by the church. The Johannine Letters reflect only a minimal engagement with Scripture and emphasize the new normative

Christian tradition that emerged with Jesus at "the beginning."

4. *Kenosis and epiphany Christology.* In the first generation, advocates of these two fundamentally different ways of interpreting God's saving act in Jesus were suspicious of each other; kenosis Christology and epiphany Christology tended to be cultivated in differing streams of tradition and different Christian communities. The Johannine community became advocates of both views.

5. *Letter and Gospel.* The Johannine community is the earliest group of churches of which we are aware that expressed its faith in both the epistolary and the Gospel form. The two literary genres do not easily mix, since they represent two fundamentally different ways of conceptualizing the Christ event.

6. *Apocalyptic and realized eschatology.* The first Christian generation had been born in the midst of fervent apocalyptic hope, which formed the framework and presupposition of its confession of Jesus, and which it continued to nourish. When the expected parousia and coming of the kingdom of God failed to appear, second- and third-generation Christian theologians developed several ways of coming to terms with the delay of the parousia. The Johannine community embraced and preserved more than one of these ways.

7. *Male and female.* The Pauline churches of the first generation had affirmed the equality of women and men in Christ, and included women among its leaders and missionaries, but second- and third-generation Paulinism in Asia was more restrictive on women's roles in the church. The Johannine community, continuing to insist that it was led by the Spirit, seems to have been more egalitarian and affirmative of women leaders.

8. *Charisma and office.* Within the broad scope and history of the Johannine churches, we see an interplay and tension between charismatic leadership and the developing ministerial offices. The Johannine community finally included both.

9. *Pauline, Johannine, and Petrine Christianity.* The Johannine community was active at the same time and in the same area as the Pauline school, and aware of other groups as well. While holding on to its devotion to the Beloved Disciple, and accepting elements of Pauline Christianity, it finally was able to embrace and be received by the emerging mainstream, with Peter as the symbolic shepherd of the whole church. The emphasis on "brotherly" love, that is, love within the community of faith thought of as a family, should be seen in the context of the struggle of the Johannine community to maintain the unity of the one church while allowing for considerable variety in both theology and practice.

25.2 The Johannine Corpus

25.2.1 Extent and Relationships

Unlike the writings of the Pauline school, the five writings of the Johannine corpus are not directly linked by claims to authorship. Only Revelation claims to have been written by "John" (Rev 1:1, 4). The first words of 2 and 3 John attribute authorship to "the Elder." The Gospel is anonymous, but a postscript in the epilogue claims the Gospel was written by the Beloved Disciple, who is not otherwise identified (John 21:24). None of the writings claims to have been written by the apostle John, son of Zebedee, though later tradition made this ascription. The Elder John (not the apostle), a leader in the churches of Asia admired by Papias, was later associated with one or more of the writings (Eusebius, *Hist. eccl.* 3.39.4).

The five documents and four possible authors have been related in a variety of ways. The letters 2 and 3 John are linked by common authorship by the Elder and the same historical context. They are then related to 1 John by their shared description of the false teachers they oppose; the only New Testament occurrences of "antichrist" is found in 2 John 7; 1 John 2:18, 22; 4:3. First John is in turn linked to the Fourth Gospel by common vocabulary, style, and theological themes. Thus the Gospel and Letters of John are a closely related collection representing the same author or group of authors.

Revelation is also associated to this group, but not in the same way they are related to each other. Revelation has numerous points of contact with the other Johannine literature, some obvious and others subtle but real. A sampling of common distinctive vocabulary and imagery illustrates both similarities and differences, and has been used as evidence for both the proximity and distance between Revelation and the Johannine school (see below, §26.1.4).

25.2.2 Authorship

The traditional view, represented in the titles of the documents in our Bible, is that all five of the Johannine writings were composed by the apostle John, son of Zebedee, who was identified with the Elder John of the Letters and the Beloved Disciple of the Gospel. The early church came to this unified view only after considerable struggle.

Revelation was a controversial document from the very beginning. We should not suppose that everyone in the seven churches to which it was originally addressed accepted it as authentic Christian teaching, for these churches contained rival prophets and teachers who opposed John and his message (Rev 2:2, 6, 14–15, 20–23). Revelation did not fit easily into the developing epistolary corpus, and became widely suspect after the Montanist controversy that caused the emerging early catholic church to distance itself from all claims to direct charismatic authority and apocalyptic revelation. Thus Gaius, an influential presbyter of the Roman church, wrote (ca. 210) a manifesto declaring that Revelation had been written by the Gnostic heretic Cerinthus. About 250, the bishop of Alexandria, Dionysius, concluded on the basis of linguistic differences that Revelation could not have been written by the same author as the Gospel of John (whom he assumed to be the apostle) and that Revelation was therefore not apostolic. His conclusion provided helpful support for those Alexandrian Christians who wanted to oppose the use of Revelation in the churches, on the basis that its literal interpretation, especially of the "millennium," was a distortion of the spiritual nature of Christianity. Thus as late as the fourth century, when Eusebius classified the Christian literature purported to be Scripture into "accepted," "rejected," and "disputed," Revelation was still classified as "disputed." When Revelation was finally accepted as authoritative Scripture, the author was identified as the apostle John.

The Gospel of John likewise was at first suspect by emerging protocatholic Christianity. Its dualism and use of gnosticizing conceptuality and language made it readily understandable in Gnostic terms, so that it was adopted by Christian Gnostic circles. The first commentary on any New Testament book was the Gnostic teacher Heracleon's commentary on the Gospel of John about 165 CE. Only in the second half of the second century do we find the Fourth Gospel being accepted in the protocatholic mainstream (Justin, *Dialogue* 81.4; Irenaeus, *Against Heresies* 2.22.5; 3.1.2; 3.3.4; 3.11.7; 5.30.1, 3). Here too, once the document was accepted as representing the apostolic faith, the Beloved Disciple was identified with the son of Zebedee, and the Fourth Gospel was granted apostolic authorship.

The Johannine writings were separated early in the canonizing process. The Gospel was joined to the emerging four-Gospel canon. The Johannine Letters finally became part of the corpus of Catholic Epistles, and the Elder was identified with John the apostle. In all this, uppermost was the theological concern of early Christianity to identity and acknowledge authentic witnesses to the apostolic faith, which they did not distinguish from the historical question of actual authorship. The modern interpreter's interest in historical understanding forces the issue of who actually wrote these texts.

Who Wrote Revelation?

Though he considers himself a prophet, the author of Revelation claims no title or office, but identifies himself simply as "John," brother, fellow servant with those in the congregations he addresses, and fellow participant in their troubles (1:1, 9; 10:7; 19:10; 22:9). Who was this John? All that we know of him is what can be inferred from his writing:

— He is not an apostle. He makes no claims to apostleship, gives no indication that he had known the historical Jesus personally, and distinguishes himself from the "twelve apostles," whom he regards as belonging to a past generation, the foundation period (Rev 21:14; cf. Eph 2:20; 3:5).

— He is not the author of the Gospel or 2 or 3 John, as indicated by the linguistic and theological features presented below (§26.1.4).

— He is a prophet, who includes himself as a member of a prophetic group in Asia, presumably as the or a leader (Rev 22:6). His own authority is direct (God → Jesus → angel → John), not derived from ordination or a chain of tradition, as in the scheme developing in other branches of the Christian movement in Asia represented in the Pastorals, 2 and 3 John, and Ignatius. He seems to understand the community as comprising "saints and prophets" (Rev 11:18; 16:6). The author gives no hint that he is a presbyter or that he is a pastor with official authority over the churches he addresses. On this point he is resistant to the tendencies that are developing in the contemporary Pauline school, and that are beginning to be disputed among the Johannine churches. The only πρεσβύτεροι (*presbyteroi*) he knows are in heaven around the throne of God; the Lamb is the shepherd (pastor) of the churches, with no earthly counterparts who exercise his pastoral authority. Yet the author has no polemic against local authorities; he resists other prophets who offer an alternative teaching (Rev 2:20; 16:13; 19:20; 20:10) but does not attack church offices.

— He is something of a "wandering charismatic," who knows and is known by a number of different congregations, but is not an individualistic freelancer. Though he travels, he is not an outsider. He seems to be like the traveling prophets in *Didache*, who assert their charismatic authority in the churches and are accepted by them, alongside the emerging institutional ministry (see Matt 10:41; *Did.* 10–11; §15.3.5 on 2 Thess 3:6–13).

— He is originally a Palestinian, a representative of one stream of pre-70 Palestinian Jewish Christianity. Although John writes in Greek to Greek-speaking churches, his Greek is peculiar and full of grammatical irregularities. The nature of his idiosyncratic Greek suggests that his native language was that of Syria-Palestine; he thinks in Aramaic, but writes in Greek. Since John is also acquainted with Palestinian prophetic traditional material, it is likely that he was originally a Palestinian Christian prophet who had immigrated to Asia, perhaps as a refugee during or just after the war of 66–70.[1]

Who Wrote the Letters?

The author of 2 and 3 John identifies himself as "the Elder," a well-known and authoritative presbyter in the Johannine school, perhaps its founder. The author of 1 John identifies himself only with the ecclesial "we" (see on 1 John 1:1–4). Once the view of apostolic authorship is

1. This thesis has been extensively argued by, e.g., Akira Satake, *Die Offenbarung des Johannes*, KEK 16 (Göttingen: Vandenhoeck & Ruprecht, 2008); Akira Satake, *Die Gemeindeordnung in der Johannesapokalypse*, WMANT 21 (Neukirchen-Vluyn: Neukirchener Verlag, 1966), 32–72 and passim. Satake argues John first became a Christian after moving to the Ephesus area ca. 70 CE, and brought with him elements of his pre-Christian Jewish prophetic experience.

abandoned, the primary issue becomes whether the Gospel and Letters have the same author, or whether two or more authors are involved. The issue is complicated by the composition history of the Gospel, which includes the evangelist, responsible for the body of the work, and the redactor, responsible for its final form. With three Letters, the evangelist, and the redactor, the possible combinations are numerous: one, two, or three authors for the Letters, one of which could be the evangelist or the redactor of the Gospel. The brevity of 2 and 3 John makes linguistic and stylistic comparisons difficult. Most are convinced that 2 and 3 John are by the Elder; opinions are divided on whether the Elder also wrote 1 John. The main question then becomes whether 1 John and the Gospel have the same author. Although general similarities in language and theology once suggested common authorship, critical research of the last hundred years has revealed significant linguistic, theological, and historical differences between 1 John and the Gospel. The majority of critical scholars of the last fifty years are convinced that these differences point to different authors, while the similarities are evidence that 1, 2, and 3 John and the Gospel derive from the same circle of teachers, the Johannine school.[2]

Who Wrote the Gospel?

Like the other Gospels, the Fourth Gospel contains materials that ultimately derive from eyewitnesses. Few contemporary scholars argue for apostolic authorship of the Gospel itself.[3] The main reasons:

1. The Gospel itself is anonymous. On any reading John 21:24 does not represent the claim of the author of the Gospel, but a claim made for him, referring to the Beloved Disciple, who has died (21:23). So also 19:35 refers to the witness at the cross in the third person, and is not a claim by the author that he was present at the crucifixion.

2. The claim that the Fourth Gospel is from the apostle seems to have originated with its Gnostic advocates in the second half of the second century CE. When the emerging protocatholic church accepted the Gospel, the apostolic claim was included. Gnostic claims to authorship were accepted, but it was now argued that the Gospel supported orthodoxy rather than heresy (Irenaeus, *Haer.* 2.22.5; 3.1.1; 3.3.4). Such second-century claims for apostolic authorship are now seen to represent a theological agenda, whether orthodox or heretical, and to be historically problematic (see above, Exc. 3.1, on evaluating patristic evidence for authorship).

3. The ancient church that attributed the Gospel to the apostle affirmed a kind of group authorship, repeatedly indicating that the Gospel was not the product of a single individual. Clement of Alexandria pictures John writing as encouraged by his companions (cited in Eusebius, *Hist. eccl.* 6.14.17). The Muratorian Canon refers to John's fellow disciples and bishops, reporting that John related "all things in his own name, aided by the revision of all." Various prefaces to ancient manuscripts and editions refer to collaborative authorship.[4] All these were apparently attempts to come to terms with the repeated "we" of the Fourth Gospel; today we would speak of the Johannine school.

4. The crucial scenes in the Synoptics at which the son of Zebedee was among the chosen few disciples present are *all* missing from the Gospel of John. These include his call to be a disciple (Mark 1:16–20 and par.), the raising of Jairus's daughter (Mark 5:37–42 and par.), the transfiguration (Mark 9:2–8 and par.), and the

2. Evidence summarized in Raymond E. Brown, *The Epistles of John*, AB (New York: Doubleday, 1982), 19–30.

3. Significant exceptions: John A. T. Robinson, *The Priority of John* (London: SCM Press, 1985); D. A. Carson, *The Gospel according to John* (Grand Rapids: Eerdmans, 1991), 40–81; Craig S. Keener, *The Gospel of John: A Commentary*, 2 vols. (Peabody, MA: Hendrickson, 2003), 1:114–15; Claus Berger, *Im Anfang war Johannes: Datierung und Theologie des vierten Evangeliums* (Stuttgart: Quell, 1997).

4. Documentation in Raymond E. Brown and Francis J. Moloney, *An Introduction to the Gospel of John*, ABRL (New Haven, CT: Yale University Press, 2003), 194–95.

Gethsemane scene (Mark 14:32–42 and par.). Since the Fourth Gospel places special emphasis on eyewitness testimony (19:35; 21:24), the absence of these stories would be very strange if the Gospel were written by John son of Zebedee, or if the apostle John were the author's primary source.

5. The distinctive presentation of Jesus in comparison with the Synoptics indicates the Fourth Gospel is not written by an eyewitness (see below, §27.1).

6. The date, sources, and compositional history of the Gospel by more than one hand are all incompatible with the theory of eyewitness authorship (see below, §§25.3; 27.2–3).

25.2.3 Relative Chronology

Since Revelation is not directly related to the Gospel and Letters in the same ways they are related to each other, the primary question is the relative order of Letters and Gospel. In the most common scenario, the Gospel was amenable to Gnostic interpretation and adopted by developing Gnostic Christianity as an authoritative document to support its docetic Christology. In this view, the Letters represent the later struggle to preserve the Gospel from misunderstanding, relating to the Gospel much as the Pastoral Letters related to Paul. So understood, the Letters are the latest products of the Johannine school.[5]

A strong minority point of view sees the Letters as the earliest witnesses to Johannine theology, with the Gospel as its ultimate climax, in the order 2 John, 3 John, 1 John, Gospel.[6] The problem is complicated by the composition history of the Gospel. It may well be that some form of the Gospel preceded the Letters, but that the canonical form came after them.

Both those who see the epistles as "Johannine Pastorals" and those who see the Gospel's final redactor as warding off misinterpretations of earlier versions of the Gospel could be right. If so, the Letters and the redactor have similar purposes: both are presupposing and giving guidelines for interpreting earlier forms of the Gospel or the traditions it came to include.

The following data support the sequence: Johannine tradition → preliminary version(s) of the Gospel → Letters → canonical Gospel.

- —The epistles do not mention the Beloved Disciple, who first appears in the Gospel.
- —The epistles do not use interpretation of the Scripture as a theological argument, which first appears in the Gospel.
- —Future eschatology and apocalypticism is stronger in the Letters, then recede in the Gospel.
- —Developing institutional structures appear in the Letters and are resisted. This struggle is overcome in the Gospel, in which more formal pastoral leadership is integrated into the larger structure of the emerging protocatholic church.
- —The Gospel's emphasis on unity looks out and back on struggles that were contemporary with the Letters. The Letters are preoccupied with internal dissensions and schism; the Gospel looks back on both internal and external troubles and pleads for unity.

The Letters provide data that suggests their relative date. The false teachers troubling the churches of 2 John 7–11 have not yet precipitated the schism manifest in 1 John 2:18–19; 4:1–3. The letter referred to in 3 John 9 seems

5. This view was argued in a brief essay that has become a classic of New Testament scholarship, Hans Conzelmann, "Was von Anfang war," in *Theologie als Schriftauslegung: Aufsätze zum Neuen Testament*, ed. Hans Conzelmann, *Beiträge zur evangelischen Theologie; theologische Abhandlungen* (Munich: Kaiser, 1974), 207–14. It has been adopted by numerous Johannine scholars, and dominates the massive 1982 commentary of Brown, *Epistles of John*.

6. Recent advocates of this view are represented by Georg Strecker, *The Johannine Letters: A Commentary on 1, 2, and 3 John*, Hermeneia (Minneapolis: Fortress Press, 1996), xxv–xli and passim; Udo Schnelle, *Die Johannesbriefe*, THKNT 17 (Leipzig: Evangelische Verlagsanstalt, 2010), 9–19 and passim; and Udo Schnelle, "Die Reihenfolge der johanneischen Schriften," *NTS* 57 (2011): 91–113, who provide detailed evidence.

to be 2 John. The order of the writings of the Johannine school thus seems to be: 2 John, 3 John, 1 John, Gospel of John.

25.2.4 Absolute Chronology: Dates of the Johannine Writings

Date of Revelation

It would seem that all uncertainty about the date would be resolved by Revelation 17:9–11, which places John and his readers during the reign of the sixth of seven Roman emperors (see Box 9, p. 78, for a list of emperors and their dates). Yet uncertainties about how John intended the emperors to be enumerated, and whether the number seven is intended literally or is a symbol for the whole series of emperors, minimizes the usefulness of the passage for ascertaining the date when Revelation was written. The "seven kings" seem to stand for the whole line of emperors, and John wants his readers to know that they stand near the end of a history that is under God's sovereign control. This mode of communication does not allow the modern scholar to base calculations of the date of Revelation on this text.

The following reasons have convinced most contemporary scholars that Revelation was written in the latter part of the reign of Domitian, about 95 CE.

— The earliest tradition is that John wrote the apocalypse "toward the end of Domitian's reign, almost in our day" (Irenaeus, *Haer.* 5.30.3. So also Eusebius, *Hist. eccl.* 5.8.6–7).

— Revelation uses "Babylon" for Rome (14:8; chaps. 17–18, esp. 17:18). Jewish and Christian literature written after the 66–70 war used "Babylon" as a transparent symbol for Rome, since Rome had besieged and destroyed Jerusalem, just as the Babylonians had done centuries before (2 Kgs. 25; cf. 2 Esd 3:1–2, 28–31; *2 Apoc. Bar* 10.1–3; 11.1, 67.7; *Sib. Or.* 5.143, 159; 1 Pet 5:13). This practice did not become common until after the destruction of the city, and would not have been appropriate before.

— The author is familiar with the letters of Paul and other sources that point to the generation after Paul.

— The social, religious, and political situation presupposed fits the reign of Domitian. The all-pervasive cultural pressure of the Caesar cult in Asia was intensified after 85 CE, when Domitian began insisting that he be addressed as "dominus et deus noster" ("our Lord and God," Suetonius, *Domitian* 10.5; 11.1–3; 13.2; 14.4; see Rev 4:11). He took action against any group suspect of challenging his authority, and expelled the philosophers from Rome. Domitian did not initiate a major persecution of the church, but in individual cases Christians were executed. The situation described by Suetonius fits the setting of Revelation.

— The Nero redivivus myth. Nero was the first emperor to persecute the churches. After his death, a legend of mythical proportions arose that he was in Parthia or in the underworld and would return with a mighty army in great wrath. This legend was especially prominent in Domitian's time; its imagery pervades Revelation, for example, 13:1–18.

— The points of contact with the emerging Johannine community point to a time around the end of the first century.

Date of the Johannine Letters

The earliest extracanonical attestation of any of the Johannine Letters is the clear allusion to 2 John 7 (and 1 John 4:2–3) in Polycarp, *Phil.* 7.1, about 120 CE. Otherwise, there are no clear data in the Letters relevant to establishing their date, and one must depend on the presumed relation to the Gospel—which has its own difficulties in regard to date.

Date of the Gospel

External data for the existence of the Gospel are ambiguous until after the middle of the second century, when Justin cites the Gospel (though not by name). If the letters of Ignatius (ca. 110) had quotations or clear allusions to the text of John, the Gospel could be dated earlier, but alleged citations seem to be only echoes of traditional language they share in common. The fragment of the Gospel found in Egypt, 𝔓[52], is often dated about 125 CE, which would argue that the Gospel was likely composed at least a decade earlier. Confidence in the precision of such an early date has eroded, and it may be as late as 175 CE (see above, §3.1). Justin, about 150, thus remains the earliest attestation of the Gospel, which is then copiously discussed by name in the writings of Irenaeus, about 180.

Internal data that might be relevant for dating the document are likewise burdened with ambiguity. If the Gospel were clearly dependent on Mark, it would be post-70. If conclusive evidence of the use of Matthew and/or Luke could be found, the Gospel would be considerably later. But the issue of the relation of the Fourth Gospels to the Synoptics remains disputed (see below, §27.3). Both the Letters and the Gospel reflect the internal disputes against false (docetic) teachers, but the date of these disputes and resulting schism is difficult to pin down. The Gospel (not the Letters) reflects conflicts with the synagogue, but whether such conflicts are related to decisions made at Jamnia in the 80s is disputed. Likewise, it is not clear whether expulsion from the synagogues is related to Jamnia decisions and, even if so, whether these conflicts form the context in which the Gospel was composed or already lie some distance in the past. The timeless metaphorical language (truth, way, life, etc.) make it difficult to locate the Gospel in a particular historical context. This has allowed responsible scholars to propose a wide range of dates, as the earliest Gospel, written before 70, to about 140, the latest writing in the New Testament.[7] It is likely, however, that John 11:48 presupposes the Jewish war and the destruction of the temple. Heracleon's commentary in the second half of the second century constitutes the *terminus ante quem*, so the range of possibilities stretches from 75 to 140 CE. Within this range, where the Gospel most probably fits depends on how one relates it to the other Johannine writings and developments within the Johannine school.

25.3 The Johannine Community and Its Conflicts: Jerusalem to Ephesus

THE EXISTENCE OF A JOHANNINE SCHOOL tradition is evidenced by the "we" that stands behind both Letters and Gospel, including the appended chapter 21, but is not so used in any other New Testament document (see on 1 John 1:1–4).[8] A large number of distinctive theological concepts and vocabulary represents the idiolect/sociolect distinctive of 1, 2, and 3 John and the Gospel (e.g., keeping Jesus' new/old command to love the brother/sister [2 John 4–6; 1 John 2:3–4; 7–8; 3:11, 22–23; John 13:34–35; 14:15, 21, 23; 15:10, 12]; the dualistic contrast between God and the world [2 John 7; 1 John 2:15–17; 4:3–6; John 14–16]; the unity of Father and Son [2 John 9; 1 John 1:3; 2:22–23; 4:14; John 5:20, 10:30, 38; 14:10]; the coming of Jesus Christ "in the flesh" [2 John 7; 1 John 4:2; John 1:14]; being "born/begotten from God" [1 John 2:29; 3:9; 4:7; John 1:13; 3:3–5]; "knowing" and "seeing" God [1 John 2:3–5, 13–14; 3:1, 6, 9; 4:6–8; 3 John 11; John 1:10, 18; 6:46;

7. Before 70: E. R. Goodenough, "John: A Primitive Gospel," *JBL* 64 (1945): 145–82; Robinson, *Priority of John*, 67; see his detailed argument in John A. T. Robinson, *Redating the New Testament* (Philadelphia: Westminster Press, 1976), 254–311; Berger, *Im Anfang war Johannes*, ca. 140; Walter Schmithals, *Johannesevangelium und Johannesbriefe: Forschungsgeschichte und Analyse*, BZNW 64 (Berlin: de Gruyter, 1992), 422.

8. Raymond E. Brown, *The Community of the Beloved Disciple: The Life, Loves, and Hates of an Individual Church in New Testament Times* (New York: Paulist Press, 1979), is the clearest and most detailed attempt to write a history of the Johannine community, but admittedly speculative ("will be pleased if 60% is verified"). Culpepper's reconstruction is less ambitious, but all the more valuable because of his historical caution (Alan Culpepper, *The Gospel and Letters of John*, Interpreting Biblical Texts [Nashville: Abingdon Press, 1998], 54–61). Both presuppose the Gospel precedes the Letters.

8:19, 55; 14:7, 9, 20; 15:24; 16:3; 17:25]; "abiding" in God, love, the truth, the teaching [μένω *menō*, 1 John 2:19; 3:9, 14; 3:24; 4:12–13, 16; 2 John 2, 9; John 6:56; 8:31; 14:10, 17; 15:4–7, 9–10]). For further examples, see on the distinctive vocabulary of the Fourth Gospel below, §27.1.3. The Johannine School tradition is also evidenced by the use of terminology associated with other schools, who referred to their members as "friends" (φίλοι, *philoi*) and their school as a "fellowship" or "partnership" (κοινωνία, *koinōnia*).[9]

Events in the history of the Johannine community can be inferred from Revelation, the Letters of John, and the Fourth Gospel. These dots can be connected in more than one way, depending, among other things, on how the relative sequence of the texts is understood. The following construction arranges the elements at work in the Johannine school into a plausible chronology.

25.3.1 The ἀρχή (*archē*, beginning, source, norm) in Judea, Samaria, and Galilee

The author(s) of the Fourth Gospel and of the Johannine epistles believed that the distinctive Johannine tradition extended back to "the beginning," that is, to the ministry of Jesus himself. Among the early disciples was one later characterized in the Gospel as "the disciple whom Jesus loved," the Beloved Disciple, regarded as primary witness of the Johannine tradition and founder of the Johannine school. He seems to have been a Judean and may have been a disciple of John the Baptist before becoming a follower of Jesus.

Some similarities to the language and theology of the Qumran writings may reflect contacts with the Essene movement in Palestine during this time. Accurate awareness of Palestinian geography, especially of Jerusalem and Judea, suggests the Johannine tradition has early Judean roots.

Samaritan mission. In the Synoptics and Acts, Jesus carries on no mission to Samaria (Matt 10:5 explicitly forbids going to the Samaritans), but after the resurrection the early Christian community successfully evangelized Samaria, partly as the byproduct of persecution by Jewish leaders in Judea (Acts 8). In Acts, this mission is the work of Hellenistic Christians. The story of the Samaritan acceptance of Jesus' message in John 4 seems to reflect the success of the Samaritan mission.

25.3.2 Centered in Ephesus

The tradition that began in Judea in the 30s had by the end of the first century spread to the Roman province of Asia, with Ephesus the hub from which the Johannine writings emanated. While Revelation is firmly located in Asia, other locations have been proposed for the Gospel and Letters (Trans-Jordan, Alexandria, Antioch, even Rome). The majority of scholars regard Ephesus as the setting of all the Johannine writings, for the following reasons:

1. The patristic tradition is unanimous in associating all the Johannine literature with Ephesus.
2. The earliest attestation of Johannine literature is from Asia: Polycarp of Smyrna, Montanism, the *Acts of John*.
3. Since Revelation was clearly written to Ephesus and other churches in Asia, connections of the Gospel and epistles with Revelation point to Ephesus.
4. Contacts with the Pauline school suggest Ephesus (e.g., nuptial imagery [Christ as bridegroom, church as bride] is only found in the Fourth Gospel, Revelation, and the Pauline tradition).
5. Explanation of Jewish customs, terms, and place names points to a predominantly Gentile church in an area some distance from Palestine (John 1:38, 41; 2:6; 4:9, 25; 11:55; 18:20, 28b; 19:40b).

9. Cf. R. Alan Culpepper, *The Johannine School: An Evaluation of the Johannine-School Hypothesis Based on an Investigation of the Nature of Ancient Schools*, SBLDS 26 (Missoula, MT: Scholars Press, 1975), 250.

All the persons named in the Letters bear Gentile names: Demetrius, Gaius, Diotrephes.

6. Ephesus was a cosmopolitan city that included numerous Jews of various types, including disciples of the Baptist (Acts 18:24–19:7). Samaritans were known far beyond Samaria.
7. "John" is the most frequent biblical name in Ephesian inscriptions, occurring eighteen times.[10]
8. The disputes among Christians over Christology and the Eucharist reflected in both Letters and Gospel are similar to the disputes in Ignatius's letters to churches in Asia at the same time.

25.3.3 Interaction with Other Religious Movements

The Johannine community began in Palestinian Judaism. While retaining its biblical and Jewish roots, in the course of its history it interacted with a number of intellectual currents. There are some indications of dialogue and debate with emerging rabbinic Judaism, but from the beginning the community seems more affected by marginal or sectarian Jewish movements that did not become mainstream Judaism: the followers of John the Baptist, Essenic elements similar to those of the Qumran community, Samaritan influences, the Hellenistic Jewish wisdom tradition as represented by Philo. During its geographical and theological pilgrimage, the community engaged and appropriated some of the conceptuality of various streams of Hellenistic religion and philosophy, the "higher Hellenism" of Stoic-Cynic philosophy and the kind of thought that later emerged in the Hermetic and Gnostic writings. The spectrum of theology that emerged in Ephesus from the Johannine school is different from its beginnings in Judea, but it has remained essentially Jewish in its orientation. The Johannine teachers had learned to formulate bridge concepts that made their theology understandable to the wider intellectual world without surrendering to it.

Along the way, three traumatic events drastically affected the life and thought of the Johannine Christians: (1) separation from the synagogue, (2) harassment and threats from the Roman government, and (3) a schism within their own ranks. Both the separation from the synagogue and the internal schism should probably be thought of as a process that extended over a considerable period, rather than a single dramatic event.

1. Separation from the Synagogue and Formation of a Separate Community

The Johannine community began as Jews within the synagogue who came to believe that Jesus is the Messiah. They had "found the Messiah" and invited others to do the same (John 1:35–39). They continued to be observant Jews; there is no suggestion in the Johannine writings that the followers of Jesus disputed with synagogue leaders about the Torah. As their Christology developed, the Johannine Christians increasingly seemed to the Jewish leaders to be in danger of making Jesus into a second God. Such claims were considered blasphemy; punishment could include the death penalty. Disputes intensified; there may have been trials and executions, or delivering of Christians over to the Romans for punishment.[11] Those followers of Jesus who now found themselves outside the synagogue believed they had been involuntarily expelled. They continued their evangelizing, within and outside the synagogue, and appealed

10. Sjef van Tilborg, *Reading John in Ephesus*, NovTSup 83 (Leiden: Brill, 1996), 2–3.

11. This is the thesis advocated by Martyn, Brown, Davies, Fortna, Kysar, Ashton, and widely accepted (see above, §7.7.6). Some scholars, e.g., Warren Carter (*John: Storyteller, Interpreter, Evangelist* [Peabody, MA: Hendrickson, 2006], 164–65) regard John 9:22; 12:42; 16:2 as "stereotypical polemic" and question whether such statements can be the basis for inferring actual history. But the first-hand accounts of an actual persecutor (1 Cor 15:9; Phil 3:6; Gal 1:13, 23), the judicial murder of James in 63 CE, and the reported attempts of the Jerusalem authorities to kill the Qumran leader, as well as the general religious ethos, give credence to the claims.

to their fellow believers in Jesus who had kept a low profile and remained within Judaism to stand up and be counted.

Exclusion from the synagogue and the formation of a distinct community separate from the Jews deeply influenced the self-understanding of the Johannine Christians. At first, they were still composed mostly of ethnic Jews with perhaps some Gentile God-fearers who had followed them out of the synagogue rather than becoming full Jews—another factor that increased the distance and ill feeling between the two communities. By the time the Gospel was written, most of the community is composed of Gentiles, who must have Jewish terms explained to them (see above list). In the story line that formed the Johannine community's self-understanding, "Jew" thus sometimes came to mean "those who had the opportunity to accept the true revelation of God, but refused."[12] But in Johannine theology, *all* have had this chance, whether Jew or Gentile (1:1–5, 10–11). "The Jews" becomes a symbolic term, like "the world," for those who do not believe in Jesus as the Messiah. The term is not racial or anti-Semitic. In a Samaritan context, Jesus is ethnically and religiously a Jew, and "salvation is of the Jews" (4:22).

The Johannine Christians now regarded themselves, with a somewhat sectarian mentality, as the true children of God, and they regarded others, including their erstwhile fellows in the synagogue, as "the Jews," "the world," even as "children of the devil." Just as the traumas and hostilities of the Reformation remained in both Protestant and Roman Catholic consciousness for generations, were celebrated in festivals, and continued to influence the perspectives and writings of both communities, so also separation from the synagogue was part of the self-understanding of the Johannine community, though it probably occurred some time before the Gospel was written. That the "parting of the ways" seems to be assumed, rather than argued for, would place the Fourth Gospel late in the trajectory of early Christianity.

2. Threats and Harassment from the Roman Government

While the Johannine Christians were still within the synagogue, the Romans regarded them with toleration, as they did the other Jews. Once they became a separate community, the Christians no longer enjoyed the protection of belonging to a legal religion. The fact that Jesus had been officially executed by the Romans, along with the Christians' talk of a new kingdom, made them targets of the pro-Roman patriotic enthusiasm that prevailed especially in Asia. Harassment by local citizens and sporadic arrests and even death sentences increased anxiety and encouraged apocalyptic eschatology among some elements of the Johannine Christians (see §26.1.4 below). When synagogues tended to deny that the Johannine group still belonged to the Jewish community, hostility and resentment increased from the Christian side, and some identified the synagogues as "synagogues of Satan" (Rev 2:9, 3:9). Others within the Johannine community, who regarded themselves as more progressive, developed ways of thinking about Jesus and the Christian faith that adapted to the culture and protected them from harassment—which the more conservative regarded as betrayal of the faith.

3. Disputes and Schism within the Community

Tensions were already evident in 2 John. These intensify in 3 John, written probably only a little later. By the time of 1 John, the

12. Ἰουδαῖος (*Ioudaios*, Jew) is a complex term in the Fourth Gospel. On the whole subject of Jews and possible anti-Judaism in the Fourth Gospel, see R. Bieringer, Didier Pollefeyt, and F. Vandecasteele-Vanneuville, "Wrestling with Johannine Anti-Judaism: A Hermeneutical Framework for the Analysis of the Current Debate," in *Anti-Judaism and the Fourth Gospel: Papers of the Leuven Colloquium, 2000*, ed. R. Bieringer, Didier Pollefeyt, and F. Vandecasteele-Vanneuville (Louisville, KY: Westminster John Knox Press, 2001), 3–44, and other essays in this collection.

Johannine community has already become two distinct and hostile groups. The author looks out and back on an us/them schism: "they" used to be part of "us." The developing christological claims of the community became one-sidedly extreme. Interacting with proto-Gnostic ideas, and with Christian teachers who had already interpreted Jesus in Gnostic-docetic categories, some in the community began to understand the deity of Christ in a way that compromised his true humanity.

Likewise, the community's realized eschatology—according to which they had already been delivered from sin, already had passed from death to life, already had eternal life—resulted in extreme claims that compromised the humanity of believers. Although they still remained in the world, some Johannine Christians began to claim they were no longer involved in human sinfulness. John 8:30–36 reflects a time in the history of the community when believing (Christian) Jews were exhorted to continue with Jesus, and not to claim to be sinless. The scene portrayed in John 8 reflects both the conflict with the Jews that led to the expulsion of the Christians, and internal conflicts among the Christians, in which the dissidents were labeled as not belonging to the truth but being children of the devil. The extremists left or were expelled (1 John 2:19; 4:1) and, in the community's dualistic theology, were considered not only as belonging "the world," but to be antichrists or children of the devil. The epistles, and the final form of the Gospel, reflect both the ordeal of separation from the synagogue and the trauma of dissension within the community's own ranks.

25.3.4 Final Dissolution and Integration of the Johannine Community

In the final edition of the Gospel of John—the only edition we actually have, of course—we see reflections of these previous crises, but also hints of their final resolution. The group(s) represented by the Elder adapted to the developing pastoral structures represented by Peter, and were integrated into the emerging protocatholic church. They brought with them the profound Christology that was to play a decisive role in the formation of the creedal orthodoxy of Nicaea and Chalcedon. Their opponents seem to have been absorbed into the Montanist and Gnostic movements.

25.4 For Further Reading

Brown, R. E. *The Community of the Beloved Disciple: The Life, Loves, and Hates of an Individual Church in New Testament Times*. New York: Paulist Press, 1979.

Culpepper, R. A. *John, the Son of Zebedee: The Life of a Legend*. Minneapolis: Fortress, 1999.

Fortna, R. T. *The Fourth Gospel and Its Predecessor: From Narrative Source to Present Gospel*. Philadelphia: Fortress Press, 1988.

———. *The Gospel of Signs: A Reconstruction of the Narrative Source Underlying the Fourth Gospel*. SNTSMS 11. Cambridge: Cambridge University Press, 1970.

Martyn, J. L. *History and Theology in the Fourth Gospel*. New York: Harper & Row, 1968.

Smith, D. M. *John among the Gospels*. 2nd ed. Columbia: University of South Carolina Press, 2001.

26

Letters from the Johannine Community: Revelation; 1, 2, and 3 John

26.1 Interpreting Revelation

REVELATION IS A PASTORAL LETTER FROM a Christian prophet to specific Christian groups in Asia in the late first century CE who were confronted with a critical religiopolitical situation about which they must make decisions that affected their very lives. The author writes to convey the message of the risen Christ to this situation, to share his vision of the transcendent world and the one sovereign God who is in control of history, encouraging his addressees to remain faithful to their confession of the one true God, despite the cultural religious pressures represented by the resurgence of the emperor cult.

The most important item in interpreting Revelation is *genre*. Three generic factors are important, all introduced in the first five verses of Revelation: letter, prophecy, apocalyptic.

26.1.1 Revelation as Letter

The pervasive apocalyptic imagery of Revelation is included within the framework of a real letter from John to the churches of Asia. We should not think of Revelation as an apocalypse that contains the "letters to the seven churches," but as a letter to the churches that contains massive apocalyptic imagery.

The epistolary features of Revelation are not incidental to its form or optional in its interpretation. Like Paul a generation earlier, the author expected his letter to be read aloud, as a whole, in the worship gatherings of the churches to which it was addressed (Rev 1:3). The letter begins (1:4–5a) and ends (22:21) with epistolary formulae that had become conventional in the wake of Paul. As in the case of Paul, the letter is a substitute for the personal presence of the prophet. In contrast to a book or essay, a letter addresses particular readers in a particular situation. The situation of the churches addressed, as perceived by John, is directly reflected in the prophetic messages of chapters 2–3.

26.1.2 Revelation as Prophecy

The author claims to prophesy (10:7, 11), to write prophecy (1:3; 19:10; 22:6, 10), and to belong to the group of church prophets (11:18; 16:6; 18:24; 22:9) who stand in the line of biblical prophets (10:7) and who, like them, are opposed by false prophets (2:20; see 16:13; 19:20; 20:10). Like the biblical prophets, he does not claim to predict the long-term historical future; rather, he addresses the divine word to his contemporaries and declares the imminent eschatological future.

26.1.3 Revelation as Apocalyptic

Revelation is filled with apocalyptic content and shares many features with other Jewish and Christian apocalypses (see above, §7.6.1): it is

FIGURE 42: Sardis, location of one of the seven churches mentioned in Revelation 2–3. USED BY PERMISSION OF DAVID PADFIELD.

crisis literature, of cosmic scope, has a penultimately dualistic perspective on the universe, communicated in mysterious, esoteric symbols. Apocalyptic is penultimately dualistic and pessimistic, portraying the present world as caught in a struggle between God and Satan, in which angels and demons play a major role. Ultimately, however, apocalyptic is monotheistic and filled with hope, for the one God will finally exercise his sovereign saving power.

Since Revelation has often been understood as predicting the long-range future, it is important to see that the author shares a key perspective of apocalypticism, its expectation that God will intervene *soon*. This motif of the nearness of the end is not incidental or optional but woven into the fabric of the Apocalypse throughout.

— 1:1. The book reveals what must soon take place; the author adds "soon" to the biblical phrase taken from Daniel 2:28.

— 1:3. The emphatic conclusion gives the basis for the obedient response to which the prophet calls his readers: "The time is near."

— 2:16. The risen Jesus warns those in Pergamum to repent, because he is coming soon.

— 2:25. The risen Jesus encourages the faithful at Thyatira to hold fast what they have "until I come." While no interval is specified before this "coming" is to occur, the word loses its function of encouragement to steadfast endurance if a long period is intended, and becomes utterly meaningless if a span of centuries is what is meant.

— 3:11. Similarly to the church at Philadelphia, "I am coming soon" functions as encouragement to faithfulness.

— 3:20. "Listen! I am standing at the door, knocking" is a temporal image, often found in apocalyptic, that reflects the shortness of time before the coming of Christ: he is already at the door (see Mark 13:29; Luke 12:36; Jas 5:9).

— 6:10–11. The souls of the martyrs already in heaven cry out for God's eschatological judgment of the world and ask "How long?" They receive the heartening response that they must wait only "a little longer."

FIGURE 43: Ephesus, location of one of the seven churches mentioned in Revelation 2–3. USED BY PERMISSION OF DAVID PADFIELD.

— 10:6–7. The "mighty angel" in the vision swears by the Creator that there is to be "no more delay," but that the "mystery of God . . . as he announced to his servants the prophets," that is, the divine plan for the establishment of God's just rule at the end of history, is about to be fulfilled.

— 11:2–3; 12:6. The longest period mentioned in Revelation is this span of time described variously as forty-two months, or twelve hundred sixty days, derived from the period of three and a half years prophesied in Daniel 7:25; 8:14; 9:27; 12:7, 11, 12. This period became a traditional apocalyptic time frame (see Luke 4:25 and Jas 5:17 vs. 1 Kgs 17:1; 18:1). While we should not think John took the period as a literally exact definition of how much time remained before the end, there is also no reason to interpret it in terms of generations or centuries, as the context in each instance makes clear.

— 12:12. The evil that John's churches are suffering will intensify, in John's view, because the devil "knows that his time is short."

— 17:10. There are to be seven emperors altogether, and John and his hearer-readers live in the time of the sixth, that is, just before the final brief period of history.

— 22:6. The angel declares that the preceding visions reveal "what must soon take place."

— 22:7. The risen Christ declares, "I am coming soon."

— 22:10. In contrast to Daniel, which was composed in the literary form of a document written centuries before the events with which it deals were to take place, and then sealed until the appropriate time, Revelation is not to be sealed, "for the time is near," that is, it deals with events of the time in which is written.

— 22:12. The risen Christ declares (again!) he is coming soon.

— 22:20. "Surely I am coming soon" are the last words from heaven that John hears.

On the variety of ways that early Christian theologians interpreted this apocalyptic nearness of the end, see the summary below at John 13–17.

Differences. In addition to its letter form and function, Revelation exhibits two fundamental differences from typical Jewish apocalypses:

1. *Not pseudonymous.* Unlike other writers of apocalyptic books, John gives his own name, writing in his own person, rather than under the assumed name of some figure of the past. John and his churches no longer believed that the prophetic gift of the Holy Spirit was only a remembered aspect of the revered past. It was a matter of their own experience that the Spirit spoke again to the churches through Christian prophets (see 1:10; 2:7, 11, 17, 29; 3:6, 13, 22; 4:2; 22:17).

2. *No retrojected preview of history.* Since John writes in his own name for his own time, there is no need for him to adopt the fictive preview of history between the time of the purported ancient author and the actual author's own time (cf., e.g., Daniel, *1 Enoch*).

26.1.4 Social and Political Setting

A good firsthand introduction to the social and political situation faced by John and his churches is provided by comparing John's letter to the exchange of letters between Pliny the Younger and the emperor Trajan (ca. 115 CE). Upon Pliny's arrival in Bithynia as the new governor from Rome, he found accusations against Christians on his court docket, but did not know how to proceed. Though writing twenty years after Revelation and in the province adjacent to Asia, Pliny indicates that a similar situation had occurred twenty-five years previously. His letter is near enough in time and place to illuminate the situation of Revelation:

> I have made it a rule, my Lord, to refer everything to you about which I am in doubt. For who could better provide direction for my hesitations or instruction for my lack of knowledge?
>
> I have never been present at the interrogation of Christians. Therefore, I do not know how far such investigations should be pushed, and what sort of punishments are appropriate. I have also been uncertain as to whether age makes any difference, or whether the very young are dealt with in the same way as adults, whether repentance and renunciation of Christianity is sufficient, or whether the accused are still considered criminals because they were once Christians even if they later renounced it, and whether persons are to be punished simply for the name "Christian" even if no criminal act has been committed, or whether only crimes associated with the name are to be punished.
>
> In the meantime, I have handled those who have been denounced to me as Christians as follows: I asked them whether they were Christians. Those who responded affirmatively I have asked a second and third time, under threat of the death penalty. If they persisted in their confession, I had them executed. For whatever it is that they are actually advocating, it seems to me that obstinacy and stubbornness must be punished in any case. Others who labor under the same delusion, but who were Roman citizens, I have designated to be sent to Rome.

In the course of the investigations, as it usually happens, charges are brought against wider circles of people, and the following special cases have emerged:

An unsigned placard was posted, accusing a large number of people by name. Those who denied being Christians now or in the past, I thought necessary to release, since they invoked our gods according to the formula I gave them and since they offered sacrifices of wine and incense before your image which I had brought in for this purpose along with the statues of our gods, I also had them curse Christ. It is said that real Christians cannot be forced to do any of these things.

Others charged by this accusation at first admitted that they had once been Christians, but had already renounced it; they had in fact been Christians, but had given it up, some of them three years ago, some even earlier, some as long as twenty-five years ago. All of these worshiped your image and the statues of the gods, and cursed Christ. They verified, however, that their entire guilt or error consisted in the fact that on a specified day before sunrise they were accustomed to gather and sing an antiphonal hymn to Christ as their god and to pledge themselves by an oath not to engage in any crime, but to abstain from all thievery, assault, and adultery, not to break their word once they had given it, and not to refuse to pay their legal debts. They then went their separate ways, and came together later to eat a common meal, but it was ordinary, harmless food. They discontinued even this practice in accordance with my edict by which I had forbidden political associations, in accord with your instructions. I considered it all the more necessary to obtain by torture a confession of the truth from two female slaves, whom they called "deaconesses." I found nothing more than a vulgar, excessive superstition.

I thus adjourned further hearings, in order to seek counsel from you. The matter seems to me in need of good counsel, especially in view of the large number of accused. For many of every age and class, of both sexes, are in danger of prosecution both now and in the future. The plague of this superstition has spread not only in the cities, but through villages and the countryside. But I believe a stop can be made and a remedy provided. In any case it is now quite clear that the temples, almost deserted previously, are gradually gaining more and more visitors, the long neglected sacred festivals are again regularly observed, and the sacrificial meat, for which buyers have been hard to find, is again being purchased. From this one can easily see what an improvement can be made in the masses, when one gives room for repentance.

The Emperor's response:

My Secundus! You have chosen the right way with regard to the cases of those who have been accused before you as Christians. Nothing exists that can be considered a universal norm for such cases. Christians should not be sought out. But if they are accused and handed over, they are to be punished, but only if they do not renounce their identity as Christians and demonstrate it by the appropriate act, i.e., the worship of our gods. Even if one is suspect because of past conduct, he or she is to be acquitted in view of repentance.

Anonymous accusations may not be considered in any trial, for that would be a dangerous precedent, and does not fit our times. *(Pliny the Younger,* Letters *X:96–97, trans. M. Eugene Boring)*

To be noted:

— Pliny is previously unaware of the Christian group. Though an informed Roman governor, he has no experience in dealing with Christians and does not know how to respond to the charges against them. There is clearly no officially established policy, no empirewide persecution of Christians, and the empire does not take the initiative against them. The initiative comes from local people who bring charges against the Christians in Roman courts.

— Worship before the image of the emperor was the litmus test of loyalty to Rome. Faithful Christians refused to comply.

— We see the precarious situation of Christians. Some Christians are killed for holding fast to their confession. Such cases, used by the Romans to "send a message" to potentially dangerous groups, had already occurred when Revelation was written. Though there was no general Roman persecution of Christians in John's time, he saw such cases as the leading edge of a general persecution shortly to come, in which all Christians would face the decision of whether to "worship the beast" or persevere in their confession of Jesus as Lord.

— The social location of the Christian community is not specifically indicated. There is no indication that it was a movement only among the poor and slaves, though the arbitrariness of Roman power is indicated when the governor tortures two slaves in order to determine whether the movement is actually politically dangerous; it turns out not to be. Christians are people who pay their debts; some are Roman citizens. Pliny refers to "wider circles" with no indication of their social or economic status. Presumably many, perhaps most, belonged to the lower socioeconomic strata, but Pliny does not consider the Christian movement a protest of have-nots against haves. There is no doubt that John's vision portrays the judgment of God against the wealthy exploiters of the world represented by Babylon/Rome (e.g., 18:3), but it is the whole world, poor and rich, slave and master, that stands under the judgment of God (see 6:15–17; 19:18).

— "Lord," "repentance," "endurance" are key words. Christians must decide whether to acknowledge Caesar as Lord. The Roman authorities insist that those who resist the emperor cult change their minds ("repent") and give them the opportunity to save their lives by doing so. Those who persist in their resistance are described as "enduring," considered arrogant and stubborn by the Romans. This vocabulary is also central to John, but the valences are reversed. Jesus is the only Lord to be confessed. Repentance is to reorient one's life away from the Roman religion and cultural values, rather than toward them. Endurance, hanging in there and holding on to the confession, is the central quality of the Christian life, rather than something to be punished.

26.1.5 Church Setting

Revelation and the Johannine Churches

Revelation is written to churches in the province of Asia, the same area in which the Johannine churches were at home, with Ephesus a central point. Some vocabulary and imagery shared by Revelation and the Gospel of John illustrate both similarities and differences:

— Christological ἐγώ εἰμι ὁ . . . (*egō eimi ho*, "I am the . . .") sayings are found only in the Gospel of John and Revelation.[1]

— "Lamb" as a central christological image, though the terminology is different: Revelation uses ἀρνίον (*arnion*) twenty-eight times for Christ, the Gospel ἀρνίον only at 21:15, elsewhere ἀμνός (*amnos*, 1:29, 36). Revelation

1. The form occurs only in Matt 22:32 (God), Matt 24:5 (those falsely claiming to be the Messiah), and as Christ's own self-predication in John 4:26; 6:35, 41, 48, 51; 8:12, 18; 10:7, 9, 11, 14; 11:25; 14:6; 15:1, 5; Rev. 1:8, 17; 2:23; 21:6; 22:16.

FIGURE 44: A carving of the goddess Nike ("Victory") at Ephesus. Nike was a popular image on Greek coins and in statuary. PHOTO CREDIT: M. EUGENE BORING.

always has absolute Lamb, Gospel always Lamb of God.

— "Word" (Λόγος, *Logos*) as central christological image: Revelation 19:13; John 1:1–2, 14. John has the absolute Word; Revelation the Word of God.

— "Dwell" (σκηνόω, *skēnoō*) for the dwelling of God/Christ with believers, Revelation 7:15; 12:12; 13:6; 21:3; John 1:14.

— "Children" as a term for disciples of a prophetic leader, Revelation 2:23/John 13:33; 1 John 2:1, 12, 28; 3:7, 18; 4:4; 5:21 (though Revelation has τέκνα [*tekna*] and John and 1 John have the diminutive τεκνία [*teknia*]).

— "Hebrew" (Ἑβραϊστί *Hebraisti*, for Hebrew or Aramaic language) only seven times in the New Testament, five in John, two in Revelation.

— "Pierce" (ἐκκεντέω, *ekkenteō*) in reference to the crucifixion only in Revelation 1:7 and John 19:37 in the New Testament, each time with reference to Zechariah 12:10. In the Gospel accounts of the crucifixion, only John refers to Jesus being nailed and his side being pierced.

— "Tribulation" (θλίψις, *thlipsis*) as a distinctive term for the eschatological sufferings of believers in the period before the end, characteristic of both Revelation (five times) and the Gospel (16:21, 33).

— Likewise the paradoxical language "conquer" and "victory" (νικάω, νίκη, *nikaō, nikē)* for the Christian life is used by both Revelation and the other Johannine literature in a distinctive sense that parallels Christ's suffering/victory on the cross with the believer's suffering/victory in testimony and martyrdom (Rev 2:7, 11, 17, 26; 3:5, 12, 21; 5:5; 6:2; 11:7; 12:11; 13:7; 15:2; 17:14; 21:7/1 John 2:13, 14; 4:4; 5:4, 5; John 16:33).

— The image of shepherding as both christological and ecclesiological (Rev 7:17/John 10:1–17; 21:16–17).

— "Living water" for eternal life (Rev 7:17; 21:6; 22:1, 17/John 4:10–11; 7:38).

— Authentic worship in the absence of the temple (Rev 21:22/ John 2:19; 4:21–24).

— The emphasis on charismatic, Spirit-led ministry rather than established offices is common to Revelation and 1 John, and is the dominant perspective of the Gospel.

— On the other hand, there are striking differences between Revelation and the other Johannine literature, e.g., ἅγιος (*hagios*, holy) is used only six times in the Gospel and Letters, always of God, Christ, or the Spirit, never of disciples. In Revelation, however, "holy" is found fourteen times, often applied to the "saints," members of the church, as in Paul. Revelation's Christology has no place for the pictures of Jesus the miracle worker, and no place in its ecclesiology for the official orders of ministry beginning to develop in some Johannine churches. John and his readers are alienated from the synagogue, but in Revelation, "Jew" is an honorable term that has not developed the symbolic connotations it often has in the Gospel (cf., e.g., Rev 2:9, 3:9 and John 9:22; 10:31).

The points of similarity and difference suggest that the author of the Apocalypse is not a direct member of the Johannine school, but is nonetheless interior to the Johannine community and has an indirect relationship with their theological leadership.

Revelation and the Pauline Churches

The early Pauline churches valued the gift of prophecy, though the later Pauline school became somewhat suspicious of charismatics (see §16.1.5). Paul had referred to prophets who delivered their revelations in the context of Christian worship (1 Cor 14:1–40, esp. vv. 6, 26). Such prophecy in the Pauline churches seems to have been an ad hoc matter; we have no indication that such prophets composed lengthy documents to be read to the congregation. John was not a prophet in the Pauline tradition in this sense. Yet Revelation is clearly within the Pauline letter tradition, sharing the Pauline kenosis Christology *and letter form*. On arriving in Asia from Palestine, John apparently preached among congregations with Pauline connections and developed a somewhat dialogical, tensive relation to the Pauline tradition. He is in relation to the Pauline churches of Asia at the end of the second century, without being interior to the Pauline school. His prophetic message takes the form of a Pauline letter, composed to be read aloud during congregational worship (Rev 1:3).

In a number of instances, Revelation shares distinctively Pauline themes, vocabulary, and conceptuality, including:[2]

— "Grace and peace to you" (χάρις ὑμῖν καὶ εἰρήνη, *charis humin kai eirēnē,* Rev 1:4) is found in all ancient literature only in Paul and the literature influenced by him (see §10.2.3).

— "In Jesus" (1:9) and "in the Lord" (14:13) reflect the Pauline "in Christ" vocabulary (see §13.3.2).

— "Firstfruits" (ἀπαρχή, *aparchē*, Rev 14:4) as a description of the Christian reality is found in the New Testament only in Paul and the literature influenced by him.

— A focus on Ephesus, a church founded by Paul, but better then than now (Rev 2:1–7). In this case, John values the earlier charismatic phase of the Pauline churches over the later developments in the Pauline school with which he is contemporary.

— The issue of eating meat sacrificed to idols is common to Paul and Revelation, but John rejects the permissive attitude initiated by Paul and developed within the Pauline school, which in his own time he regards as an

2. For detailed analysis and bibliography, see Elisabeth Schüssler Fiorenza, *The Book of Revelation: Justice and Judgment* (Philadelphia: Fortress Press, 1985), 114–32.

unacceptable compromise with idolatry (see below on Rev 2–3).

— Like Paul and the Pastorals, John resists the radical realized eschatology that reduced the resurrection to present experience (Rev 20:5–6; see 2 Tim 2:18).

— John emphasizes the political dimension of confession of Christ more than Paul and the Pauline school. He shares the key christological confession κύριος (*kurios*, Lord) with them, but with such titles as "King of kings" brings the Christian confession into more explicit opposition to the emperor cult.

26.1.6 Sources, Traditions, Influences

Prophetic revelatory experiences. As studies of Israelite and Jewish prophecy have made clear, the prophetic claim to direct revelation is combined with the use of traditional imagery and materials.[3] The original, numinous revelatory experience can be appropriated and communicated only by adapting the imagery and language already present in the mind and experience of prophet and hearers.

John's Bible. Revelation is saturated with allusions to Scripture, so that its words and images were available to provide the raw material for his visions, and the literary means by which to express them. There are no direct quotations, but the forty-eight pages of text of Revelation in the standard (Nestle-Aland[27]) edition of the Greek New Testament contain approximately five hundred allusions to the Scriptures. Scripture is not quoted as a past authority, but re-presented in new forms and combinations that break down the distance between the past of Scripture and the present of the hearer-readers in John's churches. The text of Scripture becomes in his hand the vehicle for communicating the present word of the risen Lord.

Apocalyptic tradition. John has much imagery in common with Jewish apocalypses such as *1 Enoch*, though he never cites them or quotes them directly. Revelation is not a compilation of material from other apocalyptic writings, but there can be no question but that John had read, heard, and appropriated such imagery for his own purposes.[4]

Prior Jewish and Christian prophecies. The Apocalypse is not John's first prophetic utterance as a Christian. As he composes Revelation, he is aware of his own previous oracles. Like the biblical prophets, he seems to have taken up previous prophetic material, from himself or others, and re-presented it as the present address of the risen Christ. Several scholars, for instance, regard 11:1–2 as part of the oracle of a Jerusalem Zealot prophet just prior to 70 CE, adopted and interpreted by John in his own sense.

Church liturgy. The hymns and prayers of Revelation are not ad hoc compositions, but reflect (not necessarily verbatim) the worship life of the churches of Asia.

Pauline letters. We have seen that John interacts with traditions of the developing Pauline school. He seems to have heard Paul's letters read in worship and to have adopted features of the Pauline letter form. He does not use Paul's letters as a direct source for his own writing.

Synoptic traditions. John has points of contact with traditions that appear in the Synoptic Gospels. Some sayings of the risen Jesus are similar to sayings found in the Synoptic tradition (e.g., Rev 2:7/Matt 11:15 and par.; Rev 3:3c/Matt 24:43 and par.; Rev 3:5b/Matt 10:32 and par.). In particular, the visions of Revelation 6–16 bear a striking resemblance, in general structure and content, to the "little apocalypse" of Mark 13.

3. See, e.g., Johannes Lindblom, *Prophecy in Ancient Israel* (Philadelphia: Fortress Press, 1962), 105–81.

4. Modern readers whose only encounter with such language and imagery is confined to Revelation itself would do well to browse through the selection of apocalyptic literature in Charlesworth, ed., *Pseudepigrapha*, or at least 2 Esdras/4 Ezra, found in most Bibles that contain the Apocrypha. Revelation will never look the same.

FIGURE 45: Island of Patmos, seen from monastery. PHOTO CREDIT: M. EUGENE BORING.

26.1.7 Structure

John's *apocalyptic visions* are surrounded by and included in an *epistolary frame* (1:4–8; 22:20b–21). The whole is preceded by a *titular summary*, 1:1–3. The body of the text itself is composed of two major sections. The first is set on the earthly island of Patmos (see fig. 45), where the risen Jesus appears to John and dictates messages to be sent to the seven churches of Asia (1:9–3:22).

The second scene is in the heavenly throne room, where the risen Jesus appears, opens the scroll sealed with seven seals, precipitating the final events of history and the beginning of God's eschatological reign (4:1–22:5), followed by the concluding visionary scene (22:6–20).

The general compositional scheme is clear, a narrative presentation of the broad apocalyptic pattern found in many other documents. This pattern begins with the present troubles, portrays them as intensifying just before the end, and then pictures the ultimate victory of God in the end itself. Author and readers stand at the beginning of the time of the last troubles. This means that things will get worse before they get better, and must do so, for these eschatological troubles represent the final intensification of evil just before the end, when evil is finally destroyed forever. John's and his readers' own situation is represented in chapters 1–3, the vision of the exalted Christ who communicates a message from God to the Christians in seven cities of Asia. The time of eschatological distress is portrayed in chapters 4–18, the vision of the heavenly throne room in which Christ opens the seven seals, which open in turn to seven trumpets and then to seven bowls of wrath, climaxed by the destruction of the great city, Babylon. The final victory is depicted in chapters 19–22, climaxed by the appearance of the "holy city," the heavenly new Jerusalem.

The image of *the city* plays a major role in the structure of the book. In John's time,

Christianity had become an urban phenomenon, and he addresses Christians in the major cities of Asia (chaps. 1–3). The imagery portrays the world's civilization as Babylon, ruling the present (chaps. 4–18). But the new Jerusalem is the ultimate city in which God's rule shall prevail (chaps. 19–22). The driving force of the book is the question: Should Christians in the cities of Asia orient themselves to the present lame-duck regime (Rome) or future ultimate regime (new Jerusalem)?

These considerations give the following outline:

1:1–8	Introduction
1:1–3	Titular Summary
1:4–8	Letter Opening
1:9–3:22	Part 1: Revelation to the Churches in the Cities
1:9–20	Transcendent Christ
2:1–3:22	Seven Messages to the Seven Churches
4:1–22:5	Part 2: Revelation of the City of This World and the City of God
4:1–18:24	God Judges Babylon, the City of This World
4:1–5:14	The heavenly throne room
6:1–8:1	The heavenly worship: Opening the seven seals
8:2–11:19	Sounding the seven trumpets
12:1–14:20	Exposé of the powers of evil
15:1–16:20	The seven last plagues
17:1–18:24	Fall of Babylon
19:1–22:5	God Redeems the Holy City, New Jerusalem
19:1–10	The heavenly throne room: Hallelujah choruses praise God's victory
19:11–22:20a	Seven scenes of God's ultimate triumph
19:11–16	Return of Christ
19:17–21	Last battle
20:1–3	Binding of Satan
20:4–6	Thousand-year reign
20:7–10	Defeat of Gog and Magog
20:11–15	The Last Judgment
21:1–22:5	The new Jerusalem
22:6–21	Conclusion

26.1.8 Exegetical-Theological Précis

1:1–8 Introduction

1:1–3 Titular Summary

The risen Lord is portrayed as the definitive element in a revelatory chain of command from God through Jesus Christ and the revelatory angel/Spirit, to the prophet, the churches, and ultimately to the world. The blessing pronounced on lector and hearers shows the document was not intended for private, individual reading, but was to be read forth in the worship services of the churches to which it is addressed.

1:4–8 Letter Opening

This is John's adoption and adaptation of the Pauline letter formula, exactly replicating Paul's own distinctive prescript (see above, §10.2.3).

1:9–3:22 Part 1: Revelation to the Churches in the Cities

The risen Jesus appears to the prophet John on the island of Patmos, with a revelatory message to the churches on the mainland, in the Roman province of Asia.

1:9–20 Transcendent Christ

Each of the major parts of Revelation begins with a vision of the transcendent world from which the revelatory message proceeds. The risen Christ is portrayed in ways that distinguish John's work from the typical apocalypse and make it appropriate to the particular situation to which it is addressed:

— The transcendent revealer is a recent historical figure who has been executed by the Roman government. John does not receive his revelation directly from God, as in Israelite prophecy, nor from one of the angels of the heavenly court, but from Jesus, who has already experienced the destiny to which he now calls the readers. The one now clothed in transcendent glory once stood before the authorities, was faithful to death, was killed, but now is "alive forever and ever" and has "the keys of Death and of Hades."

— "Martyr" (μαρτύς, *martus*) means the one who gave his testimony in court and also is already developing the overtones of "martyr," the one who seals his testimony by giving his life. He is the "first-born of the dead," who did not merely "survive death," but is designated by God as the preeminent One, the Heir, the Beginning of the eschatological resurrection and culmination of God's purpose. He is the "ruler of kings on earth," the "King of kings and Lord of lords" (17:14; 19:16), the rightful claimant of the title falsely claimed by the Roman emperors. Here we see the early church, through its prophets, developing new christological titles and imagery never used by the historical Jesus (see above, §9.2.2).

— The risen Christ as present and absent: John's paradoxical imagery portrays the transcendent Christ as now in heaven, to return at the end of history. But Christ is also present with his churches during their ordeal. He holds the seven stars (the angels that represent the churches) in his hands and walks among the lampstands (the churches). John draws no sharp conceptual distinction between the risen Christ and the Holy Spirit. The church's experience of the Spirit makes Christ real to them. The words of the risen Christ are identified with "what the Spirit says to the churches" (2:1, 7; repeated in each of the seven messages). John's view is akin to the Fourth Gospel's understanding of the Paraclete, who is both Christ and Holy Spirit.

2:1–3:22 Seven Messages to the Seven Churches

The messages of chapters 2–3 must be interpreted as part of the preceding vision. The so-called "letters to the seven churches" do not constitute a literary unit but belong with 1:9–20. They are not independent bits of advice to various congregations but grounded in the commission of the risen Christ portrayed in John's initial vision.

The messages to the churches are not separate letters. Revelation as a whole is a single letter, addressed to the churches of Asia, adopting the conventional forms of letter opening and closing. The whole of Revelation is read forth in the worship of each congregation. While the message to each of the seven churches is appropriate to the congregation to which it is addressed, all seven messages are addressed to all the churches (note the closing line of each message: ". . . what the Spirit is saying to the churches").

Each message has the same eightfold form: (1) address to the "angel" of each church; (2) the city in which the congregation is located; (3) the prophetic messenger formula, analogous to the "Thus says the Lord . . ." of Israelite prophecy; (4) a christological ascription, mostly reflecting features of the initial vision; (5) "I know . . . ," reflecting the divine knowledge of earthly things possessed by the risen Christ; (6) the "body" of the message, with praise and/or blame (only Smyrna and Philadelphia receive unqualified praise); (7) the call to attention and obedience, "Let anyone who has an ear listen to what the Spirit is saying to the churches"; (8) the promise of eschatological reward to the "conquerors," already setting the tone for what it means that Christ has "conquered" and calls his followers to "conquer."

FIGURE 46: Ruins at Smyrna, location of one of the seven churches addressed in Revelation 2–3. USED BY PERMISSION OF DAVID PADFIELD.

The seven messages have straightforward language that allows the modern reader insights into the life of the churches of Asia at the end of the first century CE. We see no idealized picture but the mixture of faith and unfaith, responsibility and irresponsibility reflected in Paul's letters a generation earlier. Christians are addressed not as individuals but as members of communities of mission and witness. Among the features we notice:

— *Tribulation, trouble, affliction, persecution, ordeal*. The key word θλίψις (*thlipsis*, 1:9; 2:9, 10, 22; 7:14) refers to harassment and persecution from society and government. John sees this as already having begun, and believes it will shortly intensify and engulf all Christians. He wants his hearer-readers to know they are living in the prelude to the end. John sees the great ordeal in terms of the conflict between Christian believers and the religious powers of his time, that is, the synagogue and the established, respected cultural religions, especially the Caesar cult. He sees this conflict as the this-worldly manifestation of a deeper conflict being waged in the transcendent sphere. Thus the synagogues in Smyrna and Philadelphia are "synagogues of Satan" (2:9; 3:9), and the impressive temple to the emperor in Pergamum is "Satan's throne" (2:13).

When Christians are jailed by the Romans, it is "the devil" who is really at work (2:10). On the other hand, the church is the setting where the Spirit speaks and the power of God is at work (2:7, 23; 3:8). The church is not spectator to the cosmic battle between God and the forces of evil, but experiences them in its own life. These conflicts will be pictured on a massive visionary scale in chapters 4–20, but are already presupposed in the messages to the churches in chapters 2–3.

— *Internal tensions and divisions*. John addresses the congregations as a charismatic prophet, without the authority of official status. Others in the churches he addresses also make claims to leadership, with other ideas of what the response of the church should be to the cultural pressures it is experiencing. The references to teaching (διδάσκω, *didaskō*, 2:14, 20;

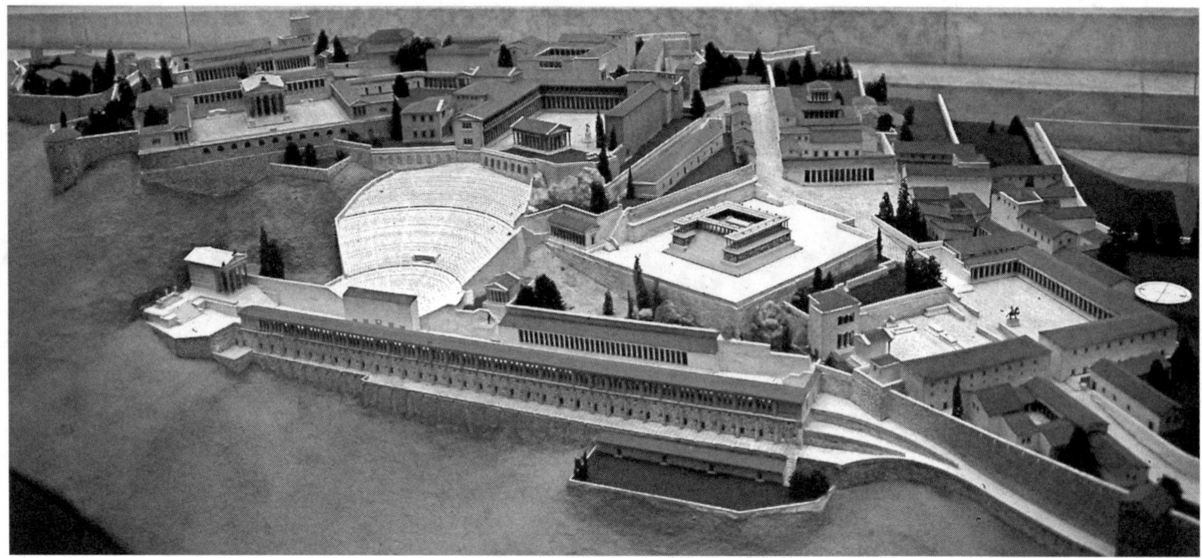

FIGURE 47: Model of the Pergamum altar to Zeus, Berlin. PHOTO CREDIT: M. EUGENE BORING.

διδαχή, *didachē*, 2:14, 15, 24) point to doctrinal disputes. The churches are visited by people claiming to be apostles (2:2). These itinerant missionaries that visited John's churches did not represent themselves as belonging to the Twelve but, as in the time of Paul, claimed to be authorized messengers, missionaries, and teachers of the church at large (see Acts 14:14; Rom 16:7; 2 Cor 8:23; Phil 2:25). Like Paul, John regards some such traveling missionaries as false apostles (cf. on 2 Cor 11:1–15). The congregations are commended for testing such claims and rejecting those that did not measure up (Rev 2:2). John also refers to rival charismatic leaders, the Nicolaitans (2:6, 15), those who follow Balaam (2:14), and the prophet Jezebel (2:20).

— *Love and spiritual gifts.* John considers love among the supreme expressions of the Christian life. As in 1 Corinthians 13, love is the active care for others manifested in Jesus' own life. It is equated with "works" in 2:4–5. The church at Thyatira is praised for its love expressed in deeds (2:19). The Ephesian church receives blame because it has abandoned the love it had at first (2:4). Like Paul earlier, John acknowledges that his churches were well supplied with charismatic phenomena, but charges them with abandoning the essential characteristic of the Christian life, the deeds of love that had characterized their initial discipleship.

4:1–22:5 Part 2: Revelation of the City of This World and the City of God—John Taken to See the Reality of the Heavenly Realm

In Part 1, the risen Christ comes to John on Patmos with messages to the churches of Asia. In Part 2, John is taken to the heavenly world to behold the world and history from the divine perspective, to see behind the scenes how things really are. Hearer-readers are taken with John into heaven and see with him; they do not remain on earth and only read his reports from the earthly perspective.

FIGURE 48: Ruins at Thyatira, location of one of the seven churches mentioned in Revelation 2–3. USED BY PERMISSION OF DAVID PADFIELD.

4:1–18:24 *God Judges Babylon, the City of This World*

4:1–5:14 *The heavenly throne room* This vision is the theological center and anchor point for the whole document. The scenes to follow are mostly horrific pictures of the woes of the end times, the terrible suffering the world and the church must endure as history comes to an end. Yet before portraying these eschatological woes, John wants the hearer-reader to see what he has seen: at the heart of things God rules in sublime majesty, the God who has defined himself as the Lamb who suffers for others. The eschatological plagues to be portrayed in chapters 6–18 unfold from the hand of the Lamb in chapter 5—the hand of the crucified and risen one, the One who suffers with and for his creation.

— *The one sovereign Creator*. Like all apocalyptic thought, Revelation is strongly influenced by dualism. Yet John emphasizes that ultimately there is one God, who created and rules all things. John is only penultimately dualistic; God vs. Satan is only the next to the last word about reality. Ultimately, all things are in one hand.

— *The book that provides the key to history*. It is in the hand of the Creator, but it is sealed. No human being, no angel, can reveal its contents and put its decrees into action. The meaning and resolution of history's pageant of suffering remains a divine mystery. John weeps.

— *The lion who is the Lamb*. The typical apocalyptic response to the problem of present evil is to point to the future saving act of God, who will send a mighty deliverer to establish justice and make things right. The good news rings through the heavenly world: there is one who can open the book, reveal its mystery, and bring history to a worthy conclusion. The divinely appointed savior of the end time, the hoped-for lion of the tribe of Judah,[5] has conquered and can open the book. John looks at the appointed place in the vision where the lion was expected to appear, *and what he sees is a slaughtered lamb.*

5. For lion imagery for the Messiah, see Gen 49:9–10; 2 Esd 12:31–32, "the lion . . . is the Messiah."

The ultimate power of the universe is not lion violence, but lamb sacrifice, the divine self-giving love manifest in the crucified Jesus. For John, this is what it means to "conquer," both for Jesus and for his followers. This is the christological redefinition of winning.

6:1–8:1 The heavenly worship: Opening the seven seals When the Lamb begins to open the seven seals, terrible violence erupts on the earth. Many readers are perplexed and repelled by these scenes, which seem to offer such a contrast to the love and grace of God revealed in Christ.

Without minimizing the problem or claiming to solve it, readers might keep in mind the following observations, perspectives, and principles in interpreting Revelation's language of violence.[6]

1. *John's and his readers' experience of suffering.* John's thought began not with visions about future suffering to be endured by others, but with the reality of present suffering experienced by himself and his readers. Apocalyptic thought gives meaning to experienced suffering by placing it in a transcendent context. It functions as interpretation of the present, not speculation about the future. As illustrated by Israel's imprecatory psalms (Pss 35; 55; 69; 109; 137), a community that feels itself pushed to the edge of society and the limits of its own endurance will, in its worship, give vent to the natural feelings of resentment, even revenge, as it anticipates the eschatological turning of the tables. Even then, cries for revenge are not personal, but a plea for the justice of God to be manifest publicly.

2. *John's use of biblical language.* The language of God's wrath (6:16–17; 11:18; 14:10; 16:19; 19:15) is not John's creation but a dimension of a deep stream of biblical theology. A sampling would include the great prophets of Israel, the Gospels, and Paul (e.g., Exod 22:21–24; Deut 9:7–8; Pss 2:5; 78:21–22; 90:7–9; Isa 1:24; 9:19; 13:9, 13; 51:17, 22; Jer 4:4; 10:10, 25; 25:15; Ezek 7:8, 12; 13:13; 20:8, 13; Hos 5:10; 13:11; Mic 5:15; Matt 3:7; John 3:36; Rom 1:18(!); 2:5; 5:9; 9:22; 12:19; 1 Thess 1:10; 2:16; 5:9). The stream of biblical theology represented by these texts pictures the relentless intolerance of sin by a God of justice.

3. *John's appropriation of tradition.* John inherited an apocalyptic tradition in which the suffering of the end times played a necessary role. In both form and content, most of it was adopted and adapted by him from his Bible and his Jewish and Christian traditions. Among these is the apocalyptic scheme of the "messianic woes" and the "birth pangs of the Messiah," which interpreted the present troubles of the faithful community as the leading edge of the period of suffering that must come just before the final victory, just as labor pains precede birth.

4. *John's use of confessional language.* It must be kept in mind that the violence in the scenes of chapters 6–16 is not literal violence against the real world, but is violence in a visionary scene of the future, expressed in metaphorical language (9:7!). The sword and fire by which the evil of the earth is judged (and even "tormented") are not literal swords and fire, but metaphors for the cutting, searing *Word of God* (1:16; 11:5). So also John's imagery portraying violent judgment upon God's enemies is the insider language of the confessing community that expresses its praise and gratitude for salvation, not an objectifying description of the fate of outsiders. Like the biblical language of the plague stories of God's deliverance of Israel from Egypt (Exod 7–12), John's visions of eschatological suffering are expressed in the confessional language of the Bible that glorifies the saving acts of God. The point is not the suffering of others, but the salvation of the faithful community.

5. *The original setting.* Revelation was intended to be read in worship, from beginning to end in one reading. This also helps place its

6. Here and elsewhere in this section, the material is adapted from Boring, *Revelation*, 113–119; and M. Eugene Boring, "The Revelation to John," in *The New Interpreter's Study Bible*, ed. Walter J. Harrelson (Nashville: Abingdon Press, 2003), 2222–23.

violent imagery in proper perspective. Analogous to the experience of watching a violent movie that "turns out right in the end," the violent scenes are not dwelt on as something significant in themselves. The hearer/viewer is taken in a relatively short time from the vision of the Creator God who holds all things in his hand (chaps. 4–5) through the terrors that precede the end (chaps. 6–18) to the dramatic victory at the coming of God's kingdom for which the community prays (chaps. 19–22).

6. *John's theology of sin and salvation*. John's theology presupposes that all human beings are sinners, including Christian victims as well as Roman oppressors (1:5). John does not picture innocent or self-righteous Christians suffering at the hands of sinful Romans, but sinful humans reeling under the judgment of the holy God. The catastrophes are not simply terrible, tragic events; they are repeatedly placed in the category of God's judgments (6:10; 11:18; 14:7; 16:5, 7; 17:1; 18:8, 10, 20; 19:2, 11; 20:12, 13). The eschatological terrors are therefore an expression of John's sense of justice. Considering the situation, this is done in a remarkably non-smug manner. The us/them mentality, while present, is relativized: *we* are also judged as sinners; *they* are not excluded from salvation.

The violent imagery is presented within a Revelation that also has scenes of universal salvation (1:7; 4:3; 5:13; 14:14; 15:4; 21:5; 21:22–22:3). Visions of absolute judgment are juxtaposed with visions of absolute mercy. The world not only staggers under the hammer blows of God's wrath; it is also redeemed and released from the power of Satan (20:1–6). The kings of the earth are not only destroyed and their flesh eaten by vultures (19:17–21); they are also redeemed and make their contribution to the new Jerusalem (21:24–26). Revelation does not advocate a theology of revenge or resentment, but a theology of justice, not just for "us" but for all.

7. *Christological transformation of traditional imagery*. The traditional imagery of apocalyptic terror is adopted and used by John, but like everything else in his revelation it is transformed within his christological perspective. Just as Martin Luther King Jr. could use the imagery of the "Battle Hymn of the Republic" in the cause of his nonviolent movement for justice, while condemning actual violence, so John can take the imagery of the lion who conquers and fill it with new content.

As each seal is broken, troubles on the earth intensify. The first five seals represent historical troubles of conquest, war, famine, plague, and death. When the sixth seal is opened, the cosmos itself begins to break up, and the reader anticipates that the seventh seal will bring the end.

8:2–11:19 Sounding the seven trumpets The seventh seal produces only a profound silence, which is then broken by the sounding of the seven trumpets. The preceding troubles are repeated and intensified. When the last trumpet is sounded (11:15–19), the final coming of the kingdom of God is announced, and the earth quakes with lightning, thunder, and hail that heralds the final theophany.

12:1–14:20 Exposé of the powers of evil Again, the anticipation of the ultimate end is thwarted. Instead of the promised new Jerusalem, the hearer-readers experience a number of visions that allow them to see behind the scenes of history, and to place their own experience in heavenly perspective. A cosmic woman gives birth to a child, a messianic figure who is threatened by a cosmic dragon but is taken to heaven, while the woman flees to a place of refuge (12:1–6). The dragon then loses the battle in the sky and is cast down to earth, where he persecutes the woman's other children (12:7–17). The dragon receives help from two beasts that represent him on earth, the beast from the sea (13:1–9) and the beast from the land (13:11–18). This beast has a number, 666.[7] The

7. The number of the beast is the sum of the numerical value of the letters of its name. Of the many possibilities, the most likely is "Nero Caesar" in Hebrew, the letters of which total 666. Nero had been the first emperor to persecute the church. Domitian, the threatening emperor

present struggles of the distressed Christians in John's situation are placed in a transcendent context, as part of a story that will conclude with the victory of God and the salvation of God's people.

15:1–16:20 The seven last plagues The seventh trumpet finally morphs into the final seven bowls, representing the sevenfold final judgment of God. This time, the seventh is final (16:17). Though chaotic terror befalls the earth, it is the expression of the orderly heavenly worship, as one by one each of the seven angels pours out his libation before God.

This section represents John's most thorough use of the exodus motif in Revelation. As Israel once stood on the banks of the Red Sea and celebrated God's liberating act of the exodus, the redeemed people of God will stand on the shore of the heavenly sea and sing the song of Moses and the Lamb. Egypt is Rome; Pharaoh is the Caesar; the plagues are eschatological woes (sores Rev 16:2 /Exod 9:10–11; sea and rivers become blood Rev 16:3–4 /Exod 7:17–21; darkness Rev 16:10 /Exod 10:22; drying up the waters Rev 16:12 /Exod 14:21–22; frogs Rev 16:13 /Exod 8:3; thunder, fire, hail Rev 16:18, 21 /Exod 9:24); the Passover lamb is the exalted Christ, the Lamb who has accomplished eschatological deliverance; the flood of troubles through which the church must pass is the Red Sea; the triumph song is the Song of Moses (and the Lamb). Even the smoke of Sinai (15:8) and the tabernacle containing the Law of God's justice appears (15:5; the heavenly sanctuary is pictured as the tabernacle accompanying Israel in the wilderness; see, e.g., Exod 40:34–38). As the Red Sea (Exod 14:21) and the Jordan (Josh 4:23) were dried up as part of God's liberating activity of the exodus, here the Euphrates is dried up to facilitate the final events (Rev 16:12).

of John's time, was thought of as heralding *Nero redivivus*, Nero back from the dead.

17:1–18:24 Fall of Babylon John's drama of history's eschatological horrors climaxes with the destruction of the "Great City" Rome, which he pictures, using biblical imagery, as both harlot and Babylon. John's original hearer-readers had known all along, from their own experience, who and what was represented in the bizarre imagery of dragon and beasts. In this concluding scene of God's judgment on the self-proclaimed Great City, he makes it unmistakably clear that he is referring to Rome (17:9, 18). He both laments and celebrates the fall of Babylon, as he anticipates its redemption in the final scenes.

19:1–22:5 God Redeems the Holy City, New Jerusalem

19:1–10 The heavenly throne room: Hallelujah choruses praise God's victory As in the corresponding section on the judgment of Babylon, the section on the redemption of Jerusalem begins with a scene of heavenly worship. John clearly intends 19:1–10 to be parallel to 4:1–5:14. Both begin with "After this," both picture the worship of the twenty-four elders, both refer to the heavenly voice and the throne.

19:11–22:20a Seven scenes of God's ultimate triumph In the final series of seven visions, God brings history to its conclusion and fulfillment in the new Jerusalem. Though the literary presentation requires that they be presented one after the other, they are not a strict chronology, but seven different pictures of the triumph of God at the end of history in which different facets of God's victory are revealed.

19:11–16 Scene 1: The Return of Christ

Throughout history, some interpretations have portrayed Jesus' second advent in contrast to his first—during his earthly life Jesus offered God's love and mercy, and suffered for others; when he returns, it will be with divine violence as the punitive Judge who makes others suffer. This is the polar opposite of John's own view.

The main point of the symbolic image of the "second coming" is that at the end of history we meet the same Christ who has already appeared in history as the loving servant of God who gave himself for others. It is the second coming of *Jesus* who is the Christ, an aspect of the fundamental Christian confession (§27.5, John 20:30–31). Even though the imagery of war and conquest is used, this imagery has been transformed by the meaning of the life and death of Jesus. The bloody robe he wears (19:13) is not stained with the blood of his enemies, but with his own redemptive blood given for others (1:5; 5:9; 7:14; 12:11). His only sword comes from his mouth (19:15), that is, is his powerful word that judges and redeems.

19:17–21 Scene 2: The last battle
For John, the victory is already won, with only mopping-up exercises in progress (see 12:7–12), but there will be a final scene portrayed as God's victory in the ultimate battle.

20:1–3 Scene 3: The binding of Satan
Jesus used the binding of Satan as an image of God's eschatological victory (Mark 3:22–27 and par.). Satan deceived not only individuals, but nations, the corporate structures that shape and condition human life. Systemic evil is here pictured in personal terms. That the idolatrous and oppressive nations are deceived shows that the cultural and institutional powers that were persecuting John's church are not the ultimate enemy. Instead, they also are God's creatures and victims of the transcendent power of evil, and must not be ultimately rejected or hated by either God or God's people. It is the transcendent power of evil that must be destroyed.

20:4–6 Scene 4: The thousand-year reign
Because of the power of Satan, God's good creation has been perverted and God's purpose thwarted, but this is not the last word. With the binding of Satan, the world finally comes into its own and enjoys the good existence for which it was created (Gen 1) and for which it sighs (Rom 8:19–24). Christ and his people reign on this good earth for a thousand years, and God's will is done on earth as it is done in heaven. This is only one of John's pictures of the end, complete in itself. To try to decide whether the millennium comes before or after the parousia or the last battle is to misunderstand the nature of John's symbolic language.

20:7–10 Scene 5: The defeat of Gog and Magog
John has in general been following the order of Ezekiel's visions. The throne and living creatures of Revelation 4 reflect the throne vision of Ezekiel 1; the eating of the scroll in Revelation 10 corresponds to the similar scene in Ezekiel 3; the sealing of God's servants in Revelation 7 is like that of Ezekiel 9; the Gog/Magog imagery of Revelation 20 is parallel to Ezekiel 38–39; and the new Jerusalem of Revelation 21–22 reflects Ezekiel 40–48. Here, John follows Jewish tradition that had reconfigured Ezekiel's Prince Gog of the land of Magog, so that Gog and Magog are not historical realities but personal transcendent beings, larger than life, who are deceived by Satan and lead the ultimate enemies of God's people against "the saints and the beloved city," to be destroyed in the eschatological battle. Evil is magnified to its fullest before being destroyed forever.

20:11–15 Scene 6: The Last Judgment
Some of John's readers have already stood before human courts and been condemned. John pictures the ultimate courtroom scene, in which justice will finally prevail. The God revealed in Christ is the final Judge. His judgment is not arbitrary. Two books play the crucial role. One book represents human responsibility, so that people are judged by what they have done. This is not "works righteousness" (see, e.g., 1:5; 5:6–14), but John's way of saying that what human beings do matters, and matters ultimately. The other book is the book of life, in which God enrolled names from the foundation of the world (3:5; 13:8; 17:8; 20:12, 15; 21:27). This is the book of grace, in which people are saved,

not by what they have done, but by what God has done. God's sovereign grace and human responsibility cannot be parceled out or harmonized in a logical system, but John can picture a scene in which both play the decisive role.

21:1–22:5 Scene 7: The new Jerusalem
The goal of history and the fulfillment of the purpose of God is a city. In the biblical story, human history started in a garden, and the first city was built by a murderer as the result of human sin (Gen 3:1–4:17). The conclusion of this story in Revelation does not nullify human history and return to the garden of Eden, but brings the garden into the city (22:1–2). A city represents human community, life together. Eschatological existence is not individualistic, but communal. The church, the community of faith, the people of God, is the anticipation of this.

The new Jerusalem is in continuity with this world and its history. The new heavens and new earth do not simply replace the old one, as though God "starts all over." This world—God's good creation—is not replaced but redeemed. God does not make "all new things" but "all things new" (21:5). The ultimate city bears the name and recognizable features of the earthly city. It is located in this world, on the transformed earth. After the thousand-year reign on this earth, John does not transfer the scene to the heavenly world, but has the heavenly city descend to this renewed earth. This world, the object of the Creator's love, is ultimately important to God (Gen 1; John 3:16).

The kingdom of God in this world is not, however, finally a matter of human achievement, but the eschatological act of God. The new Jerusalem is not built, Babel-like, toward heaven (Gen 11), but comes from God's side as the fulfillment of the divine promise and demonstration of God's faithfulness.

The final picture is true to John's paradoxically dual emphasis throughout. There are pictures of exclusion—no sinners and nothing sinful will enter the city (21:8, 27; 22:3, 14–15). There are also pictures of transformation and ultimate inclusion—the city is not for the "faithful few" but is inconceivably large (21:16); the kings and nations of the earth will be there (21:24–26); the nations are not only destroyed (19:15; 20:7–9) but finally are healed, walk by God's light, and bring their gifts to God (21:24–26; 22:2). The city has walls and gates—the boundary markers that separate insiders from outsiders, but the gates are never closed (21:12–14, 21, 25).

22:6–21 Conclusion

In contrast to the typical apocalypse (see Dan 12:4, 9), the book is not sealed like a time capsule to be opened at some future date (Rev 22:10). It is for the readers' present. The vision descends from the heavenly stratosphere to the solid earth, the literary form returns to that of the letter from John to the churches of Asia (1:4–5/22:20b–21), and its hearer-readers find themselves in this world with new hope and a job to do.

26.2 Interpreting 2 John

26.2.1 Structure

Second John is a real letter, along with 3 John following the standard Hellenistic letter form more closely than any other New Testament letter (see above, §10.2.3). It also reflects features of the Pauline letters that were circulating in the churches of Asia.

1–3	Greeting
4	Thanksgiving
5–11	Body
5–6	The Love Command
7–11	The False Teachers
12–13	Conclusion

26.2.2 Exegetical-Theological Précis

1–3 Greeting

A pronounced awareness of belonging to the church pervades the letter. The letter is addressed to the Elect Lady, that is, not to an individual but to a local Christian congregation. "Elect" ascribes the role of Israel as God's chosen people to the church, as the continuation of the biblical people of God (see below, on John 16:16). "Lady" is κυρία, *kuria*, feminine of κύριος, *kurios*, Lord. Modern English has no counterpart, but the pair of terms corresponds to the "Lord" and "Lady" of Elizabethan society (e.g., Lord and Lady Macbeth). Nuptial imagery for the church is in the biblical tradition of Israel as bride of YHWH, and was among the significant ecclesiological terms of the Johannine school (see above, on Eph 5:21–6:9). The identity of Christian believers is that they are children of this Lady, Mother Church. They are not merely individuals with their own direct relation to God, who may then decide to form an association for mutual encouragement. They inherently belong together, bound to each other, not only in a local congregation, but in a network of such congregations that exercise mutual care. The Elder assumes a certain authority for exercising this pastoral care within the network of congregations.

4 Thanksgiving

As in Paul's letters, the thanksgiving is more than the conventional wish for good health, but anticipates the theological concern of the body of the letter. Positively, the Elder is pleased to have learned that *some* members of the congregation are "walking in the truth," i.e., living according to the tradition the churches have received from the beginning.

5–11 Body

5–6 The Love Command

The brief letter uses the terms "love" and "truth" nine times. For the author, these are, if not identical, at least inseparable. Love means not only mutual care, but living by the truth, the tradition the churches have received from the beginning. This tradition was received from "the Father." The Elder understands the tradition to be derived from Christ himself, who is one with the Father. This expresses the Christology of the Johannine school (see below, §27.1.2), which is represented by the repeated "we" (see on 1 John 1:1–4).

7–11 The False Teachers

The letter is occasioned by the presence of "deceivers" (πλάνοι, *planoi*), a term often used in Jewish tradition for those who lead the people of God astray. It had been used of Jesus, and members of the Johannine community had heard it used of themselves in the synagogues (see John 7:12, 47). They now apply it to some teachers within their own community. These teachers consider themselves the "progressives" (προάγων, *proagōn*, v. 9), who are helping the church to adjust to the contemporary world by reinterpreting the faith in current categories—something the Johannine school affirmed and vigorously engaged in. The Elder regards these teachers, however, as having gone too far, having surrendered the tradition rather than interpreted it.

Their error is christological. They do not confess that "Jesus Christ has come in the flesh," that is, they deny the real incarnation, affirming the divine, spiritual Christ but rejecting his identification with the human being Jesus (see John 1:14).[8] The Elder regards the error as not merely a tolerable difference of opinion,

8. The present participle ἐρχόμενον, *erchomenon* can be literally translated "coming," and understood as referring to the parousia. In this case, the false teachers deny the future literal return of Jesus "in the flesh" in the name of a hyperrealized eschatology, which the Elder rejects, reasserting the reality of a literal second coming (so, e.g., Strecker, *Johannine Letters*, 232–41). But the syntax can readily be understood as referring not to the future parousia, but to the incarnation, as clearly in 1 John 4:2 (cf. John 1:9; 3:31; 6:14; 11:27). The NRSV and other English translations thus follow the majority interpretation, which understands the error of the false teachers to be a docetic Christology rather than a defective eschatology.

but as a threat to the faith as such. The appearance of such false teachers is an eschatological event—they represent the antichrist who was to appear just before the end (1 John 2:18; 4:3; 2 Thess 2:1–12; Jude 4–19; 2 Pet 2:1–3:10). Here we see a combination of theological motifs at work in the Johannine school: traditional futuristic eschatology is affirmed, while being demythologized at the same time. The antichrist will appear before the end—but not as a mythological figure; the harmless-looking progressive teachers already represent the antichrist.

12–13 Conclusion

The repeated "you" is plural. The Elder plans to visit the church and present his teaching personally. The letter itself is only a stopgap. Despite the serious threat of the false teachers, the letter communicates the eschatological joy and close ties that bind together the members of the Johannine churches. The sister congregation sends greetings too; the Elder does not merely write in his own authority, but represents the wider church.

26.3 Interpreting 3 John

26.3.1 Structure

Like 2 John, 3 John follows the conventional format of a Hellenistic letter. The usual greeting becomes a wish for good health, and the thanksgiving a joyful response to the report of Gaius' persistence in the truth.

1–2	Greeting
3–4	Thanksgiving
5–12	Body
5–8	The Itinerant "Brothers"
9–10	Challenge by Diotrephes
11–12	Recommendation of Demetrius
13–15	Conclusion

26.3.2 Exegetical-Theological Précis

1–2 Greeting

Though addressed to an individual, the letter is churchly. The letter greets others besides Gaius (v. 15), and deals with a community issue; it is not merely a personal letter to Gaius. That it came to be accepted as a church letter is clear from its preservation and eventual inclusion in the canon, and testifies to the stature of the Elder in the Johannine community. Gaius is a common Gentile name; the recipient is apparently an influential member of a congregation near that in which Diotrephes is the leader (v. 9), likely the owner of the house in which a congregation meets.

3–4 Thanksgiving

The repeated references to "truth" and "love" are not general abstract virtues, but designations for how the various parties in the dispute relate to the Elder's program. "My children" does not portray the aged writer condescendingly addressing a younger generation, but means "fellow church members who acknowledge my leadership." See John 1:12 and 13:33 for "children" as a designation in the Johannine school for "church members."

5–12 Body

5–8 *The Itinerant "Brothers"*

The Elder has sent out missionaries who represent his understanding of authentic theology. Like the missionaries of the earlier Q community, these itinerants are dependent on the hospitality of local congregations (see Exc. 3.5). They accept "no support from non-believers" (literally "from the Gentiles"), indicating that the Johannine churches, themselves predominately ethnic Gentiles, identify themselves as the continuing biblical people of God and contrast non-Christians (not merely non-Jews) as "Gentiles." The situation is analogous to the addressees of 1 Peter, some of whom are also in

Asia (see above on 1 Peter, esp. 2:9, 12; 4:3). A congregation in Gaius's neighborhood has rejected the Elder's missionaries, but Gaius has received them. For this he has been commended before the church.

9–10 ***Challenge by Diotrephes***

The Elder's letter to the church is probably our 2 John. Diotrephes is a church leader, a rival of the Elder, perhaps a budding monarchial bishop, who refuses to accept the Elder's representatives and excommunicates those who do receive them.

11–12 ***Recommendation of Demetrius***

Demetrius is a representative of the Elder's program he wants to commend to the churches. That he is recommended by "all," by the "we" of the Johannine school, and by "the truth itself" shows that this is not merely a personal dispute, but the clash of two differing understandings of the nature of the Christian faith. That 3 John was preserved and canonized indicates that the group represented by the Elder, Gaius, and Demetrius prevailed, that is, became part of the emerging protocatholic church that eventually became mainstream Christianity.[9]

13–15 Conclusion

The Johannine Christians refer to themselves as the community of friends of Jesus (cf. John 15:13–15).

9. This is the majority interpretation. The alternative is that Diotrephes represents the emerging orthodoxy of the protocatholic monarchial episcopate, who considered the theology represented by the Elder and the Gospel of John to be heretical, i.e., Gnostic and docetic (so Ernst Käsemann, *The Testament of Jesus: A Study of the Gospel of John in the Light of Chapter 17*, NTL [London: SCM Press, 1968]; and "Ketzer und Zeuge," in *Exegetische Versuche und Besinnungen*, ed. Ernst Käsemann [Göttingen: Vandenhoeck & Ruprecht, 1960]), 168–87.

26.4 Interpreting 1 John

26.4.1 Genre

Although 1 John has no formal marks of the typical letter, the document is not a tract dressed up as a letter, but shares some of the communicative features of Paul's letters that were read in the churches of Asia. It is not an essay, but addresses a specific situation and speaks to its hearer-readers in the second person. The document was probably circulated in the Johannine churches and assumed the place typically allotted to Paul's letters in the worship and instruction of the Pauline churches. While not formally a letter, 1 John came to function as a letter, then as quasi-Scripture, and was finally accepted into the canon as a letter of John, apostle and Beloved Disciple.

26.4.2 Addressees

Unlike 2 and 3 John, addressed respectively to a specific house church and to an individual congregational leader, 1 John is addressed more generally to "you who believe in the name of the Son of God." It is not addressed to outsiders, either to unbelievers as an evangelistic tract or to schismatic former members in order to win them back. But neither is the letter a "Catholic Epistle" addressed to the whole church. The composition addresses specific issues within the Johannine community, the network of congregations in Asia associated with the Johannine school and open to its leadership.

26.4.3 Structure

Somewhat like Proverbs in the Old Testament and James in the New, the contents of 1 John are not arranged into a clearly recognizable outline. A number of integrated subunits can be detected, but the overall pattern remains obscure, and there is no single line of argument that holds the composition together.

The following outline adapted from Schnelle[10] facilitates a coherent reading of 1 John in line with the above reflections, without claiming it has discovered "the" outline intended by the author.

1:1–4	Prologue: The Word of Life
1:5–2:17	Parenesis: Fellowship with God, Its Blessings and Hazards
2:18–27	Doctrinal Exposition: The Antichrists' Denial that the Christ Is Jesus
2:28–3:24	Parenesis: Coming of the Lord and Keeping the Commandments
4:1–6	Doctrinal Exposition: Distinguishing Truth from Error
4:7–5:4	Parenesis: God's Love, Love for Brothers and Sisters of the Community
5:5–12	Doctrinal Exposition: The Testimony of Water, Blood, and Spirit
5:13–21	Epilogue: Eternal Life and Its Hazards

26.4.4 Exegetical-Theological Précis

1:1–4 Prologue: The Word of Life

The opening words presuppose familiarity with a tradition common to both author and hearer-readers, and reflect an ongoing theological dialogue within the Johannine community. The prologue in 1 John is reminiscent of the Gospel prologue (John 1:1–18), but key words are used in different senses. Thus, for example, ἀρχή (*archē*, beginning) in John 1:1 refers to creation, the beginning of the world, but in 1 John 1:1 the same term refers to the time of Jesus and the origins of the Johannine community. There are no signs of direct literary dependence on the written Gospel of John. Both epistle and Gospel draw from the common Johannine tradition and formulate it in their own ways.

The distinctive "ecclesial we" of the Johannine writings is used in two senses. (1) It sometimes includes the whole Johannine community and the universal community of believers. It contrasts with "they," the unbelieving outsiders or deviants who have left the community, and represents the line between church and world. (2) At other times, it represents the Johannine school, the inner group of teachers and tradition bearers within the wider community, and contrasts with "you," the readers, the members of the Johannine community. This is the usage in 1:1–4; the teachers want to instruct the community, so that readers may have fellowship/ koinonia with the teachers by appropriating and sharing the same tradition. In neither case is "we" merely an editorial "we"; it refers to an actual group. The "we" of 1:1–4, who claim to have seen, heard, and touched the Word of Life, is not a claim that the author(s) were first-generation eyewitnesses, or that 1 John was written by the apostle John. This ecclesial we expresses the claim of the whole Christian community and includes, in its beginnings, those who actually saw and heard the incarnate, flesh-and-blood Christ. This claim continued to be expressed by later generations:

— About 150 CE: "with our own eyes we beheld things that have happened and are happening" (Justin Martyr, *1 Apol.* 30).

— About 180 CE: " we would not be able to know, unless we had seen our master and had heard his voice with our own ears" (Irenaeus, *Against Heresies* 5.1.1).

This ecclesial we expresses the self-understanding of belonging to the Christian community, which rests on historical beginnings. It is a continuation of the awareness of belonging to the biblical people of God, which

10. Schnelle, *Johannesbriefe*, 57.

celebrates God's mighty acts that called the community into being.[11]

1:5–2:17 Parenesis: Fellowship with God, Its Blessings and Hazards

1:5–2:6 Sinless Perfectionism and the Example of Jesus

Why begin with the issue of sin and perfectionism? Some in the Johannine community had understood that since their new being was from God and they did not belong to this world, they were sinless beings and no longer needed to take ethical standards seriously. This was probably related to the docetic Christology that did not take Jesus' humanity seriously: the Christ was understood to be a transcendent spiritual being who never really became a part of this world. If the saving event happened without actually involving a truly human being, then believers can assume a kind of spirituality that need not take their own bodily actions seriously (see 3:8–10).

The author responds: The tangibility of the incarnation calls for a faith that is visible in this-worldly deeds (2:7–11). Believers are not innocent spiritual beings, but forgiven sinners. Faith in Christ involves keeping his commands, and "walking as he walked" (2:6), that is, adopting the way Jesus lived as the believer's own pattern of life. The author refers not to particular acts of Jesus that are to be imitated, but to a life lived in union with God and determined by God's love. Such a view affirms that the life of Jesus is important for faith, that how Jesus lived is important for how believers must live.

"My children" (2:1, τεκνία, *teknia*; diminutive "little children" [NRSV and others]) is conventional, part of the Johannine sociolect, and means simply "my children" (so NIV, TNIV, REB, NAB). It is the typical address to church members within the Johannine community, also attributed to Jesus addressing the disciples (John 13:33; 1 John 2:1, 12, 14, 28; 3:7, 18; 4:4; 5:21; cf. the synonym παιδία, *paidia*, John 21:5; 1 John 2:14, 18). It is not merely a term of endearment, but reflects the Johannine theology that believers are God's children, are "of God" because they have been born of God and belong to another realm of reality than nonbelievers: they are not only "called" God's children but "that is what we *are*" (3:1; cf. John 1:12–13; 3:3–5; 1 John 2:29–3:1).

2:18–27 Doctrinal Exposition: The Antichrists' Denial that the Christ Is Jesus

The readers have heard that "antichrist" is coming. This word is found elsewhere in the New Testament only in 2 John 7; it was probably coined by the authors themselves as their term for the personified power of evil that, in apocalyptic thought, was to appear just before the end. Readers have probably heard about this figure in Revelation, which circulated in the churches of Asia at the end of the first century, though the term "antichrist" is not found in Revelation. The Johannine school demythologizes the figure. The expectation is real, but it is fulfilled not by some mythological beast or satanic world ruler. The presence of the false teachers already signals the nearness of the end.

Here we learn something new, not present in the earlier reference in 2 John 7–11. There, false teachers were loose in the world, and the churches are warned against them. Here, we learn that they are not a threat from outside the community, but formerly belonged within the Johannine churches (2:19). They have either left or been expelled, and the Johannine community has experienced a traumatic schism. They believe in the divine Christ, but deny that "the Christ is *Jesus*" (see on John 20:30–31).

The Johannine teachers instruct the community that it does not need the "advanced"

11. See Gen 17:10–11; Deut 5:1–5; 26:5–9; Num 26:4. At Passover, Jewish people confess their faith, "We were the slaves of Pharaoh" (cited in Neusner, *Way of Torah*, 88). Cf. Mishnah Pesachim 10.5, "In every generation a man must regard himself as if he came forth himself out of Egypt."

teaching of the schismatic teachers, because *all* in the community have been "anointed," that is, all have received the Spirit that guides the community as a whole, the Paraclete that leads it into all truth (see below, on John 13–17). This refers to baptism, which confers the Spirit, and which has been received by all Christians. The later practice of anointing with oil at the time of baptism may have already been practiced in the Johannine community. This anointing received by all signifies and makes real the presence of the Spirit in the community, and teaches what Christians need to know.

2:28–3:24 Parenesis: Coming of the Lord and Keeping the Commandments

3:8–10 Indicative and Imperative

The author affirms the reality that believers are already children of God, but rejects understanding it in a passive, ontological sense: "therefore we are sinless beings." He interprets it as a challenge: "therefore we must not continue to sin" (see Rom 6). As in the case of Paul, the indicative is not denied or compromised, but becomes an imperative.

"Now/not yet" (3:2): From its earliest days the Johannine community believed that the Christ had already come and was still to come. Different teachers made different emphases within this overall pattern, but realized and futuristic eschatology existed alongside each other in the community's understanding of salvation history. (Cf. the Gospel's "the hour is coming *and* now is" [John 4:23]). As for Paul, there is an eschatological reservation: believers *are* already God's children, but not yet what they *will be* at the parousia, when they become God's children in a way that cannot now be imagined or expressed. When they see Christ's glory at the parousia, they will themselves then share in it (John 14:2–3; 17:24; cf. 2 Cor 3:18).

3:11–24 "Believe . . . Love . . . Truth"

Here and elsewhere, a historical understanding of the New Testament requires that such exhortations not be reduced to general pious moralisms, but that with historical imagination the modern reader perceive their thrust and impact in the situation of the Johannine churches. In the author's situation, some members of the community had suffered economic and physical deprivation, and some had been killed as a result of their confession of faith. Some within the synagogue had apparently collaborated with Roman officials to cause Christians to be put to death (cf. Rev 2:9, 13; 3:9). The author calls on members of the community who have been spared to help by sharing their resources with needy Christians. Thus not hating, not murdering, but "laying down our lives for one another" are specific calls to respond to the needs of fellow Christians who suffer for the faith.

4:1–6 Doctrinal Exposition: Distinguishing Truth from Error

Those who belong to God and the truth can be identified by deed, not creed. Yet the Johannine community was faced with the problem of distinguishing authentic teaching from false, misleading doctrine. Alongside the test of whether the opposition manifests the love of God—a difficult criterion to apply, in any case—the Johannine teachers applied a creedal test: do the opposing teachers, who also claim to be led by the Spirit, confess that "Jesus Christ has come in the flesh" (4:2). The opposite is simply "not confessing *Jesus*" (4:3). NRSV and most English translations read "do not confess" (μὴ ὁμολογεῖ, *mē homologei*). A few translations and numerous scholars regard the variant reading found in some manuscripts (λύει, *luei*, lit. "loose," "dissolve") as original, and translate "dispense with," "omit," "dissolve." The false teachers glorify the spiritual Christ, but dispense with the human Jesus. In either case, the false teachers disregard the incarnation, and reject the human being Jesus as an essential figure in God's saving act.[12]

12. Numerous interpreters relate this to the Christology advocated by the Gnostic teacher Cerinthus, who

4:7–5:4 Parenesis: God's Love, Love for Brothers and Sisters of the Community

The strict us/them line that separates those "of God" and those "of the devil" lies in uneasy tension with the centrality of the love command. For the Johannine teachers, love (ἀγάπη, *agapē*) is not an idea, feeling, principle, or ideal, but an action, a reflex of God's act in Christ. Love is defined by God's act in sending Christ, and by Christ's voluntarily laying down his life for others (3:16–18; cf. John 3:16). Such love is the foundational command of the Johannine community, received from the very beginning (1 John 2:4–5; 3:23; 5:3; 2 John 6; John 15:10).

Perceptive readers through the centuries have been bothered by 1 John's seeming to limit love to the brothers and sisters of the Christian community; the Johannine version of the double command is not love God and neighbor (cf. Mark 12:28–34 and par.), but love God and the "brother," that is, the fellow church member. The tension with the Synoptic (and Pauline) formation remains, but three factors mitigate it somewhat: (1) 1 John is not writing philosophical ethics, but calling for Christians to care for and give concrete help to their suffering fellow believers. (2) The author's dualism conditions him to think in insider/outsider categories, those who are of God and those who are of the devil. (3) The author's dualism is transcended by his faith in the one God who is the Creator of all, and who loves the world, not just the insiders of the Christian community. God's love in the Johannine writings is not ultimately exclusive or sectarian, because it reflects the love of *God*, who loves the *world* (not just the church).[13]

5:5–12 Doctrinal Exposition: The Testimony of Water, Blood, and Spirit

The author returns to the basic creedal affirmation: God's love is manifest not merely in the spiritual realm of the heavenly world or the psychological realm of individual hearts, but in the world of humanity of which the human being Jesus was a participant. Christ came not only "by water" (empowered by the divine Spirit that came upon him at baptism), but "by blood" (he died a truly human death on the cross). The reality of this saving event is made real to believers in the sacraments of baptism and Eucharist.[14]

5:13–21 Epilogue: Eternal Life and Its Hazards

Johannine Christians had heard charges that they were idolaters, that they had violated the first commandment, that they worshiped Jesus as a second god (see John 5:18). In their own minds, they turn the accusation back on their accusers: *this* one is the true revelation of the one God. All else is idolatry.

26.5 For Further Reading

Interpreting Revelation

Aune, David. *Revelation*. WBC. 3 vols. Dallas: Word Books, 1997–1998.

Bauckham, Richard. *The Theology of the Book of Revelation*. Cambridge: Cambridge University Press, 1993.

Beale, G. K. *The Book of Revelation*. New International Greek New Testament Commentary. Grand Rapids: Eerdmans, 1999.

Blount, Brian K. *Revelation*. NTL. Louisville, KY: Westminster John Knox Press, 2009.

argued that the divine Spirit came on the man Jesus at his baptism, but left him before the crucifixion. The man Jesus was crucified, not the divine Christ (cf. Irenaeus, *Against Heresies* 1.26.1; Hippolytus, *Refutation* 7.33.1–2; Epiphanius, *Panarion* 28.1.7).

13. See the extensive discussion in Robinson, *Priority of John*, "The Charge of Introversion," 329–39.

14. At 1 John 5:7, the Textus Receptus followed by the seventeenth-century KJV and Douay versions reads, "For there are three that bear record in heaven, the Father, the Word, and the Holy Ghost: and these three are one." These words are a later gloss that appears in no ancient Greek manuscript of the New Testament.

Boring, M. Eugene. *Revelation*. Interpretation. Louisville, KY: Westminster John Knox Press, 1989.

Caird, G. B. *A Commentary on the Revelation of St. John the Divine*. HNTC. New York & Evanston: Harper & Row, 1966.

Collins, Adela Yarbro. *Crisis and Catharsis: The Power of the Apocalypse*. Philadelphia: Westminster Press, 1984.

Koester, Craig R. *Revelation and the End of All Things*. Grand Rapids: Eerdmans, 2001.

Mounce, Robert H. *The Book of Revelation*. Rev. ed. NICNT. Grand Rapids: Eerdmans, 1997.

Reddish, Mitchell G. *Revelation*. Smyth & Helwys Bible Commentary. Macon, GA: Smyth & Helwys, 2001.

Schüssler Fiorenza, E. *The Book of Revelation: Justice and Judgment*. Philadelphia: Fortress Press, 1985.

Interpreting 1, 2, and 3 John

Brown, R. E. *The Epistles of John*. Anchor Bible. New York: Doubleday, 1982.

Lieu, Judith. *1, 2, 3 John: A Commentary*. NTL. Louisville, KY: Westminster John Knox Press, 2008.

Painter, John. *1, 2, and 3 John*. Sacra pagina 18. Collegeville, MN: Liturgical Press, 2002.

Strecker, G. *The Johannine Letters: A Commentary on 1, 2, and 3 John*. Hermeneia. Minneapolis: Fortress Press, 1996.

27

Interpreting the Gospel of John

27.1 Distinctiveness of the Gospel of John

27.1.1 Structure and Story Line

The Johannine narrative has a fundamentally different shape than the Synoptic story line based on Mark.

— In the Synoptics, the story is centered in Galilee, with the seaside town Capernaum the hub of Jesus' work, and only at the end of the narrative does he make a single trip to Jerusalem and death. In John, the story is centered in Judea or southern Transjordan, Jesus is often in Jerusalem, venturing only minimally into Galilee (Cana, chaps. 2 and 4; around the Sea of Galilee, chap. 6). After 7:10, Jesus is never in Galilee again. Although Jesus is "from Nazareth," the Fourth Gospel never narrates any scene located there.

— Jesus' ministry in the Synoptics includes only one Jewish festival, the Passover at which he is killed. In John, Jesus attends the Passover twice (a third is mentioned in 6:4), as well as the festival of Booths (Tabernacles), Dedication (Hanukkah), and the unnamed feast of 5:1.

— Though portraying a longer period for the ministry, John narrates fewer events, elaborating the incidents and speeches he selects into richer, more lengthy scenes.

— In the Synoptics, Jesus does not begin his ministry until John the Baptist is arrested and off the scene (Mark 1:14–15). In John, John and Jesus have overlapping, parallel, even competitive ministries (John 3:22–23; 4:1–3).

— In the Synoptics, the cleansing of the temple occurs at the end of a one-year ministry; in John, at the beginning of a ministry that lasts two and a half years.

— In the Synoptics, Jesus disputes with Pharisees, Sadducees, Herodians, and scribes. The Johannine narrative contains many Pharisees and speaks often of "the Jews," but has no scribes, Sadducees, or Herodians.

— In the Synoptics, Jesus teaches his disciples throughout the Galilean ministry, in brief parables and aphoristic sayings, but in John Jesus never teaches his disciples until the last evening before the crucifixion, compressing all his instruction to "his own" into the Farewell Discourses of the Last Supper. John narrates two and a half years in the first twelve chapters, then takes five chapters for the last evening of Jesus' life. There is no "last week" as in the Synoptics, but only a "last night." One-third of the book is devoted to the last twenty-four hours.

— In the Synoptics, Jesus is tested by Satan at the beginning of his ministry, is transfigured before his disciples in a central scene, and agonizes in Gethsemane at the end. None of these scenes are present in the Fourth Gospel; in fact, 90 percent of John's narrative has no parallel in the other Gospels.

— In both the Synoptics and John, Jesus celebrates a last meal with his disciples on Thursday evening and is crucified the next day. In the Synoptics, this Last Supper is a Passover meal; in John, the final events of Jesus' life occur one day earlier. The Last Supper is not a Passover, but the next day Jesus the Lamb of God dies as the Passover lambs are being slain.

27.1.2 Christology: John's Distinctive Picture of Jesus

There is ultimately a deep unity between the theology of John and that of Paul, the Synoptics, and the other New Testament writers. But prior to any too-easy harmonizing talk of unity, the distinctiveness of each must be seen.[1] In addition to the different shape of the story line discussed above, we may point out these marks of the Fourth Gospel:

— No genealogy provides Jesus with a Davidic ancestry; Jesus' opponents mistakenly believe that the Messiah is to be Davidic (7:42). Not David, but Moses is the primary biblical model for the Messiah, with whom Jesus is both compared and contrasted: Moses ascends and descends, relays what he has heard from God, but—in contrast to Jesus—Moses never saw God (1:17–18).

— Jesus is from God, the Son of God, the preexistent One who has come down from heaven, but he is also from Nazareth, the son of Mary and Joseph. This simultaneous paradox is not explained in terms of a miraculous birth.

— Jesus' teaching is not about the kingdom of God, but about himself. During his ministry the Johannine Jesus refers to the kingdom of God only once, in the private nighttime meeting with Nicodemus (3:3, 5). Jesus' public teaching is about his relation to God and his role as God's revealer. Jesus does not dispute with Jewish teachers about interpretation of the Torah, but about his equality with God. He publicly calls for faith in himself as Messiah and Son of God. There is no messianic secret in the Markan sense.

— There are no parables. The brief stories and sayings of the Synoptics are replaced by long symbolic monologues. In the Synoptics, Jesus tells provocative secular stories about other people—the Prodigal Son, the Good Samaritan, the Woman Who Lost and Found the Coin, the Rich Man and Lazarus—as a way of talking about the kingdom of God. In the Fourth Gospel Jesus tells no stories; the subject of all his discourses is himself. Whereas the kingdom of God in the Synoptics is like leaven, in John, Jesus himself is the bread of life. Whereas the Synoptic Jesus speaks of the shepherd and lost sheep, in John, Jesus himself is the Good Shepherd. Whereas the Synoptic Jesus tells a parable in which the kingdom is like a vineyard that will be handed over to others, the Johannine Jesus is himself the vine.

— There are no exorcisms. God's defeat of Satan in the Christ event is conceived in cosmic terms (12:31), not as casting demons out of individuals.

— There is no citation of the "Great Commandment" from the Bible; instead, Jesus gives his own "New Commandment" (13:34).

— Both Jesus' deity and humanity are presented in emphatic, exaggerated ways. On the one hand, Jesus is often portrayed as not subject to human limitations. He does not ask questions for information (1:48–49; 6:5, 64, 71; 2:25; but cf. 11:34). He acts only unilaterally,

1. This is the value of J. A. T. Robinson's last work. Despite the idiosyncratic nature of his historical theories, Robinson saw both the distinctiveness and unity of New Testament theology. See especially his discussion of Johannine Christology, Robinson, *Priority of John*, 296–397.

not in response to requests. There is no agonized Gethsemane prayer (cf. 12:27–33). Jesus is sovereignly in charge of his own arrest, trial, and death. Miracles are elaborated and magnified: he transforms 120 gallons of water into top-quality wine (2:6–9); the royal officer's son is healed at the exact hour Jesus said (4:52), and from a distance; the man healed at the pool Beth-zatha had been sick thirty-eight years (5:5); the healed blind man had been born blind (9:2); Lazarus had been dead four days (11:17). Sick people are not healed as the expression of compassion (all the other sick people at the pool in 5:2–8 are ignored), but to show God's/Jesus' glory (2:11, 20:30–31, blind man, Lazarus). The signs are for Jesus' sake, not for the sake of the person healed. They are transparent to the divine glory, as a revelation that Jesus belongs to the world of God. On the other hand, Jesus' humanity is pointedly displayed: he gets tired, thirsts, weeps, bleeds, dies.

— Jesus as champion and friend of the lower classes and oppressed is gone. In the Fourth Gospel, there are no poor people, no wicked rich, no publicans, no sinners (7:53–8:11 is a later addition), no shepherds, no fishermen (except in chap. 21 appendix), no widows, no children, no women fellow travelers, no unclean demoniacs, no repentance or forgiveness of sins, no lepers, no prostitutes, no "other criminals" crucified with Jesus. In general, the Johannine Jesus is portrayed as without compassion, as divinely aloof. God's compassion for the world is manifest in the Christ event itself, not in the individual stories in which this ultimate act of God is symbolically portrayed.

27.1.3 Literary Perspectives and Techniques

Genre

The Fourth Gospel shares with the other canonical Gospels the distinctive generic characteristics of the Gospel form devised by Mark: composed from kerygmatic traditional units, combining kenosis and epiphany Christology, narrating the story of Jesus as the definitive segment of salvation history that stretches from creation to eschaton, fusion of perspectives that combines the Jesus "back there" in history, "up there" in the transcendent world, and "out there" in the world of the author and readers (see above, §20.1). Did John adopt and adapt the genre from Mark, or develop it independently? Some have argued that the christological dynamics inherent in the gospel message generated the Gospel form whenever Christian authors attempted to present the Christian kerygma as a narrative of Jesus' life, so John is the "second inventor" of the Gospel genre.[2] It is unlikely, however, that John was unaware of the other Gospels. A more plausible argument is that John has some familiarity with one or more of the Synoptics and shares some of their traditions, but does not use any of them as sources in the way, for example, that Matthew uses Mark. He is aware of Mark the way that 2 Peter is aware of 1 Peter, the Pauline letters, and the epistolary genre, but does not use any of them as sources. John adopts the Gospel genre from Mark, but for the most part fills the Markan form with Johannine content.

Language, Vocabulary, Style

The profound Johannine theology is expressed in a simple style and lean vocabulary. John has the smallest vocabulary of any of the Gospel writers, using only 1,011 different words in a document of 15,416 words (Mark 1,345/11,242; Matthew 1,691/18,305; Luke

2. So, e.g., Jürgen Becker, who argues John does not know the Synoptics, but has the Signs Source and the Passion Source; John creates the Gospel genre independently. "John is thus a second Mark" (Jürgen Becker, *Das Evangelium nach Johannes*, 2 vols., ÖTK 4/1 and 4/2 [Gütersloh: Gütersloher Verlagshaus, 1979, 1981], 1:40). So also Robert T. Fortna, *The Fourth Gospel and Its Predecessor: From Narrative Source to Present Gospel* (Philadelphia: Fortress Press, 1988), 205–16.

2,055/19,428).[3] Some key words that occur much more often in John than all the Synoptics together: ἀγαπάω / ἀγάπη (*agapaō/ agapē*, love, noun and verb), forty-four times John, twenty-eight times Synoptics; ἀλήθεια, ἀληθής, ἀληθινός, ἀληθῶς (*alētheia, alēthēs, alēthinos, alēthōs*, truth, true, truly), forty-six times John, twenty times Synoptics; γινώσκω (*ginōskō*, know), fifty-seven times John, sixty times Synoptics; ἀμὴν ἀμήν (*amēn amēn*, "truly truly"), twenty-five times John, not at all in the Synoptics; γραφή (*graphē*, scripture, writing [singular]), eleven times John, only twice in the Synoptics; ἐγώ ειμι (*egō eimi*, I am), twenty-four times John, five times Matthew, three times Mark, four times Luke; the series of "I am" sayings occurs only in John; ἐργάζομαι, ἔργον (*ergazomai, ergon*, work as noun and verb), thirty-five times in John, always positively, in the sense of "deeds," never in the Pauline sense of "works of the Law"; Ἰουδαῖοι (*Ioudaioi*, Jews), sixty-seven times John, in Synoptics only sixteen times, mostly in the phrase "king of the Jews"; κόσμος (*kosmos*, world), seventy-eight times John, only thirteen times Synoptics; κρίνω (*krinō*, judge, verb), nineteen times John, twelve times Synoptics; μαρτυρέω, μαρτυρία, μαρτύριον (*martureō, marturia, marturion*, witness, testify, testimony, noun and verb), forty-seven times John, fifteen times Synoptics; μένω (*menō*, abide), forty times John, twelve times Synoptics; πατήρ (*patēr*, Father, of God), one hundred eighteen times John, sixty times Synoptics; ὁ πέμψας με (*ho pempsas me*, the one who sent me), twenty-six times John, always related to God or Jesus; not at all in the Synoptics; τίθημι ψυχήν (*tithēmi psychēn*, I lay down my life), six times John, not at all in the Synoptics; φανερόω (*phaneroō*, reveal, manifest), nine times John, only once in Synoptics; φιλέω (*phileō*, love), thirteen times John, eight times Synoptics; φῶς (*phōs*, light), twenty-three times John, fifteen times Synoptics.

Characteristic items of Johannine style include (1) *parataxis*, the linking of sentences and clauses by καί (*kai*, and) rather than by subordinate clauses or participial constructions; (2) the frequent (200 times) use of οὖν (*oun*, usually translated "therefore") as a simple connective, hardly used at all in this sense in the Synoptics, and only once in the Letters (3 John 8, in the normal sense of "therefore"); (3) the demonstrative pronoun ἐκεῖνος (*ekeinos*, that one) used in the sense of the simple pronoun "he" forty-four times in John, six times in 1 John, only twenty-one times elsewhere in the New Testament (in proportion to the size of the books, this usage is nineteen times more frequent in John than in the rest of the New Testament); (4) the possessive pronoun ἐμός, *emos*, thirty-nine times, more than the rest of the New Testament put together.

Double Entendres, Inept Questions, and Misunderstanding

The evangelist sometimes intentionally uses a word that can be understood in two different ways. The character in the narrative takes it at one level, the plane of earthly, this-worldly "fleshly" reality, but the Johannine Jesus intends it in the other way, pointing to the transcendent divine level of reality. Thus the necessity of being born ἄνωθεν (*anōthen*, 3:3) can mean "from above" (as in John 3:31) or "again" (as in Gal 4:9). Jesus intends it in the former sense, Nicodemus takes it in the latter sense (John 3:3–10). So also in the same passage, ὑψόω (*hypsoō*) means "lift up," but can be understood in the sense of "crucify," being lifted up on the cross, or "exalt," being taken to heaven. Jesus' opponents suppose that *they* are *crucifying* him, but the same act is *God's exalting* Jesus to heaven. There are numerous such cases in which the pre-Easter characters in the story understand Jesus' words at one level, when the narrator, with a knowing look and stage wink at the post-Easter reader, intends them in the

3. The figures are from Morgenthaler, *Statistik*, 164, derived from Nestle, 21st ed. Statistics based on later editions of the N.-A. text vary very slightly.

other way (see 2:19–22; 3:3–4; 4:10–11, 31–34; 6:41–42, 51–52; 7:33–35; 8:18–19, 21–22, 31–33, 51–53, 56–58; 11:11–12, 23–27; 13:7–9; 14:5, 8, 22). This is an aspect of John's version of the messianic secret.

Irony

Another means by which the author invites the reader to share the narrator's point of view is the use of irony. Characters in the story make significant statements that are true at a far deeper level than the speaker realizes, or true even in the opposite sense. Caiaphas, seeing the potentially explosive effect of Jesus' preaching and the Roman reprisal, expresses the this-worldly realism of political expediency, that Jesus must die, for it is better for one person to die for the people than that the whole nation be destroyed (John 11:50). He does not realize he is voicing the profound truth of the gospel, that Jesus does indeed die for the people. The irony is deepened in that narrator and readers look back on the 66–70 war in which the Romans destroyed the nation, even though Caiaphas and Pilate had tried to save the status quo by collaborating in putting Jesus to death.

Another instance: in Jesus' trial before Pilate, the governor tries to appease the Jews by having him beaten and mocked, then brings him out, bloody and wearing the crown of thorns and purple robe, scarcely a threat to anyone, a spectacle hardly worth bothering with, and declares, "Here is the man" (traditionally, "Behold the man"). Pilate's words, at a deeper level than he could know, mean to narrator and reader: Jesus is true man, the one truly human being. This is the Johannine counterpart to the Adam Christology of Romans 5. In such statements, the narrator reaches out to include the reader in the Johannine "we" of which the characters in the story are unaware.

Symbolism

The evangelist knows that the transcendent reality of God's act in Christ cannot be expressed in literal language. He is a master of symbolic communication. Drawing on a network of metaphorical and symbolic language, he presents the significance of the Christ event in universal images enriched by biblical and Jewish tradition, or biblical and Jewish images expanded to have universal meaning. Not only does John present Jesus in paradigmatic christological symbols in terms of the life-giving images of water, bread, light, and life; he is the true vine, the true temple, the true way. In all such statements, "true" (ἀληθινός, *alēthinos*) means ultimately real as opposed to unreal, belonging to the divine world of reality instead of the relative, transient world. Major symbols such as light are expressed in multifaceted dimensions of the narrative, so that John's references to lamps, fires, torches, day and night, morning, seeing, blindness and healing, all communicate the root metaphor, the depth symbol: Jesus is the light of the world who allows human beings to see things as they truly are.

The whole christological drama is narrated as a series of *signs*, which point beyond themselves to the ultimate reality being enacted. Jesus' actions are symbolic: changing water to wine and cleansing the temple point to the transformation and fulfillment of religious ritual in the Christ event; the healing of the man born blind points to the ultimate giving of sight. When Mary anoints Jesus' feet, it is a symbolic act; when Jesus washes the disciples' feet, there is a pointer to the whole saving event of God's act in Christ. Those who see only bread and fish at the feeding of the multitudes miss the reality that can be experienced only by participation in the body and blood of Jesus (6:35–58).

Characters and Characterization

The main character. The character of Jesus is fixed from the beginning; like God, he does not change. He is the man from heaven who has received his commission from the Father, is a stranger in the world below, and carries out his mission without struggle, wavering, or gaining new insights. Like God, the Johannine

Jesus cannot learn new information, struggle with decisions, or be surprised. John's presentation of Jesus is determined by his theology, not his interest in presenting Jesus as an attractive character with whom the reader can identity.

The minor characters. John sometimes manifests more interest in the minor characters than do the Synoptics, where the demonized, paralyzed, leprous, and sick typically appear with their problems, are healed, and disappear from the narrative without a trace. John shows more interest in what happened to them and uses minor story lines to develop his theological point. He traces the story of the man born blind through several stages of increasing faith and boldness (chap. 9). The story of Nicodemus is continued through scenes in three different chapters (chaps. 3, 7, 19). Nonetheless, by such "character development" John does not approach the role of the novelist, and his portrayal of characters in the narrative still functions to make theological points. This is true even of those figures who receive relatively more space in the narrative, including Peter (the most complex character), Thomas, Lazarus, Mary, Martha, Judas, Caiaphas, and Pilate. Of these, the prime example of a narrative role expressing a theological function is "the disciple whom Jesus loved."

The Beloved Disciple. The Beloved Disciple first appears in the account of the Last Supper at John 13:23, late in the story of what is probably the latest document of the Johannine writings. The evangelist introduces the Beloved Disciple as "one of his disciples, whom Jesus loved" (13:23, not "*the* disciple"). A new character in the story is here identified. The Beloved Disciple does not appear elsewhere—not in 1, 2, or 3 John, in Revelation, or elsewhere in the New Testament. The evangelist is here creating a new role for one of the disciples. All the references to the Beloved Disciple are in the evangelist's additions to the tradition, except 21:18–25, added in the final edition of the book by the redactor. This shows the evangelist did not identify himself as the Beloved Disciple, but regarded him as the guarantor of the Johannine traditions.

— In 13:23–24, the Beloved Disciple's relation to Jesus is described in the same words as those that portray the relation of Jesus to the Father, and those words have an analogous function. As Jesus is the exegete of the Father, so the Beloved Disciple is Jesus' exegete to the other disciples and through them to the world. Jesus gives the revelation to the Beloved Disciple, and Peter must ask him what Jesus has said.

— In 18:15–16, after Jesus' arrest, Peter and "another disciple" approach the court of the high priest. The other disciple is known and admitted, but Peter is detained at the gate. The other disciple vouches for Peter, who then enters the courtyard, where he repeatedly denies Jesus. The "other disciple," of course, never wavers.

— In 19:26–27, the Beloved Disciple is the only one of Jesus' disciples at the cross. Peter and the others disappeared at the scene of Jesus' arrest, where Peter's misunderstanding of Jesus' mission caused him to try to defend Jesus with violence. From the cross, Jesus entrusts his mother to the care of the Beloved Disciple, who takes her to his own home.

— In 19:34–35, this eyewitness disciple witnessed the reality of Jesus' death, the spear thrust that brought blood and water from Jesus' side, and his testimony validates the truth of the Johannine tradition.

— In 20:2, 7–8, the Beloved Disciple and Simon Peter race to the tomb. The Beloved Disciple arrives first, and even though Peter is the first to enter the tomb, the Beloved Disciple is the first to come to faith in the risen Lord.

— In 21:7 in the epilogue, it is again the Beloved Disciple who is the first to recognize the risen Jesus and who tells Peter. Though Peter is then restored and given a kind of primacy, the Beloved Disciple does not need to be restored, but has been following Jesus throughout (21:20).

— In 21:24, the final words of the book, the circle of Johannine writers ("we") validates the Beloved Disciple as the author of the book.

— In retrospect, the reader can see that the teasingly unnamed disciple of 1:35, 40, previously a follower of John the Baptist, was one of the first to become a disciple of Jesus, and was even instrumental in bringing Peter to Jesus.

In all this, the reader becomes aware of a certain competition between the Beloved Disciple and Simon Peter, a competition in which the Beloved Disciple always comes in first (cf. the race to the tomb, 20:2, 7–8). The portrayal of the Beloved Disciple seems to represent the claims of the Johannine community over against developing protocatholic Christianity represented by Peter. Thus, for some interpreters, the Beloved Disciple is entirely a literary figure, the creation of the evangelist, representing the ideal disciple. For others, he represents Gentile Christianity, destined by Jesus to take the place of Jewish Christianity, represented by Peter. For still others, the Beloved Disciple symbolizes prophetic, charismatic leadership over against the institutionalization of ministry. The majority opinion is now that the Beloved Disciple represents an actual historical figure, a real person who was an eyewitness to events in Jesus' ministry to whom the later Johannine community looked back as founder and validating authority. Like Peter, the Beloved Disciple was a historical person who assumed a symbolic role. Beyond that, there is little unanimity. He has been identified with John son of Zebedee, Lazarus, Philip, Nathanael, Thomas, Matthias, Paul, the Benjamin figure of Deuteronomy 33:12, Andrew, John Mark, and the Elder John of Papias.[4] It is probably best to see the Beloved Disciple as a real person, not one of the Twelve, not from Galilee, but Judea. He played a formative role in the early days of the Johannine community, was idealized as a symbolic figure by the evangelist, then finally regarded as the author of the Gospel by the time of the latest edition of the Fourth Gospel.

4. All these possibilities are engagingly explored in R. Alan Culpepper, *John, the Son of Zebedee: The Life of a Legend* (Minneapolis: Fortress Press, 1999).

27.2 Addressees and Purpose

IS THE GOSPEL AN EVANGELISTIC, MISSIONary writing directed to outsiders, or an edifying composition to the Christian community addressing insiders, to deepen and clarify their understanding of the faith? Or is this a false alternative?

The primarily evangelistic purpose has been ably defended. C. H. Dodd argued that the Gospel has in view the educated Gentile outsider, the person acquainted with the religious "higher Hellenism" of the first-century Hellenistic world. The evangelist aims to show that the Christian faith did not represent a narrow Judaism but the universal religion of the incarnate Logos. The author "has in view a non-Christian public to which he wishes to appeal," and is thus reserved about some subjects, such as the sacraments, because he is writing "for a public which included pagans whom he wished to influence towards the Christian faith." Yet very often, Dodd indicates it is "the instructed Christian reader" who understands the book.[5] More recently, D. A. Carson is representative of those who understand the Gospel as directed to non-Christians and has given detailed exegetical support for the view that the Gospel is directed to outsiders who are already acquainted with Judaism but are not Christians, namely, "diaspora Jews and proselytes to Judaism."[6]

It is true enough that the Gospel presupposes a predominately Gentile readership, to whom Jewish customs and terminology must be explained (see the list above, §25.3.2) and that the Gospel has a universalistic perspective that

5. C. H. Dodd, *The Interpretation of the Fourth Gospel* (Cambridge: Cambridge University Press, 1953), 8, 310; 138, 302, 309.

6. Carson, *Gospel according to John*, 87–92. Similar views have been argued by, e.g., J. A. T. Robinson, "The Destination and Purpose of St. John's Gospel," *NTS* 6 (1960). Fortna, *Fourth Gospel and Its Predecessor*, 211–15 and passim, argues the pre-Johannine "Signs Gospel" had the evangelistic purpose of winning over other Jews in the synagogue, but the present form of the Gospel, written after the expulsion of the Johannine Christians from the synagogue, is for the community itself.

looks beyond both synagogue and church to the wider world. It is also true that the concept of the savior figure designated Christ/Messiah is assumed, and that the question is not "Who is Jesus?" but "Who is the Messiah?"; not "Is Jesus the Christ," but "Is the Christ *Jesus?*"[7] The importance of this point has been recognized and ably argued by Carson, but it does not follow from this that the document as a whole is an evangelistic message intended for outsiders. The off-putting description of "the Jews" and "the world" makes this unlikely, as does the assumption that the readers already know much Christian tradition and are struggling with Christian theological issues such as the reinterpretation of eschatology and the understanding and importance of the sacraments.

The Fourth Gospel seems to have been written for the members of the Johannine community to help them deepen and clarify the meaning of their own faith. This does not exclude, however, the evangelistic perspective. The community has a mission: it is called to bear witness to the world, to look beyond its own borders and both win new converts and be agents of uniting the scattered people of God. To be competent witnesses, the community must have a clear understanding of its own faith.

27.3 Unity, Sources, Composition History

A CLOSE READING OF THE GOSPEL PROVIDES several indications that it was written over an extended period and raises the question of sources—where did the author get his information?—and whether the text was all written by the same author. A sample list of some of the data:

— Less than 10 percent of John's text has substantial parallels in the Synoptics (vs., e.g., 95 percent of Mark found in Matthew and/or Luke).

— Of the few places where John and the Synoptics do overlap, there are some striking verbal agreements (e.g., 2:14–17; 6:5–21; 12:3–8).

— The statement that Jesus conducted a successful baptizing ministry (3:22) is corrected: Jesus baptized no one personally; it was his disciples (4:2).

— At the end of chapter 5, Jesus is in Jerusalem, but at 6:1, with no transition, he is in Galilee. Chapter 7 follows well after 5. Thus, at some stage of composition, the narrative seems to have followed the order of chaps. 4→6→5→7.

— In 11:2, the event of Mary anointing Jesus is referred to, which is not narrated until 12:3.

— Jesus' symbolic act of washing the disciples' feet receives two separate interpretations: as a symbol of the washing that happens in Jesus' death, with an oblique reference to baptism (13:2–11), and as a symbol of humble service (13:12–20).

— The Farewell Discourse comes to a proper ending at 14:31, as Jesus says, "Rise, let us be on our way." The discourse then continues for three more chapters, and they do not leave until 18:1. Some of chapters 15–16 repeats chapter 14, as though two versions of the same discourse once circulated separately. Furthermore, in 16:5 Jesus complains that no one asks him where he is going, though in the present form of the text they have just done so in 13:36 (see also 14:5).

— Some sayings material seems to float above the narrative, unconnected to the scene in which it is presently located (e.g., 3:31–36; 12:44–50).

— The Gospel comes to an end at 20:31; the narrative begins afresh and has a second ending at 21:24–25.

— This second ending itself indicates more than one compositional stage, as 21:24 distinguishes "the disciple who testifies to these things and

7. Some insiders, under the influence of the docetic teachers that still plague the community, are tempted to understand "Christ" and "Son of God" in a way that minimizes the human being Jesus.

has written them" from the "we" that composes the extant text.

An array of different theories have been developed to account for this data, but they can be represented as modifications or combinations of three basic models:

1. *The aged apostle John writes on the basis of his memory*. See above on authorship, §25.2.2. Most scholars find this theory inadequate to explain the data above.

2. *John is supplementing, revising, or replacing one or more of the Synoptic Gospels*.The common view in the early church was that John knew the other Gospels and wrote his own Gospel as a supplement, correction, or attempt to replace them.[8] Scholarship in the early twentieth century seemed to confirm this view. After a period of disfavor, the argument that John's sources included the Synoptics has been vigorously reasserted, and a number of recent studies and commentaries presuppose or argue for Johannine use of one or more of the other canonical Gospels.[9] Here are samples of some key data in the discussion:

— The general similarity of shape and proportion argues for awareness of the Synoptics, especially since John has Jesus in Jerusalem on several occasions, but still, Mark-like, has the last week of the Gospel occupy 50 percent of his text.

— In the relatively few places where John and the Synoptics overlap, the issue is whether the similarity in wording can be accounted for by common oral tradition.

— The agreements between John and the Synoptics, in wording and order, consist mainly of agreements with Mark. A smaller number coincide with Matthew. Although John has numerous thematic and perspectival agreements with Luke, there are few, if any, substantial verbal and sequential agreements between Luke and John that suggest literary dependence.

— Some unusual Markan vocabulary and phraseology are found elsewhere only in John; for example, the phrase commonly used in Mark to introduce sayings of Jesus, καὶ ἔλεγεν αὐτοῖς (*kai elegen autois*, and he said to them), is found twelve times in Mark, elsewhere in the New Testament only in Luke 6:5 in dependence on Mark 2:8, and John 5:19; 8:23. The curious colloquial diminutive "earie," typical for Mark (see Exc. 3.4) is found only in Mark 14:47 and John 18:10. "Sea of Galilee," four times in Mark, is not found outside the New Testament except in literature dependent on Mark. Elsewhere in the New Testament, however, it occurs only in John 6:1 (where it is glossed with "Sea of Tiberias," see John 21:1).

— Several components of John's narrative seem to combine and reinterpret elements in Mark's Gospel (not just his tradition). Comparison of John 5:1–16 with the events combined by Mark in the series Mark 2:1–3:6 suggests John knows the whole series as arranged by Mark, remelts the elements of this story, and reissues them in his own idiom: Jesus heals a lame man, there is a Sabbath controversy, forgiveness of sins is involved, then the Jewish authorities harass Jesus and finally decide to put him to death. Is it really likely that Mark and John independently put these elements together?

8. Famously, Clement of Alexandria in the second century: "Last of all, John, perceiving that the external facts had been made plain in the Gospel, being urged by his friends, and inspired by the Spirit, composed a spiritual Gospel" (cited, Eusebius, *Hist. eccl.* 6.14.7).

9. Among those who argue John's sources included one or more of the Synoptics: C. K. Barrett, *The Gospel according to St. John*, 2nd ed. (Philadelphia: Westminster Press, 1978), 59–71, and Thomas L. Brodie, *The Quest for the Origin of John's Gospel: A Source-Oriented Approach* (New York: Oxford University Press, 1993). A 1991 conference of international New Testament scholars was devoted to this issue. The papers are published in Adelbert Denaux, ed., *John and the Synoptics*, BETL 101 (Leuven: Leuven University Press, 1992). All the key positions and arguments are masterfully summarized and evaluated in D. Moody Smith, *John among the Gospels*, 2nd ed. (Columbia: University of South Carolina Press, 2001), who remains unconvinced that John knew the Synoptics.

— The crucial issue is whether John shows awareness of Markan (or other Synoptic) redaction. There seems to be some evidence that this is the case, that John reflects the text of Mark itself, not merely pre-Synoptic tradition. Georg Strecker, for example, argues that John clearly knows all three forms of the Synoptic Son of Man sayings, including the passion predictions in the form peculiar to Mark.[10] Some scholars regard such arguments as conclusive, but for others the evidence falls just short of proof.

— Not only presumably distinctive Markan vocabulary and style, but compositional features such as intercalation require explanation. The Markan sandwich technique is found, for example, in the story of Peter's denial, and also appears in John's version of the story. We know the technique is typically Markan (see above, Exc. 3.4); the question is whether John hit upon this structure independently or reflects Markan usage.

It thus seems likely that John knew one or more of the Synoptics, and that elements from them are reinterpreted and incorporated within his own narrative. He does not, however, consider them normative or definitive documents that constitute the basis of his own narrative.

3. *John is composing on the basis of lost written sources.* Convinced that the bulk of John's material clearly does not come from the Synoptics or any other extant sources, some scholars have posited lost sources that can be identified on the basis of evidence internal to the text of John. By far the most influential source theory of the last hundred years is that of Rudolf Bultmann (although no one today holds it in the form advocated by Bultmann).[11] In Bultmann's hypothesis, John is based on three major sources, all written: (1) the narrative was mostly provided by the signs source (Semeia-source) that presented Jesus as a powerful, miracle-working θεῖος ἀνήρ (*theios anēr*, divine man); (2) the speeches of Jesus came primarily from the Discourse source (*Offenbarungsreden*), revelatory monologues adopted and adapted from the discourses of a Mandean Gnostic revealer figure; and (3) the passion narrative derived from the passion source with similar material to the tradition behind the passion narrative in the Synoptic Gospels. Bultmann's source hypothesis was coupled with a redactional hypothesis, in which it is important to distinguish three layers of the present text: the sources used by the evangelist, the evangelist's own editing and composition, the later edition expanded by the ecclesiastical redactor.

In Bultmann's view, *the evangelist* was the theological genius who combined and elaborated these sources into a powerful expression of early Christian theology. He adopted the Gnostic-Mandean concept of the descending and ascending Revealer as the primary way of interpreting the Christ event. While the evangelist believed that Jesus' miraculous deeds actually happened, they were signs that pointed to Jesus as the Revealer. Unless one responded in faith to this Word of God encountered in the message from and about Jesus, belief in the miracle itself had no value. Similarly, the evangelist demythologized future eschatology, interpreting it entirely in terms of the present experience and self-understanding of the believer. Material sacraments involving actual water, bread,

10. Strecker, *Theology of the New Testament*, 486–87. Anton Dauer, *Johannes und Lukas: Untersuchungen zu den johanneisch-lukanischen Parallelperikopen Joh 4, 46–54/Lk 7, 1–10 - Joh 12, 1–8/Lk 7, 36–50, 10, 38–42 - Joh 20, 19–29/Lk 24, 36–49*, Forschung zur Bibel 50 (Würzburg: Echter Verlag, 1984), argues Lukan redactional material shows up not only in John, but already in his source. Not all are convinced, including scholars who think John is dependent on the Synoptics (e.g., Frans Neirynck, "John 4, 46–54: Signs Source and/or Synoptic Gospels," *Ephemerides theologicae lovaniensis* 45 [1984]: 367–75).

11. Rudolf Bultmann, *The Gospel of John: A Commentary*, trans. G. R. Beasley-Murray, R. W. N. Hoare, and John Kenneth Riches (Philadelphia: Westminster Press, 1971), 6–7 and passim; Bultmann, *Theology of the New Testament*, 2:3–14. A thorough discussion of Bultmann's source theory, with a reproduction of the postulated sources in Greek, is provided in D. Moody Smith, *The Composition and Order of the Fourth Gospel: Bultmann's Literary Theory* (New Haven, CT: Yale University Press, 1965).

and wine were disdained and spiritualized. The eschatological community is led by the Spirit with no institutional leadership.

The ecclesiastical redactor. The evangelist's original creative writing suffered some sort of accident in which passages were displaced, but the writing itself was preserved. In the later history of the Johannine community, as it began to fuse with the emerging early catholic church, an editor revised the Gospel, but was not able or interested in restoring its original order. The redactor also added chapter 21 and several other passages that brought the evangelist's writing more into line with emerging orthodox theology; future eschatology and a material understanding of the sacraments were restored.

Bultmann believed he was able to identify the additions and modifications of the ecclesiastical redactor and restore the original text of the evangelist. His classic commentary is an exegesis of this restored text, not following the canonical order.[12] Bultmann's project thus poses the important question of whether the final, canonical form of the text is to be interpreted, or whether it is to be excavated in search of its sources or an earlier form of the text that is then considered normative.

Bultmann's postulated *signs source* is the only element of his theory that still has substantial support among some Johannine scholars, represented especially by the influential monographs of Robert T. Fortna.[13] Fortna's theory contrasts with Bultmann's in two significant ways: (1) Prior to its reception by the evangelist, the *signs source* had already been combined with the *passion source*, so that it was already a *signs Gospel*. The importance of these studies bears on the issue of the origin of the Gospel genre. If Fortna is right, the Gospel form was created not by Mark but by the unknown predecessor of the Gospel of John; the *signs Gospel* is the earliest Gospel. (2) Fortna affirms only two redactional levels, the redaction of the basic document that formed the *signs Gospel* and the final redaction of the Fourth Evangelist who produced the canonical form of the text.

4. *Independent oral tradition.* The failure of research to construct generally convincing theories of written sources contributed to a reaction in favor of oral tradition. An additional factor was that research on the life of Jesus tended to favor the Synoptics and discount the Fourth Gospel, so that some scholars interested in establishing reliable information about the life of Jesus reexamined the issue of Johannine dependence on the Synoptics and concluded that John represents an independent tradition. The view that John is independent of the Synoptics became the dominant perspective for a generation, but it is now receding.[14]

5. *Successive reworkings of traditions and texts*, probably involving one or more editions of the written Gospel. It seems clear that the canonical form of the text had a compositional history involving sources and earlier forms of the Gospel, including core traditions that go back to the time of Jesus and the earliest post-Easter period, but there is little confidence in our ability either to identify these sources precisely or to chart the history of its precanonical editions. John's sources included both oral tradition and written documents. He was aware of elements of the pre-Gospel Synoptic tradition, as well as the Gospel of Mark, and perhaps Matthew and Luke. The

12. Other such attempted restorations are represented by the translation of the New Testament by James Moffatt, and by commentaries such as G. H. C. Macgregor, *The Gospel of John* (New York: Harper & Bros., 1928).

13. Robert T. Fortna, *The Gospel of Signs: A Reconstruction of the Narrative Source Underlying the Fourth Gospel*, SNTSMS 11 (Cambridge: Cambridge University Press, 1970), which prints the reconstructed Greek text, 235–45; Fortna, *Fourth Gospel and Its Predecessor*, which prints a slightly revised English text seriatim. See also Fortna's own summary of his work in Robert T. Fortna, "Signs/Semeia Source," in *Anchor Bible Dictionary*, 6:18–22.

14. The key study is the small book of Percival Gardner-Smith, *Saint John and the Synoptic Gospels* (Cambridge: Cambridge University Press, 1938). The classical works of C. H. Dodd, *Fourth Gospel, and Historical Tradition in the Fourth Gospel* (Cambridge: Cambridge University Press, 1963), embrace and extend this argument.

primary generative factor, however, was the author's own creative theological genius, guided, as he believed, by the Holy Spirit.

The Johannine community functioned with an awareness of the presence of the risen Christ, who continued to speak. The prophetic teachers of the Johannine school composed and compiled homilies and teaching documents that they regarded as expressions of the presence of the Paraclete among them (see on the Farewell Discourses below). Preliminary combinations of discourses and stories were made, but not published outside the community. There came a time, however, as the community contemplated union with the emerging protocatholic church, when a comprehensive document, embracing much of the community's history and a spectrum of its theological views, needed to be published, that is, circulated to the network of Johannine churches and other congregations with whom they were exploring closer relationships as an expression of the one church.

The final edition of the Gospel, with the addition of chapter 21, represents something of a manifesto, to itself, its sister churches, and the wider world embraced in God's mission through Jesus, the Sent One. Neither the sources used in the composition of the Fourth Gospel, nor the different stages of its decades-long process of growth and revision, can now be recovered in detail. The present tensive state of the text of the Gospel of John testifies to the dynamic history and community that produced it. Even if we could be more confident in the identification of sources and redactional stages, our exegetical attention should be focused on the canonical form of the text.

27.4 Structure and Outline

THE PRESENT FORM OF THE GOSPEL OF John is composed of two major sections with a prologue, introduction, and postscript:

Prologue, Narrative Introduction	1
Part 1: *The Book of Signs*	2—12
Part 2: *The Book of Glory*	13—20
Epilogue	21

In the *Book of Signs* Jesus, the incarnate Word who brings God's life and light, confronts the unbelieving world. The general structure is clear: Jesus performs exceptional miracles designated *signs*, which are misunderstood at the literal level, even though he interprets them as christological symbols in lengthy dialogues that modulate into monologues.

In the *Book of Glory* Jesus instructs "his own" in extensive *Farewell Discourses* at the Last Supper, and then at the crucifixion and resurrection returns to the heavenly world from which he came. The account of the Last Supper has a clear general structure: Jesus washes the disciples' feet, interprets the symbolic act, and gives the love command (chap. 13), followed by the Farewell Discourse promising the coming of the Paraclete (chap. 14), much of which is repeated in chapters 15–16. After Jesus' lengthy *intercessory prayer* (chap. 17) comes the narrative of Jesus' arrest, trial, crucifixion (chaps. 18–19), and resurrection (chap. 20).

The sign/discourse pattern seems to be important for understanding what John is about, but the enumeration of the first and second signs, both associated with Cana (2:11; 4:54) seems to be a structural signal marking off chapters 2–4 as a discrete thematic unit, rather than an indication of a lost "Signs Source." In chapters 5–10, the narrative is structured in terms of Jesus' encounter with the Jews at the principal Jewish festivals (Sabbath, chap. 5; Passover, chap. 6; Booths, 7:1–10:21; Dedication, 10:22–39). In chapters 11–12, Jesus moves toward the final conflict and resolution at the last Passover.

These considerations lead to the following outline:

1:1–18	Hymnic Prologue
1:19–51	Narrative Introduction
2:1–12:50	Part 1—*The Book of Signs*: Jesus Reveals His Glory to the World
2:1–4:54	The Cana Cycle: New Beginnings
2:1–11	Cana: Wedding Festival, New Wine
2:12–25	Jerusalem: The True Temple
3:1–21	The Discourse with Nicodemus
3:22–36	John's Final Testimony to Christ
4:1–42	Samaria: The Discourse with the Woman of Samaria
4:43–54	Cana: The Royal Official of Capernaum as Discipleship among the Gentiles
5:1–10:42	The Life That Leads to Conflict, Death, and Resurrection
5:1–47	*Sabbath*: Jesus Works as God Does, Generates Conflict
6:1–71	*Passover*: Jesus the Bread of Life, Disciples Abandon Him
7:1–10:21	*Feast of Booths*: Conflict Intensifies
10:22–42	*Feast of Dedication*: Attempted Arrest; Jesus Withdraws to Transjordan.
11:1–12:50	Climax and Conclusion of Jesus' Public Ministry: Raising of Lazarus; Decision to Put Jesus to Death
13:1–20:31	Part 2—*The Book of Glory*: Jesus Reveals the Glory of His Death and Resurrection to the Disciples
13:1–17:26	The Last Supper and Farewell Discourse
18:1–19:42	The Passion Narrative
20:1–29	The Resurrection of Jesus and Commissioning of the Disciples
20:30–31	Conclusion and Purpose of the Gospel
21:1–25	Second Conclusion

27.5 Exegetical-Theological Précis

Hymnic Prologue (John 1:1–18)

The early church created hymns with solid theological content to be used in the worship of God, in which the community confessed its faith, and as a means of instruction (Phil 2:6–11; Col 1:1–15; 3:16). Virtually all interpreters identify 1:1–18 as a hymn current in the Johannine community that expressed key aspects of its theology. The evangelist has annotated it, adding verses 6–8, 12c–13, 15, 17–19, and made it the prologue of his narrative. In its present location, this magnificent poem functions as the hermeneutical framework within which the following narrative is to be interpreted. Some key aspects are these:

A hermeneutical bridge between the Jewish Christian and Greco-Roman world. The prologue seems to reflect the structure of the original hymn, with two stanzas. The first presents the role of the Word in creation and history (1:1–13), the second the incarnation of the Word and the response of faith (1:14–18). The subject of each stanza is the Λόγος (*Logos*, usually translated "Word"). "Logos" is a key term in both the Old Testament-Jewish and Greco-Roman religious worlds. Readers with a Jewish background could not read John 1:1 without thinking of the first words of their Bible, in which "in the beginning" the whole creation came into being by the word of God. Many Gentile readers were aware of the Logos as the ultimate rational principle that permeates the universe (*logos* is the linguistic root of *logic* and the cluster of *–ology* words). Stoics spoke of the *logos* as the immanent Reason present in the whole universe, and conceived of no higher god. Platonists thought of the *logos* as the divine rational principle of an ordered universe. John will lead the reader to understand Jesus as the Christ, the Son of God, oriented to how these key terms are understood in the biblical and Jewish tradition (20:30–31), but he begins with a universally human way of thinking that already makes sense to both Jewish and Gentile readers. All the key words of the Johannine theological vocabulary (Logos, light, life, truth, Father, etc.; see on 1:38 below) have profound significance in both Jewish and Greco-Roman thought.

The myth of divine Wisdom. Already in biblical times, some Jewish thinkers had begun to interpret Jewish monotheistic faith in the one Creator in terms of universal wisdom (σοφία, *Sophia*). This *Word*/Wisdom was sometimes personified and regarded as a heavenly being present with God at creation (Prov 8:1–31; Wis 7:22–26; 9:1–2). Hellenistic Jewish philosophers such as Philo could speak of this transcendent Word in terms of deity, as the Son of God who belongs to the divine category (e.g., *Heir* 205–6; *Dreams* 1.229–30, 239–41; *Alleg. Interp.* 2.86). This divine Wisdom came to the world and was rejected by most of humanity. While the whole mythical picture is not found in any extant text, Wisdom's story can be constructed from the numerous references in the Old Testament and Jewish Wisdom literature:[15]

— Wisdom, a preexistent being (Job 28:27; Sir 24:9; Wis 7:22; Prov 3:19; 8:30; *2 Enoch* 30:8) was God's partner or helper at the creation (Prov 8:22–30; Sir 1:1–9; 24:3, 9; Wis 8:3; 9:4, 9; see also Philo).

— She sought, and still seeks, a dwelling place among human beings, but her seeking was in vain (*1 Enoch* 4:1–3; Prov 1:20–32, 9:5–6).

— Her preaching was, and is, rejected (Prov 1:23, Sir 6:23, Bar 3:12).

— She came to what was her own (for she had created it), but her own did not accept her (Sir 24:6, *1 Enoch* 42:1–3; 84:3).

— So she returned to the heavenly world, where she lives in hiding (Job 28:12–17; Bar 3:15).

— Though people seek her now, they can no longer find her. God alone knows the way to her (*1 Enoch* 5:8; 91:10; Wis 7:14, 27; Job 20–33; Bar 3:19–31).

— Nevertheless there are rare exceptions, people to whom Wisdom reveals herself, who accept her, and whom she thereby makes friends of God and prophets (Wis 7:12).

— She will reappear at the last times when her spirit will dwell in the Son of Man; he will act in the power of Wisdom and execute judgment (*1 Enoch* 49:1–4).

The Absolute God, the relativity of history, and the "scandal of particularity." Thoughtful persons of every generation have pondered how the Jewish and Christian claim could be taken seriously, the claim that the Infinite One, the Absolute, the one true God is definitively revealed in the relativity of historical events. "If there is one God, Creator of the universe and Lord of all history and all people, can we believe that this God is uniquely revealed in the history of Israel and in the one human being, Jesus of Nazareth?" How can God's universality be squared with the particularity of a historical revelation? John is clear that Christian faith deals with the Absolute, the one and only God (17:3) represented

15. Adapted from Rudolf Bultmann, "Der religionsgeschichtliche Hintergrund des Prologs zum Johannes-Evangelium," in *Eucharistérion: Studien zur Religion und Literatur des Alten und Neuen Testaments: Hermann Gunkel zum 60. Geburtstage, dem 23. Mai 1922 dargebracht von seinen Schülern und Freunden und in ihrem Namen*, ed. Hans Schmidt, FRLANT (Göttingen: Vandenhoeck & Ruprecht, 1923), 10–35. For additional parallels to the Johannine prologue, see Boring, Berger, and Colpe, eds., *Hellenistic Commentary*, §§353–68.

by the universal Logos through whom all things and all people were created (1:1–4). This transcendent Logos is the source of all light and life, wherever it may be found, not only in the history of Israel and the event of Jesus Christ (1:9–10). Whatever truth exists in the world, recognized or not, belongs to this one universal light that shines in human darkness. All truth is one, all light comes from the one God, Creator of all. John does not compromise the absoluteness of God. This is the affirmation of the first stanza of the prologue.

The second stanza makes the radical claim that this Logos has "become flesh" (1:14) and has entered into the relative, finite world of human history, that the Absolute has entered into relativity, that God has become a human being. Such statements are usually understood as representing a "high" Christology, and rightly so—John insists that in Jesus the world encounters not some lesser divine being, but the one true God, and does not hesitate to use God-language of Christ (1:1; 10:30; 20:28, at the very beginning, exact middle, and end of the book). The declaration is not only christological. It not only speaks of the significance of Christ, but of the value and worth imputed to the relativity of the world. When the Absolute does not remain absolute, does not view the relativities of human life and thought with divine aloofness from afar, but enters into our world and becomes part and parcel of it, sharing our life and experience, this not only says something about John's understanding of the Absolute Christ the Logos—he represents the Absolute God—but something about the relative world of flesh. The absolute God affirms relativity, works within and through it, affirms the human fleshly world in which God became incarnate, and thus affirms the continuing work of God in the relative, finite, human communities founded on their faith in the Christ event. John's own community was terribly human, torn by suspicion, misunderstanding and debate. John's view was that the infleshment of the absolute Word in Jesus continues in the relativity of the Christian community (see on chaps. 13–17 below). It is precisely in this stinking world that the power of the resurrection is let loose (11:39).

The dualistic structure of the story, signaled in advance. John 1:11–12 anticipates in advance the dual response to the Logos: "He came to what was his own [for all things were made through the Logos, 1:3], and his own people did not receive him." This corresponds to Part 1 of the following narrative, the Book of Signs of chapters 2–12, in which Jesus is rejected by "his own"—not only the Jewish people but the unbelieving human community as a whole, for which they stand in the story. "But to all who received him, who believed in his name, he gave power to become children of God." This corresponds to Part 2, the Book of Glory, in which the revelation of God in Jesus is accepted by "his own," those who believe in him and receive a new life through him.

The confessional, ecclesiastical "we" of the Johannine community. The "we" of the community of faith appears in the prologue (1:14, 16), binding together authors and readers with the original community of faith in the first generation, and with Christian readers of all generations (see on 1 John 1:1–4).

Cosmic drama of salvation and historical narrative. The prologue pictures a cosmic drama, from the creation through the shining of the divine light in history and the incarnation of the Logos to the response of the Christian community in the readers' own time. As in Paul's theology, the saving drama is enacted on a cosmic stage (see above, §18.4.1; 20.1.2). In contrast to Paul and the kenosis Christology, the cosmic drama is combined with details of this-worldly history, the lives of John and Jesus. The hymn is interrupted with prose sections about John (the Baptist), and the cosmic drama then becomes the encompassing framework within which the story of the earthly Jesus is told.

Narrative Introduction (1:19–51)

When the narrative curtain opens, the story is already in progress. It is a trial scene, and a witness is being cross examined. In the Synoptics, the trial comes at the end of the story, and Jesus is condemned. In the Fourth Gospel, there is no Jewish trial in the passion narrative, but the story as a whole is a courtroom scene, with witnesses, evidence, judge, and verdict. This reflects and reverses the experience of the readers, some of whom have been tried in Jewish synagogue courts and expelled from the community, and condemned in Roman courts (see above, §25.3.3).

1:19–35 Who is John? In the initial scene, John is being questioned about his identity by priests and Levites sent by the Jews. He is never called "the Baptist" in the Fourth Gospel, but he has disciples who call him "Rabbi" (3:26). The followers of John the Baptist formed a distinct community that extended into the time and place of the Johannine community (see on Acts 18:24–19:7 and §7.4.4 above). The Fourth Gospel is concerned to validate John as an authentic messenger from God, but to deprive him of any independent status. Just as the narrative insertions into the prologue had already insisted in advance that John was not the light (1:6–8), so in the opening paragraph of the narrative John himself insists that he is not the Messiah (as some of his followers in the author's time apparently claimed).

1:36–51 Who is Jesus? When Jesus appears in the narrative, John's testimony has already identified him with exalted christological titles. Although in this-worldly history John preceded Jesus, in reality Jesus existed before John, who joins with the prologue in confessing Jesus' preexistence (1:15, 30). John's baptism is unrelated to forgiveness, but Jesus is the Lamb of God who takes away the sin of the world (1:29, 36). John identifies Jesus as the promised "Coming One" (1:15, 27), the Lord (1:23), the Son of God (1:34).

John has disciples, but in the Fourth Gospel they no longer have a function. Jesus' disciples, on the other hand, form a new community of believers, and from the very beginning they enhance the confession already made by John, drawing on the whole repertoire of christological titles of the later Johannine community. Jesus is the Χριστός, *Christos* (Messiah, Christ; 1:41), the One of whom Moses and the prophets wrote (1:45), the king of Israel (1:49), the Son of Man, the bridge between heaven and earth, the mediator between God and humanity (1:51). Thus, before the narrative proper opens, the introduction has already presented Jesus as publicly known as the Messiah and Son of God, expressed in a variety of titles and concepts. This strongly contrasts with the Synoptics' way of telling the story in terms of Mark's messianic secret (see above, §20.1.2).

Yet the Fourth Gospel has its own version of the messianic secret, for here too the story is told in such a way that its real meaning is not known, and cannot be known, until the story is over and the post-Easter disciples receive the Holy Spirit (see 2:22; 7:39; 10:6; 11:11–12; 12:16; 13:7; 14:19–20; 15:26–27; 16:7, 12–18; 20:9, 22). Here too the narrator is omniscient and shares the real identity of Jesus with the post-Easter reader, who knows more or understands better than the pre-Easter characters in the story. In contrast to Mark, the Johannine Jesus reveals his identity from the beginning, in public and private, and Jesus' disciples accept and believe these claims from the beginning—but do not understand them until after Easter. Whereas Mark tells the story diachronically, withholding the disclosure of Jesus' true identity until the end of the narrative, in John it is a synchronic paradox: the revelation is given openly to all at the beginning, but their misunderstanding persists until the story is over.

1:38 "What are you looking for?" These are Jesus' first words in the Gospel of John, programmatic for all that follows. The transcendent Revealer, who shares the deity of God, has come into the world as its Savior. Yet his first words are a question. Like much of the Gospel, its meaning does not lie on the surface. It represents John's evangelistic and hermeneutical approach. His community is rooted in the Jewish tradition that anticipates God's saving act as the sending of the Messiah. In such a context, the announcement that the Messiah has come evokes faith and celebration, or unbelief and hostility. But John's community now looks beyond the synagogue, with a mission to those who are God's beloved creatures, but who are not Jews looking for a Messiah. *How does one preach Christ to those who are not looking for a Messiah?*[16] Does one first try to instruct them in the biblical and Jewish view of the world and instill in them the messianic hope? Or can one begin with them where they are? Can the Christian message, conceived and born in Judaism, be translated into new, non-Jewish terms?

Here the teachers of the Johannine school offer help to the Johannine community struggling with such questions as it engages in its mission to the world. In John's narrative, those who express their ultimate hopes in terms of Jewish messianism hear Jesus say, "I am the Christ" (e.g., 1:41; 4:26; see above, §7.6.3). By the end of the story, the author will express the meaning of the Christ event in such messianic terms (20:30–31). But to the vast majority of human beings who are not expecting a Messiah, Jesus asks, "What *are* you looking for?" If their ultimate hopes are expressed in terms of universal human longing, the Johannine Jesus will identify himself as the way, the truth, the life, as the source of true light, life, bread, water. In Jesus, the one true God comes seeking true worshipers who acknowledge God as their God (4:23). But the Revealer begins with a question, *the* question, and thus prepares for the following narrative.

16. Cf. Reinhold Niebuhr, *The Nature and Destiny of Man*, 2 vols., Gifford Lectures (New York: Scribner, 1964), 2:1–34.

Part 1: The Book of Signs: Jesus Reveals His Glory to the World (2:1–12:50)

2:1–4:54 The Cana Cycle: New Beginnings

In this subsection, the story of *Jesus* reflects the course of *early Christian history*: Galilee → Jerusalem → Judea → Samaria → Gentiles (cf. the similar pattern in Acts 1:8). The Jesus story is told as an anticipation of the ministry of the risen Lord who leads "his own" from its Jewish roots into the wider world. The unit is a ring composition, beginning and ending in Cana. The first Cana story reflects the Galilean beginnings of the Jesus movement. When the narrative moves through Jerusalem, Samaria, and back to Cana, the second Cana sign portrays Jesus' healing the member of a Gentile family, all of whom become believers. The healing is effected from a distance; the physical presence of Jesus is not necessary, as the risen Christ makes his way from Jewish territory into the Gentile world.

2:1–11 Cana: Wedding Festival, New Wine

While the Fourth Gospel has much material without direct parallels in the Synoptics, this is the only story in John that has no counterpart or point of contact whatsoever in the Synoptic Gospels, composed by the evangelist himself on the basis of traditional motifs. Johannine theological emphases present throughout the Gospel already make their appearance in this opening scene:

The hermeneutical bridging of Jewish and Gentile worlds. The image of the wedding feast, God as husband and Israel as bride, is from Jewish Scripture and tradition, taken up by early Christian teachers and applied to Christ and the church, especially prominent in Pauline tradition and in Ephesus, the setting of the Johannine school (e.g., Hos 1–3; Matt 9:15; 22:1–11; John 3:29; 2 Cor 11:2; Eph 5:25–33;

Rev 19:7, 9; 22:2, 9, 17). Pagan religion knew several stories in which a divine being changes water into wine.[17]

Jesus the transformer of Jewish ritual practices. The wine is not created ex nihilo. The water used for ritual purification is not replaced but transformed. The temple, the sacrifices, the Law, the Sabbath, the Passover and other Jewish festivals, are not replaced but fulfilled and transformed. John does not claim that Christianity is the replacement of Judaism, but repeatedly, in a variety of images, presents Jesus Christ as the transformer and fulfillment of what is sought in all religious striving, Jewish and pagan.

Eschatological extravagance. The ultimate fulfillment of God's purpose was sometimes portrayed as the end of hardship and scarcity, the time when there is plenty of food and drink for all. In the Mediterranean vineyard economy, abundance of wine symbolized eschatological fulfillment:

> That which will happen at that time bears upon the whole earth. Therefore, all who live will notice it. . . . the Anointed One will begin to be revealed. . . . The earth will also yield fruits ten thousand fold. And on one vine will be a thousand branches, and one branch will produce a thousand clusters, and one cluster will produce a thousand grapes, and one grape will produce a cor of wine. And those who are hungry will enjoy themselves and they will, moreover, see marvels every day. For winds will go out in front of me every morning to bring the fragrance of aromatic fruits and clouds at the end of the day to distill the dew of health. And it will happen at that time that the treasury of manna will come down again from on high, and they will eat of it in those years because these are they who will have arrived at the consummation of time. (2 Bar 2–8)

Jesus transforms about 120 gallons of water into the best quality wine. Salvation does not mean merely survival, but extravagant, uninhibited joy (see 12:3–8).

The presence of eschatological glory in the person of Jesus. John portrays this hoped-for eschatological glory as already present in the life of Jesus. Thus when Jesus "revealed his glory, and his disciples believed in him" (2:11; cf. 1:14!), the reference is not to glory in the celebrity sense of fame and idolization, but refers to the presence of God, the divine glory that descended on tabernacle and temple as the visible representation of God's dwelling on this earth. The issue is the location of God's presence in the world. Where does one turn to see and experience the presence of God? For John, the divine presence is not bound to the rituals and theology of any religion, whether Jewish, Gentile, *or Christian*. While John is clear that faith in the one true God cannot dispense with religion, ritual, or theology, he does not portray one religion replacing another, but the personal presence of God in Jesus as both relativizing and fulfilling all religion. This is made explicit in the next scene, in which Jesus appears for the first time in the temple.

2:12–25 Jerusalem: The True Temple

When the Johannine Jesus refers to the temple as being destroyed and raised in three days (this explanation is absent from the Synoptic account), of course the characters in the narrative cannot understand his meaning. But the readers, who look back on both the destruction of the Jerusalem temple and the death and resurrection of Jesus, guided by the Spirit and interpreting the Scripture in the light of the Christ event, can see what the story is really pointing to (2:22–23). The Johannine signs thus have an inherent ambiguity. On the one hand, the revelation of God that comes through the signs can

17. E.g., Pliny the Elder, *Natural History* 2.231. See other data and discussion in Boring, Berger, and Colpe, eds., *Hellenistic Commentary*, §§371–75.

generate authentic faith; on the other hand, the signs cannot become "evidence," the basis from which one can figure out the identity of Jesus on one's own terms. This too becomes a theme throughout the Gospel, illustrated in the next episode.

The ambiguity of signs. John affirms Jesus' signs as authentic pointers to faith; people become believers on the basis of his signs. He also sees their ambiguity and has suspicions about those whose faith rests only on miracles. In taking over the miracle story mode of communicating the faith, the Johannine community accepted the inherent ambiguity of miracles and miracle stories. This is different both from Paul, who rejected such signs, and from Paul's opponents, who affirmed them (see on 1 Cor 1:22; 2 Cor 10–13). There is a Johannine dialectic here, corresponding to the tensive combination of kenosis and epiphany Christologies in the Gospel genre.

3:1–21 The Discourse with Nicodemus

While Jesus is in Jerusalem, he is respectfully approached by "the teacher of Israel" (so NAB of 3:10), a Pharisee who is a member of the Sanhedrin. His coming at night reflects not only the light/darkness dualism of Johannine theology, but the situation of the author's time in which actual or potential believers in Jesus must keep a low profile. On the basis of Jesus' signs, Nicodemus professes to accept Jesus as a teacher sent from God. At one level, this is the correct understanding, but Jesus' response seems brusque and unrelated to Nicodemus's positive affirmation of Jesus' identity: "No one can see the kingdom of God without being born again/from above." Again the evangelist uses an episode set in the narrative framework of the life of Jesus to communicate insights of Johannine theology to the post-Easter reader. The there-and-then account of a past conversation modulates seamlessly into the here-and-now address to the reader, as the voice of Jesus to Nicodemus becomes the "we" of the Johannine community in the present (see on 1 John 1:1–4).

Kingdom of God, eternal life, and Christology. As portrayed in the Synoptic Gospels, the central message of Jesus was the proclamation of the coming-and-somehow-already-present kingdom of God (see above, §8.3). "Kingdom of God" occurs only here in the Fourth Gospel, in a private nighttime meeting with Nicodemus. Conversely, the necessity of being born again/from above does not occur at all in the Synoptics. Again, John reinterprets traditional themes into more universal categories. The kingdom of God becomes eternal life, which is inseparably bound to the revelation of God in the Christ event.

The inept question and God's revelation in Christ. The prologue had already spoken of believers as those who have entered a new life that transcends natural birth; they have been begotten or born from God. John's hearer-readers, but not Nicodemus, have heard or read the prologue. Of course Nicodemus cannot (yet) understand the revelation of God in Christ. Jesus comes from above; Nicodemus belongs to this world and can understand Jesus' words and deeds only at the this-worldly level, in terms of this-worldly logic. He thus responds with a sincere, this-worldly question that fails to grasp what Jesus is talking about, but the question gives Jesus the opportunity to teach (to the post-Easter reader, who *can* understand) about the ultimate reality that is the content of the divine revelation made present in the Christ event.

Dualism and the new birth. We have repeatedly noted that Johannine thought is shaped in dualistic categories. The apocalypticism represented by Revelation was primarily chronological and horizontal, a dualism of the two ages. Without entirely abandoning these categories, the evangelist shifts the emphasis to a vertical, simultaneous, ontological dualism. All reality is divided into two realms:

Above ⟷ below
Heaven ⟷ earth
Light ⟷ darkness
Spirit ⟷ flesh
Life ⟷ death

Good	←→	evil
Truth	←→	lie
Israel	←→	"the world" (sometimes); "the Jews" (sometimes)
God	←→	Satan

All people belong to one or the other of these realms. In the gnosticizing thought with which John is in dialogue, each person belongs to one or the other by birth. Three hermeneutical considerations are to be noted about this dualism:

1. John did not invent it. Such dualism was part of the protognostic thought of the evangelist's context. In this thought world, origin determines destiny (see above, §9.2.2). Who your father is determines your fate. Thus, when Jews are called "children of the devil" (8:44), it is a gnosticizing dualism that comes to expression, not anti-Semitism. *All* people (not just Jews) are either "children of God" or "children of the devil." This is the Johannine version of the Pauline view current in the Ephesian context of the Fourth Gospel: "All of us once lived among them in the passions of our flesh, following the desires of flesh and senses, and we were by nature children of wrath, like everyone else" (Eph 2:3).

2. Such dualism is not ultimate. There is one God, the Creator of all things, who loves *the world*. God is not the God of only the left-hand column above, but the God of all, and wills to save the whole creation (3:16).

3. The dualism is existential, not ontological; it is a dualism of decision, not a predetermined fate. Thinking within this thought world, the call to believe in God's act in Christ is the call to get a new origin, to be born again, to become a child of God by faith (1:12–13; 3:3–5). Thus John 3:16, rightly understood as a kind of summary of the Christian message, shifts from the language of new birth (God's initiative; no one can decide to be born) to the language of faith—people do decide whether or not to believe. Even so, faith is both human decision and God's gift (see on 15:16 below).

Two communities address each other. Since English "you" can be either singular or plural, English translations do not catch the interplay between the singular pronouns of verses 3:3–7a and the plural "you" of 3:7b, 11, 12. Nicodemus's initial "we" is matched by Jesus' "we" of 3:11. It is not merely two individuals speaking in a private, late-night conversation, but two religious communities that address each other.

Criteria, evidence, and faith. Nicodemus claims to accept Jesus as having come from God on the basis of good evidence: he has seen Jesus' signs and concluded that Jesus must be from God. John considers this a defective response, though it does not doom Nicodemus, who will appear later in the story as one who has come to a more authentic faith (7:50–52; 19:38–41). In John's view, the problem with Nicodemus is not that he has the wrong criteria or insufficient evidence, but the whole approach that supposes it can look Jesus over, examine him by whatever criteria, and decide on its own terms whether or not Jesus is from God (see 3:2; 6:42; 7:27, 31, 40–52; 9:16, 29, 31–33; 10:21). Coming to faith is not a matter of accumulating evidence from which legitimate deductions can be made. This is judging κατὰ σάρκα (*kata sarka*, according to the flesh), that is, according to recognized this-worldly standards, scientific, religious, and common sense (8:15). Just as evil people intent on rejecting God's will for their lives cannot justify their rejection on the basis of their false criteria, neither can honest seekers such as Nicodemus validate Jesus' claim on the basis of their good criteria. The new life is a new birth, a gift from God, not a human achievement; it is a matter of revelation from God's side, not discovery or inference from the human side. This is the significance of John's statements that sound like predestination, but John has a way of affirming both divine sovereignty and human responsibility (see below on 15:16). From John's perspective, those who want to do God's will, and only those, will recognize that Jesus comes from God (7:17).

Signs and faith. In 2:11, Jesus' disciples see his signs and believe; in 2:24, Jesus does not accept those who see his signs and believe. Early on, the Fourth Gospel presents readers with a problem to ponder. It is not Jesus in the story, but the narrator, who poses the problem—what is the difference between the two sets of believers, each of which sees the signs, each of which believes? Is it because believing must lead to public confession and identification with Jesus as a disciple? Is it because there is an inherent ambiguity in signs that can either generate authentic faith or fail to do so, even when the miracles are accepted as having actually occurred?

The post-Easter perspective of the story. This becomes explicit in 3:13, where Jesus, speaking as the Johannine community, already looks back on the resurrection and ascension (see the perspective of the Farewell Discourse chaps. 13–17, esp. chap. 17).

3:22–36 *John's Final Testimony to Christ*

Only the Fourth Gospel has the ministries of John and Jesus overlap, and only the Fourth Gospel has Jesus baptizing disciples (3:22, qualified in 4:1–2), highlighting the fact that John had not yet been imprisoned (3:24). This emphasis apparently reflects the historical situation of the Johannine community, in which the Baptist community did not cease to exist when the church began, but continued alongside it as something of a competitor. The narrative has already emphasized that John is not the light, not the Christ, but only a voice testifying to Jesus. Now the evangelist pictures the disciples of Jesus far outstripping the disciples of John in the number of baptisms; Jesus outbaptizes John.

4:1–42 *Samaria: The Discourse with the Woman of Samaria*

There is no evidence that the historical Jesus was ever in Samaria. There are no references to Samaria or Samaritans in Mark. Matthew's only reference is 10:5, in which Jesus forbids his disciples to go there (the prohibition is rescinded after Easter, when the disciples are charged to evangelize all nations). Although the Lukan Jesus is partial to Samaritans, his only effort to visit a Samaritan town is rebuffed (Luke 9:52–56), and it is only after Easter that his disciples engage in successful missionary work in Samaria (Acts 8:5–25, 9:31; 15:3). In John, this post-Easter mission under the aegis of the risen Christ is portrayed in a scene retrojected into the life of Jesus, again illustrating the dual level at which the narrative is to be read. Pertinent aspects of Johannine theology and the life of the Johannine community are disclosed in narrative form:

An inclusive community that challenged traditional boundaries. The barrier that separated Jews from Samaritans was well known from both sides, and is acknowledged in the Fourth Gospel (John 4:9b; see above, §7.4.1). Early in its history, the Johannine churches had evangelized Samaria and welcomed Samaritans into the community. This made them all the more objectionable to emerging mainstream Judaism, and may have contributed to the expulsion of some Johannine Christians from the synagogue. When mainstream Jews accuse Jesus of being a Samaritan and having a demon (8:48), we probably overhear charges made against the Johannine Christians. Either charge, if established, would disqualify them for membership in the authentic people of God. Yet the Johannine Jesus does not simply take the Samaritan side against the Jews,[18] but transcends the dispute about which community has the orthodox cult, and frees worship of God in Spirit and truth from ties to any particular place or community (4:21–24). With the Jerusalem temple in ruins, the Johannine teachers present the community of believers as a "a dwelling place of God in the Spirit" (Eph 2:22 RSV; both Ephesians and the Fourth Gospel reflect theological ideas current in the church in Ephesus at the turn of the century).

18. In Samaria, the Johannine Jesus clearly states that "salvation is of the Jews" (4:22), and John repeatedly cites the prophets, and not only the Pentateuch, as authoritative Scripture, which would not have been accepted by unconverted Samaritans. There was a sense in which Samaritans who became Christians also joined what the author saw as authentic Judaism, i.e., became "true Israelites" (1:47).

Women in leadership roles. Jesus' disciples are surprised that he talks with a woman (4:27). Yet the woman not only is a full conversation partner with Jesus who gradually comes to an authentic faith in him; she is instrumental in the conversion of many of the Samaritans (4:39). "The irony of an outcast, a Samaritan woman, coming to some understanding while the learned teacher of Israel was clueless is not lost on the author of this Gospel, nor should it be on the reader."[19] The conversation that begins on the level of physical thirst and mundane water turns out to be about the life-giving Holy Spirit (4:13–14; cf. 7:38–39). The connection between water and Spirit was already made in the conversation with Nicodemus (3:5). Like the early Pauline churches, the Johannine community valued charismatic leadership and was hesitant to accept the developing institutionalization of ministry. With the coming of a structured ministry, the cultural mores of predominantly male leadership exercised a powerful influence (see on the Pastorals and the household codes, §16.1.2; Col 3:18–4:1). But the Spirit "blows where it chooses" (3:8, with the Johannine double meaning of πνεῦμα (*pneuma*, wind/Spirit). The Spirit is not bound by structures and does not share the cultural prejudice toward male leadership, so that congregations that continued to emphasize charismatic leadership tended to retain women in leadership roles. Consider the leadership of modern Pentecostal churches in this regard. This was the case in the Johannine community and is one reason for the prominence of women in the narrative (2:1–11; 4:27; 12:1–8; 19:25–27; 20:1–18).

19. D. Moody Smith, *John*, ANTC (Nashville: Abingdon Press, 1999), 109. See "Female Characters in the Gospel of John," in Kysar, *Maverick Gospel*, 149–54. Jesus is the only main character in the Fourth Gospel. The role of all the other characters is defined by their response to him. Some are negative (e.g., Pilate), some are positive (e.g., the blind man of chap. 9), some are ambiguous and changing (e.g., Nicodemus). All the women characters respond positively and are role models for believers: the mother of Jesus, the Samaritan woman, Martha and Mary, the women at the foot of the cross, and esp. Mary Magdalene.

Contraction of christological categories. Dialogue with Samaritans and inclusion of Samaritans who came to faith in Christ in the Johannine community affected the ways it confessed its faith in Jesus. Samaritans honored Moses and the Pentateuch (see above, §7.4.1), believed in Moses as the definitive revealer of God, and Mount Gerizim was the authentic place of worship, as taught in their version of the Torah. They rejected the entire Jerusalem tradition, with its temple on Mount Zion, its celebration of Davidic kingship, and its expectation of a future Davidic Messiah. The Samaritan influx into the Johannine community may have contributed to its antipathy for Jerusalem and the distinctive shape of Johannine Christology, which is modeled on Moses instead of David. The Son of David Christology is completely missing. The Moses pattern, on the other hand, is present as both model and foil (1:17, 45; 3:14; 5:45; 6:32; 7:19; 9:28–29). Moses is honored, but it is Jesus, not Moses, who has seen God and has come down to declare his revelation from God.

4:43–54 *Cana: The Royal Official of Capernaum as Discipleship among the Gentiles*

In this concluding sign of the Cana cycle, the life-giving power of Christ comes to the son of a Gentile leader, whose whole family become believers, a model of what had happened in the house churches of the Johannine community and of its understanding of the expansion of the church from Galilee through Jerusalem, Judea, Samaria, and to the Gentiles. This history in which the Holy Spirit has been at work will now be represented in further stories from the life of Jesus that represent the Christ event as the fulfillment of the institutions of Judaism.

5:1–10:42 The Life That Leads to Conflict, Death, and Resurrection

As the evangelist composes the Fourth Gospel, Judaism is in the process of restructure in the wake of the disastrous war that had destroyed its temple, ravaged its leadership, and generated profound rethinking of Jewish theology and identity. The question of the way forward for the community of faith, the people of God, was a burning issue for both Judaism and the Johannine Christians. How should the pilgrimage festivals to Jerusalem, commanded in the Torah, be understood now that Jerusalem was in ruins? For the Johannine believers in Jesus, how to continue to understand their own relation to Sabbath and to the festivals that structured the religious year and the life of faith was a vital concern. The evangelist structures this extensive section of the Book of Signs around these issues. The general theme is introduced in 5:1, with the unspecified "feast of the Jews," then developed in relation to the Sabbath (chap. 5), Passover (chap. 6), Booths (7:1–10:21), Dedication/Hanukkah (10:22–42), climaxing in chapters 11–12 at the final, symbolic Passover.[20]

5:1–47 Sabbath: Jesus Works as God Does, Generates Conflict

At this point the narrative takes a sharp turn. In the Cana cycle 2:1–4:54, Jesus has been met with misunderstanding and lack of positive response, but not hostility. In this section overt opposition begins that immediately becomes deadly. The healing story of the man who had been sick thirty-eight years is the unilateral, sovereign act of Jesus. The man does not ask for healing, it is never said that he has faith, and after he has been healed he does not know who Jesus is and reports him to the religious authorities. Thus, in contrast to the Synoptics, the healing is not an expression of the compassion of Jesus, but the basis for the symbolic interpretation and monologue that follows. So also the problematic issue about "working on the Sabbath" is not that Jesus violates the Torah, as in the Synoptics, but that he "makes himself equal with God" (5:18). The debate moves quickly from Sabbath keeping to Christology and eschatology. It is not their view of the Sabbath that has made the Johannine Christians unacceptable to the synagogue, but their Christology.

Equal with God? In this initial conflict with the Jews, they understand the Johannine Jesus to be making himself equal with God. This charge will recur in the final conflict scene (10:30–33), forming a bracket around the clash of Jesus and Judaism, reducing it to the christological issue. Here we see a reflection of the horror of the synagogue at the christological claims the church made for Jesus. Jewish believers understood Christian claims about Jesus as making him into a second God, in violation of the most sacred conviction of Judaism: there is only one God. Elsewhere, the Fourth Gospel does not deny the "equality with God" charge—though this is not John's own way of expressing his Christology—but explains it in a way that does not compromise monotheism. Here, Jesus responds that he has not made himself anything, but has been sent by the Father, and that his unity with the Father is that of Son and Father, not a matter of "equality."

Jesus' role, which does not rest on his own claim. Jesus' act on the Sabbath had set a trial in motion. The encounter is pictured as a court scene (see on John 1:19 above). The διώκω (*diōkō*) of 5:16, usually translated "persecute," refers to legal action (REB "began to take [legal] action against Jesus"). Witnesses are called, evidence is presented, but Jesus speaks in his own defense, and only his voice is heard. Johannine Christians would think of their own experiences in the synagogue. Jesus does not testify to himself; it is God who bears witness to him, through John the Baptist, through Jesus' works, in which God is active (his words and deeds, his death and resurrection), and in the Scriptures—which must be read through the christological eyes of the Johannine community. The Johannine community does not accept the "either Moses or Jesus" alternative with which they had been presented, but claim Moses for themselves.

20. Strangely, Pentecost does not occur in the Johannine writings, despite the Johannine emphasis on the Spirit.

6:1–71 *Passover: Jesus the Bread of Life, Some Disciples Abandon Him*

Though specifically set in the time frame of Passover (6:4), in the present form of the Gospel, the story line moves away from Jerusalem and back to Galilee, where Jesus feeds the multitudes, then engages in disputes about the meaning of the miracle with both Jews and disciples. Passover motifs are reflected in the wilderness setting (6:31, 49), the references to manna, and especially in the eucharistic allusions. Jesus and his disciples do not attend this Passover, but attention is focused on the Eucharist. In the Fourth Gospel there is no institution of the Eucharist at the Last Supper; all the eucharistic language is found in the context of the feeding miracle in Galilee. This is another indication that the implied reader is the post-Easter Johannine community. The crowds, Jews, and disciples in the story could not have understood the references to eating Jesus' flesh and drinking his blood, but the Gospel's readers know that the church has been engaged in a dispute about the reality of the incarnation and the actuality of the human body of Jesus in the saving event. Some disciples have been scandalized by the crudity of such an understanding, and have left, while the evangelist represents the authentic disciples as rallying around the faith of the Twelve as expressed in Peter's confession (John 6:51c–71).[21] The dispute within the Johannine community documented in 1 John has been projected into this scene in the life of Jesus; in each case, those who objected to the confession that the divine Christ has come "in the flesh" left the community (see 2 John 7; 1 John 2:18–21, 4:1–3, and the key word σάρχ [*sarx*, flesh]). In the dualistic theology of the evangelist, the two groups are here represented by Peter and Judas. The role of Peter is another indication of the late date of the Gospel, in which the community has seen its need to unite with emerging mainstream Christianity under the symbolic leadership of Peter (see on chap. 21 below).

Jesus' "I am" sayings. Four times in this context Jesus identifies himself using the solemn revelatory "I am" formula rooted both in biblical tradition and in Hellenistic religion (6:20, 35, 41, 48). Gentiles could understand this as the definitive claim of the revealer deity to provide ultimate human needs, the universal human longing for salvation. Such declarations are found, for example, in the "I am" sayings of Isis.[22] The evangelist himself understands the sayings primarily in their biblical framework, where God speaks the revelatory "I am" (Exod 3:14; Isa 43:10–11; 45:12). In a key series of sayings, peculiar to the Fourth Gospel, "I am" is linked to a comprehensive metaphor designating the human quest for life and salvation:

— 6:35 — "I am the bread of life."

— 8:12 — "I am the light of the world."

— 10:7, 9 — "I am the door."

— 10:14 — "I am the good shepherd."

— 11:25 — "I am the resurrection and the life."

— 14:6 — "I am the way, the truth, and the life."

— 15:1, 5 — "I am the vine."

In this set of sayings—it is probably no accident that there are seven of them—the "I" is the predicate, and the longed-for saving reality is the subject, so that the sayings are to be heard in the form "The bread of life, it is I," or more colloquially, "The bread of life you're looking for—that's me" (cf. the quip attributed to Louis XIV, "L'État, c'est moi", and the notes on 1:38 above, "What are you looking for?"). In John's view, the particularity of the meaning of Passover, which could no longer be celebrated

21. John 8:31–36 also reflects the schism of 1 John: disciples believe in him, but will not continue in his word they had had "from the beginning" (cf. 8:25!). "Truth," "liar," "sin," "being from God," "freedom" are catchwords here, as in the Johannine Letters.

22. Cf. the Isis hymn and other examples cited in Boring, Berger, and Colpe, eds., *Hellenistic Commentary*, §417.

in Jerusalem, is fulfilled in the celebration of the Christ event, which is celebrated throughout the world, presented as the fulfillment of the universal human longing for authentic life, however it is expressed.

7:1–10:21 Feast of Booths: Conflict Intensifies

After the events of chapter 6, Jesus leaves Galilee for good, and the story line returns to Jerusalem and Judea. The evangelist has gathered a variety of traditions from the teaching repertoire of the Johannine school and assembled them as a series of events at the feast of Booths (cf. Exod 23:14–19; 34:22–24; Lev 23:33–36, 39–43; Num 29:12–38; Deut 16:16–17; 31:9–13). The presentation presupposes at some stage of the tradition an awareness of the particular emphases of the festival as it was celebrated in the first century, as reflected in Josephus and the Mishnah. An impressive daily ritual procession bearing a libation of water drawn from the Siloam pool focused on Israel's dependence on the beginning of the fall rains. In this context, Jesus declares that he is the source of living water (7:38).[23] A nightly ritual of lighting menorahs in the court of women (the "treasury of the temple," 8:20) symbolized the Torah as God's light for the world. In this context, Jesus declares that he is the light of the world (8:12).

Throughout this section, the disputed theme continues to be Jesus' identity. The reader overhears arguments and counterarguments formulated by the Johannine teachers in their debates with the synagogue.

Objection: Jesus (and his post-Easter followers in the Johannine school) are not authorized teachers: they have no authority as interpreters of the meaning of Scripture (7:15; cf. 7:48, "Has any one of the authorities or of the Pharisees believed in him?"). *Answer:* Jesus speaks directly by divine authority and needs no human credentials (7:28; 8:26, 38; 10:30). The charismatic teachers of the Johannine school appeal to the Holy Spirit as their teacher, not to rabbinic education.

Objection: Jesus (and the Johannine teachers) cannot be from God, since they do not respect the Sabbath (9:16; cf. 5:16). *Answer:* God works on the Sabbath; Jesus and the Johannine teachers do God's work (5:17). The Torah commands circumcision on the eighth day, which sometimes comes on the Sabbath. If circumcision can be performed on the Sabbath, healing of a whole person can be done on the Sabbath (7:20–24).

Objection: Jesus comes from Galilee, but according to the Scripture, no prophet is to come from Galilee, and the Messiah is to come from Bethlehem in Judea, not Galilee (7:41–42, 52). *Answer:* The Jews are wrong in supposing that they can judge the validity of Jesus' claim on the basis of his origin, for in fact Jesus is not from this world; his origin is in God, and this the unbelievers do not and cannot know.[24] Thus they can also claim that when the Messiah comes, people will not know his origin (contradicting their other view; see 7:27, 40–42), so that Jesus cannot be the Messiah since they do know where he is from. In John's view, all this simply shows the perversity and blindness of those who suppose they can judge the Messiah by human criteria (8:15).

Objection: Jesus, a human being, is making himself God and is guilty of blasphemy (10:33; see on 5:18). This repeated objection shows the Johannine Christians' use of God-language for Jesus was the flash point in their debates with

23. The Greek text says that "rivers of living water will flow from within him," i.e., from Jesus, the source of life (cf. 4:12–14; 13:5; 19:34). In the interest of inclusive language, some modern translations have substituted "the believer's" for "his," which misses the Johannine christological point.

24. Readers should not suppose that the evangelist here gives them a stage wink, as though we know that Jesus does come from Bethlehem and is thus qualified to be the Davidic Messiah. The Fourth Gospel never indicates Jesus was born in Bethlehem, but even this is not the real point. He does not think of Christology in Davidic categories.

the synagogue. *Answer:* The Johannine teachers combed the Scriptures to find places where God-language is used of human beings and responded to the charge with Psalm 82:6, understood to mean that certain Israelites (teachers, judges, prophets?) were called "gods." The logic of this argument is that if Israel's leaders could be called "gods" in a sense, this language is thoroughly biblical and does not infringe on the monotheistic claim of the one true God.

The evangelist, however, does not intend to argue the deity of Christ from the Bible. He begins with this conviction, and finds a biblical text that can be used to reassure Johannine Christians that their understanding of Jesus is true and biblical, despite the objections from the synagogue. The style of biblical interpretation is similar to the use of Exodus 3:6 in Mark 12:18–27. Regarded objectively, it is not convincing to the modern reader, just as it was not convincing to the ancient Jewish objectors, but this is beside the point. The Johannine teachers refuse to back down on their faith that the one true God is definitively revealed in Jesus, and that their language to express this comes from their Scriptures, which they refuse to give up.

9:1–41 The man born blind Several aspects of Johannine Christology are concentrated in this masterful story. That the man was *born* blind not only magnifies the predicament and Jesus' power in overcoming it, but shows that Jesus' life-giving power does not merely restore something that has been lost. The blind man represents the human predicament as such; human beings do not lose their sight and have it restored by the Christ event. They have never seen, but can gain (not re-gain) authentic sight (9:39). Jesus' concluding comment shows that the sign, like all his signs, is not merely a literal miracle for an individual, but the symbolic representation of the Christ event as such. The man is anointed, washed, and recovers his sight, all symbolic actions for conversion to the Sent One—John explains that "Siloam" means "sent" (see John 9:7, 39–41; 13:1–11; 1 John 2:20, 27). What Jesus does for the blind man in the story is what God does for the world in the Christ event. In this story, John emphasizes that those who receive this gift from God must take a stand; it is not enough to believe in Christ as one's "personal" savior and keep a low profile, as though the transaction were only between God and the individual. John portrays the hesitancy of the parents to acknowledge what had happened when challenged by the Jewish authorities (9:18–23), just as he condemns those who believe but will not publicly confess their faith and identify with the persecuted community (12:42–43).

John's portrayal is here transparent to his own situation, where those who do confess their Christian faith are expelled from the synagogue (9:22; cf. 16:2; Luke 6:22). The healed blind man, however, is a model of progressive deepening of faith, insight, and courage. He is the first one in the Gospel to confess Jesus in a hostile situation. His understanding of Jesus' identity does not come all at once; under examination, he moves from identifying Jesus as "a man" (9:17) to "a prophet" (9:17) who is "from God" (9:33) to the full confession of Jesus as "Son of Man,"[25] that is, the Messiah (9:35–38; see 9:22).

10:1–21 Jesus as the true Shepherd Like "way," "truth," "life," and "light," so also "shepherd" is a hermeneutical metaphor widely used in the Hellenistic world for the good ruler, a metaphor that also plays a powerful role in Jewish Scripture and tradition (e.g., Pss 23, 100; Ezek 34:11–16). Thus, when Jesus declares that he is the Good Shepherd (10:11, 14), another

25. "Son of Man" is a key title for the Fourth Evangelist, "the heart of Johannine Christology" (Kysar, *Maverick Gospel*, 40). Throughout, it is Jesus' own term for himself. It stands at the climactic place in the series of christological titles in 1:19–51. In the presupposed Wisdom myth, preexistent wisdom becomes incarnate in the Son of Man (*1 Enoch* 49:1–4, see above, §27.5 under John 1:1–18). It connotes both preexistent divinity and earthly humanity. It was probably the fundamental confession of the Johannine community, preserved from the earliest days (see above under §9.2.2).

hermeneutical bridge is constructed that facilitates an understanding of Jesus available to both Jews and Gentiles. The metaphor was the focus of intensive attention in the developing Johannine community, as the churches were threatened with heresy and schism. If Jesus himself is the church's only shepherd, who continues to lead the church through his presence in the Spirit (see on the Farewell Discourses below), does the church need authorized ministers to be its shepherds and protect it from the "wolves," the false teachers? This debate was also occurring in the Pauline school, neighbors of the Johannine community, fellow Christian communities with whom they were in dialogue (cf. Acts 20:29 and the developing institutionalization of ministry in the Pastorals). In John 10, Christ himself is the church's only shepherd, and "hirelings" are disdained (10:12–13). This may be a reflection of debates about the introduction of official, paid ministers in the charismatic Johannine community. John 21 probably represents a later, perhaps final, stage of this discussion (see below).

10:22–42 *Feast of Dedication: Attempted Arrest; Jesus Withdraws to Transjordan*

The conflict over the christological claims made for Jesus is again made explicit in the final scene of the conflict (see on 5:18 above). As Jesus withdraws to the place where John had baptized, the section forms a bracket with the opening scenes: John's baptizing and testimony, Jesus' signs, christological claims and conflict, Jesus disappears, people believe—a minidrama of the whole Gospel narrative. At one stage of the Gospel's development, this may have formed the conclusion of the Book of Signs.

11:1–12:50 Climax and Conclusion of Jesus' Public Ministry

In the present edition of the Gospel, Jesus remains in Transjordan until called to Bethany by Lazarus's sickness. The raising of Lazarus then constitutes Jesus' last and greatest sign, both pointing to Jesus' own death and resurrection and ironically becoming the occasion for a renewed attempt to put Jesus to death (11:17–53). Jesus again withdraws, this time to Ephraim, apparently the Judean village on the edge of the desert about fifteen miles northeast of Jerusalem, where he remains with his disciples until the Passover in early spring (11:54). Amid intense discussion of Jesus' whereabouts among the Passover pilgrims in Jerusalem, where a warrant for Jesus' arrest had been issued, Jesus came to nearby Bethany six days before the Passover (11:55–12:1). At a dinner party on Saturday evening in the home of Lazarus, Martha, and Mary, Jesus is anointed by Mary in anticipation of his death and burial (12:2–11). The next day, Palm Sunday, Jesus is met by a crowd of pilgrims from the city who hail him as "King of Israel." The Pharisees respond in despair that "the whole world has gone after him" (12:12–19). The apparent welcome of the Gentile world to the message of Jesus is also signaled by the coming of some Greeks to Jesus (12:20–22). Jesus responds with a summary of Johannine theology, and then withdraws into hiding for the third time (12:23–36). The narrator then gives a summary lamentation on the people's unbelief and the refusal of some believers to confess their faith (12:37–43). The Book of Signs is then concluded with a final summary of Johannine theology in the form of words of Jesus, a proclamation not located in any particular scene, but representing the word of the transcendent Lord, who is not bound by time and space. Without transition, the next scene brings the reader to the Last Supper and the Book of Glory.

Part 2: The Book of Glory: Jesus Reveals the Glory of His Death and Resurrection to the Disciples (13:1–20:31)

The Book of Glory has two parts, discourse/sign, the mirror image of the sign/discourse structure of the Book of Signs. The passion and resurrection narrative (chaps. 18–20) is preceded by the Last Supper and Farewell Discourse (chaps. 13–17).

13:1–17:26 The Last Supper and Farewell Discourse

13:1–30 The Last Supper

The narrator moves the scene abruptly to the Last Supper. In the Fourth Gospel there is no preparation for this lengthy account, which lasts through 17:26 and is by far the longest module in the narrative. It is not a Passover meal, just as there has been no preliminary contact of Judas with the high priests to arrange for Jesus' betrayal (cf. Mark 14:10–17 on all points). There is no institution of the Eucharist (specific eucharistic instruction has already been given in 6:53–58), but Jesus acts out the meaning of the whole Christ event by performing the duty of a slave, washing the disciples' feet.

The footwashing has several parallels to the Pauline hymn of Philippians 2:6–11. In both, Jesus divests himself and descends, performs the service of a slave, rises, is seated, and is then designated as "Lord." In both, Jesus is presented not merely as a humble human being, but as one who gives himself for others. This self-giving then becomes the model for discipleship. Philippians was probably written in Ephesus, a generation before the Gospel of John was written there (see above, §11.2.2). Philippians and/or the hymn probably circulated in the Johannine community. For the Johannine school, however, Jesus' laying aside his garments does not represent kenosis Christology. In the Book of Signs the preexistent Christ retains his glory as the incarnate Jesus. Here Jesus shows that the supreme sign manifests God's power as self-giving love.

As in the Synoptics, Jesus announces that one of the disciples will betray him. Jesus and the readers already know this is Judas (6:71; 12:4; 13:2), but the other disciples do not know. Peter must ask the Beloved Disciple, who is reclining at the table between Peter and Jesus, to identify the traitor.

13:31–17:26 The Farewell Discourse and Prayer

Judas goes out into the darkness, and the Light of the world begins the Farewell Discourse, which continues as monologue and prayer almost without interruption until the passion narrative begins at 18:1. Some key features:

Jesus' departure and promised return—the reinterpretation of apocalyptic. Following the Markan outline, each of the Synoptic Gospels has Jesus deliver a long speech looking ahead to the post-Easter period and the coming of the Son of Man at the consummation of history (Mark 13, Matt 23–25, Luke 21). The Markan Jesus had promised that the end was "near," would be "soon," that the generation to which Jesus spoke "will not pass away before all these things take place" (Mark 9:1; 13:29–30). In John, this language of Jesus' soon return is taken up again, as Jesus speaks to his disciples before his departure to the Father and repeatedly promises it will only be "a little while" before they see him again (14:19; seven times in 16:16–19). The perplexed disciples ask each other, "What does he mean by this 'a little while'? We do not know what he is talking about" (16:18). Here we overhear the discussions within the Johannine school struggling to reinterpret traditional eschatology.

The first generation of Christians had understood the resurrection of Jesus not as an isolated event, but as the beginning of the resurrection of all at the end of history. Jesus was the "firstfruits" (1 Cor 15:20); the remainder of the eschatological harvest was soon to follow. As history continued into the second and third generations after Jesus' death, four different responses to the hope expressed in the words "Jesus is coming soon" can be identified in early Christianity:

1. *Reaffirmation*. In times of threat and persecution, Christians of the second and third generations revived the older apocalyptic expectations with the conviction that even though earlier they had remained unfulfilled, *now* the end has indeed come near. In their situation, apocalyptic language once again made sense and supplied an urgently needed means of holding on to the faith despite all the empirical evidence to the contrary. Within the Johannine community, Revelation represents this option. In the 90s of the first century, John addresses the crisis of the churches with the renewed promise

that *now* the parousia really is coming soon (see above, §26.1.2).

2. *Rejection*. Taken literally, this renewed expectation too turned out to be mistaken. Some early Christians thus decided that apocalyptic expectation as such was an error, and simply rejected it. Gnostic streams of Christianity abandoned the conviction that God would redeem this world and exchanged the hope that God would redeem the horizontal line of history in a mighty eschatological act for a verticalism in which individual souls are saved out of this world into the transcendent realm and/or already enjoy the eschatological realities in their present religious experience (see above, §9.2.2). Such views were apparently advocated by the opponents of 2 Peter (see above, at 2 Pet 3:1–13). Within the Johannine community, this may have been the perspective of the Nicolaitans, the followers of "Jezebel" who promoted the teaching of "Balaam" (Rev 2:6, 14–15, 20). The teachers of the Johannine school adopt some of this conceptuality and language, but do not entirely reject the future eschatological hope.

3. *Reinterpretation of "soon."* Some early Christian theologians held on to the hope for the apocalyptic victory of God at the end of history, but postponed it to an indefinite future time. They reaffirmed the early Christian faith that "the end is coming soon," but reinterpreted the meaning of "soon" in a nonliteral manner. This was the view of the author of 2 Peter, who was glad to find a text in his Bible that explained a thousand years in God's sight as only a day (Ps 90:4). Similarly, Luke rewrites the story of Jesus and the church to allow for an extended period of church history, the time of the Christian mission. The Christ comes not at the end, but in the midst of history; the time of Christ is followed by the time of the church, a time of mission, which will last indefinitely before the end finally comes (see above, §23.1).

4. *Reinterpretation of the "second coming of Jesus."* In contrast to Luke, the teachers of the Johannine school responded in various ways to the death of the first Christian generation, without developing a specific periodization of salvation history (see below, on 21:20–23). Their primary approach to reinterpreting the first generation's hope that "the end is coming soon" was to redefine "end": the end did in fact come soon, as Jesus had promised, with the outpouring of the Spirit and the beginning of the church. The authors of the Letters and Gospel of John reinterpret all the realities expected to come at the eschaton as already present realities: the theology of the preexistent Logos allows the coming of the Son of Man at the end of history to be understood as the life of Jesus, the Son of Man who has already come from heaven (John 3:13); the troubles that afflict the world and the people of God just before the end ("birthpangs," "tribulation") are understood as Christian experience as such (16:20–21); the expected antichrist is understood as the false teachers already present (1 John 2:18–22; 4:3; 2 John 7); the second coming of Christ is reinterpreted as Christ's coming again as the Spirit, the Paraclete (John 14–16); the defeat of Satan happened in Jesus' ministry (John 12:31); the resurrection happens in the new life of the Christian (John 11:21–26; cf. 8:51); the cosmic, apocalyptic rebirth expected at the end (παλιγγενεσία, *palingenesia*, Matt 19:28; cf. *1 Enoch* 25.6; 50.1; *2 Bar* 51.1–10) happens in the conversion of individual Christians (John 1:11–12, 3:3–5); the Last Judgment happens in the present encounter with Christ the judge (John 3:18–19; 12:31, 48), and eternal life is already the present possession of the believer (John 3:36; 6:47; 17:3). All this can be thought of as explication of the faith that the Messiah, who was to come at the end, has already come.

Some interpreters, for example, Rudolf Bultmann and his followers, thus argue that the original author of the Fourth Gospel was a radically creative theologian who completely reduced futuristic theology to the present experience of believers. In this view, the Johannine texts that clearly affirm future eschatology are attributed to the ecclesiastical redactor, who reintroduced some elements of apocalyptic eschatology to bring Johannine theology into line with the emerging mainstream protocatholic Great Church (5:28–29; 6:27, 39–40, 44, 54; 12:25, 48; 11:24; 14:2–3, 17:24). The issue is still debated, but most scholars would now not draw such a sharp line between the final form of the Gospel and its previous edition(s), and would see the tension between present and future eschatology as present throughout the Johannine tradition—albeit with different emphases. Although the center of gravity has shifted toward present eschatology, the Johannine community retains a hope for the future consummation.

The Paraclete. The most distinctive aspect of the Johannine reinterpretation of the parousia is the understanding that the imagery of the coming of Jesus tends to be replaced by the coming of the Holy Spirit (cf. 14:23 "I will come"; 14:25, "the Holy Spirit will come"). In the Johannine school, the distinctive name for the Holy Spirit is ὁ παράκλητος (*ho paraklētos*, transliterated Paraclete, from the preposition *para-* and the adjective *klētos*, derived from the past participle of the verb *kaleō, call*). The word, which etymologically means "one called alongside," was used in a variety of senses in nonbiblical Greek: helper; one who appears in another's behalf as mediator or intercessor; occasionally in the technical legal sense "lawyer," "attorney," one who represents another in court. This last sense, though rare outside the Bible, fits the Johannine understanding: in the trials of the Johannine Christians, including their appearance before synagogue or Roman courts, Jesus does not abandon them, but stands by them as their advocate in the person of the Holy Spirit. The promise of the Synoptic Jesus (Mark 13:9–11) is thus expanded to cover Christian experience as a whole, as well as focused on the role of the Spirit as the divinely sent counselor in the forensic sense. Five "Paraclete sayings" within the Farewell Discourse portray the distinct work of the Paraclete (14:15–17, 25–26; 15:26–27; 16:7–11, 12–15). As counselor, the Paraclete is not only the defense attorney who stands by and empowers Johannine Christians when they must face hostile courts, but is also the prosecuting attorney who prosecutes God's case against the unbelieving world (16:8–11). As in the passion narrative, the apparent reality seen on the surface is not the true reality; the accused is really the judge (see on chaps. 18–19, esp. 19:13). As with Jesus, so with his followers.

The Paraclete spans the horizons of past, present, and future. As hermeneut and teacher, the Paraclete interprets the past ministry of Jesus and enables the Johannine community to remember the teaching of Jesus. The promise is not of a mechanical reproduction of the past words of Jesus, as comparison of the tradition of Jesus' sayings in the Synoptics and the Fourth Gospel makes clear. The work of the Holy Spirit is seen to be active in the creative memory of the Johannine tradition, which combines and reconfigures the teaching of Jesus inherited from the past with the new revelations from the risen Lord, in which Jesus continues to speak (cf. 16:12–14). The words of Jesus in the Gospel of John represent this fusion of past and present—Jesus-back-there-in-history with Jesus-up-there-in-heaven and Jesus-still-present-in-the-Christian-community—a fusion generated and interpreted by Christian prophets within the Johannine community.[26]

Mission and "the world." The Fourth Gospel is not a missionary or evangelistic tract addressed to unbelievers with a view to their conversion (see on §27.2, and 20:30–31 below). During the narrative of Jesus' ministry in the Book of Signs, unbelievers in general were often designated as "the Jews." In the Farewell Discourse, this often hostile, over-against community of outsiders is called "the world."[27] Just as Jesus does not

26. Boring, *Sayings of the Risen Jesus*, 48–50; M. Eugene Boring, "The Influence of Christian Prophecy on the Johannine Portrayal of the Paraclete and Jesus," *NTS* 25, no. 4 (1978): 113–23; John Ashton, *Understanding the Fourth Gospel* (New York: Oxford University Press, 1991), 182–83, 303, 515.

27. Of the sixty-three references to "the Jews" in the Fourth Gospel, the only such reference in the Last Supper and Farewell Discourse is the retrospective 13:33. Of

belong to the world, in a different sense neither do the believers (15:18–19; 16:28; 17:14–16). Jesus is the preexistent one who belongs to the divine world; believers do not belong to the world because they have been born to a new life by their decision of faith. The world is not seen merely as the hostile power dominated by the evil one, but as the beloved creation of God (1:1–2; 3:16). Jesus' disciples are not to withdraw from the world, either into their own individual experience of Jesus as their "personal savior" or into a sect that has walled itself off from the world, launching tirades not only against "the world" of unbelievers, but against other Christians who no longer belonged to their group.[28] The Johannine school understood itself to have both an ecumenical mandate to the larger church and a missionary mandate to the world. As Jesus is the Sent One, his followers are sent into the world (20:21).

Unity of believers with God, Christ, and other Christians. Jesus and the Father are one (10:30). This text, in the very center of the narrative, is also at the center of John's theology. Jesus' disciples share in this unity, they are united with each other and with Christ as the branches are united in the vine (15:1–8). Christ is the whole vine, not merely the trunk; the community has a given unity by being already united to Christ. Yet the Gospel looks back on two major conflicts, one involving the separation from their roots and fellow Christian believers who remained in the synagogue, and one involving a split in the ranks of the Johannine community itself (see on chap. 6 above). The canonical form of the Fourth Gospel, however, though it bears the scars of previous battles, is no longer in a combative mood and now wants to integrate the scattered and scattering Christians. The Gospel represents the final phase of the community's life visible to us in its writings, as it moves toward integration in the developing mainstream (see under chap. 21). Thus the Johannine Jesus prays for unity (17:21–23), and the Good Shepherd discourse concludes with the declaration, "I have other sheep that do not belong to this fold. I must bring them also, and they will listen to my voice. So there will be one flock, one shepherd" (10:16).

Predestination? In John 15:16 Jesus declares, "*You did not choose me but I chose you.*" Is this Johannine predestination? Two series of texts can easily be assembled. On the one hand, in numerous passages John indicates that salvation is entirely God's gift, that the initiative and accomplishment of salvation is entirely in God's hands. Believers are born from God, born from above (1:12–13; 3:3–5). No one decides to be born; birth is a gift. Faith is God's gift, the work of God in believers (6:29). God "gives" particular people to Christ; they cannot come to him unless drawn and granted by God (6:44, 65; 10:29; 17:2, 6, 9, 24). Only those who are already Jesus' sheep and belong to God can recognize his voice and follow him (8:47; 10:3–4). Jesus' disciples do not belong to the world because Jesus has chosen them out of the world (15:19).

On the other hand, numerous texts imply or directly state that human beings are responsible to decide for or against God, that whether or not one believes is a human decision in one's own hands, that those who do not believe could have, and should have, made the other decision, and are themselves responsible (3:16, 36; 6:27a; 10:38; 12:36, 46; 14:1, 11; 20:31). There is no way to resolve this conflict conceptually—certainly no easy and simple way. The two series of affirmations lie in two different planes and cannot be combined into one system. The one series affirms and guards God's sovereignty, the other, human responsibility. John, and the New Testament generally, affirms both, and affirms both absolutely. God cannot be "partly sovereign" and humans "partly responsible."

seventy-eight references to κόσμος (*kosmos*, world) in John, forty are in the Farewell Discourse. "The Jews" of the first half of the Gospel are analogous to "the world" of the second half.

28. The mission perspective of the Fourth Gospel is especially developed in the work of the Nigerian scholar Teresa T. Okure, *The Johannine Approach to Mission*, WUNT 2.31 (Tübingen: Mohr, 1989).

Each set of affirmations is valid in its own realm of discourse, but they cannot be combined into one logical discursive set of propositional statements. The Johannine Jesus is not making abstract philosophical statements on the problem of determinism and free will. No *essay* can affirm that both are true, but a *narrative* can do justice to each claim. Accordingly, John can compose a story in which both are present, fully present. Thus in the stories of the gathering of the disciples in 1:29–51, they become followers of Jesus in a variety of ways: some hear about Jesus from others, only one is directly called by Jesus, all are pictured as making their own decisions, and that is how they would have described their experience. Yet in retrospect they are told by Christ that they have not chosen him but he has chosen them (15:16). When I become a disciple, I think of myself as a volunteer, who could have made other choices; in retrospect, I learn that I am a draftee and, instead of congratulating myself on my good choice, I give thanks to God who has chosen me.

For John, divine sovereignty and human choice are both real, a simultaneous paradox, the necessary consequence of speaking of divine reality in human language and conceptuality, the result of the *Word* becoming *flesh*. The language of discipleship is a reflex of the language of Christology; a community that confesses the deity and humanity of Jesus Christ has been given a linguistic and theological key to how to speak of divine sovereignty and human freedom. Such matters are not theories that can be proclaimed to unbelievers in order to convert them, but the theological reflection of insiders, expressed in the confessional language of the believing community.

18:1–19:42 The Passion Narrative

The Johannine passion story follows the same general outline as the Synoptics: after the Last Supper with his disciples on Thursday evening, Jesus and his disciples go the Mount of Olives, where he is arrested, taken to a night hearing before the high priest(s), then taken to Pilate, where he is condemned to death, and taken immediately to be crucified on Friday afternoon (19:31). He is buried on Friday evening, and the empty tomb is discovered on Sunday morning. The similarity to the Synoptic account is seen not only in the similar order and structure; in several instances there is similar or identical wording (e.g., John 18:15–27/Mark 14:53–65/ Matt 26:57–68/Luke 22:54–71). Distinctive aspects of the Johannine rewriting:

The Jewish trial disappears, and the encounter is entirely with the Roman state represented by Pilate. The Romans are involved in Jesus' arrest from the beginning; Jesus is not, as in the Synoptics, arrested by Jewish police and turned over to the Romans only after the "Jewish trial" (18:3). In the Fourth Gospel, Jesus' trial before the world has extended throughout the whole narrative, and the Jewish leadership officially decided on his death at the end of the Book of Signs (11:47–54). There is thus no place for a Jewish trial that would reveal Jesus' messianic claim—this has been apparent throughout. The Johannine Jesus specifically declares that all his teaching has been public; there is no messianic secret (18:19–21). This scenario probably reflects the trials to which Christians were subject in the time of the evangelist. Suspect Christians testified that, like Jesus, they were not a secret society with esoteric teachings, but had declared their views openly in the synagogues. Jewish authorities apparently sometimes delivered Christians condemned in Jewish courts to the Roman authorities for punishment, which could mean the death penalty. The believers' experience parallels that of Jesus; the Jesus story reflects the believers' story.

The calendar is adjusted so that Jesus dies on Passover, as the lambs are being killed. The Jews will not enter the praetorium, the headquarters of the Roman governor, so that they would not become ritually unclean, which would prevent them from participation in the Passover meal (18:28). The Passover lambs would be killed Friday afternoon and the meal eaten after six o'clock; in the Jewish calendar, this is the beginning of the next day. From the beginning of the narrative, Jesus has been hailed as "the Lamb of God who takes away the sin of the world," and Jesus will die as the Passover lambs are being killed in the temple. He is spared the breaking of the legs, inflicted on the two men crucified with him, in fulfillment of the specifications for slaughter of the Passover lamb, "None of his bones shall be broken" (19:36; cf. Exod 12:46; Num 9:12). This is probably also the explanation for the use of a sprig of hyssop to reach the sponge of wine to Jesus' lips (19:29). Hyssop, mentioned only here in the Gospels, is a small, flimsy plant hardly useful for the purpose described, but it was used ritually in the Passover (Exod 12:22).

The most striking Johannine emphasis is on the sovereign authority of Jesus, who is not the victim but the sovereign victor, in charge of events throughout the passion story. In the Synoptics, following Mark, the powerful, divine Jesus appears in the first part of the story, and the weak, human Jesus in the passion narrative (see above, §21.6). John has both views simultaneously, but in the passion story the sovereign, triumphant Christ certainly prevails. Some facts of John's presentation:

— In advance of the passion, Jesus had declared that no one takes his life from him. He lays down his life of his own accord, he takes it up again by his own power; he received this authority from the Father (10:17–18).

— Jesus is not taken by surprise, but knows all things in advance.

— There is no Gethsemane prayer as Jesus faces death, agonizing about his decision, and there can be none, after the sovereign prayer of 17:1–26 (see the anticipatory comment in 12:27–28 and 18:11b).

— Jesus goes to the garden not, as in the Synoptics, in order to pray, but because Judas knows the place and Jesus can be located there.

— When the arresting officers and soldiers arrive with Judas, Jesus asks them whom they are looking for, and they respond. Jesus is not the questioned, but is himself the questioner.

— Judas does not identify Jesus. Jesus identifies himself, with the sovereign "I am," resonant with the biblical divine name. The soldiers fall down, unable to arrest him, and Jesus delivers himself into their hands.

— The disciples do not flee, but Jesus dismisses them, after instructing the arresting officers to allow them to leave.

— Jesus rebukes Peter's attempt at defending him, for he needs no defense, since he is going his own sovereign way (18:10–11).

— He refuses to be questioned by the high priest and challenges the officer who strikes him (18:20–23).

— Throughout the detailed Roman trial, as Pilate shuttles back and forth between Jesus inside the palace and the Jews outside, Jesus is calm and in control, and Pilate becomes unraveled. Jesus interrogates Pilate (18:34) and declares that Pilate has no authority over him except what God has given him (19:11). When Pilate yields to the pressure to condemn Jesus, after Jesus has been mocked with the crown of thorns and purple robe (19:2), Pilate mockingly sets Jesus on the judgment seat, as though Jesus were judge and Pilate and the Jewish accusers were being judged. Intended as mockery, the readers know this is the truth.[29]

29. The Greek verb of 19:13 can be translated either intransitively, "Pilate sat on the judgment seat" (so NRSV and most English translations), or transitively "Pilate seated him [Jesus] on the judgment seat" (so NAB, NJB, TOB, CEB, Justin, *Apology* 1.35.6, and numerous modern commentators). Either way, the scene is deeply ironic: either Pilate's attempted mockery reveals the real truth, or Pilate himself sits on the judgment seat *as if* he were the judge, when readers know the reality of the situation.

— In the Synoptics, Simon of Cyrene carries Jesus' cross (Mark 15:21/Matt 27:32/Luke 23:26); the Johannine Jesus needs no help (19:17).

— As he hangs on the cross, Jesus' words "I am thirsty" are not said to express his own need, but to fulfill the Scripture (19:28).

— There is no "My God, why . . ." cry from the cross, but his sovereign statements to the Beloved Disciple and his mother, making provision for her future (19:25–27). The ordeal is not over until Jesus himself announces, "It is finished" (19:30).

Jesus' death was real, with saving and transforming power. Alongside this portrayal of the sovereign divine Jesus who himself presides over the events of his death, John emphasizes that Jesus' death was humanly, gruesomely real. The lance thrust into Jesus' side that released blood and water not only confirmed the reality of his death, but revealed Jesus as the source of living water, whose blood takes away sin, his saving power communicated in baptism and Eucharist (cf. 3:5; 6:53–56; 7:37–39; 1 John 1:7; 5:6–8). As Jesus dies, he transmits the Spirit to the tiny community of believers around the cross, founding the church as a new family as he is lifted up and begins to draw all people to himself/God (12:32).

Just as the reality of Pentecost already pervades the Easter scenes (see 20:21–23), so here the giving of the Spirit is already anticipated on Good Friday. Joseph of Arimathea, already known in the Synoptics, in the Fourth Gospel becomes a disciple among the Jewish leadership who now dares to step forward and publicly identity himself with Jesus. John adds that Nicodemus, who had come to Jesus at night and had increasingly manifested a willingness to be associated with Jesus, steps forward to give Jesus a royal burial (19:39–40; cf. 3:1–15; 7:50–52). The Johannine school holds up Joseph and Nicodemus as models for the Jewish Christians who remain in the synagogue but are reluctant to confess Jesus publicly (cf. 7:13; 12:42–43).

20:1–29 The Resurrection of Jesus and Commissioning of the Disciples

The Johannine resurrection stories are reminiscent of the Synoptic narratives: finding the empty tomb; telling the disciples; appearances of the risen Jesus, who is at first unrecognized, then commissions the disciples. None of the four scenes in John, however, has a direct parallel in the Synoptics:

20:1–10 Discovery of the empty tomb Mary Magdalene discovers the empty tomb and runs to tell Peter and the Beloved Disciple, who then run to the tomb. The Beloved Disciple arrives first, but Peter enters the tomb first. They see the linen wrappings. The Beloved Disciple believes.

20:11–18 Appearance to Mary Magdalene Alone at the tomb, Jesus appear to Mary Magdalene, who recognizes him only when he speaks her name. She is forbidden to touch, addresses him as "Teacher," and reports to the disciples that she had seen the Lord.

20:19–23 Appearance to the disciples, in the absence of Thomas On the same Sunday evening, Jesus appears to his disciples, who are in hiding for fear of the Jews, shows them his hands and side, confers the Holy Spirit on them, and commissions them to continue his mission.

20:24–29 Second appearance to the disciples, including Thomas When Thomas learns of this, he declares that he will not believe unless he sees the pierced hands and side of Jesus. A week later, that is, the next Sunday, Jesus again appears to the disciples and invites Thomas to touch his hands and side. The Gospel concludes with Thomas's confession of faith, the most exalted in the Gospel, "My Lord and my God," forming a bracket with the opening words of the Gospel (1:1, "and the Word was God"). Jesus pronounces blessing on those who have not seen and yet have believed.

20:30–31 Conclusion and Purpose of the Gospel

This epilogue was the original conclusion of the Gospel, expressing the purpose that governs the whole. It is usually translated "that you may believe that Jesus is the Christ" (so RSV), with the alternative represented by the NRSV, "that you may come to believe that Jesus is the Christ." The difference represents the distinction between the Greek aorist tense, found in some manuscripts, and the present tense, found in others. However, even if the aorist is original, it need not be translated "that you may come to believe." The Gospel was not written to convert outsiders (see above, §27.2, on the purpose of the Gospel). It is important to see that, despite the universalistic perspective of the Gospel and its hermeneutical bridges to non-Jewish worlds of thought, belief in Jesus as the Christ is an indispensable element of Christian faith. The One sent by God as Savior of the world is the Messiah. This is an essential given of the author's thought. His faith is that this Messiah has come, that he is Jesus of Nazareth.

Second Conclusion (21:1–25)

Most scholars are convinced that chapter 21 is a secondary conclusion, not written by the author who composed chapters 1–20.[30] A selection of the evidence detailed in the critical commentaries:

1. The narrative comes to a proper conclusion in 20:30–31, so that chapter 21 seems to represent a secondary addition.

2. The vocabulary and style differ from the rest of the Gospel. This brief text contains twenty-one words not found in John 1–20, including different words for "lamb" (ἀμνός, *amnos*, 1:29, 36; ἀρνίον, *arnion*, 21:15) and "new" (καινός, *kainos*, 13:34; 19:41; νεός, *neos*, 21:18).

3. Items of content are presupposed from the general Christian tradition, but not found in John 1–20, for example, that Peter was a fisherman, that the disciples of Jesus included the two sons of Zebedee, and that resurrection appearances occurred in Galilee. Chapter 21 seems inclined to harmonize the distinctive Johannine tradition and the Synoptic tradition dominant in the wider church.

4. Historical and theological tensions between John 1–20 and John 21 include these:

- In John 1–20, the Beloved Disciple and Peter have a competitive relationship in which the Beloved Disciple is always superior (see above, §27.1.3), but in John 21 Peter is rehabilitated and given pastoral authority as the shepherd for the whole church.
- John 21 begins as though no previous resurrection appearances had occurred; the disciples return to their old lives, somewhat at loose ends. This would fit after John 19, as an independent new beginning, but not after John 20, when all the disciples have seen and joyfully recognized the risen Lord, from whom they have received the Holy Spirit and been commissioned and empowered to continue Jesus' ministry.
- Futuristic eschatology has been minimized in John 1–20 but plays the dominant role in John 21.

"Secondary" only refers to the compositional history of the Gospel and does not mean "second-rate." As the prologue presented the initial framework within which the whole narrative is to be understood, so the teachers of the Johannine school provide a conclusion that recasts the whole narrative within its ultimate hermeneutical context—note the "we" of 21:24, forming a bracket with the "we" or the prologue (1:14, 16). Here are some dimensions of this hermeneutical move:

30. Significant exceptions: Walter Bauer, *Das Johannesevangelium*, 2nd rev. ed. 1925; 3rd rev. and expanded ed. 1933, Handbuch zum Neuen Testament 2.2 (Tübingen: Mohr, 1912), 234–35; Paul S. Minear, "The Original Functions of John 21," *JBL* 102, no. 1 (1983): 85–98; Carson, *Gospel according to John*, 665–68; Berger, *Im Anfang war Johannes*, 21–25.

Charismatic leadership of the Johannine school, represented by the Beloved Disciple, is integrated into the developing structures of the Great Church, represented by Peter. By the time John 21 was written, the Johannine school was no longer driven by christological issues. The primary questions now were ecclesiological. First Peter shows that the Pauline churches of Asia were being addressed by a leading presbyter/elder in the name of Peter, inviting Christians in the Pauline tradition to see themselves as under the pastoral leadership of Peter, without giving up their Pauline tradition. John 21 represents the response of the Johannine school to this same movement. Peter had been second-best throughout the preceding narrative, finally failing and denying Jesus. The Beloved Disciple had been faithful, and at the foot of the cross it was the Beloved Disciple who had been commissioned by Jesus to care for his family.

In 21:9–19, Peter is rehabilitated. The charcoal fire recalls the scene of Peter's denial (21:9, cf. 18:18), the breaking of bread has eucharistic overtones (cf. 6:1–15), Jesus is made known in the breaking of bread (cf. Luke 24), and Peter's three denials are replaced with three affirmations of his love for Jesus. While again it is the Beloved Disciple who first recognizes Jesus, this time it is Peter who arrives first. Peter alone draws the net to shore, filled to overflowing with an incredible catch, but without breaking the net; as Jesus' one-piece tunic was not torn (19:23–24), so the net was not torn; as there is one shepherd, there is one flock (10:16).

Jesus alone had been the Good Shepherd, who gives his life for the sheep and preserves it as one flock (10:1–18), and others were considered "hirelings." Here, however, Jesus confers the pastoral responsibility for his flock on Peter alone. The Beloved Disciple is honored as a faithful follower, but his charismatic ministry is incorporated within the community that now looks to Peter as its shepherd. This community knows that Peter had been faithful to death, had been martyred in Rome, that he was indeed the good shepherd who gave his life for the sheep (21:18–20), and is encouraged to accept the developing pastoral structures he represents.

Though not written in Rome, the final version of the Gospel concluding with John 21 brings the Johannine school into the orbit of the Roman Great Church. Ephesus, outside Rome, now sees itself as included in the ecumenical church in which Peter (Rome) has a leading role. This was not a matter of Roman ecclesiastical imperialism, but a sectarian group finding its authentic identity within the larger church, somewhat like the way in which disciples of John the Baptist were integrated into the mainstream in Acts 18–19—also in Ephesus, be it noted. The Johannine school is to be seen as setting the model for emerging ecumenical Christianity; they were proactive, not reactive. The Johannine community would thus be a model of canonical Christianity in that it reinterprets older traditions without either abandoning them or being bound to them.

Futurist eschatology is reaffirmed despite the death of the first generation. The Johannine teachers take the occasion of the interchange between Jesus and Peter to correct a misunderstanding that troubled the church. The founder and leader of the Johannine school, who came to be known as the Beloved Disciple, did not die as a martyr in the persecution of the 60s, as had Peter, but lived among the Christians in Asia until he died at an advanced age. Some had thought that the Beloved Disciple would not die, but would live to see the parousia. This reflects both the conviction of the first generation that the end would come before their death (Mark 9:1; 13:30; 1 Thess 4:15), and the special place in salvation history they attributed to him. His death precipitated something of a crisis, for he was expected to live until the parousia. The Johannine teachers do not abandon the hope for the parousia, but they explain that the expectation that the first generation would live to see it was a misunderstanding. (21:20–23).

These verses should not be seen as a reintroduction of future eschatology in order to come to terms with the theology of the Great Church. Future eschatology had never disappeared from the Johannine community but had lived alongside the realized eschatology that became dominant. The second generation and the following generations of believers no longer live in the presence of eyewitnesses whose eyes have seen and whose hands have handled the Word of life (see 1 John 1:1–4; John 20:24–29). They have received the blessing of the risen Christ pronounced on those who believe without having seen. They are not adrift; their faith in the Risen One continues to be strengthened by the Scriptures (5:39; 20:9; cf. Luke 16:27–31). And they now have the written testimony of the Beloved Disciple. With the formation of the Letters and Gospel of John, it is only a step to the New Testament.

27.6 For Further Reading

Ashton, J. *Understanding the Fourth Gospel.* New York: Oxford University Press, 1991.

Barrett, C. K. *The Gospel according to St. John.* 2nd ed. Philadelphia: Westminster Press, 1978.

Brown, R. E., and F. J. Moloney. *An Introduction to the Gospel of John.* Anchor Bible Reference Library. New Haven, CT: Yale University Press, 2003.

Bultmann, R. *The Gospel of John: A Commentary.* Translated by G. R. Beasley-Murray, R. W. N. Hoare, and John Kenneth Riches. Philadelphia: Westminster Press, 1971.

Carson, D. A. *The Gospel according to John.* Grand Rapids: Eerdmans, 1991.

Carter, W. *John: Storyteller, Interpreter, Evangelist.* Peabody, MA: Hendrickson, 2006.

Culpepper, A. *The Gospel and Letters of John.* Interpreting Biblical Texts. Nashville: Abingdon Press, 1998.

Dodd, C. H. *Historical Tradition in the Fourth Gospel.* Cambridge: Cambridge University Press, 1963.

———. *The Interpretation of the Fourth Gospel.* Cambridge: Cambridge University Press, 1953.

Käsemann, E. *The Testament of Jesus: A Study of the Gospel of John in the Light of Chapter 17.* NTL. London: SCM Press, 1968.

Keener, C. S. *The Gospel of John: A Commentary.* 2 vols. Peabody, MA: Hendrickson, 2003.

Kysar, R. *John: The Maverick Gospel.* 2nd ed. Louisville, KY: Westminster John Knox Press, 1993.

Smith, D. Moody. *John.* ANTC. Nashville: Abingdon Press, 1999.

28

Epilogue: The New Testament as Word of God

THE KIND OF HISTORICAL STUDY REPRESENTED in the preceding pages has presented the New Testament as a selection from the disparate Christian literature that originated in the first hundred years of the church's life, representing various points of view within early Christianity. Authorship, sources, and dates of several documents are unknown or disputed. All testify to faith in God's act in Christ; all share the human fallibility and ancient worldview of their authors.

However, on Sunday mornings when the Scripture is read in worship, no lector says anything like, "Now let us hear a passage from a collection of ancient literature that the church selected as its normative documents." What we say and hear is "The Word of the Lord. . . . Thanks be to God."

What does it mean to call *this* kind of book the "Word of God"?

At this point in the discussion, 2 Timothy 3:16 is sometimes cited: "All scripture is inspired by God." This is an important text, but it is better not to begin here. It is the only text in the Bible that speaks explicitly of the inspiration of Scripture. Both its translation and its meaning are disputed.[1] While the church through the centuries has affirmed that the Bible is divinely inspired, the issue for thoughtful believers is not whether the statement is true, but what it means. *This* question is best not answered in advance, but only after careful examination of the kind of book the New Testament in fact is. Thus these paragraphs are *epilogue* rather than *prologue*.

28.1 The Bible Portrays the God Who Speaks.

THE FIRST SENTENCE OF THE BIBLE PORTRAYS God as the one who speaks (Gen 1:3). The God of the Bible is preeminently the God who speaks, the God who calls the worlds into being and shapes the lives of individuals, communities, and nations by the divine Word. Such phrases as "God said" and "the LORD spoke" occur hundreds of times in the Old Testament. The most common verb used with God as the subject is some form of a verb of speaking (more

1. See the critical commentaries. The key word θεόπνευστος (*theopneustos*, literally "God-breathed"), is found only here in the Bible. It can be understood to mean that the words of Scripture represent the very breath of God, though there is no other biblical instance where God breathes out Scripture. It can be understood on the analogy of Gen 2:7, in which God breathes life into the man of clay, and Ps 104:29–30, in which God's breath enlivens the whole creation. In 2 Cor 3:3, the believing community is the letter inspired by the Spirit. Since there are no biblical texts in which God's breath gives life to a book, but texts in which God breathes life into humanity, the believing community, and even animal life, 2 Tim 3:16 can be seen as an aspect of God's universal enlivening presence (cf. Acts 17:28). Furthermore, the lack of a verb means the syntax of the sentence is unclear (see above §4.2). Such considerations show this single text is a slender thread on which to hang a doctrine of Scripture.

than 2,200 times, far more than its nearest competitor). The prophetic formula "Thus says the LORD" occurs 428 times, "the word of God/the LORD" an additional 308 times.

Biblical authors portray the event of God's speaking in a variety of ways. God can be presented very *anthropomorphically* as a character in the story, who walks in the garden in the cool of the day and converses with Adam and Eve as one human being speaks to another (Gen 3:8–19). God can assemble the members of the heavenly court and dialogue with them as a human king engages the palace staff (1 Kgs 22:1–28; Job 1:6–12). God can speak *directly* from heaven, in a way that human beings hear and understand, as at the transfiguration (Matt 17:1–8). God can give the message to an *angel* or angelic group, who delivers it to human addressees, sometimes in such a way that the figure of the angel(s) and God modulate into each other (e.g., Gen 16:7–9; 18:1–19:21; 22:1–19). In Exodus 3:1–12, the angel of the Lord appears to Moses in the burning bush, but it is the Lord who speaks from the bush. God speaks in *visions* (e.g., Gen 15:1; 46:2; 1 Sam 3:1, 15; Hos 12:10; Acts 9:10; 18:10) and *dreams* (Gen 20:3, 6; 1 Kgs 3:5; Matt 2:13, 19, 22).

The image of God speaking is, like all human language for God's actions, *metaphorical*. All that human beings can denominate "speaking" requires not only the physical apparatus of speech (vocal cords, tongue, lips, not to speak of brain), but a history in which a particular language has been acquired. Thus "Word of God" is an entirely metaphorical expression, like "love of God" or "kingdom of God." To say "metaphorical," of course, does not mean "unreal"; here as elsewhere, all human language and conceptuality about the divine reality can only be metaphorical. It thus matters what kind of metaphors are utilized to portray the reality of God.

Speaking is a personal metaphor. Speaking and being spoken to are among the most fundamental aspects of human personality. Language and communication make us what we are as human beings and allow us to realize our human potential and relate to others. We are transformed by speaking and being spoken to. When we speak we share not merely information, but ourselves.

The God who speaks is the most personal God. Thus the definitive climax and center of God's revelatory speaking is a person (Heb 1:1–4). For Christian faith, the Word of God is not a book, but a person, a particular person (John 1:1, 14; Rev 19:13).

28.2 The Bible Portrays God Who Empowers and Inspires Others to Speak.

GOD NOT ONLY SPEAKS; GOD AUTHORIZES and empowers others to speak God's own word. One of the most common ways this is conceptualized is in terms of the royal messenger formula. In this model, the messenger is summoned into the royal court, the king speaks the message that is to be delivered, and the messenger repeats it to the addressees in the first person, speaking as the king. After the introductory formula "Thus says the king," the messenger speaks in the king's own words, and the hearers are addressed by the word of the king as they hear the messenger (cf. 1 Kgs 22:27; 2 Kgs 18:29, 31). Analogously, the prophet is portrayed as caught up in the visionary world of the heavenly throne room, where he or she is commissioned and hears the divine message. When the prophet delivers the message, it is the Word of God heard in the prophet's words. Thus, in the first of 428 instances of this formula, God speaks to Moses, "You shall say to Pharaoh, 'Thus says the LORD: Israel is my firstborn son . . . let my people go." This is a different pattern from the reporter model, in which Moses would have spoken God's message in the third person: "The LORD said to let his people go." In the prophetic model, the hearers are directly *addressed by* the word of God, not told *about* it.

This Old Testament prophetic model is continued to a limited extent in the early church and documented in the New Testament. Particular Christian leaders are considered to be prophets (e.g., Agabus, Acts 21:10; John of Asia, Rev 22:9), and occasionally speak or write in the first-person oracular form of the Word of God, representing their words as the very words of God or the risen Christ (Rev 2:1–3:22; 1 Cor 2:13 can also be understood this way). Those who hear the message of such Christian prophetic figures do not merely hear a report of their revelatory experiences, but are directly confronted in their preaching by the Word of God. In the New Testament, this prophetic paradigm receives two important transformations:

1. The risen Lord Jesus sometimes modulates into the figure of the one Lord God, so that it is not always clear whether "Word of the Lord" represents the Word of God or the message of the risen Christ, or whether this is a meaningful distinction.[2]

2. The prophetic role is expanded from particular chosen individuals to embrace the Christian community as a whole (see, e.g., Acts 2:17). The church as such is entrusted with the prophetic vocation and proclaims the Word of God. The Word of God is identified not only with oracular speech, but with the gospel, the Christian message as such. The prophetic form in which the Lord speaks in the first person is mostly abandoned, but the direct address is retained. In proclaiming the good news about God's act in Jesus, God speaks through the words of Christian preachers, and their message is called the Word of God that creates faith and new life (Heb 13:7; 1 Pet 1:22–25). Not only does Paul the apostle speak the Word of God to the Thessalonians; this Word continues to be at work in Thessalonian believers (1 Thess 2:13), and the Thessalonians themselves communicate the Word of God to others (1 Thess 1:8). As the Christian message is called the Word of God (Acts 18:11; 1 Cor 14:36; 1 Pet 1:25), the spread of the Christian faith can be called the growth of the Word of God (Acts 6:7; 12:24; 19:20).

Oracular and *ecclesial* mediation of the Word of God. In a helpful oversimplification, the variety of ways in which the Bible portrays the Word of God coming to human beings can be subsumed in two categories. By *oracular* I refer to the kind of revelation associated with individual prophets such as Moses and Amos, who deliver the Word of God directly, and whose words are the very words of God, received from God and delivered to the people.[3] *Oracular* revelation is direct, vertical, discontinuous with its context, an eruption into history, as the prophet stands over against the community. It is revelation "from above." *Ecclesial* mediation of the Word of God is "from below," as the Word of God wells up from within the community of faith guided by the Holy Spirit. *Oracular* revelation is associated with prophets, who stand out clearly from the community. *Ecclesial* revelation is associated with priests, elders, sages, scribes, and the community as a whole.[4] The inspired *prophet* who delivers oracles does not assemble a discussion group; prophets tend to be monological and make pronouncements in words directly from God. The inspired *community* tends to be dialogical, to reflect on a spectrum of views, to evaluate claims, and then issue a decision in its own words.

The early church and the New Testament include both types. The risen Christ of Matthew endows his church not only with prophets, but with sages and scribes (Matt 23:34). The Pauline churches, with prophets in their midst, are exhorted not only to hear them, but also to

2. Cf. Acts 15:36; 16:32; 19:10, 20; 1 Thess 1:8; 4:15; 2 Thess 3:1; 1 Pet 1:25.

3. The New Testament speaks often and typically of the Word of God in the singular, rarely of the words of God. The Word of God is typically identified not with a book, but with the gospel, the Christian message, the event of God speaking and calling people to faith. A concordance catalogues the words of the Bible, but there can be no concordance of God's Word.

4. The two types are, of course abstractions. In the real world they are overlapping, mixed categories. Biblical prophets belong to the community; the community includes prophets and evaluates their claims.

ponder and evaluate their claims, for the Spirit is given not only to prophets, but to the church as a whole (1 Cor 12–14; 1 Thess 5:19–20). The church of Acts has prophets empowered by the Holy Spirit who speak the Word of God directly (Acts 11:27–28; 13:1–2; 15:32; 21:10–11). Yet, when a crucial decision needed to be made according to the Word of God, the matter was not settled by God's sending a prophet to announce the divine will. The church convened a group of representative leaders in Jerusalem, heard various points of view, decided on the issue at hand, formulated the decision in its own words, and delivered it as a prescription to be followed in other churches, warranted by the words "It has seemed good to the Holy Spirit and to us . . ." (Acts 15:28).[5]

28.3 In Postbiblical Times, the Oracular Understanding of Word of God Began to Be Applied to the Bible as a Whole.

NONE OF THE WAYS IN WHICH THE WORD of God is described in the Bible itself results in the production of a canonical biblical text. How does it come about that the later Christian community refers to the whole Bible as "Word of the Lord"? It is one thing to compose a document that tells of God's revelation through prophets, such as Exodus, 1 Kings, or Acts. It is an entirely different thing to claim that these documents are themselves the Word of God. The church not only utters the pronouncement "the Word of the Lord" when it reads the report of the Ten Commandments delivered by God to Moses on Mount Sinai, but also when it reads the narratives of the birth and miracles of Moses or the stories about the early church in Acts. While there are hundreds of texts that picture God as speaking, there are very few that relate the Word of God to written texts, and none that identifies a canonical collection of texts as such as the Word of God. No text in the Bible speaks about the Bible as a whole. The idea that the canonical collection of Scripture texts is in some sense the Word of God is a construction of postbiblical theology.

28.3.1 The Convergence Between the Revelatory Events of God's Speaking and the Word of Scripture Begins Already in the Bible.

Although there is no biblical text that refers to a biblical document as a whole as the Word or words of God, there were already in the Old Testament some texts that related God's revelation, God's speaking, to textuality. The event of God's speaking is inscribed in silent words on a page or scroll, and again becomes living words when they are read forth to the community, so that the original linguistic event continues to happen. Later hearers are not only informed, but addressed.

Book of the Covenant. God directly wrote the Decalogue on the stone tablets (Exod 24:12; 31:18, "by the finger of God"). In Exodus 20:22–23:33 an additional collection of laws is represented as spoken directly by God to Moses on Mount Sinai. Moses wrote these in a book to be read to all the people, presumably at God's command (Exod 24:7). This composition was called the Book of the Covenant, and was later incorporated in the book of Exodus. But God is not pictured as writing or dictating the book of Exodus.

Deuteronomy. Likewise, some of Deuteronomy contains laws given to Israel, presented as the direct words of God spoken in the first person (e.g., 5:6–21). The literary form of the whole, however, is that of a series of speeches Moses gives to Israel just before they are to enter the promised land. Thus the direct speech in the Book of the Covenant in Exodus, for example, in Deuteronomy becomes Moses' citing God

5. To some scribes, it then seemed inappropriate that Luke described his own writing as based on his sources and reflection rather than inspired by the Holy Spirit, so they supplemented Luke's "It seemed good to me" with "and the Holy Spirit" (Luke 1:3).

(e.g., Exod 21:16; Deut 24:7): Moses said God said . . . These speeches of Moses, in turn, are inserted into an extensive narrative framework in which Moses is spoken of in the third person: the anonymous narrator said Moses said God said . . . This complex of materials, in turn, is placed in the comprehensive narrative of the Pentateuch. It is readily understandable how the Decalogue or Book of the Covenant could be thought of as the words/Word of God. But quite apart from the validity of the claim, what does it *mean* to call the stories and sermons in which they are embedded the Word of God? In Genesis 1:1, God speaks the world into being. But in the Bible, God does not speak *Genesis* into being.

Revelation is the most striking New Testament example of this state of affairs. The prophet-author hears the words of God and the risen Christ and presents them in direct, first-person speech (e.g., Rev 1:8; 2:1–3:22). Yet here too the direct heavenly voice is transmitted within a revelatory chain that reaches the reader as from God through Jesus, the angel, the Spirit, the prophet John, all encased in the narrative report contained in a letter (see Rev 1:1–2). Furthermore, these links in the chain do not remain distinct, but modulate into each other.[6] In Revelation, as in all canonical texts, the term "Word of God" is never applied to a text, book, or collection of books, but is reserved for Jesus Christ (Rev 19:13) and the church's message testimony to him (Rev 1:2, 9; 6:9; 20:4).

28.3.2 The Oracular Understanding of Divine Revelation Was Applied to All Scripture in Some Streams of Postbiblical Judaism.

While Israel was in its own land, the community was held together by a living tradition and culture that included sacred books, but was not embodied in or restricted to them. At the exile, this situation was disrupted, never to be restored. Israel's theologians and teachers who were among the core of Israel's deported leadership edited the documents and traditions that had become normative into a unified whole, and rallied the scattered community around the Torah, God's revealed will for the life of the people of God in an alien land. Disparate texts and traditions that had come into being in the course of generations were edited into a single, united story in which some previous differences were leveled out. In postbiblical Judaism, as the need for a level, homogenized Bible that could be considered uniformly authoritative became more pressing, some streams of Jewish tradition carried this tendency to extremes. All of Scripture became the verbally inspired Word of God, whose truth was miraculously guaranteed. This tendency can be illustrated in two texts, neither of which represent what became mainstream Judaism.

2 Esdras (4 Ezra). About 90 CE, a Jewish teacher described how the present Jewish Scriptures came into being. He writes pseudonymously under the name of Ezra, the scribal leader who lived at the end of the biblical period. In his view, all God's revelation—including not only the prophets and Wisdom literature but the extracanonical apocalyptic literature as well—had originally been given to Moses on Sinai, but the texts had been destroyed. How could the Word of God be proclaimed in the author's time and to future generations? As the author laments this sad situation, God appears to Ezra in a bush and commands him to prepare many writing tablets and secure five skilled scribes who have been trained to write rapidly:

> And you shall come here, and I will light in your heart the lamp of understanding, which shall not be put out until what you are about to write is finished. . . . So I took the five men, as he commanded me, and we proceeded to the field, and remained there. And on the next day a voice called me, saying, "Ezra, open your mouth and drink

6. For a detailed analysis, see Boring, "Voice of Jesus in the Apocalypse," 334–59.

> what I give you to drink." So I opened my mouth, and a full cup was offered to me; it was full of something like water, but its color was like fire. I took it and drank; and when I had drunk it, my heart poured forth understanding, and wisdom increased in my breast, for my spirit retained its memory, and my mouth was opened and was no longer closed. Moreover, the Most High gave understanding to the five men, and by turns they wrote what was dictated, using characters that they did not know. They sat forty days; they wrote during the daytime, and ate their bread at night. But as for me, I spoke in the daytime and was not silent at night. So during the forty days, ninety-four books were written. And when the forty days were ended, the Most High spoke to me, saying, "Make public the twenty-four books that you wrote first, and let the worthy and the unworthy read them; but keep the seventy that were written last, in order to give them to the wise among your people.[7] For in them is the spring of understanding, the fountain of wisdom, and the river of knowledge." And I did so. *(2 Esdras 14:23–48)*

The meaning is clear. The Scripture texts that had come into being through the generations of Israel's history, representing many authors and numerous perspectives, are here homogenized into one flat-surface revelation miraculously given all at once. Both Ezra and the scribes are divinely inspired. Not only the prophetic oracles contained in Scripture, but all Scripture is now verbally inspired, the infallible Word of God.

The LXX legend. The translation of the Jewish Scriptures into Greek posed serious theological issues for some. The formation of the LXX (see above, §4.3.1) forced the issue of which books were to be considered canonical, and whether a translation, no matter how accurate, could be considered as normative as the original. In Philo's version of the story, each of the translators was confined to a small cell where he worked independently on his translation, but upon completion all seventy-two translations were verbally identical. Thus once again, the centuries-long historical process that produced the Scriptures was reduced to one occasion that miraculously generated an authoritative, infallible text. In both 2 Esdras and Philo, the oracular model had been extended to the whole of the Bible, which no longer merely contained reports of oracular revelation, but was *en toto* a book of inspired oracles given from heaven all at once. Neither mainstream early Judaism nor developing mainstream early Christianity adopted this model for understanding the Bible as Word of God, but it was destined to have an afterlife in later Christian circles.

28.3.3 Later Streams of Church History Focus More Specifically on a Doctrine of Holy Scripture.

For some centuries, Christianity did not develop creedal statements regarding the nature of the Bible. The seven ecumenical creeds deal with language for God, Christ, and the Holy Spirit, but do not consider a doctrine of Scripture as part of the core faith that needed to be defined.[8] This is analogous to sacramental theology and doctrine of ministry—these were all important areas of Christian theology, but the church as a whole shared enough common assumptions that

7. The twenty-four books are the canonical texts. The seventy esoteric books intended only for the wise are the additional documents, such as 2 Esdras itself, considered authoritative by the sectarian community represented by the author.

8. The ecumenical creeds never developed an article on what Christians should believe about the Bible. The doctrine of the Word of God was subsumed under the first article of the creed, the doctrine of God. The doctrine of Scripture was subsumed under the third article, the work of the Holy Spirit in the church. It was only at the Reformation that particular denominational creeds began to specify just which books were in the Bible, how they were inspired, and what it meant to use Word-of-God terminology with respect to the Bible.

these doctrines were not topics of fundamental controversy.

In the sixteenth century and following, two revolutions in the history of church and culture shook the foundations of these fundamental assumptions and focused the spotlight of theological thought on the doctrine of Scripture as Word of God. (1) The Protestant Reformation resulted in churches that no longer considered church tradition the authoritative matrix for biblical interpretation. Inspired *Scripture* was affirmed, inspired *church* was suspect and soft-pedaled. In a way that had not been true before, churches that held to *sola scriptura* needed to clarify the meaning of the claim that the Bible is the Word of God. (2) The Renaissance, then the Enlightenment, created a gap between the worldview of the biblical authors and the modern worldview of the readers. When historical study of the Bible revealed discrepancies among biblical authors and between them and secular history and science, how could the older assumptions about the nature of the biblical revelation be maintained? When the cosmology and demonology of the Bible no longer was directly transferable to the world of the readers, what did it mean to call such a book the Word of God? If the Bible is not an infallible guide in geology and astronomy, and if it has internal tensions of both fact and doctrine, how could it be an infallible guide for Christian faith?

When the issue was posed as "science vs. the Bible," the options could be outlined in very bold strokes:

1. *Choose science and reject the Bible.* This option was taken not only by nonbelievers outside the Christian community, but by believers who continued to honor the Bible as in some respects a resource for Christian faith, but could no longer honestly affirm it as Word of God and appeal to it as authority for the church and Christian life.

2. *Choose the Bible and reject modern science.* The results of scientific study were simply rejected or understood in such a way that the assumed teaching of the Bible remained intact. In all conflicts between science and the Bible, the Bible as Word of God must be affirmed. All internal conflicts among biblical texts are only apparent, and resolvable in principle, even if in the present state of our knowledge we do not know how they can be explained. Since we know a priori what it means to call the Bible the Word of God, it can have neither conflicts with authentic science nor irresolvable contradictions.

Neither of these options, so baldly stated, was attractive to most of mainstream Christianity. The liberal theology of the nineteenth and early twentieth century attempted to accommodate biblical understanding to the modern world, classically expressed for American liberalism in such works as Harry Emerson Fosdick's 1924 *The Modern Use of the Bible* and 1938 *A Guide to Understanding the Bible*. The reaction to such accommodation among conservatives produced a full-blown doctrine of verbal infallibility, classically expressed in the late nineteenth and early twentieth centuries in the works of two Princeton scholars: *The Inspiration and Authority of the Bible*, by Benjamin B. Warfield, and *Inspiration* (1881), by A. A. Hodge and Benjamin B. Warfield. Warfield and Hodge saw themselves as the heirs of John Calvin's 1536 *Institutes of the Christian Religion* and elaborated his dynamic views of biblical inspiration in a more rigid and rationalistic manner.

Liberal theology captured most of the mainstream denominations in North America and became identified with scholarship and academic respectability; concern with the Bible as Word of God was associated more and more with fundamentalism, lack of scholarship and theological depth, focus on individual salvation, and neglect of social ethics. In the second half of the twentieth century, a renewal of evangelical scholarship focused attention on biblical authority once again, and the "battle for the Bible"[9] was renewed.

9. The phrase is from Harold Lindsell, *The Battle for the Bible* (Grand Rapids: Zondervan, 1976), a now dated defense of evangelicalism, which has developed more sophisticated expressions of its position.

28.4 Bible and Word of God in Contemporary Theology

ONCE AGAIN WITH THE RISK OF NECESSARY oversimplifications on all sides, the following positions can be delineated on the theological scene in the early twenty-first century: neo-evangelicalism, classical liberalism, and the heritage of dialectical theology and Vatican II.

28.4.1 Neo-evangelicalism

The unanimous and ubiquitous affirmation of evangelical Christianity is that the whole Bible is the infallible Word of God. What this means, however, is defined in a wide-ranging variety of ways. On the one hand, the 1960 scholarly defense of fundamentalism by James I. Packer, which found much resonance among evangelical scholars and has been recently reprinted, insists that "word of God" is not a metaphor and that the Bible is "word-for-word-God-given."[10] On the other hand, a standard evangelical systematic theology argues that "our doctrine of inerrancy maintains merely that whatever statements the Bible affirms are fully truthful when they are correctly interpreted in terms of their meaning in their cultural setting and the purpose for which they were given."[11] Likewise, while "inerrancy" is affirmed by all evangelicals, the term is defined in a startling variety of ways.[12]

10. J. I. Packer, *Fundamentalism and the Word of God* (London: Inter-Varsity Fellowship, 1960), 47, 113; J. I. Packer, *God Has Spoken: Revelation and the Bible* (Grand Rapids: Baker, 1994), 63.

11. Millard J. Erickson, *Christian Theology*, 2nd ed. (Grand Rapids: Baker, 1998), 1:221–40.

12. A spectrum of nine different positions is listed by David S. Dockery, "Variations in Inerrancy," *SBC Today* (May 1986), as cited in J. Terry Young, "The Relationship between Biblical Inerrancy and Biblical Authority," in *The Proceedings of the Conference on Biblical Inerrancy*, 1987 (Nashville: Broadman, 1987), 404. See Louis Igou Hodges, "New Dimensions in Scripture," in *New Dimensions in Evangelical Thought*, ed. David S. Dockery (Downers Grove, IL: InterVarsity Press, 1998), 212.

28.4.2 Classical Liberalism

The heritage of liberalism lives on, likewise comprising a broad spectrum of particular views. Typically, liberal theologians are hesitant to use Word of God terminology with regard to the Bible and insist that it is erroneous or meaningless to identify the whole Bible as Word of God. Fosdick was typical in using an evolutionary model, in which human understanding of God developed from primitive beginnings to the profound insights of the eighth-century prophets and the teaching of Jesus. The Bible may thus be said to "contain" the Word of God. The distinctiveness and normative authority of the Bible may be expressed in terms that are continuous with the best of human culture, such as "religious genius" (C. H. Dodd) or "religious classic" (David Tracy).[13]

28.4.3 The Heritage of Dialectical Theology and Vatican II[14]

The explosive theological power of Barthian theology in the early twentieth century and the revolutionary changes in Roman Catholic thought represented by Vatican II in the latter part of the century are not often lumped together, but in some respects they share important features with regard to the doctrine of Scripture. With evangelicalism and against liberalism, both affirmed that Word of God language is theologically appropriate to the Bible as a whole. Hearers and readers can be addressed by the Word of God that comes through any biblical text. With liberalism and

13. See C. H. Dodd, *The Authority of the Bible*, rev. 1960 ed. (New York: Harper & Row, 1928), 13–40; David Tracy, *The Analogical Imagination: Christian Theology and the Culture of Pluralism* (New York: Crossroad, 1981), 99–338. The view of neither Dodd nor Tracy should be reduced to these categories.

14. Each of these streams of theology includes considerable variety and nuance. I am here using Barth's *Dogmatics* I/1 to represent the extended shadow of Karl Barth, and the Vatican II *Dogmatic Constitution on Divine Revelation* as foundational for recent Roman Catholic understanding.

against some streams of evangelicalism, both Barthians and Roman Catholics affirmed the methods and results of historical criticism, even when they challenged traditional understandings of authorship, sources, and dating of biblical documents. Both argued that authentic biblical interpretation must take full account of the historically conditioned nature of biblical texts, which must be interpreted in terms of the worldviews and genres of the ancient world. Neither Barthian nor recent Roman Catholic exegetes understand the truthfulness or infallibility of Scripture to mean that the Bible is inerrant. The Holy Spirit utilizes human fallibility to communicate God's Word. The christological, incarnational model illuminates the nature of Scripture. For Christian faith, the definitive Word of God was spoken once for all in a person, the truly human Jesus of Nazareth, who is the truly divine Son of God. At Chalcedon, the church explicated the meaning of the Christ event such that the Christ is truly divine, but not in a way that excludes his humanity, and truly human in a way that does not exclude his divinity. Nor can the person of Christ be divided into human and divine "parts."[15] So also with Scripture: from the point of view of Christian faith, the Bible is a thoroughly human book, just as the Bible as a whole is the divine Word of God.

A most tricky issue is which verb best expresses the relation between the Word of God and the Bible. "Is" must be rejected, if it identifies the words of the Bible with the words of God. "Contains" must be rejected, if understood quantitatively, as though the interpreter could color-code the biblical text with red for Word of God and blue for merely human words. This can no more be done than the Christ can be divided into divine and human "parts." Barth and his successors have helpfully employed the language of *witness* and *testimony*: the biblical text is not itself the word of God, but points beyond itself to the Word that only God can speak, the Word spoken through prophets and apostles, and once for all in Jesus Christ. Related to this is the language of mediation and facilitation: the Bible *mediates* the Word of God, which the sovereign God may speak through it, divine Word coming through human words without being identified with them. In events of proclamation and faith, the sovereign God can speak in such a way that the Bible *becomes* the Word of God, but this cannot be manipulated by theologian or preacher.

Barth is more specific than typical Roman Catholic theologians in speaking of the threefold form of the Word of God: (1) the primal revelatory events, of which Jesus Christ as the Word of God is the defining center; (2) the Word of God as witnessed to and mediated by the Scripture; (3) the Word of God that becomes contemporary in the church's communication of the Gospel, especially in preaching. The church must do more than preach—it must do and be—but it cannot do less than preach, it cannot withhold from the world the Word with which it is entrusted. Yet this preaching cannot stand alone; it can exist only as the extension of the Word of God made known in Christ and in the Scripture.

There is thus an inherently necessary *ecclesial* aspect to all authentic Christian talk of the Word of God. The issue has too often been discussed in individualistic terms (God → Bible → me). Both evangelicalism and liberalism basically continue to operate within the paradigm that defines the Bible as Word of God in *oracular* terms, with evangelicals affirming it and liberals denying it. Barthians and Roman Catholics take the *ecclesial* option, with the work of the Holy Spirit in the life of the church as the overarching category. The Spirit is given to the community of faith, and the inspiration of Scripture is understood within the context of the inspired community. The New Testament is the church's book: "we have this treasure in clay jars, so that it may be made clear that this extraordinary power belongs to God and does not come from us" (2 Cor 4:7). Both treasure

15. Cf. Boring, *Truly Human/ Truly Divine*, 91–113.

and clay are absolutely real—truly treasure/truly clay—and both are from God.

28.5 For Further Reading

Achtemeier, Paul J. *The Inspiration of Scripture: Problems and Proposals*. Philadelphia: Westminster Press, 1980.

Barr, James. *Beyond Fundamentalism*. Philadelphia: Westminster Press, 1984.

———. *The Scope and Authority of the Bible*. Philadelphia: Westminster Press, 1980.

Barth, Karl. *Church Dogmatics*. Vol. 1, *The Doctrine of the Word of God*. Translated by G. T. Thomson. Edinburgh: T. & T. Clark, 1936.

Berkouwer, G. C. *Studies in Dogmatics: Holy Scripture*. Grand Rapids: Eerdmans, 1975.

Bonhoeffer, D. *Reflections on the Bible: Human Word and Word of God*. Translated by M. Eugene Boring. Peabody, MA: Hendrickson, 2004.

Bultmann, Rudolf. "The Concept of the Word of God in the New Testament." In *Neues Testament und christliche Existenz: Theologische Aufsätze*, edited by A. Lindemann. Tübingen: Mohr Siebeck, 2002.

———. "How Does God Speak to Us through the Bible." In *Existence and Faith: Shorter Writings of Rudolf Bultmann*, selected, translated, and introduced by Shubert M. Ogden, 166–70. New York: Meridian Books, 1960.

Calvin, John. *Institutes of the Christian Religion*. Edited by J. T. McNeill. 2 vols. Library of Christian Classics 20–21. Philadelphia: Westminster Press, 1960. Book 1, vi–xi, Book 4, viii.

Collins, Raymond F. "Inspiration." In Raymond E. Brown, SS; Joseph A. Fitzmyer, SJ; Roland E. Murphy, OCarm, eds. *The New Jerome Biblical Commentary*, 1023–33. Englewood Cliffs, NJ: Prentice Hall, 1990, 1968.

Flannery, Austin, O.P., ed. "Dogmatic Constitution on Divine Revelation," section 3, "The Divine Inspiration and Interpretation of Holy Scripture." In *The Documents of Vatican II. Constitutions, Decrees, Declarations. A Completely Revised Translation in Inclusive Language*. Northport, NY: Costello Publishing Co., 1996.

Fosdick, H. E. *A Guide to Understanding the Bible*. New York: Harper & Bros., 1938.

———. *The Modern Use of the Bible*. New York: Macmillan, 1924.

Fretheim, Terence E., and Karlfried Froehlich. *The Bible as Word of God in a Postmodern Age*. Minneapolis: Fortress Press, 1998.

Goldingay, John. *Models for Scripture*. Grand Rapids: Eerdmans, 1994.

Hodge, A. A., and B. B. Warfield. *Inspiration*. Grand Rapids: Baker Book House, 1979. (Reprint of 1881 work, one of the foundation texts of modern scholarly fundamentalism.)

Lindsell, Harold. *The Battle for the Bible*. Grand Rapids: Zondervan, 1976.

McKim, Donald K. *What Christians Believe about the Bible*. Nashville and New York: Thomas Nelson Publishers, 1985.

Packer, J. I. *Fundamentalism and the Word of God*. London: InterVarsity Fellowship, 1960.

Rogers, Jack B., and Donald K. McKim. *The Authority and Interpretationof the Bible: An Historical Approach*. New York: Harper & Row, 1979.

Warfield, Benjamin Breckinridge. *The Inspiration and Authority of the Bible*. Grand Rapids: Baker Book House, 1948. (Reprint of articles written in the nineteenth and twentieth centuries, one of the foundation texts of modern scholarly fundamentalism.)

Index

MAP 3: Palestine in the first century CE.